BREWER'S
DICTIONARY
of MODERN
PHRASE
&FABLE

BREWER'S DICTIONARY
of MODERN
PHRASE
& FABLE

COMPILED BY

ADRIAN ROOM

CASSELL&CO

Cassell & Co.
Wellington House
125 Strand
London
WC2R 0BB

First published 2000

British Library Cataloguing-in-Publication Data
A catalogue entry for this book is available from the British Library

ISBN 0–304–35381–7

Typeset in Palatino by
Gem Graphics, Trenance, Cornwall
Printed in Finland by WS Bookwell

CONTENTS

DR BREWER AND HIS
DICTIONARY OF PHRASE AND FABLE

In 1864, a middle-aged former schoolmaster and established writer of educational books offered the manuscript of a large and ambitious reference work to the London publishing house of Cassell, Petter & Galpin. His name was Dr E. Cobham Brewer (he rarely used his given name, Ebenezer), and he had already enjoyed success with a number of titles, notably his *Guide to Science*, published by Jarrold more than twenty years before. This latest offering, however, ranging as it did over an almost unimaginable multiplicity of subjects, made Mssrs Cassell, Petter & Galpin just a little nervous. But their doubts as to whether such a volume would ever repay the expense of printing must have been mitigated by some uncanny commercial intuition, for they swallowed their misgivings and agreed to risk the venture. They would not regret their decision.

Brewer's Dictionary of Phrase and Fable, as the book was called on its publication in 1870, immediately found a wide market eager to learn from its 'improving' mix of linguistic and general knowledge and to revel in the pleasures that Dr Brewer's 'alms-basket of words' afforded to the casual browser. The *Dictionary* not only sold 100,000 copies of its first edition, but remains very much alive and kicking 130 years and sixteen editions later. 'A reference book which has flourished for over a hundred years is clearly something exceptional,' states John Buchanan-Brown in his elegant introduction to successive recent editions of *Brewer*. 'But', he goes on to ask, 'what of its compiler?'

A 'brief memoir' by his grandson, Captain P.M.C. Hayman, paints an affectionate portrait of Brewer, tracing a life of quiet but substantial achievement from his birth in Norfolk in 1810, through academic successes at Trinity Hall, Cambridge, an early spell of schoolmastering, travels in Europe, middle years as a writer and publisher's editor, to comfortable landed retirement. Anecdotes testify to a character in which genial eccentricity allied with the mild testiness of the habitually exact scholar, and to working methods that bespeak the highest standards of industry and diligence. In Brewer's study at Edwinstowe Vicarage there was, Captain Hayman describes, 'a long wooden box arrangement' with an open front 'divided into pigeon-holes lettered from A to Z in which were the slips of paper on which were written the notes he made and continued to make daily'. Notes such as these were the nucleus of the material that would grow into *Brewer's Dictionary of Phrase and Fable*.

It required more than the diligence and industry of the dedicated reference book editor, however, to give *Brewer's Dictionary of Phrase and Fable* its unique breadth and addictive flavour. Dr Brewer opens his Preface to its first edition with the sceptical question supposedly asked by every reader-to-be: 'What has this babbler to say?' Dr Brewer's 'babblings' spawned well over forty books in a fifty-year writing career. His *Guide to Science* was but the first in a long and successful series of popular educational works that gained him the approbation of, amongst others, the Emperor Napoleon III of France. It was followed by a stream of titles that bear witness to the breadth of his learning and the catholicity of his interests: *A Poetical Chronology, A Guide to Roman History, Sound and its Phenomena, Theology in Science, A Dictionary of Miracles, The Political, Social and Literary History of France, Errors of Speech and Spelling* and *The Reader's Handbook* are but a modest handful of examples of his literary endeavours. Such was the eclecticism and intellectual inquisitiveness that characterized the compiler of *Brewer's Dictionary of Phrase and Fable*.

These gifts secured for Dr Brewer the position of editor-in-chief for Cassell, Petter & Galpin from the early 1860s. In this capacity he edited most of their publications and retained a room in the company's building where he wrote various educational books for the young. An eventual breakdown in his health forced him to leave London for Sussex, where he lived until his wife's death in 1878. After this time he lived with his eldest daughter, the wife of a clergyman, at Edwinstowe Vicarage in Nottinghamshire, devoting himself to study, reading and gardening until his death in 1897.

A last, very brief, vignette of the ageing Dr Brewer is provided by an unnamed acquaintance who remarked of his company, 'I can safely say that I never parted from him without learning something new or interesting.' Brewer himself would doubtless have been gratified to know that, for many, these words apply just as much to his most famous literary creation as they may have done to the man himself. They encapsulate an editorial ideal that continues to motivate the present-day editor and publishers of *Brewer's Dictionary of Phrase and Fable*. They have dictated the shape and content of *Brewer's Dictionary of Modern Phrase and Fable*, an entirely new volume, distinct from its distinguished parent in subject-matter but closely related and deeply indebted to it in aims, approach and philosophy.

Dr Brewer himself described his original Dictionary as a 'sweep-net of a book', drawing in 'curious or novel etymologies, pseudonyms and popular titles, local traditions and literary blunders, biographical and historical trifles too insignificant to find a place in books of higher pretension, but not too worthless to be worth knowing'. The idiom is that of the 19th-century scholar, and its allusion is to the Latin tags, obscure saints, sects, historical curiosities and other 'unconsidered trifles' that have long graced the pages of his *magnum opus*, but Dr Brewer's checklist remains entirely apposite to, and his spirit ever-present in, the diverse selection of modern words, names, phrases and contemporary linguistic curiosities that Adrian Room, the current editor of *Brewer's Dictionary of Phrase and Fable*, has compiled for *Brewer's Dictionary of Modern Phrase and Fable*.

EDITOR'S INTRODUCTION

Brewer's Dictionary of Modern Phrase and Fable takes the style and approach of the long-established *Brewer's Dictionary of Phrase and Fable* and focuses them on modern times, which for simple definition purposes means the 20th century, with an occasional overlap into the 19th century at one end and an essential extension into the 21st century at the other. 'Phrase' points to the many new words, terms and names that have arisen over this recent period, while 'fable', although a word redolent of ancient myths and legends, can equally apply to the tales, stories and events of modern times.

Events there have certainly been. The first decade of the 20th century saw the replacement of the horse by the car as the basic means of transport in what came to be nostalgically regarded by many as the Edwardian era. The second decade was blighted by the most horrible war the world had ever seen. The 1920s and 1930s saw the rise of mass culture on the one hand and of fascism on the other. They also witnessed a financial and industrial slump of gigantic proportions and the outbreak of history's greatest global conflict. The 1940s were largely lost in the carnage and social upheaval caused by that conflict and the struggle to restore and rebuild the fragments of shattered lives and economies after it. The 1950s saw the birth of pop music and the dawn of the space age. The 1960s was an age of rebellion by the young against the establishment. The 1970s saw a breakdown in many nations of the West of a postwar economic and political consensus and a growing awareness of damage wrought by human agency on the planet's environment. It was also a period of twofold humiliation for the West's most powerful nation, which saw a leader disgraced and the loss of an undeclared war. The 1980s ushered in the electronic revolution, while the 1990s realized the death of one of the world's two great superpowers, a global outbreak of economic anarchy, crime and civil war, and the ravages of AIDS.

Brewer's abiding concern has always directly or indirectly been with 'phrase' or language, and the 20th century has provided a rich store of new words, phrases, meanings, names and designations that have affected everyone in the English-speaking world and most outside it. The general awareness of language has been sharply increased by the mass media in its ever more sophisticated and pervasive manifestations. Radio, television, the press and the Internet have swamped the world with words and images that would have been unthinkable a century earlier, while commerce and industry have relentlessly exploited these and other media in the pursuit of financial gain and popular prestige. Advertising of all kinds has adopted and adapted language to enhance its visual and aural creations, and by sheer repetition alone has implanted its slogans and shibboleths in our brain.

The present *Brewer*, therefore, aims to reflect and re-present these two interdependent constructs of the past 100 years, the respective two sides and images of the 20th-century world coin. It does this in the traditional form of an alphabetical sequence of entries that may individually differ considerably in style, length and content. *Canyoning*, for example, requires a simple factual description and recording, while *Canteen culture* requires both a description and an etymology. An account of the film *Forbidden Planet* requires a quite different approach to an identification of the *Forces' Sweetheart*. Whatever the subject of an entry, the constant intention has been to make it both informative and interesting. It may well be sometimes entertaining as well, or even judgmental, since that is how the world usually is.

For overall ease of use, a comprehensive network of cross-references is also supplied, while the proportion of accompanying quotations for individual entries has been deliberately raised. A large number of these are entirely original, and appear here for the first time. Many are from contemporary press reports or articles, although extracts from fictional and other works are also represented.

A growing feature in recent editions of *Brewer's Dictionary of Phrase and Fable* has been the presence of 'list' entries, and this has seemed particularly pertinent for a concrete period such as the 20th century, which can be conveniently summarized in this way in one or other of its aspects. They include the following, which in themselves provide something of a bird's-eye view of the age:

> *Advertising slogans of the 20th century*
> *Aircraft names*
> *Chambersisms*
> *Commercial inventions*
> *Countries of the world*
> *Dinerese*
> *Drug nicknames*
> *Famous last words*
> *Fathers of the 20th century*
> *Film star nicknames*
> *First lines of novels*

> *Football club nicknames*
> *Goldwynisms*
> *Medical abbreviations*
> *Mispronounced words*
> *Patron saints for the 20th century*
> *Political correctness*
> *Programming languages*
> *Pseudonyms*
> *Rock group names*
> *Second World War operational code names*
> *Socionyms*
> *Soviet sayings*
> *Sporting nicknames*
> *String quartets*
> *Teletourism*
> *Titled trains*
> *Words of the 20th century*

There are also 'general' entries devoted to a particular theme but subdividing it into individual facets or instances. One such is *Fakes*, which presents a dozen noted (or notorious) cases under this heading: *Amityville Horror*; *Borley Rectory*; *Cottingley fairies*; *Drake brass plate*; *Hitler diaries*; *Piltdown man*; *Protocols of the Elders of Zion*; *Tom Keating's pictures*; *Turin Shroud*; *Vermeer forgeries*; *Vinland Map* and *Zinoviev Letter*.

In keeping with the philosophy of the original *Brewer's Dictionary of Phrase and Fable,* the present volume endeavours not only to tell the etymological 'stories' behind thousands of words, names, titles and phrases, but also to deliver information that is not generally found in more conventional works of general reference. Just as important, it also seeks to bring together in one book types of information that are rarely found within the pages of a single reference work. The effect of this approach is to create a volume with a markedly demotic flavour, one that allows slang usages to live alongside technical terms, and the titles of works of 'high' art such as literary novels alongside the names of popular cultural productions such as television sitcoms. *Mrs Dalloway* can thus cohabit with *Beavis and Butthead*, *Disgusted, Tunbridge Wells* with *Lady Chatterley's Lover*, and the devious *Tricky Dicky* of modern political folklore with his more dignified operatic avatar, *Nixon in China*.

Another happy effect of this almost promiscuous inclusiveness, and an enduring attraction of *Brewer*, is its alphabetical serendipity, so that one finds a *Black mist* verging on *Black Monday*, *Concrete poetry* adjoining a *Concrete skirting board* and *Lawrence of Arabia* hot on the heels of the *Law of the jungle*. But rather more useful to readers will be a listing of the main themes covered, together with examples of individual entries. The following is not comprehensive, either in categories or instances, but it will give a fair idea of the diversity of the material to be found.

Alternative and New Age: *Acupuncture; Age of Aquarius; Alexander technique; Couéism; Crop circles; Flower power; Feng shui; Hippie; Ley lines; New Age; Rebirthing; Reflexology; Shiatsu; Transcendental Meditation.*

Architecture: *Admiralty Arch; Airey house; Ancient monument; Barbican; Brasília; Brutalism; Coral Gables; County Hall; Granny flat; Levittown; Menin Gate; Millennium Dome; Stockbrokers' Tudor; Tudorbethan; Woolworth Building.*

Art: *Abstract expressionism; Bauhaus; Cobra; Constructivism; Cubism; Dadaism; Fantastic realism; Fauvism; Futurism; London Group; Minimalism; Op art; Pop art; Ruralism; St Ives School; Tachism; Turner Prize; Unit One; Vorticism.*

Art titles: *Angel of the North; A Bigger Splash; Christina's World; Les Demoiselles d'Avignon; Fountain; Guernica; Melancholy; Nude Descending a Staircase; The Persistence of Memory; Totes Meer; We Are Making a New World; Whaam!*

Cartoon characters: *Addams Family; Beavis and Butt-head; Blondie; Chad; Dennis the Menace; Desperate Dan; Dilbert; Donald Duck; Felix the Cat; Garfield; Jane; Keyhole Kate; Little Orphan Annie; Rupert Bear; Sheena; Bart Simpson; Spiderman; Tintin.*

Cinema: *Abby Singer shot; Best boy; Bollywood; Carry On films; Cinerama; Disaster movie; Ealing comedies; Elstree studios; Everyman Cinema; Film noir; Golden Bear; Hollywood; Horror movie; IMAX; Keystone Kops; McGuffin; Matinée idol; Merchant Ivory film; Odeon; Oscar; Pinewood Studios; Road movie; Slasher movie; Snuff movie; Technicolor; Warner Brothers; Western.*

Commemorations: *Alexandra Rose Day; Empire Day; Father's Day; Grandparents Day; Groundhog Day; Hastings Day; International Women's Day; Liberation Day; Mother's Day; Poppy Day; Remembrance Day; Sadie Hawkins Day; Veterans Day; Waitangi Day.*

Commerce: *Bait and switch; Barcode; Brand X; Hidden agenda; Impulse buyer; Loss leaders; Product placement; Sell-by date; Shopping days to Christmas.*

Commercial products (apart from those already entered under specific categories, such as food, drink or transport): *Aga; Bakelite; Catseyes; Filofax; Gannex; Hoover; IKEA; Jacuzzi; Kangol; Ladybird Books; Meccano; Nike; Post-It Notes; Pyrex; Scotch tape; Sellotape; Start-rite; Teasmade; Teflon; Tetra Pak; Tupperware; Velcro; Walkman; Xerox; Zimmer frame.*

Computers and the Internet: *Amstrad; Apple Macintosh; ASCII; Bells and whistles; CD-ROM; Clicks and mortar; Cyberspace; Default; Desktop; Dot-com; E-mail; FAQ; GIGO; Home page; HTML; Hypertext; Internet; ISP; Java; Logic bomb; Melissa virus; Net-head; Smiley face; Space Invaders; Spam; Turing machine; Virtual reality; World Wide Web; Worm; Wysiwyg; Yahoo!*

Crime: *Acid bath murders; A6 murder; Beauty in the Bath; Birmingham Six; Brides in the Bath; Brink's-Mat robbery; Copycat killing; Date rape; Dr Death; Dingo baby case; Great Train Robbery; Moors murders; Rillington Place.*

Dance and ballet: *Ballets Russes; Beguine; Beryozka; Dance of the Seven Veils; Fish dive; Fleadh; Kirov Ballet; Line dancing; Mambo; Rambert Dance Company; Sunshine matinées.*

Disasters and massacres: *Aberfan; Amritsar massacre; Columbine massacre; Dunblane massacre; Great Storm; Hillsborough disaster; Hungerford massacre; Jonestown; Katyn Massacre; Lidice; Lockerbie air disaster; Manson murders; Marchioness disaster; My Lai Massacre; Oradour-sur-Glane; St Valentines' Day Massacre; Sharpeville massacre; Three Mile Island; Torrey Canyon; Triangle Shirtwaist Fire.*

Drink: *Alcopop; Aqua Libra; Bloody Mary; Caffè latte; Coca-Cola; G and T; Harvey Wallbanger; Ice beer; Iron Brew; Manhattan; Ovaltine; Pepsi-Cola; Real ale.*

Economy: *Black Wednesday; Dutch disease; English disease; Five-year plan; Friedmanism; Great Leap Forward; Green shoots; Guns or butter; Reaganomics; Three-day week.*

Education: *Attendance teacher; Baker days; Burnham scale; Chalk and talk; Charm school; Continental day; Crammer; Dalton Plan; Early Learning Centre; Eleven-plus; Gordonstoun; Grade; Home economics; IT; Ivy League; Montessori method; Newsom Report; Ofsted; Playgroup; Plowden report; Rising fives; Slow learner; Special needs; Statemented; Summerhill.*

Environment: *Acid rain; Biodiversity; Earth Summit; Friends of the Earth; Garden city; Green belt; Greenhouse effect; Greenpeace; Genetically modified; Gaia hypothesis; Smog; Spaceship Earth.*

Famous people: *Atatürk; Theda Bara; Bonnie and Clyde; Burgess and Maclean; Al Capone; Dr Crippen; Dionne quins; Anne Frank; Harry Houdini; Fritz Hundertwasser; Ned Kelly; Kiki of Montparnasse; Kray twins; Lawrence of Arabia; Lord Lucan; Mata Hari; Rasputin; Stalin.*

Fashion: *Accessories; Afro; A-line; Bikini; Clam-diggers; Designer label; Dietrickery; Drainpipes; Hot pants; Kipper tie; Leotard; Layered look; Little black dress; Miniskirt; New Look; Pedal-pushers; Plus fours; Ra-ra skirt; Safari suit; Shell suit; Supermodel; Unisex.*

Fictional characters: *Anthony Adverse; Biggles; Lady Chatterley; Zuleika Dobson; Lord Emsworth; Fantomas; Fu Manchu; Alf Garnett; Hopalong Cassidy; Monsieur Hulot; Jeeves; Bridget Jones; Lovejoy; Pollyanna; Scarlet Pimpernel; Tarzan.*

Film titles: *All About Eve; The Battleship Potemkin; Chariots of Fire; Dances with Wolves; The Exorcist; Fatal Attraction; The Godfather; A Hard Day's Night; The Ipcress File; Jaws; The Killing Fields; Last Tango in Paris; The*

Lavender Hill Mob; On the Waterfront; Rear Window; Rosemary's Baby; Saturday Night Fever; Star Wars; The Third Man; Vertigo; Whistle Down the Wind; You Only Live Twice.

Finance: *Asset stripping; Blue chip; Decimal currency; Ethical investment; Fannie Mae; Front-end loading; Gazumping; Golden share; Greenmail; Plastic; Triple-witching hour; Venture capitalist; White knight.*

First World War: *Entente Cordiale; Fido; Gallipoli; Gotha raids; Passchendaele; Race to the sea; Room 40; Scapa Flow; Somme; Verdun; Wipers.*

Food: *All Bran; Battenberg cake; Bel Paese; Bisto; Caesar salad; Cream tea; Croque-monsieur; E-numbers; Fettuccine Alfredo; Golden Delicious; Hot dog; HP Sauce; Jaffa cake; Jammy dodger; Knickerbocker Glory; Lymeswold; Marmite; Nouvelle cuisine; Pavlova; Ploughman's lunch; Quorn; Reuben sandwich; Soldiers; Sundae; Thousand island dressing; Upside-down cake; Vichyssoise; Waldorf salad; Woolton pie; Zuppa inglese.*

Games: *Abalone; Beetle drive; Bingo; British bulldog; Cluedo; Crossword; French cricket; Grandmother's steps; Honeypot; Mah-jongg; Monopoly; Pelmanism; Ping-pong; Poohsticks; Pub quiz; Red light; Rubik's Cube; Sardines; Scrabble; Snakes and ladders; Trivial Pursuit.*

Health and fitness: *Aerobics; Bodybuilding; Callanetics; Eurythmics; Naturism; No pain; no gain; Pilates; Rolfing; Swedish massage; Weight Watchers.*

International relations: *Arcos Affair; Bamboo Curtain; Big stick diplomacy; Casablanca conference; Central Powers; Cold War; League of Nations; Lend-Lease; NATO; New World Order; The Six; Third World; Triple Entente; United Nations; Warsaw Pact.*

Ireland: *Curragh mutiny; Direct Rule; Dirty protest; Downing Street declaration; Easter Rising; Fianna Fáil; Fine Gael; Good Friday Agreement; Hillsborough Declaration; IRA; Sinn Féin; Six Counties; Sunningdale Agreement; Troubles.*

Language: *Basic English; Body language; Bokmål; Buzzword; Ebonics; Estuary English; Faux amis; Four-letter word; Fowler; Franglais; Gobbledegook; Graffiti; Hinglish; Howler; Kelvinside; Linear B; Mockney; Mummerset; Nadsat; Oxford accent; Pinyin; Tom Swifties; Valspeak; Verlan.*

Law and order: *Age of consent; Allen charge; Anton Piller order; Borstal; Cat and Mouse Act; Category A; Caution; Citizen's arrest; Crown Court; Drink-driving; Flogging and whipping; Interpol; Judges' rules; Life sentence; McKenzie friend; Megan's Law; Miranda Rights; Right to roam; Rule 43; Section 28; Stop and search.*

Literature: *Aga saga; Airport novel; Antinovel; Campus classic; Everyman's Library; Georgian Poetry; Literary type; Lubbock's Law; Magic realism; Sex and shopping; Stuffed owl; War poets; Whodunit.*

Love and sex: *Ann Summers party; Baby snatcher; Bedroom eyes; Birds and the bees; Blind date; Boyfriend; Come-hither look; Cottaging; Cover girl; Dear John; Eternal triangle; Flirty fishing; Gay; GI bride; Girl next door; Gold-digger; Goo-goo eyes; Hen night; Honey trap; Kneesies; Main squeeze; Massage parlour; Mile-high club; Missionary position; Poontang; Rumpy-pumpy; Significant other; Striptease; Sugar daddy; Sweet nothings.*

Mathematics and mechanics: *Butterfly effect; Chaos theory; Chisanbop; Googol; Mach number; Number cruncher; Richter scale; Trachtenberg system; Uncertainty principle.*

Medicine: *AIDS; Allergy; Athlete's foot; CJD; Cosmetic surgery; Cot death; Dowager's hump; Flatliner; Gerson diet; HIV-positive; Hormones; Hot flushes; Jogger's nipple; Keyhole surgery; Legionnaires' disease; Lyme disease; Morning-after pill; Panic attack; Pap test; Penicillin; Prozac; Repetitive strain injury; SAD; Sick building syndrome; Test-tube baby; Thalidomide; Twilight sleep; Viagra; Withdrawal symptoms; Yuppie flu.*

Military and terrorist groups: *Baader-Meinhof Gang; Balcombe Street Gang; Chindits; Commandos; Contras; Death squad; Eighth Army; Einsatzgruppen; ETA; Fifth Column; Forgotten Army; Freikorps; Frelimo; Gestapo; Home Guard; Irgun; Khmer Rouge; Kitchener's Army; Ku Klux Klan; Luftwaffe; Montoneros; Old Contemptibles; PLO; Red Army; Red Brigades; SA; SAS; Shining Path; Stern Gang; Taliban; Tupamaros; Ulster Volunteer Force; Waffen SS; Weathermen; Wrens.*

Military weapons and campaigns: *ABM; Agent Orange; Air raids; Armalite; Big Bertha; Claymore mine; Cluster bomb; Desert Storm; Doodlebug; Enosis; Falklands War; Flak; Gulf War; Kalashnikov; Overlord; Pershing missile; Polaris; Sea Lion; Six-Day War; Suez crisis; Tank; Tet offensive; Tommy gun; Trident; V-1.*

Music: *Amadeus Quartet; Early music; First Night of the Proms; Hammond organ; Mighty Wurlitzer; Muzak; Ondes Martenot; Signature tune; Les Six; Surtitles; Theme music; World music.*

Music titles: *Albert Herring; Belshazzar's Feast; Carmina Burana; The Dream of Gerontius; Four Saints in Three Acts; The Girl of the Golden West; Hugh the Drover; Kindertotenlieder; Land of Hope and Glory; Das Lied von der Erde; Madame Butterfly; Peter and the Wolf; Porgy and Bess; Sinfonia Antartica; Tapiola; Tosca.*

Nicknames: *Afghan Ron; the Bouncing Czech; Cheeky Chappie; Darling Daisy; Flash Harry; Gorgeous Gussie; Hanoi Jane; The Jackal; Little Willie; Mandy; Queen of the Halls; The Shrimp; Tokyo Rose; Tricky Dicky; Yorkshire Ripper.*

Novel titles: *All Passion Spent; Bonjour Tristesse; Cakes and Ale; The Day of the Jackal; East of Eden; Fahrenheit 451; Gentlemen Prefer Blondes; A House for Mr Biswas; An Ice-Cream War; The Jewel in the Crown; The Kraken Wakes; Lady Chatterley's Lover; Last Exit to Brooklyn; Lord of the Flies; Malice Aforethought; On the Road; A Passage to India; Pincher Martin; Rebecca;*

Saturday Night and Sunday Morning; Tender Is the Night; Ulysses; Vile Bodies; The War Between the Tates.

Play titles: *The Admirable Crichton; Back to Methuselah; The Caretaker; Design for Living; Endgame; The Good Person of Setzuan; Hay Fever; The Iceman Cometh; Journey's End; The Lady's Not For Burning; The Madness of George III; Pygmalion; The Rose Tattoo; A Taste of Honey; The Voice of the Turtle; Waiting for Godot; What the Butler Saw; The Zoo Story.*

Politics: *Agitprop; Black paper; Blairism; Butskellism; Chicken run; Devolution; Eisenhower Doctrine; Fascism; Feel-good factor; Fringe party; Hedgers and Ditchers; Labour Party; Loony left; Militant Tendency; Monday Club; New Labour; Paisleyites; Plaid Cymru; Powellism; Rainbow coalition; Referendum Party; Subsidiarity; Westland affair.*

Pop and rock music: *Acid house; Beatles; Boy band; Bubblegum music; Gangsta rap; Glam rock; Grunge; Heavy metal; Hip-hop; House; Indie; Jungle music; Mods and rockers; Punk rock; Ragga; Reggae; Rock 'n' roll; Rolling Stones; Spice Girls.*

Pop and rock music titles: *American Pie; Bohemian Rhapsody; Candle in the Wind; Eleanor Rigby; The Fool on the Hill; God Save the Queen; Hey Jude; I Don't Like Mondays; Jumpin' Jack Flash; Lucy in the Sky with Diamonds; Penny Lane; Rock Around the Clock; Sympathy for the Devil; Waterloo; Yesterday.*

Popular music: *Barbershop; Big band; Birdland; Dansette; Easy listening; Gibson guitar; Gold disc; Country music; Crooning; Hillbilly; Hit parade; Jazz; Jitterbug; Karaoke; Skiffle; Tamla Motown; Tin Pan Alley.*

Psychology and psychiatry: *Aha reaction; Anal-retentive; Electra complex; False memory syndrome; Gestalt therapy; Group therapy; Growing experience; Inner space; Lateral thinking; Learning curve; Love-hate relationship; Primal scene; Primal scream therapy; Psychobabble; Rorschach test; Shrink; Type A and Type B.*

Publishing and journalism: *Agony aunt; Angry Penguins; Athlone Press; Big Issue; Blurb; Centrefold; Cheque-book journalism; Column inches; Faber and Faber; Family newspaper; Fourth leader; Ghost writer; Gollancz; Gonzo journalism; Good Guides; Grauniad; ISBN; New Yorker; Nonesuch Press; Paparazzi; Penguin Books; Photo opportunity; Pulp magazines; Random House; Red-tops; Rough Guides; Stunt girl; Tabloid; Thames and Hudson; Vanity publishing.*

Race and gender relations: *Amnesty International; Apartheid; Banana; Black is beautiful; Canteen culture; Challenged; Concrete skirting board; Cricket test; Girl power; Glass ceiling; Great Society; House husband; Male chauvinist pig; Mothers and fathers; Ms; New man; New woman; Riot grrls.*

Radio: *Canned laughter; CB radio; Home Service; Light Programme; Pips; Pirate radio; Radio Caroline; Radio Doctor; Radio Luxembourg; Reith Lectures; Savoy Hill; Shipping forecast; Shock jock; Third Programme.*

Radio programme titles: *Any Questions?; Brain of Britain; Children's Hour; Desert Island Discs; Down Your Way; Family Favourites; The Hitch-Hiker's Guide to the Galaxy; Letter from America; Listen with Mother; Much-Binding-in-the-Marsh; Under Milk Wood; Woman's Hour.*

Religion: *African Christianity; Black Martyrs; Charismatic movement; Children of God; Fatima; Fundamentalism; General Synod; Good News Bible; Gideons; Happy clappy; House church; Jerusalem Bible; Jesus movement; Liberation theology; Moonies; Revised Standard Version; Scientology; South Bank religion; Vatican II.*

Royalty: *Abdication crisis; Birthday honours; Fergie; Order of Merit; Order of the British Empire; Walkabout.*

Science and technology: *Big bang; Black hole; Digital age; Dolly; Double helix; DSK; Fleming's rules; Geiger counter; Golfball; Land camera; Laser; Michurinism; Mobile phone; Primordial soup; Quark; Radiocarbon dating; Steady state theory; Time's arrow.*

Science fiction: *Aliens; Close encounter; Cyberpunk; Flying saucers; Little Green Men; Superman; UFO.*

Second World War: *Baedeker raid; Barbarossa; Battle of Britain; Belsen; Bevin Boys; Colditz; Coventry; Dachau; Dam Busters; D-Day; Desert Rats; Dresden; Enigma; Evacuee; Fighting French; Final Solution; Great Patriotic War; Gremlin; Gustav Line; Holocaust; Kamikaze; Land girls; Maquis; Panzer divisions; Second front; Sitzkrieg; Thousand-bomber raids; Vichy; Yalta Conference.*

Society: *Affluent society; A-list; Bright Young Things; Empty nester; Essex girl; Flapper; Flat cap; Girls in pearls; Hunting, shooting and fishing; In the loop; Jet set; Middle England; North-south divide; Permissive society; Skinhead; Sloane Ranger; Square; Teddy Boys; Two cultures; U and Non-U; Underclass; Wasp.*

Space exploration: *All systems go; A-OK; Apollo; Astronaut; Challenger; Mir; NASA; Skylab; Space age; Sputnik; Vostok; Voyager.*

Sport: *Admiral's Cup; All Blacks; Birdie; Bodyline bowling; Crazy golf; Davis Cup; Diamond system; Duckworth–Lewis method; Extreme sport; FIFA; Garryowen; Googly; Indy 500; Korfball; Milk Race; Nightwatchman; Off-roading; Olympic Games; Professional foul; Real Madrid; Ryder Cup; Solheim Cup; Stadium of Light; Tall Ships race; Three-day event.*

Television: *Candid camera; Dream machine; Emmy; Eurovision Song Contest; Family hour; Game show; Soap opera; Watershed.*

Television programme titles: *Absolutely Fabulous; Ballykissangel; Coronation Street; Dad's Army; EastEnders; Fawlty Towers; The Good Life; Heartbeat; Inspector Morse; Juliet Bravo; Last of the Summer Wine; Minder; The Onedin Line; Panorama; Rising Damp; The Royle Family; Star Trek; This Is Your Life; University Challenge; The X-Files; Z-Cars.*

Theatre: *Abbey Theatre; Aldwych farce; Cochrane revues; Crucible Theatre; Happening; Kitchen sink drama; Living Theatre; Manchester School; Method acting; Off-Broadway; Old Vic; Round House; Theatre-in-the-round; Theatre of Cruelty; Windmill Theatre.*

Tourism and recreation: *Adirondack country; Butlin's; Chiantishire; Club Med; Cornish Riviera; Disneyland; Eco-tourism; Emmets; Experience; Golden Mile; Golden Ring of Russia; Graceland; Grockles; Heart of England; Heritage railways; Land of a thousand contrasts; Leaf-peeping; Look and lick brigade; Ozark country; Peak District; Roller coaster; Sun, sea and sand; Theme park.*

Transport: *Black box; Black cab; Bullet train; Channel Tunnel; Concorde; Dead man's handle; Ducks; E-type; Eurostar; Fast lane; Flying Scotsman; Gas guzzler; Ghost train; Green goddesses; Hovercraft; Jalopy; Jumbo jet; Lambretta; Learjet; Mini; Mountain bike; Popemobile; Reliant Robin; Stretch limo; TGV train; Tin Lizzie.*

Youth: *Awkward age; Ballboy; Beavers; Crazy mixed-up kid; Dead end kids; 4-H Club; Gap year; Generation X; Girl Guides; Grebo; Gang show; Gymslip mum; Hitler Youth; Latchkey child; Prom queen; Street cred; Teenybopper; Tweenies; Wild child; Yoof culture; Young thing.*

In the general area of language ('phrase') there are many entries devoted to slang terms, colloquialisms, jargon, idioms, metaphors, euphemisms, general nicknames, foreign expressions and the like. Just a few are: *All dressed up and nowhere to go; Brewer's droop; Carry the can; Damaged goods; Egg on one's face; Gardening leave; Hidden agenda; Idiot savant; Johnny Foreigner; Keep up with the Joneses; Lazy eight; Mummy's boy; Nutty as a fruitcake; Out to lunch; Part of the furniture; Shotgun wedding; Suicide blonde; Talks about talks; Turkey shoot; Weird and wacky; Zut alors!*

There is also a significant representation of catchphrases, curses, quotations, sayings and slogans, such as: *Anyone for tennis?; Beam me up, Scotty!; Careless talk costs lives; Disgusted, Tunbridge Wells; Enjoy your meal; Fifty million Frenchmen can't be wrong; Happiness is a warm puppy; Hell's bells!; I couldn't care less; Just what the doctor ordered; Knock, knock!; Lovely jubbly; Pardon me for breathing!; They think it's all over; Wait and see; We shall not be moved; Wish you were here.*

It should be noted that in many cases a conscious effort has been made to date the first appearance or general use of the word or phrase in question, especially when of American origin (when it will be stated to be such). Thus *Bait and switch* dates from the 1920s, *Daylight robbery* from the 1940s, *Fag hag* from the 1960s and *Gutted* from the 1980s.

In short, there is something for everybody, and although the span of the 20th century is merely a pinprick in the history of time, there is room for both the recognizable and familiar world of the present and the nostalgically recalled or in many cases forgotten or unfamiliar world of the past.

I am indebted to four people who contributed material in certain specialized areas. David Pickering offered entries on individual plays, poems and films; Antony Kamm on novels; Ian Crofton on works of art and music; and last but hardly least, Richard Milbank, my mentor and minder at Cassell, who provided backup on topics as diverse as military history, sporting nicknames, children's literature and the songs and recordings of famous pop groups, notably the Beatles. I also owe a sincere debt of gratitude to Lydia Darbyshire, who coordinated and collated the material at all stages of the proceedings. In the final analysis, however, it is my name that accompanies Graham Rawle's collage on the cover, and the buck thus stops with me. Readers who have comments or queries on any entries are welcome to write to me c/o the publishers, whose address appears on the verso of the title page.

ADRIAN ROOM

ABBREVIATIONS USED
IN THE DICTIONARY

AD   Anno Domini
(year of Our Lord)

b.   born

BC   before Christ

Bk   book

c.   *circa* (about)

ch   chapter

d.   died

e.g.   *exempli gratia* (for example)

fl.   *floruit* (flourished)

i.e.   *id est* (that is)

No.   number

Pt   part

r.   reigned

Rev.   reverend

Vol   volume

THE DICTIONARY

A

Abalone. A popular French board game involving a hexagonal board with 15 black marbles and 15 white, the aim being for each player to position his marbles in such a way that the other's are pushed off the side. It was the invention in 1988 of Michel Lalet and Laurent Levy, who named it not after the abalone shellfish but from 'ab-' meaning 'opposite' and English 'alone', the implication being that players would never be lonely. The game first came to Britain in 1999.

Abbey Road. An album by the BEATLES, released in the UK in September 1969 and featuring, among others, the songs 'Come Together', 'Something', OCTOPUS'S GARDEN, 'Here Comes The Sun', MAXWELL'S SILVER HAMMER, MEAN MR MUSTARD and POLYTHENE PAM. The last-mentioned two tracks form part of a 16-minute 'Long Medley' of fragmentary and longer songs on the second side of the original LP.

The album's celebrated cover photograph, with no title or text, was taken on the morning of 8 August 1969 and features the four Beatles, including a shoe-less Paul McCartney, on a ZEBRA CROSSING outside the EMI Abbey Road Studios in St John's Wood, an inner suburb of northwest London. The photograph gave rise to bizarre rumours that McCartney was dead, fanatics claiming that the album's cover image carried clues to this effect. Absurdly, the registration number of a Volkswagen car captured in the photograph – LMW 281F – was identified as signifying that McCartney would have been '28 IF' he had lived. The car's number plates were stolen by hunters of Beatles memorabilia on several occasions thereafter, and the car itself was sold by auction at Sotheby's in 1986.

Abbey Theatre. Ireland's national theatre, on Lower Abbey Street, Dublin, where it was founded in 1904. It was built at the instigation of the Celtic revivalists W.B. Yeats (1865–1939) and Lady Gregory (1852–1932) and soon gained prestige for its productions of Irish playwrights such as Yeats himself, J.M. Synge and Sean O'Casey. Some stagings have caused controversy and even riots, notably the first productions of Synge's The PLAYBOY OF THE WESTERN WORLD (1907) and O'Casey's The PLOUGH AND THE STARS (1926). The latter questioned the motivations of the revered martyrs of the EASTER RISING and thus discredited the romanticized vision of Ireland that Yeats had helped to create. The original theatre was destroyed by fire in 1951, and the present building holds two auditoriums, the main one upstairs devoted to the Irish classics and new work by dramatists such as Brian Friel, and the Peacock Theatre downstairs, which is largely given over to experimental drama.

Abbott, Judy. The American orphan who is the subject of Jean Webster's sentimental novel Daddy Long-Legs (1912) and its sequel Dear Enemy (1915). She is sent to college by a mysterious 'Mr Smith', whom she subsequently meets and marries, and he turns out to be a wealthy philanthropist by the name of Jervis Pendleton. Daddy Long-Legs was made into a silent film (1919) starring Mary Pickford as Judy and later into a sound film (1931) with Janet Gaynor.

Abby Singer shot. In film production a nickname for the penultimate shot of the day. The name is that of Abby Singer, an assistant director at Universal Studios in the 1950s, who constantly promised that after the current shot only one more shot remained before the crew would move to another part of the studio or the day's shooting would end. See also MARTINI SHOT.

Abdication crisis. The constitutional upheaval in which Edward VIII (1894–1972) renounced the throne in order to marry Mrs Wallis Simpson (1896–1986), an American divorcee.

Edward became king on 20 January 1936 amid rumours of an existing romantic attachment. In the autumn came the news that the king intended to marry Mrs Simpson, who in 1927 had divorced her first husband, a US navy officer, and that same year married a London stockbroker, Ernest Simpson. The national objection to any marriage was not that Mrs Simpson was an American, or that she was a commoner, but that she was a divorcee, which would put in question Edward's relationship with the Church of England, which officially censured the whole idea of divorce. But events took their course, and on 27 October 1936 Mrs Simpson was granted a decree nisi. The king was now faced with four options: (1) he could marry Mrs Simpson and make her queen; (2) he could contract a morganatic marriage, so that neither Mrs Simpson nor any children of the marriage would share royal status or property; (3) he could abdicate and then marry; (4) he could abandon Mrs Simpson. He chose the third option, and by the Declaration of Abdication Act, 10 December 1936, Edward VIII renounced the throne and was succeeded by his brother, George VI, who created him Duke of Windsor. The marriage took place in France on 3 June 1937.

Edward VIII thus had the shortest reign of any British monarch except that of his namesake, Edward V (1470–83), one of the 'Princes in the Tower'.

Abendland (German, 'evening land'). The West, especially Western civilization regarded as in decline. The word became familiar from the title of Oswald Spengler's book *Der Untergang des Abendlandes* ('The Decline of the West'; 1918–22) in which he argues that civilizations undergo a thousand-year cycle of growth and decline.

Aberfan. A mining village in South Wales where, on 21 October 1966, a coal tip subsided on the local school, killing 116 children and 28 adults. The collapse was believed to have been caused by water pouring into the tip from a previously unknown natural spring. The subsequent enquiry blamed the tragedy on the lack of any tipping policy by the National Coal Board.

Abergele Martyrs. The name given to two members of the clandestine Welsh organization MUDIAD AMDDIFFYN CYMRU, William Alwyn Jones and George Francis Taylor, of Abergele, Denbighshire (now Conwy), who were killed when the explosive devices they were carrying were accidentally detonated on 1 July 1969, the day of the investiture of the Prince of Wales at Caernarfon Castle. Their deaths were commemorated by several poets, and their graves have become the focus for an annual ceremony.

Abide with Me. This well-known hymn by Henry Francis Lyte (1793–1847), probably written in 1847, has been sung at FA cup finals since 1927, when it was introduced at the suggestion of the FA secretary, Frederick Wall. Earlier it was much parodied by soldiers in the First World War, one common version beginning: 'We've had no beer, we've had no beer today.' The hymn gave much comfort to Edith Cavell (1865–1915), the British nurse imprisoned and condemned to death by the Germans for helping wounded soldiers to escape, and the night before she was shot, she sat in her cell singing it with a British chaplain.

Able and Baker. The names of the first animals to survive being sent into space by the United States. They were, respectively, a rhesus monkey and a squirrel monkey and were sent aloft in the nose cone of a Jupiter rocket at Cape Canaveral, Florida, on 28 May 1959. They splashed down after 90 minutes near Antigua. Their names represent the words for the letters A and B in the 1942 signalling alphabet.

Ableism. Discrimination in favour of able-bodied people or against the disabled. The concept arose in the 1980s. *See also* POLITICAL CORRECTNESS.

ABM. The abbreviation for anti-ballistic missile, a weapon designed to destroy incoming nuclear-armed missiles (*see* ICBM). Both the USA and the USSR deployed ABMs from the 1960s to give them the capacity to survive a nuclear attack and retaliate, so eroding the effectiveness of the strategy of mutually assured destruction (*see* MAD). On 26 March 1972 the two countries signed an ABM treaty that restricted the numbers of such missiles, so maintaining the power of deterrence. The SALT I treaty was signed on the same day. *See also* SALT.

Abominable No-Man. The punning nickname of Sherman L. Adams (1899–1986), chief White House aide to President Eisenhower, referring to his regular annotation 'no' on documents. The allusion is, of course, to the ABOMINABLE SNOWMAN.

Abominable Snowman. The popular name for the yeti, a large manlike or apelike animal said to inhabit the Himalayas. The term was popularized by climbing expeditions in the 1950s, and in 1960 Sir Edmund Hillary found footprints resembling those of a large bear. The phrase translates the Tibetan *metohkangmi*, from *metoh*, 'foul', and *kangmi*, 'snowman'.

Absalom! Absalom! A novel (1936) by William Faulkner (1897–1962), recounting, from three different points of view, the ultimately doomed efforts of Thomas Sutpen to become accepted in Mississippi society and found a dynasty. At the climax of this tale of dark passions, destructive relationships and murder, Sutpen's son, Henry, now old, dies in the family home, which has been set alight by his black half-sister, leaving the line to be carried on only by Henry's idiot black great-nephew. The title recalls the lament of David for Absalom: 'O my son Absalom, my son, my son Absalom! would God I had died for thee, O Absalom, my son, my son!' (2 Samuel 18:33).

Absent healing. A form of ALTERNATIVE medicine in which healers channel the 'healing forces of nature' to patients, so activating their power to heal themselves.

Absolute Beginners. A novel (1959) by Colin MacInnes (1914–76). The second book in the author's 'London Trilogy', the story, whose climax is the Notting Hill race riots of 1958, is narrated by a teenager, one of the happy-go-lucky generation who are the 'absolute beginners' of the title. The other books in the trilogy are *City of Spades* (1957) and *Mr Love and Justice* (1960). A film version of *Absolute Beginners* (1986) was directed as a musical by Julien Temple.

Absolutely Fabulous. A television SITCOM screened on BBC2 from 1992 to 1995 and centring on the lives of Edina ('Eddy') Monsoon, a jet-setting PR agent and single mother, played by Jennifer Saunders, and Patsy Stone, her chain-smoking, hard-drinking, drug-taking former schoolfriend, played by Joanna Lumley. Their outrageous behaviour is set off by Edina's strait-laced, disapproving daughter, Saffron ('Saffy), played by Julia Sawalha, and reflected in the title, colloquially abbreviated to *Ab Fab*, a typical upper-class eulogistic utterance, here employed ironically. Any notion of POLITICAL CORRECTNESS is noticeably absent.

Abstract expressionism. The dominant movement in US painting in the late 1940s and 1950s, characterized by the conveying of powerful emotions through the sensuous qualities of paint. The term was originally used in 1919 to describe certain paintings by Wassily Kandinsky (1866–1944) but in its current sense was first used by Robert Coates, art critic of the *New Yorker*, in 1946. Leading artists of the genre are Jackson Pollock (1912–56), Willem de Kooning (1904–97), Clyfford Still (1904–80), Mark Rothko (1903–70), Barnett Newman (1905–70), Franz Kline (1910–62), Arshile Gorky (1904–48), Robert Motherwell (1915–91) and Adolph Gottlieb (1903–74).

Absurd, Theatre of the. *See* THEATRE OF THE ABSURD.

Abuse. Literally, misuse, and a word current in English from the 16th century. In the latter half of the 20th century it became associated with specific areas of improper or harmful activity, notably alcohol abuse, drug abuse and solvent abuse on the one hand, as the illegal or excessive use of these substances, and child abuse on the other, as the maltreatment of a child, especially by physical violence or sexual interference. In this last sense the term effectively replaced what was earlier known as child molesting, while the subjection of very young children to physical violence was earlier familiar as 'baby battering'. All these terms are now in regular use, although certain official publications prefer 'misuse' when referring to substances. In the field of sports the word can apply to the misuse of physical equipment, so that tennis players who throw their rackets about in anger or frustration can be cautioned for 'racket abuse'.

Abwehr (German, 'repulse'). The German military intelligence organization created in 1921 as part of the Ministry of Defence. It was divided into three sections, reconnaissance, cipher and radio monitoring, and counter-espionage, and although relatively efficient in the early stages of the Second World War was continually undermined by the SS. It ceased to exist in 1944. The German word literally means 'warding off'.

Acacia Avenue. A street name evocative of suburban MIDDLE ENGLAND and its middle-class values. As the acacia flourishes in warm climates, the implication is that the street that bears its name is likely to be in the 'soft' south of England rather than the 'tough' Midlands or north. The *Greater London Street Atlas* (1998) lists a dozen genuine streets so named.

> Sales of newspapers boomed as the *Daily Mirror* went for the mass working class and the *Daily Express* for Acacia Avenue's Walter Mitty dream of success, sophistication and romance.
> *The Times* (21 January 2000)

ACAS. An acronym for Advisory, Conciliation and Arbitration Service, a UK QUANGO established by the Employment Protection Act of 1975. It can act as a mediator and/or arbitrator in industrial disputes, if both sides agree, and also advises unions and employers on a wide range of industrial-relations and employment issues.

Acceptable face. The acceptable face of something is its positive or reasonable side, as distinct from what are regarded as its negative or unpopular aspects. The expression arose in the late 1970s as the converse of an 'unacceptable face', itself popularized by Edward Heath's UNACCEPTABLE FACE OF CAPITALISM.

> Bit by bit … I was becoming the almost acceptable face of homosexuality.
>
> QUENTIN CRISP: *How to Become a Virgin*, ch vi (1981)

Accessories. In the world of fashion the term for a small article or item of clothing carried or worn to complement a garment or outfit. The term is traditionally taken to apply to items of women's dress, such as gloves or handbags, but accessories equally exist for men in the form of shoes, ties, handkerchiefs, watches, sunglasses and the like. Adornments resulting from BODY PIERCING may also be regarded as accessories. The word has been current in this sense from the 1950s.

> Accessories for women are a contradiction in terms. Everything they wear is an accessory to the natural wonder that is them. For men, accessories are like the flowers on the pine tree: small, dull and only really noticed by other pine trees.
>
> *Sunday Times* (20 February 2000)

Accidental Death of an Anarchist. A play, *Morte accidentale di un anarchico*, by the Italian playwright and actor Dario Fo (b.1926). First performed in 1970, it is about the inquiry following the death of a political activist after he falls from the window of Milan police station while being interrogated about terrorist bomb explosions. The play was based on real events, the original anarchist being Giuseppe Pinelli, a railway worker and political extremist who died in the same manner while being questioned about a terrorist bomb attack on a Milan bank in 1969. The play had to be altered on a nightly basis during its first run as more facts about the Pinelli case leaked out.

Accident waiting to happen. A potentially disastrous situation, typically caused by negligent or faulty procedures. The term is also used of a person likely to cause trouble.

> Accidents are often said to be 'waiting to happen'. It does not take much imagination to see that the chaotic start to the Whitbread round-the-world race … could easily have ended in tragedy.
>
> *The Times* (23 September 1997)

AC/DC. A slang adjective, originally dating from the 1940s, meaning bisexual. The term derives from the abbreviations for the opposite types of electric current (alternating current and direct current). *See also* ROCK GROUP NAMES.

Ace in the hole. A plan or piece of information kept hidden until the right time to use it. The expression relates to US stud poker, in which an ace, as the most valuable card, is dealt face down and not revealed. The 'hole' is simply a place of concealment. The phrase was popularized as the title of a US film of 1951 in which a journalist delays the rescue of a man (the 'ace') in a cave (the 'hole') in order to prolong the story and so boost the sales of his newspaper.

Acid bath murders. A sensational series of murders, which came to light in 1946 when John George Haigh (1909–49) was tried and convicted for the murder of an elderly widow whose body he had dissolved in a bath of sulphuric acid. He had committed similar murders and claimed to have drunk a cup of blood from each of his victims before annihilating them.

Acid house. The name of the synthesized dance music, popular in the late 1980s, is associated with 'acid' as slang for the drug LSD, although initially acid house dancers were more specifically fuelled by ECSTASY. A spin-off was acid jazz. *See also* HOUSE.

Acid rain. Rainfall made so acidic by atmospheric pollution that it causes environmental damage, mainly to forests, lakes and soils. The pollution is primarily caused by the emission of sulphur dioxide and oxides of nitrogen from combustion plants that burn fossil fuels, such as coal-fired power stations, and, in the case of the latter, gases from road vehicles. The problem became acute in the 1970s. Subsequent emission controls began to benefit the environment generally, although the recovery of the more sensitive ecosystems has been disappointingly slow.

Ack-ack gun. A name for an anti-aircraft gun in the Second World War, from the signallers' term for the letters AA. The name also happens to be imitative of machine-gun fire. *See also* PIP EMMA; ROGER.

Acol. In the game of bridge a commonly used system of bidding designed to enable partners with weaker hands to find suitable contracts, the only opening forcing to game being 2 Clubs. It was devised in the 1930s in a house in Acol Road, Hampstead, London.

Acquaintance rape. An alternative term for DATE RAPE.

Acronymic aptness. A tendency arose in the 20th century for the names of certain organizations, movements, charities and so on to spell out a meaningful or punning acronym rather than simply a meaningless word. The following are some examples current at the end of the century.

ADAPT: Access for Disabled People to Art Today

CAMPFIRE: Communal Area Management Programmes for Indigenous Resources

CHIME: Churches' Initiative in Musical Education

EUREKA: European Research Cooperation Agency

FOCUS: Financial Outstation Central Unified System

HOLMES: Home Office Large Major Enquiry System (a police computer)

SEALS: Sea, Air and Land Service

SERENDIP: Search for Extraterrestrial Radio Emissions from Nearby Developed Intelligent Populations

SMART: Special Measures Action Reform Team

STEP: Special Temporary Employment Programme

TRACE: test equipment for rapid automatic checkout and evaluation

Equally creative are the humorous reinterpretations of acronymic names of airlines, as:

Alitalia: always late in take-off, always late in arriving

BOAC: better on a camel

QANTAS: quite a nice trip, all survived

SABENA: such a bloody experience, never again

Across the board. Embracing all classes or categories; applying equally to all in a group. The expression is of US origin and dates from the 1950s. The allusion is to horse racing, where the term is used of a bet that covers all possible ways of winning money on a race: win (first), place (second) or show (third).

Action française (French, 'French action'). A far-right, proto-fascist political group in France that wielded considerable influence in the first half of the 20th century. The group expressed its ideas in *L'Action française*, a review first published in 1899, which became a daily newspaper from 1908 to 1944. The movement, led by the writer Charles Maurras (1868–1952), was anti-democratic, anti-republican and anti-Semitic, favouring instead the restoration of the monarchy and 'integral nationalism'. Its support among many Catholics was eroded when the newspaper and some of Maurras's books were placed on the Index of prohibited books by the papacy in 1926. During the Second World War the movement was closely associated with the collaborationist VICHY regime. It ceased to exist after 1944, when Maurras was given a life sentence, although he was released in 1952 on grounds of hill-health.

Action man. A man who flaunts his physical prowess by both word and deed. The phrase originates in the 'Action Man' doll created in 1965 (originally as GI JOE) as the scale model of a commando in full kit. Prior to his marriage in 1981 Prince Charles (b.1948) was dubbed 'Action Man' in allusion to his keen interest in many areas of sport, and more recently the name has been applied to Paddy Ashdown (b.1941), former leader of the LIBERAL DEMOCRATS, partly for his 'no-nonsense' manner but also specifically for his military background (he served in the Special Boat Squadron of the Royal Marines, the navy's equivalent of the SAS).

Is he [William Hague] Action Man in flesh and blood, happier on the judo mat or walking in the Yorkshire Dales than stuck in a suit in the endless meetings that go with the job of Leader of Her Majesty's Opposition?
The Times (16 August 1999)

Action painting. A technique of abstract painting in which paint is splashed or thrown at random on to the canvas. A famous exponent of the style was the US artist Jackson Pollock (1912–56), nicknamed 'Jack the Dripper', whose working methods have been captured on film by Hans Namuth (1915–90).

Action stations. The positions or posts taken up by military personnel in preparation for action. The term, frequently used as a command or a signal for action, dates from the First World War. *See also* PANIC STATIONS.

Action this day. An annotation used during the Second World War by Winston Churchill while he was at the Admiralty in 1940.

ACT-UP. The punning acronym of AIDS Coalition to Unleash Power, a direct-action protest group formed in the United States in 1987 to mount an urgent response to the AIDS crisis. The movement became noted for its guerrilla-style demonstrations, 'die-ins' and 'zaps' (sudden, coordinated acts). In 1989 members infiltrated the New York Stock Exchange and brought trading to a halt.

Acupuncture (Latin *acus*, 'needle', and English

'puncture'). Modern acupuncture developed from the technique for relieving pain developed in China some time before 2500 BC, which itself arose from the ancient dualistic theory of yin and yang. The belief is that disease is caused by an imbalance of these two forces in the human body, so that acupuncture aims to restore the person to health by bringing yin and yang back in balance with each other. The imbalance itself results in an obstruction of the *ch'i*, or life force, which flows through 12 meridians or pathways in the body, each connected with a major internal organ, such as the liver, kidneys and so on.

Acupuncture involves the insertion of needles at hundreds of points on the body, both along the 12 basic meridians and over certain other meridians. The needles may then be manipulated or linked to a low-voltage electric current. The way in which they actually relieve the pain has not yet been conclusively determined, and it is uncertain to what extent the relief is physically produced and to what psychologically. The procedure has certainly been beneficial in some cases.

Ada. *See* PROGRAMMING LANGUAGES.

Adam International Review. A literary quarterly published in London since 1941. Its name is an acronym for *Arts, Drama, Architecture, Music* and its first editor was Miron Grindea, a Romanian who settled in England in 1939. It came to be regarded as a showcase for good writing and its contributors have included Anthony Powell, Max Beerbohm, W.H. Auden, H.G. Wells, Thomas Mann and André Gide.

Adams, Alice. The heroine of Booth Tarkington's novel that bears her name (1921). She is anxious to escape her Midwestern lower-middle-class life and has dreams of a stage career or a rich marriage. She eventually falls in love with a wealthy newcomer, Arthur Russell, whom she snares by weaving a tissue of white lies about herself. This turns him against her when he sees the truth on joining her family for dinner, and the affair comes to an end. The novel was filmed twice, in 1923 with Florence Vidor as Alice and again in 1935 with a memorable performance from Katharine Hepburn in the role.

Addams Family. A macabre family in the cartoons of the US artist Charles Addams (1912–88), whose work first appeared in the *New Yorker* in 1935. A television series of the mid-1960s starred the gruesome group,

with John Astin playing Gomez Addams, Carolyn Jones as Morticia and an ageing Jackie Coogan in the role of Uncle Fester. There are also two film spin-offs: *The Addams Family* (1991) and *Addams Family Values* (1993), the latter more a series of gags than a movie.

Adidas. The proprietary name of a make of athletic equipment, and especially footwear and garments. It is that of Adolf (*'Adi'*) *Das*sler (1900–78), the German manufacturer who in 1946 founded the company that produces them.

Adirondack country. The northeastern region of New York State, the picturesque locale of the Adirondack Mountains, amid a host of gorges, waterfalls, lakes and swamps. The whole area is a popular tourist and holiday centre for New Yorkers and other East Coast Americans, and the healthy climate and in places spectacular scenery has encouraged the growth of resort villages and sanatoriums.

Adlestrop. A poem (1915) by Edward Thomas (1878–1917) evoking in rhapsodic manner the sights and sounds of the English summer. Thomas was inspired to write the poem when the train on which he was travelling stopped at the Gloucestershire village station of Adlestrop, the name of which originally meant 'outlying farmstead of a man called Tætel':

> Yes; I remember Adlestrop –
> The name, because one afternoon
> Of heat the express-train drew up there
> Unwontedly. It was late June.

Admass. A term coined by J.B. Priestley in *Journey Down a Rainbow* (1955) to describe the vast mid-20th-century proliferation of commercial advertising and high-pressure salesmanship, especially in the United States. The now dated word came to denote the vast mass of the general public to which advertisers addressed their publicity.

> Economics I do not pretend to understand, and sometimes I suspect that nobody does. But I understand people, and I know that the system I christened Admass, which we borrowed from America and did not improve, and constant inflation have made people unhappy.
>
> J.B. PRIESTLEY in *Punch* (16 July 1962)

Admirable Crichton, The. A play (1902) by J.M. Barrie (1860–1937) about a resourceful manservant who proves the salvation of his social superiors when they are all cast away on a desert island. It was filmed

(1957) under the same title, with Kenneth More in the title role, and earlier provided the basis for the Hollywood musical *We're Not Dressing* (1934), with Bing Crosby and Carole Lombard. The original of Barrie's character was the Scots adventurer, scholar, linguist and poet James 'The Admirable' Crichton (1560–82), whose brief but eventful life, culminating in his death in a brawl in Mantua, was the subject of Sir Thomas Urquhart's *Ekskubalauron* or *The Discoverie of a Exquisite Jewel* (1651) and of Harrison Ainsworth's novel *Crichton* (1837). The idea of a social inferior proving the better man on a desert island may have been suggested to Barrie by Sir Arthur Conan Doyle.

Admiral's Cup. An international yachting trophy presented in 1957 by the Royal Ocean Racing Club to encourage foreign yachts to race in British coastal waters. The event is the unofficial world championship of offshore yacht racing and is held every other summer. In 1999 nine teams contested the series of eight races, six of which were inshore in the Solent. The final race was the longest, from Cowes, Isle of Wight, to the Wolf Rock off Land's End and back on a pre-set course of some 725–805km (450–500 miles). The admiral of the title is the head of the RORC, who presents the prize.

Admiralty Arch. The imposing structure at the terminal point of The Mall in London, leading into Trafalgar Square and adjoining the Admiralty, in Whitehall. It was erected in 1910 as a memorial to Queen Victoria and consists of three identical, deep arches, each with iron-wrought gates, those in the central arch being opened only on ceremonial occasions. Offices in the south wing were occupied by the Ministry of Defence until 1994, while the north wing has two flats, one originally for the use of the First Lord of the Admiralty, the other for the First Sea Lord. The future of the building is under discussion, but in 1996 the Government vigorously denied that it planned to dispose of it.

Adoption of children. In English law adoption is effected by a court order that vests parental responsibility for a child to the adopter or adopters and extinguishes the parental responsibility of the birth parents. The effect of an adoption order is thus that the child is treated as if born as a child of the marriage of his or her adoptive parents and not as the child of anyone else. The requirements for making adoption orders are set out in the Adoption Act 1976.

Adrian Mole. *See* MOLE, ADRIAN.

Advent calendar. A calendar celebrating the approach of Christmas, with little flaps or windows that are designed to be opened each day to reveal a picture or present. The enterprise was adopted from similar calendars in Germany and Austria and first emerged in Britain in the 1950s. It was soon divorced from any religious content and is now simply part of the 'Christmas countdown', which in supermarkets usually begins in September.

Adverse, Anthony. The hero of the bestselling historical novel of 1934 named after him by Hervey Allen. He has various romantic adventures and misadventures in 19th-century Europe and America and thus lives up to his name. In a film of the same title (1936) he was played by Fredric March.

Advertising slogans of the 20th century. The ever-pervasive media of the 20th century has etched several advertising slogans on the collective consciousness, even when no actual interest is individually shown in the particular product. The most powerful have undoubtedly been those shown in television commercials, although the printed advertisements of the first half of the century also generated many memorable phrases. Rhymes, puns and wordplay are often evident. The following is a selection of some of the best known, with the name of the product and, in brackets, the date of first use, where known, and the name of the originator, if known.

> **Abbey National building society:** Get the Abbey habit (late 1970s)
> **Access credit card:** Access takes the waiting out of wanting (*c.*1973)
> **Adler Elevated Shoes:** Build up your ego, amigo (1940s, Shirley Polykoff)
> **Ajax laundry detergent:** Stronger than dirt (1960s)
> **Alka-Seltzer stomach powder:** I can't believe I ate the whole thing (1972, Howie Cohen and Bob Pasqualine)
> **Allinson wholemeal bread:** Bread wi' nowt taken out (1985)
> **Amami hair products:** Friday night is Amami night (1920s)
> **AMERICAN EXPRESS credit card:** That'll do nicely, sir (1970s)
> **AMERICAN EXPRESS credit card:** Don't leave home without it (1981)
> **Amplex breath purifier:** Someone isn't using Amplex (1950s)

Anadin analgesic tablets: Nothing acts faster than Anadin (1960s)

Andrews Liver Salts laxative: Inner cleanliness (1950s)

Andrex toilet tissue: Soft, strong and very long (1981)

Armour & Co. meat products: The ham what am (1917)

Aspro headache pills: One degree under (1960s)

Audi cars: *Vorsprung durch Technik* ('Progress through technology') (1982)

Automobile Association: ... But I know a man who can (1980s)

Avis Rent-A-Car: When you're only No. 2 [as against Hertz], you try harder (1963)

Babycham sparkling drink: I'd love a Babycham (1955)

Badedas bath additive: Things happen after a Badedas bath (1966)

Barratt shoes: Walk the Barratt way (early 1940s)

BENETTON clothing: United colors of Benetton (late 1980s)

Benson & Hedges cigarettes: Pure gold (1964)

Bic lighters: Flick your Bic (1975, Charlie Moss)

BIRDS EYE peas: Sweet as the moment when the pod went 'pop' (c.1965)

Bisto gravy browning: Ahh Bisto! (1919)

Blue Band margarine: Spreads straight from the fridge (late 1960s)

BMW automobiles: The ultimate driving machine (1981)

Bounty candy bar: Bounty – the taste of paradise (1960s)

Bournvita night drink: Sleep sweeter, Bournvita (1960s)

BOVRIL: Bovril prevents that sinking feeling (1920, H.H. Harris)

Braniff Airline: When you got it, flaunt it (1969)

Braniff airline: The end of the plain plane (1985, Charlie Moss and Phil Parker)

British Airways: The world's favourite airline (1983)

British Fruit Trades Federation: Eat more fruit (1923)

British Gas: Don't you just love being in control? (1991)

British Post Office: Someone, somewhere, wants a letter from you (1960s)

British Rail: Let the train take the strain (1970, Rod Allen)

British Rail: This is the age of the train (1980)

British Rail: We're getting there (1985)

British Telecom: It's for yoo-hoo! (c.1985)

British Telecom: It's good to talk (1994)

Brook Street secretarial agency: Brook Street Bureau got big by bothering (1980s)

Brooke Bond P.G. Tips tea: The tea you can really taste (1960s)

Brut aftershave: Splash it all over (c.1974)

Brylcreem hair cream: A little dab'll do ya (1949)

Budweiser beer: Where there's life there's Bud (1959)

Buick automobiles: It makes you feel like the man you are (1950s)

Burger King hamburger chain: Burger King – the home of the whopper (1981)

BVDs underwear: Next to myself I like BVD's best (c.1920)

Cadbury's Dairy Milk chocolate: Award yourself the C.D.M (1967)

Cadbury's Drinking Chocolate: Hot chocolate, drinking chocolate – the late, late drink (1960s)

Cadbury's Flake chocolate: Sixpence worth of heaven (1965)

Cadbury's Fruit and Nut chocolate: Everyone's a Fruit and Nut case (1964)

Cadbury's Milk Tray chocolates: And all because the lady loves Milk Tray (1968)

Cadbury's Roses chocolates: Roses grow on you (mid-1960s)

Cadbury's Snack confectionery: Bridge that gap with Cadbury's Snack (1967, Mogens Olsen)

Calvin Klein jeans: You know what comes between me and my Calvins? Nothing! (1980)

Camay soap: You'll look a little lovelier every day/With fabulous pink Camay (c.1960)

Camel cigarettes: I'd walk a mile for a Camel (early 1900s)

Campari aperitif : The first time is never the best (1981)

Canada Dry tonics and mixers: Emigrate to Canada Dry (for the sake of your Scotch) (1980)

Carling Black Label lager: I bet he drinks Carling Black Label (1990)

Carlsberg lager: Probably the best lager in the world (1973)

Carnation milk: Milk from contented cows (1906)

Castlemaine XXXX lager: Australians wouldn't give a XXXX for anything else (1986)

Castrol motor oil: Castrol. Liquid engineering (1977)

Cerebos salt: See how it runs (1919)

Chesterfield cigarettes: Blow some my way (1926)

Chevrolet automobiles: Eye it – try it – buy it! (1940)

Chock Full O'Nuts coffee: Chock Full O'Nuts is that heavenly coffee (1950s)

Chrysler Plymouth automobiles: Look at all three [low-priced cars]! (1932)

Clairol hair colouring: Does she … or doesn't she? (1955)

Colgate Dental Cream: Cleans your breath while it cleans your teeth (1946)

Colman's mustard: C'mon Colman's, light my fire (1979)

Comfort fabric conditioner: Softness is a thing called Comfort (late 1960s, Barry Day)

Commercial Union Assurance: We won't make a drama out of a crisis (early 1980s)

Condor pipe tobacco: It's that Condor moment (1970)

Consulate menthol cigarettes: Cool as a mountain stream (early 1960s)

Coppertone sun lotion: Tan – don't burn (1953)

Courage Tavern beer: Take Courage (1966)

Courage Tavern beer: It's what your right arm's for (c.1972)

Courvoisier brandy: The brandy of Napoleon (1909)

Craven 'A' cigarettes: For your throat's sake, smoke Craven 'A' (1920s)

Croft Original sherry: One instinctively knows when something is right (1982)

Cyril Lord carpets: This is luxury you can afford by Cyril Lord (early 1960s)

Daily Mail **newspaper:** *Daily Mail*, million sale (1920s)

Daily Mirror **newspaper:** Forward with the people (c.1935)

De Beers Consolidated Mines: A diamond is forever (1940s, Frances Gerety)

Del Monte canned fruit and fresh fruit: The man from Del Monte says 'yes' (1985)

Dewar's Scotch whisky: It never varies (1922)

Dial soap: People who like people like Dial (1965)

Domestos bleach: Kills all known germs (1959)

Double Diamond beer: A Double Diamond works wonders (1952)

Double Diamond beer: I'm only here for the beer (1971, Ros Levenstein)

Dr Collis Browne's Compound stomach medicine: There is no substitute (c.1900)

Dr Pepper soft drink: Good for life! (1937)

Egg Marketing Board: Go to work on an egg (1957, perhaps Fay Weldon or Mary Gowing)

Electricity Council storage heaters: Poor cold Fred (1969)

Eno's fruit salts laxative: First thing every morning renew your health with Eno's (1927)

Esso motoring fuel: The Esso sign means happy motoring (1950s)

Ex-Lax chocolate laxative: Keep 'regular' with Ex-Lax (1934)

F.W. Woolworth & Co. stores: Nothing over sixpence (1910s)

Fairy Liquid washing-up soap: For hands that do dishes (1981)

Fiat Strada cars: Designed by computer. Silenced by laser. Built by robot (1970s)

Firestone tyres: Where the rubber meets the road (1976)

Fisk Rubber Co. tyres: Time to re-tire (1907)

Fry's chocolate bars: Big Fry [as distinct from small fry] (mid-1960s)

Fry's Turkish Delight: Full of eastern promise (late 1950s)

Gas Council: High speed gas (1960s, William Camp)

Gibbs S.R. Toothpaste: It's tingling fresh (mid-1950s)

Gillette razor blades: Good mornings begin with Gillette (c.1952)

Glaxo dried skimmed milk: Glaxo builds bonny babies (1913)

Gleem toothpaste: For people who can't brush their teeth after every meal (1957)

Gloria Vanderbilt jeans by Murjani: My bottoms are tops (1980)

Golden Wonder salted peanuts: Jungle fresh (late 1970s)

Goodyear tyres: Out front. Pulling away (1980)

Gordon's gin: It's got to be Gordon's (1977)

Guinness stout: Guinness is good for you (1929, Oswald Greene)

Guinness stout: My goodness, my Guinness (1935, Dicky Richards)

Guinness stout: Pure genius (1985)

Haig whisky: Don't be vague – ask for Haig (c.1936)

Harp lager: Harp puts out the fire (c.1976, Keith Ravenscroft)

Harpic lavatory cleaner: Cleans round the bend (1930s)

Harvey's Bristol Cream: The best sherry in the world (1981)

Hat Council: If you want to get ahead, get a hat (1965)

Heineken lager: Heineken refreshes the parts other beers cannot reach (1975, Terry Lovelock)

Heinz beans: Beanz meanz Heinz (c.1967, Maurice Drake)

Homepride flour: Graded grains make finer flour (1968)

HOOVER carpet cleaners: It beats as it sweeps as it cleans (1919, Gerald Page-Wood)

Horlicks malted milk powder drink: Horlicks guards against night starvation (1930s) (*see also* NIGHT STARVATION)

Hovis bread: Don't say brown – say Hovis (mid-1930s)

Independent **newspaper:** *Independent*. It is. Are you? (1986)

John B. Stetson Co. hats: Step out with a Stetson (1930s)

John Lewis stores: Never knowingly undersold (1930s, John Lewis)

John Player & Sons cigarettes: Player's please (1927, George Green)

Johnnie Walker whisky: Born 1820 – still going strong (1910)

Keith Prowse ticket agency: You want the best seats, we have them (1925)

Kellogg's Cornflakes: The best to you each morning (1953)

Kellogg's Rice Krispies: Snap! Crackle! Pop! (c.1928)

Kentucky Fried Chicken: It's finger lickin' good (1952) (*see also* KFC)

Knirps umbrellas: You can't k-nacker a K-nirps (1981, Dave Trott)

Kruschen health salts: I've got that Kruschen feeling (1920s)

Ladies' Home Journal: Never underestimate the power of a woman (c.1941)

Lady Clairol hair colourant: Is it true … blondes have more fun? (1957)

Lay's potato chips: Bet you can't eat just one (1981)

Lifebuoy soap: Stops body odour (1933) (*see also* B.O.)

Life-Savers mints: The mint with the hole (1920);

Listerine mouthwash: Often a bridesmaid but never a bride (c.1923, Milton Feasley)

Lord Calvert custom-blended whiskey: For men of distinction (1945)

Lucas cycle lamps and batteries: King of the road (1920s)

Lucky Strike cigarettes: It's toasted (late 1920s)

Lucozade health drink: Lucozade aids recovery (c.1986)

Lux toilet soap: Nine out of ten screen stars use Lux toilet soap for their priceless smooth skins (1927)

Lyle's Golden Syrup: Out of the strong came forth sweetness [from Judges 14:14] (1930s)

Lyons Corner Houses: Where's George? He's gone to Lyonch (1936)

Mackeson beer: It looks good, tastes good and, by golly, it does you good (1950s)

Maclean's toothpaste: Did you Maclean your teeth today? (1934)

Maidenform brassieres: I dreamed I went walking [or variant] in my Maidenform bra (1949)

Maltesers chocolates: Chocolates with the less fattening centres (1965)

Marlboro cigarettes: Come to where the flavor is. Come to Marlboro Country (mid-1950s)

MARS BAR: A Mars a day helps you work, rest and play (c.1960, Norman Gaff)

Mary Quant cosmetics: Make-up to make love in (early 1970s)

Maxwell House coffee: Good to the last drop (1907)

McDONALD'S restaurants: Nobody can do it like McDonald's can (1970s)

MG motor cars: Mother wouldn't like it (1972)

Midland Bank: Come and talk to the listening bank (1980)

Milk Marketing Board: Drinka pinta milka day (1958, Bertrand Whitehead)

Milky Way confectionery: The sweet you can eat between meals (1960)

Morton Salt Co.: When it rains, it pours (1911)

Mr Kipling Cakes: Mr Kipling does make exceedingly good cakes (early 1970s)

Murray Mints: Too-good-to-hurry mints (late 1950s)

National Airlines: I'm Mandy [or variant]. Fly me (1971)

National Benzole petrol: The getaway people (1963)

National Canine Defence League: A dog is for life, not just for Christmas (late 1980s)

News of the World newspaper: All human life is there (*c*.1958)

NIKE running shoes: Just do it (1989)

Odorono toilet water: Within the curve of a woman's arm (1919)

Oldham car batteries: I told 'em, Oldham (late 1950s, Joan Bakewell)

Omo washing powder: Omo adds brightness to whiteness (late 1950s)

Orange mobile phones: The future's bright, the future's Orange (1996)

Oxo beef extract: Oxo gives a meal man-appeal (1958)

Packard cars: Ask the man who owns one (1902)

Pears' Soap: Preparing to be a beautiful lady (1932)

Pebeco toothpaste: The toothpaste for thinking people (1931)

Pedigree Chum dog food: Top breeders recommend it (1964)

Penguin chocolate biscuits: P–P–P–Pick up a Penguin (1960)

Pepsi Cola: Come alive – you're in the Pepsi generation (1964)

Pepsodent toothpaste: You'll wonder where the yellow went/When you brush your teeth with Pepsodent (1950s)

Persil washing powder: Persil washes whiter (1970s) (*see also* WHITER THAN WHITE)

Peter Stuyvesant cigarettes: The international passport to smoking pleasure (1960s)

Philips electronics: Simply years ahead (*c*.1973)

Phyllosan tonic: Phyllosan fortifies the over-forties (late 1940s)

Prudential Assurance Co.: The man from the Pru (late 1940s)

Quaker Puffed Wheat and Puffed Rice: Food shot from guns (*c*.1900, Claude C. Hopkins)

Qualcast Concorde lawnmowers: It's a lot less bovver than a hover [i.e. than a Flymo] (1981)

Remington electric razors: I liked the razor so much I [US businessman Victor Kiam] bought the company (1985)

Renault cars: What's yours called? (1985)

Rolls-Royce motors: At 60 miles an hour the loudest noise in this new Rolls-Royce comes from the electric clock (1958)

Rothman's cigarettes: The best money can buy (1981)

Rowntree's fruit gums: Don't forget the fruit gums, Mum (1958)

Rowntree's Kit-Kat chocolate biscuit: Have a break, have a Kit-Kat (*c*.1955)

Rowntree's Polo mints: The mint with the hole (1947)

SCHWEPPES: Schh … you-know-who (1960s, Royston Taylor)

SCHWEPPES tonic waters and mixers: What is the secret of Schhh? (*c*.1963)

7-Up soft drinks: Freshen up with 7-Up (1962)

Senior Service cigarettes: Senior Service satisfy (1981)

Sharp's toffee: Sharp's the word for toffee (1927)

Shell motor fuel: You can be sure of Shell (*c*.1931)

Shell motor fuel: That's Shell – that was! (late 1930s)

Shell motor fuel: Go well – go Shell (late 1940s)

Shredded Wheat breakfast cereal: Bet you can't eat three (1982)

Singapore Airlines: A great way to fly (1980)

Smarties chocolate buttons: Wot a lot I got (*c*.1958)

Smash instant mashed potato: For mash get Smash (1967)

Smirnoff vodka: I thought it was the 8.29 every morning [or variant] until I discovered Smirnoff (*c*.1973)

Smuckers preserves: With a name like Smuckers it has to be good (*c*.1960)

Society of American Florists: Say it with flowers (1917, Henry Penn and Patrick O'Keefe)

START-RITE: Children's shoes have far to go (1946)

Statler hotels: A room with a bath for a dollar and a half (*c*.1900, Ellsworth M. Statler)

Steinway pianos: The instrument of the immortals (1919, Raymond Rubicam)

Stopette spray deodorant: Make your armpit your charm pit (early 1950s)

Stork margarine: Can you tell Stork from butter? (*c*.1956)

Strand cigarettes: You're never alone with a Strand (1960, John May)

Stripe toothpaste: Looks like fun, cleans like crazy (1958)

Summer County margarine: Makes you feel like a queen (1960s)

Sun newspaper: Are you getting it every day? (1979)

Sun Oil motor oil: I can be very friendly (1973, Mary Lawrence)

Sunblest bread: Fresh to the last slice (early 1960s)

Sunday Mail **newspaper:** If it's going on, it's going in (1983)

Sunday Times **newspaper:** Sunday isn't Sunday without *The Sunday Times* (1968, Frank Page)

Surf washing powder: Hold it up to the light, not a stain and shining bright (late 1950s)

Tetley's tea: Tetley make tea-bags make tea (1970s)

The Times **newspaper:** Top people take *The Times* (1957)

Thunderbird wine: What's the good word? Thunderbird (1957)

Tide washing powder: Tide's in, dirt's out (1950s)

Tizer soft drink: Drink Tizer, the appetizer (1920s)

Toni home perms: Which twin has the Toni – and which twin has the expensive perm? (1951)

Tootal shirts: Looks even better on a man [illustrated on a woman] (1961)

Treets confectionery: Melts in your mouth, not in your hand (1967)

Triumph undergarments: Triumph has the bra for the way you are (*c.*1977)

TV Times **television listings magazine:** I never knew it had so much in it (1970s)

TYPHOO **tea:** Join the tea-set (1970s)

Virginia Slims cigarettes: You've come a long way baby (to get where you got to today) (1968)

Volkswagen automobiles: Think small (*c.*1959)

Wall's ice cream: Stop me and buy one (1922, perhaps Lionel and Charles Rodd)

Watneys beer: What we want is Watneys (1940s)

Welgar Shredded Wheat: That 'good-morning' feeling (mid-1940s)

Wendy hamburger restaurants: Ain't no reason to go anyplace else (1981)

Wheaties breakfast cereal: Breakfast of champions (1950)

Whiskas cat food: Eight out of ten cats prefer it (1980s)

White Horse whisky: You can take a White Horse anywhere (1969, Len Heath)

WONDERBRA **brassiere:** Hello boys (1994, Nigel Rose)

Woodbury's Facial Soap: The skin you love to touch (1910)

Woolwich Equitable building society: We're with the Woolwich (late 1970s)

Wrigley's Doublemint chewing gum: Double your pleasure, double your fun (1959)

YELLOW PAGES: Let your fingers do the walking (1960s)

Zubes cough sweets: Zubes are good for your tubes (1960s)

See also FLEXIBLE FRIEND; GERTCHA!; NAUGHTY BUT NICE; NICE ONE; OVALTINE; SCHOOLGIRL COMPLEXION; SUNNY JIM; TIGER IN ONE'S TANK; WHERE'S THE BEEF?

Aerial pingpong. A nickname for Australian Rules football, a variety of the game on the lines of rugby football. Players attempt to kick the ball, similar to a rugby ball, between two goalposts, which, as distinct from rugby, have no crossbars. Points may also be scored for kicking the ball between either of two outer posts and the main goalposts. The ball can be kicked or punched, and players can run with it provided that they bounce it every 9.1m (10 yards). The ball thus spends much of the time being propelled back and forth through the air, which explains the name.

Aerobics. This physical fitness programme, designed to increase the efficiency of the body's intake of oxygen, was pioneered by the US doctor Kenneth H. Cooper, a former US Airforce flight surgeon, and popularized in his books *Aerobics* (1968) and *The Aerobics Way* (1977). He took the term from the existing word 'aerobic', meaning 'existing on oxygen in the air', from Greek *aēr*, 'air', and *bios*, 'life'.

Afferbeck Lauder. *See* STRINE.

Affinity card. A cheque card or credit card for which the issuing bank donates a proportion of the money spent to a particular charity. The affinity card is a US concept, and the term primarily applies to a card owned by a member of an affinity group, i.e. a group of people having a common aim or interest, such as a club or college, whom it entitles to a range of discounts and other benefits. The affinity card relating specifically to charity dates from the late 1980s.

Affluent society. A phrase, in vogue from the 1950s, denoting the overall growth in material prosperity of British society as evidenced by the increasingly widespread ownership of cars, televisions, washing machines and the like. The term was popularized by the title of J.K. Galbraith's book *The Affluent Society* (1958). *See also* CONVENTIONAL WISDOM.

Afghan Ron. A nickname of the Scottish Labour MP Ron Brown (b. 1940), so named because of his links with the Soviet-backed regime in Afghanistan in the 1980s. He also maintained links with the Libyan leader Colonel Gaddafi. Brown was MP for Edinburgh Leith from 1979 to 1992 but was deselected following a sex scandal involving his research assistant and her underwear.

A4. A standard European size of paper. The basis of the series of sizes is a rectangle with an area of one square metre, the sides of which are in the proportion of 1:√2. The basic size of the A series is A0 (A zero), 841 × 1189mm. If this is halved, or the sheet folded in two, it produces A1, 594 × 841. Half A1 gives A2, 420 × 594, half A2 is A3, 297 × 420, and half A3 is A4, 210 × 297. This division and sub-division continues down to A10, 26 × 37. The A4 size is commonly found for standard business letters or even personal correspondence, as written, typed or computer-printed.

> Writing your [stage act] lines on your arm and sticking them to the wall on bits of A4 looks like you think the audience can just clear off.
> *Sunday Times* (15 August 1999)

African Christianity. From the turn of the 20th century many African Christians began to reject white missionary control and to form their own independent churches and sects. The result was a unique blend of orthodox Christian dogma and traditional native beliefs and customs. The Old Testament was rated more highly than the Gospels, God the Father was equated with a local god, and a sect leader would assume the persona of Jesus as a 'Black Christ'. In some churches God the Father was equated with a legendary progenitor such as Unkulunkulu ('very, very old') of the Zulus. Baptism became the main sacrament but was reserved for adults rather than the newborn. Various self-proclaimed 'prophets' arose, among the most remarkable being W.W. Harris (*c.*1860–1929), of the Glebo people of Liberia, who began his radical reforming ministry in 1910, and Simon Kimbangu (*c.*1889–1951) of the Belgian Congo (now Congo), who healed through hypnotism. A 'prophet' (or 'apostle') was often revered under the title of 'Black Messiah'.

African National Congress. *See* ANC.

African Queen, The. A film (1951) adapted by James Agee from the novel *The African Queen* (1935) by C.S. Forester (1899–1966). It depicts the changing relationship between hard-living tramp steamer skipper Charlie Allnut (played in the film by Humphrey Bogart) and domineering missionary spinster Rose Sayer (played by Katharine Hepburn) as they try to escape the Germans on the River Ulonga-Bora in Africa in 1915. Director John Huston's autocratic attitude to his actors and his preoccupation with shooting an elephant instead of getting on with the film (allegedly his reason for insisting upon filming on location in the Congo) was chronicled in the film *White Hunter, Black Heart* (1990), directed and starring Clint Eastwood, based on a book by Peter Viertel (who worked on the screenplay of Huston's film). The *African Queen* was the name of Bogart's boat. Katharine Hepburn's account of the making of the film was published as *The Making of the African Queen, or How I went to Africa with Bogart, Bacall and Huston and Almost Lost my Mind* (1987).

Afrika Korps. The German army force that arrived in North Africa in February 1941 under General Rommel to reinforce the Italians against the British.

Afro. A hairstyle in which naturally short, curly black hair is allowed to grow out in a bush around the head. The style became popular from the 1970s among black and coloured people as a supposed visual reference to their African ancestry. The name is popularly abbreviated to ''fro'.

> Mel's spectacular 'fro was just one of the looks from Fashion Week that failed to catch on.
> *heat* (16 December 1999–5 January 2000)

Afters. A colloquialism dating from the 1920s for the second, usually sweet, course of a meal such as lunch, supper or dinner, so called fairly obviously as it follows the main course. It otherwise features, especially in upper-class parlance, as 'pudding' (or 'pud') or more formally 'dessert'.

> Essentially a working-class expression.
> ALAN S.C. ROSS: *Don't Say It* (1973)

After the Fall. A play (1964) by Arthur Miller (b.1915) about the relationships between a twice-divorced lawyer and the women in his life. The character of the recently dead Maggie excited particular interest when the play was first performed, as she appeared to bear many similarities to the author's own former wife, the film actress Marilyn MONROE, from whom he was divorced in 1961 and who died in 1962. The title of the play suggests the central character's notion of Maggie having robbed him, like the biblical Eve, of his Adam-like innocence and their consequent fall from God's favour. The 'Fall' in the title also evokes the fallen stone tower of the German concentration camp in which the lawyer's lover, Holga, was incarcerated (the main feature of the stage set), although links have also been made with the Depression, mental illness and the winter of the soul.

I always preferred *This Is Your Life* as a television show.
NOËL COWARD: after the Broadway premiere
of *After the Fall*

Aga. The heavy, heat-retaining cooking stove so named
became a permanent fixture in many British kitchens
from the 1930s, especially in VILLAGE ENGLAND. It is of
Swedish origin, the letters forming an acronym of its
manufacturer, *Svenska Aktiebolaget Gasackumulator*
('Swedish Gas Accumulator Company'). It was valued
for its dependability and appreciated for its cosiness,
and they are still found in a number of middle-class
homes, especially those who savour the good life.

Contrast that with a walk in the countryside. It's an
aimless ramble with just one goal – to get back home
again, to your Aga and your noisy plumbing.
Sunday Times (7 June 1998)

Aga saga. A type of popular novel, typically set in
VILLAGE ENGLAND and devolving on the domestic and
emotional lives of middle-class characters, who are
likely to have an AGA stove in their homes. A doyenne
of the genre is the writer Joanna Trollope (b.1943),
whose novels include *A Village Affair* (1989) and *The
Rector's Wife* (1991).

Age Concern. This pressure group on behalf of the
aged evolved from the Old People's Welfare Committees that were first set up in 1940 to cope with the
problem of the elderly in the Second World War. It
adopted its present name in 1971.

Ageism. Discrimination against someone on the
grounds of age, the implication being that they are
too old for a position. Awareness of ageism arose in
the 1970s when problems associated with increased
longevity were first posed and when early retirement
began to cause hitherto unfamiliar personal difficulties. The term was coined in 1969 by Dr Robert
Butler, a US specialist in geriatrics.

Agenbite of inwit. The remorse of conscience. The
expression was a literary revival by James Joyce in
Ulysses (1922) of the title, *Ayenbite of Inwyt*, of Dan
Michel of Northgate's translation (1340) of a French
medieval moral treatise. *Ayenbite* is a Middle English
translation (literally meaning 'again-bite') of Medieval Latin *remorsum*, the source of English 'remorse',
and *Inwyt* a similar translation of Latin *conscientia*, the
source of modern 'conscience'.

His hands plunged and rummaged in his trunk while
he called for a clean handkerchief. Agenbite of inwit.
JAMES JOYCE: *Ulysses*, I (1922)

Agent Orange. A type of herbicide containing a deadly
toxin (dioxin), notorious from its use by the US forces
in the Vietnam War (1964–75) in order to defoliate
trees that might provide cover for the Viet Cong and
North Vietnamese forces and also to destroy crops
that might feed the enemy. The substance affects not
only plant life but also humans (although the users
were not aware of this at the time), as a result of which
much of Vietnam's agricultural economy was ruined
and infant birth defects subsequently appeared, both
in Vietnam and in the United States among military families. The name derives from the distinctive
orange stripe on the preparation's packaging. Similarly colour-coded herbicides are Agent White, Agent
Purple and Agent Blue.

Age of Aquarius. In NEW AGE terminology, the period
that began in the 1960s when peace, freedom, brotherhood and the conquest of space all seemed perfectly
feasible.

When the moon is in the seventh house
And Jupiter aligns with Mars,
Then peace will guide the planets,
And love will steer the stars;
This is the dawning of the age of Aquarius,
The age of Aquarius.
JAMES RADO and GEROME RAGNI: *Hair* (musical)
(1966)

Age of consent. The age at which a girl's consent to
sexual intercourse or marriage is legal. In English and
Scottish law the age is 16. There is also a homosexual
age of consent in private, which was 21 in 1967 and 18
in 1994. A Government vote in favour of a further
lowering of the latter age to 16 was overturned in 1998
by the House of Lords but again passed on a second
reading in 1999. It was rejected for a second time by
the Lords that same year, but once again passed by the
Commons in 2000, when the Government announced
its intention to invoke the Parliament Act to force it
into law. In the United States the age of consent varies
from 14 to 18, depending on the state.

Age of criminal responsibility. In England and Wales
a child of 10 is deemed to be sufficiently mature to be
prosecuted for an offence. In Scotland the equivalent
age is eight, while in Ireland it is only seven. In many
other countries the age of criminal responsibility is
significantly higher. In Canada it is 12, in France 13, in
Germany 14 and in Spain 16.

Age of puberty. In English law the age at which

puberty begins is usually reckoned as 14 in boys and 12 in girls. In practice it usually occurs between the ages of 10 and 15 in both sexes, and there are exceptions either side of this range.

Agitprop. The purveying of left-wing (usually communist) propaganda by means of theatre, cinema, art and the like. The word derives from a borrowing of the Russian *agitprop*, itself from the phrase *agitatsiya i propaganda*, ('agitation and propaganda'). The Russian term was first used by the Marxist writer Georgy Plekhanov (1856–1918), who defined and compared the two. His ideas were developed by LENIN in his 1902 pamphlet *What is to be done?* After the 1917 OCTOBER REVOLUTION special propaganda trains were sent all over the country, and in the 1920s Agitprop was the name given to the bureau of the Central Committee of the Communist Party of the Soviet Union responsible for propaganda. Subsidiary agitprop units were established throughout the USSR.

Agonizing reappraisal. A reassessment of a policy or stance that has been painfully forced on one by a radical change of circumstance or by a realization of what the existing circumstances actually are. The expression comes from a speech by the US statesman and international lawyer John Foster Dulles:

> If … the European Defence Community should not become effective; if France and Germany remain apart … that would compel an agonizing reappraisal of basic United States policy.
> Speech to NATO Council, 14 December 1953,
> in *New York Times* (15 December 1953)

Agony and the Ecstasy, The. A fictional biography (1961) by Irving Stone (1903–89) of Michelangelo (1475–1564), sculptor, painter, poet and the architect of St Peter's in Rome, in which latter capacity he had to combat fierce political infighting to achieve his aims. The book is prefaced with a quotation from Michelangelo: 'The best of artists have no thought to show which the rough stone in its superfluous shell doth not include; to break the marble spell is all the hand that serves the brain can do.' The title echoes the sonnet on liberty 'To Toussaint L'Ouverture' by William Wordsworth (1770–1850): 'Thy friends are exultation, agonies,/And love, and man's unconquerable mind', and also Walter Pater (1839–94): 'To burn always with this hard gem-like flame, to maintain this ecstasy, is success in life' (*Studies in the History of the Renaissance*). A film (1965), directed by Carol Reed and loosely based on Stone's novel, depicted the artistic

clashes between Michelangelo, played by Charlton Heston, and Pope Julius II, played by Rex Harrison, during the painting of the Sistine Chapel. The original version of the film, now rarely seen, included a 15-minute introduction about the works of Michelangelo, so that audiences would not confuse him with any other artist of the same name.

Agony aunt. A person, traditionally a woman, who conducts an advice column or page in newspapers or magazines (especially women's), answering correspondents who seek help with their problems. Many of the letters are from female readers and are concerned with such matters as family relationships, marital problems, sex and boyfriends. The male equivalent is an 'agony uncle'.

> [Former MP] Ron Brown, self-styled man of the people, yesterday embarked on his new job as an agony uncle.
> *The Times* (17 October 1998)

Agree to disagree, To. To cease discussion because neither side will compromise; to agree to differ.

Aha reaction. In psychiatric jargon the sudden achievement of insight or illumination, especially in creative thinking. The allusion is to the involuntary exclamation 'Aha!' on making some discovery. The term dates from the 1970s and replaced the earlier 'aha experience' of the 1950s. Similar is the 'aha moment', as the instant when such an insight occurs or the discovery is made.

> What followed the A-ha Moment is what I have come to think of as the technical stage.
> *The Times* (5 January 2000)

AIDS. The acronym of acquired immune deficiency syndrome, a disease in which the body loses most of its cellular immunity, so lowering the resistance to infection and malignancy. The cause is a virus known as HIV (human immunodeficiency virus) transmitted in blood and sexual fluids, and although having a lengthy incubation period, the disease is inevitably fatal. It was first identified in the early 1980s and has affected millions of people worldwide, initially spreading among homosexuals, intravenous drug users and recipients of infected blood transfusions. Its prevalence in the Western world has overshadowed its epidemic devastation in Africa, where it is chiefly transmitted through heterosexual contact. *See also* HIV-POSITIVE.

AIM. The initials of American Indian Movement, a

militant civil rights organization in the United States and Canada, founded in 1968, that sought the restoration of property and other rights granted by treaties.

Aircraft names. Many 20th-century aircraft became familiar as much from their names as from their role or appearance. The following is a selection of some of the better known, with reasons for the adoption. The first word is the manufacturer's name, with which that of the aircraft often intentionally alliterates. The date is that of the aircraft's first flight. The names themselves are in chronological order, not alphabetical.

Sopwith *Camel* (1916): for the distinctive 'hump' in front of the pilot's cockpit

Vickers *Vimy* (1917): for the Canadian victory at Vimy Ridge, France, in the First World War

Supermarine *Southampton* (1921): for Southampton Water, site of the manufacturer's works

Bristol *Bulldog* (1927): an appropriate name for the single-seater fighter

de Havilland *Gipsy Moth* (1931): Sir Geoffrey de Havilland (1882–1965) was a lepidopterist

Avro *Anson* (1933): for Sir George Anson (1697–1762), admiral and circumnavigator

Gloster *Gladiator* (1934): an appropriate name for the biplane fighter

Fairey *Swordfish* (1934): for the naval aircraft's role as a torpedo bomber

Hawker *Hurricane* (1935): for the fighter's speed and strength

Bristol *Blenheim* (1936): for the English defeat of the French at the Battle of Blenheim (1704)

Westland *Lysander* (1936): for Lysander (d.395 BC), Spartan naval and military commander

Vickers *Wellington* (1936): for Arthur Wellesley, Duke of Wellington (1769–1852)

Supermarine *Spitfire* (1936): for the fighter's aggressive role and fire power

Handley Page *Halifax* (1939): for the historic Yorkshire city

Bristol *Beaufighter* (1939): from the Bristol *Beaufort* torpedo bomber (1938) and 'fighter'

de Havilland *Mosquito* (1940): for the bomber's 'sting' (its bombs) and the whine of its engine

Avro *Lancaster* (1941): for the Wars of the Roses between the Houses of Lancaster and York

Gloster *Meteor* (1943): for the jet fighter's speed and strike power

Hawker *Hunter* (1951): for the fighter's aggressive role and speed of search for its prey

Avro *Vulcan* (1952): for the Roman god of fire, an appropriate name for the heavy bomber

English Electric *Lightning* (1958): for the fighter's high speed and strike power

Hawker *Harrier* (1966): for the fighter's ability to hunt its prey like a harrier (dog or bird)

Airey house. A house built from precast concrete sections. Houses of this type were first constructed in the 1920s by the firm of William Airey & Son Ltd, a Leeds engineering company founded by Sir Edwin Airey (1878–1955).

Air Force One. The official aircraft of the president of the United States.

Air freshener. A substance or device for making the air in a room smell fresh and clean on the one hand and masking unpleasant odours on the other, particularly in bathrooms and kitchens. Air fresheners are of US origin and were in some cases misapplied when introduced in Britain in the 1950s. The manufacturers of Airwick, a freshener operated by withdrawing and exposing an impregnated pad from a bottle of liquid, found it necessary to include in the instructions for use: 'Do not try to light wick. Wick will not burn.'

Air guitar. In a literal sense, an imaginary guitar that one goes through the motions of playing, as rock fans took to doing in the 1980s at HEAVY METAL concerts. In a figurative sense an air guitarist is a speaker of empty rhetoric or one who makes hollow promises.

Tony Blair has always been the air-guitarist of political rhetoric, standing in front of the mirror of publicity while aping the convictions of others.
Independent on Sunday (3 October 1999)

Airhead. A silly or foolish person, who has 'nothing up top'. The term arose as US teenage slang in the 1970s. *See also* BIMBO; HIMBO.

How dare any well-meaning lobbyist treat girls of 12 as if they were inevitably airheads?
The Times (12 October 1999)

Airlift. An organized manoeuvre to transport troops or stores to a destination by air. A famous example was the BERLIN AIRLIFT.

Air Miles. A proprietary incentive scheme launched in the early 1980s by which points equivalent to miles of free air travel are awarded to purchasers of airline tickets or other products.

The accumulation of air miles has become one of the ruling obsessions of modern American life.
Guardian (29 November 1995)

Airmiss. An instance of two aircraft in flight on different routes being less than a prescribed distance apart. Such incidents were an increasing cause for concern from the 1960s. An example is that of June 1999 when a Korean Air freight flight came within 183m (200 yards) of a British Airways JUMBO JET flying from London to Hong Kong. Only rapid evading action by the latter averted disaster.

Airport novel. A light novel, such as a thriller, sold at airports for passengers to purchase and read during their flight. Similar novels are sold at railway stations. The term is also applied to the genre of such fiction.

Whether Tom Wolfe's second foray into fiction [*A Man in Full*] is a huge achievement or merely the greatest airport novel since his own *The Bonfire of the Vanities* is ... debatable.
The Times (6 November 1999)

Air raids. The first offensive use of aircraft was by the Italians in Libya in 1911. The first raid on a town by a German ZEPPELIN followed in 1914, when Lunéville, France, was attacked in this way, and the first air raid on Britain by German aeroplanes came soon after. In the Second World War daily German air raids on Britain began on 18 June 1940. Attacks by V-1s followed in 1944. The Allies mounted their first heavy raids on German targets in 1943, and air raids have formed a part of almost every subsequent engagement, such as the Arab-Israeli conflict of 1948–94, the FALKLANDS WAR, the second GULF WAR and the Balkan conflicts of the 1990s. A sinister development of air weaponry was the SMART BOMB.

Aka. The abbreviation of 'also known as', as 'Cassius Clay, aka Muhammad Ali'. It dates from the early 1970s but had previously long been used in law and business and especially by police departments in the United States instead of 'alias', which denotes a false or assumed name, whereas 'aka' merely indicates another name that may or may not be used by someone to conceal his or her original identity. It is sometimes used to denote a synonym, especially when explaining slang terms or jargon, as 'rug, aka wig'.

Akela. The adult leader of a pack of Cub Scouts (formerly WOLF CUBS). The word is the name of the 'great grey Lone Wolf, who led all the Pack by strength and cunning' in Rudyard Kipling's *Jungle Books* (1894,

1895), the name itself being the Hindi word for 'single', 'solitary'.

AK-47. *See* KALASHNIKOV.

Aladdin Sane. *See* ZIGGY STARDUST.

Alamein, El. A town on the northern coast of Egypt, about 80km (50 miles) west of Alexandria, which gave its name to one of the most decisive battles of the Second World War. In June 1942 the British 8th Army, under the command of Claude Auchinleck (*see* AUK), took up a defensive position along a 65-km (40-mile) line between El Alamein and the impassable Qattara Depression. The first battle of Alamein (1–3 July) saw the 8th Army successfully repel an attack by the German AFRIKA KORPS under Erwin Rommel (*see* DESERT FOX), so preventing the Germans from reaching the Nile Delta. The British reinforced the defences through the summer, and in August Bernard Montgomery (*see* MONTY) was put in charge of the 8th Army, with Harold Alexander (1891–1969) replacing Auchinleck as overall commander in chief in the Middle East. In the second battle of Alamein, also known as the battle of Alam Halfa (30 August–6 September), the 8th Army again repelled a German advance. In the third and most significant battle (23 October–4 November) the 8th Army went on the offensive, defeating Rommel's AXIS forces and pursuing them westwards. On 8 November Allied forces landed in northwest Africa, and Rommel became caught between two large enemy armies.

It may almost be said, 'Before Alamein we never had a victory. After Alamein we never had a defeat.'
WINSTON CHURCHILL: *Second World War* vol 4, ch xxxiii (1951)

Alarmed. Fitted with an automatic alarm. The word in this usage dates from the 1960s but can still read strangely in a notice such as: 'This door is alarmed.'

The camcorders are alarmed and tied down. If you want to try and steal them, you can, I suppose, but you've got to be really good.
The Times (5 July 1999)

Alas Smith and Jones. A double-act television show of skits and sketches starring Mel Smith (b.1952) and Griff Rhys Jones (b.1953), first screened in 1982 and a mainstay of BBC comedy for the next five years. The material was at times uneven, but the 'head-to-head' sketches, between a constantly bemused Jones and a bluffingly knowledgeable Smith, were minimalist classics. The title, later shortened to *Smith and Jones*, punned on the US television comedy western *Alias Smith and Jones* (1971–3), about two outlaws, Hannibal Heyes and Kid Curry, who, under their respective aliases, try to stay out of trouble in order to earn a secret amnesty from the governor of Kansas.

Albatross. A source of misfortune or guilt; a burden. The use of the word in this sense is first recorded in the 1930s, but the allusion is to Samuel Taylor Coleridge's poem *The Rime of the Ancient Mariner* (1798) in which the Ancient Mariner shoots the albatross, a 'pious bird of good omen'. As a result, the ship is becalmed, all suffer, and his companions hang the bird around his neck as a punishment.

> This [Victoria and Albert] museum was founded on radical principles, but then got weighed down by its huge collection, which has become like an albatross round its neck.
>
> *The Times* (13 October 1999)

Albert Herring. An unusually comic opera by Benjamin Britten (1913–76) with a libretto by Eric Crozier, based on the short story 'Le Rosier de Mme Husson' (1888) by Guy de Maupassant (1850–93). It was first performed at Glyndbourne in 1947 to a mixed reception, *The Times* commenting: 'Mr Britten is still pursuing his old problem of seeing how much indigestible material he can dissolve in music … the result is a charade.' Albert Herring is a young shopkeeper who is dominated by his mother. As he is more virtuous than the local girls he is made May King, becomes drunk and liberates himself from his mother and other local puritans. In Maupassant's version the hero dies of alcoholism.

Alca. The island of penguins in Anatole France's satirical novel *L'Île des pingouins* (1908). It was originally an island in the Arctic but was then transported to the English Channel, where it became attached to the Brittany coast.

Alcatraz (Spanish *Isla de los Alcatraces*, 'island of the pelicans'). A notorious US prison on the rocky island of the same name in San Francisco Bay. First used as a place of detention for military offenders in 1868, it later accommodated civilian prisoners. From 1934 it housed the most dangerous civilian criminals, including such figures of infamy as Al CAPONE, George 'Machine Gun' Kelly and Robert Stroud, the BIRDMAN OF ALCATRAZ. A shortage of water eventually led to the abandonment of the penitentiary in 1963. Following subsequent abortive Sioux Indian claims on the island, it became part of the Golden Gate National Recreation Area in 1972 and is now open to visitors. The name has been adopted for any secure or forbidding prison or place of confinement.

> Britain's three most dangerous and disruptive prisoners are to be housed in a specially built mini 'Alcatraz' because they are considered too difficult for an existing centre for disruptive offenders.
>
> *The Times* (26 August 1999)

Alcock and Brown. The two British aviators, John Alcock (1892–1919) and Arthur Brown (1886–1948), who made the first non-stop flight across the Atlantic (14–15 June 1919). They made the flight in a converted Vickers Vimy bomber, taking off from Newfoundland and landing in a bog in Ireland 16 hours and 12 minutes later, having covered a distance of 3040km (1824 miles). The two men were knighted and received a £10,000 prize from the *Daily Mail*. A few months later Alcock died after a plane crash.

Alcoholics Anonymous. This self-help organization for those fighting the 'battle of the bottle' was founded in the United States in 1935. A branch was established in Britain in 1947, and the 3000th AA group was registered in 1992. Members identify themselves only by first name and surname initial, as did the AA's founders, 'Bill W' (William G. Wilson) and 'Dr Bob S' (Robert H. Smith).

Alcopop. A blend of 'alcohol' and 'pop', like the drinks themselves, consisting of lemonade or some other soft drink to which alcohol has been added. Alcopops emerged on the market in the mid-1990s to tempt the younger drinker and predictably drew criticism that resulted in a lowering of the alcohol content in some brands and a modification of the description in others. Many brands of alcopops bear names that smack of raffishness, such as Hooch, Two Dogs or Barking Frog.

> It would be social suicide to turn up at a party with alcopops. No one I know would even think about drinking them.
>
> *The Times Magazine* (15 May 1999)

Aldaniti. In 1981, the year that SHERGAR won the Derby, the Grand National winner was Aldaniti. His jockey was Bob Champion, fighting his way back to health after having been diagnosed with cancer and given eight months to live. While many racehorses derive their names from their sire or dam (or both), Aldaniti was named after his owner's children, Alistair, Daniel, Nicola and Timothy.

Aldeburgh Festival. The annual music festival in this small Suffolk resort was established in 1948 by Benjamin Britten (1913–76), who took up residence in the town after the Second World War. For 20 years the event was held in local village halls and churches, but in 1967 Britten and his lifelong partner, the tenor Peter Pears (1910–86), bought the Maltings, a riverside barn in the nearby village of Snape, and converted it into a concert hall. It was destroyed by fire on its opening night but was rebuilt in time for the following year's festival. Many of Britten's works were written to be performed at Aldeburgh, and the festival soon became an international event and place of pilgrimage for lovers of its founder's music.

Aldermaston. *See* CND.

Aldrich, Henry. The accident prone, middle-American teenager of this name was originally created by Clifford Goldsmith for his play *What a Life!* (1938). Its success led to a radio series, then to a film (1939) with Jackie Cooper in the lead role. Jimmy Lydon then took over the part for a further nine films, and these in turn evolved into a television series, *The Aldrich Family* (1949–53). The film critic Leonard Maltin described Henry as 'America's dumbest high-schooler – dumb, yet in an odd way endearing'.

Aldwych farce. One of 10 farces by Ben Travers (1886–1980), staged at the Aldwych Theatre, London. The first was *A Cuckoo in the Nest* (1925). *Rookery Nook* (1927) followed, and the series ended with *Dirty Work* (1932) and *A Bit of a Test* (1933). The plays combined absurdly improbable situations, eccentric characters and broad humour with social satire. Most were filmed.

Aleatory music (Latin *alea*, 'dice'). A term used in modern music for a work in which the composer deliberately allows for chance occurrences or choices by performers. The concept was introduced by the US composer Charles Ives (1874–1954), some of whose scores incorporate an intentional randomness or even unrealizable notations that invite the performer to find a solution. Other composers to adopt the construct include Karlheinz Stockhausen (b.1928), Pierre Boulez (b.1925) and, taking the technique to its extremity, John Cage (1912–92).

Alexander technique. A system of ALTERNATIVE treatment designed to improve a patient's posture so that the body can work in a more relaxed and efficient manner. It arose in the 1930s and is named after Frederick Alexander (1869–1955), the Australian-born actor who developed it.

Alexandra Rose Day. A day in June when rose emblems are sold for the hospital fund inaugurated on 26 June 1912 by Queen Alexandra (1844–1925), Danish consort of Edward VII, to celebrate the 50th year of her residence in England.

Al Fatah (Arabic, 'the victory'). The Palestinian political and military organization of this name was founded in 1958 by Yasser Arafat (b.1929) with the aim of creating a Palestinian state. The PLO evolved from it.

Alf Garnett. *See* GARNETT, ALF.

Alfie. A film (1966) based on a play by Bill Naughton (1910–92). Starring Michael Caine as the cheeky cockney misogynist, Alfie, who is permanently on the look-out for more 'birds' to add to his collection of sexual conquests, the film, with its frank confessions to camera, was considered a daring exploration of sexual morals in London of the SWINGING SIXTIES, and for a time the very title was synonymous with the so-called 'permissive society'. A sequel, *Alfie Darling* (1975), starring Alan Price in the lead role, failed to match the provocative exuberance of its predecessor.

ALGOL. *See* PROGRAMMING LANGUAGES.

Algonquin Round Table. An informal group of American literary people who met daily for lunch on weekdays at a large round table at the Algonquin Hotel, New York, in the 1920s and 1930s. The Algonquin Round Table first met in 1919, and its members soon included some of the best known writers, journalists and artists in New York, among them Dorothy Parker (1893–1967), Alexander Woollcott (1887–1943), Heywood Broun (1888–1939), Robert Benchley (1889–1945), Robert Sherwood (1896–1955), George S. Kaufman (1889–1961), Franklin P. Adams (1881–1960), Marc Connelly (1890–1980), Harold Ross (1892–1951), Harpo Marx (*see* MARX BROTHERS) and Russel Crouse (1893–1966). The gathering gradually thinned, however, and the last meeting was held in 1943.

Alice band. A flexible band used to hold back the hair, as worn by Alice in John Tenniel's illustrations for Lewis Carroll's *Through the Looking-Glass* (1872), but not those for *Alice in Wonderland* (1865), in which her hair falls free.

> A room full of elderly professors and their Alice-band wearing wives.
> *The Times* (31 May 1999)

Alice blue. A light greenish-blue colour, as that of the dresses worn at the turn of the 20th century by the dashing young American socialite Alice Lee Roosevelt (1884–1980), daughter of Theodore Roosevelt. The popular song 'Alice Blue Gown' (1919), by Joseph McCarthy and Harry Tierney, further promoted the fashion for the colour.

Alice in Wonderland. A nickname in royal circles for Princess Alice, Countess of Athlone (1883–1981), granddaughter of Queen Victoria, who was an avid reader of Lewis Carroll's books.

Alien. A well-regarded SCIENCE FICTION horror film (1979) starring Sigourney Weaver as Ripley, the human opponent of a lethal and apparently invulnerable species of alien monster. The success of the film inspired the sequels, *Aliens* (1986) and *Alien³* (1992). While the second film was considered to be on a par with the first, the third was relatively poorly received. By the end of the series one critic was moved to parody the slogan under which the films were publicized, 'In space no one can hear you scream', as 'In space no one can hear you snore'. Actors in the third film, set in a space penal colony, informally renamed the movie *Skinheads in Space*. There was another (again rather weak) sequel, *Alien Resurrection*, in 1997.

Alienation effect. *See* EPIC THEATRE.

Aliens. A blanket term for the creatures or beings from outer space that are believed by the credulous to have invaded earth at various times from the 19th century or that are expected to do so at any moment in the future. LITTLE GREEN MEN are one fairly innocuous type, but others are much more sinister and destructive, like those in SCIENCE FICTION or HORROR MOVIES. One of the latter, ALIEN (1979), was a great commercial success and did much to popularize the term. Reports of human beings abducted by aliens have mostly been met with equal scepticism, although some individual accounts of the experience have intrigued a gullible public. Budd Hopkins's book *Witnessed: The True Story of the Brooklyn Bridge Abduction* (1996) describes his investigations into the claimed abduction of Linda Cortile from a high-rise Manhattan apartment block in 1989. *See also* UFO.

> There is the problem that from H.G. Wells's *War of the Worlds* onwards there has been only one plot: aliens arrive, wreak havoc, catastrophe imminent, Achilles' heel discovered, world saved.
> *The Times* (11 May 1998)

A-line. The shape of a garment, especially a dress or skirt, that is flared from the shoulder or waist and that thus looks like a capital letter A. The design was created in the mid-1950s by the French couturier Christian Dior. *See also* DIOR LOOK.

> The rest of the outfit that you'll be craving come mid-September will involve a mid-calf, A-line skirt and a skimpy sweater.
> *The Times* (21 August 1999)

A-list. A potential or actual list of the most famous or socially sought-after people, the whole forming a super-elite or 'crème de la crème'. The letter A implies a hierarchy, so that in theory there could be a B list, a C list and even a Z list, the last consisting of the least desirable individuals. The concept is of US origin and dates from the mid-1980s.

> The other 12 [television channels] consist entirely of F-list celebrities going up the Nile in mismatched leisurewear for various lifestyle and travel causes.
> *The Times* (19 November 1999)

Alive and well. Flourishing, despite suggestions to the contrary. The 19th-century phrase came to be extended from the 1950s to include a place-name, as 'Alive and well and living in Luton' (or wherever). This formula was popularized by the title of the cabaret-style revue celebrating the songs of the Belgian composer and writer Jacques Brel, *Jacques Brel is Alive and Well and Living in Paris*, which opened OFF-BROADWAY at the Village Gate, New York, on 22 January 1968.

> Having sat through the filming of one episode of *Jerry Springer UK* I can confirm that trailer-park trash is alive and well and living in Cambridge.
> *The Times* (27 August 1999)

All About Eve. A film (1950) adapted by Joseph L. Mankiewicz from the short story 'The Wisdom of Eve' by Mary Orr. The plot concerns the vicious rivalry that develops between a fading Broadway star (Bette Davis) and the ruthless younger actress (Anne Baxter) who seeks to supplant her. Eve is not, in fact, the Davis character as might be expected, but Baxter's role. The story was later (1970) turned into a musical, *Applause*, which opened in New York with Lauren Bacall in Davis's role of Margo Channing.

> Margo (Bette Davis): Fasten your seat belts, it's going to be a bumpy night.
> JOSEPH L. MANKIEWICZ: *All About Eve*

All Blacks. The nickname of the New Zealand international rugby union team. It refers to the colour of their strip and was first made public by the *Daily Mail* at the beginning of their 1905 tour of Britain. The story goes that a reporter met the team as they landed at Plymouth and asked the colour of their shirts, shorts and socks. A player answered 'Black' to each of these, and then added by way of emphasis, 'We're all black'. The newspaper headline the following morning was: 'The All Blacks have arrived!' According to another account, the name originated during the same tour when a reporter dubbed the players 'all backs', which was subsequently misprinted. If their strip clashes with that of an opposing team the All Blacks reluctantly resort to an alternative in the form of white shirts and black shorts. This has happened when they have played against the dark colours of Scotland and in seven-a-side competitions.

All Bran. The proprietary name of a breakfast cereal invented in the 1920s by John L. Kellogg, son of W.K. Kellogg (1860–1951), founder of the Kellogg Company. The cereal arose as a convenient way of using up the bran left over from other products. It has long been discreetly promoted for its laxative properties, using euphemistic slogans such as 'Join the "regulars" with Kellogg's All-Bran'.

All dressed up and nowhere to go. Ready for action but not required. The source of the line is the title of a song by Silvio Hein and Benjamin Burt, 'When You're All Dressed Up and No Place to Go'. The song was part of Raymond Hitchcock's musical *The Beauty Shop*, first staged at the Astor Theatre on Broadway in 1913 and produced in London in 1916. 'No place', rather than 'nowhere', betrays the song's US origin.

Allen charge. In US law a charge or instruction to a hung jury in which the judge urges dissenting jurors to reconsider their views out of deference to the majority and at the same time to do their best to reach a verdict. The reference is to the case of Allen v. United States (1897) in which the charge was first used. The term itself dates from the 1950s.

Allergy. Properly a medical term for a damaging immune response by the body to a substance to which it has become hypersensitive. Foods such as eggs, shellfish and nuts cause allergies in some people as often do 'fluffy' substances such as pollen, fur or dust. The word has come to be used colloquially to denote an antipathy to something, and the corresponding adjective 'allergic' is frequently found in this role, as: 'He's allergic to work'. The term itself dates from the

early 20th century and arose from German *Allergie*, in turn from Greek *allos*, 'different', and *ergon*, 'action'. It was not until about the 1950s, however, that the word became generally familiar in English.

Alley cat. A cat that lives wild in a town. The term is of US origin so an alley here approximates to an English mews. The expression became current in the 1920s for a promiscuous woman. An alley cat scrounges for food as a prostitute touts for clients.

Alleyn, Roderick. The Old Etonian policeman who is the central character in over 30 crime novels by the New Zealand writer Ngaio Marsh (1899–1982), beginning with *A Man Lay Dead* (1934). He ages realistically throughout the series, and in *Last Ditch* (1977) his son Ricky takes over the role of detective.

All Gas and Gaiters. A television SITCOM broadcast in five series between 1967 and 1971 and making gentle fun of the church. The plot centres on the ecclesiastical rivalry at St Oggs cathedral with Derek Nimmo in the key role as a naive and accident-prone cleric. The title, expressing pomposity, comes from Dickens. Gaiters are part of a bishop's traditional costume.

All girls together. Women on terms of close friendship with one another, especially when engaged in a collective enterprise that for each individually would seem unlikely.

All God's Chillun Got Wings. A play (1924) by the US playwright Eugene O'Neill (1888–1953) about the marriage of a black man and a white woman. The play provoked a violent reaction when it first presented in New York, with one outraged newspaper carrying the headline: 'White Actress Kisses Negro's Hand.' The title refers to the truth that all humans are equal in God's eyes, no matter what their colour.

Alliance. The name used by the Liberal Party and the Social Democrats when campaigning together from 1983 until the two merged in 1988 as the LIBERAL DEMOCRATS.

All mouth and trousers. Boastful and blustering; all talk and no action. A phrase commonly used by women about men, who may be loud-mouthed and who wear the male garment mentioned.

All My Sons. A play (1947) by the US playwright Arthur Miller (b.1915) about an aircraft manufacturer, Joe Keller, whose family life falls apart after revelations that his company knowingly allowed faulty cylinder heads to be fitted to P-40 fighters, leading to the deaths of 21 pilots in the US Air Force. One of Keller's two sons has already committed suicide from shame at his father's treachery, but the 'sons' of the title is understood to refer more widely to all the young pilots who have died.

Allnutt, Charlie. The hero of C.S. Forester's gripping novel *The* AFRICAN QUEEN (1935). He is a good-for-nothing riverboat engineer in Africa at the outbreak of the First World War and is persuaded by Rose Sayer, a missionary's wife, to join combat. They turn their leaky old craft, the *African Queen*, into a 'torpedo' and finally ram and sink a German gunboat. The role of Allnutt in the film of the book (1951) was memorably played by Humphrey Bogart.

All one's Christmases have come at once. One has been specially lucky or unusually favoured. Normally 'Christmas comes but once a year' and its pleasures are thus infrequent. *See also* CHRISTMAS HAS COME EARLY.

> I have recently found the man of my dreams. ... I'm in orbit and feel as if all my Christmases have come at once.
>
> TARA PALMER-TOMKINSON in *Sunday Times* (8 August 1999)

All Passion Spent. A novel (1931) by Vita Sackville-West (1892–1962). Dedicated to her two sons 'Benedict and Nigel, who are young, the story of people who are old', it is a study of ageing and of independence in old age. The title comes from *Samson Agonistes* (1671) by John Milton:

> His servants he, with new acquist
> Of true experience from this great event,
> With peace and consolation hath dismissed,
> And calm of mind, all passion spent.

All Quiet on the Western Front. A novel (1929; in German as *Im Westen Nichts Neues*, 1929) of the First World War by Erich Maria Remarque (1898–1970). Brutally realistic and written in the first person, it is prefaced with a statement: 'This book is to be neither an accusation nor a confession, and least of all an adventure, for death is not an adventure to those who stand face to face with it. It will try simply to tell of a generation of men who, even though they may have escaped its shells, were destroyed by the war.' In 1933 the book was publicly burned by the Nazis as being 'defeatist', and Remarque was deprived of his citizenship. The title is ironic. It refers to the fact that a whole generation of his countrymen was destroyed while newspapers reported that there was 'no news in the west'. The film version (1930), directed by Lewis Milestone and starring Lew Ayres, was a landmark of America cinema.

All-singing, all-dancing. Possessing a wealth of desirable attributes or features, like an elaborate musical show. The term came to be particularly associated with technical gadgetry. Its origin may ultimately lie in a series of posters produced in the latter half of the 1920s to promote the new 'talking' cinema. One such poster advertised the first HOLLYWOOD musical film *Broadway Melody* (1929) with the words 'All talking All singing All dancing'.

> That's fashion at the end of the 1990s: an all-singing, all-dancing spectacular for shifting luggage and belts. *The Times* (5 October 1999)

All Souls' Parish Magazine. *The Times* was so nicknamed during the editorship (1923–41) of G.G. Dawson, fellow of All Souls, Oxford. He and some of his associates, who were also fellows of the college, frequently met there for discussions.

All systems go. Everything is ready for immediate action. The catchphrase was popularized in the 1960s by broadcast commentaries of the launches of US spacecraft. 'Go' does not mean 'depart' but 'correctly functioning'.

All that jazz. All that sort of thing; and so on. A phrase usually following a list of examples. 'Jazz' here has a tone of disparagement.

> I offers you this handkerchief, now set
> your left foot by my right foot,
> shoulder to shoulder, all that jazz,
> arm in arm, by the beautiful sea.
> JOHN BERRYMAN: *The Dream Songs*, 'Dream Song 76' (1969)

All the President's Men. A film (1976) about the uncovering of the WATERGATE scandal, based on a book (1974) of the same title by the *Washington Post* journalists Bob Woodward and Carl Bernstein (played respectively by Robert Redford and Dustin Hoffman). Directed by Alan J. Pakula, the film tends to glorify the role played by investigative journalists in bringing President Nixon to book and marginalizes the role of collective action on the part of government agencies and the judiciary. Its title hints misleadingly that the whole of government ('*all* the president's men') were implicated in wrongdoing. *See also* DEEP THROAT.

All You Need is Love. A musically undistinguished song by the BEATLES, credited to John Lennon and Paul

McCartney, and written specifically for a television programme entitled 'Our World', which linked 24 countries by global satellite in June 1967. Released as a single the following month (it reached number one in the charts in both the UK and America), its message of sing-along idealism and optimism made it an appropriate anthem for the SUMMER OF LOVE. Of passing interest are the musical 'quotations' contained in the song, from 'La Marseillaise' (the French national anthem), a keyboard piece by J.S. Bach, 'Greensleeves' and Glenn Miller's 'In the Mood'.

> There's nothing you can do that can't be done
> Nothing you can sing that can't be sung
> Nothing you can say but you can learn how to play
> the game
> It's easy.

Ally Pally. The nickname of Alexandra Palace in Muswell Hill, London, as the original headquarters of BBC television. The first transmission was on 26 August 1936 as *Here's Looking at You*, a variety show introduced by Leslie Mitchell, and the nickname followed soon after.

Almeida Theatre. The 300-seat London theatre of this name opened in Upper Street, Islington, in 1981 in the restored Islington Literary and Scientific Institute, built in 1837 and later a Salvation Army hostel. The theatre takes its name from Almeida Street, a short street off Upper Street here whose own name commemorates the Battle of Almeida (1811) in the Peninsular War. The theatre has attracted leading British and overseas players, such as Diana Rigg, Juliette Binoche and Kevin Spacey, but earns only 40 per cent of its required income through the box office.

Aloha State. A nickname for Hawaii, which became the 50th state of the United States of America in 1959. 'Aloha' is a Hawaiian word meaning 'love', used to express affection or kind wishes as a greeting or farewell. An 'aloha party' is thus one held on the occasion of an arrival or departure, while an 'aloha shirt' is a loose and brightly coloured sports shirt, often worn by American tourists or holidaymakers.

Along for the ride. To be, come or go along for the ride is to do so for pleasure or interest rather than active participation. The image is that of a passive passenger. The expression is of US origin; it dates from the 1950s.

Alphabet soup. A type of clear soup containing pasta in the shape of letters. In the figurative sense alphabet soup is an incomprehensible or confusing language,

especially when containing numerous abbreviations or symbols. *See also* ANIMAL CRACKERS.

Also-ran. An inferior or mediocre person or thing. Properly an 'also-ran' is a horse in a race that does not get a 'place', i.e. come second, third or fourth. The term gained its figurative sense in the 1920s.

> [Artists] Peter Gidal and Tony Sinden are Also-Rans With Film Cameras. Conrad Atkinson and Victor Burgin are Also-Rans Who Spend Much of Their Time Abroad Because There Is Nothing for Them Here. Most of the rest belong under the huge subsection: Also-Rans Who Teach.
> *Sunday Times* (13 February 2000)

Altamont. More fully Altamont Speedway, the site near San Francisco in California of a nightmarish concert by the ROLLING STONES in December 1969, regarded by some aficionados of popular culture (together with the MANSON MURDERS of the same year) as sounding a death-knell for the carefree optimism of the 1960s. The free concert, staged as a kind of second WOODSTOCK, turned to tragedy when three people died. The demise of one of the victims, stabbed to death by Hell's Angels acting as 'security guards' after he had aimed a gun at Mick Jagger as he sang SYMPATHY FOR THE DEVIL, was captured on camera. The concert can be seen in the film *Gimme Shelter* (1970).

Alte, Der (German, 'The Old One'). A nickname for Konrad Adenauer (1876–1967), Christian Democrat chancellor of West Germany, who was 73 years old when he took office in 1949 and who served for a further 14 years.

Alternative. A word fairly consistently in vogue from the late 1960s to express some cultural or other value that differs from the norm. It had its roots in the 'alternative society', associated with the world of the HIPPIES, which was dubbed 'counter-culture' by academics but 'underground' by the media. 'Alternative medicine' also appeared at this time, favouring such procedures and remedies as homeopathy and ACUPUNCTURE and today having its devotees among those who have become disillusioned with traditional medicine. The early 1970s saw the emergence of 'alternative technology' in a bid to conserve natural resources and damage to the environment. Favoured renewable energy sources in this field were wind and solar power.

The 1980s saw the evolution of both 'alternative

comedy' and 'alternative therapy'. The former, eschewing conventional comedy in favour of black or surreal humour, has been popularized on television by such performers as Dawn French and Jennifer Saunders or Vic Reeves and Bob Mortimer. Alternative therapy, a progression of alternative medicine, involves special psychiatric (or quasi-psychiatric) techniques, such as REBIRTHING, group counselling and other practices based on simplified Freudian theories and applications.

> But what of the 'alternative society' of the festivals, which are perhaps the most massive social spin-offs of modern pop?
>
> RICHARD MABEY in *Anatomy of Pop* (1970)

Altmark. In the Royal Navy an opprobrious synonym for a ship or an establishment with a reputation for very strict discipline. It derives from a famous naval exploit of February 1940, when Captain (later Admiral of the Fleet) Philip Vian, commanding the destroyer HMS *Cossack*, entered Norwegian territorial waters to effect the release of 299 British prisoners of war from the German supply ship *Altmark*, which had taken refuge in Jossingfjord.

Amadeus Quartet. One of Britain's best known string quartets in the years after the Second World War. Three of its members, Norbert Brainin, Siegmund Nissel and Peter Schidlof, were teenage refugees from Vienna in 1938 and first met in an Isle of Man internment camp in the early years of the war. The quartet was formed in 1947 with Martin Lovett as the fourth member, and it continued until Schidlof's death in 1987, when the remaining three created the Amadeus Ensemble. Its name was a tribute to Wolfgang Amadeus Mozart, whose first name furnished 'the Wolf Gang' as an affectionate nickname for the four. *See also* STRING QUARTETS.

Ambassadors Theatre. This London theatre near St Martin's Lane opened on 5 June 1913 and after an inauspicious start became famous for the COCHRAN REVUES, staged here from 1914. Its name appears to be purely prestigious, although the ambassadorial crests on the building could perhaps account for it.

Ambit. A magazine founded in 1959 by Martin Bax with the aim of breathing fresh air into British poetry. It was at first flamboyant and experimental, and the erotic and even scatological tone of some of its writing and illustrations provoked a protest from the poet Roy Fuller, who said that its Arts Council subsidy should be withdrawn on the grounds that it was 'often pornographic, occasionally obscene'. It subsequently gained the respect of many for the high quality of its prose writing and especially for its reviews.

Ambling Alp. A nickname of the Italian-born American champion heavyweight boxer Primo Carnera (1906–67), alluding to his style and country of origin.

America, Captain. *See* CAPTAIN AMERICA.

American Buffalo. A play (1975) by David Mamet (b.1947) about the bungled attempts of three small-time crooks to steal a coin collection. The title of the play, which effectively lampoons modern capitalism, refers to an old US buffalo-head nickel that one of them produces in the second act, a symbol of their preoccupation with financial gains. Mamet wrote the screenplay for the film version (1996), which starred Dustin Hoffman, Dennis Franz and Sean Nelson.

American Caesar. A nickname for the US general Douglas MacArthur (1880–1964), commander of the Southwest Pacific Area Theatre in the Second World War, supreme allied commander in occupied Japan and then commander of the US and United Nations forces during the opening months of the Korean War (1950–53). The allusion was largely to his exaggerated accounts of his own accomplishments, on the lines of those of Julius Caesar ('I came, I saw, I conquered').

American dream. The concept that the US social, economic and political system makes success possible for every American. The expression appears to have been coined by the American historian James T. Adams in *The Epic of America* (1931). It was subsequently popularized by the titles of such works as Edward Albee's play *The American Dream* (1961) and Norman Mailer's novel *An American Dream* (1965).

> In the beginning was the American Dream, and the American Dream said: you can have anything your heart desires. It's yours by right. Guess what? You can't. It isn't.
>
> ERICA WAGNER in *The Times* (11 March 1999)

American Express. The Amex credit card, as it is often known, was first issued in 1956 by the American Express Company, founded in 1850 as a company specializing in the express transportation of goods, valuables and specie between New York and Buffalo. Its first president and secretary were, respectively, Henry Wells (1805–75) and William G. Fargo (1818–81), later of Wells Fargo fame. *See also* ADVERTISING SLOGANS OF THE 20TH CENTURY.

American Gothic. Perhaps the most reproduced (and most parodied) American work of art of the 20th century was painted by Grant Wood (1891–1942) in 1930. Largely self-taught, Wood worked mainly in his native Iowa. The painting purports to be a portrait of a stern farmer-preacher and his daughter, the former holding a pitchfork, while behind is their house, with a simple Gothic window set in the gable end. Actually, Wood used his sister, Nan, and his dentist, B.H. McKeeby, as models for the painting. The title has been taken as satirical, although Wood's avowed intention was to reflect the values of provincial American life. The hard, cold style reflects the influence of north European Renaissance paint-ing that Wood absorbed during a visit to Munich in 1928.

American Graffiti. An Oscar-winning teenage rites-of-passage film comedy (1973) directed by George Lucas and starring Richard Dreyfuss. It concerns the activities of a group of teenagers in a small American town in the early 1960s and was based on the director's own experiences of growing up in Modesto, in California's Central Valley. It features an array of nostalgic pop hits of the 1960s, the rights for which constituted a significant proportion of the film's entire budget.

American in Paris, An. A classic musical film (1951) that ranks among the most popular MGM productions of the golden age of the American musical. Directed by Vincente Minnelli, it stars Gene Kelly as a frustrated artist (thereby providing an excuse for lots of backdrops based on famous French paintings) and Leslie Caron. The film was based on the tone poem 'An American in Paris' (1928) by George Gershwin, and Ira Gershwin allowed the piece's title to be used for the film provided that his brother provided all the music for the movie. The title echoes the long-established adage 'Good Americans, when they die, go to Paris', credited by Oliver Wendell Holmes to Thomas Appleton (1812–84). It was this saying that prompted Oscar Wilde in *A Woman of No Importance* (1893) to suggest that if good Americans went to Paris when they died, then bad Americans undoubtedly went to America. Ironically, the film was shot in the United States against specially built sets.

American Pie. The classic pop song of this name by Don McLean (b.1945), released in 1971 as a double-sided single lasting 8½ minutes, was a tribute to Buddy Holly (1936–59) and is full of allusions to other performers. The song is, in essence, a chronological account of American youth through the 1960s, with the emphasis on the latter years of the decade. Of the individual references, 'the Jester' is Bob Dylan; 'the King' is Elvis Presley; 'the Quartet' are the BEATLES; 'Jack Flash' is Mick Jagger of the ROLLING STONES; 'a girl who sang the blues' is Janis Joplin; and 'the Father, Son and Holy Ghost' are both the three singers who died on Holly's plane (Holly himself, Richie Valens and J.P. Richardson, the 'Big Bopper') and the three most prominent assassination victims of the 1960s, Martin Luther King, Robert Kennedy and John F. Kennedy (*see* KENNEDY CURSE). The song's non-musical allusions are less straightforward, although 'The players tried to take the field,/The marching band refused to yield' probably refers to the riots of 1968 at the Democrats' Chicago convention, while 'there we were all in one place' is almost certainly a reference to WOODSTOCK.

> So, bye, bye, Miss American Pie,
> Drove my Chevy to the levee but the levee was dry.
> Them good old boys was drinkin' whiskey and rye
> Singin' 'This'll be the day that I die.'
> DON MCLEAN: 'American Pie' (song) (1971)

American Psycho. A deeply controversial novel (1991) by Bret Easton Ellis (b.1964), recounting the murderous activities of Patrick Bateman, a 26-year-old Manhattan broker by day and psychopathic YUPPIE serial killer by night. The novel's graphic portrayal of sadistic violence against women (including torture, flaying and cannibalism) led to intense criticism from women's groups, but others chose to see the novel as a satire on the materialistic excesses of the 1980s. The novel was rejected by Simon and Schuster when they saw the manuscript, but eventually published by Vintage. A film version, starring Christian Bale as Bateman, was released in 2000.

American Tragedy, An. A novel (1925) by Theodore Dreiser (1871–1945), written as an argument that society is at fault for allowing the environment of the slums to breed a criminal instinct that is born of material ambition. The actual event on which the novel is based is one of 16 cases that Dreiser studied of a young man murdering his pregnant girlfriend in order to marry a rich girl, tragic circumstances that he felt were peculiarly American. A film version (1931), directed by Josef von Sternberg, is a worthy adaptation of the original; a remake, *A Place in the Sun* (1951), starring Montgomery Clift and Elizabeth Taylor, is less compelling.

Amityville Horror. *See under* FAKES.

Amnesty International. The organization of this name was founded in 1961 when a British lawyer, Peter Benenson, wrote an article in the *Observer* announcing the launch of an 'Appeal for Amnesty', the aim being to campaign for the release of political prisoners, meaning those imprisoned for their beliefs who had not used or advocated violence. It was the first human rights group systematically to catalogue human rights abuses worldwide, and in the 1980s it became a household name through its staging of concert tours with the participation, and implied endorsement, of celebrity performers. It publishes an annual *Report on Torture and Political Persecution Around the World* and has refined its definition of human rights over the years to include social issues, such as rape and the persecution of homosexuals. *See also* PRISONER OF CONSCIENCE.

Amos 'n' Andy. A popular US radio programme performed by two blackface clowns five nights a week during the late 1920s and early 1930s and continuing on both television and radio until 1958. Amos was eager and industrious, while Andy was a doltish slacker. In the original radio version the two were played respectively by Freeman S. Gosden and Charles V. Correll.

> Announcer: Amos and Andy, two lifelong buddies, from Dixie, have spent most of their life on a farm just outside of Atlanta, Georgia. Amos is a hard-working little fellow who tries to do everything he can to help others and to make himself progress, while his friend Andy is not especially fond of hard work and often has Amos to assist him in his own duties. As the curtain goes up we find the boys returning to the farmhouse with a bucket of milk.
>
> WMAQ RADIO: *Amos 'n' Andy* (first episode) (19 March 1928)

Amritsar massacre. An incident on 13 April 1919 (sometimes also referred to as the Jallianwallah Bagh massacre) in which 379 people died after British troops opened fire on unarmed nationalist demonstrators in the city of Amritsar in the Punjab, India. A further 1200 were injured. The British commander, Brigadier General Reginald Dyer (1864–1927), was condemned for his actions by a subsequent commission of inquiry. The incident bolstered the nationalist cause in India.

Amstrad. The home computers of this name evolved from the company originally called A.M.S. Trading set up in 1968 by the Cockney entrepreneur Alan M. Sugar (b.1947), who began his business by selling car aerials from the back of a van. By 1980 he was dealing in audio and television goods, always adhering to a 'no frills' policy to keep down costs, and in 1985 he achieved a major breakthrough when he launched a word processor for the absurdly low price of £399. The following year he shook the electronics market again when he produced a home computer for a third of the price of that marketed by IBM. The hugely successful Amstrad PC1512, launched in 1986, made IBM standard computing, previously restricted to the US market, accessible to the European home user for the first time. Amstrad enthusiasts like to point out that the registered name is an anagram of 'smart ad'.

Amtorg. A Soviet cover organization for a spy operation run in the United States in the interwar years. Its origins date from 1921 when the US businessman Armand Hammer (1899–1990) travelled to Moscow with a letter of introduction to LENIN. Lenin eased Hammer into what would become a long and profitable business arrangement with the Soviet Union, and in 1924 this led to the official establishment of Amtorg as a joint Soviet-American trading organization, its name a dual acronym for *American Trading Organization* and Russian *amerikansky torg*, 'American trade'. It remained active for many years after the United States recognized the Soviet regime in 1933. *See also* ARCOS AFFAIR.

Amtrak. The US public corporation of this name, officially the National Railroad Passenger Corporation, was set up in 1970 to run the essential intercity rail services, using federal funds, that private enterprise was unable to provide. It began to run its train services in May 1971. The name is a shortening of 'American Track'.

Anabolic steroids. The drugs so designated, available from the 1960s, have an anabolic (protein-building) effect similar to testosterone and other male sex hormones. They are used in medicine to build tissue, promote muscle recovery following injury and help strengthen bones, but they have been widely abused by athletes, sports players and others wishing to improve their strength and stamina, a controversial practice that has serious risks to health.

Anal-retentive. A term from psychoanalytical jargon adopted generally to apply to someone who is unnaturally tidy or fussy. Properly it applies to a person with a fixation for excessive orderliness and parsimony, explained as having become thus as the result of fixation at the anal stage of development, i.e. the period lasting from about the age of 18 months to three years when a child undergoes toilet training.

> My mother said, 'You're an anal retentive, aren't you?' and my father said, 'You're tight-fisted, and you've always got your perfectly groomed head in a book.'
>
> SUE TOWNSEND: *The Growing Pains of Adrian Mole* (1984)

Anarchy in the UK. *See* NEVER MIND THE BOLLOCKS, HERE'S THE SEX PISTOLS.

Anastasia. The youngest daughter (1901–18) of the last tsar of Russia, Nicholas II. She is thought to have been executed along with the rest of her family after the revolution by the BOLSHEVIKS, but over the years several women claimed to be the grand duchess, saying that they had escaped from Russia and laying claim to the Romanov fortune held in Swiss banks. One of the most notable claimants was one Anna Anderson (possibly a Polish woman called Franziska Schanzkowski), whose claim was finally rejected by a West German court in 1970. She died in 1984. The idea that Anastasia might have survived provides the theme of the US film *Anastasia* (1956), for which Ingrid Bergman won an Oscar. The film was based on a French play (1954) by Marcelle Maurette. This work's disregard for history is as nothing compared with that of the 1997 full-length cartoon of the same name.

Anatomist, The. A play (1931) by the Scottish playwright James Bridie (pen-name of Osborne Henry Mavor; 1888–1951) about the activities of the Scottish bodysnatchers William Burke and James Hare in the 1820s. The pair murdered their victims in order to provide fresh cadavers for the Edinburgh anatomist Sir Robert Knox (1791–1862), who chose not to inquire too closely into the origins of their specimens. Knox escaped official punishment, but he eventually left Edinburgh and the notoriety that had attached to his name and took up a position at the London Cancer Hospital.

ANC. The African National Congress, one of the leading political parties in South Africa. The ANC was founded in 1912 (by Gandhi among others) as the South African Native National Congress. The name echoed that of the Indian National Congress, founded in 1885. When apartheid was introduced in 1948 the ANC became one of its leading opponents, and the organization was banned in 1960. At this point it adopted a policy of armed resistance, and its leaders were either put in jail (as happened to Nelson Mandela) or were obliged to direct its activities from exile (as did Oliver Tambo). On his release from prison in 1990 Mandela took over the presidency of the just-legalized ANC from Tambo. In 1994 the ANC won South Africa's first fully democratic elections, and Mandela became president on 10 May 1994 until he retired in 1999.

Ancient monument. A building or site of special architectural, historical or archaeological interest that is protected by Act of Parliament from damage or destruction. In England such monuments are cared for by English Heritage, in Scotland by Historic Scotland, and in Wales by Cadw. There are around 30,000 scheduled sites in England alone, plus a further 450,000 or so listed buildings. It is forbidden by law to demolish, extend or alter the character of the latter without prior consent from the local planning authority, although in some cases permission may be given retrospectively.

Anderson shelter. The small prefabricated air-raid shelter became a familiar sight in many gardens during the Second World War. It took the form of a curved steel hut that was partly buried in the ground and covered with 60–90cm (2–3ft) of earth to protect the occupants against explosions. The shelters were the invention of a Scottish engineer, William Paterson, and took their name from Sir John Anderson (1882–1958), who was home secretary and minister for home security in the opening years of the war. *See also* MORRISON SHELTER.

And how! A general exclamation of agreement, made at the end of another's statement, as: 'I really enjoyed that!' 'Me too! And how!' The phrase dates from the 1920s and echoes German *und wie!*

And Quiet Flows the Don. The English title (1934) of a two-part translation of the four-volume work, *Tikhy Don* ('The Quiet Don', 1928–40), by the Russian author Mikhail Sholokhov (1905–84). The second part was *The Don Flows Home to the Sea* (1940), published in the United States as *Seeds of Tomorrow* (1935) and *Harvest on the Don* (1960). The River Don flows through central Russia into the Black Sea. The complete work covers the years 1912–22 and reflects with objectivity the effect during peace and war of the Russian Revolution on the Cossack communities in the region. Sholokhov received the NOBEL PRIZE for literature in 1965, despite charges of plagiarism levelled by, among others, Alexander Solzhenitsyn.

Andrews, Archie. The cheeky schoolboy dummy who appeared on radio from 1944 to 1960. Despite the apparent contradiction of a ventriloquist's dummy that cannot be seen, the series of programmes in which he featured proved extremely popular, the most memorable being *Educating Archie*. He was the creation of Ted Kavanagh, who gave him his name, and his operator was Peter Brough (1916–99). Many subsequently famous comedians and singers played opposite Archie Andrews, including Beryl Reid as his girlfriend.

Andromeda strain. A term for any strain of bacteria, viruses or other micro-organisms whose accidental release from a laboratory could have catastrophic effects because of its unknown biochemical composition. The term derives from *The Andromeda Strain* (1969), a SCIENCE FICTION novel by the US writer Michael Crichton (b.1942), in which an unknown type of bacteria, picked up in outer space, accidentally escapes from a returning space probe, killing a town's inhabitants and threatening to contaminate the world. A film (1970) based on the novel and directed by Robert Wise made a successful and suspenseful thriller.

And that's official. A journalistic tag to give authority to newly published facts or information, as: 'Hospital waiting lists are at an all-time high. And that's official.'

Andy Capp. *See* CAPP, ANDY.

Andy Pandy. A popular puppet, in a blue and white striped suit and matching floppy hat, which first appeared in the 1950s on the children's television programme WATCH WITH MOTHER. He was alone at first, but was later joined by a teddy bear and a rag doll called Looby Loo, with whom he shared a basket. Only 26 programmes were made, but they were repeated until the 1970s.

Angel. In the Second World War RAF slang a height of 300m (1000ft), reasonably close to heaven. For obvious reasons the word is usually found in the plural, as in the title of the film *Angels One Five* (1952) (i.e. 15,000ft) about the BATTLE OF BRITAIN.

Angel in the house. A mainly ironic term for a woman who is completely devoted to her husband. It comes from the title of Coventry Patmore's *The Angel in the House* (1854–63), a sequence of poems in praise of married love, and was introduced by Virginia Woolf in the 1930s.

> You who come of a younger and happier generation may not have heard of her – you may not know what I mean by the Angel in the House. I will describe her as shortly as I can. She was intensely sympathetic. She was immensely charming. She was utterly unselfish. She excelled in the difficult arts of family life. She sacrificed herself daily. If there was a chicken, she took the leg; if there was a draught she sat in it – in short she was so constituted that she never had a mind or a wish of her own, but preferred to sympathize always with the minds and wishes of others.
> VIRGINIA WOOLF (1931) in MICHÈLE BARRETT: *Virginia Woolf: Women & Writing* (1979)

Angel of Death (German, *Todesengel*). The nickname of Joseph Mengele (1911–79), the Nazi doctor who worked at AUSCHWITZ between 1943 and 1945. His 'racial experiments', especially involving twins, involved the most hideous cruelty. After the war he lived underground and then escaped to South America around 1949, living in Uruguay, Paraguay and Brazil under assumed identities. In 1985 an international team of forensic experts determined that the body of a man who had drowned in Brazil in 1979 was in fact Mengele.

Angel of the North. A huge sculpture of an angel with outstretched wings erected on a hillside near Gateshead in the northeast of England in 1998. It proclaims the steel and manufacturing ambition of the region and also denotes the boundary of a different country, the lands of the Venerable Bede (*c*.673–735) and St Columba (*c*.521–597) on the one hand and the largest shopping complex in Britain on the other. Its creator was Antony Gormley (b.1950).

Angels. A SOAP OPERA screened from 1975 to 1983 and following the fortunes of six student nurses at the (fictitious) St Angela's Hospital, London. It was noted for its quasi-documentary style and proved a training ground for its young actresses, including Pauline Quirke of BIRDS OF A FEATHER and Kathryn Apanowicz and Shirley Cheriton of EASTENDERS.

Angels of Mons. The 3rd and 4th Divisions of the OLD CONTEMPTIBLES under the command of General H.L. Smith-Dorrien were hard pressed in their retreat from Mons (26–27 August 1914). On 29 September that year the *London Evening News* published Arthur Machen's fantasy story *The Bowmen* crediting their preservation to St George and the angels, who, clad in white, held back the might of the German First Army by wielding longbows and raining arrows on the enemy. For some, the imaginary became a reality, and the 'Angels of Mons' became a legendary phrase.

Anglepoise. The proprietary name of a popular and innovative desk lamp, designed by George Carwardine, a motor engineer, and launched in 1933. The design used hinges that mimicked the action of a human arm, making the lamp flexible and balanced and able to hold a pose at any angle.

Anglo-Saxon Attitudes. A novel (1956) by Angus Wilson (1913–91), whose central theme is an archaeological fraud. It is also a partly satirical, partly realistic dissection of attitudes that the author sees as being prevalent among a particular group within middle-class society in England. The title comes from a remark made by the King to Alice in Lewis Carroll's *Through the Looking-Glass* (1872) as the Messenger approaches 'skipping up and down, and wriggling like an eel, with his great hands spread out like fans on each side': 'He's an Anglo-Saxon Messenger – and those are Anglo-Saxon attitudes.'

Angry Brigade. An urban guerrilla organization responsible for various acts of terrorism in the late 1960s and early 1970s. Some of their number were jailed following a bomb attack on the home of Robert Carr, the employment secretary, in January 1971, and they earlier claimed responsibility for machine-gunning the Spanish embassy in London and for planting bombs near a BBC van during the MISS WORLD contest. Their name was a loose rendering of French *Les Enragés*, a radical group of *sans-culottes* at the time of the French Revolution.

Angry Penguins. An Australian avant-garde quarterly magazine devoted to art and literature. It was first published in Adelaide in 1940 by the poet and critic Max Harris (1921–96), who named it after a line in one of his own poems. In 1944 it was the subject of an embarrassing hoax when it devoted its autumn issue to the poems of the non-existent 'Ern Malley', whose works were concocted by two traditional poets who thought the journal pretentious and wanted to test the critical judgement of its editors. The sources from which they drew quotations included an army report on mosquito control. The journal never really recovered from the adverse publicity and closed in 1946.

Angry Young Man. A name applied to certain modern British writers, and in particular to John Osborne (1929–94), whose play LOOK BACK IN ANGER (first performed 1956) prompted the reporter George Fearon to apply the term to him, although it had already occurred in 1951 as the title of a book by the Irish writer Leslie Paul. Those so dubbed were typically young and of provincial lower-middle class or working-class origin, and they gained notoriety for their satirical treatment and criticism of the ESTABLISHMENT, with its false or outmoded social, moral, political and intellectual values. The name is also sometimes applied to some American writers of protest. *See also* LUCKY JIM.

Anik. The name of one of a number of communications satellites launched by Canada in the 1970s to provide television, radio and telephone services to the country. The word is Inuit (Eskimo) for 'brother' and was proposed by a Montreal girl in a nationwide competition.

Animal crackers. Small, semi-sweet biscuits in the shape of animals, popular among American children. The confection was popularized outside the United States by Ray Henderson and Ted Koehler's song 'Animal crackers in my soup', sung with saccharine sentiment by seven-year-old Shirley Temple in the film *Curly Top* (1935). *See also* ALPHABET SOUP.

Animal Crackers. A film (1930), based on the MARX BROTHERS' stage show of the same title, in which the brothers have fun at the expense of American high society. Featuring Groucho as Captain Spaulding the explorer, highlights of the movie include some classic insults aimed at the perpetually nonplussed Margaret Dumont.

> You're the most beautiful woman I've ever seen, which doesn't say much for you.
> GROUCHO MARX: Animal Crackers

Animal Farm. A satire in fable form by George ORWELL, published in 1945 and depicting a totalitarian regime like that of Russia under STALIN. The story describes how the pigs, by cunning, treachery and ruthlessness, come to dominate the more honest, gullible and hardworking animals. Their ultimate slogan is: 'All animals are equal, but some animals are more equal than others.' The leader of the pigs is Napoleon, representing Stalin. *See also* FIRST LINES OF NOVELS.

Animated Meringue. A media nickname for Barbara Cartland (1901–2000), prolific writer of light romantic fiction and champion of healthy eating. The name alludes to her fondness for wearing pink, her 'chalky' style of writing, and specifically her fondness for driving around in a pink and white ROLLS-ROYCE. She was first so dubbed by the journalist Arthur Marshall (1910–89).

Animatronics. The technique of constructing lifelike models of humans or animals for use in films or other entertainment. The term originated in the 1970s as a shortening of animated electronics.

> To me, the kids looked like animatronics figures, robots from a ride at Disneyland.
>
> ARMISTEAD MAUPIN: *Maybe the Moon*, ch v (1992)

Anime. A genre of Japanese film and television animation, also known as Japanimation. It typically has a SCIENCE FICTION theme and sometimes includes violent or explicitly sexual material. It is usually adapted from popular MANGA comic books and in the 1990s accounted for one of the fastest growing US video markets. Its influence is not confined to the realm of pornography and is evident in the Disney film *The Lion King* (1994). The word is pronounced 'animay'.

Annabel's. A famous nightclub in Berkeley Square, London. It was opened in 1963 by Mark Birley and named after his wife, Lady Annabel Tempest-Vane-Stewart (b.1934), an Anglo-Irish heiress who in 1978 married the millionaire Sir James Goldsmith (1933–1997). Its heyday was in the 1970s, when Lady Annabel persuaded many of her well-connected friends to become members.

Anna of the Five Towns. A regional novel (1902) by Arnold Bennett (1867–1931), set within the five towns of the Staffordshire Potteries where he was born. Anna is the epitome of altruism, to the extent that she even allows herself to be married to a man she does not love. The 'five towns' themselves are Bursley (representing real-life Burslem), where Anna lives, Turnhill (Tunstall), Hanbridge (Hanley, where Bennett himself was born), Knype (Stoke-on-Trent) and Longshaw (Longton).

Anne of Green Gables. The young red-haired heroine of the novel of this name (1908) by the Canadian children's author L.M. Montgomery (1874–1942). Her full name is Anne Shirley and she is taken on by an elderly couple, making herself useful on their farm. She is somewhat precocious and outspoken, but she is winning and winsome and was described by Mark Twain as 'the dearest and most loveable child in fiction since the immortal Alice'. Her adventures have been adopted for stage, film and television, and the US child film actress Dawn Paris (1918–93) legally adopted her name after playing her in *Anne of Green Gables* (1934).

Annie Get Your Gun. A musical comedy (1946) with a score by Irving Berlin (1888–1989) about the sharpshooter Annie Oakley (1860–1926), one of the stars of Buffalo Bill's Wild West Show. The show contains many memorable numbers, including 'There's no Business Like Show Business' and 'The Girl that I Marry', but although Oakley was a real person, the plot of the musical is largely fictional. In US theatrical slang an 'Annie Oakley' became a nickname for a complimentary ticket, the punched appearance of these being reminiscent of the playing cards that the sharpshooter used to pepper with bullet-holes during her act.

Annie Hall. A film comedy (1977) portraying the angst of modern Manhattan residents. Written by, directed by and starring Woody Allen (b.1935), it featured Diane Keaton as the eponymous Annie Hall, the object of Allen's desire both on and off screen (and whose outfits in the film influenced a generation). The screenplay included some of Allen's best known and most often repeated one-liners, not least his reflections on sex ('It was the most fun I ever had without laughing') and masturbation ('Don't knock it, it's sex with someone you love').

Ann Summers party. A women's social gathering held in the home in which sex aids, 'sensual lingerie', 'naughty novelties' and similar products of the named US company are sold.

> The first couple to share their problems are Maggie, an Ann Summers party organizer and saleswoman, and Ian, her obsessively tidy (and third) husband.
>
> *The Times* (11 October 1999)

Annus horribilis (Latin, 'horrible year'). Any disastrous or unpleasant year. Such for the British royal family was 1992, which saw the divorce of Princess Anne, the Princess Royal, the separation of the Duke and Duchess of York, newspaper photographs of the latter topless and a fearful fire at Windsor Castle. Queen Elizabeth used the phrase in a speech to guests at a banquet in the Guildhall that year. The expression is itself based on Latin *annus mirabilis*, 'wonderful year'.

> Helen's *annus horribilis* [as a university student] was made worse by the flat itself. It was a dreary tenement overlooking a wrecker's yard and a railway line.
>
> *The Times* (26 August 1999)

Annus miserabilis. A pitiful year, as a neat blend of the sound of Latin *annus mirabilis*, 'wonderful year', and the sense of ANNUS HORRIBILIS. The expression was in vogue in the 1990s.

> With Ruth Rendell their highest placed representative

in 17th place, the survey continued an annus miser-abilis for British women writers.

Independent on Sunday (28 November 1999)

Anorak. A word of Greenland Inuit (Eskimo) origin for a type of waterproof jacket with a hood, as originally worn in polar regions. The garment's popularity, prac-ticality and relative cheapness caused it to be widely adopted for a number of outdoor uses, from walking to train-spotting. The latter pastime in particular gave it a 'nerdish' image, and as a result the word passed to denote a boring person or SQUARE, especially one with solitary interests. *See also* NERD.

Another Munich. *See* MUNICH.

Anschluss. In a historical context this German word, meaning 'junction' or 'union', refers to the annexation of Austria by NAZI Germany in March 1938, part of Hitler's drive to create a new German empire.

Answer's a lemon. The reply is unsatisfactory or does not exist. The saying derives from 'lemon' as a term for anything unsatisfactory, perhaps originally referring to the least valuable symbol in a FRUIT MACHINE.

Answers on a postcard. There is no neat or simple answer. The catchphrase refers to competitions in which contestants have to send in their answers on a postcard. Inevitably, there is little space for any detailed or lengthy answer, which the setters aim to deter in any case.

> What … are Vanessa [Feltz]'s talents, unique or otherwise? And how much of your money and mine is being spent on discovering a treatment that will fit them or even cure them? Answers on a postcard, please.
>
> *Sunday Times* (20 June 1999)

Answer to a maiden's prayer. An eligible bachelor, ideally young, handsome and wealthy, or generally anything that exactly meets requirements. The expres-sion dates from the 1930s.

> You're the answer to a maiden's prayer, dear heart. No need for you to do a stroke of work, you can marry money and live the life of a gentleman.
>
> JOAN M. FLEMING: *Maiden's Prayer*, II (1957)

Anthony dollar. A US one-dollar coin with raised inner borders, issued in 1979, that bore a likeness of the American social reformer and women's suffrage leader Susan B. Anthony (1820–1906). Some initially complained that in look and feel the coin was too much like a quarter (25 cents).

Anthony Eden. A black Homburg hat of the type worn in the 1930s by Sir Anthony Eden (1897–1977) when foreign secretary and one of the best dressed members of the House of Commons.

Antinovel. A novel that dispenses with conventional structures and characteristics. Such novels first came to the fore in France in the 1950s, rejecting the orderly presentation of plot and characters as not conforming to the reality of experience. Instead, the antinovel concentrated on the prosaic description of things, the theory being that the reader is thereby able to par-ticipate directly, not vicariously, and so understand the mental state of the characters. Key figures in the evolution of the *nouveau roman* were Alain Robbe-Grillet (b.1922), Nathalie Sarraute (1900–99), Michel Butor (b.1926), Claude Simon (b.1913) and Robert Pinget (1919–97).

Anton Piller order. In legal terminology a court order requiring the defendant in proceedings to permit the plaintiff or his representatives to enter the defendant's premises in order to obtain evidence essential to the case. The name is that of a German firm of electric motor manufacturers, which in 1975 was involved in legal proceedings in which such an order was granted.

Ants in one's pants. A state of nervousness or restless-ness; the fidgets or 'jitters'. A phrase of US origin, so that 'pants' here are trousers.

> What was the true explanation of yesterday's interest rate decision by the Bank of England? … The first American financier I spoke to after this astonishing move [said]: 'Why did they do it? It's simple. They've got ants in their pants.'
>
> *The Times* (9 September 1999)

Anyone for tennis? A general query based on what is regarded as a typical line in a 1920s drawing-room comedy and uttered by a well-dressed young man entering the room carrying a tennis racket. The precise provenance of the phrase is uncertain, although it has a clear pre-echo in G.B. Shaw's play *Misalliance* (1910) in which one of the characters, Johnny Tarleton, a young businessman, rises from a swinging chair and asks the assembled company, 'Anybody on for a game of tennis?' The phrase was adopted as the title of a 1968 television play by J.B. Priestley and was pastiched in John Wells's farce *Anyone for Denis?* (1981), guying Margaret Thatcher's husband.

Any Questions? A long-running radio discussion

programme, first broadcast in 1948 and transmitted weekly from a series of halls around Britain. Four people, often politicians, form a panel to answer questions on a variety of topics put by a local audience. The series came to be particularly associated with its first two chairmen, Freddie Grisewood (1948–67) and David Jacobs (1967–84), and a selection of listeners' responses to what has been said forms the basis of the following day's complementary programme, *Any Answers?*

Anything Goes. A musical comedy (1934), with a score by Cole Porter and book by Guy Bolton and P.G. Wodehouse, about a variety of characters on board an ocean liner in the 1920s. Perfectly capturing the carefree vitality of 1920s youth, the show was originally to be called *Bon Voyage* and then *Hard to Get*, with the main event in the action being a shipwreck, but the title was changed and extensive alterations to the plot were necessitated by a tragic shipwreck in real life. The phrase subsequently became uniquely associated with its time. In addition to the title song, the show contains 'I Get a Kick Out of You' and 'You're the Top'. Bing Crosby and Ethel Merman (reprising her role in the original stage show) starred in the first film version (1936).

> In olden days, a glimpse of stocking
> Was looked on as something shocking,
> But now, Heaven knows,
> Anything goes.
> COLE PORTER: 'Anything Goes'

Anzac. A word coined in 1915 from the initials of the Australian and New Zealand Army Corps. It was also applied to the cove and beach in GALLIPOLI where they landed. *See also* DIGGER; PEACEHAVEN.

Anzac biscuit. A New Zealand biscuit made with butter, golden syrup, rolled oats and coconut, named in honour of the ANZAC forces that fought at Gallipoli in 1915.

Anzac Day. 25 April, commemorating the landing of the Anzacs in Gallipoli in 1915.

Anzac Pact. The agreement reached between Australia and New Zealand in 1944 to cooperate in their policies with regard to armistices with the AXIS powers, the postwar settlement and certain other matters.

A-OK. Excellent; in good order. A US space age expression, supposedly standing for all systems OK. The term is said to be the invention of a NASA public relations officer, Colonel 'Shorty' Powers, who used it

during the suborbital flight on 5 May 1961 of the astronaut Alan Shepard. Powers misheard a simple 'OK' from Shepard as 'A-OK' and relayed it to reporters and radio listeners. Astronauts themselves are not recorded as actually using the term.

Apartheid (Afrikaans, 'separateness'). A policy adopted by the Afrikaner National Party in 1948 to ensure the dominance of the white minority. It divided South Africa into separate areas for whites and blacks, leading to the country's withdrawal from the British Commonwealth in 1961 and rioting, repression and isolation from other nations. Limited constitutional rights were granted to non-whites in 1985, and the remaining apartheid laws were repealed in 1991. *See also* PASS LAWS.

Apartment, The. An Oscar-winning bitter-sweet comedy film (1960) directed by Billy Wilder and starring Jack Lemmon and Shirley MacLaine. The apartment in question belongs to Baxter, a lonely insurance clerk, who lets his superiors use the apartment to conduct their extramarital affairs.

Ape and Essence. A dystopian novel (1948) by Aldous Huxley (1894–1963). A future is projected, looking forward from 1948, in a rejected treatment for a film, to be entitled 'Ape and Essence', in which a civilization dedicated to 'perfection' tries to suppress any rebellious desires:

> Only in the knowledge of his own essence
> Has any man ceased to be many monkeys.

Apgar score. A criterion for measuring the well-being of a baby one minute after birth. A check is made of respiratory effort, heart rate, skin colour, muscle tone and any reflex reaction to an olfactory stimulation of the nose, and each of these five signs is rated between 0 and 2, giving a maximum of 10. The resultant score is an instant indicator of whether the baby is likely to be healthy or require medical assistance. The score is named after the US obstetric anaesthetist Virginia Apgar (1909–74), who devised it in the early 1950s and published it in 1953. It has remained the world's standard assessment of newborn babies.

Apocalypse Now. A film (1979) loosely based on the short story HEART OF DARKNESS (1902) by Joseph Conrad (1857–1924). Directed by Francis Ford Coppola and starring Martin Sheen as a US Army captain detailed to assassinate the renegade Colonel Kurtz, played by Marlon Brando, it was set against the backdrop of the Vietnam War and astonished cinema audiences with such epic set-pieces as a helicopter assault conducted to the accompaniment of Wagner's 'The Ride of the Valkyries'. The massive cost of the film, which was shot in the Philippines and complicated when Martin Sheen suffered a heart attack, was compounded by the extent to which it went over schedule. In the film business it became known by the alternative title *Apocalypse Later*.

Apollo. The US space programme for landing astronauts on the Moon. The programme was announced in May 1961, but the first step of manned lunar exploration was not realized until 11 October 1968, when a team of three orbited the Moon. Apollo 11 brought the step-by-step procedure to a climax on 20 July 1969 when Neil Armstrong became the first human to set foot on the Moon. Remaining Apollo missions carried out extensive exploration of the lunar surface, and the programme came to an end with the flight of Apollo 17 in December 1972. *See also* GEMINI.

Apologies to ... . A conventional acknowledgement by an artist, illustrator or cartoonist that their work is based on that of a famous predecessor, as 'Apologies to Tenniel'. The formula is usually placed after the artist's own signature.

Appeasement. *See* MUNICH.

Appleby, Inspector. The erudite police detective, with full name John Appleby, created by Michael Innes (J.I.M. Stewart; 1906–94) for a long series of novels, beginning with *Death at the President's Lodging* (1936). He usually comes up with an appropriate literary quotation and solves every complex case with calm ingenuity.

Apple Macintosh. A popular make of personal computer and the first to replace typed commands with a graphical user interface, i.e. a mouse for pointing and clicking at windows and icons. It was introduced in 1984 by Apple Computers, founded in a garage in California in 1976 by the US computer engineers Steve Jobs (b.1955) and Stephen Wozniak (b.1950). The company was the first computer firm not to use its name as its corporate identity. The idea of selling a computer under the name and image of a fruit was conceived by Jobs, and the company motif of a multicoloured apple with a bite taken out of it is a reference to the biblical story of Adam and Eve, in which the apple (though not identified as such) represents the fruit of the Tree of Knowledge. The Macintosh model is similarly named after an American apple variety and soon became colloquially known as 'Mac'. The futuristic-looking iMac computer, launched in 1998, further promoted the name.

Après-midi d'un faune, L'. A ballet choreographed by Vaslav Nijinksy (1890–1950) using the music of the tone poem *Prélude à l'Après-midi d'un faune* by Claude Debussy (1862–1918). The ballet was first performed by Diaghilev's BALLETS RUSSES in 1912. Debussy's piece, which was first performed in 1894, had been intended as the first of three pieces, but the planned *Interlude* and *Paraphrase finale* were never written. Debussy described his piece as an 'orchestral impression' of *L'Après-midi d'un faune* (1865), a long Symbolist poem by Stéphane Mallarmé (1842–98). The title means 'the afternoon of a faun', and the poem evokes frustrated sexual desire.

Aqua Libra (Latin, 'water balance'). The proprietary name of a soft drink based on a mixture of mineral water and fruit juices with herbal and other flavourings. It was first sold in the late 1980s and is promoted as an aid to good digestion and alkaline balance.

Arabella. The heroine of Richard Strauss's opera that bears her name (1933). Strauss had asked his librettist, Hugo von Hofmannsthal, for something in the vein of his earlier *Der Rosenkavalier* (1911), as a romantic comedy with a Viennese background and an excuse to show off some waltzes. Hofmannsthal based his text on a combination of his own short story *Lucidor* (1909), a comedy of misunderstanding set in Vienna in 1860, and his play *Der Fiaker als Graf* ('The Cabby as Count') (1925). The story centres on the efforts of the impoverished Count Waldner to make a good marriage for his daughter, Arabella. He writes to his friends, one of whom, Mandryka, a Croatian landowner, expresses an interest. Meanwhile, Arabella herself rejects the young officer, Matteo, who loves her, while her younger sister, Zdenka, who has been brought up as a boy because Waldner cannot afford to have two débutantes in the family, loves Matteo and tells Arabella that it was *she* who wrote to him, pretending to be her sister. The usual misunderstandings are finally resolved with Arabella marrying Mandryka and Matteo transferring his attentions to her sister.

Arab League. The organization so named, formally the League of Arab States, was founded in 1945 in Cairo to ensure cooperation among its member states while protecting their independence and sovereignty. Egypt's membership was suspended in 1979, when the headquarters moved from Cairo to Tunis, but it was readmitted in 1989. The PLO was admitted to full membership in 1976.

Arbeit macht frei (German, 'Work sets free'). These bitterly ironical words were inscribed on the gates of DACHAU concentration camp in 1933 and subsequently on those of AUSCHWITZ in the Second World War. Their authorship is unknown.

Archer, Lew. The thoughtful private eye hero of a series of novels by 'Ross Macdonald' (Kenneth Millar; 1915–83), starting with *The Moving Target* (1949). He is based in a small, sad office in California, is familiar with modern artists and authors, and shares his creator's gift for the vivid turn of phrase.

Archers, The. The world's longest running radio serial, broadcast five days (from 1998 six days) a week from 1951, with an 'omnibus' repeat on Sunday. It was initially devised to convey useful information to the farming community, and continues to introduce themes of topical interest to its audience. The original Archers were Dan and Doris, of Brookfield Farm in Ambridge, and their descendants remain the core characters. *See also* BARWICK GREEN.

Archie Bunker. *See* BUNKER, ARCHIE.

Archies. A nickname for anti-aircraft guns and batteries in the First World War, probably from the popular song by George Robey, John L. St John and Alfred Glover, 'Archibald, Certainly Not!' (1909).

Arcos Affair. A diplomatic contretemps between Britain and the Soviet Union in 1927. It came about when MI5 suspected that personnel working for the All Russian Cooperative Society (ARCOS) in London were intelligence officers. A raid was made on ARCOS warehouses and offices and alleged evidence of espionage was found, as a result of which diplomatic ties were severed with the USSR. Britain had broken off relations three years previously after the ZINOVIEV LETTER incident (*see under* FAKES). A similar Soviet operation in the United States was run under the umbrella of AMTORG.

Are we downhearted? No! A catchphrase adopted by British troops during the First World War from the title of a popular song of 1914 by Worton David and Lawrence Wright. An earlier song of 1906 with the same title was written by George Robins.

Are You Being Served? A rude and racy television SITCOM running from 1973 to 1985 and centring on the antics of the staff at Grace Brothers, an old-fashioned department store. Much of the humour derives from unsubtle innuendo in the style of the CARRY ON FILMS.

The main characters include the brash and brassy head of ladies' fashion, Mrs Slocombe, played by Mollie Sugden, the smooth and silky-voiced floor-walker, Captain Peacock, played by Frank Thornton, the effete senior sales assistant in the menswear department, Mr Humphries, memorably camped up by John Inman, and Mrs Slocombe's assistant, Miss Brahms, played by Wendy Richard. The many *double entendres* in the script are extended to the title itself.

Are you decent? Are you dressed? This catchphrase originated in the theatre and accompanied a knock on the door of an actor's or (in particular) actress's dressing-room. It later applied to anyone who might not be fully or appropriately dressed to receive a visitor. The first part of the phrase in this wider sense is obviously variable.

Argue the toss, To. To dispute a decision already made. The phrase dates from the 1920s and alludes to a dispute over a decision reached by tossing a coin.

> The occasional irrational screaming match can benefit a marriage or relationship. A couple that argues the toss gathers no moss, if you will.
> *Sunday Times* (24 October 1999)

Arica. A training programme in self-development devised by the Bolivian-born mystic Oscra Ichaza. The Arica Institute to further the method was founded in New York in 1972, following a visit by a group of Americans to Ichaza in Arica, Chile. Hence the name. The programme is effectively a synthesis of several disciplines and is also known as 'scientific mysticism'.

Arkham. An imaginary city in Massachusetts in H.P. Lovecraft's fantasy tales *The Outsider and Others* (1939) and *Beyond the Wall of Sleep* (1943). It was founded in the 17th century but has changed very little since. It is crossed by the gloomy Miskatonic River and has a famous university, specializing in the occult. Travellers visit the city at their own risk.

Arkle. The most famous racehorse in history was foaled in Ireland in 1957 and won the Cheltenham Gold Cup three years in a row (1964–6), ridden by Pat Taaffe. He was a big bay gelding, fast and fluid over the jumps, and was a superb sprinter on the stretch. He dominated the British steeplechasing scene until a small fracture ended his career after his 35th race in December 1966. The Nottinghamshire and England cricketer Derek Randall (b.1951) was also known as 'Arkle' from the way he 'danced' at the wicket.

Armalite. The proprietary name (in the United States) of a type of lightweight, small-calibre assault rifle.

The name, based on 'arm' and 'light', was registered in 1958, and the first such rifle, the AR–10, was a 7.62mm gas-operated weapon. This paved the way for the highly successful AR–15, adopted as the standard US Army rifle known as the M16. The AR–18, similar to it, was produced in Britain but with a simpler design, enabling it to be readily manufactured in less-developed countries. The Armalite became particularly familiar as the weapon favoured by the IRA. The 'Armalite and the ballot box' was, notoriously, the stated strategy of the Irish Republican movement in the 1980s; its twin elements being violence committed against British forces by the Provisional IRA, and electoral advances made by the IRA's political wing, SINN FÉIN.

Arm and a leg. Unduly expensive, as: 'It cost me an arm and a leg to get here.'

Arm candy. A US colloquialism of the 1990s for a pretty girl or good-looking young man whose sole role is to adorn the arm of their companion of the moment. *See also* EYE CANDY.

Armistice Day. 11 November, the day set aside to commemorate the fallen in the First World War, marked by a TWO-MINUTE SILENCE at 11 a.m. and religious ceremonies. The armistice ending the war, signed at 5 a.m., came into effect 11 a.m. on 11 November 1918, the 11th hour of the 11th month. In 1946 the name was changed to REMEMBRANCE DAY. The United States has VETERANS DAY on this day as a legal holiday, while France celebrates its *Fête de la Victoire* (Victory Day).

Armitage, Jo. The middle-class Englishwoman whose marriage goes sadly awry in Penelope Mortimer's novel *The Pumpkin Eater* (1960). She is powerfully played by Anne Bancroft in the film of the book (1964), scripted by Harold Pinter

Armstrong, Jack. The young, sports-loving hero of *Jack Armstrong, the All-American Boy*, a radio series first broadcast in the United States in 1933 and running to 1951. He was the creation of scriptwriter Robert Hardy Andrews, who sends him on a series of adventures around the world with the help of his Uncle Jim. He also appeared in a comic book of the 1940s in which his motto is: 'To keep myself straight and strong and clean, in mind as well as in body.'

Army Game, The. A popular television comedy series screened from 1957 to 1961 and based on the film *Private's Progress* (1956). Recruits at a remote transit camp included Private 'Excused Boots' Bisley, so called because he was allowed to wear plimsolls on parade, Private 'Cupcake' Cook and moronic Private 'Popeye' Popplewell, whose refrain 'I only asked' became a national catchphrase. A later addition was Company Sergeant-Major Claude Snudge, played by Bill Fraser, who, with Alfie Bass's Bisley, subsequently appeared in the spin-off BOOTSIE AND SNUDGE.

Arndale Centre. The shopping malls so named arose from the business set up in Bradford in 1931 by Samuel Chippindale (1909–90), an estate agent specializing in shops. This grew into the Arndale Property Trust, taking its name from a blend of Chippindale's own name and the first name of his partner, Arnold Hargenbach. The first Arndale Centre opened in Leeds in 1967, its architecture based on a US design. The bulldozing of various town centres to make way for the malls horrified many, although the later buildings regained some of the panache of Victorian glass and wrought-iron shopping arcades. Manchester's Arndale Centre, derisively dubbed 'the longest lavatory in Europe' for its expanses of yellow tiling, was destroyed in 1996 by an IRA bomb, which devastated the city centre, but it was completely revamped and reopened in 1999.

Arnhem. *See* BRIDGE TOO FAR.

Aromatherapy. The art or science of promoting 'health and beauty' by aromatic oils extracted from plants is of French origin and was first taken up in Britain in the 1960s. Practitioners claim that it can be used to treat a wide range of disorders, especially stress-related conditions. The word itself was coined in 1937 (as French *aromathérapie*) by the chemist and perfume manufacturer René-Maurice Gattefossé.

Arrogance of power. A catchphrase used to impugn the policies of a country or organization on the grounds that they stem from the arrogance that comes from having too much power. The phrase was coined by Senator William Fulbright in the 1960s and used by him as the title of a book (1967) in which he questioned the validity of US intervention in the affairs of foreign countries.

Arsène Lupin. *See* LUPIN, ARSÈNE.

Arsenic and Old Lace. The film comedy (1941 but released in 1944) of this name was based on a play (1941) by Joseph Kesselring, which was a huge success on Broadway. The plot revolves around two kindly but deranged old ladies (hence the 'old lace') who poison (hence the 'arsenic') elderly gentlemen who visit their home, wishing to relieve them of their loneliness. They bury the bodies in their cellar. The film, which was directed by Frank Capra, starred Cary Grant as the ladies' hapless and appalled nephew, Mortimer Brewster. The title of Kesselring's play was suggested by that of Myrtle Reed's novel LAVENDER AND OLD LACE (1902), criticized by reviewers of the day for its saccharine sentimentality.

Art deco. A decorative style in painting, glass, pottery, silverware, furniture, architecture and the like, at its height in the 1930s. It is distinguished by bold colours, geometrical shapes, stylized natural forms and symmetrical designs. The name comes from French *art décoratif*, 'decorative art', itself from the *Exposition internationale des arts décoratifs et industriels modernes* held in Paris in 1925 as the first major international exhibition of decorative art since the First World War.

Arte povera (Italian, 'impoverished art'). A term coined in 1967 by the Italian critic Germano Celant to describe a form of art in which the materials used, such as soil, twigs or newspaper, are deliberately chosen for their 'worthlessness' as a reaction against the commercialization of the art world. Leading Italian or Italian-based artists in the movement are Jannis Kounnelis (b.1936) and Mario Merz (b.1925), the latter making 'igloos' of metal armatures covered in nets, mud, twigs and so on. The use of such materials has been said to have a liberating effect on the artists concerned.

Artex. A type of plaster applied to walls and ceilings to give a textured finish, usually in decorative patterns. The general effect is necessarily repetitive but blandly pleasing. The name dates from the 1950s and derives from a blend of 'art' and 'texture'.

Art nouveau (French, 'new art'). A decorative style of art flourishing in most of western Europe and the United States from the late 19th century to the outbreak of the First World War. As its name implies, it was a deliberate attempt to create a new style in reaction to the reproduction of historical forms that had been such a prominent feature of 19th-century architecture and design. Its most characteristic theme was the use of sinuous, asymmetrical lines based on plant forms, and frequent motifs were flowers, leaves and tendrils as well as female figures with flowing hair. The name itself came from a shop called *La Maison d'Art Nouveau*, opened in Paris in 1895 by the German-born art dealer Siegfried Bing (1838–1905). The genre has different names in different countries. Among English speakers it is sometimes known as 'Modern Style', while in Germany it was called *Jugendstil* (after the journal *Die Jugend*, 'Youth', founded in 1896), in Austria *Sezessionstil* (after the Vienna *Sezession*, a group of artists who had 'seceded' or broken away from the established academies), in Spain *Modernista* and in Italy *Stile Liberty* (after the Regent Street store that played an important part in promoting its designs).

As and when. When possible; eventually, as: 'I'll be in touch with you as and when.'

As before. A conventional term in fashion literature to refer to a description or details on a previous page, as: 'Grey felt boots, £89.50, Russell & Bromley, as before'. It is sometimes used illogically. A caption in *The Times* of 11 September 1999 reading 'Coat, as before (see main picture)' referred to a description beneath a large photograph to the right, the assumption presumably being that the reader would have read this first. Two smaller photographs below this main picture were also captioned 'Coat, as before' instead of a more logical 'Coat, as above'.

Ascent of F6, The. A play (1937) by W.H. Auden (1907–73) and Christopher Isherwood (1904–86) about an ill-fated British mountaineering expedition to a fictional peak identified simply as F6, on the frontier between the equally fictional British Sudoland and Ostnian Sudoland. The expedition leader, Michael Ransom, was based on the real-life soldier and writer T.E. Lawrence (1888–1935).

Ascent of Man, The. A pioneering 13-part television series broadcast in 1973 and telling the story of man's discoveries in agriculture, technology and science. It was written by the Polish-born scientist Jacob Bronowski (1908–74) and presented by him with a compelling intensity, opening the eyes of many to the broad sweep of scientific history. Bronowski's book based on the series spread far and wide his fame as an expositor and thinker.

Among the multitude of animals which scamper, fly, burrow and swim around us, man is the only one who is not locked into his environment. His imagination, his reason, his emotional subtlety and toughness, make it possible for him not to accept the environment but to change it. And that series of inventions, by which man from age to age has remade his environment, is a different kind of evolution – not biological, but cultural evolution. I call that brilliant sequence of cultural peaks *The Ascent of Man*.

JACOB BRONOWSKI: *The Ascent of Man*, ch i (1973)

ASCII. The acronym of American Standard Code for Information Exchange, representing the code of bits (binary digits) of 1s and 0s that is used in computer technology. With a particular series of bits representing the same numbers, letters and visuals, the code allows a standard exchange of files written in different computer languages.

Ashcan School. A group of American realist painters active from 1908 until the First World War. The most prominent members were those originally known as 'The Eight': Arthur B. Davies (1862–1928), William J. Glackens (1870–1938), Robert Henri (1865–1929), Ernest Lawson (1873–1939), George Luks (1867–1933), Maurice Prendergast (1859–1924), Everett Shinn (1876–1953) and John Sloan (1871–1951). Other painters who have been described as members include George Bellows (1882–1925), Glenn Coleman (1887–1932), Eugene Higgins (1874–1958), Edward Hopper (1882–1967) and Jerome Myers (1867–1940). Their style was traditional but their subjects daringly original, such as the vulgar crowds of Broadway, drunks in seedy bars and the sordid denizens of the waterfront. Hence their name, originally given derisively in a book edited by Holger Cahill and Alfred H. Barr entitled *Art in America in Modern Times* (1934). 'Ashcan' is an Americanism for a dustbin.

Ashenden. The secret agent in short stories by William Somerset Maugham (1874–1965), collected in *Ashenden, or The British Agent* (1928). The scenes are set in the First World War and are based on the author's own experience in British intelligence. Ashenden himself is something of a new type of spy in English fiction, humdrum rather than heroic. The film *The Secret Agent* (1936), starring John Gielgud and directed by Alfred Hitchcock, is based loosely on his exploits.

Ashington Group. A group of amateur artists active in Ashington, Northumberland, from 1934 to 1984. The group originated when Robert Lyon (1894–1978), an art lecturer at King's College, Newcastle upon Tyne, then part of Durham University, was asked to run an extramural class in the nearby mining town of Ashington under the auspices of the Workers' Educational Association. Lyon encouraged members to 'paint what you know', and their paintings were mainly of scenes drawn from their working, domestic and social lives.

A6 murder. In August 1961 Michael Gregsten and his lover Valerie Storie were shot in their car in a lay-by off the A6 between Luton and Bedford. Gregsten died, but Storie survived, paralysed from the waist down. The first suspect was Peter Alphon, a travelling salesman, but at an identity parade Storie picked out another man, known to be innocent. The next suspect was James Hanratty, a petty criminal. Storie picked him out from an identity parade, and her identification led to his being hanged in April 1961. The journalist Paul Foot investigated the case and in *Who Killed Hanratty?* (1971) concluded that Hanratty was innocent. Foot also revealed that Alphon had repeatedly told him he was the murderer. Either way, the crime is now believed to have been a major miscarriage of justice.

Ask me another. I don't know. The implication is that I don't know the answer to your present question, but I might know the answer to another. *Ask Me Another* was the title of an American television quiz show of the early 1950s in which panellists had to guess the identity of concealed sports celebrities by asking them questions.

> Why [in a new stage version of *Hansel and Gretel*] … does the poor woodcutter potter about with a chair on his head? Is he too poor to buy a hat, is he trying to be funny, or is this a bizarre way of symbolizing that he is in the power of his awful wife? Ask me another.
>
> *The Times* (10 December 1999)

Aslan. The great lion who is a central character in the NARNIA children's books by C.S. Lewis (1898–1963). His death and resurrection in the first book identify him as a deific or even specifically Christ-like figure. His name, which is the Turkish word for 'lion', is said to have come from Lewis's reading of the *Arabian Nights Entertainments*.

Asleep at the wheel. Inattentive; not concentrating on the task in hand. The allusion is to falling asleep while driving a car. A US equivalent of 19th-century origin is 'asleep at the switch', referring to the points lever ('switch') on a railway. The US country band Asleep at the Wheel, formed in 1970, took a name that referred to their non-stop concert travelling, much of it involving all-night drives.

Asphalt Jungle, The. A FILM NOIR (1950) based on the novel (1949) of the same name by W.R. Burnett. Directed by John Huston and starring Sterling

Hayden and Louis Calhern, it depicted the disintegration of a gang of thieves following a daring robbery attempt. The title of the film conveyed appropriate overtones of savagery in a bleak urban setting, where the paving is asphalt and the 'law of the jungle' prevails. *See also* BLACKBOARD JUNGLE; CONCRETE JUNGLE.

Aspidistra. A very tolerant member of the Convallariaceae family, with broad, lance-shaped leaves and small, inconspicuous flowers borne at soil level. It was a popular houseplant from late Victorian times until the 1920s because of its ability to survive in gas-lit rooms, and it became a symbol of lower middle-class philistinism and dull respectability. George ORWELL wrote a novel called *Keep the Aspidistra Flying* (1936), and a song by Jimmy Harper, Tommie Connor and Will E. Haines, *The Biggest Aspidistra in the World* (1938), was widely popularized by Gracie Fields (1898–1979).

As seen on TV. A stock advertising recommendation for a product that has appeared in a television commercial or documentary programme. By extension, the phrase can also apply to any TIE-IN relating to a television programme.

> The biggest section in the new Waterstone's [bookshop] in Piccadilly is devoted to the section 'As Seen On TV'. You can't move for Channel 4 and BBC books.
> *The Times* (17 December 1999)

Asset stripping. The practice of taking over a company in financial difficulties and selling each of its assets separately at a profit without regard for its future. The activity is legal but regarded with disfavour as it smacks of opportunism. The term became familiar in the 1970s but the practice itself is older.

Asta. The schnauzer bitch in Dashiel Hammett's detective story *The Thin Man* (1934), played by a male fox terrier called Skippy in the film of the same name (and same date) starring William Powell and Myrna Loy. An inferior television version of the story, starring Peter Lawford and Phyllis Kirk, was screened in 1957–8.

Asterix. The comic French cartoon hero who first appeared in 1959 as the creation of the writer René Goscinny and the artist Albert Uderzo. He is a pint-sized, moustachioed Gaul who lives in Armorica (Brittany) and does his best to keep the Romans at bay. The stories include gentle and amusing caricatures of different European peoples, ranging from stolid tea-drinking Britons professing delight in their diet of lamb and mint sauce to knife-wielding Corsicans. His friends include the obtuse and obese Obelix and the Druid Getafix. First appearing in a weekly comic, he has since featured in a number of books and animated cartoons. His name (properly *Astérix*) is based on French *astérisque*, 'asterisk', with a final *-rix* found in typical Gaulish names such as that of the Gallic chieftain Vercingetorix (d.44 BC). A film, *Astérix et Obélix contre César* ('Asterix and Obelix take on Caesar'), featuring Gerard Depardieu as Obelix and directed by Claude Zidi, was released in 1999.

As the bishop said to the actress. A response to an unintentional *double entendre*. The phrase dates from the music-hall era, when stand-up comedy abounded in 'bishop and actress' jokes. The association of the two types is either so unlikely or so potentially scandalous that the interpretation of a remark will be either innocuous or indecent. The rejoinder is often prompted by an entirely innocent reference, as: 'I've got something special to show you' ('As the bishop said to the actress'). The secondary meaning is not necessarily always improper. *See also* TOM SWIFTIES.

> Faint heart ne'er won fair lady, as the Bishop said to the Actress.
> 'ANON': *A Writer's Notebook* (1946)

As thick as a plank or **two planks** or **two short planks.** Very dull and stupid. The various versions date from the 1970s.

Aston University. The Birmingham university was formed from a college of advanced technology in 1966 and was so named to be distinguished from the existing University of Birmingham, founded in 1901. It is not actually in Aston, a district 3km (2 miles) to the north, but in Gosta Green, near the city centre, and it took the name so as to be at the top of the alphabetical list of new universities and so readily catch the eye of the University Grants Committee.

Astronaut (Greek *astron*, 'star', and *nauts*, 'sailor'). A voyager in interstellar space. This word, first used in 1929, gained popular acceptance after the first manned space flight by Major Yuri Gagarin (1934–68) of the USSR on 12 April 1961. He landed safely after orbiting the earth in 108 minutes at altitudes reaching a maximum of 327km (203 miles). *See also* COSMONAUT.

Astroturf. The proprietary name of a kind of artificial grass surface for a sports pitch. It was first developed by Monsanto in 1966 to provide a pitch for the Astrodome indoor sports stadium at Houston, Texas, where grass would not grow. Hence the name, which is sometimes taken up in other contexts, as for 'Astroturf Blonde', the journalistic byname of Alyson Rudd, writer on football for *The Times* in the 1990s.

At all at all. A supposedly typical Irish expression added for emphasis at the end of a sentence.

> Whenever she said that she always threw her eyes up to heaven as if she didn't know what she was going to do about it at all at all.
> PATRICK McCABE: *The Dead School* (1995)

Atatürk (Turkish, 'father of the Turks', from *ata*, 'father', and *Türk*, 'Turks'). A surname adopted in 1934 by Mustapha Kemal (1881–1938), the maker of modern Turkey, when all Turks were made to assume surnames. In the First World War he held the Dardanelles and subsequently ruthlessly set out to westernize the republic he had established in 1923. European dress was imposed, polygamy was abolished, women were enfranchised, and the Latin script replaced the Arabic. Atatürk died at 9.05 a.m. on 10 November 1938, and his death has been commemorated in Turkey by a minute's silence at that time each year ever since.

At Five in the Afternoon. The stark abstract painting by Robert Motherwell (1915–91) dates from 1949, the year in the artist began his series of ELEGIES TO THE SPANISH REPUBLIC. The title is a translation of *A las cinco de la tarde*, the dirge-like refrain of Federico García Lorca's great elegy, *Llanto por Ignacio Sánchez Mejías* ('Lament for Ignacio Sánchez Mejías'), in memory of a bullfighter who had been gored to death in 1934. The poem was published in 1935, and the following year Lorca himself was assassinated by nationalists shortly after the outbreak of the Spanish Civil War.

Atheists. The existence of a true atheist in the literal sense of the word is hard to rationalize. During the Second World War the Rev. W.T. Cummings, a US army chaplain in Bataan, declared in one of his sermons, 'There are no atheists in the foxholes', meaning that no one can deny the existence of God in the face of imminent death.

Athlete's foot. A popular or euphemistic name for *tinea pedis*, dating from the 1920s. The condition, a type of fungal infection, is characterized by peeling and broken skin, particularly between the toes. Its name alludes to its association with sweaty feet encased in shoes or boots, although it is frequently found among people who are anything but athletic.

Athlone Press. Formerly the publishing house of the University of London, founded in 1949 and named after the Earl of Athlone (1874–1957), then chancellor of the university. The title 'University of London Press' had been pre-empted some years earlier to a commercial house which at that time was the production and distribution channel for books sponsored by the university. The Press is now independent but preserves links with the university through an academic advisory board.

Atkins, Tommy. The once-common name of the archetypal British private soldier, often shortened to Tommy (plural Tommies). The name comes from the use of the name 'Thomas Atkins' on specimen forms in the British army in the 19th century. Tommy makes an early appearance in a poem of the same name (1892) by Rudyard Kipling (1865–1936).

> For it's Tommy this, an' Tommy that, an' 'Chuck him out, the brute!'
> But it's 'Saviour of 'is country' when the guns begin to shoot.

Atlantic, Battle of the. *See* BATTLE OF THE ATLANTIC.

Atlantic Charter. During the Second World War US President Roosevelt and Winston Churchill, the British prime minister, met on a warship in the Atlantic (11 August 1941) and made this eight-point declaration of the principles on which peace was to be based, consequent upon Allied victory. The unanswered purpose of the meeting, however, was Britain's desperate need for US support. A keynote among the pious generalities of the Charter, which can be compared to President Wilson's FOURTEEN POINTS, was that after the war 'all men shall be enabled to live in freedom from fear and want'.

Atlantic Wall. The name given by the Germans in the Second World War to their defences along the Atlantic coast of Europe, which were built to resist invasion. *See also* FORTRESS EUROPE.

Atmospheric Skull Sodomizing a Grand Piano. A calm painting of a small Spanish village by Salvador Dalí (1904–89), the peace disturbed only by the event described in the title. One rather feels for the piano, only one of whose legs remains on the ground, such is the force of the skull's phallically extended jawbone. It is to paintings such as these that James Thurber was no doubt referring when he wrote in 1945: 'The naked truth about me is to the naked truth about Salvador Dali as an old ukulele in the attic is to a piano in a tree, and I mean a piano with breasts.'

ATS. Members of the Auxiliary Territorial Service, a women's army corps formed in 1938 and serving in the Second World War. In 1949 it was succeeded by the WRAC (*see* WAAC). A single member was known as an AT.

> When shall I see the Thames again?
> The prow-promoted gems again,
> As beefy ATS
> Without their hats
> Come shooting through the bridge?
>
> JOHN BETJEMAN: *New Bats in Old Belfries*, 'Henley-on-Thames' (1945)

At Swim-Two-Birds. A modernist novel (1939) by Flann O'Brien (one of several pseudonyms of Brian O'Nolan; 1911–66). It hovers between burlesque and parody of popular fiction, and also of Irish legend, such as had been promoted in the Irish Literary Revival. Snáimh-dá-en ('Swim-two-birds') was one of the resting-places of Mad Sweeney, hero of the Early Irish legend, *Buile Shuibne* ('The Frenzy of Suibne'), and is Devenish Island, between Clonmacnois and Shannonbridge, near where O'Brien spent part of his childhood. *See also* FIRST LINES OF NOVELS.

Attaboy (probably from 'That's the boy!'). An exclamation of enthusiastic approval or encouragement, originating in the United States and widely used in the 1930s by young people in the English-speaking world. 'Attagirl' also exists when the one encouraged is female.

> 'Look at that little mite with *Attaboy*
> Printed across her paper sailor hat.
> Disgusting, isn't it? Who *can* they be,
> Her parents, to allow such forwardness?'
>
> JOHN BETJEMAN: *Selected Poems*, 'Beside the Seaside' (1948)

Attendance teacher. In the United States a term for an official charged with finding and returning truants and other absent students to school. Such officials were formerly known more realistically as truant officers.

At the end of the day. When all is said and done; when everything has been taken into account. A now hackneyed phrase that first became current in the 1970s. It was the title of the sixth volume (1973) of Harold Macmillan's monumental memoirs (1966–75), the other six being *Winds of Change* (1966), *The Blast of War* (1967), *Tides of Fortune* (1969), *Riding the Storm* (1971), *Pointing the Way* (1972) and *The Past Masters* (1975). *See also* WIND OF CHANGE.

> 'At the end of the day,' he stated, 'this verifies what I have been saying against the cuts in public expenditure.'
>
> *South Nottinghamshire Echo* (16 December 1976)

At this moment in time. Now; these days. A near meaningless phrase favoured by representatives of trade unions, sports teams and the like when interviewed by the media. The following is an example of the usage in a statement by England's football manager, Glenn Hoddle (b.1957):

> I have never said that. … At this moment in time, if that changes in years to come I don't know, but what happens here today and changes as we go along that is part of life's learning and part of your inner beliefs. But at this moment in time I did not say them things and at the end of the day I want to put that on record because it has hurt people.
>
> *The Times* (report of television interview) (2 February 1999)

Attila the Hen. A nickname of Margaret Thatcher (b.1923), Conservative prime minister from 1979 to 1990, so called for her uncompromising attitudes in punning reference to Attila (406–453), king of the Huns, noted for his ruthlessness. *See also* BLESSED MARGARET; IRON LADY; LEADERENE; TINA.

Attitude. In the 1970s this word gained a new turn of meaning to denote a resentful or antagonistic manner and hence a self-possessed stance or assertive swagger. To have the latter is thus to 'have attitude' or to be 'with attitude'. Both senses are of US origin.

> In this job, you gotta have attitude, hang loose, ready for anything.
>
> *Police Review* (28 September 1990)

Audi. The car of this name was launched in 1909 by Dr August Horch (1868–1951), founder of the German company of Horch-Werke in Zwickau. He originally manufactured the car under his own name but lost control of the company and for legal reasons could not give his name to another car. He therefore ingeniously translated his surname, as if German *horch!*, 'hark!', into Latin *audi*.

Audley, David. The British intelligence operative in a series of spy thrillers by Anthony Price, beginning with *The Labyrinth Makers* (1970). He is a BACKROOM BOY who nevertheless finds himself involved in the action. He not only works for intelligence but is himself formidably intelligent, and although he is a colonel in the early stories, the later ones go back to his days in the Second World War as a green but bright lieutenant.

Auf Wiedersehen, Pet. A television comedy series screened from 1983 to 1986 and relating the misadventures of three Geordies, Denis, Neville and Oz, persuaded by local unemployment to seek work on a Düsseldorf building site. They are joined by Cockney lothario Wayne, Bristol ex-boxer Bomber, boring Brummie Barry and Liverpudlian arsonist Moxey. The disparate characters were soon ingrained on the national consciousness, and Oz in particular, played by ex-convict Jimmy Nail, was elevated to cult status. The title represents the lads' farewell to their German girlfriends.

Auk. The regular nickname of Field-Marshal Sir C.J.E. Auchinleck (1884–1981), Commander-in-Chief in India during the Second World War. As a shortening of his surname, it derived from the bird so called and arose as an army nickname some time before the war.

Aunt Edna. A typical theatre-goer of conservative taste. The playwright Terence Rattigan introduced the character in the preface to the second volume of his *Collected Works* (1953), describing her as an average middle-class attender of matinees whom playwrights must take into account. Critics subsequently adopted the invention when complaining about the middle-class, middle-brow nature of his own plays.

Aunt Emma. An unenterprising croquet player. The appellation dates from the 1960s.

Auntie. The BBC, regarded as a conservative or 'nannyish' organization, especially by comparison with the more populist and permissive commercial television. The BBC has itself accepted the nickname and exploited it punningly in such programme titles as *Auntie's Bloomers*, a selection of mishaps during filming. In the media the tag often serves as a simple synonym. *See also* BEEB.

> The BBC is launching *Newsnight Scotland* from Glasgow on October 4. It will be Auntie's most ambitious attempt yet to reflect Britain's new political landscape.
> *The Times* (24 September 1999)

Aunt Jane. A black US nickname for an evangelical, HAPPY-CLAPPY female worshipper.

> Black Christians must relearn the whole-hearted involvement with religion that typifies the churches' 'Aunt Janes'.
> *Time* (6 April 1970)

Aunt Minnies. A US nickname for photographs taken by commercial photographers or amateurs that happen to show an object of military intelligence interest behind the human subjects. In the Second World War US intelligence officers scoured antique shops for photographs and postcards of this type, so called because someone's Aunt Minnie usually appeared in the picture.

Aunt Thomasina. A US nickname, current in the 1970s, for an obsequious black woman, especially one who did not support the cause of WOMEN'S LIB. The analogy was with 'Uncle Tom' as a name for a black man obsequious to whites, from the central character of Harriet Beecher Stowe's anti-slavery novel *Uncle Tom's Cabin* (1852).

Au pair (French, 'on an equal footing'). A young foreign person, typically female, who joins a family to take on housework and help with young children in exchange for board and lodging and a modest weekly wage. She usually does so to learn the language or to improve her knowledge of it, although some are perhaps drawn by the prospect of male company and the potential for a British boyfriend. The allure may well work the other way round, and the Swedish au pair, in particular, has come to be stereotyped as a high ranker in the sex stakes.

Auschwitz. The German name for the small town of Oświęcim in southern Poland, notorious as the site of one of the biggest Nazi death camps in the Second World War. A small camp for political prisoners (Auschwitz I) was established here in 1940, followed by a much larger camp (Auschwitz II) in 1941 close to the nearby village of Brzezinka (called Birkenau in German; hence the whole complex is sometimes called Auschwitz-Birkenau). A third camp, Auschwitz III, was a slave-labour camp. Auschwitz II was designed specifically as an extermination camp for Jews, gypsies and others. Estimates of the overall number of deaths at Auschwitz vary between 1 million and 2.5 million, and may have been as high as 4 million. *See also* ANGEL OF DEATH; BELSEN; DACHAU; FINAL SOLUTION; HOLOCAUST.

Auspasia. The imaginary kingdom that is the setting of Georges Duhamel's *Lettres d'Auspasie* (1922) and *Le dernier voyage de Candide* (1938). Its main claim to fame is the loquacity of its inhabitants, who have a passion for oratory. Its main cultural organization is the National Institute, whose distinguished members included Cussac, famous for his research on the snail, and Scrube, a noted inventor of poisons.

Aussie. A familiar name for an Australian, first in use among Australian soldiers in the First World War. Their own colloquial name for themselves was DIGGER. *See also* STRINE.

Austin, Steve. The 'bionic man' hero of Martin Caidon's novel *Cyborg* (1972). He is a test pilot who crashes, is badly injured, then rebuilt as part man, part machine. As he acclimatizes to his new body he discovers that he has superbly enhanced physical powers, which he uses to pursue various villains. The novel formed the basis of *The Six Million Dollar Man* (1973–8), a successful television series, in which Austin was played by Lee Majors (b.1940). This led to a spin-off series, *The Bionic Woman* (1976–8), with Lindsay Wagner playing the heroine, Jaime Sommers.

Austrian Corporal. A nickname of Adolf Hitler (1889–1945), the Nazi FÜHRER. Hitler was born in Austria, but moved to Munich in 1913. Although summoned for examination by the Austrian army in February 1914 he was rejected as unfit. When the First World War broke out he joined the 16th Bavarian Reserve Infantry Regiment as a volunteer. He spent much of the war serving as a runner on the front line and was wounded in 1916 and gassed in 1918. He was awarded the Iron Cross Second Class in 1914 and the Iron Cross First Class in 1918, but never rose above the rank of corporal. *See also* SCHICKLGRUBER, HERR.

Automatic pilot. To do something on automatic pilot is to do it mechanically, without conscious awareness. The allusion is to the automatic pilot or autopilot that keeps an aircraft on a set course without the aid of the pilot.

> [Clive] James ... switched himself onto automatic pilot and gently tickled himself through an asininely lacklustre programme.
> *Sunday Times* (2 January 2000)

Avengers, The. A television comedy thriller series screened from 1961 to 1968 in a blend of the chic, the sexy, the violent and the self-mocking. The hero, elegant secret agent John Steed, with bowler hat and cane, was played by Patrick MacNee, while his female, leather-clad, judo-practising sidekick was first Cathy Gale, played by Honor Blackman, then Emma Peel, her name punning on 'M appeal' ('man appeal'), played memorably by Diana Rigg, and finally Tara King, played by Linda Thorson. In 1976 MacNee returned in *The New Avengers* with Joanna Lumley.

Avenue of the Americas. The official name given in the 1940s to Sixth Avenue, New York, to honour the Latin American countries. Few New Yorkers use the appellation, preferring the briefer numerical name. The street runs from Canal Street in the south to Central Park in the north, and for many years its length was followed by an elevated 'subway' or 'el' train.

Aversion therapy. A type of behaviour therapy introduced in the 1950s. Its aim was to make a patient abandon a habit or addiction by associating it with something unpleasant, such as an electric shock. It has been used to treat self-injurious behaviour in the mentally handicapped but has now mostly been superseded by other forms of therapy.

Avon lady. A woman who calls at private houses selling cosmetics on behalf of Avon Products Inc, a US firm founded in 1886 by David H. McConnell as the California Perfume Company. The firm's advertising jingle, 'Ding dong, this is Avon calling', soon became familiar in many homes, and some of its reps have risen to impressive heights in their careers. In Britain alone 4 million women were Avon ladies in the last half of the 20th century, but the setting up of the firm's INTERNET site in 1998 was seen as a threat to the thousands still doing the domestic rounds at doorstep level. In the film *Edward Scissorhands* (1990) an intrepid Avon lady acts as good fairy to the isolated freak boy Edward and gives him a cosy home in a Florida suburb.

> In one of her most memorable cases, she discovered that an errant wife was using her job as an Avon lady to betray her husband.
> *The Times* (26 May 1999)

AWACS. The acronym of *a*irborne *w*arning *a*nd *c*ontrol *s*ystem, a system of the US Air Force for the early detection of enemy bombers. As developed by the USAF, it was carried in a specially modified Boeing 707 aircraft, with its main radar antenna mounted on a turntable housed in a circular rotodome. The first production-model AWACS entered service with the USAF in 1977 and was taken up by the RAF soon after.

Awesome Welles. A not entirely flattering nickname for the overweight actor Orson Welles (1915–85) given him by his fellow American actor Tony Curtis. Towards the end of his career Welles is said to have weighed 181kg (399lb or 28½ stone).

Awkward age. Adolescence, as a period of instability between childhood and adulthood. The term dates from the turn of the 20th century and may have been borrowed from French *l'âge ingrat*. Henry James has a novel of the English title (1899) about a young woman's emergence into an understanding of the world.

AWOL. The acronym of *a*bsent *w*ithout *l*eave (popularly, *w*ithout *o*fficial *l*eave), a military term originating in the First World War for a serviceman absent without permission from his place of duty or quarters but not intending to desert. 'To go AWOL' is to be absent thus, and the phrase can now apply to anyone or anything missing, as: 'Oh dear, Tiggy's gone AWOL again.'

Axis. A collective term for Germany, Italy, Japan and their allies in the Second World War. The term was coined by the Italian fascist leader Benito Mussolini to describe the military alliance with NAZI Germany (also known as the Pact of Steel or the Rome–Berlin Axis) of 22 May 1939. The roots of the Axis go back further: Germany signed the Anti-Comintern Pact with Japan in 1936 and with Italy in 1937. In September 1940 the three countries signed the Tripartite Pact, committing them to a 10-year military alliance. During the Second World War Hungary, Bulgaria, Romania, Slovakia and Croatia all fought on the side of the Axis powers.

Axis Sally. The name given by US servicemen to the radio propagandist Mildred Elizabeth Gillars (1900–88), the first woman in US history to be convicted of treason. Her career began in the Second World War on German radio, when in a sultry voice she tried to persuade the homesick soldiers that Germany was unbeatable, that their chances of surviving death were slim and that some draft dodger back in the United States was making off with their girlfriend. After the war she was convicted for treason for a single broadcast that she made on 11 May 1944, on the eve of the Normandy invasion. She was sentenced to 10 to 30 years' imprisonment and in 1950 was sent to the Federal Reformatory for Women in Alderson, West Virginia, where TOKYO ROSE also served part of her sentence. Gillars converted to Catholicism in 1960, was released on parole the following year and spent the rest of her working days teaching languages and music at a convent school. *See also* HAW-HAW, LORD.

Ayatollah. A title given to any of a class of Shi'ite religious leaders in Iran, most notably the fiercely anti-Western Ayatollah Ruholla Khomeini (1902–89), leader of the 1979 Islamic revolution. Since then the ayatollahs have wielded considerable political power. The term is also sometimes pejoratively used for any sinisterly powerful political or morally prescriptive figure. The word derives from the Arabic for 'miraculous sign of God'. *See also* FATWA; GREAT SATAN; SATANIC VERSES.

Azania. The African name of South Africa, introduced by the African National Congress. It is of classical origin and initially applied to East Africa. Its origin lies in the root word, meaning 'land of blacks', that gave the name of Zanzibar. In Evelyn Waugh's novel *Black Mischief* (1932) Azania is an imaginary island empire off the east coast of Africa, its name and location clearly inspired by those of Zanzibar. Its capital is Debra-Dowa and it has many churches and places of worship of all denominations.

Aziz, Dr. The gentle Indian doctor in E.M. Forster's novel *A* PASSAGE TO INDIA (1924). He is accused of assaulting the Englishwoman Adela Quested in the Marabar Caves and is made to stand trial. He is acquitted, but remains permanently embittered. Forster based him on his friend Syed Ross Masood (1889–1937), director of public education in Hyderabad State from 1916 to 1928. In the 1984 film of the novel he is played by Victor Bannerjee.

AZT. The abbreviation of azidothymidine, the tradename of zidovudine, an antiviral drug used in the treatment of AIDS. It was introduced in 1986.

Aztec two-step. *See* MONTEZUMA'S REVENGE.

B

Baa-Baas. The Barbarians, the rugby football club that distinguished players are invited to join. Founded in 1890 in Bradford, it has no clubhouse or ground of its own. There are six fixtures a year against English and Welsh clubs, and since 1948 international teams have usually concluded a tour of Britain with a game against the Barbarians. A classic moment in the history of the Baa-Baas was in 1973, when in a match against the ALL BLACKS a run was made almost the length of the field involving six passes and ending in a try by the Welsh player Gareth Edwards.

Baader-Meinhof Gang. A German terrorist group active from 1968 against US and German capitalist targets. It was also known as the Red Army Faction and was named after two of its founders, Andreas Baader (1943–77) and Ulrike Meinhof (1934–76). Both were arrested and jailed. Meinhof hanged herself in her cell. Baader and two other gang members were found shot in their cells, presumably suicides. Their deaths on 18 October 1977 came the day after West German commandos stormed a hijacked Lufthansa plane in Mogadishu, Somalia, and blocked a ransom attempt to free the terrorists. *See also* URBAN GUERRILLA.

Babar. The elegantly dressed African elephant in the books for young children by the French writer and illustrator Jean de Brunhoff (1899–1937), first published in 1931 with the author's handwritten text and original watercolours. Other characters are Céleste, whom Babar marries, and her cousin Arthur. Babar has inspired works in unexpected quarters, including a sequence of piano pieces by Francis Poulenc (1899–1963) and a study by the Marxist critic Ariel Dorfman entitled *The Empire's Old Clothes* (1983). His name appears to derive from Hindi *babar*, 'lion'.

Babbitt. The leading character in the novel of this name (1922) by Sinclair Lewis (1885–1951). He is a prosperous realtor (estate agent) in the western city of Zenith, a simple, likeable fellow, with faint aspirations to culture that are forever smothered in the froth and futile hustle of US business life. Drive (which takes him nowhere), hustle (by which he saves no time) and efficiency (which does not enable him to do anything) are the keynotes of his life. Babbitt came to typify the business man of orthodox outlook and virtues, with no interest in cultural values, and the name has become a synonym for a certain type of American Philistinism.

Babe, The. George Herman 'Babe' Ruth (1895–1948), a US professional baseball player, was so known when he joined his first team, the Baltimore Orioles. He was a record-breaking hitter for the Boston Red Sox from 1914 to 1919 and thereafter for the New York Yankees (1920–34). The Yankee stadium, built shortly after he joined the club, has since been known as the 'House that Ruth Built'.

Baby blues. (1) A nickname for post-natal depression. (2) Also a nickname for eyes, irrespective of their colour.

Baby boom. A sudden increase in births in the period following the Second World War, when husbands and fathers returned home and there was a sudden increase or 'boom' in the birth rate. A person born at this time is sometimes known as a 'baby boomer'.

> They are stressing the importance of the baby-boomers, roughly the generation now over 25 and under 40.
>
> *Observer* (5 January 1986)

Baby Born. One of the most popular and commercially successful dolls of the 1990s, designed by Victor M.

Pracas and made by Zapf Creation of Germany. It was created to resemble a real baby and had a realistic appeal in its multitude of 'bodily functions', which included eating, crying and soiling its nappy. Joints at its hips, shoulders and neck also gave realistic flexibility and movement.

Baby Doc. *See* PAPA DOC.

Baby doll dress. A short, high-waisted, short-sleeved, diaphanous dress, such as worn by a doll or young child. Young women who took to wearing such dresses in the early 1990s were seen as making a somewhat ambivalent statement about fashion and gender roles.

Babygro. The all-in-one stretch garment for babies was the invention in the 1950s of the Viennese businessman Walter Artzt, who also designed the fabric. The suit was designed for comfort and practicality and given a name to denote its prime function.

Baby-kisser. A US nickname for a politician, especially a campaigning one, who meets families and admires their babies (but without necessarily kissing them).

Baby M. The label name of the baby girl who was the centre of a court case of 1987. Her real name was either Melissa Stern or Sara Whitehead. Matters began when a New Jersey couple, William and Elizabeth Stern, engaged Mary Beth Whitehead as a SURROGATE MOTHER to bear Mr Stern's child via artificial insemination. When the child was born in 1986, however, Whitehead refused to part with her. The Sterns sued, and the resultant case raised important questions about business ethics and the bond between mother and child. The judge originally decided for the Sterns, but the New Jersey Supreme Court overturned the decision, granting Mr Stern custody and Whitehead parental rights, while at the same time declaring surrogacy contracts illegal.

Baby snatcher. Someone who enters into an amorous relationship with a much younger person. The expression is first recorded early in the 20th century, preceding the later 'cradle snatcher'.

Baby Yar. A large ravine near Kiev in Ukraine that became the site of a mass grave of more than 100,000 victims, mainly Jews but also Communist officials and Russian prisoners of war, killed by German SS squads between 1941 and 1943. The massacre was carried out partly in obedience to Hitler's order to exterminate all Jews and Soviet officials, but partly also in retaliation for an explosion earlier in 1941 that had rocked the German command post in Kiev, killing many German soldiers. When the Germans subsequently retreated from the Soviet Union, they attempted to hide the evidence of the slaughter. The massacre was depicted in novels by Ilya Ehrenburg and Anatoly Kuznetsov and was the subject of Yevgeny Yevtushenko's moving poem *Baby Yar* (1961).

Bachelor gay. A former stock term for a young man of independent means who lived mainly for 'wine, women and song'. The expression was popularized by a song of this title by James W. Tate from Harold Fraser-Simson's musical *The Maid of the Mountains* (1916). The change in sense of GAY essentially killed any currency that the phrase retained, except in frivolous or facetious use.

Bachelor girl. A now somewhat dated term for an unmarried professional young woman. The expression dates from the early 20th century.

Bach Flower Remedies. A form of ALTERNATIVE medicine using a series of 38 preparations made from wild flowers and plants to treat 'negative emotions' that manifest themselves as illness. The treatment was devised by the Harley Street homeopathist Dr Edward Bach (1880–1936).

Backbeat. *See* FIFTH BEATLE.

Back in the USSR. A rollicking rock 'n' roll song by the BEATLES, credited to John Lennon and Paul McCartney. It appears on the so-called WHITE ALBUM, released in November 1968. The title of the song was originally to have been 'I'm Backing Britain' (inspired by the slogan of a contemporary pro-British industry campaign) but was playfully turned on its head to become 'Backing the USSR' and finally 'Back in the USSR' (probably by analogy with Chuck Berry's 1959 hit 'Back in the USA'). Released in the year that the Soviet Union invaded Czechoslovakia (*see* PRAGUE SPRING), the song and its title led to the Beatles being accused by the extreme right-wing JOHN BIRCH SOCIETY of promoting communism.

Back of a bus. To look like or have a face like the back of a bus is to be at best unprepossessing and at worst plain or ugly. The back of a bus, with its dirt and exhaust fumes, is an unpleasant public sight.

> As a cynical police inspector said at the time: 'It's harder to get press help [in a murder enquiry] when the woman looks like the back of a bus'.
>
> *The Times* (7 December 1999)

Backroom boys. A name given to the unpublicized scientists and technicians in the Second World War who contributed much to the development of scientific warfare and war production, and since applied generally to any BOFFINS of this kind. Nigel Balchin's novel *The* SMALL BACK ROOM (1943) is an exciting story of such research, with its many challenges and frustrations. It was filmed in 1948 by Michael Powell and Emeric Pressburger. The ultimate source of the phrase was the song 'See What the Boys in the Back Room Will Have', sung by Marlene Dietrich in the film DESTRY RIDES AGAIN (1939). Her spirited rendering of this inspired Lord Beaverbrook to use the words in a speech on war production (24 March 1941):

> Now who is responsible for this work of development on which so much depends? To whom must the praise be given? To the boys in the back rooms. They do not sit in the limelight. But they are the men who do all the work. Many of them are Civil Servants.

Back-seat driver. One who criticizes without responsibility or who attempts to control from a subordinate position, like a passenger in the back seat of a car who tries to direct the driver. The phrase originated in the United States in the 1920s, when many cars were chauffeur-driven and their passengers sat in the back seat, quite legitimately directing the chauffeur where to go.

> Aides … emphasized that he [retiring Liberal Democrat leader Paddy Ashdown] had no ambition to be a 'back-seat driver' for Mr Kennedy's leadership.
> *The Times* (22 September 1999)

Backstage. This word's sense of 'behind the scenes' dates only from the 1920s. Originally the back stage was a recess in the rear wall of a stage used for pieces of scenery in a deep-set vista or otherwise for storage. The term then came to apply to all parts of the theatre behind the stage, including the actors' dressing rooms.

Back to basics. A return to 'ground rules' and traditional values. The catch-all slogan was coined by the then prime minister, John Major, at the Conservative Party Conference of 1993. A succession of minor sex scandals involving Tory MPs in the months that followed gave the dictum an unfortunate resonance.

> It is time to get back to basics: to self-discipline and respect for the law, to consideration for others, to accepting responsibility for yourself and your family, and not shuffling it off on the state.
> JOHN MAJOR: Speech at Conservative Party Conference (8 October 1993)

Back to Methuselah. A play (1921) by the Irish play-

wright George Bernard Shaw (1856–1950) consisting of five loosely linked plays on a variety of philosophical themes, including that of old age. Methuselah is the oldest man mentioned in the Bible, in which he is said to have lived to the age of 969. Shaw himself lived to the age of 94. He once ascribed his long life to the location of his home in the village of Ayot St Lawrence, Hertfordshire, explaining that he had decided 'this is the place for me' after spotting a gravestone with the legend: 'Jane Eversley. Born 1825. Died 1895. Her time was short.'

Back to square one. Back to where one started. The expression apparently gained currency from the early days of broadcast commentaries on football matches when, in order to make the course of the game easier to follow, a diagram of the pitch, divided into numbered squares, was printed in radio programmes. The idea may have been derived from earlier board games such as SNAKES AND LADDERS.

> The film [*Girl*] goes back to square one every time [Dominique] Swain goes back to her man. Who needs a coming-of-age story that suffers from arrested development?
> *Sunday Times* (26 September 1999)

Back to the drawing board. Back to begin again, especially after the aborting of an enterprise. The implication is that the venture was not properly or adequately planned. The expression may have originated with aircraft designers in the Second World War, when tests revealed faults in some models.

> His message is brutal and blunt. 'We've got to go back to the drawing-board and no longer scrabble around in the hope of winning short-term engagements and battles.'
> *New Statesman* (10 May 1999)

Bad hair day. A day on which nothing seems to go right, as when one's hair proves to be quite unmanageable. The expression dates from the 1980s.

Bad news. An unpleasant person or thing. More specifically, in US usage, the bad news is the bill in a café or restaurant, as: 'OK, let's see what the bad news is.' *See also* GOOD NEWS AND THE BAD NEWS.

Bad trip. A bad or frightening experience while taking psychedelic drugs. The phrase dates from the 1960s.

Baedeker raid. A phrase originating in 1942 to describe a German air attack on a historic or culturally important British city, and specifically one listed in a Baedeker guidebook, such as Bath, Canterbury or

Norwich. The raids were made in reprisal for British raids on Cologne and Lübeck. The guides themselves were originally issued by Karl Baedeker (1801–59) in Coblenz.

BAFTA award. An annual award of the British Academy of Film and Television Arts, founded in 1976 to promote British films and television. It is subdivided into categories such as 'best actress', 'best actor', 'best original screenplay' and the like. The awards ceremony is televised live by the BBC as a glittering show overlaid with a gloss of mutual admiration and mawkish sentimentality. *See also* OSCAR.

Baggins, Bilbo. The hero of J.R.R. Tolkien's children's novel, *The* HOBBIT (1937). He is a small, hairy-footed being who, accompanied by the wizard GANDALF and a dozen 'dwarves', helps slay a dragon and recover a lost treasure. He reappears in *The* LORD OF THE RINGS (1954–5). *See also* FRODO.

Bag lady. A homeless woman who wanders the streets carrying all her possessions in shopping bags. The phrase originated in the United States.

Bag of nerves. *See* BUNDLE OF NERVES.

Bagpuss. An award-winning children's television cartoon, first shown in 1974, in which Emily, a Victorian girl who owns a magic shop, leaves various objects for her beloved eponymous cloth cat and his friends to mend. After the item was restored to its former glory, it was put in the window for its owner to collect. The pink-and-white striped Bagpuss, so named because he was 'baggy and a bit loose at the seams', would then yawn and go to sleep until the next episode.

Bail bandit. A colloquialism of the 1990s for a person who commits a crime while on bail awaiting trial.

Bailey bridge. A temporary bridge made of prefabricated steel parts that can be erected speedily, invented by the engineer Sir Donald Bailey (1901–85). In the Second World War such bridges were a major factor in the rapidity of Allied advances, especially in northwestern Europe.

Bailie Vass. A nickname used by *Private Eye* for Sir Alec Douglas-Home (1903–95), Conservative prime minister (1963–4). The nickname arose from a miscaptioning of a photograph in a Scottish newspaper (a bailie is a municipal magistrate in Scotland). To everybody's surprise Douglas-Home succeeded Harold Macmillan (SUPERMAC) as prime minister when the latter resigned at the time of the PROFUMO AFFAIR. To do so he renounced his title of 14th earl of

Home, and the Labour leader Harold Wilson (1916–95) observed. 'The whole process of democracy has ground to a halt with a fourteenth earl.' Douglas-Home responded: 'I suppose, if you come to think of it, Mr Wilson is the fourteenth Mr Wilson.' In 1974 Alec Douglas-Home became a life peer as Baron Home of the Hirsel.

Bait and switch. A deceptive and generally illegal commercial ruse by which customers are induced to visit a store by an advertised sale item (the 'bait'), only to be told that it is out of stock or that it is inferior to some more expensive item (the 'switch'). The expression dates from the 1920s.

Baked Alaska. The name of this tasty dessert, combining hot meringue and cold ice cream on a sponge cake base, is first recorded in the 1909 edition of Fannie Farmer's *Boston Cookery Book*. It existed some time before this, however, and is said by some to have been created by the chef Charles Ranhofer, who called it 'Alaska, Florida' in his cookbook of 1893.

Bakelite. The material course of modern life was altered significantly in 1909 when Leo Baekeland (1863–1944), a Belgian-born American chemist, announced his invention of Bakelite, the first synthetic polymer, basing its name on his own. It was hard, indissoluble, able to be moulded into different shapes and, above all, inexpensive. Commercial production began within a year, and soon everything from billiard balls to electrical insulators was made from the new plastic.

Baker days. Days set aside in term time for teacher training in state schools. Such days, also known as INSET (in-service training), were introduced in 1987 by Kenneth Baker (b.1934), secretary of state for education, originally to acquaint teachers with new policies and classroom practice and to prepare them for the National Curriculum. With the pupils absent, some schools have taken advantage of such days to send teachers on 'educational' visits to museums or even on day trips abroad by way of 'team-building exercises'.

> Parents hate them. Children don't understand them. Even teachers have come to resent them. So why do we shut down our schools for five 'Baker days' a year?
>
> *The Times* (26 February 1999)

Bakerloo Line. A line of the London Underground that, when opened in 1906, ran only between Baker

Street and Waterloo. Hence its portmanteau name, said to have been coined by 'Quex' (G.H.F. Nichols) of the *Evening News*.

Bakewell tart. The name of this baked pie dates only from the early 20th century. It was formerly known as Bakewell pudding, and is still so called in Bakewell, Derbyshire, its town of origin.

Balance of nature. An ecological equilibrium, produced by the interaction of living organisms. The expression dates from the turn of the 20th century.

Balance of payments. The difference over a given period between a nation's gross receipts from other countries and its gross payments to them, the result being adverse or favourable.

Balance of terror. A state of equilibrium between nations based on their mutual possession of nuclear weapons or some other means of mass terror. The expression dates from the COLD WAR and is said to have been coined in 1955 by the Canadian prime minister, Lester Pearson.

Balcombe Street Gang. An IRA group, which terrorized London in the early 1970s in a campaign of bombings and shootings. The name is that of the Marylebone street where the four gunmen, Joseph O'Connell, Harry Duggan, Eddie Butler and Hugh Doherty, took a husband and wife hostage in December 1975 following a car chase and running gun battle in the West End. The men were jailed for life in 1977.

Bald Eagle of Foggy Bottom. A nickname of Robert A. Lovett (1895–1986), US secretary of state and undersecretary of defence under President Truman. The name alludes to his baldness, but also invites comparison with the bald eagle that is the national symbol of the United States. The latter part of the name refers to his time in the State Department, known as FOGGY BOTTOM.

Bald Prima Donna, The. A one-act play (*La Cantatrice chauve*) by the Romanian-born French playwright Eugène Ionesco (1912–94), which was first performed in Paris in 1950 to an audience of three. Described by the author as an 'anti-play', it is an apparently nonsensical entertainment in which the words exchanged by the characters seem to have no relation to each other, and it owed its genesis to the author's fascination with examples of bizarre English phrases in language books. The 'bald prima donna' herself is the subject of just one obscure reference in the text,

which actually came about in rehearsal when the Fire-chief garbled the words Ionesco had originally written. *See also* THEATRE OF THE ABSURD.

Fire-chief: By the way, what about the Bald Prima Donna?
Mr Smith: Ssh!
Mrs Smith: She always wears her hair the same way!

Balfour Declaration. A letter expressing the views of the British government, written on 2 November 1917 by the foreign secretary Arthur Balfour (1848–1930) to Lionel Walter, 2nd Baron Rothschild (1868–1937), chairman of the British ZIONIST Federation. The letter stated the British government's support for 'the establishment in Palestine of a national home for the Jewish people' but specified that 'nothing shall be done which may prejudice the civil and religious rights of existing non-Jewish communities in Palestine' and that the political status of Jews in other countries should not be compromised. The Balfour Declaration was incorporated into the British mandate over Palestine (formerly part of the Turkish Ottoman empire) awarded by the League of Nations in 1922, but the British abandoned the policy in 1939 and severely limited further Jewish immigration.

Balfour's poodle. The House of Lords. From 1906 the Conservative leader Arthur Balfour (1848–1930) exploited his party's majority in the Lords to block the legislation of Campbell-Bannerman's Liberal government, which had an overwhelming majority in the House of Commons. When the Lords rejected the Licensing Bill of 1908, Henry Chaplin, MP, claimed that the House of Lords was the 'watchdog of the constitution', to which Lloyd George replied: 'It is the right honourable gentleman's poodle. It fetches and carries for him. It barks for him. It bites anybody that he sets it on.' The expression was popularized by the title of Roy Jenkins's book *Mr Balfour's Poodle* (1954), an account of the struggle between the House of Lords and Asquith's government. This came to a head when the Lords vetoed Lloyd George's 'radical budget' of 1909 and led to the Parliament Bill of 1911, ending the power of the upper house to veto.

Ballad of the Sad Café, The. The title piece of *The Ballad of the Sad Café and Other Stories* (1951) by the US novelist Carson McCullers (1917–67). The café of the title is created as an evening retreat for the people of a small Georgia town by Amelia, the muscular 30-year-old who owns the store. It was done at the suggestion of her cousin, a hunchback, who becomes fascinated with Amelia's husband of 10 days, now released from prison after an orgy of vandalism following her refusal to sleep with him. Amelia and her husband have a fight, which she loses when her cousin intervenes, the café is wrecked, and Amelia is psychologically and physically isolated. The rather Gothic story, with its stark effects and changes of mood, reflects the techniques of the traditional ballad form. There was a stage version (1963) by Edward Albee and a disappointing film version (1990) directed by Simon Callow. *See also* HEART IS A LONELY HUNTER.

Ballboy or **ballgirl.** A young person employed to retrieve balls that go out of play in tennis or some other game. Ballboys and ballgirls are particularly associated with the annual international tennis championships at Wimbledon, where they are constantly in the public eye. They were long recruited from Barnardo's foster homes but are now selected from year 10 (14- and 15-year-olds) at local comprehensive schools. They receive six months of disciplined coaching, including instruction in rolling and feeding balls to the players, and are issued with smart green uniforms. For many years only boys were engaged. They were joined by their female counterparts in 1979, but girls were not admitted into the elite Centre Court team of 12 until 1985.

Ballet des Étoiles de Paris. This Paris ballet company first appeared as the *Ballets 1956 de Paris* at the Festival of Lyon-Charbonnières in the year stated. Two years later it changed its name to *Ballet 1958 des Étoiles de Paris*, changing the year in the title annually until 1961, when it abandoned the practice. Its aim was to concentrate on what it called the *danseur étoile*, 'star dancer', while infusing its performances with the contemporary spirit and tastes of the French capital.

Ballet Rambert. *See* RAMBERT DANCE COMPANY.

Ballets Russes. The world's first modern ballet company was born on 18 March 1909 at the Théâtre du Châtelet, Paris, when a troupe of top-class Russian dancers, brought by Sergei Diaghilev (1872–1929) from St Petersburg and Moscow, staged *Le Pavillon d'Armide*, the *Polovtsian Dances* from *Prince Igor* and *Le Festin*. The event was a sensation with the public and launched Diaghilev himself as the greatest producer and impresario of the modern theatrical world. The company dissolved in 1929 following Diaghilev's death, and in 1932 it was succeeded by the Ballets Russes de Monte Carlo, with Colonel de Basil (originally Vasili Voskresensky; 1888–1951) as director.

Ballgirl. *See* BALLBOY.

Ball is in your court, The. It is up to you to make the next move. A metaphor from tennis dating from the 1950s.

Ballpark figure. An approximate figure, especially of a financial amount. A ballpark is a US baseball stadium. Since the playing area is large, a ballpark figure will not be narrowly defined. The term, which dates from the 1950s, equally relates to the practice of estimating the crowd attendance at a baseball game. *See also* IN THE RIGHT BALLPARK.

Ball-tampering. In cricket the illegal alteration of the surface of a ball to affect its motion through the air when bowled. 'Tampering' of this kind is usually effected by fingering or rubbing the seams of the ball, as when a bowler rubs a ball on his trousers before a delivery.

Ball the jack, To. To travel fast; to hurry. The expression originated in US railway jargon, in which a 'highball' was a signal to get under way or to increase speed and 'jack' was a locomotive. 'Ballin' the Jack', by Roy Burris, was a popular song in the ZIEGFELD FOLLIES 1913 revue.

> No sooner were we out of town than Eddie started to ball that jack ninety miles an hour out of sheer exuberance.
> JACK KEROUAC: *On the Road*, Pt I, ch iii (1957)

Ballyhoo. Fuss and bother. The word is of US origin and caught on in the early 20th century. Its source is disputed. A connection with the name of Ballyhooly, a village in Co. Cork, Ireland, has not been sustained, and even less likely is a blend of 'ballet' and 'whoop'. It is possible the initial 'bally' may be the same as the now old-fashioned euphemism for 'bloody'.

Ballykissangel. A popular and picturesque television comedy series, first screened on BBC1 in 1996 and set in the fictional Irish village of the title name, supposedly meaning 'town of the banished angel' but in fact based on the real Irish village of Ballykissan. It is a clerical comedy centring originally on the triumphs of a newly arrived English priest, Peter Clifford, whose secular travails include the landlady Assumpta Fitzgerald and the local fixer and businessman Brian Quigley. The series happened to coincide with an explosion of interest in things Irish, and 'Bally-K', as it came to be affectionately known, opened the eyes of many viewers to the changing role of religion in Irish society at the close of the 20th century, as typified by the loss of faith in many of the characters.

Baloney or **boloney.** Nonsense. The word dates from the 1920s and is said on dubious ground to derive from the Bologna sausage. The connection between the two remains obscure, although the sausage so named is traditionally said to have originally been stuffed with odds and ends ('rubbish') from slaughterhouses. When the United States went off the gold standard in 1933 the devalued dollar was nicknamed the 'baloney dollar', the reasoning being that no matter how thinly the sausage is sliced it still retains its basic characteristics.

Bambi. A young deer who lives in a German forest. He originated as the creation of Felix Salten (real name Sigmund Salzmann) in his gentle children's novel *Bambi* (1926), which is a more or less realistic depiction of forest life. Bambi gained his greatest fame, however, from the Walt Disney feature-length cartoon named after him, released in 1942. His name, a shortening of Italian *bambino*, 'baby', was applied by the media to Tony Blair when he became leader of the Labour Party and, later, prime minister. The allusion was to his youthfully innocent appearance.

> Walt Disney made no more drastic or mistaken change than when he showed Bambi as a cute, lisping celluloid puppet titupping through a rainbow-hued landscape. A child who came to the book after seeing Disney's cartoon would find it hard to believe that Salten's young deer was the same character.
> MARGERY FISHER: *Who's Who in Children's Books* (1975)

Bamboo Curtain. Formed by analogy with IRON CURTAIN to denote the veil of secrecy and mistrust drawn between the Chinese communist bloc and the non-communist nations. The expression dates from the late 1940s. *See also* GARLIC WALL.

Bampopo. The fictional British colony in Equatorial Africa that is the setting of Norman Douglas's novel *South Wind* (1917). It is inhabited by various tribes, the most noteworthy being the Bulanga, the Bilongo and the M'tezo. Bampopo is a diocese of the Church of England, and Anglican missionaries have successfully converted the Bilongo. The M'tezo have firmly declined to follow the new faith, however, and have retained their traditional customs of going naked, filing their teeth and eating their relatives.

Banana. A derogatory term for an Asian who has chosen to adopt white, Western values. Such a person is 'yellow outside but white inside'. The term dates from the 1960s.

Banana belt. A US term for a winter resort with a relatively mild climate. It was originally applied on Baffin Island in the 1960s to mainland North America as a region ('belt') regarded as being warm enough to grow bananas.

Banana King. Roger Ackerley (1863–1929), chief salesman of the banana importers Elders & Fyffes, was so known. He did much to make Britain 'banana-conscious' in the early 20th century.

Banana oil. A phrase used colloquially in Australia and America for 'nonsense' or 'insincere talk'.

Banana republic. A small state, especially one in Central America, whose economy centres solely on the export of bananas. In consequence, the country is heavily dependent on foreign capital. The expression, which dates from the mid-1930s, came to gain a pejorative ring.

Banana skin. A cause of upset and humiliation. Fake banana skins are stock devices in pantomime for causing a 'pratfall'.

> The man who slips on the cunningly placed banana-skin does not laugh so soon as those who set the harmless trap and so, from the first, observe the whole scene.
> JOHN RUSSELL BROWN: *Shakespeare's Plays in Performance*, ch x (1966)

Band Aid. A series of charity projects undertaken by the rock singer Bob Geldof after seeing a television documentary about the famine in Ethiopia in 1984. He contacted Midge Ure of the group Ultravox and they booked an array of stars from the world of pop to record a song of their own composition, 'Do They Know It's Christmas?'. Profits from the sales of the single, together with those from related projects such as the sale of T-shirts and videos, went to the famine victims. Geldof went to Ethiopia himself in 1985, then on 13 July 1985, under the name of Live Aid, arranged a huge simultaneous concert linking the Wembley Stadium in London with Philadelphia. The money raised by all this amounted to some £60 million by mid-1987. Meanwhile a similar US enterprise, American Band Aid, released the hit song 'We Are the World' on 1 April 1985. The name itself puns on 'Band Aid', the proprietary name of a US brand of adhesive sticking plaster similar to ELASTOPLAST. *See also* COMIC RELIEF.

Bandit Country. A name given to the southern part of the county of Armagh, Northern Ireland, by the then Labour secretary of state for Northern Ireland, Merlyn Rees, in November 1975. Rees used the name in a statement after the shooting by the IRA of three British soldiers at Drummuckavall, near Crossmaglen:

> There has never been a cease-fire in South Armagh for a variety of reasons – the nature of the countryside and the nature of the people. It is an unusual area – there is little support for the security forces in South Armagh. The government is not trying to buy off terrorism by the release of detainees as the number of terrorists arrested and charged shows. The release of detainees has nothing to do with the violence of the bandit country of South Armagh. There is wholesale gangsterism there.

The term was resented by nationalists, who saw it as typical of British efforts to portray as the actions of thugs and outlaws what they regarded as blows for Irish freedom. Some Republicans, however, revelled in it as a 'badge of honour' and as triumphant proof of the effectiveness of the IRA's military strategy in the area.

South Armagh is bordered on three sides by the Irish Republic and its largely Catholic population is historically sympathetic to the Republican cause. From the outset of the TROUBLES it was dominated by the Provisional IRA, who operated here with a greater freedom of action than in any other part of Northern Ireland. Attacks by the local brigade of the IRA included the sectarian massacre at Kingsmills, near Newry, in January 1976 of 12 Protestants (itself a revenge attack for the slaughter of three Catholics by Loyalists), the ambush and murder of 18 British soldiers at Narrow Water, near Warrenpoint, in August 1979, and the mysterious abduction and assassination in 1977 of Captain Robert Nairac, a maverick Grenadier Guards officer, whose body has never been found. *See also* NO-GO AREA; PROVOS.

Bandito, El. A nickname given by the Argentinian press to the Manchester United and England footballer Nobby Stiles (b.1942) on account of the supposed brutality of his tackling in Argentina's quarter-final defeat by England in the 1966 World Cup. The unprepossessing Stiles was also known as the 'Toothless Tiger' because of his committed style of play and his wearing of false teeth. Stiles is affectionately remembered for his dancing a spontaneous jig of delight around Wembley stadium after England's victory over West Germany in the 1966 World Cup Final.

B and K. A shorthand used by journalists to refer to the Soviet leaders Nikolai Bulganin (1895–1975) and Nikita Khrushchev (1894–1971) when they visited the UK in 1956.

Bangers and mash. Sausages and mashed potatoes. The former are presumably so called because their skins are liable to burst when they are being cooked. The dish is popularly regarded as quintessentially British, although other nations equally enjoy the combination. 'Bangers' as a word for sausages has been current from the early 20th century, but the vogue for bangers and mash themselves began mainly after the Second World War.

Bang to rights. Caught in the act; arrested with positive proof of guilt. The slang expression is of US origin, dating from the 1920s, and derives from 'bang', denoting a sudden action, in this case the apprehending of a criminal, and 'to rights', meaning 'according to the law', 'good and proper'.

Banker's hours. Short working hours. The allusion is to the former usual opening hours of a bank, in Britain 9.30 a.m. to 3.30 p.m., in the United States 10.00 a.m. to 2.00 p.m. Bankers themselves actually work longer hours.

Bankroll, To. To provide financial backing for a project, as if offering rolls of bank notes. The term is of US origin and dates from the 1920s.

Ban the bomb. An anti-nuclear slogan of the 1950s of US origin, adopted subsequently by the CND. The alliterative brevity of the phrase made it memorable.

Bantustan. The name given to each of the supposedly independent areas set aside for black people in South Africa in the 1970s on the basis of ethnic and linguistic groupings. The first of the homelands, as they were also known, was Transkei, set up in 1976. Bophuthatswana followed in 1977, Venda in 1979, and Ciskei in 1981. Their independence did not receive international recognition since the areas were clearly set up to allow the white government to control the blacks and exclude them from the political process. Six further black states, containing approximately a third of South Africa's total black population, were 'self-governing' but non-independent: Gazankulu, KwaZulu, Lebowa, KwaNdebele, KaNgwane and Qwaqwa. Since 1994 all the Bantustans have rejoined the 'new' South Africa under the democratically elected black-majority government led by the African National Congress. Bantustan meant 'Bantu country', just as Hindustan means 'Hindu country'.

Banzai. In the Second World War a nickname for a reckless military attack by the Japanese. The word represents the shout or cheer given by the Japanese when greeting the emperor or going into battle. The literal meaning is '10,000 years', as a wish that the person may live that long.

Bara, Theda. The exotic US film actress who became intimately associated with the term VAMP was born Theodosia Goodman in Cincinnati, Ohio, c.1885, the daughter of Bernard Goodman, an immigrant Polish Jew, and Pauline Louise de Coppet, a Frenchwoman. Her press agents put it about that she was born an Arab princess in the Sahara desert, further claiming that her name was an anagram of 'Arab Death'. However, the Goodman family were already calling themselves Bara when she began her career, taking the name from Coppet's Swiss father, Francis Bara de Coppet, and Theda was simply a pet form of the actress's first name. She died in 1955.

Barbarella. The blonde space voyager in a comic strip by Jean-Claud Forest, originally published in the French *V Magazine* from 1962. Her piquant adventures were collected in a 1964 book of her name that was translated into several languages. A film of the same title directed by Roger Vadim was produced in 1967 in which she was played by Jane Fonda.

Barbarossa. The code name for the German invasion of the Soviet Union on 22 June 1941. It was originally to have been called Fritz, but on 18 December 1940 Hitler renamed the operation after the byname, meaning 'Redbeard', of Emperor Frederick I (c.1123–90), who it was said would rise from his deathlike sleep and restore Germany to power. The intention was to capture three key cities, Leningrad, Moscow and Archangel, but although the operation began with tactical gains, it ultimately failed. Leningrad never fell, the Germans were checked before Moscow, and Hitler's forces were totally unprepared for the onset of winter.

Barbershop. A popular style of close harmony singing, revived in the 1930s in the United States from its former 19th-century vogue. The origins of the name are somewhat obscure. It may date from a time when US barber's shops were social and musical centres for the males of the locality or else refer back to British 'barber's music', meaning an extempore performance put on by patrons in a barber's shop as they waited their turn to be shaved.

Barbican. The word is most familiar as the proper name of the London Barbican, a complex of high-rise apartment blocks grouped around the Barbican Centre, a large and brutish building opened in 1982 as a major cultural and exhibition centre. The complex takes its name from a former street, which was itself named after a watchtower in the city walls. The word represents Medieval Latin *barbacana*, but the origin of this is unknown.

Barbie doll. The progenitor of the curvaceous blonde doll was the German toy manufacturer Rolf Hausser, who launched her on the market on 12 August 1955, basing his creation on a cartoon character called Lili, who had first appeared in the German newspaper *Bild Zeitung* in 1952. In 1956 Ruth and Elliot Handler, co-founders of the US toy manufacturers Mattel, were on holiday in Lucerne with their daughter Barbara and son Ken when Barbara, then aged 15, pointed out the Lili doll in a shop window. Mrs Handler bought one and took it home. A manufacturer for a clone was found, and on 9 March 1959 Barbara Millicent Roberts, otherwise Barbie, named for the young girl who had spotted her prototype, was launched at the American Toy Fair in New York. In 1961 she was joined by a 'boyfriend', Ken, named after Barbara's brother.

Barcelona chair. A stainless steel chair with leather cushions and usually without arms. A chair of this type was originally exhibited in Barcelona in 1929 by the German architect Ludwig Mies van der Rohe, who designed it.

Barcode. The first machine-readable code in the form of figures and parallel lines was introduced in supermarkets in 1973. All countries have their individual authority for numbering, and each uses the first two or three digits for the full sequence of 13 figures. In Britain the prefix is 50. When a company seeks a barcode for a branded product it is given a number beginning with 50 followed by five more digits. The company then allocates a further five figures, making a total of 12. The 13th digit is a check, calculated from the other 12 to ensure that the overall number is correct.

Bare-faced cheek. One of a number of standard phrases adopted as humorous euphemisms to denote nudity, in this case of the backside as when MOONING.

Others of a more general nature are 'revealing one's assets', 'disclosing one's secrets', 'showing one's charms'. 'presenting one's credentials' and 'displaying one's wares'. The punning phrases are typical of tabloid journalism.

Barefoot doctor. A paramedical worker with basic medical training, especially one working in rural China. The phrase, dating from the 1970s, translates Chinese *chìjiǎo yīshēng*.

Barefoot in the Park. A play (1963) by the US playwright Neil Simon (b.1927) about a newly married couple who experience their first fallings-out as they move into their first home, a tiny flat at the top of five flights of stairs. The title relates to the wife's complaint that her lawyer-husband is too strait-laced when he turns down an invitation to walk barefoot in the park in the freezing weather (he subsequently does so, despite a raging cold). Simon also wrote the screenplay for the film (1967), which starred Jane Fonda and Robert Redford as Corie and Paul Bratter and Ethel Banks as Corie's mother, Mildred.

> *Ethel*: I feel like we've died and gone to heaven – only we had to climb up.

Barfly. A person who spends much time in a bar, as if 'buzzing' around it.

Bargaining chip or **counter.** A potential concession or other factor that can be used to advantage in negotiations. The expression dates from US diplomatic usage of the mid-1960s and relates to the gambling chip. A poker player or gambler will obviously be at an advantage if he has a good supply of chips when bluffing or bidding against other players. The term became prominent during arms limitation talks between the United States and the USSR.

> The Government has taken a positive step to help industry in Scotland without giving up any bargaining chips in relation to the real battle.
> *The Times* (Letter to the Editor) (10 September 1999)

Barking mad. Completely crazy. The allusion is to an uncontrollable dog.

Barmy army. A phrase used of enthusiastic sports spectators, especially at cricket and football matches. Rowdy cricket fans were nicknamed the 'Barmy Army' on the Ashes tour of Australia in 1994–5. A Scottish equivalent is the TARTAN ARMY.

> As tension mounted and the drinks flowed, a huge man wearing a Union Jack T-shirt stepped forward:
> 'Barmy Army! Barmy Army!' he cried, immediately joined in this chorus by several hundred voices.
> *The Times* (4 July 1998)

Barnacle Bailey. The nickname of the Essex and England cricketer Trevor Bailey (b.1923), a notably obdurate and 'clinging' batsman, whose celebrated partnership with Willie Watson to save England from defeat against Australia in the 1953 Ashes series made him a national hero.

Barnes, Jake. The impotent hero of Ernest Hemingway's famous first novel *The Sun Also Rises* (1926). As a war-wounded American living in Paris he becomes embroiled with the fascinating Lady Brett Ashley, and both are archetypes of the LOST GENERATION. In the film of the book (1957), which was directed by Henry King, he was played by Tyrone Power, and Ava Gardner played the aristocratic love interest.

Barrel of fun or **of laughs.** A source of much fun or merriment. The expression is mostly found in the negative, as: 'It wasn't exactly a barrel of laughs.' A barrel contains beer, which is conducive to merriment. The expression is of US origin.

> Roll out the barrel,
> We'll have a barrel of fun!
> JAROMIR VEYVODA, WLADIMIR TIMM and LEW BROWN: 'The Beer Barrel Polka' (song) (1939)

Barrow Boy. A nickname, punning on his surname, of the colourful Conservative politician Sir Gerald Nabarro (1913–73), MP for Kidderminster from 1950 to 1973 and owner of several cars with a CHERISHED NUMBER beginning NAB.

Barrow Poets. A group of poets founded in 1951 with the aim of selling their books of verse from street barrows in London during the FESTIVAL OF BRITAIN. When refused a licence for outdoor trading they turned to poetry readings in pubs and other places of public entertainment. By 1969 they had become sufficiently accepted to give a lunchtime reading in Westminster Abbey and had official approval to sell from their barrows in the Queen Elizabeth Hall on the SOUTH BANK.

Barton, Dick. The doughty hero of the BBC's first daily radio serial, *Dick Barton – Special Agent!*, running from 1946 to 1951. With the help of his trusted sidekicks, Snowey White and Jock Anderson, he foiled a host of criminal enterprises in a stream of thrilling adventures. A short television series based on the stories was screened in 1979. The series had a memorable signature tune in the form of Charles Williams's pounding 'Devil's Galop' (1944).

> I like Dick Barton and listen to him when I get the chance. I listen because I like it, which seems a good reason for doing a thing provided you don't get yourself into trouble. There are too many people going round publicly trying to psycho-analyse other people.
> HERBERT MORRISON quoted in E.S. TURNER: *Boys Will Be Boys*, ch xvii (1948)

Bart Simpson. *See* SIMPSON, BART.

Barwick Green. The catchy signature tune to the radio series *The* ARCHERS, one of the most familiar pieces of music in the whole of British broadcasting. It is the last segment of Arthur Wood's four-part suite *My Native Heath* (1922), composed in honour of his native Yorkshire.

> Even now, 15-or-so years later, this friend shivers on hearing the opening bars of Barwick Green.
> *Sunday Times* (31 October 1999)

Base or **BASE jump.** A parachute jump from a high point on land, such as the roof of a tall building or a clifftop, instead of from an aircraft. The acronym represents four such points: 'building, antenna tower (of a radio station), span (of a bridge), earth.' The sport evolved in the United States in the 1970s. One of its champions was the daredevil parachutist Thor Alex Kapperfjell (1967–99), known as the 'Human Fly', who once jumped from the Eiffel Tower. His favourite launch sites were Manhattan's tallest buildings, and his conquests included the Empire State Building, World Trade Center, Chrysler Building and Trump Tower. He was planning a leap from Chicago's Sears Tower when he was killed in an accident on a cliff in Norway after losing his bearings in fog.

Bash Street Kids. A group of unruly schoolchildren in a picture strip in the BEANO comic.

BASIC. *See* PROGRAMMING LANGUAGES.

Basic English. A fundamental selection of 850 English words designed in the 1920s by C.K. Ogden (1889–1957) as a common first step in the teaching of English and as an auxiliary language. The name comes from the initials of the words British, American, Scientific, International, Commercial.

Basil Brush. A fox puppet possessed of a gap-toothed grin, an upper-class voice and a prominent, highly mobile tail. Basil Brush first appeared on British television in 1964 and had his own Saturday children's show from 1968 to 1980, accompanied by a variety of straight men. His hallmark was a raucous cry of 'boom boom', which accompanied his usually execrable jokes. His operator was Ivan Owen.

Basin Street. A street in the red light district of the French quarter of New Orleans, which is possibly the original home of US JAZZ. The well-known 'Basin Street Blues' was composed by Spencer Williams in 1928.

Basket case. Originally, a soldier who had lost all four limbs in the First World War and thus had to be carried in a litter ('basket'). Hence, generally, any useless or incapable person or thing, especially when needing the support of others.

> There seems no other option but to find someone else to run the company, but what could persuade any credible retailer to put their name to the worst basket-case in the sector?
> *The Times* (28 September 1999)

Basket of currencies. A group or range of currencies, especially as used for calculating values in certain international financial transactions. The term is economic jargon and dates from the 1970s. The image is presumably of a shopping basket that holds a collection of similar things.

Bataan Death March. The forced march of some 70,000 US and Filipino prisoners of war, captured by the Japanese in the Philippines in the early stages of the Second World War. The march started on 9 April 1941 at Mariveles, at the southern end of the Bataan Peninsula, and covered 88km (55 miles) to San Fernando. From there the marchers were taken by rail to Capas, from where they marched the final 13km (8 miles) to Camp O'Donnell. The marchers were constantly starved and beaten, and many who fell by the wayside were bayoneted. Only 54,000 reached the camp. After the war, the Japanese commander of the invasion forces in the Philippines, Lieutenant General Homma Masaharu, was charged with responsibility for the death march, tried by a US military commission and executed on 3 April 1946.

Bates, Norman. The mad murderer in charge of a lonely motel in Robert Bloch's novel PSYCHO (1959). He believes that he is his own mother and in a fit of sexual frenzy kills a young woman who has unwittingly aroused him. The story was the basis for one of Alfred Hitchcock's most memorable movies (1960), in which Bates is played by Anthony Perkins. In *Psycho 2*

(1982), Bloch's sequel to his original novel, Bates escapes from the hospital for the criminally insane in which he has been confined and once more goes on the rampage. A film loosely based on this was produced in 1983, again starring Perkins, and he also played him in a further sequel, *Psycho 3* (1986), with himself as director.

Bates method. A system of simple eyesight exercises designed to keep the eyes strong and healthy without the use of lenses or surgery. The technique was devised in the 1920s by the US ophthalmologist William H. Bates (1860–1931).

Bathing beauty. An attractive young woman in a bathing costume, especially one taking part in a beauty contest at a seaside resort. The now dated expression arose in the 1920s. An alternative was 'bathing belle'.

Bathing Towel. A punning nickname dating from his Charterhouse schooldays for Lord Baden-Powell (1857–1941), founder of the BOY SCOUTS. He in fact held bathing in high esteem and recommended its merits to his charges and followers in *Scouting for Boys* (1908).

Batman. The costumed superhero of US comics, in popular regard almost as famous as SUPERMAN himself. He first appeared in 1939, conceived and drawn by Bob Kane (1915–98) for *Detective Comics*, issue number 37. His real name is Bruce Wayne, and in day-to-day life he is a Gotham City socialite, but dons his special bat suit, with cape and mask, in order to unmask villains incognito. His assistant is Robin, the Boy Wonder, alias Dick Grayson. He has appeared in most popular media, including books, films and television, and has inspired a female equivalent, Batgirl, alias Babs Gordon, who made her debut in *Detective Comics* in 1967. Batman's heroic deeds and escapades can be said to have classical antecedents in heroes such as Hercules (Heracles) and Ulysses (Odysseus). *See also* CAPED CRUSADER.

Battenberg cake. The name of this distinctively coloured cake is first recorded in 1903. It must have existed earlier, however, and the cake itself is said to have been created to mark the marriage in 1884 of Princess Victoria of Hesse-Darmstadt, granddaughter of Queen Victoria, to Prince Louis of Battenberg. The Prince later took British nationality and in 1917 anglicized his name to Mountbatten. One of their four children was Earl Louis Mountbatten of Burma (1900–79).

Batten down the hatches, To. To prepare for trouble. The term originated in naval parlance, when a ship's crew would prepare for a storm by fastening tarpaulins over hatches with battens (strips of wood).

> *Blue* was about getting through a tough time. ... Basically I battened down the hatches, got my head down, sorted it out and came out the other side with better songs.
>
> MICK HUCKNALL in *heat* (7–13 October 1999)

Battered baby. A young child who has been subjected to repeated injuries by one or more parents or some other adult. The injuries typically include bruises, burns and fractures, but their full extent may not be apparent until the child is examined medically and the complete skeleton X-rayed. The syndrome was first identified by social workers in the early 1960s. The concept was later extended to the battered wife and, although to a lesser extent, battered husband.

Battered Cherub. An amusingly descriptive nickname for the miner and trade union leader Joe Gormley, later 1st Baron Gormley (1917–93), who used it as the title of his autobiography (1982).

Battleaxe. A colourful term of US origin dating from the turn of the 20th century for a formidably aggressive and typically middle-aged or even elderly woman, who is figuratively seen as hacking her way through opponents and obstacles by wielding an axe. According to Christine Hamilton's *The Book of British Battleaxes* (1997), listing 33 representatives of the class (including herself), examples include the Conservative prime minister Margaret Thatcher (*see* IRON LADY), the dog trainer Barbara Woodhouse (*see* WALKIES), Queen Victoria (1819–1901), Viscountess Rothermere (*see* BUBBLES), the brothel-keeper Cynthia Payne (*see* MADAM CYN), and the fictional Ena Sharples, played by Violet Carson in the SOAP OPERA CORONATION STREET.

> The term Battleaxe was first used around 1910 and it referred then to a very closely defined type: elderly, probably a spinster, aggressive, resentful towards the world, thoroughly unpleasant and pretty ugly to boot! Cast aside that image! For the purposes of this book, the word Battleaxe covers a multitude of talents, attributes and attitudes.
>
> CHRISTINE HAMILTON: *The Book of British Battleaxes*, Introduction (1997)

Battlebus. The special bus in which a political leader tours marginal and other key constituencies in order to rouse the electorate in the run-up to a general election. *See also* WHISTLE-STOP TOUR.

Battle of Britain. The attempt of the German LUFT-WAFFE by their prolonged attack on southeastern England (August to October 1940) to defeat the RAF, as a prelude to invasion. RAF Fighter Command gained the victory and won universal admiration. The name arose from Sir Winston Churchill's speech (18 June 1940): 'What General Weygand called the Battle of France is over. I expect that the Battle of Britain is about to begin.' The words 'The Battle of Britain is about to begin' appeared in the order of the day for RAF pilots on 10 July. *See also* FEW; SEA LION.

Battle of Highbury. The nickname of the so-called friendly football match between England and Italy at Highbury on 14 November 1934, which England won 3–2. The name alludes to the behaviour of the Italian team, who, promised exemption from military service if they won, resorted to physical confrontation, leaving a number of English players injured and provoking retaliation.

Battle of the Atlantic. The continuous struggle for control of the sea routes around the British Isles in the Second World War.

Battle of the Bogside. The name given to the savage rioting that took place in the Catholic BOGSIDE area of Londonderry on 12–15 August 1969, during the first 'long hot summer' of Northern Ireland's modern TROUBLES. Sectarian clashes arising from the annual march of the (Protestant) Apprentice Boys of Derry turned into a serious confrontation between the ROYAL ULSTER CONSTABULARY and Catholics. When the police, accompanied by Protestant rioters, chased Catholics back into the Bogside, they were attacked by a hail of petrol bombs from enraged residents. The intervention of the B SPECIALS, hated by Catholics, exacerbated an already volatile situation. A semblance of order was restored when a British Army regiment stationed nearby took over the police lines. The 'Battle of the Bogside' was the first time that CS gas was used as a riot control in the United Kingdom. Rioting erupted elsewhere in Northern Ireland, particularly Belfast, where hundreds of Catholics were burned out of their homes on the night of 14 August. The events of 12–15 August led directly to the despatch of British troops to Northern Ireland, partly in response to the pleadings of moderate nationalist politicians for protection for their communities.

Battle of the Bulge. (1) The final chief German counter-offensive in the Second World War, also known as the Ardennes offensive, when the Allied forces were pushed back into Belgium in 1944, the 'bulge' being the wedge driven into their lines. The Germans were repulsed by the end of January 1945.

(2) The expression is also in colloquial use for a struggle to lose weight, a 'fight against flab', as well as for a fight by the visibly pregnant to maintain a regular routine.

Battle of the Somme. *See* SOMME.

Battleship Potemkin, The. A film (1925) commissioned by the Russian BOLSHEVIK regime to commemorate the 20th anniversary of the unsuccessful 1905 Revolution. Director Sergei Eisenstein focused on a single crucial episode of the 1905 Revolution, namely the mutiny of sailors on board the battleship *Potemkin* in the seaport of Odessa. The ruthless crushing of the rebellion by tsarist troops was encapsulated in the most famous scene of Eisenstein's film, that of the massacre of civilians on the ODESSA Steps (one of the most famous images in 20th-century cinema). In fact, this and many other scenes in the film diverged sharply from historical fact, and there is little real evidence of any such massacre taking place outside the imagination of Bolshevik propagandists.

Bauhaus. The 20th century's most important movement in art and design opened in 1919 when the German architect Walter Gropius (1883–1969) established the school of this name in Weimar. His aim was to return to first principles in every form and so end the 19th-century division into 'art' on the one hand and 'craft' on the other. The name itself means literally 'house of building'.

Bay of Pigs (Spanish *Bahía de los Cochinos*). The bay on the southwest coast of Cuba that on 17 April 1961 was the scene of an abortive invasion by a large group of anti-Castro dissidents. The operation was financed by the US government, which had been planning it for some months. The incident led to the installation of Soviet missile sites on Cuba and to the threat of nuclear war between the superpowers in October 1962. The crisis was resolved only when Russia agreed to dismantle the rocket bases and ship them home.

Baywatch. This highly popular and melodramatic US television series, with its sun-drenched beaches, swimwear-bursting bathing beauties and mainly moralistic but wholly sexless plots, was first screened in 1990. It centres on a group of male and female Malibu lifeguards and has unsurprisingly generated a number of lucrative commercial spin-offs.

Bazooka. (1) A trombone-like instrument invented by the US comedian Bob Burns (1896–1956). The name is perhaps modelled on 'bazoo' or 'kazoo', a once popular, submarine-shaped toy producing sounds of the 'comb and paper' variety.

(2) A portable, tubular rocket-launcher used as an anti-tank weapon in the Second World War. This sense of the word was introduced in 1943 by Major Zeb Hastings of the US Army to name the new rocket gun, which when fired went 'bazoooom'.

B.B. The pseudonym of the British writer and illustrator Denys James Watkins-Pitchford (1905–90), the author of the fantasy novel *The* LITTLE GREY MEN (1942). Watkins-Pitchford chose the initialism for *The Sportsman's Bedside Book* (1937) and derived it from the designation of the particular size of lead shot he used for shooting wild geese, BB being 0.18 inches in diameter.

BBC. The British Broadcasting Company, as it was originally called, was formed by six electrical companies and broadcast its first programme, a news bulletin, at 6 p.m. on 14 November 1922 from 2LO, a studio in Savoy Hill, London. Two days later this was followed by the first entertainment programme. It lasted an hour, opening with Leonard Hawke, a baritone, performing 'Duke Goes West' and 'Tick' and concluding with Dorothy Chalmers performing 'Hymn to the Sun' and Schubert's *Rosamunde* on the violin. Its charter expired on 31 December 1926, and the following year it became a corporation. Television was first broadcast from Alexandra Palace in 1936, and foreign broadcasts began the following year. The BBC's television monopoly was broken in 1954 with the introduction of the first commercial channel, and its radio monopoly was similarly lost in the 1970s. The BBC's contribution and finances are governed by royal charter, and its broadcasting is funded by an annual television licence fee. Increasing competition from commercial channels has latterly obliged the BBC to lighten its 'fuddy-duddy' image without losing its long-held respected public status.

Beached whale. A stock epithet for a large and ungainly person. A real whale in this situation is more likely to be described as 'stranded' or 'left high and dry'.

He [R.A. Butler] seemed like a benign and decent beached whale washed up on the harder shores of modern Conservatism.

PETER HENNESSY in the *Independent* (8 May 1987)

Bead shoes. A type of ornate women's shoes in fashion at the turn of the 20th century. They combined a high upper with the slightly waisted heel of a COURT SHOE, and the pattern cut into the leather was enhanced by an arrangement of tiny steel beads.

Béal na mBláth (Irish, 'the mouth of flowers'). A valley in West Cork, Ireland, between Bandon and Macroom, notorious in Irish folk memory as the location of the assassination on 22 August 1922 of the nationalist leader Michael Collins (1890–1922). As commander of the army of the newly created Irish Free State (*see* FREE-STATERS), Collins had travelled to the west of Ireland, where Republican 'Irregulars' opposed to the treaty that he had signed with Britain, which had brought the new state into being, were holding out against the forces of the Free State government. Travelling in an armoured convoy, Collins was ambushed and killed in a gun battle with anti-treaty IRA men, plunging Ireland into mourning and exacerbating the bitterness of the civil war. The assassination was graphically and movingly recreated in Neil Jordan's film *Michael Collins* (1996).

Collins's near-legendary status in nationalist Ireland and the dramatic circumstances of his death, ensured that myth and controversy attached to the events of 22 August 1922. In particular, the presence in the vicinity of Béal na mBláth at the time of Collins's death of Éamon de Valera, Collins's former comrade-in-arms, Republican arch-opponent of the Anglo-Irish Treaty and future Irish prime minister (*see* DEV; TAOISEACH), gave rise to conspiracy theories implicating de Valera in the assassination, but these have long since been discredited. *See also* BIG FELLA.

Beam me up, Scotty! Get me out of this! An expression of the desire to be elsewhere, originating on US campuses in the 1960s. The phrase quote Captain Kirk's supposed habitual request to the chief engineer, Lieutenant Commander 'Scotty' Scott, in the television series STAR TREK, to activate a 'beam' that can return him from a planet to the starship *Enterprise*. According to 'Trekkers', however, he never actually says this, his nearest equivalent words being 'Beam us up, Mr Scott'.

Beam someone up, To. To extricate someone from a

difficult situation. The allusion is to the misquotation BEAM ME UP, SCOTTY! from STAR TREK.

> 'Life on the road is very, very tough,' says Olson ...
> 'But this is the way the chips fell, and, until they can
> find a way to beam us up, we're just going to have to
> deal with it.'
>
> *The Times* (10 December 1999)

Beanie. A small, close-fitting hat worn on the back of the head, something like a skullcap. The word dates from the 1940s and presumably derives from 'bean' as a slang term for the head.

Beanie Babies. Soft, bean-filled toys launched in 1994. They existed in about 200 different types of animals and characters and became an all-consuming craze for collectors, first in the United States, where they originated, then in Britain. Each type had a different name, such as Quackers the Duck, Chilly the Polar Bear and Waddle the Penguin, and collectors attended regular Beanie Fairs or traded their toys on the INTERNET. In 1999 their creator, Ty Warner, unexpectedly discontinued the toys, whose immense popularity had made him the richest toy-maker in the world.

Beano. A popular children's comic, published weekly since 1938. Its memorable characters include the little terror DENNIS THE MENACE, who first appeared in 1951, and at the top of the social scale, the top-hatted Lord Snooty. The latter was disposed of in 1992, however, in the interests of POLITICAL CORRECTNESS.

Bean Town. A nickname for Boston, Massachusetts, where the staple diet is supposedly Boston baked beans, i.e. baked beans with salt pork and molasses.

Bear, The. *See* STORMIN' NORMAN.

Beastly Beatitudes of Balthazar B, The. A picaresque novel (1968) by the US-born Irish author J.P. Donleavy (b.1926). The story is set in France, England and Ireland and concerns the protagonist's romantic misadventures:

> 'Name, please.'
> 'Balthazar B.'
> 'What's that.'
> 'Balthazar. B is for B.'
> 'O. Is it just one.'
> 'O no it was for two.'
> 'A double eh.'
> 'Yes, I think so, please, with bath.'

A school friend of Balthazar's, named Beefy, recurs throughout the narrative, on one occasion announcing his arrival by telegram: 'am en route please

chill champagne for rather unblessed man without beatitude.'

Beast of Belsen. In the Second World War the name given to Josef Kramer (1906–45), commandant of the infamous BELSEN concentration camp. Kramer was hanged on 13 December 1945 after being tried by a British military court.

Beast of Bodmin Moor. The nickname for a wild animal, possibly a black panther, that has attacked sheep and calves on farms in the region of Bodmin Moor, Cornwall, since the early 1980s. It was first sighted in 1983 but has still not been captured or even fully identified. Speculation exists that the beast may be a big cat released into the countryside by its former owner when it grew too big to be kept as a pet. A legendary beast of Dartmoor forms the subject of Sir Arthur Conan Doyle's tale *The* HOUND OF THE BASKERVILLES (1902). *See also* RUTLAND PANTHER.

Beast of Bolsover. The nickname given by parliamentary correspondents to Dennis Skinner (b.1932), the hard-line, left-wing Labour MP since 1970 for Bolsover, Derbyshire, notorious for his forthright and personally abusive language in the Commons. He has more than once been asked by the Speaker to withdraw his comments and even to leave the Chamber. Skinner describes himself in *Who's Who* as of 'good working-class mining stock' and he is generally held in public affection, even gaining admiration for his integrity and honesty.

Beast of Jersey. A journalistic nickname for E.J.L. (Ted) Paisnel, convicted of 13 sex offences against children in Jersey, Channel Islands, and sentenced to 30 years' imprisonment in 1971. The name was applied to him during the 11 years in which he evaded arrest on the island.

Beat a path to someone's door, To. To seek them out as important or of interest. The image is of trampling down the undergrowth to gain access to the remote home of a person who normally lives a quiet or anonymous life but who has suddenly become 'hot news'.

> Michael Crick's classic work on Jeffrey Archer –
> *Stranger Than Fiction* – was withdrawn from its list by
> the publishers ... and is now out of print. The rights
> to it have, however, reverted to its author and I
> imagine publishing houses are now beating a way to
> his door.
>
> *The Times* (24 November 1999)

Beat Generation. The generation of the 1950s and early 1960s, who rejected traditional Western values by turning to drugs, living communally and generally adopting an anarchic attitude towards society. More specifically, the name refers to a group of US writers at this time, among the most notable of whom were Jack Kerouac (1922–69), Allen Ginsberg (1926–97) and William Burroughs (1914–97). The use of 'beat' in this sense is generally said to have been coined by Kerouac, who related it to the word 'beatitude'. Recent authorities, however, claim it was the creation of the writer and drug addict Herbert Huncke (1916–96). He was the template for Elmer Hassel in Kerouac's ON THE ROAD (1957), for an 'angel-headed hipster' in Ginsberg's *Howl* (1956) and for Herman in Burroughs's *Junkie* (1953). *See also* NAKED LUNCH.

Beatlemania. A term that entered into the English language in 1963 to describe the frenziedly enthusiastic popular response to the BEATLES and their music. The term was specifically coined by the *Daily Mirror* in the aftermath of a successful appearance by the Beatles on 'Sunday Night At the London Palladium' on 13 October 1963, which was seen by an estimated 15 million television viewers in the UK. 'Beatlemania' soon became an established word. It was also briefly considered as a possible title for the film that eventually came to be called *A* HARD DAY'S NIGHT.

Beatles. Probably the world's most famous pop group, formed in 1959 by four young Liverpool musicians: Paul McCartney (b.1942), John Lennon (1940–80), George Harrison (b.1943) and Ringo Starr, real name Richard Starkey (b.1940). They broke up in 1970, but the demand for their music has continued unabated. In their day they were worshipped by the young, respected by the not so young, and even compared by one music critic (William Mann, of *The Times*) to Schubert. Their name, while punning on 'beetle', perhaps partly in reference to their black jackets, was more obviously an allusion to the BEAT GENERATION with which their heyday coincided. *See also* ABBEY ROAD; BEATLEMANIA; FIFTH BEATLE; LET IT BE; REVOLVER; SERGEANT PEPPER'S LONELY HEARTS CLUB BAND; WHITE ALBUM.

> The easiest way to account for the lasting impact of the … Beatles is to praise the genius of their music, and, in particular, their songwriting. This scarcely needs reiterating.
> *Sunday Times* (15 January 1995)

Beatnik. A member of the BEAT GENERATION or, loosely, any person with long hair and scruffy clothes. The Yiddish suffix *-nik* is of Russian origin, as for SPUTNIK.

Beat or **scare the living daylights out of someone, To.** To beat or scare them severely. The daylights were originally the eyes but the word then came to be understood as meaning any vital organ.

> The ghost train was the first funfair attraction to scare the living daylights out of me during my Blackpool boyhood.
> *The Times* (3 January 2000)

Beau Geste. A novel (1924) by P.C. Wren (1875–1941) about the French Foreign Legion, in which he himself served. The three GESTE brothers, Michael (Beau), John and Digby, have joined the Legion, taking upon themselves the opprobrium of having stolen a diamond that their aunt has sold and replaced by a fake so that she can preserve the reputation of her wastrel husband. The novel opens with an account of how a French officer, going to the relief of a desert fort manned by legionnaires, which has been surrounded by rebel Tuaregs, finds it defended only by corpses. The sequels included *Beau Sabreur* (1926) and *Beau Ideal* (1928). The title of the first book means 'fine deed' in French. A silent film version (1926) was directed by Herbert Brenon. A stylish sound version directed by William Wellman followed in 1939. It starred Gary Cooper as Beau, Ray Milland as John and Robert Preston as Digby and was filmed in Buttercup Valley, west of Yuma, Arizona, not Africa. A 1966 remake, starring Telly Savalas and Guy Stockwell, stressed the violence of the original and allowed Beau to survive at the end.

Beaujolais Nouveau (French, 'new Beaujolais'). The annual promotion of young Beaujolais, sold in the first year of a vintage, crossed from France to Britain and then to the United States in the 1970s. Beaujolais sold within the first few months of a vintage is known as *Beaujolais Primeur*, 'early season Beaujolais'. When demand for Beaujolais Nouveau in Britain reached its peak in 1992 nearly half of all regular Beaujolais was sold in this youthful state for immediate consumption, thereby generating a welcome cash flow for the producer.

Beautiful game. Football. The description is attributed to the Brazilian footballer Pelé (b.1940), whose autobiography was entitled *My Life and the Beautiful Game* (1977). *See also* FUNNY OLD GAME.

Generations of Scottish football fans have treasured a piece of vintage film footage as the first recording of the beautiful game north of the border.

The Times (17 November 1999)

Beautiful people. Originally, a nickname for the colourfully dressed HIPPIES of the 1960s, but subsequently a term for those moving in fashionable or glamorous circles.

How does it feel to be one of the beautiful people,
Now that you know who you are?

JOHN LENNON and PAUL MCCARTNEY: 'Baby You're a Rich Man' (song) (1967)

Beauty contest. In the context of US politics, a primary election contest in which the actual selection of delegates to the nominating convention is determined by party caucuses rather than votes. The term evolved in the 1960s from the traditional use of the phrase for a competition of women for a prize awarded to the most beautiful. *See also* CATTLE SHOW.

Beauty in the Bath. A media nickname for the long unsolved murder of Cynthia Bolshaw, a 50-year-old beauty consultant of Heswall, Merseyside (now Wirral), found dead in her bath in 1983. In 1999 advances in DNA profiling techniques enabled police to charge John Taft, a 49-year-old company director, with the crime. He was found guilty by a majority verdict and jailed for life.

Beaver. An early 20th-century children's game, which involved being the first to spot a bearded man and shout 'Beaver!'. The word was earlier a nickname for a beard, probably referring to the animal's thick fur rather than to the beaver as a medieval term for the lower part of the face-guard of a helmet in a suit of armour. The game would hardly have been played in Victorian times since men were normally bearded then. In the 1920s, however, they were increasingly clean-shaven.

Beaver, The. The name given in journalistic circles to Lord Beaverbrook (William Maxwell Aitken; 1879–1964), Canadian-born politician and newspaper magnate. The term obviously derives from his title, but according to Tom Driberg, then 'William Hickey' columnist on Beaverbrook's *Daily Express*, it was equally apt as 'a zoological symbol of tireless industry'.

Beavers. Young boys, aged from six to eight, who are members of the youngest group in the Scout Association. The group was inaugurated in 1971 in Canada, a country where beavers are well known and where they were formerly exploited for their fur. *See also* BOY SCOUTS; EAGER BEAVER.

Beavis and Butt-head. The two teenagers who are the central characters of the television cartoon series that bears their name. They first appeared in 1992 as the creation of the former US musician, Mike Judge, who provides most of the voices. Their keynote is their sneering cynicism, regularly applied to the television and videos that they are invariably watching. In this role they are essentially caricatures of US youth and its obsession with these particular media.

Because it's there. The reply of the mountaineer George Leigh Mallory (1886–1924) when asked in 1923 why he wanted to climb Mount Everest. He was killed on that mountain the following year.

Bed and breakfast, To. In Stock Exchange parlance 'to bed and breakfast' shares is to sell them after hours one evening and buy them back as soon as the market opens the following morning. The procedure establishes a loss for tax purposes.

Bed-hopping. A succession of casual sexual encounters. *See also* JUMP INTO BED WITH SOMEONE.

Bedknob and Broomstick. A novel by the British children's author Mary Norton (1903–92) concerning the relationship between three village children and Miss Price, a spinster who is training to be a witch. It was originally published in two parts, *The Magic Bedknob* (1945) and *Bonfires and Broomsticks* (1947), appearing as one volume with the title *Bedknob and Broomstick* in 1957. A musical film based on the book, *Bedknobs and Broomsticks*, was released by the Disney studios in 1971.

Bed of nails. In the figurative sense an extremely difficult or uncomfortable situation. The term dates from the 1960s, when it was used by Ray Gunter (1909–77), minister of labour under Harold Wilson from 1964 to 1968, to describe the ministry itself. The phrase puns on 'bed of roses' while alluding to the literal bed of nails on which fakirs lie.

Bedroom eyes. Eyes expressing a sensual or sexual invitation. The phrase dates from the 1950s.

Bedroom farce. A popular play in which sexual infidelity and amorous escapades both in and out of marriage are normally required ingredients. The type owes much to the works of the French playwrights Eugène Labiche (1815–88) and Georges Feydeau (1862–1921), and the latter's name is synonymous with the French genre.

Beeb, The. A familiar nickname for the BBC, from the pronunciation of the initials. It is often used by the media as a simple synonym. *See also* AUNTIE.

> *Newsnight Scotland* was born out of the Beeb's realization that it could not stand still if it was to keep pace with political devolution and serve all of the UK properly.
> *The Times* (24 September 1999)

Beeching Axe. The drastic modernization and 'rationalization' of Britain's railways in the 1960s, executed by Dr (later Lord) Richard Beeching (1913–85) when chairman of the British Railways Board (1963–5). Britain had previously been traversed by a dense network of railway lines that reached even the smallest towns. Many of the lines were barely profitable, while others had simply been allowed to deteriorate or been abandoned. The answer was a radical reorganization of the system. Beeching called for the closure of 2128 stations in a single sweep, decimating the service and all but erasing the rural railways that served the country's less populous communities. The operation was traumatic but highly effective, saving the exchequer millions of pounds. Some of the closed stations were later converted into private houses as an unusual type of DES RES.

Beefcake. A colloquial term for pictures or photographs of men displayed for their muscular bodies or 'hunkiness'. *See also* CHEESECAKE.

Beef Wellington. A dish dating from the 1960s in the form of roasted filet of beef covered with pâté de foie gras and baked in a pastry crust. It is presumably named after the Duke of Wellington (1769–1852), who is known to have enjoyed a hearty meaty meal.

Beefy. A nickname given to the swashbuckling Somerset, Worcestershire, Durham and England cricketer Ian Botham (b.1955). A powerfully built all-rounder, Botham's batting and bowling feats in the Ashes series of 1981 (and in particular his performance in what became known as 'Botham's match' in the third test match of the series at Headingley), made him a national hero. He was also known, more prosaically, as 'Both' (pronounced as in 'moth').

Beehive. A woman's domed and lacquered hairstyle in fashion in the 1960s, so named as suggesting the appearance of a beehive. It gained the nickname in the southern United States of 'B–52', after the huge US Air Force bomber so called. Hence the name of the B–52s, the US pop group formed in 1976, whose two female members, Kate Pierson and Cindy Wilson, sported outsize bouffant hairdos.

Been there, done that. A stereotyped phrase indicating that the speaker already has personal experience or knowledge of the thing mentioned, such as a visit to a place abroad or a new type of sport. The words also have sexual overtones, implying that the speaker has 'done it all'. An extended form, 'Been there, done that, bought the T-shirt', introduces a jaded touristic touch.

> Severed cows' heads? Pickled sharks? Elephant dung? Darling, we have been there, done that, bought the T-shirt – or at least a mop and bucket.
> *The Times* (28 September 1999)

Beer and sandwiches. Informal negotiations. The phrase became associated with last-ditch talks between trade unionists and politicians at 10 Downing Street when a strike or stoppage was in the offing, as frequently happened in the 1960s and 1970s. The named fare is regarded as typical of the negotiators. *See also* SMOKE-FILLED ROOM.

Beer belly. A stomach that protrudes as a result of the excessive consumption of beer. The unpleasant spectacle is also known as a 'beer gut'.

Beer goggles. US campus slang for the condition that results from an excess of beer drinking, when hitherto unremarkable people start to look sexually alluring. The expression dates from the 1980s.

Beer Hall Putsch. A failed NAZI rising in Munich on 8–9 November 1923, led by Adolf Hitler. It is also known as the Munich Putsch, *Putsch* being the German word for a sudden, violent political uprising. In association with General Erich Ludendorff (1865–1937), the right-wing military strong man who had become the 'silent dictator' of Germany towards the end of the First World War, Hitler and his small Nazi Party successfully persuaded a right-wing meeting in a Munich beer hall to join them in marching on Berlin to seize power, as Mussolini had done the previous year with his MARCH ON ROME. The next day some 3000 marchers set off for the centre of Munich, but were stopped when the police opened fire, killing 16 marchers. Realizing that the government was not going to cave in, the marchers abandoned their project. Ludendorff was acquitted at the subsequent trial, while Hitler received the minimum five-year sentence for treason. He served only eight months, however, during which he wrote MEIN KAMPF.

Bee's knees. Said of someone or something excellent or outstanding. The term, in the singular, was earlier used of a small or insignificant thing, but in the 1920s, in the plural, gained its present sense. The reference may be to the pollen containers on a bee's legs. The process of removing the pollen involves much bending of the bee's knees and is performed with great precision.

> The specs that speak 'prat' at Cowes or 'dork' at a festival may well scream 'bee's knees' at Eton.
> *Sunday Times* (29 August 1999)

Bee-stung lips. Lips, especially a woman's, that are full, red and pouting, as if swollen from a bee-sting. The US film actress Mae Murray, whose real name was Marie Adrienne Koenig (1889–1965), was known as 'The girl with the bee-stung lips', and this was the title of an article about her by Alfred A. Cohn in the November 1917 number of *Photoplay*.

Beetle. An affectionate name for the Volkswagen saloon car, first in production after the Second World War, suggested by the vehicle's rounded body. The name translated German *Käfer*, additionally a word for an attractive girl or young woman, something like English 'chick'. A 'new look' Beetle was launched in 1999.

> Men of all ages, it seems, cannot resist curves. Or a well-rounded bottom. Or buxom front. Or wide-eyed look. Or a brash red exterior. And the new VW Beetle has them all.
> *The Times* (22 May 1999)

Beetle drive. A session of the game of beetle, in which a picture of this insect is drawn or assembled. The build-up of the image is determined by the throw of a dice, six giving a body, five a head, four two eyes, three two feelers, two six legs and one a tail. A player must throw a six before beginning, but cannot draw eyes or feelers until a five is thrown. Play stops as soon as one player completes a picture. The game was first popular in the 1930s.

Be good! A friendly exhortation not to misbehave, usually said on parting. It is sometimes expanded to: 'If you can't be good, be careful!' Another addition is: 'Don't do anything I wouldn't do!'

Beguine. A popular dance in bolero rhythm of the 1930s originating in Martinique. It was the inspiration for Cole Porter's song 'Begin the Beguine' (1935) and takes its name from French *béguin*, 'flirtation', 'fancy', itself perhaps from the cap worn by members of the Beguine sisterhood of nuns.

Behind the bike shed. Secretly; illicit. The reference is to a school bicycle shed, behind which clandestine sexual encounters and furtive smoking sessions are or were carried on. 'Bike shed' alone may suffice for the allusion.

> Celebrities' bike-shed confessions are mixed with some beautiful footage from tobacco plantations and facts about the political history of smoking.
> *The Times* (20 July 1999)

Behind the eight ball. In a dangerous position from which it is impossible to escape. The phrase comes from the game of pool, in one variety of which all the balls must be pocketed in a certain order, except the black ball, numbered eight. If another ball touches the eight ball, the player is penalized. Therefore, if the eight ball is in front of the one which he intends to pocket, he is in a hazardous position. The expression dates from the 1930s.

Behind the sofa. The place from which one supposedly watches a scary television programme. A DOCTOR WHO fan club among Bristol University students calls itself 'Behind The Sofa'.

> Adequate slasher/horror flick [*I Know What You Did Last Summer*] but a little too formulaic for proper behind-the-sofa material.
> *The Times* (11 January 2000)

Being for the Benefit of Mr Kite! A song that appears on the celebrated BEATLES album SERGEANT PEPPER'S LONELY HEARTS CLUB BAND, credited to John Lennon and Paul McCartney. The inspiration for the song's title comes from a Victorian poster bought by John Lennon in an antiques shop in Kent, which advertised a variety show starring a Mr Kite.

Beirut. The name of Lebanon's capital city became synonymous with bloody internecine strife during Lebanon's devastating civil war (1975–90), which not only involved an array of domestic factions but also attracted baleful interventions by outside parties including Israel, Syria and the USA. Until the mid-1970s Beirut had been an international financial centre, but subsequent struggles for power between left-wing Muslims and conservative Christian groups (mainly members of the PHALANGE) devastated the city. There was also conflict between pro-Iranian Shi'ite Muslims and Syrian-backed Druse (an Islamic sect). An already chaotic situation was exacerbated by the presence in Lebanon of the forces of the Palestine Liberation Organization (*see* PLO), who used southern Lebanon as a base for guerrilla raids into northern Israel. In 1976 Syria was invited by the Lebanese government to intervene in the fighting. The presence of the PLO and the Syrians led to a horrific escalation of the conflict in the early 1980s, when Israel invaded Lebanon (1982) and demanded the removal of Syrian and Palestinian forces from Beirut. An evacuation was overseen by a US-led international force but, following its departure, Israel moved into Muslim west Beirut and sent Christian Phalangist militias into the Palestinian refugee camps of Sabra and Chatila, where they killed hundreds of civilians, provoking an international outcry. The nightmare continued in 1983 as 300 US servicemen were killed in an attack on the US military headquarters by a suicide bomber of the militant Islamic Jihad faction after the US navy had shelled Muslim positions in Beirut. The year 1984 saw a new and sinister development: the abduction of Europeans and Americans in Beirut by Muslim extremists. Prominent among those abducted were the US journalist Terry Anderson, the British journalist John McCarthy, the Irish teacher Brian Keenan and the Archbishop of Canterbury's envoy Terry Waite. Keenan later wrote a book about his experiences, *An Evil Cradling* (1992). *See also* GREEN LINE.

To compare any scene of strife to Beirut in the 1970s and 1980s was to suggest that it was reaching an extreme level of violent chaos. A graphic eye-witness account of the savagery of the Lebanese civil war and its effect on Beirut was provided by *Pity the Nation* (1990), by the journalist Robert Fisk.

Belfast Child. A folk-influenced song by the Scottish rock group Simple Minds, released in 1989 and based on a traditional Irish air entitled 'She Moves Through the Fair'. The creative prompting for the song was the TROUBLES in Northern Ireland and, in particular, the deaths at Enniskillen in 1987 of 11 people in the Remembrance Day bomb attack by the IRA. The song's wistful refrain, bracketing an apocalyptic middle section, looks forward to a peaceful time beyond the Troubles: 'One day we'll return here, when the Belfast Child sings again.' The song is the longest, other than the Beatles HEY JUDE, to reach number one in the UK singles charts.

Believe it or not. Said of something that seems incredible but that is actually true. The US illustrator Robert L. Ripley (1893–1949) gained considerable popularity with his syndicated newspaper features entitled *Believe It or Not!* His first contribution appeared in the New York *Globe* of 19 December 1918 in the form of nine small drawings of sports oddities, including a Canadian who ran 200 yards backwards in 14 seconds, a Frenchman who remained under water for 6 minutes and 29.8 seconds, and an Australian who skipped 11,810 times in four hours. They appeared under the heading 'Believe It or Not!' and launched Ripley into his lucrative career.

Be like Dad, keep Mum. This punning security slogan was launched by the Ministry of Information in the Second World War, the message being that younger members of a family should follow the example of the serviceman father and not talk about war-related matters. *See also* CARELESS TALK COSTS LIVES; LOOSE LIPS SINK SHIPS.

Belisha beacon. A flashing light in an amber-coloured globe mounted on a black-and-white banded pole, the sign of a pedestrian crossing. It is named after Leslie Hore-Belisha (1893–1957), minister of transport from 1934 to 1937, who introduced it.

Belle of the ball. The most beautiful girl or woman at a particular event or in a particular group. The French word *belle*, 'beautiful', came into English in the 17th century but the alliterative phrase quoted here dates from much later and was popularized by G.W. Hunt's song *The Belle of the Balle* (1873) as sung by George Leybourne. Modern usage may be ironic.

Bell jar. An environment in which one is protected or isolated from the outside world, as in the laboratory bell-shaped glass cover of the name, used for preserving samples. The figurative sense derives from Sylvia Plath's novel *The Bell Jar* (1963), published under the pseudonym Victoria Lucas, telling of the mental breakdown, attempted suicide and eventual recovery of a college girl, and based on the author's own experiences.

Bells and smells. Anglo-Catholic or High Church. The allusion is to the use of altar bells and incense in the service of the Eucharist, in the Roman Catholic manner.

Bells and whistles. In computing jargon, additional attractive features, gimmicks or 'gizmos'. The allusion is to a fairground organ with its multiplicity of bells and whistles. *See also* VANILLA.

You don't need to spend any more than this on a computer ... £700 will get you on the way, £1,000 will add bells and whistles and £1,500 will buy you a state-of-the-art machine.

The Times (18 November 1998)

Belly dance. A dance originating in the Middle East, usually performed by a woman and involving undulating movements of the belly and rapid gyration of the hips. The English name dates from the turn of the 20th century for the dance that is more properly known as *raqs sharqi*, 'oriental dance'. There are belly-dancing circles in Britain and elsewhere in the Western world.

If you're interested in learning 'belly dancing', it is best to be aware of one thing: many of its practitioners don't like that name, preferring 'Arab-Egyptian' as a catch-all for the variety of styles available.

Sunday Times (14 November 1999)

Bel Paese (Italian, 'beautiful country'). This well-known Italian cheese was not made until the 20th century. It was the creation of Egidio Galbani in 1906 at Melzo, near Milan. The name does not allude directly to the beauty of the north Italian landscape, as many suppose, but was taken from the title of a book, *Il bel paese* (1875), by Antonio Stoppani (1824–91), an Italian priest, geologist and writer. The book does, however, describe the charms of the local countryside. The cheese wrapper depicts the head of Abbot Stoppani and a map of Italy. The Bel Paese made in the United States has what appears to be the same wrapper but its map is actually that of America.

Belsen. A Nazi concentration camp near the villages of Belsen and Bergen in Hanover, northwest Germany. It was also known as Bergen-Belsen. Although not built as an extermination camp, some 37,000 inmates, including Anne FRANK, died there during the Second World War as a result of starvation, disease or exhaustion. Its particular notoriety derives from the fact that it was the first such camp liberated by the Western Allies (on 15 April 1945). *See also* AUSCHWITZ; BEAST OF BELSEN; DACHAU; FINAL SOLUTION; HOLOCAUST.

Belshazzar's Feast. A noisy oratorio by William Walton (1902–83) setting words from the Bible that had been selected by Sacheverell Sitwell (1897–1988). It was first performed in 1931 and at the time must have seemed daringly modernist, but now rather seems to strain for its effects. Belshazzar, the last king of Babylon, was the son of Nebuchadnezzar. At the king's feast an unseen hand writes the words 'Mene, mene, tekel, upharsin' on the wall, which the prophet Daniel claims is a divine warning of the destruction of Babylon and Belshazzar's own death (Daniel 5:25).

Belt and braces. Doubly safe; extra secure. The phrase is usually said of a policy offering twofold security. Trousers that are kept up by both belt and braces are hardly likely to fall down. The expression dates from the 1920s.

Belt out, To. To sing or play loudly or vigorously. The term dates from the 1950s.

Belt the grape, To. To drink heavily; to 'hit the bottle'. The expression dates from the 1930s.

Belt up, To. To be quiet; to shut up. The expression evolved from RAF slang of the 1930s.

Beltway. A US term for a ring road, and in particular a nickname for the ring road around Washington, D.C., used allusively for Washington itself, especially with regard to the perceived insularity of the US government.

[Presidential contender Pat] Buchanan's declaration yesterday was framed as a 'last chance' by the pugnacious right-winger. 'Let me say to the money boys and the Beltway elite, who think that at long last they have pulled up the drawbridge and locked us out forever, you don't know this peasant army,' he said.

The Times (26 October 1999)

Be my guest. Do as you wish; help yourself. The expression dates from the 1950s, when it was a slogan advertising Hilton hotels. The words were also used as the title of a book of 1957 by the company's founder, Conrad Hilton (1887–1979).

Bend or **lean over backwards, To.** To make every effort to accommodate someone or something; to do all one can to be fair. The image is of a person who deliberately adopts a stance contrary to their natural 'inclination'. The expression dates from the 1920s.

Judges are now taught how to avoid offence and ... how to deal with litigants in person. Usually, they bend over backwards to try to find a good point put forward by the litigant.

The Times (29 June 1999)

Bend Sinister. A novel (1947), set in a fictional totalitarian state, by the US writer Vladimir Nabokov (1899–1977), who was born in St Petersburg. It centres on the ultimately fruitless efforts of a philosopher to oppose a new and brutal regime whose manifesto is mediocrity and whose administration is incompetent. The title is name of the heraldic device that denotes bastardy.

Bend someone's ear, To. To talk to them at length or in order to request a favour. The image is of getting the person to incline their ear towards one's mouth. The phrase dates from the 1940s.

Benetton. This well-known fashion-wear company began as a small family enterprise producing woollen jumpers in a depressed postwar Italy. The nominal founder of the business was Luciano Benetton, a truck driver from Treviso, who died of malaria in 1945. His eldest son, Luciano, obtained work at the age of 15 in a fabric shop, while the youngest child, 13-year-old Giuliana, worked in a garment shop, knitting sweaters by night to sell to customers. Orders started coming in and by 1965 the Benettons had enough money to start a firm of their own. The company has gained notoriety by its controversial advertisements, with its logo, 'United Colors of Benetton', seen affixed to giant photographs of a dead AIDS victim, a slimy newborn baby, a Mafia victim, close-ups of genitalia and a black woman nursing a white baby.

Ben-Hur. A film epic (1959) based on a novel (1880) by Lew Wallace. Directed by William Wyler for MGM, it told the story of a rebellion against the Romans led by gladiator Ben-Hur. Starring Charlton Heston, it won particular acclaim for its breathtaking chariot race sequence, in which it was widely (but erroneously) believed that one participant was killed (legend has it that crew members can be seen racing to the stricken chariot in the film itself). A cash prize was put up for the charioteers hired for the film to encourage them to take greater risks. The full title of the original novel was *Ben-Hur: A Tale of the Christ*.

Bennies. An uncomplimentary nickname for inhabitants of the Falkland Islands, introduced by members of the British forces stationed there during the FALKLANDS WAR. The name derives from a 'loveable half-wit' character called Benny played by Paul Henry in the television SOAP OPERA *Crossroads* (1964–88).

Benny Hill Show, The. A consistently popular television comedy show, first screened on ITV in 1969 and featuring the cheerfully risqué comedian Benny Hill (1925–92). It was in the revue tradition, combining visual gags, slapstick sketches and corny jokes, and was the making of Hill, who won worldwide fame in consequence. Hill's lecherous leers at the bevies of scantily clad women brought mounting criticism, however, and although he claimed his humour was in the mould of Donald McGill's SEASIDE POSTCARDS (a trifle disingenuously, since the girls chased Hill, not Hill the girls), the show was eventually cancelled in 1989.

Be prepared. The motto of the BOY SCOUTS and GIRL GUIDES, taken from the initials of the movement's founder, Sir Robert Baden-Powell, known familiarly as 'B.P.'

Bergen-Belsen. *See* BELSEN.

Berlin airlift. The operation by British and US aircraft to airlift food and supplies to Berlin in 1948, when the Soviet occupying army in eastern Germany blockaded all road, rail and water links between Berlin and the West. The Russians had taken this action in retaliation for the Western powers' decision to unite their German occupation zones into a single economic entity. When the blockade was lifted in 1949 the city was formally divided into East and West.

Berliner. A German word for a kind of doughnut, a lexical curiosity that escaped President J.F. Kennedy (JFK) when he gave his famous COLD WAR speech in Berlin on 26 June 1963: 'All free men, wherever they may live, are citizens of Berlin, and, therefore, as a free man, I take pride in the words *Ich bin ein Berliner*.'

Berlin Wall. On 13 August 1961 the East German authorities sealed off the border between East and West Berlin and began constructing a barrier along it. The purpose was to halt the large number of defections from East to West and to prevent impoverished East Berliners from travelling to relatively wealthy West Berlin. The original barbed wire was eventually replaced by concrete topped with wire. Would-be escapers were shot on sight, one tragic example being that of 18-year-old Peter Fechter, who was machine-gunned in the back as he tried to climb the wall in August 1962 and left to bleed to death while the East German guards looked on. On 9 November 1989, after hundreds of East Germans had fled to the West through Hungary and Czechoslovakia, the beleaguered East German regime lifted travel restrictions and, within days, began dismantling the wall. By January 1990 the authorities were selling large slabs of it for hard currency and had set December that year for its total demolition. In October, however, East Germany was formally absorbed into the German Federal Republic and only short sections of the wall remained standing as memorials. The name became emblematic for any disuniting barrier or artificial divide. *See also* CHECKPOINT CHARLIE.

Bermuda shorts. Casual knee-length shorts, as originally worn by US tourists on the island of Bermuda in the 1950s.

Bermuda Triangle. The triangular sea area between Bermuda, Florida and Puerto Rico, said to be a region of profound danger for anyone venturing into it. The story began in December 1944 when five bombers of the US Navy were lost while on a routine training mission from the Fort Lauderdale air base. A sensational book by Charles Berlitz, *The Bermuda Triangle* (1974), brought this to the attention of the public. Various other ships and aircraft were subsequently said to have vanished in the area. However, these either did not exist, or sank or capsized elsewhere, or simply went down from natural causes, such as the violent storms and rough seas for which the Bermuda Triangle is notorious. Mystics and occultists believe that the lost world of Atlantis lies beneath the Bermuda Triangle, and that the fire crystals that powered the city still emit energy beams that send ships and aircraft to their doom.

Berni Inns. These popular steakhouses or restaurants were the inspiration of Aldo Berni (1909–97), the son of an Italian-born café proprietor in South Wales. He spent some years working for his father but in 1948, together with his brother Frank (1903–2000), opened his first restaurant at Hort's in Bristol. From there the two went from strength to strength, buying up and transforming old coaching inns such as the Mitre at Oxford and the Rummer in Bristol. The latter became their first Berni Inn steakhouse in 1955. They went on to build up an empire of more than 300 restaurants, becoming the biggest chain outside the United States, and their enterprise brought 'dining out' within reach of many in 1950s Britain.

Bertram Mills. At one time Britain's best known circus, founded by Bertram Mills (1873–1938), owner of a coach-building firm, after a bet with a friend that he could put on a better show than that currently available at Olympia in London. From 1920 his circus was the regular Christmas show at Olympia, and from 1929 it toured annually in a big top. It was continued after his death by his two sons, Cyril and Bernard, and held its final season in the winter of 1966.

Beryozka. This Russian ballet company was founded in 1948 by the dancer Nadezhda Nadezhdina (1908–79) and originally consisted only of women. Its name is Russian for 'young birch', referring to a round dance in which the women glide round the stage, their feet invisible under long *sarafan* skirts, carrying birch

branches in their hands. Men first joined in 1961. The company soon built up a wide repertory of dances and scenes based on Russian folklore and first visited England in 1954.

Best-before date. The date by which a food product must be used to ensure that it is still in good condition. In 1980 new regulations were introduced in Britain for the labelling of foodstuffs, and it became obligatory for perishable goods to be marked with the 'best-before' formula and a date. It was later realized that the phrase was too vague for certain perishables, and 'use-by' or 'sell-by' was preferred instead. Even so, the term is still widely used. The phrase has subsequently been adopted to indicate the age constraints on the employability of some job applicants, who thus have a 'best-before date' after which they will seem less attractive to employers. *See also* SELL-BY DATE.

Best boy. In cinematography a name for the principal assistant to the chief electrician or 'gaffer' in a film crew. The term is of US origin.

Best of British luck. An ironic wish to someone in an enterprise that is expected to fail. The expression, also abbreviated as 'the best of British', arose as a military catchphrase in the Second World War.

Best Years of Our Lives, The. An Oscar-winning film (1946) directed by William Wyler about three war veterans returning to civilian life in a middle-American town after war service in the Second World War. The film is critical of the casual attitude held by many Americans to the sacrifices made on their behalf. The film was based on a novel, *Glory For Me*, by MacKinlay Kantor.

Best thing since sliced bread. The best thing or person ever. A general term of commendation dating from the late 1960s and referring, tongue in cheek, to the great technological innovation that enabled bread to be bought wrapped and already sliced. Such bread was already available as early as the 1930s.

Betamax. A video format introduced by SONY in the 1970s. It soon lost out to Matsushita's VHS (video home system), which is now standard. The name represents Japanese *beta*, 'all over' and English *maximum*.

Bête blanche (French, 'white beast'). A slight cause of aversion; a minor annoyance. The term dates from the 1960s as a variant on the familiar *bête noire* ('black beast') as a particularly disliked person or thing.

Better 'ole. Old Bill, a disillusioned old soldier with a WALRUS MOUSTACHE in the First World War, portrayed by Captain Bruce Bairnsfather (1887–1959), artist and journalist, in his publications *Old Bill* and *The Better 'Ole*. As depicted in the *Bystander* of 24 November 1915, a younger Bill, cowering in a wet and muddy shell hole in the midst of a withering bombardment, says to his pal Bert, 'Well, if you knows of a better 'ole, go to it.' The joke and Old Bill struck the public fancy, and Old Bill became the embodiment of a familiar type of patient old grouser. It is probably from this that the 'Old Bill', or simply the BILL, became a nickname for the police, and the Metropolitan Police in particular. The precise connection is uncertain, but it may be either because many ex-servicemen joined the Metropolitan Police after the war or because such servicemen were recruited by posters showing Bairnsfather's Old Bill in a Special Constable's uniform.

Better red than dead. Better to live under Communist domination than be exterminated. The phrase arose among nuclear disarmament campaigners in the late 1950s. The words may have been an inversion of a counter-cliché, 'Better dead than red'. A similar sentiment was expressed by the US revolutionary and statesman Patrick Henry in a speech to the Virginia Convention on 25 March 1775: 'I know not what course others may take; but as for me, give me liberty or give me death.' The international chain of shoe shops Red or Dead, presumably inspired by the phrase, was founded in 1982 by Wayne and Geraldine Hemingway and grew from a market stall in London. *See also* PEACENIK.

Better than sex. Very good or exciting. A general term of approval dating from around the 1950s, the comparison notionally being with an act of sexual intercourse.

Betty Boop. *See* BOOP, BETTY.

Between a rock and a hard place. In a dilemma; faced with a difficult decision. The expression has a biblical ring but is of US origin and first recorded in the 1920s. The image is of being caught or crushed between two rocks.

Between the sticks. Football jargon for the position of the goalkeeper, between the goalposts. The phrase dates from the 1950s.

Beulah. The cheery black housemaid who first appeared in the US radio show *Fibber McGee and Molly* in 1944. Her voice was, in fact, provided by a white male actor, Marlin Hurt. She soon graduated to her own

radio series, then moved to television. Her persona would subsequently be seen as a racial stereotype, but she was nevertheless one of the most popular comedy characters of the 1940s and 1950s.

Beveridge Report. The popular name of *Social Insurance and Allied Services*, a report written in 1942 by Lord Beveridge (1879–1963) that became the basis for the social-reform legislation of the Labour government of 1945–50. It identified five prime 'giants', illness, ignorance, disease, squalor and want, and proposed a scheme of social insurance 'from the cradle to the grave', recommending a national health service, social insurance and assistance, family allowances and policies to implement full employment.

Beverly Hills. A fashionable district of Los Angeles, near HOLLYWOOD, famous for its individualistic or extrovertly eccentric residences, the homes of film and television stars and of millionaires of all kinds. Its opulent mansions and winding drives form an elegant oasis of some 31,000 residents, cocooned from the hurly-burly of downtown Los Angeles, which completely surrounds it. It adopted its present name in 1911, before which it was simply Beverly. The name comes from Beverly Farms, where in 1906 a newspaper report claimed President Taft was staying.

In more recent times the name has become associated with the popular SOAP OPERA *Beverly Hills 90210*, about a group of well-heeled high school students, first shown in 1990. The number in the title is the highly desirable ZIP CODE of their residential quarter.

Bevin Boys. A nickname for the young men directed to work in coal mines in the Second World War instead of doing military service. The name comes from that of Ernest Bevin (1881–1951), minister of labour and national service, who devised the scheme. Some 21,000 men were conscripted, the figure at the end of their call-up number determining their selection as miners rather than military men. The nearest they thus got to a uniform was the miner's helmet and safety lamp, and they were denied the protection of the buttonhole badge that identified members of the Merchant Navy. Although literally out of the public eye, their contribution to the war effort was fully recognized by Winston Churchill:

> One will say: 'I was a fighter pilot'; another will say: 'I was in the Submarine Service'; another: 'I marched with the Eighth Army'; a fourth will say: 'None of you could have lived without the convoys and the

Merchant seamen'; and you, in your turn, will say, with equal pride and with equal right: 'We cut the coal.'

Report (22 April 1943)

Bewitched. A classic US SITCOM running from 1964 to 1972 and depicting the adventures of an 'ordinary guy', Darrin Stephens, played by Dick York and Dick Sargent, and his wife, Samantha, who happens to be a witch, played by Elizabeth Montgomery. The immensely popular series, also shown in Britain, did much to promote a vogue for the names Darren and Samantha and to a lesser extent for Tabitha, the Stephens' magical daughter.

Beyond the black stump. Beyond the limits of civilized life; in the 'back of beyond'. The expression is Australian in origin and alludes to the ubiquitous fire-blackened stump used as a marker when pointing out a route to travellers in the outback. Similarly 'this side of the black stump' means in the civilized world or at any rate the world familiar to the speaker.

Beyond the Fringe. The pioneering satirical show, which was first staged in 1960, owed its inspiration to Robert Ponsonby, director of the annual Edinburgh Festival, who sought a way of beating the FRINGE at its own game. Accordingly he invited four young Oxbridge writers and performers, Alan Bennett (b.1934), Dudley Moore (b.1935), Peter Cook (1937–95) and Jonathan Miller (b.1936), to present a revue show. The result was a smash hit, and the show's vein of quirky satire established the four as the dominant force in British comedy for the following decade.

I go to the theatre to be entertained, I want to be taken out of myself, I don't want to see lust and rape and incest and sodomy and so on, I can get all that at home.

ALAN BENNETT: *Beyond the Fringe*, 'Man of Principles' (1963)

B-girls. Bar girls, as young women employed by a bar to mix with male customers, chat to them and encourage them to buy drinks. B-girls were prevalent in US bars in the Second World War.

Biafra. The name of a short-lived West African state. Fears that the Nigerian government was becoming dominated by the rival Hausa tribe led to the secession of the predominantly Ibo Eastern Region of Nigeria in 1967. In the ensuing civil war federal Nigerian forces confined the Biafrans to a shrinking area of the interior by 1968 and by 1970 Biafra had

ceased to exist. The sufferings of the Biafrans led to their name becoming synonymous with the ravages of warfare, famine and disease.

Bible. *See* GOOD NEWS BIBLE; JERUSALEM BIBLE; REVISED STANDARD VERSION.

Bible-basher. An aggressive evangelical preacher, so called from his blows on his Bible as he rams home his text. Alternative names are Bible-thumper and Bible-puncher.

Bible Belt. A name emerging in the 1920s for those areas of the southern and Midwestern United States and western Canada where Protestant fundamentalism is widely practised. Nashville, Tennessee, is generally reckoned to be the capital of the US Bible Belt, and several Protestant religious denominations have publishing headquarters there, including the United Methodist Publishing House, one of the largest of its kind in the world.

Bic. *See* BIRO.

Bicycle shot. In football a shot made by a player kicking the ball back over his head with both legs off the ground when facing away from the goal. The effect somewhat resembles the motion of the legs when pedalling a bicycle.

Bidonville. A French term, literally meaning 'container town', applied in the 1950s to a shanty town built of oil drums or other metal containers, especially on the outskirts of a North African city, and typically an oil port such as Mohammedia in Morocco. *See also* CARDBOARD CITY.

Biffo. A nickname given to the Tory politician John Biffen (b.1930), who, despite being to the left of Margaret Thatcher, served in the IRON LADY's cabinet from 1979 to 1987 (as leader of the House of Commons from 1982). He then served as a backbencher until he was awarded a peerage in 1997. The name derives from Biffo the Bear, a cartoon character in *The* DANDY. The name was also applied to the rightwing Tory backbencher Geoffrey Dickens by the Labour MP Joe Ashton (b.1933), who explained it as an acronym for 'Big ignorant fool from Oldham'.

Big Apple. New York City. The name was first popularized in the 1920s by John J. FitzGerald, a reporter for the *Morning Telegraph*, who used it to refer to the city's racetracks and who claimed to have heard it used by black stable-hands in New Orleans in 1921. Black jazz musicians in the 1930s took up the name to refer to the city (and especially Harlem) as the jazz capital of the world. The nickname then faded from use but was revived in 1971 as part of a publicity campaign by Charles Gillett, president of the New York Convention and Visitors Bureau. The general allusion is to a city that is the 'big apple' or (punningly) 'apple core' sought as an ultimate prize by anyone after world fame.

Big band. The big band era of popular music dates from the 1930s, the age of SWING, when augmented dance and jazz bands came into vogue, with reed and brass sections having separate parts and playing against one another while leaving space for soloists. The style was perfected by the US bandleader and composer Don Redman (1900–64).

Big Bang. (1) In cosmology a theory explaining the origin of the universe. It postulates that a small, super-dense mass exploded, hurling matter in all directions in a cataclysmic explosion. As the fragments slowed down, the stars and galaxies formed, although the universe is still expanding.

(2) The major modernization of the Stock Exchange, in the City of London, which took place on 27 October 1986, was also known as the Big Bang. The distinction between stockjobber and stockbroker was abolished, and operations became fully computerized. The aim was to maintain London's position as a leading inter-national financial centre.

Big Bertha. The name given by the French to the large howitzers used by the Germans against Liège and Namur in 1914. They were made at the Škoda works, but were mistakenly assumed to be manufactured by Krupp, the famous German armament firm. Hence the allusion to Bertha Krupp (1886–1957), great-granddaughter of the firm's founder, Friedrich Krupp (1787–1826), to whom control of the works had passed on her father's death in 1902. In 1918 Paris was shelled from a range of 122km (76 miles) by the 142-ton 'Paris' gun, to which the name Big Bertha was again applied.

Big Brother. A person or organization that exercises dictatorial control, supposedly for one's own welfare and in one's best interests. The name is that of the invisible state machinery in George ORWELL's *Nineteen Eighty-Four* (1949) (*see* 1984), representing the real-life political leader of the USSR:

> On each landing, opposite the lift shaft, the poster with the enormous face gazed from the wall. It was one of those pictures which are so contrived that the eyes follow you about when you move. BIG BROTHER IS WATCHING YOU, the caption beneath it ran.
>
> ch i

Round-the-clock scrutiny by unseen watchers became a reality for contestants in the voyeuristic television game show *Big Brother*, which enjoyed success in Britain and many other countries in the summer of 2000.

Big bug. A BIG WHEEL.

Big C. Cancer, which one is reluctant to name in full.

> Shortly after an appearance at the Academy Awards ceremony in April ... [John] Wayne succumbed to what he had termed 'The Big C'.
>
> JOHN H. LENIHAN in *American National Biography* (1999)

Big cheese. The boss or someone in an important position. 'Cheese' here is either an alteration of 'chief' or a borrowing via Urdu from Persian *chiz*, 'thing'.

Big Cyril. A friendly nickname for Cyril Smith (b.1928), the genial and generously proportioned Liberal (and subsequently Liberal Democrat) MP for Rochdale for 20 years from 1972.

Big Daddy. The nickname of Idi Amin (b.1925), the massively built Ugandan president (1971–79), known to his people as Idi Amin Dada. Amin seized power in Uganda in 1971 and committed numerous gruesome atrocities against his own people until overthrown in 1979. The nickname was also sometimes applied to President Lyndon Johnson (*see* LBJ). Big Daddy was also the professional name of the powerfully figured all-in wrestler Shirley Crabtree (1930–97).

Big day. The day of an important or decisive event, and especially that of a marriage or wedding. The mental, moral, emotional, physical and social preparations involved for the latter can combine to make it the 'biggest' of a lifetime.

Big deal! An ironic exclamation belittling a supposedly fine offer or proposal. *See also* NO BIG DEAL.

Big E. An unceremonious dismissal or rejection; 'the push'. The 'E' stands for 'elbow'.

Big Enchilada. The nickname of John M. Newton (1913–88), US attorney general, who led President Nixon's re-election campaign in 1972 and was sub-sequently jailed for his role in the WATERGATE affair. An enchilada is a Mexican dish. The name was given by a Nixon aide, John Erlichman, during a taped con-versation of 1973 when he sought to describe the size of the 'sacrificial lamb' who was being thrown to the wolves. The British would probably have seen him in terms of a BIG CHEESE.

Big Fella. A nickname of the Irish nationalist guerrilla leader and politician Michael Collins (1890–1922), so called for his impressive physical stature. *See also* BÉAL NA MBLÁTH; DEV; FREE-STATERS.

Big fish in a small pond. A person regarded as important only within the limited scope of their own social or other group.

> [Footballer] Ally McCoist would be the first to admit that he's a big fish in a small pond.
> *The Times Magazine* (27 November 1999)

Big five-o. One's 50th birthday. The phrase dates from the 1980s and may be applied to similar landmark decade birthdays, such as 'the big four-o', 'the big six-o'.

Big Four. (1) The four main Allied powers and/or their leaders at the Paris Peace Conference after the First World War: the USA/Woodrow Wilson; Britain/Lloyd George (WELSH WIZARD); France/Georges Clemenceau (TIGER); Italy/Vittorio Orlando.

(2) The four major Allied powers in the Second World War and/or their leaders: the USA/Franklin Roosevelt (FDR); the USSR/Stalin (UNCLE JOE); the UK/Churchill (FORMER NAVAL PERSON; WINNIE); China/Chiang Kai-shek (General CASH-MY-CHEQUE). It was these four powers who drew up the Charter of the United Nations at the San Francisco Conference in April 1945. *See also* BIG THREE.

Big Freeze. A nickname for the unusually cold winter of 1962–3 in Britain. It seriously disrupted the football league programme, and many matches were cancelled or postponed.

Bigger Splash, A. The best known of the many swimming-pool pictures by David Hockney (b.1937), painted in 1967. It was the third of a series, which explains the title, as Hockney himself recalls: '*The Little Splash*, which is a tiny painting ... was the first of three paintings ... from a photograph I found in a book about how to build swimming pools I found on a news stand in Hollywood. It was a nice little subject, a splash ... And I thought, it's worth making this bigger, doing it a little differently, and so I did a slightly bigger one, *The Splash*, and I took a bit more care with it. But then I thought the background was perhaps slightly fussy, the buildings were a little too complicated, not quite right. So I decided I'd do a third version, a big one using a very simple building and strong light.'

Biggin Hill. The site near Westerham in Kent (now in the unitary authority of Bromley) of an RAF aerodrome that played a major part in the BATTLE OF BRITAIN. The airfield was first established in the First World War and was affectionately known as 'Biggin on the Bump'. The name later became a byword for the heroic spirit of 1940. *See also* FEW; MOVING CHURCH.

Big girl. A teenage girl whose physical development suggests that she is older and more mature than she really is.

> Georgina Brundle looks like a big girl. In a clinging top that does her curves no favours ... she looks about 25 at first glance. In fact she is 15.
> *The Times* (29 July 1999)

Big girl's blouse. A weakling; an ineffectual person. The expression originated in the north of England in the 1960s and was popularized by northern-based television programmes such as the SITCOM *Nearest and Dearest* (1968–72), featuring Hylda Baker and Jimmy Jewel as brother and sister Nellie and Eli Pledge who inherit a pickle-bottling factory. *See also* BIG GIRL.

> I find it bizarre that, while men are praised to the skies every time they come over all big girl's blouse, women are still penalized for getting in touch with their masculine side.
> INDIA KNIGHT in *Sunday Times* (17 October 1999)

Biggles. The most famous aviator in boys' fiction was the creation of Captain W.E. Johns (1893–1968), who drew on memories of his experiences in the Royal Flying Corps during the First World War. His hero's full name is James Bigglesworth, DSO, DFC, MC, and he made his bow in magazine stories of the early 1930s. He also starts his flying career in the First World War and eventually becomes commander of a flying squadron. In the Second World War he plays a major role in the BATTLE OF BRITAIN. His GUNG-HO exploits continued until his creator's death.

Big hair. A bouffant hairstyle, especially one that has been teased, permed or sprayed to produce an impressive profusion. The term and style arose in the United States in the 1970s.

> In eighties Britain, women wore in-yer-face shoulder pads and big hair to demonstrate their enthusiasm for money, power and the yuppie dream.
> *Sunday Express* (27 February 2000)

Big-hearted Arthur. The comedian Arthur Askey (1900–82) so called himself, alluding to his cheery willingness to help where no others would, and the name was generally adopted for him in billings.

Big Heat, The. A film (1953) adapted by Sidney Boehm from a mystery novel by William P. McGivern (1924–83). It starred Glenn Ford as Sergeant Dave Bannion, a police officer and family man determined to wreak vengeance on the gangsters who had killed his wife in mistake for him. Directed by Fritz Lang, it caused a considerable stir at the time for its violent content, notably an incident (not actually shown to the audience) in which gangster Lee Marvin throws scalding coffee in heroine Gloria Grahame's face. The title refers to the heat generated by the police as a result of US Senate crime investigations against organized crime in the early 1950s.

Big Issue. A magazine launched in 1991 to 'help the homeless help themselves'. The homeless make money by selling the magazine on town and city streets, and its profits are used in grants to them. In content it deals with the arts and current affairs as well as issues relating more specifically to housing and unemployment, which are implicitly the key subject of its punning title.

Big lie. A gross distortion or misrepresentation of the facts, especially when used by a politician or political party. In the Second World War the expression was specifically applied to NAZI propaganda as disseminated by Hitler and Goebbels, the theory being that the bigger the lie and the more often it is told, the greater the number of people who will accept it. *See also* PROTOCOLS OF THE ELDERS OF ZION *under* FAKES.

Big Look. A fashion in women's clothes introduced in 1974 and characterized by loose, broad, voluminous designs. It involved the elimination of linings and interfacings and meant that the clothes could be worn on top of one another in layers without making the wearer look unduly huge.

Big Mac. A proprietary name for the largest hamburger in the range served by MCDONALD'S fast-food outlets. *See also* MAC OUT.

Big Mal. A nickname for anyone called Malcolm who is outstanding in some way, either physically or in status. Two so known are Malcolm Allison (b.1927), manager of Manchester City football club and later of Crystal Palace and Middlesbrough, and Malcolm Fraser (b.1930), prime minister of Australia from 1975 to 1983, who is over 1.8m (6ft) tall.

Big Man. The great Scottish football manager Jock Stein (John Stein; 1922–85), who led Glasgow Celtic to nine consecutive Scottish League championships (1966–74) and the European Cup (1967).

Big man on campus. A US term for a male college student leader or idol. The phrase is usually abbreviated to BMOC.

Big Momma. A not unkind nickname for the champion golfer Laura Davies (b.1964), who is 1.7m (5ft 10in) tall and who when the name was given in the early 1980s weighed 73kg (161lb or 11½ stone).

Bigmouth. A noisy or indiscreet person.

Big noise. A BIG WHEEL.

Big O. The nickname of the US singer Roy Orbison (1936–88). Also the nickname of the US basketball player Oscar Robertson (b.1938), a prodigiously talented guard for the Cincinatti Royals from 1960 to 1970 and later for the Milwaukee Bucks.

Big of you. Generous of you. A phrase invariably used ironically, as: 'So you won't charge me for the stamp? That's big of you!' The phrase dates from the 1940s.

Big one. Something promoted to be bigger and better than any of its kind before. Also, a major or daunting undertaking, typically prefaced by a remark such as: 'This is the big one.'

Big pot. A BIG WHEEL.

Big shot. A BIG WHEEL.

Big Sleep, The. The first crime novel (1939) by the US writer Raymond Chandler (1888–1959). It is set in Los Angeles and introduces the detective Philip MARLOWE, a man of sentiment, wit and morality, as well as toughness. Chandler's aim was to present criminals as they really were, not as the writers of detective novels represented them. The title refers to a passage at the end of the book: 'What did it matter where you lay once you were dead? … You were dead, you were sleeping the big sleep.' A complex but pacy film version (1946), with Humphrey Bogart as Marlowe, was directed by Howard Hawks. A remake (1978), directed by Michael Winner and starring Robert Mitchum, lacked the subtlety of Howard Hawks's version

Big stick diplomacy. The backing of negotiations with the threat of military force. The term was popularized by Theodore Roosevelt's declaration in 1900 that he had always been fond of the West African proverb 'speak softly and carry a big stick'. He used such tactics successfully (1902–4) in the Alaskan boundary dispute and the second Venezuelan crisis.

Big Three. Winston Churchill, Franklin D. Roosevelt and Joseph Stalin, heads of government of Britain, the United States and the Soviet Union, were so called when they met at the YALTA CONFERENCE in 1945. *See also* BIG FOUR.

Big time. Success in a profession, especially show business.

Big Train. The nickname of the tall and well-built US baseball player and manager Walter Johnson (1887–1946), so called from the power of his deliveries. He first received the name in 1910.

Big wheel. An important or conceited person.

Big white chief. An important person, or the head or leader of an organization. The expression dates from the 1930s and supposedly represents Native American speech.

Big Yin. The regular nickname of the Scottish comedian Billy Connolly (b.1942), as Scots dialect for 'Big One'.

Bikini. This atoll in the Marshall Islands, the scene of US nuclear weapon testing in 1946, gave its name to a scanty two-piece swimming costume worn by women. The allusion is supposedly to the devastation of the atom-bomb test and the 'explosive' effect caused by a woman wearing such a costume (*see also* BLONDE BOMBSHELL; SEX BOMB). The garment was pioneered in the year of the test by the French couturiers Jacques Heim and Louis Réard, and the term first appeared in the magazine *Le Monde Illustré* in 1947. The initial 'bi-' was later amusingly taken to mean 'two', with reference to the two parts of the costume, so that a one-piece or topless swimsuit (the lower half of a bikini) came to be called a monokini. There is also a trikini, with two top parts. A more recent development is the 'tankini', a combination of a TANK TOP and a bikini.

Bikini line. The area of the thigh along the bottom edge of a BIKINI, especially with regard to its cosmetic depilatory treatment. The term need not specifically apply to the wearing of a bikini.

> While investigating the new, superbly thorough Brazilian bikini wax you should maintain a roughly natural outline on your bikini line.
> *The Times* (26 June 1999)

Biko affair. A scandal arising from the death while in police custody of Steve Biko (1946–77), founder of the Black Consciousness Movement in South Africa. Biko's death came after 24 days during which he was held naked and shackled and suffered three brain lesions. Despite a postmortem finding that these were caused by 'application of force to his head', the subsequent inquest absolved the police from any responsibility for his death. This led to an international outcry, and to Biko becoming an important martyr in the anti-APARTHEID cause. The affair featured in Richard Attenborough's 1987 film *Cry Freedom*.

Bilbo Baggins. *See* BAGGINS, BILBO.

Bilko. The bespectacled US Army master sergeant played by Phil Silvers in the anarchic television comedy series *You'll Never Get Rich*, later known as *The Phil Silvers Show* and *Bilko* (1955–9). With the full name Ernest G. Bilko, he is a loveable conman who is forever fooling his superior officers. His creator was Nat Hiken. The show became cult viewing, and some enthusiasts regard Sergeant Bilko as the most memorable comic creation on US television.

Bill, The. The police force, or a member of it. The term is a shortening of OLD BILL (*see* BETTER 'OLE) and was adopted as the title of a polished television crime series about the lives and loves of personnel at the fictional Sun Hill police station in London's East End, first screened in 1984.

Billi-bi. A type of soup made from fresh mussels, cream and white wine. It name is of French origin and dates from the 1960s, when it was complimented by Billy B. Leeds, a US businessman who was a regular diner at Maxim's in Paris, where the soup was served.

Billy Budd. An all-male nautical opera by Benjamin Britten (1913–76) with a libretto by the novelist E.M. Forster and Eric Crozier, based on the novel *Billy Budd* (1891; not published until 1924) by Herman Melville (1819–91). It was first performed in London in 1951. Billy Budd is an innocent sailor on board an 18th-century man-of-war. He is tormented by Claggart, the master at arms, whom he accidentally kills, and then goes willingly to his execution. There is another opera on the subject by Giorgio Ghedini (1892–1965), with a libretto by the Nobel laureate Salvatore Quasimodo (1901–68); it was first performed in 1949. There is also a film (1962) written and directed by Peter Ustinov (b.1921), who starred alongside Terence Stamp (b.1940) as Billy.

Billy Bunter. *See* BUNTER, BILLY.

Billy Williams' Cabbage Patch. The English Rugby

Football Union's ground at Twickenham, the head-quarters of the game, also known as Twickers. It is popularly so called after William (Billy) Williams (1860–1951), who discovered the site and who persisted until it was acquired for rugby in 1907. The latter part of the name refers to the ground's former use as a market garden. The first match played there, on 2 October 1909, was between Harlequins and Richmond, and the first international was England v. Wales the following year. The nearby Railway Tavern changed its name to the Cabbage Patch in 1959 when England and Wales played Scotland and Ireland in a centenary match. The ground is now also the site of the Museum of Rugby, and tours of the stadium are held six days a week.

> Billy Williams's cabbage patch has never staged a more momentous game than this afternoon's match between England and the All Blacks.
> *The Times* (9 October 1999)

Bimbo. A superficially attractive but essentially shallow or unintelligent young woman. The word, from the Italian for 'baby', was first used in the 1920s as a derogatory term for a person of either sex. It then came to apply to a 'loose' woman before gaining its present nuance in the 1980s and duly spawning the HIMBO as a male equivalent.

Bindle. The henpecked husband in a series of comic novels by Herbert Jenkins, beginning with the one that bears his name (1916). Joseph Bindle spends much of his time on the dole and his wife is forever berating him with the cry of 'Lorst yer job?'

Bing Boys. The nickname of the Canadian troops in the First World War, from the name of their commanding officer, Lord Byng of Vimy (1862–1935). The name was also popularized by the revue, *The Bing Boys Are Here*, which opened at the Alhambra in 1915.

Bingo. A lastingly popular gambling game, played typically by pensioners in bingo halls converted from cinemas. The game is simple. Players have a card printed with a selection of numbers, and they cover the numbers as they are announced at random by a caller. The player who first covers all the numbers on his or her card calls 'Bingo' (or 'House') and wins a prize. The allure of the game is in its conviviality and in the caller's patter, which until electronic technology took over had traditional rhymes for the various numbers, such as 'legs eleven' for 11, 'dinkie doos' for 22, 'all the threes' for 33, 'clickety-click' for 66

and 'two fat ladies' for 88. The usual call at the start of the game is 'Eyes down, look in!' The word bingo itself probably imitates the 'ping' of a bell formerly rung to announce a win.

Binkie. The regular first name, perhaps originally a childhood nickname, adopted by Hugh (originally Hughes) Beaumont (1908–73), managing director of the theatre group H.M. Tennant and an influential force in West End theatre. He was always known thus in theatrical circles.

Biodiversity. A BUZZWORD of the 1980s for the variety of plant and animal life in a particular location or even as taken worldwide. Generally speaking, a high level of biodiversity is regarded as both desirable and important, and its implementation often involves conservation action, especially in areas where particular plants or animals are close to extinction. In Britain the establishment of the NATIONAL FOREST is just one part of the programme.

Biofeedback. In a literal sense, biofeedback is simply feedback about the body, such as may be obtained by weighing oneself on the bathroom scales or taking one's temperature with a thermometer. 'Feedback' itself is a term that first gained currency among radio pioneers at the turn of the 20th century and that was defined by the US mathematician Norbert Wiener as 'a method of controlling a system by reinserting into it the results of its past performance'. In the light of this, biofeedback is now used for the electronic monitoring of a person's normally automatic bodily function, such as blood pressure, in order to train them to acquire voluntary control of that function. Once this is done, the procedure can have various beneficial applications. The biofeedback of BRAINWAVE activity, for example, can aid insomniacs and epileptics.

Biological clock. A supposed natural mechanism inside the body that controls the rhythm of the body's functions, whether they occur on a daily basis, such as sleeping, monthly, such as the menstrual cycle, or seasonally, such as the growth rate of children. The term is popularly misunderstood to denote the inexorable 'ticking away' of a woman's fertile years. *See also* CIRCADIAN RHYTHMS.

> Kate's biological clock ticks away as she trawls around in increasing desperation for a father. … And all the while, the millennium is ticking towards its own inexorable close.
> *The Times* (2 October 1999)

Birdie. A hole at golf that the player has completed in one stroke less than par (the standard for the course). Two strokes less is an eagle. Three strokes less is an albatross.

The story goes that one day in 1903 A.B. ('Ab') Smith was enjoying a game of golf in Atlantic City, USA. Endeavouring to improve his already good game, he made a shot that enabled him to sink his ball one under par. The success prompted his cry of delight, 'That's a bird of a shot!' The term caught on and in due course became affectionately known as a 'birdie'. The eagle and the albatross followed logically, since a stroke two under par is rare, like the eagle, and one three under par even rarer, like the albatross.

Birdland. A former famous jazz club in New York, named after the saxophonist Charlie 'Bird' Parker (1920–55), who played there. It opened in a Broadway basement in 1949 and was a venue for many leading jazz musicians. Rising rents forced it to close in 1965. It gave its name to George Shearing's song 'Lullaby of Birdland' (1952), and the name was subsequently appropriated by an unrelated jazz club at another Broadway address.

Birdman of Alcatraz. The US murderer Robert Stroud (1887–1963) was so called from his study of canaries while awaiting execution in ALCATRAZ. His sentence was commuted in 1916 and he died of old age in prison.

Birds and the bees. A euphemism for sexual activity or reproduction, alluding to the fanciful stories told to young children on the subject.

> Ten years ago, my friend was listening to his parents explaining the 'birds and the bees', now he finds himself extolling the virtues of the Femidom and ISAs to an astounded, clueless mother.
> *Sunday Times* (15 August 1999)

Birds Eye. The proprietary name of a make of frozen foods, from Clarence Birdseye (1886–1956), a US fur trapper, who, while trading in furs in Labrador over the five years from 1912, noticed that frozen fish and caribou meat tasted as good as fresh food even after being frozen for several months. He experimented with re-creating the natural conditions of freezing at his home, and in the early 1920s devised a system of quick-freezing that could have commercial applications. In 1924, at Gloucester, Massachusetts, he founded the General Seafoods Corporation, and a development of this was Birdseye Frosted Foods,

formed in 1930. The first products to appear under the name were first commercially available in 1932.

Birds of a Feather. A popular television SITCOM first broadcast on BBC1 in 1989 and based on the sibling rivalry and affection that exists between Sharon Theodopolopoudos and Tracey Stubbs, two ESSEX GIRL types, played by the real-life friends Pauline Quirke and Linda Robson. The series did much to promote the stereotypes associated with the names SHARON and TRACY.

Birdwatching. The practice or hobby of watching birds in their natural habitat. The term is first recorded as the title of a book by E. Selous, *Bird Watching* (1901), as a 'homelier' equivalent of the specifically scientific ornithology, and it in turn prompted various other 'watching' activities, such as those studied by the ethologist Desmond Morris in *Manwatching* (1977), *Bodywatching* (1985), *Catwatching* (1986) and even *Christmas Watching* (1992).

Birmingham Six. The six Irishmen who were arrested following the IRA bombing of two crowded Birmingham pubs on 21 November 1974, killing 21 and wounding more than 150. Billy Power, Gerry Hunter, Hugh Callaghan, John Walker, Paddy Joe Hill and Dick McIlkenny were tried in 1975, convicted on 21 murder counts and sentenced to life imprisonment. Subsequent appeals against the sentence failed until 1991, when they were said to have been wrongly convicted and freed. *See also* BRIDGEWATER THREE; GUILDFORD FOUR; WINCHESTER THREE.

Biro. A name that soon became generic for any make of ball-point pen but that began with the commercial model introduced in 1945 by the Hungarian László Biró (1899–1985), who had patented his invention two years before. Working with a magazine, he had realized the advantage of quick-drying ink, and in 1940 had moved to Argentina on the rise of Nazism to perfect his idea. The Frenchman Marcel Bich (1914–94) took over the invention in 1958 and created a disposable version, the Bic. As with its predecessor, the name soon came to be used for any ball-point.

Birthday Boys, The. A historical novel (1991) by Beryl Bainbridge (b.1934), the second of three successive books that centre on a national disaster. The inspiration for this recreation of the doomed Antarctic expedition of Captain Robert Falcon Scott (1868–1912) was the letter written by Scott to the dramatist and novelist James Barrie (1860–1937) as he and his companions waited for death: 'We are very near the end, but have not and will not lose our good cheer.' The title refers to the birthday party for Petty Officer (Taff) Evans just before the attempt on the Pole and to the fact that Captain Oates walks out of the tent to his death on his birthday. *See also* I MAY BE SOME TIME; SOUTH POLE; YOUNG ADOLF.

Birthday honours. The honours awarded on the date that is the sovereign's official birthday (as distinct from the actual one). For Elizabeth II, this is a Saturday in June. Most of the honours, in the form of peerages, knighthoods, military and civilian awards, are made from a list drawn up by the Prime Minister, which includes about 50 individuals recommended 'for political services'. The vast majority of those honoured, however, receive an OBE (ORDER OF THE BRITISH EMPIRE). The BEM (British Empire Medal) was also awarded until 1993, when it was discontinued. Only the highest honours are received personally from the sovereign, and the junior award is presented by royal representatives. A similar system operates for the New Year honours.

Birthday Party, The. A play (1958) by the British playwright Harold Pinter (b.1930) in which two menacing strangers disrupt the banality of life in an ordinary seaside boarding house. The celebration of the birthday of the lodger Stanley (including present-giving and party games) provides a connecting theme for the drama, as well as the title.

Birth of a Nation, The. An early film epic (1915), directed by D.W. Griffith and based on a racist novel, *The Clansman*, by the Southern Baptist minister Thomas Dixon. In bald cinematic terms *The Birth of a Nation* is a film following the fortunes of two families during the American Civil War (1861–5), and it was the most ambitious motion picture released to date. Ideologically, it is probably the most controversial film ever released in the United States, justifying and celebrating the white South's 'redemption' from Reconstruction (the liberal political reorganization of the Southern states (1865–77) that followed the Northern victory in the Civil War), the end of which process saw the disenfranchising of blacks and the imposition of rigid racial segregation in the southern states of the old Confederacy. The nation 'born' in the title is thus a white-dominated society that has turned its back on the perceived fratricidal folly of the Civil War and the supposed black despotism of Reconstruction.

The film portrays the KU KLUX KLAN as triumphant defenders of white America, and blacks as an inferior race.

> It is like writing history with lightning. And my only regret is that it is all so terribly true.
> PRESIDENT WOODROW WILSON at the White House
> (18 February 1915)

Birtism. The style of management and organizational culture named after John Birt (b.1944), who was director general of the BBC from 1993 to March 2000. Birt was much criticized for stifling creativity by excessive layers of management and by the introduction of an internal market within the BBC, all at great expense, although with the intention of ensuring a culture of accountability.

Biscuit cough. A cough caused by a mere irritation or 'tickle' in the throat, as from biscuit crumbs. The term was popularized, or even invented, by A.A. Milne.

> 'Nasty cold day,' said Rabbit, shaking his head. 'And you were coughing this morning' ... 'It was a Biscuit Cough', said Roo, 'not one you tell about.'
> A.A. MILNE: *The House at Pooh Corner* (1928)

Bish-bash-bosh. A phrase descriptive of any rapid or routine manual or mechanical operation, as: 'The double-glazing people put the new window in bish-bash-bosh.' The implication is generally that the operation was efficient, although taken individually the three elements of the phrase suggest the opposite.

Bismarck. The Second World War German battleship, named after the 'Iron Chancellor' Otto von Bismarck (1815–98), who played the leading role in unifying Germany in the mid-19th century. Intended as a commerce raider, the immensely powerful *Bismarck* was completed in 1940. It made its first foray into the Atlantic in May 1941, accompanied by the heavy cruiser *Prinz Eugen*. A British fleet anticipated their course and met up with them in the north Atlantic on 24 May, when, during a brief encounter, the German ships sank the Royal Navy battleship *Hood* and damaged another, the *Prince of Wales*. The British heavy cruisers *Norfolk* and *Suffolk* continued to shadow the *Bismarck*, and later that day an attack by Fairey Swordfish torpedo-bombers from the carrier *Victorious* failed to inflict much damage on the German battleship. Then the British lost contact with the *Bismarck*, which was heading south, until it was spotted again on 26 May. Another attack by torpedo-bombers from the

Ark Royal damaged the Bismarck's steering gear. The next morning the battleships *King George V* and *Rodney*, together with the *Norfolk*, caught up with the *Bismarck* and reduced it to a blazing wreck. It was then dispatched to the bottom by a torpedo from the cruiser *Dorsetshire*. All but 110 of the *Bismarck*'s crew died. The German claim that it was scuttled is not generally accepted. The epic British pursuit of the German battleship was the subject of the 1960 film *Sink the Bismarck* starring Kenneth More.

Bisto. The proprietary name of a gravy powder first sold in 1910. It was popularized by the 'Bisto Kids', a group of urchin children who breathe 'Ah! Bisto!' as they savour the gravy's aroma. The name is probably arbitrary but has been explained as an anagrammatized acronym of the product's advertising slogan, 'Browns, Seasons, Thickens In One'.

Bitch, The. A nickname of the film actress Joan Collins (b.1933), partly from the reputation she has gained in her colourful private life, as a four-times married MANEATER, partly from the image of herself that she has projected in the films *The Stud* (1978) and *The Bitch* (1979) and as 'superbitch' Alexis Colby in the television melodrama DYNASTY.

> Joan Collins is NOT 'The Bitch'. You'd better believe it. Or she will chew you into small pieces, spit you out and stamp on you. Then she'll sue the pants off you. That's official.
> CHRISTINE HAMILTON: *The Book of British Battleaxes* (1997)

Bitch goddess. Material or worldly success as an object of attainment. The phrase comes from a letter of 11 September 1906 written by William James to H.G. Wells, in which he refers to 'a symptom of the moral flabbiness born of the exclusive worship of the bitch-goddess *success*'.

Bite on, To. To copy; to imitate, especially in matters of fashion. The phrase arose on the US campus in the 1980s.

Bits and bobs. Odds and ends; small diffuse amounts. Weather forecasters sometimes refer to 'bits and bobs of rain' meaning scattered showers.

Bitten by a bug. Keenly interested in an activity. The phrase usually names the bug in question, as 'bitten by the railway bug'. The expression dates from the 1930s but 'bug' as a word for an enthusiast goes back to the 19th century.

> I was bitten by the bug in my native California at the age of 12 when a girlfriend taught me to body surf with flippers. I've been a wave rider ever since.
> *Independent on Sunday* (3 October 1999)

Blackadder. A wise-cracking but cynical character created by Rowan Atkinson in successive television series, each set in a different historical period. The first, *The Black Adder* (1983), was supposedly during the War of the Roses. The second, *Blackadder II* (1985), was a comic version set in Elizabethan times. In the third, *Blackadder the Third* (1987), Blackadder is butler to the Prince Regent in the period 1760–1815. The saga ended magnificently with *Blackadder Goes Forth* (1989), bringing the tale into the 20th century and set in the First World War. In all of these Blackadder's long-suffering, dim-witted servant, Baldrick, is played by Tony Robinson.

Black and Tans. The name of a pack of hounds in County Limerick, applied to the specially recruited armed force of ex-servicemen sent to Ireland by the British government in 1920 during the Anglo-Irish War (War of Independence) to supplement the Royal Irish Constabulary. This force was so called from the colour of the mixed uniforms, which consisted of army khaki combined with the black belts and dark green caps of the RIC. Their main objective was to put down Republican rebels, which they proceeded to do with much bloodshed. The Irish for their part were merciless in their treatment of crown forces or suspected informers. *See also* IRA; TROUBLES.

Black and White Minstrel Show, The. A popular Saturday night television variety show running for 20 years from 1958 and featuring white men blacked up as nigger minstrels. The show finally faded from the screen when its incongruously racist nature was realized.

Black bag job. A US slang term for the surreptitious entry of an office or home in order to obtain files or other materials of intelligence interest. Although such break-ins were illegal, they were undertaken by the FBI in the interwar years, mainly for the benefit of code-breakers who wanted photographs of code books or diagrams of cipher machines. Another purpose was the installation of 'bugs' and telephone wire-taps. Black bag jobs, so called from the notional black (i.e. secret) carrier used, were outlawed by J. Edgar Hoover in 1966 but were again sanctioned in 1981 by President Reagan as long as they were conducted against a foreign power or its agents.

Blackboard Jungle, The. The first novel (1954) of the US writer Evan Hunter (b.1926) was based on his personal experience. It is a somewhat sensationalized account of an American urban high school where the boys are rough, the headmaster a bully, and the teachers overworked and plagued additionally by personal problems. As a result of the book, the expression blackboard jungle became a popular idiom for any undisciplined school of this type. A film version (1955), directed by Richard Brooks, was more notable for its introduction of Bill Haley and the Comets' ROCK AROUND THE CLOCK behind the credits than for any intrinsic interest. *See also* ASPHALT JUNGLE; CONCRETE JUNGLE; ROCK 'N' ROLL.

Black bottom. A popular dance of the 1920s, of US origin. It involved a sinuous rotation of the hips ('bottom').

Black box. An aircraft's flight data recorder, today usually orange in colour, not black. The term has a broader sense to apply to any complex piece of equipment whose workings remain a mystery. Here 'black' alludes to the arcane nature of its functions.

Black Bradman. A nickname of the Jamaica and West Indies cricketer George Headley (1909–83), whose batting feats in the 1930s led to inevitable comparisons with Australia's champion batsman, Don Bradman (*see* DON).

Black cab. A licensed London taxi, whether black in colour or not. Their drivers are required to be proficient in the KNOWLEDGE.

Black dog. Winston Churchill's name for the severe depressions to which he was sometimes prone. The term originally dates from the early 19th century, and appears in the writings of Sir Walter Scott and Robert Louis Stevenson, among others.

Black Forest gateau. A rich chocolate sponge cake with layers of morello cherries or cherry jam and whipped cream, topped with chocolate icing. The name translates German *Schwarzwälder Kirschtorte*, the latter word referring to the kirsch with which the cake layers are sometimes sprinkled. The confection is said to have originated in Berlin in the 1930s and its name almost certainly alludes to its dark colour rather than to the Black Forest itself.

Black Friday. 15 April 1921 in Britain, when the alliance between the three main trade unions broke down over the refusal of transport workers and railwaymen to strike in sympathy with the miners. The miners thus struck alone but were forced to return to work in June. The decision of two of the main workforces not to join the strike marked a watershed in postwar industrial relations. *See also* RED FRIDAY.

Black Hand. The popular name of the Balkan terrorist organization that was founded in 1911 with the aim of uniting Serbia with Bosnia and Herzegovina and was largely responsible for contriving the assassination of the Archduke Franz Ferdinand in SARAJEVO on 28 June 1914. This was the event that precipitated the First World War. The name was also that of a group of Sicilian blackmailers and terrorists operating in the United States in the early 20th century.

Blackhawk. The US vigilante hero of *Military Comics* and of his own book, *Blackhawk*, from 1941 to 1969. He begins his career as an anti-NAZI freedom fighter and ends it as a CIA agent. He was the creation of Chuck Cuidera, and was perpetuated by Reed Crandall and other artists. He appeared on radio in the 1940s and was played by Kirk Allyn in a film serial, *Blackhawk* (1952).

Black hole. In astronomy a hypothetical region of collapsed stars whose gravitational pull is so extreme that not even light can escape. In 1974 the physicist and cosmologist Stephen Hawking caused a stir in scientific circles by asserting that small black holes emit radiation.

Black is beautiful. A black civil rights slogan of US origin, dating from the mid-1960s. The words have a biblical resonance: 'I am black, but comely, O ye daughters of Jerusalem, as the tents of Kedar, as the curtains of Solomon' (Song of Solomon 1:5).

Black Jack. John J. Pershing (1860–1948), commander-in-chief of the American Expeditionary Force in the First World War, was so known with reference to his leadership of black troops in Cuba and the Philippines early in his career.

Black knight. The converse of a WHITE KNIGHT, as an individual or company making an unwelcome take-over bid for another company. The term dates from the 1980s.

> Lance was styling himself as a 'friendly suitor' for the moment, but he would turn into a 'black knight' if he got an unfavorable answer from the boss.
> MILTON MOSKOWITZ, MICHAEL KATZ and ROBERT LEVERING (eds): *Everybody's Business*, ch xv (1980)

Black List, Section H. A semi-autobiographical novel

(1971) by the Australian-born Irish novelist Francis Stuart (1902–2000). The protagonist and narrator is called simply H, and the metaphorical black list to which the title refers is people's attitude to his going to work in Germany in 1940, as did Stuart himself. 'He was thinking now of himself as a writer, published, and for the most part, read in England, rather than an Irishman. This was a kind of malefactor whose rejection was seldom rescinded because the crime was not merely against an individual but that society as a whole.' The novel also deals with his relations with the poet W. B. Yeats (1865–1939) and the actress Maud Gonne (1866–1953), and Stuart's disastrous marriage to Gonne's illegitimate daughter Iseulte (1894–1954).

Black Martyrs. A general name for the 22 Africans of Uganda who died for their Christian faith in the late 1880s. They included Joseph Mkasa, who reproached the ruler, Mwanga, for debauchery and for murdering a missionary bishop, James Hannington, in 1885, Charles Lwanga, in charge of the royal pages, most of whom were also killed, Matthias Murumba, a judge, and Andrew Kagwa, a catechist. They were all canonized in 1964 and their feast-day of 3 June was included in the Roman calendar of 1969 as that of the proto-martyrs of Black Africa. *See also* FORTY MARTYRS.

Black mist. A corrupt business or political practice. The term dates from the 1960s and specifically applies to such practices in Japan, so translates Japanese *kuroi kiri*, from *kuroi*, 'black', and *kiri*, 'fog', 'mist'. A black mist obscures the vision and thus figuratively serves as an intentional cover-up of such a practice.

Black Monday. 19 October 1987, when £50 billion was wiped off the value of publicly quoted companies. The crash followed Wall Street's panic performance the previous Friday and heavy selling in Tokyo. In the United States the fall was the greatest since the GREAT DEPRESSION. Black Monday was also the nickname given by Conservative right-wingers to 3 February 1960, the day when Harold Macmillan gave his WIND OF CHANGE speech in Cape Town. *See also* MONDAY CLUB.

Black Muslims. *See* NATION OF ISLAM.

Black October. A nickname among economists for the time of year when there is often a financial crisis. During the 13 years from 1986 to 1999 there were six such stock market panics or 'mini-crashes', including BLACK MONDAY. BLACK THURSDAY was also in October, and BLACK WEDNESDAY the previous month. The incidence is linked to the perception that

autumn is, in effect, a 'new year' after the summer holiday, when personal strategies and life plans are reviewed.

Blackout. The term was first used in the theatre, when the lighting was extinguished to darken the whole stage. It is now mainly associated with its use in the Second World War as an air-raid precaution. From the outbreak of war (3 September 1939) until 23 April 1945 (coastal areas, 11 May), it was obligatory throughout Britain to cover all windows, skylights and the like before dark so that no gleam of light could be seen from outside. Moving vehicles were allowed only the dimmest of lights.

Black Panther. A nickname applied by the popular press to Donald Neilsen, convicted in 1975 of the kidnap and murder of the young heiress Lesley Whittle and of the killing of three sub-post office officials. The name referred to the black hood worn by Neilsen during the nine-month police search for him.

Black Panthers. A group of extremists in the United States set up to fight for the rights of black people. The organization was founded in 1966 in Oakland, California, by Huey Newton (1942–89) and Bobby Seale (b.1936) and began by setting up armed 'self-defence' patrols to resist police harassment.

Black paper. An unofficial paper criticizing or censuring an official document or policy. The contrast is with the White Paper that is a government report giving information or proposals on a particular issue. The term dates from the 1960s.

> Yet, as spending on education rises, so, too, does public concern or bafflement about its aims and method, as shown in the acrimonious debate initiated by the Black Paper on education.
> *The Times* (30 December 1970)

Black Pearl. The great Brazilian footballer Pelé (Edson Arantes do Nascimento; b.1940), regarded by many as the most talented player of all time. *See also* BRAZILIAN FOOTBALLERS.

Blackpool. The north of England resort's earthy name derives from a peaty pool that existed here before the present town arose in the 19th century. In some ways it evokes the down-to-earth pleasures and entertainments that are on offer. They include the golden sands of its Pleasure Beach; the famous Blackpool Tower, a scaled-down version of the Eiffel Tower, housing a zoo, a circus, a ballroom and a large organ; and a promenade, the GOLDEN MILE, thronged with holiday-makers and trundling trams by day and illuminated by strings of gaudy lights at night, when it is often populated by drunks and prostitutes. The Pleasure Beach, with its four ROLLER COASTERS, including the famous Pepsi Max Big One, is the apotheosis of sheer corporeal pleasure. Blackpool is in many ways the Brighton of the north, and on the serious side shares with its southern counterpart the privilege of hosting major political and trade union conferences.

> Blackpool is less cool Britannia than gruel Britannia. It is 1960s Britain minus the rock'n'roll.
> *Sunday Times* (10 October 1999)

Black Power. An emotive concept originating among certain sections of black opinion in the United States since 1966, whose advocates aim at redressing racial injustice by militant black nationalism that allows for violence and race war. *See also* NATION OF ISLAM.

Black Sash. An organization of black South African women founded in 1955 to sponsor research into racial questions and oppose APARTHEID. Their original official title was the Women's Defence of the Constitution, but they soon came to be known by their nickname, alluding to the broad black diagonal sash worn during picketing or other demonstrations.

Black September. A Palestinian terrorist group formed when the Palestine Liberation Organization (*see* PLO) was driven from Jordan in September 1970.

Blackshirt. The gentleman thief or amateur cracksman, real name Richard Verrell, in Bruce Graeme's bestselling novel named after him (1925). He is always scrupulously dressed in black, his evening dress complemented by black hood, black silk gloves, black shoes, black socks and black shirt. He has a special pocket from which, after his derring-do, he springs out an opera hat to set rakishly on his head as he sets out for home. The elegant hero appeared in many more books by Graeme, whose real name was Graham Montague Jeffries, and after the Second World War Graeme's son, writing as Roderic Graeme, began a new series of Blackshirt tales.

Blackshirts. Mussolini's Italian Fascists, who wore black shirts, as did their English imitators. The name was also used in NAZI Germany for Himmler's SS, by contrast with the Brownshirts (*see* SA). *See also* FASCISM; MOSLEYITE; WAFFEN SS.

Black Sox scandal. A scandal in the world of sport when in 1919 eight members of the Chicago White Sox, subsequently nicknamed the 'Black Sox', were accused of accepting bribes to lose the World Series

that year to the Cincinnati Reds. The eight were acquitted through insufficient evidence but were later banned from baseball for life. *See also* SAY IT AIN'T SO, JOE.

Black spot. A place on a road where accidents often occur, such as a bend or crossing. *See also* CATSEYES.

Black Thursday. 24 October 1929, the first day of the WALL STREET CRASH, when nearly 13 million shares changed hands. The panic continued on Black Monday (28 October) and Black Tuesday (29 October), when 16 million shares were traded and the stock market collapsed completely, leading to the GREAT DEPRESSION.

Black Wednesday. 16 September 1992, when Britain pulled out of the Exchange Rate Mechanism (ERM), allowing sterling to float. The Chancellor of the day, Norman Lamont, raised interest rates by 2 per cent and then by 3 per cent, but without improving sterling's value. The day was subsequently dubbed White Wednesday by those opposed to Britain's entry to the ERM.

Bladder diplomacy. A ploy to extract a concession from the other party in a discussion. The hapless visitor is plied with drinks until he feels constrained to agree to the point at issue in order to excuse himself. The ruse was notoriously resorted to by President Assad of Syria (1930–2000) who, in an apparently generous gesture, offered his guests small cups of black coffee to this end. Presidents, secretaries of state and foreign ministers alike were all subjected to the treatment.

Blade Runner. A bleak SCIENCE FICTION film (1982) directed by Ridley Scott, starring Harrison Ford and Rutger Hauer, and set in Los Angeles in the year 2019. Ford plays a detective who is hunting down escaped androids or 'replicants'. It is based on a short story by Philip K. Dick entitled *Do Androids Dream of Electric Sheep?*

Blah. A representation of words that are too tedious or obvious to give in full, the degree of tedium or obviousness usually indicated by repetition. The word itself dates from the early years of the 20th century and is simply imitative while suggesting 'blather' or 'blether'.

> Yes, I know sexy clothes perpetuate sexual stereotypes and can be hell to wear, blah, blah, blah.
> *The Times* (20 September 1999)

Blair Babes. Originally a derisory term for the women

Labour MPs supposedly cosseted by Tony Blair and devoted to him as fawning loyalists after Labour's victory in the 1997 general election. The phrase was suggested by a subsequent photocall, one of whose shots showed a grinning Blair amid a large group of such MPs looking up adoringly. The term was later extended to all backbenchers who were 'on-message' (*see* OFF-MESSAGE) and unquestioningly loyal to Blair and his policies.

Blair babes threaten to quit the Commons.

The Times (headline) (3 April 2000)

Blairism. The political and economic policies of Tony Blair (b.1953), leader of the LABOUR PARTY from 1994 and prime minister from 1997. The personalized term corresponded largely in import to the general party policy implicit in the designation NEW LABOUR.

Blaise, Modesty. The strip cartoon adventuress created by Peter O'Donnell made her maiden bow in the *Evening Standard* in 1963. She is popularly regarded as a sort of female James BOND, and she rose to fame in the 1960s, when spy fiction was all the rage. She 'wrote' a number of novels (the author was actually O'Donnell), the first of which, *Modesty Blaise*, appeared in 1965. She featured in a single somewhat uncharacteristic film of this name (1966), directed by Joseph Losey, in which she was played by Monica Vitti. Her cartoon adventures continue to be syndicated in newspapers around the world.

Blake, Sexton. A fictional detective who first appeared in the adventure paper MARVEL in 1893. The first author to write a Sexton Blake story was Harry Blyth (1852–98), writing under the pen-name Hal Meredith. According to *The Oxford Companion to Children's Literature* over 100 writers have written stories featuring Sexton Blake, and he appeared in a wide variety of magazines, adventure papers and popular novels in the first half of the 20th century. Blake's appearance and manner gradually came to resemble that of Sherlock Holmes.

Blake's 7. A cult television SCIENCE FICTION serial screened from 1978 to 1981. It followed the fortunes of a band of freedom fighters against the Terran Foundation led by Roj Blake in the second century of the third calendar. The motley 'magnificent seven' in question were Blake himself, played by Gareth Thomas, smuggler Jenna Jannis, computer expert Kerr Avon, thief Vila Restal, alien warrior Cally, 'gentle giant' Gan and the master computer of Blake's ship, Zen.

Blandish, Barbara. The millionaire's daughter who is kidnapped, tortured and raped by the villainous Slim Grissom in James Hadley Chase's salacious novel *No Orchids for Miss Blandish* (1939). The strange thing is that she enjoys it. 'Chase' was in fact an Englishman, named René Raymond, who attempted to write in the American vernacular. The story subsequently spawned stage and screen versions of dubious merit.

Miss Blandish belongs forever in the Forties schoolboys' prurient pantheon as part of the unholy trinity completed by Fanny Hill and Lady Chatterley: to be joined shortly after the war by Amber St Clair. Their names were enough to raise a laugh in any desperate music-hall comedian's act.

PHILIP FRENCH in *New Statesman* (5 November 1971)

Blanket protest. A protest beginning in 1980 by IRA prisoners in Northern Ireland's MAZE Prison during the TROUBLES. The protest aimed at achieving political status for the prisoners and involved a refusal to wear prison clothing, the prisoners wrapping themselves in prison blankets instead. Some prisoners went on to hold a DIRTY PROTEST. The protest culminated in a hunger strike in 1981 in which Bobby Sands, followed by nine more Republican prisoners, died, the British government having refused to give in to their demands. Nevertheless, the protests served to increase nationalist support for the Republican cause.

Blankety Blank. A weekly television GAME SHOW first screened in 1977 in which members of the public had to guess the missing word, the 'blank' of the title, in a given sentence and hope that the six celebrity guests present had written the same. It was originally hosted with Irish geniality by Terry Wogan, then by a world-weary, sarcastic Les Dawson. In the 1990s the host was the drag artist and comedian Lily Savage (real name Paul O'Grady). The title is the stock euphemistic oath, as: 'I wish you'd leave my blankety-blank pen alone.'

Blast. The title of a British MODERNIST magazine, of which only two issues were produced, both in 1914. The magazine was founded by the British writer and painter Percy Wyndham Lewis (1882–1957) and the American poet Ezra Pound (1885–1972) and was subtitled 'the Review of the Great English Vortex' (Lewis being heavily involved in the art movement known as VORTICISM). The magazine was noted for its aggressive geometrical graphics, innovative typography and wild challenges to received ideas and values, echoing FUTURISM and in some ways anticipating DADAISM.

Blast from the past. Anything suddenly or powerfully nostalgic, especially an old pop song.

> These thigh-length leather boots are a real blast from my past. I bought them in Chester in the 1970s because my friend had a pair, so I just had to follow suit.
> *Sunday People Magazine* (25 April 1999)

Blaue Reiter, Der (German, 'The Blue Rider'). A group of German expressionist painters formed in 1911 and based in Munich. Leading members were Wassily Kandinsky (1866–1944), Franz Marc (1880–1916) and Paul Klee (1879–1940), and the organization took its name from Kandinsky's drawing of a blue horseman on the cover of an *Almanac* published in May 1912 as the first number of a proposed annual although in fact the only issue to appear. *See also* BLAUE VIER.

Blaue Vier, Die (German, 'The Blue Four'). A group of four painters formed in 1924 at the instigation of the German art dealer Galka Scheyer (1889–1945) with the aim of promoting their work abroad. They were Lyonel Feininger (1871–1956), Alexei von Jawlensky (1864–1941), Wassily Kandinsky (1866–1944) and Paul Klee (1879–1940), and their name indicated their association with the BLAUE REITER.

Blaxpoitation. A blend of 'black' and 'exploitation', with particular reference to films made with black performers and aimed at black audiences but usually made by white producers. Such films were popular in the 1970s. They took the form of every established genre but were particularly prominent in the form of violent crime films such as *Shaft* (1971), in which a black PRIVATE EYE, played by Richard Roundtree, finds himself at odds with a racketeer. The US actress Pam Grier (b.1949) is generally regarded as the 'blaxploitation icon' of the period.

Bleeding heart. A person regarded as being excessively soft-hearted, especially in terms of financial generosity or political liberalism.

> Cut-throat competition in the credit card market has meant that it is even possible for conspicuous consumers and bleeding hearts [holding AFFINITY CARDS] to benefit from the lower rates.
> *The Times* (28 June 1999)

Bleed someone white, To. To submit them to extortion, so depriving them of all their money ('blood'). The expression dates from the 1930s.

Bless! A somewhat cloying exclamation current in the 1990s in response to a tweely touching sight or utterance, especially one involving a young child or pet. It is a shortening of 'bless you', 'bless her heart', 'bless his little cotton socks' or some similar soppiness.

Blessed Margaret. A nickname given Margaret Thatcher (b.1923), Conservative prime minister from 1979 to 1990, by the Conservative politician and prominent Roman Catholic Norman St John Stevas, later Lord St John of Fawsley (b.1929), while Leader of the House and Arts Minister. He saw her as the saviour of Britain from Socialism. *See also* ATTILA THE HEN.

Blighty. A colloquial name for England used by soldiers serving overseas in the First World War but originating among those who had served in India some years before. It represents Urdu *bilāyatī*, 'foreign', from Arabic *wilāyat*, 'dominion'. A highly popular song during the First World War was A.J. Mills, Fred Godfrey and Bennett Scott's 'Take Me Back to Dear Old Blighty' (1916). A magazine called *Blighty*, specializing in PIN-UPS and cartoons, was a former favourite with the troops, particularly in and after the two world wars. Its last issue appeared in 1958. *See also* FIRST WORLD WAR SLANG.

> As far as ageing romantics are concerned Dover is the only way to return to good old Blighty.
> *The Times* (17 August 1999)

Blimp (apparently a coinage based on *limp*, perhaps from the code name *Type B-limp*). A word originally applied to an observation balloon in the First World War. 'Colonel Blimp' was created after the war by the cartoonist David Low as a plump, pompous ex-officer who was rigidly and blindly opposed to anything new. Hence Colonel Blimp or blimp as a now rather dated term for a military officer, or any person with stuffy or reactionary views. *See also* LIFE AND DEATH OF COLONEL BLIMP.

> He [Tony Blair] must also be the first party leader since Neville Chamberlain ... to have the whole-hearted support of Colonel Blimp. What can one hear the old boy saying? 'Gad sir, it's good to have a public school man back at the helm.'
> WILLIAM REES-MOGG in *The Times* (29 August 1994)

Blind date. An appointment to meet a person of the opposite sex whom one has never met before, the expectation adding excitement to the romantic allure. The popular television programme *Blind Date* was first screened in 1985 as a sort of combined dating service and GAME SHOW. In the world of espionage a blind date is a meeting by an intelligence officer and an agent at the time and place of the latter's choosing.

Blind someone with science, To. To confuse or over-awe them with technical jargon or learned talk.

Bliss out, To. To achieve a state of such supreme content that one is oblivious to all else. The phrase dates from the 1960s and the drug-draped world of HIPPIES.

> Still slightly blissed-out after a shave and face massage, I acquiesce. The guy is John Major's barber, after all.
>
> *The Times* (21 August 1999)

Blithe Spirit. A play (1941) and film (1945) by British playwright, actor and composer Noël Coward (1899–1973). The plot revolves around the haunting of novelist Charles Condomine by the ghost of his first wife. The film, directed by David Lean, starred Rex Harrison as Charles, Kay Hammond as Elvira, the first Mrs Condomine, Constance Cummings as Ruth, the second Mrs Condomine, and Margaret Rutherford as the wholly memorable medium Madame Arcati. The title of the play is a quotation from Percy Bysshe Shelley's 'To a Skylark' (1820), with a pun on 'spirit':

> Hail to thee, blithe Spirit!
> Bird thou never wert,
> That from Heaven, or near it,
> Pourest thy full heart
> In profuse strains of unpremeditated art.

Blitz. The name (an abbreviation of BLITZKRIEG) given to the intensive German air raids on London during the Second World War. The bombardment was initiated by Hitler in retaliation for RAF attacks on Berlin and began on 7 September 1940, when 450 people were killed by a raid over the East End. The raids continued almost nightly until 10 May 1941, by which time there was an estimated casualty rate of over 1000 civilian deaths a day. Londoners were not the only ones to suffer, and most of Britain's major cities were bombed, COVENTRY suffering particularly badly. The final toll was an estimated 40,000 civilians killed and 46,000 injured. More than a million homes were destroyed and an immense amount of damage caused to industrial installations. *See also* BATTLE OF BRITAIN; BLACKOUT; EVACUEE; WIREWALKERS.

Blitzkrieg (German, 'lightning war'). A concentrated military offensive designed to produce a knockout blow. The term was particularly applied to the attacks by Hitler's Germany on various European countries between 1939 and 1941. In 1940 in western Europe the

Germans captured Copenhagen on 9 April, Oslo on 10 April, The Hague on 14 May, Brussels on 17 May and Paris on 14 June, resulting in the British withdrawal at DUNKIRK. *See also* D-DAY.

Blobbo. A nickname of the powerfully built US professional golfer Jack Nicklaus (b.1940) who has won more than 80 tournaments in his career.

Blockbuster. Anything of great power or size, such as an epic film or a bestseller. The term derives from the heavy high-explosive bombs dropped in the Second World War, which were capable of destroying a whole block of buildings.

Blonde bombshell. A dated term for a strikingly good-looking, fair-haired young woman, especially when exuding a lively sexuality. The allusion is to her 'explosive' effect (*see also* BIKINI). The expression dates from the 1930s and was notable applied to the film actress Jean Harlow (1911–37), one of whose films was actually titled *Blonde Bombshell* (1933). The actress Betty Hutton (b.1921) was also sometimes so known. One of her own films was *Incendiary Blonde* (1945).

> Do you remember that 1960s school sitcom, Please Sir!? The one with John Alderton as the nice teacher who'd get into a ... tizzy when confronted by the blonde bombshell of 5C?
>
> *Sunday Times* (17 October 1999)

Blondie. The heroine of the US cartoon strip of the same name by Chic Young, first published in 1930. She began as the flapper Blondie Boopadoop, but subsequently became the wife of the ineffectual Dagwood Bumstead and mother of the precocious Baby Dumpling. Her domestic dramas burgeoned into a series of more than 20 films with Blondie in the title, such as *Blondie Brings up Baby* (1939). The last was *Blondie's Hero* (1950), after which she moved to television. The name of the US rock group Blondie (1975–82) was directly associated with its charismatic blonde lead singer Deborah Harry (b.1945), although she never adopted the name for herself.

Blood, Captain. The medical doctor turned pirate captain in Rafael Sabatini's historical novel *Captain Blood* (1922) and its sequels. His full name is Peter Blood. Unjustly sentenced by Judge Jeffreys, Dr Blood is transported to the Spanish Main but there escapes captivity and becomes a privateer. The film of the same name (1935) was a great success and made a star of its leading man, Errol Flynn. Further films followed, with *Son of Captain Blood* (1962) appropriately starring Sean Flynn, Errol's son.

Blood and Guts. A nickname given by the soldiers in the Second World War to the US General George Smith Patton (1885–1945), with reference to his ungovernable temper. His career ended when he struck an enlisted man. The name is also a disrespectful term for the red ensign. A spectacular film, *Patton*, dealing with Patton's military career from 1943 to 1945, was released in 1970. It was directed by Franklin J. Schaffner and starred George C. Scott as Patton.

Blood and Guts in High School. An impressionistic novel (1984) by the US writer Kathy Acker (1948-97) incorporating experimental techniques of presentation, for which she has been described as a postmodernist feminist.

Bloodbath. The earliest sense of the word, dating from the 19th century, was a literal bath in warm blood taken by a debilitated person as a supposed tonic. The term then came to denote a massacre, borrowing the sense from German *Blutbad*. In the 20th century a figurative meaning evolved for a mass dismissal of employees or wholesale sacking of staff.

> I hear of a bloodbath in Crédit Lyonnais, which has just fired eight analysts.
> *The Times* (8 December 1999)

Blood group. A classification of blood according to the two types of antigens, known as A and B, on the surface of blood cells. According to whether a person's blood contains one or other of the two types, both or neither, it is classified as type A, B, AB or O. In Britain, the most common group is A, followed by O, then B, and finally AB.

Blood on the carpet. A heated debate or verbal wrangle, as if a fierce fight causing bloodshed.

> The main publishing casualties of a judging process said to have involved 'blood on the carpet' and resignation threats are Penguin, Orion … and Cape.
> *Sunday Times* (26 September 1999)

Blood Orange. The partly punning, partly descriptive nickname of Lieutenant-General Sir George Gorringe (1868–1945), given by soldiers in the First World War on the grounds that he needlessly expended men's lives on the WESTERN FRONT.

Blood Wedding. The play, *Bodas de sangre*, by the Spanish playwright Federico García Lorca (1898–1936), first performed in 1933. It is about the tragedy and bloodshed that result after a bride elopes with a former lover on the day fixed for her marriage to

another man. Lorca based his story on a real incident reported in the newspapers of Almería in 1928, in which a bride and her lover were hunted down by the family of the thwarted bridegroom. It was first staged in New York in 1935 under the title *Bitter Oleander* and subsequently in London as *The Marriage of Blood*.

Bloody Friday. 21 July 1972, when 11 people were killed and 130 injured by IRA bombs in Belfast.

Bloody Maria. A drink made with tequila and tomato juice. The name dates from the 1970s as a variant on the earlier BLOODY MARY.

Bloody Mary. The cocktail of vodka and tomato juice is said to have gained its name in 1927 when the US vaudeville comic, George Jessel (1898–1981), mixed a mid-morning tomato drink for himself in a Palm Beach bar. He offered a taste to Mary Brown Warburton, a Philadelphia socialite, who promptly spilt it down the front of her white gown, 'thereby christening herself and the drink "Bloody Mary"' (*American National Biography*, 1999). The allusion is to Mary I (1516–58) of England and Ireland, nicknamed 'Bloody Mary' for her persecution of Protestants.

Bloody Saturday. 15 August 1998, when an IRA splinter group planted a car bomb that killed 29 and injured more than 200 in Omagh, Northern Ireland.

Bloody Sunday. (1) 22 January 1905. A deputation of workers led by Father Gapon marched to the Winter Palace in St Petersburg to present a petition to the Tsar. After giving warnings to disperse, the troops fired into the crowd. More than 100 people were killed and many hundreds more wounded.

(2) 21 November 1920. Fourteen undercover British intelligence agents were shot by SINN FÉIN in Dublin, and in the afternoon of the same day the BLACK AND TANS opened fire on a Gaelic football crowd at Croke Park, killing 12.

(3) 30 January 1972. Paratroops of the British army opened fire on a banned civil rights march in Londonderry, killing 13. BLOODY FRIDAY followed six months later. *See also* BOGSIDE.

A wry twist to the term was given by the title of the award-winning film *Sunday, Bloody Sunday* (1971), written by Penelope Gilliatt.

> Didn't I know there was a famous Irish Bloody Sunday … Didn't I know about the Russian Bloody Sunday? Yes, I said. But it still wasn't the English bloody Sunday.
> PENELOPE GILLIATT: *Making Sunday Bloody Sunday*, Introduction (1986)

Bloom, Leopold. *See* BLOOMSDAY; ULYSSES.

Bloomsbury Group. The name given to a group of writers, artists and intellectuals, who lived and worked in Bloomsbury, central London, from about 1907 to 1930. They included Leonard (1880–1969) and Virginia (1882–1941) Woolf, Clive (1881–1964) and Vanessa (1879–1961) Bell, Roger Fry (1866–1934), E.M. Forster (1879–1970), Lytton Strachey (1880–1932), Duncan Grant (1885–1978) and John Maynard Keynes (1883–1946). They saw themselves as advocates of a new rational, civilized society and many of them had Cambridge links. They have been criticized by some as an overexposed group of serial adulterers and second-raters who, famously, 'lived in squares and loved in triangles', but the honesty of their intentions to some extent redeems them from such charges. They were influenced by the anti-Hegelian G.E. Moore's *Principia Ethica* (1903), which analyzed the moral concept of goodness and commended the value of friendship and aesthetic experience.

Bloomsday. 16 June 1904, the day in the life of Leopold Bloom described by James Joyce in his novel ULYSSES (1922). It is marked annually in Dublin with a tour of pubs, hotels and shops where Bloom stopped, beginning with the South Bank Restaurant in Sandycove. It was David Norris, a senior lecturer in English at Trinity College, Dublin, who in the late 1960s revived interest in Bloom's journey:

> I dressed up in a straw hat and, with a silver cane, walked through Dublin and read from the book. Everyone thought I was mad, but it seems to have caught on.
>
> *The Times* (17 June 1994)

Blot one's copybook, To. To commit an error that spoils one's hitherto unblemished record or stains one's reputation. A copybook was originally a book containing models of handwriting for young people to copy. The expression dates from the 1930s.

Blot on the landscape. Anything that mars the beauty or perfection of something. 'Blot' as a blemish has been current since at least the time of Shakespeare, but the full phrase emerged only in the early 20th century. The reference is to a mark or stain that spoils a painted landscape. The term was punningly adapted by Tom Sharpe for his black farce *Blott on the Landscape* (1975), in which Blott is a handyman who halts the construction of a motorway through the grounds of a stately home. A televised version by Malcolm Bradbury was screened in 1985.

Blow a fuse, To. To explode with rage, especially unexpectedly, as when the fuse in an electric circuit suddenly melts through overloading. The expression dates from the 1920s.

> One of my teachers has an irritating habit. After teaching us very difficult pieces of information she asks, 'Does anyone have any questions?' Then if any confused pupil raises their hand … the teacher automatically blows a fuse! Now everyone is so terrified to ask a question that they're left confused, and when test time arrives she blows another fuse at the fact that we got it wrong!
>
> *The Times* (11 September 1999)

Blow a raspberry, To. To show contempt for someone or something by putting one's tongue between closed lips and expelling air forcibly with a resulting rude noise. The action is also known as a BRONX CHEER. 'Raspberry' is short for 'raspberry tart', rhyming slang for 'fart'. The expression is frequently applied figuratively. *See also* GOLDEN RASPBERRY.

> She [singer Shelby Lynne] finally blew a raspberry to the country music fame factory, went back home, and at 30, has recorded an album of monumental versatility and élan.
>
> *The Times* (4 October 1999)

Blow away the cobwebs, To. To banish a condition of lethargy; to refresh or reinvigorate oneself. 'Cobweb' as a metaphor for an accretion that needs to be cleared dates from the 16th century.

Blow by blow account. One describing events in minute detail. The expression is of US origin and comes from radio boxing match commentaries, where one would have 'a left to the body, a right to the chin' and so on.

Blowin' in the Wind. A song by Bob Dylan, one of the most famous protest songs of the 1960s, released in 1963 on the album *The Freewheelin' Bob Dylan*. Its gentle and wistful melody, sung to guitar and harmonica accompaniment, is based on the tune of the black spiritual 'No More Auction Block For Me'. The song asks nine questions about peace and civil rights (including 'How many years can some people exist before they're allowed to be free?'), all of which are answered by the forlorn response 'The answer, my friend, is blowin' in the wind, the answer is blowin' in the wind.' The song became an anthem of the civil rights movement in America.

Blow one's top, To. To lose one's temper; to become angry. There are various alternatives for 'top' in this phrase, all originating in the 20th century, and including 'cool', 'cork', 'gaff', 'lid', 'roof', 'stack'. The general image is of a volcano erupting. *See also* FLIP ONE'S LID.

> When ... [David] Mellor heard what had occurred, he blew his top. A few days later an account of his temper tantrum appeared in *The Observer*.
> *The Times* (17 November 1999)

Blow someone out, To. To abandon a romantic relationship. An expression dating from the 1960s.

> We had a girl ... who came up and said, 'Ooh, is this [the television dating show] *Streetmate*? Can I do it? Can I do it?' So we found her someone, and she blew us out the next day.
> *heat* (16 December 1999–5 January 2000)

Blow someone's mind, To. To induce hallucinatory experiences by means of drugs; to impress or affect keenly.

Blow someone's socks off, To. *See* KNOCK SOMEONE'S SOCKS OFF.

Blow the whistle on, To. To inform on someone; to bring a stop to something. The allusion is either to the policeman's whistle or to that of the referee in a football match. *See also* WHISTLE-BLOWER.

> Professor Davies was also found guilty of asking a junior colleague ... to 'violate' study protocol, threatening him that he would be 'finished' if he blew the whistle on his boss.
> *The Times* (2 October 1999)

Bludger. An Australian term of abuse for someone drawing unemployment pay; the equivalent of the British 'scrounger'. The word is a shortened form of 'bludgeoner', originally meaning someone who lives off the earnings of a prostitute.

Blue Angel, The. A film (1930) adapted by Carl Zuckmayer from the novel *Professor Unrat* (1905) by Heinrich Mann (the brother of Thomas Mann). Shot under the direction of Joseph von Sternberg simultaneously in German and English (the German title is *Der blaue Engel*), the film made an international star of Marlene Dietrich, playing nightclub singer Lola, who was subsequently sometimes referred to as 'the blue angel'. Today it is best remembered for Dietrich's memorable rendition of 'Falling in Love Again', one of the tunes with which she was destined to become most closely associated.

Blue baby. A baby with a blue complexion resulting from a lack of oxygen in the blood. The cause is usually a congenital defect of the heart or the major blood vessels.

Bluebell Girls. A troupe of high-kicking young women in the Folies-Bergère tradition, established in the 1930s by the Anglo-Irish dancer Margaret Kelley, known as Miss Bluebell from the colour of her eyes as a baby. They actually began their career at the Folies-Bergère and still perform mainly in Paris, although many of the troupe are British.

Blue Berets. A nickname for members of the multinational UNITED NATIONS Peacekeeping Force, whose uniform includes such headgear. The UN Security Council has established several such forces since its foundation, each known by an acronymic name. Those still active at the close of the 20th century ranged from the UN Truce Supervision Organization (UNTSO) in Israel, founded in 1948, to the UN Transitional Administration in East Timor (UNTAET), set up in 1999.

Blue bird of happiness. A visionary concept elaborated from Maurice Maeterlinck's play *L'Oiseau bleu* (1908), first produced in London as *The Blue Bird* in 1910. It tells the story of a boy and girl seeking 'the blue bird', which brings 'the great secret of things and of happiness'.

Blue chip. Said of anything dependable or of high quality, with particular reference to a company or its shares when regarded as a reliable investment. The source is in gambling games such as poker, in which the blue chip usually has the highest value. The term dates from the early years of the 20th century and is now frequently found in job advertisements.

> Blue Chip Secretary for Blue Chip Co.
> *The Times* (advertisement heading) (21 July 1999)

Blue-collar worker. A manual industrial worker, who at one time traditionally wore blue overalls. The term dates from the 1950s and arose from a contrast with the WHITE-COLLAR WORKER. *See also* GREY-COLLAR WORKER; PINK-COLLAR WORKER.

Blue corner. One of the two opponents ('corners') in a boxing match, the other being the red corner. The terms are used metaphorically for any two views or approaches, not necessarily in opposition.

> Roll up, roll up, for what promises to be one of the most entertaining fights in British banking history. In

the blue corner we have one of Edinburgh's financial elite, Peter Burt; while in the red, there is the career banker from Newcastle, Derek Wanless.

The Times (25 September 1999)

Bluegrass. A form of COUNTRY MUSIC influenced by JAZZ and BLUES. It represents the earliest, traditional style of HILLBILLY string bands and is most familiar from its high-harmony vocals. It takes its name from the bluegrass grown for fodder in the southern states of the United States and especially in Kentucky and Virginia, the former of which is nicknamed the Bluegrass State. *See also* COUNTRY MUSIC.

Blue Guides. The well-known series of guidebooks to Britain and foreign countries was launched in 1915, when Finlay and James Muirhead published their *Blue Guide to London and its Environs*. This was later issued by Hachette in French as a *Guide Bleu*. Hachette then went on to produce its own *Guide Bleu* to Paris, which was in turn published by Muirhead in English. The two-way arrangement lasted until 1933. The series has since continued, published by A & C Black, and in 1993 the 50th *Blue Guide*, to Tuscany, appeared.

Blue movie. A pornographic film. The name is fancifully derived from the custom of Chinese brothels being painted blue externally.

Blue Peter. One of the longest lasting and best of children's television programmes, broadcast by the BBC from 1958. Aimed mainly at the under-12s, it covers a wide range of subjects, many of them practical, and has made charitable appeals a special feature. Some of its presenters were almost family friends, such as Valerie Singleton (1962–71), John Noakes (1965–79) and Peter Purves (1967–79). Animals regularly featured, and the mongrel Petra, born in the year of *Blue Peter*'s launch, was a firm favourite until her death in 1977. The programme takes its name from the blue peter, a blue flag with a white centre, which a ship flies when about to leave port. *See also* CHILDREN'S HOUR.

Blue plaque. A blue ceramic plaque set into the façade of a building in London where a famous person lived, giving the relevant dates and details. The first was placed by the London County Council in 1903 on the house, Holly Lodge, Kensington, in which Thomas Macaulay died. In recent years plaques have commemorated events as well as lives. One set on an East End railway bridge in 1988 reads: 'The first Flying Bomb on London fell here, 13 June 1944.'

Blueprint. Strictly, a photographic print of a detailed plan, technical drawing or the like, in white lines on a blue background. The word is now used generally for any project, scheme or design.

Blue Riband. The liner gaining the record for the fastest Atlantic crossing was said to hold the Blue Riband of the Atlantic, and from 1907 to 1929 it was held by the Cunard liner *Mauretania*. It then passed to the *Europa* (1930) and *Bremen* (1933) of Germany, to the *Rex* of Italy (1933), and to the French liner *Normandie* in 1935. After that it was held by the *Queen Mary* of Britain from 1938 until its capture by the American-owned *United States* in 1952. A trophy offered in 1935 by H.K. Hales (1868–1942) was first accepted by the United States Lines in 1952.

Blue rinse brigade. A slighting term for elderly, well-to-do women, who sometimes use a special rinse to give their grey or white hair a temporary blue tint. The phrase gained currency towards the end of the Second World War and came to be particularly associated with women at the annual Conservative Party conference, partly because of the party's identifying colour. The use of 'brigade' in the term implies that those so designated are a force to be reckoned with.

He also goes traipsing across the United States ... reciting poems to the blue-rinsed brigade.

Manchester Guardian Weekly (1 August 1970)

Blues. A traditional form of US folksong, expressive of the unhappiness of blacks in the Southern states. The usual subject matter is love, the troubles that beset the singer or a nostalgic longing for home, coupled with an acceptance of life as it is. Blues usually consist of 12 bars made up of three four-bar phrases in 4/4 time. They can be vocal or instrumental and have had significant influence on JAZZ.

Blueshirts. An Irish fascist organization under General Eoin O'Duffy, former Commissioner of the Garda, which developed from the Army Comrades Association in the early 1930s. A Blueshirt battalion led by O'Duffy fought for General Franco in the Spanish Civil War (1936–9). *See also* FASCISM.

Blue Sky Laws. In the United States laws passed to protect the inexperienced buyer of stocks and bonds against fraud. The name is said to have its origin in a phrase used by one of the supporters of the earliest of these laws, who said that certain business operators were trying to capitalize 'the blue skies'.

Blue Suede Shoes. A classic pop song about teenage fashion, written and sung by the country singer Carl Perkins and released in 1956. The song's title has its roots in an incident at a dance in which Perkins heard a boy tell a girl not to tread on his blue suede shoes. He wrote the song immediately afterwards. There was an almost simultaneous version of the song by Elvis Presley.

Blurb. A publisher's promotional description on the dust jacket or cover of a book. The word is said to have originated from the name 'Miss Belinda Blurb', coined in 1907 by the US humorist Gelett Burgess for the figure of a pulchritudinous young lady on a comic book jacket. Burgess later defined the word as follows:

> 1. A flamboyant advertisement; an inspired testimonial. 2. Fulsome praise; a sound like a publisher.
>
> *Burgess Unabridged* (1914)

B-movie or **B-picture.** A low-budget film of poor quality and often cheaply sensational content made as a supporting feature for the main film (the implied 'A-movie') in a cinema programme. A good example of the type is Val Newton's *I Walked With a Zombie* (1943), with a plot that is a tongue-in-cheek adaptation of Charlotte Brontë's *Jane Eyre* (1847).

> It could be a scene from a B movie. Picture a remote comprehensive school in the bleak industrial valleys of Wales. It is 5 pm, the children have gone home and the site is deserted. The deputy head is finishing his paperwork when suddenly two burly men barge into his office.
>
> *The Times* (3 November 1999)

B.O. Body odour, caused by the bacterial decomposition of sweat in unwashed areas of the body, especially the armpits and feet. The euphemistic abbreviation was invented and promoted by the manufacturers of Lifebuoy soap in the 1930s, originally in the United States. Hence 'B.O. juice' as US campus slang for deodorant.

> A club-less man is sure to be regarded with some misgiving. Was he blackballed? Doesn't he know anyone to put him up? Has he B.O.?
>
> GUY EGMONT: *The Art of Egmontese*, ch i (1961)

Boanerges (Greek, 'sons of thunder'). The name given by T.E. Lawrence, LAWRENCE OF ARABIA, to the Brough Superior motorbike on which he was killed in an accident in 1935. Boanerges was originally the nickname given by Jesus to the apostles James and John

(Mark 3:17), perhaps because of their excessive zeal (as in Mark 9:38 and Luke 9:54).

Boarding-house reach. Reaching across fellow diners for food instead of asking them to pass it. The term is of US origin and dates from the early 20th century, alluding to the former boarding-house practice of seating all the residents at a single large table, where some would rudely stretch across others to help themselves.

Boat people. A group term for refugees who have left their native country by sea. The expression became particularly associated with those Vietnamese who fled in small boats to Hong Kong, Australia and elsewhere following the conquest of South VIETNAM by North Vietnam in 1975.

Bob-a-Job Week. A fund-raising week instituted by the BOY SCOUTS in 1949. All kinds of jobs were undertaken, some for their publicity value, for the payment of one shilling. It became an annual effort but with the declining value of the 'bob' and the advent of DECIMAL CURRENCY, Scout Job Week took its place in 1972.

Bobbetty. A nickname of the Conservative politician Robert Cecil, Lord Cranbourne (1893–1972), later the 5th marquess of Salisbury, who resigned from Baldwin's government in 1938 over its appeasement policy, but later served as leader of the Lords until 1957.

Bobbsey Twins. Two sets of twins in a long series of books for young children by Laura Lee Hope, beginning with *Bobbsey Twins; or, Merry Days Indoors and Out* (1904). The older pair are called Bert and Nan, the younger Freddie and Flossie. The books have been read by generations of American children and in 1950 Hope revised the original, amending its genteel racism.

Bobby socks. White ankle-length socks commonly worn by teenage girls in the United States in the 1940s and 1950s. Hence bobby-soxers for the adolescent girls who wore such socks, especially as fans of popular singers. 'Bobby' here denotes the length of the socks, as if cut short or 'bobbed'.

> Fair Elaine the bobby-soxer,
> Fresh-complexioned with Innoxa.
> JOHN BETJEMAN: *A Few Late Chrysanthemums*,
> 'Middlesex' (1954)

Boche. A FIRST WORLD WAR SLANG word for a German,

or the Germans collectively, from a French word originating as a shortening of *Alboche*, an alteration of *Allemoche*, an argot form of *Allemand*, 'German'. The *b* is from *caboche*, a slang word for 'head', or from *tête de boche*, 'wooden head'.

Bodice-ripper. A sexually explicit romantic novel or film in a historical setting, the latter serving as a supposedly acceptable vehicle for the lubriciously narrated or portrayed seduction. The bodice is the old-fashioned type of undergarment worn by the heroine and torn by her lover in his passion.

Bodmin Moor, Beast of. *See* BEAST OF BODMIN MOOR.

Body, The. A promotional name for the US film actress and former model Marie McDonald (1923–65). Her physical allure first drew the public in *Pardon My Sarong* (1942). Not surprisingly, the tag has also been applied to other actresses and models, notably the US actress Victoria Principal (b.1945), prominent in the television series DALLAS, and the Australian SUPERMODEL and actress Elle MacPherson, real name Eleanor Gow (b.1964).

Body art. A type of art in which the artist's own body is the medium. Much of it is overtly sexual or sadomasochistic in nature, an example of the former being the American Vito Acconci's *Seedbed* (1972), involving a daily display of masturbatory activity, and of the latter being the Italian Gina Pane's *Nourishment* (1971), in which she forced herself to regurgitate meat. Extreme examples of the genre have been exploited by the Californian Chris Burden, who in the name of art was kicked down two flights of concrete stairs in 1974. The term itself is also used for BODY PIERCING, as a public exhibition of a similar form of potentially harmful self-expression.

Body bag. A bag for carrying a corpse from the scene of warfare or an accident, such as a plane crash. In the plural the term has become something of a journalistic euphemism for war casualties, and US strategy and tactics in the second GULF WAR clearly recognized in advance the importance of the so called 'body bag factor' and the need to limit one's own losses at all cost.

Body beautiful. An ideal of physical beauty. The form of the phrase, with inverted noun and adjective, suggests a patterning on a legal term such as 'the body politic'.

Body blow. In boxing a punch to the body; figuratively, therefore, a shattering blow, a severe setback or shock.

Bodybuilding. The carrying out of regular exercises designed to enhance the body's muscular development. The modern form of the practice grew out of 19th-century strong-man theatrical and circus acts. The first US physique contest took place in New York in 1903, staged by the physical culturist Bernarr Macfadden (1868–1955), dubbed 'the most perfectly developed man in America'. (He was born Bernard McFadden but respelled his name to make it sound 'stronger'.) The activity was widely promoted through mail-order lessons from the 1920s by Charles Atlas, original name Angelo Siciliano (1894–1972), and more recently the premier figure in the art was the Austrian-born US film actor Arnold Schwarzenegger (b.1947), formerly Mr Universe. Women bodybuilders began to emerge in the 1970s.

Body count. A tally of the people present or of those participating in a particular situation. The term originated in the VIETNAM War (1955–75) when it was used for the count of enemy soldiers killed by US and Allied forces. The HORROR MOVIE *Friday the 13th Part II* (1981) was advertised with the words 'The body count continues', referring to its forerunner, *Friday the 13th* (1980).

Body double. A stand-in for a film actor or actress in a stunt or nude scene. Thus Shelley Michelle was Julia Roberts's body double in certain scenes in *Pretty Woman* (1990).

> The film [*The Thomas Crown Affair*] makes only brief use of body doubles – the well-toned stand-ins who earn their living imitating someone else's body – but not, apparently, for reasons of vanity.
> *Sunday Times* (22 August 1999)

Body language. The use of movements of the body or gestures, mostly unconsciously, to convey a meaning or information. Thus crossing the legs and folding the arms are defensive gestures, expressing the desire to protect oneself. Different races have differing body languages. The term itself dates from the 1960s and apparently arose as a translation of French *langage corporel*.

Bodyline bowling. In cricket fast bowling aimed at the batsman's body rather than the wicket. Such bowling was originally known as leg theory, the aim being to bowl short and fast so that the batsman was obliged to use his bat as a shield to protect his upper body and in so doing lob a catch to a knot of expectant fielders on the leg side. In England's 1932–3 tour of Australia the captain, Douglas Jardine, encouraged his fast bowlers, Harold Larwood and Bill Voce, to use body-line tactics as a counter to the threat posed by the prodigious Australian batsman Don Bradman. The strategy won the Ashes for England but aroused such a storm of indignation in Australia that diplomatic relations between the two countries were almost suspended. One positive result was a modification in the laws of cricket. *See also* DON; PULL A FAST ONE.

Body piercing. The piercing of holes in parts of the body other than the ear lobes in order to insert rods, rings and other objects, a form of adornment fashionable among young people in the 1990s. Visible organs favoured for the treatment include the nostril, the eyebrow, the lip and, among females, the navel. The tongue and nipple may also be so embellished, and for the enhancement of sexual pleasure more intimate parts. The art became socially acceptable but the risk of serious infection makes it medically hazardous. *See also* BODY ART.

Body popping. A dance popular in the 1980s, involving jerky and robotic arm and head movements and originating as a form of urban street display among Los Angeles teenagers in the late 1970s.

Body search. A search, especially by customs officials or the police, of a person's body for illicit weapons, drugs, and the like. The procedure can be unpleasant and degrading.

> I have considerable sympathy for [popular singer] Ms Diana Ross's outrage about the body search she endured at Heathrow. It is a revolting experience, and quite unnecessary.
> *The Times* (Letter to the Editor) (24 September 1999)

Body Shop. The cosmetics company and shops of this name owe their origin to Anita Roddick (b.1942) who in 1976, together with her husband, Gordon Roddick, opened a shop in Brighton under this name to sell cosmetics made from natural materials and 'stripped of the hype'. The name was not original, but had been suggested by a car bodywork repair shop called 'The Body Shop' that Roddick had seen in the United States. Following the opening of the shop, two undertakers with premises in the same street, Kensington Gardens, sent Roddick a solicitor's letter claiming that her enterprise would adversely affect their business. The local paper ran a story that she, a defenceless woman, was being harassed, and the incident served instead as welcome start-up publicity.

Body stocking. A woman's undergarment covering the torso and legs. It is similar to a bodysuit, or body, a close-fitting one-piece garment worn for sports and exercising.

Boer Wars. Two wars (1880–81 and 1899–1902), also known as the South African Wars, fought between the British and the Boers (or Afrikaners) for mastery in southern Africa. The second conflict began with early British reverses that culminated in three celebrated sieges, at Ladysmith, Mafeking and Kimberley, the relief of which entered British imperial folklore (*see* MAFEKING NIGHT). Thereafter the British used scorched-earth tactics to quash the Boer COMMANDOS and CONCENTRATION CAMPS to intern their families. The war was ended by the Treaty of Vereeniging (1902), which included a British promise to the defeated Boers that they would deny the franchise to Africans until the Boer republics were returned to representative government.

Boffin. A nickname used by the RAF in the Second World War for a research scientist, one of the BACK-ROOM BOYS. It passed into general use in the 1940s. Its origin is uncertain. One theory derives it from an obsolete torpedo bomber, the Blackburn Baffin, itself named after the navigator William Baffin (*c.*1584–1622), discoverer in 1616 of Baffin Bay in the North Atlantic. The word has now passed into school slang to mean a studious person or 'swot'.

Bofors gun. A light, rapid-firing 40-mm double-barrelled anti-aircraft (AA) gun made by the Swedish firm of Bofors (named after the town of Bofors in south-central Sweden). Regarded as the most effective light AA gun of the Second World War, it was widely used by both British and US forces, both on land and at sea. In 1987 a political corruption scandal erupted in India when it was discovered that the Bofors firm had been involved in giving financial kickbacks in return for arms orders. *Events While Guarding the Bofors Gun* is the title of a play (1966) by the Scottish playwright John McGrath (b.1935).

Bogside. One of the most resonant place-names in the geography of Northern Ireland's TROUBLES, sometimes colloquially shortened to 'the Bog'. The Bogside is a low-lying area beneath the city walls of Londonderry (Derry), and one of two Catholic estates that dominate the city (the other being the Creggan). Police incursions into the Bogside after a civil rights march from Belfast to Londonderry in October 1968 led to the birth of 'Free Derry', the Bogside becoming a NO-GO AREA for the security forces. The BATTLE OF THE BOGSIDE in August 1969 led to the deployment of British troops on the streets of Northern Ireland. On 29 March 1970, following a commemoration of the 1916 EASTER RISING, young Catholics were involved in clashes with the British army and the police, who replied to bricks and petrol bombs with tear gas, rubber bullets and Saracen armoured cars. The district was subsequently sealed off, and on 10 April the army announced the adoption of a 'get tough' policy in Northern Ireland, adding that anyone throwing a petrol bomb after a warning would be shot dead in the street. The Bogside was also the scene of the horrific events of BLOODY SUNDAY in January 1972. *See also* STROKE CITY.

Bog-standard. Ordinary and unremarkable. 'Bog' is an intensive suggesting a basic or rudimentary quality.

> They may polish off a million bottles of bog-standard vodka a day in Moscow, but that's economic chaos for you.
> *Sunday Times* (30 May 1999)

Bohemian Rhapsody. A flamboyant and operatic rock song, with teasingly allusive lyrics, by the pop group Queen. One of the most commercially successful pop releases of all time, it remained at number one in the UK charts for nine weeks in 1975–6 and again in 1991 when it was re-released following the death of the group's lead singer Freddie Mercury from AIDS. The song appeared on the album, *A Night at the Opera*. Its lyrics, heavily overlaid with images of death, and including allusions to fictional and historical characters (Scaramouche and Galileo), have long intrigued the public. Freddie Mercury said of the song: 'People should listen to it, think about it, and make up their own minds as to what it says to them.' *See also* ROCK GROUP NAMES.

Boho. An abbreviation of 'Bohemian' current from the 1950s to describe anyone with an unconventional lifestyle or a strikingly unusual or theatrical mode of dress.

> All that boho tragedy and minimalism of the Nineties [fashions] never sat very happily in Milan.
> *The Times* (28 February 2000)

Bokmål (Norwegian, literally 'book language'). The written language derived from Danish that is now the more common of the two official languages of Norway, the other being Nynorsk ('new Norwegian').

The name was officially adopted in 1929 to replace the earlier *Riksmål* ('state language'). Nynorsk was itself known before this date as *Landsmål* ('language of the land'). Plans to merge the two tongues into a common Norwegian language remain highly controversial.

Boléro. A long, slow and mesmeric orchestral crescendo by Maurice Ravel (1875–1937), unremittingly utilizing the rhythm of the traditional Spanish dance of the same name. Originally the music was for a ballet (1928), but it immediately became a very popular concert piece. *Boléro* featured on the soundtrack of the romantic film comedy *10* (1979), in which Dudley Moore lusts after Bo Derek, and was also used by the British ice-dancers Jayne Torvill and Christopher Dean (*see* TORVILL AND DEAN) in their performance at the 1984 Winter Olympics, for which they won the gold medal.

Bolly. Bollinger champagne. The casual colloquialism conceals the prestigious origin of the top quality wine, taking its name from Jacques Joseph Placide Bollinger, the youngest son of a noblewoman and a legal officer in Württemberg, who in 1829 formed a partnership with Amiral Comte Athanase Louis Emmanuel de Villermont and Paul-Joseph Renaudin to form the house of Champagne Renaudin, Bollinger & Cie. In 1837 Bollinger married de Villermont's daughter, Louise Charlotte, and became a French citizen. The champagne is a favourite for a celebratory occasion.

> And to drink? For someone [pop singer Gabrielle] with a recent number one single and album to celebrate, perhaps a bottle of Bolly? 'Herbal tea, please,' she says.
> *heat* (2–8 March 2000)

Bollywood. A nickname for the Indian popular film industry, which is based in Bombay. The word is a blend of 'Bombay' and HOLLYWOOD. The standard product of such companies as Bombay Talkies Ltd was originally garish imitation of Hollywood entertainment.

> The new productions are pure Bollywood from the studios of Bombay. There are battle scenes and Pakistanis dying by the platoon. But there is also singing, dancing and romancing in the meadows.
> *The Times* (17 July 1999)

Boloney. *See* BALONEY.

Bolshevik. Properly a member of the Russian revolutionary party under LENIN, which seized power in

1917, aiming at the establishment of the supreme power of the proletariat and declaring war on capitalism. The Bolsheviks were so called from the fact that at the party conferences of 1902–3 the Leninists were the majority group (Russian *bol'she*, 'more'). The defeated minority were called MENSHEVIKS. *See also* WHITE RUSSIAN.

Bolshie or **Bolshy.** A contraction of BOLSHEVIK, used to denote a person with left-wing tendencies, or a rebellious or 'difficult' person generally.

Bolsover, Beast of. *See* BEAST OF BOLSOVER.

Bomba. The hero of the novel *Bomba the Jungle Boy* (1926) by 'Roy Lockwood', a member of Edward L. Stratemeyer's writing syndicate, and of its many sequels. He lives in the Amazon basin and engages in exploits similar to those undertaken by TARZAN. He was played by Johnny Sheffield in the low-budget film *Bomba the Jungle Boy* (1949) and 11 sequels.

Bomb Alley. A description applied in the Second World War to a corridor through Kent and Sussex that was badly damaged by German V-1 flying bombs aimed at London in 1944–5. The hits were either caused by the DOODLEBUGS' notorious inaccuracy or as a result of being shot down by RAF fighters or anti-aircraft fire (out of 9521 fired at southern England, 4621 suffered this fate).

Bomber Harris. The apt nickname of Marshal of the RAF Sir Arthur Harris, Bt (1892–1984), commander-in-chief of Bomber Command in the Second World War and advocate of strategic bombing. He directed a huge bombing offensive in the form of a relentless nightly attack on German cities and manufacturing centres, ports and railways. His aggressive tactics have since been criticized and the effectiveness of the assault questioned. In 1992 demonstrators marred the unveiling by the Queen Mother of a statue to Harris at St Clement Danes, London, a church handed over to the RAF after the war and now a memorial to those killed in air battles. *See also* DRESDEN.

Bomber jacket. A short jacket tightly gathered at the waist and cuffs and usually having a front zip. It was modelled on the flight jackets worn by US Air Force crews. Hence the name.

> Both my three-year-old son and my father wear bomber jackets and jeans and I go to parties where 60-year-olds chat to 20-year-olds on something like equal terms.
>
> JOHN DIAMOND in *The Times Magazine* (1 January 2000)

Bomb-happy. An expression current in the Second World War to describe someone in a state of near-hysteria induced by bombing, which often took the form of irrational euphoria. *See also* TRIGGER-HAPPY.

Bomfog. Pompous rhetoric. The term was coined in the 1970s by Vice-President Nelson A. Rockefeller as an acronym of '*b*rotherhood *of m*an and *f*atherhood *of G*od', a phrase said to be frequently used by preachers.

Bon chic, bon genre (French, 'good style, good form'). Well-bred and elegant; smart and stylish; PREPPY. The phrase describes the sophisticated, understated style of dress and manner seen in the British SLOANE RANGER. In France itself the expression is usually abbreviated as *BCBG*.

> She was a little unsure about it when I wrote the story a few months back, unconvinced that she wanted to share ... our bilious bust-ups with the UK's well-heeled *bon chic, bon genre*.
>
> *Sunday Times* (24 October 1999)

Bond, James. The ultimate superspy, famous from the novels by Ian Fleming (1908–64) and from the gripping films based on them or inspired by them. He is intelligent and resourceful, a technological adept, a lover of fast cars and a wily seducer. Wherever his adventures and misadventures take him, he is always ultimately the victor and the avenger. He first appears in *Casino Royale* (1953). His persona is an amalgam of some of the men whom Fleming met when he was serving in British Naval Intelligence in the Second World War. The 'double-O' prefix of his secret agent number, 007, declares he is 'licensed to kill'. His name, more prosaically, was taken from that of James Bond, ornithologist author of *Birds of the West Indies*, who was one of Fleming's neighbours in Jamaica. The title of the 19th Bond film, *The World Is Not Enough* (1999), neatly epitomizes his appeal to his fantasy-struck fans, for whom the real world is never enough. The words are the 1658 motto of the wealthy financier Sir Thomas Bond (d.1685), who gave his name to Bond Street, London, and they appear on the dust cover of Ian Fleming's novel *On Her Majesty's Secret Service* (1963), in which Bond comments that 'it is an excellent motto which I shall certainly adopt'. The words themselves translate Latin *Non sufficit orbis*, the tag end of a cynical line in Juvenal's *Satires* (2nd century AD), about Alexander the Great: *Unus Pellaeo juveni non sufficit orbis*, 'For a young fellow from Pella a single world was not enough.' Juvenal in turn derived the phrase from the poet Lucan, who put the words in the mouth of Julius Caesar in a passage in his *Civil War* (1st century AD) in which Caesar quells a mutiny in the ranks. Bond can thus claim a classical pedigree of a sort. *See also* DIAMONDS ARE FOREVER; DR NO; FROM RUSSIA WITH LOVE; GOLDFINGER; NEVER SAY NEVER AGAIN; VIEW TO A KILL; YOU ONLY LIVE TWICE.

Bondage trousers. Black leather trousers hung with chains, safety pins, zips and the like, of the kind favoured by PUNK rockers and others in the 1970s.

Boneless Wonder. A nickname given by Winston Churchill on 28 January 1931 to Ramsay MacDonald (*see* RAMSAY MAC) while the latter headed the Labour government of 1929–31. Churchill recalled that as a child he had been prevented by his parents from viewing an exhibit at Barnum's Circus known as 'the Boneless Wonder': 'My parents judged that the spectacle would be too revolting for my youthful eyes, and I have waited fifty years to see the Boneless Wonder sitting on the Treasury bench.'

Bonfire of the Vanities, The. A novel (1987) by Tom Wolfe (b.1931). It is a panoramic study of aspects of New York society, embracing Manhattan and the ghettoes of the Bronx, the art world, journalism, socialites and the legal profession. The title refers to the two occasions in the 1490s when, at the urging of the reformer Girolamo Savonarola (1452–98), the citizens of Florence made a huge 'bonfire of vanities' on which they immolated their worldly goods. A misguided attempt at a film version (1990) was directed by Brian de Palma.

Bongo Bongo Land. The term notoriously applied to the Third World collectively by the laid-back lothario of the Conservative Party, Alan Clark (1928–99). His use of the term while serving in Margaret Thatcher's government in the 1980s caused an uproar. As it happens, there is a Massif des Bongos in the Central African Republic, the bongo being a species of antelope.

Bonjour Tristesse. The first novel (1954; in English, 1955) by Françoise Sagan (pen-name of Françoise Quoirez; b.1935). The title translates as 'Good morning, sadness', and the book, written in less than three months in a deserted family apartment after a tiff with her mother, is about the self-discovery of a precocious 17-year-old girl, Cécile, who is obsessed with life and love. The title quotes words from a poem by Paul Éluard:

Adieu tristesse
Bonjour tristesse
Tu es inscrite dans les lignes du plafond
Tu es inscrite dans les yeux que j'aime
Tu n'es pas tout à fait la misère
Car les lèvres les plus pauvres te dénoncent
Par un sourire
Bonjour tristesse.
(Farewell sadness/Good morning sadness/You are written in the lines of the ceiling/You are written in the eyes that I love/You are not entirely misery/For your weakest lips betray you/By a smile/Good morning sadness)
PAUL ÉLUARD: *La vie immédiate* (1932)

Bonk, To. To engage in an act of sexual intercourse. The sense evolved in the 1970s from the earlier meaning 'to hit' and has had various claimed originators.

'I [television personality Jeremy Beadle] remember the Sun headlines used to claim that the Sun created the word bonking, but *I* used to use the word bonking *regularly* on my show [in the late 1970s]

... I used to say to callers, Done any good bonking lately? It was a real laugh. It's a bit much of the Sun to take credit for putting that word in the dictionary.'
Q (March 1990)

Bonkbuster. A type of popular novel in which the characters engage in explicit sexual encounters (*see* BONK). A notorious female pioneer of the genre was the US writer Jacqueline Susann, notably in her best-sellers VALLEY OF THE DOLLS (1966), *The Love Machine* (1969) and *Once Is Not Enough* (1973). The word itself puns on BLOCKBUSTER. *See also* SEX AND SHOPPING.

A quick romp through the sexual fantasies of politicos can be exhausting, but writing a bonkbuster is at least a way of becoming noticed.
The Times (15 November 1999)

Bonkers. Mad; crazy. The colloquial term dates from the 1950s and perhaps came from the identical naval slang word meaning 'slightly drunk', itself probably alluding to a 'bonk' on the head. The term tends to be used by politicians of one another. 'Stark raving bonkers' is an elaboration.

In a series of 'foul remarks' about Baroness Thatcher, Mr Major described her as 'bonkers', 'mad' and 'loopy', according to a secret diary kept by one of his closest aides.
The Times (20 September 1964)

Bonnie and Clyde. The first names of the American bandits Bonnie Parker (1911–34) and Clyde Barrow (1909–34). They first met in 1930 and moved into a small room in Dallas, Texas. Soon afterwards, Barrow was arrested for robbery and sentenced to two years in jail. He escaped with the aid of a pistol, probably smuggled in by Parker, but was recaptured and sent to a more secure unit. He was released on parole in 1932 and later that year the pair began a criminal career, taking a number of hostages, robbing banks and killing those who seemed to pose a threat. This continued until February 1934, when the head of the Texas prison system hired Frank Hamer, a former Texas ranger, to hunt the pair down. On 23 May 1934 a trap was set up on a road near Gibsland, Louisiana, and when the two arrived at the site Hamer and his posse riddled their vehicle with gunfire, killing them instantly. The exploits of the pair both appalled and enthralled America.

A film (1967) with a screenplay by Robert Benton and David Newman and directed by Arthur Penn was loosely based on their escapades, although the real robbers were much less attractive than their cinematic equivalents, played in the film by Faye Dunaway and Warren Beatty. The romance between them, suggested in the movie, was rendered unlikely by virtue of Barrow's homosexuality. The couple's murderous progress across the American Midwest has long been the subject of modern legend and has inspired several other movies, among them *You Only Live Once* (1937), *They Live by Night* (1948), *Gun Crazy* (1949), *The Bonnie Parker Story* (1958) and *Thieves Like Us* (1974).

Bonus Army. A gathering of unemployed American war veterans who in 1932 set up camp in Washington, D.C., and vowed to stay put until Congress authorized the immediate distribution of bonuses for military service in the First World War, although these were not scheduled for payment until 1945. They were dispersed by cavalrymen and their shantytown demolished.

Bonzo. The comically shaped puppy in the drawings by George E. Studdy, the first of which appeared in *The Sketch* for 8 November 1922. The name was invented by Captain Bruce Ingram, editor of *The Sketch*, and gained a place in the public consciousness as a typical dog name long after its original bearer had vanished from the printed page. It was further popularized by the eccentric musical group known as the Bonzo Dog Doodah Band, formed in 1965.

Boob tube. An expression of two meanings: first, a television set, as watched by a boob or COUCH POTATO; second, a woman's tight-fitting strapless top, encasing the 'boobs' or breasts. It is likely the latter sense arose (in the 1970s) as a pun on the former, which dates from the 1950s.

> If you want to do the tube top thing, a word of advice: boob tubes tend to be too tight and ultra tarty.
> *The Times* (31 July 1999)

Boogaloo. A popular dance of US origin that arose in the 1960s. It is (or was) performed to ROCK 'N' ROLL music with swivelling and shuffling movements of the body and presumably bases its name on BOOGIE-WOOGIE.

Boogie-woogie. A style of piano JAZZ in which the left hand maintains a heavy repetitive pattern of eight beats to the bar while the right hand improvises. It was probably developed in the American Midwest early in the 20th century. The name seems to have originated in Clarence 'Pinetop' Smith's 'Pinetop's Boogie-Woogie' (1928). Boogie already existed as a slang word for a party. Its origin is uncertain. Woogie was then added as a rhyming element. *See also* BLUES; SWING.

Booker Prize. The leading British annual literary prize, launched in 1968 by the firm of Booker McConnell Ltd (now Booker plc) and in 1999 worth £20,000. It is for a novel first published between 1 October and 30 September in the year of the award and since 1981 has been presented live on television. A winner did not enter the bestseller lists until 1982, when Salman Rushdie's MIDNIGHT'S CHILDREN was the choice. Some awards have been controversial, such as that of 1995 for James Kelman's *How Late It Was, How Late*, with its proliferation of FOUR-LETTER WORDS. More generally, criticism has been expressed regarding the quality of the selected writing, and Ian McEwen's short novel *Amsterdam*, awarded the prize in 1998, was felt by many to be inferior to earlier works such as *The Comfort of Strangers* (1981), *The Child in Time* (1987) and *Black Dogs* (1992). The only double winner to date is the South African writer J.M. Coetzee, for LIFE AND TIMES OF MICHAEL K (1983) and *Disgrace* (1999).

Boondocks. A US colloquialism for rough or isolated country. The term dates from the 1940s when it was adopted by US Marines from Tagalog *bundok*, 'mountain', to apply to any remote region where they were required to operate.

Boondoggle, To. A verb of US origin meaning to do

useless or futile work. The word is of uncertain origin. According to one account it was invented in the 1930s by an American scoutmaster, Robert H. Link, for a type of braided lanyard. This took time or trouble to make, hence the word passed to a futile task in general.

Boop, Betty. A supposedly sexy star of short cartoon films produced by Max Fleischer in the 1920s and 1930s. She had big sparkling eyes, a button nose and a squeaky voice and often appeared in various degrees of undress. Her tagline was 'Boop-Boop-a-Doop'. She was the first cartoon character to be censored and by the mid-1930s had abandoned her provocative garter, short skirt and décolletage.

Boots and Slippers. The two black Aberdeen terriers or Scotties who live in the country with their 'Gods', Master-Missus, and Smallest, the baby, in Rudyard Kipling's novel *The Servant a Dog* (1930). The story is narrated by Boots.

Bootsie and Snudge. An army private and his irascible sergeant, played by Alfie Bass and Bill Fraser in the popular television series *The* ARMY GAME. The pair also appeared in the film *I Only Arsked* (1958) and made sporadic returns subsequently. Their humour was very much in the mould of the CARRY ON FILMS.

Booze-and-bash fiction. A term formerly applied to novels in which drunkenness and violence prevailed, such as a number of American crime novels, the James BOND stories of Ian Fleming and certain realistic novels in vogue after the Second World War, such as Alan Sillitoe's SATURDAY NIGHT AND SUNDAY MORNING (1958).

Booze cruise. A one-day visit to France by ship to stock up with alcoholic drink and tobacco at favourable prices. The traditional route for the enterprise, because the shortest, is Dover to Calais.

> Last-minute 'booze cruises' to buy cheap drink for Christmas and millennium parties are leading many motorists to risk their lives in search of a bargain, warn police.
> *The Times* (18 December 1999)

Bore the pants off someone, To. To bore them to a state of desperation. The expression, which dates from the 1930s, may be a variant of 'to charm the pants off', meaning to ingratiate oneself with a person. The implication is that they will do anything for you, even take their trousers off. If the charmer is female, as seems the most likely scenario, the guile will have achieved its purpose.

Borley Rectory. *See under* FAKES.

Borrowers, The. The family of little people who live beneath the floorboards in Mary Norton's highly rated children's novel that bears their name (1952). Individually they are Homily, Pod and little Arriety, and they are so called as they survive by 'borrowing' essentials from the household above. There were four sequels and a subsequent television version.

Borscht Belt. A showbusiness nickname dating from the 1930s for a Jewish resort area in the Catskill Mountains, New York State, so called from the popularity of borscht (Russian-style beetroot soup) among Jews of eastern European origin.

> The Borscht Belt, they call this corridor of kosher kitsch, dotted with holiday bungalow complexes and resort hotels famous for generations for their matchmakers, big dinners, and fast-talking comedians.
> HOWARD JACOBSON in *Sunday Times* (29 August 1999)

Borstal. A prison or detention centre for young male offenders, since 1982 officially designated a youth custody centre and subsequently a young offender institution. The centres took their name from the location of the first, which opened at Borstal, near Rochester, Kent, in 1902. By a strange linguistic coincidence, the Anglo-Saxon place-name Borstal means 'security place'. Brendan Behan's *Borstal Boy* (1958) gives a vivid fictionalized autobiographical account of life in such a centre.

Bosie. An Australian nickname for the GOOGLY in cricket, after the name of its inventor, the Middlesex player B.J.T. Bosanquet (1877–1936).

Boss, The. A nickname that has been applied to a number of political figures, including Margaret Thatcher (*see* IRON LADY), Franklin Roosevelt (*see* FDR), Charles Haughey (prime minister of Ireland 1979–81, 1982, 1987–92), and to his wife by Harry S. Truman (*see* GIVE-'EM-HELL HARRY).

BOSS. The sinisterly appropriate acronym for the Bureau of State Security, formerly a branch of the South African security police. It was notorious for its ruthless campaigns, including assassinations, against anti-APARTHEID activists at home and abroad.

Boston Pops. The US orchestra of this name is drawn from members of the Boston Symphony Orchestra, founded in 1881. It began giving an annual series of light music concerts in 1885 and from 1900 these were known simply as 'Pops', short for 'Popular Concerts'. The name then passed to the orchestra itself.

Boston Strangler. Albert de Salvo (1933–73), who strangled 13 women in Boston, Massachusetts, in the early 1960s. He was jailed for life and stabbed to death by a fellow prisoner.

Bottle bank. A large metal container in which empty bottles are deposited (as if in a bank) by the public so that the glass can be recycled. There are also 'paper banks' for newspapers and magazines, 'can banks' for used drinks cans and 'clothes banks' for old clothing, curtains and the like.

Bottleneck. A narrow stretch of road where the smooth flow of traffic is impeded; any impediment that holds up production or trade.

Bottle out, To. To lose one's nerve or 'bottle'. The latter word apparently comes from 'bottle and glass', rhyming slang for 'arse', perhaps with a reference to the temporary incontinence experienced by an apprehensive or 'shit-scared' person.

Bottle party. A party to which guests are expected to bring a bottle of wine or some similar drinkable contribution.

Bottom line. The grand total; the final assessment. The expression arose in the 1970s as a translation of Yiddish *di untershte sture*, meaning the final profit or loss figure on an account.

> That is apparently what motivates Mr Michael Ashcroft. That is the bottom line. Not political convictions. … Not public interest, but the ruthless pursuit of his bottom line – of his profit.
>
> PETER BRADLEY (speech in House of Commons, 21 July 1999) in *The Times* (22 July 1999)

Bottom out, To. To reach the lowest point before stabilizing or recovering. The phrase is typically associated with a country's economy or with a person's or organization's popularity ratings.

> In the last 18 months of 'phoney war' election run-up the Tories have constantly sought evidence that they have 'bottomed out'.
>
> ROBIN OAKLEY in *The BBC News General Election Guide* (1997)

Bottoms up! A drinking toast of naval origin. The bottoms are those of the glasses as they are tilted up over the drinkers' mouths.

Boudoir biscuits. The sponge biscuits or sponge fingers now so known were originally eaten at funerals. In the early 20th century they received their present name, from a much more agreeable association

with a lady's boudoir. The name is often found embossed on the bottom of the biscuit.

Bounce an idea off someone, To. To put it to them in order to get their reaction or opinion. The degree of 'bounce' will indicate its potential.

Bounce back, To. To recover well after a setback or difficulty. The analogy is more with a toy figure that rights itself after being pushed over rather than with a rebounding ball.

> Elton [John] has bounced back so many times he is pop's original India Rubber Man.
>
> *The Times* (6 September 1999)

Bouncing Czech. A punning nickname applied to the crooked and litigious media tycoon Robert Maxwell (1923–91), who was born in Czechoslovakia as Jan Ludvik Hoch. He was also known as Captain Bob, and featured as such in a long-running cartoon strip in *Private Eye*. Maxwell was Labour MP for Buckingham (1964–70). Although a 1973 report by the Department of Trade and Industry had declared that he was unfit to hold the stewardship of a public company, he went on to build a huge publishing empire. The full depths of his fraudulent dealings, including the embezzlement of the Mirror Group's pension funds, did not emerge fully until after his apparent suicide.

Bouncy castle. A large inflatable toy castle for children to play on, chiefly by jumping and bouncing. The device was a standard attraction of the British fete from the late 1980s.

Bounding Basque. The nickname of the French tennis player Jean Borotra (1898–1994), one of the FOUR MUSKETEERS. He was born in the département of Basse-Pyrénées in the French Basque country and was known for the swiftness of his movement over the tennis court.

Bourbon biscuits. The chocolate-flavoured 'sandwich' biscuits have no connection with the French royal house of Bourbon apart from bearing its name, which is first recorded for them in the 1930s.

Bovril. This well-known concentrated beef extract was the invention in 1889 of John Lawson Johnston (1839–1900), a Scot who had studied with a view to entering the medical profession but who instead turned his attention to dietetics. He named his new food from a combination of Latin *bos, bovis*, 'ox', and Vril, a substance described in Lord Lytton's novel *The Coming Race* (1871) as an 'electric fluid … capable of being raised and disciplined into the mightiest agency of all forms of matter'. This name itself suggests Latin *virilis*, 'manly', so that the overall name implies 'beefiness'.

Bovver boots. Heavy laced boots extending to the mid-calf, as typically worn by BOVVER BOYS and SKINHEADS or any young male out to cause 'bovver', a Cockney pronunciation of 'bother'.

Bovver boy. A young hooligan of the SKINHEAD type prevalent in the 1960s, especially one wearing BOVVER BOOTS.

Bowler hat. In the armed forces to get one's bowler hat is to be demobilized and return to civilian life, a bowler hat at one time being regarded as an essential accoutrement of a civil servant.

Bowles, Sally. An English nightclub singer in Germany just before the coming of the NAZIS in Christopher Isherwood's novella named after her (1937). Although very young, she cultivates a brash air of sexual sagacity. Isherwood's work was subsequently incorporated in the volume GOODBYE TO BERLIN (1939), itself made into a stage play of 1951 by John Van Druten and a film of 1955 directed by Henry Cornelius, both bearing the title *I Am a Camera*. The film starred Julie Harris as Sally. Following another title change, to CABARET, the rather slight story became a stage musical of 1961 and a highly praised musical film of 1972. In the latter Sally was played with great verve and nervous vitality by Liza Minnelli.

Bowl of cherries. A pleasant or enjoyable situation or experience. The expression is frequently used ironically in the catchphrase 'Life is a bowl of cherries', popularized by Lew Brown's song 'Life is Just a Bowl of Cherries' (1931). The ironic twist is already present in the title of Erma Bombeck's humorous book *If Life Is a Bowl of Cherries, What Am I Doing in the Pits* (1979).

Box clever, To. To act so as to outwit someone. A boxer has to use his wits to deliver and dodge punches. The metaphor dates from the 1930s.

Boxed in. Restricted in one's movements or ability to act, as if enclosed in a box.

> He [former prime minister John Major] urged the Tory leader [William Hague] to widen the appeal of his party … and not allow himself to be boxed in by either wing of the party.
> *The Times* (30 December 1999)

Boxers. Members of a nationalistic Chinese secret society, which took a prominent part in the rising against foreigners in 1900 and which was suppressed by joint European action. The group practised certain boxing and callisthenic rituals in the belief that this gave them supernatural powers and even made them impervious to bullets. Their Chinese name was accordingly *Yihéquán*, 'righteous harmony fists', and it was the last word of this that gave their English name of Boxers.

Box junction. An area at a road junction marked out with a yellow grid. Drivers are supposed to enter the box only if their exit is clear. However, a driver may enter if intending to turn right and only prevented from doing so by oncoming traffic or by other vehicles waiting to turn right.

Box of Delights, The. A fantasy novel (1935), subtitled *When The Wolves Were Running*, by John Masefield (1898–1967). It concerns the involvement of Kay Harker, hero of *The* MIDNIGHT FOLK, with Cole Hawlings, the owner of a magic box that can transport people into the past.

Boy band. A purpose-created pop group whose members are young, male, clean-cut and likely to appeal to adolescent (and younger) girls. Examples of the boy band are Take That, highly successful in the early 1990s, and, more recently, the Irish groups Boyzone and Westlife.

Boy David, the. A *Private Eye* nickname for David (now Lord) Steel (b.1938), leader of the Liberal Party (1976–88). He was the youngest MP in the Commons when returned at a by-election in 1965, and was only 38 when he took over the leadership of his party. The nickname was justified by his enduringly boyish looks, and the phrase alludes to the biblical David, who as a youth slew Goliath (1 Samuel 17), a giant-killing feat that Steel and his party never quite managed to pull off. The direct source of the name was perhaps the title of J.M. Barrie's play *The Boy David* (1936).

Boyfriend. A person's regular male companion or lover, more likely to be a man than an actual boy. The same holds for a girlfriend, as the female equivalent.

> Some people like the idea of having a boyfriend or girlfriend more than the actuality of it. They want intimacy without commitment.
> *Sunday Times* (28 June 1998)

Boyo. A boy or young man, especially a Welsh one, or a Welshman of any age. The term is mildly deprecatory. In UNDER MILK WOOD (1954) Dylan Thomas has a character Nogood Boyo: 'I want to be *good* Boyo, but nobody'll let me.'

Who could really blame him [Welsh popular singer Tom Jones] for occasionally fancying what the tabloids invariably describe as a 'boyo-loving blonde' on the side?
Sunday Times (28 November 1999)

Boy Scouts or **Scouts.** A popular youth movement started by General Sir Robert Baden-Powell (Lord Baden-Powell of Gilwell) in 1908. The aim was to train boys to be good citizens with high ideals of honour, service to others, cleanliness and self-reliance, based essentially on training in an outdoor setting. The movement became worldwide. There are four branches: Beaver Scouts (aged 6 to 8), Cub Scouts, formerly WOLF CUBS (8 to 10½), Scouts (10½ to15½) and Venture Scouts, formerly Rover Scouts (15½ to 20). About one-third of Venture Scouts are now girls, and in 1990 younger girls were admitted to the Scouts. *See also* BEAVERS; BE PREPARED; GIRL GUIDES.

Boysenberries. The hybrid of blackberries, loganberries and raspberries takes its name from Rudolph Boysen (d.1950), the US horticulturist who developed it in California in 1920.

Boys from the Black Stuff, The. *See* YOSSER.

Boys in blue. The police, from the colour of their uniforms.

Boy's Own Paper, The. Known as the BOP, this boys' magazine appeared from 1879 to 1967. First published by the Religious Tract Society, the BOP strove to provide its mainly middle-class readership with such appropriately uplifting subject matter as historical and military adventure stories, articles on sport and natural history as well as puzzles and competitions. Its prevailing white, Christian and imperialist ethos was memorably summed up by the writer Wyndham Lewis, who described the BOP as being: 'full of tough, hairy, conquering Nordics plundering through trackless forests and lethal swamps, wrestling with huge apes and enormous cobras, foiling villains of Latin origin, crammed with experience and philosophy and knowing practically everything.' The last issue of the BOP was published in February 1967. That its Baden-Powellish values had long since ceased to be fashionable is reflected with unconscious irony in the BOP having as its final cover feature the 21-year-old Manchester United footballer George Best, described as a role model who 'doesn't smoke, drinks only occasionally and restricts his card-playing to sessions which ease the boredom of travelling'. The title of the BOP is ironically reflected in the gay rites-of-passage novel *A BOY'S OWN STORY* by the US writer Edmund White, and punningly in Boyzone, the name of a highly successful Irish BOY BAND of the 1990s. *See also* GIRL'S OWN PAPER; RIPPING YARNS.

Boy's Own Story, A. The first (1982) in a trilogy of semi-autobiographical novels by the US novelist Edmund White (b.1940). It charts a boy's growing awareness of his homosexuality. The others are *The Beautiful Room is Empty* (1988) and *The Farewell Symphony* (1997). *See also* BOY'S OWN PAPER.

Boystown. A nickname for the predominantly gay neighbourhood in West Hollywood, California. In 1985 the city was the first in the United States to elect a council with a majority of openly gay or lesbian members. The name itself puns on BOYS TOWN.

Boys Town. This unusual settlement near Omaha, Nebraska, was the brainchild of Father Edward J. Flanagan (1886–1948), an Irish-born Roman Catholic priest who was ordained in Austria in 1912. In 1913 he was appointed assistant pastor at St Patrick's Church, Omaha, and began to devote his life to improving the lot of the destitute and delinquent young people he saw on the streets. In 1917 he founded a home for homeless youths and when it became crowded moved outside the town to establish Boys Town the following year. Despite financial difficulties, the undertaking was a success and brought Flanagan worldwide fame as an expert on juvenile delinquency. The village is governed by the boys themselves and maintained by voluntary contributions. Girls were first admitted in 1979 and by the end of the 20th century Boys Town numbered some 800 residents. The enterprise was introduced to a wide public by the MGM film *Boys Town* (1938), with Spencer Tracy as Father Flanagan and Mickey Rooney as a troubled youth.

Boy toy. *See* TOY BOY.

Boy wonder. A nickname dating from the 1920s for an exceptionally talented young man or boy, especially when in the public eye. The jockey Lester Piggott (b.1935) was so known after riding his first winner in 1948. The term suggests a variant on the earlier 'wonder boy'.

B-picture. *See* B-MOVIE.

Bra. An abbreviation of brassière first current in the 1930s, originally in the form 'bras'. 'Brassière' itself dates from the early years of the 20th century, and in 1914 Mary Phelps Jacobs used two handkerchiefs with ribbon straps as a basic design for a garment to flatten the bust. 'Burn your bra' was an American Women's Liberation slogan of the 1970s and bra-burning itself became the image most widely associated with feminism on both sides of the Atlantic. The analogy was with the burning of a draft card as a protest against the Vietnam War (1955–75).

> Just as the scale and coherence of suffragette militancy had been hidden from view, so the smokescreen of the 'burning bra' helped to obscure the real nature of the women's liberation movement.
>
> ANNA COOTE and BEATRIX CAMPBELL: *Sweet Freedom: The Struggle for Women's Liberation* (1982)

Bradbury. A £1 note, as issued by the Treasury in 1914–28, bearing the signature of J.S. Bradbury (1st Baron Bradbury), who launched the issue as Joint Permanent Secretary to the Treasury.

Bradshaw. A famous British railway guide, first issued in Manchester in 1839 by George Bradshaw (1801–53), a printer and engraver. The 'Monthly Guide' was first issued in January 1842, and consisted of 32 pages, giving tables of 43 railway lines. Publication ceased in 1961.

> 'There are difficulties, Watson. The vocabulary of Bradshaw is nervous and terse, but limited. The selection of words would hardly lend itself to the sending of general messages. We will eliminate Bradshaw.'
>
> SIR ARTHUR CONAN DOYLE: *The Valley of Fear*, Pt I, ch i (1915)

Brady Bunch, The. A US television comedy series running from 1969 to 1974 and subsequently syndicated. Its story line centred on two broken families, a widower with three sons and a widow with three daughters. The six children of various ages mix and match to heal the break and the two adults marry. The plot was predictable but the programme struck a chord in a generation with a high divorce rate, and almost every young viewer could identify with one or other of the characters. A series of increasingly improbable spin-offs, including *The Brady Brides* (1981), was less successful.

Brain drain. A phrase used to denote the drift abroad,

which occurred from the early 1960s, of British-trained scientists, technologists, doctors and university teachers (especially to the United States), attracted by higher salaries and often better facilities for their work. See also BRAIN GAIN.

Brain gain. An increase in the professional and skilled workforce of a country as a result of the immigration of foreign scientists and scholars seeking better job opportunities. The term dates from the 1960s and puns on BRAIN DRAIN.

Brain of Britain. A radio quiz show first broadcast in 1967 with mostly abstruse general knowledge questions put to selected members of the public. The overall annual winner is deemed 'brain of Britain'.

Brains Trust. The name was originally applied by James M. Kieran of the New York Times to the advisers of Franklin D. Roosevelt (1882–1945) in his election campaign. It was later used for the group of college professors who advised him in administering the NEW DEAL. In Britain it was the name of a popular BBC programme (1941–9), in which a regular panel of Dr Julian Huxley, Professor C.E.M. Joad and Commander A.B. Campbell aired their views on questions submitted by listeners. The term is now in general use for any such panel or team that answers questions.

Brainwashing. The subjection of someone to an intensive course of indoctrination in order to transform their opinions and political loyalties.

Brainwave. 'Brain wave' was originally a term for a hypothetical telepathic vibration in the brain that announced the occurrence of a remote event. This 19th-century sense evolved into the 20th-century 'brainwave' that is a sudden idea or 'flash of inspiration'. In the 1930s 'brainwaves' became a scientific term for the electrical impulses in the brain, as now measured by the electroencephalogram, an essential tool in BIOFEEDBACK. Four frequency bands of such waves have been classified: delta, with a frequency of 0.5–3.5 cycles per second (c/s), as occurring in sleep; theta, 4–7 c/s, as in dozing or deep meditation; alpha, 8–12 c/s, as in relaxed wakefulness or meditation; and beta, 13–22 c/s, as in thinking or when focusing on the external world.

Bramble, Colonel. The British army officer in the First World War who is the central character of André Maurois's humorous novel *Les Silences du Colonel Bramble* (1918). He is a sort of Colonel BLIMP seen through French eyes, and he endeared himself to French Anglophiles in the interwar years. In Saul Bellow's novel *Mr Sammler's Planet* (1970) the elderly Polish-born protagonist Artur Sammler recalls how 'he had reconsidered the whole question of Anglophilia, thinking sceptically about Salvador de Madariaga, Mario Praz, André Maurois and Colonel Bramble'.

Brand image. The impression that a commercial product or brand makes in the mind of consumers, whether actual or potential. The term arose as advertising jargon in the late 1950s with reference to the enhancement of a product's image at the expense of its true description or actual value. The general aim of the brand image is to link words, statements, pictures, sounds and even smells to the brand in question.

> Ray Kroc's vision was to establish in the consciousness of all McDonald's customers a brand image whose essential characteristics and appeal never wavered.
> ANDREW TAYLOR in *Brands* (1998)

Branding. The 20th-century business of selecting brandnames for new products is fraught with problems. One hazard is the meaning of a name in a language other than that of the manufacturer. In 1992 the London advertising agency Euro RSCG ran an advertisement with pictures of a can of French orange drink named 'Pschitt', a packet of Spanish bubblegum called 'Bang Bang', a roll of Swedish toilet paper called 'Kräpp' and a packet of Turkish biscuits named 'Bum!' Yet all these are simply imitative words except the Swedish name, which means 'crêpe'.

Brand X. An arbitrary designation for an unnamed brand when contrasted unfavourably with a product of the same type that is currently being promoted. The term dates from the 1930s.

Branestawm, Professor. The absent-minded, spectacles-bedecked professor who is always building crazy, impractical machines in Norman Hunter's children's book *The Incredible Adventures of Professor Branestawm* (1933), which was perfectly illustrated by William HEATH ROBINSON. Many more stories followed, and he was still going strong in *Professor Branestawm's Perilous Pudding* (1980), which was written when Hunter was 81.

Brasília. The purpose-built capital of Brazil, and one of the world's finest architectural realizations of the 20th century. It lies on the banks of an artificial lake near the geographical centre of the country and was designed by Lúcio Costa in 1957. It has the outline of an aeroplane, with the federal and civic buildings as the fuselage, the residential areas as the wings and the triangular Square of Three Powers as the nose. The executive, judicial and legislative buildings are grouped around the square, and the federal government began its move there from Rio de Janeiro in 1960. It is purely an administrative city, and has no industry of any kind.

Brassed off. Fed up, as if reprimanded by a senior officer or 'brass hat'.

Brass monkey weather. Weather that is 'cold enough to freeze the balls off a brass monkey'. The full phrase, of 19th-century origin, is probably not as ribald as it sounds. A brass monkey was a term for the plate on a warship's deck where cannon balls were stacked. In cold weather, the brass would contract, causing the stack to collapse. 'Monkey' has long been a general word for an object or person, especially when active in some way.

Brat, The. One of many uncomplimentary nicknames earned by the US tennis champion John McEnroe (b.1959) as a result of his childish tantrums and abusive language when on court. Others include 'The Incredible Sulk' (from the INCREDIBLE HULK), 'King Sneer' (after Shakespeare's *King Lear*), 'The Merchant of Menace' (his *Merchant of Venice*), 'The Prince of Petulance', 'The Rude Dude' and 'Superbrat'.

Brat pack. A group or clique of rowdy or ostentatious young people. The term originally applied to Hollywood stars of the mid-1980s such as Emilio Estevez, Matt Dillon, Patrick Swayze and Tom Cruise and is a pun on RAT PACK. The term itself was coined in 1985 by David Blum in an article about the film *St Elmo's Fire* (1985), in which one of the characters was played by Estevez.

Braveheart. The title of a film (1995) about the Scottish national hero William Wallace (*c*. 1270–1305), directed by the Australian-born actor Mel Gibson, who also played the title role. The film, although broadly faithful to Wallace's story (including his gruesome hanging, drawing and quartering in London), took considerable historical liberties. For example, it portrayed Wallace as the son of a Highland peasant, whereas his father was Sir Malcolm Wallace, a small landowner in Renfrewshire, in the Central Lowlands. The film also inaccurately depicts Wallace dallying romantically with Isabella of France, wife of the future

Edward II of England. Nevertheless, the film struck a chord in Scotland, and became something of an icon of national pride and resistance at a time when most Scots felt oppressed by almost two decades of Conservative government from London. The term 'Braveheart spirit' has been used in relation to Scottish national football and rugby teams. The film won Oscars for best picture and best director.

Brave New World. A DYSTOPIAN novel (1932) by Aldous Huxley (1894–1963). Its portrayal of an imagined future world state in which men and women are processed into standardized batches by genetic engineering and lifelong conditioning was originally conceived as a challenge to the claims of H.G. Wells (1866–1946) for the desirability of eugenics. The title derives from Miranda's exclamation in Shakespeare's *The Tempest*:

> O brave new world,
> That has such people in't!
> V.i

See also FIRST LINES OF NOVELS.

Brazil, Angela. The prolific author (1869–1947) of girls' school stories. Her name is now associated with the schoolgirl crushes and adventures with which her novels, rejoicing in titles such as *A Terrible Tomboy* (1904) and *A Fourth Form Friendship* (1911), were crammed. The schoolgirl slang used by Brazil's heroines, typified by words and phrases such as 'blossomy', 'top-hole' and 'jinky', provoked the censure of contemporary educationists and the mirth of posterity.

Brazilian footballers. Many Brazilian footballers play under their nicknames. The following are some of the best known, with real names and dates of birth.

> *Bebeto*: José Roberto Gama de Oliveira (b.1964)
>
> *Didi*: Valdir Pereira (b.1928)
>
> *Garrincha*: Manoel Francisco dos Santos (1933–83)
>
> *Jaïrzinho*: Jaïr Ventura Filho (b.1944)
>
> *Juninho*: Giulio Botelho (b.1929)
>
> *Pelé*: Edson Arantes do Nascimento (b.1940)
>
> *Tostão*: Eduardo Gonçalves de Andrade (b.1947)
>
> *Vava*: Edvaldo Izidio Neto (b.1934)
>
> *Zico*: Artur Antunes Coimbra (b.1953)
>
> *Zito*: José Eli de Miranda (b.1932)

Bread. A television comedy series screened from 1986 to 1991. It featured the Boswells, a Catholic working-class family of two adults and five grown-up children,

living in Liverpool and all unemployed, and centred on their expert 'working of the system' in order to obtain state handouts. The punning title alluded both to the table on which Nellie Boswell laid food for her children and around which she insisted they gathered, and to 'bread' as a slang term for money.

Bread-and-butter letter. A term of US origin dating from the turn of the 20th century for a letter expressing thanks for hospitality. One's host has provided one with sustenance, a basic form of which is bread and butter.

Bread and Butter State. A nickname for the state of Minnesota. It originated in 1901 at the time of the Pan-American Exposition in Buffalo, New York, where wheat and dairy products from Minnesota were displayed, giving the impression that the state was the 'nation's granary'. Agriculture still plays an important part in Minnesota's economy, although manufacturing displaced it in the early 1950s as the major source of income.

Break a leg! Good luck! A traditional wish to an actor going on stage in the theatre. The expression is said to relate to the assassination of Abraham Lincoln in his private box at Ford's Theatre, Washington, D.C., on 14 April 1865. The murderer, John Wilkes Booth, a Shakespearean actor of some repute, made good his escape after firing the shot by leaping down onto the stage, breaking his leg. 'Break a leg!' then arose as an example of black humour. This story is dismissed by many, if only on the grounds that the phrase is not recorded before the 20th century. It may be a translation of German *Hals und Beinbruch*, 'Neck and leg break'. Other languages have their equivalents, extended to good luck wishes in general, such as Italian *In bocca di lupo*, 'Into the wolf's mouth', and Russian *Ni pukha ni pera*, 'Neither fur nor feather'.

Break-dancing. This style of street dancing, both energetic and acrobatic, evolved among American blacks in the 1970s. It was typically danced to HIP-HOP and was so called as it was designed to fill a gap or break in a piece of rap music.

Breakfast at Tiffany's. A novella (1958) by the US writer Truman Capote (1924–84) about the uninhibited exploits in New York of 18-year-old Holly GOLIGHTLY. She has a homespun cure for the 'reds', worse than the mere 'blues [which] are because you're getting fat or maybe it's been raining too long':

> Reds are horrible. You're afraid and you sweat like hell

... something bad is going to happen and you don't know what.

The remedy is 'to get into a taxi and go to Tiffany's', the upmarket jewellery store. A bland, asexual film version (1961), directed by Blake Edwards, starred Audrey Hepburn as Holly.

Breathe down someone's neck, To. To pursue them closely; to watch or monitor them constantly. The two senses date from the 1940s.

Breathless. An influential film (1959) based on a story suggested by François Truffaut (1932–84). The first film of the French NOUVELLE VAGUE director Jean-Luc Godard and well known under its French title, *À Bout de souffle*, it starred Jean-Paul Belmondo and Jean Seberg in a largely improvised (and indeed 'breathless') plot about small-time gangsterism and helped to establish a new genre in European cinema. A lacklustre 1983 remake with the same title, directed by James McBride, starred Richard Gere and transferred the action to Los Angeles.

Breath of fresh air. A refreshing change. The figurative sense of the literal term evolved in the mid-20th century. 'Breath' should be understood as a wafting of fresh air, not an inhalation of it.

> At King Edward VII School, Lytham, he was a breath of fresh air, replacing endless performances of Gilbert and Sullivan with Shakespeare.
>
> *The Times* (Obituary of headmaster David Baggley) (10 January 2000)

Breckenridge, Myra. The transsexual who narrates her lurid adventures in Gore Vidal's novel that bears her name (1968) and in its sequel, *Myron* (1975). Both deal with HOLLYWOOD myths. A film of the first book was released in 1970 with Raquel Welch in the title role.

Brenda. A *Private Eye* nickname for Queen Elizabeth II (b.1926), who came to the throne in 1952. The name represents a deliberate down-grading of the royal status. A similar suburbanization was arranged for Charles, Prince of Wales, rechristened by the magazine as BRIAN.

Bren gun. The lightweight quick-firing machine-gun made its first appearance in the years immediately preceding the Second World War. It was originally made in Brno, Czechoslovakia, then in Enfield, England. Bren is a blend of Brno and Enfield. *See also* STEN GUN.

Bretton Woods. The idyllic resort in New Hampshire, USA, where in the summer of 1944 economic ambassadors of 44 countries met to negotiate the shape of postwar world trade. The resulting Bretton Woods agreements established the WORLD BANK. *See also* IMF.

Brewer's droop. Impotence resulting from the consumption of alcohol. This and brewer's goitre are expressions of Australian origin.

Brewer's goitre. A BEER BELLY.

Brewster, Bobby. The boy hero of a series of children's books, published between the 1940s and 1970s, by the British writer H.E. Todd (1908–88), who is visited by strange and magical happenings.

Brezhnev doctrine. A policy formulated by the Soviet leader Leonid Brezhnev (1906–82). The Brezhnev doctrine declared the right of the Soviet Union and its allies to intervene in Eastern Europe to 'defend socialism', where 'the essential common interests of other socialist countries are threatened by one of their number'. This doctrine was used to justify the Warsaw Pact invasion of Czechoslovakia in 1968 (*see* PRAGUE SPRING).

Brian. A male forename sometimes used to evoke an earnest but tedious person or a lower-middle-class nonentity. Examples are common in the media, as in joking references to the television sports commentator Brian Johnston, who always seemed to be interviewing a sportsman of the same name, so that the conversation was peppered with 'Well, Brian ...', 'Yes, Brian ...' and so on. The television comedy series MONTY PYTHON'S FLYING CIRCUS has a famous sketch centring on the name, and the programme's creators further exploited it in their film *Monty Python's Life of Brian* (1979), in which Brian is taken to be Jesus and crucified instead of him. *See also* MAGIC ROUNDABOUT.

> Winston Churchill, the grandson of the Prime Minister and former Conservative MP, might have chosen a different and happier career path had he been christened Brian.
>
> *The Times* (17 July 1999)

Bricks and clicks. A nickname of US origin arising in the 1990s for the two basic types of business company. 'Bricks' companies do not use the INTERNET and rely on traditional 'bricks and mortar' business methods. 'Clicks' companies, named after the click of a computer mouse, use nothing but the Internet. A third type are the 'bricks and clicks' companies that combine online and traditional methods. Analysts believe that eventually there will be only 'bricks' and 'clicks' companies, all others having been eliminated by competition or bought by rivals. *See also* CLICKS AND MORTAR.

Brideshead Revisited. A family saga novel (1945) by Evelyn Waugh (1903–66) about the aristocracy and the Catholic faith in the years 1923–39, subtitled *The Sacred and Profane Memories of Captain Charles Ryder*. It is told in retrospect by Charles Ryder, whose army unit in the Second World War is billeted at Brideshead Castle, seat of the Marchmain family. When he was a student at Oxford, Charles was romantically involved with Sebastian Flyte, the charming but dissolute younger Marchmain son, owner of a TEDDY BEAR called Aloysius. In his letters, Waugh referred to the evolving novel as his 'M.O.' (Magnum Opus) and 'G.E.C.' (Great English Classic). The lavish and highly acclaimed television series (1981) was scripted by John Mortimer.

Brides in the Bath. In 1915 a Bristol antiques dealer, George Joseph Smith, was sentenced to death for the murder of three young women. He had bigamously married each one, using an alias, then insured his new wife's life or persuaded her to make a will in his favour. As the final stage in his plan he took each to a different lodging house and drowned her in the bath. A colourful story was long current that while the body of one of his victims was still in the bath, Smith went into the next room and played 'Nearer, my God to Thee' on the harmonium.

Bride Stripped Bare by Her Bachelors, Even, The. This painting on two large panels of glass by the DADAIST Marcel Duchamp (1887–1968) is also called *The Large Glass*. The work consists of meticulously painted but indecipherable fragments of machinery (although a coffee grinder is apparent). Duchamp worked on the piece between 1915 and 1923, in search of an ideal of 'painting of precision and beauty of indifference'. The painting is said by some to satirize the frustrations of physical love, and by others to satirize the cult of the machine.

Bridge of San Luis Rey, The. A novel (1927) by the US writer Thornton Wilder (1897–1975), which won the PULITZER PRIZE for fiction. 'On Friday noon, July the twentieth, 1714, the finest bridge in all Peru broke and precipitated five travellers into the gulf below.' Brother Juniper, a witness to the accident, works for six years, 'knocking at all the doors in Lima, asking thousands of questions', to investigate why God should have chosen those five to die. In the end his

book is burned and he goes to the stake for heresy. The conclusion of the abbess, who as a nun brought up one of the victims, is that: 'There is a land of the living and a land of the dead, and the bridge is love, the only survival, the only meaning.' An interminable film version (1944) was directed by Rowland V. Lee.

Bridge on the River Kwai, The. A film (1957) adapted by Carl Foreman and Michael Wilson from the novel *The Bridge over the River Kwai* by Pierre Boulle. Directed by David Lean, it starred Alec Guinness as Colonel Nicholson, the commanding officer of British prisoners of war forced by the Japanese to build a railway bridge over the River Kwai in Burma during the Second World War. Nicholson was based on the real Lieutenant-Colonel Philip Toosey (d.1975), who was the senior officer in a Japanese prisoner of war camp at Tamarkan. Unlike the film character, Toosey actively assisted those who tried to escape and sanctioned various attempts to sabotage the two bridges his men were obliged to build. The two bridges, one wood and one metal, were disabled by Allied bombers but never totally destroyed as they are in the film.

Bridge Over Troubled Water. The title of a song and album by Simon and Garfunkel, released in 1970. The song, a gospel-influenced pop classic written by Paul Simon and sung by the angelic-sounding tenor of Art Garfunkel, can be compared with a number of late 1960s pop anthems (the Beatles' LET IT BE, Cat Stevens's 'Morning Has Broken' and George Harrison's 'My Sweet Lord') for its striving after a tone of almost religious tranquillity (the song had the working title of 'Hymn'). The title comes from the phrase 'I'll be your bridge over deep water', which Paul Simon had heard in a version of the gospel song 'Mary Don't You Weep' sung by the Rev. Claude Jeter and the Swan Silvertones.

Bridges of Madison County, The. A romantic novel (1993) by the US writer Robert James Waller (b.1939). The story, a novel within a novel, concerns Francesca, a housewife whose life is suddenly transformed, while her family is away, by Robert Kincaid, a man who asks for directions. He has come to Madison County, Iowa, to photograph the seven covered bridges in the location. They have a fleeting affair. Blaise Aguirre's *The Fridges of Madison County* (1997) is a parody. A handsomely crafted film version (1995) was directed by Clint Eastwood, who also took the role of Kincaid, playing opposite Meryl Streep. Many judged it an improvement on the original.

Bridget Jones. *See* JONES, BRIDGET.

Bridge too far. A position reached that is too risky; a step that is 'one too many'. The phrase comes from the title of Cornelius Ryan's book *A Bridge too Far* (1974), made into a memorable film (1977), about the 1944 Allied airborne landings in Holland. These were intended to capture 11 bridges needed for the Allied invasion of Germany but the enterprise failed grievously at Arnhem. In advance of the operation General Frederick Browning is said to have protested to Field-Marshal Montgomery, who was in overall command: 'But, sir, we may be going a bridge too far.' The cliché is mainly found in journalistic use. An item in *The Times* of 20 June 1990 about a plan to build a new bridge over the Ironbridge Gorge, Shropshire, was headed, 'A bridge too near'.

Bridgewater Three. Michael Hickey, Vincent Hickey and Jimmy Robinson, on the basis of evidence of a fourth man, Patrick Molloy, were jailed in 1978 for the murder of a 13-year-old newspaper boy, Carl Bridgewater, when he disturbed their alleged robbery at Yew Tree Farm, Staffordshire. Molloy died in custody in 1981. The remaining three were released in 1997 when their convictions were declared unsafe following the discovery that the police had forged Hickey's signature. *See also* BIRMINGHAM SIX; GUILDFORD FOUR; WINCHESTER THREE.

Brief Encounter. A romantic film (1945) based on the play *Still Life* by Noël Coward, and with a screenplay by Coward, David Lean, Ronald Neame and Anthony Havelock-Allan. Directed by David Lean, it starred Trevor Howard and Celia Johnson as star-crossed lovers who meet by chance on a railway station but subsequently deny themselves the opportunity to share an extra-marital affair. Such was the iconic status of the film with postwar British audiences that the very phrase 'brief encounter' became virtually synonymous with a short-lived sexual liaison.

Brigadoon. The imaginary village in the Scottish Highlands that is the setting of the musical play by Frederick Loewe and Alan Jay Lerner of the same name (1947). It is a strange place of the past, discovered by two American tourists on the one day of its reawakening in the 20th century, when one of its inhabitants, disappointed in love, tries to leave it. Its name suggests a blend of 'Bridge of Doon', a genuine-sounding Scottish place-name, and 'rigadoon', a lively dance for couples.

Brigg Fair. An 'English rhapsody' for orchestra by Frederick Delius (1862–1934). The work, which was first performed in 1907, consists of variations on a Lincolnshire folksong to which Delius had been introduced by Percy Grainger. Not everyone shared their enthusiasm for folksongs. In 1934 Constant Lambert complained: 'The whole trouble with a folksong is that once you have played it through there is nothing much you can do except play it over again and play it rather louder.'

Bright-eyed and bushy-tailed. Alert and lively; RARIN' TO GO. The phrase, dating from the 1940s, is a stereotypical image of a squirrel. It was popularized by Bob Merrill's song 'Bright Eyed and Bushy Tailed' (1953), which has the lines:

> If the fox in the bush and the squirr'l in the tree be,
> Why in the world can't you and me be
> Bright eyed and bushy tailed and sparkelly as we
>   can be.

Bright lights. The glitter and glamour of city life, especially as a lure to the country dweller. The phrase, of US origin and dating from the 1920s, is familiar from the film *Bright Lights* (1935) and from Jay McInerney's novel *Bright Lights, Big City* (1984), about the frenzied life of a young fact checker in Manhattan. The latter was filmed under the same title in 1988.

> Despite his apparent eligibility [as a potential husband], Peter's problem is that he's a farmer who lives far from the bright lights.
> *The Times* (18 August 1999)

Brighton Rock. An 'entertainment' (1938) by Graham Greene (1904–91), centring on crime and corruption in the seaside resort of Brighton, Sussex, with Pinkie, a young scarfaced hoodlum, as the antihero. It was the first of Greene's novels to explore the dilemmas he experienced in observing the Catholic faith, to which he had converted in 1926 in order to marry. 'Rock' here is the confection in the form of a cylindrical stick of hard peppermint-flavoured sugar, often pink on the outside, sold at holiday resorts, with the name of the place worked round the inside all the way down the stick. A successfully 'seedy' film version (1947), to whose script Greene contributed, was directed by John Boulting, with Richard Attenborough in the role of Pinkie.

Brighton Run. An annual rally for veteran cars (*see* VINTAGE CAR) from Hyde Park in London to the promenade at Brighton in Sussex, a distance of 85km (53 miles). It is held on the first Sunday in November and commemorates the so-called 'Emancipation Run' made by 33 motorists between the two towns on 14 November 1896, the day of repeal of the Locomotive Act of 1865, limiting the speed of steam carriages to 6.4kph (4mph) in the country and 3.2kph (2mph) in the town.

On the 1996 centenary run, a record 600 cars took part, of which 540 finished. Speeds ranged from just over 11kph (7mph) by an 1896 Lutzman to almost 121kph (75mph) by a 1903 Mercedes. The run is commemorated in the film GENEVIEVE.

Brighton School. A group of pioneer film-makers who were based in the Brighton area at the beginning of the 20th century, among them G.A. Smith (1864–1959) and J.A. Williamson (1855–1933). They attached great importance to the close-up and are best remembered for *Rescued by Rover* (1905), a seven-minute drama showing a collie rescuing his master's baby from kidnappers.

Bright young things. The YOUNG THINGS or FLAPPERS who originally made their presence known in fashionable society in the 1920s and 1930s. They were 'bright' in meretriciousness rather than mentality, and their heirs continue to thrive in the form of PARTY GIRLS and other 21st-century socialites.

> By 8pm on Friday the mood in the club has completely transformed. The main bar is spilling over with bright young things ordering vodka martinis.
> *The Times* (7 January 2000)

Brilliant pebbles. A code name for small heat-seeking missiles designed to intercept and destroy enemy weapons. The term originated as part of the STAR WARS vocabulary of the late 1980s, when a series of code names was employed to indicate the different levels of intelligence shown by weapons of different sizes. The largest and least intelligent were thus 'moronic mountains', the smaller and more intelligent were 'smart rocks' (*see* SMART BOMB), and those yet smaller and smarter were 'brilliant pebbles'. A fourth category in the series was 'savant sand'.

> The Pentagon has been pushing the smart rocks, while Congress has been championing the ground-based missiles. Mr Edward Teller advocates 'brilliant pebbles'.
> *Economist* (4 February 1989)

Bring home the bacon, To. To provide the necessities of life; to achieve success. The suggestion is of earning enough to feed one's family. The expression dates from the 1920s but may allude to a much older game of catching a greased pig at a country fair, the winner gaining the pig.

Bring tears to someone's eyes, To. To evoke such sympathy or empathy from them that they weep. The phrase is frequently used ironically.

> 'The block vote? That's got to go – actually,' said [Tony] Blair in opposition. So in power he keeps it to fix Labour's mayoral selection. ... It is enough to bring tears to the eyes of an old trade union boss.
> *Sunday Times* (19 December 1999)

Brinkmanship. A term coined by Adlai Stevenson (1900–65) in 1956 (although he disclaimed originality), with particular reference to the policy of US secretary of state J. Foster Dulles as leading to the brink of war. The term, based on Stephen Potter's GAMESMANSHIP, found a subsequent general application in the field of politics.

Brink's-Mat robbery. A robbery that took place in November 1983 when a gang stole gold bars worth £26 million, belonging to Johnson Matthey, a firm of dealers in precious metals, from the Brink's-Mat security warehouse at Heathrow Airport. It was Britain's biggest robbery at the time. The confession of a corrupt security guard gave police their first lead in an investigation which lasted almost ten years and resulted in charges against some 30 people.

Britain, Battle of. *See* BATTLE OF BRITAIN.

Britain, Festival of. *See* FESTIVAL OF BRITAIN.

Britain can take it. These morale-boosting words were promulgated by the Ministry of Information during the early months of the Second World War. They were regarded as patronizing, however, and as portraying Britons in a humourless 'stiff upper lip' stereotype, and the slogan was soon dropped.

Britain plc. Business jargon for Britain regarded as a unified commercial concern or 'corporation' formed from all its registered companies. UK PLC is similarly used. *See also* PLC.

> The message for Britain plc is very blunt and clear. The markets will not come to us; we have to go and find them.
> *The Times* (Letter to the Editor) (20 September 1999)

Brit Awards. Annual awards made in various

categories for British pop and rock music, with 'Brit' both short for 'British' and an acronym of 'British Record Industry'. The first awards were held as the British Record Industry 'Britannia Centenary' Awards at the Wembley Conference Centre on 18 October 1977, the winners receiving recognition for their achievements over the previous 25 years. They included the groups Queen and Procol Harum, the cellist Jacqueline du Pré and the singers Cliff Richard and Julie Covington. It was intended to hold the ceremony annually, but this happened only from 1982. The formal title British Record Industry Awards was shortened to its present form in 1989. The occasion that year, televised live, was something of an embarrassment, with the presenters confusing stars, talking over videos and battling with lengthy pauses, but in the 1990s the event became much slicker and more high-profile. The awards are colloquially known as 'the Brits'.

> The Brits have gone from a national laughing-stock to a must-be-there event ... Appear on The Brits and you are guaranteed to sell albums.
> *Sunday Express* (27 February 2000)

British bulldog. A team game formerly popular among boys. Members of one team dash across a field or other space and attempt to break through a line formed by the other team, who in turn attempt to catch them. A caught player is hoisted off the ground with the cry 'British bulldog!' and then joins the opposing team. The name dates from the jingoistic days of the early 20th century, but the game was still being played in the 1960s.

British disease. An uncomplimentary term used abroad with reference to the prevalence of strikes and industrial action in Britain during the 1970s.

British invasion. The transformation of the US popular music scene by British performers, first in the 1930s and 1940s by singers and players such as Ray Noble, Vera Lynn and George Shearing, but especially by ROCK 'N' ROLL in the 1950s and then almost single-handedly by the BEATLES in 1964. Other British bands to cross and conquer included the ROLLING STONES, the Dave Clark Five, Herman's Hermits, Gerry and the Pacemakers, the Animals, the Searchers, the Zombies, the Kinks, Wayne Fontana and the Mindbenders and Freddie and the Dreamers. Some acts, such as Chad and Jeremy, were famous in the United States but virtually unknown at home. The 'second British invasion' was by PUNK ROCK and NEW WAVE in the early 1980s, but this time no single group led the charge.

British Legion. An organization for promoting the welfare of ex-service personnel, especially the aged, sick and disabled. It was founded in 1921 largely through the exertions of Field Marshal Earl Haig (1861–1928), and it became the Royal British Legion in 1971. There are many local branches, and much of the money is raised by the sale of artificial poppies on POPPY DAY. *See also* ARMISTICE DAY; REMEMBRANCE DAY.

British Library. The British national library, formed in 1973 from the British Museum library. It opened in new premises at St Pancras, London, in 1998.

British restaurant. A government-subsidised restaurant operating in Britain in the Second World War. The designation 'Communal Feeding Centre' was originally proposed, but Winston Churchill suggested 'British restaurant' as more appropriate and attractive.

Britpop. British pop music, particularly of the type that emerged among the young bands of the mid-1990s such as Supergrass, Oasis and (especially) Blur and was influenced by the BEATLES. To a large extent Britpop was a reaction against US GRUNGE.

> There is an eagerness to accept that our national culture is exemplified by Britpop, even at a time when the 'Brit' is as meaningless as the pop.
> ROGER SCRUTON in *The Times* (14 April 1999)

Brittas Empire, The. A television SITCOM screened from 1991 to 1996. It is set in a leisure centre and depicts the goings-on among the staff under the manager and his wife, the unlikeable and disaster-prone Gordon Brittas, played by Chris Barrie, and his dazed and confused wife, Helen, played by Pippa Haywood. The punning title contains a rather obvious historical allusion.

Broad in the beam. Well fleshed around the hips and buttocks. The expression dates from the 1940s and derives from the nautical expression for a ship that is 'wide in the waist'.

Broadway Boogie-Woogie. This painting (1942–3) represented a major stylistic breakthrough for the Dutch painter Piet Mondrian (1872–1944). For decades Mondrian had been painting 'neo-plasticist' abstracts consisting of no more than a few rectangles and lines with provocative titles such as *Composition in Yellow and Blue* (1929). Indeed, latterly colour itself had begun to absent itself from his works. Then, when the Second World War forced him to New York in 1940, the shock of being separated from his native polders seems to given him a much-needed shot in the arm. The daringly entitled *Broadway Boogie-Woogie* not only brings back primary colours, but includes more lines and rectangles than you could count in one glance. It is regarded as one of his finest works. Mondrian was to become even less inhibited in his *Victory Boogie-Woogie*, in which the geometrical shapes are much more loosely painted. This work was unfinished at the time of Mondrian's death.

Brockton Bomber. The nickname of the US heavyweight boxer Rocky MARCIANO, who hailed from Brockton, Massachusetts. He was also known as the Blockbuster and as the Rock from Brockton.

Brompton cocktail. A powerful painkiller and sedative consisting of vodka or other liquor laced with morphine and sometimes also with cocaine. The preparation is used to relieve pain caused by cancer and is said to be named after Brompton Hospital, London, where it was first applied to this end.

Bronx cheer. The rude sound made by those who BLOW A RASPBERRY to express their contempt. The allusion is to the uncouth behaviour of residents of the Bronx, New York. The expression dates from the 1920s.

Brooklands. The site of the world's first custom-built motor-racing circuit, near Weybridge in Surrey. It was the enterprise of Hugh Locke-King, a Surrey landowner, who in 1907 paid £150,000 to build a concrete racetrack in the form of an oval course with heavily banked curves. It was soon widely used by car manufacturers for testing new models. In its first year a record was set up by Selwyn Edge for travelling 2546km (1582 miles) in 24 hours at an average speed of 106kph (66mph), a figure that remained unbeaten for 18 years. Racing continued until the Second World War, during which the track was given over to aircraft production. It was not restored subsequently.

Brooklyn Dodgers. This famous baseball team was formed in Brooklyn, New York, in 1883. Around the turn of the 20th century it added the name 'Dodgers', from 'Trolley Dodgers', a general nickname for the residents of Brooklyn, referring to their reputed skill at evading ('dodging') the streetcars on the growing trolley system. Other names for the team included the Bridegrooms, following a run of marriages by team members in 1889; the Superbas, from 'Hanlon's Superbas', a popular theatrical group at the turn of the century, as a compliment to Ned Hanlon, their manager at this time; and the Robins, after their manager from 1914 to 1931, Wilbert Robinson.

Brothel creepers. Soft-soled suede shoes, suitable for creeping into and out of a brothel. Footwear of this type was popular among TEDDY BOYS in the 1950s.

> Look at photographs of [violinist Nigel] Kennedy six years ago and you see a straight-laced young chap with awfully sensible hair and polite shoes (none of the brothel creepers or cowboy boots he favours today).
>
> *Q* (September 1990)

Brother Cadfael. *See* CADFAEL, BROTHER.

Brown, Father. The priest and detective who appears in the short stories by G.K. Chesterton (1874–1936), which were collected in *The Innocence of Father Brown* (1911) and other books. Although outwardly meek and modest, he has a shrewd understanding of the criminal mind. His most fearsome adversary is the French thief Flambeau. His most powerful assistant is his God. Chesterton based him on the Irish priest Monsignor John O'Connor (1870–1952), a well-known figure in Catholic literary circles and the author's lifelong friend.

Brown, William. *See* WILLIAM.

Brown bagger. An Americanism for a person who carries their lunch to school or work in a brown paper bag. Brown-bagging is also the carrying of drink in such a bag to a club or restaurant, a concealment necessary to conform to the law in some states.

Brown Bomber. Joe Louis (1914–81), undefeated heavyweight champion of the world from 1937 until his retirement in 1949. On his return in 1950 he was defeated by Ezzard Charles and Rocky MARCIANO. He turned professional in 1934, winning 27 fights, all but 4 by knockouts. The phrase comes from his being black and from the great power of his punches.

Browned off. Fed up, disgruntled, disheartened. The slang phrase became popular in the Second World War. The reference is probably to a dish that has been overcooked. *See also* CHEESED OFF.

Brown envelope. An anonymous envelope in which personal or intimate information is delivered or illicit cash payments made, the latter typically to MOON-LIGHTERS.

Michael Stacpoole handed [Monica] Coghlan a sealed

brown envelope containing £2000 in £50 notes to help her leave the country.
Sunday Times (21 November 1999)

Brownfield site. A site for potential building development that has already had some development on it, as distinct from a GREENFIELD SITE. The green grass has gone, leaving the brown earth.

Brownie. A make of box camera manufactured by Kodak. The first model was introduced in 1900 and was named by George Eastman, the founder of Kodak, from the 'Brownies', the miniature humanoids who populated the children's books of the Canadian-born writer and illustrator Palmer Cox (1840–1928). Eastman's camera was cheap, simple and easy to operate and was especially aimed at children. Hence the appropriate name. *See also* BROWNIES.

Brownie points. Notional credit for something done to please or win favour. The expression probably relates to BROWN-NOSE but has become popularly associated with the BROWNIES, and is thus often spelt with a capital letter.

> [Culture secretary Chris] Smith should come off the fence more as he did when he said the Turner prize had become too narrow. That won him brownie points.
> *Sunday Times* (2 January 2000)

Brownies. Members of the junior section of the GIRL GUIDES, ostensibly so named from the colour of their uniform (now brown and yellow), but apparently originally alluding to the benevolent elves of Scottish folklore so called who haunted houses and carried out housework by night. Such duties would have accorded with the domestic tasks and 'good deeds' that the modern uniform wearers would have been encouraged to carry out.

Browning Version, The. A play (1949) by the British playwright Terence Rattigan (1911–77) about an ailing public school teacher who is humiliated both by his failure in his career and by his wife's infidelity. The title refers to a copy of Browning's translation of Aeschylus' *Agamemnon* that is presented to the teacher, Andrew Crocker-Harris, by one of his few admiring pupils. The character of Crocker-Harris was based on one of Rattigan's teachers at Harrow School, Coke Norris, who was similarly presented with a copy of the 'Browning version' (although possibly not by Rattigan himself). The role of Crocker-Harris was memorably played by Michael Redgrave in the 1951 film version and, less memorably, by Albert Finney in the 1994 remake.

Brown-nose, To. To curry favour; to behave sycophantically. The term relates to 'arse-licking'. *See also* BROWNIE POINTS.

Brown Owl. The name of the adult leader of a group of BROWNIES, her assistant being Tawny Owl. The names still popularly persist, although since 1968 the two posts have been formally designated Brownie Guider and Assistant Brownie Guider respectively. The idea is that owls are wise, while brown (or tawny) is the colour of the Brownie uniform. Brown owl and tawny owl are alternative names for the same bird, *Strix aluco*.

Brownout on Breadfruit Boulevard. A satire (1995), set in Southeast Asia, on international political and academic organizations, by the Hong Kong-born novelist Timothy Mo (b.1950). Breadfruit Boulevard is a highway in Manila. A brownout is a reduction in electrical power causing a partial blackout, such as occurs in her hotel room just before one of the participants decides to introduce a computer virus into the records of a conference. The word also reflects Professor Pfeidwengeler's particular perversion, coprophilia.

Brownshirts. *See* SA.

Brown sugar. A US black slang term for an attractive black woman which crossed over into white slang vocabulary following the success of a rock song of the same title by the ROLLING STONES. The term also came to denote the drug HEROIN. The song, credited to Mick Jagger and Keith Richards, appears on the album STICKY FINGERS, released in 1971.

> Gold coast slave ship bound for cotton fields
> Sold in a market down in New Orleans
> Scarred old slaver knows he's doing alright
> Hear him whip the women, just around midnight
>
> Ah, brown sugar how come you taste so good?
> Ah, brown sugar just like a young girl should.

Brown v. Board of Education of Topeka. A legal case in which on 17 May 1954 the US Supreme Court ruled unanimously that racial segregation in public schools violated the 14th Amendment to the Constitution, which says that no state may deny equal protection of the laws to any person within its jurisdiction. Although the decision was limited to the public schools, it was believed to imply that segregation was not permissible in other public facilities.

Brücke, Die (German, 'The Bridge'). A group of German expressionist artists founded in Dresden in 1913 by four students of architecture: Fritz Bleyl (1880–1966), Erich Heckel (1883–1970), Ernst Ludwig Kirchner (1880–1938) and Karl Schmidt-Rottluff (1884–1976). The name was suggested by this last with reference to the group's admiration for the philosopher Nietzsche, who in *Also sprach Zarathustra* (1883–92) wrote: 'What is great about man is that he is a bridge and not a goal.' This dictum indicated the faith of the four in a happier and more creative future, to which their own work would lead as a bridge.

Bruderhof (German, 'band of brothers'). A Christian sect founded in Germany in 1921 who stressed the importance of communal property. They journeyed to Gloucestershire in England in 1937 when they were driven out by the NAZIS but to avoid internment in the Second World War left for Paraguay in 1941. They re-established themselves in Sussex in 1971. The men wore beards and dark trousers with braces. They supported themselves by making quality wooden toys in community workshops, and the women were clad in long skirts and headscarves or caps. Children first left the community at the secondary school stage. They later became known simply as the Christian Community. There are four other groups in the eastern United States.

Bruges Group. A group of anti-European (mainly Conservative MPs), named after a strongly worded speech made on 20 September 1988 by Margaret Thatcher, the IRON LADY, in Bruges, Belgium, in which she spoke out against closer European integration. In the 1992 general election some of the group stood as 'anti-federalists' against Conservative candidates. *See also* F-WORD.

Brutalism. A style of architecture created by the French architect Le Corbusier and his leading fellow architects, the German-born Ludwig Mies van der Rohe and the American Frank Lloyd Wright. It demanded a strictly functional approach to architectural design and was so named in 1954 by the English architects Peter and Alison Smithson with reference to Le Corbusier's post-1930 style, with its use of monumental sculptural shapes and raw, unfinished moulded concrete, by contrast with Mies van der Rohe's use of glass and steel. Typical of the style are the 1960s building of the SOUTH BANK, especially the depressing Queen Elizabeth Hall and Purcell Room and the Smithsons' own Hunstanton secondary modern school, Norfolk, built in 1950–53.

Brylcreem Boy. The Middlesex and England cricketer and Arsenal footballer Denis Compton (1918–97), who became one of the first British sportsman to boost his appeal by appearing in advertisements, in his case for the hair preparation Brylcreem. Compton was one half of the MIDDLESEX TWINS.

Brylcreem Boys. A nickname for young Royal Air Force officers in the Second World War, famous for their well-groomed appearance and dashing exploits. One such young officer was pictured in advertisements for the named brand of hair cream. Hence the name, chiefly current among their army counterparts. *See also* GLAMOUR BOYS.

BSE. *See* MAD COW DISEASE.

B Specials. Members of the Ulster Special Constabulary, created in 1920 during the Anglo-Irish War (War of Independence) of 1919–21, and drawing many of its recruits from Edward Carson's Ulster Volunteers. They were paid an allowance for their one night's duty a week and were retained until late 1969, when following the outbreak of the TROUBLES they were disbanded and replaced by the ULSTER DEFENCE REGIMENT. There were also A Specials, on regular duty and full pay, and C Specials, unpaid auxiliaries. *See also* ROYAL ULSTER CONSTABULARY; ULSTER VOLUNTEER FORCE.

BTM. A colloquialism for the posterior, from 'bottom' as if written euphemistically 'b–t–m'. The term dates from the early years of the 20th century.

> No friendly wallop on the B.T.M.
> No loving arm-squeeze and no special look.
> JOHN BETJEMAN: *Selected Poems*, 'Beside the Seaside' (1948)

Bubble dancer. A woman who dances as if in the nude but actually covered by one or more balloons. A noted performer was the US actress Sally Rand, originally Helen Gould Beck (1904–79), who was long a fan dancer, using large fans made of ostrich feathers, before creating an alternative dance with 1.5m (5ft) elastic 'bubbles'.

Bubblegum music. Bland or repetitive pop music, designed to appeal to children and young teenagers, who blow bubblegum. Middle of the Road's 'Chirpy Chirpy Cheep Cheep' (1971) is an example. Bubblegum itself was first on sale in the United States in 1928, as Fleer's 'Dubble Bubble'.

> Pop tends to divide between the highly commercial 'bubble-gum' songs, which almost exclusively have lyrics of complete banality, and the heavy or pro-

gressive rock in which the singer is there but his lyrics cannot be made out.

PETER COLE in *Anatomy of Pop* (1970)

Bubbles. A childish substitution for the first name Beverly, as for the US soprano Beverly Sills (b.1929) and the actress Beverley Brooks, otherwise Patricia, Viscountess Rothermere (1929–92).

Buchmanism. An alternative name for MORAL RE-ARMAMENT, from the name of the movement's founder, Frank Buchman (1878–1961).

Bucket shop. A firm or travel agency that sells cheap airline tickets, especially illegally. The term originated as US slang in the 1970s but has a much longer history, a bucket shop earlier being an unauthorized stock-broking firm that speculates fraudulently with its clients' funds. The original bucket shops of the late 19th century were low-class liquor stores selling small quantities of spirits that had been dubiously distilled in buckets.

Buck House. SLOANE RANGER jargon for Buckingham Palace. The expression, with its pun on 'buck' as a devilish dandy and its degrading of 'palace' to 'house', is vulgar rather than voguish, although Buckingham Palace actually was Buckingham House originally.

Buck Rogers. The famous spaceman hero was created by Philip Francis Nowlan for his magazine serial 'Armageddon: 2419' in *Amazing Stories* in 1928. The cartoonist Dick Calkins then seized on the character for his newspaper strip 'Buck Rogers in the 25th Century', and this ran continuously from 1929 until the late 1960s, becoming so well known that he essentially personified the whole SCIENCE FICTION genre. In 1932 Buck made the transition to radio and subsequently to a cinema serial (1939), starring Buster Crabbe. His avowed intent, while planet warred against planet with death rays, fleets of spaceships and the like, was to save the universe from total destruction.

Buck stops here. The responsibility rests with me. The expression dates from the 1940s and alludes to the 19th-century phrase 'to pass the buck', meaning to evade blame or responsibility or shift it on to someone else. The US term comes from the game of poker, in which it is said to refer to the buckhorn knife that was placed in front of a player to indicate that he was the next dealer. When he had dealt, he 'passed the buck' to another player. President Harry S. Truman famously

had a sign on his desk in the Oval Office saying 'The buck stops here.'

Buck the trend, To. To oppose or run counter to a general tendency, as of a company whose shares rise on the market while most are falling. There is an allusion to 'buck' as a male horned animal such as a deer or (originally) a goat, and probably also to 'butt', the way in which such an animal combats another. The term is usually applied positively and approvingly.

> *The Blair Witch Project* ... bucks one of the most sustained cinema trends by setting out to scare audiences through suggestion rather than crude shocks.
>
> *The Times* (13 September 1999)

Buddha of Suburbia, The. A novel (1990) by Hanif Kureishi (b.1954) about racial attitudes in southeast London. The Buddha of the title is the narrator's Indian father, who precipitates a round of sexual musical chairs by leaving his English wife and setting up home with another Englishwoman, becoming regarded as a guru at her parties in the suburbs of south London. Karim, the novel's bisexual narrator, becomes an actor, goes to New York, but yearns for London, to which he eventually returns, full of hope for a less complicated future.

Buddy movie. A US term dating from the 1960s for a film centring on comradeship between two men, i.e. between 'buddies'. Good examples are *Butch Cassidy and the Sundance Kid* (1969) and *The* STING (1973), both directed by George Roy Hill and both starring Paul Newman and Robert Redford.

Buffy the Vampire Slayer. A young American girl who wants to be normal but instead has been chosen as 'The Slayer', and given the power to hunt and destroy vampires. Her full name is Buffy Summers, and she first appeared in the rather feeble film of this name (1992), in which she was played by Kristy Swanson. She made a much more effective transfer to the television screen in 1997, with her role taken by the 'scream queen' Sarah Michelle Gellar and the location changed from Los Angeles to Sunnydale. Here, in between homework and dating, she wrangles with bloodsuckers, Inca mummies and the like. A spin-off, *Angel* (1999), followed the trail of the eponymous vampire who had now renounced evil to become Buffy's main love interest.

Bugger Bognor! A retort allegedly made by George V in his last illness when a courtier, seeking to lift His Majesty's spirits, remarked that if he continued to make good progress he would soon be able to enjoy a few weeks' recuperation at Bognor Regis, a salubrious seaside resort in West Sussex. The town was originally plain Bognor but in 1929 was granted its royal suffix, Latin for 'of the king', as a token of appreciation by the king after spending an earlier period of convalescence there.

Buggins' turn. The principle of awarding promotion by rotation rather than on individual merit. Buggins is a supposedly common surname, but there were only two in the 1980 London telephone directory. The name itself is familiar in another context from 'Grandma Buggins', a tiresome old lady played by Mabel Constanduros in a radio series that ran from 1925 to the late 1940s.

Bughouse Square. A US nickname for any city park or centre where tramps, vagrants and the mentally deranged gather. The sobriquet is particularly associated with Union Square, New York, and Washington Square Park, Chicago. The latter gained fame in the 1920s and 1930s for its numerous public speakers on political and philosophical subjects, with the orators standing on boxes or crates to be better seen and heard over the heads of the listeners and participants below. *See also* SPEAKERS' CORNER.

Bugs Bunny. The cartoon rabbit made his first appearance in a Warner Brothers animated short in 1938. He was the creation of Chuck Jones and Tex Avery, and his inimitable voice was produced by Mel Blanc. He went on to star in comics and on television. His catchphrase, 'What's up, Doc?', was used for the title of a comedy film of 1972. He was to have been called Jack Rabbit, but in the end was named after the infamous West Coast gangster, Benjamin 'Bugsy' Siegel (*c*.1906–47), whose colourful life and violent death were the subject of the film *Bugsy* (1991).

Bulge, Battle of the. *See* BATTLE OF THE BULGE.

Bull Connor. A nickname of Eugene Connor, Commissioner of Public Safety in Birmingham, Alabama, whose brutal line with civil-rights protestors in 1963 caused a national outcry among liberal elements in the USA.

Bulldog Drummond. An adventure thriller (1920), the first in a series, by Sapper (pen-name, from his war service in the Royal Engineers, known as Sappers, of Lieutenant-Colonel H.C. McNeile; 1888–1937). Subtitled *The Adventures of a Demobilized Officer Who Found Peace Dull*, it features a hard-drinking, athletic, ex-

army, amateur anti-crime agent of the Robin Hood school, who always manages somehow to keep on the right side of the law, although his actions and attitudes are hopelessly racist, protofascist and anti-Semitic. The nickname Bulldog (his real name is Hugh), denoting tenacity, comes from 'We are the boys of the bulldog breed', in a jingoistic music-hall song of the times by Ian Colquhon and Arthur Reece, 'Sons of the Sea, All British Born' (1897). Drummond was based on the soldier and writer Gerard Fairlie (*c*.1900–83), but his character also displays traits of 'Sapper' himself. A silent film version (1922), with Carlyle Blackwell in the title role, was followed by a lengthy series of British and US Bulldog Drummond films of varying quality. The last was *Some Girls Do* (1970), a feeble sequel to *Deadlier than the Male* (1967), with Richard Johnson as Drummond played *à la* James BOND, for whom he was undoubtedly the inspiration.

Bullet train. A type of Japanese high-speed train, so nicknamed in the West because of its shape. The first such train ran on the *Shinkansen* ('new trunk line') between Osaka and Tokyo in 1964. There are two types of service: the fast limited-stop trains called *Hikari* ('Lightning') and the fast stopping trains called *Kodama* ('Echo').

Bullfrog of the Pontine Marshes. A derisive nickname used by Winston Churchill in the Second World War for the Italian Fascist leader Benito Mussolini (1883–1945).

Bullying-Manner. A nickname of Sir Reginald Manningham-Buller (later Lord Dilhorne, 1905–80), the Conservative attorney general from 1954 to 1962.

Bump and grind. The thrusting of the pelvis and rotating of the hips by a dancer, typically a striptease artist, imitating an act of sexual intercourse.

> Endless chorus lines of fascistic showgirls executing a lurid bump-and-grind.
> *The Times* (19 October 1999)

Bump off, To. To murder. The allusion is to giving someone a 'push'. The expression originated in the US underworld in the early years of the 20th century.

Bum rap. A false accusation; an unfair criminal sentence. The expression arose as US underworld slang in the 1920s. 'Bum' means 'bad', and 'rap' is the charge with which one is 'hit'.

Bums on seats. A paying audience viewed as a source of income.

> The massed Partick Thistle fans in the audience were

ecstatic, everyone else looked a mite baffled. But that's your fragmented post-modern culture, isn't it? It makes no claims to universality; just puts neatly-labelled bums on seats.
Guardian (11 May 1993)

Bum's rush. Forcible ejection from a room or building. An expression of US origin with reference to the throwing out of an undesirable customer (as a bum might be) from a bar. To give someone the bum's rush is by extension to dismiss a person regarded as unsuitable or useless.

Bundle of fun or **laughs.** Something amusing or enjoyable. The expression is mostly encountered in the negative.

There is no way in which Poulenc's opera [*The Carmelites*] can be dressed up in a review as a bundle of laughs. Quite the opposite.
The Times (22 May 1999)

Bundle of joy. A baby, especially one not yet born and lovingly longed for.

Both men will see their lives altered in the early summer – both bundles of joy are due within days of each other.
The Times (18 December 1999)

Bundle of laughs. *See* BUNDLE OF FUN.

Bundle or **bag of nerves.** In a tense or apprehensive state, as: 'He was a real bundle of nerves before his driving test.'

Bungee-jumping. An EXTREME SPORT that came into vogue in the early 1990s, consisting of jumping off a bridge or other high point with a strong elastic cord tied to one's ankles. The potentially lethal activity soon spread commercially to fair and amusement park operators, who used construction cranes to raise up metal cages for the jumpers. The word derives from bungie or bungy as a familiar term for an India rubber or eraser at the turn of the 20th century, the name itself perhaps being imitative of the object's 'squashiness'. Bungee-jumping is said to have had its beginnings on Pentecost Island in the South Pacific, where vines were used for similar jumps made by native boys in an ancient rite of passage.

Bun in the oven. A foetus in the womb. The concept is of having something 'cooking' within. *See also* IN THE CLUB; UP THE DUFF.

Bunker, Archie. The US equivalent of Alf GARNETT in the television comedy series *All in the Family* (1971–9)

and the subsequent *Archie Bunker's Place* (1979–83). He is a loud-mouthed bigot who is not slow to voice his low opinion of ethnic minorities. His impact on American viewers was if anything more shocking than Garnett's on his British counterparts.

Bunny girl. A nightclub hostess whose somewhat skimpy costume includes a fluffy, rabbit-like tail and a head-dress with long ears, like those of a rabbit. They were introduced by Hugh Hefner and Victor Lownes in the PLAYBOY Club on Park Lane, London, in 1966. Thousands of young women applied for the £34-a-week job, which involved wearing the cruelly boned costume, serving drinks with a special 'Bunny Dip', retaining a fixed smile for hours on end and keeping the fluffy tail fluffy. Miscreants were made to stand in a corner facing the wall. The name apparently derived from the notion that the girls provided male clients with an evening's chase.

Hugh Hefner might never have made it to the big time if he had called his girls rabbits instead of bunnies. He probably chose bunny because he wanted something close to, but not quite so obvious as, kitten or cat – the all-time winners for connotating female sexuality.
ALLEEN PACE NILSEN: *Sexism and Language* (1977)

Bunny hug. A type of dance in ragtime rhythm in which the couple hold each other closely, popular in America in the early 20th century.

Bunter, Billy. A fat or greedy boy or man. The name is that of the fat and greedy schoolboy in the stories by 'Frank Richards' (Charles Hamilton) published between 1908 and 1961. His full name is William George Bunter. He is bespectacled, wears check trousers and attends GREYFRIARS, where he is known to his friends as the Fat Owl of the Remove. His favourite exclamation is 'Yarooooh!' He has a sister, Bessie Bunter, whose adventures are chronicled separately.

Burgess and Maclean. Two notorious British traitors, Guy Burgess (1911–63) and Donald Maclean (1913–83), who secretly worked as agents of the Soviet Union while serving as diplomats in the Foreign Office. Both had been recruited to the communist cause while at Cambridge in the 1930s (*see* CAMBRIDGE SPY RING), and served Soviet interests throughout the Second World War and the early part of the COLD WAR. Warned in 1951 that British and US agents were becoming suspicious of Maclean, both men disappeared, nothing being heard of them until 1956 when they emerged in Moscow. It turned out in 1963 that they had been warned by a 'third man' from their Cambridge circle, the intelligence officer Kim Philby (1912–88), who that year defected to the Soviet Union.

In 1979 it was made public that a 'fourth man' from the same Cambridge circle, Anthony Blunt (1907–83), had confessed in 1964 to helping to arrange the flight of Burgess and Maclean. Blunt had served in MI5 during the war, before resuming a career as a distinguished art historian and becoming surveyor of the Queen's pictures. There was a public outcry that his role had been kept secret while he was still serving the Queen, and he was stripped of his knighthood. In 1991 John Cairncross, who had served in the Treasury, at Bletchley Park (*see* ULTRA) and with MI6 during the Second World War, confessed to being the FIFTH MAN in the spy ring, Soviet intelligence sources having spoken of 'the magnificent five'. *See also* MAGNIFICENT SEVEN.

Burkitt's lymphoma. A cancer of the lymphatic system particularly prevalent among children in central Africa. It takes its name from Denis P. Burkitt (1911–93), a Northern Ireland surgeon and nutritionist who first identified the disease in 1957 when at Mulago Hospital, Kampala, Uganda.

Burlington Bertie. A would-be elegant 'man-about-town' or 'masher', personified by Vesta Tilley in a popular song of this name by Harry B. Norris (1900). The song below is a parody, written by William Hargreaves for his wife, the male impersonator Ella Shields.

> I'm Burlington Bertie:
> I rise at ten thirty
> And saunter along
> Like a toff;
> I walk down the Strand
> With my gloves on my hand,
> And I walk down again
> With them off.
> WILLIAM HARGREAVES: 'Burlington Bertie from Bow' (1914)

Burma Road. The route that was made in 1937–9 to open up the western interior of China by communication with the sea and that ran from Lashio to Kunming in Yunnan, a distance of 1240km (770 miles). It was the chief highway for supplies to China during the Second World War until the Japanese cut it in 1941. It was recaptured in 1945.

Burn, baby, burn. A black extremist slogan current during the riots of August 1965 in the Watts district of Los Angeles, in which 34 people were killed and whole blocks destroyed by fire. The words were adopted for the title of a popular song of 1974 by the duo Hudson-Ford, but here they had a sexual connotation.

Burn bag. A receptacle for secret documents that are to be officially destroyed by burning. The term has long been in use in intelligence work but was brought before the public in connection with the WATERGATE investigations.

Burnham scale. The standard salary scale for teachers in state schools, named after Harry Lawson Webster Levy-Lawson, 1st Viscount Burnham (1862–1933), chairman of the Standing Joint Committee of Education Authorities and Teachers that was set up on 12 September 1919.

Burrell Collection. In 1944 the shipping magnate William Burrell (1861–1958) endowed Glasgow with a magnificent collection of 9000 artefacts and paintings, ranging from Greek and Egyptian antiquities to European medieval stained glass and paintings spanning 500 years. The bequest, one of the greatest to a city, stipulated that the works be displayed in a rural setting close to Glasgow. Since 1983 they have been housed in a museum designed to admit natural light and afford parkland views through high glass walls.

Bury My Heart at Wounded Knee. An historical study (1971) by Dee Brown (b.1908) of the conquest of the American West and the destruction of the Native American tribes. The title comes from the last verse of a poem, 'American Names' (1927), by Stephen Vincent Benét:

> I shall not rest quiet in Montparnasse.
> I shall not lie easy in Winchelsea.
> You may bury my body in Sussex grass,
> You may bury my tongue at Champmédy.
> I shall not be there, I shall rise and pass.
> Bury my heart at Wounded Knee.

Wounded Knee was the site of the battle between US army forces and Native Americans on the Sioux reservation in South Dakota in 1890, in the course of which Chief Sitting Bull was killed.

Busboy. In the United States a young man who clears dirty dishes from tables in a restaurant or cafe, so called from the four-wheeled cart or trolley that he manoeuvres, as if driving a bus.

Busby's Babes. A nickname for the younger members

of Manchester United football team, coached into a new winning side by Matt (later Sir Matthew) Busby (1909–94) after the loss of eight of their number in an air crash at Munich on 6 February 1958. Busby was himself badly injured in the disaster.

Business as usual. A phrase indicating that normal business carries on as best it can under difficult circumstances. The expression was current before the First World War but became familiar in the Second World War when shops and businesses aimed to keep going in bomb-damaged premises. The term is something of a hyperbole, since conditions were hardly usual. The expression is also used, sometimes ironically, of any recurring event.

> Tuesday's coup was business as usual in Pakistan.
> *The Times* (14 October 1999)

Busted flush. A person or thing that shows signs of great promise and fulfilment but that ultimately lets one down as a failure. The term comes from the game of poker, in which a busted flush is a flush (a hand of five cards all of the same suit) that one fails to complete.

> An insider said yesterday that a decision to limit [Mo] Mowlam's media appearances [as cabinet office minister] had already been taken. 'Mo is a busted flush,' he said.
> *Sunday Times* (6 February 2000)

Buster. A US nickname for a boy or young man, especially a 'beefy' one. The name sometimes replaces an individual's first name, as for the actor Buster Keaton (1895–1966), whose original names were Joseph Francis, the swimmer Buster Crabbe (1908–83), originally Clarence, and Buster Edwards (b.1931), one of the gang involved in the GREAT TRAIN ROBBERY, born Ronald Edwards.

Butcher of Baghdad. A nickname given by the Western press to Saddam Hussein (b.1937), president of Iraq, after his invasion of Kuwait in 1990, which was purportedly accompanied by widespread atrocities.

Butcher of Broadway. The nickname of the feared and corpulent New York drama critic Alexander Woollcott (1887–1943), described by *Life* magazine as 'testy as a wasp and much more poisonous' (30 October 1939).

Butcher of Lyons (French, *boucher de Lyon*). Klaus Barbie (1913–91), head of the GESTAPO in Lyons from 1942 to 1944, was so nicknamed because of his alleged torture and murder of French Resistance fighters and others (*see* MAQUIS). Barbie was held responsible for

the deaths of 4000 people, including French Resistance leader Jean Moulin (1899–1943), and the deportation of 7500 others. He was sentenced to life imprisonment by a French court in 1987, having been extradited from Bolivia.

Butcher of Prague. *See* HANGMAN.

Butlin's. The popular holiday camps of this name were the enterprise of Sir William ('Billy') Butlin (1899–1980), who opened the first on the site of a former sugarbeet field near Skegness, Lincolnshire, on Easter Saturday, 11 April 1936. The camps evolved into modern holiday centres, with a variety of amenities and entertainments on tap for both residents and visitors. Regular features were the broadcast call 'Wakey, Wakey!' to begin the day and the presence of REDCOATS to entertain and organize. The original at Skegness is now Butlins Holiday Centre.

Butskellism. Consensus politics characteristic of the 1960s and 1970s, when there was a measure of agreement between the left wing of the Conservative Party and the right wing of the LABOUR PARTY. The name combines two representative MIDDLE-OF-THE-ROAD figures, RAB Butler and the Labour leader Hugh Gaitskell (1906–63).

Butterflies. An unusually poignant television SITCOM shown from 1978 to 1980. It centres on Ria Parkinson, an attractive woman approaching middle age and worrying that she has not made the most of her life, and her worthy but dull dentist husband Ben, who collects butterflies. The two are played to the letter by Wendy Craig and Geoffrey Palmer. Humour of the usual sitcom type is present but there is also a darker tone, centring on Ria's frustration, marital ennui and ageing. The fine script was by Carla Lane and the title perhaps alludes to the evanescence of human existence.

Butterflies in one's stomach or **tummy.** A nervous fluttering sensation in one's body experienced before a formidable venture. The expression dates from the turn of the 20th century and is often shortened to simply 'butterflies'.

> 'I always have butterflies when I open Parliament,' she [Queen Elizabeth II] said.
> *Sunday Times* (25 January 1959)

Butterfly effect. The notion, in CHAOS THEORY, that a very small difference in the initial state of a physical system can make a significant difference to the state at some later time. The allusion is to the title of a paper delivered by the meteorologist Konrad Lorenz to the American Association for the Advancement of Science on 29 December 1979 in Washington: 'Predictability: Does the flap of a butterfly's wings in Brazil set off a tornado in Texas?'

Buy the farm, To. To die. The expression is of US origin and dates from the Second World War. The origin may lie with fighter pilots, whose pipe dream was to give up flying, buy a farm and settle into peaceful retirement. Alternatively, the allusion may be to training flights crashing in a farmer's field, causing the farmer to sue for damages. As the pilot usually dies in such a crash, he has effectively bought the farm with his life.

Buzz bomb. A nickname for the V–1 flying bomb in the Second World War, so called either from the buzzing of its engine or because it came in at a low altitude, like an aircraft 'buzzing' the ground.

Buzz off, To. To go away quickly, like a busy, buzzing bee. As an imperative ('Buzz off!'), the phrase has a connotation of abruptness or even vulgarity, perhaps from its suggestion of 'bugger off' or the somewhat similar-sounding 'piss off'.

Buzzword. A fashionable or vogue word, especially one originating as a technical term. Many terms from computer technology have become buzzwords, such as 'mainframe' and 'peripheral'. Even 'buzzword' has become a buzzword. The word itself relates chiefly to 'buzz' in the sense of being excited or purposeful, but the influence of 'business' is also probably present. Those using buzzwords in their everyday speech are usually happily ignorant of the original technical sense.

BVDs. A type of lightweight long underwear for men, popular in the first half of the 20th century. They are of US origin and the abbreviated name is that of the manufacturers, Bradley, Vorhees and Day Co., although popularly interpreted as 'babies' ventilated diapers'. They now exist as a type of boxer shorts.

By Grand Central Station I Sat Down and Wept. A novel (1945), in the form of a prose poem, by the Canadian novelist Elizabeth Smart (1913–86). It reflects some of the circumstances of her long-term affair with the British poet, George Barker (1913–91), with whom she had four children while Barker was married to another woman. The title plays on the first verse of Psalm 137: 'By the rivers of Babylon, there we sat down, yea, we wept, when we remembered Zion.' It refers to the narrator's reaction at Grand Central Station in New York when a meeting is missed and the affair appears to be over. There are further biblical references, drawn from the Song of Solomon, in an exchange between the police and the narrator, who has been arrested, with her lover, on a charge of crossing a state boundary for an immoral purpose.

Byker Grove. A phenomenally popular teenage SOAP OPERA first screened in 1991 and set in the (fictional) Tyneside youth centre of the title. Its story lines included such themes as puppy love, anguished bereavement, drug-taking, 'girl-only nights' and arson attacks, and in 1995 it outraged the tabloid press by featuring a gay kiss. It also spawned the pop duo Ant and Dec (Ant McPartlin and Declan Donnelly) who returned in 1995 with a chat show series, *The Ant and Dec Show*.

C

C. *See* PROGRAMMING LANGUAGES.

'C'. The traditional code name for the head of MI6, deriving from the name of its first director, Captain Mansfield Cumming (1859–1923).

Cabaret. A stage musical (1968) and film (1972) adapted from John Van Druten's stage play *I am a Camera* (1951), which was in turn based on the short stories published as GOODBYE TO BERLIN (1939) by Christopher Isherwood. Drawing parallels between the overt decadence of the Berlin cabaret scene in the early 1930s and the more sinister moral decadence of the growing NAZI movement, the film starred Liza Minnelli as the cabaret singer Sally BOWLES to whom a young Englishman (Michael York) is attracted. Isherwood drew heavily for his book on his own memories of the years (1929–34) he spent in Berlin, supporting himself by giving English lessons. The original for Sally Bowles was Jean Ross (1912–73), the daughter of a Scottish cotton merchant who rebelled after a childhood in Egypt and went to Berlin to sing in cabaret.

Cabbage Patch dolls. Dough-faced, chinless dolls, representing children born from the heart of a cabbage, that were all the rage of 1983 in the USA and to a lesser extent in Britain. They were created by Xavier Roberts of the Original Appalachian Artworks Inc in Cleveland, Georgia, and were commercially marketed as Cabbage Patch Kids. In 1996 Mattel updated and relaunched them for a new generation.

Cabbages and Kings. The first volume of stories (1904) by O. Henry (pen-name of William Sydney Porter; 1862–1910). They are set in Latin America, where Porter took refuge from justice after having been accused of embezzling funds from the chaotically organized bank for which he worked. He returned home because of his wife's illness and gave himself up to the authorities in 1897 when she died. Found guilty on a technicality, he served three years in prison, and he began writing stories to support his young daughter during this period. The title of the first collection is from 'The Walrus and the Carpenter' by Lewis Carroll (1832–98) in *Through the Looking-Glass* (1872):

> 'The time has come,' the Walrus said,
> 'To talk of many things:
> Of shoes – and ships – and sealing wax –
> Of cabbages – and kings.'

Francis Spufford's 1989 book of 'Lists in Literature' was titled *Cabbages and Kings*.

Cabin fever. A colloquial term of US origin dating from the early 20th century for the lassitude, irritability and similar symptoms that result from long confinement or isolation indoors during the winter.

> Nobody has attempted a year in cyberspace. Some observers believe that after a few months DotCom-Guy's perception of reality will become distorted and he will suffer cabin fever.
> *Sunday Times* (19 December 1999)

Cab-rank rule. In legal parlance the rule by which barristers are expected to accept any instructions offered to them at a fair and proper fee and not select the clients for whom they act. The analogy is with a taxi rank, where a passenger is expected to hire the next vehicle available.

> Alun Jones, QC, is the barrister instructed by the Crown Prosecution Service (CPS) on behalf of the Spanish Government on the extradition of General Augusto Pinochet. How did you get the case? The CPS asked me to conduct it after the arrest. Why did you

agree to take it on? By virtue of the cab-rank principle. I specialize in extradition and I was given instructions. *The Times* (12 October 1999)

Cactus Jack. A nickname of John Nance Garner (1868–1967), the Texan Democrat who was speaker of the House of Representatives (1931–3) and Franklin D. Roosevelt's vice-president (1933–41).

Cadfael, Brother. The medieval Welsh monk in the series of historical detective novels by Ellis Peters (real name Edith Pargeter), beginning with *A Morbid Taste for Bones* (1977). He lives at Shrewsbury Abbey where he tends the herb garden and uses his wise powers of deduction to solve murder mysteries. The stories were transferred to television in 1994 with Derek Jacobi in the role of Brother Cadfael.

Caesar salad. A salad of cos lettuce and croutons served with a dressing of olive oil, lemon juice, raw egg, Worcester sauce and seasoning, the whole the invention in 1924 at Tijuana, Mexico, of the restaurateur Caesar Cardini.

Café society. A term of US origin dating from the 1930s for the frequenters of fashionable restaurants and nightclubs.

> Rather like the new Covent Garden … the new South Bank will mix culture with café society.
> *Sunday Times* (2 January 2000)

Caffè latte (Italian, 'milk coffee'). A drink of frothy steamed milk to which a shot of espresso coffee has been added, popular from the 1960s and often known simply as 'latte'.

> Tourists sit and sip caffelattes, clatter through the smart shopping malls and throng to worship at the new John Lewis building.
> *Sunday Times Magazine* (19 September 1999)

Cagney and Lacey. The female American cops, 'First Ladies of the New York Police Department', played respectively by Loretta Swit and Tyne Daly in the television movie *Cagney and Lacey* (1981) and in the popular subsequent television series of this title (1982–8), in which Cagney was played by Meg Foster and Sharon Gless but Lacey still by Daly. Detective Mary Christine Cagney and Detective Mary Beth Lacey are THIRTYSOMETHING professionals whose remit takes them out of the squad room into areas such as alcoholism, DATE RAPE and other social evils.

Caine Mutiny, The. A novel (1951) by Herman Wouk (b.1915), which won the PULITZER PRIZE for fiction. It centres on the court-martial of a naval officer who

has been persuaded to take command of the minesweeper USS *Caine* on the grounds that its paranoid captain is unfit to continue at his post. It was made into a play (1953) by Wouk, and a film version (1954), directed by Edward Dmytryk, starred Humphrey Bogart as Captain Queeg.

Cairo crud. *See* MONTEZUMA'S REVENGE.

Cakes and Ale. A novel (1930) by W. Somerset Maugham (1874–1965), in which the author satirized the British literary establishment. Of the novelists portrayed, Edward Driffield was said to be based on Thomas Hardy (1840–1928), Grand Old Man of Literature, and Alroy Kear on Hugh Walpole (1884–1941), while Willie ASHENDEN is in some respects Maugham's *alter ego*. The title comes from a remark by Toby Belch to the Clown in Shakespeare's *Twelfth Night*:

> Dost thou think, because thou art virtuous, there shall be no more cakes and ale?
> II.iii

Calamity Jane. A nickname for anyone with a permanently gloomy outlook or doom-ridden view of life. It comes from the popular name of Martha Jane Burke, *née* Cannary (*c.*1852–1903), an American frontierswoman famed for her skill at riding and shooting, particularly during the Gold Rush days in the Black Hills of Dakota. It is claimed that she threatened 'calamity' to any man who tried to woo her, although she did in fact marry.

California über Alles. The title of the début single of the American PUNK rock group, the Dead Kennedys, released in 1979. The title plays on the words *Deutschland über alles* ('Germany above all'), which appear in the German national anthem. The song's lyrics, written by the group's lead singer, Jello Biafra, savage the perceived NEW AGE modishness of life in the Golden State ('You will jog for the master race / and always wear the happy face'). The song appears on an album entitled *Fresh Fruit for Rotting Vegetables* (1980), the snarling anti-bourgeois invective of which is epitomized by such tracks as 'I Kill Children' and 'Let's Lynch the Landlord'.

Caligari, Doctor. The mysterious villain of the famous German HORROR MOVIE *The Cabinet of Dr Caligari* (1919). He is a magician and hypnotist who uses a sleepwalking victim to commit murders on his behalf, and was played by Werner Krauss. A later US film, *The Cabinet of Caligari* (1962), bore little relationship to the original.

Callanetics. A system of physical exercises based on small repeated muscular movements and squeezes, designed to improve muscle tone. It takes its name from Callan Pinckney (b.1939), the fitness trainer who devised it, and was the subject of a book of the same name published in 1984, subtitled *Ten Years Younger in Ten Hours*. Although perhaps partly based on 'athletics', the name overall also fortuitously suggests 'callisthenics', gymnastic exercises to achieve gracefulness and strength, from Greek *kallos*, 'beauty', and *sthenos*, 'strength'.

Calling bird. In the late 20th century an increasingly common replacement for the colly bird in the familiar 'Twelve Days of Christmas' rhyme, giving thus 'four calling birds' in the countdown. The colly bird, as a dialect name for the blackbird (literally 'coaly bird'), was presumably felt to be too obscure to hold its place. But a calling bird lacks the specificity of the other birds in the verselets: the three French hens, the two turtle doves and the single partridge in a pear tree.

Call Me Madam. A musical comedy (1950) with a book by Howard Lindsay (1889–1968) and Russel Crouse (1893–1966) and a score by Irving Berlin (1888–1989) about the domineering Sally Adams, US ambassador to the tiny country of Lichtenburg. Made immortal by Ethel Merman, Sally Adams was based originally on the Washington society hostess Perla Mesta, who served as an ambassador under Harry S. Truman and instructed her staff to 'call her madam' when they asked how she should be addressed. Ethel Merman was much irritated by changes that Irving Berlin continued to make to the score very late in rehearsal for the show: when he tried to introduce a new verse for one of the songs she refused point-blank to take it on board, with the quip: 'Call me Miss Bird's Eye. The show is frozen.'

Call me stupid. A phrase, usually followed by 'but', used to point out a truth that others seem to have overlooked. The speaker implies that the adjective, although at other times perhaps applicable, is not so in this instance. The adjective itself is variable.

> Call me old-fashioned, but it seems to me that one of the great things to be said for being married is the combination of company and privacy.
> LIBBY PURVES in *The Times* (12 January 1999)

Call of the Wild, The. An animal novel (1903) by the US writer Jack London (1876–1916) about a domestic dog, Buck, which, out of grief at his master's death, takes to the wild and joins a pack of wolves.

Call the shots, To. To dictate a course of action; to be in charge. The allusion is to dice gambling. The phrase dates from the 1960s.

> In the best tradition of this resistant-to-change genre, the shots are still being called by a man, though not a terribly Nashville type of one – actually the [female country music] singer's personal trainer.
> *The Times* (3 December 1999)

Call-waiting. A commercial service that advises a person making a telephone call that someone else is trying to call them. It usually arranges for the call being made to be placed on hold so that the incoming caller can be connected. The system was first introduced in the United States in 1976.

Cambridge Mafia. A term of the early 1990s for a group of senior Conservatives who were at Cambridge together in the early 1960s and active there in university politics. Five were in John Major's cabinet of 1992: Kenneth Clarke, John Gummer, Michael Howard, Norman Lamont and Peter Lilley. A sixth, Norman Fowler, was then party chairman. Yet another of the group, Leon Brittan, was in the cabinet somewhat earlier (1981 6). *See also* PORTILLISTAS.

Cambridge Spy Ring. The popular name for the spies recruited by the NKVD (*see* KGB) at Cambridge University in the 1930s. The five main agents were Kim Philby (1912–88), Donald Maclean (1913–83), Guy Burgess (1911–63), John Cairncross (1913–95) and Anthony Blunt (1907–83). Most accounts consider the first recruit to have been Blunt, who in turn won over Cairncross, although their Soviet handler, Yuri Modin, in his book *My Five Cambridge Friends* (1994), says that Burgess was the man who recruited Blunt. According to Modin, code names for the five were Söhnchen ('Sonny'), Tom and Stanley for Philby; Mädchen ('Missy') and Hicks for Burgess; Johnson, Tom and Yan for Blunt; and Stuart, Wise, Lyric and Homer for Maclean. These last three were members of the Apostles, a secret Cambridge society founded in 1826 and including such famous figures as Roger Fry, Bertrand Russell, Desmond MacCarthy, Lytton Strachey, E.M. Forster, Leonard Woolf and J.M. Keynes. The Apostles sequestered themselves from their fellow students, not only because they believed in their intellectual superiority but also because many espoused Marxism and were homosexuals. *See also* BURGESS AND MACLEAN; SMILEY, GEORGE.

Camden Town Group. A group of artists formed in 1911 by Walter Sickert (1860–1942), who had painted many of his nude studies in drab boarding-house rooms in Camden Town, then a largely working-class area of north London. In the group's first show he included two such paintings, *Camden Town Murder Series No. 1* and *No. 2*, although the link with any recent murder was more for publicity than for actuality. Other members of the group were Robert Bevan (1865–1925), Harold Gilman (1876–1919), Charles Ginner (1878–1952), Spencer Gore (1878–1914), Augustus John (1878–1961) and Wyndham Lewis (1882–1957). They had no real identity of style although most shared Sickert's liking for everyday subjects. In 1913 they merged with others to form the larger and more disparate LONDON GROUP.

Camelot. A nickname in the early 1960s for the members of John F. Kennedy's administration, casting the stylish young president himself in the role of King Arthur and his glamorous wife as Queen Guinevere. Kennedy's inauguration in 1961 gave promise of brighter and better things to come after the sober Eisenhower years. Although ultimately deriving from the medieval legend, the name was directly prompted by the Lerner and Loewe musical *Camelot*, depicting King Arthur's court, which had opened on Broadway the previous year. Camelot was later familiar in Britain as the name of the consortium operating the National Lottery from 1994. The same associations of glamour and glitter are present, but there is also a verbal pun on 'lottery' and perhaps even on 'came a lot'.

> At several Cambridge dinner parties one heard faculty-types discuss … institutional politics, the glory days in Washington when Camelot reigned, their books or research career frustrations.
> *Harper's* (October 1970)

Camel's nose. A small part of something very large, especially when difficult or unpleasant to deal with; the TIP OF THE ICEBERG. The term is of US origin, dating from the 1960s, and derives from the fuller phrase 'to let the camel's nose into the tent'.

Camford. A blend of the names of Oxford and Cambridge to suggest a university city, on the lines of the currently more familiar 'Oxbridge'. Both were used by Thackeray in *Pendennis* (1848) but Camford also features in Conan Doyle's story 'The Adventure of the Creeping Man' in *The Case Book of Sherlock Holmes* (1927), in which it is famous for its chair of Comparative Anatomy, held in 1903 by Professor Presbury. Holmes duly reveals the secret of the professor's claim that a man can be transformed into an ape by being injected with monkey serum.

Camillo, Don. The tough rural priest in a series of humorous stories by the Italian writer Giovanni Guareschi (1908–68). His adversary is Peppone, the local communist mayor. The stories first appeared in the Italian magazine *Candido* in the late 1940s and were subsequently collected in a number of books. The first of these in English translation was *The Little World of Don Camillo* (1950), and film and television versions have followed.

Camp. Ostentatiously and extravagantly effeminate; exaggerated or theatrical in style or manner. The origin of the word in this sense is uncertain, and it is not likely to derive directly from the military camp. A connection with French *se camper*, 'to adopt a proud pose', has been suggested.

> Not only is there a Camp vision, a Camp way of looking at things. Camp is as well a quality discoverable in objects and the behavior of persons. There are 'campy' movies, clothes, furniture, popular songs, novels, people, buildings.
> SUSAN SONTAG: 'Notes on Camp', *Partisan Review* (Fall 1964)

Campbell's Soup. The well-known brand of comestible was multiply immortalized by Andy Warhol (1928–87) in his 1962 stencilled picture *100 Cans of Campbell's Soup* and again in *Four Campbell's Soup Cans* (1965). Typically, Warhol's idea was not original: in 1960 Jasper Johns (b.1930) had made his sculpture of two cans of Ballantine Ale entitled *Painted Bronze*. But then, as Warhol predicted in 1963: 'Some day everybody will be thinking alike.'

Camp David. The rural retreat of US presidents, in Catoctin Mountain Park, Maryland, some 112km (70 miles) from Washington, D.C. It was established under the name SHANGRI LA in 1942 by F.D. Roosevelt and was made an official retreat by Harry S Truman in 1945. In 1953 Dwight D. Eisenhower renamed it Camp David after his grandson (b.1947), who grew up to marry Richard M. Nixon's younger daughter Julie (b.1948).

Camp David Agreements or **Accords.** The two agreements between Israel and Egypt that led to a negotiated peace between those two countries, the first between Israel and any of its Arab neighbours. The agreements were signed on 17 September 1978 between the Israeli prime minister, Menachem Begin, and the Egyptian president, Anwar Sadat, under the aegis of the US president, Jimmy Carter, at the latter's government retreat, CAMP DAVID. Hence the name.

Campfire Girls. A youth organization for girls founded in the USA in 1910, the same year as the British GIRL GUIDES. As the name implies, camping is an important activity. Boys have been admitted from 1975.

Campion, Albert. The upper-class detective in the crime novels of Margery Allingham, beginning with *The Crime at Black Dudley* (1929). He is initially a somewhat foppish character but grows in strength and maturity as the series progresses.

Campus classic. A novel whose phenomenal success is due to its cult adoption by university students. The attraction is usually in a mix of entertainment with philosophy or of profundity with naivety. Examples of writers who produced such books are Hermann Hesse (*see* NARZISS UND GOLDMUND), J.R.R. Tolkien (*see* LORD OF THE RINGS), Mervyn Peake (*see* GORMENGHAST) and J.D. Salinger (*see* CATCHER IN THE RYE).

Canard Enchaîné, Le (French, 'The Fettered Duck'). A French satirical weekly, first published in 1915, when it arose from an anti-militarist tract of troops in the trenches. It is famous for its exposés of scandals and abuses of power and is the *bête noire* of the authorities, who bugged its new offices in the 1970s. Its name alludes to its beleaguerment.

Candid camera. An unseen camera which is used to photograph an unsuspecting subject. Candid camera shots have long been used in pictorial journalism. In the 1950s a US television series of the name, subsequently taken up in Britain, set up scenes putting people in an embarrassing situation and then filming their reaction. The British version ran from 1960 to 1967 with Jonathan Routh as the host and returned briefly in 1974 under Peter Dulay. The stunts varied. In one scenario a secretary on her first day at work found the office collapsing around her, while in another a man was asked to hold up a wall for moment, then abandoned. In one classic example a car without an engine was 'driven' to a garage with a request for a repair to be carried out.

Candle in the Wind. A eulogy in song for the sex symbol Marilyn MONROE produced by the successful combination of Bernie Taupin (an avid collector of Monroe memorabilia, who wrote the lyrics) and Elton John (who wrote the music). Released in 1973, the song appeared on the album GOODBYE YELLOW BRICK

ROAD. The inspiration for the title appears to have come from Taupin's reading a description of the hell-raising rock star Janis Joplin as a 'candle in the wind', an allusion to the vulnerability of the latter's lifestyle (Joplin 'blew herself out' with drink and drugs at an early age).

After the death in a car crash of Diana, Princess of Wales in 1997, Taupin (at Elton John's suggestion) revised the lyrics to create a eulogy for the PEOPLE'S PRINCESS. The resulting version of the song (in which the original opening line 'Goodbye Norma Jean' becomes 'Goodbye England's rose') was sung by Elton John at Diana's funeral and went on to become the fastest-selling, best-selling single ever.

Candy. The innocent heroine of Terry Southern and Mason Hoffenberg's comic-cum-pornographic novel named after her (1958). As her name implies, she is a latter-day Candide-style character in a modern, sexually liberated setting. A film of the book was produced in 1968 with Ewa Aulin in the title role.

Canned laughter. Pre-recorded laughter that is dubbed on to radio and television comedy programmes. It is the modern equivalent of the claques who were hired to clap and cheer at theatre performances and is a device of US origin. It was first heard in Britain in the US television comedy show *I Love Lucy*, starring Lucille Ball, screened when ITV began broadcasting on 22 September 1955.

> The trend in TV has been to the canned laugh, a laugh reproduced by recording from some previous happy crowd, or synthetically manufactured.
> VANCE PACKARD: *The Hidden Persuaders*, ch xviii (1957)

Canned music. Music recorded and reproduced, as opposed to live music, played by musicians present in person. The comparison is with canned foods, since such music can be stored and used when required.

Cannibal, The. The nickname of the Belgian cyclist Eddie Merckx (b.1945), five times winner of the Tour de France and probably the greatest cyclist ever. He owed his nickname to his ability to 'eat up' his opponents through a combination of speed and strength.

Can of worms. A complex and unappetizing situation. The phrase dates from the 1950s and is found in the fuller form 'to open a can of worms', meaning to reveal a situation that is bound to lead to trouble. The image is of a container of maggots for use as fish bait.

Can't do something for toffee. Cannot do it at all. Said of someone who quite clearly lacks a particular ability, as: 'He can't sing for toffee.' 'For toffee' may have evolved as a variant of 'for nuts', referring to the bruised nuts that are a proper ingredient of toffee (hence walnut toffee and the like).

Canteen culture. A term for the male chauvinist and racist attitudes that are said to exist within the ranks of the British police force. The phrase dates from the late 1980s and alludes to the off-duty expression and exchange of opinions of this type in police station canteens.

> 'I've been in the canteen culture in the Seventies, I've told dirty jokes, I've used inappropriate language, I've sworn, because it was the norm. But I watch my words now.'
>
> *The Times Magazine* (21 August 1999)

Can't pay, won't pay. This doughty device was adopted in 1990 by those objecting to the new COMMUNITY CHARGE or 'poll tax', as well as by some other protest groups. The words were adopted from the title of Lino Pertile's English translation (1981) of Dario Fo's Italian play *Non si paga! Non si paga!* (1974).

Canyoning. An EXTREME SPORT that consists in launching oneself, appropriately clad in protective clothing, down a series of natural rapids and waterfalls. The undertaking is hazardous if proper precautions are not taken, and in 1999 21 participants were swept to their deaths by a swollen stream in the Swiss Alps after ignoring a severe storm warning.

Caped crusader. A person who fights to uphold moral right and decency and who champions the underdog. The allusion is to Robin and BATMAN, as virile vigilantes who combat villains.

> In the past, caped crusaders fought for truth, justice and the American way. Now gay rights will be added to their muscle-bound repertoire. The 21st-century gender pioneers are called Apollo and Midnighter, a loving couple who cohabit in a giant spaceship.
>
> *Sunday Times* (27 February 2000)

Capone, Al. A notorious Chicago gangster of Sicilian origin (1899–1947). He rose to power in the PROHIBITION era and made himself master of the rackets in the city by organizing the killing of most of the rival gunmen. After the ST VALENTINE'S DAY MASSACRE of 1929 he was left in supreme control of the protection rackets, speakeasies, brothels and so on. The suburb of Cicero was completely dominated by him.

Capp, Andy. The cloth-capped working man from the northeast of England who is the lazy and loutish anti-hero of the popular comic newspaper strip by Reg Smythe (1917–98). He and his nagging wife, Flo, first appeared in the *Daily Mirror* in 1957. He survives today, but with a nod in the direction of POLITICAL CORRECTNESS, so that, for example, a cigarette no longer dangles from his lower lip. But he still keeps his cap on indoors, even when snoozing on the sofa. His name is an obvious pun on 'handicap', a racing word instantly appreciated by his gambling cronies.

Capri pants. Tight-fitting trousers for women, with tapering legs ending below the knee. They were first in vogue in the 1950s, when they were worn by fashion-conscious visitors to the Italian island of Capri and other Mediterranean resorts.

> Capri pants still make us think of St Tropez, Brigitte Bardot and Audrey Hepburn at their best, and chic summer holidays involving Vespas and kitten-heeled shoes.
>
> *The Times* (17 April 1999)

Captain America. The costumed superhero of this name was the creation of Joe Simon and Jack Kirby for a comic book that first appeared in 1941. He begins as a weakling by the name of Steve Rogers, but is then injected with a wonder drug, acquires mighty muscles, and starts to set about the NAZIS. He goes on to win the Second World War almost single-handed. His usual dress is a Stars-and-Stripes costume and a tight-fitting hood with a letter A on the brow. He rather lost direction after the war but then reappeared in various Marvel Comics.

Captain Blood. *See* BLOOD, CAPTAIN.

Captain Bob. *See* BOUNCING CZECH.

Captain Corelli's Mandolin. A novel (1994) by Louis de Bernières (b.1954), set in the Greek island of Cephalonia. The major part of the action takes place during the Second World War and concerns the romance between the local doctor's daughter and Captain Antonio Corelli, a member of the occupying Italian forces, who is a skilled performer on the mandolin. A survey in 2000 revealed that the book was one of the ten sources most used for readings at weddings. *See also* FIRST LINES OF NOVELS.

Captain Future. The space-travelling hero of the SCIENCE FICTION pulp magazine that bears his name (1940–44). His real name is Curt Newton, and his main task is to pursue interstellar criminals, which he does accompanied by a robot, an android and a 'living brain'. Most of the stories in which he features were written by Edmond Hamilton, sometimes using the pen-name Brett Sterling.

Captain Marvel. (1) The red-suited, tough-muscled superhero of American comics, nicknamed 'the Big Red Cheese'. He first appeared in Fawcett's *Whiz* comics in 1940. His real name is Billy Batson, implying he is a son of BATMAN, who made his début the previous year. He begins as a weedy youth but is transformed when he meets a wizard who gives him a magic word to say. This is Shazam, an acronym of the names of six traditional heroes: Solomon, Hercules, Atlas, Zeus, Achilles and Mercury.

(2) The nickname of the West Bromwich Albion, Manchester United and England footballer Bryan Robson (b.1957), a talented midfielder of great stamina and courage during the 1980s and early 1990s. He made 89 appearances for England, earning his nickname by analogy with the US comic-strip superhero by captaining the side on 45 occasions.

Captain Midnight. A US radio hero created by Robert M. Burtt and Wilfred G. Moore. He is a daredevil pilot of the Secret Squadron and his 'real' name is Captain Jim 'Red' Albright. His chief role is as a NAZI-hunter and crime-buster, and his adventures livened the airwaves from 1940 to 1953. He also appeared in film and television serials as well as in comic books and strips.

Captain Pugwash. A cartoon pirate created by the British illustrator John Ryan (b.1921), who first appeared in picture books and on television (1957–75). The bombastic and cowardly Pugwash, captain of the ramshackle vessel the *Black Pig*, is terrified of his mortal enemy, the villainous Black Jake, and has to be rescued by cabin boy, Tom.

Captain's chair. A style of wooden chair with a saddle seat, a low curved back and arms supported on vertical spindles, the whole having a somewhat magisterial or 'commanding' appearance. Such chairs came into vogue from the 1970s and are mainly sought after by the aspiring and affluent.

[In the study] there will be a leather-topped desk, a green banker's lamp, some pretentious non-fiction books and perhaps a 'captain's chair' of manly mahogany.

The Times (18 November 1999)

Cap the Knife. A nickname given to Caspar Weinberger (b.1917) because of his slashing of spending and lowering of taxes when running the finances of California during Ronald Reagan's governorship (1966–74). Once he became secretary of defence in Reagan's cabinet in 1981, however, the enormous hike in military expenditure earned him the nickname Cap the Ladle. *See also* GREAT COMMUNICATOR; MAC THE KNIFE.

Car bomb. A terrorist weapon consisting of a car packed with explosives parked near to the target and detonated by timer or remote control. Car bombs have been used by the IRA during the TROUBLES, both in Northern Ireland and in mainland Britain.

Cardboard City. A grimly descriptive nickname for an area on London's SOUTH BANK, in particular its concrete undercroft, neighbouring railway arches and 'Bull Ring' subway, which in the 1980s became the home of the homeless, who devised a makeshift residence in discarded cardboard cases and other packing materials. The term came to apply to similar 'cities' elsewhere. *See also* BIDONVILLE.

Careless talk costs lives. A British government security slogan in the Second World War. *See also* BE LIKE DAD, KEEP MUM; LOOSE LIPS SINK SHIPS.

Caretaker, The. A play (1960) by Harold Pinter (b.1930) about the disruption that ensues when two brothers befriend a rascally tramp and offer him shelter in the room they share. The title refers to the post of caretaker that the brothers independently offer the tramp, who rewards them by trying to drive them apart. *See also* THEATRE OF THE ABSURD.

Carey, Philip. The central character of William Somerset Maugham's semi-autobiographical novel OF HUMAN BONDAGE (1915). He has a club foot and endures a lonely childhood, and grows up to become a doctor but is led into trouble by his infatuation with a waitress. The story has been filmed more than once, with Leslie Howard in the name part in the 1934 version, Paul Henreid in 1946, and Laurence Harvey in 1964. Carey's club foot equates to Maugham's own stammer.

Carjacking. A crime, said to have begun in Detroit, in which a car driver is ordered out of their car at knife or gun point and the vehicle driven off by the 'jacker'. *See also* JOYRIDING.

Carlos. *See* JACKAL.

Carmina Burana. The highly rhythmic and lyrical 'scenic cantata' by Carl Orff (1895–1982) was first performed in 1937. The title means 'Songs of Beuron', and the subtitle *cantiones profanae* means 'profane songs'. The text consists of poems in Old French, Old German and Latin about love, drink and other pleasures; they come from a 13th-century manuscript found in the Benedictine monastery of Beuron in Bavaria. In Britain the work is usually given in a concert version, but in Germany it is often staged.

Carnaby Street. In the SWINGING SIXTIES the much publicized clothing centre for fashion-conscious young people, east of London's Regent Street. Its connection with youthful fashion began in the late 1950s, when John Stephens, John Vince and Andrea Spyropoulos opened 'Vince', a boutique selling colourful clothes to young people of both sexes. It subsequently became associated with trendy UNISEX costumes generally. It was showily refurbished by Westminster City Council in 1973, but its popularity had declined by 1975 when boutiques in the King's Road, Chelsea, began to attract this type of custom.

Carpetbagger. Originally a US term for a political candidate in an area where they had no local connections, but simply a 'carpet bag' of personal belongings, the word subsequently came to be used generally of an unscrupulous opportunist, especially in politics or the financial market. Its recent application to building society members dates from 1995, when it was adopted by Peter Robinson, a former building society executive, to describe speculators who joined a society purely in the hope of a 'windfall' payment made when it converted from a mutual organization to a bank.

> Societies may have more than enough carpetbaggers to defeat loyalists who favour remaining as mutuals owned by their members, rather than by shareholders.
> *Financial Times* (16 January 1999)

Carpetbaggers, The. A novel (1961) by Harold Robbins (born Francis Kane; when he was adopted in 1927 he took the name Harold Rubin, which he later changed to Robbins; 1916–97). 'And behind the Northern Armies came another body of men. They came by the hundreds, yet each travelled alone. ... And on their back, or across their saddle, or on top of their wagon was the inevitable faded multicoloured bag made of worn and ragged remnants of carpet into which they had crammed all their worldly possessions. It was from these bags that they got their name.

The Carpetbaggers.' The novel is about big business and sex and is clearly based on the career of the US industrialist, film producer and aviator Howard Hughes (1905–76). The action, set between 1925 and 1945, with flashbacks, mainly concerns Jonas Cord, whose outward interests are 'airplanes, explosives and money and, when the spirit moves him, occasionally [making] a motion picture'. A melodramatic film version (1964) was directed by Edward Dmytryk and starred George Peppard.

Carpet bombing. The systematic intensive bombing of an area. Hence, in less serious vein, the delivery by the postman of unsolicited advertising matter ('junk mail') or any other relentless 'bombardment'.

> [The television quiz show *Who Wants to Be a*] *Millionaire*'s power isn't in its individual figures though, more its carpet-bombing of 12 consecutive nights of rival output.
> *heat* (23–29 September 1999)

Carpet treader. Estate agents' jargon for a person who asks to look round a house for sale with neither the inclination nor the money to buy.

Carrie. *See* PROM QUEEN.

Carrot and stick. A method of coercion that consists in alternating or combining the offer of an enticement with the threat of a punishment. The allusion is to the proverbial method of persuading a donkey to move by dangling a carrot before it one moment and beating it with a stick the next. The expression dates from the early 20th century.

> Human resources managers would argue that the best combination is usually a mixture of carrot and stick.
> *The Times* (19 October 1999)

Carry a torch for someone, To. To suffer from unrequited love for them. The picture is of a 'light of love' that still burns. A torch is also an emblem of marriage, from the old custom of forming wedding processions in the evening by torchlight.

Carry On films. A long-running series of film comedies that began with *Carry On Sergeant* in 1958. Their humour was mostly unsubtle or even 'blue', but they won a loyal following and still have their devotees, despite their complete lack of POLITICAL CORRECTNESS. There were 31 in the sequence, all with titles beginning *Carry On*, such as *Carry On Doctor* (1960) and *Carry On up the Khyber* (1968), and regular members of the cast included Kenneth Williams, Charles Hawtrey, Sid James, Joan Sims, Barbara Windsor and Hattie Jacques. The latter two, in their respective roles as busty blonde nurse and formidable hospital matron, long etched the stereotypes in the public consciousness. The series proper ended in 1978 although the formula was temporarily revived for *Carry on Columbus* (1992), in which Julian Clary injected his own brand of CAMP.

> New generation falls for Carry On classics.
>
> *The Times* (headline) (1 March 1999)

Carry the can, To. To take the responsibility or blame for the mistakes or misdeeds of others. The phrase dates from the 1920s and is said to refer to the can of beer that a soldier carried for all his companions.

Carry the flag, To. *See* SHOW THE FLAG.

Carter, John. The hero of Edgar Rice Burroughs's swashbuckling interplanetary fantasy *A Princess of Mars* (1912) and its nine sequels. He is a Confederate army officer who finds himself transported by magical means to Barsoom (Mars), where he fights giant green men and other monstrosities and falls in love with a red-skinned princess, Dejah Thoris.

Carve Her Name with Pride. A film (1958) based on the heroic wartime career and ultimate death of Violette Szabo, who was executed in 1945 by the Germans as an Allied spy following her capture on active service in France during the Second World War. The film starred Virginia McKenna as Szabo, and the title refers to the carving of Violette Szabo's name on a memorial after the war. Szabo, who was awarded a posthumous George Cross, was the daughter of a London taxi driver and a French woman. She was recruited into the Special Operations Executive (SOE) and was only 23 years old when she was executed. The screenwriter Leo Marks wrote a poem by which her radio messages from France were recognized:

> The life that I have
> Is all that I have
> And the life that I have
> Is yours.
> The love that I have
> Of the life that I have
> Is yours and yours and yours …

Carve-up. A distribution of spoils or ill-gotten gains. The term dates from the 1930s.

Casablanca. A classic romantic melodrama (1942), based on a script by Julius and Philip Epstein, largely set in a bar in wartime Casablanca. Starring Humphrey Bogart as bar-owner Rick and Ingrid Bergman as his old flame, the film defied all expectations for its success. Originally intended as a vehicle for George Raft, it was demoted to a B-MOVIE when he was unavailable, and the parts were passed to Bogart and Bergman only after being first offered to Ronald Reagan and Ann Sheridan. The performers were the key to the film's success rather then the plot. A remake in 1983, starring David Soul, was greeted with derision, as was another version in 1990, when Sydney Pollack produced *Havana*, set in Cuba and starring Robert Redford. *See also* PLAY IT AGAIN SAM.

> *Rick*: We'll always have Paris.
>
> JULIUS and PHILIP EPSTEIN: *Casablanca*

Casablanca conference. On 14–24 January 1943 Winston Churchill and Franklin D. Roosevelt met at Casablanca, Morocco, to determine Allied strategy as the Second World War took its course. STALIN refused to attend as he was overseeing operations at STALINGRAD. The prospect of opening a SECOND FRONT in northern France was discussed, but Churchill considered this premature. Instead, the invasion of Sicily ('Operation Husky') was planned. Agreement was also reached to increase the bombing of Germany and to give priority to defeating the U-BOATS in the North Atlantic.

Case the joint, To. To survey a building such as a store with the aim of subsequently robbing it. 'Case' here has the sense 'cover', while 'joint', although now applied to any building or premises, was earlier one where criminals met or joined up. The phrase dates from the early 20th century.

Cash cow. A business or investment that provides a steady income or profit, like a cow that yields a regular supply of milk. The expression dates from the 1970s.

Cash for questions. A phrase arising from a series of parliamentary incidents in the mid-1990s, when a number of Conservative MPs admitted having received money from private individuals in return for asking specific questions in the House of Commons. In 1997 the Parliamentary Commissioner investigated claims that the Conservative MP Neil Hamilton had taken cash for questions from Mohamed al Fayed, the multi-millionaire owner of Harrods. Hamilton was found guilty and in 1999 lost a sensational libel action against his donor. *See also* SLEAZE FACTOR.

Cash-my-cheque, General. A nickname given to General Chiang Kai-shek (1887–1975), the Chinese

Nationalist leader who headed the KUOMINTANG government of China from 1925 until defeated by the communists in 1949. He subsequently set up a government-in-exile in Taiwan. The nickname was originally a joke by the GOONS.

Casper. The cute little ghost of this name first appeared in the short animated film *The Friendly Ghost* (1945), based on a short story by Seymour Reitt. His search for a hospitable American family to haunt is continued in later films and in his own comic book from 1949.

Casper Milquetoast. A nickname for a timid person. The name is that of the central character in H.T. Webster's cartoon 'The Timid Soul', first published in the *New York World* in May 1924.

Cassidy, Hopalong. *See* HOPALONG CASSIDY.

Casualty. A top-ranking television medical drama screened on BBC1 from 1986 and set in the accident and emergency department of the fictional Holby City Hospital. Most episodes opened with an innocent member of the public about to experience a tragedy that puts them in hospital. The series was noted for its frequent changes of cast with the exception of the caring charge nurse, Charlie Fairhead, played by Derek Thompson.

Cat, The. The Chelsea and England goalkeeper Peter Bonetti (b.1941), famed for the feline agility that allowed him to save apparently unreachable shots. Bonetti is unfortunately remembered for letting in the three goals that Germany scored against England in the quarter-finals of the 1970 World Cup, which removed England from the competition.

Cat and Mouse Act. The popular name of the Prisoners (Temporary Discharge for Ill Health) Act of 1913, which was passed by the Liberal government during the SUFFRAGETTE disturbances to avoid the imprisoned lawbreakers from achieving martyrdom through hunger strikes. They were released on licence when necessary, subject to re-arrest when their health recovered. To play cat and mouse with someone is to treat them cruelly or teasingly before a final act of cruelty. A suffragette poster of the day depicted a cat with a drooping suffragette in its mouth, like a mouse, and the caption: 'The Liberal Cat. Electors Vote Against Him! Keep the Liberal Out!'

Cat and the Canary, The. A stage thriller (1922) by John Willard (1885–1942) that has inspired a host of film adaptations and imitations. As mourners gather for the reading of a will in an old, dark house, several of them fall victim to the maniac who haunts its spooky corridors, preying on them as a cat might tease and kill a canary. Most film adaptations played the story for laughs, including the best known 1939 version, which did much to establish comedian Bob Hope as a major star.

Catbird seat. A favourable position. The American expression is said to derive from James Thurber's short story *The Catbird Seat* (1942) where the phrase 'sitting in the catbird seat' is explained as referring to a baseball player in the fortunate position of having no strikes and therefore three balls still to play. The phrase came into common usage in the 1940s when the Mississippi-born sports commentator Red Barber used it. The image is rather of a cat perched in a tree eyeing a bird below as its potential prey than of the bird actually called a catbird (*Dumetella carolinensis*).

> I get you. If we swing it, we'll be sitting pretty. In the catbird seat.
> P.G. WODEHOUSE: *Cocktail Time*, ch xiii (1958)

Cat burglar. A thief who enters a building by climbing to an upper storey. Cats are famed for their ability to negotiate heights. The term dates from the early 20th century.

> Detectives believe that a professional cat burglar carried out the theft. ... The thief reached the gallery on the first floor by crossing a series of roofs from a building site. Once above the large skylight, the burglar cut through the glass, let down a rope ladder and then climbed down.
> *The Times* (3 January 2000)

Catch a tiger by the tail, To. *See* RIDE A TIGER.

Catcher in the Rye, The. The first novel (1951) by J. D. Salinger (b.1919), about a mixed-up teenager called Holden CAULFIELD. The character first appeared in a story published in the *New Yorker* in 1946, in which year Salinger withdrew an earlier version of the book. The title of this CAMPUS CLASSIC is alluded to in ch xxii, when Holden's younger sister goads him into naming 'something you'd like to be'. It transpires that he has misread the line in the song by Robert Burns (1759–96), 'Gin a body meet a body/Comin thro' the rye', as 'catch a body':

> 'I keep picturing all these little kids playing some game in this big field of rye. ... And I'm standing on the edge of some crazy cliff. ... I have to catch

everybody if they start to go over the cliff. ... I'd just be the catcher in the rye. I know it's crazy.'

Catch-23. A colloquial term for a situation that is new to or more intricate than that of CATCH-22.

> The speech showed that Kissinger ... has come to accept what Washington insiders call the 'Catch-23' of the oil business. Put simply, the idea is that to escape the political clutches of the cartel, the West will have to develop vast new sources of energy ... The catch is that the very act of producing all this new energy may lead to a glut of oil.
>
> *Newsweek* (17 February 1975)

Catch-22. A 'no-win' situation: whichever alternative you choose, you will lose or be in trouble. *Catch-22* is the title of Joseph Heller's novel, published in 1961. The story centres on Captain Yossarian of the 256th United States (Army) bombing squadron in the Second World War, whose main aim is to avoid being killed.

> There was only one catch and that was Catch-22, which specified that a concern for one's own safety in the face of dangers that were real and immediate was the process of a rational mind. Orr was crazy and could be grounded. All he had to do was to ask; and as soon as he did, he would no longer be crazy and would have to fly more missions.
>
> ch v

Category A. In the British system of justice the highest category of security, for the most dangerous type of prisoner. Category B is for prisoners who should not be allowed to escape, C for those who are unlikely to attempt a difficult escape, and D for those suitable for open prison.

Caterpillar Club. An unofficial club started by the Irvin Parachute Company during the Second World War. The caterpillar is that of the silkworm, which supplied the material from which parachutes were formerly made. The company presented a small gold caterpillar pin to any RAF airman who had baled out in action, on his supplying the number of the parachute that had saved his life. Similarly the Goldfish Club existed for those who had been forced to resort to their rubber dinghies. Since then, similar clubs have been formed to encourage the wearing of protective clothing by industrial workers.

Cathedral of light. The lighting effects, using searchlights, designed by Hitler's personal architect, Albert Speer (1905–81), for the 1934 NUREMBERG RALLY. It was this rally that featured in Leni Reifenstahl's film, *The Triumph of the Will* (1936).

Catherine. The beautiful medieval French heroine of the somewhat salacious historical novels by Juliette Benzoni. In her adventures she meets Joan of Arc, Gilles de Rais and other memorable people of the period. The first five titles of the English translations were *One Love Is Enough* (1964), *Catherine* (1965), *Belle Catherine* (1966), *Catherine and Arnaud* and *Catherine and a Time for Love* (1968).

Cat on a Hot Tin Roof. A play (1955) by Tennessee Williams (1911–83) that was subsequently turned into a successful film (1958) starring Elizabeth Taylor, Paul Newman and Burl Ives. The title echoes the old English saying 'like a cat on hot bricks', which dates back to at least the 17th century, and this link is interestingly furthered by the fact that one of the main characters in Williams's story is named Brick. The play began life as a short story entitled 'Three Players of a Summer Game', but Williams changed it when he developed the tale for the stage, during the course of which he first introduced Brick's wife Maggie ('Maggie the Cat'). The author later explained that his own father had coined the phrase, habitually complaining to his wife that she made him 'nervous as a cat on a hot tin roof'.

Cats. A musical comedy (1981) with a score by Andrew Lloyd Webber (b.1948) in which all the main characters are cats. It was based on poems from T.S. Eliot's *Old Possum's Book of Practical Cats* (1939).

Catseyes. The proprietary name of reflective studs set in rubber pads in the road as a guide to drivers when it is dark or foggy. They were the invention in 1934 of Percy Shaw (1889–1975), when 50 were laid at Brightlington crossroads, a notorious BLACK SPOT near Bradford, Yorkshire. 'Cat's Eyes Cunningham' was the nickname given to Group Captain John Cunningham (b.1917), RAF night fighter pilot in the Second World War. Even when flying without navigational aids he managed to shoot down some 12 German aircraft.

Cat's pyjamas. Something excellent or praiseworthy. The term dates from the 1920s and is said to have been coined by the US cartoonist and sportswriter Tad Dorgan (1877–1929), who may also have originated HOT DOG and LOUNGE LIZARD, among other colourful expressions, and who certainly popularized them. A similar expression is the BEE'S KNEES. *See also* CAT'S WHISKERS.

Catsuit. A one-piece, close-fitting trouser suit, so called from its resemblance to the costume worn by a panto-mime cat.

Cat's whisker. In the old 'crystal' wireless sets or radio receivers, this was the name given to the very fine pointed wire that made contact with the crystal.

Cat's whiskers. An excellent person or thing. There is a real allusion to the whiskers of a cat, since their extreme sensitivity enable it to pass through narrow spaces in total darkness.

Cattle show. In US politics a term for a public gathering of presidential candidates running in a primary election campaign. *See also* BEAUTY CONTEST.

Catwalk. A narrow pathway or gangway over a theatre stage or along a bridge. Also an extended stage at a fashion show. Cats are able to walk safely along a raised narrow surface such as the top of a wall.

> Bare all you dare is the message from the New York catwalk.
>
> *The Times* (20 September 1999)

Caucasian Chalk Circle, The. A play (1948) by Bertolt Brecht (1898–1956), with the German title *Der kaukasische Kreidekreis*, set in Caucasia in the aftermath of the Second World War, in which the competing claims of a child's biological mother and its foster mother are decided by a bogus judge (actually a thief and poacher). The judge, Azdak, orders that the matter be settled by the two women having a tug of war with the child within a chalk circle. The foster mother lets go first, fearing the child will be hurt, thus demonstrating her greater love, and is granted custody of the child. *See also* EPIC THEATRE.

Caudillo. The title adopted by General Franco, head of the Falangist government in Spain, in imitation of Mussolini's DUCE and Hitler's FÜHRER. Like them it means 'leader'. The slogan *Una Patria, Un Estado, Un Caudillo* ('one people, one state, one leader'), in imitation of the Nazi slogan EIN VOLK, EIN REICH, EIN FÜHRER, was invented for Franco by Millán Astray (*see* GLORIOSO MUTILADO). *See also* FALANGE.

Caught with one's pants down. Caught unprepared or in an embarrassing situation. Pants (trousers) are normally lowered for two private purposes, one in the bedroom, the other in the bathroom. Despite this origin, the expression, which dates from the 1930s, is not considered vulgar. *See also* PADDY PANTSDOWN.

Caulfield, Holden. The young protagonist of J.D. Salinger's CAMPUS CLASSIC *The* CATCHER IN THE RYE (1951). He runs away from school and has a number of adventures and encounters in New York. He narrates his experiences in a part-cynical, part-innocent style and expresses his dismay at the 'phoniness' of everything. Salinger, a notorious recluse, has not permitted any film or television version of the novel to be made.

Caution. In its modern sense a formal warning given by a police officer to someone suspected of an offence. The warning in use from the 1960s was: 'You do not have to say anything unless you wish to do so but what you say may be given in evidence.' In 1995 a modified version was introduced: 'You do not have to say anything. But it may harm your defence if you do not mention when questioned something which you later rely on in court. Anything you do say may be given in evidence.'

Caution, Lemmy. The G-man hero (*see* G-MEN) of a series of pseudo-American thrillers by the British writer Peter Cheyney, beginning with *This Man is Dangerous* (1936). He is notable for his willingness to use violence and he subsequently appeared in various French films of the 1950s, as well as in Jean-Luc Godard's unusual SCIENCE FICTION movie *Alphaville* (1965), in which he is played by Eddie Constantine.

Cautionary Tales for Children. A book of comic tales in verse (1907) by the French-born British writer Hilaire Belloc (1870–1953), with illustrations by 'B.T.B.' (Belloc's friend Lord Basil Blackwood). Belloc's stories are a conscious parody of 19th-century 'Cautionary Tales', 'improving' parables intended to demonstrate the dangers that lie in wait for children who act disobediently.

In Belloc's verses an array of often minor childhood misdemeanours attract comically severe punishments. The stories include the tales of 'Jim, Who ran away from his nurse, and was eaten by a lion', 'Henry King, Who chewed bits of String, and was early cut off in Dreadful Agonies', 'Matilda, Who Told Lies, and was Burned to Death', 'Lord Lundy, Who was too Freely Moved to Tears, and thereby Ruined his Political Career', 'Rebecca, Who slammed doors for Fun and Perished Miserably' and 'George, Who played with a dangerous Toy, and suffered a Catastrophe of considerable Dimensions'. The last memorably describes the destruction of a wealthy town house and most of its residents by the explosion of a balloon purchased for George by his doting grandmother:

The Lights went out! The Windows broke!
The Room was filled with reeking smoke.
And in the darkness screams and yells
Were mingled with electric bells,
And falling masonry and groans,
And crunching, as of broken bones,
And dreadful shrieks, when, worst of all,
The house itself began to fall!
It tottered, shuddering to and fro,
Then crashed into the street below –
Which happened to be Savile Row.

Cavern Club. A cellar-club in Liverpool that owes its principal fame to the many lunch-time appearances made there by the BEATLES in the early 1960s and which led to their attracting a cult following.

C-B. A nickname for Sir Henry Campbell-Bannerman (1836–1908), British Liberal prime minister (1905–8).

CB radio. Citizens' Band radio originated in the United States in 1958 as a narrow airwave band for businesses and emergencies. It was taken up by truckdrivers in the mid-1970s and soon became a national craze, developing its own idiosyncratic language. Typically, a CB-er might broadcast the alert that there were 'smokies' (police) ahead, avoid going over 'double nickel' (55mph/88kph), and receive a '10–4' (affirmative acknowledgement). A hit song devoted to the system was 'Convoy' (1976) by the country singer C.W. McCall. Its words were in CB jargon and the record was released with a printed 'translation' so that DJs could pass on the meaning to their listeners.

CD-ROM. The abbreviation of compact disc read-only memory, as a computer-linked medium capable of storing information equivalent to about half a million pages of text (one gigabyte). The system took off from the early 1990s and has the obvious advantage of storing facts and figures that had hitherto been obtained from bulky reference works such as encyclopedias and law volumes.

Ceiling. The term is figuratively applied to the maximum height to which an aircraft can rise under certain conditions, or to an upper limit for prices or wages. In meteorology, the ceiling is the highest level from which the earth's surface can be seen, which is effectively the height of the cloud base above ground level.

Ceiling zero. An expression meaning that the clouds or mist are down to ground level.

Celie. The long-suffering heroine of Alice Walker's novel *The* COLOR PURPLE (1982). She is a black girl growing up in the American South, where she is cruelly treated by her father and her husband. She subsequently finds solace in female companionship.

Cellulite. A substance made up of fat, water and wastes that is supposed to form unsightly lumpy pockets beneath the skin or dimples on its surface like orange peel, especially on women's hips and thighs. Methods of removing it are varied but it cannot generally be burned off by dieting since it remains after slimming. The word dates from the 1970s and was coined by the French dietician Nicole Ronsard, from French *cellule*, 'cell'.

Celtic Sea. This area is formally defined as 'that part of the continental shelf lying between the 200 fathom contour, southern Ireland, the southwestern tip of Wales, Land's End and Ushant'. The term derives from the surrounding Celtic areas, i.e. Brittany, Cornwall, Wales and Ireland, and was first used by E.W.L. Holt in 1921.

Cement Garden, The. A novella (1978) by Ian McEwan (b.1948). The death of the teenage narrator's father, and then of his mother, leaves him, his two sisters and their small brother alone. Rather than tell anyone, with the risk that they will be taken into care and separated, they conceal their mother's body in the cellar in a tin trunk, filled with cement ('the cement garden'). A gamut of sexual deviation propels the action to its dark denouement. An unsettling film version (1993) was directed by Andrew Birkin.

Cenotaph (Greek *kenotaphion*, from *kenos*, 'empty', and *taphos*, 'tomb'). A monument raised to the memory of a person or persons buried elsewhere. By far the most noteworthy to the British is that in Whitehall, designed by Sir Edwin Lutyens, which was dedicated on 11 November 1920 to those who fell in the First World War. It is a slightly curved block of Portland stone, adorned with the flags of the three services and the merchant navy, and with the simple inscription 'To the Glorious Dead'. It has since been adapted to commemorate the fallen of the Second World War.

Central Powers. A term for the coalition in the First World War formed mainly of the German Empire and Austria–Hungary, as the 'central' European states that were at war from 1914 against France and Britain on the WESTERN FRONT and against Russia on the Eastern Front. *See also* SARAJEVO.

Centrefold. A printed and usually illustrated sheet that has been folded to form the centre spread of a magazine. The term was extended to the model, usually naked or at best skimpily clad, whose photograph features there. This sense became specifically associated with Hugh Hefner's PLAYBOY, where the spread first appeared in February 1954, the subject being Margaret Scott.

> The concept of the centerfold became world famous and added a new word to the language. 'Centerfold' became another way of referring to a picture of a beautiful girl, just as 'pin-up' had the decade before.
>
> HUGH HEFNER in GRETCHEN EDGREN: *The Playmate Book*, Introduction (1996)

Centre 42. An organization of writers, painters, composers, actors and others set up by the playwright Arnold Wesker in 1961 to promote festivals of the arts, exhibitions of craft work and other activities designed for working people. It had trade union support and took its name from the numerical position it held on the agenda of a trades union meeting that solicited greater union involvement in artistic work. Its base was the building that became the ROUND HOUSE theatre. It closed in 1970.

Century of the Common Man. The 20th century, the age of democracy. *The Century of the Common Man* (1940) was the title of a book by Henry A. Wallace, vice-president of the United States (1941–5) under F.D. Roosevelt. The phrase speedily became popular on both sides of the Atlantic and was much favoured by Nancy, Viscountess Astor.

Cha-cha or **Cha-cha-cha.** This popular dance of the 1950s, like the MAMBO from which it evolved, was of Latin American origin. Its small steps and swaying hip movements, as well as its infectious music, made it a craze on both sides of the Atlantic.

Chad or **Mr Chad.** A character whose bald head and large nose were depicted appearing over a wall and inquiring, 'Wot, no [word filled in to suit the circumstances]?', as a comment on a shortage of some commodity during and after the Second World War. Chad was particularly popular among the forces and offered scope for light relief in many a difficult situation. He was the creation in 1938 of the cartoonist 'Chat' (George Edward Chatterton). *See also* GRAFFITI; KILROY.

Chaff. In modern usage, 'chaff' was adopted in the Second World War as a term for the thin strips of metallic foil that were released into the atmosphere from aircraft to deflect radar signals and prevent detection. The strips were scattered in the air like chaff blown in the wind.

Chain letter. A letter, frequently anonymous, that the recipient is asked to copy and send to a stated number of friends or acquaintances, requesting them to do likewise, the aim being to secure a large sum of money or some other material reward. The pernicious practice seems to have begun at the turn of the 20th century, and the *Daily Chronicle* for 27 July 1906 tells how a Miss Audrey Griffin of Hurstville, New South Wales, Australia, initiated such a letter with the aim of collecting a million used postage stamps. By the end of the century the chain letter had become a chain E-MAIL, and *The Times* of 13 May 1999 relates how a brewer offered to give away 2 million SIX-PACKS for the MILLENNIUM if a message by this method reached the same number of recipients. The initiator was purportedly one Gary D. Anderson, but no such person existed.

Chain reaction. A series of events in which each event is caused by the previous one. The expression is of scientific origin, applied first in the 1920s to a chemical reaction in which the products themselves promote the reaction, which may in some cases accelerate dramatically, and second in the 1940s to a process of nuclear fission that occurs in nuclear reactors and bombs.

Chain smoker. One who smokes continuously, lighting a new cigarette from the one being finished, so that they form a chain. The term dates from the 1930s.

Chalet School. The fictional international school in the Austrian Tyrol that features in a series of girls' stories by Elinor Brent-Dyer (1895–1969). The first in the series was *The School at the Chalet* (1925); the last, published posthumously, was *Prefects of the Summer School* (1970).

Chalk and talk. The traditional method of teaching, with the teacher using the blackboard to illustrate what he says, as distinct from more informal or interactive methods. The phrase dates from the 1930s or even earlier.

Challenged. A word used euphemistically to indicate that a person has a disability or impairment in a particular respect, its precise application being indicated by a preceding adverb. The original intention was to introduce a term that was more positive than 'handicapped' or 'disabled' in an expression such as 'physically challenged'. The usage was mocked by the media, however, who applied it whimsically to other areas, so that a short person was 'vertically challenged', one with bad teeth was 'dentally challenged', and a bald man was 'follicularly challenged'. The original usage arose in the United States in the 1980s. *See also* POLITICAL CORRECTNESS.

> [The US television series] *Freaks [and Geeks]* tells it like it really was, giving centre stage to the misfits, losers and athletically challenged.
>
> *heat* (23–29 September 1999)

Challenger. The name of the US space shuttle that on 28 January 1986 exploded 73 seconds after blast-off from Cape Canaveral, instantly killing all seven astronauts, including a high-school teacher, Christa McAuliffe, the first private citizen to take part in the US shuttle programme. The American public was shocked to see such a disaster take place live on their TV screens but was comforted by the words of the GREAT COMMUNICATOR, President Ronald Reagan, who in a national television broadcast quoted (without crediting his source) from the 1941 sonnet 'High Flight' by John Gillespie Magee (1922–41), a US-born pilot who served with the Royal Canadian Air Force in the Second World War and who died while on a bombing raid over Germany:

> Oh! I have slipped the surly bonds of earth,
> And danced the skies on laughter-silvered wings …
> And, while with silent lifting mind I've trod
> The high, untrespassed sanctity of space,
> Put out my hand and touched the face of God.

The inquiry into the disaster, headed by the distinguished physicist and Nobel laureate Richard Feynman (1918–88), found that the rubber seals in the booster rocket had failed because of low overnight temperatures on the Cape the night before launch. The shuttle programme was suspended for two years until the fault was rectified.

Challenger, Professor. The irascible black-bearded scientist created by Arthur Conan Doyle as the central character of his novel *The Lost World* (1912). Together with the explorer Lord John Roxton and the young newspaper reporter Edward Malone he goes in search of MAPLE WHITE LAND, where they discover living dinosaurs and ape-men. He subsequently appeared in two further novels, *The Poison Belt* (1913) and *The Land of Mist* (1926).

Chambersisms. Such may be called the idiosyncratic

definitions that have regularly appeared in the various editions of *Chambers Dictionary* since its original publication in 1901. Their number has declined over the years, presumably under the constraints of POLITICAL CORRECTNESS or simply on grounds of accuracy, but the following remain in the 1998 edition:

> *double-locked*: locked by two turns of the key, as in some locks and many novels
>
> *éclair*: a cake, long in shape but short in duration
>
> *he-man*: a man of exaggerated or extreme virility, or what some women consider to be virility
>
> *Japanese cedar*: a very tall Japanese conifer (*Cryptomeria japonica*) often dwarfed by Japanese gardeners
>
> *jaywalker*: a careless pedestrian whom motorists are expected to avoid running down
>
> *middle-aged*: between youth and old age, variously reckoned to suit the reckoner
>
> *Pict*: one of a dwarfish race of underground dwellers, to whom (with the Romans, the Druids and Cromwell) ancient monuments are generally attributed
>
> *picture restorer*: a person who cleans and tries to restore old pictures
>
> *sea serpent*: an enormous marine animal of serpent-like form frequently seen and described by credulous sailors, imaginative landsmen and common liars

Champagne socialist. A person who practises and advocates socialist beliefs while patently seen to be a consumer of the best things in life. The writer John Mortimer (b.1923), the Labour MP Barbara Follett (b.1942) and the newspaper tycoon Robert Maxwell (1923–91) are examples of the type cited in the media. The term came to be more generally associated with the NEW LABOUR image promoted by Tony Blair following the 1997 general election. *See also* LIMOUSINE LIBERAL.

> In a time which has given bachelors a bad name, he [Labour MP Frank Field] has preserved his good one. In a party of champagne socialists, he is the champagne monk.
>
> *The Times* (31 July 1998)

Champers and hampers. Champagne and choice comestibles, especially when consumed to mark a special occasion or celebrate a victory.

> Lawrie Mayer, Mr Al Fayed's media spokesman, broke the news by telephone. 'It's champers and

hampers,' an elated Mr Al Fayed bellowed in reply. 'Christmas has come early.'

The Times (22 December 1999)

Chan, Charlie. The Chinese-American detective who works for the Honolulu Police was created by the US writer Earl D. Biggers and first appeared in *The House Without a Key* (1925). He is wise and impassive and solves many murder mysteries, usually with the help of his 'Number-One Son'. He went on to feature in a number of popular films and was memorably played by the Swedish actor Warner Oland in *Charlie Chan Carries On* (1931) and its many sequels. His adventures on British television in the 1950s were rather less successful.

Chance would be a fine thing. If only... . A phrase expressing the speaker's regret that the desired opportunity is unlikely to present itself. The expression is a stock reply by a married woman to a single who says that she does not wish to marry.

> I am a smug married. But in case you thought that I had entirely retreated into the couple's world of John Lewis, joint accounts and Saturday nights in, let me add that chance would be a fine thing.
>
> *The Times* (26 May 1999)

Changi. A notorious Japanese prisoner of war camp in the Second World War, near the town of this name in eastern occupied Singapore. In 1945 the prisoners were released by the British, who stripped the Japanese guards of their uniforms and made them kneel naked and kowtowing in submission before the liberators.

Channel Tunnel. A plan to link Britain and France by a tunnel under the English Channel had been discussed long before 1986, when an Anglo-French agreement was signed and work began. French and British teams met up in 1990 and the official opening took place in 1994, attended by Queen Elizabeth II and President Mitterrand of France. The route runs from Folkestone to Sangatte near Calais and there are three tunnels, each 50km (31 miles) long, two for rail traffic and a third in the centre for services and security. The enterprise has been not without cost. Six British workers died during construction, and a fire closed the tunnel for two weeks in 1996.

Chaos theory. A branch of mathematics that deals with so-called chaotic systems, an example of one such system being a engineered structure such as an oil platform that is subjected to irregular and unpredict-

able wave stress. The science is also sometimes known as chaology. *See also* BUTTERFLY EFFECT.

Chaplinesque. In the style of the highly popular film actor Charlie Chaplin (1889–1977), whose roles usually involved an affecting blend of comedy and pathos, especially in the depiction of unrequited love. His most memorable character and mythic alter ego was the Tramp.

Chappaquiddick. A tiny island off the Massachusetts coast that gained worldwide notoriety on 18 July 1969 when Senator Edward Kennedy, brother of the late President John F. Kennedy, was involved in an accident in which a 28-year-old woman, Mary Jo Kopechne, was trapped and drowned when a car he was driving ran off a small bridge. After an initial attempt to conceal the whole incident, Kennedy was eventually exonerated, despite a legal ruling that he had probably been driving negligently and had thus contributed to Miss Kopechne's death. Popular opinion claimed that Kennedy had escaped penalty through his social standing and political power, and the whole episode left a bitter taste in the mouth of the US public. *See also* KENNEDY CURSE.

Chariots Offiah. The rugby league and union wing Martin Offiah (b.1966). His nickname, punning on the title of the film CHARIOTS OF FIRE, reflects his speed and strength as a runner.

Chariots of Fire. A film (1981) about the rivalry between two British runners competing in the 1924 Olympics. Written by Colin Welland (b.1934) and starring Ben Cross and Ian Charleson, it featured a memorable soundtrack by Vangelis, which quickly became a signature tune for sporting enthusiasts everywhere. The title came from William Blake's poem 'Jerusalem', the preface to his epic poem *Milton* (1804–08), which is best known today as an anthemic hymn with strong patriotic overtones:

> Bring me my bow of burning gold!
> Bring me my arrows of desire!
> Bring me my spear! O clouds, unfold!
> Bring me my chariot of fire!
> WILLIAM BLAKE: 'Jerusalem'

Charismatic movement. A fundamentalist movement within many leading Christian churches that emphasizes group worship and the exercise of the spiritual 'gifts' of divine healing and glossolalia, or 'speaking in tongues'. It began in North America in the 1960s and is now worldwide. It has much in common with Pentecostalism, although since the 1970s its 'enthusiastic' features have become less evident. By the early 1980s it had become one of the main lay movements in the Roman Catholic Church, as well as the Church of England, and was recognized as such by the Vatican. Underlying the movement is an implicit understanding of 'charisma' itself as a word that in the original Greek means 'gift of grace'.

Charleston. A dance popular in the first half of the 1920s, apparently originating as a back-kicking dance among young blacks in South Carolina, where Charleston is the main seaport. Dancers swivelled on the balls of their feet, swayed their body from side to side and knocked their knees with their hands in a furious frenzy, motions condemned by some killjoys as 'immoral'.

Charlie. See VICTOR CHARLIE.

Charlie and the Chocolate Factory. A fantasy novel (1964) by Roald Dahl (1916–90), in which Charlie Buckett wins a ticket that allows him to visit a chocolate factory owned by Mr Willy Wonka and manned by pygmies called Oompa-Loompas. It was filmed as *Willy Wonka and the Chocolate Factory* (1971), with Gene Wilder as Willy Wonka.

Charlie's Angels. A popular US television crime drama series screened from 1977 to 1982. It centred on three glamorous PRIVATE EYES, played by Farrah Fawcett-Majors, Kate Jackson and Jaclyn Smith, who are sent out 'crime-busting' by Charlie Townsend, the wealthy head of Townsend Investigations. The series was derided by many for its blatant sexism, and each episode opened with the following foreword: 'Once upon a time there were three little girls who went to the police academy and they were each assigned very hazardous duties, but I took them away from all that and they now work for me. My name is Charlie.' Viewers never saw Charlie, who communicated with his trio by office intercom.

Charm and cheek. A disarming combination of 'niceness and nerve' that is popularly believed to enhance a person's prospects in an enterprise, especially in politics. *See also* CHARM OFFENSIVE.

> If charm and cheek were the sole qualifications for public office the Labour Party would have no need for any cumbersome electoral college in London: Ken Livingstone would be selected by acclamation.
> *The Times* (9 November 1999)

Charm bracelet. A bracelet hung with charms, as small ornaments or trinkets fancifully believed to protect the wearer on the one hand and attract admirers on the other.

Charm offensive. The calculated use of personal charm or assumed amiability to achieve a particular end, especially in politics. The expression dates from the 1970s. *See also* CHARM AND CHEEK.

> The BBC's marketing department is launching a 'charm offensive' to persuade Greg Dyke, Director-General-in-waiting, that its job is worth doing.
> *The Times* (19 November 1999)

Charm school. An educational establishment where young women are taught social graces such as deportment and etiquette. Such schools burgeoned in the 1950s at a time when the Western world was anxious to return to civilized values after the brutalization and degradation of the Second World War.

Charter 88. A pressure group that in 1988 published a document arguing that several specific reforms were needed in Britain. Among them were a written constitution, a bill of rights, devolution to a Scottish assembly, proportional representation and freedom of information. Some of these aims are no longer mere aspirations. In 1993 a private member's Freedom of Information bill came before parliament, proportional representation was adopted for the European elections of 1999, and that same year more significantly saw the opening of a Scottish parliament. The group's name relates both to the year in which its charter appeared and to 1688, the year of the Glorious Revolution, which introduced constitutional monarchy.

Charter 77. A petition drawn up in Czechoslovakia in January 1977 by a group of intellectuals, listing their grievances over the human-rights abuses of the communist regime. Many of the signatories were subsequently detained by the authorities, but the group remained active over the next decade or so, and played a key role in the VELVET REVOLUTION that toppled the communist regime in late 1989. Among the signatories was the playwright Václav Havel (b.1936), who during the revolution became spokesman for the main opposition group, Civic Forum, and by the end of the year had become president.

Chase one's tail, To. To indulge in a futile pursuit; to go round in circles. Dogs when excited or frenzied may literally chase their tails. The expression dates from the 1960s.

Chase the dragon, To. To smoke HEROIN. The drug is placed on a folded piece of tinfoil, which is heated with a taper. As the fumes are inhaled through a tube or roll of paper, they waft up and down the tinfoil with movements resembling the undulating tail of a dragon. Hence the term, reputedly translated from the Chinese.

Chat room. An area on the INTERNET or other computer network where users can communicate with one another, typically on a particular topic.

Chatterbox. A British children's magazine published between 1866 and 1948. Its contents included a mixture of 'improving' material such as factual articles and religious instruction.

Chattering classes. A slighting term for educated people, especially those in academic, artistic or media circles, who enjoy 'chattering' in print on issues of topical interest. The implication is that although writing extensively on such matters they have little or no first-hand knowledge of them. The phrase dates from the early 1980s, when it mainly applied to city-oriented, left-wing intelligentsia, who held forth over the dinner table. *See also* HAMPSTEAD SET.

> Who are these 'chattering classes'? … This phrase, like 'PC', is now common in Australia – used by the lazy and arrogant to abuse people and ideas they don't like without having to justify their contempt.
>
> *Times Literary Supplement* (Letter to the Editor)
> (15 January 1999)

Chatterley, Lady. The repressed aristocratic woman who finds sexual release with her gamekeeper, Oliver Mellors, in D.H. Lawrence's often misunderstood novel LADY CHATTERLEY'S LOVER (1928). Her name subsequently entered the language as something of a smutty joke. She is said to have been based on Lady Cynthia Asquith (1887–1960).

Chat-up line. An enquiry or remark used as a flirtatious or seductive gambit, such as the hackneyed 'Do you come here often?'

> The Shaftesbury Theatre is hosting a singles night for its musical *Rent*, a chance for audiences in search of a partner to try their best chat-up lines.
>
> *The Times* (6 September 1999)

Cheap and cheerful. Simple and inexpensive but not unattractive, as of a garment or fashion detail but also applied to a restaurant.

> 'There has been an absolute change in the way customers react … In the past they expected to go either

somewhere cheap and cheerful for low prices or somewhere else for quality. Now they see low prices as consistent with good quality and service.'
>
> *Sunday Times* (20 June 1999)

Check. An exclamation of assent or agreement, with a sense on the lines of 'OK', 'That's right' or 'Just as I thought'. It is of US origin and dates from the 1920s.

> The main murder victim is someone disliked by many people with varied motives. Check. Poirot sports foolish facial fur and refers to himself in the third person. Check. Someone with vital information gets a knife in the neck, just as they are about to blab. Check.
>
> *heat* (review of television drama *Poirot: Lord Edgware Dies*)
> (17–23 February 2000)

Check out the plumbing, To. A US euphemism, one of many, meaning to visit the toilet.

Checkpoint Charlie. The most notorious of the official crossing-points between East and West Berlin, at the junction of Friedrichstrasse and Kochstrasse in the US sector. It took its name from the NATO phonetic code for the letter C as it was the third crossing point in order. The others were Checkpoint Alpha, at Helmstedt-Marienborn, and Checkpoint Bravo, at Dreilinden-Drewitz. Checkpoint Charlie was the only crossing-point to be open round the clock. It became familiar to the public at large as much from spy fiction and thrillers such as Len Deighton's *Funeral in Berlin* (1965) as from its real existence in the COLD WAR. It was dismantled in 1990. *See also* BERLIN WALL.

Cheeky Chappie. A billboard byname for the comedian Max Miller, whose original name was Thomas Henry Sargent (1894–1963), alluding to his JACK THE LAD persona and his love of innuendo and double entendres. His PLUS FOURS, black and white CO-RESPONDENT SHOES, snow-white HOMBURG and gaudy KIPPER TIE enhanced his brash image.

Cheerio! Goodbye! A parting expression of good wishes dating from the early years of the 20th century. The word derives from 'to cheer' in the sense 'to take courage', but later became associated with 'cheery'. A use as a friendly wish before drinking was also current but has now been largely superseded by 'cheers!'

> And 'cheerioh' and 'cheeri-bye'
> Across the waste of waters die.
>
> JOHN BETJEMAN: *New Bats in Old Belfries*, 'Henley-on-Thames' (1945)

Cheerleaders. In the United States a team of girls who as their name implies 'lead the cheers' or perform organized cheering, chanting and dancing in support of a sports team at a match. Every high school has such a team, with members chosen for their looks, ability and enthusiasm, and professional sports teams have similar supporters in the form of well-paid dancers. Their colourful costumes with eye-catching MINI-SKIRTS or HOT PANTS provide much of the attraction. The cheerleaders of the Dallas Cowboys American football team are particularly noted for their poise and panache.

Cheese and wine party. A social gathering at which cubelets of cheese and glasses of wine are served but where the emphasis is on business rather than pleasure, as at a fundraising event.

> The disclosure of Mr Dyke's presence at the most expensive cheese and wine party in British political history will be seized on by opponents of his candidacy within the BBC.
> *The Times* (17 May 1999)

Cheesecake. Pictures or photographs of women displayed for their sex appeal (*see* BEEFCAKE). A literal cheesecake is a type of rich tart, filled with a mixture of cream cheese, cream, sugar, and sometimes fruit, with or without a fruit topping. The colloquial equation of sweet and succulent food with attractive women is common. This particular example dates from the 1930s, while others are 'cookie', 'crumpet' and 'cupcake'. *See also* TWINKIE.

Cheesed off. Fed up, disgusted, disgruntled, like milk that has gone sour in the process of becoming cheese. *See also* BROWNED OFF.

Cheka. *See* KGB.

Chelm. The fictional Jewish town that is the setting of Samuel Tenenbaum's novel *The Wise Men of Chelm* (1965). It is probably in the former USSR, although held by some authorities to be connected with the real city of the same name in eastern Poland. It has a magnificent but windowless town hall and horses and carts go along the pavements while pedestrians walk in the streets. The logic for the latter is simple. Human beings are more important than animals and so should have the wider walkway. The inhabitants of Chelm have a foolproof method of distinguishing a drake from a duck. They throw the bird a piece of bread. If he runs after it, it is a drake, but if she runs after it, it is a duck.

Chelsea Flower Show. An annual summer display organized by the Royal Horticultural Society in the grounds of the Royal Hospital, Chelsea, since 1913. The exhibits range from prize vegetables to whole gardens, all housed on the 4.5ha (11 acres) of lawn. Opening night is a major occasion, attended by the royal family and other celebrities. The event lasts four days and on the final day a bell is rung at 5 p.m., when remaining exhibits are sold to the public.

Chemin des Dames (French, 'Ladies' Way'). A ridge between the rivers Aisne and Ailette in northern France that was the scene of desperate fighting in the First World War. On 16 April 1917 the French advance under General Nivelle met with failure here after earlier successes at Laffaux, Hurtebise and Berry-au-Bac, in which French tanks were used for the first time, and on 27 May 1918 the German advance towards the Marne under General Ludendorff finally won through here. The ridge itself, an old Roman road, is said to take its name from the daughters of Louis XV (1710–74), the 'Ladies of France'. *See also* TIGER.

Cheongsam (Chinese, 'long dress'). A figure-hugging traditional Chinese dress that came into vogue among Western women in the mid-1990s as stylish evening wear. It is usually made from lustrous flower-patterned silk, closed in front by a 'frog' closure and topped with a round mandarin collar.

Cheque-book journalism. A phrase first current in the 1960s for the practice of securing exclusive rights to newspaper stories by offering large sums of money to anyone who can provide them, with scant regard for any ethical or moral considerations.

> Newspapers ... should ... come to a self-denying ordinance to abandon the cheque-book journalism of confession stories by criminals, prominent divorcees and others who have won notoriety.
> *New Statesman* (24 May 1963)

Cheque is in the post, The. A time-honoured excuse for failure to make a payment.

> When you are owed £200, you hear that great lie about the cheque being in the post a lot. When you are owed £20,000, the cheque is posted early. £2 million and they will probably send it by courier with a bouquet.
> *The Times* (17 January 2000)

Chequers. The official country residence of the prime minister, in the Chilterns near Wendover, Buckinghamshire, was presented to the nation for this purpose by Lord Lee of Fareham in 1917 and was first so used by Lloyd George in 1921. The house itself is Tudor in origin but with Victorian additions and substantial remodelling by Lee over the period 1909–12. Its formal name is Chequers Court and the Tudor house was built on the site of a 13th-century one owned by Laurence de Scaccario, whose own name probably meant that he was an official of the medieval Court of Exchequer, the court of law that dealt with matters of revenue. 'Scaccario' was thus rendered as the medieval equivalent of modern 'Exchequer' and subsequently shortened to 'Chequers'. The history of the name is in the event appropriate, since the prime minister is also First Lord of the Treasury.

Cherished number. A vehicle registration number that has been specially selected by the vehicle's owner to represent some personal whim or characteristic, as expressed by a legally prescribed combination and arrangement of letters and figures. The latter are often exploited as letters, so that 0 is O, 1 is I or L, 2 is Z, 5 is S, 6 is G, 13 is B and so on. CLA 55Y could thus be seen as 'classy'. The most common device is to represent one's own name or initials.

A pioneer of the game was the Scottish comedian Harry Tate (1872–1940) who had T8 on his old Ford. Lord Brabazon of Tara (1884–1964), the first pilot to obtain the Royal Aero Club Flying Certificate, later secured FLY1, while Brigadier-General A.C. Critchley (1890–1963) acquired all the numbers GRA1 to GRA36 for himself and his Greyhound Racing Association colleagues. Celebrities continue to adopt the dodge, so that the comedian Jimmy Tarbuck is COM 1C, and when the flamboyant Conservative MP Jeffrey Archer made his first appearance in Parliament in 1969 his personalized number plate was SOM 1 while that of his wife was ANY 1. Cars of ambassadors and high commissioners in Britain usually have a registration number 1 before or after the country's abbreviated name. Thus Australia has AUS 1, Canada has CAN 1, France has FRA 1, Norway has 1 NWY and so on. Spain, truer to the spirit, has SPA 1N. *See also* NAB; VANITY PLATE.

Chernobyl. A town near Kiev, Ukraine, where the world's worst nuclear accident occurred on 26 April 1986. Huge amounts of radioactive material were released into the atmosphere when one of the nuclear power station's four reactors exploded during attempts to install a safety system. The accident caused the deaths of 30 and radiation sickness among a further 200, some of whom later died. The radioactivity was spread by the wind over Belarus and Ukraine and traces of it reached as far as France and Italy. The disaster dealt a grave blow to the Soviet Union's nuclear power programme.

Cherry on the cake. The finishing touch to something that is already agreeable. An iced cake is often decorated with a single cherry on top.

Cherry reds. A colloquial term for DOC MARTENS or BOVVER BOOTS, especially those of this colour worn by a SKINHEAD as part of his 'uniform'.

> Their [skinheads'] hair is shaved within an eighth of an inch from the scalp, and they are dressed in oversized workpants, thin red suspenders and hobnailed, steeltoed boots costing about $10 and known as 'cherry reds'.
> *Time* (8 June 1970)

Chew the carpet, To. To lose emotional control; to suffer a tantrum. The image is of a person falling to the floor and biting the carpet in anger or frustration. The expression is of US origin and dates from the 1950s.

> He won't chew the carpet, but Sir Neil Cossons will still radicalize English Heritage.
> *Sunday Times* (5 December 1999)

Chiantishire. A media name for the area of Tuscany in Italy where Chianti wine is produced, especially in its role as a holiday resort for the English middle classes, who may even purchase a home there. The term is sometimes attributed to the writer and barrister John Mortimer (b.1923).

> The British are coming, flooding into Pisa airport, known as Pizza to the BA hostesses. They're invading Tuscany, part of Italy which has become part of England, so that it's known as Chiantishire to the natives.
> JOHN MORTIMER in *Mortimer in Tuscany* (television programme) (17 May 1988)

Chicago Bears. A record-breaking professional American football team, with a home base at Wrigley Field, Chicago. They hold the record for the greatest number of consecutive wins, 18 (twice), in the National Football League, and their star player, George Blanda, played in a record 340 games in a record 26 seasons between 1949 and 1958.

Chicago Seven. The seven defendants convicted in 1970 of conspiracy to incite a riot following disturbances during the Democratic National Convention at Chicago in 1968: Rennie David, David T. Dellinger, John Froines, Thomas Hayden, Abbie Hoffman, Jerry C. Rubin and Lee Weiner. They were originally dubbed the Chicago Eight but an eighth defendant,

Bobby Seale, was tried separately. The name set a pattern for subsequent groups of protesters or activists, especially when allegedly wrongly convicted. *See also* BIRMINGHAM SIX; GUILDFORD FOUR; WINCHESTER THREE.

Chicken à la King. Cooked chicken breast served in a cream sauce with mushrooms and peppers. The name is said to compliment E. Clark King, the New York hotel proprietor who devised the dish at the turn of the 20th century.

Chicken-and-egg situation. An unresolved problem as to which of two things caused the other. The allusion is to the old riddle: 'Which came first, the chicken or the egg?' If the answer is 'chicken', then how was it hatched? If the answer is 'egg', then how was it laid? 'Chicken-and-egg' in this sense arose in the 1950s. An earlier equivalent dating from the 1930s was 'hen-and-egg'.

Chicken Kiev. Chicken breast fried or baked and filled with garlic butter. The dish first emerged in the 1960s and was one of the first successful supermarket ready-made meals. The original name was chicken cutlet Kiev, translating Russian *kotlety po kievski*, 'cutlets in the Kiev manner'.

Chicken out, To. To back down through fear or loss of nerve. The chicken is traditionally regarded as a nervous or cowardly creature. Hens will flee clucking in panic if approached unless the approacher is bringing their regular feed.

Chicken run. A term of the mid-1990s for the abandonment by a sitting MP of a marginal seat for a safer one. The specific application was to Conservative MPs who fled to safer seats in this way in anticipation of a rough ride in the forthcoming general election (1997). The phrase puns on 'chicken' in the sense of coward, a chicken run normally being an enclosure for domestic fowls. An earlier chicken run existed as a derisory term used in Rhodesia (now Zimbabwe) for the flight from the country of whites in the 1970s in anticipation of black rule.

Chicken Soup with Barley. A play (1958) by the British playwright Arnold Wesker (b.1932) about the life of the Jewish Kahn family in East London in the 1930s. The first part of a trilogy, completed by *Roots* (1959) and *I'm Talking About Jerusalem* (1960), in which the central theme is that of caring, the play owed its title to the chicken soup young Ada Kahn is brought by a kind neighbour when she is ill.

Chick flick. A colloquialism for a TEARJERKER with an all-female cast and a story line involving much expression of emotion, mainly in the form of weeping, laughing, hugging and the like. Examples of such films, also known as 'sisterhood dramas', are *Boys on the Side* (1995), *The First Wives Club* (1996), *A Thousand Acres* (1997) and *Hanging Up* (1999).

> The actress's [Diane Keaton's] most beloved vehicle for her emoting talents – the out and out 'chick flick' – is of no interest to the studio executive boys' club.
> *The Times* (21 February 2000)

Chick index. A sexist colloquialism for the degree to which attractive and desirable young women are represented in an organization, especially one that is usually male-dominated.

> The conference 'chick index' is based on the theory that the upward mobility of a party can be gauged by the quality of the female interest.
> *Sunday Times* (10 October 1999)

Chief, The. The nickname of Herbert Hoover (1874–1964), 31st US president. The hardly original name for a boss or leader here specifically related to Hoover's influence as secretary of commerce (1917–21). The public appearance of a US president is traditionally greeted with 'Hail to the Chief', James Sanderson's music to verses from Sir Walter Scott's *The Lady of the Lake* (1810), beginning with the line: 'Hail to the Chief who in triumph advances!'

Chien Andalou, Un. *See* SURREALISM.

Child-bearing hips. Broad hips, which in a girl or young woman popularly promise the birth of several children. The term is really a misnomer, since all girls at puberty develop wider hips than boys to provide for the future bearing of children.

Child of Our Time, A. A wartime oratorio by Michael Tippett (1905–98) with a libretto by the composer. The work was written in 1939–41 and first performed in 1944. The 'child' of the title is Herschel Grynszpan, a Polish-Jewish student whose assassination in Paris of the German diplomat Ernst vom Rath on 7 November 1938 led to *Kristallnacht*, a night of violence against Jews and their property in Germany (*see* HOLOCAUST). Escalating official persecution followed. Tippett uses Negro spirituals at important points in the score, as Bach had used chorales in his Passions.

Children of a Lesser God. A play (1979) by the US playwright Mark Medoff (b.1940) about the efforts of a hearing therapist to develop a relationship with a profoundly deaf young woman who refuses all offers of help. The title comes from Tennyson:

> For why is all around us here
> As if some lesser god had made the world,
> But had not force to shape it as he would.
>
> *Idylls of the King*, 'The Passing of Arthur' (1869)

Children of all ages. Everyone, including adults. A jocular formula popular with local radio broadcasters and first current in the 1950s. 'From nine to ninety' is sometimes added.

> Obscenities are so frequently used on television that they are regarded as acceptable parlance; children of all ages and classes use obscene language in public.
>
> *Daily Telegraph* (Letter to the Editor) (16 May 1994)

Children of God. A controversial religious group that grew out of the JESUS MOVEMENT of the 1960s. It was founded in 1968 in California by David Berg and from the first its DROPOUT members adopted a strict communal lifestyle. Centres were set up in cities across the United States, but then some of the 'Children' made their way to London, and the group set up its headquarters there in 1971, using donated properties. The 'communities' or colonies formed the foundation of the group's activities and total commitment was required by each member. Emphasis was placed on the sharing of everything, and all members were expected to give up their personal possessions in accordance with the teaching of Jesus. Their political platform was 'godly socialism' and their creed that the world was in the 'last days'. The collapse of America in particular was prophesied.

Children's Corner. The set of six charming piano pieces by Claude Debussy (1862–1918) was dedicated to his daughter and written in 1906–8. The titles of the pieces are in English, presumably influenced by the family's English governess. The first piece is 'Doctor Gradus ad Parnassum', a parody of a series of studies by Clementi from 1817 (*Gradus ad Parnassum* is Latin for 'steps to Parnassus', the home of the classical Greek muses); the other pieces are 'Jimbo's Lullaby' (thought to be an error for 'Jumbo', given that Jimbo is a toy elephant), 'Serenade for the Doll', 'The Snow is Dancing', 'The Little Shepherd' and 'Golliwogg's Cakewalk'. A cakewalk was a kind of black American competitive dance with complex steps, for which a cake was awarded as a prize, and the 'Golliwogg's Cakewalk' includes a satirical musical quotation from Wagner's love-and-death music drama, *Tristan und Isolde* (1865).

Children's Hour. The popular radio programme for children was broadcast continuously by the BBC from 1922, the first year of its existence, to 1964. It went out early each weekday evening and for many years had regional editions. Its presenters came to seem like members of the family, and were accordingly known as Aunt or Uncle. The best known was Uncle Mac, in real life Derek McCulloch (1897–1967), and it was he who played LARRY THE LAMB in the programme's famous TOYTOWN. There were protests from adults and children alike when the programme was brought to an end, but audiences were falling as a result of the rise of television and the success of programmes such as BLUE PETER. The 'hour' of the title was not intended literally and the programme lasted a true hour for only two years The title itself came from the first verse of a poem by Longfellow:

> Between the dark and the daylight,
> When the night is beginning to lower,
> Comes a pause in the day's occupations,
> That is known as the Children's Hour.
>
> H.W. LONGFELLOW: *Birds of Passage*, Flight the Second, 'The Children's Hour' (1860)

Children's Hour, The. A play (1934) by US playwright Lillian Hellman (1905–84) about the scandal that erupts after a teacher is accused of lesbianism by a revengeful pupil. Filmed in 1936, the play was based on an a real case that was reported in Scotland in the 19th century, pointed out to the author by her close friend, the crime novelist Dashiell Hammett.

Children's Newspaper, The. A newspaper for children published from 22 March 1919 until 1 May 1965 and edited by Arthur Mee (1875–1943) until his death. Mee was also editor of *The Children's Encyclopaedia*, also published by Alfred Harmsworth's (Lord Northcliffe's) Amalgamated Press. Like *The Children's Encyclopaedia*, *The Children's Newspaper* concentrated on stories of heroism and individual achievement and also featured serial stories, photo pages and maps.

Chill out, To. To relax; to take it easy. The phrase was originated by black US teenagers in the 1970s but later spread to blacks and whites on both sides of the Atlantic. The concept is of being COOL.

> Tammy's dad gives us a lift back to her house for about 2.30am and if we're lucky he brings a curry. Then we chill out, drink the half bottle of vodka left … and eventually go to sleep.
>
> *The Times* (5 June 1999)

Chilly bom-bom. A pleasant phrase to indicate that it is unpleasantly cold. The words come from Cliff Friend's song 'I Love My Chili Bom-Bom' (1923), which also gave the name of the actress Chili Bouchier (1909–99), born Dorothy Boucher, on beginning her career as a teenage model.

Chinaman. A cricketing term (not to be confused with GOOGLY) denoting an offbreak bowled by a left-handed bowler to a right-handed batsman. It is said that the name derives from the Trinidadian bowler Ellis Achong (1904–86), who, although he played for the West Indies, was actually Chinese and who practised this kind of bowling, although not the first to do so. The term first became current in the 1930s.

China syndrome. A hypothetical series of events following the meltdown of a nuclear reactor, the fantastic premise being that the meltdown would pass through the earth's core from the United States and come out on the opposite side of the world in China. The term was popularized by the film *The China Syndrome* (1979) about attempts to conceal a nuclear danger, and the catastrophe at CHERNOBYL in 1986 gave it greater relevance.

No-one was yet mentioning the words 'China Syndrome', but US nuclear power industry regulators have discovered that around one third of the nation's 103 nuclear power stations have yet to resolve all of their Y2K [MILLENNIUM BUG] problems.
The Times (25 August 1999)

Chindits. The long-range penetration force commanded by the maverick Major General Orde Wingate in the Second World War. In 1943 they entered Japanese-held Burma from the west, crossed the River Chindwin and, with supplies dropped by air, conducted guerrilla operations against the Japanese until they reached the River Irrawaddy. Finding the terrain unfavourable on crossing that river, however, they were obliged to make a circuitous return to India. They took their name from the *chinthe*, the fabulous lion that guards Burmese pagodas, and adopted the creature as their emblem. The name of the Chindwin itself may have influenced the choice.

Chinese restaurant. A restaurant specializing in Chinese 'take-away' dishes, a regular outlet on the British High Street. The first Chinese restaurant in Europe opened in London in 1908, when Chung Koon, a Chinese ship's cook, left his vessel and, marrying an English girl, set up an eating establishment in

Piccadilly Circus. The restaurant, the Cathay, catered mainly for old colonial types who had returned to England from the Orient. Its popularity increased in the Second World War, when US GIs began taking their girlfriends there. Other family-run restaurants started to open elsewhere in London and in cities such as Liverpool and Manchester, their chief clientèle after the war being British soldiers who had returned from the Far East. The aroma of CHOP SUEY and CHOW MEIN is now familiar in even the smallest market town.

Chinese restaurant syndrome. A short-lived malady that can appear in a small number of people after eating in a CHINESE RESTAURANT. Symptoms include headache, dizziness and flushing and the cause is an excessive use of the flavouring agent monosodium glutamate. The illness is also known as Kwok's disease, after Robert Kwok, the US doctor who first described it in the 1960s.

Chinese slavery. Effective slavery in the form of much hard work for negligible rewards. The phrase became widely used as a political slogan by the Liberals from 1903, when Arthur Balfour's Conservative government (1902–5) introduced coolies from China to combat the shortage of Kaffir labour in the Rand gold mines after the dislocation caused by the South African War. They were kept in compounds and allowed out only under permit.

Chinese wall. On the Stock Exchange a ban on the passing or leak of confidential financial information from one department to another, especially when detrimental to a client. The allusion is to the Great Wall of China.

The Law Lords have ruled that there can be no guarantee that Chinese walls constructed on an ad hoc basis are leak proof. That will pose problems at dozens of institutions where Chinese walls owe more to jerry building techniques than brilliant architecture.
The Times (19 December 1998)

Chinese water torture. A form of torture in which water drips steadily onto a bound victim's forehead with the aim of driving him insane.

Chinese whispers. Mistakes caused by faulty communication. The reference is to the party game in which a message is passed in a whisper to all the participants in turn. By the time it reaches the last player, it is so distorted that it might as well be in Chinese. A famous example is the military message

'Send reinforcements, we are going to advance', which emerged as 'Send three and fourpence, we are going to a dance.'

Chingford Skinhead or **Chingford Strangler.** A media nickname for Norman (now Lord) Tebbit (b.1931), the rightwing populist Europhobe MP for Chingford from 1974 (he had previously represented Epping, 1970–4) until his elevation to the peerage in 1992. He is known for his abrasive manner and robust invective and was a leading figure in the cabinets of Margaret Thatcher in the 1980s. He famously told the unemployed to get on their bikes to find work, as his own father had done in the GREAT DEPRESSION. *See also* EUROPHILE; SKINHEAD.

Chinless wonder. A vacuous upper-class male, who typically or supposedly has a receding chin, a feature that when firm is indicative of strength or determination. The expression dates from the 1960s and probably puns on the BONELESS WONDER, the contortionist of classic circus repute.

Chippendales, The. The US male striptease group was formed in 1979 by Somen Banerjee, an Indian garage owner from Los Angeles, who in 1975 had bought a failing bar called Destiny II and turned it into a nightclub. It is uncertain what gave him the inspiration for the enterprise, but he realized the potential of such a show following an initial 'male exotic dance night for ladies only' at the club, which he renamed Chippendales, for its mock-English furnishings. The name was in turn adopted by the hunky he-men. Their act is 'strip' and 'tease' in equal measure, and although full frontal nudity is strictly speaking off limits there are times when a view beyond the veil is apparently or even actually afforded, to the delight of the delirious female audience.

Chips, Mr. The archetypal bachelor public schoolmaster, who devotes his life to his school and his boys, and is fondly regarded by all. His full name is Arthur Chipping, and he was the creation of James Hilton (1900–54), who introduced him in the sentimental story GOODBYE, MR CHIPS (1934), in which his life is told in flashback. Long a bachelor, he had once met a young woman on a mountaineering holiday and married her, but she died after two years. He is an amalgam of Hilton's own headmaster father and a housemaster at the Leys School, Cambridge, which Hilton had attended.

Chips Channon. The nickname of Sir Henry Channon (1897–1958), American-born Conservative MP for Southend-on-Sea, better known as a London society figure and diarist. The reason for the name remains uncertain. One unlikely suggestion attributes it to the potato chips he introduced at a cocktail party. Another claims that he once shared bachelor quarters with a friend named or nicknamed Fish.

Chisanbop (Korean, 'finger counting'). The proprietary name of a system of calculating by using the fingers and thumbs. It was invented by the Korean mathematician Sung Jin Pai in the 1970s and adopted in particular for the teaching of basic arithmetic. The fingers are used to count to 99 with larger numbers carried over by memory or written down. The right-hand thumb stands for one unit with a place value of five, while each finger represents an additional unit. The left-hand thumb stands for 50, with each finger representing 10.

Chitty-Chitty-Bang-Bang. A series of children's stories (1964) about a magical car by the thriller writer Ian Fleming (1908–64), creator of James BOND. Chitty-Chitty-Bang-Bang is a 'supercharged Paragon Panther', boasting 12 cylinders and owned by the inventor Commander Caractacus Potts. It is capable of flying and can perform exciting stunts. A successful film adaptation, with a screenplay by Roald Dahl, was released in 1967.

Chopper. A helicopter. The colloquialism or military jargon is part corruption of 'helicopter' (or 'copter'), part reference to the machine's 'chopping' blades.

Chop suey. A Chinese-style dish of meat, bean sprouts and the like, served with rice. From Chinese *tsap sui*, 'mixed bits'.

Chorus Line, A. A musical (1975) with a score by Marvin Hamlisch (b.1944) and lyrics by Edward Kleban (1939–87) about the trials and tribulations of the hopeful actors and actresses as they present themselves for an audition. The show was based on a collection of taped interviews made with 24 dancers in 1974. It was filmed, not entirely successfully, in 1985.

Chow mein. A Chinese-style dish of fried noodles with shredded meat or shrimps and vegetables. The name represents Chinese *chao miàn*, 'fried flour'.

Christ and Carrots. A nickname given by Winston Churchill to the Labour politician Sir Stafford Cripps (1889–1952) on account of his Christian socialism and asceticism, which were reflected in the rigorous austerity of his policies during his time as chancellor of the exchequer (1947–50).

Christina's World. One of the best known and most popular works of the US artist Andrew Wyeth (b.1917), *Christina's World* (1948) is an eerily lit, sharply delineated but featureless farm landscape, with two farm buildings on the high horizon, while in the foreground is the mysterious figure of Christina, a thin-limbed girl propping herself up on the grass. Christina, whose view of the landscape we share, was a crippled neighbour of Wyeth's in the Brandywine Valley, Pennsylvania.

Christingle. A lighted candle, often set in an orange, that symbolizes Christ as the light of the world and that is given to children in a special children's service held during Advent. The custom originated in the Moravian Church but was taken up in the mid-20th century by other churches and in particular by the Church of England Children's Society. The name probably derives from German dialect *Christkindl*, 'Christ child', meaning Baby Jesus, who brings presents to children on Christmas Eve. The second part of the word has probably been influenced by 'ingle'.

Christmas disease. Not the consequence of an annual festive overindulgence but a serious condition that can make life difficult all the year round for its sufferer. It is a rare type of bleeding disorder, also known as haemophilia B, that is caused by a defect in the blood coagulation mechanism. It takes its name from Stephen Christmas, one of the first patients to be diagnosed with it in 1952.

Christmas has come early. An unexpected bonus or benefit has been received. The catchphrase often applies to the provision of something usually associated with the materialistic side of Christmas, such as money, food or drink. *See also* ALL ONE'S CHRISTMASES HAVE COME AT ONCE.

> One [pub] regular said: 'It was like Christmas come early. The beer was already flowing when I arrived and no one was asking for any money.'
> *The Times* (22 October 1999)

Christmas tree bill. In US political jargon a legislative bill that provides benefits for various special-interest groups, especially as a result of numerous amendments not directly related to the main part of the proposed law. The term was originally applied to a tax bill affecting foreign investors that was passed in 1966

and signed 'with reservations' by President Lyndon B. Johnson (*see* LBJ), who noted that it would 'confer special tax windfalls and benefits [like Christmas presents] upon certain groups'.

Christmas truce. The spontaneous and unofficial truce that broke out along much of the WESTERN FRONT on the first Christmas of the First World War, in 1914. At various places along the line soldiers of both sides emerged out of their trenches into no-man's land to exchange small gifts and sing carols together. Between Frelinghien and Houplines the Seaforth Highlanders and a Saxon regiment played each other at football (the Scots losing 2–3). However, such fraternization was frowned on by senior officers, who made sure that such contact between their troops never occurred again for the rest of the war.

Christopher Robin. The little boy who shares adventures with WINNIE-THE-POOH and other animal friends in the stories and poems by A.A. Milne. He represents Milne's son, Christopher Robin Milne (1920–96), who was also the model for E.H. Shepard's illustrations. In his autobiography *The Enchanted Places* (1974) the original Christopher Robin tells how he grew up to wish his name were Charles Robert.

Chuck it down, To. To rain heavily, as distinct from the more common steady or gentle fall of rain.

Chuffed. A word of opposite meanings, both current from the 1950s: on the one hand pleased or satisfied, on the other displeased or disgruntled. The former sense is commoner. *See also* JANUS WORD.

Chump change. A small or insignificant amount of money, i.e. small change fit only for a chump or fool. The expression arose from black American English in the 1960s.

Chums. A magazine for boys, along the lines of *The* BOY'S OWN PAPER, published from 1892 until 1934.

Chunnel. A nickname for the CHANNEL TUNNEL first recorded in 1928, several years before the long projected project finally became a reality.

Church in Wales. Following lengthy agitation, an Act of 1914 finally disestablished the Church in Wales and this took effect in 1920, when a separate province was created. The Church in Wales is thus no longer *Eglwys Loegr* (the 'English Church'), over-dependent on the landowners, and it provides regular services in Welsh as well as in English. After 1920 it increased in both numbers and influence.

CIA. The Central Intelligence Agency, established by President Truman to coordinate US intelligence in 1947. It became a global agency for collecting and evaluating intelligence and for extending US influence through covert action, especially in the early years of the COLD WAR, when it was still largely unknown to the US public. Although subject to fiascos, such as the BAY OF PIGS, the CIA performed well during the Cuban Missile Crisis (*see* HAWKS AND DOVES). Its reputation was badly tarnished, however, in the WATERGATE scandal, and it was almost annihilated in the revelations of abuses of power that followed. In 1995 President Clinton redefined its mission as the countering of weapons of mass destruction, drug trafficking and international organized crime, a brief far removed from its original mission of combating communism.

Cicciolina, La (Italian, 'the little plump one'). The nickname of Hungarian-born Italian porn star and politician Ilona Staller (b.1955), who campaigned with the slogan 'less nuclear energy, more sexual energy', and became a Radical Party member of the Italian parliament in 1987.

Cider with Rosie. An autobiographical account (1959) of his early years by the poet Laurie Lee (1914–97), evoking the landscape and innocent rural life of the Slad valley in Gloucestershire where he was born and brought up. He and Rosie Burdock 'sat very close, breathing the same hot air. We kissed only once, so shy and dry, it was like two leaves colliding in the air. ... Rosie, having baptized me with her cidrous kisses, married a soldier, and I lost her for ever.' Whether or not Rosie actually existed, Lee would never reveal. *See also* FIRST LINES OF NOVELS.

Cigarette cards. Picture cards on various thematic subjects inserted by manufacturers into cigarette packets. They first emerged in the late 19th century and remained a strong promotional device until well after the Second World War. The collection of complete sets of cards became a popular pastime and specialists in the subject became known as cartophilists, a designation coined by C.L. Bagnall in the April 1936 issue of *Cigarette Card News*.

Cinderella services. A US term for medical and social services provided to the mentally and physically handicapped, the aged and the chronically sick. The expression dates from the 1970s and alludes to the name of the fairy-tale heroine in its use as a term for a neglected or despised person.

Cinecittà (Italian, 'Cine-city'). A complex of film studios opened in 1937 on the outskirts of Rome and the source of such BLOCKBUSTERS as BEN-HUR (1959) and *Cleopatra* (1963).

CinemaScope. A patent cinematographic process using anamorphic lenses to compress a wide image into a standard frame and then expand it again during projection. The result was a picture almost two and half times as wide as it was high. The system was introduced by Twentieth Century-Fox in 1953 with its production of *The Robe* and the technique itself was based on that of Henri Chrétien (1879–1958), French inventor of the anamorphic lens.

Cinerama. A wide-screen cinematographic technique created by the US research technician Fred Waller (1886–1954), who saw it open commercially only two years before his death in *This Is Cinerama* (1952). The system employed three projectors, each projecting on a separate third of the huge 'wraparound' screen that filled the viewer's peripheral vision, giving the sense of being in the centre of the scene and actually involved in the action. One famous scene was a thrilling rollercoaster ride that invariably elicited screams of terrified delight from the audience.

Circadian rhythms. The daily periodicity of physiological processes and states such as metabolism, sleep patterns and variation in body temperature as controlled by the BIOLOGICAL CLOCK. The term arose in the 1950s and derives from Latin *circa*, 'about', and *dies*, 'day'.

Circuit breaker. A US term for a rebate on property tax or income tax granted by a state to a low-income homeowner or renter to help them cope with rising property taxes. The term dates from the 1970s and derives from the name for the automatic device that stops the flow of current in an electric circuit as a safety measure.

Circus, The. A nickname for the British Secret Service, allegedly from Cambridge Circus, London, although the organization's headquarters were actually at Broadway from 1924 to 1966. The similarity between 'Circus' and 'Service' may have further prompted the name, which was made familiar to the public by the novels of John Le Carré such as *The Honourable Schoolboy* (1977). *See also* SMILEY, GEORGE.

Cisco Kid. A romantic Latin cowboy and Robin Hood of the American Southwest, who first appeared as a Mexican bandit in 'The Caballero's Way', a short story by O. Henry included in *Heart of the West* (1907). The character became a long-running hero of HOLLYWOOD silent and sound films and in the 1950s featured in a radio show and in television serials named after him.

Citius, altius, fortius (Latin, 'faster, higher, stronger'). The motto of the OLYMPIC GAMES, introduced *c*.1908 by Baron Pierre de Coubertin, founder of the modern games. He apparently spotted the words over the entrance to a French school, although they have also been attributed to the Rev. P. Didon, a friend and colleague of Coubertin.

Citizen Kane. A film (1941) based on a screenplay by Herman J. Mankiewicz (1897–1953) that looks back on the life and career of fictional newspaper magnate Charles Foster Kane (played by Orson Welles, who was also the director). Commonly listed among the best films ever made, it was a thinly disguised biography of the real-life media baron William Randolph Hearst (1863–1951). Hearst was sharply aware of this fact, particularly of the similarity between the relationship between Kane and his wife, who dreams of a career in opera, and that between himself and his wife actress Marion Davies, and he tried to prevent the film's release but failed when Welles himself threatened to sue RKO Pictures if they withheld his masterpiece.

> There, but for the Grace of God, goes God.
> HERMAN J. MANKIEWICZ: referring to Orson Welles
> during the filming of *Citizen Kane*

Citizen's arrest. Any British citizen has the legal right to arrest someone committing or suspected of committing an arrestable offence, i.e. one carrying a prison sentence of five years or more, but in practice the right is rarely exercised and usually hits local or even national headlines when it is.

> The driver pulled off the road and the lorry drivers forced him to stop, making a citizen's arrest.
> *The Times* (6 November 1999)

Citizen's Charter. The document so named was launched by the Conservative government in 1991 as a statement of the British citizen's rights of redress in cases where a public service failed to meet a certain standard. The aim was to raise that standard and make the service more responsive to its users. In 1998 the LABOUR PARTY launched its successor, known as Service First. The term was originally coined by C.E. Innes and used in 1913 as the title of a book in which he set forth his 'scheme of national organization'.

Cittabella. The imaginary city of uncertain location that is the setting of Lia Wainstein's Italian novel *Viaggio in Drimonia* (1965). It is full of holes of various shapes and sizes, but despite this considerable hazard has a name that is Italian for 'beautiful city'. *See also* DRIMONIA.

City of Dreadful Knights. Cardiff. After the First World War Lloyd George, prime minister of the COALITION GOVERNMENT, made lavish grants of honours in a cynical and blatant fashion. In 1922 Lord Salisbury opened an attack, and it was alleged that the government had fixed prices for the sale of titles, the money being put into party political funds. The Conservatives profited, as did Lloyd George's private party chest. As a consequence, a Royal Commission was set up in 1922 to recommend future procedure. Three people connected with prominent South Wales newspapers were among the recipients of these honours, hence Cardiff was dubbed the City of Dreadful Knights, a punning allusion to James Thomson's poem 'The City of Dreadful Night' (1874).

Civvy Street. Civilian life, especially as reverted to after military service or on 'demob'. The phrase dates from the Second World War, but 'civvy' in combination with other words, such as 'civvy life', dates from the First World War, and 'civvies' as civilian clothes are of similar vintage.

CJD. *See* MAD COW DISEASE.

Clam-diggers. Casual trousers reaching to the middle of the calf, so called because they were originally worn for digging clams. The term dates from the 1940s and was revived when the trousers (pants) were again in fashion from the 1970s.

> These boots are perfect for showing off dance-toned calves. Whether you team them with an A-line skirt or clam-diggers, they're bold, bare and beautiful.
> *heat* (23–29 September 1999)

Clangers, The. A children's television puppet programme screened from 1969 to 1974. The Clangers were a band of pink, knitted, mouse-like creatures who inhabited a small blue moon, which they shared with the Soup Dragon and the Froglets. They wore small suits of gold armour and communicated in whistles, and they were so named from the sound the metal dustbin-lid entrances to their burrows made when they dived inside to escape meteorites. One of their favourite pastimes was eating Blue String Pudding.

Clapped-out. Worn out from age or heavy use. A term usually applied to something mechanical, such as a car. The suggestion is that it has been disabled or disempowered by the clap, or venereal disease. The expression dates from the 1940s.

Claudine. The lively young heroine of four semi-autobiographical novels by Colette, in their English versions known as *Claudine at School* (1900), *Claudine in Paris* (1901), *Claudine Married* (1902) and *Claudine and Annie* (1903).

Clause Four. A clause originally in the LABOUR PARTY's constitution of 1918. It was written by Sidney Webb and embodied an affirmation of the party's commitment to the common ownership of industry and services. The clause was rewritten in 1995, and the commitment to common ownership was dropped from the party's constitution during the evolution of NEW LABOUR.

Clause 28. A clause in the Local Government Act of 1988, now an Act, that makes it illegal for local authorities to 'promote homosexuality' by publishing material or by encouraging the teaching of the acceptability of homosexuality as a 'family relationship'. It has provoked considerable controversy, not only because it implicitly attacks gay rights but also because it threatens the sponsorship of a number of cultural activities that could be said to have some kind of homosexual content or association. In 1999 the Conservatives vigorously opposed Labour's plans to annul the Act.

Claymore mine. A type of anti-personnel mine introduced by the US Army in the 1960s. It was horseshoe-shaped and produced a directionalized, fan-shaped pattern of fragments. It was so named on an analogy with the claymore, as a large double-edged broadsword formerly used by Scottish Highlanders.

Clean one's act up, To. To improve one's conduct or way of life. The phrase dates from the 1970s.

Clean someone's clock, To. To beat or defeat them decisively. The term is of US military origin and arose in the Second World War. A person's 'clock' is probably their face ('dial').

Clear blue water. A tag touted by Conservative leaders in the mid-1990s to express the ideological gap between themselves and other parties, and especially the LABOUR PARTY. The phrase blends 'clear water', the distance between two boats, with 'blue water', the open sea, while rather obviously evoking blue as the traditional colour of the Conservative Party, then in power. The expression subsequently appeared in other contexts.

> The once-great Marks & Spencer is finding it increasingly difficult to show clear blue water between itself and leading rivals.
> *Sunday Times* (29 August 1999)

Clear one's desk, To. To leave one's job, usually as a result of dismissal. The phrase may have been suggested by the much older 'to clear the decks'.

> The *Mirror* share-tipping scandal claimed its first casualty last night when the broker who bought £20,000 shares for the Editor was asked to clear his desk.
> *The Times* (18 February 2000)

Cleckheckmondsedge. A semi-serious portmanteau name for the former Yorkshire (now Kirklees) conurbation of Cleckheaton, Heckmondwike and Liversedge, south of Bradford.

Clerihew. The name given to a particular kind of humorous verse invented by E. Clerihew Bentley (1875–1956). It is usually satirical and often biographical, consisting of four rhymed lines of uneven length. The first examples of the genre appeared in Bentley's book *Biography for Beginners* (1905), published under the name of 'E. Clerihew', and the name was applied to the form soon after by some unknown reader. A classic specimen from this first collection is:

> Sir Christopher Wren
> Said 'I am going to dine with some men.
> If anybody calls,
> Say I'm designing St Paul's.'

A more recent clerihew, not by Bentley, is:

> Prime Minister John Major
> Was hardly an old stager;
> He cut little ice
> By simply being nice.
> A.R.

Clicks and mortar. In computer jargon a commercial operation that combines a retail store with an online business using the INTERNET. The 'clicks' are those of the mouse to exploit the latter; the 'mortar' is that of the bricks and mortar (on which the phrase puns) of the actual retail store. *See also* BRICKS AND CLICKS.

> 'Clicks-and-mortar has a lot of inherent advantages,' says Seema Williams, e-commerce analyst at Forrester Research. … 'It's going to be awful tough for an online retailer to maintain its lead once the clicks-and-mortar people get their act together.'
> *Time* (27 December 1999)

Cliffhanger. Figuratively, a state of affairs producing anxiety. The term derives from early US serialized adventure films, in which the hero or heroine was left in a perilous plight at the end of an episode in order to whet the audience's appetite for the next instalment. A classic exponent of the art was Pearl White, the star of *The Perils of Pauline* (1914), who frequently finished up dangling from the Palisades over the Hudson River. The suspense, in both senses of the word, made sure that the audience returned.

> There are enough cliffhangers this week to fill a wardrobe as Grant and Tiffany lurch from one marital crisis to another.
>
> *Radio Times* (12–18 September 1998)

Clio. A statuette presented annually in the USA as an award for the best production, acting or the like in commercial advertisements during the year on US television. It was first awarded in 1967 and takes its name from the Greek muse of history.

Clippety-clop. An imitative phrase dating from the 1920s for the sound of a horse's hoofs.

> Horsey, horsey, don't you stop,
> Just let your feet go clippety-clop;
> Your tail goes swish and the wheels go round,
> Giddy-up, we're homeward bound.
>
> DESMOND COX: 'Horsey, Horsey' (song) (1937)

Clippies. Bus conductresses in London and other large cities were so known in the Second World War when they took over the clipping of tickets from male conductors. The occupation was continued by women for some time after the war.

Cliveden set. The name given to the right-wing politicians and journalists who gathered for weekend parties in the late 1930s at Cliveden, the Buckinghamshire home of Lord and Lady Astor. They were alleged to favour appeasement with NAZI Germany.

Cloche hat. A woman's close-fitting bell-shaped hat, in fashion in the EDWARDIAN ERA and undergoing periodic revival since, for example in the 1950s.

Clock in or **on, To.** To start work; to begin a session of activity. The literal sense is to register one's arrival at a workplace by recording the time on a clock-like device. The converse is 'to clock out' or 'to clock off'. *See also* LOG IN.

Clockwork Orange, A. A futuristic, dystopian novel (1962) by Anthony Burgess (pen-name of John Anthony Burgess Wilson; 1917–93). Told in the first person in NADSAT, it describes an attempt to turn its young criminal hero, Alex, into a 'mechanical man' by means of therapy and brainwashing. The title derives from the Cockney expression 'queer as a clockwork orange', meaning 'homosexual'. The relevance of this to the novel or any of its characters is uncertain, although in the narrative itself it is the title of a book being typed up by a writer whose house Alex and his mates burst into. A film version of the novel was directed by Stanley Kubrick (1971). Burgess had reservations about changes made in film adaptation of his novel and suggested that the film should be retitled *Clockwork Marmalade*. Withdrawn after its original release, the film was re-released in 2000. *See also* COPYCAT KILLING.

> Then I looked at its top sheet, and there was the name – A CLOCKWORK ORANGE – and I said: 'That's a fair gloopy [silly] title. Who ever heard of a clockwork orange?' Then I read a malenky [little] bit out loud in a sort of very high type preaching goloss [voice]: ' – The attempt to impose upon man, a creature of growth and capable of sweetness, to ooze juicily at the last round the bearded lips of God, to attempt to impose, I say, laws and conditions appropriate to a mechanical creation, against this I raise my sword-pen –'
>
> ch ii

Close, but no cigar. A formula for a commiseration or 'nice try'. The allusion is to the 'Highball', a fairground 'try-your-strength' machine with a pivot that the contestant hit with a hammer in the hope of sending a projectile up high enough to ring a bell. Those who succeeded were awarded a cigar by the proprietor. The expression, like the machine itself, derives from US carnivals. *See also* RING A BELL.

Closed book. A person or thing about which one knows nothing, as distinct from an 'open book', about which one knows everything The analogy is with an unopened book, whose contents remain undiscovered. The phrase dates from the early years of the 20th century and is sometimes taken to refer to an awkward or delicate matter, as if a book that one hesitates to open.

> 'Who ... catching sight of a book with that title, could resist opening it?' Almost anyone, I should think, but Adair clearly can't resist congratulating himself on the idea: a closed book with *A Closed Book* written on it. Trouble is, the phrase does not mean ... an embarrassing subject, it means an unknown quantity. Although people do make such slips in everyday

speech, a novelist shouldn't erect a big intellectual joke on such a feeble premise.

Sunday Times (Review of Gilbert Adair, *A Closed Book*) (24 October 1999)

Close encounter. Journalistic jargon for any meeting, whether personal or professional. The phrase was popularized by the title of the SCIENCE FICTION film *Close Encounters of the Third Kind* (1977), itself referring to contact with ALIENS from a UFO. A 'close encounter of the first kind' is thus simply a sighting of a UFO, while a 'close encounter of the second kind' is evidence of an alien landing. A 'close encounter of the fourth kind' is an abduction by aliens. The categories were proposed in J. Allen Hynek's *The UFO Experience: A Scientific Enquiry* (1972).

Closet queen. A clandestine male homosexual, who has not COME OUT OF THE CLOSET. 'Queen' as a term for a male homosexual dates from the late 19th century.

Cloth cap. A man's flat woollen cap with a peak, regarded from the 1950s as an essential attribute of a working-class person. Andy CAPP always wears one in his day-to-day doings, even indoors. *See also* FLAT CAP.

Today … new Labour celebrates that great event [the founding of the LABOUR PARTY 100 years earlier]. Don't expect too many cloth caps or misting NHS specs among the cheesy grins.

Sunday Times (27 February 2000)

Cloth ears. To be cloth-eared is to be unable to hear or understand clearly, as if one's ears were made of cloth. The derogatory term dates from the early 20th century. *See also* TIN EAR.

How cloth-eared can you get? Or rather, how cloth-eared can you contrive to make yourself by affecting literary youthfulness?

Times Literary Supplement (Letter to the Editor) (11 February 2000)

Cloud nine. To be on cloud nine is to be elated or very happy. The expression derives from terminology used by the US Weather Bureau. Clouds are divided into classes, and each class into nine types. Cloud nine is cumulonimbus, a cumulus cloud of great vertical extent, topped with shapes of mountains or towers.

[Television presenter] Sally [Gray] was particularly excited because Edinburgh is her home town … Everything was going well and Sally was on cloud nine.

The Times (2 February 2000)

Clouseau, Inspector. The accident-prone French police inspector enjoyably played by Peter Sellers in the comedy film *The* PINK PANTHER (1963). He appeared in four sequels, with Sellers continuing in the role in the first three and Alan Arkin taking the part in the fourth. After Sellers' death in 1980, a final Clouseau film, *Trail of the Pink Panther* (1982), was stitched together from footage left over from the earlier movies.

Club car. A railway coach furnished as a lounge, often with a refreshment bar. Club cars, reserved for passengers paying a premium over the season ticket rate, were formerly provided on so-called club trains, long-distance commuter trains operating until the Second World War between Manchester and the North Wales coast, Manchester and the Fylde coast and Manchester and the Lake District, among other routes.

Club Med. The popular short name of the *Club Méditerranée*, 'Mediterranean Club', a French holiday firm founded in 1950 and a pioneer in the all-inclusive or 'package' holiday. It has established holiday camps or *villages* worldwide, but primarily on the Mediterranean coast of North Africa. Although now international in scope, the French flavour remains. The camp director is the *chef de village* and the camp staff, the equivalent of REDCOATS at BUTLIN'S, are *GOs* or *gentils organisateurs*, 'gentle organizers'. The name has become a byword for SUN, SEA AND SAND and all that goes with it, or for hedonism generally.

Club sandwich. A US term for a 'three decker' sandwich of meat (especially chicken and bacon), tomato, lettuce and mayonnaise, usually with two layers of filling between the three layers of bread (or toast). The comestible dates from the turn of the 20th century.

Cluedo. This classic WHODUNNIT board game was the invention in 1949 of Anthony Pratt, an English solicitor's clerk, later a concert pianist. The object is to discover which of six suspects, using which of six weapons, murdered Dr Black, found dead after a dinner party, and in which of the nine rooms of his country house the murder took place. The characters, their names representing their colours, are the actress Miss Scarlett, aged 29; the retired Colonel Mustard, 66; the village vicar Reverend Green, 48; the socialite Mrs Peacock, 41; the archaeologist Professor Plum, 38; and Dr Black's housekeeper and cook Mrs White, 57.

The weapons are a dagger, a length of lead piping, a candlestick, a rope, a spanner and a revolver; the rooms are the kitchen, the lounge, the ballroom, the billiard room, the hall, the dining room, the study, the library and the conservatory. In North America the game is known as Clue and the victim is Mr Boddy.

Clueless. *See* POPSOCKS; VALSPEAK.

Cluster bomb. A type of anti-personnel bomb containing numerous mini-bombs which radiate over a wide range on impact. It evolved in the mid-1960s as a 'refinement' of the conventional bomb during the VIETNAM War (1964–75). The name does not mean that such bombs are dropped in 'clusters', like sticks of incendiary bombs, but refers to the mass of projectiles discharged. Cluster bombs were widely used in the Kosovo War of 1999.

> If there are still an estimated 14,000 unexploded cluster bombs [in Kosovo] from 355 cluster bomb attacks, each containing 147 bomblets, the crude failure rate is 27 per cent if dropped one at a time, or around 7 per cent if dropped four at a time.
> *The Times* (Letter to the Editor) (18 August 1999)

Clydesiders. A loose association of left-wing MPs representing Glasgow and Clydeside constituencies, who enlivened British politics and Parliament from 1922 until they were much diminished in numbers following the 1931 general election. Notable among them were John Wheatley, of Housing Act fame, Campbell Stephen, Emanuel Shinwell and, best known of all, James Maxton (1885–1946), who became chairman of the Independent Labour Party, founded by Keir Hardie in 1893. They acted as a ginger group for the LABOUR PARTY and were noted champions of the poor and unemployed.

The term 'Red Clydeside' is generally applied to the strongly socialist working-class movement in and around Glasgow, particularly associated with the (now largely defunct) ship-building industry. Revolutionary socialism first appeared on Clydeside during the First World War, when a number of left-wingers were jailed after they called for strike action. Early heroes of the movement included the pacifist Maxton, who was one of those imprisoned, and the communist school teacher John Maclean. In January 1919 English troops and tanks were deployed in Glasgow in the expectation of an imminent Bolshevik revolution. Red Clydeside again came to national notice in the early 1970s, when workers at one of the shipyards, led by the shop steward Jimmy Reid, staged a work-in to stop the yard being closed down. A right-wing perspective on Red Clydeside unrest in the First World War is to be found in John Buchan's novel MR STANDFAST (1919).

CND. The Campaign for Nuclear Disarmament was launched in 1958 and immediately gained prominence with its BAN THE BOMB marches from London to the Atomic Weapons Research Establishment at Aldermaston, Berkshire. Its first chairman (to 1964) was Canon Collins and its first president Bertrand Russell. The latter resigned in 1960, however, to form the more militant Committee of 100. The CND was committed to UNILATERAL NUCLEAR DISARMAMENT and the banning (or removal) of US cruise missiles from Britain but its influence waned after the end of the COLD WAR and even further following the demise of the Soviet Union in 1991. The CND symbol is an inverted V bisected by a vertical line within a circle. The inverted V represents the semaphore signal for the letter N (both flags held down at an angle of 45 degrees from the horizontal), and the vertical line that for D (one flag held straight up and the other straight down), i.e. ND, the initials of *n*uclear *d*isarmament.

Coalition government. A government formed of normally opposed parties, usually in times of crisis, when party differences are set aside. Examples in the 20th century are Liberals, Unionists and Labour under Asquith (1915–16) (reformed under Lloyd George, 1916–22), MacDonald's NATIONAL GOVERNMENT (1931–5) and Winston Churchill's wartime Coalition Government (1940–45).

Coastal Command. The RAF command that operated over the sea from coastal bases in Britain in the Second World War.

COBOL. *See* PROGRAMMING LANGUAGES.

Cobra. A group of expressionist painters formed in Paris in 1948 by various Dutch and Scandinavian artists. Leading figures among the founders were the Dutchman Karel Appel (b.1921), the Belgian Corneille (full name Corneille Beverloo) (b.1922) and the Dane Asger Jorn (1914–73). They aimed to give free expression to the unconscious, unimpeded and undirected by the intellect, and set store by spontaneous gesture. Their name derives from the first letters of the capital cities of the three countries of the artists involved: *Co*penhagen, *Br*ussels and *A*msterdam.

Coca-Cola. The carbonated drink was the invention in 1886 of John S. Pemberton, a US pharmacist. It is uncertain how he concocted the blend of ingredients that first went into the product, but his bookkeeper, Frank Robinson, devised a name that indicated the source of two of the extracts: coca leaves and the cola nut. Coca leaves yield cocaine, a form of which was originally present in Coca-Cola. Hence the curative claims initially made for it, so that people took it for dyspepsia, headaches and similar malaises. The drink came to be nicknamed Coke, and the manufacturers registered this as an alternative name in 1920 as their exclusive property. Thus, while cola can be used as a general name for any carbonated drink made from cola nuts, Coca-Cola and Coke cannot. *See also* PEPSI-COLA; REAL THING.

Cochran revues. The impresario Charles Blake Cochran (1872–1951) started his career in America but back in England soon became famous for his intimate revues, beginning with *Odds and Ends* (1914) at the AMBASSADORS THEATRE. In 1918 he began a remarkable run of revues at the London Pavilion, including Noël Coward's *On With the Dance* (1925) and *This Year of Grace* (1928). The former was the first to star Cochran's famous 'Young Ladies'. His revues were distinctive from those of the EDWARDIAN ERA in that they relied more on witty dialogue than on dress and dancing.

Cockaigne. The boisterous concert overture by Sir Edward Elgar (1857–1934) is subtitled 'In London Town'. It was first performed in 1901 and was intended to be an evocation of Edwardian London. 'Cockaigne' or 'Cockayne' (from which the word 'Cockney' is popularly derived) refers to a land of idleness and luxury that features in medieval European folklore and that is the subject of a painting by the Flemish painter Pieter Bruegel the Elder (*c*.1525–69). The word derives from Middle Low German *kokenje*, a small cake, from which the houses in this idyllic land were supposed to be made. The idea is a persistent one: in the 1930s Depression in the United States, hobo lore evoked the land of the 'Big Rock Candy Mountain'. Despite expectations, the word 'Cockaigne' bears no etymological relationship to 'cocaine'; the latter derives from 'coca', as in COCA-COLA.

Cocktail Party, The. A poetic drama (1949) by the Anglo-American poet T.S. Eliot (1888–1965) in which the personal relationships among a small group of friends are explored and discussed. The drama begins with a cocktail party hosted by Edward Chamberlayne shortly after his wife Lavinia has left him; it ends with another cocktail party with Edward and Lavinia reunited and their various friends having moved on in their lives. The cocktail party itself thus becomes a symbol of human existence, full of compromise and banality.

Cock-up. A muddle; a mess-up. An allusion to something that is turned from the true, with a suggestion of the vulgar sense of 'cock'.

Coconut ice. The name of this confection of grated coconut and sugar syrup dates from the early years of the 20th century. The precise sense of 'ice' is uncertain. The confection is not frozen, and it is not made with or served with ice or even ice cream. The allusion may perhaps be to its natural colour or its somewhat crystalline texture.

Coffee-table book. A large, expensive and lavishly illustrated book, supposedly placed on a low table in a sitting-room to be glanced at rather than read or to impress a visitor. The term dates from the early 1960s and may have originally been intended to mean a book that was simply too large to be shelved normally. Such books were earlier sometimes known as 'grand-piano books'. In 1999 the German art publishers Taschen published a limited edition of a book of 400 photographs by Helmut Newton that was so large and heavy that it came with its own coffee table.

Cog in the wheel or **machine.** A person who holds a small but necessary post in a large organization. The allusion is to the cog on a small wheel that engages with that on a larger wheel, which in turn may engage with that on an even larger wheel. The expression dates from the 1930s.

Colbred sheep. This highly fertile sheep, a cross between the Border Leicester, Clun, Friesland and Dorset Horn, takes its name from the Gloucestershire company of H.A. Colburn and Son, who first had the idea of developing such a breed in 1954. The process took nine years, and the first Colbred was shown by H.A. Colburn himself in 1963 at the Royal Show, Newcastle upon Tyne.

Cold calling. The calling of someone by telephone in an attempt to sell them something. The usual culprits are double-glazing firms. The call is 'cold' because the one called is unprepared for it.

Cold Comfort Farm. A novel (1932) by Stella Gibbons (1902–89), parodying the rural novels of D.H. Lawrence (1885–1930) and Mary Webb (1881–1927), and in particular the latter's PRECIOUS BANE (1924). The author noted in her foreword: 'Because I have in mind all those thousands of persons not unlike myself ... who are not always sure whether a sentence is Literature or whether it is just sheer flapdoodle, I have adopted the method perfected by the late Herr Baedeker, and firmly marked what I consider the finer passages with one (*), two (**) or three (***) stars.' The title was suggested to the author by the writer Elizabeth Coxhead, who took the name from a real farm so called near her home at Hinckley, Leicestershire. Farms of the name still exist today, and 'cold comfort' as a phrase for little cheer goes back to medieval times. A film version (1995), written by Malcolm Bradbury and directed by John Schlesinger, was shown on television in Britain as an enjoyable comedy that never quite captured the spirit of the original.

> If she intended to tidy up life at Cold Comfort, she would find herself opposed at every turn by the influence of Aunt Ada ... Persons of Aunt Ada's temperament were not fond of a tidy life.
> ch v

Cold Duck. A name in the USA for an inexpensive mixture of sparkling burgundy and champagne. The name translates German *Kalte Ente*, 'cold duck', a fanciful alteration of *kalte Ende*, 'cold ends', meaning left-over wines mixed and served at the end of a party.

Colditz. A byword for a bleak prison or for any generally forbidding or unwelcoming edifice. Colditz Castle, in the town of this name about 48km (30 miles) from Leipzig, Germany, was a notorious prisoner of war camp in the Second World War and the site of many daring escape bids by Allied officers. The building and its name became widely known to the postwar generation from the highly popular television series *Colditz* (1972–4). Its 28 episodes were based on the books by Major Pat Reid and re-enacted the ruses devised by British officers to effect a breakout.

Cold turkey. The unpleasant effect produced by suddenly and completely giving up a drug to which one had been addicted. The reference is perhaps to a cold and unappetizing uncooked turkey by comparison with a warm and appetizing cooked one, although when this particular sense emerged in the 1920s 'cold

turkey' already existed to mean 'directly', 'without any warning', and this may be the actual source. *See also* WITHDRAWAL SYMPTOMS.

Cold War. A state of tension, distrust and mutual hostility between states or groups of countries, without recourse to actual warfare. The state existed between the Soviet bloc countries and the Western world from the end of the Second World War until 1990. The term was first used in a speech made on 16 April 1947 by the US financier Bernard Baruch (1870–1965), when US ambassador to the United Nations Atomic Energy Commission, and is said to have been suggested to him by Herbert B. Swope, former editor of the *New York World*. *See also* NATO; WARSAW PACT.

Cold Warrior. A US term for a politician or statesman who played an active part in the COLD WAR. The term first arose in the late 1950s.

Collateral damage. A euphemism for unintended casualties and damage caused among civilians in the course of a military operation. The term is of US origin and arose during the VIETNAM War (1964–75). More recently it was again before the public in the second GULF WAR.

College of cardinals. Properly the College of Cardinals is the Roman Catholic body of cardinals responsible for electing the pope. In a general sense the term is also used for any select group of people authorized to elect a person as their leader, especially in politics.

Colombey-les-deux-Églises. A village in eastern France, where the French soldier and statesman Charles de Gaulle (1890–1970) had his private residence. As the location of de Gaulle's periodic withdrawals from political life, first in 1946, then again from 1953 until 1958, when he returned to national politics first as prime minister then as president at the height of the Algerian crisis, it has become synonymous with the voluntary exile of the elder statesman, waiting in landed isolation for his country's call. *See also* FIGHTING FRENCH; GAULLIST.

Colombian necktie. A euphemism for a particularly unpleasant method of killing whereby the throat is cut below the chin and the tongue then pulled through the resulting gash. The drastic measure is usually inflicted on someone who has betrayed the killer or his boss, and originated in the Colombian drug wars of the 1980s.

Colonel Bogey. A bracing march tune composed in 1914 by a military bandmaster, Kenneth Alford, whose real name was Frederick Ricketts (1881–1945). It is familiar in its whistled form from the film *The* BRIDGE ON THE RIVER KWAI (1957), set in the Second World War, and in the war itself was enthusiastically adopted for an anonymous bawdy quatrain about the NAZI leadership:

> Hitler has only got one ball,
> Goering has two but very small,
> Himmler is somewhat similar,
> But poor old Goebbels has no balls at all.

Colonel Bramble. *See* BRAMBLE, COLONEL.

Color Purple, The. A novel (1982), written in the form of letters, by the US writer Alice Walker (b.1944), which won the PULITZER PRIZE for fiction. A young black woman, CELIE, having been raped as a child by her father and borne him two children, who are then taken away from her, is married off to a violent bully. She is helped by her husband's mistress, a blues singer, to appreciate herself, the pleasures of sexual love and the role of God in the proliferation of love and beauty. His presence is especially evident in the colour purple. A film version (1985) was directed by Steven Spielberg, with Whoopi Goldberg as Celie.

Columbia Pictures. A US film company founded in 1924 by Harry Cohn (1891–1958), a former song plugger in vaudeville. It produced many B-MOVIES but also had its share of successful major features, especially films directed by Frank Capra in the 1930s and starring Rita Hayworth in the 1940s. Elia Kazan's ON THE WATERFRONT (1954) and David Lean's LAWRENCE OF ARABIA (1962) were both Columbia films. Cohn's wife second wife, Joan Perry, provided the face of the statue of Columbia that serves as the studio's logo on pictures.

Columbine massacre. On 20 April 1999 two teenagers ran amok in Columbine High School, Littleton, Colorado, killing 12 students and a teacher before turning the gun on themselves. Many of their victims were shot at random, but the killers specially picked out 'jocks' (athletes) and blacks. The pair were obsessed with the NAZIS and timed the shooting to coincide with Hitler's birthday. The massacre rekindled the bitter debate about gun control in the USA. *See also* DUNBLANE MASSACRE; HUNGERFORD MASSACRE.

Columbo. The dishevelled, one-eyed Italian-American police lieutenant in the television series of the 1970s named after him, played by the squint-eyed Peter Falk. His trademarks are his shabby raincoat and his trick of talking inconsequentially about his dragon wife, then turning back at the door to ask one final, vital question.

Column inches. Press publicity. A column inch is properly a one-inch length of a column in a newspaper or magazine. The greater the number of inches, either in a single issue or over several, the greater the prominence of the subject of the article or report.

> In the month she vanished there were 492 women and 544 men reported as missing ... but Suzy [Lamplugh] got the column inches.
> *The Times* (7 December 1999)

Come or **fall apart at the seams, To.** To lose emotional control. The image is of a disintegrating costume as a garment representing one's physical figure. The expression dates from the 1940s.

Comeback kid. Anyone who returns to their former activity, especially in the world of sport or entertainment or the media generally. President Bill Clinton so described himself after coming second in the New Hampshire primary in the 1992 presidential election. (Since 1952, no presidential candidate had won the election without first winning in New Hampshire.) Clinton successfully overcame allegations of sexual impropriety, draft-dodging and cannabis use ('I didn't inhale') to win the presidential election. His nickname continued to be justified by his riding of such storms as the WHITEWATER real-estate scandal and the MONICA Lewinsky affair, the latter leading to an unsuccessful attempt to impeach him in February 1999.

> One mystery taxing everyone in the media is how Alan Yentob, the BBC's Director of Television, managed to become 'the comeback kid', rehabilitating himself.
> *The Times* (4 June 1999)

Come clean, To. To confess to a crime; to tell the whole truth. The phrase, of US origin and dating from the early 20th century, became a cliché in murder mysteries. A similar expression of earlier origin is 'to make a clean breast of'.

Come from behind, To. To win after lagging; to advance from a losing position. The metaphor originated in horse racing and has a general application in sport as well as a figurative usage.

Come-hither look. A flirtatious or seductive look. The second part of the phrase is variable.

> They make, in front of their looking-glasses, haughty or come-hithering faces for the young men in the street outside.
> DYLAN THOMAS: *Under Milk Wood* (1954)

Come in from the cold, To. To return to shelter and safety; to be welcomed back to a group. The expression has a literal origin but is almost always used figuratively. It was popularized by the title of John Le Carré's novel *The Spy Who Came in from the Cold* (1963) about a secret agent in the COLD WAR who longs to abandon his dubious and dangerous profession.

Come out of the closet, To. To admit something openly; to let it be known that one is homosexual. The 'closet' is the metaphorical cupboard in which one keeps one's private information. *See also* CLOSET QUEEN; OUTING.

> Celebrity make-up artist Kevyn Aucoin [is] calling for more gay stars to come out of the closet.
> *heat* (16 December 1999–5 January 2000)

Come out of the kitchen, To. To abandon one's traditional domestic role as a housewife for a career as a businesswoman, especially when successful and of senior status.

> Women are not just coming out of the kitchen in the small business sector. Sly Bailey ... has achieved a boardroom position in a more established company.
> *Sunday Times* (9 January 2000)

Come out of the woodwork, To. To be revealed; to emerge from obscurity. The expression is frequently used in connection with someone or something unpleasant. The allusion is to beetles, cockroaches and other 'creepy-crawlies', which are seen only when they emerge from their hidden habitat (not necessarily woodwork). The converse is to vanish or disappear into the woodwork. The phrase dates from the 1970s.

> We are anticipating that people will come out of the woodwork [to sell fake shades for viewing the total eclipse of the sun] and create what we call the crisp packet option.
> *The Times* (21 July 1999)

Come the acid, To. To be unpleasant or offensive; to speak in a sarcastic or caustic manner. The expression dates from the 1920s.

Come the raw prawn on or **over someone, To.** To attempt to deceive them or impose on them. The Australian expression dates from the 1940s and derives from 'raw prawn' as an act of deception. A raw prawn is hard to swallow.

Come to a grinding halt, To. *See* GRIND TO A HALT.

Come up roses, To. To develop favourably; to turn out perfectly. The phrase dates from the 1960s and derives from the song 'Everything's Coming Up Roses' from Stephen Sondheim's musical GYPSY (1959), based on the life of the dancer and STRIPTEASE artist Gypsy Rose Lee (1914–70). *See also* COME UP SMELLING OF ROSES.

Come up smelling of roses, To. To emerge unscathed from an unpleasant experience and find oneself in a better position than before. The image is of a person who has fallen into the mire but been 'fertilized' in the process of clambering out of it. Roses grow well in enriched soil. *See also* COME UP ROSES.

Comfort food. Food that comforts because it is associated with one's childhood or home cooking. The word can be used in similar applications, so that a comfort book is one that was perhaps first read some time ago but that is now reread with pleasure, especially if one is feeling 'low'.

> Beginning university is a time when young people put on excess fat, not just because they are enjoying themselves, but because they may be comfort eating.
> *Sunday Times* (8 August 1999)

Comic Relief. The first television programme so titled was screened in 1986, the aim being to entertain the viewer while raising money for famine relief. Many famous comedians were involved, offering their services free. The concept sprang from the charity BAND AID, organizers of Bob Geldof's rock-music event Live Aid staged for the same purpose the previous year. Subsequent Comic Relief programmes have been of marathon length with the scope widened to raise money for all kinds of needy causes both at home and abroad. *See also* RED NOSE DAY.

Comics. Although comic strips had been appearing in US newspapers since the closing years of the 19th century, it was not until the 1930s that comic books were published in non-newspaper form. The first, a newspaper-style Sunday section containing only comics, was a failure. The second, a 68-page publication introduced by the Dell Publishing Company in 1934, was a success. It was called *Famous Funnies*, promised 'games, puzzles, magic' and cost 10 cents. It was through SUPERMAN that the world of comics subsequently burgeoned into films and television.

Coming out of one's ears. In great abundance; very plentiful. The notion is that one is so full that one overflows through the only orifice that does not normally serve as an outlet. The phrase is of US origin and dates from the 1960s.

Comintern. The popular name of the Third (Communist) International (1919–43), formed in Moscow by the Soviet leader LENIN. From 1933 the Comintern advocated a POPULAR FRONT of communists, socialists and liberals against the German dictator Adolf Hitler. Germany signed the Anti-Comintern Pact with Japan in 1936 and with Italy in 1937 (see AXIS). The Internationals were coordinating bodies established by labour and socialist organizations. The First International or International Working Men's Association (1864–72), formed in London under Karl Marx, lasted from 1868 until 1872; and the Second International, founded in Paris, from 1889 until 1940. An abortive Trotskyist Fourth International was founded in 1938.

Commando (Afrikaans *kommando*, from Dutch *commando*, 'command'). Originally, an armed unit of Boer horsemen on military service active in the Kaffir or Frontier Wars (1779–1877). Boer commandos raided isolated British units and lines of communication in the Second BOER WAR (1899–1902). In the Second World War the name was adopted for a member of the specially trained British assault troops formed from volunteers to undertake particularly hazardous tasks and originally, in 1940, to repel a German invasion of England.

> Plans should be studied to land secretly by night on the islands and kill or capture the invaders. This is exactly one of the exploits for which the Commandos would be suited.
>
> WINSTON CHURCHILL: *The Second World War*, ii (1948: these words written in 1940)

Commercial inventions. The 20th century saw the emergence of several now familiar household names and branded products. The following, with year of introduction, is a selection of 50. *See also* ROWNTREE MACKINTOSH.

> Gillette safety razor (1901)
> Crayola crayons (1902)
> Campbell's pork and beans (1904)
> Palmolive soap (1905)
> L'Oréal perfume (1907)
> Ex-Lax chocolate-flavoured laxative (1908)

> Lipton's tea (1909)
> Hallmark greetings cards (1910)
> Hellmann's mayonnaise (1912)
> Quaker Puffed Wheat (1913)
> Wrigley's Doublemint chewing gum (1914)
> PYREX (1915)
> Lucky Strike cigarettes (1916)
> BMW cars (1917)
> Kotex sanitary towels (1918)
> Bentley cars (1919)
> Maidenform bras (1923)
> Wonder bread (1927)
> Lithiated Lemon (now 7-Up) (1929)
> Snickers chocolate bars (1930)
> Alka-Seltzer (1931)
> Ritz crackers (by Nabisco) (1933)
> Toyota cars (1935)
> Tampax tampons (1936)
> SPAM (1937)
> Nescafé instant coffee (1938)
> M&Ms chocolates (1940)
> Cheerios (1941)
> TUPPERWARE (1945)
> Timex watches (1946)
> Ajax cleanser (1947)
> VELCRO (1948)
> LEGO (1949)
> Tropicana products (1951)
> No-Cal ginger ale (1952)
> Kentucky Fried Chicken (1955) (*see* KFC)
> Pampers disposable nappies (1956)
> BankAmericard (now VISA) (1958)
> BARBIE DOLL (1959)
> Pentel felt-tip pens (1960)
> Coffee-Mate coffee whitener (1961)
> Kodak Instamatic camera (1963)
> Nutra-Sweet artificial sweetener (1965)
> MasterCharge credit card (now MasterCard) (1966)
> JACUZZI bath (1968)
> NIKE shoes (1972)
> Miller Lite beers (1975)
> WALKMAN (1979)
> POST-IT NOTES (1980)
> PROZAC (1988)

Common Market. The former popular name for the economic association of certain European countries that has now grown to be the EUROPEAN UNION.

Community Charge. The official euphemistic name for the controversial local tax introduced by the Conservative government in 1990. It was levied on every adult in a community and took no account of ability to pay, apart from a few categories of people eligible for an 80 per cent reduction. Popularly dubbed the 'poll tax', a term dating from medieval times, it led to a riot in West London in the spring of 1990 followed by an orchestrated campaign of non-payment. It was abandoned in 1993 in favour of the more equitable 'council tax', similar in structure to the earlier 'rates'. *See also* CAN'T PAY, WON'T PAY.

Companion of Honour. An order instituted in 1917 by George V for recognized services of national importance, sometimes regarded as a junior class of the ORDER OF MERIT. It may be conferred on men or women and restricts its membership to 65, excluding honorary members.

Compassion fatigue. Indifference to charitable appeals brought about by the frequency or number of such appeals. The expression dates from the early 1980s and came to reflect a concern that repeated images of starving and suffering people would lead to a deadening of the public's sympathy and generosity, especially towards THIRD WORLD countries affected by famine.

Comper. A fanatic or devotee of 'comps' or competitions, especially those of the type advertised on the back of products such as breakfast cereals. At the close of the 20th century the British 'comper king' was 78-year-old Leslie Jerman, a retired journalist, who over a three-year period alone won 150 prizes, from holidays to champagne. Many 'comps' involve the writing of original or punning advertising slogans, and Mr Jerman won a microwave oven from Iceland Frozen Foods for 'It's the finest food you ever thaw.'

Compiègne. A town about 65km (40 miles) northeast of Paris. It was in the adjacent forest of Compiègne, in the railway carriage of Marshal Foch, the Allied commander-in-chief, that on 10 November 1918 a delegation of moderate German politicians agreed to the punitive armistice terms set out by the Allies to end the First World War. All hostilities ceased the next day, at 11 a.m. on the eleventh day of the eleventh month (*see* ARMISTICE DAY). In the Second World War, after the fall of France, Hitler deliberately chose to re-enact the ceremony in reverse, and Foch's railway carriage was brought from a museum to the forest of Compiègne for General Jodl to dictate the German armistice terms to the French delegation on 22 June 1940. *See also* PÉTAINISTS; VICHY.

Comstockery. The rigid suppression of books, plays and other literature deemed to be salacious or corrupting, as advocated by the New York Society for the Suppression of Vice, whose moving spirit was the moral crusader Anthony Comstock (1844–1915). The word was coined in 1905 by George Bernard Shaw, writing in the *New York Times* of 26 September, when he defined it as 'the world's standing joke at the expense of the United States'.

Conan the Barbarian. The mighty-muscled warrior from Cimmeria created by the Texan writer Robert E. Howard and first appearing in short stories written for *Weird Tales* magazine in the early 1930s. He is big on brawn and small of brain, and slashes his way with his trusty sword through a fantastic world of magic and monsters. He continued to appear in a large number of later stories, many of them written by other hands.

Concentration camp. A guarded camp for non-military (usually political) prisoners. Concentration camps were first used by the British to intern Boer families in the Second BOER WAR (1899–1902), but the most infamous were the camps set up by the NAZIS after 1933 for the detention and persecution of their political opponents. *See also* HOLOCAUST.

Concept album. An oft-ridiculed development in the history of the pop music album, in which the tracks on the album, rather than being a series of discrete songs, together form a supposedly coherent series of songs on a related theme. The ROCK OPERA can be seen as a further development of the idea. *See also* SERGEANT PEPPER'S LONELY HEARTS CLUB BAND; ZIGGY STARDUST.

Concerning the Eccentricities of Cardinal Pirelli. A novel (1926) by Ronald Firbank (1886–1926), written while he was dying of tuberculosis. It has just two pieces of action, both of which take place in the cathedral. In the first, Pirelli ceremonially baptizes a young dog. In the second, he chases Chicklet, a young boy of dubious morality, around the cathedral before falling dead beneath a sacred painting, naked but for his mitre. The whole is presented in Firbank's distinctive style, which he suggested 'calls to mind a frieze with figures of varying heights all trotting the same way'.

Concert pitch. The pitch, internationally agreed in 1939 and renewed and extended in 1960, to which musical instruments are usually tuned, a frequency of 440 hertz (vibrations per second) for the A above middle C. It replaced the standard of 435 Hz fixed in Paris in 1859 and confirmed in Vienna in 1885. Figuratively, 'concert pitch' is a state of alertness or keen readiness.

Concorde. The world's first supersonic passenger aircraft was built jointly by Britain and France at a cost of some £360 million. The French aircraft, Concorde 001, made its maiden flight on 2 March 1969, and the British version, 002, a month later, on 9 April. It entered regular service on 21 January 1976. The name represents the combined Anglo-French enterprise. The most popular route for the aircraft is the transatlantic, the flight from London to New York taking about 3 hours 40 minutes, roughly half the time required by a conventional jet. The first fatal accident involving Concorde occurred on 25 July 2000 when a French Concorde, bound from Paris to New York, crashed 60 seconds after take-off, killing all 109 people on board.

Concordia. The fictional smallest country in Europe that is the setting of Peter Ustinov's play *Romanoff and Juliet* (1956). It was at one time a Roman Catholic land but it subsequently reverted to the Holy Unorthodox Church, headed by a deaf bishop aged over 100. It has an army with no cannon and a general atmosphere of indolence prevails.

Concordski. A media nickname, especially in the tabloid press, for the Soviet Tupolev Tu–144 supersonic transport aircraft, particularly at the time of its crash at the Paris Air Show on 23 June 1973. The name is a 'russified' version of CONCORDE.

Concord Sonata. A strikingly discordant work for piano, with solos for viola and flute, by Charles Ives (1874–1954). It was composed between 1909 and 1915. The title refers not to the harmoniousness of the piece, which is highly experimental and features note-clusters, but to Concord, Massachusetts, home of the New England Transcendentalists. The full title of the work is *Sonata No. 2 (Concord Mass., 1840–1860)*, and the four movements are 'Emerson', 'Hawthorne', 'The Alcotts' and 'Thoreau'.

Concrete jungle. An expression dating from the 1960s for a city, or area of a city, with a high proportion of large, unattractive, modern buildings, making it unpleasant as a living environment. The term was popularized by the ethologist Desmond Morris. *See also* ASPHALT JUNGLE; BLACKBOARD JUNGLE.

> The city is not a concrete jungle, it is a human zoo.
> DESMOND MORRIS: *The Human Zoo*, Introduction (1969)

Concrete poetry. A form of poetry arising in the 1960s in which the meaning or effect is conveyed partly or even entirely by visual means, either by using patterns of words or letters or by drawing on other typographical devices. British exponents include Edwin Morgan (b.1920), George MacBeth (1932–92) and Bob Cobbing (b.1920). The technique was to some extent foreshadowed by the US poet e.e. cummings (1894–1962).

Concrete skirting board. A barrier on the career ladder for female members of minority groups, especially Asian women. The imagery is based on the GLASS CEILING but is presented as a much tougher obstacle, involving bias not only against gender but also race and culture.

Confederacy of Dunces, A. A satirical comedy (1980) by the US novelist John Kennedy Toole (1937–1969). Thanks to the efforts of his mother it was published more than ten years after he committed suicide, and won the PULITZER PRIZE for fiction. It is set in New Orleans, and the central character, Ignatius Reilly, is an overweight, argumentative layabout, who interrelates with a cast of equally eccentric and accident-prone characters. The title comes from Jonathan Swift:

> When a true genius appears in the world, you may know him by this sign, that the dunces are all in confederacy against him.
> *Thoughts on Various Subjects, Moral and Diverting* (1711)

Confessional poetry. A term used mainly by literary critics for a distinctive type of autobiographical poetry that emerged in the United States in the 1960s. The designation was first applied to Robert Lowell's *Life Studies* (1959), in which he wrote of his marital problems, his psychiatric difficulties and his sometimes ambivalent feelings towards his family. Later examples of the genre are Anne Sexton's *To Bedlam and Part of the Way Back* (1960), describing her depressive illness, and Sylvia Plath's *Ariel* (1965), whose 40 poems express her personal responses to the world about and within her.

Conk out, To. To fail or stop running suddenly, as of an engine or motor. The word conk here is of uncertain origin. It may be simply onomatopoeic. The verb also means to collapse suddenly, as from exhaustion, or even to die. The actor John Le Mesurier, familiar as Sergeant Wilson in the DAD'S ARMY television series, arranged for the following announcement to be placed in *The Times* on his death (in 1983): 'John Le Mesurier wishes it to be known that he conked out on November 15th. He sadly misses family and friends.'

Conscientious objector. A person who objects to serving in the armed forces on grounds of conscience. The expression in this sense dates from the First World War. Colloquial names for a conscientious objector are 'CO' or (sometimes disparagingly) 'conchie' ('conchy').

Conservative with a small 'c'. Favouring traditional attitudes and values coupled with an aversion to change, as distinct from Conservative, belonging to the Conservative Party, which also espouses such attitudes and values but claims to do so selectively in order to conserve the best. *See also* WITH A CAPITAL.

> In popular opinion, independent schools are the Establishment, conservative with a small 'c', if not a larger one.
> *The Times* (13 October 1999)

Constructivism. A movement or trend in abstract art that originated in Russia *c*.1914, became dominant there after the 1917 Revolution, and spread to the West in the 1920s, where it has had considerable influence on a wide spectrum of artists. The founding father of the style, in which assorted mechanical objects are combined into abstract mobile structural forms, was Vladimir Tatlin (1885–1953), but his gigantic *Monument to the Third International*, intended to celebrate his faith in a communist society, never progressed beyond a wooden model, exhibited in 1920.

Contemptibles, Old. *See* OLD CONTEMPTIBLES.

Continental day. A school day common in many countries of mainland Europe, in which the timetable runs from early morning to early afternoon, typically 8 a.m. to 2 p.m. A day of this kind was adopted by some British schools from the 1980s, one prime advantage being the availability of greater time for after-school activities.

Continuity girl. The technique of filming allows a scenario to be shot in scenes that are not necessarily in sequence, and each shot may even be made several times. It is the task of the continuity girl to ensure that all details of costume, make-up, scenery and the like are correctly and consistently repeated each time. If this is done well the audience will be carried smoothly from one scene to the next without disturbing breaks or lapses of detail. The post has always been traditionally held by a woman.

Contras. Members of a guerrilla force in Nicaragua that opposed the left-wing SANDINISTA government of 1979 to 1990 and that was supported by the United States for much of that time. The force became widely known from the 'Iran-Contra' affair or Irangate of 1986 (*see under* GATE). It was officially disbanded in 1990, following the Sandinistas' electoral defeat. The name is an abbreviation of Spanish *contrarrevolucionario*, 'counter-revolutionary'.

Control freak. A person obsessed with controlling and manipulating others. The expression is of US origin and dates from the 1960s.

> Labour's control freaks will pay a high price for their paranoia over Red Ken [Livingstone].
> *The Times* (14 October 1999)

Conventional wisdom. An ironic term for a widely held belief on which most people act. The expression comes from J.K. Galbraith's *The Affluent Society* (1958) to describe economic ideas that are familiar and predictable and therefore accepted by the general public, or as he put it: 'the beliefs that are at any time assiduously, solemnly and mindlessly traded between the conventionally wise'. *See also* AFFLUENT SOCIETY.

> According to conventional wisdom, oppositions do well when governments run into trouble.
> *Sunday Express* (27 February 2000)

Convergence of the Twain, The. A poem (1914) by the British poet and novelist Thomas Hardy (1840–1928) about the sinking of the TITANIC in 1912. The 'twain' of the title are the ship and the iceberg with which it collided, an event that to Hardy was dictated by the mysterious Fate that governs the universe:

> Well: while was fashioning
> This creature of cleaving wing,
> The Immanent Will that stirs and urges everything
> Prepared a sinister mate
> For her – so gaily great –
> A Shape of Ice, for the time far and dissociate.

Convict # 2273. A name applied to himself by the US socialist Eugene Debs (1855–1926) during his campaign for the presidency in 1920 (his fifth attempt). He ran this campaign from Atlanta Penitentiary, where he was serving a 10-year sentence for a 1918 speech in which he had defended three socialists who refused to serve in the First World War; this was judged a violation of the 1917 Espionage Act. Despite these difficulties, Debs still won nearly a million votes. The following year President Harding released Debs from jail, but his US citizenship was not restored until 1976, 50 years after his death.

Coochy coochy coo. A nonsense phrase expressing affection as one tickles or cossets a young child or, depending on the circumstances, an adult. The words have a vaguely sexual suggestion, partly by association with the type of belly dance known as the hootchy-kootchy.

> Most cheering of all … was the novelist A.N. Wilson's recollection of [television cook Jennifer] Paterson coiling a lock of Enoch Powell's hair around her heavily jewelled finger and crooning 'coochy coochy coo' at him during one of the Spectator lunches she used to cook for.
> *Sunday Times* (15 August 1999)

Cookie Lady Affair. In 1970 US naval intelligence was informed that a Vietnamese national working at the US Navy offices in Saigon was selling discarded Navy documents to a woman who sold cookies (biscuits) on a nearby street corner. Expecting to uncover the early stages of a major spy ring, the Naval Investigative Service sent an officer to look the lady over. He bought three cookies from her, and she obligingly wrapped them in what the officer immediately recognized as a US Navy confidential message. It turned out that the cookie lady had been buying scrap paper from the employee to wrap her cookies, and that neither of them spoke a word of English. Security was subsequently tightened following this embarrassing blunder.

Cook on the front burner, To. To be on the right lines; to be on the road to success. The front burners (hotplates, rings) of a stove cook more rapidly than those at the back. The expression is an Americanism dating from the 1940s. *See also* ON THE BACK BURNER.

Cool. Fashionably attractive; smartly up-to-date and desirable. The colloquialism was as widely current in the 1990s as it first was in the 1930s, when it seems to have evolved from jazz slang, alluding to jazz that was restrained and relaxed, as distinct from 'hot' jazz, which is strongly rhythmical and played with verve. A record of Charlie Parker's *Cool Blues* was released in 1947.

> A formal white shirt without the conventional tie is both casual and smart, a sort of provisional definition of cool.
> *Sunday Times* (26 December 1999)

Cool Britannia. A vogue phrase, punning on the patriotic song 'Rule, Britannia', for the revitalized Britain that many saw emerging in 1997 on the election of a Labour government under Tony Blair. The watchword was 'new' by contrast with the staleness and paleness of John Major's previous Conservative administration. The phrase fell from favour as LUVVIES began to criticise BLAIRISM. *See also* NEW LABOUR.

> '[Britain and China] are two old and arrogant powers who know each other only too well', said one diplomat. 'It will take a lot more than Blair's New Labour and Cool Britannia to change fundamentally such a long, complex and often acrimonious relationship.'
> *The Times* (5 October 1998)

Cooling-off period. A period in which two sides in a dispute consider their position before resuming negotiations or discussions. The term is also used for the period of 14 days in which the signatory to a contract or agreement has the right to cancel. *See also* COOL IT.

> Ten years ago the annual England-Scotland home matches were called off after running battles in the streets and mayhem on the terraces. What has happened in between could hardly be called a cooling-off period.
> *The Times* (21 October 1999)

Cool it. Relax, calm down. An injunction to someone who has become overheated. *See also* COOL.

Cop, To. An old verb meaning 'to catch' that in the 20th century formed a number of phrases, many of them of black American origin. Examples are 'cop a drag', to smoke a cigarette, 'cop a nod', to have a nap, 'cop a packet', to be killed or wounded, 'cop a squat', to sit down, 'cop a steal', to steal. *See also* COP A FEEL; COP A PLEA.

Copacabana. A famous New York nightclub on East 60th Street, opened in 1940. For the next two decades it was a glamorous venue for performances by such well known names as Frank Sinatra, Ella Fitzgerald,

Nat King Cole and Jimmy Durante. It then declined in popularity and closed in 1973. The name is that of the main beach of Rio de Janeiro in Brazil, a magnet for foreign tourists.

Cop a feel, To. To fondle sexually or FEEL UP. *See also* COP.

Cop a plea, To. To engage in plea bargaining, i.e. to plead guilty to a lesser charge in return for the dropping of a greater one. The device is a peculiarity of the US legal system. *See also* COP.

Cop out, To. To abandon an attempt; to go back on one's word; to avoid one's responsibility. Hence a cop-out as a cowardly or feeble evasion.

Copper's copper. A senior police officer respected and trusted by his men, who see him as 'one of us'. The phrase may have arisen by contrast with 'copper's nark', a police informer, who is obviously not to be trusted.

> [Sir John Stevens, Metropolitan Commissioner of Police] ... variously described as 'the best detective in the country', 'a man with a CV to die for' and 'a copper's copper'.
> *Sunday Times* (30 January 2000)

Copycat killing. A killing carried out in imitation of another, whether real or fictional. The increasing incidence of murders of this type in the latter half of the 20th century raised concern about the lurid publicity lavished on such crimes by the media and generated debate regarding the extent to which scenes of violence on television and in the cinema are capable of influencing the young and susceptible. Stanley Kubrick's controversial film version of Anthony Burgess's novel *A* CLOCKWORK ORANGE (1962), first screened in 1971, was banned by Kubrick in 1973 in response to criticism that it could lead to copycat killings, and several rapes and murders were linked to the film. A gang chanting 'Singing in the Rain', a tune accompanying a vicious mugging in the film, was said to have raped a girl in Lancashire, and a judge condemned the film after a teenage boy wearing the 'droog' uniform of white overalls and black bowler hat beat a younger child. The film was re-released only in 2000. *See also* NADSAT.

Coral Gables. A superb example of a planned city adjoining Miami, Florida. It was developed by George E. Merrick on his family's farmland and at its incorporation in 1925 named for the family's house of coral rock walls and gables. It is noted for its blend of Spanish and contemporary architecture and for its unique 'villages' with houses built in French, South African Dutch and Chinese styles, and although originally exclusively residential now contains several offices of large corporations, especially those trading with Latin America. To a large degree it is a visible realization of Merrick's ambition to build 'a place where castles in Spain are made real'.

Co-respondent shoes. Men's two-toned shoes, fashionable in the 1930s. They were so called because they were supposedly worn by a man cited in a divorce case, in other words by a 'cad'. They are sometimes erroneously called 'correspondent shoes', e.g. in Michael Tambini's study of 20th-century design, *The Look of the Century* (1999), presumably for their matching tones.

> In no circumstances should he [the 'Egmonter', or well-mannered male] wear 'co-respondent's shoes'.
> GUY EGMONT: *The Art of Egmontese*, ch v (1961)

Corgi and Bess. A broadcasting nickname for the Christmas message given annually on radio and television by Queen Elizabeth II, noted for her pet corgis, the pun being on PORGY AND BESS.

Corn circles. *See* CROP CIRCLES.

Cornelia Gray. *See* GRAY, CORNELIA.

Corn is Green, The. A play (1938) by the British playwright Emlyn Williams (1905–87) about the experiences of a schoolmistress in the Welsh valleys at the turn of the century. The title evokes not only the rural surroundings but also the 'unripeness' of Miss Moffat's star pupil, Morgan Evans, and his preparation by her for the great deeds she hopes he will perform in later life. Williams himself played the schoolboy in the first production, recreating on stage the close relationship he himself had had as a boy with his own teacher, Miss Cooke, who nurtured his burgeoning talents.

Cornish Alps. A humorous local nickname for the clay spoil tips that are a prominent feature of the landscape surrounding St Austell in Cornwall. Viewed on a sunny day they do in fact bear a fancied resemblance to snow-covered peaks.

Cornish Riviera. A touristic name, based on that of the French Riviera, for the southern coast of Cornwall, and in particular Mounts Bay, from Penzance in the west to the Lizard in the east. The name is familiar from the Cornish Riviera express train from

Paddington to Penzance. It first ran in 1904, when it was named the Riviera Express by J.C. Inglis, General Manager of the Great Western Railway. The south Devon and Dorset coast, further east, is sometimes similarly known as the English Riviera.

Coronation chicken. Cold chicken with a curry sauce, accompanied by a salad of rice and peas and named for the coronation of Elizabeth II in 1953. The supreme advantage of the cold dish was that it would avoid the need for cooking on the day.

Coronation Street. An enduringly popular television SOAP OPERA about working-class life in the (fictional) Manchester district of Weatherfield, first screened on 9 December 1960. The locale is the street so named, and most of the action takes place in a pub, the Rover's Return, at one end and a corner shop at the other. The cast and the characters they play have become household names, and the series has been lauded by prime ministers (Harold Wilson) and poets (John Betjeman). Its early story lines tended to be largely devoid of political or social issues, their content mostly concentrating on tales of petty scandals and illicit relationships, but in recent years social issues as diverse as teenage pregnancy and even transsexualism have found their way into the programme.

Corridors of power. A collective term for the ministries in Whitehall with their top-ranking civil servants. The phrase was popularized (but not invented) by C.P. Snow in his novel *Homecomings* (1956) and gained wide acceptance. He later used it for the title of the novel *Corridors of Power* (1964).

> Boffins at daggers drawn in corridors of power.
> *The Times* (headline) (8 April 1965)

Cosa Nostra (Italian, 'our thing'). A name for the Mafia crime syndicate in the USA. It was originally used as a secret name but was made public by the informer Joseph Valachi in 1962.

> A former member of organized crime's ruling body, Mr Joseph Valachi, has named names and drawn a master plan of the Syndicate (which the underworld refers to as *Cosa Nostra*).
> *Economist* (17 August 1963)

Cosmetic surgery. An operation performed to enhance an individual's appearance rather than to cure disease. It is chiefly undergone among women and typically involves an alteration of the size or shape of the nose (rhinoplasty), breasts (mammoplasty) or chin (mentoplasty) or a FACE LIFT. The first two of these are known colloquially and respectively as a 'nose job' and a 'boob job'.

Cosmic Bob. A nickname given to Senator Bob Kerrey (b.1943) of Nebraska owing to his interest in other-worldly matters. He briefly and unsuccessfully ran for the Democratic presidential nomination in 1992.

Cosmonaut (Russian *kosmonavt*, from Russian *kosmos*, 'space', and Greek *nautēs*, 'sailor'). A Soviet ASTRONAUT. The word was first popularized in the late 1950s, when the USSR and the United States began their rivalry for space, and continued to be used for Russian astronauts in the post-Soviet era.

> Russia's endangered space programme was rescued yesterday by the skill of one of its cosmonauts.
> *The Times* (3 September 1994)

Costa del Crime. A nickname for the southeast coast of Spain, used by several British criminals as a bolt-hole from the law. The name punningly reflects those of various stretches of holiday coastline such as *Costa Brava* or *Costa del Sol*. The expression was the invention of the popular press and dates from the 1980s. The Costa Brava itself was so named in 1918 by the Spanish poet and journalist Ferran Aguiló in recognition of its ruggedness.

> Jack Took … said he expected that Harry Harris was at that very moment living it up on the Costa del Criminal [*sic*] with Miss Eddon Gurney.
> FAY WELDON: *The Heart of the Country* (1987)

Costa Geriatrica. A jocular name dating from the 1980s for the south coast of England, as a region with a large residential population of old and retired people, who seek sunny summers, sea air and mild winters. The name imitates those of Spanish coastal regions such as *Costa Brava*.

> Affectionately derided for decades as the 'Costa Geriatrica', even by the geriatric residents themselves, the Dorset resort [Bournemouth] must now have more nightclubs than Manhattan.
> *The Times* (29 July 1999)

Cost an arm and a leg, To. To be very expensive. The loss of both an arm and a leg is clearly too great a price to pay.

Cosy up to, To. To ingratiate oneself by creating a mutually agreeable or 'cosy' relationship. The expression is of US origin and dates from the 1930s.

> The BBC will do itself no harm by cosying up to the culture secretary.
> *Sunday Times* (6 June 1999)

Cot death. The unexplained death of a baby in its sleep, more formally known as sudden infant death syndrome (SIDS). It is the most common form of death between the ages of one month and one year, and is slightly more common among boys, among second children, and in winter. There may be no single cause for the death, which often cannot be explained even after autopsy.

Cottage industry. An industry in which employees work in their own homes, using their own equipment. The term dates from the 1920s.

Cottaging. In gay jargon the act of waiting or loitering in a public toilet or 'cottage' for the purpose of a sexual encounter. The adoption of this particular word is said to derive from the particulars of an eccentric 19th-century will in which the testator left a large sum to be expended on the construction of 'cottages of convenience', so called as public lavatories are small buildings. The verbal noun dates from the 1960s.

> Two adult men caught 'cottaging' in a public toilet are likely to be given advice about inappropriate behaviour.
>
> *The Times* (25 August 1999)

Cottingley fairies. *See under* FAKES.

Couch potato. A person who prefers lounging at home watching television to engaging in any purposeful activity, especially if it involves any physical effort. The expression is of US origin and probably puns on BOOB TUBE as slang for a television, the potato being a plant tuber. There may further be a punning reference to the fact that such a person is 'all eyes'.

> The interactive potential of the new medium is the kiss of death for the couch potato. Your [digital] television will no longer be just a 'dumb instrument' dealing out whatever the programme planners have on their set menus.
>
> *Sunday Times* (4 October 1998)

Couéism. A system of therapy by auto-suggestion popular in the 1920s. It was propounded by the French pharmacist and hypnotist Émile Coué (1857–1926) and was encapsulated in the formula familiar in English as: 'Every day, in every way, I am getting better and better.' Coué recommended his patients mouth the mantra 15 to 20 times every morning and evening.

> *Tous les jours, à tous points de vue, je vais de mieux en mieux* ('Every day, from every point of view, I am getting better and better').
>
> ÉMILE COUÉ: *De la suggestion et de ses applications* ('On Suggestion and its Applications') (1915)

Countdown. A simple light entertainment television programme first screened in 1982 that somewhat curiously became cult afternoon viewing. Two contestants were required first to construct as long a word as possible from nine randomly drawn letters of the alphabet and then to manipulate numbers, also randomly selected, to arrive at a stated total. Part of the attraction lay in the cheerfully bumbling banter of the host, Richard Whiteley, on the one hand, and the photogenic charms of the letters and numbers drawer, Carol Vorderman, on the other.

Count one's blessings, To. To be grateful for what one has. Edith Temple and Reginald Morgan's song 'Count Your Blessings One by One' became a hit in the late 1940s through such singers as Josef Locke, Harry Secombe and the Luton Girls Choir.

Countries of the world. Most of the nation-states in the world gained their independence as republics or sovereign states in the 20th century. The following is a tally of the situation at the close of the century, with the year in which each nation-state gained or declared independence and a brief note on the circumstances of the change of status. There were two great waves in this respect: the liberation from colonial rule in the WIND OF CHANGE that blew across Africa from the late 1950s, and the establishment of independent states in eastern Europe resulting from the formal dissolution of the Soviet Union in 1991. Some states, notably in Africa, took a new name on gaining independence, such as Ghana, formerly Gold Coast.

> **Albania** (1912): independence from the Turkish empire
>
> **Algeria** (1962): independence from France
>
> **Andorra** (1993): Andorra's first formal constitution
>
> **Angola** (1975): independence from Portugal
>
> **Antigua and Barbuda** (1981): independence from Britain
>
> **Armenia** (1991): secession from the Soviet Union; Armenia was briefly independent 1918–20 after Turkish (16th century) then Russian (1916) conquests
>
> **Austria** (1955): recognition of Austrian sovereignty by the former Allied powers; Austria had previously become a republic in 1920 following the collapse of

the Austro-Hungarian Empire, but was absorbed into the German Reich 1938–45

Azerbaijan (1991): secession from the Soviet Union; Azerbaijan became an independent republic in 1918 but was occupied by Russia in 1920

Bahamas (1973): independence from Britain

Bahrain (1971): independence from Britain

Bangladesh (1971): secession from PAKISTAN, of which Bangladesh was formerly the eastern province

Barbados (1966): independence from Britain

Belarus (1991): secession from the Soviet Union; Belarus was a Soviet Republic from 1919 (as Byelorussia)

Belize (1981): full independence from Britain

Benin (1960): independence from France (Benin was known as Dahomey until 1975)

Bosnia-Herzegovina (1992): international recognition of Bosnia's secession from Yugoslavia, of which it had been a constituent part since 1918

Botswana (1966): independence from Britain

Brunei (1984): full independence from Britain

Bulgaria (1946): proclamation of a communist republic; Bulgaria had previously been an independent kingdom from 1908 after 500 years of Turkish domination

Burkina Faso (1960): independence from France

Burundi (1962): independence from Belgium

Cambodia (1953): independence from France; known as Kampuchea 1976–89

Cameroon (1960): independence from France

Cape Verde (1975): independence from Portugal

Central African Republic (1960) independence from France

Chad (1960): independence from France

Comoros (apart from Mayotte) (1975): independence from France

Congo (1960): independence from Belgium; full name Democratic Republic of Congo; known as Zaire 1971–97

Congo-Brazzaville (1960): independence from France

Côte d'Ivoire (1960): independence from France

Croatia (1991): secession from Yugoslavia, of which it had been a constituent part since 1918

Cuba (1901): proclamation of republic; Cuba had been ceded to the USA by Spain in 1898 and was administered by the USA 1898–1901 and 1906–9

Cyprus (1960): independence from Britain

Czech Republic (1993): became a sovereign state when Slovakia (*see below*) seceded from Czechoslovakia, which had existed since 1918

Djibouti (1977): independence from France

Dominica (1978): independence from Britain

Egypt (1953): proclamation of republic; Egypt was granted nominal independence by Britain in 1922

Equatorial Guinea (1968): independence from Spain

Eritrea (1993): secession from Ethiopia

Estonia (1991): secession from the Soviet Union, of which it had been a constituent republic since 1945; previously Estonia had been a democratic republic 1919–40 and was occupied by Germany 1941–44

Fiji (1970): independence from Britain

Finland (1917): independence from Russia, which had ruled Finland since 1809

Gabon (1960): independence from France

Gambia (1965): independence from Britain

Georgia (1991): secession from the Soviet Union, of which it had been a constituent republic since 1922

Ghana (1957): independence from Britain

Grenada (1974): independence from Britain

Guinea (1958): independence from France

Guinea-Bissau (1974): independence from Portugal

Guyana (1966): independence from Britain

Hungary (1918): became an independent republic, stripped of much of its former territory, after the collapse of the Austro-Hungarian empire

Iceland (1944): independence from Denmark

India (1947): independence from Britain; the partition of British India created the states of India and PAKISTAN

Indonesia (1949): independence from the Netherlands

Iran (1979): proclamation of an Islamic republic

Ireland (1921): limited independence as a dominion of the British empire; constitution of 1937 declared Ireland to be a sovereign nation (*see* EIRE); became the Republic of Ireland in 1949

Israel (1948): proclamation of the state of Israel after the end of the British LEAGUE OF NATIONS mandate in Palestine (*see* MANDATE)

Jamaica (1962): independence from Britain

Jordan (1946): independence as the Kingdom of Jordan; as Transjordan it had been a British MANDATE 1920–23, then a separate emirate.

Kazakhstan (1991): secession from the Soviet Union

Kenya (1963): independence from Britain

Kiribati (1979): independence from Britain

Kyrgyzstan (1991): secession from the Soviet Union

Laos (1954): independence from France

Latvia (1991): secession from the Soviet Union, of which it had been a constituent republic since 1945; previously Latvia had been an independent republic 1919–40 and was occupied by Germany 1941–44

Lebanon (1944): independence from France, which had ruled the area as a LEAGUE OF NATIONS mandate since 1920 (*see* MANDATE)

Lesotho (1966): independence from Britain

Libya (1951): independence gained after Italian rule (from 1911) and Anglo-French administration after the Second World War

Lithuania (1991): secession from the Soviet Union, of which it had been a constituent republic since 1945; previously Lithuania had been an independent state 1919–40 and was occupied by Germany 1941–44

Macedonia (1992): secession from Yugoslavia

Madagascar (1960): independence from France

Malawi (1964): independence from Britain

Malaysia (1963): formed from a group of former British colonies which had gained independence in 1957 as the Federation of Malaya, plus territories in northwestern Borneo and Singapore (*see below*)

Maldives (1965): independence from Britain

Mali (1960): independence from France

Malta (1964): independence from Britain

Mauritania (1960) independence from France

Mauritius (1968): independence from Britain

Micronesia (1990): recognition of independence

Moldova (1991): secession from the Soviet Union

Mongolia (1924): establishment of republic following centuries of Chinese domination

Morocco (1956): independence from France

Mozambique (1975): independence from Portugal

Myanmar (Burma) (1948): independence from Britain; the country's name was changed to Myanmar in 1989

Namibia (1990): independence from South Africa, which in 1966 had ignored the cancellation by the United Nations of the MANDATE under which South Africa had ruled Namibia since 1919

Nauru (1968): recognition of independence

Niger (1960): independence from France

Nigeria (1960): independence from Britain

North Korea (1948): declaration of a People's Republic; the state was created from the zone north of the 38th parallel occupied by Soviet troops after Japan's surrender at the end of the Second World War

Pakistan (1947): independence from Britain (*see also* India *above*)

Panama (1903): independence (with US support) from Spain

Papua New Guinea (1975): recognition of independence

Philippines (1946): independence from the USA, of which the islands had been a colony since 1898

Poland (1918): restoration of statehood after the First World War; Poland had been carved up between Russia, Austria and Prussia in the second half of the 18th century

Rwanda (1962): independence from Belgium

St Lucia (1979): independence from Britain

St Vincent and the Grenadines (1979): independence from Britain

Samoa (1962): recognition of independence

São Tomé e Príncipe (1975): independence from Portugal

Saudi Arabia (1932): state created from the kingdoms of Najd and Hejaz; Arab rulers had fought over the area after the demise of the Turkish empire in 1918

Senegal (1960): independence from France

Seychelles (1976): independence from Britain

Sierra Leone (1961): independence from Britain

Singapore (1965): secession from the Federation of Malaya (*see* Malaysia above)

Slovakia (1993): secession from Czechoslovakia (*see* Czech Republic *above*)

Slovenia (1991): secession from Yugoslavia, of which it had been a constituent part since 1918

Solomon Islands (1978): independence from Britain

Somalia (1960): creation of an independent republic by a merger of former British Somaliland and Italian Somaliland

South Africa (1961): declaration of a republic outside the British Commonwealth; South Africa achieved independence within the British empire in 1910

South Korea (1948): republic formed out of the zone

south of the 38th parallel of latitude, the area occupied by US troops after Japan's surrender in 1945 at the end of the Second World War

Sri Lanka (1972): independence from Britain

Sudan (1955): independence from Britain; under Anglo-Egyptian administration from 1899

Suriname (1975): independence from the Netherlands

Swaziland (1968): independence from Britain

Syria (1946): independence from France, which had ruled the area as a LEAGUE OF NATIONS mandate since 1920 (*see* MANDATE)

Tajikistan (1991): secession from the Soviet Union

Tanzania (1961): independence from Britain as Tanganyika, which united with Zanzibar to become Tanzania in 1964

Togo (1960): independence from France

Tonga (1970): independence from Britain

Trinidad and Tobago (1962): independence from Britain

Tunisia (1956): independence from France

Turkey (1923): proclamation of a Turkish republic

Turkmenistan (1991): secession from the Soviet Union

Tuvalu (1978): independence from Britain

Uganda (1962): independence from Britain

Ukraine (1991): secession from the Soviet Union

United Arab Emirates (1971): independence from Britain

Uzbekistan (1991): secession from the Soviet Union

Vanuatu (1980): recognition of independence

Vatican (1929): the Vatican City State came into being through the LATERAN TREATY of 1929

Vietnam (1976): proclamation of the Socialist Republic of Vietnam after the VIETNAM War

Yemen (1990): merging of North and South Yemen; previously the North became independent of Turkey in 1918, and the South independent of Britain in 1967

Yugoslavia (1918): creation of the Kingdom of Serbs, Croats and Slovenes, consisting of Serbia, Montenegro, Macedonia, Bosnia, Croatia and Slovenia; renamed Yugoslavia in 1929; reduced in size by the secession of Slovenia, Croatia, Bosnia and Macedonia in the early 1990s

Zambia (1964): independence from Britain

Zimbabwe (1980): independence from Britain

Country. The 20th century has seen the burgeoning of this word as the name for a geographical region associated with a particular writer or artist. Shakespeare Country is thus the region around Stratford-upon-Avon, Hardy Country is historical Wessex, where Thomas Hardy's novels are set, and Constable Country is the Stour Valley, Suffolk, where John Constable lived and painted. More recent than any of these is Catherine Cookson Country, or South Tyneside, where the prolific and long-lived popular novelist lived. Charles G. Harper's *The Hardy Country* appeared as early as 1904 in a series published by A & C Black that also included *The Burns Country*, *The Dickens Country* and *The Scott Country*. These regions are also promoted by local tourist authorities, as are such obvious literary shrines as the Brontë Country around Haworth, Bradford, while famous persons have given rise to themed areas such as Captain Cook Country between Whitby, North Yorkshire, and Middlesbrough. Many recent 'Countries' have drawn tourists as the settings of filmed fiction. Herriot Country is thus the region around Askrigg in North Yorkshire where the televised version of James Herriot's novel of veterinary life *All Creatures Great and Small* (1972) was filmed. *See also* TELETOURISM.

> Small is beautiful. Never have these words been more apt than when applied to the Forster Country of North Hertfordshire, which adjoins Rooks Nest, childhood home of the writer E.M. Forster.
> MARGARET ASHBY: *Forster Country*, Introduction (1991)

Country and western. A form of COUNTRY MUSIC that in the 1940s and 1950s added cowboy songs to the generally rural music of southern American states. The name is popularly abbreviated to C&W. *See also* WESTERN.

Country fit for heroes. A phrase derived from a speech that the British prime minister David Lloyd George, the WELSH WIZARD, made at Wolverhampton on 24 November 1918, less than two weeks after the end of the First World War. His exact words were slightly different: 'What is our task? To make Britain a fit country for heroes to live in.' Lloyd George's COALITION GOVERNMENT swept back to power in the general election the following month. However, the phrase came to have a notoriously hollow ring, as, once the brief postwar economic boom was over, many former servicemen found themselves without a job, to the apparent indifference of those in power.

Country mile. A very long way. A mile in the country can take longer to traverse than in the town. The term is of US origin.

Country music. A form of popular or folk music originating in the southern states of the United States in the early 20th century. It can be ultimately traced back to British immigrants who brought with them a tradition of narrative Celtic ballads and string-instrument playing, especially fiddling, and came to be known by different genre names depending on dominant elements or geographical factors. *See also* BLUEGRASS; COUNTRY AND WESTERN; HILLBILLY.

Countryside Alliance. A lobby of some quarter of a million country residents from all over Britain who organized a demonstration in London on 1 March 1998 to protest against certain government policies and proposals that would adversely affect their way of life. Chief among their concerns were a possible ban on blood sports and especially fox-hunting, the prospect of more building on GREEN BELT land and the hesitant handling of the MAD COW DISEASE crisis. Protesters also called for an end to the decline of rural services such as village shops and country buses.

Count sheep, To. To imagine sheep crossing an obstacle and count them one by one as a supposed aid to inducing sleep. The dodge was known to the Victorians but became popular as an insomniac's soporific recourse only in the 20th century. The choice of this particular animal for the purpose may have arisen from a verbal association between 'sheep' and 'sleep'.

Count to 10, To. To pause when heated or angry in order to recover one's composure. The idea is that a mental count of one to 10 will give one enough time to cool down. The expression is often used as an imperative, sometimes to oneself, as: 'He was a proper – count to 10! – rascal.'

County Hall. This impressive building on the south bank of the Thames in London was opened by George V in 1922 to house the London County Council, which until then had occupied crowded premises off Trafalgar Square. Construction took 13 years, partly because of the size of the building, partly because marshland on the site had to be reclaimed. On the demise of the LCC in 1965 County Hall became home to its successor, the Greater London Council, until that body in turn ceased to exist in 1986, leaving London as the only European city without any elected authority. The future of the building remained uncertain for some years until it reopened in 1998 as a luxury hotel, complete with conference facilities, an aquarium and a health and fitness club.

Couples. A novel (1968) by the US writer John Updike (b.1932) about eight couples in suburban Massachusetts. Piet, who is married to Angela, has an affair with Georgene, and also with a pregnant Foxy, whom he impregnates immediately after she has had the baby. Georgene's husband lusts after Angela, who agrees to sleep with him in return for his having procured an abortion for Foxy. And so on. In the end, some normality is achieved. Piet and Foxy, now married to each other, 'live in Lexington, where, gradually, among people like themselves, they have been accepted, as another couple'.

Coupon Election. During the general election of 1918 Prime Minister David Lloyd George and Chancellor of the Exchequer Bonar Law sent a certificate or coupon to all candidates supporting the COALITION GOVERNMENT. The coupon was not accepted by the Asquith Liberals or by the Labour Party. A 'couponeer' was a politician who accepted the coupon.

Courtesy. A word applied variously to a product or service provided with the intention of being helpful or solicitous. A 'courtesy car' is thus one supplied free of charge by a commercial organization to someone already paying for other services, while a 'courtesy phone' in a supermarket or hotel enables customers or guests to call a taxi or hire a car, which itself may have a 'courtesy light', automatically switching on when a door is open. A 'courtesy call' is a telephone call made by a commercial organization to a private individual with the aim of selling something, usually double glazing, and as such is often intrusive and so anything but courteous.

Court shoes. Low-cut shoes for women, without laces or straps, and so called from their use as part of court dress. The US equivalent name for such shoes is 'pumps'.

> 'Elfine, *whatever* you do, always wear court shoes. Remember – c-o-u-r-t.'
> STELLA GIBBONS: *Cold Comfort Farm*, ch xi (1932)

Coventry. A city in the English Midlands, which during the Second World War was a centre for the manufacture of military vehicles, munitions and armaments. On the night of 15 November 1940 the city was extensively damaged by 449 Luftwaffe bombers in an operation codenamed Moonlight. Over 1000 civilians were killed or badly injured, 50,000 houses damaged, and the famous medieval cathedral was almost completely destroyed. Another raid followed in April 1941. The burnt remains of the cathedral now stand alongside the new cathedral, designed by Sir Basil Spence (1907–76), which was consecrated in 1962. *See also* WAR REQUIEM.

Cover girl. A now dated term for an attractive young woman whose photograph appears, or deserves to appear, on the front cover of a magazine. The phrase is of US origin and dates from the early years of the 20th century.

Cowboy. An unqualified and usually unscrupulous provider of goods and services, especially in the building trade. The word in this sense dates from the 1960s and derives from an earlier term for a reckless driver, especially a lorry driver. This in turn goes back to a US slang term of the 1930s for any reckless young man, comparing him to the 'wild and woolly' original cowboys who were the cattle-herders of the American West. *See also* WHITE VAN MAN.

Crack down on something, To. To repress it; to take strong measures against it. The expression dates from the 1930s.

Crackerjack. A long-running children's television programme screened from 1955 to 1984. It based its content largely on the music hall, and mixed slapstick sketches with pop music numbers, interspersed with 'boys v. girls' competitions. Many of its presenters, such as Eamonn Andrews, Leslie Crowther and Michael Aspel, subsequently became famous names on adult television. 'Crackerjack' itself is an evocative slang word for anyone or anything regarded as excellent.

Crammer. A type of private (independent) secondary school that concentrates on preparing its students for examinations and university entry. They are so called since they 'cram' their fee-paying candidates with the appropriate subject knowledge and the 'tricks of the trade'. They are less in evidence now than they once were, but are by no means defunct, since there are always schools where pupils are poorly taught and always pupils who lack application or intellect.

Cramp someone's style, To. To prevent them from acting freely or naturally. The image is of physically restricting one's manner of writing. The expression dates from the early 20th century.

Crash and burn, To. To fail disastrously in a romance or some other experience or enterprise. The allusion is to an aircraft or car that crashes and catches fire. The phrase is of US campus origin and dates from the 1970s.

> Many start-ups [newly established businesses] will crash and burn.
> *The Times* (16 August 1999)

Crash out, To. To go to sleep, especially suddenly or in a place other than one's usual bed.

> We never actually go to sleep in Leeds, we just crash out, then get up the next morning and think about doing it all again.
> *The Times* (15 May 1999)

Crash pad. A place where one can CRASH OUT.

Crazy Foam. The proprietary name of a type of foam for children sold as a pressurized foam in an aerosol container and a popular toy or joke device in the 1960s.

Crazy Gang. The lunatic lot so named first formed up in 1932 for a performance of the revue *Crazy Month* at the London Palladium. It consisted of three pairs of already famous comics: Flanagan and Allen, otherwise Bud Flanagan (Robert Wintrop, originally Reuben Weintrop) (1896–1968) and Chesney Allen (1894–1982), Nervo and Knox, viz. Jimmy Nervo (James Henry Holloway) (1897–1975) and Teddy Knox (1896–1974), and the Scots pair Naughton and Gold, i.e. Charlie Naughton (1887–1976) and Jimmy Gold (James McGonigal) (1886–1967). They remained together until 1960. The name Crazy Gang was applied in the 1980s and 1990s to the players of Wimbledon Football Club, for their vigorous style of play and antics both on and off the football field.

Crazy golf. A form of putting in which balls have to negotiate a number of obstacles such as humps, tunnels, bends and bridges in order to reach the hole. *See also* CLOCK GOLF.

> Until recently crazy golf was regarded as a quaint relic of the 1950s: now, with a glut in conventional 18-hole courses, long-nurtured plans for wilder alternatives are beginning to emerge.
> *Sunday Times* (26 July 1998)

Crazy like a fox. Very shrewd or cunning. An ungrammatical phrase of US origin, and the title of an anthology of prose pieces by the American humorist S.J. Perelman published in 1944.

Crazy mixed-up kid. A young person whose mind is confused by conflicting emotions. The expression dates from the 1950s.

Crazy paving. Paving composed of irregularly shaped stone or concrete slabs, used for ornamental effect on terraces, garden paths and the like.

Cream of the crop. The best of anything. The alliterative phrase may owe something to the similarly alliterative and virtually synonymous French *crème de la crème*.

Cream tea. Afternoon tea that includes scones with clotted cream and jam. The name of the meal is first recorded only in the mid-1960s but must have existed some time before this. The homeland of the cream tea is the southwest of England, hence its alternative name of 'Devon cream tea', but the repast is now found in all parts of the British Isles as a leading staple in a variety of teashops.

Creature of habit. A person who follows an unvarying routine. The implication is that the one so described is governed by the routine and cannot break free of it.

Credibility gap. The disparity that can exist between a claim or statement on the one hand and the reality of the situation on the other. If this is constantly experienced, it results in a loss of confidence in those making such statements. President Nixon created a credibility gap in the 1960s when he asked black Americans 'to judge him by his deeds and not his words'. They did, and were disappointed.

CREEP. An acronym for Committee for the Re-Election of the President, the inner circle that organized President Richard Nixon's campaign for a second term in the White House in 1972. After the WATERGATE scandal broke CREEP was revealed to have been involved in various illegal activities, such as funding the actual burglars. *See also* TRICKY DICKY.

Crest of a wave. To be on the crest of a wave is to be 'riding high' or making good progress in one's affairs, while more generally it is to be optimistic or OVER THE MOON. Ralph Reader's song 'Riding Along on the Crest of a Wave' (1937) was the theme tune of his GANG SHOW.

Crew cut. A form of haircut popularized by US athletes, particularly college rowing crews at Harvard and Yale universities, in the decade following the Second World War. The hair is closely cropped and brushed upright.

Crew neck. A close-fitting round neckline on a sweater. Its origin is similar to that of the CREW CUT.

Cribb, Sergeant. The bowler-hatted police detective in the crime novels by Peter Lovesey, beginning with *Wobble to Death* (1970). The stories are pastiche Victorian tales mostly set against a background of sports and outdoor pastimes. A television series based on the books, *Cribb* (1979–81), starred Alan Dobie in the title role.

Cricket in Times Square, The. A children's novel (1960) and the best known book by the US writer George Selden (1929–89). It tells the story of Chester, a cricket, who travels to New York from rural Connecticut. *See also* TIMES SQUARE.

Cricket test. A hypothetical indicator of the national loyalty of new immigrants to Britain, and of their degree of integration into the British way of life. The phrase was prompted by a controversial contribution by Norman Tebbit (*see* CHINGFORD SKINHEAD) in April 1990 to a debate in the House of Commons on immigration from Hong Kong. He suggested that a way of determining whether immigrants from the Indian subcontinent were fully integrated into British society was to see whether they supported England or their country of origin in cricket test matches between the two.

> Those right-wing ideologues – who define patriotism by a 'cricket test' – completely fail to understand our true strengths.
> GORDON BROWN in *The Times* (10 January 2000)

Crimbo. Christmas. A child's word adopted in the 1980s by adults, especially those in the armed services and the popular media, who took to wishing all and sundry a 'Happy Crimbo'. Variants are Crimble and even just Crim.

> What with their Boxing Day feast of fun and this video for new single *Say You'll Be Mine*, Steps are going to be ever-present this Crimble.
> *heat* (16 December 1999–5 January 2000)

Cringe-making. Embarrassing enough to produce a physical reaction, as if cringing. The expression dates from the 1980s.

> A New Year's Eve show from my childhood ... is seared on my memory as one of the most cringe-making in television history.
> *The Times* (16 April 1999)

Crippen, Dr. The still redolent name of Hawley Harvey Crippen (1862–1910), an American doctor whose poisoning of his wife, an amateur music-hall artiste calling herself Belle Elmore, was one of the most sensational cases of the early 20th century. The remains of her body were discovered in 1910 in the coal cellar at 39 Hilldrop Crescent, north London, where Crippen had been living with his mistress, Ethel Le Neve. The pair had meanwhile fled to Canada on board the SS *Montrose*, Crippen calling himself Mr Robinson and Le Neve disguising herself as his son. The ship's captain was suspicious, however, and sent a message to Scotland Yard by wireless telegraphy. Chief Inspector Dew set off in pursuit in another ship and boarded the *Montrose* in the St Lawrence River. The use of telegraphy, the first known use of radio in making an arrest, meant that newspapers were able to report every stage of the chase before the murderer was even aware that he had been discovered. Crippen was hanged but Le Neve acquitted, living until 1967.

Crisp packet option. A cheap and shoddy alternative to a proper or genuine article. The allusion is to crisp packets as one of the cheapest forms of packaging, serving simply as a basic container for its rapidly consumed contents.

Croft, Lara. The feisty, busty heroine of the *Tomb Raider* computer game series. She is the dreamchild of Jeremy Heath-Smith, who created her in 1996, and is produced by his company, Core Design. In the manner of her kind she has a fantasy 'biography' which records that she was born on 14 February (Valentine's Day) in Wimbledon, the daughter of Lord Henshingley Croft, attended Wimbledon High School for Girls, GORDONSTOUN and a Swiss finishing school, and went out in the world with the occupation of 'adventurer'. In 1998 the model Nell McAndrew assumed her PIN-UP persona for a promotional tour in Europe.

> There is no doubt that Lara Croft is a lot more than a mere computer character. She has touched a nerve in the same way that James Bond does, and has become the first icon of the digital age.
> *The Times* (27 November 1999)

Cronyism. The preferential treatment of one's friends or colleagues, and especially the awarding of political posts through friendship rather than on ability. The charge of cronyism was levelled at Tony Blair, Labour prime minister from 1997, whose INNER CABINET members were dubbed TONY'S CRONIES by the media.

> The re-election of Jacques Diouf as Director-General of the Food and Agricultural Organization is bad news. It is a victory for machine politics and cronyism.
> *The Times* (15 November 1999)

Crooning. A sentimental type of humming or singing in a low subdued voice that originated in the United States in the 1920s and that soon became popular. The word itself is ultimately imitative.

> The principle of crooning is to use as little voice as possible and instead to make a sentimental appeal by prolonged moaning somewhere near the written notes, but preferably never actually on those notes.
> ERIC BLOM: *Everyman's Dictionary of Music* (1947)

Crop circles. Also known as corn circles, these are circular areas of standing crops that have been neatly but mysteriously flattened, apparently by some kind of scything motion or vortex. They first appeared in the early 1980s in the south of England and have baffled scientists. They have been ascribed to supernatural forces, to UFOs, to freak whirlwinds and to the orchestrated handiwork of hoaxers, but no explanation for their appearance has been fully convincing or conclusive. The phenomenon subsequently surfaced in other countries.

> If crop circle investigator Paul Vigay is right, the mysterious force which creates intricate patterns in fields doesn't just flatten corn – it genetically improves it.
> *The Times* (12 August 1998)

Croque-monsieur (French, literally 'munch-sir'). The French equivalent of a toasted cheese and ham sandwich. When served with a fried egg on top, it is known as a *croque-madame*. It is said to have first appeared in the early 20th century on the menu of a café on the Boulevard des Capucines in Paris. The name itself may have arisen as a whimsical variant of *croque-mitaine*, literally 'munch-mitten', a term for a bogeyman or ugly monster formerly used by French nurses and parents to frighten children into good behaviour.

Cross of Lorraine. *See* MAQUIS.

Cross one's heart, To. To promise or pledge. The words are often accompanied by a sign of the cross made over the heart.

> 'Let's both swear.' 'Cross my heart and hope to die. Now what about bed?'
> ROSE MACAULAY: *Crewe Train*, ch x (1926)

Crossword. The popular pastime or obsession has its origins in the puzzle devised in 1913 by the British-born American editor Arthur Wynne for the Christmas issue of the 'Fun' supplement to the *New York*

Sunday World. It appeared on 21 December as a diamond-shaped device with 31 words to be entered and straightforward clues such as 'What bargain hunters enjoy' ('sales'). The First World War hampered the spread of the new craze, but it was taken up soon after in Britain and continental Europe, and on 1 February 1930 *The Times* published its 'Crossword Puzzle No. 1', compiled by the rural novelist Adrian Bell, who was paid 3 guineas a puzzle. Its clues were rather more sophisticated, one being 'The final crack' ('doom') and another 'Retunes (anag.)' ('tureens').

Cryptic clues soon became a regular feature of most British crosswords, based on the compiler's classic principle, 'I need not mean what I say, but I must say what I mean', a tenet first propounded by 'Afrit' (A.F. Ritchie). An example of such a clue, in *The Times* crossword No. 21,302 for 3 January 2000, is 'Not feeling pain in leg, as broken in two areas', in which 'in leg as' is 'broken' (anagrammatized) between two letters 'a', the mathematical abbreviation for 'area', producing 'analgesia', defined as 'not feeling pain'. Crosswords that have become institutions include the cryptic 'Everyman' and harder 'Mephisto' in the *Sunday Times*, and the notoriously difficult *Listener* crossword, published weekly in *The Times* after that journal's demise in 1991.

Croucher, The. The nickname of the Gloucestershire and England cricketer Gilbert Laird Jessop (1874–1955), so called for his idiosyncratic stance at the crease. Jessop was probably the consistently fastest scorer in the history of cricket.

Crow. A sequence of poems (1970) by the British poet Ted Hughes (1930–98). The image of a mocking, predatory crow runs through the poems, which are mostly on the themes of birth and creation. The symbol of the crow was originally suggested to Hughes by a meeting with the US illustrator Leonard Baskin, with whom he had worked on several previous publications.

Crown Court. A court of criminal jurisdiction for England and Wales, set up in 1971, when it superseded the assize courts and quarter sessions. It deals with the most serious offences, such as murder, manslaughter, rape and robbery, amounting to some 3 per cent of all criminal cases, and is presided over by a judge sitting with a jury of 12 members of the public. Lesser offences, such as burglary and some assaults, are tried by magistrates.

Crucible, The. An historical drama (1953) by the US playwright Arthur Miller (b.1915) about the witchcraft hysteria that swept through Salem, Massachusetts, in 1692. As well as suggesting the cauldrons and other utensils indispensable to traditional magic-making, the title also suggests that the incident should be attributed largely to the social conditions that prevailed at the time (fear of war with France, a bad winter, a smallpox epidemic, raids by pirates and the like) and the unconscious desire to find scapegoats to blame for such ills. Treated by Miller as a parallel for the McCARTHYITE investigations of the 1950s, the original witchcraft trials created a furore at the time and several of the jurors involved went so far as to publish a public 'Confession of Error':

> We confess that we ourselves were not capable to understand, nor able to withstand, the mysterious delusions of the Powers of Darkness and Prince of the Air; but were, for want of knowledge in ourselves and better information from others, prevailed with to take up such evidence against the accused, as on further consideration and better information we justly fear was insufficient for the touching the lives of any.

Crucible Theatre. This noted Sheffield theatre opened in 1971 as a new building to replace the old Sheffield Playhouse, which had been set up in a converted British Legion hall. It takes its name from the crucible process of steel production, which was invented in Sheffield by Benjamin Huntsman in 1740, and has staged many memorable productions. The semicircular shape of the building, with its steeply rising banks of seats, further suggest an actual crucible as well as a metaphorical theatrical 'melting pot'. The theatre is also the venue for the world professional snooker championship.

Cruella De Vil. *See* DE VIL, CRUELLA.

Cruellest month. T.S. Eliot's memorable phrase 'April is the cruellest month' in *The* WASTE LAND (1922) has been freely adopted and adapted by journalists for application to other months. One of the more frequent substitutions is 'August' for 'April', either because that month, although traditionally in the 'silly season', often chances to be newsworthy, or else by confusion with the title of Edna O'Brien's novel *August is a Wicked Month* (1965). There may also be a false association of sound between the second syllable of 'August' and that of 'cruellest'.

> June is the cruellest month in politics.
> *The Times* (5 June 1993)

Cruel Sea, The. A novel (1951) by Nicholas Monsarrat,

about the officers and men, and their wives, of HMS *Compass Rose*, a corvette on convoy duties in the Second World War, and, after its sinking, HMS *Saltash*. 'The men are the stars of this story. The only heroines are the ships: and the only villain the cruel sea itself.' Monsarrat himself commanded a frigate during the war, and was mentioned in dispatches. A memorable and successful film version (1953) was directed by Charles Frend.

Cruelty, Theatre of. *See* THEATRE OF CRUELTY.

Cruelty-free. A BUZZWORD of the 1980s for consumer goods produced without involving any cruelty to animals in their manufacture or development.

Cruising for a bruising. Asking for trouble. A US phrase current from the 1940s.

Crush bar. A bar in a theatre or opera house where members of the audience can buy a drink in the interval, so named because people are pressed close together in its confined area.

Crusties. A nickname of the 1990s for the homeless and vagrant young people who live by begging in towns and cities. They typically wear rough, dirty clothes, have matted or dreadlocked hair and are often visibly unwashed. Several have a dog on a string lead, and a number play rudimentary musical instruments in the hope of eliciting a few pennies from pedestrians. The name alludes to the patina of grime that characterizes their appearance.

Crying game. An exaggerated show of grief or mourning in order to win sympathy. The expression was popularized by Neil Jordan's acclaimed film *The Crying Game* (1992), a moving study of the ambiguity of human relationships against the background of Northern Ireland's TROUBLES. The public expression of grief following the death of Diana, Princess of Wales in 1997 was felt by some to be contrived or media-enhanced and so little more than a 'crying game'.

> When we witness a real human tragedy such as the devastating Turkish earthquake, it should put Britain's silly little crying games into some sort of perspective.
> *The Times* (23 August 1999)

Cryonics. The science of deep-freezing the bodies of people who have died with the aim of bringing them back to life in the future if and when medical knowledge makes this possible. It is practised in particular in cases where someone has died of an incurable disease, and arose in the 1960s. The term itself is a

contraction of 'cryogenics', the first element meaning 'cold' and deriving from Greek *kruos*, 'frost'.

Crystal-gazing. Attempting to forecast the future, as a fortune teller or clairvoyant does when gazing into her crystal ball.

> M&S is still buying nine months into the future. They are still crystal ball-gazing there at Baker Street.
> *The Times* (3 November 1999)

Cry, the Beloved Country. A novel (1948) by the South African writer Alan Paton (1903–88), in which he suggested a Christian resolution of the problem of racial APARTHEID in South Africa. It was influential also in promoting an awareness abroad of the country's political policies. The beloved country is Africa. A recurring motif is the 'forlorn crying' of the titihoya, a bird of the veldt. A film version (1951; US title *African Fury*) was directed by Zoltan Korda.

C2. A skilled manual worker. The term is a socio-economic category taken from a five-point scale that runs from A as top management, through B as middle management and C1 as supervisory and clerical workers, to D as unskilled and semi-skilled workers. C2s were the subject of special debate by political commentators in the 1980s and early 1990s, when their defection from a traditional Labour allegiance to THATCHERISM was held to be a major factor in successive Labour defeats.

> The C2s, regarded by pollsters and political parties as 'crucial' to electoral success, are important because they are the point where Mr Pooter gives way to Alf Garnett.
> DOMINIC HOBSON: *The Wealth of the Nation* (1999)

Cuban Missile Crisis. *See* HAWKS AND DOVES.

Cubism. The style of an early 20th-century school of painters who depicted surfaces, figures, tints, light and shade, and so on, by means of a multiplicity of shapes of a cubical and geometrical character. The name was introduced in 1908 by the French art critic Louis Vauxcelles, who took up a remark attributed to Matisse about Braque's 'little cubes'. The genre was essentially abstract and divorced from realism. It rejected any attempt to depict actual appearances and turned its back on traditional canons of art. It paved the way for much of modern art subsequently. Its chief exponents were Georges Braque (1882–1963), André Derain (1880–1954), Fernand Léger (1881–1955) and, notably, Pablo Picasso (1881–1973). *See also* DADAISM; FAUVISM; FUTURISM; MODERNISM; ORPHISM; RURALISM; SURREALISM; SYNCHROMISM; TACHISM; VORTICISM.

Cuckoo in the nest. An unwelcome intruder. The allusion is to the cuckoo's habit of laying its eggs in the nests of other birds, who then incubate them as their own. After hatching, the young cuckoos eject their adoptive parents' own eggs and chicks and so effectively 'rule the roost'.

> The growth of offshore finance has been so dramatic that some micro-states risk it emerging as a cuckoo in the nest, not only crowding out existing industries, but also dominating the state apparatus.
> *The World Today* (August/September 1999)

Cullinan Diamond. The largest known diamond, named after Sir Thomas Major Cullinan (1862–1936), chairman of the Premier Diamond Mine, Johannesburg, where it was found in 1905. Its uncut weight was 3025¾ carats (about 624g or 1lb 6oz). It was presented to King Edward VII by the South African government and was cut into a number of stones (the largest weighing some 516 carats), which now form part of the Crown Jewels.

Cultural cringe. A nickname for the supposed sense of inferiority experienced by the British when compared to the peoples of continental Europe, where all roads lead to Rome and where edicts promulgated by rulers and notions proposed by philosophers seem to carry greater weight and have greater influence than in Britain. The awareness was particularly acute following Britain's entry to the Common Market in 1973 and subsequent involvement with the EUROPEAN UNION.

Cultural Revolution. The political upheaval in China of 1966–9, largely promoted by the youthful RED GUARD, aimed to effect a return to revolutionary Maoist doctrines. It involved attacks on intellectuals, a wide-ranging purge in party posts, and a burgeoning personality cult of Mao himself. It resulted in economic disruption and dislocation and was eventually stemmed by the Chinese prime minister Chou En-lai.

Culture shock. A feeling of disorientation on being suddenly subjected to an unfamiliar culture, such as a Westerner in the Far East or a country-dweller in a city. The theme has been variously treated in fiction, and was amusingly presented in the film *'Crocodile' Dundee* (1986), about the experiences of an outbacker in New York. *See also* FUTURE SHOCK.

> Bill Bryson found himself suffering the indignity of culture shock when he took his English wife and kids to live in his homeland, America, after an absence of nearly 20 years.
> *The Times* (11 September 1999)

Culture vulture. A person obsessively interested in the arts. The expression dates from the 1940s.

> There is a vulture
> Who circles above
> The carcass of culture.
> OGDEN NASH: Free Wheeling (1931)

Curate's delight. *See* CURATE'S FRIEND.

Curate's egg. Among the catchphrases that *Punch* has introduced into the language, 'Good in parts, like the curate's egg' is proverbial. The original cartoon showed a timid young curate at his bishop's breakfast table.

> I'm afraid you've got a bad egg, Mr Jones.
> Oh no, my Lord, I assure you! Parts of it are excellent!
> Vol 109 (9 November 1895)

Curate's friend or **delight.** A cakestand with two or more tiers, as at one time placed next to a curate when visiting a family and offered afternoon tea. The expression dates from the EDWARDIAN ERA. The otherwise puzzling stage direction below abbreviates the term.

> [*They sit down, ill at ease, whilst he places the tray on the table. He then goes out for the curate*].
> GEORGE BERNARD SHAW: *Fanny's First Play*, III (1911)

Curl up, To. To shrink with shame, horror, embarrassment or the like. The reference is either to the pose adopted by a young child when shocked or scolded, or to the similar instinctive reaction of an animal or insect such as a hedgehog or woodlouse. An extended form of the phrase, 'to curl up and die', again alludes to animals. The expression dates from the early 20th century.

> I could have curled up and died when I realized that the extremely plain girl who had just walked into one of my favourite restaurants ... must be my blind date.
> *Sunday Times* (15 August 1999)

Curragh mutiny. In March 1914 a number of officers at the Curragh camp near Dublin offered their resignations rather than face the possibility of being ordered to act against Ulstermen to impose the Irish HOME RULE Bill. They succeeded in obtaining a written assurance from their commander-in-chief that they would not be expected to do this. The following month a successful gun-running operation provided arms for the ULSTER VOLUNTEER FORCE.

Curse, The. A euphemism for menstruation, dating from the 1920s. The reference is apparently to the curse that God put on Eve when she ate the forbidden fruit in the Garden of Eden (Genesis 3).

Curtains. The end; death. An allusion to the closing of the stage curtains at the end of a theatrical performance.

> That two minutes of compelling television [a viewer's grilling of Margaret Thatcher] in 1983 may well have meant curtains for *Nationwide* and the spirit of Lime Grove.
>
> *The Times* (15 October 1999)

Curtis, Olivia. The heroine of Rosamond Lehmann's novels *Invitation to the Dance* (1932) and *The Weather in the Streets* (1936), in the latter of which she has an unhappy love affair with a man called Rollo. Nicola Beauman, in *A Very Great Profession: The Woman's Novel 1914–39* (1983), describes Olivia as striking a chord with 'anyone who has ever loved foolishly and recklessly'.

Customer is always right. A general rule of retail tacitly adopted by most shops and stores from the turn of the 20th century, and explicitly stated by Gordon Selfridge, founder in 1909 of the London department store that bears his name. A year or two earlier the Swiss hotelier César Ritz (*see* RITZY) was quoted as saying, '*Le client n'a jamais tort*' ('The customer is never wrong'), which amounts to exactly the same thing.

Cut and dried. Completely settled; finally arranged. The term arose in the early 20th century from an earlier literal sense applied to herbs sold in herbalists' shops, as distinct from fresh, growing herbs.

Cut-and-paste. Patched-up; rough and ready. An allusion to the simple artwork done by children in which pictures or shapes are cut out and glued (pasted) to paper. In computer jargon to cut and paste is to delete (and save) a section of text from a page or document and insert it elsewhere.

Cuthbert. A name coined by 'Poy' (Percy Hutton Fearon; 1874–1945), cartoonist of the London *Evening News* from 1913 to 1935, for the fit men who avoided military service in the First World War by securing a post in a government office or in the Civil Service. He depicted them as frightened-looking rabbits. The particular name perhaps intentionally echoes the children's taunt of 'cowardy custard', while its lisping sound suggests a womanish wimpishness. *See also* PERCY.

Cut it out! Stop it! That's enough! To cut an action is to stop it. To cut it out is to stop it for good.

Cut the mustard, To. To do something well and efficiently, especially when it is suspected that one may lack the ability. The expression derives from 'mustard' as a slang word for a thing that is the best and the 'cutting' refers to the harvesting of the plant, garnering the best. *See also* HOT STUFF.

> When you have to come up with the goods almost daily without allowing your standards to slacken, the pressure must be unbearable. Day after day you have to cut the mustard.
>
> *The Times* (16 October 1999)

Cut the rug, To. To dance, especially when jitterbugging. The image is of one's vigorous steps gashing or tearing the floor covering. The expression comes from 1930s jive talk.

Cutting edge. The forefront of new developments. The analogy is with the sharp edge of a knife or tool. The term arose in the field of scientific and technological research in the 1950s.

> Something has changed. Sex … is no longer at the cutting edge of politics, especially for women.
>
> *Guardian* (14 March 1989)

Cut to the chase, To. To come to the point. The allusion is to a silent film in which the preliminary action is edited (cut) so that one immediately gets to the exciting chase scene.

Cybercafé. A café where customers can sit at computer terminals and log on to the INTERNET while enjoying a drink or a snack.

> Just beyond the entrance lobby, the cybercafé beckons: coffee and food on one side, PCs and laptop docking on the other.
>
> *The Times* (24 May 1999)

Cybernetics. This name for the science of communications and automatic control systems, in both machines and animate beings, was the invention of the US mathematician Norbert Wiener, who introduced it in his book, *Cybernetics: Control and Communication in the Animal and the Machine* (1948). Its derivation is in the Greek word for 'helmsman'. It was cybernetics that brought terms such as 'feedback' and 'input' into common usage, and it has itself spawned such offspring as CYBERCAFÉ, CYBERPUNK, CYBERSEX and CYBERSPACE.

Cyberpunk. A literary movement of the 1980s as a

form of SCIENCE FICTION in which typically the human mind or body is invaded and controlled by computer-generated forces. The scenario is usually that of a lawless subculture, and the characters are often hackers or computer freaks. The term itself, combining CYBERNETICS and PUNK, was first used in the early 1980s by Gardner Dazois, editor of *Isaac Asimov's Science Fiction Magazine*.

Cybersex. Sexual arousal obtained by exchanging messages with another person on the INTERNET or by using VIRTUAL REALITY techniques, both erotic diversions of the 1990s. *See also* CYBERNETICS.

> Most [chat] rooms seem to be about sex. Far from being full of nerdy sociopaths, they are overrun by married men … looking for cybersex.
> *The Times* (29 June 1999)

Cyberspace. The notional environment in which communication over computer networks occurs. It is conventionally perceived as being 'space' inside the computer system but in fact has no real existence. The concept evolved in the 1980s. *See also* CYBERNETICS; INTERNAUT.

Cybersquatter. In computer jargon a person who registers the DOMAIN name of an existing company or individual with the aim of forcing the rightful owner to pay an exorbitant price for it. The practice is banned in American law as are variant ruses. When the oil companies Exxon and Mobil announced in 1998 that they were in merger talks, for example, five speculators registered addresses that joined their names in combinations such as 'exxonmobil.com', 'mobilexxon.com', 'exxon-mobil.net' and 'exxon-mobil.org'. There are also cybersquatters who deliberately try to mislead INTERNET users by registering names that are very close to existing names and that may be accidentally accessed by a slip of the finger on the keyboard. Thus 'wwwcitibank.com', as distinct from 'www.citibank.com', led to a lurid eyeful before Citibank closed it. Similarly 'microsift.com', rather than 'microsoft.com', used the adjacency of 'i' to 'o' on the keyboard to take the hasty to a site called 'geek-guy.com' run by a 24-year-old GEEK in SILICON VALLEY.

Cymru am byth (Welsh, 'Wales for ever'). The motto of the Welsh Guards, formed in 1915. The words are also generally in use as a rallying call for the principality as a whole.

Czar. *See* DRUGS CZAR.

D

Da. A play (1973) by the Irish playwright Hugh Leonard (pen-name of John Keyes Byrne; b.1926) about the attempts of an adopted son to come to terms with the death of a beloved, but exasperating father, his 'da'. Leonard wrote the play as a recognition of the personal debt he owed his own father, only to find that the success of the play, which was a hit on Broadway and was made into a film (1987), meant that he felt he owed his parent even more.

DA. *See* DUCK'S ARSE.

Dachau. The first Nazi concentration camp, built near the town of Dachau in Bavaria in 1933, with the slogan ARBEIT MACHT FREI ('work brings freedom') over the gateway. Dachau became the model for later camps, and controlled a network of sub-camps throughout southern Germany and Austria. Although it was not an extermination camp, some 32,000 prisoners died from starvation, disease, maltreatment and the effects of horrendous medical experiments. Many of the inmates were transported on to death camps such as AUSCHWITZ. *See also* BELSEN; FINAL SOLUTION; HOLOCAUST.

Dadaism. An anarchic and iconoclastic art movement, which began at Zurich in 1916 and arose from indignation and despair at the catastrophe of the First World War. Its supporters, writers and painters, sought to free themselves from all artistic conventions and what they considered cultural shams. Dadaism was influenced by CUBISM and FUTURISM, and after about 1922 it was succeeded by SURREALISM. The origin of the name is surrounded in confusion, but one of the more plausible accounts tells how the German poets Hugo Ball (1886–1927) and Richard Huelsenbeck (1892–1974) were leafing through a German–French dictionary when they came across the French word *dada*, meaning 'hobbyhorse'. Partly because of its nonsensical sound and partly through its associations with the freedom of childhood, they decided to adopt it. Jean Arp (1888–1966), Max Ernst (1891–1976) and Marcel Janco (1895–1984) were among their number. There was a similar wave in New York at the same time associated with Marcel Duchamp (1887–1968), Francis Picabia (1879–1953) and Man Ray (1890–1977). A plaque showing a human navel was unveiled in Zurich in 1966 to commemorate the 50th anniversary of the movement. *See also* FAUVISM; ORPHISM; RURALISM; SYNCHROMISM; TACHISM; VORTICISM.

Daddy-and-daughter. A nickname for a relationship or enterprise involving a middle-aged man and a young woman, in some cases commercially staged to suggest a true family relationship.

> Others complain in turn to the BBC that its coverage was presented in strangely dated daddy-'n'-daughter format by wrinkly old men and fresh young blondes.
> *The Times* (4 January 2000)

Dad's Army. A nickname for the HOME GUARD, many of whose members were middle-aged fathers. The name was popularized by the enjoyably nostalgic television comedy series so titled, screened on BBC from 1968 to 1977 and centring on the Second World War adventures of a disparate group of men who formed part of Britain's 'last line of defence' in the fictional south-coast town of Walmington-on-Sea. Memorable characters included Arthur Lowe as the pompous Captain Mainwaring, John Le Mesurier as the vague but cultured Sergeant Wilson, Clive Dunn as the madcap Lance-Corporal Jones, John Laurie as the pessimistic Private Frazer and Arnold Ridley as the frail Private Godfrey. 'Dad's army' is now used for any body of middle-aged or elderly volunteers. *See also* CONK OUT.

Daggers. A nickname supposedly awarded to Margaret Thatcher, the IRON LADY, by members of her cabinet, not because she 'looked daggers' at them, but as an abbreviation for Dagenham, 'two stops on from Barking' (as in BARKING MAD).

Dagwood. A large thick sandwich of mixed ingredients, of the type made by Dagwood Bumstead, the lazy husband of BLONDIE in the cartoon strip by Chic Young.

Dáil. The lower house of the parliament of the Republic of Ireland, in full *Dáil Éireann* (Irish, 'Assembly of Ireland'). It was first established in 1919, when SINN FÉIN proclaimed an independent Irish republic.

Daily double. A mainly US term for a bet on the winners of two stated horseraces, usually the first and second, on a particular day of a meeting.

Daily dozen. A short session of daily physical exercises, traditionally performed in sets of 12. The phrase originally referred to a set of 12 callisthenic exercises devised by the famous Yale University American football coach Walter C. Camp (1859–1925) and came into general use in the early 20th century.

Daisy chain. Originally referring to a garland made by threading daisies together through slits in their stalks, the term has subsequently come to apply to various kinds of linked arrangements. One such is a group of dealers who agree to buy and sell a particular commodity, typically crude oil, among themselves as a way of inflating the price at which it is finally sold to an outside buyer. Another is a group of people who act as partners to each another simultaneously in sexual activity.

Daleks. The tin robots, resembling pepperpots on wheels, in the children's television series DOCTOR WHO, made their first appearance in 1963. They were the invention of the scriptwriter Terry Nation, who denied a claim that their name came arbitrarily from an encyclopedia volume titled DAL–LEK. They were famous for their threatening vocalization 'Exterminate! Exterminate!' and their ability to floor a foe with a ray beamed from their antennae.

Daley, Arthur. *See* HER INDOORS; MINDER; NICE LITTLE EARNER.

Dallas. A US television melodrama screened from 1978 to 1991 that rapidly gained worldwide cult status. It centred on the everyday life of the Ewings, a Texan oil-rich family, consisting of patriarch Jock, matriarch Miss Ellie, and sons JR, Gary and Bobby. The show soon focused on JR, a scheming businessman and seducer of women, married to the alcoholic Sue Ellen, and the high point of the series was his attempted murder in 1980. The assassin was subsequently revealed to be Sue Ellen's sister, Kristin, pregnant with JR's child.

Dalloway, Mrs. *See* MRS DALLOWAY.

Dalton Plan. A US system of secondary education based on individual learning. It divided each subject into monthly assignments, with pupils free to plan their own work schedules. The scheme was developed by Helen Parkhurst in 1919 and first used at a school for the handicapped. It was then introduced in 1920 at a high school in Dalton, Massachusetts. Hence the name.

Damaged goods. A derogatory term for a person who is inadequate or impaired in some way and specifically for an unmarried woman who is no longer a virgin. Goods that have been damaged are reduced in value. The expression dates from the early 20th century.

Damart. The thermal underwear of this name was the creation in the 1950s of three French brothers named Despature, who had a weaving business in the town of Roubaix. They experimented with a new type of chlorofibre that had good insulation and water-repellent properties and that also generated triboelectricity, a form of static electricity generated when fibres rub during wear. This latter attribute was believed by some to have therapeutic value in the treatment of rheumatism, arthritis and muscular complaints generally. They called their new material 'Thermolactyl', from 'thermo-', the Greek root meaning 'warm', and 'lactyl', a chemical radical derived from lactic acid used in the manufacturing process. The name of the product itself is said to come from the Rue Dammartine, where the three sat in a café discussing their breakthrough, while the red 'lightning flash' through the 'D' of the name represents a charge of triboelectricity.

Dam Busters. This special squadron of the RAF derived its name from the bombing raid it undertook in May 1943 to destroy the Sorpe, Eder and Moehne dams and so flood the Ruhr valley and disrupt German industry. The specially fitted Lancaster bombers achieved their aim, quite literally, with a unique 'bouncing bomb' designed by Sir Barnes Wallis (1887–1979). The mission was not an unqualified success, however, as the dams were soon repaired and 42 per cent of the bombers were lost. On the ground at least 1500 people died, many of them foreign 'slave' labourers. A film of the same name reconstructing the exploit was released in 1954.

Damsel in distress. A mainly humorous term for a young woman in difficulties, especially when of a trivial or mildly embarrassing nature. The image is of the imprisoned maiden or captive princess of medieval stories and fairy tales who was rescued by a KNIGHT IN SHINING ARMOUR. *See also* WHITE KNIGHT.

> Phil Willis … received an SOS pager message ('Ring home – flat flooded') while on his feet in a debate. … 'I then zoomed to the flat, got a plumber, and zoomed back to the Commons just in time for the end of the debate', he says. His excuse to the powers that be: 'A damsel in distress.'
>
> *The Times* (20 December 1999)

Dance of the Seven Veils. The popular title of Salome's sensuous dance before Herod in Richard Strauss's opera *Salome* (1905), in which she removes her seven veils one by one, in a sort of oriental striptease. There is no evidence of such a dance in the Bible, which does not refer to Salome by name, although Matthew 14:6 states that 'the daughter of Herodias danced before them'. The particular dance of this kind is, however, specified in Oscar Wilde's play *Salomé* (1893), on which the opera is based. In her role as Salome at a Covent Garden performance in 1988 the US mezzo-soprano Maria Ewing performed the sequence to its logical conclusion.

Dances with Wolves. A film (1990) about a US army officer who wins the trust of the Sioux Indians he has been sent to fight. It was directed by and starred Kevin Costner (b.1955). As well as winning acceptance by the Sioux, Lieutenant Dunbar (played by Costner) also wins the friendship of a wolf, hence the name given to him by the Sioux and the title of the film. While the film was still in production many people in the film business doubted that it would enjoy the success it eventually did, and it was commonly referred to as *Kevin's Gate*, drawing parallels with the disastrous HEAVEN'S GATE (1980).

Dance to the Music of Time, A. A *roman fleuve* (1951–75) by Anthony Powell (1905–2000). The title of the 12-novel sequence is that of the painting so known by Nicolas Poussin (1594–1665). The starting point of the first novel, *A Question of Upbringing*, is the narrator, Nicholas Jenkins, seeing in the attitude of some workmen gathered around a bucket of coke a suggestion of 'Poussin's scene in which the Seasons, hand

in hand, facing outward, tread in rhythm to the notes of the lyre that the winged and naked greybeard plays'. The books have a chronological framework corresponding to Powell's own experience and times, and verge between the tragic and the comic. Poussin's painting was given its title by the Italian art theorist and collector Giovanni Pietro Bellori, originally: *Le quattro stagioni che ballano al suono del tempo* ('The four seasons that dance to the music of time'). Powell has described how the painting inspired him:

> I found myself in the Wallace Collection, standing in front of Nicolas Poussin's picture there given the title *A Dance to the Music of Time*. An almost hypnotic spell seems cast by this masterpiece on the beholder. I knew at once that Poussin had expressed at least one important aspect of what the novel must be.
>
> ANTHONY POWELL: *To Keep the Ball Rolling* (1976–82)

See also FIRST LINES OF NOVELS.

Dan Dare. The space pilot in the boys' comic EAGLE from 1950 to 1967. He serves as a colonel in the Interplanetary Space Fleet and has adventures on Venus and beyond. His great enemy is the dread MEKON. The cartoon strips featuring him were the work of Frank Hampson. Attempts to revive Dan Dare in comics of the 1970s and 1980s proved disappointing.

Dandy. A British comic first published in December 1937. Its most famous character is DESPERATE DAN. *See also* KEYHOLE KATE.

Dangerous dog. A dog legally defined as dangerous to the public by the Dangerous Dogs Act 1991, which set out restrictions on the importation, breeding and keeping of a number of named breeds, notably pit-bull terriers, following a series of attacks on children by such dogs.

Danny the Red. A nickname of Daniel Cohn-Bendit (b.1945), one of the leaders of the student revolt in Paris in May 1968. He was subsequently deported to his native West Germany.

Dansette. A make of record player found in many households in the 1950s at a time when popular music had become a major industry. With the advent of ROCK 'N' ROLL, commercial opportunities were beginning to emerge for the growing teenage culture, and the player, with its colourful modern styling, appealed to many youthful music fans, its name suggesting its purpose.

Dark is Rising, The. The name of a five-volume sequence of novels for young adults by Susan Cooper (b.1935), the first of which was *Over Sea, Under Stone*

(1965). *The Dark is Rising* is also the title of the second book (1973) in the series, which draws on Celtic and Arthurian mythology but in a modern setting. Will Stanton discovers that he is the last born of the 'Old Ones', a line of immortal guardians, opposed by an evil force, the 'Dark'. The Dark is rising for a final assault on humanity.

Dark Materials. A highly praised trilogy of fantasy novels for children by Philip Pullman (b.1946) consisting of *Northern Lights* (1995), *The Subtle Knife* (1997) and *The Amber Spyglass* (2000). The trilogy's title comes from John Milton's *Paradise Lost* (1667), of which it is in part a re-working: '... Unless the almighty maker them ordain/His dark materials to create more worlds ...'. The novels themselves move between different universes: one 'which is like ours but different in many ways; the universe we know; and a third universe, which differs from ours in other ways again'.

Dark matter. A term used by astronomers for material that has not been directly detected but whose existence is postulated to account for the motions of stars and galaxies. It is thought that some 90 per cent of the mass in the universe resides in some form of dark matter.

Darkness at Noon. A novel (1940) by Arthur Koestler (1905–83), originally written in German. It draws on his experience as a member of the Communist Party from 1931 to 1938, during which time he was commissioned by the Communist International to write a book on the first FIVE-YEAR PLAN in Russia. The novel follows an earlier one, *The Gladiators* (1939), in which Spartacus is doomed because he did not apply the 'law of detours', whereby leaders should be 'pitiless for the sake of pity' and execute dissidents. In *Darkness at Noon* an elderly BOLSHEVIK follows the 'law' and sends people to their execution without compunction, until he himself is deemed expendable and is forced to sign a confession that consigns him to his death. The title echoes words from Milton's *Samson Agonistes* (1671) relating to the blindness of Samson:

O dark, dark, dark, amid the blaze of noon,
Irrecoverably dark, total eclipse
Without all hope of day!

An anonymous booklet was published in Boston in 1806 and entitled *Darkness at Noon, or the Great Solar Eclipse of the 16th June 1806*, and it is possible that Koestler was aware of this.

Dark Side of the Moon, The. A commercially success-

ful album by the rock group Pink Floyd, released in 1973. Its cover, featuring a prism that creates a spectrum of colours, is one of the best known of all pop album sleeves. The bleak and portentous title introduces a suite of songs that dwell on the themes of materialism, madness, ageing and death, and include 'Time', 'Brain Damage', 'Money' and 'Us and Them'. *See also* ROCK GROUP NAMES.

Darling Buds of May, The. A comic novel (1958) by H.E. Bates (1905–74), the first of several about the carefree LARKIN FAMILY in rural England. Other titles featuring the Larkin family are the faintly punning *A Breath of French Air* (1959) and *Hark, Hark, the Lark* (1960), *Oh! To be in England* (1963) and *A Little of What You Fancy* (1970). In 1991–3 the books became the basis of a popular television series. The title comes from Shakespeare:

Rough winds do shake the darling buds of May,
And summer's lease hath all too short a date.
Sonnet 18 (1609)

See also SUMMER'S LEASE.

Darling Daisy. Frances Evelyn Greville, Countess of Warwick (1861–1938), adulterous wife of the 5th Earl of Warwick and for nine years mistress of Edward VII, whom he often addressed in his letters to her as 'My Darling Daisy wife'. In 1914 she sought to make money by threatening to publish her memoirs, which would include the late king's letters. This was prevented by three prominent courtiers acting on behalf of George V. Her entry in the *Dictionary of National Biography* makes no mention of her infidelity, preferring instead to praise her beauty, her interest in socialism and her love of birds and animals.

Darren. A forename that came to be regarded as rather NAFF in the 1980s. It is of 20th-century origin and was popularized by the husband in the US television comedy series BEWITCHED (1964–71). He was actually 'Darrin', but British viewers took to the name, assuming it was typically American, and respelled it 'Darren'. As such, it seemed a suitable male counterpart to the female SHARON and Karen, then rising in favour. However, the US film actor Darren McGavin (b.1922) was an earlier bearer of the name and possibly the first to be emulated.

Darren Tackle. *See* TACKLE, DARREN.

Darth Vader. *See* STAR WARS.

Dashing White Sergeant. A lively Scottish country dance performed in sets of three. It was devised by David Anderson of Dundee *c*.1890 and takes its name from the title of a song composed *c.*1792 by General Burgoyne and subsequently incorporated into the libretto of an operetta by Sir Henry Bishop. The music of the dance is set to Bishop's tune.

Date rape. Rape by a person whom the subject is dating or with whom she has gone on a date. Although hardly a new phenomenon, date rape first emerged as a particular issue on US college campuses in the early 1980s. There may be fine legal implications in the act, since to an extent the person dated has implicitly or explicitly agreed to 'go with' the potential rapist.

Daughter of Time, The. A crime novel (1951) by Josephine Tey (pen-name, that of her great-great-grandmother, of Elizabeth Mackintosh; 1897–1952). A police detective, hospitalized after an accident, conducts a long-distance investigation into the murder of King Richard III's two nephews, the 'Princes in the Tower'. The title is from the old proverb, 'Truth is the daughter of time.'

Davis Cup. The international tennis trophy of this name was donated in 1900 by the US doubles champion Dwight F. Davis (1879–1945), the first tie being played between the United States and Britain on 7 August that year at the Longwood Cricket Club in Boston, Massachusetts. The cup is competed for annually on a knockout basis by teams from different countries but has not been won by Britain since a triumph over Australia in 1936.

Dawes Plan. An arrangement for Germany's payment of reparations after the First World War. On the initiative of the British and US governments, a committee of experts, presided over by Charles G. Dawes (1865–1951), a US financier, produced a report on the question of reparations for Germany's presumed liability for the war. The report was accepted by both the Allies and Germany on 16 August 1924 and payments began. The scheme worked so well that by 1929 it was felt reasonable to remove the stringent controls over Germany and fix total reparations instead.

Dawn raid. A surprise visit by police at daybreak, usually made when searching for criminals or illicit goods or weapons. In stock exchange parlance a dawn raid is an operation in which a large proportion of a company's shares are suddenly bought at the start of a day's trading at a price much higher than their prevailing market rate, usually as a preliminary to a takeover bid.

> Bankers caught on the hop by dawn raid.
>
> *The Times* (headline) (25 September 1999)

Day in the Death of Joe Egg, A. A play (1967) by Peter Nichols (b.1927) about the struggles of a man and woman to cope with life with a severely disabled daughter. Based largely upon Nichols's own experiences as the father of a similarly handicapped child, the play took its title from a children's rhyme:

> Joe Egg's a fool,
> He tied his stocking to a stool.

Day in the Life, A. A highly imaginative and moving song, ending with a famous 42-second chord, that appears on the celebrated BEATLES album SERGEANT PEPPER'S LONELY HEARTS CLUB BAND. Credited to John Lennon and Paul McCartney, it is sometimes described as their finest musical achievement. The first verse of the song was inspired by the death in a car crash of the Beatles' society friend Tara Browne and, more famously, an item in the *Daily Mail* newspaper concerning holes in the road in the Lancashire town of Blackburn.

> There are 4000 holes in the road in Blackburn, Lancashire, or one twenty-sixth of a hole per person, according to a council survey. If Blackburn is typical, there are two million holes in Britain's roads and 300,000 in London.
>
> *Daily Mail* (17 January 1967)

Like LUCY IN THE SKY WITH DIAMONDS, the song was banned by the BBC for its alleged references to drugs. The song has been the subject of enormous critical attention, focusing on such matters as disenchantment with the limits of conventional perception and the alienating effects of the media.

Daylight robbery. A blatantly excessive charge. The analogy is with a robbery committed in broad daylight, with no attempt at concealment or subterfuge. The expression dates from the 1940s.

Daylight saving. *See* SUMMER TIME.

Day of the ... . A popular formula for a novel title, especially when indicating some sinister person or force. Examples are Nathanael West's *The Day of the Locust* (1930), John Wyndham's *The* DAY OF THE TRIFFIDS (1951), Paul Scott's *The Day of the Scorpion* (1968) and Frederick Forsyth's *The* DAY OF THE JACKAL (1971).

Day of the Jackal, The. The first novel (1971) by Frederick Forsyth (b.1938). This thriller established his basic formula: an international crisis and a mixture of fictional and historical characters. The narrative follows the progress of an international plot to kill the French President, General de Gaulle (1890–1970), at the hands of a professional killer known as the JACKAL. An exciting film version (1973) was directed by Fred Zinnemann. A less exciting remake, *The Jackal*, appeared in 1997.

Day of the Triffids, The. A SCIENCE FICTION novel (1951) by John Wyndham (1903–69). An agricultural experiment has produced giant, man-eating, per-ambulating plants, which threaten a civilization that has already been hit by blindness after a stellar ex-plosion. Wyndham himself invented the word 'triffid' for the plants, apparently basing it on 'trifid', meaning 'divided into three parts', since he describes the plants as being supported on 'three bluntly-tapered projec-tions extending from the lower part [of their bodies]'. An unsubtle film version (1962) was directed by Steve Sekely.

Day one. The beginning, as: 'I never liked him from day one.' The concept is of the first ever day.

> From Day 1, fashion has dictated that women's tender toes be squeezed into a pointed-toe shoe that ignores the realities of human anatomy.
>
> *New York Times Magazine* (2 February 1979)

Day person. Someone who is at their best in the day and who tires early in the evening. The opposite is a 'night person', who finds it hard to function in the morning. There is also a 'morning person' and an 'evening person'. Every person is to an extent an amalgam of these. *See also* LARKS AND OWLS.

Dayton Agreement. The agreement on measures aimed at ending hostilities in the former Yugoslavia, reached in Dayton, Ohio, in November 1995. The accord was signed by the presidents of the three coun-tries involved, Bosnia, Serbia and Croatia.

Dazed and confused. Bemused; disturbed; discon-certed. The phrase was in vogue in the 1990s as an expression of the turbulence of the social and cultural scene and of general unease concerning the approach-ing MILLENNIUM with its attendant MILLENNIUM BUG. The words were widely popularized as the title of a film of 1993 about a group of 1960s US high school students who celebrate their last day by victimizing their juniors. They also became familiar as the title of a CUTTING EDGE music, fashion and arts magazine, first published in 1992. A similar sense of uncertainty and insecurity was voiced half a century earlier by Lorenz Hart's song 'Bewitched' (1941) with its memorable line 'Bewitched, bothered, and bewildered am I'.

> Appearing somewhat dazed and confused, Keith Richards, the hell-raising Rolling Stones guitarist,

accepted a lifetime achievement honour at the tenth annual *Q Magazine* awards.
> *The Times* (4 November 1999)

D-Day. In the Second World War the day appointed for the Allied invasion of Europe and the opening of the long-awaited second front. It was eventually fixed for 5 June 1944 but because of impossible weather con-ditions was postponed at the last moment until 6 June. D simply stands for Day. *See also* LONGEST DAY; OVERLORD; SECOND WORLD WAR OPERATIONAL CODE NAMES.

Dead cat bounce. In stock exchange jargon a tempor-ary recovery in share prices after a substantial fall, caused by speculators buying to cover their posi-tions. A live cat on falling will spring up or 'bounce back', but a dead one will not, although it may seem to do so.

Dead end kids. Children from poverty-stricken back streets for whom the future seems to hold little promise. The Dead End Kids were a popular group of young American film actors who first appeared as 'hooligans' in *Dead End* (1937). This was set in New York's East Side, where slum kids and gangsters lived next to a luxury apartment block. They went on to appear in such films as *Angels with Dirty Faces* (1938) and *On Dress Parade* (1939). They subsequently split up into the Little Tough Guys, the East Side Kids and the Bowery Boys. The original Dead End Kids were Billy Halop, Leo Gorcey, Bernard Punsley, Huntz Hall, Bobby Jordan and Gabriel Dell.

Dead from the neck up. Noticeably stupid. Such a person is 'brain-dead'.

Dead heart. The remote interior of Australia. The phrase comes from the title of J.W. Gregory's book *The Dead Heart of Australia* (1906).

Dead in the water. Unable to function effectively. The reference is not to a drowned person but to a ship that is unable to move for some reason, either because there is no current or no wind or because her engine has failed.

> He [Ken Livingstone] said that if Mr Dobson won the nomination contest with the backing of less than half the Labour membership, he would be 'dead in the water as mayoral candidate'.
>
> *The Times* (11 February 2000)

Dead letter. A law or regulation no longer acted upon. A letter that the post office has been unable to deliver either because of an incorrect address or because the person addressed is untraceable.

Dead letter box or **drop.** In espionage a place where messages can be left by one person for another without either of them meeting. In 1985 Chief Warrant Officer John A. Walker Jr, a retired US naval officer, was arrested following months of observation by the FBI during which he left 129 classified documents at a dead drop in Poolsville, Maryland, for a KGB agent. The plan involved Walker dropping a 7-Up can at a prearranged spot to signal that he had placed the material at the drop, near a specified tree. On seeing the signal, the agent was to proceed to the drop, pick up the bag and leave Walker a packet of cash. Walker was tried and sentenced to life imprisonment in a case that was one of the most damaging spy episodes in the history of the US Navy.

Deadly Derek. The nickname of the Kent and England cricketer Derek Underwood (b.1945), a left-arm medium-pace spin bowler whose bowling was unplayable on any wicket that was conducive to spin.

Dead man's handle. A handle on the controls of an electric train, so designed that it cuts off the current and applies the brakes if the driver releases his pressure from illness or some other cause. It is now officially called a driver's safety device and is usually in the form of a plate depressed by the foot. It was invented in 1902 by the American Frank J. Sprague.

Dead meat. To be dead meat is to be in serious trouble, as if as good as dead. 'Dead meat' is 19th-century slang for a corpse.

> It was taken for granted by news editors that by 9 am we had read our own paper, its main rival and a couple of the broadsheets. We were dead meat if we hadn't.
> *The Times* (1 October 1999)

Dead Poets Society. A film (1989) written by Tom Schulman and directed by Peter Weir about the disturbing events that unfold after an unconventional English teacher (played by Robin Williams) arrives at a conservative Vermont prep school in 1959. Inspired by their teacher to develop an interest in literature, the pupils assemble their own anarchic 'Dead Poets Society', which becomes a focus of their rebellion against the educational establishment.

Dead Sea scrolls. In 1947 a Bedouin goatherd made the first scroll discoveries in a cave at the northwest end of the Dead Sea, since when some hundreds more have been found. The scrolls are in Hebrew and Aramaic, and most scholars accept them as originating from the monastery of the Jewish sect of the Essenes at Qumran. There is still much controversy over their interpretation. In 1991 RADIOCARBON DATING established that most of the scrolls date to the last two centuries BC, making them the earliest extant manuscripts of the Old Testament and Apocrypha.

Dead sheep. A description of the then shadow chancellor Geoffrey Howe, MOGADON MAN, by chancellor of the exchequer Denis Healey, the GROMYKO OF THE LABOUR PARTY. Healey used the phrase in a Commons debate in 1978, when he declared that 'That part of his speech was rather like being savaged by a dead sheep.' Healey claimed the phrase was derived from Winston Churchill's likening of an attack by Clement Attlee, LORD LOVE-A-DUCK OF LIMEHOUSE, to 'being savaged by a pet lamb'. Churchill himself denied ever describing Attlee as 'a sheep in sheep's clothing'.

Dead soldier. An expression of US origin for an empty bottle, answering to the earlier 'dead marine'. Full bottles, especially in the mass, suggest soldiers on parade, but when they are empty they are isolated and abandoned.

Dead white European male. The stereotype on which literary, cultural and philosophical studies have been traditionally centred, as distinct from (say) a living black African female. The expression became familiar in the 1990s as the acronymic form DWEM.

Deafening silence. An oxymoronic term for a significant or 'pregnant' silence, especially in a situation where one would have expected to hear something, such as a response to a question or a comment on a particular matter. The expression is first recorded in the 1960s.

> On the eve of today's deadline for challenging this summer's results, examination boards reported a 'deafening silence' from schools involved in the Government's pilot scheme.
> *The Times* (20 September 1999)

Dear John. A letter ending a personal relationship. The expression dates from the Second World War, when US servicemen were separated from their partners, who then wrote to terminate the relationship. The words, a typical opening, have served as the title of various American and British comedies in which a hapless husband arrives home to find such a letter awaiting his return.

> 'Dear John,' the letter began. 'I have found someone else whom I think the world of. I think the only way out is for us to get a divorce,' it said. They usually

began like that, those letters that told of infidelity on the part of the wives of servicemen.

Democrat and Chronicle (Rochester, New York) (17 August 1945)

Dear Prudence. A song by the BEATLES, concerning the mental dilemmas of Prudence Farrow, a sister of the actress Mia Farrow and friend of the Beatles, who became serious and withdrawn as a result of the meditation she undertook at the chalet of the Maharishi Mahesh Yogi at Rishikesh in India. Credited to John Lennon and Paul McCartney, the song appears on the so-called WHITE ALBUM, released in November 1968. *See also* TRANSCENDENTAL MEDITATION.

Death, Angel of. *See* ANGEL OF DEATH.

Death by a thousand cuts. A succession of slight injuries whose cumulative effect is fatal. The expression comes from one of the 'thoughts' in Chairman Mao's LITTLE RED BOOK: 'He who is not afraid of death by a thousand cuts dares to unhorse the emperor.'

> 'I don't think we are out of the woods until next June,' he said. 'If something does go wrong, it [the MILLENNIUM BUG] won't be an apocalypse. It will be death by a thousand cuts.'
>
> *Sunday Times* (26 December 1999)

Death in Venice. A novella, originally *Der Tod in Venedig* (1912), by the German novelist Thomas Mann (1875–1955), which was published in Britain in 1928. It is a study, overlaid with symbolism, of the fatal attraction of an ailing and ageing writer, Gustav von Aschenbach, for a beautiful 13-year-old boy, Tadzio. He remains in Venice even in the face of a cholera epidemic, in which he dies. In the notable film version (1971) von Aschenbach, sensitively played by Dirk Bogarde, is reimagined as a composer. The latter is transparently based on Gustav Mahler, and the moving *Adagietto* from his Fifth Symphony (1901) accompanies the slow evolution of the story. Tadzio was played by the young Swedish actor Björn Andresen (b.1955), and the boy's mother by Silvana Mangano. *See also* FIRST LINES OF NOVELS.

Deathless prose. Immortal prose. The cliché, which dates from the 1960s, is almost always used ironically.

> I had imagined that my jumbled speech would be translated into deathless prose.
>
> QUENTIN CRISP: *How to Become a Virgin*, ch v (1981)

Death of a Salesman. The PULITZER PRIZE-winning play (1949) by US playwright Arthur Miller (b.1915) is about the tortured relationships between the failed salesman Willy Loman and his two sons. The play,

which culminates in Loman's suicide, was originally titled *The Inside of His Head*, a reference to the salesman's delusions about himself and his family.

Death on the Nile. A detective novel (1937) by Agatha Christie (1890–1976), involving Hercule POIROT. The setting is a cruise ship, and the background stemmed from the author's interest in the work of her archaeologist husband, Max Mallowan (1904–78), whom she married in 1930 after a divorce from her first husband. A film version (1978) was capably directed by John Guillermin and starred Peter Ustinov as Poirot.

Death on the Rock. A popular name, from a television documentary on the incident, for the killing by the SAS of three IRA members, Sean Savage, Daniel McCann and Mairead Farrell, in Gibraltar on 6 March 1988. In 1995 the European Court of Human Rights condemned the killing. The undercover SAS men claimed that the three had been about to detonate a car bomb.

Death row. A 20th-century Americanism, but hardly a euphemism, for the section of a prison that contains the condemned cells.

> Last month David Martin Long tried to commit suicide on death row but was nursed back to health so that he could be flown from intensive care to execution.
>
> *The Times* (4 January 2000)

Death squad. A term that was first applied in the 1970s in Latin America to groups of military or police personnel who, working out of uniform and with or without official sanction, eliminate anybody perceived of as a threat to the government in power. Death squads usually operate under right-wing military regimes; notable examples include Argentina in the period 1976–83 (*see* DISAPPEARED) and El Salvador in the 1980s, where the death squads' victims included Archbishop Oscar Romero, assassinated in 1980. Sometimes the victims have been the target of a personal grudge, and in Brazil death squads have operated against homeless children.

Debs' delight. An eligible or elegant young man in fashionable society. 'Debs' are debutantes.

Debunk, To. To expose the falseness of; to reduce the inflated reputation of. The word, based on 'bunk', was invented by the US editor and writer William E. Woodward (1874–1950) in his book *Bunk* (1923). The new verb was adopted unwillingly by some Britons.

> The origin of *to debunk* is doubtless the same as that of American jargon in general – the inability of an ill-educated and unintelligent democracy to assimilate

long words. Its intrusion in our own tongue is due partly to the odious novelty of the word itself, and partly to the prevailing fear that to write exact English nowadays is to be put down as a pedant and a prig.

Daily Telegraph (2 March 1935)

Decimal currency. This was introduced in Britain on 15 February 1971, the new pound consisting of 100 pence. The new coins were the seven-sided 50p piece, the 10p piece (the same size as the former florin), the 5p piece (the same size as the former shilling), the 2p piece, the 1p piece and the ½p piece. The first three coins were silver in colour and the remainder copper-coloured. The introduction of a decimal currency was first mooted in 1816 by the Tory MP John Croker.

Decline and Fall. The first novel (1928) by Evelyn Waugh (1903–66), a comic, but embroidered and extended, reprise of some of the author's own experiences at Oxford University and as a teacher at a private school. A theological student, Paul Pennyfeather, innocently embroiled in a drunken incident, is sent down from Scone College, Oxford and becomes a master at an eccentric public school. Further misfortune follows when, on the morning of his wedding to the glamorous Margot Best-Chetwynde, he is arrested and imprisoned for his wife-to-be's involvement in the white slave-trade. An escape is engineered that allows Pennyfeather to resume his studies in the guise of a distant cousin. The title echoes that of *The Decline and Fall of the Roman Empire* by Edward Gibbon (1737–94). An only moderately amusing film version (1968), with Robin Phillips as Paul Pennyfeather, was directed by John Krish. *See also* FIRST LINES OF NOVELS.

Decommissioning. Generally, the process of putting something out of commission or closing it down, such as a nuclear power plant. More specifically the word has been applied to the handing over or destruction of weapons held by the various paramilitary groups in Northern Ireland under the terms of the GOOD FRIDAY AGREEMENT.

Deely Bobbers. These bobbing headsets resembling insect antennae were all the rage of 1982. They were the invention of John Mincove, a US novelty manufacturer. The origin of their name remains a mystery.

Deep six, To. To get rid of; to destroy. The phrase originated as US naval jargon for to throw overboard. The reference is ultimately to SIX FEET UNDER.

Deep Throat. A code name for the anonymous source in the White House during the presidency of Richard M. Nixon who supplied *Washington Post* journalists

Carl Bernstein and Bob Woodward with information that aided them in their WATERGATE investigations of 1972–4. The rumour that 'Deep Throat' did not in fact exist was hotly denied by Woodward. The name came from the title of a celebrated pornographic movie of 1972 starring Linda Lovelace. *See also* ALL THE PRESIDENT'S MEN; CREEP; TRICKY DICKY.

Default. In computer jargon a pre-selected option that a program will adopt if none other is selected by the user or programmer. The specialized sense dates from the 1960s and can bemuse neophytes since the word normally denotes a failure and suggests 'falter' and even more 'fault'.

'Default' to me implies that something is seriously wrong. It has connotations of debt, failure and wretchedness and yet, to the writers of the manual it has another meaning entirely.

Sunday Times (12 September 1999)

Defence of the Realm Acts. *See* DORA.

Defining moment. An event which typifies or determines all subsequent related occurrences. The term gained common currency from the 1980s.

Def jam. Excellent music. 'Def' may be short for 'definitive' or possibly a Jamaican English form of 'death' as a general intensifier. A television programme for younger viewers, *DEF II*, first shown on BBC 2 in 1988, introduced the word to an initially baffled British audience.

Deir Yassin. The name of a Palestinian village (in what is now the state of Israel) that was the scene of a massacre, on the morning of 9 April 1948, of 254 Arab civilians by IRGUN and STERN GANG terrorists, who included amongst their number the future prime minister of Israel, Menachem Begin (1913–92). Deir Yassin was situated outside the area assigned by the United Nations to the Jewish State. However, it was located in the 'corridor' between Tel Aviv and Jerusalem and was targeted for occupation by the HAGANAH, who authorized the Irgun and Stern Gang to carry out the takeover. The panic engendered by the massacre contibuted to the exodus from Palestine of hundreds of thousands of Arabs. After the attack the leaders of the Haganah distanced themselves from the events at Deir Yassin and issued a statement denouncing the dissidents of Irgun and the Stern Gang, as they had done after the attack on the King David Hotel in July 1946.

Arabs throughout the country, induced to believe wild takes or Irgun 'butchery', were seized with limitless panic and started to flee for their lives. This mass flight soon developed into a maddened, uncontrollable stampede. The political and economic significance of this development can hardly be overestimated.

MENACHEM BEGIN

Déjà lu (French, 'already read'). A phrase dating from the 1960s for the feeling that one may have read the present passage before, or an identical passage elsewhere. The phrase is based on *déjà vu*, 'already seen', as a term for the illusory feeling of having experienced the present situation before.

Delaney amendment or **clause.** An amendment of the US Food, Drug and Cosmetic Act which forbids the use of any food additive that has been shown to cause cancer in animals or people. The name is that of the US Congressman James J. Delaney (b.1901), the amendment's author. Although some 20 years old at the time, the amendment became the centre of controversy in the 1970s when scientists pointed out that minute quantities of an additive might not necessarily be harmful and could, in fact, be useful. Others maintained that even the smallest quantities of such substances should be banned.

Delhi belly. *See* MONTEZUMA'S REVENGE.

Delia. A name synonymous with good, simple cooking (rather than *haute cuisine*), from Delia Smith (b.1941), author and broadcaster on the subject from the 1970s. Guests invited to dinner may welcome or sample a dish with an enquiry on the lines of 'Is this Delia?'

Deliver the goods, To. To come up with what was expected; to fulfil one's promise.

Delusions of grandeur. An exaggerated estimation of one's own importance; megalomania. The term dates from the early 20th century.

Demoiselles d'Avignon, Les. It was with this stunning canvas that Pablo Picasso (1881–1973) heralded the arrival of CUBISM. The austere simplicity of the work, painted in 1907, incorporates Picasso's discovery of African and ancient Iberian art: it features five nudes, four of whom are standing, and three of whom have mask-like faces. Surprisingly, given that the painting has become such an icon of modernism, the work was not reproduced until 1925 and not exhibited in public until 1937. The title was jokingly given to the work by the critic André Salmon, who suggested that the young ladies in the painting might be *demoiselles* ('young ladies') in a brothel in the Carré d'Avinyo (Avignon Street) in Barcelona.

Denishawn School of Dancing. This dance school

and company opened in Los Angeles in 1915, taking its name from its founders, Ruth St Denis (1879–1968) and her husband, Ted Shawn (1891–1972). Its main attention was devoted to modern dance, and it fostered such leading modern dancers as Martha Graham (1894–1991), Doris Humphrey (1895–1958) and Charles Weidman (1901–75). The company closed in 1931 after St Denis and Shawn separated. *See also* JACOB'S PILLOW.

Dennis the Menace. There are two cartoon characters of this name and title, one British, the other American. The British Dennis has featured in the BEANO since 1951 and was the creation of cartoonist David Law. He has a shock of black hair, wears a red striped jersey and is accompanied by a fearsome dog called Gnasher. His female counterpart is Beryl the Peril. His US namesake was created the same year by artist Hank Ketcham as a four-year-old brat. He has appeared in various cartoon stories, including a televised version in the early 1960s.

Denver boot. A wheel clamp used to immobilize an illegally parked car. The colloquialism is now dated but was current in Britain from the late 1960s when this solution to illegal parking was first discussed. The allusion is to Denver, Colorado, where wheel clamping was introduced in 1949.

Derek and Clive. *See* NOT ONLY ... BUT ALSO ... .

Derivative. In stock market parlance a financial contract whose value derives from, and is dependent on, the value of an underlying variable asset, such as a commodity, currency or security. Many such contracts are highly speculative, since an investor can potentially make a huge profit by a minimal outlay. In consequence, some banks and individuals have made and lost vast sums in such speculations, one of which led to the collapse of Barings Bank in 1995.

Desaparecidos, Los. *See* DISAPPEARED.

Desert Fox. The nickname of Field Marshal Erwin Rommel (1891–1944), German commander of the AFRIKA KORPS in North Africa in the Second World War. The allusion was to his audacious surprise attacks, which won him early successes in 1941–2. The name was used equally by the Germans as *Der Wüstenfuchs*. There is no actual such animal. *See also* ALAMEIN, EL; DESERT RATS.

Desert Island Discs. The enduringly popular radio programme was created in 1942 by Roy Plomley (1914–85) and had its 2000th 'castaway' (the actor John Thaw) in 1990. Each celebrity is allowed to choose eight gramophone records and a single luxury and book (except the Bible or Shakespeare) that they would wish to have on their desert island. The first subject was the comedian Vic Oliver, and the only celebrity to be 'shipwrecked' four times was the comedian Arthur Askey. Plomley himself presented the programme until his death.

Desert Rats. The name associated with the British 7th Armoured Division in the Second World War, whose divisional sign was the desert rat (jerboa), which was adopted during its 'scurrying and biting' tactics in Libya. The final design of the badge was a red rat outlined on a black background. The division served throughout the North Africa campaign of 1941–2 and in northwestern Europe from Normandy to Berlin. The name was later associated with the 7th Armoured Brigade, and was again to the fore when this force was in action in the Middle East during the second GULF WAR.

Desert Shield. The name adopted for the US contribution to the UN military coalition against Iraq in the second GULF WAR. *See also* DESERT STORM.

Desert Storm. The name of the air and land campaign waged by the US-led UN military coalition against Iraq in the second GULF WAR. In some contexts the name is used for the land battle only.

Desiccated calculating machine. A phrase coined by Aneurin Bevan, usually thought to refer to Hugh Gaitskell (1906–63), his successful rival for the LABOUR PARTY leadership in 1955. Earlier, when Gaitskell was chancellor of the exchequer in 1950–51, Tory politician Iain Macleod (1913–70) had dubbed Gaitskell 'Mr Rising Price'. *See also* NYE.

Designer drug. A drug deliberately synthesized ('designed') to circumvent drug laws. A structure is used which is not illegal but which mimics the chemistry and effects of an existing banned drug.

> Some of these people obviously use cocaine, marijuana and some exotic designer drugs.
> *New York Times* (23 September 1989)

Designer label. A label on an expensive or modish item of clothing that bears the name of a famous fashion designer, such as that of Calvin Klein on the back of jeans in the 1970s.

Designer stubble. The short hairs and beard on a man's face that has been deliberately left unshaven for a day or so with the aim of appearing attractively macho. The fashion became current from the late 1980s among models and media celebrities.

> A 20th-century Jack-the-lad, all designer stubble, shy smiles and off-the-shoulder shifts – an expert at pulling birds.
> *The Times* (11 October 1999)

Design for Living. A play (1933) by Noël Coward (1899–1973) about a successful *ménage à trois* established by three friends, Leo (a writer), Otto (a painter) and Gilda (a designer). The idea of writing about such a threesome was suggested to Coward both by Eugene O'Neill's *Strange Interlude* (1928) and by his own close friendship with the actors Alfred Lunt and Lynn Fontanne.

Desire Street. A street in New Orleans made famous by Tennessee Williams's play *A* STREETCAR NAMED DESIRE (1947), in which the central character, Blanche Du Bois, visits her sister Stella, who lives with her husband Jack in the French Quarter of the city near the stop of two streetcars (trams) that run on the same track. Each is named for its destination, respectively 'Desire' and 'Cemetery', and these names are taken symbolically, Blanche contending that Stella's marriage is a product of lust, as aimless as the 'streetcar named Desire' that shuttles through the narrow streets. The name of the street does not denote a place of pleasure but derives from the French girl's name Désirée. A monument, the 'Streetcar Named Desire', now stands on the site near the French Market.

Desire Under the Elms. A play (1924) by the US playwright Eugene O'Neill (1888–1953) about the tragic events that transpire when an elderly patriarch brings home a new, much younger wife who has designs on the farm that he owns. The elms of the title are two huge trees that loom over the farmhouse where the action takes place. The desire is the incestuous love affair that develops between the wife and her new husband's youngest son. There was a depressing film version (1957) with Burl Ives, Sophia Loren and Anthony Perkins.

Desktop. In computer jargon the working area of a computer screen thought of as the equivalent of a desktop and containing ICONS representing items such as files and a waste bin, as normally found respectively on and under a conventional desk.

Desperate Dan. The brawny, stubble-chinned westerner who has appeared in the DANDY comic (which his name matches) since 1937. His favourite dish is cow pie, which he eats with the horns protruding from the pastry. He was the creation of the artist Dudley D. Watkins.

Des res. A 'desirable residence', former estate agents' jargon for any house that they wish to sell. Since the mid-1980s the expression has generally been an ironic colloquialism.

> The ultra rich and famous can now leave dry land for the ultimate des res – an apartment on the ResidenSea liner.
>
> *heat* (18–24 November 1999)

Destry Rides Again. A WESTERN (1939) directed by George Marshall and adapted from a novel of the same title (1930) by Max Brand about peace-loving marshal Tom Destry, who relies on his wits rather than his gun to keep law and order in the unruly town of Bottleneck. He refuses to carry a gun, much to the alarm of the inhabitants, and his favourite tipple is sarsaparilla. The film starred James Stewart and Marlene Dietrich, but this was not the first time Destry had 'ridden again': Brand's novel had already been filmed in 1932, starring Tom Mix, and in 1954 it was adapted for the screen once more, called simply *Destry*, and starring Audie Murphy. *See also* BACK-ROOM BOYS.

Détente (French, 'relaxation'). A term describing the reduction in COLD WAR tension between the United States and the Soviet Union during the 1970s. Attempts to achieve a measure of peaceful co-existence began in 1968 during the VIETNAM War peace talks, and in 1972 President Richard Nixon re-established friendly relations between the USA and communist China. This Sino-US rapprochement in turn led the Soviet Union to improve its relations with the USA. Among the results of détente were the ABM and SALT treaties, in which the USA and the Soviet Union agreed to limitations in the nuclear arms race. *See also* NIXON IN CHINA.

Dev. A nickname of the Irish politician Éamon de Valera (1882–1975), prime minister of Ireland (1932–48, 1951–4 and 1957–9) and president (1959–73). Born in the USA of a Spanish father, de Valera was also called the 'Long Fellow' because of his tall and gaunt appearance. A biography of de Valera by the Irish journalist Tim Pat Coogan was entitled *De Valera: Long Fellow, Long Shadow* (1993). *See also* BIG FELLA.

De Vil, Cruella. The wicked heroine of Dodie Smith's children's novel *The Hundred and One Dalmatians* (1956), who kidnaps puppies with the aim of turning their fur into coats for humans. Her name, subsequently a byword for female heartlessness, implies that she is a cruel villainess or cruel deviless. The story was made into a popular Disney cartoon film, *One Hundred and One Dalmatians* (1961). Cruella De Vil was also a nickname given to the Conservative politician Edwina Currie (b.1946). Currie's appearance in the Commons provoked in one Tory minister a 'brief bat-squeak of desire'. Her short career in government (1986–8) ended when, as a junior health minister, she announced, to the fury of the farming lobby, that most of the UK's egg production was infected with the salmonella bacteria. She has subsequently had a successful career as a radio broadcaster and writer of political BONKBUSTERS, while continuing to sit on the back benches.

Devil's Dictionary, The. A glossary of aphorisms (1911), first published as *The Cynic's Word Book* (1906) by Ambrose Bierce (1842–?1914). Typical entries are:

> APOLOGIZE, *v.* To lay the foundation for a future offence.
>
> INSURANCE, *n.* An ingenious modern game of chance in which the player is permitted to enjoy the comfortable conviction that he is beating the man who keeps the table.
>
> MARRIAGE, *n.* The state or condition of a community consisting of a master, a mistress and two slaves, making two in all.

Bierce is believed to have died in battle at the age of 71, having been caught in Ojinaga, on the Rio Grande, when it was besieged and taken by rebels.

Devil's Island (French *Isle du Diable*). A former French penal colony, notorious for the harshness of its conditions, situated on a tiny island off the coast of French Guiana. The island's most famous prisoner was Albert Dreyfus (1859–1935), wrongly convicted of espionage and held there from 1895 to 1899 (*see also* DREYFUS-ARD). In 1969 another prisoner, Henri Charrière (1906–73), published a best-selling book, *Papillon* (the title referring to his own nickname), about his attempts to escape from the island, the last try in 1944 being successful. The 1973 film version, starring Steve McQueen and Dustin Hoffman, drew the following barb from one critic: '*Papillon* offers torture as entertainment but winds up making entertainment a form of torture.' The penal settlement was closed down in 1953, and the island is now a tourist resort.

Devolution. A term adopted in the 20th century for the transfer of certain powers from central government to provincial assemblies in Scotland and Wales. In 1974 the Labour government proposed setting up a new Scottish parliament and a Welsh assembly. Referendums were held in 1979, with the Welsh voting against. The Scots narrowly voted in favour, but the support of at least 40 per cent of the electorate was required and was not obtained, so no action resulted. The intervening Conservative governments stood fast against devolution, but in 1997 the NEW LABOUR government held new referendums. This time both countries voted in favour. The Scottish parliament and Welsh assembly, both elected in 1999, received authority and legislative power over domestic issues, such as health, housing and social services, while Westminster retained control over defence, economic policy, employment, taxation and foreign affairs.

Di, Lady. See LADY DI.

Diamond Lil. A nickname of the US film actress Mae West (1892–1980), from her play thus titled (1928) in which she took the main role. The heroine is so called because of the large amount of 'ice' (jewellery) her pimp has lavished on her.

Diamonds Are Forever. The eighth film (1971) in the James BOND series, starring Sean Connery as Bond and based on a book of the same title by Ian Fleming (1908–64). The title (which was reinforced by a theme tune sung by Shirley Bassey) was inspired by a slogan devised in 1939 by US advertising writer B.J. Kidd on behalf of De Beers Consolidated Mines in South Africa as part of a campaign to promote diamond engagement rings.

Diamond system. A system of play in football in which the formation of the midfield players is in the shape of a diamond. One player operates at the tip in the role of part-midfielder, part-striker, two players take up wider positions behind, and an anchor midfielder locates himself at the base in front of the defence. The task of the middle two players is to push forward when in possession of the ball and track back when the opposition has it.

Dianetics. A system designed to relieve or remove psychosomatic disorders by cleansing the mind of harmful images. It was developed in 1950 by L. Ron Hubbard (1911–86) founder of the Church of SCIENTOLOGY, and takes its name from Greek *dianœtikos*, 'relating to thought'.

Dice with death, To. To take serious risks. The expression dates from the 1940s and was long a journalistic cliché used in connection with motor-racing. The concept is of playing a game of dice with Death. If he wins, one will lose one's life.

Dick Emery Show, The. A long-running television comedy series screened from 1963 to 1981 and starring Dick Emery (1918–84) in a series of enjoyable impressions that included a toothy vicar, an ageing BOVVER BOY and a bouncy blonde, Mandy, who always ended a radio interview by giving her interviewer a saucy punch and saying: 'Ooh, you are awful – but I like you.'

Dicky bow. A bow tie. The name alludes to 'dicky' as a former slang term for a shirt collar and a still current colloquialism for a false shirt front.

Dief the Chief. A nickname awarded by his colleagues to Canadian politician John G. Diefenbaker (1895–1979), who became prime minister (1957–63) following his Progressive Conservative Party's landslide victory over the Liberals.

Die Hard. A film thriller (1988) starring Bruce Willis as a New York policeman pitted against a ruthless gang of terrorists with whom he is trapped in a high-rise Los Angeles office block (actually the headquarters building of 20th Century-Fox, makers of the film). The title of the film, and its sequels *Die Hard 2* (1990) and *Die Hard with a Vengeance* (1995), had been used previously in a variety of contexts over the years. 'Die Hard' was, for instance, the regimental nickname bestowed on the 57th Foot, later the 1st Battalion Middlesex Regiment and later still the 4th Battalion The Queen's Regiment, after their heroic but bloody stand at the Battle of Albuera in 1811. As the French enemies attacked, Colonel Inglis exhorted his men: 'Die hard, my men, die hard.'

> Die harder.
> Publicity slogan for *Die Hard 2*

Diehards. The nickname of those Conservative lords who rebelled against the party line in 1911 to vote against the Parliament Act, saying they would 'die fighting' the provisions of the act that restricted the veto power of the House of Lords. Their actions led to the resignation of party leader Arthur Balfour. *See also* BALFOUR'S POODLE; HEDGERS AND DITCHERS.

Dien Bien Phu. A village in VIETNAM, some 320 km (200 miles) west of Hanoi, near the border with Laos. It was chosen as the site of a heavily fortified forward base by the French in their war against the nationalist and communist VIET MINH, who had been fighting for Vietnamese independence since 1946. The Viet Minh, having cut off all roads into Dien Bien Phu, began to besiege the base in March 1954, which now could only be supplied from the air. The Viet Minh artillery outgunned that of the French, who, in the words of one soldier, were in a chamber pot with the enemy in the process of unfastening his trousers. A series of offensives culminated in an all-out Viet Minh attack launched on 1 May, and on 7 May the base was completely overrun. It was the end of French rule in Vietnam, and the former colony was divided into communist North Vietnam and American-sponsored South Vietnam.

Dietrickery. A nickname for the women's fashion for wearing men's clothes inspired in the 1930s by the German-born American actress Marlene Dietrich (1901–92). Amelia Bloomer's attempt to introduce trousers for women at the close of the 19th century had largely ended in failure, but 40 years on Dietrich set a trend popular with her female fans when she took to wearing men's clothes in public, typically in the form of a suit and tie topped by a slanting hat. Women did not wear trousers on a daily basis until after the Second World War, and by the 1960s women were buying more trousers than skirts.

Different strokes. A short form of 'different strokes for different folks', meaning that different people have different requirements. There is probably a sexual reference here. The phrase is of black US origin. *Diff'rent Strokes* (1978–86) was a US television comedy, shown subsequently in Britain, about a millionaire white widower who adopts two black boys.

Dig for victory. A Ministry of Agriculture exhortation disseminated in the earliest days of the Second World War, when the shortage of foodstuffs was an immediate concern. One consequence was a rise in the number of allotments from 815,000 in 1939 to 1.4 million in 1943. In the United States the equivalent call was 'Garden for victory', but somehow the British byword was beefier.

Digger. An Australian. The name was in use before 1850, consequent upon the discovery of gold, and was applied to ANZAC troops fighting (and digging in) in Flanders in the First World War and again in the Second World War.

> Burly, slouch-hatted, independent and profane, the Digger bestrides the battlefields of Gallipoli and the Western Front just as jauntily as his bronze monument looks down from Mont St Quentin above Péronne. It is integral to the Australian sense of nationhood and national character.
>
> *Times Literary Supplement* (review of Alistair Thomson,
> *Anzac Memories*) (16 September 1994)

Digital age. A nickname for the 1990s, in which rapid advances in technology resulted in the transfer of many items of electrical or electronic equipment to digital operation, among them compact discs (CDs), digital cameras, digital radio, digital video discs (DVDs) and not least DIGITAL TELEVISION. The revolution owed much to the burgeoning of the INTERNET, which enabled people to download digital images, information, music and the like and to switch from traditional shopping to HOME SHOPPING and from High Street banking to online banking.

> Jimmy and Doug's Farm Club, 'a worldwide record label for the digital age'.
> *The Times* (10 December 1999)

Digital television or **DTV.** Television in which sound and images come to a screen via a digital (as distinct from analogue) signal broadcast from space The result is an improvement in sound and picture quality and the possibility of interactive services such as HOME SHOPPING and banking and the sending of E-MAILS without the use of a computer. Digital television came to Britain in the late 1990s and can be received by dish (satellite), aerial (terrestrial) or cable. It was at first regarded with caution by the public, who were wary of this revolution in their favourite medium.

Dig one's own grave, To. To cause one's own downfall. The phrase is first recorded in the 1930s.

> Far from staging a renaissance, the Conservatives dug their own grave last week.
> *Independent on Sunday* (10 October 1999)

Dilbert. The comic strip character of this name, an engineer NERD working for The Company, is the invention of the US cartoonist Scott Adams. He appears with his dog Dogbert, much smarter than he is, his mother Dilmom, a SCRABBLE addict, his colleagues Wally, Alice and Loud Howard, and The Pointy-Haired Boss. The strip is one of the most popular in the world, reaching 150 million readers daily, with spin-off bestsellers and its own WORLD WIDE WEB site, which attracts 4 million visits a month.

Dimbledom. A nickname for the dominant role played by the three members of the Dimbleby family in British radio and television for half a century. Richard Dimbleby (1913–65) was a noted radio reporter in the Second World War, and it was his voice that listeners heard describing airborne forces taking off for Normandy and the horrors of BELSEN. His elder son, David (b.1938), presented the current affairs programme PANORAMA for many years and anchored the BBC coverage of every general election from 1979 to

1997. David's brother, Jonathan (b.1944), became associated with major documentary programmes, including a report on the Ethiopian famine in 1973 and a documentary on Prince Charles, *Public Person, Private Man*, in 1994.

Diminished responsibility. A legal term from the Homicide Act 1957, which exempts a person suffering from an unbalanced mental state from full liability for a crime, especially murder.

Dimsie. A fictional schoolgirl of the traditional JOLLY HOCKEYSTICKS type. She loves games and forms an 'Anti-Soppist Society' opposed to love, sentimentality and the use of cosmetics. She appeared in a lengthy series of stories by Dorita Fairlie Bruce, beginning with *The Senior Prefect* (1921) and was very popular among schoolgirl readers in the 1920s and 1930s. Her full name is Dorothy Maitland.

Dinerese. American diners of the 1940s were a source of many colourful expressions relating to customers' orders. Several are still current. A selection follows:

Abbott and Costello: frankfurters and beans (after the comedy film partners)
Adam and Eve on a raft: two poached eggs on toast
All the way: a sandwich with 'the works', i.e. every condiment in the kitchen
BLT: bacon, lettuce and tomato sandwich
Bowl of red: a serving of chilli
Burn it: cook it until well done
Cowboy with spurs: a western omelette (with minced ham and onions) with French fries (chips)
Eve with the lid on: apple pie
Haystack: strawberry pancakes ('hay' for 'straw')
High and dry: a sandwich without any condiments
Hold the grass: without lettuce
Hold the mayo: without mayonnaise
Murphy carrying a wreath: ham and potatoes (murphies) with cabbage
On the hoof: rare meat
OVER EASY
Put out the lights and cry: liver and onions (to put out someone's lights is to punch them in the liver)
Red lead: tomato ketchup
Wreck a pair: two scrambled eggs

Diners Club. The first all-purpose credit card came into being in 1950. It was launched by a US business executive, Francis X. McNamara, who embarrassingly discovered he had left his wallet at home on coming to settle the bill after entertaining clients to lunch at a fashionable Manhattan restaurant.

Dingbat. A North American and Australian term for a stupid or eccentric person. The origin may be in 'ding' in the sense 'to beat' with 'bat' subsequently associated with 'batty'. The word has also been used for various rather vaguely specified objects. In printing and computer jargon dingbats are special characters and symbols, i.e. those that differ from the standard letters and numerals.

Dingo baby case. An extraordinary Australian legal case originating in an incident at a campsite near Ayer's Rock, Alice Springs, in 1980, when a young baby, Azaria Chamberlain, disappeared from her parents' tent. Initially it was thought that the baby must have been taken by a dingo (the Australian wild dog), but various pieces of circumstantial evidence led to suspicion falling on the mother, Lindy Chamberlain. Suspicion was increased by the fact that Azaria's parents belonged to the millenarian Seventh-Day Adventist cult, and it was said that the name they had given their daughter, Azaria, meant 'carrier of sin' (although the conventional meaning of the Hebrew Azariah is 'helped by God'). From this the rumour emerged that the mother might have sacrificed her daughter in some bizarre ritual. Lindy Chamberlain was arrested, tried, convicted and sentenced to hard labour for life. However, many believed that there had been a gross miscarriage of justice, and the case was reopened in 1986, resulting in the release and pardon of Lindy Chamberlain. The story became the subject of the 1989 film *A Cry in the Dark*, starring Meryl Streep and Sam Neill.

Dinky Toys. The model vehicles and figures so named were the creation of Frank Hornby, the inventor of MECCANO. They were introduced in 1934 as 'Modelled Miniatures' for use with Hornby's toy railway system but soon gained a distinct identity among their delighted schoolboy owners.

Dinner lady. A term current from the 1960s for a woman who serves meals and supervises children at mealtimes in a school. The term derives from young children themselves, for whom a midday meal is 'dinner' and any adult woman a 'lady'.

Dionne quins. The five daughters, Marie, Émilie, Yvonne, Cécile and Annette, born prematurely on 28 May 1934 to Oliva and Elzire Dionne near Callander, Ontario. They became wards of the state in 1935 and were exploited by the government for promotional purposes but their father regained control in 1941. Émilie died in 1954 and Marie in 1970. In 1998 the three surviving sisters accepted a settlement of $2.8 million from the Ontario government and promises of an inquiry into their treatment during their childhood.

Dior Look. The narrow-waisted, tightly fitting bodices and full-pleated skirts designed by the French couturier Christian Dior (1905–57) were launched in Paris on 12 February 1947, as the first postwar fashion fad, later known as the NEW LOOK. *See also* A-LINE.

Dip one's beak, To. To drink beer or some other alcoholic beverage; to visit a pub or bar.

Dip one's wick, To. Of a man, to engage in sexual intercourse. To dip a wick in the literal sense is to make a candle by immersing a wick repeatedly in hot wax. In the modern phrase 'wick' is short for 'Hampton Wick', rhyming slang for 'prick'.

Directoire knickers. Straight, full, knee-length knickers with elastic at waist and knee. They are a development of the late Victorian 'Directoire' style of dress adopted from that worn at the time of the French Directory (1795–9), itself characterized by extravagance of design and imitative of Greek and Roman costume. The garment is still worn by some women, especially the elderly.

Direct Rule. The direct government of Northern Ireland from Westminster, introduced in 1972, the year of BLOODY SUNDAY, following the outbreak of the TROUBLES four years earlier. Direct rule was abandoned in December 1999 as an outcome of discussions proceeding from the signing of the GOOD FRIDAY AGREEMENT and the setting up of the Northern Ireland Assembly. It was reimposed in February 2000 amid bitter recriminations between SINN FÉIN and the British authorities over the issue of the DECOMMISSIONING of paramilitary weapons. The Assembly recommenced its functions, however, in the summer of 2000.

Dire straits. Desperate trouble; impecuniosity. The phrase is probably based on the older 'dire necessity' and was popularized by the pop group of this name formed in 1977. *See also* ROCK GROUP NAMES.

Dirty dancing. A form of dancing to pop or disco music involving gyratory movements and hip-to-hip contact. It was craze of the 1980s and was popularized by a film of 1987 of this title starring Jennifer Grey and Patrick Swayze. The LAMBADA was a natural development.

> Flirting is the agenda, with dirty dancing and chat-up techniques on the side.
>
> *The Times* (27 November 1999)

Dirty Dozen, The. A war film (1967) directed by Robert Aldrich and adapted from a novel of the same title by E.M. Nathanson about a squad of 12 military prisoners who are challenged to perform a suicidal mission in occupied France during the Second World War in exchange for the chance of freedom. Starring Lee Marvin and Telly Savalas, among others, the film's title deliberately evoked the classic western *The* MAGNIFICENT SEVEN, made seven years earlier.

Dirty dozens. A ritual game among black Americans of insulting various relatives, especially their mother, with 12 'rounds' of attack. The barbs are usually sexual or scatological. Hence 'dirty'.

Dirty Harry. The film (1971), written by John Milius and directed by Don Siegel, is about a San Francisco police detective whose hunt to find a vicious serial killer becomes a personal quest. 'Dirty Harry' is Detective Harry Callahan, played by Clint Eastwood, who has little compunction about using illegal methods to get to his quarry. The film includes Callahan's gloating words to a terrified bank robber as he holds a .44 magnum to his temple:

> I know what you're thinking, punk. You're thinking, 'Did he fire six shots or only five?' Now, to tell you the truth, in all this excitement, I've kind of lost track myself. But being as this is a .44 Magnum, the most powerful handgun in the world, and would blow your head clean off, you've got to ask yourself one question: 'Do I feel lucky?' Well, do ya, punk?

Dirty mac or **raincoat brigade.** A term for men who frequent sex shops, watch BLUE MOVIES in seedy cinemas, and buy pornographic magazines from the TOP SHELF of newsagents. The name alludes to the dirty macintosh they supposedly wear to achieve anonymity. The expression dates from the 1970s.

> Much has been made of the sex and nudity in the film [*Eyes Wide Shut*], but the dirty raincoat brigade will be disappointed if they hope for rampant coupling all the way through.
>
> *The Times* (1 September 1999)

Dirty money. Money acquired by dishonest or disreputable means. Such money can decriminalized by 'laundering' it through a legitimate business such as a bank.

> Lawyers in at least 60 firms are suspected by detectives and customs officers of laundering millions of pounds of dirty money for criminals.
>
> *The Times* (7 December 1998)

Dirty old man. A lecherous one, not necessarily old.

Dirty protest. A form of protest by mainly Republican paramilitary prisoners in Northern Ireland in the 1970s. They refused to wash and fouled their cells with the aim of gaining political, as opposed to criminal, status. *See also* BLANKET PROTEST.

Dirty raincoat brigade. *See* DIRTY MAC BRIGADE.

Dirty realism. A term and concept introduced in 1987 by Bill Buford, editor of *Granta*, in an issue devoted to contemporary US fiction. 'Dirty realist' fiction typically includes laconic dialogue, seedy settings, explicit descriptions of violence and sordid sex and characters that are downbeat and drearily hopeless. Leading writers of the genre are Raymond Carver (1938–88), Richard Ford (b.1944) and Tobias Wolff (b.1945).

Dirty tricks. A term dating from the 1940s for undercover or clandestine operations and deceitful schemes in politics and espionage. 'Dirty' here means 'unethical'. The term originally applied to covert intelligence operations carried out by the CIA, whose planning directorate was nicknamed 'Department of Dirty Tricks'. The expression was subsequently extended to underhand activities aimed at undermining political opponents or commercial rivals.

> A Dirty Tricks campaign designed to paint Ken Livingstone as an 'enemy of Israel' was instigated … at the behest of a government minister.
> *The Times* (19 November 1999)

Dirty War. *See* DISAPPEARED.

Dirty weekend. A weekend spent with someone other than one's spouse or with one's spouse but without one's children. 'Dirty' expresses a Victorian or puritanical attitude to sex. The phrase dates from the 1930s.

Dirty work. Although literally meaning an unpleasant or distasteful physical task, in which one is covered in dirt, the phrase more usually refers to an underhand or dishonourable action, in which the dirt is metaphorical. A fuller form is 'dirty work at the crossroads', perhaps alluding to the crossroads as a place where suicides were buried. The expression dates from the early years of the 20th century.

Disappeared, The (Spanish *los desaparecidos*). Those persons who disappeared in Argentina during the so-called 'Dirty War' under the military government of 1976–1983. The Dirty War was aimed at suspected left-wing guerrillas, the MONTONEROS, but widened to target anybody regarded as an enemy of the state. The disappeared, numbering between 6000 and 15,000 people, were assumed to have been murdered by state-sponsored DEATH SQUADS. 'The disappeared' is also used to refer to those people murdered by the IRA during the Northern Ireland TROUBLES who were buried in unknown places.

Disaster movie. A film in which a group of people are involved in a natural or 'manmade' disaster of some kind. The genre is of US origin and arose in the 1970s. Classic examples are *The Poseidon Adventure* (1972), with passengers trapped inside a capsized luxury liner, *Airport 1975* (1974), in which a stewardess has to manoeuvre a jumbo jet to safety after it collides with another plane, *Earthquake* (1974), set in Los Angeles, and *The Towering Inferno* (1974), in which the world's tallest building is destroyed by fire on the night of its inauguration. *See also* HORROR MOVIE.

Discovery. The bright green and crimson apple of this name is so called because it arose as a chance discovery by an amateur grower. It was first marketed commercially in the 1970s.

Discworld. The setting of the comic fantasies by the novelist Terry Pratchett (b.1948), as a flat planet supported by four elephants riding through space on a giant tortoise. There is no central character in the stories, although Death appears in each and is prominent in several. The first book in the sequence, *The Colour of Magic* (1983), was essentially a parody of H.P. Lovecraft (1890–1937) and other fantasy writers, but the series went on to create a world of its own, each of the volumes being self-contained. Much of the enjoyment of the stories derives from the strange names of characters and places, such as the wizard Igneous Cutwell, the kingdom of Djelibeybi, the Unseen University in Ankh-Morpork, Discworld's most ancient city, and Lady Sybil Deirdre Olgivanna Ramkin, the latter's richest resident, married to Commander Samuel Vimes.

Disgusted, Tunbridge Wells. A byname for a disgruntled resident of the named Kent town, a worthy and respectable community famed as a bastion of morality and decency. The name is supposedly used by those penning anonymous letters of complaint or objection to the press, especially on any matter relating to falling standards. It is uncertain where the phrase originated, but it is unlikely to have been Royal Tunbridge Wells itself.

> Disgusted of Tunbridge Wells would not have been

pleased to hear that the South Bank is playing host to the world's most famous rabbit.

The Times (10 June 1998)

Dish the dirt, To. To reveal or spread malicious gossip. 'To dish' is to dish up or serve to an eager audience, while the 'dirt' is the damaging information. The phrase dates from the 1950s.

A close friend of Sir Edward Heath is planning to dish the dirt on Baroness Thatcher.

The Times (19 November 1999)

Dishy. Very attractive. The notion is that the person so described is 'tasty' or 'good enough to eat'. The term dates from the 1960s and can also be applied to things, such as a 'dishy car' or a 'dishy dress'.

'Mm, is *that* him?' said the girl, all velvet. 'He's dishy.'

JOHN GARDNER: *The Liquidator*, ch iii (1964)

Disneyland. One of various THEME PARKS centring on the world created by the US animator and film producer Walt Disney (1901–66) and thus featuring MICKEY MOUSE and DONALD DUCK, among other characters, as well as replicas of the fairytale world of the cartoons themselves. The first such park of the name was opened in Anaheim, California, in 1955, with themes including Frontierland, tropical exploration, fairy tales, and space travel and the future. A second, larger complex, Walt Disney World, was opened near Orlando, Florida, in 1971. In 1983 a Japanese version, Tokyo Disneyland, opened near Tokyo. Its themes replicated all those at Anaheim except Frontierland, which became Westernland, stocked with cowboys and Indians in retro fancy dress. In 1992 Disneyland Paris opened its gates at Marne-la-Vallée, east of Paris.

Displaced persons. A phrase applied to the millions of homeless and uprooted people in Europe, India and Asia whose misfortunes resulted from the havoc produced by the Second World War and subsequent events. They were colloquially referred to as DPs.

Ditchers. *See* HEDGERS AND DITCHERS.

Divine Callas. The American-born operatic soprano of Greek parentage Maria Callas (1923–77) was so known, the descriptive being traditional for a grand (or temperamental) opera singer. Her original surname was Kalageropoulos.

Divino, Il. The nickname of the Brazilian footballer Paolo Roberto Falcao (b.1953), one of the best players in the world in the early 1980s. *See also* BRAZILIAN FOOTBALLERS.

Dixiecrats. The nickname of a group of southern conservatives from 'Dixie' (the American South) who left the Democratic Party because of President GIVE-'EM-HELL HARRY Truman's policy of desegregation. In the 1948 US presidential election they put forward Strom Thurmond as a candidate, but he was overwhelmingly defeated by Truman.

Dixie Dean. The popular footballer William R. Dean (1907–80) was so nicknamed from a rhyme on 'sixty', the number of goals he scored for Everton in the 1927–8 season.

Dixon of Dock Green. The longest running police series on British television, shown on the BBC from 1955 to 1976. Its star was the kindly police constable George Dixon, played by Jack Warner, and the programme provided cosy, non-violent family entertainment. Each episode opened with Dixon saluting the viewer with the words 'Evening, all' and closed with a homily from him to the effect that crime does not pay. He would walk then off into the night whistling 'Maybe It's Because I'm a Londoner'.

Dizzy heights. In the figurative sense a position of worldly importance, as: 'He reached the dizzy heights of company director.' The usage is often ironic.

DNA. *See* DOUBLE HELIX.

D notice. An official notice sent to newspapers and the media generally forbidding them from publishing or broadcasting particular security information. D is the initial of the Defence, Press and Broadcasting Committee, the government body that sends out the notice. There have been suspicions that the security in question might be that of the government rather than that of the nation.

Do a disappearing act, To. To vanish suddenly, as: 'When the children saw the policeman looking they did a disappearing act.' The reference is to the familiar magician's trick of making people and objects disappear. The phrase dates from the early 20th century.

Do a foreigner, To. To work for one's own gain in one's employer's time or using their materials or facilities, or to do so without declaring one's earnings to the relevant authorities, such as the tax office. The expression originated in Second World War military slang and implies a betrayal of one's normal allegiance to one's employer and the state.

Do a runner, To. To abscond from the police; to run away; to leave without paying. The expression spread from semi-criminal jargon in the 1970s.

Do bird, To. To serve a prison sentence. 'Bird' is short for 'birdlime', rhyming slang for 'time'. The phrase dates from the 1920s. 'Birdlime' is itself old slang for a thief, who has 'sticky fingers'.

Dobson, Zuleika. The young woman who wins the hearts of Oxford undergraduates in Max Beerbohm's novel ZULEIKA DOBSON (1911). Her beaux are so smitten that they all drown themselves in sorrow. She is said to have been based on the actress Constance Collier (1880–1955), who was briefly engaged to Beerbohm and who spent the summer of 1903 with him in Dieppe.

Dockers' KC. A press nickname for the Labour Minister Ernest Bevin (1881–1951) when he was national organizer of the dockers' union during the period 1910–21. 'KC' is 'King's Counsel'.

Docklands. London's dockland region has changed dramatically since the flourishing trade of the 18th and 19th centuries, when the British empire was expanding and the Thames was full of cargo vessels of all types, with the enclosed docks handling hundreds of ships a year. The docks were originally in private hands but were taken over by the Port of London Authority in 1909. By the end of the 1960s the docks began to close, partly as a result of the demise of the empire but also because of competition from other ports, labour troubles and other adverse factors. In the mid-1970s it was proposed to redevelop the dockland site for commercial and residential use, and in 1981 the London Docklands Development Corporation was set up to oversee this. By 1990 areas such as the Surrey Commercial Docks and Isle of Dogs had been transformed, as had Canary Wharf, now a massive office development. The area is served by the Docklands Light Railway, which opened in 1987 and links with the main Underground system. The whole enterprise has not been without its financial fiascos, exacerbated by the recession of the early 1990s, and some developers were unable to sell their completed schemes.

Doc Martens. A type of footwear invented in 1945 by Klaus Maertens, a German doctor who needed a comfortable shoe after a skiing accident. He formed a rubber sole from a tyre and sealed it to an upper, so trapping a cushion of air. The boots was first produced in England under licence in 1960 by R. Griggs & Co. and were soon adopted by SKINHEADS, who saw their potential when 'putting the boot in'. PUNK rockers revived the fashion for 'Docs' in the 1970s, and the shoes subsequently became a youth-culture fashion staple and simultaneous anti-fashion statement.

Dr Aziz. See AZIZ, DR.

Doctor Caligari. See CALIGARI, DOCTOR.

Dr Death. A media nickname for a murderer, especially a real or sham doctor who kills elderly people for financial or material gain. An example was the confidence trickster Sydney Noble, imprisoned in 1978 for drugging old ladies in order to ransack their homes. Another was the genuine family doctor Harold Shipman, Britain's worst SERIAL KILLER, convicted in 2000 of murdering 15 women patients and suspected of killing 100 during his 30-year career as a GP. The name owes its impact to its alliterative sound and oxymoronic sense. Doctors are expected to preserve life, not deprive their patients of it. The politician David Owen (b.1938), a Labour foreign minister and one of the founders of the Social Democrats (see LIBERAL DEMOCRATS), was known as Dr Death in *Private Eye*, because he was a medical doctor and for his dark looks.

> While horror stories about 'Dr Deaths' proliferate, few hear about modern hero stories like that of the Australian doctor Barry Marshall.
> *The Times* (28 December 1999)

Dr Dolittle. See DOLITTLE, DR.

Doctor Faustus. A novel, originally *Doktor Faustus* (1947), by the German novelist Thomas Mann (1875–1955), published in English in 1949. Subtitled *The Life of the Composer Adrian Leverkühn as Told by a Friend*, it is a study of the rise and fall of Nazism in the Second World War, which Mann implies was caused by the same Faustian (or demonic) energy that impels and ultimately destroys the composer who is the protagonist of his novel. The ultimate reference is to Goethe's verse tragedy *Faust* (1808–32), telling how the legendary ageing philosopher so named sells his soul to Mephistopheles in return for eternal youth and the beautiful Marguerite.

Dr Feelgood. A nickname for a doctor who readily dispenses mood-enhancing drugs, such as amphetamines, for non-medicinal use. Hence also a term for a doctor who provides short-term palliatives rather than a more efficacious treatment or cure. The term was apparently first used, although not in the sense described, as a designation for himself by the US blues pianist Piano Red (real name William Perryman), who recorded 'Dr. Feelgood and the Interns' in 1962. The current sense is implicit, however, in the words of a song recorded soon after by the US soul singer Aretha Franklin and her husband and manager, Ted White, and this popularized the term.

Don't send me no doctor
Filling me up with all those pills
Got a man named Dr. Feelgood
That man takes care of all my pains and my ills.
ARETHA FRANKLIN and TED WHITE: 'Dr. Feelgood'
(1967)

Dr J. The nickname of the flamboyant and articulate US basketball player Julius Winfield Erving II (b.1950). A star player with the Philadelphia 76s from 1976, he acquired his nickname when playing for the University of Massachusetts early in his career.

Dr Kildare. *See* KILDARE, DR.

Dr No. A thriller (1958) by Ian Fleming (1908–64), set largely on an island in the Caribbean, where he had a second home, and featuring the agent James BOND. Bond's adversary is known as Dr No. The book is notable because Fleming, having killed off Bond at the end of FROM RUSSIA, WITH LOVE (1957), by having him ingeniously hacked with a poisoned toe-cap, had to resurrect him, as Conan Doyle did with Sherlock Holmes. The film of *Dr No* (1962), produced by Harry Saltzman and Albert R. Broccoli, was the first of a long series and marked the first appearance as Bond of Sean Connery.

Doctor Robert. A song by the BEATLES alluding to a contemporary New York doctor who freely prescribed amphetamines and other drugs. Credited to John Lennon and Paul McCartney, the song appeared on the album REVOLVER, released in August 1966.

Doctors and nurses. A game played by very young children, involving make-believe treatment such as bandaging or massaging on the one hand or rudimentary sexual investigation on the other.

> For many, playing doctors and nurses and other dirty games is as much a part of childhood as swings and Play-Stations.
> *The Times* (30 August 1999)

Dr Seuss. *See* SEUSS, DR.

Dr Strangelove. A film (1963) based on the novel *Red Alert* by Peter George about the threat of global nuclear destruction. Titled in full *Dr Strangelove: or, How I Learned to Stop Worrying and Love the Bomb*, it was directed by Stanley Kubrick and starred Peter Sellers in three roles, notably that of the US president who finds himself helpless to stop events spiralling out of control. Such was the success of the film that subsequently any militarist leader or defender of nuclear weapons was liable to be dismissed as a 'Strangelove'.

Doctor Who. The Time Lord hero of the children's television SCIENCE FICTION series first shown in 1963. He travelled through time and space in a vehicle called the Tardis, disguised on the outside to resemble a London police telephone box, and was invariably accompanied by a winsome female assistant. The first actor to take the part was William Hartnell, who portrayed him as a testy elderly academic. One of the most memorable depictions was by Tom Baker, whose Doctor was a tousle-headed eccentric sporting a long scarf. The series was originally intended as a children's educational programme.

Doctor Zhivago. A historical film epic (1965), lasting over 190 minutes, based on a novel of the same title (1957) by the Russian writer Boris Pasternak (1890–1960). Set against the background of the Russian Revolution and the ensuing civil war, it was filmed with Omar Sharif as the poet and physician Zhivago, whose love for the beautiful Lara (Julie Christie) causes pain for all involved. Many critics accused the film, directed by David Lean, of being too pretentious for its own good and saw MGM's insistence that the word 'Dr' be spelled out in full in the title as symptomatic of this weakness. The book brought Pasternak himself little happiness. Following his award of the NOBEL PRIZE for Literature, he was pilloried by literary rivals, who accused him of plagiarizing other works, and his companion Olga Ivinskaya, on whom Lara was based, was thrown into prison by the Soviets. The first Russian publication of the novel did not take place until 1987. *See also* FIRST LINES OF NOVELS.

Dodgems. Bumper cars at a funfair. The name dates from the 1920s and originated in the United States as the proprietary term 'Dodg'em', so called because the aim is to avoid the other cars ('dodge 'em') while simultaneously trying to bump them.

Dodge the column, To. To shirk one's duty; to avoid work. The original reference was to the avoidance of military service in the First World War.

Dog and pony show. An elaborate display or presentation, as for a political party's new manifesto. The allusion is to a travelling variety show in which the performers are the named animals. The expression dates from the 1950s.

Dog Day Afternoon. A film (1975) written by Frank Pierson and directed by Sidney Lumet about a bisexual man (played by Al Pacino) who stages a bank robbery in order to fund a sex-change operation for his transsexual lover (played by Chris Sarandon). The plot was based on an article about a real incident. The 'dog days' have been identified since Roman times as the hottest days of the summer, between early July and mid-August, when the dog star Sirius is reputed to add its heat to that of the sun.

Dogger Bank. The battle of the Dogger Bank, during the First World War, was fought in the North Sea on 24 January 1915 when a raiding force of German battle cruisers was intercepted and shelled by a British squadron under the command of Admiral Beatty. The action convinced the Germans that they had been right to adopt a cautious strategy.

Doggy bag. A bag provided by some restaurants for customers to put uneaten food in, ostensibly to take home for their pet dog. The phrase and practice date from the 1960s.

Dogsbody. A person who does all the menial jobs that no one else wants to do, typically a young person or trainee employee. The term dates from the 1920s and presumably alludes to the simple tasks such as fetching and carrying that a dog can perform.

> I worked as a receptionist, general dogsbody and teamaker. ... I was 18 at the time and in charge of the phones, photocopiers, plants, fridge, dishwasher, couriers and fruit bowl.
> *The Times* (10 January 2000)

Dog's dinner or **breakfast.** A mess; a confused mixture. A dog's meal is often a mishmash of scraps. The expression dates from the 1930s. *See also* DRESSED UP LIKE A DOG'S DINNER.

Dogs of War, The. A thriller (1974) by Frederick Forsyth (b.1938). The theme is the attempt by a band of mercenaries to overthrow an African dictator. The title comes from Shakespeare: 'Cry *Havoc*, and let slip the dogs of war' (*Julius Caesar* III.i). A film version (1980), directed by John Irvin, lacked the tension of the original.

Do it, To. To engage in sexual intercourse; to urinate or defecate. *See also* 'IT' GIRL.

> Everybody's Doin' It Now.
> IRVING BERLIN: (song title) (1911)

Do-it-yourself. A post-1945 phrase applied primarily to the efforts of the amateur house repairer, home improver and the like, but also more widely applied to many forms of self-help. A do-it-yourself (DIY) shop is one that caters for the needs of people who like making and repairing things themselves rather than having someone else do it for them.

Dolby. The tradename of an electronic noise-reduction system used in tape recording to reduce hiss. It accomplishes this by compressing the sound range during recording and decoding the signal by expansion during playback at a level greater than the level of the hiss. It was developed in the 1970s by the US engineer Ray A. Dolby (b.1933) of the Ampex Corporation and found a ready application in the provision of stereophonic sound for cinemas and television sets.

Dolce Vita, La. A film (1960) co-written and directed by Federico Fellini (1920–93) about the meaninglessness of an Italian gossip writer's life among the rich, bored young of Rome. The title, meaning 'the soft life', is an ironical reference to the apparent ease and comfort of life among the jet-set. *See also* PAPARAZZI.

Dolittle, Dr. The genial and eccentric doctor who is the central character of the stories by Hugh Lofting (1886–1947). He has the special gift of speaking the language of most animals and eventually gives up his human practice to become an 'animal doctor'. He lives in Puddleby on the Marsh, but his adventures take him all over the world and even as far as the Moon. His companions include Polynesia the Parrot, Chee Chee the Monkey and Gub Gub the Pig. The first book in the series is *The Story of Doctor Dolittle* (1920) and the middle volumes of the series are generally regarded as the best. Lofting illustrated the stories himself.

Dollar diplomacy. A term applied to governmental support and furtherance of commercial interest abroad for both political and economic ends. The phrase, popular with critics of US policy, stems from the Taft administration (1909–13), which fostered such policies in the Far East and Latin America. Their intention was to control as well as to promote enterprise abroad by substituting dollars for bullets and lending 'all proper support to every legitimate and beneficial American enterprise abroad'.

Dolly. The world's first cloned sheep, born on 5 July 1996 at the Roslin Institute near Edinburgh. She was grown from an embryo created from an egg cell whose nucleus had been replaced by the nucleus of a cell from an adult Finn-Dorset ewe, and was named after the full-figured US country singer Dolly Parton (b.1946) because the cell was taken from the sheep's udder. The scientific breakthrough raised the real possibility of the cloning of human beings.

Dolly-bird. An attractive and stylish young woman, considered only with regard to her appearance. She was an essential ingredient of the SWINGING SIXTIES and was typically a secretary or shop assistant in her late teens or early 20s. The usage is thus now chiefly historical.

Dolly mixture. A mixture of small sweets of various shapes and colours, such as a doll might eat.

Domain. In computing, the sequence of words, abbreviations and the like that identifies a specific computer or network on the INTERNET and that serves as its address. A domain name appears in the form 'username@computer.domain' and common organizational domains are 'com' (commercial organization), 'edu' (educational organization), 'gov' (governmental organization), 'int' (international organization), 'net' (network organization) and 'org' (private organization). For countries other than the USA country domains may combine with organization domains, e.g. 'co.uk' (UK commercial organization), 'edu.ca' (Canadian educational organization). Domain names have been the object of fanciful and mostly illegal manipulation by CYBERSQUATTERS.

Do me or **us a favour!** You must be joking! Do you think I would do that? A phrase denying the implications of a situation, as: 'So will you be living abroad?' 'No way! Do us a favour!'

Dome Secretary. *See* MANDY.

Domino effect. An inescapable succession of related and usually undesirable events, each caused by the preceding one. The allusion is to the successive collapse of a row of upended dominoes, caused when the first falls onto the one behind it. The analogy was first voiced in the 1950s by President Eisenhower with reference to the theory that a political event or development in one country would lead to its occurrence in others. In the 1960s the concept was cited by US strategists as a justification for the VIETNAM War, the reasoning being that if one Southeast Asian country fell to communism, the rest would follow. This in turn could then lead to the subjugation of Australia and countries elsewhere in the world.

Don, The. The Australian batsman Sir Donald Bradman (b.1908), whose prodigious feats of run-making in the 1930s make him the greatest batsman who ever lived. Bradman was also known as the 'Little Master' on account of his diminutive size.

Donald Duck. The ill-tempered cartoon duck in a sailor suit, second in fame only to MICKEY MOUSE, was created by the Walt Disney studios in 1934, his first appearance being in the *Silly Symphony* cartoon *The Wise Little Hen*. His popularity was due in no small measure to his distinctive quacking voice, the creation of Clarence Nash.

Don Camillo. *See* CAMILLO, DON.

Done and dusted. Ready and prepared. A mainly domestic metaphor, as: 'So, all set for the big day?' 'Yes, all done and dusted!' The literal sense could relate either to a clearing and cleaning procedure or to a culinary one, where a cake, for example, has been dusted with icing sugar. The former is the more likely, but the duality is possible due to the contrary meanings of 'to dust': on the one hand to remove dust, on the other to add it.

Donkey jacket. A thick jacket, often blue in colour, worn by manual workers as a protection against the weather. The name alludes to the donkey as a working animal. The jacket was first adopted in the 1920s and was later turned into a general fashion garment.

Donmar Warehouse. The London theatre of this name, famous for its experimental productions, opened in 1960 in a warehouse for ripening bananas and was at first known simply as the Warehouse. 'Donmar' was then added from the names of its original purchasers, Donald Albery (1914–88) and his friend Margot Fonteyn (1919–91), the ballet dancer. Albery was the son of Bronson Albery (1881–1971), who gave his name to the Albery Theatre, and step-grandson of Charles Wyndham (1837–1919), after whom Wyndham's Theatre is named.

Don't ask. Do not question me about it. The question may be merely potential rather than actual, and the unspoken answer left to the imagination, as: 'We found it was a nudist beach. Don't ask.'

Don't ask, don't tell. A pithy summary of the US military policy on homosexuality adopted in 1994, whereby personnel were not asked about their sexual orientation and gays and lesbians were allowed to serve providing they did not openly reveal their sexuality. The usage spread subsequently to other areas.

Don't ask me. A statement disclaiming knowledge or responsibility, as: 'I wonder how that happened?' 'Don't ask me. I wasn't there.'

Don't call us, we'll call you. A traditional expression of dismissal, arising from the formula of rejection used by producers or directors when auditioning actors. They naturally never do call.

Don't give me that. That's no excuse. You can't fool me. A phrase from the 1920s.

Don't give up the day job. Don't take up another

career at which you might not succeed. The 'day job' is one's regular NINE-TO-FIVE JOB. The catchphrase is often humorously directed at someone who thinks they can make their fortune by pursuing a hobby or alternative interest.

> If [pop musician and writer Stuart] David ever gives up the day job, pop music's loss could well be literature's gain.
> *The Times* (13 November 1999)

Don't hold your breath. Don't expect the thing in question to happen immediately. The implication is that it may not happen at all. The phrase is of US origin and dates from the 1970s.

Don't make me laugh. Don't be stupid. A stock ironic phrase from the 1920s.

Don't strain yourself. A stock ironic caution addressed to someone who is conspicuously failing to pull their weight.

Doodlebug. A nickname in the Second World War for the V-1 flying bomb. The word itself goes back to the 19th century and combines *doodle*, 'ninny', with *bug*.

Doolally. An army expression of the early 20th century for an unbalanced state of mind or mental derangement. British time-expired soldiers in India were formerly sent to a camp at Deolali, near Bombay, to await passage home. There were often long, frustrating delays, when boredom and the climate may have led to some odd behaviour, which caused some of them to become 'doolally'. The full phrase was 'doolally tap', the latter word being Urdu *dap*, 'fever'.

Doolittle, Eliza. The Cockney heroine of G.B. Shaw's play PYGMALION (1914). She is a simple FLOWER GIRL until she is taken in hand by Professor Henry Higgins, who gives her an intensive course in elocution and introduces her to high society. The story was adapted as the successful Lerner and Loewe stage musical MY FAIR LADY (1945), and this was in turn made into a film of the same name (1964) with Audrey Hepburn in the leading role.

> *Higgins*: Eliza: you are to live here for the next six months, learning how to speak beautifully, like a lady in a florist's shop. If youre good and do whatever youre told, you shall sleep in a proper bedroom, and have lots to eat, and money to buy chocolates and take rides in taxis. If youre naughty and idle you will sleep in the back kitchen among the black beetles, and be walloped by Mrs Pearce with a broomstick.
> GEORGE BERNARD SHAW: *Pygmalion*, II (1914)

Doom and gloom or **gloom and doom.** Despondency and despair; a state of depression regarding the future. The expression and its variant are of US origin and arose in or soon after the Second World War. Both were given prominence by their occurrence in E.Y. 'Yip' Harburg's popular stage musical FINIAN'S RAINBOW (1947).

Doomsday Machine. A hypothetical machine designed to trigger automatic nuclear destruction under certain conditions without the possibility of human intervention to stop it. The term dates from the 1960s, and the concept of such a machine was first formulated by Herman Kahn in *On Thermonuclear War* (1960).

Do one's best, To. To do all one can. The call of a WOLF CUB leader to the assembled pack was 'Dyb, dyb, dyb, dyb!' standing for 'Do your best'. The chanted reply was 'We'll dob, dob, dob, dob!' ('Do our best').

Do one's bit, To. To make a useful contribution to an effort or cause. The expression first came to the fore in the First World War when it specifically related to serving in the armed forces. G.B. Shaw used the phrase in this sense in the title of his play *Augustus Does His Bit* (1919), as at a different level did Richmal Crompton in *William Does His Bit* (1940) (*see* WILLIAM). It then broadened to apply to any public-spirited action. In 1999 the government embarked on a publicity campaign called 'Are You Doing Your Bit' to encourage simple methods of environmental management.

Doonesbury. The NERD college graduate hero of a satirical comic strip by the US artist Garry Trudeau. He first appeared in the *Yale Daily News* in 1968 but two years later went national. His full name is Mike Doonesbury, his surname being a combination of 'Doone', Yale slang for an amiable fool, and 'Pillsbury', Trudeau's New Haven room-mate. Other characters include the star American football player B.D. (named after the real Yale quarterback Brian Dowling) and the would-be radical Megaphone Mark. It was the first comic strip to win a PULITZER PRIZE (1975).

> 'Say, B.D., as your new *roommate*, I'm most naturally very curious to learn what your interests are.' 'I play football.' '*Oh, wow! Really*? Football! Just think of that! *Wow! Boy*, what a pair we're going to make! A football player and a *lover boy*! I could get you girls, and you

could get me football tickets. It certainly has *amazing advantages.'*

GARRY TRUDEAU: *Doonesbury* (extract) (26–28 October 1970)

Do one's head or **nut in, To.** To harass; to aggravate; to bemuse or confuse. The sense is that one's mental processes become disturbed or deranged. The expression dates from the 1970s and is of US student origin. *See also* DO ONE'S NUT.

The pop star Shaun Ryder was so high on drugs that he could not be bothered with a contract's small print. 'It did his nut in,' the Court of Appeal was told.

The Times (16 December 1999)

Do one's homework, To. To make adequate preparation for the task facing one, especially to acquaint oneself thoroughly with the relevant material for a discussion, debate or speech, as a school pupil is expected to do work at home for the following day or later in the week. The expression dates from the 1930s.

Do one's nut, To. To lose one's temper; to fly into a rage; to become worked up. The 'nut' is the head. The expression dates from the early 20th century.

Do one's nut in, To. *See* DO ONE'S HEAD IN.

Dora. The popular name of the Defence of the Realm Acts (DORA), which imposed many temporary restrictions. The first of the series was passed in 1914 and the legislation was extended to the supply and sale of liquor in 1921. The name passed into common speech after being used in the Law courts by Mr Justice Scrutton (1856–1934). In newspaper cartoons Dora was often portrayed as a long-nosed elderly female, the personification of restriction.

Dorothy bag. A woman's handbag gathered at the top by a drawstring and slung by loops from the wrist. Such bags came into vogue in the early years of the 20th century. The identity of the Dorothy in question, if she ever existed, is unknown.

Do's and don'ts. Recommendations what to do and what not to do. The phrase dates from the early 20th century. A more recent equivalent is 'do's and taboos', especially with reference to international etiquette, business procedures and the like.

Do someone in, To. To injure or kill them.

Dot and the Kangaroo. An Australian fantasy novel, much influenced by Lewis Carroll, by Ethel C. Pedley (*c*.1860–98). Although it was published in Britain in 1899, it was not published in Australia until 1906. It tells the tale of a little girl, Dot, who is befriended by the Kangaroo when she becomes lost in the outback. With the Kangaroo's assistance she eventually reaches home, a double satisfaction since the Kangaroo discovers that her lost baby is being kept by Dot's parents after a kangaroo hunt. The novel is critical of the brutality of humans towards animals and features a 'trial' of Dot by assorted animals for crimes committed against them by white settlers.

Dot-com. A colloquialism for a company with a site on the INTERNET, alluding to its DOMAIN name, which will include 'com' (for 'commercial') preceded by a dot, such as the booksellers Amazon.com.

Unlike established advertisers such as household goods and car manufacturers, the dot-coms care more about being on air [on television] by a certain date than the cost.

The Times (10 December 1999)

Do tell. Is that so? Really? A phrase of opposite meanings: on the one hand, as an ironic response to a piece of information in which one has no interest; on the other, as an exhortation to the speaker to impart a piece of juicy gossip. Both date from the 1950s.

Do the decent thing, To. To behave honourably or appropriately, especially when the action is not in one's own interest.

If the Prime Minister is not ashamed of his broken promise, he ought to be. If he is ashamed, he should do the decent thing and withdraw the legislative Sword of Damocles that overhangs some of the finest schools in this country.

The Times (Letter to the Editor) (13 October 1999)

Do the dirty on someone, To. To cheat or betray them. The implication is that one plays a dirty trick on them. The expression dates from the First World War.

Directors can destroy new plays very easily. ... So says Simon Stokes, artistic director of the Theatre Royal, Plymouth – although we can assume he has never done the dirty on [writer] Snoo Wilson.

The Times (13 October 1999)

Do the math, To. To estimate people's ages and surmise their salaries at a social gathering, especially with a view to finding a sexual partner. The expression, but hardly the practice, is of US origin, as obvious from American 'math' for British 'maths'.

Double helix. The structure of the DNA molecule, which consists of two linked spirals. The molecular structure of DNA, the 'blueprint of life', was established by Francis Crick (b.1916) and James Watson (b.1928) in 1953 while working at Cambridge

University. As Watson said: 'A structure this pretty just had to exist.' Their exposition demonstrated how the molecule could carry the genetic code unique to every individual organism. The discovery marked the foundation of modern genetics. The two men shared the NOBEL prize for their work in 1962, along with Maurice Wilkins (b.1916), who developed the method of X-ray diffraction that helped in their discovery. A fourth scientist, Rosalind Franklin (1920–58), is thought by many to have played an equally important role, but she died of cancer before the Nobel prize was awarded. In 1968 Watson published a popular account of the discovery under the title *The Double Helix*.

Double Indemnity. A classic FILM NOIR (1944) adapted by Raymond Chandler and Billy Wilder (who also directed) from a novel of the same title by James M. Cain (1892–1977). It starred Fred MacMurray as the insurance salesman who becomes the lover of the scheming Barbara Stanwyck. She persuades him to help her murder her husband for the insurance money she will receive but does not allow for the interference of insurance investigator Edward G. Robinson. The title refers to the clause in the insurance policy that promises payment of a double benefit in the case of accidental death. The plot was based on an actual murder case, the notorious Snyder Gray affair of 1927.

Double take. An actor's trick in which one looks away from the person who has addressed a remark to one and then looks back at them quickly when the purport of the remark sinks in. The term is also used for a second look prompted by surprise or admiration. The phrase dates from the 1930s.

> A tall, rangy drunk with gravestone teeth and 1973 hair lolls past and does a double, no, triple take ... 'The only time I don't have my bloody camera! Can I have your autograph?'
>
> *The Times Magazine* (27 November 1999)

Doublethink. A term used by George ORWELL in his *Nineteen Eighty-Four* (1949) (*see* 1984) to describe what unscrupulous propagandists achieved by NEWSPEAK. It denoted the mental ability to hold simultaneously two entirely conflicting views or beliefs, a state achieved by political indoctrination.

> His mind slid away into the labyrinthine world of doublethink. To know and not to know, to be conscious of complete truthfulness while telling carefully constructed lies, to hold simultaneously two opinions which cancelled out, knowing them to be contradictory and believing in both of them, to use logic

against logic, to repudiate morality while laying claim to it, to believe that democracy was impossible and that the Party was the guardian of democracy.

> GEORGE ORWELL: *Nineteen Eighty-Four*, Pt I, ch iii (1949)

Double whammy. A twofold blow ('wham') or setback. The phrase came into vogue in the political field in the general election campaign of 1992, when the Scottish Secretary, Ian Lang, would have lost both his seat and his job if he had not been re-elected. Lang himself told his supporters: 'Scotland has rejected separatism. Britain has rejected Socialism. It's a double whammy!' The term itself dates earlier than this, however, and is familiar from Al Capp's strip L'IL ABNER in which the character Evil-Eye Fleegle explains it:

> *Evil-Eye Fleegle* is th' name, an' th' *'whammy'* is my game. Mudder Nature endowed me wit' eyes which can putrefy citizens t' th' spot! ... There is th' *'single whammy'! That*, friend, is th' full, *pure power* o' one o' my evil eyes! It's *dynamite*, friend, an' I do not t'row it around lightly! ... And, lastly – th' *'double whammy'* – namely, th' *full power* o' *both eyes* – which I hopes I never *hafta* use.
>
> *Al Capp's Li'l Abner* (July 1951)

Doughnutting. The practice whereby MPs in the House of Commons sit close to an MP making a speech while the proceedings are being televised. The aim is to give the viewer the impression that the speaker is well supported or that the House is well attended, although the clustering MPs may simply wish to be seen on television themselves. The term is said to have been originally used of televised debates in the Canadian parliament. It became current in Britain after 1989 when parliamentary proceedings were first televised. The allusion is presumably to the circular shape of a ring doughnut, the speaker being at its centre.

Do us a favour. *See* DO ME A FAVOUR.

Dover Patrol. A naval patrol based in Dover that was formed in the First World War to maintain communications across the English Channel, comprising a varied collection of warships and fishing vessels. Both *Dover Patrol* and *L'Attaque* later became the names of popular board games.

Dowager's hump. A term for a forward curvature of the spine caused by osteoporosis. It is more common in older women than in men (hence its name) and can be avoided or retarded if the person concerned receives enough calcium in their adult diet.

Down and Out in Paris and London. The autobiographical study (1933) by George ORWELL was the author's first published book. It is an account of working with the poor in London's East End, and doing menial jobs in a working-class district of Paris, while trying to get his writing published.

Down below. *See* DOWN THERE.

Downing Street declaration. An agreement between the British and Irish governments, formulated in 1993 and intended as the basis of a peace initiative in Northern Ireland. The declaration, issued from the Prime Minister's residence at 10 Downing Street, was a further step along the road initiated by the Anglo-Irish Agreement of 1985. *See also* GOOD FRIDAY AGREEMENT.

Down memory lane. A nostalgic reminiscence or sentimental journey into the past. Some local newspapers run a regular feature under this heading. *Down Memory Lane* (1949) was the title of a compilation of Mack Sennett comedy shorts, while earlier 'Memory Lane' (1924) was a popular waltz by Buddy De Sylva, Larry Spier and Con Conrad.

> Since I was a child, my fantasies have been fueled by the images of beautiful women in newspapers, magazines and on the movie screen. But this book is more than that. It is a trip down memory lane.
> HUGH HEFNER in GRETCHEN EDGREN: *The Playmate Book,* Introduction (1996)

Downshifter. A person who changes a financially rewarding but stressful career or lifestyle for one that is less pressurized and less well paid but more fulfilling. The trend for downshifting arose in the United States during the early 1990s, when those in stressful occupations such as the computer industry started to re-evaluate their priorities. The general conclusion was that quality equated with simplicity, so that people began moving to smaller houses and halving their workloads.

> So has she downshifted? 'Yes, I was in a job people envied,' she says, 'and I earned more money in London but I've built a better life for myself here. There's the countryside ... plus it's only a mile away from work and my job is full of potential.'
> *The Times* (26 January 2000)

Down the hatch! A drinking toast of nautical origin, dating from the 1930s. The hatch is the throat.

Down there or **down below.** A maidenish euphemism for the genital and excretory region. *See also* NETHER REGIONS.

> A programme devoted to problems 'down there' was too shy for anything but innuendo.
> *Radio Times* (Letter to the Editor) (12–18 September 1998)

Down to the wire. Said of a situation in which the outcome is not known until the last minute. The allusion is to the imaginary line marking the end of a horse race, where the winners notionally pass 'under the wire'. The phrase is also heard in the variant 'up to the wire'.

> Cannes went right down to the wire last night in one of the most surprising and dramatic finishes in the [film] festival's history.
> *The Times* (24 May 1999)

Down Your Way. A BBC radio programme first broadcast in 1946 in which the presenter visited a different town or village in Britain each week and talked to colourful local figures about their community and history. In return they were rewarded with the playing of their favourite piece of music. For many *Down Your Way* became regular Sunday teatime listening. There were only four presenters during the programme's long run: Stewart MacPherson (1946–50), Richard Dimbleby (1950–5), Franklin Engelmann (1955–72) and Brian Johnston (1972–87).

DP. *See* DISPLACED PERSON.

Drag. Female dress worn by men; transvestite clothes. The allusion is to a long dress, which drags along the ground. The term originated as theatrical slang in the early 20th century.

> You would never have the fag
> Of dressing up in drag,
> You'd be a woman at the weekend.
> JOHN OSBORNE: *The World of Paul Slickey,* II, x (1959)

Dragged kicking and screaming. Obliged to do something against one's will. The image is of a stubborn child forced to perform some necessary task. A regular full form of the phrase has long been 'to drag kicking and screaming into the twentieth century'. The precise source of this is uncertain.

> Labour had to be dragged kicking and screaming to accept the privatization of public transport.
> *The Times* (19 July 1999)

Dragon boat. A long and slender rowing boat with a dragon's head at its bows, used for racing with a mixed crew of 18. The sport of dragon-boat racing became popular worldwide in the 1990s, especially in Canada, and was adopted from the much older annual contests held in China and Hong Kong on the fifth day of the fifth lunar month as an occasion for driving off evil spirits. Britain first hosted the world championships in 1999.

Dragon lady. A domineering or fearsome woman. The image is oriental, and the phrase had its origin in the name of the mysterious Asian chieftainess in Milton Caniff's popular cartoon strip *Terry and the Pirates* (1934–73), featuring Terry LEE. The name was also used as a nickname for the American U–2 strategic reconnaissance aircraft.

Drain, The. A nickname for the Waterloo and City Line on the London Underground, opened in 1898. The designation, at first derogatory but now almost affectionate, dates from the 1920s and refers to the deep and dingy route. It was the only Underground line run by British Rail.

Drainpipes. Narrow-legged, tight-fitting trousers, an essential part of the garb of TEDDY BOYS in the 1950s.

> There are still sufficient ancient aficionados [of SKIFFLE] to get out their drainpipes and winklepickers to fill the Albert Hall for the occasional tribute concert.
> *The Times* (11 January 2000)

Drake brass plate. *See under* FAKES.

Drake's Drum. A drum that once belonged to the Elizabethan sea dog and English national hero Sir Francis Drake (1540–96), who played a key role in the defeat of the Spanish Armada in 1588. As he died Drake apparently ordered that the drum be taken back to his home at Buckland Abbey near Plymouth. As Sir Henry Newbolt (1862–1938) put it in 'Drake's Drum' (1897):

> Take my drum to England, hang et by the shore,
> Strike et when your powder's runnin' low;
> If the Dons [Spaniards] sight Devon, I'll quit the port o' Heaven,
> An' drum them up the Channel as we drummed them long ago.

The drum is said to have sounded on three momentous occasions in the 20th century. It was reportedly heard on the outbreak of the First World War in 1914, and again at the end of the war in 1918, when it apparently sounded aboard the *Royal Oak*, flagship of the British Grand Fleet anchored at SCAPA FLOW in the Orkneys while the German fleet arrived to surrender. Finally, a drum roll was heard during the desperate British evacuation from DUNKIRK in 1940.

Draw a line in the sand, To. To define a limit or boundary; to state a level of tolerance beyond which one will

not go. The expression is perhaps an elaboration of 'to draw the line' and was first current in the United States in the 1970s. It was seized on gratefully by politicians and diplomats, one of whom was probably responsible for the added imagery in the first place.

Dreaded lurgy. An illness or indisposition of uncertain or unstated nature. The phrase became popular in the 1950s following its use by the GOONS in *The Goon Show*. The origin of 'lurgy' is unknown, although it suggests a thing that lurks on the one hand or an ALLERGY on the other. A spelling 'lergy' also exists to support the latter association.

> The Goon Show. ... Poor Arnold Fringe is suddenly stricken with the Dreaded Lurgi.
> *Radio Times* (4 November 1954)

Dreadlocks. The hairstyle favoured by RASTAFARIANS, in which the hair is washed but not combed and then twisted while wet into braids or ringlets that hang down on all sides. Rastafarians outlawed the combing or cutting of hair in obedience to the biblical injunction: 'They shall not make baldness upon their head, neither shall they shave off the corner of their beard' (Leviticus 21:5), and they coined the term 'dreadlocks' to mock the aversion of non-believers to the look.

Dreadnought. A battleship launched on 18 February 1906 as the prototype of a class of Royal Navy battleships so named. They were larger and faster than their predecessors and equipped entirely with large-calibre guns. In 1960 the name passed to the first British nuclear-powered submarine.

Dreamboat. A very attractive person, especially a man from the point of view of a woman, as the 'vessel of one's dreams'. The expression, redolent of HOLLYWOOD, dates from the 1940s. Alma Cogan's 'Dreamboat' was a hit song of 1955.

Dream come true. A journalistic cliché for any stroke of luck or success experienced by a member of the public. It is equally resorted to by such people when interviewed by the media.

> But the Sheikh's first words after [winning] the race [the Derby] were not for himself. He said: 'This is a dream come true, but my thoughts are now of Alex.'
> *Independent on Sunday* (11 June 1995)

Dream machine. A nickname for the television industry. The term derives from *The Great American Dream Machine* (1971), a US television programme of topical satire. *See also* AMERICAN DREAM.

Dream of Gerontius, The. This heavy-going choral piece (the composer rejected the label 'oratorio') by Edward Elgar (1857–1934) uses a text taken from a long mystical poem by Cardinal Newman (1801–90). The work was first performed in 1900 at the Birmingham Festival. Newman's poem, published in 1866, concerns the agonizing death of Gerontius and his experiences in the afterlife. A copy of the poem was found near the body of Gordon of Khartoum, covered in Gordon's jottings, and it was a copy of this annotated text that inspired Elgar. Newman's poem includes such tin-eared lines as:

They sing of thy approaching agony,
Which thou so eagerly didst question of

which Elgar nevertheless managed to set to music. George Moore described Elgar's piece as 'Holy water in a German beer barrel', while Charles Villiers Stanford complained that it was 'stinking of incense'. Frederick Delius opined that '*Gerontius* is a nauseating work', although Pope Pius XIII believed it to be 'a sublime masterpiece'.

Dresden. A city in eastern Germany that was destroyed by bombing during the Second World War. It was formerly one of the world's most beautiful cities, referred to as 'the Florence on the Elbe', but on the night of 13–14 February 1945 a massive raid by 800 RAF bombers created a firestorm in the city that killed between 30,000 and 60,000 civilians (some estimates go as high as 135,000). During daylight on 14 February 400 USAAF bombers took over from the RAF, followed by 200 the next day, 400 on 2 March and 572 on 17 April. The raid has been the subject of controversy ever since. It was part of an Allied strategy, requested by the Soviet Union, to block the movement of German troops by bombing major cities such as Berlin, Chemnitz, Leipzig and Dresden. However, critics point out that the destruction of Dresden achieved little militarily and that the actual intention was to terrorize the German population into submission, so that they would not resist following the imminent Allied military victory. It has also been suggested that the Western Allies used the raid as a demonstration to the Soviet Union of the strength of their air power. In 1999 the citizens of Dresden objected strongly when a statue of Arthur BOMBER HARRIS, wartime head of RAF Bomber Command, was raised in London.

Dresden china. A term used of anyone or anything delicately pretty or attractive, the comparison being with the fine porcelain so called, made originally at Dresden or at nearby Meissen. The figurative sense dates from the turn of the 20th century and is mostly used of women.

Dress down, To. To dress informally. Dressing down at work or in the office on Fridays arose as a US innovation, the idea being that the wearing of casual clothes would improve staff morale and increase productivity. Psychologists deny any connection, however, and for many employees, especially the more mature, obligatory dressing down can be an imposition. The practice is sometimes coupled with a fund-raising effort for charity, and school students may also have the occasional 'non-uniform day' set aside for this purpose. UNICEF capitalized on the trend by setting aside the first Friday in February as 'Non-Uniform Day' with the aim of encouraging schools to raise funds for needy children worldwide.

Dressed up like a dog's dinner. Dressed in smart but ostentatious clothes. The allusion is to a (literal) DOG'S DINNER that outwardly looks appetizing but that is really a mishmash of scraps. The expression dates from the 1930s.

Dreyfusard. An advocate of the innocence of Capt. Alfred Dreyfus (1859–1935), a French artillery officer of Jewish descent who was convicted in 1894 on a charge of betraying military secrets to Germany and sent to DEVIL'S ISLAND. In 1898 Clemenceau and Zola took up his case and Zola wrote his famous open letter *J'accuse*. In 1899 he was retried, again condemned, but shortly afterwards pardoned. In 1906 the proceedings were finally quashed.

Drimonia. The fictional European country that is the setting of Lia Wainstein's Italian novel *Viaggio in Drimonia* (1965). To understand its language, the traveller need command only two words: *trunca*, meaning 'yes', although literally translated as 'If-thus-be-the-will-of-the-great-and-all-powerful-Oskutchawa-thus-be-my-will-as-well', and *narta*, meaning 'no', although with a literal sense 'As-I-cannot-know-whether-it-will-rain-today-or-tomorrow-I-cannot-pledge-my-answer'.

Drink-driving. The criminal offence of driving a vehicle with an excess of alcohol in the blood. In 1998 in Britain the legal blood alcohol limit for drivers was 80 milligrams per 100 millilitres. The expression itself dates from the 1960s.

Drive a coach and horses through something, To. To nullify its effectiveness. The earlier form of the phrase, which dates from the 17th century, was invariably 'to drive a coach and six (or four) through', and in 1672 Sir Stephen Rice, a Roman Catholic Chief Baron of the Exchequer, is quoted as saying: 'I will drive a coach and six horses through the Act of Settlement.' The present form of the expression arose in the 20th century and still frequently has a political or legalistic reference.

> 'The school's code of conduct is to respect the right of others to learn. This is a child who drives a coach and horses through that code.'
> *The Times* (7 December 1999)

Drive by the seat of one's pants, To. *See* FLY BY THE SEAT OF ONE'S PANTS.

Drive or **send someone up the wall, To.** To frustrate or infuriate them. The suggestion is that they are driven insane and attempt to climb the wall in order to escape.

Droopy drawers. A nickname for a sloppy, depressing or dull person. 'Drawers' are knickers or underpants.

Drop a bombshell, To. To deliver unpleasant or disappointing news, especially when the opposite was expected. The expression dates from the First World War, when bombs were dropped by hand from aeroplanes.

> Jean loved dropping bombshells. Sometimes he thought she kept him for the sake of dropping them and watching him jump. ...
> 'Harrix went bust,' she told him.
> FAY WELDON: *The Heart of the Country* (1987)

Drop a brick, To. To make an indiscreet or embarrassing remark. The expression is said to relate to a group of builders in Cambridge who dropped their bricks in surprise on seeing an extraordinarily inept column of student volunteers on the march one day in 1905. The actor and playwright Robert Morley edited an entertaining collection of verbal gaffes in *Robert Morley's Book of Bricks* (1978).

Drop a clanger, To. To commit a social gaffe or an embarrassing blunder which draws ringing attention to itself. Enjoyable examples of 'clangers' are those depicted by the cartoonist H.M. Bateman (1887–1970) in his drawings with titles beginning 'The Man Who ... ', such as 'The Man Who Lit His Cigar Before the Loyal Toast' or 'The Man Who Threw a Snowball at St Moritz'.

Drop a dime on someone, To. To inform on them or betray them. The expression is of US origin and dates from the 1960s, when a public telephone call cost 10 cents (a dime). Such a call could be made by an informer to the police.

Drop dead! An expression of irritation or contempt, and short for 'Why don't you drop dead!'

Drop-dead. Strikingly beautiful; excellent. The term dates from the 1970s and is frequently encountered with the adjective 'gorgeous'. The stunning effect is enough to make one drop dead.

> [Popular singer Shania] Twain is a bit of a conundrum. In the flesh, she is petite and slim ... and pretty rather than the drop-dead stunner of her photos and videos.
> *The Times Magazine* (11 September 1999)

Drop one's trousers, To. To lower one's trousers, especially in a public place for purposes of urination or defecation.

Dropout. A student who fails to complete a college or university course, or more generally a person who has 'opted out' of conventional society.

> An international gathering of misfits and drop-outs, smoking pot and meditating in the Buddhist temples.
> *New Statesman* (15 December 1967)

Drop someone in it, To. To do or say something, often deliberately, that places another in difficulties. 'It' is tacitly understood as 'the shit'.

Drop the dead donkey, To. To abandon a project. The phrase was popularized or even originally introduced by the television satirical SITCOM *Drop the Dead Donkey* (1990–94), set in a newsroom, where the reference was to a last-minute decision to drop a news story.

Drug Czar. The popular title of the Anti-Drugs Coordinator, appointed by the Labour government in 1997 to coordinate the fight against drug abuse in Britain. The first to hold the post was Keith Hellawell. The term itself is of US origin, as the spelling implies (rather than British 'tsar'). The designation was subsequently extended to officials with similar responsibilities in other areas.

> The Government will appoint a cancer 'czar' today to take charge of efforts to bring about big improvements in the way Britain treats people who have the disease.
> *The Times* (25 October 1999)

Drug nicknames. Drug users and dealers have evolved a jargon of their own, and most drugs, whether legal or not, have their individual nicknames. They include the following:

Amphetamine: bennies, dexies, goof balls, ice, speed

Cannabis (marijuana): baby, black, boo, bush, doobie, draw, ganja, grass, green, hash, hemp, Mary Jane, pot, reefer, shit, tea, weed

Cocaine: bennies, C, Charlie, coke, crack, dust, flake, freebase, leaf, nose, rock, snow

HEROIN: beast, black tar, H, horse, poison, scag, scat, schmeck, smack, stuff, sugar

LSD: A, acid, chief, purple

MDMA: Adam, E, ECSTASY, XTC

Phencyclidine: angel dust, corn flakes, goon, hog, loopy dust, rocket fuel

Drum majorette. A girl or young woman who marches at the head of a procession, twirling and tossing a baton. Her uniform and prominent position to some extent mirror those of a drum major, who commands the corps of drums of a military band. She first made her appearance in America in the 1930s.

Drummond, Bulldog. *See* BULLDOG DRUMMOND.

Dry out, To. To undergo treatment for alcoholism or drug abuse; to go into 'rehab'.

Dry run. A rehearsal of a performance or procedure before the actual one. It is 'dry' because it is unproductive, just as a dry cow yields no milk. The term is of US military origin and was first used in the Second World War for simulated bombings in which no bombs were dropped.

Dry White Season, A. A novel (1979) by the South African writer André Brink (b.1935), originally written and published in Afrikaans as *'n Droë wit seisoen*, and translated by himself. It is one of six novels he wrote between 1958 and 1967, using modern narrative techniques, as a counterblast to those Afrikaans novels that he described as a 'literature of drought and poor whites'. The message of this one, in which a white teacher, believing himself to be apolitical, embarks on a quest for justice after the death in custody of a black colleague, is that in the prevailing situation in South Africa it was impossible for anyone to remain politically uncommitted. A passionate film version (1989) was directed by Euzhan Palcy.

DSK. The abbreviation of 'Dvorak simplified keyboard'. In 1932 Dr August Dvorak, professor of education and director of research at the University of Washington, Seattle, devised a simplified typewriter keyboard which, he claimed, would accelerate the speed of typing on the traditional QWERTY arrange-

ment by some 35 per cent. He based it on the frequency of letters in the English language, which is generally agreed to be as follows: E T A O N R I S H D L F C M U G Y P W B V K X J Q Z. The vowels A E I O U make up 39 per cent of all letters used and the five most common consonants are H N R S T. Dr Dvorak's layout was thus PYFGCRL in the top row, AOEUIDHTNS in the middle row, and QJKXBMWVZ in the bottom row. Despite the obvious advantages, however, the simplified keyboard never caught on and modern computer keyboards still adhere to the awkward and illogical QWERTY display.

DTV. *See* DIGITAL TELEVISION.

Duce (Italian, 'leader'). The title adopted by Benito Mussolini (1883–1945), the Fascist dictator of Italy from 1922 to 1943. *See also* CAUDILLO; FASCISM.

Duchess of Pork. *See* FERGIE.

Duck and dive, To. To use one's ingenuity to escape from an undesirable or difficult situation. The metaphor may come from a boxer's agile attempts to avoid his opponent's blows, although the expression has also been explained as rhyming slang on 'skive'.

> He [MP Neil Hamilton] was on the wrong side of the wavering line of decency. ... Worst of all, he became involved with the emir of duckers and divers [Harrods owner Mohamed al Fayed].
> *Sunday Times* (26 December 1999)

Duck or grouse. A standing pleasantry for a notice on a low lintel warning people not to bump their head on passing beneath. A variant at one time in an Oxford bookshop was 'Mind Your Egghead'.

Ducks. American army-sponsored amphibious vehicles active in the Second World War. Their name arose as a fortuitous adaptation of the official designation DUKW, representing the factory code letters D for boat, U for lorry body and KW for lorry chassis. The vehicle moved on rubber tyres ashore and was propeller-driven when afloat.

Duck's arse or **DA.** A men's hairstyle in which the hair is swept back to a point at the nape of the neck, so that it looks like a duck's tail. The style was popular among TEDDY BOYS in the 1950s.

Duck soup. An easy task; a 'doddle' or 'cinch'. The allusion may be to a 'sitting duck' as an easy target. The expression is American in origin and was popularized by the MARX BROTHERS' film *Duck Soup* (1933).

Duckworth–Lewis method. An intricate method of

revising targets in one-day cricket matches when rain stops play, devised in the 1990s by Frank Duckworth, a statistician, and Tony Lewis, a mathematics lecturer. The system is based on the principle that the teams must know two figures in order to make as many runs as they can, namely the number of overs they have still to receive and the number of wickets they have in hand. The new targets are reached using a table and a calculator.

The system has baffled the media and the public as well as official scorers but was adopted as the 'rain rule' for the 1999 World Cup hosted by the England and Wales Cricket Board.

> New Zealand would almost certainly have won under the Duckworth–Lewis method, but then the rain came down even harder and they called the match off.
>
> *The Times* (8 June 1999)

Duff someone up, To. To beat them up. The verb is probably Scottish dialect *duff*, 'to hit'.

Dulce et Decorum Est. A poem (1918) by the WAR POET Wilfred Owen (1893–1918) in which he describes the horrors of a gas attack in the trenches of the First World War. The poem was informed by Owen's personal experiences of the trenches and made doubly poignant by his own death in the last week of the war, when he was himself killed in action on the Sambre Canal. The title, with which the poem also ends, is a quotation from Horace's *Odes*, usually translated as: 'It is sweet and becoming to die for one's country.'

> If you could hear, at every jolt, the blood
> Come gargling from the froth-corrupted lungs,
> Obscene as cancer,
> Bitter as the cud
> Of vile, incurable sores on innocent tongues, –
> My friend, you would not tell with such high zest
> To children ardent for some desperate glory,
> The old Lie: Dulce et decorum est
> Pro patria mori.
>
> WILFRED OWEN: 'Dulce et Decorum Est' (1918)

Dullsville. A dull state or condition, as if caused by living in a town so named. The term dates from the 1960s.

Dumbarton Oaks. The 'little concerto in the style of the Brandenburg Concertos' by Igor Stravinsky (1882–1971) was commissioned in 1938 by Mr and Mrs R.W. Bliss, who lived in the mansion of Dumbarton Oaks

in Georgetown, near Washington, D.C. Between 21 August and 7 October 1944 the same mansion played host to a conference of Allied powers (China, the Soviet Union, the United States and the United Kingdom) that laid the foundations of what was to become the UNITED NATIONS.

Dumb blonde. This now rather dated expression for a conspicuously attractive but stupid young blonde woman, the BIMBO of today, seems a contradiction in terms, since such a female is not normally noted for her silence. The term was used to typecast the film actress Marilyn MONROE (1926–62) but was in fact an unfair stereotype that troubled her throughout her career. The first word of the US phrase has probably been influenced by German *dumm*, 'stupid'.

> Aged just seventeen and the daughter of a Blackpool landlady, she [television personality Sabrina] was the original dumb blonde. Indeed, part of her gimmick was that she never said a word on screen.
>
> HILARY KINGSLEY and GEOFF TIBBALLS: *Box of Delights* (1989)

Dumb cluck. A stupid person. 'Dumb' suggests German *dumm*, 'stupid' and 'cluck' Yiddish *klotz*, 'blockhead', the phrase as a whole perhaps influenced by German *Dummkopf*, 'idiot'.

Dumb down, To. To reduce to a lower level of understanding. Dumbing down was perceived by some in the 1990s as increasingly pervasive in the media, in which 'serious' newspapers re-presented their material in a more populist fashion while the more subtle points of television dramas and documentaries were demotically 'spelled out' for the benefit of the hedonistic viewer.

> Dumbing down, levelling down, politically correct, progressive – one word summarizes the history many children are being taught: bunk.
>
> *The Times* (Letter to the Editor) (25 August 1998)

Dumbo. A baby elephant whose large ears enable him to fly. The Walt Disney cartoon film of 1941 was based on the book *Dumbo, the Flying Elephant* by Helen Aberson and Harold Pearl. In addition to Dumbo, the film introduced the Crows, who have the best song in the movie, 'When I see an Elephant Fly', and Dumbo's savvy 'manager' Timothy Mouse.

Dunblane massacre. On 13 March 1996 a lone gunman, Thomas Hamilton, a former Scout leader, entered the local primary school at Dunblane, central Scotland, killing 16 young children and their teacher before turning the gun on himself. The massacre led to the banning of all privately held handguns in Britain and further tightening of the gun laws. *See also* COLUMBINE MASSACRE; HUNGERFORD MASSACRE.

Dunkirk. This once notorious haunt of pirates and privateers in northern France has acquired fresh associations since the Second World War. The name is now used figuratively to denote a forced military evacuation by sea to avoid disaster, a speedy and complete withdrawal, an entire abandonment of a position. The allusion is to the heroic evacuation of the main British expeditionary force (26 May to 4 June 1940), in the face of imminent disaster, by Vice-Admiral Ramsay's motley force of destroyers, yachts and other craft, with essential air cover from RAF Fighter Command. The phrase 'Dunkirk spirit' gained general currency to describe any sudden confrontation or crisis, especially one that is handled by 'rising to the occasion'.

> As our bank balance dwindled to £2.40, we developed a Dunkirk spirit and set about doing creative things with marrows and potato peelings.
> *Sunday Times* (23 May 1999)

Dunroamin. A typical punning name for the home of a family that has finally found its nest or niche. Names of this type proliferated in the housing boom of the interwar years, when families sought a secure and comfortable base after the disruption and destruction of the First World War. Such names are still found today for the suburban semi and the country cottage, but council estates and retirement homes mostly eschew the characteristically British label in favour of a faceless number.

> Dunroamin – a declaration to the world that a family has settled in the home of its choice; an innocent exposure of poor taste and puerile humour; or the epitome of middle-class bourgeois complacency?
> PAUL OLIVER, IAN DAVIS and IAN BENTLEY: *Dunroamin*, Introduction (1981)

Dunsterforce. The nickname during the First World War of a 1000-strong British and Commonwealth force, under the command of General L.C. Dunsterville (1865–1946), which in January 1918 marched north from Persia to support the establishment of an independent Transcaucasia. The aim was to keep the oil-rich region free from the BOLSHEVIK Russians, Turks and Germans and to prevent any German–Turkish invasion of India. Dunsterville himself was a Russian speaker, a childhood friend of Rudyard Kipling, and the model for Corkran in Kipling's *Stalky & Co.*

(1899), and the expedition was a notable episode in the GREAT GAME. By August, after various adventures, Dunsterforce had reached Baku (now the capital of Azerbaijan) but was obliged to withdraw on 14 September as 14,000 Turkish troops prepared to attack. Although Dunsterville reoccupied Baku after the armistice, he was ordered to withdraw. The region was subsequently absorbed by the Soviet Union.

Durex. The proprietary name of a well-known make of condom. The name, presumably based on 'durable', was registered in 1932 and was coined by A.R. Reid, chairman of the London Rubber Company, its manufacturers. The name is a potential pitfall for Australian visitors to Britain since in their home country 'Durex' is the equivalent of SELLOTAPE.

Dust and ashes. A disappointment or disillusionment. The expression dates from the turn of the 20th century and alludes to the legend of the Dead Sea Fruit or Apples of Sodom, as the fruit of trees reputed to grow on the shores of the Dead Sea, described by Josephus as of fair appearance externally but dissolving, when grasped, into smoke and ashes.

Dust Bowl. An area of Oklahoma and other prairie states of the United States. The name arose from the severe drought that affected the region in the early 1930s. Thousands of families were forced to leave the area at the height of the GREAT DEPRESSION.

Dust bunny. An Americanism for a ball of dust and fluff, as found in an undusted area of the home, typically under a bed.

> From now on, she said, you must keep your eyes firmly fixed at table height. Try never to look below knee level. 'Oh?' I said, grateful but puzzled. 'Dust bunnies,' she said, shortly. 'If you don't look at them, eventually they won't seem so bad.'
> *The Times* (15 October 1999)

Dust something down or **off, To.** To bring it out again for use after a long period of neglect. The expression dates from the 1940s.

> A similar argument [that pornography corrupts] has often been used on behalf of the fairer sex. Most famously, it was dusted off in the *Lady Chatterley's Lover* obscenity trial 39 years ago, when the jury was asked: 'Is it a book you would wish your wife or your servants to read?'
> *The Times* (31 July 1999)

Dutch. A nickname of President Ronald Reagan (b.1911). According to his autobiography, the name was given him as a baby when his father described him as 'a little bit of a fat Dutchman' (*Where's the Rest of Me?*, 1965). Edmund Morris's *Dutch* (1999) is a memoir of Reagan. *See also* GIPPER; TEFLON.

Dutch cap. A contraceptive diaphragm for women, so named because the shape it assumes when in position bears some resemblance to the cap with triangular flaps that forms part of Dutch women's national dress.

Dutch disease. A term used by economists for the failure of a country's economy to develop properly as a result of the plundering of its natural resources, a situation typified by the Netherlands following the discovery of massive reserves of natural gas in 1959. The immediate effect of the find was to boost the economy but it was subsequently depressed when capital was diverted away from more productive investments, in particular manufacturing.

Dutch elm disease. The popular name of *Ceratocystis ulmi*, a disease in which a suffocating fungus grows beneath the bark of elm trees to be spread by beetles. It was first identified in Holland in 1919 and was particularly virulent in Britain in the 1970s, so that by the early 1980s two out of three British elms had perished as a result of the infestation. When the disease killed the elms it produced forests of suckers from the roots, and these may be seen in hedgerows across Britain. The suckers grow to at least 6m (20ft), by which time they have developed a heavy enough bark to attract the beetles that carry the fungus. The cycle then recurs: the stems are re-infected and die, and the plants once again start from suckers.

Dutching. The practice of sending food destined for the British market for irradiation (exposure to gamma rays to kill micro-organisms) in a country where this is permitted, such as the Netherlands, in order to mask any bacterial contamination before it is put on sale. The technique was first applied in the 1980s.

DVM. Dead vegetable matter, a derisory nickname for the mass of dried flowers, dyed leaves, curling bark, twisted willow twigs, desiccated fruit and the like proliferating as supposedly essential accessories in the homes of the affluent. The term was introduced by the sociologist Tony Chapman in his study of new homes in Britain, *Stage Sets for Ideal Lives* (1999).

Dvorak simplified keyboard. *See* DSK.

Dweeb. A contemptible or puny person; a NERD. The term is of US origin and suggests a blend of 'dwarf' and 'feeble'.

DWEM. *See* DEAD WHITE EUROPEAN MALE.

Dwile flonking. A supposedly ancient but in reality entirely modern rustic contest that might otherwise be known as 'flannel flinging'. It became a nationwide craze in the 1960s after it featured on the television programme *It's a Square World* and is still held intermittently in Suffolk and elsewhere. Its rules and entertainingly esoteric vocabulary involve the formation of a 'girter' (circle) by one team, who dance round a member of the opposition, the 'flonker'. He holds a 'driveller' (stick) on the end of which is a 'dwile' (cloth) soaked in 'flonk' (ale). When the music stops the flonker flings the dwile and tries to hit the girter, scoring points depending on which part of their body is struck. If he fails to score the flonker is faced with the penalty of rapidly downing six pints. In 1967 in a match between Beccles and Bungay, the latter won 16–1.

Dying Swan, The. A ballet dance that became intimately associated with the great Anna Pavlova (1881–1931), for whom it was created by Michel Fokine, as a setting of *Le Cygne* from Camille Saint-Saëns's *Le Carnaval des animaux* (1886). It is essentially a poignant poem about the final struggle for life of a dying bird. Pavlova first danced it at a gala performance in St Petersburg on 22 December 1907. She interpreted the role dramatically but simply, using her arms to simulate the beating of the swan's wings as its struggled helplessly to fly, while the quivering movements of her body and head suggested its death throes. At the end, the fluttering ceased, and the dancer slowly sank upon the stage. *See also* PAVLOVA.

Dyke. A lesbian. The word, dating from the 1940s, is of disputed origin. It may be a shortening of *morphodyke*, a dialect form and sub-standard pronunciation of 'hermaphrodite'.

Dynasty. A US television melodrama on the lines of DALLAS, screened from 1982 to 1989 and centring on the Carringtons, a Colorado oil-rich family comprising the slick, smooth Blake Carrington, his beautiful new wife Krystle and a mixed bag of offspring. Blake's ex-wife, Alexis, had a key role as the 'villain of the piece'.

Dystopia. A modern coinage signifying the opposite of Utopia, the imaginary island in Sir Thomas More's political romance of the same name (1516) where all is perfect. The word is often used to describe the nightmare futures depicted in such novels as BRAVE NEW WORLD and *Nineteen Eighty-Four* (*see* 1984).

E

Eager beaver. A US expression in the Second World War for an over-zealous recruit whose keenness was marked by volunteering on every possible occasion. It was subsequently applied in civilian life to any glutton for work. The beaver is noted for its industry and hard work, but not specifically for its eagerness.

> It would be futile to play that game against Republican Earl Warren, one of the foremost spokesmen of the eager-beaver West.
>
> *Time* (5 July 1948)

Eagle. A British comic published between 1950 and 1969. It was initiated by the Rev. Marcus Morris and the illustrator Frank Hampson, and it was under Hampson's influence that *Eagle* moved away from the Christianity-imbued BOY'S OWN PAPER that Morris had envisaged to something more exciting. It featured the character DAN DARE, Pilot of the Future, and the villainous MEKON, as well as a comic-strip version of PC 49. An equivalent for girls had the imaginative title *Girl*.

Eagle Has Landed, The. A film (1976) adapted by Tom Mankiewicz from a bestselling novel by Jack Higgins (1975) about a fictional Nazi plot to kill Winston Churchill during the Second World War. The film starred Donald Sutherland as the Irish Republican hitman detailed to execute the assassination. In the original novel Heinrich Himmler receives the message that 'the eagle has landed' and thereby knows that his agent is safely on British soil. Higgins himself claimed that at least half of his story was based on truth, but left it to the reader to decide what was true and what was fiction. Coincidentally, in 1969 the phrase became the first words spoken by a human being on the surface of the moon, when it was quoted by US astronaut Neil Armstrong reporting the safe touchdown of the lunar module *Eagle*:

> Tranquillity Base here – the Eagle has landed.
>
> NEIL ARMSTRONG: radio transmission (1969)

Eagle of the Ninth, The. A children's historical novel (1954) by Rosemary Sutcliff (1920–92), describing the search north of Hadrian's Wall by a retired centurion, Marcus, for a lost legion (the Ninth) and its standard (a silver eagle).

Eagle's Nest. Adolf Hitler's private retreat high on the Obersalzburg mountain above Berchtesgaden in Bavaria, near the Austrian border. It was linked by a lift cut through the rock to Hitler's mountain chalet, the Berghof, home to his mistress Eva Braun from 1936 until she joined him in Berlin in 1945. Although the Eagle's Nest was private, Hitler used the Berghof for important meetings, such as that with Neville Chamberlain in mid-September 1938, before the MUNICH AGREEMENT. The Berghof was destroyed by Allied bombing in April 1945, and the ruins were levelled in 1952 to prevent the site from becoming a shrine. However, the Eagle's Nest survives as a tea room. *See also* FÜHRER.

Ealing comedies. Comedy films produced by the Ealing Studios, west London, from the late 1940s. They typically feature a downtrodden group rebelling against authority and are regarded as quintessentially 'English'. Among the best are WHISKY GALORE (1948), in which a ship with a cargo of whisky is wrecked on a small Scottish island, *The* LAVENDER HILL MOB (1951), centring on a timid clerk who plans and executes a bullion robbery, and *The Titfield Thunderbolt* (1952), telling how villagers take over a railway branch line when it is faced with closure.

Ealing Studios itself was founded in 1907 and five

years later its studios were the biggest in Britain. The company's fortunes began to fail in the 1950s, when tastes were changing, and after releasing The LADY-KILLERS (1955) it sold its studios to the BBC. Film stages and offices were subsequently rented out for independent productions, and in 1995 the site was sold to the National Film and Television School. *See also* ELSTREE STUDIOS; PASSPORT TO PIMLICO.

Early bath. If a sports player is ordered to have an early bath he is sent off the pitch before the end of the game for an infringement. The reference is to the bath or shower taken by players at the end of the game, with perhaps also a hint of a child sent to bed early for misbehaving.

> A referee took an early bath after being confronted in the tunnel at half-time. Eddie Green … quit during a non-league match fixture between Farnborough and Purfleet.
>
> *The Times* (22 October 1999)

Early Learning Centre. The firm of this name, running shops to sell educational toys for pre-school children and give advice to their parents, was set up in 1974 by the educationalist John Beale (b.1945), when the first shop so called opened in Reading. The name itself is an Americanism for a pre-school centre. A second shop followed in 1977, a third in 1978 and many more subsequently. Beale sold the business off to Fine Art Development in 1984 and two years later founded Past Times, a firm also with a chain of shops specializing in historical replicas and nostalgic artefacts.

Early music. A name originating in the 1940s for medieval, renaissance and baroque music, especially as revived and played on 'authentic' instruments of the appropriate period. A pioneer in the field was David Munrow (1942–76), founder of the Early Music Consort in 1967.

Early night. An occasion on which one goes to bed earlier than usual, especially in order to catch up on sleep. The term is necessarily subjective, since what is 'early' for one person will be normal for another. The same holds for a late night.

Early retirement. Retirement from one's occupation earlier than the statutory pension age. From the 1980s many have been able to retire early on favourable terms. At the turn of the 21st century the pension age was 65 for men and 60 for women, but in 1995 legislation was introduced to equalize the age for both sexes at 65. The change will be phased in over two years starting from 2010.

Earthsea. The fictional archipelago that is the setting of Ursula LeGuin's fantasy quartet A WIZARD OF EARTH-SEA (1968), *The Tombs of Atuan* (1971), *The Farthest Shore* (1972) and *Tehanu* (1990). It is roughly circular and at its heart lies the group known as the Inner Isles, which cluster round the Inmost Sea. To the north of this sea lies Havnor, the seat of the King of all the Isles. To the south is Wathort, a key post for trading with the southern islands. At the heart of the Inmost Sea is Roke, the centre for the teaching of the magic that is crucially important to the life of Earthsea.

Earth Shoes. The proprietary name of a type of square-toed shoes with soles that are thicker in the front than at the back, the aim being to lower the heel for greater comfort. They are so called because they were first imported to the United States from Denmark, their country of origin, on 22 April 1970, the first Earth Day, a day set aside by environmentalists to promote the importance of pollution control.

Earth Summit. An unofficial name for the United Nations Conference on Environment and Development, held in Rio de Janeiro in 1992. The basic purpose of the summit conference was to discuss matters of environment and development regarded as essential to the future of the Earth, such as BIODIVERSITY.

EastEnders. A BBC SOAP OPERA launched in 1985 and soon challenging and even bettering the veteran CORONATION STREET in viewing figures. As its title implies, it is set in the East End of London, in the (fictitious) borough of Walford, and centres on Albert Square and its Queen Vic pub, originally run by Den Watts and his wife Angie. The chief theme of the series has been the love triangle, and an early story line involved the seduction of a schoolgirl by the lecherous 'Dirty Den'. The episode in which Den gave Angie divorce papers for Christmas was watched by a record 30 million viewers. The soap's success has been largely due to its bold treatment of 'tough' issues such as rape, prostitution, unemployment, HIV infection, abortion and homosexuality.

Easter Rising. The most dramatic of the events in the struggle for HOME RULE in Ireland. The uprising had been planned by a number of radical nationalist groups and began with the seizing of the General Post Office in O'Connell Street, Dublin, on Easter Monday, 24 April 1916. From its pillared portico Patrick Pearse, a leader of the Irish Republican Brotherhood, read out a proclamation announcing the birth of the Irish republic. British troops soon arrived to put down the rebellion and for almost a week Dublin was paralyzed by street fighting. British artillery bombardments compelled Pearse and his colleagues to surrender on 29 April, and he and 14 other leaders of the rebellion were subsequently court-martialled and executed, their martyrdom creating much sympathy for their cause. The rebellion was a contributory factor in the establishment of the Irish Free State in 1921 (*see* FREE-STATERS).

W.B. Yeats's (1865–1939) poem 'Easter 1916' was inspired by the Rising, and mythologized its very considerable impact on modern Irish history.

> I write it out in a verse – Macdonagh and MacBride
> And Connolly and Pearse
> Now and in time to be,
> Wherever green is worn
> Are changed, changed utterly:
> A terrible beauty is born.

The phrase 'terrible beauty' is frequently quoted as a pithy yet poetic encapsulation of the violent nature of Ireland's ascent to nationhood, and makes regular appearances in the titles of books on Irish themes, such as *Ireland: A Terrible Beauty* (1976), by Jill and Leon Uris. *See also* IRA; PROVOS; TROUBLES.

East of Eden. A novel (1952) by John Steinbeck (1902–68). The story follows two families in the Salinas Valley, California, through three generations of discord. It centres on Adam Trask, his murderous wife Kathy, who abandons her family and becomes the madam of a brothel, and their twin sons, Aron and Caleb, whose rivalry recalls the biblical story of Cain and Abel. The title is drawn from that account: 'And Cain went out from the presence of the Lord, and dwelt in the land of Nod, on the east of Eden' (Genesis 4:16). A rousing film version (1955), starring James Dean, was somewhat over-directed by Elia Kazan.

Easy listening. A term dating from the 1960s for recordings of popular music that are undemanding to listen to and that thus serve well for background music in a working or social environment. The style is typified by the US singer Andy Williams (b.1928) with songs such as 'Music to Watch Girls By' and 'On the Street Where You Live'.

Easy on the eye. Pleasing to look at. A phrase dating from the 1920s and usually applied to a beautiful girl or woman. A somewhat earlier equivalent was 'easy to look at'.

Easy-peasy. Childishly simple. The second word is simply a rhyming jingle. The phrase dates from the 1970s.

> But do I hear our ludic masochist asking for more? Univocalics? Easy. Lipograms? Peasy.
> DAVID CRYSTAL: *Language Play*, ch iii (1998)

Easy rider. A sexually satisfying lover. The reference is to 'riding' one's partner. The title of the acclaimed film *Easy Rider* (1969), in which two dropouts ride across America on motorcycles, has overtones of the earlier sense.

Easy street. A secure and comfortable life; a place or position where living is easy. The US expression dates from the turn of the 20th century.

Eat, drink and sleep something, To. To be fully and continuously absorbed in it, not only in one's every waking moment but also as if when asleep. The expression is usually applied to an all-consuming occupation or interest. In 1996 COCA-COLA was promoted during the European Championship football tournament in England with the slogan 'Eat football, sleep football, drink Coca-Cola', and the same formula was subsequently used with regard to cricket in India.

> 'I've seen what a physically and mentally grinding job the leadership [of the Liberal Democrats] is to do. It is a job that you can only do if you eat, drink and sleep it.'
> CHARLES KENNEDY in *The Times* (10 August 1999)

Eat out of someone's hand, To. To be entirely submissive or obedient. The allusion is to a pet or tame animal, which will eat from a human hand. The expression dates from the early 20th century.

Eat someone for breakfast, To. *See* HAVE SOMEONE FOR BREAKFAST.

E-boat. In the Second World War an abbreviation for enemy torpedo boat, i.e. a German one. See also U-BOAT.

E-boat alley. The name given to the coastal convoy route off the coast of East Anglia, which was the scene of much successful E-BOAT activity in the early years of the Second World War.

Ebonics. American black English regarded as a language in its own right rather than as a dialect of English. In 1996 it was recognized as a legitimate language variety by school officials in Oakland, California. The term combines 'ebony' and 'phonics'. *See also* LYIN' AND TESTIFYIN'.

Ecological footprint. A term dating from the early 1990s for the amount of land required to sustain a particular society or the human race in general. 'Footprint' as a word for the area covered by something, such as that under a vehicle or aircraft, dates from the 1960s.

Economical with the truth. A euphemism for untruthful, brought before the public in 1986 as a result of a statement by the then Cabinet Secretary, Sir Robert Armstrong, to the Supreme Court, New South Wales, Australia, in the SPYCATCHER TRIAL. Referring to a letter, Sir Robert said: 'It contains a misleading impression, not a lie. It was being economical with the truth' (*Daily Telegraph*, 19 November 1986).

The phrase can be traced back to a similar statement by Edmund Burke: 'Falsehood and delusion are allowed in no case whatsoever. But, as in the exercise of all the virtues, there is an economy of truth' (*Two Letters of Proposals for Peace*, 1796). Cross-examined at the Old Bailey in 1992, the Conservative politician Alan Clark referred to 'our old friend economical ... with the *actualité*'.

Eco-tourism. Tourism directed towards an exotic natural environment, especially one under threat such as the Amazon rainforest, in order to support conservation efforts and view wildlife. Such tourism is distinct from the conventional kind, which frequently despoils the natural environment.

Eco-warrior. An activist who takes direct and often illegal action on an environmental issue, 'eco-' representing 'ecology'. Like 'eco-terrorist', the term has two diametrically opposed senses: on the one hand, one who takes action to further environmental ends; on the other, one who wreaks politically motivated damage to the natural environment. Both terms date from the 1990s.

> The ring road plan sparked massive protests. Dr Margaret Jones abandoned her academic career to become a full-time eco-warrior to fight the road scheme.
> *Sunday Express* (27 February 2000)

Ecstasy. The name of a drug that acts as a stimulant and can cause hallucinations, as a state of supposed ecstasy. Its chemical name is methylenedioxymethamphetamine, usually abbreviated as MDMA. It was originally designed in 1917 as an appetite suppressant, but in the late 1980s played a key role in the rise of RAVE culture in Britain, and in the early 1990s in California, USA.

Eddie the Eagle. The nickname of Eddie Edwards (b.1964), a short-sighted Gloucestershire plasterer who without any official back-up competed for Britain in the ski-jumping event in the 1988 Winter Olympics at Calgary. To no one's great surprise he came last, but the eagle had momentarily soared, winning the instinctive support of thousands for the plucky underdog.

Edge of one's seat. To sit or be on the edge of one's seat is to be in a state of attentive or expectant excitement, as when watching an absorbing spectacle. The phrase may be hyphenated as a synonym for 'exciting', 'thrilling'.

> This [Mozart's opera *Don Giovanni*] is an edge-of-your-seat production, definitely worth catching in London this week.
> *The Times* (11 October 1999)

Edible Woman, The. The first novel (1969) by the Canadian writer Margaret Atwood (b.1939). Its theme is survival in the face of destruction. The title refers to a cake in the form of a woman, which the main character, Marian McAlpin, bakes and then eats in celebration of her release from her suffocating life, engaged to be married to a young man who drains or 'eats' her emotionally.

Edinburgh Group. A group of Scottish painters who exhibited together in 1912, 1913, 1919, 1920 and 1921. Leading members were John R. Barclay (1884–1963), William Oliphant Hutchison (1889–1970), Dorothy Johnstone (1892–1980), Mary Newbery (1892–1985), Eric Robertson (1887–1941), J.G. Spence Smith (1880–1951), A.R. Sturrock (1885–1953), who was married to Newbery, D.M. Sutherland (1883–1973) and Cecile Walton (1891–1956). They painted in a variety of figurative styles and attracted a good deal of public and critical attention, not least because of the notoriously involved love lives of many of their number, notably Robertson.

Edinburgh Tattoo. The display of music and marching is a high point of the annual Edinburgh Festival, although not officially part of it. It was introduced in 1947 as a celebration of ethnic piping and dancing, organized by the Army's Scottish Command, and in 1950 was officially retitled the Edinburgh Military Tattoo. The show is held on the esplanade of Edinburgh Castle, the core of the entertainment being provided by pipes and drums. A lone piper concludes the programme.

To you it may be taboo
To poo-poo the Tattoo.
But to me the Tattoo
Is something to say ta-ta to.
JOHN HEGLEY: 'Edinburgh' (1986)

Edsel. A nickname for a manufactured product that is old-fashioned or that does not answer to the requirements of its time. The allusion is to the Ford Edsel, an unpopular make of Ford car made from 1957 to 1962 and named after the US car manufacturer Edsel B. Ford (1893–1943), only son of Henry Ford, founder of the Ford Motor Company. It did not help that the name suggests German *Esel*, 'donkey'.

Educated guess. A guess based on knowledge and past experience, and therefore likely to be correct. Many guesses are random or at best speculative, so lack the attributes of any kind of education.

Education, education, education. The avowed priority of NEW LABOUR in the mid-1990s, as declared by its leader Tony Blair at the Labour Party Conference on 1 October 1996: 'Ask me my three main priorities for government and I tell you: education, education and education.' Inevitably, party priorities became more diffuse following Labour's election to power in 1997, although education remained, at least nominally, a front runner. It is uncertain to what extent the pronouncement was based on that of an earlier labourite, LENIN, who in an article of 1923 advocating the importance of scientific education in the furtherance of communism, voiced the prime objectives of the *apparat* as: 'first – to study, second – to study and third – to study.' The threefold clarion call became a slogan of Soviet youth in its pursuit of politically correct learning.

Edutainment. An activity or product in an electronic medium such as a video or computer game that is intended to be both educational as well as enjoyable. The term is a blend of 'education' and 'entertainment' and arose in the 1980s on an analogy both with 'docutainment', as a documentary film that seeks to inform as well as entertain, and with 'infotainment', as any kind of broadcast material that seeks to inform and entertain at the same time.

Edwardian era. The decade of the reign of King Edward VII (1901–10), an age of fashion and style, of households with servants, of personal maids, of comfortable trains, of grand hotels, of richly stocked department stores, and of general opulence and leisure.

The period has been regarded with nostalgia by many ever since, and accounts for the popularity of such television series as UPSTAIRS, DOWNSTAIRS and of the meticulous re-creations of MERCHANT IVORY FILMS. *See also* SERVANT PROBLEM; TEDDY BOYS.

> Imagine you can stop the clock at any decade in the 20th century, and make it last for ever. Which would you choose? My guess is that two periods would be favourite choices: the 1960s and the Edwardian era.
> *Sunday Times* (10 May 1998)

Ee bah gum. A supposedly characteristic Yorkshire exclamation, made up of *ee*, a northern form of 'oh', and *bah gum*, 'by God', with the *u* pronounced short as in 'good'. Although widely known, the phrase was curiously absent from dictionaries until the *Concise Oxford Dictionary* included it in its 1999 edition. A Second World War pleasantry had a Yorkshireman emerging from an air-raid shelter with the rueful words: 'Bah gum, chum, ma bum's numb.'

> Eeeh bah gum, Bradford's glum.
> *Independent on Sunday* (headline) (28 November 1999)

Eejit. A fool, as a spelling representing a supposedly typical Irish pronunciation of 'idiot'.

> He could have phoned someone downstairs at the reception desk and asked: 'Where's the minibar?' But he'd have felt like an eejit.
> DERMOT BOLGER (ed.): *Finbar's Hotel*, 'Room 101 – Benny does Dublin' (1997)

Effing and blinding. Swearing; using coarse language. 'Effing' is using the F-WORD (*see also* FOUR-LETTER WORD); 'blinding' is using a word based on 'blind' such as 'blimey' or 'gorblimey'.

Egghead. An academic or intellectual, popularly envisaged as having a head as bald as an egg. The term is of US origin and dates from the early years of the 20th century. *See also* POINTY HEAD.

Egg on one's face. An appearance of embarrassment or foolishness resulting from a gaffe. Eating a soft-boiled egg may well leave yolk stains around the mouth. The expression dates from the 1950s.

> Fondly remembered are the technical hitches … 'Night after night we were left with egg on our faces. But we persisted,' Barratt recalls.
> *The Times* (15 October 1999)

Eight Days a Week. A song by the BEATLES, credited to John Lennon and Paul McCartney and released in Britain in December 1964. The title is based on the casual use by the group's drummer, Ringo Starr, of a Liverpudlian phrase denoting hard work.

Eighteenth law. Common sense. The laws (not rules) of football have been condensed to 17 in number and the modern referee is expected to be familiar with all of them, not least the addition.

Eighth Army. The most familiar of the seven British Armies during the Second World War, formed in Egypt in 1941 for the North African and subsequent Italian campaigns. The others were the First Army, formed in Britain to invade North Africa in 1942, the Second Army, also formed in Britain and taking part in northwest European campaigns, the Ninth Army, formed behind the Eighth Army in the Levant, the Tenth Army, formed in Iraq in 1941 and controlling Syria, Persia and Iraq, and the Twelfth Army, raised in Burma in 1945 and joining the Fourteenth Army, also raised there, in retaking Burma and Malaya. The numbering defies logic and is generally seen as a way of duping the enemy into thinking there were more fighting men than was actually the case. *See also* ALAMEIN, EL; FORGOTTEN ARMY; MONTY.

Eight-page. Sexually titillating; 'steamy'. The allusion is to the eight-page pornographic booklets of the 1930s in which cartoon characters such as MICKEY MOUSE, POPEYE and BLONDIE were depicted in smutty scenarios far removed from their usual 'good clean fun'.

> A truck-load of movie offers followed on from *Wild Things*, including … the Lara Croft gig in *Tomb Raider*. 'And lots of films with eight-page lesbian scenes', she [Denise Richards] adds.
>
> *heat* (18–24 November 1999)

Eighty-six. In US restaurants and 'eateries' an expression indicating that the requested item is 'off' or not available, or that the customer is not to be served. The number is probably simply rhyming slang for 'nix'.

Einsatzgruppen (German, 'task forces'). The groups of SS troops formed in 1939 to follow the German armies into Poland, with the purpose of killing national leaders and rounding up Jews. By the time Hitler invaded the Soviet Union the Einsatzgruppen were 12,000 strong and were charged with the 'resettlement' (i.e. extermination) of all Jews and Soviet political commissars and the elimination of civilian resistance. The initial method was shooting, and then other methods were tried, such as pumping exhaust fumes into sealed lorries in which the victims were locked. By 1943 more than 600,000 Soviet Jews had

been 'resettled' by the Einsatzgruppen, but their productivity did not satisfy the Nazi hierarchy, who decided it would be more efficient to build purpose-built extermination camps. *See also* FINAL SOLUTION.

Ein Volk, ein Reich, ein Führer. A NAZI slogan meaning 'One people, one realm, one leader'. It also appears in the form *ein Reich, ein Volk, ein Führer*. *See also* CAUDILLO; FÜHRER.

Eire. A former name of Southern Ireland. The new Irish constitution of 1937 changed the name of the country from the Irish Free State (*see* FREE-STATERS) to Eire (the Gaelic name for Ireland). In 1949, when Southern Ireland became a republic and withdrew from the Commonwealth, it became the Republic of Ireland.

Eisenhower Doctrine. A foreign policy pronouncement by President Dwight D. Eisenhower on 5 January 1957, during the COLD WAR period. It promised military or economic aid to any Middle Eastern country needing help in resisting communist aggression and was intended to check the increase of Soviet influence in the Middle East resulting from the supply of arms to Egypt by communist countries, as well as from strong communist support of Arab states against an Israeli, French and British attack on Egypt in October 1956 (*see* SUEZ CRISIS). The pronouncement did not represent a radical change in US policy, since the TRUMAN DOCTRINE had pledged similar support to Greece and Turkey ten years before.

El Alamein. *See* ALAMEIN, EL.

Elastoplast. The proprietary name of a type of adhesive sticking plaster for covering cuts and wounds, first put on the market in 1928 by the firm of Smith and Nephew, founded in 1856. The name simply denotes an 'elastic plaster'.

El cheapo. Very cheap; shoddy. The pseudo-Spanish expression came into vogue in the 1960s. Spanish *el*, 'the', has long been familiar to English speakers from its occurrence in personal and place-names such as *El Cid, El Greco, El Paso, El Dorado*. *See also* EL NIÑO.

Elder statesman. While now denoting a respected and experienced politician, the term originally specifically applied in the 1920s to a member of the Japanese *Genro*, a body of retired statesmen consulted when necessary by the emperor. The Japanese word itself means 'principal elders', from *gen*, 'root', and *ro*, 'old'.

Eleanor Rigby. A poignant lyric (to the accompaniment of a string quartet) by the BEATLES, credited to John Lennon and Paul McCartney and released in Britain in

August 1966 on the album REVOLVER. Eleanor Rigby is a lonely spinster who dies alone without ever having been able to tell anyone about her feelings of personal despair. The name may derive from the name of a clothes shop in Bristol combined with the first name of the actress Eleanor Bron, or may alternatively be taken from a real-life Eleanor Rigby (1895–1939) who lived in Liverpool. The song's lyrics have a depth and resonance unusual for a pop single. Particularly memorable is the image of Eleanor keeping her face 'in a jar by the door', an expression of her stoic refusal to show her real emotions publicly.

Electra complex. The psychoanalytical term for a daughter's feelings of sexual attraction towards her father and hostility towards her mother. The allusion is to Electra in Greek tragedy, the daughter of Agamemnon and Clytemnestra, who incited her brother Orestes to kill their mother in revenge for the latter's murder of their father. *See also* OEDIPUS COMPLEX.

Elegies to the Spanish Republic. The title of a series of paintings by the great abstract expressionist Robert Motherwell (1915–91), characterized by vertical bands and ovals in black, white and subdued colours. Motherwell began the series in 1949, on the tenth anniversary of the final defeat of the Spanish Republic by Franco's Nationalists. Over the next three decades he painted almost 150 of these *Elegies*. *See also* AT FIVE IN THE AFTERNOON.

Elephant Man, The. A much-admired film (1980), shot in black and white and directed by David Lynch, about a man whose elephantine features (resulting from disease) sentence him to a life as a carnival-show freak until he attracts the attention of a sympathetic member of the medical establishment. The film, starring John Hurt, was based on the life story of the real Joseph Merrick (1867–90), who was thus disfigured and who became the subject of medical curiosity in Victorian England.

Eleven-plus. The name formerly given to the examination set to primary schoolchildren at the age of 11 or 12 and used as a means of judging their suitability for the various types of secondary education provided by the Education Act of 1944 (secondary modern, secondary technical, secondary grammar, etc). The unreliability of testing children at this age and so determining the type of school to which they should be sent resulted in the 1976 Education Act, which compelled local authorities to draw up plans for comprehensive reorganization, although this was later repealed. The term is still loosely used for the age at which children leave primary school.

Eleventh commandment. An ironical addition to the Ten Commandments, usually interpreted as 'Thou shalt not be found out'.

Elfhame. An Elfin Kingdom in Sylvia Townsend Warner's novel *Kingdoms of Elfin* (1972). It lies beneath a hill near the Eskdalemuir Observatory on the Scottish border and its inhabitants are not small and immortal, as might be expected, but more or less human-sized and mortal. A peculiarity is that they rarely have children but steal them instead, leaving changelings in their place.

Elidor. A fantasy (1965) for children by Alan Garner (b.1934). A collection of everyday objects becomes the means of saving the mythical world of Elidor, to which four children have been transported from the back streets of Manchester. The name of Elidor suggests that of El Dorado, the fictitious country or city abounding in gold, at one time believed to exist in South America.

Eligible bachelor. A bachelor who is desirably available for marriage, as distinct from a 'confirmed bachelor', who for reasons known or unknown is not.

> With February 29 fast approaching, the day women may traditionally propose, Nicole Swengley asked ten eligible bachelors where they would like to receive a marriage request.
> *The Times* (12 February 2000)

Eliza Doolittle. *See* DOOLITTLE, ELIZA.

Elk Hills scandal. *See* TEAPOT DOME SCANDAL.

Elm Street. The fictional location of a hugely successful series of SLASHER MOVIES that began with *A Nightmare on Elm Street* (1984), directed by Wes Craven. Five similarly blood-spattered sequels followed. The films centre around the nightmarish events that take place at 1428 Elm Street, involving the terrorizing of a group of suburban teenagers by the hideously scarred figure of Freddy Krueger (played by Robert Eklund), who has knives for fingernails.

El Niño. The irregularly occurring weather system that is characterized by warm ocean temperatures in the Equatorial Pacific. Its name is short for Spanish *El Niño de Navidad*, 'the Christmas Child', since it warms the water off the north Peruvian coast at Christmas. The name became generally familiar in the latter half of the 20th century when marked changes in the global climate became a matter of increasing concern. *See also* LA NIÑA.

Elstree Studios. Films at Elstree date from 1914, when Neptune Studios opened on the rural Hertfordshire site, chosen for its proximity to London. They closed in 1917 but were succeeded by a sprawling complex of studios soon dubbed 'the British HOLLYWOOD'. The first British 'talkie', *Blackmail*, was directed by Alfred Hitchcock at Elstree in 1929 and in the 1930s a stream of thrillers, comedies and musicals poured from the site. Following the Second World War Elstree produced such British classics as *The* DAM BUSTERS (1954) and also attracted American stars such as Gregory Peck in *Moby Dick* (1954) and Cary Grant in *Indiscreet* (1957). Its fortunes then flagged, but Stanley Kubrick kept the studios busy with 2001: A SPACE ODYSSEY (1968) and George Lucas even more so with STAR WARS (1976). The huge success of *The* FULL MONTY (1997), also shot at Elstree, ensured financial stability for the studios into the 21st century.

Elvis Lives. An anagrammatical slogan claiming the immortality, at least in spirit, of the extraordinarily popular singer Elvis Presley (1935–77). So-called 'Elvis sightings', or supposed physical manifestations of 'the King', were still being proclaimed by devotees some 20 years on. *See also* KING.

Elvis the Pelvis. A rhyming nickname of Elvis Presley (*see* ELVIS LIVES), alluding to the gyration of his hips on stage. It was sometimes shortened to simply 'Pelvis'. *See also* GRACELAND.

E-mail. Electronic mail, sent by one computer user to one or more others over a network. Communications sent by e-mail have attracted their own etiquette, differing from that of letters sent by SNAIL MAIL and in some ways closer to that of a telephone call. The prefix is also applied to other areas such as e-trade and e-commerce, meaning trade or commerce over the INTERNET. See also SMILEY FACE.

> If you have no e-mail address you're a walking piece of history, as out of date as papyrus.
> *The Times* (2 March 1999)

Emergency – Ward 10. The first British medical television SOAP OPERA, screened on ITV from 1957 to 1967. It was set in the (fictitious) Oxbridge General Hospital and was initially to have been titled *Calling Nurse Roberts* after the original main character, Nurse Pat Roberts, played by Rosemary Miller.

Emil and the Detectives. A novel, originally *Emil und die Detektive* (1929), by the German writer Erich Kästner (1899–1974). A much-imitated 'children-against-villains' tale, it tells the tale of 10-year-old Emil Tischbein who, travelling from Neustadt to Berlin to stay with relations, is robbed of his money on a train. He embarks on a hunt for the thief with the assistance of a group of children. The thief turns out to be notorious bank-robber, long sought by the police, and Emil is handsomely rewarded for his efforts.

Emily's list. A group launched in the United States in 1985 to raise funds for women wishing to become Democratic candidates, especially those who are pro-abortion. The name is an acronym of 'Early Money Is Like Yeast', the last word of this being a punning allusion to an agent that makes 'dough rise'. The movement spread to Britain in the early 1990s with the aim of increasing the representation of women in the LABOUR PARTY.

> In the run-up to the last election, the 'Emily's List' campaign and women-only shortlists were knocked off course by a challenge at an industrial tribunal.
> *Sunday Express* (27 February 2000)

Eminent Victorian. Any famous or worthy Briton active in the reign of Queen Victoria (1837–1901). The expression derives from the title of Lytton Strachey's *Eminent Victorians* (1918), containing biographical studies of Cardinal Manning (1808–92), Florence Nightingale (1820–1910), Thomas Arnold (1795–1842) and General Gordon (1833–85). *See also* LEGEND IN ONE'S LIFETIME.

> Queen Elizabeth [the Queen Mother] is our last eminent Victorian, born in the middle distance of history during the last year of that monarch's life.
> *The Times* (31 July 1999)

Emmanuelle. The eponymous heroine, played by Sylvia Kristel, of a soft-core French pornographic film, released in 1974. Emmanuelle, the bored wife of a French diplomat based in Thailand, is urged by her friends to embark on a journey of sexual discovery. The film spawned a number of equally tawdry sequels.

Emmets. An expression commonly applied in Cornwall to tourists and holidaymakers. 'Emmet' is an old word for an ant, and such insects swarm everywhere. *See also* GROCKLES.

Emmy. The television equivalent of the OSCAR, first awarded by the American Academy of Television

Arts and Sciences in 1949. The awards, in the form of winged statuettes, are divided into comedy series, drama series and miniseries, with each of these subdivided into individual actors and actresses. The name itself is a form of Immy, a nickname for the image orthicon camera tube that formed part of early television sets. *See also* GRAMMY.

Emoticon. *See* SMILEY FACE.

Empire Day. A memorial day instituted by the Earl of Meath in 1902, after the end of the second Boer War, as a way to encourage schoolchildren to be aware of their duties and responsibilities as citizens of the British Empire. The day set aside was 24 May, Queen Victoria's birthday. In 1916 it was given official recognition in the United Kingdom, and it was renamed Commonwealth Day in 1958. Since 1977 this has been observed on the second Monday in March.

Empty nester. A parent whose children have grown up and left home or 'flown the nest'. The expression is of US origin and dates from the 1960s. *See also* HOME ALONE.

> High-quality conversions appeal to discerning empty-nesters. These are people who have always lived in big houses and who still want imposing rooms where they can put their large furniture.
> *The Times* (7 July 1999)

Emsworth, Lord. The pig-loving peer who resides at Blandings Castle in the novels and short stories of P.G. Wodehouse (1881–1975). In his full glory he is Clarence Threepwood, 9th Earl of Emsworth, and he and his idiotic son, the Hon. Freddie Threepwood, first appear in the novel *Something Fresh* (1915). Many of the stories involve daring plots to abduct the Empress of Blandings, Lord Emsworth's prize pig.

Endgame. A play (1957) by the Irish playwright Samuel Beckett (1906–89) in which four enigmatic characters, Hamm, Clov, Nagg and Nell (the last two of whom are encased in dustbins), inhabit a bare room with just two small curtained windows. The play is said to be the author's favourite among his works. Its meaning is obscure, but the title refers to chess, in which the endgame is the final series of moves in which a victor completes his opponent's inevitable defeat.

End in tears, To. To have a unhappy or painful outcome. The phrase is often by way of a warning: 'It will all end in tears.'

Where almost nobody will speak to her, she falls for a middle-aged poacher who does at least involve her in his murderous rivalry with a gamekeeper. You can be sure it will all end in tears.
Sunday Times (12 September 1999)

End is nigh. Traditional doom-laden words familiar from the placards of religious fanatics. The precise source of the prediction is uncertain, and although 'nigh' is very much a biblical word, the statement is not found in the Bible. Approximations exist, however, in 'But the end of all things is at hand' (1 Peter 4:7), 'The day of the Lord cometh, for it is nigh at hand' (Joel 2:1), and 'Know ye that the kingdom of God is nigh at hand' (Luke 21:31).

End of civilization as we know it. The total collapse of ordered society. The expression, a supposed cinematic cliché uttered in a SCIENCE FICTION movie when the world is threatened by invasion from outer space, appears to originate in a line from the film CITIZEN KANE (1941) spoken by the newspaper magnate Charles Foster Kane at a press conference before the Second World War:

> 'I've talked with the responsible leaders of the Great Powers – England, France, Germany and Italy. They're too intelligent to embark on a project which would mean the end of civilization as we now know it. You can take my word for it: there'll be no war!'

End of story. There is nothing more to add. A phrase indicating that the speaker has said all that needs to be said and that further words are superfluous. *See also* FULL STOP.

> He has not only discovered that most duodenal ulcers … are caused by a bug living in the stomach lining; he has proved it by publicly drinking the bug … and then eradicating it with a simple course of three drugs. End of story, end of surgery.
> *The Times* (28 December 1999)

End of the Affair, The. A novel (1951) by Graham Greene (1904–91) about a wartime love affair during the BLITZ. It is said to have been inspired by Greene's own extra-marital affair with Catherine Walston (1916–78), the promiscuous wife of a wealthy banker, Henry Miles, whose first name was the same as that of the cuckolded husband in the novel. In the novel Sarah, the wife, ends the affair, and dies from the complications of a cold, aggravated by the harassment of her former lover, who is a novelist. The affair between Greene and Walston carried on until the late 1950s.

There have been two films: in 1954, directed by Edward Dmytryk, and 2000, directed by Neil Jordan.

End of the world. To say that something is not the end of the world is to recognize that although apparently calamitous, it is not finally disastrous. The expression dates from the beginning of the 20th century.

> Lomax [*with studied coolness*]: My good fellow: you neednt get into a state of nerves. Nothing's going to happen to you; and I suppose it wouldnt be the end of the world if anything did.
>
> GEORGE BERNARD SHAW: *Major Barbara*, III (1907)

Enemy within. *See* KING ARTHUR.

English disease. A term current in continental Europe in the 1960s and 1970s (French, *la maladie anglaise*) to explain the sluggish state of the British economy. The symptoms were seen as strikes, restrictive practices, absenteeism and extended tea breaks. The same term was applied in the 1980s to soccer hooligans and LAGER LOUTS. Historically 'English disease' was a term current in continental Europe for melancholy or 'spleen' and also for rickets, a disease first identified in 17th-century England.

English Patient, The. A novel (1992) by Michael Ondaatje (b.1943), which was joint winner of the BOOKER PRIZE with *Sacred Hunger* by Barry Unsworth (b.1930). Set in 1945 in Tuscany, in the last months of the Second World War, it is a study of an intriguing foursome in a battered villa surrounded by unexploded mines. One of them, the 'English patient', has been burned in a plane crash. A glossily romantic film version (1996), with Ralph Fiennes and Juliette Binoche in key roles, was directed by Anthony Minghella.

English rose. This term for a typically attractive light-complexioned English girl dates from the turn of the 20th century and is found in Basil Hood's poetic drama *Merrie England* (1902) in which he describes a garden where 'women are the flow'rs' and in which 'the sweetest blossom' or 'fairest Queen' is 'the perfect English rose'. The phrase has subsequently been associated with royal princesses, fair-skinned portrait posers and fine-boned film actresses, among others.

> Despite the fiery talk she [dancer Darcey Bussell] is at heart a delicate English rose, unlikely to be stirred by anything other than ballet.
>
> *The Times* (2 October 1999)

Enigma. Germany's device for the encoding of strategic messages before and during the Second World War. The Enigma machine had a set of revolving drums that could scramble the alphabet into millions of combinations, generating a mass of gibberish that could be decoded only by another Enigma. A Polish mechanic working on the machine in 1928 took notes of the components before being repatriated, and with the help of the British and French secret services constructed a wooden mock-up. Later, a British cryptographer managed to smuggle a completely new Enigma machine to England, where a team of decoders found a way of cracking the ciphers. In 1939 the secret service set up the Ultra project at Bletchley Park, Buckinghamshire, for the purpose of intercepting the Germans' Enigma signals. The intelligence received was crucial in the BATTLE OF BRITAIN, the DUNKIRK evacuation and the Normandy landings on D-DAY. The Ultra project provided the subject-matter for *Enigma* (1995), a successful thriller by Robert Harris.

Enjoy your meal. A stock expression of goodwill made by a waiter in a restaurant after serving an opening course at table. The formula is virtually meaningless and is intended to suggest that whatever the reality the meal will indeed be a success and that the waiter will benefit as a result. *See also* HAVE A NICE DAY.

Enola Gay. The name of the Boeing B-29 Superfortress bomber that on 6 August 1945 dropped 'Little Boy', the atomic bomb that destroyed HIROSHIMA, killing nearly 80,000 people instantly. It was piloted by Colonel Paul Tibbets (b.1915) and was named after the pilot's mother. A second bomb, 'Fat Man', was dropped by *Bock's Car*, another B-29, on Nagasaki three days later. Shortly afterwards Japan surrendered, ending the Second World War. *Enola Gay* has been restored and is now on display at the Smithsonian's National Air and Space Museum in Washington, D.C.

A film, *Fat Man and Little Boy*, simplistically pinning the blame for the increase in nuclear weapons on militarists who bullied right-thinking scientists into creating weapons of mass destruction, was released in 1989. It was directed by Roland Joffe and starred Paul Newman and Dwight Schultz.

Enosis (Greek, 'union'). The campaign of this name for the union of Cyprus and Greece originated in 1912 and continued until the establishment of the Republic of Cyprus in 1960. *See also* EOKA.

Ensa. The Entertainments National Service Association, which in the Second World War provided concerts and shows for British troops abroad and for camps and factories at home. Many famous figures in the entertainment world took part, greatly helping to boost morale. The acronym was affectionately interpreted as Every Night Something Awful.

Entente Cordiale (French, 'cordial understanding'). The agreement signed between Britain and France in 1904, forming the basis of Anglo-French cooperation in the First World War. It covered matters ranging from policies in North Africa to fishing rights off Newfoundland and proved that the former enemies could work together after all in the face of German military expansion. *See also* SARAJEVO.

Entertaining Mr Sloane. A play (1964) by the British playwright Joe Orton (1933–67) about an attractive young murderer whose attempts to establish a comfortable life for himself in the home of a doting woman and her brother only results in him becoming their sexual plaything. Sloane is the murderer 'entertained' by the brother and sister. This was the first of Orton's full-length plays, and its transfer to the West End of London was largely due to the efforts of Terence Rattigan, an apparently unlikely supporter. A film version appeared in 1969.

E-numbers. Code numbers preceded by the letter E on food products denote additives numbered in accordance with EUROPEAN UNION directives. There are just over 300 listed additives and about 3000 flavourings. E-numbers are divided into five groups: colourings (E100–180), preservatives (E200–290), antioxidants (E300–321), emulsifiers (E322–394) and sweeteners (E420–421). E-numbers are popularly associated with JUNK FOOD, which has many additives and flavourings.

EOKA. The Cypriot guerrilla force organized in 1954 to fight for ENOSIS. It was active until the mid-1970s. The name is an acronym of Greek *Ethnikē Organōsis Kupriakou Agōnos*, 'National Organization of Cypriot Struggle'.

Epic theatre. A type of anti-naturalistic theatre developed in the 1920s by the German dramatists Erwin Piscator and Bertolt Brecht. In plays such as MOTHER COURAGE and *The* CAUCASIAN CHALK CIRCLE, Brecht sought deliberately to distance audiences from the characters and action on stage through stylized dialogue and the use of songs, thereby encouraging them to focus on understanding the political contexts of the action. Brecht later described this technique as the *Verfremdungseffekt* (German, 'alienation effect').

Equivalent VIII. *See* TATE BRICKS.

Equus. A play (1973) by the British playwright Peter Shaffer (b.1926) about a young stable boy who undergoes psychiatric analysis after he blinds six horses following a frustrated sexual liaison. The play was based on an actual case, reported in the press in 1973, in which a young man blinded several horses apparently without motive. The play was filmed in 1977 starring Richard Burton as the psychiatrist. The young man's obsession with horses is reflected in the title, which is Latin for 'horse'.

ER. A television medical drama series of US origin, first screened on Channel 4 in 1995 and set in the Emergency Room (ER) of Cook County Hospital, Chicago. Its draw lies in its frantic pace, gory scenes and high emotional tension, with most of the action centring on the doctors and nurses rather than the patients.

ERNIE. The Premium Bonds genius, more formally designated the electronic random number indicator equipment. ERNIE is thus not a computer, as is it sometimes described. The first prize was drawn in 1956, and ERNIE was still in high favour with 'investors' 40 years on, despite the competing allure of the National Lottery from 1994. At the turn of the 21st century ERNIE offered thousands of prizes ranging from £50 to a single top prize of £1 million.

Escape film. A film whose main story deals with some kind of entrapment. A narrative of this type has long been popular in the cinema since its effect is naturally enhanced by the confined area of the auditorium and even the spatial restriction of the screen, creating a sense of oppression for the audience and their own increased desire for freedom. Examples of such films are Jean Renoir's *La Grande Illusion* (1937), about three French pilots captured by the Germans in the First World War, and John Sturges's *The* GREAT ESCAPE (1963), in which Allied prisoners break out of a German prison camp. *See also* COLDITZ.

Eskimo pie. A proprietary name for a bar of chocolate-coated ice cream introduced in the United States in 1921.

Essex girl. A type of unintelligent and materialistic young woman who emerged in the late 1980s as the female equivalent of ESSEX MAN. Her supposed promiscuity and tarty appearance made her the butt of a variety of politically incorrect jokes. *See also* BIRDS OF A FEATHER; SHARON.

> It was soon obvious I had a blue-green algae problem. The stuff spreads faster than an Essex girl joke in a bar full of salesmen.
> *Practical Fishkeeping* (April 1992)

Essex man. A type of socially ungraced and culturally deprived Conservative voter, typically a self-made businessman, who lives in Essex or southeast England and who in the late 1980s worshipped the consumer-oriented gospel of THATCHERISM. The expression was coined in an article headed 'Mrs Thatcher's bruiser' that appeared in the *Sunday Telegraph* for 7 October 1990. It defined Essex man as ruthlessly self-interested, philistine, lager-swilling, racist and the potential owner of a Rottweiler, if only he had time to walk it. The specific link with Essex is that the county is the nearest for the upwardly mobile to move to from London's East End. The Essex town of Basildon reinforced the stereotype when in the 1992 general election it was the first constituency to declare a result that accurately implied a stronger level of Conservative support in the country than the polls had predicted. The term itself evokes an anthropological label such as Neanderthal man or PILTDOWN MAN (*see under* FAKES). *See also* ESSEX GIRL.

> Essex Man, one of Britain's most strident class warriors with his mobile phone, Ford Escort XR3i and 'loadsamoney' mentality, is a doyen among consumers.
> GREG HADFIELD and MARK SKIPWORTH: *Class*, ch viii (1994)

Establishment, The. A term long used to denote in particular the established Church of England, but now a popular designation for the group or class of people who have authority within a society, especially, in Britain, those who control not only the Church of England but the government, the Civil Service and the armed forces. It has a somewhat derogatory significance associated with reaction, privilege and 'stuffiness'.

> By the 'Establishment' I do not mean only the centres of official power – though they are certainly part of it – but rather the whole matrix of official and social relations within which power is exercised.
> HENRY FAIRLIE in *Spectator* (23 September 1955)

Estádio da Luz. The home ground of the Portuguese football club Benfica, on the outskirts of Lisbon, where it was opened in 1954. The name happens to mean 'Stadium of Light' but actually derives from the suburb, Luz, in which the ground and its surrounding sports facilities are located. *See also* STADIUM OF LIGHT.

Estuary English. A type of English accent identified as spreading out from London to the southeast of England, the area of the Thames Estuary, and containing a blend of received (standard) pronunciation and that of Cockney or London speech. The term was coined in 1984 by the linguist David Rosewarne. The accent is regarded as typical of a supposedly growing classless society. *See also* MOCKNEY.

> In contrast with Eliza Doolittle, who had to re-engineer her accent to become socially acceptable, the prime minister [Tony Blair] descended into estuary English in an attempt to reach out to the masses.
> *Sunday Times* (7 June 1998)

E.T. The gentle but rather grotesque creature from outer space, which befriends the children of a Californian household in Steven Spielberg's SCIENCE FICTION fantasy film *E.T.: The Extra-Terrestrial* (1982). He comes to earth looking for plant specimens but is stranded. The children care for him, and he teaches them how to fly. He then devises equipment enabling him to phone home. He finally falls ill and apparently dies, but is reborn just before a spacecraft arrives to take him back. The sentimental story, which has a quasi-religious undertone, is curiously moving.

ETA. An armed Basque separatist organization that aims to create a Basque state made up of four northern Spanish provinces and parts of southwest France. It arose in 1959 from the Basque Nationalist Party and has bases in both France and Spain but since 1968 has made the Spanish side its main battleground. It has pursued a campaign of violence in various parts of Spain, but a plot to assassinate King Juan Carlos in 1995 was unsuccessful. It declared a unilateral cease-fire in 1998 but in 1999 restarted its campaign of bombings, shootings and kidnappings. The name is an acronym of Basque *Euzkadi ta Azkatasuna*, 'Basque homeland and liberty'.

Eternal triangle. The comic or tragic situation of the amorous involvement of one of a married couple with another member of the opposite sex. The phrase occurred as the title of a book review in the *Daily Chronicle* for 5 December 1907: 'Mrs. Dudeney's novel … deals with the eternal triangle, which, in this case, consists of two men and one woman.' 'Eternal' implies that the situation dates from times of old.

Ethical investment. Investment in companies that meet ethical criteria specified by the investor. Typical areas of exclusion are the arms industry, tobacco manufacture, trade with a country that operates an oppressive regime, as formerly South Africa in the days of APARTHEID, or with a country that damages or despoils the natural environment, as the rainforests of South America. The term is of US origin and arose in the early 1980s.

Ethnic cleansing. A euphemistic term for the mass expulsion or extermination of people from a minority ethnic group within a particular country or region. The phrase came to be particularly associated with the bitter fighting between Bosnian Serbs and Bosnian Muslims in the former Yugoslavia in the 1990s and with the mass expulsion by ethnic Serbs of ethnic Albanians from Kosovo in 1999.

> The discovery of a detailed Serb plan to drive ethnic Albanians out of Kosovo … shows that the blueprint for President Milosevic's ethnic cleansing was drawn up shortly before the Second World War.
> *The Times* (9 April 1999)

Eton crop. A short boyish hairstyle, fairly popular among English women in the 1920s, called after the boys at Eton College. The name was doubtless prompted by the Eton jacket, Eton collar and Eton suit, originally worn by the younger Eton boys but adopted and adapted for feminine wear before the First World War and returning to fashion after it.

> Sylvia was wearing Etons at Monckley's suggestion.
> COMPTON MACKENZIE: *Sylvia Scarlett*, I, ii (1918)

Etrog. An award presented annually since 1967 by the Canadian Film Awards Committee for film-making achievements. It is in the form of a gold-coated statuette mounted on a marble base and takes its name from the statuette's designer, the Romanian-born Canadian sculptor Sorel Etrog (b.1933).

E-type. A stylish model of Jaguar car launched in 1961. It became the instant motif of the SWINGING SIXTIES, attracting celebrity owners such as George Harrison of the BEATLES and the film actor Peter Sellers. It was produced until 1974 and although still sought after as a male dream car in the 1980s had generally declined as an object of desire by the close of the century, when even so speculation persisted about a revival.

The name evolved as a serial letter. The E-type was originally intended to be a racing replacement for the D-type of 1955-7, which in turn replaced the C-type, itself designed as a special racing two-seater for the 1951 LE MANS race. Because its engine and transmission were based on those of the XK120, the latter was originally called the XK120C, with C standing for 'Competition'. Enthusiasts began calling it the 'C-type', however, and the name stuck.

Eurhythmics (Greek, 'good rhythm'). A method of expressing the rhythmic aspects of music by physical movement, essentially a blend of dance and gymnastics. It was developed *c.*1905 by Émile Jaques-Dalcroze (1865-1950), a Swiss music teacher, composer and professor of harmony, who first applied it to schoolchildren. In 1910 he established an institute near Dresden in Germany and others followed in various European capitals and also in New York. The method still has its adherents and has influenced modern ballet and the dance of the theatre. Eurythmics was later familiar as the name of a highly successful British pop duo formed in 1980 by Annie Lennox and David Stewart.

Euro. The name of the single currency that in 1999 began to circulate alongside the national currencies of 11 countries (but not Britain) in the EUROPEAN UNION and that is due to replace those currencies in 2002. It was first minted as a coin by France in 1998.

Euroland. An American name for the EUROPEAN UNION as the 'superpower of the future'.

> The creation of the magic kingdom of Euroland feeds the kind of statistical comparison beloved of US opinion makers.
> *The Times* (11 May 1998)

European Pelé. The Portuguese footballer Eusébio Ferreira da Silva (b.1942). A star forward, he appeared for the Portuguese club Benfica during the 1960s and early 1970s. Eusébio was, in fact, African, and was born in Portuguese East Africa (now Mozambique).

European Union. The economic grouping of western European countries that evolved in 1993 from the old European Community (EC), itself incorporating (and alternatively known as) the European Economic Community (EEC), or Common Market, which itself came into being in 1958 following ratification of the Treaty of Rome. It originally consisted of Belgium, France, Federal Germany, Italy, Luxembourg and the Netherlands, collectively known as The SIX. These were joined by Britain, Denmark and Ireland in 1973, by Greece in 1981, by Spain and Portugal in 1986, by the former East Germany in 1990 and by Austria, Sweden and Finland in 1995. A single European currency is planned for 2002 with a complete replacement of national currencies by the EURO.

Europhile. Any person who is in favour of the EURO-PEAN UNION (EU) and of closer European integration. A Eurosceptic is any person who is generally sceptical about the benefits of EU membership, and about the desirability of closer European integration, while a Europhobe is completely hostile to all things relating to the EU, seeing the organization as a threat to national sovereignty and national identity. *See also* F-WORD.

Eurosceptic. *See* EUROPHILE.

Eurostar. The high-speed passenger service provided by the railways of Belgium, Britain and France to link London with Paris, Brussels and other cities via the CHANNEL TUNNEL. The service first operated in 1994, and the journey from Waterloo to Paris Nord takes about four hours.

Eurotrash. An epithet originally applied to rich foreigners living in the United States, especially those from titled or ancient families. The term was popularized and personally epitomized by the society writer Taki Theodoracopoulos ('Taki') (b.1937) in columns for *Vanity Fair* and the *Spectator*. By the 1990s, however, the word came to be used for any 'foreign-looking' person, such as one who spoke with a foreign accent, whose clothing was markedly different from the norm, who sported a deep tan, who frequented fashionable nightclubs, or who displayed un-British (or un-American) signs of affectation or preciousness. *Eurotrash* is also the title of a teasingly tasteless Channel 4 programme, introduced by Antoine de Caunes.

Eurovision Song Contest. This popular annual television event, in which a number of European countries compete for the best popular song of the year, was first seen on the Eurovision network in 1956, but Britain did not enter until 1957, when 10 countries took part. By the end of the century this figure had more than doubled. Each country awards points from 0 to 12 to the others, the results being announced in French and English. The ability of some countries to be awarded *nul points* (pseudo-French for *nul point*) is a frequent feature, and the disgrace has been particularly associated with Norway, whose song *Mil etter mil* ('Mile after Mile') in the 1978 contest failed to pick up a single vote. Although not in Europe, Israel participates by virtue of its membership of the European Broadcasting Union.

Eustace and Hilda. A novel (1947), and also the title of a trilogy of which it is the third part, by L.P. Hartley (1895–1972). The trilogy follows the course of the relationship between the sickly Eustace and

his elder sister, symbolically represented in the first book, *The Shrimp and the Anemone* (1944), when Hilda tears a shrimp from the grip of an anemone, killing the shrimp and disabling the anemone. The second volume, *The Sixth Heaven* (1946), continues their story, and at the end of the third novel, Eustace dies in his sleep, and Hilda, whom he has cured from psychosomatic paralysis after a disastrous affair, retires into a nunnery.

Euston Road School. A name coined in 1938 by the art writer Clive Bell for a group of British painters centred round the School of Drawing and Painting that opened in a studio at 12 Fitzroy Street, London, in 1937, soon transferring to nearby 316 Euston Road. Founding members were William Coldstream (1908–87), Victor Pasmore (1908–98) and Claude Rogers (1907–79). They advocated a move away from modernist styles to a more straightforward naturalism and laid stress on the training of observation in the teaching of art. *See also* FITZROVIA.

Evacuee. A person who has been moved from a place of danger to one of safety. The word first became familiar in Britain on the eve of the Second World War, when the government decided that more than 2 million children could be killed if left in the cities and organized their evacuation. Operation Pied Piper began at 7.30 p.m. on 1 September 1939, two days before war broke out. Children gathered at schools ready to be taken to the country, their parents equipping them with spare clothing, a toothbrush, comb, handkerchief, their gas mask and enough food for the day. Billeting was compulsory, and all evacuees were found homes within three days. Fosterers were often shocked by the poverty of their new charges, many of whom were lice-ridden and innocent of basic hygiene. Evacuation was voluntary, but over 3 million went.

Evans of the Broke. The byname of Admiral Edward Evans, 1st Baron Mountevans (1881-1957), famed in the First World War for defeating six German destroyers when in command of HMS *Broke*. The ship herself was named for Rear-Admiral Sir Philip Broke (1776–1841), a post captain commanding the frigate *Shannon* in a famous duel with the US frigate *Chesapeake* in 1813.

Eventide home. A euphemism for a home for the elderly, who are in the evening of their lives. In *My Commonplace Book* (1970) Baroness Stocks famously described the House of Lords as 'a perfect eventide home'.

Everage, Edna. Dame Edna Everage, a falsetto-voiced, larger-than-life Australian matron, with butterfly-winged spectacles, is the persona of the comedian Barry Humphries (b.1934). She (he) first appeared on television in the 1970s, and shocked a delighted audience by the way she alternately teased and insulted the star guests invited on her show. Her sidekick is Madge Allsop, a little woman who is as dour and dumb as Edna is cheery and chatty. Humphries was also the creator of the gross Sir Les PATTERSON.

Everyman Cinema. London's oldest repertory cinema, in Hollybush Vale, Hampstead. It specializes in double and triple bills of classic or cult films and opened in 1933 in the former Everyman Theatre here, established in 1919 and named for Ben Jonson's comedy *Every Man in His Humour* (1598).

Everyman's Library. This popular standard edition of reprints of masterpieces of world literature was first published by J.M. Dent in 1906. The first volume to appear was Boswell's *Life of Johnson*, originally published in 1791. The following words spoken by Knowledge in the 15th-century morality play *Everyman* were the inspiration for the name and appear in every volume:

> Everyman, I will go with thee, and be thy guide,
> In thy most need to go by thy side.

Everyone I Have Ever Slept With. A tent constructed by Britart *enfant terrible* Tracey Emin (b.1963), embroidered with the names of the 102 people she had ever shared a bed with. She followed this up with *My Bed*, featuring soiled sheets, empty vodka bottles and used condoms, which failed to win the 1999 TURNER PRIZE.

Every picture tells a story. An evocative truism popularized by the caption for an advertisement of 1904 for Doan's Backache Kidney Pills, showing a person bent over with pain. The phrase may have been current before this but has been put to good use ever since, as for the title of John Hadfield's illustrated commentary on a selection of Victorian paintings, published in 1985.

Everything but the kitchen sink. Everything imaginable. The expression apparently arose in the Second World War as a humorous reference to the varied uses to which different articles could be imaginatively put in times of need. A kitchen usually has the widest range of such objects, but the uses to which the sink can be put are limited, if only on account of its size and fixedness.

Everything in the garden is lovely. All is well. The catchphrase originated in a song of 1898 by John P. Harrington and George Le Brunn popularized in the early 20th century by Marie Lloyd.

Everything you always wanted to know about sex but were afraid to ask. This formulaic phrase, as the title of a book of 1970 by David Reuben, spawned a host of similar mesmeric strings and titles. Among the latter, of books published down to 1984, are the following:

> *Everything That Linguists Have Always Wanted to Know About Logic But Were Ashamed to Ask*
>
> *Everything You Always Wanted to Know About Drinking Problems And Then a Few Things You Didn't Want to Know*
>
> *Everything You Always Wanted to Know About Elementary Statistics But Were Afraid to Ask*
>
> *Everything You Always Wanted to Know About Mergers, Acquisitions and Divestitures But Didn't Know Whom to Ask*
>
> *Everything You Wanted to Know About Stars But Didn't Know Where to Ask*
>
> *Everything You Wanted to Know About the Catholic Church But Were Too Pious to Ask*
>
> *Everything You Wanted to Know About the Catholic Church But Were Too Weak to Ask*

Everywoman. A typical woman; the prototype of womanhood. The word arose in the 1960s as a variant of 'Everyman', the name of the hero of a 15th-century morality play.

> A political wife, in a sense, is a contradiction in terms … She must be the model of purity and probity at home, but she must be Everywoman outside, with a ready smile and a cheerful word for all the importuning bores on the campaign trail.
> *Time* (7 October 1974)

Evil Empire. A description of the Soviet Union coined by President Ronald Reagan, the GREAT COMMUNICATOR, in a speech to US evangelical church leaders in March 1983. The phrase, summing up the Manichaean approach to the COLD WAR of the American religious right, is assumed to have been drawn from the STAR WARS films, especially *The Empire Strikes Back* (1980). Earlier, in 1981, Reagan made an equally undiplomatic gaffe: while believing he was testing a radio microphone prior to a live broadcast he announced 'My fellow Americans, I have signed legislation to outlaw Russia for ever. We begin bombing in five minutes.' Unfortunately, he was on air. However, after 1985 Reagan found himself able to do business with the new Soviet leader, Mikhail Gorbachev, GORBY, as the Cold War drew to a close.

Evita. A musical (1978) with a score by Andrew Lloyd Webber (b.1948) and words by Tim Rice (b.1944) depicting the life and death of María Eva de Perón (1919–52), the wife of General Juan Perón, president of Argentina. Her sympathy with the poor, whom she called *los descamisados* ('the shirtless ones'), helped her husband to win the 1946 election, but after her death from cancer his popularity declined. Evita was her nickname, and the musical touches on her rise from being a minor actress and model to her death from cancer, when she was regarded as almost a saint and idolized by the poor. The film version (1996) starred Jonathan Pryce as Perón and Madonna as Evita, with Antonio Banderas as Che Guevara, taking the part of a Greek chorus.

Exclusion zone. A term dating from the 1970s for an area where an authority has banned a particular activity. The original application was to a maritime zone forbidden to enemy ships. The sense was then extended to an area out of bounds because a hazardous substance has been released, as at CHERNOBYL in 1986. Finally, the term was taken up for any generally 'unacceptable' area.

> If the card manufacturers are unwilling – for fashionable 'exclusion zone' reasons – to wish us 'A merry Christmas', why can't they at least hold out the prospect of 'A happy new year'?
> *The Times* (15 December 1999)

Executioner's Song, The. A 'true life' novel (1979) by Norman Mailer (b.1923), which won the PULITZER PRIZE for fiction. Gary Gilmore (1941–77) was paroled from prison in 1976 and immediately committed two murders. He was rearrested and demanded the death penalty, which was carried out by firing squad. He was the first person to be executed in the United States for more than 10 years. Mailer fashioned a narrative of the affair and a portrait of Gilmore from more than a thousand hours of taped interviews with those involved in the case and hundreds of pages of notes. The title recalls the quotation from John Donne: 'I am mine own executioner', from *Devotions Upon Emergent Occasions*, Meditation No. 17 (1624).

Exhibit A. The chief evidence; the prime proof. The allusion is to the first document or object, labelled 'A',

produced for the inspection of the court in a court case, or shown to a witness when giving evidence.

> My sister's Exhibit A for favouritism in our grown-up lives … is that my mother sent parcels of second-hand baby clothes to me when I had my children.
> *Sunday Times* (24 October 1999)

Exit. The popular name of the Voluntary Euthanasia Society, formed in 1935 by a group of doctors. Their purpose was to campaign for a change in the law so that doctors could legally help terminally ill patients who wanted to die. Suicide ceased to be illegal in Britain in 1961, but it remains a criminal offence to assist anyone to commit suicide. The society distributes a LIVING WILL. The whole subject of voluntary euthanasia remains highly controversial and continues to remain a topic of impassioned debate in the media.

Exocet. The British public first became aware of this French-made guided anti-ship missile in 1982 when it was launched by Argentina against British ships in the FALKLANDS WAR. Its name derives from Greek *ekokoitos*, 'fish that comes up on the beach' (literally 'out of bed'). Exocoetidae is the family name of the various species of flying fish, *Exocoetus volans* being one of the most widely distributed.

Exopotamia. A vast deserted country in Boris Vian's novel *L'Automne à Pékin* (1956). It can be reached (from Paris) in only two ways, either by train, ship, train and taxi successively, or by a 975 bus from the railway terminus. The climate of Exopotomia is mild, and the atmosphere is healthy owing to the complete lack of air. Its name, reminiscent of the ancient region of Mesopotamia in southwest Asia, indicates that it is 'outside the river'.

Exorcist, The. A notorious HORROR MOVIE (1973), directed by William Friedkin, about the satanic possession of a 12-year-old girl and the efforts of various priests to drive the Devil out of her body. The film, which provoked huge controversy at the time of its release, was based on a bestselling novel (1970) by William Peter Blatty, who also wrote the screenplay.

Experience. A BUZZWORD from the 1980s for a range of promotional ventures, especially those regarded as coming under the umbrella of HERITAGE. Thus Land's End has a trivializing display called the 'Land's End Experience', Whitby, North Yorkshire, has the 'Dracula Experience' as a sort of 'horror show', and for the MILLENNIUM London drew many to the 'Millennium Experience' by the Thames. In its issue for 27 August 1995 the *Observer* had an advertisement inviting readers to 'leave your worries and the traffic behind and enjoy the Cotswold Experience'. The fashion for the word may owe something to the Jimi Hendrix Experience, a 1960s rock group.

Expletive deleted. A US expression indicating the omission in a printed text of an obscene word or phrase. The term dates from the 1970s. Transcripts of President Nixon's testimony during the WATERGATE enquiry contain many editorial amendments using this annotation.

> To an outsider to the field of astronomy, the range of reactions to the term 'Janus', listed in many references as the 10th moon of Saturn, is often a bit of a shock. Responses range from acceptance to tolerant smiles to expletive deleted.
> *Science News* (29 January 1977)

Explore every avenue, To. To investigate every possibility; to try all ways of reaching a solution. The trees that line an avenue can conceal its course and one may need to explore several before finding the one that leads to the desired destination. The expression is first recorded in the 1920s and the issue of *Punch* for 2 December 1931 had a cartoon captioned: 'Fancy picture of an eminent politician in search of a formula, leaving no stone unturned while exploring every avenue.'

Expressionism. *See* BLAUE REITER, DER; BLAUE VIER, DIE; BRUCKE, DIE.

Extra-virgin. A commercial term for olive oil that is not only 'virgin', i.e. obtained from the first pressing of the olives, but 'extra', i.e. of an especially fine grade.

Extreme sport. A term coined in the early 1990s for any sport involving a high risk. Many extreme sports evolved as variants of already existing standard sports, examples being snowboarding (from skiing), sky-surfing (from parachuting), free climbing (without the aid of climbing devices) and barefoot water-skiing (without skis). Others, such as BUNGEE-JUMPING and ZORBING, arose independently. *See also* CANYONING.

Exxon Valdez. While leaving the port of Valdez, the terminus of the Alaskan oil pipeline, on 25 March 1989, the tanker of this name ran aground on a reef in Prince William Sound, holing her hull and releasing 238,000 barrels of crude oil into the sea. The resulting damage to the rich marine wildlife was considerable. The subarctic environment severely hampered clean-up operations and Exxon, the company responsible, was further criticized for its allegedly slow response to the disaster. The spillage was the worst in US history. *See also* TORREY CANYON.

Eyeball to eyeball. Face to face. The image is of two people staring aggressively at each another without either giving way. The expression is of US origin and dates from the 1950s.

Eye candy. A US term originating in the 1980s for visual images that are attractive and enjoyable but intellectually undemanding. The term has been applied to elegantly or scantily dressed women in advertisements and to various television programmes, notably scenically attractive ones such as BAYWATCH, which are both entertaining and EASY ON THE EYE. *See also* ARM CANDY.

Eye in the sky. A term for an electronic ground surveillance apparatus used in aircraft or artificial satellites. The name dates from the 1960s and while descriptively appropriate may have been suggested by PIE IN THE SKY.

Eyeless in Gaza. A novel (1936) by Aldous Huxley (1894–1963), in which some of the circumstances reflect those of the author; its writing heralded his final, philosophical phase, in which pacifism and mysticism are predominant influences. The novel's theme is that freedom without values is a form of blindness. It follows the journey of an able man, who is incapable of forming personal relationships, to self-discovery in the unlikely environment of a revolution in Mexico. The title is from *Samson Agonistes* (1671) by John Milton:

> Ask for this great deliverer now, and find him
> Eyeless in Gaza at the mill with slaves.

Eyes out on stalks. Eyes figuratively or even actually protruding through inquisitiveness, amazement, fear or other strong emotion or reaction. The allusion is to the eyes of a snail, which are at the end of retractable stalks and suggest alertness. The phrase dates from the 1930s.

> There was genuine shock at the amount of venom dripping from the page. It is not an exaggeration to say jaws hit the ground and eyes were out on stalks.
> *The Times* (13 December 1999)

F

Faber and Faber. In 1924 Geoffrey Faber (1889–1961) was invited to become chairman of the Scientific Press. The following year he established his own publishing firm of Faber and Gwyer, the latter name representing the original owners of the Scientific Press. In 1929 the firm was reconstituted under its present name, the Gwyer interest being entirely withdrawn. The second Faber was fictional, and rumour has it that the repetition of the name was suggested by the writer Walter de la Mare, father of Richard de la Mere, one of the original directors, 'because you can't have too much of a good thing!'

> So if you 'ave business with Faber – or Faber –
> I'll give you this tip, and it's worth a lot more:
> You'll save yourself time, and you'll spare yourself
>   labour
> If jist you make friends with the Cat at the door.
> T.S. ELIOT: *Old Possum's Book of Practical Cats*, 'Cat Morgan Introduces Himself' (1939)

Fab Four. A nickname for the BEATLES at the height of their fame in the 1960s. 'Fab' is 'fabulous'.

Façade. The series of technically brilliant, supposedly avant-garde but fundamentally facile poems by Edith Sitwell (1887–1964), which are intended to be recited to music by William Walton (1902–83). The first performance was in 1923, but considerable revisions and rearrangements followed. A few lines will suffice to give a taste of the fun:

> When
> Sir
> Beelzebub called for his syllabub in the hotel in Hell
>   Where Proserpine first fell ...

Face fits. If one's face fits a situation figuratively one is judged as being suitable for it. The expression typically relates to a job application or interview. The idea is that that one's credentials or qualifications are acceptable but that one needs to complete the picture with the right 'image'.

> The only safe way to make sure that your face fits the bill is being a defendant in a television soap trial.
> *The Times* (12 October 1999)

Face lift. An operation by COSMETIC SURGERY to smooth out wrinkles and lift sagging skin on an ageing face to make it look younger. It is commonest among women and produces a result that usually lasts about five years, when it may need to be repeated.

Factor. A vogue word from the 1980s for any influential force or agent, beginning with the FALKLANDS FACTOR, whose alliterative appeal may have encouraged similar coinings. *See also* FEEL-GOOD FACTOR; FUDGE FACTOR; KRYPTON FACTOR; SLEAZE FACTOR.

Fag hag. A slighting term of US origin dating from the 1960s for a heterosexual woman ('hag') who prefers or seeks out the company of a homosexual man ('fag').

Fahrenheit 451. A fantasy of the near future by Ray Bradbury (b.1920), it was the author's first published novel, appearing in 1953. The theme is the triumph of the imagination under the threat of obliteration, and in particular the destruction by fire of all books. The title represents the temperature at which book paper is said to ignite and burn. Dissidents respond by memorizing the texts. A suitably futuristic film version (1966) was directed by François Truffaut.

Fail-safe. A seemingly oxymoronic term that arose in aeronautical jargon of the 1940s to apply to a mechanism that can revert to a safe condition in the event of breakdown. In the COLD WAR the term was extended to apply to precautions and procedures agreed beforehand to ensure against escalation to a nuclear war. More recently the expression has found wider application.

> The Prime Minister was looking at proposals … to toughen the so-called 'fail-safe' mechanisms to ensure that Sinn Fein does not continue in government if the IRA fails to disarm.
>
> *The Times* (14 July 1999)

Fair crack of the whip. A reasonable chance to attempt something or prove oneself. The allusion is to having a chance to drive a horse-drawn vehicle. The expression dates from the 1920s and is first recorded in Australia.

Fair Deal. The liberal domestic reform programme of US President Harry S. Truman, originally outlined by him as early as 1945. In his first postwar message to Congress that year, Truman called for expanded social security, new legislation on working hours and wages and a permanent Fair Employment Practices Act that would prevent racial or religious discrimination in the engagement of workers. Congress paid little attention at the time but the following year did pass the Employment Act, clearly stating the government's responsiblity for maintaining full employment and establishing a Council of Economic Advisers to help assure a continuing healthy national economy. Truman reasserted his reform proposals in 1949 under the catchphrase, but Congress agreed to legislation on only some of his recommendations.

Fairies at the bottom of the garden. Said of anything seemingly ideal or idyllic, especially of a place to live or stay. The phrase comes from the opening line of Rose Fyleman's best known poem 'The Fairies' (1918): 'There are fairies at the bottom of our garden!'

> We imagined we were in the money. Mortgage sorted, deposit in the bank, fairies at the bottom of the garden. So sweet, so naive, so stupid.
>
> *The Times* (4 December 1999)

Fairy cycle. A type of small-wheeled low bicycle for children, first seen in the 1920s. Its small size and 'dinkiness' suggested the fancy that it might have been made for fairies to ride, just as a fairy cake is a small cake and fairy lights are small coloured lights.

Fairy godmother. Originally, in Victorian children's stories, a fairy who becomes godmother to a mortal child. The term was subsequently applied to a benefactress of any kind, especially a longed-for one.

If the proverbial fairy godmother could wave a wand,

he says, he [comedian Rainer Hersch] would still choose to make a career as a concert pianist.

The Times (27 December 1999)

Fakes. The difference between a fake and a forgery is a fine one. Generally speaking a fake is a thing that is not genuine, whether its perpetrator intended to deceive or not, whereas a forgery is an attempt to pass off as genuine some piece of spurious work or writing with the intent to deceive or defraud. All the following are 20th-century fakes or hoaxes, although some are more patently forgeries. *See also* ANGRY PENGUINS; FALSE MEMORY SYNDROME.

Amityville Horror. A sensational case of an alleged diabolical presence in a house at Amityville, Long Island, New York. The Lutz family of five moved into a large Dutch colonial house in Amityville on 18 December 1975, undisturbed by the report that it had been the scene of a mass murder the previous year. They were soon subjected to a series of ghostly apparitions and other evil manifestations, forcing them to flee on 14 January 1976. A lurid account of their experiences was published by Jay Anson as *The Amityville Horror* in 1977, becoming an instant bestseller and spawning a top-grossing film of 1979 as well as a host of similar stories and movies based on the theme of a possessed house. It eventually emerged that the Lutzes had fabricated the whole ghoulish scenario with a view to having a book published and reaping the reward of the ensuing publicity. The case resulted in a string of lawsuits.

Borley Rectory. The rectory at Borley, Essex, near the Suffolk border, was the subject of an exhaustive series of 'ghost hunts' conducted between 1929 and 1938 by Harry Price, founder of the National Laboratory of Psychical Research. The manifestations were supposedly in the form of poltergeist activity, with interest in the phenomena first fuelled by the *Daily Mail*. Price himself stayed at the rectory for a year from 1937 and assiduously documented his investigations using remote-control cine-cameras, still cameras, fingerprinting paraphernalia and other equipment. The rectory burned down in 1939 and the following year Price published his sensational account *The Most Haunted House in England*. Critics pointed out, however, that the incumbents of the rectory had not reported any unusual incidents, and Price was accused of having faked or fabricated them. Legends of the hauntings lingered even so, and the site continues to draw the curious.

Cottingley fairies. In 1917 two little girls living at Bingley, Yorkshire, Elsie Wright and her cousin Frances, claimed they had seen fairies in nearby Cottingley Dell and said they had even taken photographs of them. The story came to the attention of Sir Arthur Conan Doyle, by then a convert to spiritualism. He believed the girls and vouched for the veracity of the photographs, even taking lantern slides made from them to America as part of a lecture tour. In 1983 Frances Griffiths, now aged 76, admitted that the pictures had been faked by photographing cut-outs of fairies from *Princess Mary's Gift Book*, a popular children's book. Two films have recreated the events, the British-made *Photographing Fairies* (1997) and the US *Fairytale: A True Story* (1997), the former on a more philosophical plane than the latter.

Drake brass plate. Sir Francis Drake, during his voyage of circumnavigation (1577–80), anchored off the Californian coast in 1579 and set up a brass plate naming the territory New Albion and claiming it in the name of Queen Elizabeth I. In 1936 the plate was said to have been found near San Francisco and the inscription seemed to be reasonably authentic, although some authorities expressed doubt. A replica was, in due course, presented to Queen Elizabeth II, which is kept in Buckland Abbey, Drake's Devonshire property, now a museum. In 1977 a reported analysis of the composition of the brass by the Lawrence Berkeley Institute of the University of California and the Research Laboratory for Archaeology at Oxford found that it was of late 19th- or early 20th-century manufacture.

Hitler diaries. In April 1983 the *Sunday Times* reported the discovery of 60 volumes of Hitler's diaries, which had been acquired by the Hamburg magazine *Stern* for £2,460,000 and delivered to them by their reporter Gerd Heidemann. They were said to have been salvaged from an aircraft wrecked in 1945 and found in a hayloft. Professor Hugh Trevor-Roper (Lord Dacre) had vouched for their authenticity and the *Sunday Times* (after paying *Stern* for publication rights) obtained two volumes (1932 and 1935) for testing. Dr Julius Grant, a chemical expert, proved that the paper in the diaries was not in use until after the Second World War. Two weeks after their alleged discovery the Bonn government also declared them to be forgeries. Heidemann revealed that he had obtained them from a Stuttgart dealer in military relics, Peter Fischer, real name Konrad Kujau, and the latter confessed to forgery. Both were imprisoned in May 1983, brought to trial in August 1984 and sentenced in July 1985. Kujau was jailed for 4 years 6 months for forgery and Heidemann for 4 years 8 months for fraud. A black television comedy based on the hoax, *Selling Hitler*, based on Robert Harris's book of the same title (1987), was screened in 1991.

Piltdown man. In 1908 and 1911 Charles Dawson of Lewes, Sussex, 'found' two pieces of a highly mineralized human skull in a gravel bed at Piltdown near Lewes. By 1912 he and Sir Arthur Smith Woodward had discovered the whole skull. This was thought to be that of a new genus of man and was called *Eoanthropus dawsoni*. It came to be accepted as such by prehistorians, archaeologists and others, although a few were sceptical. In 1953 J.S. Weiner, K.P. Oakley and W.E. Le Gros Clark issued a report (*Bulletin of the British Museum* (Natural History), Vol II, No. 3) announcing that the Piltdown mandible was a fake, in reality the jaw of a modern ape, the rest of the skull being that of *Homo sapiens*. The hoax, which duped most of the experts, was apparently planned by William Sollas, Professor of Geology at Oxford, through his dislike of Woodward.

Protocols of the Elders of Zion. Forged material published by Serge Nilus in Russia in 1905 and based on an earlier forgery of 1903, purporting to outline secret Jewish plans for achieving world power by undermining Gentile morality, family life and health and by securing a monopoly in international finance, among other things. Their falsity was first exposed by Philip Graves, *The Times* correspondent in Constantinople, in 1921 and later judicially, at Berne (1934–5). Their influence in inciting anti-Semitism, notably among the Russians, and later providing Hitler and his associates with an excuse they knew to be a myth, provide tragic evidence of the power of the BIG LIE.

Tom Keating's pictures. Keating (1918–84), beginning as a picture restorer, produced about 2000 drawings and paintings and sold them as originals by Samuel Palmer (1805–81) and other English artists. He admitted his works were fakes in 1976, and in the last years of his life enjoyed brief fame on television as an expert on painting generally and Impressionism in particular.

Turin Shroud. The shroud of twill linen kept in Turin Cathedral since 1578 and claimed to be the one in which the body of Christ was wrapped after the crucifixion. The pope agreed to RADIOCARBON DATING in 1987, and in 1988 the archbishop of Turin appointed the Oxford Research Laboratory for Archaeology, the

Department of Physics of Arizona University and the Swiss Federal Institute of Technology at Zurich to date the shroud, pieces of which were given to these institutes in April 1988. The results were announced on 13 October and the cloth was dated to the 14th century. There is no firm historical evidence that it was known earlier than this. Although not accepted by all, the general conclusion is that the shroud is a medieval fake.

Vermeer forgeries. Hans (Henri) van Meegeren (1889–1947) began his series of brilliant fakes of Dutch masters in 1937 with *Christ at Emmaus*, which was sold as a 'Vermeer' for 550,000 gulden. Experts duly acclaimed it. His intention seems to have been to indulge his contempt and hatred of the art critics by a superlative hoax, but the financial success of his first fake led to others, mostly 'Vermeers'. Discovery came only in 1945 when Allied commissioners were seeking to restore to their former owners the art treasures that had found their way to Germany during the Second World War. Among Goering's collection was an unknown Vermeer, *The Woman taken in Adultery*, and its original vendor was found to be van Meegeren. Sale of such a work of national importance involved a charge of collaboration with the enemy. To escape the heavy penalty, van Meegeren confessed to faking 14 Dutch masterpieces, nine of which had been sold for a total of 7,167,000 gulden, and to prove his story agreed to paint another 'old masterpiece' in prison in the presence of the experts. He was sentenced to one year's imprisonment in October 1947 but died on 30 December.

Vinland Map. In *c.*1000 the Norse explorer Leif Eriksson visited and named an area of wooded land in North America. According to the Norse Saga, *Flateyjarbók*: 'When spring came they made ready and left, and Leif named the land after its fruits, and called it Vinland.' In 1957 the discovery of a map of the northeast American coast was announced and said to be the most exciting cartographic find of the century. Supposedly drawn *c.*1440, it substantially preceded the voyages of Columbus (1492) and of John Cabot (1497), thus conclusively establishing the extent of the Viking explorations. It was presented to Yale University by an anonymous donor in 1965. In 1974 Yale announced that it was a fake. The pigment of the ink with which it was drawn was found to contain titanium dioxide, first used in the 1920s.

Zinoviev Letter. A letter purportedly signed by the Russian Communist leader Grigory Zinoviev

(1883–1936), president of the COMINTERN. It summoned the British Communist Party to intensify its revolutionary activities and to subvert the armed forces, and after being leaked to the *Daily Mail* it was published on 25 October 1924, four days before a general election. It helped to promote a 'red scare' and contributed to the fall of Ramsay MacDonald's first Labour government. Many Labour leaders held it to be a forgery, and its authenticity was denied by the Russians. In December 1966 the *Sunday Times* published an article establishing that the letter was a forgery perpetrated by a group of WHITE RUSSIAN *émigrés*. At the same time it was suggested that certain leaders at the Conservative Central Office knew that it was a fake, although the Conservative party as a whole assumed it to be genuine. The 'informant' was paid for his services. The letter itself, headed 'VERY SECRET' and dated 15 September 1924, had the following opening paragraph:

> Dear Comrades, The time is approaching for the Parliament of England to consider the Treaty concluded between the Governments of Great Britain and the S.S.S.R. [sic] for the purpose of ratification. The fierce campaign raised by the British bourgeoisie around the question shows that the majority of the same, together with reactionary circles, are against the Treaty for the purpose of breaking off an agreement consolidating the ties between the proletariats of the two countries leading to the restoration of normal relations between England and the S.S.S.R.

Falange (Spanish, 'phalanx'). At first the title of a right-wing party in Spain formed in 1933 by José Antonio Primo de Rivera (1903–36) to uphold his father's memory against republican criticism but later adopted by General Franco as the name of the one official party in the state. It basically represented a combination of European FASCISM and Spanish nationalism and was used to counterbalance royalist, army and church influence. In 1937 it forced the Carlists to join with it. The Falange lost its unique position after the CAUDILLO's death in 1975 and was formally disbanded in 1977.

In Lebanon, the 'Phalange' is a right-wing Christian militia, the political and military force of the Maronite Christian Church in Lebanon, formed in 1936 on the model of Franco's movement. The resistance of the Phalange to the introduction of democratic institutions in Lebanon contributed greatly to that country's civil war (1975–90). *See also* BEIRUT.

Falklands factor. The effect of the FALKLANDS WAR on the popularity of political parties, and in particular the electoral impetus it was believed to give to Margaret Thatcher and her Conservative administration, which had previously been experiencing a period of unpopularity.

Falklands War. A brief and in many eyes needless armed conflict between Britain and Argentina in 1982. It was sparked off when General Galtieri's military junta sent Argentinian forces to invade the Falkland Islands, a British Crown Colony in the South Atlantic, in support of Argentina's claim to sovereignty. (The Argentinians know the islands as the Malvinas.) In response Britain sent a TASK FORCE of ships and aircraft, which forced the Argentinians to surrender six weeks after its arrival. Major losses included Argentina's only cruiser, the GENERAL BELGRANO, with the loss of 362 lives, and Britain's HMS *Sheffield*, sunk by an EXOCET, with a loss of 21. The overall death toll was 652 on the Argentinian side and 255 on the British. *See also* GOTCHA!

Fall about, To. To collapse in laughter. The expression is of US origin and dates from the 1960s.

> 'Eastern audiences tend to fall about at every mention of cheese. They just think it is ludicrously funny stuff to think of eating.'
> *The Times* (17 August 1999)

Fall apart at the seams. *See* COME APART AT THE SEAMS.

Fall guy. A person who readily falls for a trick; a sucker; a scapegoat.

Fall off the back of a lorry, To. Said of stolen goods or of something acquired fortuitously or by somewhat dubious means. The allusion is to the traditional bogus excuse given to the police by someone caught in possession of stolen goods.

> On the pavement in front of every shop are stalls offering exactly what the shop behind them sells. Their goods are all off the back of a lorry and they are in business for themselves.
> *The Times* (31 May 1999)

Fall off the wagon, To. To resume drinking after a period of abstinence ON THE WAGON.

Fall on one's sword, To. To commit metaphorical suicide; to step down from a post. The phrase is curiously absent from dictionaries and the *Oxford English Dictionary* has only the literal sense, as in the biblical original: 'Then said Saul unto his armourbearer, Draw thy sword, and thrust me through therewith. ... But

his armourbearer would not; for he was sore afraid. Therefore Saul took a sword, and fell upon it. And when his armourbearer saw that Saul was dead, he fell likewise upon his sword, and died with him' (1 Samuel 31:4–5).

> Yesterday's [Cabinet] reshuffle tipped the balance to those who believe in Mr Blair's project. ... [Minister for the Cabinet Office] Jack Cunningham, with due decency, fell on his sword.
> *The Times* (12 October 1999)

Fallout. The descent of radioactive dust from a nuclear explosion. Figuratively, fallout is used of the secondary consequences of some action.

Falls Road. An almost exclusively Catholic working-class street of industrial west Belfast in Northern Ireland. A potent element, like the nearby Protestant SHANKILL ROAD, in the sectarian geography of the city, during the TROUBLES 'the Falls', the road and its adjacent streets, became synonymous with hard-line republicanism. The Divis Flats, a flashpoint in the early years of the Troubles, lie in the 'Lower Falls', at its eastern end. *See also* BOGSIDE.

False memory syndrome. A term, often abbreviated FMS, that came into use in the 1990s following many cases in which individuals 'recall' child or adult sexual abuse or ritual satanic abuse that has not actually taken place. Such 'memories' have been coaxed out of children or those accused of abusing children by over-eager therapists or prosecutors, with the result that many lives have been blighted, not least those of parents, falsely implicated by their adult children. Cases of FMS first came to light in the United States in the late 1980s, when 22-year-old Ericka Ingram, of East Olympia, Washington, was obliged to 'admit' that she had been abused as a child by her father, an accusation supposedly supported by her 18-year-old sister, Julie, who 'evidenced' tales of satanic rituals involving their family and their father's friends. In 1993 Robert Kelly, of Edenton, North Carolina, was found guilty of some of the 183 charges of satanic paedophilia he was accused of committing at his day-care centre, despite the fact that some of the tales involved children being microwaved or thrown into tanks full of ravenous sharks. Most of the accusations came from stay-at-home mothers, and no one visiting the centre had ever noticed anything unusual. That same year 35-year-old Peter Ellis, of New Zealand, was accused of abusing over 50 young children at a similar centre. Much of the children's evidence was shown to be patently false, but Ellis was found 'guilty' of sexual violation and indecent assault and jailed for 10 years. The whole murky phenomenon subsequently surfaced in Britain, where in 1996 a man was acquitted of sexually abusing a woman thanks to psychological assessments concluding that the plaintiff was probably suffering from FMS, and that her 'memories' had in fact been suggested by story lines in television dramas.

Falun Gong. A Chinese method of spiritual healing introduced by Li Hongzhi (b.1951) in China in 1992. It is based on the ancient mystical and healing principles of *qigong* (literally 'energy exercise') said to balance and enhance the body's *qi* or energy force and takes its name from the *falun* ('law wheel'), a wheel of energy believed to revolve continuously inside the lower abdomen of its practitioners, who are exhorted to abstain from such 'vices' as homosexuality, premarital sex and even marital sex unless for procreation, as well as alcohol and tobacco. Its bible, written by its founder, is *Zhuan Falun* ('Rotating the Law Wheel'). In 1999 the Chinese government outlawed Falun Gong as an 'evil and dangerous cult' and issued a warrant for the arrest of Li, by then living in New York, on a charge of disruption of public order and conspiring to undermine the country's communist hegemony, a crime that carries the death penalty.

Family Favourites. A popular weekly record request show on the BBC's Light Programme linking London with the British Forces Network in Germany. *Family Favourites* began in 1945 and went out for an hour at Sunday lunchtime, thereby becoming intimately associated with the aroma of roast meat and gravy wafting from the kitchen. The programme was presented by Jean Metcalfe in London and Cliff Michelmore in Germany, but the two did not meet until 1949. They married the following year. The title became *Two-Way Family Favourites* in 1960 and the programme continued until 1984.

Family from One End Street, The. A children's novel (1937) by the British author Eve Garnett (1900–91) recounting the adventures of the working-class Ruggles family who live at No. 1, One End Street in the fictional Midlands town of Otwell. It was one of the first children's novels to describe the lives of working-class children but has since been criticized for its allegedly patronizing attitudes. The Ruggles family also appear in *Further Adventures of the Family from One End Street* (1956) and *Holiday at the Dew Drop Inn* (1962).

Family hour. A US term for a television viewing period, usually from 7 p.m. to 9 p.m., when programmes containing excessive violence or explicit sexual material are barred and only programmes suitable for family viewing are shown. In British terms this generally equates to viewing time before the WATERSHED.

Family jewels. (1) A euphemism dating from the 1960s for the male genitalia, as the precious means of generating a new family.

(2) In the world of US espionage the Family Jewels was the nickname of a list of illegal activities carried out by the Central Intelligence Agency (*see* CIA). It was compiled at the direction of James Schlesinger in 1973, appointed head of the CIA in the wake of the WATERGATE scandal, and first went to William E. Colby, Schlesinger's successor. The preliminary summary was called 'Potential Flap Activities', and the CIA's director of security, passing his files to the inspector general for inclusion in the report, jokingly called them 'the Family Jewels'. The name caught on and was soon applied to the entire list.

Family newspaper. Any regular newspaper regarded as an unsuitable medium for explicit sexual language. In some cases the phrase is introduced expressly to titillate the prurient reader.

> The neurotic nature of the British can be seen in the colourful lexicon we've developed to cope with bodily functions. … New to me this month is the gay phrase 'taking a trip up Shaftesbury Avenue' and (for women only) 'riding the cotton pony'. This is a family newspaper. You work it out.
> *Evening Standard* (27 September 1999)

Family Reunion, The. A poetic drama (1939) by the Anglo-American poet and playwright T.S. Eliot (1888–1965) about a husband's sense of guilt over his wife's mysterious death. The play was based upon the *Oresteia* of Aeschylus.

Family values. A catch-all phrase for social conservatism, chiefly embodying a range of 'anti-' attitudes, such as opposition to abortion, gay rights, feminism and sexual permissiveness. In many ways the term has become the antonym of ALTERNATIVE.

Famous Five. (1) The four children and their dog who have unlikely adventures at various holiday locations around Britain in the novels of Enid Blyton (1897–1968). They are the two brothers Julian and Dick, their sister, Anne, and their tomboy cousin Georgina, known as 'George', together with the mongrel dog

Timmy. They first appeared in *Five on a Treasure Island* (1942) and continued their exploits in a further 20 volumes, all with a title beginning *Five*. The tales were the inspiration for television farces in the *Comic Strip Presents* ... series of the 1980s, the first being *Five Go Mad in Dorset* (1982). *See also* SECRET SEVEN.

(2) There are popularly said to be only five famous Norwegians: the composer Edvard Grieg (1843–1907), the playwright Henrik Ibsen (1828–1906), the explorer Fridtjof Nansen (1861–1930), the writer Knut Hamsun (1859–1952) and the traitor Vidkun QUISLING.

Famous for 15 minutes. Enjoying a brief period of fame before slipping back into obscurity. The expression comes from a remark made by the US artist Andy Warhol: 'In the future everybody will be world famous for 15 minutes' (*Andy Warhol*, 1968). Brief celebrity is thus sometimes referred to as '15 minutes of fame'. In 1988 BBC Radio 4 presented a series entitled *Famous for Fifteen Minutes* in which people who had tasted instant fame spoke of its effect on their lives and the obscurity to which they mostly returned. The first interviewee was Erika Roe, a Hampshire second-hand bookshop assistant, who became a sensation overnight when she ran topless across the pitch at Twickenham during a rugby international in 1982 (*see* STREAKING). She revealed that she had earned only £8000 during the whole six-year period from her fame and that she was now living on social security.

> A must is the Valley of the Geysers, Kamchatka's party piece, where Costa achieved his 15 minutes of fame as Michael Palin's interpreter during the *Full Circle* TV series.
>
> *The Times* (18 December 1999)

Famous last words. A phrase now used as an ironical or facetious comment on an over-confident statement that may well be proved wrong by events, as: 'I'm bound to pass my driving test first time – famous last words!' Many 'famous last words' in the sense of dying utterances are either apocryphal or have survived in inaccurate versions. The following, spoken or written at or shortly before the named person's death, are among the more noteworthy of the 20th century:

William S. Burroughs (1914–97; US writer): 'Love? What is it? Most natural painkiller. What there is ... love.'

Edith Cavell (1865–1915; English nurse) before facing the German firing party: 'Patriotism is not enough. I must have no hatred or bitterness towards anyone.'

Anton Chekhov (1860–1904; Russian dramatist and short story writer): 'It's been so long since I've had champagne.'

Erskine Childers (1870–1922; Anglo-Irish writer and nationalist) to the firing squad at his execution: 'Come closer, boys. It will be easier for you.'

Stephen Crane (1871–1900; US writer): 'When you come to the hedge that we must all go over, it isn't so bad. You feel sleepy, you don't care. Just a little dreamy anxiety, which world you're really in, that's all.'

Isadora Duncan (1877–1927; US dancer) uttered in French when her shawl caught in a car wheel in Nice, breaking her neck: 'Farewell, my friends, I go to glory.'

Kathleen Ferrier (1912–53; English contralto): 'Now I'll have eine kleine Pause.'

Charles Frohman (1860–1915; US theatre manager) before drowning in the *Lusitania*: 'Why fear death? It is the most beautiful adventure in life.'

George V (1865–1936; king of Britain) to his private secretary on the morning of his death: 'How's the Empire?'

O. Henry (1862–1910; US author; real name William Sydney Porter): 'Turn up the lights. I don't want to go home in the dark.'

Timothy Leary (1920–96; US drug-culture GURU): 'Why not, why not, why not. Yeah.'

Katherine Mansfield (1888–1923; British writer): 'I believe ... I'm going to die. I love the rain. I want the feeling of it on my face.'

Lawrence Oates (1880–1912; English polar explorer): 'I am just going outside and may be some time.'

Sylvia Plath (1932–63; US poet) in the opening lines of her last poem, written a week before her suicide: 'The woman is perfected/Her dead/Body wears the smile of accomplishment.'

Dennis Potter (1935–94; English dramatist) in the face of imminent death from cancer: 'The nowness of everything is absolutely wondrous.'

Alan Pryce-Jones (1908–2000; English editor and conversationalist): 'What are they saying?'

Cecil John Rhodes (1853–1902; British colonial administrator): 'So little done, so much to do.'

Ken Saro-Wiwa (1941–95; Nigerian writer and minority rights activist) when about to be hanged: 'Lord take my soul, but the struggle continues.'

Robert Falcon Scott (1868–1912; English polar

explorer) in his last diary entry: 'For God's sake look after our people.'

Lytton Strachey (1880–1932; English writer): 'If this is dying, then I don't think much of it.'

Queen Victoria (1819–1901; queen of Britain) referring to the Boer War then in progress: 'Oh, that peace may come.'

Sergei Yesenin (Russian poet; 1895–1925) writing in his own blood the day before he hanged himself: 'In this life there's nothing new in dying,/But nor, of course, is living any newer.'

Fan club. An organization catering for the admirers of a celebrity, usually one in a field such as the cinema or pop music. Devotees send their adulatory comments and requests to a given address, where they may or may not be passed on and replied to by the idol in question. In modern times most such 'celebs' have their individual web site on the INTERNET. The first fan club is generally reckoned to be the Keen Order of Wallerites, founded in London in 1902 for fans of the popular actor-manager Lewis Waller (1860–1916). Members wore a badge showing on one side Waller in a powdered wig as Monsieur Beaucaire and on the other his favourite flower, a pansy.

Fancy dress. A fanciful costume put on when masquerading as a different person or as an animal. Fancy dress plays a popular part in children's parties and adults readily don it to raise money for charity at fêtes and the like.

> More than 40 volunteers marked the [sick] boy's birthday by abseiling down the City Hospital in fancy dress. The organizers hope the stunt will have raised money for a physiotherapy and exercise room for Jack.
>
> *Ceefax, BBC East Midlands* (12 December 1998)

Fannie Mae. An acronym based on the name of the Federal National Mortgage Association, set up by the US government in 1938 to trade in mortgages. It is now privately owned. *See also* FREDDIE MAC; GINNIE MAE.

Fanny. The heroine of a trilogy of plays by Marcel Pagnol (1895–1974). They are set in Marseilles, where Fanny is abandoned by her lover, Marius, when he goes to sea. She goes on to marry another, much older man in order to provide her child with a father. The three plays were made into successful French films: *Marius* (1931), *Fanny* (1932) and *César* (1935).

Fantasia. An animated film (1940) produced by Walt Disney to the music of Bach, Tchaikovsky, Stravinsky, Mussorgsky, Ponchielli, Schubert, Beethoven and Paul Dukas. The project was acclaimed for its ambitious scope, if not for the kitschy nature of many of the images, but in reality the film was not originally intended to be of feature length. Disney's original project was to render an animated version of 'The Sorcerer's Apprentice', with Leopold Stokowski conducting Dukas's music and MICKEY MOUSE as the over-ambitious apprentice, but when this went badly over-budget, Disney realized the only way to get his money back was to make it part of a full-length work. The sorcerer's name is Yen Sid.

Fantastic realism. A style of painting that developed in Vienna in the late 1940s. Its adherents, mainly pupils of Albert Paris von Gütersloh (1887–1973), depicted a fairy-tale world of fantasy and imagination with minute detail, the paintings themselves often being literary and anecdotal by nature. The best known representative of the genre is Ernst Fuchs (b.1930).

Fantasy football. A competition in which entrants select imaginary teams of real football players in an actual league and score points according to the actual performance of the players selected. The concept arose in the United States in the 1980s using American football players, but it soon spread across the Atlantic to British soccer teams. The *Daily Telegraph* was the first national newspaper to publish a fantasy football league, and its first season, in 1993, attracted around 300,000 entries. The contest has since been extended to other sports, such as cricket and basketball.

Fantippo. A fictional kingdom in West Africa in Hugh Lofting's children's novels *Doctor Dolittle's Post Office* (1923) and *Doctor Dolittle and the Secret Lake* (1948). Its capital, of the same name, is a bright and cheerful city at the mouth of the Little Fantippo River. The country itself is remarkable for two things: its postal system and its celebration of Christmas. The postal system, introduced by King Koko, at first failed to work because people believed in the magical power of the stamps and did not see the need for postmen. The problem was dealt with by Dr DOLITTLE, and the celebration of Christmas was a direct result of the re-organization of the postal services, which introduced a delivery of presents at this season.

Fantomas. A French master criminal who turns over a new leaf and decides to use his skills for good causes instead of bad. He first appears in the novel (1911) named after him by Pierre Souvestre and Marcel

Allain. His fame became international when he was played by René Navarre in 1913 in a series of silent films, and there have been various comic books and strips starring him. His name is based on French *fantôme*, 'phantom', 'ghost'.

FAQ. In computing jargon the abbreviation or acronym of 'frequently asked questions', as a text file containing a list of questions and answers relating to a particular subject, especially one that gives basic information for users of an INTERNET newsgroup (a group of users who exchange E-MAIL messages on a topic of mutual interest). The term dates from the early 1990s.

Farewell, My Lovely. A crime novel (1940) by Raymond Chandler (1888–1959), of which the theme is police corruption. He originally intended it to be called 'The Second Murderer' from Shakespeare's *Richard III*, in which that character, after showing some reluctance to carry out his commission, steels himself: 'Zounds, he dies: I had forgot the reward.' After his publisher had rejected this title and the author's second choice, 'Zounds, He Dies', Chandler settled for *Farewell, My Lovely*, referring to the suicide of a character who has caused his hero, Philip MARLOWE, a great deal of trouble. It was made into a masterful FILM NOIR (1944), directed by Edward Dmytryk and with Dick Powell as Marlowe. A remake (1975), with Robert Mitchum as Marlowe, was tightly directed by Dick Richards.

Fascism. Originally an Italian political movement, taking its name from the old Roman *fasces*, a bundle of rods with a projecting axe blade carried by a lictor as a symbol of a magistrate's power. It was founded in 1919 by Benito Mussolini (1883–1945), who took advantage of the discontent in Italy after the First World War to form a totalitarian nationalist party against left-wing radicalism and socialism. In 1922 the Fascists marched on Rome and demanded power, and Victor Emmanuel III made Mussolini prime minister. He styled himself DUCE (leader) and made himself dictator in 1925, suppressing all other political parties the following year. The Fascists controlled Italy until 1943. The term soon came to be applied to similar totalitarian movements in other countries. Ruthlessness, inhumanity and dishonest and disreputable practices were notable characteristics of its adherents. *See also* FÜHRER; HITLERISM; MARCH ON ROME; NAZI.

Benito Mussolini provided Italy with a new theme of government which, while it claimed to save the Italian people from Communism, raised himself to dictatorial power. As Fascism sprang from Communism, so Nazism developed from Fascism.

WINSTON CHURCHILL: *The Second World War*, Vol I, *The Gathering Storm*, ch i (1948)

Fashion victim. A person who blindly follows or adopts the latest fashion merely for the sake of it. The term dates from the 1980s.

Fast or **quick buck.** To make a fast or quick buck is to make money easily and quickly, also possibly illicitly. A buck is a dollar. The origin of the word is uncertain, but it may be a shortening of 'buckskin', as deerskins were used as a unit of exchange by Native Americans and frontiersmen in 19th-century America.

Today's speculators may wear jeans and Nikes rather than a wig and frock-coat, but their game is essentially the same: how to make a quick buck.

The Times (5 January 2000)

Fast food. Food that can be served up fast, since it requires little preparation. Most types of cooked JUNK FOOD are available at fast food outlets.

Fast forward. The control that rapidly advances the tape on a tape or video player. The term is used figuratively to denote a jump ahead in a narrative, as: 'Fast forward to a London café a few months later' (*The Times*, 2 October 1999).

Fast lane. The outer, right-hand lane of a motorway, where traffic overtakes or travels at high speed. Metaphorically, to be or live in the fast lane is to have a busy or even hectic lifestyle.

Being in the fast lane means using the internet, voice mail, pagers and video conferencing.

Sunday Times (26 December 1999)

Fast Show, The. A fast-paced television comedy show first screened on BBC2 in 1994 and consisting of a series of brief unrelated sketches based on individual characters who reappear in their clearly identifiable roles every week. It was created and compiled by Paul Whitehouse and Charlie Higson, who took most of the main roles, one of the most memorable being the repressed homosexual country squire Lord Ralph Mayhew, played by Higson, and his Irish estate worker, Ted, played by Whitehouse. Many of the show's catchphrases, such as 'Suits you, Sir!' and 'Which was nice', soon became part of the national vocabulary.

Fast track. Metaphorically, a route or method that provides rapid results or promotion in business, especially when up against keen competition. The expression evolved from a US term for a racing track that is hard and dry, enabling horses to run fast.

Fast worker. A colloquialism for a person who achieves quick results, especially in a love affair.

Fatal Attraction. A film thriller (1987) directed by Adrian Lyne that depicted the vengeance wreaked on a successful lawyer and family man (Michael Douglas) by his lover (Glenn Close) after he refused to have any more to do with her after their ONE-NIGHT STAND. The ferocity of the tale caused a furore on the film's release and was alleged to have led to a sharp (if short-lived) drop in such extramarital activity on both sides of the Atlantic for some time afterwards. Subsequently the press relished reports that Michael Douglas himself was being treated for 'sex addiction'.

Fat cat. A rich and influential person, especially a businessman, politician or civil servant. In Britain in the 1990s the term came to be particularly associated with directors of privatized public utilities, some of whom were awarded spectacularly large pay rises or pay-offs. A fat cat is one that gets the 'cream'.

> Licking up the cream may have become more sophisticated over the years, but Britain's fat cats are in better health than ever.
> *The Times* (17 July 1999)

Fat city. Success or wealth, especially from criminal activity. The phrase dates from the 1940s and was popularized by the film *Fat City* (1972), about a boxer who makes a final bid for success.

Fat Controller. A nickname for any heavyweight manager or supervisor, such as a nightclub bouncer. The name is that of the boss of THOMAS THE TANK ENGINE in the children's picture books by the Rev. W. Awdry (1911–97), first published in 1946.

Fat farm. A US colloquialism for a health farm for overweight people.

Father and Son. An autobiography (1907) of his early years, subtitled *A Study of Two Temperaments*, by the literary critic Edmund Gosse (1849–1928). Gosse was the only son of Philip Gosse (1810–88), the FUNDAMENTALIST writer on zoology, with whom, after his mother's death in 1857, Gosse went to live in Devon. The book explores the conflict between generations caused by a restricted upbringing. *See also* OSCAR AND LUCINDA.

Father Brown. *See* BROWN, FATHER.

Fathers of the 20th century. The title 'Father of' has long been traditionally applied to a leader, inventor or pioneer of some kind, such as Hippocrates (460–377 BC), the Father of Medicine, or George Washington (1732–99), the Father of America. The following are some 20th-century 'Fathers' in various fields:

Father of American Music: Charles Ives (1874–1954), US composer

Father of Australia: Sir Edmund Barton (1849–1920), the first Australian prime minister (1901–3)

Father of Country Music: Jimmie Rodgers (1897–1933), US singer and guitarist

Father of Daylight Saving: William Willett (1856–1915), English advocate of SUMMER TIME

Father of English Football: Sir Stanley Rous (1895–1986), sixth president of FIFA (1961–74)

Father of Europe: Jean Monnet (1888–1979), French proposer of a plan for the European Community (*see* EUROPEAN UNION)

Father of Geomorphology: William M. David (1850–1934), US geographer and geologist who discovered the cycle of erosion of land masses

Father of Greyhound Racing: Brigadier-General Alfred Critchley (1890–1964), who built the first track at Belle Vue, Manchester, in 1926

Father of Indian Nationalism: Dababhai Naoroji (1925–1917), who in 1906 claimed the right of India to self-government

Father of Modern American Gangsterism: Johnny Torrio (1882–1957), US bootlegger, brothel-keeper and killer

Father of Modern English Criminology: Dr Hermann Mannheim (1889–1974), German-born British founder of the study of criminology

Father of Modern Navigation: Admiral of the Fleet Sir Henry Oliver (1865–1965), English sailor

Father of Nuclear Physics: Ernest Rutherford, 1st Baron Rutherford (1871–1939), New Zealand physicist who split the atom

Father of Published Ragtime: Irving Berlin (1888–1989), US composer

Father of Ragtime: Scott Joplin (1886–1917), US jazz pianist and composer

Father of Television: John Logie Baird (1888–1946), Scottish electrical engineer, the first demonstrator of a television image (1926)

Father of the Atomic Bomb: Dr Robert Oppenheimer

(1904–67), US physicist who supervised the construction of the atomic bomb in the Second World War

Father of the Blues: William C. Handy (1873–1958), US composer of 'The Memphis Blues' (1909); the title was also that of his autobiography (1941)

Father of the Chin: Major-General Sir John Bagot Glubb (1897–1987), English commander of the Arab Legion in Transjordan (1938–56), also known as 'Glubb Pasha'; he was badly wounded in the jaw in 1917. The sense of 'Father' here derives from Arabic usage, and the English title is a loose translation of the Arabic original, *Abu Hunaik*, literally 'Father of the Little Jaw'

Father of the Comic Strip: Richard Outcault (1863–1928), US creator of the 'Yellow Kid' (*see* YELLOW PRESS)

Father of the Four-letter Word: Henry Miller (1891–1980), US author of *Tropic of Cancer* (1934) and *Tropic of Capricorn* (1938), novels notorious for their explicit sexual content; *see also* FOUR-LETTER WORD

Father of the Gossip Column: Walter Winchell (1897–1972), US journalist, who began such a column in the *Evening Graphic* in 1924

Father of the Helicopter: Igor Sikorsky (1889–1972), Russian-born US aeronautical engineer, who constructed his first helicopter in 1909

Father of the Irish Republic: Éamon de Valera (1882–1975), Irish president of SINN FÉIN, which set up the first (unrecognized) Irish Republic in 1919; *see also* DEV

Father of the King's African Rifles: Frederick Lugard, 1st Baron Lugard (1858–1945), English soldier and colonial administrator, who raised the regiment of this name in 1891

Father of the Royal Air Force: Air Marshal Hugh Trenchard, 1st Viscount Trenchard (1873–1956), English officer, who helped found the RAF in 1918

Father of the Twentieth Amendment: Senator George W. Norris (1861–1944), who advocated the amendment to the Constitution that the inauguration of the president should take place on 20 January instead of 4 March (1933); the amendment ended 'lame-duck' sessions of Congress

Father of the United Nations: Cordell Hull (1871–1955), US secretary of state (1933–43), whose proposals at the Moscow conference of 1943 led to the formation of the UNITED NATIONS in 1945; his endeavours won him the NOBEL PRIZE for Peace in 1944

Father of Westerns: Thomas Ince (1882–1924), US film producer who introduced the WESTERN to the film industry (*War on the Plains*, 1912)

Father's Day. A day devoted to fathers in the annual calendar, falling on the third Sunday in June. Britain imported the occasion from the United States, where it was devised by Mrs John Bruce Dodd of Spokane, Washington, in 1910 as a counterpart to MOTHER'S DAY. It was not widely observed, however, until almost a quarter of a century later.

Father Ted. The Irish Roman Catholic priest, played by Dermot Morgan, who was the central character of the television SITCOM named after him, first screened in 1995. The action took place in the priests' home on a remote island, where Father Ted was forever struggling to control his two fellow priests, the young Dougal, played by Ardal O'Hanlon, and the old Jack, acted by Frank Kelly. Overseeing the three was the housekeeper, Mrs Doyle, a larger-than-life figure played by Pauline McLynn. Morgan's early death aged 45 in 1998 brought the series to a premature end.

Fatima. The small town of this name in west central Portugal became a centre of Roman Catholic pilgrimage after the reported sighting of the Virgin Mary in 1917. On 13 May that year three country children, Lucia dos Santos and her two cousins, Francisco and Jacinta, claimed to have seen a vision of a woman standing on a cloud in an evergreen tree. In a conversation heard only by the two girls, the woman asked the children to return to the site on the 13th of each month until October. Despite attempts to refute the children's evidence, the story drew increasing numbers of devotees, so that by October 50,000 pilgrims assembled with the children at the site. Many claimed to have witnessed a 'miracle of the sun', but the woman herself was visible only to the children, identifying herself as 'Our Lady of the Rosary'. In 1930 the bishop of Leira proclaimed the legitimacy of the apparitions and authorized the cult of Our Lady of Fatima.

The name itself is remote from Christianity as it derives from a 12th-century Moorish princess, a namesake of Fatima (*c*.606–632), youngest daughter of the prophet Muhammad.

Fat Man. *See* ENOLA GAY.

Fatty Pang. A nickname given to Chris Patten (b.1944) while governor of Hong Kong (1992–7), prior to the handover of the colony to the People's Republic of China. The comfortably but by no means excessively built Patten had been chairman of the Conservative Party, but lost his seat in the 1992 general election. He is now a European commissioner, and has produced contentious recommendations for the reform of the Royal Ulster Constabulary.

Fattypuffs and Thinifers. The English title of *Patapoufs et Filifers* (1930) by the French writer André Maurois (1885–1967). It tells of two brothers, one fat, one thin, who discover two contrasting nations beneath the surface of the earth. The suitably obese Fattypuffs do little but eat and sleep, while the slender and fastidious Thinifers work six days a week and do without lunch. An invasion of the land of the Fattypuffs by the Thinifers sets in train a reconciliation between the two peoples, who eventually agree to unite.

Fatwa. A legal decision given by a Muslim religious leader. The word became familiar in the West in 1989 when AYATOLLAH Khomeini of Iran issued a fatwa sentencing the writer Salman Rushdie (b.1947) to death for publishing *The* SATANIC VERSES (1988), a novel condemned as blasphemous and highly offensive. The Arabic word, which does not itself specifically mean a death sentence, is related to 'mufti'.

Fauvism. The name given to the work of a group of young French artists of the first decade of the 20th century, whose leader was Henri Matisse (1869–1954), and which included André Derain (1880–1954), Georges Braque (1882–1963), Maurice de Vlaminck (1876–1958), Raoul Dufy (1877–1953), Albert Marquet (1875–1947), Othon Friesz (1879–1949) and Georges Rouault (1871–1958). The corresponding German movement was *Die* BRÜCKE. The French school derives from the influence of Van Gogh, and the work was characterized by the imaginative use of brilliant colour, decorative simplicity, vitality and gaiety. The name Fauves ('wild beasts') arose from a remark of the French art critic Louis Vauxcelles, *Donatello au milieu des fauves!* ('Donatello among the wild beasts'), occasioned by the sight of a quattrocento-like statue amid their spectacularly coloured paintings at an exhibition of their work in 1905. *See also* CUBISM; DADAISM; FUTURISM; ORPHISM; RURALISM; SURREALISM; SYNCHROMISM; TACHISM; VORTICISM.

Faux amis (French, 'false friends'). A term adopted in English in the 1950s for words that appear the same or that are identical in two different languages, especially English and French, but that have quite different meanings. The phrase comes from *Les Faux Amis ou Les Trahisons du vocabulaire anglais* ('False Friends or The Treacheries of English Vocabulary'), by Maxime Kœssler and Jules Derocquigny, published in 1928 as a study of the subject. The following, based on Philip Thody and Howard Evans's *Faux Amis & Key Words* (1985), are some of the more egregious Anglo-French confusions. The French word is followed by the apparent meaning, then the actual.

abusif: not 'abusive' but 'incorrect', 'illegal', 'unauthorized'

achever: not 'to achieve' but 'to finish off'

appointer: not 'to appoint' but 'to pay a salary to'

apte: not 'apt' but 'able'

avertissement: not 'advertisement' but 'preface'

bande: not 'band' but 'gang'

brassière: not 'brassiere' but 'baby's vest'

car: not 'car' but 'bus'

carpette: not 'carpet' but 'rug'

carton: not 'carton' but 'cardboard'

casserole: not 'casserole' but 'saucepan'

cave: not 'cave' but 'cellar'

chasser: not 'to chase' but 'to drive away', 'to hunt'

château: not 'castle' but 'country house'

colon: not 'colon' but 'colonial'

commode: not 'commode' but 'chest of drawers'

complaisant: not 'complacent' but 'indulgent'

conforter: not 'to comfort' but 'to support', 'to encourage'

courtier: not 'courtier' but 'broker'

curé: not 'curate' but 'parish priest'

débonnaire: not 'debonair' but 'easy-going'

défiance: not 'defiance' but 'distrust'

demander: not 'to demand' but 'to request'

déranger: not 'to derange' but 'to disturb'

disposer: not 'to dispose of' but 'to have at one's disposal'

droguerie: not 'drugstore' but 'hardware store'

écolier: not 'scholar' but 'pupil'

engin: not 'engine' but 'machine'

express: not 'express train' but 'fast train'

fourniture: not 'furniture' but 'furnishing', 'act of supplying' *froc*: not 'frock' but 'monk's cowl'

fuel: not 'fuel' but 'fuel oil'

futile: not 'futile' but 'frivolous', 'trivial'

galoches: not 'galoshes' but 'clogs'

génial: not 'genial' but 'full of genius', 'masterly'

grief: not 'grief' but 'grievance'

hasard: not 'hazard' but 'luck', 'chance'

humeur: not 'humour' but 'bad temper'

industrieux: not 'industrious' but 'skilful'

ingénuité: not 'ingenuity' but 'simple-mindedness'

instamment: not 'instantly' but 'urgently'

isolation: not 'isolation' but 'insulation'

issue: not 'issue' but 'exit', 'way out'

jaquette: not 'jacket' but 'morning coat'

labourer: not 'to labour' but 'to plough'

large: not 'large' but 'wide'

lecture: not 'lecture' but 'reading'

librairie: not 'library' but 'bookshop'

location: not 'location' but 'renting', 'hiring'

magot: not 'maggot' but 'nest-egg'

monnaie: not 'money' but 'change'

opportunité: not 'opportunity' but 'opportuneness'

outrage: not 'outrage' but 'insult'

pantomime: not 'pantomime' but 'mime show'

peine: not 'pain' but 'sadness'

pétrole: not 'petrol' but 'petroleum'

pétulant: not 'petulant' but 'lively'

pondérer: not 'to ponder' but 'to weigh', 'to balance'

préservatif: not 'preservative' but 'condom'

prétendre: not 'to pretend' but 'to claim'

professeur: not 'professor' but 'teacher', 'lecturer'

prune: not 'prune' but 'plum'

raisin: not 'raisin' but 'grape'

recette: not 'receipt' but 'recipe'

relaxer: not 'to relax' but 'to acquit', 'to discharge'

rente: not 'rent' but 'unearned income'

reporter: not 'to report' but 'to postpone', 'to transfer'

résumer: not 'to resume' but 'to summarize'

romance: not 'romance' but 'song'

rude: not 'rude' but 'coarse'

séculaire: not 'secular' but 'age-old'

sensible: not 'sensible' but 'sensitive'

store: not 'store' but 'window blind'

sympathique: not 'sympathetic' but 'pleasant', 'agreeable'

trivial: not 'trivial' but 'vulgar', 'rude'

vacances: not 'vacancies' but 'holidays', 'vacation'

veste: not 'vest' but 'jacket'

vicaire: not 'vicar' but 'curate'

vivace: not 'vivacious' but 'long-lasting', 'tough'

volontiers: not 'voluntarily' but 'willingly'

Fave rave. A now dated term for an infatuation with a popular performer, especially a singer. 'Fave' is 'favourite'. *See also* RAVE.

As soon as he [popular singer David Cassidy] was seen on screen he was snatched by the US fan magazine market, always at the ready to replace a current fave rave.

The Times (30 July 1973)

Fawlty Towers. A classic television SITCOM that has long claimed an indelible place in the British collective memory. It consisted of 12 half-hour programmes, the first series of 6 screened in 1975, the second in 1979. It was written by John Cleese and Connie Booth, married at the time, with Cleese playing Basil Fawlty, the manic, hen-pecked owner of the hotel of the title, and Booth taking the part of the winsome waitress Polly. Prunella Scales played Basil's formidable wife Sybil, while Andrew Sachs was the spectacularly incompetent but well-meaning Spanish waiter Manuel. The glory of the series lay in its beautifully crafted plots, its realistic dialogue with many memorable lines, and its perfectly cast characters, in both major and minor roles. The programme had its genesis in an occasion in 1971 when Cleese and some other members of the MONTY PYTHON'S FLYING CIRCUS team stayed in a Torquay hotel with a highly irascible manager.

FBI. The Federal Bureau of Investigation evolved in 1935 from a Department of Justice force of 'special agents' set up in 1908 as the Bureau of Investigation. It was most prominent in its anti-communist activities in the COLD WAR years following the Second World War, but its role in counter-espionage was gradually taken over by the CIA from the 1960s.

FDR. An affectionate nickname of Franklin Delano Roosevelt (1882–1945), the Democratic statesman who was elected an unprecedented four times to be president of the USA (1933–45), and who led America through the GREAT DEPRESSION and the Second World War. He was also known as Franklin D. His high-spending NEW DEAL policies to deal with the Depression earned him the hostile nickname Franklin Deficit

Roosevelt. Alistair Cooke (*see* LETTER FROM AMERICA) later observed that he 'saved the capitalist system by simply forgetting to balance the books'. In his secret communications with Winston Churchill before America's entry into the Second World War Roosevelt adopted the code name POTUS (President of the United States), while Churchill was FORMER NAVAL PERSON. *See also* JFK; LBJ.

Fear and Loathing in Las Vegas. A documentary account (1972) by Hunter S. Thompson (b.1939) of the drug scene in Las Vegas. Under an alias and with a companion, Thompson, himself much of the time under the influence, confronted casino operators, bartenders, tourists, police officers and other members of the community. A surreal film version (1998), directed by Terry Gilliam, was unable to match the cult status of the original.

Fear of Flying. The first novel (1973) by Erica Jong (b.1942). Isadora Wing (29), who is scared stiff of aeroplanes, flies with her psychiatrist husband to a convention in Vienna. From there she embarks with a lover on a sexual odyssey, fantasizing about the 'zipless fuck', which 'has all the swift compression of a dream and is seemingly free of all remorse or guilt; because there is no talk of her late husband or of his fiancé; because there is no talk at all'. At the end Isadora returns to her husband, having survived her adventures and conquered her fear. The title works on a deeper level than mere travel in an aircraft, however, since although sex for Isadora is a means of 'flying', it is an illusory escape from reality and an illusory freedom and one that she fears.

Fearsome foursome. A nickname for any formidable quartet. In sport the designation was used of Roosevelt Grier, Deacon Jones, Lamar Lundy and Merlin Olsen, members of the defensive line of the Los Angeles Rams American football team in the mid-1960s.

Federast. *See* F-WORD.

Fédération internationale de football association. *See* FIFA.

Feeding frenzy. A concentrated period of frantic commercial competition or rivalry, as in the media for readers, listeners or viewers or among firms aiming at an identical market. The allusion is to sharks or piranhas, which launch an aggressive and competitive group attack on their prey. The figurative phrase dates from the 1970s.

To what extent is Britain succumbing to an Eighties-style feeding frenzy [in the property market] as portrayed in the media?
The Times (28 July 1999)

Feed the fishes, To. To vomit over the side of a ship when suffering from seasickness. The euphemism is a 20th-century US addition to the earlier colloquial sense to die by drowning.

Feel-good factor. A feeling of well-being in people, especially in a financial or material context. The phrase is frequently used in the media by political commentators with regard to an economic recovery following a downturn of some kind, the theory being that the political party achieving such a recovery will make the electorate feel good and so win their votes.

Merger mania is threatening to take over the big City law firms just as the mambo dance craze is threatening to take over our pop charts. Both are products of the 'feel-good' factor.
The Times (14 September 1999)

Feel or **look like death warmed up, To.** To feel (look) very unwell. An expression often used by those suffering from a hangover. The expression dates from the 1930s.

Feel no pain, To. To be drunk, so that one is insensitive to physical hurt.

Feel someone's collar, To. To arrest them. An allusion to a policeman's grip on a person's collar.

Feel the earth move, To. To experience sexual ecstasy. The expression is first found in Ernest Hemingway's *For Whom the Bell Tolls* (1940):

'Oh,' she said. 'I die each time. Do you not die?'
'No. Almost. But did thee feel the earth move?'
'Yes. As I died. Put thy arm around me, please.'
ch xiii

Feel up, To. To fondle sexually, especially surreptitiously or without the subject's permission.

It is no accident, I have often thought, that men seem so exceptionally keen on feeling one up while one is bent over a sink full of washing up in one's yellow rubber gloves.
The Times (22 September 1999)

Feldenkrais method. A system designed to promote bodily and mental efficiency. It involves the analysis of neuromuscular activity through special exercises and was devised in the 1930s by the Russian-born physicist Moshe Feldenkrais (1904–84).

Felix the Cat. The feline hero of early animated film cartoons produced by Pat Sullivan in the 1920s. Throughout his many adventures, 'Felix kept on walking', and thus originated the formerly familiar catchphrase. Felix was introduced in the film *Feline Follies* (1919) and was designed and animated by Sullivan's associate, Otto Messmer, who stated that he based his black tomcat's mannerisms on those of Charlie Chaplin. His name was intended to suggest 'felicity', by contrast with the bad luck normally associated with black cats.

Fellow traveller. A person in sympathy with a political party but not a member of that party. The term, which came to be chiefly used of communist sympathizers, is a translation of Russian *poputchik*, first used by Trotsky in this sense to refer to non-communist writers who sympathized with the Revolution. *See also* SPUTNIK.

Femidom. A proprietary name for a contraceptive sheath worn by women. Hence the name, a shortening of 'feminine condom'. The word should not be confused with 'femdom', the term for a dominatrix or dominating female in a sexual practice such as bondage and discipline (B & D).

Feng shui. In Chinese thought a system of good and evil influences in the natural surroundings, now increasingly taken into account in the West when designing buildings or simply when deciding where to sit. The words represent Chinese *fēng*, 'wind' and *shui*, 'water'. For the Chinese *feng shui* is both an art and a science, the former as a means of counteracting evil influences by good ones, the latter by determining the desirability of sites from the configuration of natural objects such as rivers, trees and hills. Many Chinese were at first concerned that the introduction of railways and telegraph lines would seriously damage the *feng shui* or prosperity of the districts through which they were laid.

Ferdinand the Bull. The gentle, peace-loving bull in the children's tale *The Story of Ferdinand* (1936) by Munro Leaf. He is chosen for the bullring, but the matador is disappointed when all that Ferdinand wants to do is to sniff the scent of the flowers in the hats of the women spectators. An award-winning Disney cartoon, *Ferdinand the Bull* (1938), was based on the story, which has a simple moral: peace and gentleness are better than fighting and death.

Fergie. A nickname of Sarah Ferguson (b.1959), who married Queen Elizabeth II's second son, Andrew, in 1986, becoming Duchess of York. Known for her extravagant lifestyle and fullish figure, she has also unkindly been dubbed the Duchess of Pork. Her marriage to the Duke of York ended in divorce in 1996.

Ferry Across the Mersey. A nostalgic Liverpudlian pop anthem by Gerry Marsden, performed by Gerry and the Pacemakers and released in 1964. The name of the song was chosen as the title of a film about Gerry and the Pacemakers by Tony Warren, creator of the title CORONATION STREET for the popular soap opera.

Festival of Britain. This grand, government-sponsored celebration was staged on an area of derelict ground on London's SOUTH BANK in 1951 ostensibly to mark the centenary of the Great Exhibition of 1851. In reality it was a morale-boosting exercise, a gesture of faith in a brighter future for Britain after the deprivations of the Second World War and the years of austerity that followed. Three of its most striking structures were the Dome of Discovery, the world's largest dome at the time, the Skylon ('sky pylon'), a spindle-shaped filigree spire with no visible means of support, and the Royal Festival Hall, the only permanent building, now one of London's main concert venues. *See also* BRUTALISM; MILLENNIUM.

> We believe in the right to strike,
> But now we've bloody well got to like
> Our own dear Festival of Britain.
> NOËL COWARD: *The Lyric Revue*, 'Don't Make Fun of the Fair' (1951)

Fettuccine Alfredo. A dish made with fettuccine (pasta shapes), butter, Parmesan cheese, black pepper and cream. The name slightly alters the Italian original, *fettucine all'Alfredo*, taking its name from Alfredo, the owner of a restaurant in Rome noted for the dish.

Fever Pitch. A popular sociological study (1992) by Nick Hornby (b.1957), subtitled *A Story of Football and Obsession*. It charts the author's personal relationship with the game as a fan (from the age of 10) of Arsenal Football Club. The book, which soon became a best-seller, gave an insight into the thinking and attitude of the typical NEW LAD. The title has obvious punning connotations. A film version (1996), directed by Michael Carlin, presented the original as a romantic comedy. *See also* HIGH FIDELITY.

Few, The. The RAF pilots of the BATTLE OF BRITAIN, so called from Winston Churchill's memorable tribute in the House of Commons on 20 August 1940: 'Never in the field of human conflict was so much owed by so many to so few.' A myth centring on the devil-may-care courage of the fur-collared British public-school airman was disseminated by the film *First of the Few* (1942) starring David Niven. In reality, British victory in the Battle of Britain owed just as much to the efforts of non-commissioned sergeants of the Volunteer Reserve and to the skills and bravery of the many foreign nationals, Czechs, Poles and others, who flew with the RAF.

Few well-chosen words. This phrase originally meant what it said in a positive or approbatory sense. In the 20th century, however, it took on an ironic tone. The words were still well-chosen but selected in order to reprehend, denounce or abuse.

FFI (*Forces françaises de l'intérieur*, 'French Forces of the Interior'). The grouping together in February 1944 of the various forces fighting for liberation after the fall of France in 1940. It was subsequently merged with the army (November 1944). *See also* MAQUIS.

FFL (*Forces françaises libres*, 'Free French Forces'). The forces organized by General de Gaulle from June 1940, after the German occupation of France, to continue the struggle in cooperation with the Allies. They were later called the FIGHTING FRENCH. *See also* MAQUIS.

Fianna Fáil. One of the two main political parties in Ireland, sometimes loosely called the Republican Party. It was formally constituted in 1926 under Éamon de Valera as a grouping of those opposed to the terms of the treaty with Great Britain that in 1921 brought the Irish Free State into existence. Its name derives from Irish *fianna*, 'band of warriors' and *Fáil*, the genitive form of *Fál*, an old name of Ireland, popularly understood to mean 'Destiny'. *See also* DEV; FINE GAEL; FREE-STATERS; SINN FÉIN; TAOISEACH.

Fiddler on the Roof. A stage musical (1964) and film (1971), with a book by Joseph Stein, score by Jerry Bock and lyrics by Sheldon Harnick, that relate the story of a Jewish milkman who is forced to leave pre-revolutionary Russia and emigrate to the United States. Based on the short story collection *Tevye and His Daughters* by Sholom Aleichem, the significance of the title is obscure. It may be based on a proverbial expression meaning to 'eat, drink and be merry', but it may be taken generally to signify a person who cheerfully makes the best of things, whatever the circumstances.

Fidel Castro in a miniskirt. A description of the fiery young Northern Irish civil rights campaigner

Bernadette Devlin (now McAliskey; b.1947) as she made her striking maiden speech in the House of Commons in 1969, having been elected a Unity Party MP for Mid-Ulster. The phrase was coined by the Ulster Unionist MP Stratton Mills (b.1932). The identification with the Cuban communist politician Fidel Castro (b.1927) reflects the perceived radicalism of her politics.

Fido. The name of a system developed by the Allies in the First World War for dispersing fog by means of petrol burners on the ground. It is an acronym of *fog intensive dispersal operation* and was probably suggested by the dog's name Fido, meaning 'I trust'.

Fiery Fred. A nickname of the fast-bowling Yorkshire and England cricketer Freddie Trueman (b.1931), whose autobiography was titled *Ball of Fire* (1976).

FIFA. The Fédération Internationale de Football Association, the world governing body of amateur football, named after the Football Association (FA) created in 1863 to standardize the rules of the game. By the end of the 19th century it became clear that football needed a governing body to encourage international development. The English, who had pioneered modern football, were not keen on the globalization of the game when a Dutch banker, C.A.W. Hirschmann, first proposed such a federation in 1902. They were equally cautious when a similar suggestion was made the following year by the Union des Sociétés Françaises de Sports Athlétiques. The English were thus absent when, on 21 May 1904, delegates from Belgium, Denmark, France, Holland, Spain, Sweden and Switzerland met in Paris to found FIFA. In due course England relented, and D.B. Woodfall became FIFA's second president. It was his French successor from 1921, Jules Rimet, who in 1932 moved FIFA to its present neutral headquarters in Zurich.

Fifth Beatle. A nickname used for a number of individuals associated with the four BEATLES. The original and most 'authentic' Fifth Beatle may be said to be Stuart Sutcliffe, the group's original bass guitarist, who left the group in 1961. Sutcliffe died in Hamburg in 1962 at the age of 21 and later became the subject of a film, *Backbeat* (1993). Brian Epstein (1934–67), the Beatles' manager, was so dubbed in 1964 by the US disc jockey 'Murray the K' (Murray Kaufman), but did not readily take to the appellation. George Martin (b.1926), the Beatle's recording manager, was also so named. The term was subsequently applied to anyone who has missed out on success.

Fifth Column. Traitors, those within a country who are working for the enemy, often by infiltrating into key positions and seeking to undermine the body politic from within. The phrase is attributed to General Emilio Mola, who, in the Spanish Civil War (1936–9), said that he had four columns encircling Madrid, and a fifth column (Spanish *quinta columna*) working for him in the city.

Fifth Estate. Jocularly applied to various 'authorities', such as the BBC, the trade unions, and so on, following on from the Fourth Estate as a term for the press. The term dates from the 1960s.

Fifth Man. In 1991 John Cairncross (1913–95) was identified as the long-sought 'Fifth Man' in the CAMBRIDGE SPY RING. His role as a 'masterspy' was described in various books in the 1980s but he always denied having been the Fifth Man. He was backed in his rebuttal by Graham Greene, who, like Cairncross, had acted as an agent for MI6 in the Second World War, but the evidence against him was conclusive.

Fifth Republic. *See* FOURTH REPUBLIC.

Fifty-fifty. In equal amounts or proportion; 50 per cent each. The expression dates from the early 20th century and has been adopted untranslated by other languages, such as French and German *fifty-fifty*, Russian *fifti-fifti*.

> 'We share everything fifty-fifty. Well, it's probably about seventy-thirty actually, he is so adept.'
> *The Times* (17 November 1999)

Fifty-first state. An epithet of Puerto Rico, a commonwealth whose citizens have US citizenship. Hawaii was formerly so known until it became the 50th US state in 1959. The name is also sometimes applied to Britain, seen as following the fashions and trends of the United States. The ordinal number may vary in this sense, especially in British use.

> [The MILLENNIUM DOME] may be proof of Britain as the 53rd United State, and it may be a waste of money, but it's also a great day out.
> *The Times* (3 January 2000)

Fifty million Frenchman can't be wrong. This catch-phrase was popular with US troops in the First World War, the stated number being that of the population of France. When the US nightclub personality Texas Guinan and her troupe were refused entry into France in 1931, she was quoted as saying: 'Fifty million Frenchmen *can* be wrong.' She promptly renamed her revue *Too Hot for Paris* and toured the United States with it instead.

Fighting French (French *La France Combattante*). All those Frenchmen at home and abroad who combined with the Allied nations in their war against the AXIS powers after the fall of France (June 1940). General de Gaulle and others escaped to England and he formed them into the FFL. The name was later changed to the Fighting French (14 July 1942). One of their most noted feats was the march of General Leclerc's column across the Sahara, from Lake Chad, to join the EIGHTH ARMY in Libya. These men were honoured by being the first formation to enter Paris on 23 August 1944. The Fighting French supported the Allies in Africa, Italy and elsewhere and together with the FFI made a valuable contribution to the liberation of France

Fight or flight. The instinctive physiological response to a threatening situation, which alerts a human or animal either to mount an instant vigorous defence or to run away. It was first described in Walter Cannon's *The Wisdom of the Body* (1914).

Figure of eight. An outline of the figure 8, especially as traced in the ice by a skater or flown by an aircraft in the air. The figure can be repeated endlessly without a break. Hence the adoption of a horizontal figure of eight (∞) as the symbol for infinity in mathematics.

Fill someone in, To. To inform them more fully in a particular matter. The concept is of filling in the blanks in the knowledge. The expression dates from the 1940s.

Fill someone's shoes, To. To assume their role and fulfil it perfectly. One identifies with the other person not just by wearing their shoes but also by sharing their shoe size.

> Children and the young at heart all know Madeline … a mischievous, resourceful pupil at a Paris convent school. Nine-year-old Hatty Jones fills her shoes on screen without a problem.
> *The Times* (5 August 1999)

Film noir (French, 'black film'). A term based on *roman noir*, 'black novel', as originally applied to the 19th-century English gothic novel. The term is generally used to apply to a HOLLYWOOD film of the late 1940s and early 1950s that presents a dark and brutal urban world of crime and corruption, peopled by sordid figures and presented in a style that emphasizes bleak settings, heavy shadows and sharp contrasts between light and dark. An archetypal example is the sinister world portrayed in Billy Wilder's DOUBLE INDEMNITY (1944), telling how an insurance salesman connives with a client's glamorous wife to kill her husband and reap the ill-gotten reward.

Film star nicknames. Many stars of the silver screen gained one or more nicknames, some more ephemeral than others. The names were not usually given by the public but mostly originated as promotional labels. The following is a selection.

America's Boy Friend: Charles 'Buddy' Rogers (1904–99)

America's Sweetheart: *see* World's Sweetheart *below*

Anatomic Bomb: Silvana Pampanini (b.1927)

Biograph Girl: Florence Lawrence (1886–1938)

BODY

Bogey: Humphrey Bogart (1899–1957)

Brazilian Bombshell: Carmen Miranda (1913–55)

Clothes Horse: Joan Crawford (1904–77), who 'suffered in mink'

Empress of Emotion: Elissa Landi (1904–48)

FIRST GENTLEMAN OF THE SCREEN

First Lady of the Screen: Norma Shearer (1900–83)

Handsomest Man in the World: Francis X. Bushman (1883–1966)

HANOI JANE

ICEBERG

IRON BUTTERFLY

'IT' GIRL

KING OF HOLLYWOOD

King of the Cowboys: (1) Tom Mix (1880–1940); (2) Roy Rogers (1912–98)

King of the Serials: Buster Crabbe (1907–83), the original FLASH GORDON in serials

Lolla, La: Gina Lollabrigida (b.1927)

Magnificent Wildcat: Pola Negri (1897–1987)

Man of a Thousand Faces: Lon Chaney (1883–1930), a master of macabre make-up

MAN YOU LOVE TO HATE

OOMPH Girl

PEEKABOO Girl

PLATINUM BLONDE

SEX KITTEN

Sex Thimble: Dudley Moore (b.1935), a mere 5ft 2½in tall

Sexy Rexy: Rex Harrison (1908–90)

Singing Capon: Nelson Eddy (1901–67), partner of the IRON BUTTERFLY

SWEATER GIRL

Threat: Lizabeth Scott (b.1922), a sultry leading lady of the 1940s

World's Greatest Actor: John Barrymore (1882–1942)

World's Greatest Actress: Marie Dressler (1869–1934)

World's Sweetheart: Mary Pickford (1893–1979), originally America's Sweetheart

Filofax. The loose-leaf notebook or personal organizer so called, as a respelling of 'file of facts', dates from 1930, when the name was registered by its inventor, Grace Scurr, a 36-year-old shorthand typist with a London firm of printers. The product was originally a personal filing system, and as such was in demand by clerics, scientists and certain regiments. In the Second World War Filofaxes were standard issue at Sandhurst, and in military circles they were often known as vade-mecums. In the early 1980s Filofaxes suddenly became a necessary item for business people or an indispensable fashion accessory for YUPPIES. By the mid-1990s, however, they had largely been superseded by various computerized gadgets.

Final Solution (German *die Endlösung*). The term coined by the NAZIS for the extermination of the Jews of Europe. The term emerged at the Wannsee Conference, held on 20 January 1942 in the Berlin suburb of Grossen-Wannsee. The conference, attended by 15 senior Nazis headed by Reinhard Heydrich (the HANGMAN), was called to determine 'the final solution of the Jewish question'. Although EINSATZGRUPPEN extermination squads had been active in eastern Europe since the beginning of the Second World War, their rate of killing did not satisfy the Nazi leadership, who now set in motion the mass transportation of European Jews to specially built death camps such as AUSCHWITZ, where extermination could be carried out on an industrial scale (*see* ZYKLON-B). Those deemed fit to work would be used as slave labour until they were exhausted, at which point they would be killed. The strategy was carried out with ruthless efficiency, resulting in the deaths of some 6 million Jews, the HOLOCAUST.

Fine and dandy. Excellent; perfect. The phrase is frequently applied ironically.

Fine Gael. One of the two main political parties of Ireland, together with FIANNA FÁIL, its name being Irish for 'tribe of Gaels'. It arose in 1933 from William Thomas Cosgrave's *Cumann na nGaedheal* (Society of Gaels), whose members had supported the terms of the Anglo-Irish treaty of 1921 that brought the Irish

Free State into existence. Little now separates it politically from FIANNA FÁIL, of which it is even so a distinctive rival. *See also* FREE-STATERS.

Fine or **small print.** In the strict sense, printed matter in small type. The phrase subsequently came to denote the disadvantageous details of a situation. The specific allusion is to the conditions stipulated in an agreement or contract, which are often printed in such small print that they may be overlooked at the time of signing.

Finest hour. The words from a celebrated speech by Winston Churchill (18 June 1940), given at the time when the collapse of France was imminent and the BATTLE OF BRITAIN about to begin.

> Let us therefore brace ourselves to our duty, and so bear ourselves that, if the British Commonwealth and its Empire lasts for a thousand years, men will still say, 'This was their finest hour.'

Finger on the pulse. To have or keep one's finger on the pulse is to be aware of all the latest news or developments, just as the rate of a person's heartbeat and so the state of their health can be monitored by feeling their pulse with one's fingertips.

> 'I think I'm the hippest dude in town,' he [film actor Tom Hanks] laughs. 'I think I'm on the cutting edge of gangsta rap mentality right now. I have my finger on the pulse of what we are in this society.'
> *Sunday Express* (27 February 2000)

Fingers or **hand in the till.** To have one's fingers or hand in the till is to appropriate money from one's place of work. The expression is open to elaboration as required.

> Mr Lilley was not so much fired from the Shadow Cabinet but [*sic*] chucked out like some shop assistant caught with both hands, both legs and several other body parts in the till.
> *The Times* (25 November 1999)

Finger trouble. A colloquial term for an error caused by operating a control wrongly or pressing a wrong key on an electronic instrument, such as a television or a computer.

Fings Ain't Wot They Used T'Be. A musical (1959) with a score and lyrics by Lionel Bart (1930–99) and book by Frank Norman about the gamblers and prostitutes who inhabit low-life London. The success of the title song, which reflects the changes that overtake the lives of all the main characters, was enough to establish it as a popular catchphrase.

Finian's Rainbow. A musical comedy (1947) with a score by Burton Lane (1912–97) and book by E.Y. Harburg (1898–1981) and Fred Sady about an Irish immigrant to the United States called Finian McLonergan who tries to get rich by burying a crock of gold he has stolen from a leprechaun. The title refers not only to the legend of the crock of gold at the end of the rainbow but also to the fact that Finian buries his crock of gold, hoping it will multiply, in a place called Rainbow Valley.

Finnegans Wake. A MODERNIST novel (1939) by James Joyce (1882–1941). He began work on it in 1922, but was too superstitious to reveal the title; sections of it were published (1927–30) in New York as 'Work in Progress'. Whereas ULYSSES is concerned with a single day, *Finnegans Wake* is a record of a night, in which the mind of the sleeping H.C. Earwicker is interpreted with great virtuosity and invention of language. Joyce illustrated his literary method by saying that he was tunnelling through a mountain from two sides. And all the while he added layers of meaning. The structure largely follows the Italian philosopher Giovanni Battista Vico (1668–1744), who divided human history into three ages, divine, heroic and human, to which Joyce added a fourth, return, emphasizing Vico's theory of evolutionary cycles in civilizations. The punning title derives from an Irish-American ballad about Tim Finnegan, a drunken hod-carrier who falls from his ladder and is killed. A splash of whiskey at his wake awakes him, and he exclaims, 'Do ye think I'm dead then?' It also suggests the return of Fionn mac Cumhaill, mythical hero of the Ossianic cycle of stories. *See also* FIRST LINES OF NOVELS.

Fireball. The nickname of the fast and furious US motor-racing champion Edward G. Roberts (1929–64). Ironically, he died of burns following a crash on a circuit in North Carolina.

Fire in one's belly. Ambition; 'drive'. The belly is popularly regarded as the 'engine' that drives the body and the emotions, food being the fuel that 'stokes' it.

> It is high time the girls got a bit of fire in their belly and stopped depending on all that gentle singer-songwriter stuff to see them through.
> *The Times* (25 February 2000)

Fire on all cylinders, To. To work at peak level. The allusion is to an internal combustion engine, in which a cylinder 'fires' when the fuel inside it is ignited. A fuller form of the phrase is 'to fire on all four cylinders'. Hence 'to fire on one cylinder' in the sense to work badly.

> After a period in which the world economy has been sputtering along … it is now starting to fire on all cylinders.
>
> *Sunday Times* (28 November 1999)

Fireside chats. The name adopted by President F.D. Roosevelt (see FDR) for his broadcasts to the American people on topics of national interest and importance. They began in 1933 and became customary during his administration.

Fire-walker. A person who walks barefoot over hot stones or smouldering ashes, often as part of a ceremony. The act depends as much on strength of will as on the strategic placing of the feet, and wood ash in fact has a low 'specific heat' in any case. In modern times fire-walking has been adopted by some business companies as a test to foster leadership skills.

> After an intensive course of at least 10 12-hour days, participants are invited to a spectacular finale which involves fire-walking, breaking bricks with bare hands or group hypnosis.
>
> *The Times* (15 July 1998)

Fire watcher. The name given to those volunteers in Britain who kept watch for fires started by enemy air raids during the Second World War.

Firm, The. A nickname for any influential or authoritative organization, especially as current among its members, such as the Royal Family or the CIA. The former was reputedly first so called by George VI.

First Gentleman of the Screen. A nickname of the English-born US film actor George Arliss (1868–1946), so called from his elegance and the monocle that he sported.

First Lady. A name applied to the wife of the president of the USA. The term came into general use in the early 20th century. Eleanor Roosevelt (1884–1962), wife of FDR, became known as the First Lady of the World, owing to her work on behalf of peace and the poor with the UNITED NATIONS after her husband's death. She was perhaps the most influential and politically involved first lady prior to Hillary Rodham Clinton (b.1947), long-suffering wife of Bill Clinton, the COMEBACK KID.

First Lady of … . The title 'First lady of … ' has been given to the following:

> First Lady of Broadway: a nickname of the US actress Katherine Cornell (1893–1974)

First Lady of Country Music: the nickname of the US singer Tammy Wynette, born Virgina Wynette Pugh (1942–98)

First Lady of Fleet Street: the nickname of the journalist Jean Rook (1931–91), chief columnist and assistant editor of the *Daily Express*

First Lady of Hollywood Fashion: the nickname of the US costume designer Edith Head (1907–81), who created opulent dresses for many famous HOLLYWOOD actresses as well as the stylish suits worn by Robert Redford and Paul Newman in *The Sting* (1973)

First Lady of the Stage: the US actress Helen Hayes (1900–93), who won an OSCAR in 1932, an EMMY in 1954 and a TONY in 1958; she was also known as 'The First Lady of the American Theatre'

First light. A term used in the armed forces for the earliest time (roughly dawn) at which light is sufficient for the movement of ships or for military operations to begin. Similarly last light is the latest time when such movements can take place. The expression was current in the Second World War.

First lines of novels. There follows a selective list of the first lines of some of the most celebrated novels and other works of fiction, in alphabetical order, written since 1900. Novel titles in small capital letters indicate that a separate entry for the novel or work in question can be found elsewhere in the dictionary.

> **Age of Innocence, The** (1920) by Edith Wharton: 'On a January evening of the early seventies, Christine Nilsson was singing in Faust at the Academy of Music in New York.'
>
> **All the Pretty Horses** (1992) by Cormac McCarthy: 'The candleflame and the image of the candleflame caught in the pierglass twisted and righted when he entered the hall and again when he shut the door.'
>
> **ANIMAL FARM** (1945) by George Orwell: 'Mr Jones, of the Manor Farm, had locked the hen-houses for the night, but was too drunk to remember to shut the pop-holes.'
>
> **AT SWIM-TWO-BIRDS** (1939) by Flann O'Brien: 'Having placed in my mouth sufficient bread for three minutes' chewing, I withdrew my powers of sensual perception and retired into the privacy of my mind, my eyes and face assuming a vacant and preoccupied expression.'
>
> **BRAVE NEW WORLD** (1932) by Aldous Huxley: 'A squat grey building of only thirty-four storeys.'

Cancer Ward (1968) by Alexander Solzhenitsyn: 'On top of it all, the cancer wing was "number thirteen".'

CAPTAIN CORELLI'S MANDOLIN (1994) by Louis de Bernières: 'Dr Iannis had enjoyed a satisfactory day in which none of his patients had died or got any worse.'

Casino Royale (1953) by Ian Fleming (the first James BOND book): 'The scent and smoke and sweat of a casino are nauseating at three in the morning.'

Castle, The (1926) by Franz Kafka: 'It was late evening when K. arrived.'

CATCH-22 (1961) by Joseph Heller: 'It was love at first sight.' (Yossarian falls in love with the Chaplain.)

CIDER WITH ROSIE (1959) by Laurie Lee: 'I was set down from the carrier's cart at the age of three; and there with a sense of bewilderment and terror my life in the village began.'

DANCE TO THE MUSIC OF TIME, A, volume 1, *A Question of Upbringing* (1951) by Anthony Powell: 'The men at work at the corner of the street had made a kind of camp for themselves, where, marked out by tripods hung with red hurricane-lamps, an abyss in the road led down to a network of subterranean drain-pipes.'

DEATH IN VENICE (1912) by Thomas Mann: 'Gustave Aschenbach – or von Aschenbach, as he had been known officially since his fiftieth birthday – had set out alone from his house in Prince Regent Street, Munich, for an extended walk.'

DECLINE AND FALL (1928) by Evelyn Waugh: 'Mr Sniggs, the Junior Dean, and Mr Postlethwaite, the Domestic Bursar, sat alone in Mr Sniggs's rooms overlooking the garden quad at Scone College'.

DOCTOR ZHIVAGO (1957) by Boris Pasternak: 'On they went, singing "Eternal Memory", and whenever they stopped, the sound of their feet, the horses and the gusts of wind seemed to carry on their singing.'

Earthly Powers (1980) by Anthony Burgess: 'It was the afternoon of my eighty-first birthday, and I was in bed with my catamite when Ali announced that the archbishop had come to see me.'

Edwardians, The (1930) by Vita Sackville-West: 'Among the many problems that beset the novelist, not the least weighty is the choice of moment at which to begin his novel.'

Farewell to Arms, A (1929) by Ernest Hemingway: 'In the late summer of that year we lived in a house in a village that looked across the river and the plain to the mountains.'

FINNEGANS WAKE (1939) by James Joyce: 'riverrun, past Eve and Adam's, from swerve of shore to bend of bay, brings us by a commodius vicus of recirculation back to Howth Castle and Environs.'

Glass Bead Game, The (1943) by Hermann Hesse: 'It is our intention to preserve in these pages what scant biographical material we have been able to collect concerning Joseph Knecht, or Ludi Magister Josephus III, as he is called in the Archives of the Glass Bead Game.'

Good Soldier, The (1915) by Ford Madox Ford: 'This is the saddest story I have ever heard.'

Grand Meaulnes, Le (1913) by Alain-Fournier: 'He appeared at our house on a Sunday in November 189…'

GRAVITY'S RAINBOW (1973) by Thomas Pynchon: 'A screaming comes across the sky.'

GREAT GATSBY, THE (1925) by F. Scott Fitzgerald: 'In my younger and more vulnerable years my father gave me some advice that I've been turning over in my mind ever since.'

HEART OF DARKNESS (1902) by Joseph Conrad: '*Nellie*, a cruising yawl, swung to her anchor without a flutter of sails, and was at rest.'

HERZOG (1964) by Saul Bellow: 'If I am out of my mind, it's all right with me, thought Moses Herzog.'

HOBBIT, THE (1937) by J.R.R. Tolkien: 'In a hole in the ground there lived a hobbit.'

Honorary Consul, The (1973) by Graham Greene: 'Doctor Eduardo Plarr stood in the small port on the Paraná, among the rails and yellow cranes, watching where a horizontal plume of smoke stretched over the Chaco.'

House at Pooh Corner, The (1928) by A.A. Milne: 'An Introduction is to introduce people, but Christopher Robin and his friends, who have already been introduced to you, are now going to say Good-bye.' (opening sentence of the introductory 'Contradiction')

Invisible Man (1952) by Ralph Ellison: 'I am an invisible man.'

Jazz (1992) by Toni Morrison: 'Sth, I know that woman.'

JEWEL IN THE CROWN, THE (1966), first novel of the *Raj Quartet* by Paul Scott: 'Imagine, then, a flat landscape, dark for the moment, but even so conveying to a girl running in the still deeper shadow cast by the wall of the Bibighar Gardens an idea of immensity, of distance, such as years before Miss Crane had been conscious of standing where a lane ended and cultivation began: a different landscape but also in the alluvial plain between the mountains of the north and the plateau of the south.'

Kind of Loving, A (1960) by Stan Barstow: 'It really begins with the wedding – the Boxing Day Chris got married – because that was the day I decided to *do* something about Ingrid Rothwell besides gawp at her like a love-sick cow or something whenever she came in sight.'

LADY CHATTERLEY'S LOVER (1928) by D.H. Lawrence: 'Ours is essentially a tragic age, so we refuse to take it tragically.' (*See also* CHATTERLEY, LADY; LADY CHATTERLEY TRIAL.)

Light in August (1932) by William Faulkner: 'Sitting beside the road, watching the wagon mount the hill toward her, Lena thinks, "I have come from Alabama: a fur piece. All the way from Alabama a-walking. A fur piece."'

LION, THE WITCH AND THE WARDROBE, THE (1950) by C.S. Lewis: 'Once there were four children whose names were Peter, Susan, Edmund and Lucy. This story is about something that happened to them when they were sent away from London during the war because of the air-raids.'

LOLITA (1955) by Vladimir Nabokov: 'Lolita, light of my life, fire of my loins.'

Look Homeward, Angel (1929) by Thomas Wolfe: 'A destiny that leads the English to the Dutch is strange enough; but one that leads from Epsom into Pennsylvania, and thence into the hills that shut in Altamont over the proud coral cry of the cock, and the soft stone smile of an angel, is touched by that dark miracle of chance which makes new magic in a dusty world.'

LORD OF THE FLIES (1954) by William Golding: 'The boy with fair hair lowered himself down the last few feet of rock and began to pick his way towards the lagoon.'

LORD OF THE RINGS, THE, volume 1, *The Fellowship of the Ring* (1954) by J.R.R. Tolkien: 'When Mr Bilbo Baggins of Bag End announced that he would shortly be celebrating his eleventy-first birthday with a party of special magnificence, there was much talk and excitement in Hobbiton.' The Prologue prior to

Chapter 1 begins: 'This book is largely concerned with hobbits ...'

LUCKY JIM (1954) by Kingsley Amis: '"They made a silly mistake, though," the professor of history said, and his smile, as Dixon watched, gradually sank beneath the surface of his features at the memory.'

MAGIC MOUNTAIN, THE (1924) by Thomas Mann: 'An unassuming young man was travelling, in midsummer, from his native city of Hamburg, to Davos-Platz in the Canton of the Grisons, on a three weeks' visit.'

Magus, The (1966/1977) by John Fowles: 'I was born in 1927, the only child of middle-class parents, both English, and themselves born in the grotesquely elongated shadow, which they never rose sufficiently above history to leave, of that monstrous dwarf Queen Victoria.'

Malone Dies (1951) by Samuel Beckett: 'I shall soon be quite dead at last in spite of all.'

Man Without Qualities, The, volume 1 (1930) by Robert Musil: 'There was a depression over the Atlantic.'

Metamorphosis (1915) by Franz Kafka: 'When Gregor Samsa awoke one morning from troubled dreams he found himself transformed in his bed into a monstrous insect.'

MIDNIGHT'S CHILDREN (1981) by Salman Rushdie: 'I was born in the city of Bombay ... once upon a time.'

MORE PRICKS THAN KICKS (1934) by Samuel Beckett: 'It was morning and Belacqua was stuck in the first of the canti in the moon.'

MYRA BRECKINRIDGE (1968) by Gore Vidal: 'I am Myra Breckinridge whom no man will ever possess.'

NAKED AND THE DEAD, THE (1948) by Norman Mailer: 'Nobody could sleep.'

NAKED LUNCH, THE (1959) by William Burroughs: 'I awoke from The Sickness at the age of forty-five, calm and sane, and in reasonably good health except for a weakened liver and the look of borrowed flesh common to all who survive The Sickness.'

Nights at the Circus (1984) by Angela Carter: '"Lor' love you, sir!" Fevvers sang out in a voice that clanged like dustbin lids.'

Nineteen Eighty-Four (1949) by George ORWELL: It was a bright cold day in April, and the clocks were striking thirteen.' (*See also* 1984)

ON THE ROAD (1958) by Jack Kerouac: 'I first met Dean not long after my wife and I split up.'

OSCAR AND LUCINDA (1988) by Peter Carey: 'If there was a bishop, my mother would have him to tea.'

Our Lady of the Flowers (1943) by Jean Genet: 'Weidmann appeared before you in a five o'clock edition, his head swathed in white bands, a nun and yet a wounded pilot fallen into the rye one September day like the day when the world came to know the name of Our Lady of the Flowers.'

PASSAGE TO INDIA, A (1924) by E.M. Forster: 'Except for the Marabar Caves – and they are twenty miles off – the city of Chandrapore presents nothing extraordinary.'

PETER PAN (1911) by J.M. Barrie: 'All children, except one, grow up.'

Plague, The (1947) by Albert Camus: 'The unusual events described in this chronicle occurred in 194…, at Oran.'

PORTRAIT OF THE ARTIST AS A YOUNG MAN, A (1916) by James Joyce: 'Once upon a time and a very good time it was there was a moocow coming down along the road and this moocow that was coming down along the road met a nicens little boy named baby tuckoo …'

RAILWAY CHILDREN, THE (1906) by E. Nesbit: 'They were not railway children to begin with.'

REBECCA (1938) by Daphne du Maurier: 'Last night I dreamt I went to Manderley again.'

REMEMBRANCE OF THINGS PAST, volume 1, Swann's Way (1913) by Marcel Proust: 'For a long time I used to go to bed early.'

RIDDLE OF THE SANDS, THE (1903) by Erskine Childers: 'I have read of men who, when forced by their calling to live for long periods in utter solitude – save for a few black faces – have made it a rule to dress regularly for dinner in order to maintain their self-respect and prevent a relapse into barbarism.'

ROOM AT THE TOP (1957) by John Braine: 'I came to Warley on a wet September morning with the sky the grey of Guiseley sandstone.'

SATANIC VERSES, THE (1988) by Salman Rushdie: '"To be born again," sang Gibreel Farishta tumbling from the heavens, "first you have to die." '

Scoop (1938) by Evelyn Waugh: 'While still a young man, John Courteney Boot had, as his publisher proclaimed, "achieved an assured and enviable position in contemporary letters".'

SEA, THE SEA, THE (1978) by Iris Murdoch: 'The sea which lies before me as I write glows rather than sparkles in the bland May sunshine.'

Sons and Lovers (1913) by D.H. Lawrence: '"The Bottoms" succeeded to "Hell Row".'

SWALLOWS AND AMAZONS (1930) by Arthur Ransome: 'Roger, aged seven, and no longer the youngest of the family, ran in wide zigzags, to and fro, across the steep field that sloped up from the lake to Holly Howe, the farm where they were staying for part of the summer holidays.'

Sword of Honour Trilogy, The, volume 1, Men at Arms (1952) by Evelyn Waugh: 'When Guy Crouchback's grandparents, Gervase and Hermione, came to Italy on their honeymoon, French troops manned the defences of Rome, the Sovereign Pontiff drove out in an open carriage and Cardinals took their exercise side-saddle on the Pincian Hill.'

Tailor of Gloucester, The (1902) by Beatrix Potter: 'In the time of swords and periwigs and full-skirted coats with flowered lappets – when gentlemen wore ruffles, and gold-laced waistcoats of paduasoy and taffeta – there lived a tailor in Gloucester.'

Tale of Samuel Whiskers, The (1908) by Beatrix Potter: 'Once upon a time there was an old cat, called Mrs Tabitha Twitchit, who was an anxious parent.'

Tale of the Flopsy Bunnies, The (1909) by Beatrix Potter: 'It is said that the effect of eating too much lettuce is "soporific".'

Tale of Tom Kitten, The (1907) by Beatrix Potter: 'Once upon a time there were three little kittens, and their names were Mittens, Tom Kitten, and Moppet.'

THIRTY-NINE STEPS, THE (1915) by John Buchan: 'I returned from the City about three o'clock on that May afternoon pretty well disgusted with life.'

TIN DRUM, THE (1959) by Günter Grass: 'Granted: I am an inmate of a mental hospital; my keeper is watching me, he never lets me out of his sight; there's a peephole in the door, and my keeper's eye is the shade of brown that can never see through a blue-eyed type like me.'

Titus Groan (1946), the first of the GORMENGHAST trilogy by Mervyn Peake: 'Gormenghast, that is, the main massing of the original stone, taken by itself would have displayed a certain ponderous architectural quality were it possible to have ignored the circumfusion of those mean dwellings that swarmed like an epidemic around its outer walls.'

TOWERS OF TREBIZOND, THE (1957) by Rose Macaulay: '"Take my camel, dear," said my aunt Dot, as she climbed down from this animal on her return from High Mass.'

TRAINSPOTTING (1993) by Irvine Welsh: 'The sweat wis lashing oafay Sick Boy; he wis trembling.'

ULYSSES (1922) by James Joyce: 'Stately, plump Buck Mulligan came from the stairhead, bearing a bowl of lather on which a mirror and a razor lay crossed.'

Unnamable, The (1953) by Samuel Beckett: 'Where now?'

Wonderful WIZARD OF OZ, The (1900) by L. Frank Baum: 'Dorothy lived in the midst of the great Kansas prairies, with Uncle Henry, who was a farmer, and Aunt Em, who was the farmer's wife.'

WORLD ACCORDING TO GARP, THE (1976) by John Irving: 'Garp's mother, Jenny Fields, was arrested in Boston in 1942 for wounding a man in a movie theater.'

First Night of the Proms. The first evening of the annual Promenade Concerts at the Royal Albert Hall, London, in July, an eagerly awaited event for many concert-goers. The music chosen varies from year to year, and thus lacks the predictability of the pieces at the LAST NIGHT OF THE PROMS. A performance of Sir Michael Tippett's choral epic *The Mask of Time* (1982) at the opening night of the 1999 season was unusually demanding.

> In 30 years of Promming I cannot recall a 'tougher' First Night … Nor can I remember a more absorbing curtain-raiser.
> *The Times* (19 July 1999)

First past the post. Said of a voting system in which a candidate is elected by means of a simple majority. British parliamentary elections are run on the first-past-the-post system. The allusion is to horse-racing, in which the horse that reaches the winning post first is the one that wins.

> Since the election of a mayor for London is breaking new ground, perhaps there should be a box on the ballot paper for those who do not want one. If they were first past the post it would stop the gravy train.
> *The Times* (Letter to the Editor) (25 August 1999)

First World War slang. British troops in France and Belgium during the First World War picked up certain French phrases and corrupted them after their own fashion. The following examples are from Basil Hargrave's *Origins and Meanings of Popular Phrases and Names* (1925):

> 'Ally toot sweet' (*Allez tout de suite*): Go away; clear off. (A *Punch* cartoon of 5 December 1917 showed a

'Tommy' shooing away a group of inquisitive French children with the words: 'Nah, then, alley toot sweet, an' the tooter the sweeter.')

'Apree ler gare finee' (*Après la guerre finie*, or more correctly *Après que la guerre sera finie*): After the war; when the war is over

'Aunt Mary Ann': a variant of *Sanfaryan*

'Come on tally plonk?' (*Comment allez-vous?*): How are you getting on?

'Cum-sah' (*Comme ça*): What's-its-name

'Na-poo'd' (*Il n'y en a plus*): Done for; put out of action; killed (*see* NAPOO)

'Sally-fairy-ann' (*Cela ne fait rien*): a variant of *Sanfaryan*

'Sanfaryan' (*Ça ne fait rien*): It doesn't matter

'Tres beans' (*Très bien*): Very good; very well

'Wulla' (*Voilà*): There you are

See also WIPERS.

Fish Called Wanda, A. A film comedy (1988) written by and starring John Cleese (b.1939) and based on a story by Cleese and Charles Crichton about a repressed English barrister who becomes chaotically involved in a jewel robbery. Wanda is the sexually alluring thief Wanda Gershwitz (played by Jamie Lee Curtis) for whom Cleese develops a passion (although a pet fish does also play a significant role in the convoluted plot).

Fish dive. A position in ballet in which the male dancer holds the ballerina almost vertically upside down, as if diving towards the floor. It is particularly effective for a *pas de deux*, such as that in Act III of *The Sleeping Beauty*. The term dates from the 1940s and is known in French as *pas poisson*.

Fishing expedition. An attempt to find information by asking questions at random rather than directly. A fisherman hopes for a catch but may not have one. The expression is of US origin and dates from the 1930s.

Fistful of Dollars, A. A Western (1964), written and directed by Sergio Leone (1921–89), about a nameless gunfighter (played by Clint Eastwood) who becomes involved in the struggle for power between two rival families. The title refers to the gunfighter's mercenary status, hired first by one family and then by the other. The basic plot of the film, which helped establish the SPAGHETTI WESTERN genre and spawned the sequels *For a Few Dollars More* (1965) and *The* GOOD, THE BAD AND THE UGLY (1967), was derived from Akira Kurosawa's *Yojimbo* (1961), in which the mysterious stranger is a samurai warrior. *See also* MAN WITH NO NAME.

Fit the frock, To. Of a woman, to wear conventional female dress, or more generally to conform to the supposedly traditional feminine norm. The expression is often found in the negative.

> I was always a tomboy at heart, so there were times when I didn't really feel like I fitted the frocks. It wasn't too much of a problem, though, because I love clothes.
> KIM WILDE in *heat* (6–12 January 2000)

Fitzrovia. A region of London north of Oxford Street and west of Tottenham Court Road, so called after Fitzroy Square there. The name became associated in the 1930s with impecunious artists and writers and gained a somewhat dubious reputation.

> After leaving school he emigrated into what he calls Fitzrovia – a world of outsiders, down-and-outs, drunks, sensualists, homosexuals and eccentrics.
> *Times Literary Supplement* (10 January 1958)

Five-finger discount. US teenagers' slang for shoplifting, in which one puts the five fingers to nefarious use. The expression dates from the 1960s.

Five-finger exercise. Anything easy or straightforward. The allusion is to a piece of music composed specially to give a piano player practice in using all five fingers. This invariably involves running up and down a series of five notes and the execution of scales, as entertainingly exampled by the piece 'Pianists' in Camille Saint-Saëns' *The Carnival of the Animals* (1886).

Five o'clock shadow. The beginnings of a new beard on a man's clean-shaven face, visible at about this time of day. The expression dates from the 1930s when it was first used in an advertising campaign for Gem razor blades. One such advertisement contained the lines: 'Gem Blades are made by the makers of your Gem Razor. They fit *precisely*. This famous combination positively prevents "5 o'clock Shadow"; it's the last word in shaving comfort.' *See also* TRICKY DICKY.

> His make-up varies in each shot, ensuring that he blends with the bodies he has invaded. At the same time, though, he makes no attempt to hide his five o'clock shadow.
> *The Times* (12 January 2000)

Five Percenters. An offshoot of the black Muslim NATION OF ISLAM, who see themselves as possessing 'self-knowledge' of the racial superiority of blacks. They take their name from their belief that en-

lightened followers of Islam make up just 5 per cent of the population, a minority charged with educating the majority 85 per cent, who are oppressed by the remaining 10 per cent of corrupt 'white devils'. Their credo became the theme of many black American RAP artists in the 1990s.

Five-star. Of the highest standard or class. The reference is to the system used to grade hotels. Sometimes crowns are substituted for stars, especially for hotels, but otherwise the system can be adopted for any type of rating. In some gradings the highest is four-star.

> Five stars denote large, luxury hotels offering the highest international standards of accommodation, facilities, services and cuisine.
> *AA All-In-One Guide: London* (1998)

Five Towns. Towns in the Potteries that Arnold Bennett (1867–1931) used as the scene of the best known of his novels and stories, one of the earliest being ANNA OF THE FIVE TOWNS (1902). They are Tunstall, Burslem, Hanley, Stoke-on-Trent, Longton and Fenton. These actually number six, but for artistic purposes Bennett called them five, giving them the respective fictional names of Turnhill, Bursley, Hanbridge, Knype and Longshaw. All are now part of Stoke-on-Trent.

Five-year plan. In the former USSR one of a series of plans for developing the whole of the nation's economy in a coordinated effort by a five-year programme. The first such plan was launched by STALIN in 1929 with the aim of making the Soviet Union self-supporting. Further plans followed, and the example was copied by some other countries. The strategy was subsequently discredited and abandoned after the dissolution of the USSR in 1991.

Fizzbo. An Americanism for the selling of a house without the services of a real-estate broker (estate agent). The word is an attempt at pronouncing the abbreviation 'fsbo', standing for 'for sale by owner'.

Flag. The painting of the US flag by Jasper Johns (b.1930), dating from 1954, is regarded by some as marking the beginning of the POP ART movement. Although clearly depicting the Stars and Stripes, the work's richly textured encaustic surface raises the question as to whether it is a painting or a flag. Johns later recalled (in a 1972 documentary): 'One night I dreamt I painted a large American flag, and the next morning I went out and bought the materials to begin it.'

Flag of convenience. The national flag flown by a ship that has registered in that country in order to avoid legal or tax commitments. The phenomenal growth in the mid-1950s of merchant fleets registered under the flags of such non-maritime countries as Liberia and Panama caused considerable concern. The ownership of such vessels was mainly vested in Greek and American countries as well as citizens of other nationalities. As a result of this system Panama had the world's largest merchant fleet in the mid-1990s while less than one-third of British shipping was actually registered in Britain.

Flak. Anti-aircraft fire. The expressive word is an abbreviation of German *Fliegerabwehrkanone*, literally 'flyer defence cannon'. A development was the flak-jacket, worn as protection against gunfire. Later came the figurative flak-catcher, as a person who deals with and deflects hostile comments or questions aimed at another. The word is sometimes spelt 'flack'.

Flaky. Liable to behave eccentrically; unreliable. The term is of US origin and became current in the 1960s. The suggestion is that the person could 'flake' or 'fall apart'. The word became widely known following President Reagan's use of it in a speech at the beginning of January 1986 to describe the Libyan head of state, Colonel Gadaffi.

Flambards. A fictional house in Essex that lends its name to the first (1967) of a series of novels for teenagers by K.M. Peyton (b.1929). The books were later (1979) adapted for television.

Flannelled fools. Cricketers. This term, used derisively or humorously, is taken from Rudyard Kipling:

> Then ye returned to your trinkets; then ye contented
>   your souls
> With the flannelled fools at the wicket or the
>   muddied oafs at the goals.
> 'The Islanders' (1903)

Flapper. A term applied in the early years of the 20th century to a teenage girl, from her plaited pigtail tied at the end with a large bow. As she walked along, the pigtail flapped on her back. Her hair was subsequently 'put up' in a bun or other hairstyle. The term later became synonymous with the BRIGHT YOUNG THINGS of the 1920s and 1930s. It gained an added punning sense since it referred to a young woman who was 'flighty'. *See also* YOUNG THING.

Flapper vote. A contemptuous name for the vote granted to women of 21 by the Equal Franchise Act of 1928, sponsored by Stanley Baldwin's Conservative government.

Flash. Ostentatious or gaudy, as: a 'flash wedding', a 'flash hotel'.

Flashback. A scene in a film or novel set earlier than the current action. It is a useful narrative device that allows a writer to be flexible in the temporal structure of the plot. Some films have a flashback within a flashback. In *The Barefoot Contessa* (1954) Humphrey Bogart, while attending Ava Gardner's funeral (in the present), reminisces about the night when she visited his hotel (flashback) to tell him about her wedding night (flashback within a flashback). *The Locket* (1946) famously has a fourfold flashback, i.e. a flashback within a flashback within a flashback within a flashback.

In psychotherapy a flashback is a disturbing sudden vivid memory of an event in the past, especially as the result of a psychological trauma such as that resulting from an accident. A flashback of this kind may be accompanied by hallucinations and can be precipitated by circumstances similar to those of the original event. Thus for a person who has undergone a wartime experience, a flashback could be induced by a clap of thunder.

Flash Gordon. The spaceman hero created in imitation of Buck ROGERS by the American strip cartoonist Alex Raymond in 1934. Together with his girlfriend, Dale Arden, he has a series of adventures on the planet Mongo and elsewhere, and subsequently moved to other media, notably the cinema but also in novel form.

Flash Harry. A name for a loudly dressed and usually boorish man. The nickname was applied more kindly and specifically to the orchestral conductor Sir Malcolm Sargent (1895–1967), famous for his debonair manner and dapper appearance. Sargent himself claimed the name referred to the way he flashed round the world. When Sir Thomas Beecham heard that Sargent was conducting in Tokyo, he is said to have remarked, 'Ah! Flash in Japan!'

> 'He's no Flash Harry,' says a friend. 'You won't see a fleet of Ferraris in his drive.'
> *heat* (13–19 January 2000)

Flat cap. A man's cloth cap with a peak, similar to a CLOTH CAP but unlike it worn by an upper-class male or a member of the aristocracy. The names differentiate the two types of wearer.

> A Barbour, green wellies and a flat cap are perfectly sensible garb for the country but they also convey a

certain set of Countryside Alliance values, of a person at ease with old landowner hierarchies.

Sunday Express (27 February 2000)

Flat Earth Society. An ALTERNATIVE scientific organization that emerged at the turn of the 20th century from the 19th-century Universal Zetetic Society and that developed under the guidance or misguidance of Samuel Shenton (d.1971), an Englishman. Members hold that the earth is patently flat, as one can see with one's own eyes, that there are many references to the fact in the Bible, in which the Old Testament implies that the earth is flat and in which the New Testament tells how Jesus 'ascended' into heaven, that one has long spoken of 'the four corners of the earth' and that the landings on the moon in the 1960s were faked by HOLLYWOOD. The North Pole is thus at the centre of the earth and not, as its name implies, at its most northern point. At the close of the 20th century the society's president was an American, Charles K. Johnson, of Lancaster, California.

Flatland. The setting of Edwin A. Abbott's novel of the same name (1952). It is a land where all objects, both animate and inanimate, appear two-dimensional. It has no sun and its houses are windowless, since light mysteriously appears inside and out, day or night. The size and shape of the inhabitants depend on age and status. Women, at the bottom of the social stratum, are straight lines, while the rest of society vary from soldiers and workmen, as isosceles triangles, to priests, who are perfect circles.

Flatliner. Medical jargon for a person whose heart has stopped beating. The reference is to the flat line that appears on an electrocardiograph screen when this occurs. The term was popularized by the film *Flatliners* (1990), in which medical students experiment to see if there is life after death.

Flat spin. To be in a 'flat spin' is to be very flurried, to be in a panic. In flying, a flat spin is when the longitudinal axis of an aircraft inclines downwards at an angle of less than 45°. In the early days this inevitably involved loss of control. It later came to be an aerial manoeuvre performed at low level in air combat as an evasive action.

Flat top. A style of haircut in which the hair is cut short on the top of the head so that it stands up and appears flat.

Flattop. A colloquial US term for an aircraft carrier.

Flaubert's Parrot. A novel (1984) by Julian Barnes (b.1946), in which the life and literary pursuits of the French novelist Gustave Flaubert (1821–80) are investigated by Geoffrey Braithwaite, a retired English doctor, as a means of coming to terms with the suicide of his wife. Parallels are drawn between Flaubert's eight-year affair with the poet Louise Colet (1810–76) and the unfaithfulness of Braithwaite's wife. The title refers to a stuffed parrot that Flaubert borrowed from a museum and set on his desk while writing the story 'Un Cœur Simple', in which a parrot, alive and then stuffed, is an object of reverence to the heroine.

Flavour of the month. A person or thing that is temporarily fashionable or in favour. The term evolved in the 1970s from an advertising phrase of the 1940s aimed at US ice cream consumers.

> When last she worked there she had been young, attractive, unattached. She had been 'flavour of the month'. But returning she was in a rather different situation: 'married, a mother, with outside commitments'.
>
> *The Times* (2 June 1998)

Fleadh (Irish, 'feast', 'banquet'). A festival of Irish or Celtic music, dancing and culture, as staged in various parts of Britain in the 20th century. The best known is the one first held in Finsbury Park, London, in 1990 and now having its equivalent in New York and other US cities. It attracts top Irish bands and performers and was the creation of the Irish rock promoter Vince Power (b.1947). The word is pronounced 'flah'.

Flea market. A street market selling second-hand goods and the like, so called because the clutter of bric-à-brac and old clothes is conducive to fleas. The term was adopted in the 1920s from the French *marché aux puces*, the oldest and best known being that at St Ouen, on the northern edge of Paris, which has stalls selling clothes, shoes, records, books and junk of all kinds, as well as expensive antiques. *See also* FLEA PIT.

Flea pit. A colloquialism dating from the 1930s for a cinema, some of which were cheaply constructed and poorly furnished with dusty seats and floor coverings that literally bred fleas.

Fleet's lit up. One of the earliest and most famous of broadcasting gaffes came in 1937, when Lieutenant Commander Tommy Woodrooffe (1899–1978) commentated live for the BBC on the Spithead Naval Review. The commander, who appears from the recording to a be a little the worse for wear ('lit up' in the slang of the time), slurred: 'At the present moment the whole fleet is lit up. When I say "lit up" I mean lit up by fairy lamps. It's fantastic. It isn't a fleet at all … it's Fairyland. The whole fleet is in Fairyland,' and so on for a few more moments, during which the lights went off and Woodrooffe appeared to be convinced that the fleet had actually disappeared into thin air, at which point the broadcast cut to the studio announcer. This did not quite end Woodrooffe's broadcasting career. Commentating on the FA Cup Final in 1938 he announced 'If there's another goal now I'll eat my hat.' There was, and he kept his word.

Fleming's rules. Memory aids for recalling the relative directions of the magnetic field, current and motion in an electric generator or motor, using one's fingers. Extend the hand vertically with the thumb pointing upwards, the first finger forwards, and the second finger at right angles to it. The three directions are represented by the thumb (*m* for *m*otion), first finger or forefinger (*f* for *f*ield) and second finger (*c* for *c*urrent). The left hand is used for motors, and the right for generators and dynamos. The devices were the invention of the English physicist John Fleming (1849–1945).

Flexible friend. A punning name for a credit card, which is 'flexible' because it allows its bearer to negotiate varying amounts of money and because the PLASTIC of which it is made can be bent. The phrase originated in the early 1980s as an advertising slogan for the Access credit card.

Flicks. The cinema, a film show, an expression deriving from the early days of such shows in the 1920s, when the pictures 'flickered' on the screen. 'Flick' is still current as a colloquial term for a film.

Flimsy. An old journalists' term for newspaper copy, arising from the thin paper (often used with a sheet of carbon paper to take a copy) on which reporters and others wrote up their matter for the press. The white £5 Bank of England note, which ceased to be legal tender in March 1961, was known as a flimsy. In the Royal Navy the name is also given to the brief certificate of conduct issued to an officer by his captain on the termination of his appointment to a ship or establishment. The derivation is again from the thin-quality paper.

Flintstones, The. The animated television series of this name (1960–66), a Hanna-Barbera production, recounted the day-to-day adventures of the Stone Age couple Fred and Wilma Flintstone and their neighbours, Barney and Betty Rubble, who lead a suburban existence in a world of Palaeolithic vehicles and dinosaur-powered machines. There have been various comic books and strips continuing the stories, and Fred Flintstone, in particular, is remembered for his exultant cry, 'Yabba-dabba-doo!'

Flip one's lid, To. To throw a fit of temper; to lose one's self-control. The image is that of a pot boiling over. The phrase dates from the 1940s. *See also* BLOW ONE'S TOP.

Flip side. The converse; the undesirable aspect of something. The allusion is to the reverse or less important side of a gramophone record, especially a pop single, as the side the listener 'flips' over to after hearing the main side. The original sense dates from the late 1940s.

> The book [Victoria Griffin's *The Mistress*] describes how most mistresses fall into their role passively. … The flip side of this is that most approaches are initiated by men.
> *Sunday Times* (19 September 1999)

Flirty fishing. A method of attracting potential members to a religious cult by beguiling them with expressions of love and friendship, as a sort of CHARM OFFENSIVE. The modern colloquialism in fact has biblical overtones: 'I will make you fishers of men' (Matthew 4:19). A more direct equivalent expression for such recruitment is LOVE-BOMBING.

Float someone's boat, To. To appeal to them or excite them. The picture is of a grounded boat being freed by rising water or the incoming tide, an image that is perhaps ultimately sexual.

> Sitting … on one's own eating microwaveable Swedish meatballs washed down with aquavit does not exactly float my boat.
> *Sunday Times* (21 November 1999)

Flogging and whipping. Powers of the British courts to pass a sentence of corporal punishment were abolished by the Criminal Justice Act 1948, both for adults and juvenile offenders.

Flook. A bear-like beast with a trumpet-like snout and magical powers created for his strip cartoons in the *Daily Mail* by the artist Wally Fawkes (b.1924) under the pen-name 'Trog'. He appeared from 1949 to 1984 when he was transferred for a time to the *Daily Mirror*. The series was originally intended for children but soon evolved into a vehicle of adult satire and comedy at the expense of SWINGING LONDON.

Flower girl. Originally a woman or girl who sold flowers in the streets, but more recently a young girl who carries flowers at a wedding or scatters them before the bride.

Flower of Scotland. A song written and performed in the late 1960s by the Corries, a Scottish folk music duo, and taken up as the favourite song at football and rugby matches north of the border, replacing SCOTLAND THE BRAVE as the unofficial Scottish national anthem. In 1998 the *Herald* newspaper of Glasgow ran a competition for a new Scottish anthem. The winner, announced in January 1999, was William Jackson's *Land of Light*.

Flower people. Supporters of a garishly clad youth cult of the mid-1960s who advocated peace and love, FLOWER POWER, as a substitute for materialism.

Flowerpot Men, The. Two flowerpot-dwelling identical puppets named Bill and Ben who first appeared on BBC children's television in 1952–4 as part of the WATCH WITH MOTHER programmes. They have since achieved a kind of cult status. Bill and Ben emerge from their pots to play when the gardener goes home for lunch and are warned of his imminent return by their friend Little Weed. The Flowerpot Men speak in a kind of gibberish, involving frequent use of the nonsense word 'flobbalot'.

Flower power. The power of the FLOWER PEOPLE or Flower Children, based on the precept 'Make love, not war'. The Flower Children, also known as the BEAUTIFUL PEOPLE, were a new form of HIPPIE movement, whose adherents were characterized by the wearing of bells and flowers. They appeared in Britain in 1967, taking their pattern from San Francisco. The term itself may have been suggested by BLACK POWER. *See also* SUMMER OF LOVE.

Fluff. The nickname of the Australian-born disc jockey Alan Freeman (b.1927), not as might be supposed for his 'fluffs' or mistakes on air but apparently from the old fluffy pullover that he wore.

Flute-playing. The English footballer Paul Gascoigne (*see* GAZZA) twice pretended to play the flute when playing for Rangers against Celtic. The act was seen as provocative, as it could be interpreted as a symbol of militant Protestantism and thus likely to inflame the age-old sectarianism that still exists among some fans of the two Glasgow clubs. (Flute bands are particularly associated with the Protestant Orange Order, which still flourishes in Northern Ireland.) On the first occasion Gascoigne claimed he was unaware of the response that his action could provoke. The second incident occurred as he was warming up

before playing as substitute in the 1998 New Year match. He was reported to Strathclyde police and substantially fined by Rangers.

Flutter one's eyelashes at someone, To. To flirt with them. The eyes play an important role in the art of seduction.

Fly a desk, To. In RAF parlance, to take up a civil service or other office job after retiring as a pilot.

> Stanic found work in the Valuer's Department of the Treasury, based first in Whitehall and subsequently in Notting Hill. It was 'flying a desk' – but it paid the bills.
>
> *The Times* (7 February 2000)

Fly blind, To. To pilot an aircraft solely by means of instruments, the opposite of visual navigation.

Flyby. A flight past a particular object, especially for purposes of observation, as a spacecraft past a planet or satellite.

Fly or **drive by the seat of one's pants, To.** To rely on instinct rather than on knowledge. The phrase originated with US Air Force pilots in the Second World War. The concept is of sitting in the pilot's or driver's seat but being unprepared for what one may encounter as one proceeds.

> He'll be interviewing three guests, but won't know who they are until they walk on to the set; no researchers' notes, no autocue to remind him of their achievements: he'll be flying by the seat of his no doubt immaculately-ironed pants.
>
> *The Times* (29 May 1999)

Flyer, The. *See* KITTY HAWK.

Flying bedstead. A nickname of the experimental wingless and rotorless VTOL (vertical takeoff and landing) jet aircraft demonstrated in Britain in 1954. Its official designation was the Rolls-Royce Thrust Measuring Rig (TMR). The nickname was inspired by its appearance.

Flying bishop. An informal term dating from the 1990s for an Anglican bishop appointed to minister in another bishop's diocese to those who do not accept the ordination of women. The formal title of such bishops is 'Provincial Episcopal Visitors'. The analogy is with a FLYING PICKET.

Flying circus. An exhibition of aerobatics, as by aircraft at an air show. *See also* MONTY PYTHON'S FLYING CIRCUS.

Flying Duchess. Mary du Caurroy Russell, Duchess of Bedford (1865–1937). After making record-breaking return flights to India (1929) and South Africa (1930) with Captain Barnard, she obtained an 'A' pilot's licence in 1933 and disappeared on a solo flight over the North Sea in March 1937.

Flying Finn. The Finnish runner Paavo Nurmi (1897–1973) earned this apt nickname following his successes in the 1924 Olympics in Paris, in which he won a record nine gold medals. More recently the title has been accorded to Hannu Mikkola (b.1942), world rally champion in 1983. The name has since been adopted for almost any famous Finn, especially one who travels, as the following, describing the Finnish conductor and composer Esa-Pekka Salonen (b.1958):

> The flying Finn … has had seven great years in Los Angeles, where his meticulous musicianship has disciplined the Philharmonic.
> *The Times* (26 June 1999)

Flying Fortress. A nickname for the Boeing B–17, a US long-range bomber developed in the 1930s and widely deployed in the Second World War.

Flying Peacemaker. US Secretary of State Henry Kissinger (b.1923) was so dubbed by the press in the 1970s from his frequent journeys to world trouble spots and his SHUTTLE DIPLOMACY in the Middle East and Africa.

Flying picket. A picket that moves from one site to another in an industrial dispute. In the miners' strike of 1984 many flying pickets went to Nottinghamshire to support their colleagues in Britain's second largest coalfield. As a result of their activities, flying pickets were declared illegal under the 1980 Employment Act, and striking miners were confined to their own pits. *See also* KING ARTHUR.

Flying saucers. Mysterious objects supposedly resembling revolving, partially luminous discs that shoot across the sky at a high velocity and at a great height. They were largely brought to public attention by the US writer George Adamski, who in books such as *Flying Saucers Have Landed* (1953) told of travelling into space with extraterrestrials. The landing or sighting of flying saucers was reported on several occasions in the 1950s and 1960s, but their cult has now mostly faded.

The term itself is said to owe its origin to the American Kenneth Arnold, who after seeing a formation of objects in the Cascade Mountains, Washington, in June 1947 described them as moving 'like a saucer would if you skipped it across water'. A local reporter

picked up the phrase and coined the term 'flying saucer'. *See also* UFO.

Flying Scotsman. Designed by Sir Nigel Gresley, locomotive No. 4472 of this name was built in 1923 in Doncaster, Yorkshire, for the London and North-Eastern Railway. It was soon breaking new ground, and on 1 May 1928 made the first non-stop express run from London to Edinburgh in eight hours and three minutes. Its moment of glory came on 30 November 1934, when on a test run between London and Leeds it reached a speed of 160kph (100mph) over a stretch of 548m (600 yards) between Grantham and Peterborough. It was withdrawn in 1963 and after touring the United States for four years was bought by Sir William McAlpine of the building firm. It proved prohibitive to run, however, and in 1995 was retired with a cracked firebox before being rescued and lovingly restored by Tony Marchington, a computer software millionaire. On 4 July 1999, its expensive renovation completed, it once again steamed out of King's Cross station bearing its familiar engine number. The name *Flying Scotsman* had been in use for the service itself since 1862. *See also* TITLED TRAINS.

Flying squad. A police detachment able to proceed rapidly to the scene of a crime such as a robbery. In the Metropolitan Police, the Flying Squad became the best known department of Scotland Yard. It was set up in 1918 to patrol dangerous areas of London and in 1920 acquired two motor vans to help in the task. These brought it the name of Flying Squad. The department was reorganized in 1978 as the Central Robbery Squad, but its old name is still in use. *See also* SWEENEY.

> Macavity's a Mystery Cat: he's called the Hidden Paw –
> For he's the master criminal who can defy the Law.
> He's the bafflement of Scotland Yard, the Flying Squad's despair:
> For when they reach the scene of the crime –
> *Macavity's not there!*
> T.S. ELIOT: *Old Possum's Book of Practical Cats*, 'Macavity: The Mystery Cat' (1939)

Fly low, To. To have one's trouser fly undone or gaping. A punning but rather dated phrase.

> 'You are flying rather low, old boy' used to be the warning.
> *The Times* (5 June 1999)

Fly on the wall. A hidden observer, who can overhear discussions or watch events unnoticed. A fly-on-the-wall technique, recording events as they happen without any overt artistic direction, is used by some makers of film and television documentaries. A pioneer example of the genre was the BBC's *The Family* (1974), a 12-part serial following the day-to-day life of the Wilkins family of Reading. The phrase dates from the 1940s.

> You and I would think that if there is a [television] cookery programme on one side, then perhaps they'd better put a frock show or a medical fly-on-the-wall on the other.
> *Sunday Times* (20 June 1999)

Flyover zone. A virtual synonym for MIDDLE AMERICA, consisting of states that one mostly passes over in an aircraft flying from coast to coast without ever actually visiting.

> The campaign trail is a nasty, brutish place for a candidate's advisers, forced to visit dull states in the 'flyover zone' of middle America, and stay in bad motels.
> *The Times Magazine* (27 November 1999)

Flypast. A ceremonial flight of aircraft over a particular building or area.

Flyposting. The posting of bills or advertisements on unauthorized places, such as the windows of empty shops. The expression presumably alludes to the fact that the posters fly as soon as they have stuck up their bills. *See also* FLY-TIPPING.

Fly the flag, To. *See* SHOW THE FLAG.

Fly-tipping. The tipping of refuse in unauthorized sites. *See also* FLYPOSTING.

FMS. *See* FALSE MEMORY SYNDROME.

Foggy Bottom. A nickname for the US State Department, whose headquarters, to the southwest of the White House in Washington, D.C., are in a locality subject to fogs from the neighbouring Potomac River. The name has become punningly synonymous with political routine and government bureaucracy.

Foleys. In film-making a slang term for sound effects, especially as devised by the US expert Jack Foley, who established modern techniques for creating sounds recorded to fit the images on the screen. A 'Foley walker' is thus a technician who walks on boxes of gravel or starch to represent the sound of someone walking on gravel or snow out of doors.

Fond farewell. A tender or affectionate (or affecting) parting. The phrase owes much to its alliterative appeal and appears to have become popular only in the 20th century, when it became associated with funerals and memorial services. The *Daily Mirror* of 2 May 1995 tells how more than 500 admirers of the satirist and humorist Peter Cook 'gathered for the fond farewell in a London church'.

Fonz. The teenage hero of the US SITCOM *Happy Days* (1974–84), in full Arthur Fonzarelli. With his black leather jacket, slangy speech and 'thumbs up' gesture he was the epitome of 1950s COOL. He was played by Henry Winkler.

Fool on the Hill, The. A song about isolation by the BEATLES, credited to John Lennon and Paul McCartney and released in Britain in November 1967. The Fool on the Hill is a kind of *idiot savant*, a 'man with a foolish grin' living 'alone on the hill' in a world of child-like ignorance. His intrinsic wisdom of the ways of the world is implied by the words of the chorus:

> But the fool on the hill
> Sees the sun going down,
> And the eyes in his head,
> See the world spinning round.

The song appeared in the film of MAGICAL MYSTERY TOUR.

Football club nicknames. Several English football clubs have nicknames that are not of immediately obvious origin. The following is a selection of those in use at some time in the 20th century. The majority of the clubs themselves were founded in the late 19th century, and the year of formation is given in brackets after the club name. Each name is usually preceded by 'The'.

> **Addicks:** Charlton Athletic (1905). A corruption of the second word of the club name. *See also* Latics *below.*
>
> **Baggies:** West Bromwich Albion (1879). Said to refer to the baggy working clothes worn because of the heat by supporters from the local ironworks. *See also* Throstles *below.*
>
> **Bantams:** Bradford City (1903). From the club's colours, supposedly those of a Bantam chicken.
>
> **Bees:** Brentford (1889). 'B' for 'Brentford', as well as the insect, with its deadly sting.
>
> **Biscuitmen:** Reading (1871). For the Huntley and Palmer biscuit factory in the town until 1974.
>
> **Blades:** Sheffield United (1889). For the city's famous steel industry, and especially its cutlery.
>
> **Blues:** (1) Ipswich Town (1878); (2) Manchester City (1894); (3) Chelsea (1905). From the clubs' colours.

Other club sides thus nicknamed include Birmingham City, Carlisle United and Chester City.

Canaries: Norwich City (1902). From the city's former fame as a centre for the breeding and exhibition of canaries and other cage birds, reflected in the team's yellow and green strip.

Chairboys: Wycombe Wanderers (1884). From High Wycombe's furniture-making industry.

Cherries: AFC Bournemouth (1899). From the team's red and black strip.

Clarets: Burnley (1882). From the team's claret, blue and white strip.

Cobblers: Northampton Town (1897). For the city's boot and shoe manufacture.

Cottagers: Fulham (1879). From their home ground, at Craven Cottage.

Dons: Wimbledon (1889). From the district's name, punning on the academic sense.

Filberts: Leicester City (1884). From their home ground, at Filbert Street.

Glaziers: Crystal Palace (1905). From the Crystal Palace, the exhibition building resembling a giant greenhouse, originally in Hyde Park but then moved to Sydenham, where the team's ground was.

GRECIANS

Gulls: Torquay United (1910). From the birds at this seaside town. *See also* Seagulls *below*.

Gunners: Arsenal (1886). For the club's original location near Woolwich Arsenal.

Hammers: West Ham United (1895). From the district name, punning on the punishing instrument.

Hatters: Luton Town (1885). From the town's fame as a centre of straw-hat manufacture.

Hornets: Watford (1891). From the club's yellow and black strip.

Imps: Lincoln City (1883). From the 'Lincoln Imp', a famous carving high up in Lincoln Cathedral.

Iron: Scunthorpe United (1899). From the ironstone beds that brought the town industrial fame.

Ironsides: Middlesbrough (1876). From the heavy industries formerly based in the area.

Latics: (1) Oldham Athletic (1895); (2) Wigan Athletic (1932). A corruption of the second word of the club name. *See also* Addicks *above*.

Magpies: (1) Newcastle United (1881); (2) Notts County (1862). From the black and white strip of each.

Mariners: Grimsby Town (1878). From the town's once famous fishing harbour.

Merry Millers: Rotherham United (1884), From the team's home ground, at the Millmoor Ground.

Minstermen: York City (1922). From York Minster, the city's crowning glory.

Owls: Sheffield Wednesday (1867). The club's ground is located in a district divided into the localities of Hillsborough and Owlerton. The latter gave the punning nickname. *See also* HILLSBOROUGH DISASTER.

Pilgrims: Plymouth Argyle (1886). From the 'Pilgrim Fathers' who set sail for America from Plymouth in 1620.

Pirates: Bristol Rovers (1883). From the club's 'roving' style without a home base, and for Bristol's fame as a port from which pirates set sail.

POSH

Potters: Stoke City (1863). From the location of Stoke-on-Trent at the heart of the Potteries.

Quakers: Darlington (1883). From Darlington's former fame as a railway centre, thanks to the financial backing of John B. Pease, one of the town's prominent Quaker residents.

Railwaymen: Crewe Alexandra (1877). From Crewe's once famous railway junction and workshops.

Rams: Derby County (1884). From the mythical Derby Ram, a beast so huge that it covered an acre with every stride, while eagles built their eyries in its horns. The annual Derby Tup plays, with a man dressed as a tup (a castrated ram), are performed in Derbyshire on Boxing Day.

Robins: Bristol City (1894). From the team's red and white strip.

Red Devils: Manchester United (1892). From the club's colours.

Reds: (1) Nottingham Forest (1865); (2) Liverpool (1892). From the clubs' colours.

Rokermen: Sunderland (1879). From the club's former home ground, Roker Park; following the club's move to the STADIUM OF LIGHT in 1997 supporters were asked to choose a new name.

Saints: Southampton (1885). From the club's original name, Southampton St Mary's.

Seagulls: Brighton and Hove Albion (1901). From the club's seaside location. *See also* Gulls *above*.

Seasiders: BLACKPOOL (1887).

Sky Blues: Coventry City (1883). From the club's sky-blue strip, itself reflecting 'Coventry blue' as an old name for a type of blue thread made at Coventry.

Spurs: Tottenham Hotspur (1882). From the club name, punning on the device to urge on a horse.

Throstles: West Bromwich Albion (1879). From the thrushes (throstles) that reputedly flocked in the bushes of the area known as the Hawthorns, now the team home ground. *See also* Baggies *above*.

Toffeemen or **Toffees:** Everton (1878). From the former well known 'Everton toffee' brandname.

Trotters: Bolton Wanderers (1874). From the team's nomadic style before they had a home ground.

Tykes: Barnsley (1887). From the 'Yorkshire tyke', a nickname for a Yorkshireman.

Valiants: Port Vale (1876). From the club name, punningly.

Villans: Aston Villa (1874). From the club name, punningly.

Whites: Leeds United (1919). From the club colours.

Wolves: Wolverhampton Wanderers (1877). From the club name, punning on the voracious animal.

Outside England colourful nicknames exist for African football teams, many adopted from animals, as the following:

Atlas Lions: Morocco

Bafana Bafana: South Africa ('The Boys'; the women's team is Banyana Banyana, 'The Girls')

Black Panthers: Angola

Black Stars: Ghana

Cranes: Uganda

Crocodiles: Lesotho

Desert Rats: Namibia (*see also* DESERT RATS)

Desert Warriors: Algeria

Eagles: Mali

Elephants: Côte d'Ivoire (former Ivory Coast)

Indomitable Lions: Cameroon

Leopards: Congo Democratic Republic

Lions: Senegal

Lone Star: Liberia (referring to the single white star in the Liberian flag)

Mambas: Mozambique

Mighty Zambia: Zambia

Pharaohs: Egypt

Red Devils: Congo

Scorpions: Gambia

Super Eagles: Nigeria

Warriors: Zimbabwe

Zebras: Botswana

Jamaica's nickname, the Reggae Boys, is said to have been coined by a journalist in 1995 when the team travelled to Africa to play Zambia in a friendly. *See also* BRAZILIAN FOOTBALLERS.

Football pools. An organized system of betting on the results of football matches. Participants bet by postal coupon or through a collection agent (or point) on which matches will finish in a score-draw, i.e. a drawn match in which the sides score at least one goal each. The total prize money, or pool, is distributed to those who have a winning entry, the size of the pay-out depending on the number of winners and the amount of money in the pool. Football pools were launched by Littlewoods in 1923, originally in Manchester. The first £100,000 prize was won in 1950 and the first £1 million prize in 1987. The biggest pay-out by the end of the 20th century was £2,924,622 on 19 November 1994 by Littlewoods Pools to a syndicate from Manchester.

Foot in both camps. To have a foot in both camps is to have an interest or stake concurrently in two parties or sides. The expression dates from the 1930s.

> One initiative has planted a foot squarely in both camps. *New Beginnings* targets the nowness of the young while proclaiming that the Bard really carries the cultural flame.
> *The Times* (28 December 1999)

Foot-in-mouth disease. The perennial bane of making grossly tactless or embarrassing remarks. The expression dates from the 1960s and puns on both 'foot-and-mouth disease' as the contagious disease of livestock and the continual knack of 'opening one's mouth and putting one's foot in it'. A punningly pedantic term for the affliction is 'dontopedology'.

Foot in the door. To get a foot in the door is to gain a first introduction to a business or organization. The allusion is to a door-to-door salesman or canvasser, who when the door is opened, or is about to be closed, blocks it ajar with one foot. *See also* TOE IN THE DOOR.

Footsie. The acronym of the Financial Times-Stock Exchange 100 share index, influenced by footsie, the amorous sport of feeling out a person's foot with one's own under the table. One can play footsie just as one 'plays' the stock market. The nickname dates from the mid-1980s.

Forbidden Planet. A SCIENCE FICTION film (1956) adapted by Cyril Hume from a story by Irving Block and Allen Adler about a space mission that lands on the remote planet Altair-4 to check on the welfare of the scientist Morbius and his daughter Altaira only to be terrorized by an invisible monster. The film, which many years later inspired the hit stage musical *Return to the Forbidden Planet*, was loosely based on Shakespeare's *The Tempest*, Morbius equating with Prospero, Altaira with Miranda, Robby the Robot with Ariel, and the monster with Caliban.

Forces' Sweetheart. The nickname of the popular singer Vera Lynn (originally Vera Margaret Welch) (b.1917), who became a household name in the Second World War with her radio show *Sincerely Yours* (1941–7) and who went to Burma in 1944 to entertain the British troops. She is specially associated with sentimentally patriotic songs such as 'The WHITE CLIFFS OF DOVER' (1941) and 'We'll Meet Again' (1939). She was made a Dame of the British Empire in 1975.

> Jim Davidson conjured up a new vision of the Forces' sweetheart yesterday, with Vera Lynn ... replaced by Geri Halliwell [of the SPICE GIRLS].
> *The Times* (7 May 1999)

For colored girls who have considered suicide when the rainbow is enuf. A play (1974) by the US playwright Ntozake Shange (b.1948) consisting of 20 'choreopoems' about the experiences of African-American women in modern Western society. One of the longest running shows in Broadway history, the play's extraordinary title, with its unconventional spellings and rejection of accepted grammatical rules, was intended by the author to represent the independence of African-American culture from Western influence. The mutilation of words throughout the title and text are reportedly meant to remind the reader of the mutilation of African slaves through branding and other punishments.

For crying out loud! An exclamation of frustration or anger, arising in the early 20th century as a US euphemism for 'For Christ's sake!'

Forget it! An exclamation dating from the 1960s to imply dismissal of an idea or proposal, or to waive an apology or expression of gratitude, or to imply that the previous speaker did not understand the gist of the conversation.

> 'Get real! Grow up!' he says at the suggestion that his intentions are strictly mercenary. 'Anything to do with exploitation, forget it.'
> *The Times* (15 June 1999)

Forgotten Army. A name for the British army in Burma after the fall of Rangoon in 1942 and the evacuation west and subsequent cutting by the Japanese of the supply link from India to Nationalist China. The words are said to derive from Lord Louis Mountbatten's encouragement to his troops when he took over as Supreme Allied Commander Southeast Asia in late 1943:

> Right, now I understand people think you're the Forgotten Army on the Forgotten Front. I've come here to tell you you're quite wrong. You're not the Forgotten Army on the Forgotten Front. No, make no mistake about it. Nobody's ever *heard* of you.
> LORD LOUIS MOUNTBATTEN, quoted in Richard Hough *Mountbatten: Hero of Our Time* (1980)

Former Naval Person. A code name used by Winston Churchill to refer to himself in his secret communications with US President Franklin Roosevelt (FDR) prior to America's entry into the Second World War. Churchill had been first lord of the Admiralty (1911–15, 1939–40).

Formula One. Until 1906 international motor racing was open to all kinds of automobile. When it became clear that driving ability could not be fairly tested in cars of different types, races were organized for cars with similar specifications. Types of vehicles were grouped into various formulas, each defined by the characteristics of a car's performance. Formula One eventually applied to cars weighing not less than 505kg, with a maximum width of 200cm, a four-stroke engine with a maximum 12 cylinders, an engine capacity of 3500cc and no turbocharger.

For Pete's sake! A mild exclamation of annoyance, exasperation or the like, dating from the 1920s. It may be a euphemistic form of 'For pity's sake!'

Forrest Gump. A film (1994) directed by Robert Zemeckis and adapted by Eric Roth from a novel of the same title by Winston Groom about an intellectually challenged Southerner who largely by accident witnesses many of the great events of his time and comes face to face with many of the great figures of postwar US history. Played by Tom Hanks, Forrest

Gump became a symbol of well-meaning American conservatism whose good nature won the plaudits of leading Republican politicians. However, the film was described by one exasperated critic as 'a well-meaning celebration of stupidity'.

Fortnum–Mason line. A jocular name for the imaginary geographical line that marks off the supposed 'lush' south of England from the 'lean' north and that thus pinpoints the NORTH-SOUTH DIVIDE or separates the south from all parts of the country north of WATFORD. The phrase adopts the name of the prestigious London store Fortnum and Mason as a pun on the Mason–Dixon Line that is the boundary between Maryland and Pennsylvania in the United States.

FORTRAN. *See* PROGRAMMING LANGUAGES.

Fortress Europe (German *Festung Europa*). A Nazi propaganda image of a heavily fortified mainland Europe, impregnable to attack, especially by the USA and Britain. The propaganda image was not entirely without foundation. The Allied campaign up through Italy had to overcome a succession of heavily fortified positions, such as the GUSTAV LINE and the GOTHIC LINE. Any Allied invasion of northwest Europe had to face the so-called ATLANTIC WALL along the French and Belgian coasts, although German newsreel footage leaked to Allied countries via neutrals carefully exaggerated the strength of the coastal defences. Finally, there were the WEST WALL and SIEGFRIED LINE along Germany's western frontier. Before the D-DAY landings, Nazi radio propagandist AXIS SALLY (US citizen Mildred Gillars) broadcast to Allied troops, warning them of the dire consequences of trying to invade Fortress Europe. (It was this broadcast that led to Gillars serving twelve years for treason.) As it turned out, the German defences in Normandy were much less strong than in the Pas de Calais, where the invasion had been expected.

Fortune 500. A list of the 500 largest US industrial corporations, published annually in *Fortune* magazine. From 1970 there has also been a Fortune 1000, including the next 500 largest.

Forty Martyrs. The short name of the Forty Martyrs of England and Wales, a group of representative English and Welsh Roman Catholics who were martyred between 1535 and 1679. They were canonized by Pope Paul VI on 25 October 1970 after being selected from 200 already beatified by earlier popes. They include 13 seminary priests, 10 Jesuits, three Benedictine monks, three Carthusian, one Brigettine, two Franciscans and one Austin Friar. The remaining seven, four men and three women, were lay folk. *See also* BLACK MARTYRS.

42nd Street. A street in Manhattan running east from the Hudson through a notorious RED-LIGHT DISTRICT near TIMES SQUARE. Its name is sometimes used for similar districts elsewhere. It is also the title of a film musical (1933) with a score by Harry Warren (1893–1981) about life backstage at a Broadway theatre. 42nd Street is the street in Broadway where the biggest theatres are situated.

For Whom the Bell Tolls. A novel (1940) by Ernest Hemingway (1899–1961). It was written out of his experiences as a war correspondent in 1937 during the civil war in Spain. He was in the company of the book's dedicatee, his mistress Martha Gellhorn (1908–98), who during the conflict also acted as a war correspondent (they married in 1940). The mainspring of the plot is the blowing up of a bridge, symbolizing also the futility of the politicization of a country. A stolid film version (1943), directed by Sam Wood, starred Gary Cooper and Ingrid Bergman in key roles. The title is a quotation from John Donne:

> Any man's death diminishes me, because I am involved in Mankind; And therefore never send to know for whom the bell tolls; it tolls for thee.
>
> *Devotions Upon Emergent Occasions.* Meditation No. 17 (1624)

Fosbury flop. In athletics a style of high jump in which the jumper clears the bar headfirst and backwards. It is named for its deviser and perfecter, the US athlete Dick Fosbury (b.1947), who won a gold medal at the 1968 Mexico Olympics using this technique.

Foucault's Pendulum. The second novel (1989; in Italian as *Il Pendolo di Foucault*, 1988) by Umberto Eco (b.1932), which he wrote 'because one novel could have been an accident'. Experimental in form, it features computer science and Rosicrucianism. The pendulum devised by Léon Foucault (1819–68) to demonstrate the rotation of the earth is the motif with which the novel opens: 'The sphere, hanging from a long wire set into the ceiling of the choir, swayed back and forth with isochronal majesty.'

Foul-mouthed Joe. A nickname of US Republican politician Joseph ('Joe') Gurney Cannon (1836–1926). As speaker of the House of Representatives (1903–11) he controlled Congress in a highly partisan manner with his profane and lashing tongue. Despite his tyrannical methods, he was personally liked by many, earning the fonder nickname Uncle Joe.

Fountain. The inspirational title given by the DADA artist Marcel Duchamp (1887–1968) to one of his 'ready-mades': a urinal placed on its side (1917). It was signed 'R. Mutt', the name of a firm of sanitary engineers. As a member of the jury of the first New York *Salon des Indépendants*, Duchamp submitted this work to his fellow jurors for consideration. Predictably enough they rejected it with indignation, and Duchamp resigned. Its shock value wore off in time, however, and at a Dada exhibition in the 1950s it hung over the main entrance, filled with geraniums.

4×4. Shorthand for 'four by four', as a colloquialism for a four-wheel drive vehicle, i.e. one that provides power directly from all four wheels, as distinct from the usual two front wheels or, less commonly, the rear two. Such vehicles were originally designed for driving over rugged terrain or OFF-ROADING generally but by the 1990s became the almost exclusive preserve of middle-class mothers in suburban residential areas, who used them for transporting their children to school and elsewhere and who came to look on them as a social accessory or STATUS SYMBOL.

> A 4×4 at the school gate has, in recent years, become as *de rigueur* as organic vegetables and DKNY jeans.
> *The Times* (1 December 1999)

Four-colour problem. A problem first posed in the early 1850s but not solved until 1976. The puzzle was to find the minimum number of colours required to colour a map in such a way that no two adjacent regions were of the same colour. Three colours are not enough, as can be seen in a map of four regions with each region contacting three others. It had been proved mathematically that five colours would serve, and in practice no map had ever been found in which four colours would not do. The problem was solved by a group of mathematicians at the University of Illinois by creating a catalogue of 'unavoidable' configurations that must be present in any graph, however large it is. They then showed how each of these configurations could be reduced to a smaller one in such a way that if the smaller one could be coloured with four colours, so could the original catalogue configuration. Thus if a map existed that could not be coloured with four colours, they could use their catalogue to find a smaller map that could not be so coloured, then a smaller one still, and so on. Such a

reduction process would lead to a map with only three or four regions, which supposedly could not be coloured with four colours. This absurd result, deriving from the hypothesis that a map coloured with more than four colours might exist, led to the conclusion that no such map exists. All maps can thus in fact be coloured with four colours.

Four Feathers, The. A novel (1902) by A.E.W. Mason (1865–1948). The four white feathers, symbols of cowardice, are given to Harry Feversham by three fellow officers and by his fiancée, when, fearful that he cannot measure up to his father's standards of bravery, he resigns his commission after his regiment is ordered to Egypt on active service. Harry follows after the regiment and in disguise performs two acts of incredible heroism, as a result of which the feathers are taken back, and he gets his girl after all. The story has been filmed several times, notably in 1939 under the direction of Zoltan Korda. This was remade in 1956 as *Storm over the Nile*, while an effective television version (1977) starred Beau Bridges, Robert Powell, Simon Ward, Richard Johnson and Jane Seymour.

4.50 from Paddington. A detective novel (1957; in USA as *What Mrs McGillicuddy Saw*, 1957; as *Murder She Said*, 1961) by Agatha Christie (1890–1976), featuring her spinster sleuth Jane MARPLE. From the 4.50 train from London's Paddington Station, Elspeth sees a man strangling a woman in a compartment in another train that is running alongside hers. Then the other train draws away. A disappointing film version, *Murder She Said* (1961), directed by George Pollock, was not even saved by a gallantly British Margaret Rutherford as Miss Marple.

Four Freedoms. The formulation of worldwide social and political objectives enunciated by Franklin D. Roosevelt in a message delivered to Congress on 6 January 1941. The president stated the freedoms to be the freedom of speech and expression, the freedom of every person to worship God in his own way, the freedom from want, and the freedom from fear.

4-H Club. One of a number of US clubs for young people aged 10 to 21 who pursue programmes of 'learning by doing' in farming, rearing livestock and the like. Their emblem is the four-leaf clover with the letter H on each leaf, and the designation itself derives from the vow: 'I pledge my head to clearer thinking, my heart to greater loyalty, my hands to larger service, and my health to better living, for my club, my community and my country.' The clubs originated among rural youth in the early 20th century and are sponsored by the Department of Agriculture.

Four-letter man. An obnoxious man, best summed up by the FOUR-LETTER WORD 'shit'.

Four-letter word. One of various short English words relating to sex or excrement. The two words commonly regarded as the grossest are those that came to be widely known in the 1990s as the F-WORD and the 'C-word'. The otherwise liberally minded *Oxford English Dictionary* did not even admit these two to its pages until it issued the first volume of its Supplement (A–G) in 1972. Although such words are still not used in polite society, they have gained an increasing degree of acceptance in the media and in literature. However, many newspapers still resort to dashes or asterisks when printing them, and their occurrence in literature, even of the 'serious' type, still offends many. *The F-Word*, edited by Jesse Sheidlower, was published in 1995 as a study of the history and usage of this particular expletive from the 15th century to the present day, and in 1999 Channel 4 screened *A Brief History of the F-Word*, a 60-minute documentary on the subject.

Four-letter words are sometimes referred to as 'Anglo-Saxon words', although some are not of Old English origin. 'Crap', for example, comes from Medieval Latin *crappa*, 'chaff', and PISS from Old French *pisser*. The term itself is also sometimes punningly applied to everyday words with four letters. Henry Livings' play *Eh?* (1965) was turned into a film under the title *Work is a Four-Letter Word* (1968), while Nicholas Monsarrat's two-volume autobiography was presented to the public as *Life is a Four-Letter Word* (1966, 1970). *See also* FOUR-LETTER MAN; F-WORD; SHIT.

> Good authors too
> Who once used better words
> Now only use four-letter words.
> COLE PORTER: 'Anything Goes' (song) (1934)

Four-minute men. The name given in the United States during the First World War to the members of a volunteer organization some 75,000 strong who, in 1917–18, set out to promote the sale of Liberty Loan Bonds and stir up support for the war in Europe. They gave talks of four minutes' duration to church congregations, cinema audiences, lodges and the like.

Four-minute mile. The running of a mile in 4 minutes was for many years the eagerly sought goal of professional athletes. The rigorous training and timed pacing of P.J. Nurmi (*see* FLYING FINN) achieved a time of 4 minutes 10.4 seconds in 1924, but Roger Bannister (b.1929) was the first man to achieve the ambition in 1954, when he breached the barrier at Oxford with a time of 3 minutes 59.4 seconds. In 1979 Sebastian Coe set a new world record of 3 minutes 49 seconds, only to be beaten almost immediately by Steve Ovett, who reduced this time by one-fifth of a second. The time has subsequently been gradually eroded. Coe beat his own record in 1981 with a running of 3 minutes 47.33 seconds. In July 1999 the Moroccan athlete Hicham El Guerrouj notched up a new world record with a mile in 3 minutes 43.13 seconds.

4' 33". A controversial and certainly unusual work by the US composer John Cage (1912–92), scored for any instrument or any combination of instruments. The piece consists of 4 minutes and 33 seconds of silence. It was first performed in 1952. Ten years later Cage went one better with 0' 00", designed 'to be performed in any way to anyone'. In his book entitled *Silence* (1961), Cage observed:

> nothing is accomplished by writing a piece of music
> nothing is accomplished by hearing a piece of music
> nothing is accomplished by playing a piece of music

Four Musketeers. The flamboyant French tennis players Jean Borotra (1898–1994), Jacques 'Toto' Brugnon (1895–1978), Henri Cochet (1901–87) and René Lacoste (1904–96) were thus known. They won the Davis Cup for France in six successive years (1927–32). *See also* BOUNDING BASQUE.

Fourpenny one. A blow; a hit; a 'clip round the ear'. The term may have its origin in rhyming slang, 'fourpenny bit' giving 'hit', although no coin of this value was current in the 1930s, when the expression is first recorded.

Four Saints in Three Acts. The teasingly misleading title of an opera by Virgil Thomson (1896–1989) to a libretto by Gertrude Stein (1874–1946). The opera, which is set in Spain, actually has four acts, and more than four saints (among whom are St Theresa and St Ignatius). Its first performance in 1934 was given by an all-black cast dressed in Cellophane.

Fourteen Points. The 14 conditions laid down by President Woodrow Wilson as those on which the Allies were prepared to make peace with Germany on the conclusion of the First World War. He outlined them in a speech to Congress on 8 January 1918, and they were eventually accepted as the basis for the peace. They were: (1) the renunciation of secret diplomacy; (2) freedom of navigation of the high seas; (3) freedom of trade; (4) the reduction of arms; (5) a settlement accommodating the peoples of the colonies as well as the colonialist powers; (6) respect for Russia's right of self-determination; (7) the restoration of Belgium; (8) German withdrawal from France and a settlement of the Alsace-Lorraine dispute; (9) a readjustment of the frontiers of Italy along ethnic lines; (10) the prospect of autonomy for the peoples of Austria-Hungary; (11) the restoration of Romania, Serbia and Montenegro, including free access to the sea for Serbia and international guarantees for the Balkan states; (12) the prospect of autonomy for the non-Turkish peoples of the Ottoman Empire and the unrestricted opening of the Straits, but at the same time sovereignty for the Turks in their own areas; (13) independence for Poland with access to the sea; and (14) 'a general association of nations' to guarantee every state's integrity. *See also* LEAGUE OF NATIONS; OPEN DIPLOMACY.

Fourteenth of October, The. A historical novel (1954) about the Norman invasion of Britain by Bryher, the name adopted in 1918 from one of the Scilly Isles by the feminist writer Winifred Ellerman (1894–1983). The Battle of Hastings was fought on 14 October 1066.

Fourth dimension. As a mathematical concept, a hypothetical dimension, whose relation to the recognized three of length, breadth and thickness is analogous to their relation with each other. Albert Einstein in 1921 introduced time as the fourth dimension in his Theory of Relativity. The expression is also occasionally used to describe something beyond the limits of normal experience.

Fourth leader. The fourth leading article in *The Times* from 1922 to 1966, usually light or humorous in nature. The role has subsequently been irregularly filled by the third leader.

Fourth man. *See* BURGESS AND MACLEAN.

Fourth Reich. A disparaging nickname for those who wish to see Britain fully integrated in the EUROPEAN UNION and her subsumption into EUROLAND. The analogy is with the THIRD REICH.

> 'We're giving England to the Fourth Reich, the Euro-loonies. In the last war, if you wanted to give your country to the Germans you got hung; these days you get prizes.'
>
> *Sunday Times* (21 November 1999)

Fourth Republic. The French Republic established in 1946 to replace the provisional governments that followed the collapse of the VICHY regime after D-DAY. It gave way to the Fifth Republic in 1958.

Fourth World. A name for those countries and communities of the THIRD WORLD that are regarded as the poorest and most underdeveloped. The tag was coined in 1974 by Robert McNamara (b.1916), US president of the World Bank.

Four Weddings and a Funeral. An astonishingly successful British comedy film (1994), written by Richard Curtis and directed by Mike Newell, about a reserved young Englishman's abiding love for an American called Carrie, which survives the four weddings and a funeral of the title before its consummation. Hugh Grant plays the young Englishman in his trademark 'charmingly diffident' manner. The film begins, famously, with the repetition by Grant of the word 'fuck', and it includes a moving reading of W.H. Auden's 'Funeral Blues' (1936), which briefly took a collection of the poet's verse into the bestseller lists, just as the film of The ENGLISH PATIENT engendered a short-lived interest in Hesiod.

Fowler. The short name of *A Dictionary of Modern English Usage*, by H.W. Fowler (1858–1933), first published in 1926 and soon established as a 'bible' for settling matters of dispute in the use of English. Fowler first made his name in 1906 with *The King's English*, a book about good and bad English written together with his brother, F.G. Fowler. A second edition of the *Dictionary*, revised by Sir Ernest Gowers, appeared in 1965, and a much more radical revision, edited by R.W. Burchfield, was issued in 1996 under the title *The New Fowler's Modern English Usage*. Fowler's name often occurs in the phrase 'according to Fowler'. The original Fowler was a well-balanced blend of fogeyish pedantry, sound advice and good-natured humour, and the distinctive style was evident from the headings of some of the general articles, which included 'Battered ornaments', 'Facetious formations', 'Novelty-hunting', 'Pairs & snares', 'Pride of knowledge', 'Sturdy indefensibles', 'Unequal yoke-fellows' and 'Worn-out humour'. The following is the opening sentence of the general article headed 'Hackneyed phrases':

> When *Punch* set down a heading that might be, & very likely has been, the title of a whole book, 'Advice to those about to marry', & boiled down the whole contents into a single word, & that a surprise, the

thinker of the happy thought deserved congratulations for a week; he hardly deserved immortality, but he has – anonymously, indeed – got it; a large percentage of the great British people cannot think of the dissuasive 'don't' without remembering, &, alas! reminding others, of him.

Fox, The. The nickname, sometimes self-applied, of various 20th-century criminals, among them the US child murderer Edward Hickman (1907–28), the British murderer, rapist and robber Arthur Hutchinson (b.1928) and the British rapist and burglar Malcolm Fairley (b.1952). The fox is a prime symbol of cunning and trickery.

Foxhole. A small slit trench or pit for one or more men.

Foxtrot. A short, quick walking pace, as of a fox. A foxtrot is also a ballroom dance originating in America, popular from the 1920s until the 1950s.

Foxy. As well as meaning 'crafty', as a fox is traditionally said to be, the word has also been used from the early 20th century to mean 'sexually attractive'.

> W/f [white female] … 21 years old and foxy, would like to hear from a gorgeous man with a terrific body.
> *Easyriders* (February 1983)

Foyle's. A name synonymous with bookshops. The store of W. & G. Foyle Ltd in Charing Cross Road, London, arose from the textbook-selling business set up by the brothers William and Gilbert Foyle in 1903. Their initial stock was second-hand, but they added new books in 1912. In 1930 William's daughter, Christina Foyle (1911–99), inaugurated monthly literary luncheons, held at the Grosvenor Hotel, to enable the reading public to meet distinguished writers and artists. She was managing director until her death, running the business traditionally and ignoring advances such as computerized billing even into the 1990s. William Foyle died in 1963, Gilbert in 1971.

Fraffly. Accordong to the writer Alistair Morrison, the brand of English spoken in London's West End, humorous examples of which are provided in *Fraffly Well Spoken* (1968) and *Fraffly Suite* (1969), under the supposed authorship of a Professor Afferbeck Lauder. Both volumes present comic dialogues in which upper-class English speech is spelled out phonetically to demonstrate its drawling absurdities. Thus 'York air scissors good as mine' translates as 'Your guess is as good as mine', 'Egg-wetter gree' as 'I quite agree', and 'Rilleh quettex trod nerreh!' as 'Really quite extraordinary!' *See also* STRINE.

F Plan Diet. The proprietary name of a type of high-fibre diet devised by Audrey Eyton in the early 1980s. F stands for 'fibre', meaning food material such as bran and cellulose that is not broken down by the process of digestion, otherwise what was formerly known as 'roughage'.

Franglais (blend of French *français*, 'French', and *anglais*, 'English'). A blend of French and English, either in the form of French speech that makes excessive use of English expressions, or as pidgin French spoken by an English person, as sometimes rather unsubtly guyed by humorists. The term itself was proposed in 1949 by Maurice Rat in an article reproduced in René Étiemble's seminal study of the subject, *Parlez-vous franglais?* (1964). Similar blends are denoted by names such as Japlish (Japanese + English), Spanglish (Spanish + English) and the like. *See also* HINGLISH.

Frank, Anne. A German Jewish girl (1929–45) who kept a lively and moving diary when in hiding from the Nazis with her family in Holland and who perished in the Bergen-BELSEN concentration camp. The only surviving member of her family was her father. Her diary was first published in abridged form in 1947 (in English in 1952). Many of the original entries relating to her repressed sexual feelings were issued separately in 1989 and a full 'definitive' edition appeared in 1997.

> I see the world gradually being turned into a wilderness, I hear the ever approaching thunder, which will destroy us too, I can feel the sufferings of millions and yet, if I look up into the heavens, I think that it will all come right, that this cruelty too will end, and that peace and tranquillity will return again.
> ANNE FRANK: *The Diary of a Young Girl* (from entry for 15 July 1944) (1952)

Frasier. The central character of the highly popular US SITCOM named after him, first screened in 1994. He is the psychiatrist Dr Frasier Crane, played by Kelsey Grammer, and appearing earlier in the equally enjoyable comedy *Cheers* (1993). He now returns home to Seattle to start a new life following his divorce from his wife Lilith, originally played by Bebe Neuwirth, and embarks on a career as a radio phone-in psychiatrist. A key motif is the volatile relationship between Frasier and his brother Niles, a fellow psychiatrist, played by David Hyde Pierce. *Frasier* was the first television series to win five consecutive EMMY awards for 'Outstanding Series'.

Freak out, To. To react in a wild and irrational way, as under the influence of drugs or when mentally unbalanced. The expression dates, unsurprisingly, from the SWINGING SIXTIES.

Freddie Mac. A US nickname for the Federal Home Loan Mortgage Corporation. *See also* FANNIE MAE; GINNIE MAE.

Fred Karno's army. A humorous nickname applied to the new British army raised during the First World War, in allusion to Fred Karno, the popular comedian and producer of stage burlesques, whose real name was Frederick John Westcott (1866–1941). Fred Karno's company was a household name at the time through its high-spirited and eccentric performances. The well-known army chorus, sung to the tune of 'The Church's One Foundation', runs:

> We are Fred Karno's army,
> Fred Karno's infantry;
> We cannot fight, we cannot shoot,
> So what damn good are we?
> But when we get to Berlin
> The Kaiser he will say
> Hoch, hoch, mein Gott
> Vot a bloody fine lot,
> Fred Karno's infantry.

There are variants, of course, and in the Second World War 'Old Hitler' was substituted for 'The Kaiser'. The name is also applied derisively to other nondescript bodies. Karno himself adopted his stage name when he and two gymnast colleagues filled in at a music-hall for an act called 'The Three Carnos'. His agent, Richard Warner, suggested they change the 'C' to a more distinctive 'K'.

Free and easy. Casual and carefree. The expression has an implication of moral laxity.

> 'It's just that I don't believe in this – whatever you call it – this free-and-easy way of going on. It –'
>   'Anticipation of marriage is probably how they put it in your – in the advice columns.'
>   KINGSLEY AMIS: *Take a Girl Like You*, ch iv (1960)

Free association. In psychology a method of investigating a person's unconscious by eliciting spontaneous associations with ideas or words proposed by the examiner. The word 'chair' might thus prompt a response 'table' in one subject, 'high' in another and 'electric' in a third. The second and third of these would alert the examiner more than the first.

Freebie. A colloquialism for something provided free, especially as a bonus, 'perk' or inducement. The increasing prevalence of freebies by way of corporate hospitality in the business world has met with some criticism. *See also* FRINGE BENEFITS.

> The freebie-culture of certain professions – journalism, showbiz, PR – causes people to start believing, against all reason, that they shouldn't have to pay full price for *anything*.
> *The Times* (24 October 1994)

Free fall. A downward movement due solely to gravity, as of a parachutist before the parachute opens. The term is also used for any state of falling rapidly, as of a 'dive' of share prices on the stock market.

Free French. *See* FFL; FIGHTING FRENCH.

Free-Staters. The Irish supporters of the Anglo-Irish treaty signed on 6 December 1921, which set up the Irish Free State in the southern 26 counties of Ireland as a dominion within the British Commonwealth. The treaty continued to demand an oath of allegiance to the British crown, and left Northern Ireland (six of the nine counties of Ulster) as an integral part of the United Kingdom. The Free-Staters were led by Michael Collins (the BIG FELLA), and opposed by Republicans led by Éamon de Valera (DEV or the Long Fellow), who refused to accept any outcome other than complete independence for the entire island of Ireland. This led to a bloody civil war in which Collins was assassinated (*see* BÉAL NA MBLÁTH). The civil war came to an end in 1923, and in 1937 a new constitution renamed the country EIRE. In 1949 the Republic of Ireland was established, and withdrew from the Commonwealth. *See also* FIANNA FAIL; FINE GAEL.

Free, white and 21. A descriptive term, now dated and regarded as racist, for a young white person who has reached their majority and who is thus a free agent. The phrase originally applied to both sexes but subsequently became specifically associated with a young American woman.

> We're all of us free, white, twenty-one, and hairy-chested, and we know how to be kind to a pretty girl.
> JOHN BUCHAN: *The Courts of the Morning*, Pt II, ch xiv (1929)

Free world. A nickname for themselves given collectively by non-communist countries during the COLD WAR.

Freikorps (German, 'free corps'). Any of a number of far-right German paramilitary groups that first emerged in December 1918, just after Germany's defeat in the First World War. The Freikorps were made up of ex-soldiers and unemployed youths, and their numbers grew through 1919. They were used unofficially by the WEIMAR REPUBLIC government to assist in the suppression of left-wing revolts but developed a taste for looting and vandalism. When the government resolved to disband the Freikorps brigades, one brigade marched on Berlin (13 March 1920) and set up a government under the right-wing Prussian politician Wolfgang Kapp (1858–1922), the so-called Kapp Putsch (*Putsch* being the German word for a sudden and violent seizure of power). However, Kapp's government fell within days in the face of a general strike by Berlin workers. Kapp himself fled to Sweden, but then returned to Germany and died awaiting trial. Many Freikorps personnel subsequently joined the NAZI Party, and one Freikorps commander, Ernst Röhm, became head of the BROWN-SHIRTS.

Frelimo. An acronym for Frente de Libertação de Moçambique (Portuguese, 'Mozambique Liberation Front'), the armed political group led by Samora Machel (1933–86) that fought for independence from Portugal from 1963. With independence achieved in 1975, Frelimo set up a one-party socialist state, and from 1977 fought a civil war against the South African-backed Renamo. Renamo is an acronym for Resistência Nacional Moçambicana (Portuguese, 'Mozambican National Resistance'). Renamo is also referred to as the MNR. Multi-party democracy was introduced in 1990, and a peace treaty between the warring factions was signed in 1992.

French and Saunders. A television comedy series featuring and written by Dawn French (b.1957) and Jennifer Saunders (b.1958), first screened in 1987. The programmes mix satire and slapstick from a female perspective and essentially bridge the gap between ALTERNATIVE and mainstream comedy. As with many memorable comic couples, much of the humour derives from the contrast between the two and their adopted personalities, French being short, dark, plump and frivolous while Saunders is tall, fair, slim and serious. The two originally created and honed their double act on stage.

French Connection, The. A film (1971) adapted by Ernest Tidyman from a book of the same title by Robin Moore about a detective's efforts to combat the illegal drug trade in New York. Starring Gene Hackman as Detective 'Popeye' Doyle and Roy Scheider as his partner, both characters were based on actual drug squad officers. The film contains one of the most memorable chase scenes ever filmed. The title refers to the link between drug dealers in Marseilles and New York that the two detectives uncover, the word 'connection' being doubly significant in that it is also slang for a drug dealer or pusher.

French cricket. A simplified form of cricket without stumps in which the 'bowler' gets the 'batsman' out if the ball hits the latter's legs. The name, first mentioned in the early 20th century, is a slighting allusion to the French, who supposedly cannot understand the rules of cricket.

French flu. A passion for all things French. The phrase was invented by Arthur Koestler (1905–83).

> The managerial class on Parnassus ... have lately been affected by a new outbreak of that recurrent epidemic, the French 'Flu.
> ARTHUR KOESTLER: *The Yogi and the Commissar* (1945)

French kiss. A kiss with one's tongue in the other's mouth, as said to be favoured by the French.

French knickers. A type of loose-fitting, wide-legged women's knickers that are usually trimmed with lace and generally made of silk or satin. The style is supposedly typically French.

French Lieutenant's Woman, The. A novel (1969) by John Fowles (b.1926), in which a deliberate blend of styles supports an exploration into the historical and subconscious worlds. It opens in Lyme Regis in the 1860s, at a spot overlooked by the 18th-century house in which Fowles has lived since 1965. Several alternative endings are suggested. The 'woman' is Sarah Woodruff, believed to have been deserted by a French lieutenant. She is unsuccessfully pursued by Charles Smithson, at the cost of his own engagement. A rather unsatisfactory film version (1981) was directed by Karel Reisz from a screenplay by Harold Pinter.

French Resistance. *See* MAQUIS.

French tickler. A type of condom with ribbed protrusions. The term evolved in the 1960s from the earlier 'French letter' as a colloquial term for a condom. This and expressions such as FRENCH KISS and FRENCH KNICKERS preserve the traditional British notion, not entirely groundless, that the French attach a particular importance to the sensual aspects of sexual pleasure, just as they do to those of food and drink.

Freudian slip. An unintentional mistake that appears to reveal a subconscious intention. It takes its name from the Austrian neurologist and psychotherapist Sigmund Freud (1856–1939), famous for his interest in the sexual subconscious. This last gave the term a popular or facetious usage for a slip of the tongue that reveals thoughts of a sexual nature. The term dates from the 1950s.

Friday Club. An information association of progressive artists founded in 1905 by the painter and designer Vanessa Bell, its members initially meeting on Fridays at her home, 46 Gordon Square, London. For some years there was a strong BLOOMSBURY GROUP presence and exhibitions were held down to 1922.

Friedmanism. An economic doctrine named after the US economist Milton Friedman (b.1912), who won the 1976 Nobel Prize for economics. Friedman opposed KEYNESIANISM, emphasizing the importance of the free market and control of the money supply. His theories, also known as monetarism, strongly influenced the Conservative government of Margaret Thatcher. *See also* IRON LADY.

Friendly fire. A military euphemism for fire coming from one's own side, especially when it results in accidental injury or death among one's own forces. The phrase was current in the VIETNAM War (1964–75) but came into prominence during the second GULF WAR, when many fatal casualties among Allied troops were attributed to it. 'Friendly bombing' is also found as a variant.

> Come, friendly bombs, and fall on Slough
> It isn't fit for humans now.
> JOHN BETJEMAN: *Continual Dew*, 'Slough' (1937)

Friendly persuasion. Gentle coercing; gradual inducement. The phrase became popular from the Western film of 1956 so titled, itself based on Jessamyn West's novel *The Friendly Persuasion* (1945). The sense there is quite different, however, since the book is a series of sketches of the life of a Quaker family during the American Civil War, with 'friendly' punning on the official name of the Quakers as the Society of Friends and 'persuasion' relating to religious beliefs.

Friend of Dorothy. A euphemism for a male homosexual. The allusion is to Dorothy Gale, the young heroine of L. Frank Baum's children's novel *The WIZARD OF OZ* (1900), who in the film version of 1939 was played by Judy Garland (1922–69), an actress who subsequently gained cult status in the gay community. The variant 'Dorothy's friend' is also current. *See also* STONEWALL.

Friends. A popular US television SITCOM first shown in 1995 and depicting a sextet of good-looking YOUNG THINGS, three men and three women, the action mainly taking place in a local coffee bar and the penthouse apartment of two of the women. The pleasure of the series lies chiefly in the evolving relationships and the fast-paced repartee. The friendships between the characters are enhanced by the real affection that the cast members clearly have for one another.

Friends of the Earth. An environmental pressure group, originating in the United States and existing in Britain since 1970. It first became publicly prominent in a campaign of 1971, in which thousands of disposable bottles were dumped on the doorstep of the soft drinks manufacturers Schweppes. By the mid-1990s it had branches in more than 30 countries. Protests and propaganda are furthered by public meetings, demonstrations and so on. Members are actively against all forms of pollution, developments that ruin the countryside and the destruction of wildlife. *See also* GREENPEACE.

Friends thought I was mad. A journalistic cliché dating from the first half of the 20th century and used when describing some apparently foolhardy venture, such as moving from a spacious and well-appointed town house to the sparse amenities of an isolated country cottage. The pronoun is obviously variable.

> Friends thought they were mad. Family shook their heads as they surveyed the mildew-spotted wall, peeling plaster, rusty radiators, and the gull droppings on the parquet floor.
> *Daily Mail* (28 May 1994)

Frighten the horses, To. To alarm people. The words are attributed to Mrs Patrick Campbell (1865–1940) in Daphne Fielding's *The Duchess of Jermyn Street*, ch ii (1964): 'It doesn't matter what you do in the bedroom as long as you don't do it in the street and frighten the horses.'

> What is equally certain is that Labour's strategy of doing nothing which could 'frighten the horses' will mean their tactics pin-point the 'soft' voters.
> BILL BUSH in *The BBC News General Election Guide* (1997)

Fringe. The secondary festival held on the periphery ('fringe') of the annual Edinburgh Festival. It was first held in 1947 when eight companies presented plays in venues which they hired themselves. The enterprise has remained faithful to the original open policy and there is no censoring of performers. The result is originality of the highest order on the one hand and time-wasting trivia on the other. At the 1999 Fringe 14,562 performers, mostly struggling or at best self-supporting students, staged 1346 shows. *See also* BEYOND THE FRINGE; HAPPENING.

Fringe benefits. Concessions and benefits given to employees; 'perks' that go with a job or appointment such as free fuel, use of a car, pensions, insurances, medical benefits and so forth. *See also* FREEBIE.

Fringe party. A British political or quasi-political party with a small or ephemeral membership, as distinct from the Conservative Party, LABOUR PARTY or Liberal Democrats. Many such parties emerge only at the time of a general election and are of narrow, local or frivolous appeal, with policies that may be specific or deliberately nebulous. As such, they add a note of eccentricity to an otherwise serious and even portentous event. One of the best known fringe parties is the MONSTER RAVING LOONY PARTY, its name aptly echoing its affinity with the LUNATIC FRINGE.

In the General Election of 1997 the following were among the 150 or so fringe parties that fielded one or more candidates:

> All Night Party
> British Democratic Party
> Care in the Community
> Christian Unity
> Common Sense Sick of Politicians Party
> Fancy Dress Party
> Hemp Coalition
> Independent No to Europe
> Independent Royal Forest of Dean
> Legalize Cannabis Party
> Lord Byro versus the Scallywag Tories
> Miss Moneypenny's Glamorous One Party
> None of the Above Parties
> Rainbow Dream Ticket Party
> Ronnie the Rhino Party
> Socialist Equality Party
> Space Age Superhero from Planet Beanus
> Top Choice Liberal Democrat
> UK Pensioners Party
> Universal Alliance
> Wessex Regionalist
> West Cheshire College in Crisis Party

Fringe theatre. A form of British theatre corresponding to the American off-off-Broadway (*see* OFF-BROADWAY), i.e. devoted to productions that because of their political content or experimental nature are usually staged in non-theatrical buildings such as converted warehouses or factories, or even rooms in pubs. Their audiences have mostly been young and anti-ESTABLISHMENT. The term itself probably derives from the Edinburgh FRINGE.

Frisbee. The concave disc designed for skimming through the air evolved in 1957 from the pie tins used similarly that themselves came from the Frisbie bakery in Bridgeport, Connecticut. Frisbees were commercially produced by Wham-O Manufacturing, makers of the HULA HOOP, and they now serve as a fitness fetish in Ultimate Frisbee, a seven-a-side team game invented by students at a New Jersey high school in the late 1960s. The game has been billed as a cross between football, basketball and hockey, and its name implies that it is 'the ultimate sports experience'. The governing body is the World Flying Disc Federation, and a key rule is that a player must not hold the Frisbee for more than 10 seconds before passing it to another member of the side.

Fritz. A nickname for a German, from the pet form of the common German forename Friedrich (Frederick). It was widely used by British forces in the First World War but in the Second World War was largely replaced by JERRY. Walter Mondale (b.1928), whose middle name is Frederick, was known as Fritz when US vice-president (1977–81) in allusion to his Germanic ancestry. *See also* NORWEGIAN WOOD.

Frodo. A HOBBIT in J.R.R. Tolkien's *The* LORD OF THE RINGS (1954–5) who went on a quest to destroy a ring that could make the wearer all-powerful, lest it fall into the hands of an evil lord. 'Frodo Lives' was a HIPPIE slogan of the 1960s.

Frog in one's throat. A temporary hoarseness or phlegm in the throat. The allusion may be to the 'croaking' of the voice, although frog is also an old term for various diseases of the mouth or throat. The expression dates from the early 20th century.

Frog march. A method of carrying an obstreperous prisoner face downwards by his four limbs, like a frog. The term is now more generally used, however, for a way of making a person walk somewhere by pinning his arms behind him and hustling him forwards.

Frogmen. In the Second World War strong swimmers dressed in rubber suits with paddles on their feet resembling the feet of frogs, who operated in enemy harbours by night attaching explosives to shipping etc. They are now used in salvage operations, searches for submerged bodies and the like.

From hell. A tag applied to a person or group of people regarded as unusually bad or dangerous, as 'the au pair from hell' or 'the neighbours from hell'. A television exposé of consultants and GPs who continued practising although struck off the register was entitled *Doctors from Hell* (1999).

> She also found herself sharing with three flatmates from hell: three lads, who were pleasant individually, but they never washed up.
> *The Times* (26 August 1999)

From Here to Eternity. The first novel (1951) by James Jones (1921–77). He was serving in the US infantry in Hawaii when the Japanese bombed PEARL HARBOR in 1941. Twice promoted and twice reduced to private, he fought at Guadalcanal and was wounded in the head by a mortar fragment. The novel, which won a National Book Award, draws on his own experiences in Hawaii and caused a sensation for its exposé of army brutality and its outspokenness about sex and military mores. The film (1952) was a slick, 'cleaned-up' version directed by Fred Zinnemann. The title comes from the poem 'The Gentlemen-Rankers' (1889), about oppressed junior ranks, by Rudyard Kipling:

> Gentlemen-rankers out on the spree,
> Damned from here to Eternity,
> God ha' mercy on such as we.

From Russia with Love. The second film (1963) in the long-running series of movies about British secret agent James BOND derived from the spy novels of Ian Fleming (1908–64). Starring Sean Connery as Bond and Robert Shaw as Red Grant, one of the best of all Bond villains, its title was inspired by a standard formula on British holiday postcards.

From soda to hock. From beginning to end. The phrase dates from the turn of the 20th century and derives from the game of faro, in which 'soda' is the exposed top card at the beginning of a deal and 'hock' the last card remaining in the box after all the others have been dealt.

From the get-go. From the beginning. A phrase of black American origin dating from the 1960s, with 'get-go' a shortened form of 'get going'.

> Let's get one thing straight from the get-go: anyone after a good narrative thriller would be better off reading a book.
> *heat* (16 December 1999–5 January 2000)

From the House of the Dead. A surprisingly uplifting opera by Leoš Janáček (1854–1928), *Z Mrtvého Domu* has a text by the composer based on Fyodor Dostoyevsky's prison reminiscences, *Memoirs from the House of the Dead* (1862). The 'House of the Dead' in question is a Siberian prison camp. Nothing much happens, although the Dostoyevsky figure (called Alexander Goryanchikov in the opera) arrives at the beginning and departs at the end. At the head of the score Janáček wrote: 'In every human being there is a divine spark.' He left the work unfinished at the time of his death; it was completed by Břetislav Bakala and O. Zitek and first performed in 1930.

Front-end loading. In financial jargon the repayments of a loan arranged in such a way that service charges relating to the whole period of the loan are recovered in the early payments and so form a large proportion of such payments by the investor. The term dates from the 1960s. In literal terms a front-end loader is a machine with a bucket or scoop on an articulated arm at the front for digging and loading earth.

Fruit machine. A coin-operated gaming machine or ONE-ARMED BANDIT that spins symbols of fruit on a dial. If when the spin stops all the symbols are identical, such as three pears, the player usually wins. The use of fruit as a reward or prize is in a tradition dating from classical times, and fruit has an equally venerable association with the classical cornucopia as a symbol of plenty.

Fuddy-duddy. An irredeemably old-fashioned person; an inveterate old fogey. The expression dates from the turn of the 20th century and is probably of dialect origin.

> RIBA, the fuddy-duddy architects' body, has recruited Naomi Campbell's friend to introduce razzle-dazzle into an otherwise dry event.
> *The Times* (19 July 1999)

Fudge and mudge, To. To gloss over differences or blur distinctions; to prevaricate. The phrase is first recorded in a speech made by the politician David Owen at the 1980 LABOUR PARTY Conference. 'Mudge' is simply a rhyming jingle on 'fudge'.

We are fed up with fudging and mudging, with mush and slush. We need courage, conviction, and hard work.

Guardian (3 October 1980)

Fudge factor. A factor speculatively included in a calculation to compensate for the lack of accurate information.

The market soon recognized the fudge factor – half a point tacked on for the drought effect – and settled back into more familiar expectations on growth.

Financial Times (22 February 1989)

Führer (German, 'leader'). The title assumed by Adolf Hitler (1889–1945) when he acceded to supreme power in Germany on the death of Hindenburg in 1934. *See also* CAUDILLO; DUCE; EIN VOLK, EIN REICH, EIN FÜHRER.

Fulbright scholar. A student receiving an educational grant under an international exchange scholarship programme conceived by US Senator William Fulbright (1905–95) of Arkansas and implemented by the Fulbright Act of 1946, which authorized funds from the sale of surplus war materials overseas to be used for the purpose. Candidates for a Fulbright grant must be under 35 years old, have a Bachelor of Arts degree or equivalent, be proficient in the language of the country in which they plan to study and be generally competent scholastically. Most exchanges to date have been made by university or college students, but teachers and researchers have also qualified.

A picture of that year's intake

Of Fulbright Scholars. Just arriving –

Or arrived. Or some of them.

Were you among them?

TED HUGHES: *Birthday Letters*, 'Fulbright Scholars' (1998)

Full Fathom Five. The wild action painting by Jackson Pollock (1912–56) dates from 1947. Most of Pollock's subsequent works had numerical titles such as *Number One*, *Number Thirty Two*, or, marginally more original, *Black and White Number Five*. However, this one is a quotation from *The Tempest* (I.ii):

Full fathom five thy father lies;

Of his bones are coral made;

Those are pearls that were his eyes …

These are the words that Ariel sings to Ferdinand, who believes his father has drowned in the storm. While he was still in his teens, Pollock had lost his own father. As he himself said, 'Every good painter paints what he is.'

Full frontal. A painting or photograph of a nude person with genitals exposed to full view or an actual person standing thus.

Full Metal Jacket. A film (1987) about the training of a squad of US Marines and their subsequent experiences in VIETNAM. It was based on the novel *The Short Timers* by Gustav Hasford and was filmed by Stanley Kubrick entirely in the UK (a gasworks in the East End doubling up for Vietnam, complete with imported palm trees). The title is army slang for full combat gear. The reality of the film was heightened by the presence of R. Lee Ermey as Gunnery Sergeant Hartman. Ermey was a former army drill instructor who was hired initially just to advise but who persuaded Kubrick into letting him play the part himself.

Full monty. Everything; the lot; 'the works'. Said of anything done to the utmost or fullest degree. The origin of the expression is uncertain. It may derive from 'the full amount' or the Spanish card game monte (literally 'mountain', i.e. heap of cards), or allude to a full three-piece suit from the men's outfitters Montague Burton. One explanation traces the term to Field Marshal Bernard Montgomery, nicknamed MONTY (1887–1976), said to have begun every day with a full English breakfast when campaigning in the North African desert in the Second World War. Yet another derives it from the city of Montevideo, Uruguay, on the grounds that fleece-packers shipping sheepskins from there graded them as 'full Monte'. The British phrase became familiar generally in the English-speaking world from its use as the title of a comedy film (1997) about a group of unemployed British factory workers who raise money by staging a strip act at a local club.

Full stop. And that's that; there is no more to be said. A tag placed at the end of a sentence to indicate that further elaboration on a topic is unnecessary. The implication is that a final full stop has been written. 'Period' is used similarly. *See also* END OF STORY.

Jeff Clark … said: 'Road signs are put up by the relevant divisions. … Any other signs are illegal and have to be removed. We do not put advertising up, full stop.'

The Citizen (4 January 2000)

Fu Manchu. The Chinese master villain who is head of the dreaded 'Si-Fan' secret society. He was the creation of Sax Rohmer (real name Arthur Sarsfield Ward) in a series of stories that ran in the *Story-Teller Magazine* from 1912. These were soon collected to form best-selling novels such as *The Mystery of Dr Fu Manchu* (1913). Fu operates internationally, his ultimate aim apparently being to gain mastery of the world, but his evil plans are constantly foiled by the doughty Englishman Dennis Nayland Smith. Fu Manchu's adventures were later transferred to the screen, and he became established as the 'YELLOW PERIL incarnate', a familiar racial stereotype.

Fun and games. Enjoyable goings-on. The phrase dates from the early 20th century and is often used to apply to sexual play.

Fun City. A nickname, sometimes ironic, of any place of potential or actual pleasure. It came to be associated with New York during the term of office of John V. Lindsay as mayor (1966–73), and was coined in January 1966 by Dick Schaap, a columnist for the New York *Herald Tribune*.

Fundamentalism. The maintenance of traditional Protestant Christian beliefs based on a literal acceptance of the Scriptures as fundamentals. Fundamentalism as a religious movement arose in the United States about 1919 among various denominations. What was new was not so much its ideas and attitudes, but its widespread extent and the zeal of its supporters. It opposed all theories of evolution and anthropology, holding that God transcends all laws of nature and that He manifests Himself by exceptional and extraordinary activities, belief in the literal meaning of the Scriptures being an essential tenet. In 1925, John T. Scopes, a science teacher of Rhea High School, Dayton, Tennessee, was convicted of violating the state laws by teaching evolution, an incident arousing interest and controversy far beyond the religious circles of the United States. Their leader was William Jennings Bryan (1860–1925), the lawyer and politician.

Fungus the Bogeyman. The lovably loathsome hero of Raymond Briggs's illustrated book for children so titled (1977). Fungus and his family live underground in a dank and noxious world where all things dry and clean are outlawed. The book is full of (literal) dirty jokes and puns that have given it a certain additional appeal to adults.

Funny bone. A pun on the word *humerus*, the Latin name for the arm bone. It is the inner condyle or knob at the end of the bone where the ulnar nerve is close to the surface of the skin at the elbow. A knock on this part is naturally painful and produces a tingling sensation.

Funny business. Suspicious behaviour; craftiness.

Funny-face. A term of endearment.

Funny farm. A colloquial or facetious term for a psychiatric hospital. The expression is said to refer to Friern Hospital, the former mental hospital at Friern Barnet, London, which had a working farm. Noël Coward has a song 'All the Fun of the Farm' in his musical play *Cavalcade* (1931).

Funny foreigners. A typical British catch-all deprecation of other races as quaint or eccentric, the British themselves being paragons of normality and rationality.

Funny Girl. A film musical (1968) based on the stage musical of the same title (1964) by Jule Styne, Bob Merrill and Isobel Lennart about the life of vaudeville star Fanny Brice (1891–1951), who was at one time the wife of the gangster Nicky Arnstein. Brice was played on both stage and in the film and in the sequel, *Funny Lady* (1975), by Barbra Streisand, with whom the title became virtually synonymous.

Funny money. Counterfeit or worthless money, especially when associated with crime or dubious practices. The term dates from the 1940s. 'Funny' here does not mean amusing but relates to 'funny business' as a term for deceitful or underhand practices.

Funny old game. Football. A journalistic cliché that sometimes omits the 'old'. It is frequently used by footballers themselves. *See also* BEAUTIFUL GAME.

> Funny old game football, as Greavsie [footballer Jimmy Greaves] might have said … even when it's TV's fantasy kind.
> *Today* (30 August 1994)

Funny old world. Said of anything strange or unexpected. The phrase was adopted from the quip spoken by W.C. Fields in the film *You're Telling Me* (1934): 'It's a funny old world – a man's lucky if he gets out of it alive.' Margaret Thatcher also memorably commented 'It's a funny old world' on being persuaded to withdraw from the contest for leadership of the Conservative Party in 1990.

Funny-peculiar or funny-ha-ha? A question put to someone who uses the word 'funny' without making it clear which of the two senses is meant.

Chris: That's funny.

Button: What do you mean, funny? Funny-peculiar, or funny ha-ha?

IAN HAY: *Housemaster*, III (1936)

Funny Thing Happened on the Way to the Forum, A. A film musical (1966) based on a stage show of the same title (1962), with music by Stephen Sondheim and book by Burt Shevelove and Larry Gelbart, about a Roman slave's farcical attempts to gain his freedom. Starring Zero Mostel, Phil Silvers and Buster Keaton, the film was, like the stage show, derived ultimately from the comic writings of Plautus.

Fun run. A long run undertaken by a large number of people for pleasure and exercise, and especially a sponsored run, as a marathon to raise money for charity. The term and the activity itself originated in the United States in the mid-1970s.

Furby. A furry toy animal with a microchip implant that enables it to make sounds (including those of bodily functions) and respond to and imitate external stimuli. Furbies were the invention of the American Dave Hampton and were the Christmas present craze of 1998.

> Furby fever is an exercise in supply-side economics: fuel the hunger and then drip-feed the victims.
>
> *Sunday Times* (25 October 1998)

Future, Captain. *See* CAPTAIN FUTURE.

Future shock. A state of distress or disorientation resulting from rapid social or technological change. The expression is first defined by Alvin Toffler in *Horizon* (1965) as 'the dizzying disorientation brought on by the premature arrival of the future'. *See also* CULTURE SHOCK.

Futurism. An art movement that originated at Turin in 1909 under the influence of Filippo Tommaso Marinetti (1876–1944). Its adherents sought to introduce into paintings a 'poetry of motion' whereby, for example, the painted gesture should become actually 'a dynamic condition'. The Futurists tried to indicate not only the state of mind of the painter but also that of the figures in the picture. It was another movement to shake off the influence of the past. Original members apart from Marinetti included Umberto Boccioni (1882–1916), Carlo Carrà (1881–1966), Luigi Russolo (1885–1947) and Gino Severini (1883–1966), and they first exhibited in 1912 at the Galérie Bernheim-Jeune in Paris. 'Futuristic' is often used as a general term for any 'modern' art, even when not strictly Futurist. *See also* CUBISM; DADAISM; FAUVISM; ORPHISM; RURALISM; SURREALISM; SYNCHROMISM; TACHISM; VORTICISM.

Fuzz. The police. The colloquialism is of US origin and dates from the 1920s. The source may lie in 'fuss', as a reference to an over-particular person.

F-word. A term usually used euphemistically to denote the taboo slang word 'fuck', but adopted by UK Europhobes and Eurosceptics (*see* EUROPHILE) to denote 'federalism', i.e. political union, in the context of the European Union. Supporters of federalism are dubbed Federasts (playing on 'pederast'). *See also* FOUR-LETTER WORD.

> Where once use of a four-letter F-word at meetings would have had managers coughing up their coffee, now we hear the word is almost de rigueur. These days the corridors ring blue with managers showing off their verbal machismo.
>
> *The Times* (16 June 2000)

Fylingdales. The moorland site near the coast in North Yorkshire of a US early-warning station, built in 1963. It was notable for its radar installations shaped like giant golf balls, designed to give early warning of a nuclear attack. So striking were these structures that it was suggested in some quarters that they be made listed buildings. However, the golf balls have now been replaced by solid-state phased-array radar (SSPAR) in the form of a three-sided truncated pyramid *c*.36m (120 ft) high.

G

Gaia hypothesis. The theory that the Earth is not a collection of independent mechanisms but a single living organism in which everything interacts to regulate the survival and stability of the whole. The hypothesis was put forward in 1969 by the British scientist James Lovelock and at the suggestion of the novelist William Golding was named after Gaia, Greek goddess of the Earth, whose name is sometimes used of the Earth itself, especially when viewed holistically and reverentially. Adherents of the principle are known as Gaians. Some scientists object to the religious overtones of the theory, but it has gained acceptance among many conservationists. As a girl's name Gaia became fashionable for its environmental connotations from the 1990s and was given among others to the daughter (b.1999) of the OSCAR-winning actress Emma Thompson.

> Gaia is a tough bitch. People think the earth is going to die and they have to save it, that's ridiculous ... There's no doubt that Gaia can compensate for our output of greenhouse gases, but the environment that's left will not be happy for any people.
> LYNN MARGULIS in *New York Times Biographical Service* (January 1996)

Gallipoli. A disastrous campaign of the First World War. The plan was for the British fleet to bombard its way through the heavily defended Dardanelles, a narrow strait between Europe and Asiatic Turkey, while an Allied army captured the Gallipoli peninsula, on the European side. Neither happened owing to miscalculation and incompetence. The fleet withdrew after three battleships were sunk in an undetected minefield, and the troop landings on 25 April 1915 were gallant but ineffectual. The Allies withdrew in January 1916 with the loss of more than 200,000 men. A film of the same name, directed by Peter Weir and starring Mel Gibson, was released in 1981. Despite some inaccuracies, it depicts in moving fashion the courage in the face of death of members of the Australian Tenth Light Horse Regiment. *See also* ANZAC.

Galloping Gourmet. A semi-facetious nickname for Graham Kerr (b.1934), the popular British-born cookery expert, whose television programmes were made in Canada but were shown in many countries in the late 1960s and early 1970s. He earned the name from his alacrity in the kitchen and his nimbleness in the preparation of dishes.

Gallup Poll. The best known of the public opinion surveys, instituted by Dr George H. Gallup (1901–84) of the American Institute of Public Opinion in 1935. Trained interviewers interrogate a small but carefully selected cross-section of the population. For the British general election of 1945, out of 25 million voters, 1809 were interviewed, but the Gallup Poll forecast was within 1 per cent. The forecast was, however, wrong for the US presidential election of 1948. A Labour victory was correctly forecast for the British general elections of 1964 and 1966. It is held that such polls in themselves influence the result. Straw polls and market research surveys were the forerunners of the Gallup Poll. Most electoral polls in Britain are now conducted by MORI (Market and Opinion Research Institute), a joint Anglo-American organization, founded in 1969. *See also* MASS OBSERVATION.

Game Boy. The proprietary name of a hand-held, battery-operated device for playing computer games. It has a small screen, direction and function buttons, and a slot where various game cartridges, such as that for POKÉMON, can be inserted. It was launched on the market in the late 1980s by the Japanese firm Nintendo as a portable version of its popular video game. Its name indicates its function and its usual owner and operator, while also suggesting its small size.

Game over. The situation is hopeless. A phrase of US origin probably deriving from the announcement at the end of a computer game.

Game plan. A strategy worked out in advance, especially in sport, politics or business. The original sense specifically related to a plan of fixed 'plays' prearranged by the coach and the team for winning a game of American football. The term was taken up in Britain in the 1980s when this sport became more familiar from television.

Game show. The popular genre of television programme, in which members of the public compete to win prizes, has its origin in US radio shows of the 1930s. American television then adopted the game show in the 1950s, using large cash rewards for correct answers. An indication of the quantum increase was the escalation of one radio programme's highest prize, the SIXTY-FOUR DOLLAR QUESTION, to a sixty-four thousand dollar question on television. The television game show in Britain was launched in the 1960s with series such as The GOLDEN SHOT, The GENERATION GAME, Sale of the Century (1972–83), Celebrity Squares (1975–9) and the more complex 3–2–1 (1978–87). The following transcript of an extract from an early episode of this last, compered by the comedian Ted Rogers, offers a taste of the ingredients:

> Ted Rogers: 'This is a composer, German by birth, English by adoption, best known for an oratorio published in 1741.' Short pause. 'It was called … Messiah.' Longer pause. 'You're bound to know … his handle.'
> Both teams press buzzers.
> Ted: 'Who is it?'
> Female contestant (shutting eyes): 'Oh God, I used to have it at school … Handel's Water Music.'
> Ted: 'So who's the composer?'
> Female contestant: 'Chopin.'
> Uproar from audience.
> Ted (turning to other team): 'So I can offer it to you.'
> Male contestant: 'Beethoven?'
> MARCUS BERKMANN: Brain Men (1999)

Gamesmanship. A term popularized by Stephen Potter, whose book The Theory and Practice of Gamesmanship (1947) defines the meaning in its subtitle: 'The Art of Winning Games without actually Cheating.'

Gandalf. In J.R.R. Tolkien's epic The LORD OF THE RINGS (1954–5), the tall, good magician who sends FRODO on his quest and who helps him whenever possible.

G and T. Gin and tonic, a drink mostly favoured by the better off or those priding themselves on their discernment. See also GIN AND IT; GIN AND JAG.

> The main lounge … is stuffed full of elderly Colonel Mustard types sipping G&Ts and muttering incomprehensible golf jargon.
> The Times (7 January 2000)

Gang of four. (1) The leaders of a Chinese radical group who unsuccessfully attempted to seize control after the death of Mao Zedong in 1976. The gang, who were imprisoned in 1981, consisted of Jiang Qing (Mao's widow and third wife), Zhang Chungqiao, Wang Hongwen and Yao Wenyuan.

(2) In Britain the name was given to the four MPs who left the Labour Party in 1981 to form the Social Democratic Party (SDP), namely Roy Jenkins (party leader until 1983), David Owen, Shirley Williams and Bill Rodgers.

Gang saw. A number of power-driven circular saws mounted together so that they can reduce a tree trunk to planks at one operation. Gang is similarly applied to various collections of tools, machines and the like working in combination. Other examples are a gang mower, used for mowing large areas of grass, and a gang plough, used for ploughing a field.

Gang show. A variety show formerly performed annually by BOY SCOUTS and GIRL GUIDES. The first Boy Scout Gang Show was held in 1932 as the brainchild of the theatrical actor and producer Ralph Reader (1903–82). The last such show ran for a fortnight and closed in October 1974, when Reader retired. He then revealed that that he had worked for British Intelligence in the Second World War and had used Gang Shows as a cover to recruit former Scouts to track down enemy agents. Local gang shows have since been staged intermittently in support of charitable causes.

Gangsta rap. A type of RAP MUSIC that evolved in south central Los Angeles in the 1990s. 'Gangsta' is a black American slang word, first appearing in the 1980s, denoting a rebellious individual who refuses to accept the authority of the (white) establishment. The 'gangsta' lifestyle embraces sex, violence, drugs and money. The deliberate misspelling of 'gangsta' ('gangster' in Standard English) reflects the anti-establishment pose. See also HIP-HOP.

Gang up, To. To form a closely knit group, usually in a spirit of antagonism.

Gannex. The trademark name of a make of raincoat much favoured by Labour politician Harold Wilson (1916–95), prime minister (1964–70, 1974–6). The maker of Gannex, Joseph Kagan (b.1915), became Lord Kagan in Wilson's controversial 1976 resignation honours list (the LAVENDER LIST) and was subsequently given a prison sentence for evading excise duties.

Gap year. A year between secondary and further or higher education, when some school-leavers go out 'into the world' to travel or to find work before resuming their studies. Those who travel often go hitch-hiking or backpacking abroad, especially to exotic or even dangerous places. By the late 1990s many such travellers had become something of an unattractive phenomenon, cocooning themselves in a bubble of self-centred hedonism and spurning a genuine voyage of discovery for the ersatz attractions of touristic commercialism and the purely animal pleasures of drugs and sex.

> The gap year has come of age. It is now an established rite of passage for British school-leavers.
> *The Times* (21 August 1999)

Garden city. The garden city movement in England was the inspiration of Sir Ebenezer Howard (1850–1928), who coined a name for his vision in *Tomorrow: A Peaceful Path to Real Reform* (1898), later republished as *Garden Cities of Tomorrow* (1902). His aim was to combine the best aspects of town and country in an environment appropriate for all members of society, and in practical terms planned a scheme whereby six 'satellite' cities would encircle a central metropolis, each having its own allotments, hospitals and leisure areas. His ambition resulted in the formation of the Garden City Association in 1899 and to the laying out of Letchworth on a green-field site in Hertfordshire in 1903. The new city prospered and others followed, among them Hampstead Garden Suburb in 1907 and Welwyn Garden City in 1919. *See also* NEW TOWN.

Gardening. A term used in British espionage for the carrying out of an activity that will force the enemy to send a message in cipher or code, thus giving cryptographers a crib to help their work. A typical ruse in the Second World War was to lay ('plant') mines in an area that the Germans thought they had cleared. When the Germans discovered a new mine, they would report it and deploy minesweepers until the signal 'route cleared' was transmitted. Interception of this single message was enough for cryptographers to isolate the text and discover the daily change in the cipher.

Gardening leave. A euphemism for suspension from work on full pay, as if to enable an employee to stay at home and garden. Such suspension is typically made to prevent the employee from seeking work with another employer before the end of their contractual notice period.

> Tony Greig, the former England cricket captain, has been suspended from his sports commentating job after making derogatory remarks about mail-order Asian brides. … The result: a flood of complaints and gardening leave for Tony.
> *The Times* (2 November 1999)

Garden of Remembrance. A garden commemorating the dead of either or both world wars, typically found in a town that lost many local people thus. Sometimes a whole road or avenue may be so dedicated, and Folkestone, Kent, has a Road of Remembrance planted with rosemary ('That's for remembrance', *Hamlet*, IV.v).

> Across the Garden of Remembrance? No,
> That would be blasphemy and bring bad luck.
> JOHN BETJEMAN: *A Few Late Chrysanthemums*, 'Original Sin on the Sussex Coast' (1954)

Garden suburb. *See* GARDEN CITY.

Garfield. The fat and lazy ginger cartoon cat created by the American illustrator Jim Davis first appeared in a comic strip in 1978 and proved one of the most popular of all cartoon characters over the following decade. Davis gave the cat his grandfather's middle name.

Garlic Wall. The satirical name applied by Gibraltarians to the Spanish barrier, which closed the frontier to La Linea in 1969 as a consequence of Spain's claim to the Rock. Spain reopened the frontier in 1985.

Garnett, Alf. The working-class Londoner played by Warren Mitchell in the television series *Till Death Us Do Part* (1964–74). He is an archetypal royalist and racist, and his forthright pronouncements had the unusual effect of simultaneously endearing him to the viewing public, who secretly agreed with some of his views, yet alienating him from them because of his bigoted attitude and his bad language. His appearance in a sequel, *In Sickness and in Health* (1985–6), seemed much less shocking. His US equivalent was Archie BUNKER in *All in the Family* (1971–8), a television series based on *Till Death Us Do Part*.

Garp. The mother-fixated hero of John Irving's bestselling novel *The World According to Garp* (1978). He is the offspring of Jenny Fields, a New England heiress, and a brain-damaged aircraft gunner who can only shout the meaningless exclamation 'Garp!' His initials are T.S., standing for Technical Sergeant, as the rank of his father at the time of his conception. Garp grows up to become an author, marries a bookish woman and fathers two children, while his wife, Helen, becomes a leader in a women's rights movement. A series of grim accidents follows, and both mother and son are murdered.

Garryowen. In rugby football a very high kick that keeps the ball in the air long enough for the kicker and other members of his team to run up and take it where it falls among the opposition. It is also known as an 'up and under', for obvious reasons, and takes its name from the Irish rugby club in Limerick where it was first deployed. Garryowen is also the name of a 'mangy mongrel' in James Joyce's ULYSSES (1922). The name itself puns on Owen Garry, a legendary 3rd-century king of Leinster.

Gas guzzler. A nickname for a large car with a high fuel consumption, especially an American one, which 'guzzles the gasoline'. Cynics claimed that the second GULF WAR was fought to make the world safe for the gas guzzler.

Gastarbeiter (German, literally 'guest worker'). A person who has temporary permission to work in another country, otherwise an immigrant worker. The term arose from those encouraged into West Germany after the Second World War, many of them Turks and Yugoslavians, to assist in its postwar economic revival.

Gate. As *-gate*, this is the second element of a noun denoting a scandal associated with the person, animal or place named in the first element. The analogy is with WATERGATE. Irangate was thus a scandal of 1986 following the revelation that members of the Reagan administration had sanctioned arms sales to Iran in exchange for the release of hostages in Lebanon, the proceeds being used to give arms to the CONTRAS in Nicaragua, while Lawsongate was a British scandal of 1988 caused by allegations that the Chancellor of the Exchequer, Nigel Lawson, had deliberately deceived the public about the economy. The format was still in active use in the late 1990s.

The cumulative effect of Squidgygate, Fergiegate and Camillagate [in the royal family] has been to replace deference with popular disdain.

GREG HADFIELD and MARK SKIPWORTH: *Class*, ch i (1994)

Gatsby, Jay. The central character of F. Scott Fitzgerald's classic novel *The* GREAT GATSBY (1925), a wealthy but mysterious man who gives lavish parties but whom nobody really knows. He epitomizes the type of man who has little or no self-esteem and who relies on wealth to enhance his social status.

Gaudy Night. A detective novel (1935) by Dorothy Sayers (1893–1957). The gaudy is an Oxford college reunion for former undergraduates. Harriet Vane returns to her college for the occasion and finds herself in a maelstrom of obscene graffiti and poison pen letters. She asks Lord Peter WIMSEY for help. He manages not only to identify the perpetrator but also to overcome Harriet's feminist objections to marriage.

Gaullist. A supporter of the French politician Charles de Gaulle (1890–1970) or, more specifically, of any of the various right-wing political parties claiming to represent his political philosophy after his death. Present-day Gaullists follow the RPR or *Rassemblement pour la République* (French, 'Rally for the Republic'), which came into being in 1976.

Gay (Old French *gai*). Light-hearted; merry; brightly coloured.

Belinda smiled and all the world was gay.

ALEXANDER POPE: *The Rape of the Lock*, ii (1714)

French *gai* became associated with effeminate roles in French burlesque theatre, and the English theatre similarly began to apply the word 'gay' to saucy or 'promiscuous' characters. These mock female roles were always played by men, because in Elizabethan times women were not allowed on the stage in either country. It was this use of the word that gave the general current one of 'homosexual', a use favoured by male homosexuals themselves.

Gay plague. A US nickname for AIDS dating from the early 1980s. When the disease was first identified it seemed to be spreading rapidly and uncontrollably exclusively among GAY men.

Gaza Strip. The strip of territory in Palestine that includes the city of Gaza was administered by Egypt from 1949 until 1967, when it was occupied by Israel (*see* SIX-DAY WAR). It became a self-governing enclave under the PLO–Israel accord of 1994 and elected its own legislative council in 1996. *See also* WEST BANK.

Gazelle Boy. In 1961 Jean-Claude Armen, travelling by camel through the Spanish Sahara in west Africa, was told by nomad tribesmen of the whereabouts of a young boy living with a herd of gazelles. In due time he sighted the boy and eventually attracted him to close quarters by playing a Berber flute. The boy fed on the same plants as the animals, sometimes eating worms and lizards. On a subsequent expedition in 1963, this time in a Jeep, the speed of the boy when galloping with the herd was established at 50kph (over 30mph).

Gazumping. A colloquial term from the early 1970s relating to the property market. It denotes the dubious practice of raising the selling price of a house after agreement has been reached with an intending purchaser. After agreeing a price with the vendor, the purchaser finds that he is gazumped because the vendor has accepted a higher offer from another buyer before contracts have been signed and exchanged. The origin of the word is uncertain. It may derive from a Yiddish verb meaning 'to swindle'. GAZUNDERING is a later variant.

> Gazumping, one of the ugliest words in the English language, is enjoying a revival.
> *The Times* (7 July 1999)

Gazundering. Essentially the converse of GAZUMPING, as the practice of lowering the selling price of a house shortly before the exchange of contracts and threatening to withdraw from the sale if the new offer is not accepted. The term dates from the 1980s and substitutes 'under' for the '-ump' of 'gazump', interpreted humorously as 'up'.

Gazza. The popular nickname of the English footballer Paul Gascoigne (b.1967), who played for his local team, Newcastle United, before being transferred for £2 million to Tottenham Hotspur in 1988. He gained fame in the semi-final of the 1990 World Cup in Italy, when the referee showed him a YELLOW CARD after a foul against Berthold of West Germany. It was his second card of the tournament and would have prevented his playing in the final if England had won this match. In front of the millions watching on television, Gascoigne wept. The event was a milestone in the maverick player's career and endeared him to many. *See also* FLUTE-PLAYING.

GB's GB. Gordon Brown's Great Britain, a media tag for Britain and the British as viewed by the NEW LABOUR Chancellor of the Exchequer in his 1997 *Spectator*

Lecture. According to Brown, British qualities include adaptability and creativity, a belief in tolerance and liberty, a strong sense of fair play and the common good at home and an outward-looking internationalism abroad.

GCHQ. The Government Communications Headquarters at Cheltenham, and the centre of Britain's global intelligence-gathering network. After the Second World War it established a partnership with the US National Security Agency and in the 1990s had some 10,000 employees. In 1982 a linguist at GCHQ, Geoffrey Prime, was convicted of handing the secrets of US spy satellites to the USSR and two years later the organization was again in the news when the Conservative government announced that workers there could no longer belong to a trade union. A compensation of £1000 was offered instead to each employee, and within a month 9 out of 10 employees had accepted. A small minority, however, refused to give up membership. Their case was rejected by the European Court of Human Rights in 1987 but the rights of all GCHQ employees to have union representation were restored by the Labour government in 1997. *See also* ROOM 40.

Gear. Clothing, equipment and the like, as, for example, sports gear. The word also applies to the combination of toothed wheels and levers, which connect a motor with its work. 'High gear' is the arrangement whereby the driving part moves slowly in relation to the driven part, while 'low gear' is when the driving part moves relatively more quickly than the driven. Colloquially, 'gear' signifies illegal drugs.

Geddit? Do you get it? A journalistic device to draw the reader's attention to a pun or joke that might otherwise be missed, or to a particularly 'corny' or unoriginal one.

> Her [Kathy Lette's] paperback titles ... have all the subtlety of tabloid bad-pun headlines: Foetal Attraction, Altar Ego. 'Geddit? Geddit?' you can hear her screaming.
> *Sunday Times* (6 June 1999)

Geek. A knowledgeable and obsessive enthusiast, or more generally a NERD. The US word originally meant a simpleton or dupe and arose as a variant of 'geck', an English dialect term for a fool. The late 20th-century application is typically to technology.

> 'Most people on my team work for me because I am a geek,' he claims in *Computer Weekly*. 'Geeks like

working for geeks. Geeks don't like working for accountants.'

The Times (21 October 1999)

Geiger counter. The German nuclear physicist Hans Geiger (1882–1945) produced the first primitive version of his famous radiation detector in 1908 while working with Ernest Rutherford at Manchester University. His invention was subsequently improved through collaboration with his colleague Walther Müller, and the device is still sometimes known by both men's names.

G8. *See* GROUP OF EIGHT.

Gemini. The name of a series of US spacecraft launched into orbit round the Earth between 1964 and 1967, so called from its two-man crew (Latin *gemini*, 'twins'). The programme was chiefly designed to test the ability of astronauts to manoeuvre their spacecraft by manual control and to develop techniques for docking with a target vehicle. Such procedures were vital to the success of the ensuing APOLLO programme.

Gender bender. A colloquial term for a person who dresses and behaves in a manner characteristic of the opposite sex, or more generally for an androgyne. The term evolved in the early 1980s in the context of an androgynous fashion among NEW ROMANTIC pop singers such as Boy George.

Gender gap. The difference in attitudes or viewpoints that can exist between men and women, especially in the political field.

> The gender gap – the marked difference between the political views of men voters and the increasingly sizeable body of women voters – rang out as the theme of the convention.
>
> *The Times* (25 July 1983)

Gene pool. Literally, the stock ('pool') of different genes in an interbreeding population. More generally the term is used for the total of all people in a group or of a kind, especially one of highly rated individuals of varied origin.

> Some of modelling's biggest names have learned the hard way that a beautiful face and big name aren't a passport to Oscar glory … 'Julia Roberts is pretty enough to satisfy most audiences. Hollywood's gene pool just isn't clamouring for a transfusion from the catwalks.'
>
> *heat* (17–23 February 2000)

General, The. The English footballer and manager Sir Alf Ramsey (1920–99), under whom England won the World Cup in 1966. Cool, taciturn and somewhat superior in manner, and often criticized for a lack of tactical imagination, Ramsey's achievement earned him a knighthood and the enduring gratitude of a hitherto sceptical nation.

General Belgrano. An old Argentinian cruiser named after Manuel Belgrano (1770–1820), a military leader in the Argentinian war of independence against the Spanish. The ship had previously belonged to the US navy, under the name USS *Phoenix*, and had survived the Japanese attack on Pearl Harbor. But on 2 May 1982 it was sunk with the loss of 362 lives by a British submarine, HMS *Conqueror*, in what turned out to be the most controversial incident in the FALKLANDS WAR. Margaret Thatcher (*see* IRON LADY) and her ministers told the Commons that it had been on course for the Falklands at the time, but it turned out that it had been steaming in the opposite direction for some eight hours. The Labour MP Tam Dalyell (b.1932) campaigned to expose the truth, believing the sinking was a deliberate attempt to scupper the peace plan proposed by Peru; like many, he believed that Thatcher was determined to fight a war to restore her electoral fortunes (*see* FALKLANDS FACTOR). Dalyell's case was strengthened in 1984 when a senior civil servant, Clive Ponting, passed documents to his member of Parliament suggesting there had indeed been a cover-up. Ponting was charged under the Official Secrets Act, but in March 1985 was acquitted by the jury against the direction of the judge, establishing the principle that the interests of the state are not necessarily identical with the interests of the government.

General Strike. Britain's first and only nationwide strike was called by the Trades Union Congress at midnight on 3 May 1926 in support of the miners' union, which was resisting the mine-owners' demands for longer hours and lower wages. Stanley Baldwin's Conservative government used troops, volunteers and special constables to maintain food supplies and basic services, and it held a monopoly on the media, including BBC radio. The TUC ended the strike after nine days, leaving the miners, who felt betrayed by them, unsuccessfully continuing the strike until 12 November. The Trades Disputes Act of 1927 made general strikes illegal.

General Synod. The governing body of the Church of England, established in 1969 to achieve a more effective system of control, to give a greater role to the laity, and to avoid the delays caused by the previous diarchy of the Convocations and Church Assembly. Members of its three houses, bishops, clergy and laity, meet twice a year to discuss doctrine and worship. It also has a pastoral role and speaks for the Church on political, social and moral issues. In 1995 a synod committee urged the abandonment of the phrase 'living in sin'. Members voted to 'take note' of the request but emphasized the Christian ideal of marriage.

Generation Game, The. A popular GAME SHOW screened from 1971 to 1982 and hosted first by a cheery Bruce Forsyth, then by a CAMP Larry Grayson. Two pairs of contestants, related to each other and of different generations, performed 'arts and crafts' feats such as throwing pots and icing cakes after watching an expert. Predictably this rapidly degenerated into farce. The winning couple were then placed beside a 'conveyor belt' and challenged to memorize the GOODIES that passed before them. The items recalled could be taken home as prizes. The show was relaunched in 1990 and from 1995 was hosted by the comedian Jim Davidson.

Generation gap. The years that separate an older generation from a younger, especially as discernible in a difference of outlook, values and attitudes. In some instances the disparity can lead to a lack of understanding or empathy between the two.

Generation X. The generation born after that of the baby boomers (see BABY BOOM), i.e. in the 1960s and 1970s, distinguished by their disaffection and general lack of direction. The name comes from a sociological survey of 1964 by Charles Hamblett and Jane Deverson, whose front cover blurb ran: 'What's behind the rebellious anger of Britain's untamed youth? Here – in their own words – is how they really feel about Drugs, Drink, God, Sex, Class, Colour and Kicks.' The theme was continued in a book by the Canadian writer Douglas Coupland, *Generation X: Tales for an Accelerated Culture* (1991), in which he coined the term McJOB to describe 'low-pay, low-prestige, low-benefit, no-future jobs in the service industry'.

> They are Generation X – resigned to insecure working and wanting a flexible lifestyle, which they see as incompatible with homebuying.
> *Observer* (10 May 1998)

Genetically modified. Of foodstuffs, containing or consisting of genetically altered plant or animal material. The stocking of supermarket shelves with genetically modified (GM) food products in the late 1990s caused widespread concern among consumer organizations and consumers themselves, since the latter had been largely kept uninformed about the ethical and health implications of such products. Moreover, many foods made with GM organisms were initially not even labelled as such. Members of environmental groups such as FRIENDS OF THE EARTH and GREENPEACE protested by destroying fields where GM crops were being experimentally grown, and the public became increasingly confused and concerned about the issue, despite certain reassurances from politicians and food manufacturers.

Genetic fingerprinting. The pattern of DNA unique to each person that can be analyzed in a sample of blood, saliva or tissue, and that is used as a means of identification as conventional fingerprints are.

Genevieve. A good-natured film (1953) written by William Rose and directed by Henry Cornelius about two rival couples who enter their classic cars in the annual BRIGHTON RUN rally. Genevieve was the name of the car (a 1904 roadster) owned by Alan and Wendy McKim (played by John Gregson and Dinah Sheridan). Their rivals, Ambrose Claverhouse and Rosalind Peters, were played by Kenneth More and Kay Kendall.

Genocide. A word invented by the American jurist Raphael Lemkin, and used in the drafting of the official indictment of NAZI war criminals in 1945. It is a combination of Greek *genos*, 'race', and Latin *caedere*, 'to kill'. It is defined as acts intended to destroy, in whole or in part, national, ethnic, racial or religious groups, and in 1948 was declared by the General Assembly of the UNITED NATIONS to be a crime in international law. *See also* HOLOCAUST.

Gentle giant. A nickname for a tall and strong but kindly person that is first recorded in the 19th century but that came into its own in the 20th. A policeman killed by an IRA bomb outside Harrods store in London in 1983 was so dubbed by the media, and the name has been accorded to various sportsmen, among them the footballer John Charles (b.1931), centre-half for Leeds United, who helped Wales to the World Cup finals, the US track and field champion James R. Mason (b.1945) and the world heavyweight champion Larry Holmes (b.1950). In the film *The Gentle Giant* (1967) a small boy in Florida befriends a bear that later saves the life of the boy's hitherto disapproving father. The alliteration of the phrase makes it memorable and thus apt for advertising purposes, as in the following jingle promoting Pickfords Removals in the 1930s:

A note from you, a call from us,
The date is fixed, with no worry or fuss,
A Pickfords van, a gentle giant,
The work is done – a satisfied client.

Gentleman friend. A woman's regular male companion; a BOYFRIEND.

Margy: I'm sick of this town and everything that goes with it. Damn him.
Gregg: Oh, the gentleman friend, eh?
Margy: Gentleman, hell. You're the first one to ever call him that.
MAE WEST: Sex (1926)

Gentleman's agreement. An arrangement or understanding that is based on trust or honour rather than a legal obligation. The Oxford English Dictionary dates the earliest occurrence of the term as 1929 and claims that it is of US origin.

Gentlemen Prefer Blondes. A novel (1925) by Anita Loos (1888–1981), subtitled The Diary of a Professional Lady. Breathless, ungrammatical entries record the heroine's picaresque search for a broader mind, a living and, she hopes, a rich husband. It is said that some of its popularity was due to the fact that young women took it seriously as a how-to-get-rich handbook. The success of the musical comedy (1949) based on the novel made both the title and its best known number, 'Diamonds are a Girl's Best Friend', into popular catchphrases. The updated film (1953), directed by Howard Hawks, starred Jane Russell and Marilyn MONROE. In 1974 Carol Channing, who had starred as Lorelei LEE when the musical first opened, appeared in a revival of the show entitled Lorelei, advertised under the slogan 'Gentlemen Still Prefer Blondes'.

Gentrification. The process by which a working-class or decayed urban area, especially in the inner city, is made middle-class. The term has been ascribed to the Marxist urban geographer Ruth Glass, who used it in an article of 1964, but it did not become generally familiar until the early 1970s, when the professional middle classes began to buy homes in traditional working-class city areas. Their aim was to restore and renovate the properties to suit their tastes, and this in turn led to a change in character of the area as a whole, so that shops went upmarket and pubs and cafés became bistros or wine bars.

Geography. One of many euphemisms for the lavatory. One may have to explore a building in order to find it. A considerate hostess in a private house would thus tell guests: 'Let me show you the geography.' The now obsolescent (though not obsolete) expression dates from the 1920s.

Geometry of Fear. A term coined by the art critic Herbert Read to describe the angst-ridden look of the work of a group of eight British sculptors who exhibited together at the 1952 Venice Biennale. They were Robert Adams (1917–84), Kenneth Armitage (b.1916), Reg Butler (1913–81), Lynn Chadwick (b.1914), Geoffrey Clarke (b.1924), Bernard Meadows (b.1915), Eduardo Paolozzi (b.1924) and William Turnbull (b.1922). Many of them were influenced by the 'Existentialist' sculptures of Giacometti and Richier, which seemed to encapsulate the anguish and bewilderment of the postwar generation.

George Cross and **George Medal.** The George Cross is second only to the Victoria Cross. It consists of a plain silver cross with a medallion showing St George and the Dragon in the centre. The words 'For Gallantry' appear round the medallion, and in the angle of each limb of the cross is the royal cipher. It hangs from a dark blue ribbon. The George Cross was instituted by George VI in 1940 for acts of conspicuous heroism, primarily by civilians. It is awarded to service personnel only for acts of heroism not covered by existing military honours. In 1999 there were 38 surviving holders of the George Cross, one of these being the island of Malta (see GEORGE CROSS ISLAND). In 2000 the George Cross was controversially awarded to the ROYAL ULSTER CONSTABULARY.

The George Medal (red ribbon with five narrow blue stripes) is awarded for similar but somewhat less outstanding acts of bravery.

George Cross Island. Malta is so called from the award of the GEORGE CROSS to the island by George VI in April 1942 in recognition of the steadfastness and fortitude of its people while under siege in the Second World War. It had suffered constant aerial attacks from Italian and German bombers.

George Medal. See GEORGE CROSS.

Georgia Mafia. A disparaging label applied to the group of advisers that Democratic President Jimmy Carter (b.1924) assembled around him when he went to the White House in 1977. Most of the group had worked with him while he was governor of Georgia

(1970–74), and their inexperience in national politics led to considerable problems.

Georgian Poetry. This was originally the title of a series of five poetry anthologies published between 1912 and 1922 and named after George V, whose reign began in 1910. The term has since been applied more generally to rural and stylistically conventional verse of the kind the original books mostly contained. Major poets so categorized include W.H. Davies, Walter de la Mare, John Masefield, Ralph Hodgson, Edward Thomas, James Stephens, Andrew Young, Siegfried Sassoon, Rupert Brooke, Wilfred Owen, Robert Graves, Edmund Blunden and D.H. Lawrence. While many of these poets produced works of great merit, much verse of the genre was characterized by pedestrian rhythms, rural sentimentality and imaginative banality, so that 'Georgian' has gained something of a pejorative sense in the modern critical armoury. *See also* WAR POETS.

Georgia Peach. A nickname for the outstanding US baseball player Ty Cobb (1886–1961), who was born in Georgia. He played for the Detroit Tigers and the Philadelphia Athletes. The name alludes to his popularity and is said to have been coined by a Detroit sportswriter.

Geronimo! This cry of exultation, first used by US paratroops in the Second World War, is the name of the Apache Indian chief Geronimo (1829–1900), who warred against the Mexicans when they killed his mother, wife and three children. His Indian name was Goyahkla, 'One Who Yawns'.

Gerson diet. A vegetarian diet of fresh fruit and raw food, used successfully in the 1920s by the German physician Max Gerson (1881–1959) to treat patients with chronic conditions such as tuberculosis, arthritis and vascular disease, and later also cancer. It is based on the diet of apes and was first applied by Gerson to himself to cure the severe migraine from which he suffered in his youth.

Gert and Daisy. The pair of Cockney gossips were created as a comic duo for BBC radio in the 1930s by the sisters Elsie (*c.*1895–1990) and Doris (*c.*1904–78) Waters. They became national institutions in the Second World War to the extent that Lord HAW-HAW, in a broadcast from Germany, declared: 'the good folk of Grimsby should not expect Gert and Daisy to protect them from attacks by the Luftwaffe.'

Gertcha! GET AWAY WITH YOU! This colloquial form of the phrase, dating from the 1930s, was adopted from a popular song by the Cockney trio Chas and Dave for a television commercial for Courage Best Bitter in the early 1980s. The scene was set in an East End pub, and the drinkers shouted the word out during breaks in the music.

Gestalt therapy. A psychotherapeutic approach developed *c.*1950 in New York by Fritz Perls (1893–1970) and his wife Laura. It focuses on insights into so-called gestalts in patients and their relations to the world, and frequently uses role-playing in order to help resolve past conflicts.

The German word *Gestalt* literally means the way a thing has been *gestellt*, i.e. 'placed', and in English use the term was adopted by psychologists to mean an organized whole whose attributes are not deducible from analysis of the parts in isolation.

Gestapo. A name shortened from German *Geheime Staatspolizei*, 'secret state police', which acquired sinister fame in NAZI Germany after 1933. It was formed by Hermann Goering (1893–1946) and later controlled by Heinrich Himmler (1900–45), and it was responsible for terrorizing both the Germans and the peoples of occupied territories. It was declared a criminal organization by the Nuremberg Tribunal in 1946.

Geste, Beau. Michael Geste, a bold young Englishman who joins the French Foreign Legion and has a number of adventures in North Africa. He is the hero of P.C. Wren's BEAU GESTE (1924). His name puns on the French phrase *beau geste* (literally, 'fine gesture') used for a display of magnanimity.

> He gave in, but he gave in with a passionate reservation. He was not going to quarrel with a *beau geste*.
> WARWICK DEEPING: *Sorrell and Son*, ch xv (1925)

Get a handle on, To. *See* HAVE A HANDLE ON.

Get a life! An adjurement to someone to start living a more purposeful existence, the implication being that their present life is empty or boring. *See also* GET REAL!

> 'I'm approaching 40 and I've been told by my doctor to get my life in balance; I have been told by my wife to get my life in balance; I've been told by my 12-year-old to get a life.'
> *The Times* (2 October 1999)

Get away with you! You can't be serious! You're having me on! Don't make me laugh! *See also* GERTCHA!

Get a wiggle on, To. To get a move on; to hurry up; to 'look lively'. An expression of US military origin dating from the turn of the 20th century.

'I [novelist Greg Williams] heard a woman the other day saying to a friend, "Come on, we're late. Get a wiggle on." I thought "I'll have that. What a great way to say hurry up".'

The Times (7 August 1999)

Get cracking, To. To get started; to begin work speedily and efficiently. The phrase dates from the 1930s and alludes to cracking one's whip when mustering cattle or geeing-up a team of horses.

Get in on the act, To. To involve oneself in an enterprise or activity, especially one that promises kudos or reward.

Get it on with someone, To. To seduce them, especially after a long period of time. An expression of US origin dating from the 1960s. *See also* HAVE IT OFF WITH SOMEONE.

After six years of will they, won't they, did they, didn't they, Mulder and Scully [of *The* X-FILES] finally got it on. David Duchovny and Gillian Anderson managed a screen kiss.

heat (9–15 December 1999)

Get knotted! Go away! An expression of contemptuous rejection, perhaps alluding to a sexual liaison.

Get lost! Go away! Clear out! A term dating from the 1940s.

Rover says that all their press demonstrators are booked out until February. And no more reservations are being taken. Roughly translated, this means, 'Get lost, sunshine'.

Sunday Times (5 December 1999)

Get nowhere fast, To. To make no headway after making every effort to do so. The phrase dates from the 1950s.

Get off the ground, To. To make a successful start. The allusion is to the take-off of an aircraft or the launch of a spacecraft. The expression dates from the 1960s.

Get one's act together, To. To organize or reorganize one's life or business. The phrase implies an under-rehearsed or poorly performed part in a play that has been worked on until right. The expression dates from the 1960s and originated in American black slang.

You want a caring, self-confident, successful, adventurous, travelled, sporting man, who has got his act together.

The Times (personal advertisement) (31 July 1999)

Get one's feet under the table, To. To become established in a job. The image is of sitting down

to work at a desk and settling oneself there.

This is the time of the year when foreign diplomats new to London are getting their feet under the table.

The Times (9 October 1999)

Get one's finger out, To. To get a move on or to make an effort, especially when one is slow or idle, or prevaricating. The allusion is to a male finger and a female anatomy. Perhaps because of the crude reference, the expression has undergone mock-pompous variants, such as 'to dedigitate'. The phrase startled some when it was used by Prince Philip in a speech about British industry on 17 October 1961: 'It is about time we pulled our fingers out!'

Get one's hands dirty, To. To do manual or menial work, especially when normally one is, or regards oneself to be, above such basic labour.

Get one's head down, To. To sleep; to concentrate on the task in hand. In the former case one lays one's head on the pillow; in the latter one lowers one's head over one's task.

As I had only five and a half weeks to write the book, I rented a cottage in Buckinghamshire to get my head down and meet my deadline.

Sunday Times (17 October 1999)

Get one's head round something, To. To puzzle it out; to make sense of it. The expression is usually found in the negative.

Nic and Allan said they were still stuck trying to get their heads round that worrying 300-plus figure.

The Times (25 September 1999)

Get one's jollies, To. To have fun; to get a thrill. 'Jollies' is probably a shortening of 'jollifications'.

Get one's kit off, To. To remove one's clothes, especially as part of a stage or film performance or as an artistic model. The expression dates from the 1970s and partly suggests a sports player's undressing at the end of a game in order to wash or shower and then re-dress in ordinary clothes. Compare the word 'strip' in its dual sense of 'act of undressing' and 'sports player's identifying outfit'.

The sporting world has been assaulted by a rash of alarming calendars featuring teams ... eager to mark the months of the coming sporting season by getting their kit off.

The Times (2 December 1999)

Get one's knickers in a twist, To. To become unduly concerned or excited about a matter, especially when frustrated. The allusion is to a woman who misaligns the named garment when hastily dressing (or re-dressing). The expression dates from the 1960s.

> Strange behaviour from *Hello!* and *OK!* magazines … Both have been getting their sequinned knickers in a twist over press releases each issued after a High Court case this week.
> *The Times* (19 November 1999)

Get one's leg over, To. To achieve sexual intercourse. The allusion is to the position adopted. The expression dates from the 1970s, although 'to lift one's leg over' in the sense of to seduce is found in the 18th century.

Get one's rocks off, To. To experience an orgasm, 'rocks' here being the testicles, as a pun on medieval 'stones' in this sense. The vulgar expression has gained a wider and more generally acceptable meaning 'to enjoy oneself', 'to obtain satisfaction'. Both senses date from the 1940s.

> Last year I did 17 concerts in Asia … In Beijing, for the Chinese people to get their rocks off was extraordinary.
> *The Times* (9 July 1999)

Get or sink one's teeth into something, To. To become fully engaged or engrossed in it. The analogy is with an animal biting deeply and vigorously into food. The expression dates from the early years of the 20th century.

Get out more, To. To gain greater experience of life and people; to emerge from one's cocooned existence and see the REAL WORLD. The expression is mainly used of a naive or narrow-minded person, or someone so involved in their own interests that they miss the wider picture of things.

> She [television cook Delia Smith] offers up a veritable paean of praise and love to the cauliflower, the dismembering of whose florets is declared to be 'fun'. She should really get out more.
> *The Times* (7 February 2000)

Get out of someone's face, To. To stop pestering them. The expression dates from the 1960s and as may be expected is mostly found in the imperative. *See also* IN YOUR FACE.

> 'People would ask me, "Is your name Mena [Suvari] because you're mean?" What should I say? "Yeah, I'm a bitch. Now get out of my face!"'
> *heat* (16 December 1999–5 January 2000)

Get out of third gear, To. To get going properly; to move towards one's peak. The third gear is the one the driver of a motor vehicle engages for manoeuvring before changing up to top gear.

> Fans will enjoy the usual details … and the clever conceit, but for once he [novelist Iain Banks] never gets out of third gear.
> *The Times* (7 August 1999)

Get real! Be realistic! An admonition of US campus origin current from the 1970s. *See also* GET A LIFE!

> Are we shouting from the rooftops because Bheke Makhubu … was arrested last month in Mbabane and charged with criminal defamation? Get real. That's Africa.
> *The Times* (16 October 1999)

Get someone's goat, To. To irritate them. A somewhat fanciful story explains the phrase as an allusion to the goat that was traditionally stabled with a racehorse as its 'comforter'. To nobble the horse the trick was to creep into its stable the night before a big race and steal the goat. It would then be restless all night and off form the following day. But one can irritate a person by constantly butting in, and this may be a more likely reference.

Get the message, To. To understand; to take a hint. A phrase dating from the 1950s and originating in jazz jargon.

Get the show on the road, To. To get going; to get started. The expression is of US origin and refers to the times at the turn of the century when companies presenting plays, vaudevilles, circuses and the like toured all over the country.

Get up someone's nose, To. To irritate or annoy them. The allusion is to a bad smell, which offends the nostrils. The expression dates from the 1950s.

Get weaving, To. To begin an action; to GET CRACKING. The expression dates from the Second World War and derives from RAF slang. An aircraft was said to 'weave' when flying a devious course, especially to avoid or escape danger.

Ghetto-blaster. A large portable radio, especially one used to play loud pop music. The term dates from the early 1980s and alludes to the prevalence of such radios in the black quarters ('ghettos') of US cities.

Ghost in the machine. The mind ('ghost') as distinct from the body ('machine'). The expression was coined by the philosopher Gilbert Ryle in *The Concept of Mind* (1949). The phrase is sometimes used in a derogatory sense by critics of the dualism exemplified by

Descartes' distinction between the material body and the immaterial soul.

Ghost town. A town that once prospered but that is now in decay with few inhabitants.

Ghost train. A train seen running at a time when none is scheduled, especially silently or after dark. Arnold Ridley's comedy thriller *The Ghost Train* (1925) was one of the most successful ever written, and formed the basis of many films, the best being *Oh Mr Porter* (1937). At a fun fair a ghost train is a miniature train that takes riders on a round trip of ghoulish sights, sounds and special effects. In railway jargon a ghost train is a night-running de-icing train on electric railways equipped with conductor rails.

Ghost writer. An anonymous author who writes speeches, articles or books, and especially autobiographies, for which another, better known person gets the credit. The term dates from the 1920s.

Ghote, Inspector. The Indian police detective created by H.R.F. Keating for his novel *The Perfect Murder* (1964). He lives and works in Bombay and is amiable and unassuming, but he always cracks his cases. Of his subsequent involvements *Inspector Ghote Trusts the Heart* (1972) is reckoned to be one of the best.

GI. During the Second World War American enlisted men called themselves GIs, from an abbreviation of Government (or General) Issue. After becoming accustomed to GI shirts, GI blankets and other army issues, the soldiers began to apply the term to themselves.

GI bride. A woman who married a US serviceman (GI) after meeting him when he was stationed in England (or some other country) in the Second World War. An estimated 75,000 women became GI brides, and a third of all births in the war were illegitimate.

Gibson Girl. A representation of female beauty characteristic of its era depicted by Charles Dana Gibson (1867–1944) in several series of black-and-white drawings dating from 1886 and continuing well into the 20th century. His picture books with drawings of the modern and staunchly American girl enjoyed an enormous vogue. One of the best known was *The Education of Mr Pip* (1899), chronicling the adventures in high society of the wealthy and amiable Mr Pip, his socially ambitious wife and his Gibson Girl daughter, and *A Widow and Her Friends* (1901), following the emergence from mourning of a beautiful young widow and the antics of her six suitors. The Gibson Girl was portrayed in various poses and occupations, her individuality accentuated by the sweeping skirts and large hats of the period. She was based on his wife Irene (née Langhorne), one of whose sisters was Nancy, Viscountess Astor (1879–1964).

Gibson guitar. The US guitarist Les Paul (b.1915) took his new solid-bodied electric guitar to the famous Gibson company in 1947. Nicknamed 'the log', it was an adaptation of Adolph Rickenbacker's version of 1931, known as 'the frying pan'. The Gibson was the required instrument for rock 'n' roll guitarists from the late 1960s.

Gideons. The organization of Christian business and professional men, familiar to the traveller and tourist from the Bibles they place in hotel rooms, was founded in Janesville, Wisconsin, in 1899. It began placing Bibles in 1908, and during the Second World War supplied the US armed forces with service Testaments. The work of the Gideons is supported by voluntary donations, and their emblem is a two-handled pitcher and torch, in memory of the biblical Gideon's victory over the Midianites (Judges 7:15–23).

Gidget. The nickname of Francine Lawrence, a sporty teenage 'California girl' who is the main character in several novels by Frederick Kohner, beginning with *Gidget* (1957). She appeared in a series of films based on the books from 1959, played in turn by Sandra Dee, Deborah Walley and Cindy Carol. In US slang, a gidget is a lithe, pert young woman.

GIFT. The semi-punning acronym of *gamete intrafallopian transfer*, as a technique developed in the 1980s for facilitating human conception. The procedure involves transferring sperm and ova directly into the Fallopian tubes of the mother-to-be.

Gigi. The pet name of Gilberte, the young Parisian girl who is the heroine of Colette's novel titled after her (1944), in which she is trained by her aunt to become a courtesan. The story inspired a film of 1948, in which Gigi is played by Danièle Delorme, and a successful screen musical by Frederick Loewe and Alan Jay Lerner (1958), with Leslie Caron in the lead role. The later film has the popular numbers 'Thank heaven for little girls' and 'I remember it well'.

GIGO. In computer jargon, the acronym, pronounced to rhyme with 'my go', of 'garbage in, garbage out'. The sense is that faulty input will always result in faulty output.

GI Joe. A Second World War nickname for a US infantryman. It was the name of the soldier in Lieutenant Dave Breger's comic strip for *Yank*, the US Army magazine, and first appeared in the issue of 17 June 1942. Breger chose 'Joe' as the name for its alliteration with 'GI'. *See also* ACTION MAN.

Gilded cage. A luxurious but restrictive environment. The expression dates from the turn of the 20th century. It was popularized and possibly introduced to the language by Arthur J. Lamb and Harry von Tilzer's song 'A Bird in a Gilded Cage' (1899) about a young girl who marries for wealth instead of love and pays for the luxury with a life of regret.

Giles. The pen-name of the cartoonist Carl Ronald Giles (1916–95), whose work appeared regularly in the *Daily Express* and *Sunday Express* from 1943 until his death. His wartime cartoons, often featuring Hitler and Mussolini, were crowded with detail and incident, but he is most closely associated with the large and chaotic 'Giles Family', dominated by Grandma, a squat figure with a bespectacled, pugnacious face only partly visible between her black coat and hat.

Gill Sans. This elegant sans serif typeface was created in 1928 for the Monotype Company (later Monotype Corporation) by the sculptor Eric Gill (1882–1940). It was commissioned by the company's consultant, Stanley Morison, as was Gill's subsequent typeface, Perpetua, created in 1930. Both are classics of 20th-century typography. Morison himself designed the typeface now known as Times New Roman for *The Times*, where it first appeared on 3 October 1932.

Gimmick. The first use of this word in US slang in the 1920s was to describe some device by which a conjurer or fairground showman worked his trick. In later usage it applied to some distinctive quirk or trick associated with a film or radio star, then to any device. The origin of the word is uncertain. It may be an alteration of 'gimcrack' or even a form of 'magic'.

Gin and it. Gin and Italian (bitter-sweet) vermouth, a drink mostly favoured by the aspiring or actual upper-middle classes. Slightly higher in the social scale is a gin and French (dry) vermouth. *See also* G AND T.

Gin and Jag. Gin and a Jaguar car, two of the desirable perquisites of the upper-middle class and an encapsulation of their lifestyle. The 'gin' is likely to be G AND T or GIN AND IT. The jingle dates from the 1960s.

The 'gin and Jag' brigade has mobilized against Alan Shearer. ... After snobbish mutterings in the clubhouse, he has been stuck on a waiting list stretching well into the next millennium.
The Times (14 June 1999)

Ginger Man, The. The first novel (1955; 1963 unexpurgated) by J.P. Donleavy (b.1926). Sebastian Dangerfield, both a redhead and a man of action ('ginger'), rollicks and frolics drunkenly through Dublin and its society. The play (1959), adapted by the author, was withdrawn from the Dublin stage because of clerical opposition.

Ginnie Mae. A US nickname for the Government National Mortgage Association, based on the earlier FANNIE MAE. *See also* FREDDIE MAC.

Gioconda smile. An enigmatic smile, as that of the *Mona Lisa*. Leonardo da Vinci's famous painting (1503–6), also known as *La Gioconda* or *La Joconde*, is a portrait of the wife of Francesco del Giocondo. The expression was popularized or even coined by Aldous Huxley, who has a short story, 'The Gioconda Smile', in *Mortal Coils* (1922).

Gipper. A regular nickname for Ronald Reagan (b.1911), film actor and 40th president of the United States (1981–9). The reference is to the part of George Gipp that he played in the film *Knute Rockne – All American* (1940). Gipp himself (1895–1920) had been an American football star coached by Knute Rockne when at Notre Dame University, Indiana. Following Gipp's early death from a mysterious illness, a press story circulated that on his deathbed he had urged his team to 'win one for the Gipper', a phrase that subsequently became legendary. It was famously repeated by Ronald Reagan in the film and subsequently exploited by him at political rallies. *See also* GREAT COMMUNICATOR.

Gippy tummy. *See* MONTEZUMA'S REVENGE.

Gipsy Moth IV. The 16.75-m (55-foot) yacht in which Francis (subsequently Sir Francis) Chichester (1901–72) made the first solo sailing voyage around the world, making only one stop. The voyage, in 1966–7, took a total of 226 actual sailing days. The gipsy moth (*Lymantria dispar*) is a species of European moth, which also gave its name to a biplane, popular as a trainer. It was in such a plane that Chichester had made a solo flight from Britain to Australia in 1929. In 1960 Chichester won the first transatlantic solo yacht race in *Gypsy Moth III*.

Girl Friday. A dated term for a female 'clerk of all work' or personal assistant. The term is a 1950s adman's alteration of Man Friday, as the name of the young savage found on a Friday by the hero of Daniel Defoe's *Robinson Crusoe* (1719) and kept as his servant and companion on the desert island. The name is appropriate for someone whose working week ends (and weekend begins) on this day. The term was popularized by the film *His Girl Friday* (1940) starring Cary Grant and Rosalind Russell, but fell from favour in the 1980s as being sexist.

> Person Friday required for this busy Interior Design and Architectural Practice.
>
> *The Times* (advertisement) (26 October 1994)

Girl Guides. The female counterpart to the BOY SCOUTS, organized in 1910 by Lord Baden-Powell (1857–1941) and his sister Agnes (1858–1945). Their training and organization is much the same as the Scouts and is based on similar promises and laws. The three sections of the movement, since 1992 officially named Guides rather than Girl Guides, were originally BROWNIES, Guides and Rangers, but the names and groupings have now been modified to: Rainbow Guides (aged 5–7), Brownie Guides (7 and over), Guides (10 and over), Ranger Guides (14 and over) and Young Leaders (15–18).

In the United States they are called Girl Scouts (formed 1912), with names and age groups: Daisies (5–6), Brownies (6–8), Juniors (8–11), Cadettes (11–14) and Seniors (14–17).

Girl meets boy. The paradigm of a conventional love match, fictional or in fact.

Girl next door. A young woman, especially one known from childhood, regarded as a pleasant and decent but in the main conventional marriage partner.

> Her appearance in *Playboy* marked the beginning of the 'girl-next-door' concept that separated *Playboy* from the other glamour magazines of the time.
>
> *The Times Magazine* (27 November 1999)

Girl of the Golden West, The. The heroine of Puccini's opera *La Fanciulla del West*, which was first performed in New York in 1910 with a libretto by Carlo Zangarini and Guelfo Civinini based on David Belasco's play of the same title (1905). The story is set in California in 1850 at the time of the first big gold rush. Minnie, keeper of the Polka Saloon and a friend of the gold miners, falls in love with the stranger Dick Johnson, who turns out to be the wanted bandit Ramírez. When Dick is wounded by the guns of a posse she hides him in her cabin, but the sheriff, Jack Rance, discovers him there. Minnie and Rance agree to a game of poker to decide Johnson's fate, and she wins by cheating. Rance leaves, but Johnson is captured by the miners and is about to be hanged. Minnie begs them to spare the man she loves and they release him. Minnie and Dick ride off into the sunset. The Italian opera title lacks the 'Golden' glow of Belasco's English original.

Girl power. The social and economic power of young women as individuals in their own right, rather than as sexual stereotypes. The feministic stance of the 1990s was based on the need for young women to make their voices heard and was expanded and expounded in such books as Patty Ellis's *Girl Power: Making Choices and Speaking Out* (1994) and Hillary Carlip's *Girl Power: Young Women Speak Out* (1995), the latter a variety of viewpoints by 'cowgals, lesbians, teen mothers, sorority sisters and girls in gangs'. The 'official book' of the SPICE GIRLS was entitled *Girl Power!* (1997), and the phrase became associated with the group, whose lyrics purported to extol its virtues.

> Girl Power! Girls can do whatever they like, and it's all Girl Power! And as Girl Power is feminism with added fun and hair-mascara, so women dressed as teenagers are feminist statements on sexuality.
>
> CAITLIN MORAN in *The Times* (3 August 1999)

Girls in pearls. A colloquial term for a 'society portrait' of a fashionably dressed young woman, such as that appearing weekly in *Country Life*.

> Sophia Burrell, 25, posed in a replication of Botticelli's *Birth of Venus* on what is usually the 'girls in pearls' page.
>
> *The Times* (9 September 1999)

Girl's Own Paper, The. A magazine for girls first published in 1880, a year after *The* BOY'S OWN PAPER. Like its companion publication, it featured material in keeping with contemporary ideas about the correct upbringing of juveniles: features on women's fashions, articles on homemaking skills, such as sewing and cooking, and accounts of 'suitable' female role-models such as Queen Victoria and Florence Nightingale. It ceased publication in 1965.

Giro. The word has come to have two main applications, one formal, the other informal. Formally, it is the name of the Girobank, a clearing bank set up as part of the Post Office in 1968. It operates like any other bank, but uses post offices as its outlets. Informally, as an abbreviation for girocheque, it is the name of the social security payment sent by post to those entitled, who then cash the cheque at a post office. The word ultimately goes back to Italian *giro*, 'circulation'.

> 'That my lager?' he inquired, feeling mean even as he uttered the question. 'Yeah, d'you mind?' said Raymond. 'I'll replace it when I get me next giro.'
> DAVID LODGE: *Nice Work*, Pt III, ch ii (1988)

Give-'em-hell Harry. A nickname of the forthright Democratic politician Harry S. Truman (1884–1972), president of the USA (1945–53). In the 1948 presidential election campaign his supporters shouted 'Give 'em hell, Harry'. Truman responded: 'I never give 'em hell; I just tell 'em the truth and they think it's hell.' During his presidency he earned the nickname High-Tax Harry from his opponents (*compare* FDR's nickname of Franklin Deficit Roosevelt). An earlier nickname was Haberdasher Harry; after the First World War Truman had opened a haberdashery store in Kansas City, which failed after two years. He was also known as the Man from Missouri (as indeed he was). The 'S' in his name does not stand for anything (as with the 'H' in General H Norman Schwarzkopf, STORMIN' NORMAN). *See also* NMI.

Give me strength! A 'prayer' uttered on hearing some stupid statement. The invocation is for the strength to restrain oneself. The phrase dates from the 1920s.

Give someone a bell or **a buzz, To.** To telephone or call them.

Give someone grey hairs, To. To cause them worry or trouble; to annoy or pester them persistently. The expression is logically best applied to a young person whose hair has not yet naturally begun to turn grey.

> I would prefer to have a property empty for a month than spend six months putting up with tenants who give me grey hairs.
> *The Times* (13 October 1999)

Give someone something on a plate, To. *See* HAND SOMEONE SOMETHING ON A PLATE.

Give someone the finger, To. To make a gesture of contempt. In the United States, and now also in Britain, the gesture is an upward jerk of the middle finger. More commonly in Britain it is a V-SIGN.

Give someone the large, To. To give them their freedom. The expression can equally be applied to ani-

mals or to anything living, such as flowers or plants.

> I did a little audition at home planting some clematis, giving it the large, you know, and got the job.
> *heat* (6–12 January 2000)

Glad eye. An amorous glance; a look of sexual interest. The phrase dates from the early 20th century and has been humorously associated with the first name Gladys and *vice versa*.

Glad rags. One's best clothes, and specifically formal dress. The expression is of US origin.

Glagolitic Mass. A setting of the Ordinary of the Mass for solo voices, chorus, organ and orchestra by Leoš Janáček (1854–1928). The title of a piece is a misnomer: the composer thought 'Glagolitic' referred to the Old Slavonic language of the 9th century, the time of St Methodius and St Cyril, but the term only refers to the Old Slavonic alphabet, supposedly invented by St Cyril. Of the work, which was first performed in 1927, Janáček wrote: 'I wanted to portray the faith in the certainty of the nation, not on a religious basis but on a basis of moral strength which takes God for witness.'

Glamour boy. A nickname for a Royal Air Force pilot in the Second World War. The RAF had a glamorous image, not only for their exploits but for their appearance. *See also* BRYLCREEM BOYS; FEW.

Glamour puss. A glamorous person, usually female but also sometimes male. The expression dates from the 1950s.

Glam rock. A style of rock music of the early 1970s, characterized by the wearing of extravagantly coloured clothes and make-up by the male performers. The aim was perhaps to make a statement about decadence, or simply to draw attention away from the unoriginality of the words and music. 'Glam' is 'glamorous'. *See also* ZIGGY STARDUST.

> We are not here to discuss the [David] Bowie icon of 1970s legend, the glam-rock icon with red hair, white face, and seven-league platform boots.
> *Sunday Times Magazine* (19 September 1999)

Glasnost (Russian, 'openness'). The practice of more open consultative government and wider dissemination of information in the former Soviet Union was initiated from 1985 by Mikhail Gorbachev (*see* GORBY). The policy had been only partially implemented by the time of the country's collapse as a communist state in 1991. *See also* PERESTROIKA.

Glass ceiling. An invisible barrier on the career ladder that some employees, in particular women and members of minority groups, find they can see through but which they cannot surmount. *See also* CONCRETE SKIRTING BOARD.

> If there are still glass ceilings in some offices, they are likely to shatter at the collective impact of the confident, well-qualified generation of girls now emerging from the nation's schools.
>
> *The Times* (7 September 1998)

Glasshouse. Army slang for a military prison. It was originally applied to the prison at North Camp, Aldershot, which had a glass roof.

Glass menagerie. A diverse but meretricious or insubstantial display of people or things. The allusion is to the title of Tennessee Williams's play *The Glass Menagerie* (1944), in which a collection of small glass animals owned by the daughter of the central character, Tom Wingfield, symbolizes the Wingfields themselves as the 'little people', whose poor world is falling apart.

> One aim is to prevent the new second chamber [the reformed House of Lords] looking like a glass menagerie assembled by No. 10.
>
> *The Times* (3 November 1999)

Glastonbury Festival. The short name of the Glastonbury Festival of Contemporary Performing Arts, better known as an annual rock festival, held at the end of June on Worthy Farm in the village of Pilton near the ancient Somerset town of Glastonbury, itself a centre of pagan and Christian legend and a magnet for droves of NEW AGE adherents. The festival was the enterprise of a local farmer, Michael Eavis, who in September 1970 leased out his land for a combination of pop festival, country fair and harvest festival. The event has evolved from a fairly primitive affair with rudimentary facilities and an attendance of only 2000 to a highly organized occasion, complete with roads laid specially for the three days, cash points, retail outlets, proper restaurants and flush lavatories for the convenience of the thousands of HIPPIES, music fans and performers.

Glastonbury Romance, A. A novel (1933) by John Cowper Powys (1872–1963), set in the Somerset town of Glastonbury. To illustrate his central theme of self-fulfilment, Powys draws on the local legend that Joseph of Arimathea came to convert the British, choosing Glastonbury as his base and placing the Holy Grail, the cup used by Christ at the Last Supper, beneath a spring on a hill by the town. The attitude to a symbolic grail of each of the main characters is examined. A climax of the narrative is a pageant depicting details from Arthurian legend and the story of the Crucifixion. *See also* GLASTONBURY FESTIVAL.

Gleam in one's eye. *See* TWINKLE IN ONE'S EYE.

Glengarry Glen Ross. A film (1992), directed by James Foley, based on a play (1984) by David Mamet (b.1947), who also wrote the screenplay. It is about the pressures sales staff at a real estate office find themselves under when they learn that the two least successful among them will be sacked. Glengarry Glen Ross refers to the useless areas of land that the staff compete to sell.

> Put that coffee down. Coffee's for closers only.
>
> DAVID MAMET: *Glengarry Glen Ross*

Glitterati. A name for fashionable people, especially those conspicuously involved in show business or some other glamorous activity. The term arose in the 1950s as a blend of 'glitter' and 'literati', the latter being a 17th-century word for literate or well-educated people, as the plural of Latin *literatus*, literally 'acquainted with letters'.

Global village. The world regarded as a unified community linked by telecommunications. The implication of the term, originally coined by Marshall McLuhan in 1960, is that the mass media reduces national distinctions and creates an element of economic and social interdependence, as in a small village, where everything is accessible to everyone. *See also* McLUHANISM.

Global warming. The gradual increase in the overall temperature of the Earth's atmosphere due to the GREENHOUSE EFFECT. The two terms are sometimes confused in the public mind.

Gloom and doom. *See* DOOM AND GLOOM.

Gloomy Dean. The nickname of W.R. Inge (1860–1954), dean of St Paul's Cathedral, London, from 1911 to 1934. The sobriquet sprang from his resistance to current trends and his forcefully expressed doubts regarding political and social reforms that most saw as beneficial.

Gloriana. A controversial opera by Benjamin Britten (1913–76) with a libretto by William Plomer. It was commissioned by Covent Garden to celebrate the coronation of Elizabeth II and was first performed in the queen's presence in 1953. It was criticized at the time both for its music and for its depiction of its subject. Gloriana was the name that Edmund Spenser (c.1552–99) gave to Queen Elizabeth I in *The Faerie Queene*, and Britten's opera concerns the relationship between Elizabeth I and the Earl of Essex.

Glorioso mutilado, El. (Spanish, 'the glorious mutilated one'). The nickname given by his followers to the extreme right-wing Spanish soldier José Millan Astráy y Terreros (1879–1954), a profoundly sinister, death-obsessed henchman of General Franco and creator of the Spanish Foreign Legion. The brutal methods of the latter under Astray's leadership contributed much to Franco's victory in the Spanish Civil War. He owed his name to the fact that he was maimed by a number of old war wounds, having but one arm, one eye, a shattered jaw and mutilated fingers on his remaining hand. *See also* CAUDILLO.

Gloves are off. A journalistic cliché to describe a worsening dispute. The metaphor is from boxing, in which removal of the gloves signifies a more serious bare-knuckle fight.

> If Murdoch can offer big bucks and get them, then so can we. The gloves are off now.
> *Guardian* (29 April 1995)

Glutton for punishment. A person who welcomes hard or unpleasant tasks. The phrase is often used humorously for a repeated imposition that one is obliged to undergo, such as a training routine or a regular round of domestic chores. The expression dates from the 1970s as an altered form of the earlier 'glutton for work'.

Glyndebourne. The country estate, near Lewes in Sussex, where John Christie (1882–1962) opened the Glyndebourne Festival Theatre in 1934 for operatic and musical performances, which became an annual summer event. A new opera house opened to general acclaim in 1994.

G-men. Government men or agents of the FBI. The term originally applied to the agents of the Department of Justice's Bureau of Investigation under J. Edgar Hoover and continued after the establishment of the FBI in 1935.

Gnomes of Zurich. An uncomplimentary name given to those financiers of Zurich controlling international monetary funds. The phrase became popular after its use in 1964 by George Brown, then Labour Minister of Economic Affairs, at the time of a sterling crisis. The

expression had been used before this, however, by Harold Wilson, when in a speech in the House of Commons on 12 November 1956 he had referred to 'all the little gnomes in Zurich and other finance centres'.

> What most infuriated George Brown, and Labour MPs such as John Mendelson and Ian Mikardo ... was that the men they disparaged as the 'gnomes of Zürich' were really giants.
> T.R. FEHRENBACH: *The Gnomes of Zürich* (1966)

Go a bundle on, To. To be very keen on. The original sense was to bet a large sum of money (a 'bundle' or 'packet') on a horse. The expression is of US origin and dates from the 1930s.

Go ape, To. To go crazy; to lose one's self-control; to display strong emotion or reaction. The allusion is to the frenzied and panic-stricken behaviour of monkeys and apes when captured and caged, typically involving screaming and defecation.

Go ballistic, To. To fly into a rage. The image is of the launch of a ballistic missile. The expression is of US origin and dates from the 1980s. A stronger variant is 'go nuclear'. *See also* GO INTO ORBIT.

> He went 'ballistic', terrifying the women and keeping them imprisoned for five hours, the court was told.
> *The Times* (20 July 1999)

Gobbledygook. A word invented by the Texan lawyer Maury Maverick, a descendant of the cattle-owner Samuel A. Maverick, eponym of the *maverick*, to describe the convoluted, pretentious and often meaningless language of bureaucracy.

> People ask me where I got gobbledygook. I do not know. It must have come in a vision. Perhaps I was thinking of the old bearded turkey gobbler back in Texas, who was always gobbledy-gobbling and strutting with ludicrous pomposity. At the end of this gobble there was a sort of gook.
> *New York Times* (21 May 1944)

Go belly up, To. To go bankrupt. The allusion is to the posture of a dead fish in the water. The expression dates from the 1920s.

Go-Between, The. A novel (1953) by L. P. Hartley (1895–1972). The go-between is a boy holidaying at the stately home in Norfolk of his schoolfriend. He agrees to take messages between his friend's elder sister and the local farmer with whom she is in love. The main themes are the destruction of a child's innocence in an adult world and the dangers of sexual relationships between classes in the context of 1900.

The film version (1970), an almost palpable re-creation of the EDWARDIAN ERA in the mould of a MERCHANT IVORY FILM, with haunting music by Michel Legrand, was directed by Joseph Losey from a script by Harold Pinter.

> The past is a foreign country: they do things differently there.
>
> *The Go-Between* (Prologue)

Gobsmacked. Astounded; speechless with amazement. The allusion may be to a slap on the face, or to the involuntary act of clapping a hand over one's mouth ('gob') when taken aback. The term originated in North of England dialect speech but entered general usage only in the 1980s.

> I remain, as [former governor of Hong Kong] Chris Patten once famously put it, 'gobsmacked' by the Earl of Snowdon's decision to accept a nomination for a life peerage.
>
> ANTHONY HOWARD in *The Times* (10 November 1999)

Godfather, The. (1) A film (1972) adapted from a novel (1969) by Mario Puzo (1902–99) about an Italian Mafia family in New York. Directed by Francis Ford Coppola and starring Marlon Brando as the head (or 'Godfather') of the powerful Corleone clan, it inspired two equally acclaimed sequels and firmly established the use of 'the Godfather' to describe any person at the head of an organization, particularly one suspected of employing dubious, underhand or plain illegal methods. In business circles a takeover bid for a company that is so generous no one can afford to turn it down is commonly referred to as a 'godfather offer', with reference to the tradition of Mafia gangsters making 'an offer you can't refuse'.

(2) The football manager Don Revie (1928–89), so called for his autocratic style of management. The allusion is to the Mafia boss played by Marlon Brando in the 1972 film. Revie made Leeds United into one of the best club sides in Europe in the early 1970s but was subsequently less successful as manager of the English national side.

Go down a storm, To. To be enthusiastically received by an audience, who react to one's speech or performance with a storm of applause.

> [Chancellor Gordon] Brown's speech went down a storm. … In a barnstorming performance, Brown set out the future direction of the Government.
>
> *The Times* (29 September 1999)

Go down like a lead balloon, To. To be poorly received, as of a speech, proposal or the like. A balloon normally goes up, but weighted with lead will do the reverse. The expression is of US origin and dates from the 1950s.

> I do not know [who] … came up with this crazy scheme but it would have been catastrophic politics – going down like a lead airship with the vast majority of the electorate if ever implemented.
>
> *The Times* (25 November 1999)

God Save the Queen. A scabrously anarchic song by the short-lived PUNK rock group the Sex Pistols, which was released in 1977, the year of the Silver Jubilee of the accession to the throne of Queen Elizabeth II. The song's provocative title (the name of the national anthem of the UK) and lyrics (at one point the UK is described as a 'fascist regime') led to its being banned by the BBC on grounds of taste, and a number of High-Street shops refused to stock it. The sleeve of the single featured a photograph of the queen defaced with the name of the group and the song's title. *See also* ROCK GROUP NAMES.

God's Eye. A small cross made of twigs, branches and the like around which coloured yarn or threads is wound in geometric patterns. The artefact is popular in Mexico and the southwestern United States as a decoration or a symbol of good luck. The name translates Mexican Spanish *ojo de dios*, 'eye of a god', and the symbol is so called because it originally represented the eye of a deity among certain Native American peoples.

God's gift. A person regarded as a 'godsend', especially a man irresistible to women. The term is often used ironically, as (of an idiosyncratic teacher): 'He thinks he's God's gift to education.' The phrase is sometimes expanded to 'God's own gift'.

> Jessica Hatfield thought she was 'God's gift' to advertising when she dreamt up a scheme to link point-of-sale promotional material across supermarkets in Britain.
>
> *Sunday Times* (7 November 1999)

God slot. A period in a broadcasting schedule regularly reserved for a religious programme, such as BBC radio's daily *Morning Service* or BBC television's *Songs of Praise* each Sunday evening.

> They thought he [BBC chief political correspondent John Sergeant] might like a change of pace. Someone suggested he present the late Sunday night God slot *Everyman*.
>
> *The Times* (21 January 2000)

God squad. A nickname for an evangelical Christian group, especially one proselytizing among college students.

Godzilla. A fearsome dinosaur of the cinema that is awakened from its primordial slumbers by H-bomb tests and menaces Tokyo. It first appeared in the film that bears its name, in the original Japanese *Gojira* (1955). The name itself is a blend of Japanese *kujira*, 'whale', the nickname of a film production company employee at the time, and 'gorilla'. The monster reappeared in a number of sequels, some even more ridiculous than the original, including *King Kong vs. Godzilla* (1962), *Godzilla vs. the Thing* (1964) and *Destroy All Monsters* (1964). An all-new, all-American recreation was *Godzilla* (1998).

Go for broke, To. To risk everything in a venture; to commit oneself unreservedly. The reference is to gambling, when one stakes all. The expression is of US origin and dates from the 1960s.

Go for the burn, To. To push one's body to the extreme when undergoing physical training or 'working out'. Although recommended by such manuals as *Jane Fonda's Workout Book* (1981), the practice is not automatically applicable to all and is positively ill-advised in some cases.

Go for the jugular, To. To be aggressive when making an attack. The allusion is to the jugular vein in the neck, which carries blood from the head and face. A predator such as a wolf will literally go for the jugular when seizing the throat of a larger animal with the aim of killing it.

> The [*Daily*] *Mail* is successful because it goes for the emotional jugular and plays on prejudice.
> *The Times* (7 January 2000)

Go-go dancer. A scantily dressed female dancer who performs energetic and often erotic dances in a nightclub or the like. The term is based on a reduplication of 'go' influenced by French *à gogo*, 'aplenty', 'galore'.

> The fourth floor resembled a hi-tech Bangkok jazz bar, with conveyor belts of Thai nibbles whirring past the stockinged go-go dancers who were gyrating to booming r'n'b.
> *heat* (17–23 February 2000)

Go great guns, To. To go well; to perform vigorously. The expression dates from the early 20th century and apparently originated in horse racing, 'great gun' already existing as a term for an eminent or 'go-ahead' person, a BIG SHOT.

Going on. Getting on for; nearly. Said of ages, as: 'He must be going on 60.' The phrase, earlier 'going on for', is often used to compare a person's actual age with an apparent one, especially when a young person displays an ability or maturity ahead of their years.

> 'The guy [golfer Sergio García] is hugely talented. I cannot think of any weaknesses in his game. He is 19 going on 30.'
> *The Times* (16 August 1999)

Go into a flat spin or **tailspin, To.** To become agitated; to panic; to lose control. A flat spin is one in which an aircraft descends in tight circles while remaining almost horizontal. In a tailspin the aircraft falls nose first, its tail describing a spiral. Both expressions date from the early years of the 20th century.

Go into orbit, To. To lose one's temper. The expression dates from the 1960s and the start of space exploration proper. *See also* GO BALLISTIC; IN ORBIT.

> I was once brutally criticized ... for not setting a case down for final hearing. The barrister I instructed had specifically advised me not to. The judge did not know this and went into orbit.
> *The Times* (11 January 2000)

Golan Heights (Arabic *Al Jawlān*, Hebrew *Ha-Golan*). A strategically important range of hills in southern Syria. From here the Syrian army was able to shell settlements in northern Israel, making it an important objective for the Israelis in the SIX-DAY WAR (1967). They succeeded in capturing most of the Golan Heights, and Israeli settlements were established there. Israel's annexation of the area in 1981 was not recognized internationally, and the status of the Golan Heights has since proved a stumbling block to peace negotiations between Israel and Syria.

Gold Beach. The Allied code name for the stretch of beach on the Normandy coast running west from JUNO BEACH at La Rivière to Arromanches. On D-DAY it was where the British XXX Corps came ashore.

Gold-digger. A young woman who courts or marries an older man for his money.

> One 41-year-old met and wed a 78-year-old millionaire; but the marriage was not consummated and she took a younger lover. In court she was called a gold-digger and she emerged with relatively little.
> *The Times* (3 November 1999)

Gold disc. A record, usually of popular music, that has sold a specified high number of copies. In Britain the term applies to an album that has sold 100,000 copies or a single that has sold 400,000. In the United States the honour is awarded to either an album or a single that has sold 500,000 copies.

Golden Arrow. A famous Pullman train service from London to Paris, with a ferry crossing from Dover to Calais. On the French side of the English Channel the train had the equivalent name, *Flèche d'Or*. A train had been leaving Victoria Station at 11 a.m. daily for many years on this route before the name was adopted in 1929. The service was withdrawn in 1972. The name itself comes from folklore, in which the Golden Arrow was the one sought by a pair of lovers in the land of their dreams. The legend is alluded to in the title and story of Mary Webb's early novel *The Golden Arrow* (1916). The name was apt for a train that took passengers to Paris, the 'City of Lovers'. *See also* TITLED TRAINS.

Goldenballs. A *Private Eye* nickname for Sir James Goldsmith (1933–97), who filed numerous libel suits against the magazine. The name itself is an old abusive appellation, recorded in the Domesday Book (1086) as *gildyn ballokes*. In the modern adoption it was naturally suggested by the surname. *See also* REFERENDUM PARTY.

Golden Bear. An annual award for the best feature film made by the Berlin Film Festival since 1956, when it went to Gene Kelly's *Invitation to the Dance* (1956). According to legend, Berlin takes its name from the medieval margrave Albert the Bear (Old High German *bero*, modern German *Bär*), and a black bear appears on the city arms. Hence the name of the award.

Golden boy or **girl.** A popular or successful person, especially in sport or business. In the former, it is usually implicitly connected with one who wins gold medals, especially when handsome or attractive. Thus the good-looking US boxer Oscar De La Hoya was dubbed the 'Golden Boy of Boxing' after winning the gold medal in the 1992 Olympics. In Clifford Odets's play *Golden Boy* (1937) the hero, a violinist, is also a successful boxer. *The Golden Girls* (1985–92) was an US television SITCOM featuring three middle-aged women and one clearly older. The title was deliberate, as one can still be a 'golden girl' when no longer really young in years. *See also* GOLDEN OLDIE.

> [Michelle] Smith, the golden girl of Ireland, the swimmer who improved … enough to win three gold medals at the last Olympic Games, has paid the inevitable price.
> *The Times* (9 June 1999)

Golden Cockerel Press. A publishing business founded in 1920 by Harold Taylor (d.1924) to produce works of a high typographic quality. Its first book was A.E. Coppard's collection of short stories, *Adam and Eve and Pinch Me* (1921), and its most famous work was *The Four Gospels* (1931), with wood engravings by Eric Gill, a magnificent quarto volume bound in white pigskin. The much later Golden Cockerel Press, founded in 1980, is quite distinct, as a distributor of titles for the US firm of Associated University Presses. The golden cockerel symbolizes a new dawn or sunrise.

Golden Delicious. The greenish-yellow (rather than obviously golden) apple of this name should not be confused with the 'Delicious'. The Golden Delicious is a US apple that appeared as a chance seedling on a West Virginia farm at the turn of the 20th century. It is now the most widely grown variety in many countries. The 'Delicious', a red apple, began as a chance seedling on the farm of Jess Hiatt of Peru, Iowa, in 1872. He marketed it as 'Hiatt's Hawkeye', but a fruit-growing company, Star Brothers, bought Hiatt out and renamed the variety 'Delicious'. It has been the leading US apple since the 1940s and is now widely grown elsewhere. The similarity between the names arose because the same nursery firm bought the rights to both varieties.

Golden farewell. *See* GOLDEN GOODBYE.

Golden Gate Bridge. Until the completion of the Verrazano-Narrows Bridge in New York in 1964, the Golden Gate Bridge, completed in 1937 across the Golden Gate, California, was the longest suspension bridge in the world. Its construction involved many difficulties, including frequent storms and fogs, but it remains an inspiring sight in its magnificent setting.

Golden girl. *See* GOLDEN BOY.

Golden Globe. An annual film award made since 1944 by the Hollywood Foreign Press Association, an organization of journalists and photographers founded in 1943 to cover HOLLYWOOD film and television for foreign publications. It first went to Henry King's *The Song of Bernadette* (1943).

Golden Gloves. The amateur boxing competition of this name was initiated by Arch Ward, sports editor of the *Chicago Tribune*, and first sponsored by that paper in 1926. Annual tournaments between Chicago and New York were held from 1927, the New York organizer being Paul Gallico of the *New York Daily News*. The idea was subsequently taken up by other cities. Many Golden Gloves champions went on to become professional world champions, among them Joe Louis (1914–81), Sugar Ray Robinson (1920–89), Floyd Patterson (b.1935) and Sugar Ray Leonard (b.1956). Cassius Clay, later Muhammad Ali (b.1942), won six Golden Gloves titles, the first at the age of 14.

Golden goal. In football, the first goal scored in extra time following a draw. This wins the game under a 'sudden death' system, as distinct from a penalty shoot-out. The modification to the rules was introduced in the first half of the 1990s and has now been extended to hockey. The German striker Oliver Bierhoff was the first player to score a golden goal in the final of a major international tournament in the 94th minute of the 1996 European Championship final against the Czech Republic at Wembley.

> France became the first team in World Cup history to win a game under the new golden goal rule when they beat Paraguay 1–0 yesterday.
> *The Times* (29 June 1998)

Golden goodbye or **farewell.** A compensation payment similar to a GOLDEN HANDSHAKE made to a company executive on transferring to non-executive status or to any employee leaving employment under certain conditions. *See also* GOLDEN HELLO.

> Police officers who lose interest in their jobs in mid-career will be offered a golden farewell under reforms to the pension scheme to be announced by Jack Straw, the Home Secretary.
> *The Times* (23 August 1999)

Golden handcuffs. Payments to an employee that are deliberately deferred over a number of years in an attempt to make them stay with a particular company. *See also* GOLDEN HANDSHAKE.

> Jeremy Paxman was named yesterday as the new presenter of Radio 4's *Start the Week* after signing a 'golden handcuffs' deal that will keep him at the BBC until 2002.
> *The Times* (28 July 1998)

Golden handshake. A phrase that is applied to the often considerable terminal payments made to individuals, especially business executives, whose services are prematurely dispensed with. It was coined by Frederick Ellis (d.1979), City Editor of the *Daily Express*. *See also* GOLDEN GOODBYE.

> The average 'golden handshake' to departing directors has risen for the first time since 1994, from

£328,000 for the year to October 1997 to £463,000 over the past 12 months.
> *The Times* (2 October 1998)

Golden hello. A special payment made by a company or other body to a sought-after recruit when they sign a contract of employment. *See also* GOLDEN GOODBYE; GOLDEN HANDSHAKE.

> The Government's 'golden hello' scheme to attract graduates into teaching has failed to halt the recruitment crisis, a head teachers' leader said yesterday.
> *The Times* (26 April 1999)

Golden hour. In medical jargon the hour following a person's serious head injury, as in boxing, during which prompt treatment may limit brain damage or prevent death.

Golden Lion. An annual award made since 1980 by the Venice Film Festival for the best feature film. The first award went jointly to John Cassavetes' *Gloria* (1980) and Louis Malle's *Atlantic City* (1980). The award's full title is the Golden Lion of St Mark, after the winged lion that appears on the coat of arms of the city, whose patron is St Mark.

Golden Mile. The popular name for a promenade or street for strolling in some cities, especially one with places of evening entertainment such as cinemas, theatres, pubs and clubs. One of the most familiar is the seafront promenade at BLACKPOOL, and in particular the section between the Tower and the South Pier. Another Golden Mile is in Belfast, leading down from the Opera House on Great Victoria Street to Queen's University, the Botanic Gardens and the Ulster Museum. The area buzzes with activity most evenings, especially in term time, and its attractions include the Crown Liquor Saloon, a famous Victorian gin palace. 'Golden' refers both to the glamour and glitter of such streets and to the amount of money that changes hands.

Golden oldie. Something that is an old favourite, such as a nostalgic song or piece of music. Also a person who is no longer young but still successful in a particular field.

> We are not here to discuss the golden oldies, more numerous than one realizes, that [David] Bowie sometimes omits completely from his concerts.
> *Sunday Times Magazine* (19 September 1999)

Golden Palm (French *Palme d'or*). An annual award for the best film of the year made at the Cannes Film festival since 1955, when the winner was Delbert Mann's *Marty* (1955).

Golden parachute. A clause in a senior executive's contract that grants him special benefits if he loses his post as the result of a take-over. There is a pun on 'bale out' and 'bail out' here. *See also* GOLDEN GOODBYE; GOLDEN HANDSHAKE.

Golden Raspberry. One of a number of semi-serious annual awards made for the worst film, actor or actress of the year or some similar category as a counter to the OSCAR awards. Colloquially known as the 'Razzies', the nominations in February 2000 included not only the worst film, actor and actress of the decade but also the worst actor and actress of the century. The latter included Sylvester Stallone (b.1946) and Kevin Costner (b.1955). *See also* BLOW A RASPBERRY.

Golden Ring of Russia (Russian *Zolotoye kol'tso Rossii*). A famous tourist route northeast of Moscow. It was laid out in the 1970s and takes a looping clockwise course through the medieval cities of Sergiyev Posad (formerly Zagorsk), Pereslavl-Zalessky, Rostov, Yaroslavl, Kostroma, Suzdal and Vladimir. The name reflects the unique historical and architectural interest of the towns and also mirrors the dazzling golden cupolas of the many churches and monasteries seen along the route.

Golden share. A share in a company that controls at least 51 per cent of the voting rights. Such shares are usually those held by the government on the occasion of a privatization. The figure of 51 per cent is a token one, indicating just over half of the total. In the closing years of the 20th century the Labour government held a golden share in 10 companies.

> When [transport minister] John Prescott announced his plans to sell off more than half of Britain's air traffic control network, much stress was laid on the golden share that the Government would stash away in the national safe.
>
> *The Times* (29 July 1999)

Golden Shot, The. An early television GAME SHOW screened from 1967 to 1975. Contestants were required to guide a blindfolded cameraman on a 'telebow' and instruct him with commands such as 'left a bit', 'up a bit' to fire at targets in return for prizes. The ultimate prize was won by piercing a thread hung before an apple, whereupon a hoard of coins spilled over the studio floor. The idea was adopted from the German game *Der Goldene Schuss* and the series was hosted for most of its run by an unctuous Bob Monkhouse. 'Golden girl' hostesses also participated.

Golden Triangle. An approximately triangular area of southeast Asia, consisting of parts of Myanmar (Burma), Laos and Thailand, where most of the world's raw opium is grown. The name is also found elsewhere for any geographical area characterized by high productivity or social superiority, such as the industrial area that extends from the Midlands of England to the Gulf of Genoa or the wealthy residential region that centres on Wilmslow in Cheshire.

> Cheshire's so-called Golden Triangle owes its existence not to mindless materialists but to its better weather and the beautiful countryside unblemished by the industrial revolution.
>
> *Sunday Times* (Letter to the Editor) (31 October 1999)

Goldfinger. A thriller (1959) by Ian Fleming (1908–64), featuring his secret service agent James BOND. His adversary has gained the sobriquet Goldfinger, not just because he has a passion for the metal but because he has a habit of painting his girlfriends all over with it. The plot includes a classic golf match. A lively film version (1964), directed by Guy Hamilton, had Sean Connery as Bond and Honor Blackman as the sexy Pussy Galore.

Goldfish bowl. A place or situation in which one has no privacy and in which one can thus be publicly viewed and watched, like goldfish in a bowl. This sense of the term evolved in the 1930s and originally applied specifically to a police interrogation room, where the prisoner is isolated among his interrogators and where a one-way mirror is also often in operation.

> Theatrical props are exactly what a star's clothes must be. They are the wardrobe of the dream and no star should step into the goldfish bowl unless they are perfect.
>
> *Sunday Times* (2 January 2000)

Goldilocks. *See* TARZAN.

Goldwynisms. The US film producer Samuel Goldwyn (1882–1974) is credited with uttering a number of unwitting witticisms, often in the form of an absurdly mixed metaphor or a colourful contradiction. Some are undoubtedly apocryphal, but the following is a selection of the better known, quoted in Richard Lederer's *Anguished English* (1989).

Include me out.

A verbal contract isn't worth the paper it's written on.

In two words: im-possible.

Every director bites the hand that lays the golden egg.

Anyone who goes to a psychiatrist should have his head examined.

I had a monumental idea last night but I didn't like it.

Tell me, how did you love my picture?

We have all passed a lot of water since then.

I'll give you a definite maybe.

We're overpaying him, but he's worth it.

I never liked you, and I always will.

Don't talk to me when I'm interrupting.

I may not always be right, but I'm never wrong.

The scene is dull. Tell him to put more life into his dying.

This book has too much plot and not enough story.

It's more than magnificent – it's mediocre.

A bachelor's life is no life for a single man.

Go see it and see for yourself why you shouldn't see it.

It's spreading like wildflowers!

If I could drop dead right now, I'd be the happiest man alive!

You've got to take the bull by the teeth.

This makes me so sore it gets my dandruff up.

When I want your opinion, I'll give it to you.

Colour television! Bah, I won't believe it until I see it in black and white.

I read part of it all the way through.

William? What kind of a name is that? Every Tom, Dick and Harry is called William.

Golfball. A nickname for the type-ball or spherical printing element formerly found in some electric typewriters. It was the invention of IBM, which introduced it in the 'Selectric' model of 1961. The innovation was a technological breakthrough in that the machine itself had no type-bars and no movable carriage. The type-ball bore 88 alphabetic characters, numerals and punctuation symbols and was mounted on a small carrier which ran along a cylindrical metal bar while in use. Because the type-ball moved, not the paper-carrying unit, the need for the familiar carriage was eliminated. The 'Selectric' thus required less

space, minimized vibration and abolished altogether the noisy and disruptive carriage return jolt.

Golightly, Holly. The fascinating young heroine of Truman Capote's novella BREAKFAST AT TIFFANY'S (1958). She has a calling card which states, 'Miss Holiday Golightly. Travelling', and it turns out that she is a farmer's child bride on the run. Her name marks her role as a carefree roving girl. She was memorably portrayed by Audrey Hepburn in the film version of the book.

Gollancz. The British publishing house of this name was founded in 1927 by Victor Gollancz (1893–1967) with the stated aim of steering between 'the Scylla of preciousness and dilettantism and the Charybdis of purely commercialized mass production'. Its initial list consisted of histories, biographies and fiction, and it soon established itself on a sound commercial footing, its editions drawing the eye with their distinctive bright yellow dust jackets. It attracted authors such as Daphne du Maurier, A.J. Cronin, Dorothy Sayers and George ORWELL and began to specialize in socialist and pacifist books, a development that led to the formation of the LEFT BOOK CLUB. From the mid-1940s many of its authors were Americans such as John Updike, Vladimir Nabokov, James Agee and John Cheever, and in the 1960s it became noted for its SCIENCE FICTION titles.

Golliwog. The black-faced doll with a shock of black hair began life as a character in a children's picture book by Bertha and Florence Upton, *The Adventures of Two Dutch Dolls – and a 'Golliwogg'* (1895), with Florence illustrating the verse text written by her mother, Bertha. The character became immensely popular, and a 'golliwogg' (*sic*) craze soon developed. Debussy even included a 'Golliwogg's Cake-Walk' in his CHILDREN'S CORNER suite (1905–6). The doll also caught on as a rather incongruous commercial symbol for Robertson's jam. However, 100 years after his creation, the golliwog became a serious victim of POLITICAL CORRECTNESS, and his centenary was only mutely marked, if at all. The origin of the name is uncertain. It may be a blend of 'golly' (what a sight!) and 'polliwog', a US term for a tadpole. It is perhaps itself the source of the also subsequently outlawed slang word WOG.

Golliwogg's Cakewalk. *See* CHILDREN'S CORNER.

Gollum. A creature in J.R.R. Tolkien's novels *The* HOBBIT (1937) and *The* LORD OF THE RINGS (1954–5). First encountered by Bilbo BAGGINS under the Misty Mountains, he is so named by Bilbo because of the curious glottal noises he makes in his throat. It is revealed in *The Lord of the Rings* that Gollum was formerly a hobbit-like being, originally named Sméagol, who had fled hearth and home after murdering his friend Déagol to gain possession of what turns out to be the One Ring. Gollum succumbs to the power of the ring (which he refers to as 'the Precious'), losing his original appearance and becoming a repellent, slimy, crawling thing.

Golly gosh. A form of overblown juvenile exclamation, combining two mild euphemisms for 'God', often used by adults in a facetious or ironic sense.

> The government's Women's Unit has concluded that they [women] find it difficult to strike a balance between home and work. Well, golly gosh; who would have thought it?
>
> *Sunday Times* (10 October 1999)

Gondor. A kingdom of MIDDLE-EARTH in J.R.R. Tolkien's *The LORD OF THE RINGS* (1954–5). Gondor contains the greatest cities of Middle-Earth and stands in contrast to MORDOR, the Land of Shadow. There are Arthurian echoes in Tolkien's depiction of Gondor as a quasi-medieval realm of chivalrous knights. Its capital, Minas Tirith (the Tower of Guard) was formerly known as MINAS ANOR (the Tower of the Sun) and was the twin city of Minas Ithil (the Tower of the Moon), later renamed MINAS MORGUL. At the time of the events recounted in *The Lord of the Rings* Gondor has fallen into decline, but its fortunes revive spectacularly with the victory of the army of the West over the forces of SAURON described towards the end of the trilogy.

Gone to the big or **great ... in the sky.** A light-hearted formula to state that someone has died and 'gone to heaven'. The missing word depends on the person's occupation or interest, thus an actor might go 'to the big theatre in the sky', a seasoned drinker to 'the big pub in the sky' and a horticulturist to 'the great garden in the sky'.

> To Reid Miles, Barney Bubbles, Neon Park and Mike Doud – gone to the great studio in the sky.
>
> STORM THORGERSON and AUBREY POWELL: *100 Best Album Covers*, Dedication (1999)

Gone With the Wind. A highly acclaimed film (1939) based on a romantic historical novel (1936) of the same title by Margaret Mitchell (1900–49). The film, which depicts the experiences of thrice-married Southern belle, Scarlett O'Hara, during the US Civil War, starred Vivien Leigh as Scarlett O'Hara and Clark Gable as her lover, Rhett Butler, and has long been the stuff of Hollywood legend. The title comes from a line in Ernest Dowson's poem 'Non sum qualis eram' (1896):

> I have forgot much, Cynara! Gone with the wind,
> Flung roses, roses riotously with the throng,
> Dancing, to put thy pale, lost lilies out of mind.

This was itself based on the refrain in one of Horace's *Odes* (IV.i), with the lines *Non sum qualis eram bona / Sub regno Cynarae* ('I am not as I was when good Cynara was my queen'). To Dowson, Cynara represented a 12-year-old Polish girl, Adelaide Foltinowicz ('Missie'), with whom he fell in love after seeing her serving in her parents' restaurant in Sherwood Street, London. While still working on the novel, Mitchell used the working title 'Pansy', the original name of her heroine. Other titles she considered included 'Tote the Weary Land', 'Tomorrow Is Another Day' and even 'Ba! Ba! Black Sheep'.

> There was a land of Cavaliers and Cotton Fields called the Old South. Here in this patrician world the Age of Chivalry took its last bows. Here was the last ever seen of the Knights and their Ladies fair, of Master and Slave. Look for it only in books, for it is no more than a dream remembered, a Civilization gone with the wind.
>
> *Gone with the Wind* (Prologue) (1939)

Gonzo journalism. Journalistic writing of an exaggerated, subjective and fictionalized style, as a feature of the US press from the 1970s. The word perhaps derives from Italian *gonzo*, 'foolish' or Spanish *ganso*, 'fool', literally 'goose'.

Goodbye, Mr Chips. A novella (1934) by James Hilton (1900–54) about a gruff master of the old tradition at a minor English public school, Mr Chipping. His response, on his deathbed, to hearing a colleague say that it was a pity that he had had no children, is, 'Yes – umph – I have ... Thousands of 'em ... all boys.' Equally celebrated is the parting remark, after one of Chipping's intimate tea-parties, by a small new boy, who has only heard him referred to by his nickname: 'Goodbye, Mr Chips.' A classic film version (1939), in MGM's best sentimentally romantic style and with Robert Donat as the schoolmaster, was directed by Sam Wood. A less appealing musical version (1969), with Peter O'Toole in the title role, was directed by Herbert Ross. *See also* CHIPS, MR.

Goodbye to Berlin. A novel (1939) by Christopher Isherwood (1904–86), who as himself is the observer and narrator: 'I am a camera with its shutter open, quite passive, recording, not thinking.' The book begins and ends with extracts from 'A Berlin Diary' respectively for Autumn 1930 and Winter 1932–3, the period that he was teaching English in Berlin. The four linked sketches in between reflect the situations of various characters and their reactions to the brittle political situation. Elements concerning the promiscuous cabaret performer, Sally BOWLES, were made into a play, *I Am a Camera* by John van Druten (1901–57), from which were derived a musical, CABARET (1966), and a film of the same title (1972).

Good Friday Agreement. An agreement between the British and Irish governments regarding the future of Northern Ireland, reached on Good Friday, 10 April 1998. At the core of the agreement was the principle of consent that Northern Ireland is part of the United Kingdom and would remain so for as long as the people who live there wish it. Conversely, it was agreed that if the people of Northern Ireland were formally to consent to the establishment of a united Ireland, the government of the day would bring forward proposals to implement this. The agreement thus resulted in a formal resolution of the historic differences between Britain and Ireland, a development in principle welcomed by SINN FÉIN. *See also* DIRECT RULE.

Good girl, bad boy. Two converse expressions whose alliterative appeal has contributed to the sexual stereotyping of the children (or animals) in question.

Good Guides. An alliterative basis for many titles of informative books and radio programmes, the two words sandwiching the subject in question. First and foremost in the field was *The Good Food Guide* (1951), edited by Raymond Postgate. Others to follow, as listed in *British Books in Print* (1982), have included *Good Beer Guide, Good Birth Guide, Good Boat Guide, Good Caff Guide, Good Camera Guide, Good Camps Guide, Good Con Guide, Good Cook's Guide, Good God Guide, Good Health Guide, Good Hotel Guide, Good Job Guide, Good Life Guide, Good Move Guide, Good Museums Guide, Good Pets Guide, Good Plants Guide* and *Good Toy Guide*. A four-part radio series broadcast in 1988 using words and music to celebrate parliament, the law, the church and royalty was entitled *The Good Establishment Guide*. The format is more subtle than it seems, since 'Good' relates not only to the guide, as being supposedly superior to others on the subject, but to the subject itself, singled out for selective appraisal as the best of its kind.

Goodies. A term for any tasty titbits. 'Goody' or 'Goody goody' is still used as a sign of approval and a once popular childish expression of satisfaction was 'Goody goody gum drops'. A goody-goody is a smug or unduly virtuous person, however. In a story or film, the 'Goody' is the hero or heroine, as contrasted with the 'Baddy'. There may well be several 'Goodies' lined up against the 'Baddies'. *The Goodies* was the collective name adopted by three comics in the television series so titled, running from 1970 to 1982. They were Graeme Garden, Tim Brooke-Taylor and Bill Oddie. 'Goodies' actually represented letters from the beginning, middle and end of their surnames: Garden, Brooke-Taylor and Od*die*

> Mr Benn never ceases to amaze. He is like those Christmas crackers packed with mystery surprises. You pull the taper, there is a flash, a bang, and out pops a selection of weird goodies.
> *The Times* (1 November 1994)

Good Life, The. A television SITCOM running from 1975 to 1978. It depicted a middle-class suburban couple, Tom and Barbara Good, and their efforts to go 'back to the land', growing their own food, keeping animals and making their own tools and equipment. Inevitably, the enterprise creates friction with their next-door neighbours, Jerry and Margo Leadbetter. The series owed much to its topicality, its clever scripts and its first-rate acting and casting, with Richard Briers and Felicity Kendal as the Goods and Paul Eddington and Penelope Keith as the Leadbetters.

Goodman Memorial Theatre. The oldest regional theatre in the United States, in Chicago, Illinois. It opened on 22 October 1925, when it was donated to the Arts Institute of Chicago by the parents of the playwright Kenneth S. Goodman (1883–1918), author of *Dust of the Road* (1913) and *The Wonder Hat* (1913), the latter one of eight plays written in collaboration with Ben Hecht. The theatre was meant to combine a school of acting with a resident professional company, but the GREAT DEPRESSION forced the company to disband in the 1930s. In the 1960s the Goodman once again housed a fully professional company and in 1977 was incorporated as the Chicago Theatre Group.

Good Neighbour Policy. A popular name for the Latin-American policy of President Franklin D. Roosevelt (*see* FDR). It was suggested by his commitment 'to the policy of the good neighbour', as outlined in his first inaugural address of 4 March 1933, and resulted in a renunciation by the United States of its right to intervene in the internal affairs of Latin American states. The success of the policy was measured by the rapidity with which most Latin-American countries rallied to the Allies in the Second World War.

Good news and the bad news. The mixed consequences of an action; an outcome that has both a good and a bad side. The implication is generally that the news is good but that it is tempered by an unexpected disadvantage. The dual consequence is typically implied in the question: 'Do you want the good news or the bad news?' The formula dates from the 1970s.

> The good news is that British Telecom has just conducted the world's first live GPRS data call, and announced that it will be introducing the service next year. The bad news is that things rarely happen when they're supposed to.
> *Sunday Times* (5 December 1999)

Good News Bible. An illustrated version of the Bible, produced by the American Bible Society and designed to be easily understood, including by those whose first language is not English. The New Testament was published in 1966 and the complete Bible in 1976. It follows the traditional numbering of chapter and verse. The modernized text was not to everyone's taste and was criticized by some for the quality of its translation.

> The accuracy of the latest and much-heralded translation of Holy Scripture, the Good News Bible, the millionth copy of which has just been presented to the Queen, has been challenged by Dr Eric Kemp, Bishop of Chichester. He says he finds it incredulous [*sic*] that those famous words of St Paul about 'flesh' and 'lower nature' have, in his episcopal view, been altogether mistranslated.
> *Manchester Guardian Weekly* (6 February 1977)

Goodnight Sweetheart. A television SITCOM serial created by Laurence Marks and Maurice Gran and first shown on BBC1 in 1993. It is essentially a love story and centres on the double life of Gary Sparrow, a television repairman who discovers he can escape from his dull marriage to Yvonne by being magically transported back to the London of the BLITZ and having an affair with Phoebe, a landlord's daughter. The three main characters are respectively played by Nicholas Lyndhurst, Michelle Holmes (later Emma

Amos) and Dervla Kirwan (later Elizabeth Carling). *See also* SHINE ON HARVEY MOON.

Good ole boy. A typical American Southerner, easygoing, unpretentious and friendly. 'Ole' is 'old', as GRAND OLE OPRY.

> This is the world of the Good Ole Boy, the country hick from down in the hollow, his innocent, God-fearing eyes scanning the world of corruption laid out before him at every crossroad grocery store, supermarket, and shopping center.
> *Harper's* (September 1976)

Good on you. An Australian equivalent of 'good for you', dating from the early 20th century.

Good Person of Setzuan, The. A play, originally entitled *Der gute Mensch von Sezuan* and sometimes rendered as *The Good Woman of Setzuan* (1938–41), by the German playwright Bertolt Brecht (1898–1956), first performed in 1943. Three gods travel the globe in search of a good person, and they eventually find Shen Te, a prostitute of Setzuan, who uses the money she wins to set up a cigar factory (which she runs in the guise of a man, employing various underhand means). The idea of three gods descending on a town and finding it wanting is an ancient literary device, but in Brecht's mind it became linked with a visit he and two friends made to Dresden, where they got a cool welcome. He took his revenge by savaging the city in a poem. *See also* EPIC THEATRE.

Good question. One that requires careful consideration before answering. A common evasive response to a question which one cannot answer is, 'That's a good question.'

Goodtime George. A nickname for George Melly (b.1926), jazz singer, critic, connoisseur of excess and devotee of SURREALISM. The name derives from John Chilton's song 'Goodtime George', a Melly favourite.

Good-time girl. A young woman who seeks pleasure and 'plenty of action' to go with it, often at the expense of a more mundane commitment such as working, studying or domestic duties. The term, of US origin and dating from the 1920s, can also euphemistically imply sexual promiscuity.

Good time was had by all, A. Everybody enjoyed themselves. A supposed traditional conclusion of a descriptive account of a social event in a parish magazine. The words were adopted as the title of a collection of poems by Stevie Smith published in 1937.

Good Vibrations. A song by the Beach Boys, one of the classic songs of the 1960s. Written by Brian Wilson (over a period of six months) and released in 1966, it marries the HIPPIE notion of 'vibes' (meaning variously atmosphere, feeling or intuition, as in 'I'm getting bad vibes off her') with the time-honoured pop music theme of boy-meets-girl. Glen Campbell, later famous as a star of country music, who worked as a session guitarist on the single, is reported to have remarked to the Beach Boys' Brian Wilson: 'What were you smokin' when you wrote that?' *See also* ROCK GROUP NAMES.

Goody bag. A little bag containing GOODIES or other small presents, given to children to take home after a party or to adults at the end (or start) of a social event, conference, business presentation or the like. In the latter case the bag may be big rather than little, and the presents large rather than small. The aim is to express goodwill or hospitality. The concept is of US origin.

> Guests, including 50 MPs and four ministers, were handed a sombrero and goody bag with bottles of tequila as they arrived at a marquee festooned with cactus plants and helium balloons.
> *The Times* (30 September 1999)

Go off the deep end, To. To succumb to anger; to vent one's emotions violently. The allusion is to a swimmer diving or jumping in where the water is deepest, not simply paddling in the shallows. The expression dates from the 1920s.

Googly. A cricketing term dating from the early 20th century for an off-break bowled with an apparent leg-break action. The delivery was particularly associated with the Middlesex bowler B.J.T. Bosanquet (1877–1936) but the origin of the word is uncertain. It may have been so called because it made the facing batsman goggle. Australians know it as a BOSIE. *See also* CHINAMAN.

Googol. This word for the number 1 followed by 100 zeroes (10^{100}) is explained in *Mathematics and the Imagination* (1940), by the US mathematician Edward Kasner and his student James Newman, as having been invented by Kasner's nine-year-old nephew, who was asked to think up a name for a very big number. The boy may have subconsciously based the word on the name of the comic strip *Barney Google* (*see* HEEBIE-JEEBIES). The name is not in formal use.

Goo-goo eyes. Amorous glances. The expression probably relates to 'goggle' although 'goo-goo' is associ-

ated with babies and SWEET NOTHINGS on the lines of COOCHY COOCHY COO. The phrase came into vogue at the turn of the 20th century, and Carl Smith and Fanny Wentworth's *The Goo-Goo Song* (1900) popularized the general idea.

Gook. US slang (now regarded as highly offensive) for any East Asian person. It was used extensively by the US military during the VIETNAM War to refer to the Vietnamese (of whatever political persuasion). However, its use among the US military dates back to the 1920s, when it was used to refer to Filipinos, and subsequently was also applied to Japanese and Koreans. A number of not entirely plausible etymologies have been proffered. One relates it to the Filipino word *gugu*, meaning 'spirit'. Another suggestion is that it mimics the sound of an incomprehensible language, just as the ancient Greek *barbaros* ('uncivilized', 'barbarian') mimicked the 'ba-ba' sound attributed to foreign speech.

Goons, The. A team of four comics who won a wide following for their absurd sense of humour in the weekly radio series *The Goon Show* (1951–60). The crazy quartet comprised Spike Milligan (b.1918), Peter Sellers (1925–80), Harry Secombe (b.1921) and Michael Bentine (1921–96). The name Goon betrayed the wartime influence on Milligan and Secombe, who had first met in the North African desert. It was a word often used by prisoners of war for their German guards, as which it may have been a blend of 'gorilla' and 'baboon'. Milligan claimed, however, that he took the name from the creature called Alice the Goon in the POPEYE comic strip by the US cartoonist Elzie C. Segar. The former origin may have prompted one of the programme's catchphrases: 'Neddie Seagoon' (Secombe) would offer a cigarette with the words 'Have a gorilla', to which the reply was, 'No thanks, I only smoke baboons.'

Go overboard, To. To be very enthusiastic; to overreact. The evocation is of a vigour or action so extreme that one throws oneself over the side of a ship. The expression dates from the 1930s.

Go over the wall, To. To escape from prison; to leave a religious order; to defect to another country. In all three instances an actual wall may have to be traversed in order to make one's way out. In *I Leap Over the Wall* (1950) Monica Baldwin, a niece of the prime minister Stanley Baldwin, describes her return to the outside world after having spent 28 years in a monastery. She based the title on the Baldwin family motto, *Per Deum meum transilio murum*, 'By the help of my God I leap over a wall', itself from the biblical words, 'By my God have I leaped over a wall' (2 Samuel 22:30; Psalm 18:29). Miss Baldwin recounts in the book how some 400 years earlier her ancestor, Thomas Baldwin of Diddlesbury, had leapt to freedom from behind the walls of the Tower of London, where his name with an inscription 'July 1585' can still be seen where he carved it on the wall of his cell in the Beauchamp Tower.

Go over to Rome, To. To join the Roman Catholic Church, especially of an Anglican.

> Sources close to the late Tory MP [Alan Clark] ... are insisting that he definitely would have gone over to Rome before he died, were it not for the deterioration in his health.
> *The Times* (14 October 1999)

Go pear-shaped, To. To go wrong. The term became current in the 1980s but was earlier found in RAF slang with humorous reference to the shape of an aircraft that has crashed nose-first. A pear-shaped person is noticeably BROAD IN THE BEAM.

> Things do go pear-shaped sometimes. Video conferencing can be tricky to patch in. Food doesn't arrive. You've got to be on hand all the time.
> *The Times* (11 October 1999)

Go places, To. To succeed; to do well. The concept is of gaining seniority by moving to different posts. The phrase is of US origin and dates from the 1920s.

Go public, To. To seek a quotation on the stock market. This specific sense, as applied to a privately owned company, came to give a general meaning to reveal oneself, to come out into the open.

Gorblimey. A rakish hat, as supposedly worn by a Cockney or anyone prone to exclaiming 'gorblimey', as a slurring of 'God blind me'. ('Blimey' is a short form of this.) The hat so named evolved in the early years of the 20th century as a type of unconventional military headgear in the form of a floppy field-service cap. Gorblimey trousers were in similar style, and both terms were directly inspired by a ribald Liverpool folk ditty, 'My Old Man's a Fireman on the Elder-Dempster Line', which had the couplet, 'He wears Gorblimey trousers/An a little gorblimey 'at'. This same song was adapted by Lonnie Donegan for his No. 1 hit, 'My Old Man's a Dustman' (1960), which again popularized the garments.

Gorby. The nickname of the Soviet communist politician Mikhail Gorbachev (b.1931), general secretary of the Communist Party (1985–91) and president of the Soviet Union (1989–91). The liberalizing reforms he unveiled under the slogans GLASNOST and PERESTROIKA made him popular in the West, and led to a surge of 'Gorbymania'.

Gordon, Flash. *See* FLASH GORDON.

Gordonstoun. The Scottish public school near Lossiemouth, renowned for its emphasis on physical self-reliance, was founded in 1934 by the German educationist Kurt Hahn after he was forced to flee from NAZI Germany. His aim was to counteract what he saw as the 'four social declines' of physical fitness, initiative, care and compassion. To combat the problems of puberty, he instigated a rigorous routine of morning runs and cold showers. He later devised the Duke of Edinburgh Award scheme. The school won royal approval, and no fewer than three royal princes, Charles, Andrew and Edward, were educated here, the first of these letting it be known subsequently that his time there had not been a happy one. The school has now toned down its ruggedness and rigidity, but much of Hahn's legacy survives. Gordonstoun became coeducational in 1972.

Gorgeous Gussie. The nickname of the US tennis star Gussie Moran (b.1923), whose lace-trimmed panties caused a sensation on the courts of Wimbledon in 1949. They were designed for her by the Wimbledon fashion expert Teddy Tinling. The name has appropriate overtones of GUSSIED UP.

Gorky Park. A crime novel (1981) by Martin Cruz Smith (b.1942) in which a Soviet policeman sets out to solve the mystery of a murder in Moscow's Gorky Park, named after Maxim Gorky (1868–1936), Russian novelist, dramatist and communist social and political agitator. A film version (1983), directed by Michael Apted and shot in Helsinki, failed to capture the authentic detail of Moscow life in the original.

Gormenghast. The second novel (1950) in a trilogy of grotesque fantasies by Mervyn Peake (1911–68). The first, *Titus Groan* (1946), was begun in 1941–42 'to escape the tediousness and pettiness of army life', just before he was invalided out because of a nervous breakdown. It was completed, and the other two written, after he had, as an official artist, visited the concentration camp at Bergen-BELSEN shortly after its liberation and also sketched, in their cells, Nazi prisoners accused of war crimes. His son has suggested, however, that 'all his writings, all his ghoulish illustrations, were because of something that was in his nature anyway'. A controversial televised version was screened in 2000. *See also* FIRST LINES OF NOVELS.

Gormenghast Castle. The hereditary seat of the Lords of Groan in Mervyn Peake's Gothic fantasy trilogy (*see* GORMENGHAST). Its aspect is fearful, and the landscape between Gormenghast Mountain and the castle is bleak and desolate. Its inhabitants are simply part of it and have no idea of the world that exists outside. It is also so vast that members of the household may not see each other for weeks on end.

Gort Na Cloca Mora. The home of the leprechauns in James Stephens's best known novel *The Crock of Gold* (1912). It lies on the edge of a wood, where a rough field is scattered with grey rocks. Hence its name, which in Irish means 'Field of the Great Stones'.

Gory details. An explicit account of some unpleasant episode, such as a business deal or a divorce. A humorous allusion to the 'bloody' content.

Gotcha! Got you! Caught you! A notorious frontpage headline in the *Sun* newspaper on 4 May 1982, referring to the sinking of the Argentinian cruiser GENERAL BELGRANO in the FALKLANDS WAR. The word itself, dating from the 1930s, was earlier familiar in the form 'gotcher'.

Go Tell It on the Mountain. The first novel, published in 1953, with autobiographical undertones, by the black US writer, James Baldwin (1924–87), the climax of which is the religious conversion of a 14-year-old Harlem boy. At the centre of the book are the boy's troubled relations with his stepfather, a preacher of the store-front Temple of the Fire Baptized. Aspects of the slave era and of life in a dysfunctional family are recounted in flashbacks. Various biblical passages are reflected in the title, the closest perhaps being the following: 'O Zion, that bringest good tidings, get thee up into the high mountain; ... say unto the cities of Judah, Behold your God!' (Isaiah 40:9).

Gotha raids. The air raids on Britain by German Gotha G-IV and G-V bombers in the First World War. The Gothas were twin-engined biplanes, with a pencil-shaped fuselage suspended from the upper wing and 'pusher' engines attached to the rear of the lower wing. They had a three-man crew, a range of 480km (290 miles) and could carry 500kg (1100 lb) of bombs on external racks. They were manufactured by the Gothaer Waggonfabrik and named after the

town of Gotha in central Germany. The Gotha raids began on 13 June 1917, taking over from the earlier ZEPPELIN raids. The Gothas caused little damage, but caused a public uproar in Britain. Fighters were withdrawn from the WESTERN FRONT to meet the threat, but in fact it was the number of losses due to accidents and anti-aircraft fire that led the Germans to abandon the raids in May 1918.

During the First World War the British royal family changed their surname from Saxe-Coburg-Gotha to WINDSOR.

Go the distance, To. To carry through an action to completion. The expression originated in boxing, in which a boxer who 'goes the distance' lasts for all the scheduled rounds. In baseball the same phrase means to pitch for the entire length of the game. The distance is thus of time, not space.

Go the extra mile, To. To make a special and often prolonged effort to achieve one's aim, especially on behalf of another. The idea is that one is prepared to do more than just GO THE DISTANCE. The expression dates from the 1950s but has a biblical resonance: 'And whosoever shall compel thee to go a mile, go with him twain' (Matthew 5:41).

> For Bill Hitzig, lifelong friend, who has gone more extra miles for more people than even the poets dreamed possible.
> NORMAN COUSINS: *Human Options*, Dedication (1981)

Go the whole nine yards, To. To do everything; to GO THE DISTANCE. The US term dates from the 1960s and probably uses nine as a 'mystic' number rather than referring to some specific nine-yard measurement. 'The whole nine yards' is also used independently to denote 'the lot', as: 'This part of the world has been hit by fires, floods, famine, the whole nine yards.' The expression was popularized by the title of the comedy film *The Whole Nine Yards* (1999) starring Bruce Willis as a HITMAN in suburbia.

> I went to the City and Islington sixth-form college after that. ... I was there to retake my GCSEs but I left after five months. Stupid. I wanted to go the whole nine yards, be a total graduate.
> *Sunday Times Magazine* (2 January 2000)

Gothic Line (German *Gotisch Linie*). A heavily fortified defensive line built across Italy by the Germans during the Second World War. The line crossed the Italian peninsula north of Florence, running between La Spezia on the west coast to Pesaro, south of Rimini, on the east coast. The Allied operation to breach the line took place in August–September 1944. The name refers to the ancient Gothic tribes, fearsome warriors who were regarded as the ancestors of modern Germans. *See also* FORTRESS EUROPE; GUSTAV LINE.

Go through a bad patch, To. To undergo a period of difficulty. The allusion is to a period of time that does not accord with the normal course of events, like a rough or poorly worked patch in an otherwise smooth and continuous length of fabric. 'Patch' in this sense dates from the 1920s.

> The bad patch that Russian relations with the West underwent earlier this year ... has passed.
> *The Times* (30 July 1999)

Go through the roof, To. To lose one's temper suddenly. *See also* HIT THE CEILING.

> On the same statement that revealed the surcharge, I discovered that Lloyds TSB had, without my permission, 'promoted' me to a fee-paying Gold Service Account. I went through the roof.
> *The Times* (16 October 1999)

Go to town, To. To do something thoroughly or extravagantly; to enjoy oneself greatly. The concept is of a rural resident finding reward and fulfilment in 'the big city'. The expression is of US origin and dates from the 1930s.

Gottle o' geer. A representation of the words 'bottle of beer' said without moving the lips, as a supposed typical utterance of a ventriloquist and so a byword for their art.

Government Communications Headquarters. *See* GCHQ.

Governor Moonbeam. A nickname given to Jerry Brown (b.1938), governor of California (1975–83), because of his environmentally aware policies, regarded by some as eccentric. His beliefs had developed into a kind of NEW AGE philosophy (he studied Zen in Japan) by the time he tried for the Democratic presidential nomination in 1992, earning him the new nickname, the SPACE CADET.

Go West, Young Man. A film (1937) whose title contains a reference to its star Mae West (1892–1980) while punning on a well-known exhortation to new arrivals in the United States in the mid-19th century, when the western territories of the country were being opened up to settlers. The slogan is usually attributed to the newspaperman Horace Greeley, who ran unsuccessfully for the presidency, but it was, in fact, coined by John Babsone Lane Soule, writing in the Terre Haute (Indiana) *Express* in 1851:

> Go west, young man, and grow up with the country.

Go while the going is good, To. To get away while one can; to proceed while conditions are favourable. The US expression appears in many popular novels of the first half of the 20th century and relates to horse racing, which is best held when the 'going' or condition of the ground is good.

Go with a bang, To. To be highly successful; to be a 'hit'. *See also* WITH A BANG.

Go with a swing, To. To be a great success; to be lively and enjoyable. The phrase dates from the 1970s and typically applies to a party or other social function where there is vigorous activity or animated conversation. At its height such a party would be in full swing.

Go with the flow, To. To accept a situation rather than trying to control it. The phrase dates from the 1960s and is a succinct resumé of the teaching of the US psychologist Carl R. Rogers (1902–87) that life involves 'floating with a complex streaming of experience'.

Graceland. The mansion and burial site of Elvis Presley (1935–77), the KING, at Memphis, Tennessee, opened as a shrine to his adoring public in 1982. 'Graceland' is also the title of a song and album by Paul Simon, released in 1986, the inspiration behind the song being an actual trip that Simon made to Graceland with his young son. *See also* ELVIS LIVES; ELVIS THE PELVIS.

Grade. This word is commonly used to denote a student's assessment or mark of attainment in schools and colleges, as the seven grades A to G in the GCSE (General Certificate of Secondary Education) examination. From 1994 there has been an additional 'starred' A grade (A*) to cater for the highest attainers.

Graduate, The. A film (1967) adapted by Calder Willingham and Buck Henry from the autobiographical novel by Charles Webb about a young man's confusion as he approaches adulthood in suburban southern California. Starring Dustin Hoffman and directed by Mike Nichols, the film's title refers as much to his seduction by an older married woman (played by Anne Bancroft) and his grappling with what he wants from life as it does to the recent completion of his college studies. The soundtrack, by Paul Simon and Art Garfunkel, includes such classic songs as 'Mrs Robinson', 'The Sound of Silence' and 'Scarborough Fair'.

Graffiti (Italian *graffito*, 'scratching'). A name applied originally to the 'wall scribblings' found at Pompeii and other Italian cities, as the work of schoolboys, idlers and the like, many of them obscene and accompanied by rough drawings. Modern graffiti are found on walls, in public toilets, on posters and in other clearly visible places. They are sometimes crude and erotic, but some are genuinely witty. One seen in Manchester in 1978 read: 'If you hate graffiti, sign a partition.'

Political graffiti were formerly common in the 1930s and so-called graffiti art, also known as 'spraycan art', evolved in the 1980s as a semi-abstract, quasi-pictorial manifestation in the New York subway system. A leading exponent of the technique was Jean-Michel Basquiat (1960–88). His brief but bright career was ended by a drugs overdose. *See also* CHAD; KILROY.

Grammy. One of a number of annual awards given by the American National Academy of Recording Arts and Sciences for achievement in the record industry, first made in 1958 and taking its name from a blend of 'gramophone' and EMMY. It was introduced largely as a publicity stunt. The award itself is in the form of a gold-plated disk.

Granadaland. The area around Manchester, where Granada Television is based, typically regarded as brash and affluent. The company takes its name from the Granada chain of cinemas opened in 1930 by Sidney Bernstein (1899–1993), who so called them after a holiday in the Spanish city of Granada, where he had much admired the Alhambra Palace.

In 1987 Bernstein received a silver pomegranate from the governor of the Spanish province of Granada in recognition for his company's achievement in 'putting Granada on the map'. *Granada* is the Spanish for 'pomegranate'.

[Cheshire's STOCKBROKER BELT] is home to Granadaland's rich, famous and garish, from *Coronation Street* actors to Manchester United footballers.
The Times (10 June 1999)

Granddaddy of them all. The first, oldest or greatest example of something, as: 'That old TV set is the granddaddy of them all.' The expression dates from the 1950s.

Grandmother's steps or **footsteps.** A children's game in which one player stands with his back to the others who approach him stealthily and try to touch his back without him seeing them move. The player

at the front is allowed to turn round often and without warning and anyone he sees moving is sent back to the starting line. The name takes a grandmother as a person supposedly hard of hearing or dimly sighted and so unlikely to be aware of anyone's approach. The game dates from the 1920s. *See also* RED LIGHT.

We, who remember, look back to the blossoming
    May-time
On ghosts of servers and thurifers after Mass,
The slapping of backs, the flapping of cassocks, the
    play-time,
A game of Grandmother's Steps on the vicarage
    grass.
JOHN BETJEMAN: *High and Low*, 'Anglo-Catholic
Congresses' (1966)

Grand Ole Opry. This country music show at Nashville, Tennessee, began weekly radio broadcasts in 1925, playing traditional country or hillbilly music. The show was originally known as the 'WSM Barn Dance', but gained its familiar name, a dialect form of 'Grand Old Opera', in 1926. In 1941 the Opry became a live stage show, and in 1974 moved to the Opryland amusement park and entertainment centre in Nashville.

Grandparents Day. MOTHER'S DAY and FATHER'S DAY had been observed for much of the 20th century before National Grandparents Day was inaugurated in the United States in 1979 to complement the family commemoration on the day after the first Sunday in September.

Grand slam. A sports term for a win in each of a group of major championships or matches in a given year, and especially in tennis, golf or rugby union. The tennis grand slam refers to winning the four most prestigious tournaments: the Australian Open, the French Open, the US Open and Wimbledon. The golf grand slam refers to winning all four MAJORS in a single year. The rugby union grand slam refers to winning all the matches in the six nations championship, which is contested by England, Scotland, Wales, Ireland, France and Italy. This 20th-century usage evolved from the specific 19th-century term for the bidding and winning of all 13 tricks in the game of bridge. 'Slam' here is not the same as the word for a loud bang but the name of an old card game.

Grange Hill. A pioneering children's SOAP OPERA first screened in 1978 and set in the (fictional) London comprehensive school of the title. Plot lines included a teenage boy's HEROIN addiction and a teenage girl's pregnancy, and the regular scenes of hair-pulling and shop-lifting outraged many. The producers countered criticism, however, by claiming that the tales were cautionary ones.

Granny dumping. The deliberate 'dumping' of an elderly relative, usually female, especially one suffering from fits of confusion or other troubling habits, by taking them to a hospital or care centre and abandoning them there. The practice was first observed in the United States in the early 1990s.

Granny flat. A self-contained flat or annexe inside or built on to a house, designed as a modest home for an elderly relative. Such flats became less common in the closing years of the 20th century, the elderly largely living in sheltered housing or similar residential accommodation. The term granny annexe is sometimes contracted as 'grannex'.

> The house may have a family room ... but despite the demographic predictions of an ageing population it is never built with a granny flat.
> *The Times* (18 November 1999)

Granny glasses. Spectacles with small circular lenses, which were in fashion in the 1960s during the heyday of the BEATLES and the FLOWER PEOPLE. Their popularity was largely due to John Lennon, who wore glasses of this type.

> The [album] sleeve reveals Rennie minus her kooky granny specs, wearing a nice black top.
> *Sunday Times* (27 February 2000)

Grapes of Wrath, The. A novel (1939) by John Steinbeck (1902–68), which won the PULITZER PRIZE for fiction. It charts the vicissitudes of a farming family, which migrates from the dustbowls of Oklahoma in search of a better future in California during the GREAT DEPRESSION. The title comes from 'The Battle Hymn of the Republic' by Julia Ward Howe (1819–1900): 'Mine eyes have seen the glory of the coming of the Lord, / He is trampling out the vintage where the grapes of wrath are stored' (lines 1–2). A superb film version (1940) was memorably directed by John Ford. *See also* OKIES.

Grasshopper mind. One unable to concentrate on any single subject for long. The grasshopper is quick to leap from one resting place to another.

Grassy knoll. An area in Dallas that was just ahead of President John F. Kennedy when he was assassin-ated on 22 November 1963. Those conspiracy theorists who do not accept that Lee Harvey Oswald was a lone gunman interpret various bits of evidence to indicate that the shots that killed Kennedy came from the grassy knoll and not from Oswald in the Texas School Book Repository, as the official WARREN COMMISSION concluded. *See also* JFK.

Grauniad. A mostly affectionate media nickname for the *Guardian* newspaper, dating from the 1970s and originating in *Private Eye*. The name is an anagrammatic travesty of the paper's title and alludes to its legendary misprints. In 1997 the *Guardian* launched an entertaining and instructive 'corrections and clarifications column' to set the record straight in such instances. One such item read: 'The film starring Errol Flynn ... was *The Master of Ballantrae*, not *The Mask of Gallantry*' (quoted in *The Times* of 10 December 1999).

Graveyard shift. In the Second World War the name given by shift workers in munitions factories and other workplaces to the shift covering the midnight hours. The allusion is perhaps to the watchmen who at one time patrolled the graves of the wealthy in order to deter grave robbers. The second word is variable for any similar night work or schedule.

> The so-called 'graveyard' slot for the 11pm *Nightly News* has proved quite lively at times.
> *The Times* (23 July 1999)

Gravity's Rainbow. A novel (1973) by Thomas Pynchon (b.1937). Set in Europe towards the end of the Second World War and immediately after it, the main plot concerns a US soldier who has erections in places in London that are due to be hit by V-2 missiles, which in turn would become the method of delivering the nuclear armaments that were being developed in the United States at the same time. 'Gravity's Rainbow' refers both to the arc of the missile and to the metaphorical trajectory of civilization as it moves towards its own destruction. The novel shared the National Book Award. It was selected for the PULITZER PRIZE only to be thrown out by the advisory board as 'obscene' and 'unreadable', but won the Howells Medal, which the author refused. *See also* FIRST LINES OF NOVELS.

Gravy train. A sinecure; a simple situation or nominal position that will give ready profit. The image is of a train of 'gravy' as a pleasing addition to the 'meat' that is one's daily sustenance. There is doubtless also an association in sense between a 'gravy boat', so called from its shape, and a 'gravy train', both alluding to forms of transport. The expression dates from the 1920s.

> Since the election of a mayor for London is breaking new ground, perhaps there should be a box on the ballot paper for those who do not want one. If they were first past the post it would stop the gravy train.
> *The Times* (Letter to the Editor) (25 August 1999)

Gray, Cornelia. The woman detective who appears in P.D. James's novels *An Unsuitable Job for a Woman* (1972) and *The Skull Beneath the Skin* (1982). She is independent, single-minded and intelligent and, in an appealing way, entirely guileless. In a television version (1985) of the former novel she is played by Pippa Guard, and in a later and better version of 1998 by Helen Baxendale.

Graziano, Rocky. The US middleweight boxing champion, born Thomas Rocco Barbella (1919–90), who helped to popularize the nickname 'Rocky' for boxers. He was at his best in the 1940s and 1950s, when his brawling style made him popular with the public. He was a model for the ROCKY films starring Sylvester Stallone. *See also* MARCIANO, ROCKY.

Grease. A film musical (1978) based on a stage show (1972) with music by Jim Jacobs and Warren Casey about a group of lively teenagers during the ROCK 'N' ROLL era of the 1950s. Starring John Travolta and Olivia Newton-John, the film was a massive international success, spawning several major pop hits. The title, referring to the grease most young men put in their hair at that time, was changed to *Glease* when the film was released in Japan, to *Vaselino* when released in Mexico, and to *Brilliantine* when shown in France. A sequel, *Grease 2* (1982), was entirely unmemorable.

Greasy pole. A form of outdoor entertainment dating from the 19th century in which two people try to knock each other off a horizontal pole covered with an oily substance that makes it difficult to keep one's feet. The traditional 'weapons' for this purpose are pillows. Figuratively a greasy pole is a difficult 'career ladder' that one has to climb. Here the pole is envisaged as vertical.

> In 1984–5 he took a year out to return to academia … but on his return he began the serious ascent of the 'greasy pole'.
> *Sunday Times* (30 January 2000)

Greasy spoon. A nickname for a cheap café or restaurant, so called from its unwashed cutlery. The expression is of US origin and dates from the 1920s.

> Had I seen him, as people sometimes do, in a greasy spoon, I would not have recognized him.
> *The Times* (8 November 1999)

Great American Nude. The series of paintings and mixed-media works by the US Pop artist Tom Wesselmann (b.1931) includes *Great American Nude No. 10* (1961) and *Great American Nude No. 54* (1964). In some of the works the flatly painted nude contrasts with the actual room fittings in the assemblage, such as a radiator, a telephone that rings, a window and curtains. The title is a SWINGING SIXTIES dig at the 'great AMERICAN DREAM' and the 'great American novel'.

Great and the good. Those who are distinguished and worthy. The term also occurs as 'the good and the great' and frequently has an ironic implication. Further adjectives may be added.

> The great, the good and the ghastly of the Tory party slid over one another to cast the first stone at [Lord] Archer and his lie.
> *Sunday Times* (28 November 1999)

Great Balls of Fire. A rock 'n' roll song released in 1958, written by Otis Blackwell and performed with manic energy and intensity by Jerry Lee Lewis (nicknamed the 'backwoods wildman'). The 'balls of fire' in question are the fires of passion, but such was the devilish frenzy of Lewis's way with the song (and the piano) that they came in some people's minds to have an almost satanic implication.

> Man, I got the devil in me.
> JERRY LEE LEWIS (after recording 'Great Balls of Fire')

Great Communicator. A nickname of Republican politician Ronald Reagan (b.1911), president of the United States (1981–9). Reagan had been an actor in numerous Hollywood B-movies before entering politics and successfully used his communication skills to present himself as a man of humility, warmth, integrity, homespun wisdom and gentle wit, which won him enormous support for his right-wing policies from the American people, including many former Democrats (*see* REAGAN DEMOCRATS). During his tenure of office wags referred to Washington, D.C. as Hollywood East. Reagan's ability to extricate himself from political scrapes led to another nickname, the Great Rondini, after the escapologist Harry HOUDINI. *See also* EVIL EMPIRE; GIPPER; MURDER, INC.

Great Depression. The economic slump that began in 1929 in North America, Europe and other industrialized regions of the world. It originated in the United States, where it was triggered by a catastrophic collapse of stock market prices on BLACK THURSDAY, resulting in the insolvency of many banks. As the US was the major creditor and financier of postwar Europe, whose economies had been weakened by the war itself, its effects were soon felt across the Atlantic. *See also* DUST BOWL; NEW DEAL.

Great Dictator, The. A film comedy (1940) written by, directed by and starring Charles Chaplin (1889–1977) about a nameless Jewish barber who protests against the persecution of the Jews in the fictional country of Tomania under its dictator Adenoid Hynkel (Chaplin playing both main roles). It was the physical similarity between Chaplin's celebrated tramp, complete with toothbrush moustache, and the German dictator Adolf Hitler that inspired the making of the film, Chaplin's first 'talkie'.

Great Escape, The. A film (1963) adapted by James Clavell and W.R. Burnett from a book of the same title by Paul Brickhill about a mass escape of Allied prisoners from a German prisoner of war camp during the Second World War. The plot was based on a real mass break-out staged by Allied prisoners from POW camp Stalag Luft III in 1942. *See also* ESCAPE FILM.

Greatest Story Ever Told, The. A biblical film epic (1965) that attempted to make great cinema of the life of Christ, the 'greatest story' of the title. Starring Max von Sydow as Christ and filmed largely in Utah rather than Palestine, it was generally considered a failure, chiefly because of the distracting appearance of well-known HOLLYWOOD stars in bit parts. One such was John Wayne as a Roman centurion, whose drawling delivery of the line 'Truly, this man was the Son of God' provoked hilarity.

Great game. Spying. A term dating from the turn of the 20th century but found earlier, in a quite different context, as a nickname for golf. The colonial civil servant Tom Rogers gave an entertaining account of his time as a diplomat in his memoirs *Great Game, Grand Game* (1991).

> When he comes to the Great Game he must go alone – alone, and at peril of his head.
> RUDYARD KIPLING: *Kim*, ch vii (1901)

Great Gatsby, The. A classic novel (1925) by F. Scott Fitzgerald (1896–1940), set on Long Island, New York. Jay GATSBY, one of the wealthy criminal class, has an affair with Daisy, who is married to Tom, rich, dim and violent. Tom takes as his lover Myrtle Wilson, whose husband works in a garage. Daisy, driving Gatsby's car, accidentally kills Myrtle and does not stop. Tom tells Myrtle's husband that it was Gatsby who was driving. Wilson shoots Gatsby and then turns the gun on himself. There have been two rather unsatisfactory film versions, directed respectively by Elliott Nugent (1949) and Jack Clayton (1974), while a televised version (2000) was a handsomely glossy costume drama that never really came to life. *See also* FIRST LINES OF NOVELS.

Great Leap Forward. The attempt by Mao Zedong in 1958–60 to speed up the process of industrialization in China and improve agricultural production. The population was organized into large collectives and labour-intensive methods were introduced. The 'great leap' was more a small hop, however, and progress was slow. The CULTURAL REVOLUTION followed soon after.

Great Masturbator, The. The probably self-referential painting by Salvador Dalí (1904–89) was executed in 1929. Dalí was himself a lifelong devotee of onanism, an enthusiasm happily tolerated by his wife Gala. Among the more identifiable features of the painting is the head of an attractive young woman sniffing with apparent pleasure at the scantily covered genitalia of an adolescent boy.

Great Patriotic War (Russian, *Velikaya Otechestvennaya voyna*). The designation of the course of the Second World War from the Russian point of view following NAZI Germany's invasion of the Soviet Union on 22 June 1941 (*see* BARBAROSSA). The war ended in 1945 with the USSR in control of Eastern Europe and East Germany. According to the *Great Soviet Encyclopedia* (1971), the Great Patriotic War was the 'just, liberating war of the Soviet people for the freedom and independence of the Socialist homeland against Fascist Germany and its allies (Italy, Hungary, Romania, Finland, and in 1945, Japan)'. *See also* SOVIET SAYINGS.

Great Rondini. *See* GREAT COMMUNICATOR.

Great Satan. A term applied to the USA by AYATOLLAH Ruholla Khomeini (1902–89), the spiritual leader of the anti-Western Islamic fundamentalist regime in Iran.

Great Society. The vision of the USA presented by President Lyndon Johnson during a speech at the

University of Michigan in May 1964: 'We have the opportunity to move not only toward the rich and the powerful society, but upward to the Great Society … The Great Society rests on abundance and liberty for all. It demands an end to poverty and racial injustice.' To this end Johnson pursued a 'war on poverty', introduced sweeping civil-rights reforms and established subsidized health care in the USA via the Medicaid and Medicare schemes. Unfortunately his immersion in the VIETNAM War deflected attention from his achievements in social reform. *See also* LBJ.

Great Storm. A media nickname for the ferocious winds that battered the southeast of England on the night of 15–16 October 1987. The onslaught caused considerable destruction, uprooting some 15 million trees and inflicting costly ecological damage. At the Royal Botanic Gardens, Kew, the storm destroyed 500 trees and damaged 1000 others, including some rare specimens. The death toll of 18 was relatively low but insurance losses to property amounted to some £800 million.

Great Train Robbery. The most audacious crime in British history was committed on 8 August 1963 when a gang hijacked a Royal Mail train in Buckinghamshire and escaped with mailbags containing £2.6 million in the form of used banknotes on their way to being destroyed. The robbers stopped the train by turning off a green signal and replacing it with a red signal rigged up with batteries. During the raid itself the train driver, Jack Mills, was clubbed over the head and received injuries from which he never fully recovered. Twelve of the fifteen were caught and convicted but one of the gang, Ronnie Biggs, escaped from prison, picked up his share of the haul and made his way to Brazil, which did not then have an extradition treaty with Britain. He was still there at the close of the century. Media accounts of the long-running story were inspired by *The Great Train Robbery*, the title of a famous silent US film of 1903.

Great Wallendas. A famous family of American tight-rope walkers, founded by Karl Wallenda (1905–78) and involving his children, grandchildren, cousins, nephews and nieces. The troupe first gained fame in Europe for their four-man pyramid and high-wire cycling act. They then worked in circuses, where they developed a seven-man pyramid in 1947. From then on, they performed independently, always working without a net. Two members of the troupe were killed in a 1962 performance, another in 1963, and yet another in 1972. Karl himself lost his life in 1978 when a gust of wind blew him off the cable he was walking between two hotel buildings in Puerto Rico.

Great War. The war of 1914–18 was so called until that of 1939–45, when the term First World War or World War I largely replaced it, the latter becoming the Second World War or World War II. The French call the latter *La Seconde Guerre mondiale*, the adjective *second* being used for the second of only two (as distinct from *deuxième*, which implies a higher count).

Great white hope. A US expression for a person or thing that is expected to succeed. It dates from the early 20th century and alludes specifically to the black heavyweight boxing champion Jack Johnson (1878–1946), who seemed invincible. The phrase was thus used for any white hopeful who might defeat him. The term was popularized by the title of Howard Sackler's play *The Great White Hope* (1968), based on Johnson's life, and by a 1970 film version of this.

Great White Way. A once popular name for Broadway, New York, especially the part that passes through TIMES SQUARE. The name is associated with the area's multitude of electric advertising signs and brilliant street lighting, but was actually given by journalists in December 1901 following a heavy snowfall, as an adoption of the title of Albert Bigelow Paine's novel *The Great White Way* (1901), a tale of adventure at the South Pole.

Grebo. A member of a 1980s urban youth cult in Britain characterized by musical tastes ranging from HEAVY METAL to PUNK ROCK, an aggressive or anti-social manner, and long hair and clothes reminiscent of the earlier 'biker' generation. The term is also used for the cult itself and is probably based on 'greaser', as a scruffily dressed member of a motorcycle gang, with '-bo' as in 'dumbo' or 'jumbo'.

Grecians. The nickname of Exeter City football club, founded in 1904. In 1726 a re-enactment of the Siege of Troy was held at an Exeter fair, with the attacking Greeks played by the residents of St Sidwells, outside the city walls. A tradition of football matches developed between the city dwellers (Blues) and St Sidwells inhabitants (Greeks, subsequently Grecians). A football ground with a 'Grecian' entrance gate was built off Sidwell Street for the matches and the team playing there, originally St Sidwell's Old Boys, became Exeter City and adopted their long-established nickname. *See also* FOOTBALL CLUB NICKNAMES.

Grecian 2000. The proprietary name of a hair colouring lotion that 'restores' dark tones to a male head whose locks have greyed with age. The name is invoked slightingly or mockingly of various celebrities who are deemed to have resorted to the product. The name itself is presumably intended to evoke the dark hair of the ancient Greeks in 2000 BC, perhaps with a hint of 'grease'.

> Science is galloping to the rescue of the exhausted armies of ageing politicians and pop stars who ... keep bottles of Grecian 2000 hidden in their bathroom cupboards in the hope that they can convincingly dye their grey locks back to the lustrous darkness of a lost youth.
>
> The Times (29 December 1999)

Greek Colonels. The three senior army officers who were placed in key posts under prime minister Konstantinos Kollias in the military government of Greece from 1967 to 1974. They were Lieutenant-General Gregorios Spandidakis, Brigadier Stylianos Patakos and Colonel Georgios Papadopoulos. King Constantine fled to Rome in December 1967, whereupon General Georgios Zoitakis was appointed regent while Papadopoulos and Patakos, relinquishing their military ranks, took over as prime minister and deputy prime minister respectively. In 1972 Papadopoulos replaced Zoitakis as regent and in 1973 became president, the junta decreeing the monarchy to be abolished. A civilian government under Konstantinos Karamanlis resumed office in 1974.

Green belt. A stretch of country around a large urban area that has been scheduled for comparative preservation and where building development is restricted. The concept was introduced in the 1930s but was adopted only in the 1950s in response to the pressure to expand towns regarded by many to be large enough already. Green belts have no statutory authority and their demarcation is under constant challenge from the conflicting interests of developers, farmers, conservationists and existing residents. See also GREENFIELD SITE.

> Green belts should no longer be regarded as sacred cows in a rural pasture in which no development is allowed. Those surrounding our cities have slowly been turning into brown belts.
>
> The Times (Letter to the Editor) (10 January 2000)

Green Berets. A nickname for British or US commandos.

Green card. A green-coloured document issued by various authorities in the 20th century, including: (1) a card filled in by a visitor to the Houses of Parliament, requesting an interview with an MP; (2) an international insurance document for motorists taking their cars abroad, and confirming that the driver holds the necessary insurance cover; (3) a permit issued by the US government enabling a foreign national to live and work permanently in the United States. This last is formally known as an 'alien-registration-receipt card', and provided the title for an off-beat 1990 film comedy.

Green Cross Code. A code of road safety for children, first published in 1971 and now included in the HIGHWAY CODE as a guide to crossing the road for all pedestrians. A green traffic light or pedestrian crossing light is associated with safety.

Greenfield site. A rural or undeveloped site that has potential for the building of private houses or for commercial exploitation. See also BROWNFIELD SITE; GREEN BELT.

Green fingers. To have green fingers is to be unusually successful in making plants grow. The phrase dates from the 1920s and was popularized by Reginald Arkell's book so titled (1934).

Green form. The form on which application is made for legal advice and assistance in England and Wales. It is completed by the client and the solicitor then assesses the client's means by referring to a 'key card'. Those whose income and capital are within certain limits are entitled to free advice on most legal matters. The scheme provides initially for up to three hours' work for matrimonial cases where a petition is drafted, and two hours for other work.

Green goddesses. A nickname for the green military fire engines that are brought in when crews of the regular fire services are out on strike. The name has been similarly given to other vehicles, such as the double-decked trams running in Liverpool in the 1930s. In this case the adoption seems to have been suggested by William Archer's popular melodrama The Green Goddess (1921), then playing at a theatre in the city. The Green Goddess was also a name for the keep-fit demonstrator Diana Moran, who wore a lurid green body stocking on breakfast television in 1983.

Greenham Common. A village near Newbury, West Berkshire, that was the site of a United States cruise missile base and that from 1981 until its closure in

1991 was the focal point of a camp of 'peace women' protesting against nuclear weapons. At the peak of the protest in December 1982 some 30,000 women encircled the perimeter fence. The camp was not disbanded until 1999. The 'green' place-name was coincidentally appropriate for the stance. *See also* CND.

Greenhouse effect. Literally, an effect occurring in greenhouses in which radiant heat from the sun passes through the glass and, trapped inside by the glass, warms the contents. The term came to apply to an analogous effect on the Earth's atmosphere in which carbon dioxide and other gases in the atmosphere absorb the infrared radiation emitted by the Earth's surface through being exposed to solar ultraviolet radiation. As a result, the Earth's mean temperature rises. The term is first found in G.T. Trewartha's *Introduction to Weather and Climate* (1937). *See also* GLOBAL WARMING.

Green light. Permission to proceed. The image is that of a green traffic light or railway signal, authorizing one to go ahead. The phrase dates from the 1970s.

> The Emap team seemed a bit doubtful when I showed them a cover that I'd mocked up on my kitchen table with scissors and glue. But they gave me the green light, and 'Project Nora' was born.
>
> *The Times* (17 September 1999)

Green Line. A boundary line established in the 1970s in the Lebanese capital, BEIRUT, to separate Christian and Muslim factions in East and West Beirut. It became a dangerous barricade permanently dividing the city, somewhat in the manner of the BERLIN WALL.

Greenmail. The stock market practice of buying enough shares in a company to threaten a take-over, so forcing the company concerned to buy them back at a higher price in order to retain control of the business. The term is a variant of 'blackmail' with 'green' here in the sense of money, as in 'greenback', a US $1 bill, so named from its colour.

Green man. A popular name, especially as used to children, for the outline of a human figure on the green light of a PELICAN CROSSING, signifying that it is safe to cross the road.

> 'She was absolutely amazed when we came out of Debenham's and she saw the little green man flashing on the lights at the crossing.'
>
> *The Times* (10 December 1999)

Greenmantle. A thriller (1916) by John Buchan (1875–1940), employing some of the same characters as in

The THIRTY-NINE STEPS, including the protagonist Richard Hannay. The setting is the Middle East, and the theme, the danger of Germany sponsoring a Muslim uprising which would destabilize India, was a real one which Buchan knew from his work in Intelligence and from writing the history of the First World War as it happened. The title is the code name for the seer Zimrud ('Emerald'), after a Turkish miracle play, found on a scrap of paper on the body of a dead British agent. Reading the book cheered up the family of Tsar Nicholas II (1868–1918) of Russia as they awaited their fate in captivity. *See also* MR STANDFAST.

Green Paper. In British parliamentary parlance, a command paper containing policy proposals for discussion in the Houses of Parliament. When the proposals have been discussed by all the parties concerned, they are published as a White Paper. This in turn usually leads to the introduction of a Bill and finally to an Act of Parliament. An example is the Green Paper introduced by the Home Secretary after the Southall riots of 1979. This led in 1985 to a White Paper called 'The Review of Public Order', which in turn led to the introduction of the Public Order Bill and Act of 1986. The Green Paper, so called from the colour of its cover, was introduced by the Department of Economic Affairs in 1967, and was defined by Michael Stewart, Senior Economic Adviser to the Treasury, as 'a statement by the Government not of policy already determined but of propositions put before the whole nation for discussion' (*The Times*, 1 March 1969).

Green Party. In Britain a political party founded in 1973 after the publication of *Blueprint for Survival*, a work issued by the editors of the *Ecologist* magazine by way of offering radical solutions to environmental problems. The party was known as the Ecology Party until 1985. Despite the importance attached to environmental issues, the party has made only a minimal impact on the political scene. It fielded 95 candidates in the 1997 general election and polled 63,991 votes, just 0.2 per cent of the total.

Greenpeace. A movement originating as an anti-nuclear group in British Columbia, Canada, in 1971, initially to oppose US nuclear tests in Alaska. It now aims to persuade governments to change industrial activities that threaten natural resources and the environment. It supports direct non-violent action and has gained wide attention by its efforts to protect whales and to prevent the killing of young seals.

When acting against French nuclear tests in the South Pacific in 1985, its ship *Rainbow Warrior* was sunk by a French saboteur. A successful campaign in 1995 forced the Shell oil company not to sink an obsolete oil platform, the Brent Spar, in the North Atlantic. *See also* FRIENDS OF THE EARTH.

Green pound. The exchange rate for the pound applied to payments for agricultural produce in the EUROPEAN UNION.

Green revolution. A term dating from the 1970s for the introduction of new and more productive agricultural techniques in developing countries. New hybrid wheats were first bred in Mexico in the 1950s and new rice varieties in the Philippines in the 1960s. Such new varieties have since spread to other THIRD WORLD countries and have had considerable success, in some cases more than doubling the yields of traditional varieties. It remains unlikely, however, that the green revolution will ever fulfil its original promise because of lack of capital and expertise, lack of time and the will to act quickly, and lack of cooperation on the part of farmers. The degree of resistance of the new strains to attacks of insects and plants diseases is also uncertain.

Green Shield Stamps. A popular brand of British trading stamps in the 1960s. They were given to customers with purchases as an incentive to buy more goods and were redeemable for cash or merchandise. They were introduced in 1957 on the lines of the green stamps issued in the United States by the firm of Sperry and Hutchinson.

Greenshirt. A supporter of the Social Credit Movement established in England by Major Douglas in the 1920s, and so named from the green uniform shirt adopted.

Green shoots. Signs of growth or renewal as part of a country's economic recovery. The phrase was brought before the public in 1991 when the Chancellor of the Exchequer, Norman Lamont, speaking at the Conservative Party Conference, said: 'The green shoots of economic spring are appearing once again.' This optimistic view was not, however, supported by subsequent events.

Green wellies. Green wellington boots, as typically worn by SLOANE RANGERS, or those members of the upper classes who practise the country sports of HUNTING, SHOOTING AND FISHING. The 'green welly brigade' is a term dating from the 1970s for such people in the mass.

Greenwich Village. The residential area of lower Manhattan, New York, gained a reputation from the early years of the 20th century for its bohemianism, and became established as a meeting-place of unconventional writers, artists and musicians, especially members of the BEAT GENERATION and of students generally. In more recent times it has lost much of its sense of creative originality, although its alternative lifestyle continues to be represented in that of its gay community. Many New Yorkers now wax lyrical about 'the Village', with its former feel of excitement and vitality.

Gremlin. One of a number of imaginary gnomes or goblins humorously blamed by the RAF in the Second World War for everything that went wrong in an aircraft or an operation. The name was probably coined at the end of the First World War or in the 1920s and was apparently in use on RAF stations in India and the Middle East in the 1930s. The name is first traced in print in *The Aeroplane* (10 April 1929). One explanation claims that a gremlin was the goblin that came out of Fremlin's beer bottles (Fremlin being a Kent brewer), although there are numerous other origins, some more plausible than others.

Gremlins. A comedy horror film (1984), directed by Joe Dante, about a small furry creature called the mogwai that spawns a race of ferocious monsters called gremlins when accidentally wetted. Chris Columbus, who wrote the screenplay, derived the basic idea for the film from a nightmare in which he dreamed his feet were being nibbled by mice. *See also* GREMLIN.

Grey area. Generally, an area or situation where distinctions cannot be clearly made or rules precisely determined. In a more specific sense, a grey area is a region of relatively high unemployment, first so called in Britain in 1966. The official term for such a region is a development area. The description 'grey' may have owed something to maps of Britain showing such areas shaded grey.

Grey-collar worker. A mostly US term for a mechanic or maintenance man, who usually wears grey overalls. The expression dates from the 1960s and contrasts with the WHITE-COLLAR WORKER and BLUE-COLLAR WORKER. *See also* PINK-COLLAR WORKER.

> By 1975, only one out three jobs is expected to be in production ... Blue-collar, gray-collar, and farm employment combined will just barely exceed the white-collar total.
>
> *World Year Book* (1968)

Greyfriars. The imaginary school that is the setting of the long series of school stories by 'Frank Richards' (Charles Hamilton). Its most colourful pupil is Billy BUNTER, but its shining light is the brave, energetic and resourceful Harry Wharton, whose inner circle of friends consists of Frank Nugent, Bob Cherry, Johnny Bull and the rather more exotic Hurree Jamset Singh, the youthful Nabob of Bhanipur.

> The year is 1910 – or 1940, but it is all the same. You are at Greyfriars, a rosy-cheeked boy of fourteen in posh tailor-made clothes, sitting down to tea in your study on the Remove passage after an exciting game of football which was won by the odd goal in the last half-minute. There is a cosy fire in the study and outside the wind is whistling. The ivy clusters thickly round the old grey stones. The King is on his throne and the pound is worth a pound. ..., Everything is safe, solid and unquestionable. Everything will be the same for ever and ever. That approximately is the atmosphere.
> GEORGE ORWELL in *Horizon* (1940), quoted in
> E.S. TURNER: *Boys Will Be Boys*, ch xiii (1948)

Grey market. In the Second World War a transaction regarded as a lesser breach of the rationing regulations than the black market. In Stock Exchange parlance, a grey market is a market in the shares of a new issue by investors who have applied for the shares but not actually received them.

Grey Owl. The pen-name of the Canadian author and conservationist Archibald Stansfeld Belaney (1888–1938), who adopted the name when he became a blood brother of the Ojibwa people in 1920. A former trapper, he later became interested in conservation and, in addition to setting up a beaver sanctuary, wrote a novel for children, *The Adventures of Sajo and Her Beaver People* (1935).

Gricer. A nickname for a railway enthusiast, especially one who turns a hobby into an obsession. The origins of the term are obscure, but it apparently emerged in northern England in the 1940s. A variant of 'grouser' has been suggested by some, as has a pun on 'grouse', since train-spotting is an activity bearing a supposed resemblance to grouse-shooting. Further speculative etymologies are given in the June 1970 number of *Railway World*.

Grim Grom. A popular media nickname for the Soviet foreign minister Andrey Gromyko (1909–89), who invariably had a solemn expression. English 'grim'

and Gromyko's Ukrainian surname, deriving from *grom*, 'thunder', are linguistically related, so the name is not mere alliteration. *See also* GROMYKO OF THE LABOUR PARTY.

Grin and bare it, To. To brave a social function in a revealing costume. A punning expression based on 'grin and bear it' applied mostly to BRIGHT YOUNG THINGS or PARTY GIRLS.

> All four girls not only grinned and bared it, they even managed to smile warmly at onlookers.
> *Sunday Times* (2 January 2000)

Grind to a halt or **come to a grinding halt, To.** To come laboriously to a standstill. The reference is to the clogging up of a piece of machinery until it can no longer function. In the days of the windmill, when the wind dropped, the grinding action of the millstones on the grain stopped the mill, and it literally ground to a halt.

> [You would] be better off on Mars when it [the MILLENNIUM] happens. Everything here will grind to a halt.
> *New Scientist* (29 August 1998)

Grits and Fritz. A nickname for the successful Democratic ticket in the 1976 US presidential election, comprising Jimmy Carter (b.1924) and his running-mate Walter Mondale (b.1928). Coming from Georgia, Carter was 'Grits' (a kind of maize porridge popular with Southerners), while in the Senate Mondale was known as FRITZ. *See also* GEORGIA MAFIA; NORWEGIAN WOOD.

Grocer, The. A *Private Eye* nickname for Sir Edward Heath (b.1916), Conservative prime minister from 1970 to 1974. There is a twofold allusion. The first is to Heath's role as secretary of state for trade and industry in the 1960s, when he was negotiating British entry into the Common Market and so discussing the prices of eggs, butter, bacon and the like. The second is to his modest social background. The name was enthusiastically seized on by the *Guardian* newspaper.

Grocer's Daughter (French *fille d'épicier*). A description of Margaret Thatcher, the IRON LADY, by Valéry Giscard d'Estaing (b.1926) while president of France (1974–81), referring not only to the fact that her father was a grocer in Grantham, Lincolnshire, but also to her petit-bourgeois outlook on the world. It should be noted that she followed Edward Heath, the GROCER, as Conservative leader.

Grockles. A term used in Devon for visiting tourists and holidaymakers, especially when from the Midlands or north of England. The word is said to derive from the clown Grock, implying someone who is a 'little clown'. It apparently arose in 1963 from comments about holidaymakers made at the Globe Inn, Brixham, and was used by Peter Draper in his film *The System* (1964), shot at Brixham, Torquay and other parts of the English Riviera. The film itself centres on the system adopted by seaside layabouts for collecting and sharing female visitors. *See also* EMMETS.

Gromyko of the Labour Party. A description of himself by the Labour politician Denis (now Lord) Healey (b.1917). Andrey Gromyko (1909–89) was Soviet foreign minister (1957–85) and president (1985–8). Like Healey, despite his enormous power and influence over several decades, he never obtained the job of party leader. Healey himself was secretary of state for defence (1964–70), chancellor of the exchequer (1974–9) and deputy leader of the Labour Party (1981–3). *See also* DEAD SHEEP; GRIM GROM; LADY WITH THE BLOWLAMP.

Groovy. Successful; fashionable, exciting. The allusion is to the accurate reproduction of music by a needle in the groove of a gramophone record. The term originally related to the SWINGING SIXTIES but in the 1980s took on the converse sense of passé, out-of-date, referring to that era.

Gross out, To. To disgust or repel. The expression arose in the 1980s from 'gross' in the US campus sense of 'disgusting'. 'Gross me out!' thus became an exclamation of disgust.

> Director David O. Russell appeared to be saying that he has used a real bullet-ridden [*sic*] corpse for one scene. ... [George] Clooney's co-star, Mark Wahlberg, has admitted that the scene was so realistic that 'when I first saw it, I got grossed out'.
> *The Times* (2 October 1999)

Grouch bag. A hidden pocket or purse where one can keep one's money safe. The implication is that one grouches when spending or revealing one's money. The comedian Groucho Marx, born Julius Henry Marx, was perhaps so nicknamed because he carried a bag of this type around with him. *See* MARX BROTHERS.

Groucho Club. A London club founded in 1985 for writers, artists, publishers and those working generally in the arts and media. Its name alludes to the celebrated comment by the comedian Groucho Marx (1890–1977) that he would never join any club that would have him as a member. *See* MARX BROTHERS.

Ground control. The personnel and equipment at an airbase or launch site that monitor and control the flight of aircraft or spacecraft.

Groundhog Day. A film comedy (1993) adapted by Danny Rubin and Harold Ramis from a story by Rubin about an obnoxious television weather presenter (Bill Murray) who finds himself reliving the same day over and over again until he becomes a better person. In the United States Groundhog Day is Candlemas Day (2 February), the name deriving from the saying that the groundhog first appears from hibernation on that day. If he sees his shadow, he goes back to his burrow for another six weeks, indicating six more weeks of winter weather. The general idea is that a sunny day (when he sees his shadow) means a late spring, whereas a cloudy day (when he does not see it) means an early spring.

Groundnut scheme. Figuratively, an expensive failure or ill-considered enterprise. The reference is to a hastily organized and badly planned British government scheme (1947) to clear large areas of hitherto unprofitable land in Africa to grow groundnuts. The venture was abandoned three years later at considerable cost to the taxpayer.

Group of Eight. A name for the eight leading industrialized nations: Canada, France, Germany, Italy, Japan, Russia, the United Kingdom and the United States. Until Russia joined in 1998 the group was known as the GROUP OF SEVEN, a label still current for the original seven as a financial entity. The name is often abbreviated to G8.

Group of Seven. A name for the seven leading industrialized nations: Germany, Canada, the United States, France, the United Kingdom, Italy and Japan. Russia joined the group in 1998 to form the GROUP OF EIGHT but the finance ministers of the original countries still meet independently to coordinate their economic policy and as such continue to be known as the Group of Seven or G7.

> Human chain increases debt pressure on G7.
> *The Times* (headline) (14 June 1999)

Group therapy. A form of psychiatric therapy originally introduced in the United States by Joseph H. Pratt (1872–1942). Instead of meeting the therapist individually, several patients come together in a group to describe and discuss their problems. A therapist usually guides the proceedings and in many cases patients have a problem in common, such as alcoholism or bereavement.

Grove Family, The. The first authentic British SOAP OPERA, screened from 1954 to 1957 and centring on the domestic and social concerns of a lower middle-class family from Hendon. The family, named after the BBC's Lime Grove studios, consisted of Mr and Mrs Grove, librarian daughter Pat, National Serviceman son Jack, younger son Lenny and irascible Gran.

Grovel, grovel. A phrase first current in the 1960s to express an apology or a fawning request.

Growing experience. American PSYCHOBABBLE for a salutary factor extracted from a misfortune, 'bad turned to good'. The American show business couple David and Talia Shire were quoted in 1984 as saying of their 'very loving separation': 'We're going to rotate the house and we even rotate the cars. We've been separated for four months and it's a growing experience' (quoted by William Safire in *New York Times Magazine*, 20 January 1980). The reference is to the lessons that a growing child can learn from his or her mistakes.

Growing pains. A figurative expression dating from the early 20th century for the difficulties experienced in the early stages of an enterprise, such as the setting up of a new business. Literal growing pains are the vague aches and pains occurring in the limbs of young children. Their cause is unknown, and they do not seem to be related to the process of growth itself. The term is also used for sexual stirrings in one's teens.

Gruesome twosome. A phrase originating with black Americans in the 1940s to express two people in a relationship, neither of them necessarily gruesome. A FEARSOME FOURSOME is also sometimes similarly heard for a group of four, as in mixed doubles at tennis.

Grumbling appendix. One that gives intermittent discomfort without actually flaring into appendicitis. The term dates from the 1930s.

Grunge. A style of rock music characterized by a raucous guitar sound and lazy vocal delivery. It emerged in the United States in the early 1990s and was typified by Nirvana's 1992 hit 'Smells Like Teen Spirit'. The term was subsequently extended to apply to clothing evoking impoverishment, such as ill-fitting jackets, moth-eaten sweaters, ripped jeans or 'clumpy' shoes. The word was originally adjectival, as 'grungy', and seems to have evolved as a blend of 'grubby' and 'dingy' with, at least in Britain, a further touch of 'gunge'.

Grunt work. Any dull but necessary work, especially when menial or undemanding. The phrase is associated with 'grunt' as a US slang word for an infantry soldier, perhaps referring to his endless muttering and complaining. There is also perhaps a suggestion of 'groundwork', as preliminary or basic work which can be physically and mentally wearing but which is essential for the building of a firm and durable edifice, whether literal or figurative.

G7. *See* GROUP OF SEVEN.

G-spot. A sensitive area, literal or figurative, that reacts uncontrollably to excitation or stimulation. The origin is in the Gräfenberg spot, a site in the vagina identified by the German-born American gynaecologist Ernst Gräfenberg (1881–1957) as highly erogenous. The transferred use of the term evolved in the late 1980s.

Guardian Angels. A citizen vigilante group founded in New York City in 1979. Wearing their maroon berets they ride the subway system in order to deter crime. Chapters have been founded in other US cities, but an attempt to establish a chapter in London in 1989 came to nothing.

Guernica. Perhaps the most famous painting of the 20th century, the great mural was painted by Pablo Picasso (1881–1973) in 1937 in horrified protest at a notorious atrocity in the Spanish Civil War. On 27 April 1937 bombers of the German Kondor Legion, in support of Franco's nationalists, destroyed the ancient Basque capital of Guernica, causing many civilian casualties. Picasso's stark monochromatic painting has become a symbol of the barbarity of modern warfare. The name of the village itself happens to evoke its subject: Spanish *guerra* and French *guerre* both mean 'war'. There is a (probably apocryphal) story that while Picasso was living in Paris in the Second World War, a Gestapo officer visited his studio. Looking at the canvas of *Guernica*, the Nazi asked, 'Did you do that?' 'No,' Picasso replied, 'You did.'

Guerrilla Girls. A group of women artists founded in New York in 1984 to combat what they saw as sexism and racism in the art world. Members appeared on television, wearing gorilla masks to hide their identity, and distributed leaflets and posters to advertise their cause. One of their posters showed a reclining female nude by Ingres with the woman's head replaced by that of a gorilla and an accompanying text: 'Do women have to be naked to get into the Met.

Museum? Less than 5 per cent of the artists in the Modern Art Sections are women, but 85 per cent of the nudes are female.' The group's activities were documented in a book called *Confessions of the Guerrilla Girls (Whoever They Really Are)* (1995).

Guest beer. A term dating from the 1970s either for a beer available only temporarily in a pub which is a free house, or in the case of a tied house for a beer offered in addition to those produced by the particular brewers. In the latter case the guest beer is usually an independent REAL ALE.

Guide dogs. Dogs were first specially trained to guide the blind in the First World War, when they were schooled to work with blinded German soldiers. Special organizations were later set up to provide such dogs, two of the best known being the SEEING EYE in the United States and, from 1931, the Guide Dogs for the Blind Association in Britain. Several breeds have been trained for the work, but German shepherds (Alsatians) are generally favoured as the most proficient.

Guildford Four. On 5 October 1974 two IRA bombs killed five people in two Guildford pubs. A month later two were killed in an IRA bomb attack on a Woolwich pub. Patrick Armstrong, Gerald Conlon, Paul Hill and Carole Richardson were subsequently arrested, charged with murder in both incidents and sentenced to life imprisonment. Irregularities in police evidence resulted in the release of all four in 1989. *In the Name of the Father*, a 1993 film based on the case, explored movingly the relationship between Gerald Conlon and his sick father, but was described by one critic as 'unashamed Irish myth-making' on account of the inaccuracies of its court-room denouement. *See also* BIRMINGHAM SIX; BRIDGEWATER THREE; WINCHESTER THREE.

Guinea pig. A person or thing used as a subject for experiment, as guinea pigs were formerly by vivisectionists. The use of the animal's name in this way dates from the 1920s. In the Second World War the term was specifically applied to RAF pilots suffering from burns when treated at the Queen Victoria Hospital, East Grinstead, under the pioneering plastic surgeon Sir Archibald McIndoe. A Guinea Pig Club, headed by a Chief Guinea Pig, was subsequently formed to care for their welfare.

> We're all of us guinea pigs in the laboratory of God. Humanity is just a work in progress.
> TENNESSEE WILLIAMS: *Camino Real*, Block xii (1953)

Guinness Book of Records. An annual record of the superlative or 'mostest' in every conceivable field, first published in 1955. The germ of its creation was a shooting party in County Wexford, Ireland, in 1951, during which Sir Hugh Beaver, managing director of the brewery Arthur Guinness & Co. Ltd, was involved in a dispute as to whether the golden plover was Europe's fastest game bird. He realized that the answer was best found among people in pubs, and that a book which provided the answers for similar pub debates would be of benefit to licensees. The future athlete Chris Chataway, then an underbrewer with Guinness, recommended two friends to produce such a book, the twins Norris and Ross McWhirter, whom he had met at athletics events. They were duly commissioned and the first copy of the book was bound on 27 August 1955. It now appears in its own pages as an all-time bestseller. The 1999 MILLENNIUM edition was retitled *Guinness World Records*.

Gulag. The abbreviation of Russian *Glavnoye upravleniye ispravitel'no-trudovykh lagerey*, 'Chief Administration for Corrective Labour Camps'. Such camps were a notorious feature of the Soviet Union from 1930 to 1955 and resulted in the deaths of thousands of prisoners. Their true nature was revealed to the public at large by Alexander Solzhenitsyn's *The* GULAG ARCHIPELAGO (1973).

Gulag Archipelago, The. A three-volume history (1974–78; in Russian as *Arkhipelag Gulag*, 1973–76) of the GULAG, the Soviet administrative department responsible for maintaining prisons and forced labour camps, by Alexander Solzhenitsyn. Having been awarded the NOBEL PRIZE for Literature (1970), the author was in 1974 deported after the publication in Paris of the first two volumes and the suicide of his former assistant who, after five days of interrogation by the KGB, had revealed where she had hidden a copy of the complete work.

Gulf War. A term for two conflicts in the Persian Gulf. The first, also known as the Iran–Iraq War, was that of 1980–88 between the named countries. It ended inconclusively after considerable hardship and losses on both sides. The second Gulf War was that of January and February 1991, when an international coalition of forces assembled in Saudi Arabia to force the withdrawal of Saddam Hussein's Iraqi forces from Kuwait, which they had invaded the previous year. *See also* DESERT RATS; DESERT SHIELD; DESERT STORM; GULF WAR SYNDROME.

Gulf War syndrome. A name for a disorder of the nervous system alleged to have been contracted by soldiers serving in the second GULF WAR (1991). It was initially questioned whether such a syndrome actually existed, but when physical evidence was produced, a search for a possible physical cause began. Attribution was made either to anti-nerve-gas medication administered to troops before service in the Gulf or to exposure to harmful chemicals during such service.

Gummidge, Worzel. (1) The scarecrow who comes to life in the children's books by Barbara Euphan Todd, beginning with the one that bears his name (1936). He normally stands in the Ten-Acre Field at Scatterbrook Farm but in his alter ego becomes involved in a host of comic adventures. He was a popular figure on CHILDREN'S HOUR and in a television series (1978–81) was convincingly played by Jon Pertwee.

(2) The nickname Worzel Gummidge was at one time applied to Michael Foot (b.1913), left-wing leader of the LABOUR PARTY (1980–83), admired for his convictions, oratory, writings and intellect, but not for his powers of leadership (his stewardship saw Labour at its most divided) or for his sartorial elegance. It was the absence of the latter characteristic that led *Private Eye* and others to confer the nickname. In 1982 Foot appeared at the REMEMBRANCE DAY ceremony dressed in what his opponents unkindly described as a donkey jacket, recalling the shock caused almost a century before when QUEER HARDIE turned up to take his seat in the Commons wearing a cloth cap. The American novelist Norman Mailer likened his appearance to that of 'an eccentric professor of ornithology'.

Gunboat diplomacy. A foreign policy supported by the use or threat of military force. Gunboats go back to the 18th century, but the phrase dates only from the 1920s and was originally applied in the US press to foreign intervention in China.

Gun for, To. To 'have it in for' someone. The image is of a Western gun-fighter pursuing his prey.

Gung-ho. Excessively or unthinkingly eager, especially in the context of patriotism and military aggression. The term dates from the Second World War when it was adopted as a slogan by US Marines as a pidgin English form of Mandarin Chinese *kung, gonghé*, literally 'work together'.

Guns of Navarone, The. A thriller (1957) by Alistair Maclean (1922–87). An international team of commandos in the Second World War attempts to destroy a battery of heavy naval guns at the Greek fortress of Navarone, with the Germans on their trail, before an Allied invasion fleet passes within range. An ambitiously heroic film version (1961) was directed by J. Lee-Thompson.

Guns or butter. When a nation is at war a choice of priorities has to be made between material comforts and a contribution to the war effort. In NAZI Germany Hermann Goering summarized the situation in a speech at Hamburg in 1936: 'We have no butter … but I ask you – would you rather have butter or guns? … Preparedness makes us powerful. Butter merely makes us fat' (quoted in W. Frischauer, *Goering*, ch x, 1951). Joseph Goebbels had earlier made the same specific comparison in a speech in Berlin on 17 January 1936:

> Ohne Butter werden wir fertig, aber nicht, beispielsweise, ohne Kanonen. Wenn wir einmal überfallen werden, dann können wir uns nicht mit Butter, sondern nur mit Kanonen verteidigen. ('We can manage without butter but not, for example, without guns. If we are attacked we cannot defend ourselves with butter, only with guns.')
> *Deutsche Allgemeine Zeitung* (18 January 1936)

Gurrelieder. An early Wagnerian-style extravaganza by Arnold Schoenberg (1874–1951). It was completed in 1911 and is scored for five solo singers, three male choruses, one mixed chorus, a narrator and a vast orchestra, which includes a set of iron chains. The title means 'Songs of Gurra', and the text is a German translation of poems by the Danish poet J.P. Jacobsen (1847–85). Gurra itself is a 14th-century castle, in which lives the heroine Tove, who is loved by the Danish king, Waldemar IV. In his memoirs *The Tongs and the Bones* (1981) Lord Harewood wrote of the piece: 'A proof if you want it – and I often do – that Schoenberg could, as they used to say about Picasso, draw when he wanted to.'

Guru. Properly, a Hindu spiritual teacher, from a Sanskrit word meaning 'grave', 'weighty', but in modern times a general term for any influential teacher, leader or expert.

> [Theatre director Peter] Brook does not like being called a guru, but in its pure sense as a guide to inner equilibrium, a collaborator in the search for a way to conduct yourself in your vocation, the word applies to him perfectly.
> *Sunday Times* (10 May 1998)

Gussied up. Dressed up in one's best clothes, as for a night out. The origin may lie in Gussie, a pet form of the name Augustus, current in the early 20th century for an effeminate man. Some see a source in 'gusset', as a piece of material sewn into a garment to allow for freedom of movement. *See also* GORGEOUS GUSSIE.

Gustav Line (German *Gustav Linie*). A heavily fortified defensive line built across Italy by the Germans in the winter of 1943–44. The line stretched across Italy south of Rome and north of Naples, extending from the mouth of the River Garigliano on the west coast to the mouth of the Sangro on the east coast, and included the key position on the hilltop monastery of Monte Cassino, the capture of which cost so many Allied lives in the first half of 1944. *See also* GOTHIC LINE.

Gut reaction. An instinctive or emotional reaction, as opposed to a rational or considered one. A 'gut feeling' is similarly instinctive or intuitive. Expressions of this type date from the 1960s.

> [*Yorkshire Evening Post* editor Neil] Hodgkinson also admits to a gut feeling that a tabloid was the right solution for Britain's ninth bestselling evening paper serving a vibrant city.
> *The Times* (17 September 1999)

Gut rot. A colloquial term for stomach ache or an upset stomach.

Gutted. Bitterly disappointed; devastated. A colloquialism dating from the 1980s that came to be mainly associated with sports players and media celebrities. The sensation is similar to receiving a blow in the guts.

> They all really wanted to see Gizz's band, but due to Break for the Border's policy of only admitting over 21s, they couldn't go. They were gutted, and we were gutted for them.
> *Stamford Herald and Post* (10 June 1999)

Guys and Dolls. A musical comedy (1950) with music and lyrics by Frank Loesser (1910–69) and book by Jo Swerling and Abe Burrows about the romance that develops between a Salvation Army worker (representing the 'dolls') and gambler Sky Masterson (representing the 'guys'). Filmed in 1955 with Frank Sinatra, Marlon Brando and Jean Simmons, it was based on stories by Damon Runyon (1884–1946).

Guzzle guts. A greedy person. A term used mainly among children and dating from the 1950s, when it arose as a variant of the much older 'greedy guts'.

Gymslip mum. A teenage girl who bears a child while still at school. Gymslips or gym tunics were invented in 1893 by a student at Hampstead College of Physical Education and although originally designed specifically for physical activities in a gymnasium rapidly became a standard girls' school uniform. Their use declined in the Second World War although they were still worn in some of the more traditional schools well into the 1950s. The stock phrase preserves the memory of their existence.

> Today, Clare, Chris and Linda open their hearts to *The People* to reveal how they coped from the moment Linda discovered her daughter was about to become a gymslip mum.
> *People* (30 April 1995)

Gypsy. A musical comedy (1959) with a score by Jule Styne (1905–94), lyrics by Stephen Sondheim (b.1930) and book by Arthur Laurents, telling the story of a vaudeville entertainer who with the encouragement of her ambitious mother builds a reputation as a striptease artist. The show, which furnished Ethel Merman with one of her best roles as the mother, was based on the career of the real-life striptease dancer Gypsy Rose Lee (1914–70).

H

Haberdasher Harry. *See* GIVE-'EM-HELL HARRY.

Hackette. A mostly derogatory media nickname for a female journalist, with the feminine suffix '-ette', as in 'usherette', added to 'hack' as term for a male journalist who produces dull or unoriginal work, just as a hack is or was an ordinary horse for riding. The word was popularized by its use in *Private Eye*. The gossip columnist Lady Olga Maitland (b.1944) was nicknamed the 'Fragrant Hackette'.

> Perhaps Mr Cameron was misquoted, or plied with drink and led on by a *Sunday Times* hackette.
> *Listener* (16 May 1985)

Haganah (Hebrew, 'defence'). A Zionist military organization set up by Jewish settlers in Palestine in 1920 to protect themselves from attacks by Palestinian Arabs. When the British authorities began to take harsh measures to restrict Jewish immigration after the Second World War the Haganah embarked on a sabotage campaign. In 1947, after the United Nations determined on the partition of Palestine, the Haganah became involved in open conflict with the British and with Palestinian Arabs. On the creation of the Jewish state of Israel in 1948 the Haganah was turned into the official army. The Israeli armed forces are called Tzva Haganah le Yisra'el (Hebrew, 'Israel defence forces'). *See also* DEIR YASSIN; IRGUN; STERN GANG.

Haigspeak. Obfuscatory or convoluted speech, of the kind supposedly typified by Alexander Haig (b.1924), especially in his dealings with the press when US secretary of state (1981–82).

Hair. *See* ROCK OPERA.

Hairdressers' names. Many modern hairdressers devise a punning name for their salon that is as artistically apt as the styles they pride themselves on creating. One need only look under 'Hairdressers' in the local YELLOW PAGES to find premises called 'Cut Above', 'Face Value', 'Hair We Go', 'In the Pink', or 'Turning Heads'. The following real examples of American and British salons with names of this type are from Paul Dickson's *What's In a Name?* (1996):

> About Faces, Best Little Hairhouse in Town, Beyond the Fringe, Clip Joint, Curl Up 'n Dye, Do Yer Nut, Hair Apparent, Headmasters, Julius Scissors, Kiss My Act, Lockworks, Loose Ends, Makin' Waves, Mane Attraction, Off the Top, Shear Artistry, Short Cut, Streaks Ahead.

Haka. A Maori ceremonial war dance involving chanting. The ALL BLACKS rugby team dance a version of it before a match as a challenge to the opposing team and first performed it internationally in 1888, when the 'Natives' toured New Zealand, Australia and Britain. The chanted words are: 'Ka mate ka mate, ka ora ka mate ka mate, ka ora tenie tengata, puhuru huru nana e piki mai, whaka whiti te ra hupanei, hupanei, hupanei kaupanei whiti te ra' ('There is going to be a fight between us. May it mean death to you and life to us. We will fight on, or until our side is vanquished. So long as the daylight lasts. We are here to continue the battle. To be either killed or to be victorious.')

HAL. The computer on board the spaceship *Discovery* in Arthur C. Clarke's novel 2001: A SPACE ODYSSEY (1968), based on his early story 'The Sentinel' (1951), and widely popularized by the spectacular film released simultaneously with it. HAL 9000, as an artificial intelligence, has been sent with a three-man crew to locate the origin of an alien monolith found on the Moon. HAL malfunctions, plans to take over the mission, and murders two of the crew members. The remaining member, David Bowman, dismantles the computer's memory, effectively 'killing' HAL. The scene in which HAL regresses to infancy, singing 'Daisy, Daisy', is curiously moving. HAL's name is an acronym of '*h*euristically programmed *a*lgorithmic computer', and the letters themselves are one alphabetical place short of IBM.

Haldane principle. The principle that government research agencies should be completely separated from government departments that benefit from their research. The name is that of the geneticist J.B.S. Haldane (1892–1964), chairman of the committee that formulated the principle in 1966.

Half a Sixpence. A musical comedy (1963) with music and lyrics by David Heneker (b.1906) about a poor young man who wins a fortune, loses it and is finally redeemed by his love for his wife. Based on the novel *Kipps* by H.G. Wells, the title refers to the sixpence that the two lovers split in two, each keeping half to remind themselves of the other.

Halitosis Hall. A nickname given to the House of Commons in *Private Eye*'s 'Dear Bill' letters, purportedly written by Denis Thatcher (b.1915), husband of the IRON LADY, to William (now Lord) Deedes (b.1913), editor of the *Daily Telegraph* (1974–86). The name echoes the titles of various satirical novels by Thomas Love Peacock (1785–1866), such as *Headlong Hall* (1816), *Nightmare Abbey* (1818), *Crotchet Castle* (1831) and *Gryll Grange* (1860).

Hall of Fame. A place where famous persons are commemorated by busts or plaques, as especially in the USA. Two of the best known are the Hall of Fame for Great Americans in the Bronx, New York City, founded in 1900 and dedicated on 30 May 1901 by Henry M. MacCracken, president of New York University, and the National Baseball Hall of Fame and Museum at Cooperstown, New York, founded in 1936 and dedicated on 12 June 1939, the centenary of the supposed invention of baseball by the US Army officer Abner Doubleday (1819–93).

Hamas (Arabic, 'zeal'). The Palestinian Islamic fundamentalist movement so named, calling for the creation of a Palestinian state founded on religious principles, first came to prominence in the GAZA STRIP in the 1980s. An impetus to its campaign came in 1988 when the Palestinian Liberation Organization (PLO) recognized Israel's right to exist. It has consistently opposed both the PLO and Israel, and boycotted the first Palestinian elections in 1996. Its name has also been interpreted as an acronym of *harakat al-Muqawama al-Islamiyya*, 'Islamic Resistance Movement'.

Hamburger. This popular American dish of fried minced beef, onion, egg and so forth, made into a flat cake, takes its name from Hamburg in Germany. It appears to have originated in the Baltic region some centuries ago, and it was introduced into America in the 19th century by immigrants from the port of Hamburg and subsequently 'naturalized'. The beefburger came to be so called by caterers to avoid confusion by association with ham. There are now various types of burgers with the first part of the name indicating the chief constituent. Examples are cheeseburger, chickenburger, steakburger, vegeburger. *See also* BIG MAC; FAST FOOD; JUNK FOOD; McDONALD'S.

Hammer, The. A nickname given by the *Scottish Daily Express* to Sir David McNee (b.1925), Commissioner of the Metropolitan Police from 1977 to 1982, for his tough approach to law and order when a senior detective in Glasgow. The name alludes to the historical 'Hammer of the Scots', otherwise Edward I of England (1272–1307).

Hammer, Mike. The tough and amoral detective in a series of violent thrillers by Mickey Spillane, beginning with I, THE JURY (1947). He butts and bludgeons his way through the various cases, is brutal towards women, and has a particular antipathy for communists. Film and television versions of some of the stories followed in due course. *See also* KISS ME DEADLY.

Hammer and sickle. The emblem of the former USSR, symbolic of the union under communism of workers in the factory and peasants on the land. The Russians themselves always referred to the emblem as 'Sickle and Hammer' (*Serp i molot*).

Hammer Films. In financial terms one of the most successful companies in the history of the British cinema. It was founded in 1947 by Will Hammer (real name William Hinds) and Sir James Carreras and first won fame in 1956 when it launched a cycle of low-budget HORROR MOVIES that quickly captured wide markets in Britain and the United States. It emphasized blood and gore in vivid colour and revived such figures from the American cinema as Frankenstein and Dracula. It then expanded into other genres such as SCIENCE FICTION, psychological thrillers and costume dramas. In 1980 it produced an anthology of spine-chilling 'shockers' for television under the title *Hammer House* *of Horror*. The name is a byword for any 'grim' situation, literal or metaphorical.

Hammond organ. The once ubiquitous electric organ of this name was the invention in 1929 of the American mechanical engineer Laurens Hammond (1895–1973), who in the same year set up the Hammond Instrument Co. of Chicago to manufacture it. It was favoured by dance bands since its varying tones could be used to back a small group of players, while it was popularized as a solo instrument by performers such as Ethel Smith in America and Harry Farmer in Britain. Several variations on the original model were subsequently produced.

Hampstead set. A term originally applied in the 1950s to a group of supporters of Hugh Gaitskill (1906–63), leader of the Labour Party (1955–63). The group, opposed by NYE Bevan and his followers, lived, like Gaitskill, in the wealthy area of Hampstead in north London. The group included Anthony Crosland, Denis Healey (*see* GROMYKO OF THE LABOUR PARTY), Douglas Jay, Roy Jenkins (*see* WOY) and Frank Pakenham (*see* LORD PORN). Subsequently, journalists have used the term more generally and collectively for liberal and/or left-leaning intellectuals living in and around Hampstead, such as the playwright Harold Pinter (b.1930) and historical biographer Antonia Fraser (b.1932), who have been involved in fashionable causes such as CHARTER 88, and are deemed a subset of the CHATTERING CLASSES.

Hamptons, The. The popular name of the eastern end of Long Island, New York City, where the resort villages of Westhampton, Southampton, Bridgehampton, East Hampton and Hampton Bays are located, among others. Nicknamed 'Hollywood East' (*see also* GREAT COMMUNICATOR), the area is a summer retreat for wealthy New Yorkers, including many celebrities, and the leading summer social event is a glittering charity benefit. The August 1999 issue of *The Tatler* somewhat unexpectedly nominated West Wittering, West Sussex, as the English answer to the Hamptons, but 'without its pretentiousness'.

Hancock's Half-Hour. A classic television comedy series screened from 1956 to 1961 and starring the popular actor Tony Hancock (1924–68), famous for his lugubrious buffoonishness. His gradual decline and early death from alcoholism added a note of genuine poignancy to his finely judged roles, one of the most memorable being that of a timorous blood donor.

Hancock's fictitious address, 23 Railways Cuttings, East Cheam, was equally savoured by his fans.

Handbag, To. To attack. The colloquialism relates specifically to women (who carry a handbag) and became associated in particular with the prime ministerial period of office (1979–90) of Margaret Thatcher (*see* IRON LADY), who was depicted in cartoons as hitting opponents with her omnipresent handbag. This method of assault is not of course new, and in *The* MUPPET SHOW the leading lady, Miss Piggy, although normally composed, was prone to felling with her handbag anyone who offended her.

Hand in the till. *See* FINGERS IN THE TILL.

Hand it to someone, To. To recognize their achievement, as: 'I've got to hand it to you, you were easily the best.' The image is of handing the person an award. The phrase is of American origin.

Handlebar moustache. A wide, thick moustache with the ends curving slightly upwards. The term dates from the 1930s and probably relates more to the motorcycle than the bicycle.

> Handle-bar moustaches show the extrovert or suggest an inferiority complex.
> GUY EGMONT: *The Art of Egmontese*, ch i (1961)

Hand of God. A name for the goal scored in the 51st minute by the Argentine player Diego Maradona in the football World Cup quarter-final against England at Mexico City in 1986. Maradona quite clearly punched the ball into the net ahead of the England goalkeeper Peter Shilton. The infringement enabled Argentina to win 2–1 and Maradona was quoted afterwards as saying that the goal was 'a little bit of Maradona's head [*sic*], a little bit of the hand of God'.

Hand-Reared Boy, The. A novel (1970) by Brian Aldiss (b.1925), the first in a trilogy. It unashamedly charts the early life and progress of Horatio Stubbs, a compulsive masturbator who eventually achieves relief through a torrid affair with his school matron, an experience apparently enjoyed also by Aldiss, according to his autobiographical study, *The Twinkling of an Eye* (1998). In Stubbs's case, the romance has an unhappy conclusion. 'Hand-Reared' has punning connotations. *See also* PORTNOY'S COMPLAINT.

Hands Across America. A human chain of some 6 million people was formed on 25 May 1986 to raise money and awareness in the cause of homelessness. Apart from some unavoidable breaks in desert areas, the hand-to-hand line extended from New York to Long Beach, California.

Hand or **give someone something on a plate, To.** To give it to them with little or no effort on their part. The allusion is to a plate of food served up ready to eat. The phrase dates from the 1920s.

Hands-on. A term originating in the late 1960s and at first applied to the direct operation of a computer by using a keyboard, as distinct from a theoretical understanding of the process. The term then extended in meaning to apply to active participation in any area of knowledge, whether actually using the hands or not, especially one traditionally regarded as academic.

> 'Hands-on archaeology' is being offered [to young people] at Bignor Roman Villa and the Fishbourne Roman Palace, both in West Sussex.
>
> *The Times* (19 July 1999)

Hang in there, To. To stick with it, even when the going is tough. The allusion is probably to the boxing ring, where a boxer getting the worst of it may seek relief by clinging on to his opponent or to the ropes. After such a brief respite, he is better able to continue.

> 'No, no,' said Simon. 'I'll hang in there now that I've waited this long.'
>
> JEFFREY ARCHER: *First among Equals*, ch xii (1984)

Hang left or **right, To.** To make a left or right turn, especially in motoring or skiing. A variant is 'to hang a left' etc. The expression is of American origin and dates from the 1960s.

> 'Hang a right on Santa Monica Freeway, hang a left on Harbour and another right on Sixth Street.' If you hang lefts where you were told to hang rights, the freeway system is unforgiving.
>
> *Sunday Telegraph* (29 July 1984)

Hang loose, To. To have a relaxed attitude to everything. The expression probably originated in sport, where one often performs better if one is not tense.

Hangman, The. A nickname given to the high-ranking SS officer Reinhard Heydrich (1904–42), also known as the Butcher of Prague. He became Reichsprotektor for Bohemia and Moravia in 1941, and within five weeks he had ordered the execution of some 300 Czechs. He also headed the notorious Wannsee Conference, which determined the so-called FINAL SOLUTION. His assassination in 1942 by Czech resistance fighters led to hundreds of Czechs being executed in retaliation, and the wiping out of the entire village of LIDICE.

Hang or **hold on to your hat!** Stand by for a surprise! Get ready for a shock! A stock warning of unexpected news dating from the early years of the 20th century and perhaps having its origins in a rollercoaster ride, where one would indeed need to hold on to one's hat, if wearing one.

Hangover Square. A thriller (1941) by Patrick Hamilton (1904–62), subtitled *A Story of Darkest Earl's Court*, an area in west London. A schizophrenic haunts the streets and public houses in an almost perpetual hangover, obsessed, in his lost periods, with murdering the woman he loves. The title puns on London's Hanover Square.

Hang right, To. *See* HANG LEFT.

Hang-up. An emotional problem or inhibition; a mental block. A phrase dating from the counterculture of the 1960s.

Hannay, Richard. *See* THIRTY-NINE STEPS.

Hanoi Jane. A hostile nickname given by right-wing US critics to the film star Jane Fonda (b.1937), whose support for radical and left-wing causes included a visit to Hanoi, the capital of communist North Vietnam, at the time of the VIETNAM War. She made a documentary about this visit, *Introduction to the Enemy*, in 1974. Earlier she had formed the Anti-War Troupe with Canadian actor Donald Sutherland, which gave performances at army bases despite the Pentagon's attempts to stop them. Her documentary about this tour (1972) was entitled *F.T.A.* (*Free the Army*).

Happening. An all-embracing word describing a partly improvised or spontaneous piece of theatrical or pseudo-theatrical performance, especially when involving audience participation. The term arose in the 1950s in the world of American avant-garde art. Happenings became a regular feature of FRINGE performances at the Edinburgh Festival. One such, organized by the American director Kenneth Dewey, involving the wheeling of a naked model on a trolley across the organ gallery of the McEwan Hall in the midst of the 1963 International Drama Conference. The conference organizer, John Calder, and the model, Anna Kesselaar, were charged with indecency. The event caused a publicity storm but was a landmark of its kind. The concept of the happening was seized on internationally and the term adopted untranslated, as French *le happening*, German *das Happening*, Italian *il happening*, Russian *kheppening*, Japanese *hapuningu*.

Happiness is a Warm Gun. A darkly ironic and ambiguous song by the BEATLES, credited to John Lennon and Paul McCartney. It appears on the so-called WHITE ALBUM, released in November 1968. The title originally derives from a slogan used by the US

National Rifle Association ('Happiness is a warm gun in your hand'), which greatly shocked Lennon. Given that 'gun' is an established slang term for both the male member and a hypodermic syringe, the song's title (and its lyrics) are clearly open to a variety of interpretations. *See also* HAPPINESS IS A WARM PUPPY.

Happiness is a warm puppy. A twee truism made popular by the title of Charles M. Schulz's bestselling book of 1962 centring on his cartoon puppy SNOOPY and itself evolving from a caption to a panel in an earlier strip showing a small child hugging the dog. The phrase spawned a raft of advertising slogans, since 'happiness' is the goal of all manufacturers and service providers. Among them were 'Happiness is egg-shaped' (British eggs), 'Happiness is a quick-starting car' (Esso petrol), 'Happiness is a cigar called Hamlet' (first in 1964), 'Happiness is a warm ear-piece', 'Happiness is being elected captain – and getting a Bulova watch', 'Happiness is a $49 table' (Brancusi furniture), 'Happiness is giving Dad a Terry Shave Coat for Christmas' (Con Sporterry), 'Happiness is the Sands' (a Las Vegas hotel), 'Happiness is a bathroom by Marion Wieder' (a firm of US decorators) and 'Happiness can be the color of her hair' (Miss Clairol). The words equally suggested themselves to motorists as suitable bumper-sticker fodder, as 'Happiness is being single', 'Happiness is seeing Lubbock, Texas, in the rear view mirror' (a line from a COUNTRY AND WESTERN song), 'Happiness is Slough in my rear-view mirror', HAPPINESS IS A WARM GUN (title of a song of 1968 by John Lennon), 'Happiness is Wren-shaped' (i.e. in the mould of the WRENS rather than the birds) and dozens on the same lines.

> We have lived through the era when happiness was a warm puppy, and the era when happiness was a dry martini, and now we have come to the era when happiness is 'knowing what your uterus looks like'.
> NORA EPHRON: *Crazy Salad*, 'Vaginal Politics' (1975)

Happy as Alice. Very happy. A phrase varying the gender of the male HAPPY AS LARRY.

> For two days I panicked. Then they ran another scan and it had gone. I have been as happy as Alice ever since.
> *The Times* (26 May 1999)

Happy as Larry. Very happy. An Australian expression. It is suggested that the original Larry may have been Larry Foley (1847–1917), the noted boxer, but the word may actually derive from 'larrikin', an Australian term for an unruly young man.

Happy birthday! A greeting to someone on their birthday. The birthday greeting song 'Happy Birthday to You', with the person's name inserted in the third line after 'Dear', was originally a children's song, 'Good Morning to You', written in 1893, with words by the American kindergarten educator Patty Smith Hill (1868–1946) and music by her sister, Mildred J. Hill. The present words by Clayton F. Summy were substituted in 1935.

Happy camper. US campus slang of the 1980s for a contented person, the reference being to a holiday camp. The expression is frequently found in the negative for a dissatisfied or unhappy person, 'not a happy camper'. The flippancy of the phrase may hide a heaviness of heart.

Happy clappy. A term descriptive of a type of evangelical religious worship, with joyful hymn singing accompanied by rhythmic clapping. The phrase caught on in the early 1990s.

> Holy Trinity, Brompton, one of the largest happy-clappy (and one of the poshest) churches in London.
> *Independent* (21 July 1992)

Happy Days. A play (1961) by the Irish playwright Samuel Beckett (1906–89) in which the two characters, Winnie and her husband Willie, babble incoherently but evocatively as they are gradually buried up to their necks in sand. The deeper Winnie is buried in the sand, the more ludicrous her chaotic optimism becomes:

> Oh this is a happy day, this will have been another happy day!

Happy hour. An hour when a pub or bar sells drinks at reduced prices, the idea being that patrons will consume more than usual and stay on to buy drinks when they revert to full price. The period may well be longer than just a single hour. The phrase originated in the 1950s as a US Navy term for a scheduled time of entertainment and refreshment.

Happy landings! A toast when drinking, especially among aircraft pilots.

Happy Valley. A place where people live or work in peace and contentment. The term can be applied ironically. In the Second World War RAF pilots so named the Ruhr, as a much bombed area. In Hong Kong, on the other hand, Happy Valley is the site of a famous racecourse, its Chinese name being Wong Nei Chong Valley, while in Labrador, Canada, Happy

Valley is a residential district established in 1970 for families of a local military base. The name ultimately comes from Dr Johnson's prose romance *Rasselas* (1759), the story of a prince of Abyssinia who, weary of the joys of the 'happy valley' where the inhabitants know only 'the soft vicissitudes of pleasure and repose', travels far and wide in search of true happiness. In the ROARING TWENTIES Happy Valley was the name of a loose gathering of dissolute aristocrats and playboys in colonial Kenya headed by the handsome philanderer Lord Erroll, otherwise John Carberry, formerly Baron Carbery of Castle Freke, Ireland, whose murder by Sir Jock Delves Broughton in 1941 was a *cause célèbre* of the day, and formed the subject of the 1987 film *White Mischief*. *Happy Valley* (1939) is also the ironic title of the first novel of the Australian writer Patrick White.

Happy Warrior. The nickname of the US Democratic politician Al (Alfred Emmanuel) Smith (1873–1944). When Franklin Roosevelt, FDR, spoke in support of his bid to win the Democratic nomination to run for president in 1924, he described Smith as 'the happy warrior of the political battlefield'. Smith's bid was unsuccessful.

The nickname was later applied to the liberal Democratic politician Hubert Humphrey (1911–78). Humphrey was Lyndon Johnson's vice-president (1965–9), and ran unsuccessfully for president against Richard Nixon in 1968. When paying tribute to Humphrey in 1980 President Jimmy Carter eulogized him thus: 'The great president who might have been – Hubert Horatio Hornblower!' (inadvertently confusing Humphrey with the fictional naval hero of C.S. Forester's historical novels, set during the Napoleonic Wars). Humphrey himself was prone to gaffes: on hearing of the failed assassination attempt against President Gerald Ford in 1975 he commented: 'There are too many guns in the hands of people who don't know how to use them.' *See also* TRICKY DICKY.

Hard or **tough act to follow.** A performance or feat which it is difficult to emulate. The expression arose in the early 20th century from American vaudeville, originally as a description of a particularly good act that would make the one following it seem mediocre by comparison.

> [David] Attenborough, more than anyone else, has ensured that the second century of the broadcasting age has a hard act to follow.
> *Sunday Times* (2 January 2000)

Hard Day's Night, A. The name of a BEATLES film, its soundtrack album and title track, all of which were released in 1964. The film was still without a title when shooting began in March 1964, and 'A Hard Day's Night' is usually credited to the Beatles' drummer Ringo Starr, who apparently used the phrase to describe a particularly tiring day of filming. Other titles that were considered for the film included 'It's A Daft, Daft, Daft, Daft, Daft World', BEATLEMANIA and 'What Little Old Man?', the last being one of the first lines uttered in the film. The song is credited to John Lennon and Paul McCartney. The soundtrack album included the songs 'Can't Buy Me Love', 'Tell Me Why' and 'And I Love Her'.

Hard hat. American slang for someone with reactionary or conservative views. The allusion is to construction workers, known from their protective headgear as 'hard hats', who took a conservative stance during the social upheaval of the 1960s.

Hard Rain's A-Gonna Fall, A. An anti-war song by Bob Dylan, released in 1963 in the aftermath of the Cuban Missile Crisis, at the height of the COLD WAR. The 'hard rain' of the title is nuclear fallout, and prefigures the concept of NUCLEAR WINTER.

> Oh, where have you been, my blue-eyed son?
> Oh, where have you been, my darling young one?
> I've stumbled on the side of twelve misty mountains,
> I've walked and I've crawled on six crooked highways,
> I've stepped in the middle of seven sad forests,
> I've been out in front of a dozen dead oceans,
> I've been ten thousand miles in the mouth of a graveyard,
> And it's a hard, and it's a hard, it's a hard, and it's a hard,
> And it's a hard rain's a-gonna fall.

Hard rock. A type of highly amplified rock music with a heavy beat, popular in the latter half of the 1960s.

Hardy perennial. Horticulturally a herbaceous plant with a perennial rootstock, i.e. one that lasts for several years and that dies back in winter. Metaphorically a hardy perennial is a thing that irrevocably recurs, especially annually.

> We still have two other foolhardy perennials to look forward to: the [holiday] pictures of the PM's wife in a bikini … and pictures of the Prime Minister in slightly unflattering trousers.
> *The Times* (11 August 1999)

Hare Krishna. A sect devoted to the worship of the Hindu deity Krishna. It arose in the United States in 1966 as the International Society for Krishna Consciousness and claims a lineage of spiritual masters dating back to Caitanya (1485–1533), whom it regards as an incarnation of Krishna. It has become familiar to the public from the shaven-headed, saffron-robed young people who chant and clash cymbals as they weave their way along the city streets. The chant, known as the Maha ('Great') Mantra, gave the present name, and in full runs: 'Hare Krishna, Hare Krishna, Krishna, Krishna, Hare Hare.' This is repeated, substituting Rama, as the name of the second most popular Hindu deity, for Krishna every second verse. 'Hare' means 'O god'.

Harker, Kay. The hero of John Masefield's *The* MID-NIGHT FOLK (1927). He is an orphan who is brought up by an unpleasant governess. He also appears in the sequel *The* BOX OF DELIGHTS (1935).

Harkness Ballet. A noted American ballet company founded in 1964 by the composer and philanthropist Rebekah Harkness (1915–82). Its aim was to promote young American talents, but although much admired for the vitality of its dancers it was often criticized for its lack of artistic integrity. It was disbanded in 1970 but succeeded by a group of junior dancers from the Harkness House for Ballet Arts, founded in 1965, now granted senior status. This in turn disbanded in 1975. *See also* JOFFREY BALLET.

Harlem Globetrotters. The black professional American basketball team of this name was founded in 1927 by Abe Saperstein, a sports promoter. As players had no home base, they originally began touring the USA in Saperstein's car but later, as their name implies, travelled widely abroad. They are known for their spectacular ball handling and amusing antics, and play against a team called the 'Opposition', largely made up of white players, which never wins. Famous Globetrotters include Marques Haynes (b.1926), 'Meadowlark' Lemon (b.1933), the 'Clown Prince of Basketball', and Wilt 'the Stilt' Chamberlain (1936–99), 2.18m (7ft 2in) tall, regarded by many as the greatest basketball player of all time.

Harlem Renaissance. A term applied to a mainly literary artistic movement centred on New York's Harlem district in the 1920s. During this period, writers and artists generated a new aesthetic within African-American culture, one that reflected the opportunities and challenges facing a younger generation that was moving away from the rural south to northern districts of the city such as Harlem.

The idea of a 'Harlem Renaissance' gained currency following the publication in 1925 of *The New Negro* by Alain Locke (1885–1954). Locke studied at Oxford as the university's first African-American Rhodes Scholar (1907–10), and identified in the work of Harlem's artistic community 'a spiritual coming of age'. The Renaissance attracted criticism from conservative black community leaders and, at least briefly, the interest of white intellectuals. Always primarily concerned with the aesthetics of self-expression, the Renaissance lost momentum during the GREAT DEPRESSION.

Harlequin romances. The American equivalent of MILLS & BOON, in the form of cheaply priced romantic novels, first issued for the mass market in 1949. The protagonists were long in the mould 'dominant male, submissive female', but have recently become more of an equal match.

> The traditional Harlequin heroine is young, vulnerable, in a dead-end job; the hero is ten years older, arrogant and moody, as well as being rich and powerful. Sometimes he's brutal as well, alternating between kissing and hitting. But in the end the heroine learns that he's mocked her because he really loves her.
>
> EMILY TOTH in *Women's Review of Books* (February 1983)

Harley-Davidson. The famed American motorcycle, first produced in Milwaukee, Wisconsin, in 1903, is named after its designers, William Harley and the brothers Arthur, Walter and William Davidson. The low, loud Harley 'hog' became a lasting symbol of the wide-open American road.

Harry Lime. *See* LIME, HARRY.

Harry Potter. A boy-wizard whose adventures are chronicled in a commercially successful sequence of children's novels by J.K. Rowling (b.1965). The first novel in the series, *Harry Potter and the Philosopher's Stone* (1997), describes the orphaned Harry's rescue from the everyday world of boorish 'Muggles' (ordinary human beings) by Rubeus Hagrid, Keeper of Keys and Grounds at Hogwarts School of Witchcraft and Wizardry, and his subsequent experiences during his first year at the magical boarding-school. *Harry Potter and the Chamber of Secrets* (1998) and *Harry Potter and the Prisoner of Azkaban* (1999) describe, respectively, Harry's second and third years at Hogwarts. They were followed by *Harry Potter and the Goblet of*

Fire, a massive print-run of which was published amid a blaze of publicity in the summer of 2000.

The novels combine elements of the school story, the adventure story and the fantasy novel, and their imaginative richness and playful humour attracted an adulatory readership, both child and adult, from the outset. Hogwarts is both a fully realized imaginary world and a humorous reflection of the 'real', non-magical, world. It has its own house system (the four houses are Ravenclaw, Hufflepuff, Slytherin and Gryffindor, the last-named being Harry's house); school sport (a fast and violent game known as Quidditch, played in the air by teams mounted on broomsticks); and a curriculum that includes Potions (a nightmare version of chemistry), History of Magic, Charms, Divination, Transfiguration, and Defence Against the Dark Arts.

Hogwarts's strange blend of slapstick and menace is evident in its endlessly inventive nomenclature. Albus Dumbledore, the school's affable headmaster, combines Latin *albus* and the dialect word *dumbledore* to produce a name meaning, literally, 'white hedgehog'; Cornelius Fudge is the aptly named 'Minister of Magic'; Draco Malfoy, Harry's rival in Slytherin house, hints at Transylvanian malevolence and bad faith; while Voldemort, sinister 'fallen' alumnus of Hogwarts and mortal enemy of Harry Potter, translates from the French as 'flight of death'.

Harry Ramsden's. A name synonymous with fish and chips, and with the palatial fish and chip restaurant at White Cross, Guiseley, Yorkshire, where in 1928 Harry Ramsden (1886–1963) started his business in a small wooden hut with a loan of £150. In 1931 he opened the plushest 'chippie' yet seen in Britain, and in 1989 the restaurant was the first of its kind to be floated on the stock market. There are now Harry Ramsden branches elsewhere in Britain, all in the opulent style of the Guiseley prototype.

Harry starkers. Stark naked. The prefixing of a word by *Harry*, the word itself taking the ending *-ers*, evolved from upper-class forces slang in the Second World War as a British linguistic quirk. Some words attracted the form more than others. Also common was *Harry flakers*, 'flaked out'. In naval usage *Harry flatters* for a calm sea was popular. The style is still sometimes heard.

Har-Tru. The American proprietary name of an artificial surface for tennis courts, made of crushed greenstone. The name represents the physical attributes of such courts, 'hard' and 'true', the latter word in the sense 'level'. *See also* ASTROTURF.

Harvey. The invisible six-foot rabbit who befriends the drunken Elwood P. Dowd in Mary C. Chase's comedy of his name (1944). In the delightful film (1950), adapted by Chase and Oscar Brodney from Chase's play, Dowd is played by James Stewart. The imaginary rabbit's name has entered American parlance and in the 1980s the military programme to develop a STEALTH BOMBER was nicknamed 'Project Harvey'.

Harvey Nicks. SLOANE RANGER slang for the London fashion store Harvey Nichols, in Knightsbridge, famous for its cosmetics department.

> Money is never available to pay, for a million reasons – out playing golf, having hair, feet, nails done, coffee mornings, going to Henley, Ascot, Harvey Nicks, Wimbledon.
> *Sunday Times* (Letter to the Editor) (31 October 1999)

Harvey Smith. A V-SIGN. At the Hickstead show-jumping finals in August 1971, it was alleged that the horseman Harvey Smith (b.1938), on completing his last, winning round, made the sign at Douglas Bunn, one of the judges. He was threatened with the loss of all prize money but claimed he had merely made a V FOR VICTORY sign to mark his triumph. The matter was subsequently dropped but his name became attached to the gesture.

Harvey Wallbanger. A cocktail of gin or vodka and orange juice. It emerged in the United States in the late 1960s and has a name that presumably compliments and commemorates its inventor and alludes to its disorientating effect on those who drink it.

Háry János. The central character of Zoltán Kodály's opera that bears his name, set to a libretto by Béla Paulini and Zsolt Harsányi and premièred at Budapest in 1926. It is the composer's best known opera, mainly for its incidental music rather than its story, and contains long stretches of spoken dialogue. Háry János himself is the great liar of Hungarian folklore, and the plot centres on his love for Napoleon's second wife, Archduchess Maria-Louisa of Austria.

Hashbury. A nickname for the district of Haight-Ashbury in San Francisco, celebrated as a centre of the alternative, drug-using HIPPIE culture in the late 1960s. By the 1970s, however, it had declined into a squalid drug-dealers' paradise. 'Hash' is a slang abbreviation of hashish (cannabis resin).

Hastings Day. An eight-day celebration held every October in Hastings, East Sussex, since 1968. The event had its genesis in 1966, the 900th anniversary of the town's foundation. The current festivities include music, sports and flag ceremonies, with all in the town contributing. A recent addition is the revival of a bonfire tradition, and a torchlight procession culminates in a bonfire and fireworks, featuring the 'largest Guy Fawkes in England', on the Saturday nearest 14 October.

Hatchet job or **work.** A vicious verbal attack on someone, especially in print. The term frequently applies to a critic's dismissive review of a new book. The person who carries out such an attack is thus a 'hatchet man', in turn so called from the Chinese assassin of old who used a real hatchet.

Hate mail. Hostile and sometimes threatening letters sent, usually anonymously, to an individual or group. The subject of the letters is often controversial and the style of writing frequently crudely abusive. The term is first recorded in the 1960s, but the practice dates from considerably earlier. *See also* POISON PEN LETTER.

> A Cambridge professor has received hate mail after producing a report that led to staghunting being banned on National Trust land, he said last night.
> *The Times* (3 January 2000)

Hatterji. A nickname given to Roy (now Lord) Hattersley (b.1932), who served in the Labour cabinet (1976–9) and was deputy leader of the Labour Party (1983–92), by analogy with the Indian name Chatterji. The nickname derived from the large number of Indians and Pakistanis in his Birmingham Sparkbrook constituency, which he represented from 1964 to 1997. Hattersley was crudely depicted as an Asian in a long-running *Private Eye* cartoon strip. He has also been lampooned for his alleged fondness for good lunches (Tory politician Norman Fowler observed that he was 'the only man to move from the cabinet table to the restaurant table and consider it a promotion'), and for his somewhat salivating manner of speech. Once regarded as being on the right of the Labour Party, since Tony Blair's government came to power in 1997 Hattersley has presented himself as the guardian of the party's socialist conscience.

Hattonistas. The supporters of Derek Hatton (b.1948), the Trotskyite MILITANT TENDENCY deputy leader of Liverpool City Council (1983–6). The term was coined in allusion to the SANDINISTAS, the left-wing guerrilla movement that had seized power in Nicaragua in 1979. The sharp-suited Hatton was expelled from the Labour Party in 1987 along with other members of the Militant Tendency, and subsequently embarked on a career in public relations. *See also* PORTILLISTAS.

Have a ball, To. To have a good time; to enjoy oneself uninhibitedly. The ball here is a dance. The expression is of American origin and dates from the 1940s.

> 'I was having a ball being single when I met James five years ago,' she says. 'I had a job that took me to the hippest destinations in the world.'
> *Sunday Times* (29 August 1999)

Have a bash, To. To attempt something; to give it a go. A phrase from the 1940s.

Have a good war, To. To achieve satisfaction or success during a war. The expression dates from the 1960s and is mostly ironic, as in the title of the musical *Oh, What A Lovely War!* (1963), a documentary satire about the First World War, set in a holiday camp.

Have or **get a handle on, To.** To possess a means of understanding or controlling a person or thing, as if 'grasping' them. The expression is of American origin and dates from the 1970s.

> It is Cameron Diaz ... who has, perhaps, a better handle on him [film director Oliver Stone]. 'He is,' she says, 'a mad genius'.
> *Sunday Times* (31 October 1999)

Have a lot on one's plate, To. To have much to occupy one. The reference is to a large plateful of food that one has to consume. The expression dates from the 1920s.

> Can you tell me how many times in all she has forbidden you the house? – No, sir. Half a dozen times? – It might have been. I cannot say. I have a lot on my plate ... Mr. Justice Horridge: A lot on your plate! What do you mean? Elton Pace: A lot of worry, my lord.
> *Daily Express* (4 July 1928)

Have a nice day. A stock expression of goodwill to one departing that reached its heyday in the United States in the 1950s and also subsequently crossed the Atlantic to Britain. The phrase is purely a token politeness, since the speaker does not really care what sort of day the other will have. *See also* ENJOY YOUR MEAL.

Have a tiger by the tail, To. *See* RIDE A TIGER.

Have by the short and curlies, To. To have at a disadvantage or under one's complete control. The 'short and curlies' are pubic hair.

Have had one's chips, To. To be dead; to be dying; to be out of the running. The metaphor is from gambling. When one no longer has any chips, as counters representing money, one has lost.

Have I Got News For You. A satirical comedy show first screened on BBC2 in 1990, in which the host, Angus Deayton, puts questions on the previous week's news to two regular panellists, Ian Hislop and Paul Merton, and to the celebrity guest accompanying each, usually a politician or entertainer. The programme's popularity lies in the wit of the three regulars and their put-downs of the hapless guests. *See also* NEWS TO ME.

Have it away with someone, To. *See* HAVE IT OFF WITH SOMEONE.

Have it made, To. To be in an excellent position; to be set up for life. The idea is that all the necessary work or preparation has been done for one and one can now reap the reward. The phrase dates from the 1920s.

Have it off or **away with someone, To.** To have sexual intercourse with them. The phrase seems to imply a success or 'score', as if one has won a prize. *See also* GET IT ON WITH SOMEONE.

'What's his wife like?'
'She's been having it off with Arthur, on Tuesday and Thursday afternoons, back of the shop.'
FAY WELDON: *The Heart of the Country* (1987)

Have kittens, To. To be extremely nervous or apprehensive. Pregnant cats are sometimes scared into premature kittening.

Have or **eat someone for breakfast, To.** To deal with them or defeat them with consummate ease.

Dismissed in some quarters as a clever-clever sloppy-jeaned hippy band, ... Gomez are actually the sound of the Nineties eating the rest of the century for breakfast.
The Times (31 December 1999)

Have the hots for someone, To. To be sexually attracted to them, 'hots' alluding to the physical arousal involved. The expression dates from the 1940s.

Prince William has got the hots for Holly Branson, daughter of the bearded entrepreneur.
The Times (2 August 1999)

Have what it takes, To. To possess the necessary qualities or commodities that enable one to succeed. The implication is that it may have taken a lot. The phrase dates from the 1930s.

Haw-haw, Lord. In the Second World War the name given by Jonah Barrington, a journalist with the *Daily Express*, in allusion to his upper-class accent, to the American-born William Joyce (1906–46) who broadcast anti-British propaganda in English from Germany. His broadcasts usually began 'Germany calling! Germany calling!' with 'Germany' pronounced more like 'Jairmany'. Joyce was hanged for treason. *See also* AXIS SALLY; TOKYO ROSE.

Hawks and doves. In foreign affairs the hawks are those who favour war and resolute military action, the doves those who support peace or compromise and negotiation. The pairing became particularly associated with the Cuban Missile Crisis of October 1962, a COLD WAR confrontation that brought the United States and the USSR close to war over the presence of Soviet nuclear missiles in Cuba. American 'hawks' favoured an air strike to eliminate the missiles, while the 'doves' opposed such strikes and favoured a naval blockade. The 'doves' won the day and after an exchange of messages between John F. Kennedy and Nikita Khrushchev, amidst extreme tension on both sides, the Soviet premier eventually backed down. The terms are also used for similar stances generally.

'Doves' on the MPC [Monetary Policy Committee] will also draw comfort from yesterday's ... survey, which pointed to a moderation of growth in confidence. However, MPC 'hawks', who would like to see higher rates, will point to recent evidence of stronger economic growth.
The Times (5 October 1999)

Hay Fever. A play (1925) by the British playwright Noël Coward (1899–1973) about a family of sharp-tongued eccentrics who make a habit of treating visitors to their home with total indifference to the normal rules of etiquette and hospitality. Coward reportedly based his portrait of the delicious but impossible Bliss family on the actress Laurette Taylor (1884–1946), who treated visitors to her New York home with similar indifference to their wants and needs, instead obliging them to take part in parlour games.

Hazel. The rabbit hero of Richard Adams's best-selling children's novel WATERSHIP DOWN (1972), telling how he and his second-sighted brother Fiver lead a small band of rabbits from their doomed warren to go in search of a new home. An animated film of the book was released in 1978, with Hazel voiced by John Hurt.

H-Block. *See* MAZE.

Head for the hills, To. To make for the rolling open countryside, especially to escape the stress of modern life. The expression is in the American pioneering spirit and may be applied figuratively to allude either to a retreat from the rat-race or to a venture into a major new enterprise.

> Then the school tests, the constant assessments, the looming exams, the league tables. ... I'd be there on the sidelines as ambitious and watchful as every other modern parent. Why on earth didn't I ever shout, 'Let's head for the hills'?
>
> *The Times* (31 August 1999)

Headhunt, To. To identify and approach a person in a senior managerial post and offer them a similar but usually enhanced position with another company. Such individual recruitment is usually carried out by a special agency. The jargon relates to the practice among some peoples of cutting off the heads of slain enemies and keeping them as trophies. The modern, metaphorical sense dates from the 1960s.

Heads will roll. People will be dismissed. A journalistic catchphrase denoting that senior members of an organization will be obliged to resign because of some form of gross mismanagement or scandal. In other words, they will be 'axed'. The *Daily Herald* of 26 September 1930 quoted Adolf Hitler as saying: 'If our movement is victorious there will be a revolutionary tribunal which will punish the crimes of November 1918. Then decapitated heads will roll in the sand.'

> Would it be indelicate to ask what this debacle has cost, and if any heads will roll in the greatest corporate cock-up for years?
>
> *The Times* (Letter to the Editor) (7 June 1999)

Health warning. In the figurative sense a warning that a thing is not what it should be or normally is. The term applies in particular to radio reports made under restrictive conditions. A more literal health warning is the one placed by law on tobacco products and in tobacco advertising.

> The BBC precedes all Mr Simpson's dispatches with a 'health warning' explaining that they are being monitored by the Serbs.
>
> *The Times* (16 April 1999)

Hearing dog. A dog trained to alert a deaf or hard-of-hearing person to a meaningful sound in the home such as a knock at the door, the bleep of a smoke alarm, the crying of a baby or the ringing of an alarm clock.

The name and function are based on those of the SEEING EYE dog.

Hear My Song. A film (1991) based on a story by Peter Chelsom about the attempts of a nightclub owner to persuade the legendary Irish tenor Josef Locke (1917–99) to return from Ireland to make a single comeback appearance, despite the risk of arrest for tax evasion. The film was based on fact, Locke having fled Britain at one point in his career after he got into difficulty with the tax authorities.

Heartbeat. A television drama series first screened in 1992. It is set in the 1960s and opens when a London policeman, PC Nick Rowan, is transferred to the (fictional) Yorkshire village of Aidensfield, where his wife sets up practice as a rural GP. Its nostalgic tone, picturesque settings, upbeat story lines and period pop music brought it high ratings from the first. Its title is a gently subtle pun on a country bobby's beat in the heart of the community, and on the human heart that needs both a doctor's physical care and the loving support of friends and family.

Heartbeat away from the presidency. A description of the circumstance of the US vice-president, who, by the US Constitution, succeeds to the presidency on the death of the incumbent and serves for the rest of the term. The phrase has been current since the 1950s, when Richard Nixon was Eisenhower's vice-president. Since that time only one vice-president, Lyndon Johnson (LBJ), has succeeded to the presidency in this fashion. America was luckily spared the likes of Spiro Agnew and T. Dan Quayle; indeed, there was a probably apocryphal story that Quayle was always accompanied by two CIA men with orders to shoot him should anything happen to President Bush.

> The young man [Richard Nixon] who asks you to set him one heart-beat from the presidency of the United States.
>
> ADLAI STEVENSON: Speech at Cleveland, Ohio
> (23 October 1952)

Heartbreak Hotel. A moody rock 'n' roll song performed by Elvis Presley, written by Tommy Durden and Mae Axton. Released in 1956, it was the first song recorded by Elvis to reach the top of the US charts. The song had its roots in a real-life newspaper report in the *Miami Herald* of a suicide victim who left a note containing the words 'I walk a lonely street'. Fittingly, the hotel of the title is metaphorically located at the end of 'Lonely Street'.

Heartbreak House. A play (1919) by George Bernard Shaw (1856–1950) about the disastrous consequences that result from the arrival of the youthful Ellie Dunn in the household of the 88-year-old Captain Shotover. The play, which may be interpreted as an allegory for the state of modern civilization, was inspired in part by the chaotic home life of Hubert Bland (1856–1914), a brush manufacturer and member of the Fabian Society who divided his time between his wife, writer Edith Nesbit, and his mistress Alice Hoatson and had several children by both, all three of them living in the same house at one point.

> *Ellie* [musically]: This silly house, this strangely happy house, this agonizing house, this house without foundations.
>
> GEORGE BERNARD SHAW: *Heartbreak House* III

Heart is a Lonely Hunter, The. A novel (1940) by Carson McCullers (1917–67) of the 'Southern grotesque' school. It features a deaf-mute, to whom the other main characters wrongly attribute the faculty of inner serenity which they lack. The title is from the poem 'The Lonely Hunter' (1896) by Fiona Macleod (pen-name of William Sharp; 1855–1905): 'My heart is a lonely hunter that hunts on a lonely hill.' A rather pale film version (1968) was directed by Robert Ellis Miller. *See also* BALLAD OF THE SAD CAFÉ.

Heart of Darkness. A short story, written in 1899 and first published in *Youth: a Narrative with Two Other Stories* (1902), by Joseph Conrad (1857–1924). It is based on the author's own experience of a voyage up the Congo River in 1890 and is told by Marlow, commander of a French coasting steamer. He finds a corrupt and depraved regime under the control of the monstrous figure of Kurtz, who finally dies on board Marlow's boat. In an epilogue, Marlow tells of visiting Kurtz's fiancée and pretending that he died with her name on his lips. The story ends: 'The offing was barred by a black bank of clouds, and the tranquil waterway leading to the uttermost ends of the earth flowed sombre under an overcast sky – seemed to lead into the heart of an immense darkness.' Kurtz's words 'The horror! The horror' (ch iii) inspired Francis Ford Coppola's controversial film APOCALYPSE NOW (1979) set during the VIETNAM War, which has parallels with Conrad's story. *See also* FIRST LINES OF NOVELS.

Heart of England. A touristic name for the West Midlands of England, extending north to Cheshire with its GOLDEN TRIANGLE, west to the Welsh borders, east to Shakespeare Country (*see* COUNTRY) and south to the Cotswolds, the whole presenting an idyllic image of picturesque houses, pubs and churches, despite the presence of industrial Birmingham and Stoke-on-Trent. The implication is that this is the 'essence' of England. Geographically the region lies more or less in the centre of the country, and politically may even be identified with MIDDLE ENGLAND.

Hearts and flowers. Mawkish sentimentality. The named objects are traditional symbols of love and affection. The phrase dates from the early 20th century and was popularized by a song of 1891 by Mary C. Brine so titled. *See also* MILLS & BOON.

Heart-to-heart. An intimate talk. A phrase of American origin dating from the early years of the 20th century. The idea is that each speaks openly, 'from the heart'.

Heath Robinson. A term sometimes applied to an absurdly complicated mechanical contraption, especially one performing a basically simple function. The name is that of William Heath Robinson (1872–1944), whose amusing drawings of such absurdities appeared in *Punch* and elsewhere. *See also* BRANESTAWM, PROFESSOR; RUBE GOLDBERG.

> It seems extremely unlikely that this [the MILLENNIUM BUG] will be a problem suffered by our lift, a particularly ancient model which wheezes and rattles on a Heath Robinson series of pulleys and chains.
>
> *The Times* (27 December 1999)

Heathrow. London Airport, as it is officially known, takes its popular name from the small settlement that was formerly in that place, west of London, itself so called as it was simply a row of cottages at the western edge of Hounslow Heath. The site was acquired by the Ministry of Civil Aviation in 1946, and in 1955 Queen Elizabeth II opened the Europa Building, the first of the airport's permanent buildings, now Terminal 2. The Oceanic Terminal, now Terminal 3, opened in 1962, and Terminal 1 was formally opened in 1969. Terminal 4 followed in 1986, but a long-planned fifth terminal is not due for completion until 2006. *See also* THIEFROW.

Heave-ho. Expulsion or dismissal by a person or organization. The phrase is most commonly used of a jilted lover or a sacked employee: 'I was given the old heave-ho.' As 'heave-ho' is associated with pulling, so there is an analogy with pushing: 'I was given the push.' The original 'heave-ho' was a cry of sailors when hauling on a rope to raise the anchor, pull in sails or the like.

> Opera audiences are celebrated for giving performances the old heave-ho.
> *Sunday Times* (31 October 1999)

Heaven's Gate. The WESTERN film (1980), written and directed by Michael Cimino (b.1940), is set against the 1892 Johnson County wars in Wyoming. Starring Kris Kristofferson, the film cost somewhere between $35 million and $50 million but lost more than any other film ever made. It was slated by critics and public alike but the doomed extravagance of the project entered movie legend. Within the film 'Heaven's Gate' is the name of a local roller-skating rink popular with settlers in Wyoming in the early 1890s. The phrase Heaven's gate also crops up in the Bible, Shakespeare and William Blake's 'Jerusalem' (1815):

> I give you the end of a golden string;
> Only wind it into a ball:
> It will lead you in at Heaven's gate,
> Built in Jerusalem's wall.

See also DANCES WITH WOLVES.

Heavies. A colloquial term dating from the 1950s for the serious newspapers, which contain weightier or more intellectually demanding material than the others. Such papers, especially the Sunday editions, have now also become physically heavier, with many having several parts or sections and usually including one or more magazines. *See also* TABLOID.

Heavy hitter. An important person or celebrity, especially in business, politics or the social world. The metaphor is from baseball and dates from the 1970s.

> Most modern actresses are what would have been called starlets in the days of the real Hollywood heavy-hitters.
> *Sunday Times* (2 January 2000)

Heavy metal. A type of rock music emerging in the early 1970s. It is characterized by its high amplification, its harsh, brutal sound, its repetitive rhythms, and its frequent use of violent or fantastic imagery. 'Heavy' may relate to the music's heavy beat and 'metal' either to its metallic sound or to the metal decorations of the leather gear worn by its performers and adherents. The words are to some extent reflected in the names of some of the genre's most prominent bands, such as Steppenwolf, Black Sabbath, Iron Maiden and Led Zeppelin, although the last-named eschewed the label. *See also* ROCK GROUP NAMES.

Heavy water. Water that has been enriched with deuterium oxide. Deuterium, or 'heavy hydrogen', is an isotope of hydrogen with two neutrons in its nucleus (rather than the one neutron found in common hydrogen). Heavy water is used as a moderator in some nuclear reactions. During the Second World War the Germans, as part of their programme to develop atomic weapons, prepared stocks of heavy water at a plant in Norway. This was destroyed by a British commando raid on 19–20 November 1942. The operation was the subject of the film *The Heroes of Telemark* (1965).

Heavy weather. To make heavy weather of something is to do it ineptly or magnify its difficulties, which may hardly exist in the first place. The expression dates from the early 20th century and derives from the nautical sense relating to the hard passage of a ship in a storm or rough seas.

Hedgers and Ditchers. The two opposing Conservative groups in the House of Lords that split over the bill that was to become the 1911 Parliament Act, which restricted the Lords' power of veto over bills passed by the Commons. The Hedgers, also known as the Judas group, were prepared to 'hedge' (hedge their bets or dodge expressing their true feelings) by voting in favour of the bill, by which they hoped to avoid the government's threat to create a large number of new Liberal peers. The Ditchers, also know as the DIE-HARDS, claimed that they would die in 'the last ditch' rather than give in. Hedging and ditching are important activities in the countryside, maintaining hedgerows and clearing ditches. In the Commons, meanwhile, the bill's Conservative opponents, whom Lady Violet Bonham Carter later described as behaving 'like mad baboons', were known as Hughligans, after their leader Lord Hugh Cecil.

Heebie-jeebies. An American slang term for a state of nervousness or jitters, attributed to the cartoonist Billy DeBeck and first noted in his strip *Barney Google* in the *New York American* on 26 October 1923.

Heffalump. A child's (and now also adult's) word for an elephant, popularized if not actually invented by A.A. Milne in his books about WINNIE-THE-POOH. The apt name ('lump') provides a challenge for translators of these stories into other languages. One Russian version has the Heffalump as a *Slonopotam*, blending *slon*, 'elephant', with *gippopotam*, 'hippopotamus'. The word is sometimes applied to a large person or animal in general.

I could not help feeling more than my usual desperation to lose the extra 15lb that clings to me as tenaciously as a limpet. ... I am a Heffalump.

The Times (16 August 1999)

Heidelberg man. A type of prehistoric man found near Heidelberg, Germany, in 1907, possibly of the genus *Pithecanthropus*. A single lower jaw was found along with other extinct mammal fossils of the Pleistocene period.

Heidi headscarf. A peasant-style red headscarf fashionable in the late 1990s like that worn by the young Swiss orphan Heidi in illustrations for Johanna Spyri's novel that bears her name (1881).

The summer's Heidi headscarf trend reinvents itself for autumn with Toast's embroidered pashmina version.

The Times (17 September 1999)

Heil Hitler (German, 'Hail Hitler'). The familiar salutation to the FÜHRER, often used derisively of one adopting dictatorial methods or attempting dictatorial policies. *See also* HITLERISM; SIEG HEIL.

Heimlich manoeuvre. An emergency technique to treat someone who is choking. The rescuer embraces the choking victim from behind, beneath the rib cage, then presses a closed fist under the breastbone with a quick upward thrust. This should dislodge food or any other object from the person's windpipe. There is also a 'Heimlich's sign' to indicate that one is choking, made by grasping one's neck between the thumb and index finger of one hand, a natural reaction for many victims in any case. The name is that of Henry J. Heimlich (b.1920), the American surgeon who devised the procedure.

Hell is other people. A line, which has since become proverbial, from the play *Huis Clos* (1944; known as *In Camera* in Britain, and *No Exit* in the USA) by the French existentialist philosopher Jean-Paul Sartre (1905–80): '*Vous vous rappelez: le soufre, le bûcher, le gril ... Ah! quelle plaisanterie. Pas besoin de gril, l'Enfer, c'est les Autres.*' ('Do you remember, brimstone, the stake, the gridiron? ... What a joke! No need of a gridiron, Hell is other people.') The play involves three people shut together in a room for eternity. The French term *huis clos*, like the English 'in camera', is used to describe a trial or judicial hearing from which the public are barred.

Hello, sailor! A camp greeting born of sailors' reputation for homosexuality induced by long spells at sea, but no doubt originally a prostitute's call to a sailor on shore leave. The phrase was made familiar by various radio and television programmes, such as *The Goon Show* (*see* GOONS) and MONTY PYTHON'S FLYING CIRCUS (1969–74).

Hell's Angels. Members of a group of unruly motorcyclists originating in California in the 1950s. They typically wear denim or leather jackets, and their symbol is a death's head. In due course Hell's Angels appeared in Britain and Europe. They are often tattooed, flaunt NAZI symbols and badges and are noted for their lawlessness and initiation rites. Hell's Angels are depicted in the film *The Wild One* (1954), starring Marlon Brando, although they are here called 'Black Rebels'. *See also* MODS AND ROCKERS.

Hell's bells! A fairly mild expletive dating from the 1920s, expressing irritation or disappointment. The phrase is sometimes expanded to 'Hell's bells and buckets of blood!' *See also* LIKE THE CLAPPERS.

Hell's Corner. The triangle of Kent centring on Dover was so called in the Second World War from being both the recipient of German bombardment from across the English Channel and the scene of much of the fiercest air combat during the BATTLE OF BRITAIN.

Helpline. A telephone service that can provide specialized information, advice or assistance. The facility originated in the United States in the 1970s and soon spread to other countries. Although the service can be provided by a commercial company or organization, it is most familiar as that available from a charity or government authority, usually in the form of a name incorporating the nature or scope of the help and with a memorable number. Examples of British helplines at the end of the 20th century were thus DrinkLine, ChildLine, Parentline and Seniorline.

Help the police with their enquiries, To. To be interviewed by the police in connection with a crime. A nice euphemistic turn of phrase dating from the 1950s.

A 17-year-old girl ... was found battered to death. ... Later, a man was helping police with their enquiries.

Sunday Times (14 October 1973)

Helter-Skelter. An undistinguished foray into heavy rock by the BEATLES, credited to John Lennon and Paul McCartney. It is one of the tracks on the so-called WHITE ALBUM, released in November 1968. Bizarre to relate, the psychopathic HIPPIE godfather Charles Manson (notorious for the grisly murders of the actress Sharon Tate and four others at the

California home of the film director Roman Polanski in August 1969; *see* MANSON MURDERS), unaware that 'helter-skelter' signifies in British English a type of spiral fairground slide, interpreted the term as having something to do with 'hell' and used it as a codeword for the mayhem he hoped to unleash.

Henderson the Rain King. A novel (1959) by the US novelist Saul Bellow (b.1915). Eugene Henderson, a disillusioned millionaire, journeys to Africa on an impulse, yearning for some new forms of satisfaction. He causes a disastrous mishap in one village when trying to cleanse its water supply. He then reaches another village where he befriends the local chief and is declared to be 'Sungo', the official rainmaker, after apparently causing a deluge by moving the goddess out of the clouds. He then becomes involved in the tribal rites of the chief's succession, becoming the chief himself on the incumbent's death. Fearing for his safety, Henderson then escapes from the village and returns home having successfully opened new chapters in his life.

Hen night. An all-women party for a bride the night before her wedding. *See also* STAG NIGHT.

> I was the hen at a hen night. Consider it, your Honour, a case of high jinx [*sic*] and hilarity rather than debauchery. We ordered no stripagrams [*sic*], we frequented no dive bars. I was simply the victim of a girls' night out.
> *The Times* (5 November 1994)

Here be dragons. A cliché indicating a hidden risk, from the supposed traditional indication on early maps that a region was unexplored and potentially dangerous.

> No doubt there are problems ... with new techniques. But if we are denied the benefits of experiment by a culture which pins a 'Here Be Dragons' warning on anything new, we will never know.
> *The Times* (28 December 1999)

Here's looking at you. A drinking toast. A clichéd variant, 'Here's looking at you, kid', has its origin in words addressed by Humphrey Bogart (as Rick Blaine) to Ingrid Bergman (as Ilse Lund) in the film CASABLANCA (1942).

Here's mud in your eye. A jocular drinking toast dating from the First World War and perhaps originating among army officers, with reference to the mud of the trenches.

Here's one I made earlier. A catchphrase popularized from the 1960s by the children's television programme BLUE PETER, as the culmination of a set of directions for making a model from everyday household items, such as empty yoghurt pots and coat hangers.

Her Indoors. A person's wife, especially when regarded as taking charge or 'wearing the trousers'. The expression was popularized by the television series MINDER, in which the leading character, Arthur Daley, regularly refers to his wife (who never appears on screen) by this name. The phrase is sometimes spelt ''Er Indoors' to suggest a Cockney tone. *See also* NICE LITTLE EARNER.

> Observe the following rules. One: bear in mind that builders never, I repeat, never, mean what they say or say what they mean. Two: 'her indoors' should do the talking.
> *The Times* (26 June 1999)

Heritage. A vogue word from the 1970s for any feature of historical, cultural or touristic interest regarded as worth protecting and preserving for future generations before it is destroyed or damaged by the present one. A heritage coast is thus a section of officially protected coastline, and a heritage centre is a museum of local cultural 'heritage'. *See also* HERITAGE INDUSTRY; HERITAGE RAILWAYS.

> 'Heritage' – a word he [Sir Neil Cossons, chairman of English Heritage] dislikes, but for which, like all of us, he cannot think of a good synonym.
> *Sunday Times* (5 December 1999)

Heritage industry. A term arising in the 1980s for the commercial exploitation of historic buildings or sites, or anything loosely termed HERITAGE. Opinions are divided regarding the activity. On the positive side it may be said that such commercialization preserves and popularizes evidence of the country's history. On the negative side the argument is often made that it cheapens and distorts it, reducing all to the level of a mere tourist attraction. The latter view tends to predominate, and the expression is thus usually understood in a dismissive sense. 'Heritage', according to this view, is not simply that which is inherited but that which additionally can be packaged and marketed. *See also* EXPERIENCE.

Heritage railways. Special privately owned railways catering for the tourist and holidaymaker. They mostly run through scenic regions and some are known by nicknames. The Bluebell Line, first so named in c.1955 by a journalist, runs between Sheffield Park and Kingscote in Sussex, while the Watercress Line runs between Alton and Alresford in Hampshire, the latter town being noted for its watercress beds. The Tarka Line, though no longer taking passengers, is named after Henry Williamson's *Tarka the Otter* (1927) (*see* TARKA) and runs between Exeter and Barnstaple in Devon, where the novel is set. There are many heritage railways in Wales, mostly narrow gauge, while Kent has the famous Romney, Hythe and Dymchurch 15in-gauge miniature railway. The Snowdon mountain railway, opened in 1896, is Britain's only rack and pinion railway. The majority of such trains are powered by steam or vintage diesel, adding to their nostalgic appeal.

Herland. The imaginary country populated solely by women that is the setting of Charlotte Perkins Gilman's feminist Utopian novel of the same name, published serially in 1915. Its inhabitants are strong and athletic, while the older women have an ageless quality of power and beauty. All wear their hair short, and their clothes are comfortable and practical, in the form of close-fitting tunics worn over knee-breeches. The culture of Herland revolves around motherhood and the raising of children, and the language is simple and rational.

Heroin. The so-called RECREATIONAL DRUG was introduced in the 1890s by Friedrich Bayer & Co. in Germany as a substitute for morphine. It gives an extraordinary sense of euphoria, suggesting that its name may derive from Greek *hērōs*, 'hero'. It can be 'snorted', injected into veins, or smoked. It is produced from the opium poppy, grown extensively in the GOLDEN TRIANGLE. The hazards of heroin use are appalling and involve loss of appetite, convulsions, vomiting, loss of bowel control, sleeplessness, impotence in men, infertility in women and ultimately death. *See also* DRUG NICKNAMES; HEROIN CHIC; JUNKIE.

Heroin chic. A term evolving in the mid-1990s for the glamorization of the culture and appearance of HEROIN users, characterized in particular by the use of thin, wan models. The film TRAINSPOTTING (1996) furthered the cult.

Herrenvolk. A German word meaning broadly 'master race'. In NAZI usage it implied the superiority of the German peoples. *See also* UNTERMENSCHEN.

Hershey bar. In the United States a well-known make of chocolate bar, which was available only to the troops in the Second World War. The name is that of Milton S. Hershey (1857–1945), who founded the Hershey Chocolate Corporation in 1903. General Lewis B. Hershey (1893–1977) was Director of the Selective Service System (1941–70), the agency that drafted millions of young American men into the armed forces. In US army slang the term Hershey bar was thus applied to the narrow gold bar worn by troops on the left sleeve to indicate that they had done six months' overseas service.

Herzog. A novel (1964) by Saul Bellow (b.1915), in which Moses Herzog, a Jewish scholar, addresses a voluminous series of letters to the living and the dead, which are never sent. His sufferings reflect the break-up of Bellow's second marriage, to Sondra Tschacbasov, a Catholic convert. *See also* FIRST LINES OF NOVELS; HENDERSON THE RAIN KING.

He/she. A combination of 'he' and 'she' sometimes used as a pronoun of common gender, to save a cumbersome 'he or she', as in: 'If the worker tires quickly, he or she must be encouraged to rest'. There is in fact no need for an artificiality of this kind, as a resort already exists in the form of the genderless pronoun 'they', used in such circumstances in this dictionary.

Hey Jude. A song by the BEATLES with weighty orchestral backing, one of their longest (7 minutes and 15 seconds in length). Credited to John Lennon and Paul McCartney, it was released in Britain in November 1968. The title was originally intended to be 'Hey Jules' (after Lennon's son Julian) but later became 'Hey Jude'.

Hezza. A not unaffectionate nickname for the Conservative politician Michael Heseltine (b.1933), more dashingly and originally known as TARZAN. The name is similar to that of GAZZA.

Hi-de-Hi! A period-piece television SITCOM running from 1981 to 1988 and centring on the trials and tribulations endured by an entertainment troupe at a typical British holiday camp in the late 1950s. The series was in effect a pastiche of real-life camps such as BUTLIN'S and PONTIN'S with their respective REDCOATS and Bluecoats, as implied by the fictional Maplin's and its Yellowcoats. Much of the humour lay in the relations between the troupe's newly appointed manager, the dreamy academic Jeffrey Fairbrother, played by Simon Cadell, and the individual members of his team. The title represents the campers' rallying call, broadcast over the public address system. The response, at first enthusiastic, soon lapsed into a weary 'Ho-de-Ho'.

Hidden agenda. An ulterior or secret motive for something; an 'agenda' that is deliberately not spelt out. The term originated in the jargon of business management training in the mid-1970s. The agenda of a meeting is normally the official, written statement of issues for discussion.

> Greek-accented Katina Kangaris serenades us with a cod-operatic *Love is a Many-Splendored Thing*. It is an amusing send-up of kitsch romanticism, but what is this ingratiatingly funny foreigner's hidden agenda?
> *The Times* (13 September 1999)

Hidden persuaders. Those involved in the advertising business. The term is from Vance Packard's book *The Hidden Persuaders* (1957) which sets out to demonstrate how advertisers influence and manipulate consumers by means of psychological techniques, many of which take place below the level of human awareness. The appeals that prompt a response are thus largely 'hidden'.

Hiding to nothing. To be on a hiding to nothing is to be unlikely to succeed, or to be unlikely to gain much advantage if one does. The expression dates from the early 20th century and apparently derives from horse racing, in allusion to giving a horse a 'hiding' (whipping) to no avail.

> It is here … that [Conservative leader] Mr Hague is on a hiding to nothing. Not because he is an inadequate politician, far from it, simply an unconvincing actor.
> *The Times* (6 October 1999)

Hi-fi. *See* HIGH FIDELITY.

Highbrow. In the literal sense, having a lofty brow or forehead, a supposed sign of superior intellectual powers or the possession of esoteric cultural interests. The term is of American origin and dates from the turn of the 20th century. Lowbrow, denoting the converse, followed soon after, while middlebrow, relating to average or moderate cultural interests, dates from the 1920s.

> Dickens's blend of sentiment, melodrama, gritty realism and grotesque humour make him the apotheosis of the 'middle-brow' entertainer.
> *The Times* (6 November 1999)

Highbury, Battle of. *See* BATTLE OF HIGHBURY.

High fidelity or **hi-fi.** Sound reproduction on electronic equipment that gives faithful reproduction with a minimum of distortion. High-fidelity sound systems assembled by specialists from individual components were first in use in the 1920s, while complete systems housed in cabinets appeared in the 1950s.

High Fidelity. The first novel (1995) by Nick Hornby (b.1957). It follows the varied route towards self-discovery of its NEW LAD, THIRTY SOMETHING narrator, a pop-music obsessive and struggling record shop owner, after he has been discarded (on the first page) by Laura. The title reflects fidelity of musical reproduction as well as faithfulness in relationships. *See also* FEVER PITCH.

High five. A form of greeting or mutual congratulation of American origin in which two people slap each other's raised right hand. 'Five' refers to the five fingers. The term and practice originated among American basketball players in the late 1970s, although a similar, palm-slapping ritual at waist height, first with one hand, then with the other, existed earlier among American blacks.

> 'And what are these girls after, O knowledgeable one?' McDermott asks, bowing slightly as he walks. Van Patten laughs and still in motion they give each other high-five.
> BRET EASTON ELLIS: *American Psycho* (1991)

High Noon. A WESTERN film (1952), based on the story 'The Tin Star' by John W. Cunningham. It stars Gary Cooper as a marshal deserted by all his fellow-townsfolk as he awaits the hour (noon) when he will have to fight a returning desperado and his gang. The importance of the hour of noon in the film was underlined by the fact that the film takes place in 'real' time, beginning at 10.40 in the morning and ending at five past midday. Although director Fred Zinnemann denied it, the writer of the screenplay, Carl Foreman, claimed it was an allegory of the need for individual opposition to the work of the House Un-American Activities Committee (*see also* McCARTHYISM), which was then busy rooting out suspected communists in HOLLYWOOD (including Foreman himself). The phrase 'high noon' has since been quoted on innumerable occasions whenever someone or something faces a moment of crisis.

High society. The fashionable sector of the upper classes. *The Philadelphia Story* (1940), one of America's finest comedy films, was remade as *High Society* (1956) in a musical version that fell far short of the wit and glamour of the original.

High-Tax Harry. *See* GIVE-'EM-HELL HARRY.

Highway Code. A booklet giving guidance and rules on all aspects of road use in Britain, from drivers and passengers to cyclists and pedestrians, although intended primarily for motorists. It was first published in 1931. Knowledge of the *Highway Code* forms an essential part of the driving test.

> If you have to herd animals after dark, wear reflective clothing and ensure that white lights are carried at the front and red lights at the rear of the herd.
> *Highway Code* (Rule 215) (1996)

High, wide and handsome. Happy; carefree. The expression is of American origin and became specifically associated with cowboys at a rodeo.

High Wind in Jamaica, A. The first novel (1929; in USA as *The Innocent Voyage*) by Richard Hughes (1900–76) was inspired by a real event in 1822, recounted in a manuscript that was passed on to his mother. Seven amoral children, whose parents think they will be safer in England after a high wind and storm have ravaged their Jamaican home, are unintentionally hijacked by a band of incompetent pirates. The film version (1965) was directed by Alexander Mackendrick.

High-wire act. One requiring great skill or judgement, like that demanded of a tightrope walker.

Hijacker. A term of American origin now applied to a person who seizes a vehicle in transit to force it to go to a different destination or to commandeer it for another purpose. The name is popularly said to derive from the gunman's command to his victim, 'Stick 'em up high, Jack,' meaning that the arms were to be raised well above the head. *See also* CARJACKER; SKYJACKER.

Hill, The. A shorthand used by US politicians to refer to Congress, which is situated on Capitol Hill in Washington, D.C.

Hillbilly. A nickname from the turn of the 20th century for an inhabitant of a remote or rural region of the United States and in particular of the southeastern states of Alabama and Georgia. The name became attached to a form of COUNTRY MUSIC in which string bands with banjos and guitars predominate, such bands themselves originating in the Appalachian mountains of the southeast. The basic meaning of the name is a 'Billy' or person who comes from the hills.

Hillsborough Declaration. The joint statement in April 1999 by Tony Blair and Bertie Aherne, the respective British and Irish prime ministers, at Hillsborough Castle near Belfast. It proposed a plan to break the impasse in the Northern Ireland peace process by removing any connotations of surrender in the looked-for DECOMMISSIONING of weapons by the IRA. The latter rejected the plan. The 1985 Anglo-Irish Agreement was signed at Hillsborough, and the mansion was the residence of the governor of Northern Ireland from 1925 to 1973. The village owes its name to Sir Arthur Hill, who built the fort here in 1650. Its Irish name is Cromghlinn, 'winding valley'.

Hillsborough disaster. The death of 96 football fans on 15 April 1989 at the FA Cup semi-final between Liverpool and Nottingham Forest at Hillsborough in Sheffield was caused when Liverpool supporters rushed onto the already crowded centre section of the west stand. Victims were crushed in the entrance tunnel, on the steps up to the terraces and against the perimeter fence. The tragedy resulted in the removal of fences from all football fields.

Himbo. A male BIMBO, whose main asset is good looks rather than intelligence, 'brawn' rather than 'brain'.

Hindenburg Line. The German fortified line of defence in northeastern France set up by Field Marshal Paul von Hindenburg (1847–1934) in the First World War. It resisted all Allied attacks in 1917 and was not breached until late 1918. *See also* SIEGFRIED LINE.

Hinglish. A blend of Hindi and English spoken in India. It uses English parts of speech for more complicated functions, as in the following: 'Dekho great democratic institutions kaise India main develop ho rahi hain', meaning 'See how the great democratic institutions are developing here in India' (quoted in *New Yorker*, 9 September 1967). The name itself is a blend of 'Hindi' and 'English'. *See also* FRANGLAIS.

Hip-hop. A street subculture originating among black American urban teenagers in the late 1970s and involving RAP MUSIC, GRAFFITI art and BREAK-DANCING as well as particular codes of dress and speech. The term combines 'hip' in the sense of fashionable (*see* HIPPIE) and 'hop' in the sense of dance. *See also* GANGSTA RAP.

Hippie. Hippies originated in San Francisco in the late 1960s among young people who were anarchists but with a regard for the environment. The movement spread to Britain where they adopted fantastic styles of dress, travelled around in ramshackle vehicles, and were often given to drink and drugs. They lived to some extent by begging, scrounging and with the help of Social Security payments. By the 1990s they had largely been superseded by an amorphous group of young unemployed or homeless people, the most positively motivated of whom are the NEW AGE travellers, who prefer a life in the natural environment of the countryside to one in the polluted prison of the cities. The word probably comes from 'hip' in the sense of fashionable. *See also* BEATNIK; DROPOUT; HELL'S ANGELS; SUMMER OF LOVE.

Hire and fire, To. To engage and dismiss employees, especially as a way of indicating one's authority.

Hired gun. A person with special knowledge or expertise employed to resolve a complex problem, especially in business. The allusion is to a gunman or HITMAN employed to kill someone, not always a straightforward task. The expression is of American origin and dates from the 1950s.

Hiroshima. A Japanese city and military base, the target of the first atomic bomb dropped in warfare (6 August 1945). More than 160,000 people were killed or injured and far more rendered homeless. The flash of the explosion was seen 275km (170 miles) away, and a column of black smoke rose over the city to a height of 12,190m (40,000ft). Hiroshima remains a solemn portent of the fate overshadowing mankind in the event of major world conflict. There is now an annual Peace Festival at Hiroshima. *See also* ENOLA GAY.

Hiss affair. An early episode in the REDS UNDER THE BED scares in the USA as the COLD WAR got under way. On 3 August 1948 Whittaker Chambers (1901–61), an ex-communist, testified before the House Un-American Activities Committee (HUAC), that Alger Hiss (1904–96), a former employee of the US State Department, had given secret documents to him to pass on to the Soviets in the 1930s. A prominent member of HUAC, Richard Nixon (*see* TRICKY DICKY), used the allegations to smear the State Department, anticipating Senator Joe McCarthy's subsequent allegations of communist infiltration of government (see McCARTHYISM) and to vaunt his own red-baiting credentials. Hiss denied the charges and sued Chambers for slander when he repeated them outside the privileged setting of the House. However, Chambers produced documents that he alleged Hiss had supplied to him; Chambers had hidden the documents in a pumpkin on Chambers's Maryland farm. Hiss was indicted on two charges of perjury and, after a first trial in 1949 ended with a hung jury, was retried and sentenced in 1950 to five years in prison. He was released in 1954. In 1992,

at Hiss's request, Russian officials went through the Soviet archives and could find no evidence of Hiss's involvement in a spy ring, although experts did not regard this as conclusive.

His Shadowship. A nickname given to the US politician and civil-rights activist Reverend Jesse Jackson (b.1941) when in 1990 he became one of the two Washington, D.C. 'shadow senators' (officially 'statehood senators'), posts created by Washington City Council to campaign for statehood for the District of Columbia. It was Jackson's first elective office, as he had failed to win the nomination as Democratic candidate for the presidential election in both 1984 and 1988. His 1984 bid had been damaged by his reference to New York City as 'Hymietown', which was taken as evidence of anti-Semitism.

History Man, The. A novel (1975) by Malcolm Bradbury (b.1920) that, like his two earlier books, *Eating People is Wrong* (1959) and *Stepping Westward* (1965), has a university campus setting. He has described Howard Kirk, the trendy Marxist lecturer who is its principal character, as a 'sociologist, but also a "history man" because he believes he can act to change history and transform individual lives, challenging humanism as an old philosophy of individualism and innocence'. The novel was brilliantly adapted for television (1981) by Christopher Hampton, with Anthony Sher, sporting a ZAPATA MOUSTACHE, as the sexually adventurous Kirk.

History of Mr Polly, The. A comic novel (1910) by H.G. Wells (1866–1946). The book is intended as a reflection on the popular education of the times. Mr Polly goes from dissatisfaction with his shop and his marriage to freedom in an unexpected way, and finally, through a stroke of good fortune, to contentment. A gentle film version (1948), typically 'English' in style, starred John Mills in the title role and was directed by Anthony Pelissier.

History of the World in 10½ Chapters, A. A novel (1989) by Julian Barnes (b.1946) consisting of 10 linked pieces and a 'half-chapter' inserted two-thirds of the way through, in which the author expounds his theories on the nature of love. The biblical, historical and imaginative incidents which are chosen to illustrate his thesis have thematic links.

Hit-and-run. Descriptive of a road accident in which the driver of a motor vehicle has hit or knocked down a person, then driven on without stopping.

Hitch-Hiker's Guide to the Galaxy, The. A cult radio classic by Douglas Adams (b.1952), broadcast in 1978 and 1979. The story begins with the imminent destruction of Earth to make way for a hyperspace express route and centres on the attempts of the Earthling Arthur Dent and his friend Ford Prefect to escape the apocalypse by hitching a ride on the Vogon spacecraft. The programme combined the comic with the surreal and introduced a host of eccentric characters. In 1981 it transferred less successfully to television but books based on the original were bestsellers.

Hit for six, To. *See* KNOCK FOR SIX.

Hitler diaries. *See under* FAKES.

Hitlerism. A generic term for the whole doctrine and practice of FASCISM as exemplified by the NAZI regime of Adolf Hitler (1889–1945), who became German Chancellor in 1933 and ruled until his death. His regime was marked by tyranny, aggression and mass persecution of communists and Jews.

Hitler moustache. A narrow moustache in the centre of the upper lip, as regularly worn by Adolf Hitler (*see* HITLERISM).

Hitler Youth. The *Hitlerjugend* was initiated by Hitler in 1933 for the education and training of male youth in NAZI principles. By 1935 it included almost 60 per cent of all German boys, and in 1936 it was decreed that all young 'Aryan' Germans were expected to join. On reaching his 10th birthday, a German boy was registered and investigated for 'racial purity' and, if qualifying, was inducted into the *Deutsches Jungvolk* or German Youth People. At the age of 13 he became eligible for the Hitler Youth, from which he graduated when he was 18. He then progressed to membership of the Nazi Party and served in the state labour service and the armed forces until he was at least 21. The *Bund Deutscher Mädel* or League of German Girls was a parallel organization.

Hit list. Originally, a list of people to be assassinated for criminal or political reasons. The term, dating from the 1970s, then passed to a list of people against whom action is to be taken, as typically a dismissal or demotion.

> Jonathan Powell, Mr Blair's chief-of-staff, is understood to have drawn up a 'hitlist' of ministers who are performing poorly or need to be moved to make room for new talent.
> *The Times* (5 July 1999)

Hitman. A hired assassin, especially one engaged by a criminal or political organization. *See also* HIRED GUN.

> A hitwoman broke down in tears at the Old Bailey yesterday as she described shooting a roofing contractor in the face in return for the money to buy a mobile home.
> *The Times* (8 November 1994)

Hit Man. The nickname of US welterweight, light-middleweight, middleweight and light-heavyweight boxer Thomas Hearns (b.1958), who possessed a devastatingly effective punch.

Hit parade. Formerly, a list of the most popular songs, as the forerunner of the TOP 10. The term is American in origin and dates from the 1930s, but was used by the *New Musical Express* to announce Britain's first 'Record Hit Parade' in its edition of 14 November 1952. There were actually 15 records occupying 12 positions in this prototype 'Top Ten', with Al Martino and 'Here in My Heart' at number one and Johnnie Ray with 'Walkin' My Baby Back Home' at number 12. The chart was extended to a Top 20 in 1954 and to a Top 30 in 1956, the year generally regarded as that of the birth of ROCK 'N' ROLL in Britain. A Top 50 ensued in 1983 and has remained since.

Hit the ceiling or **roof, To.** To lose one's temper. The image is of leaping so high in one's rage that one hits the object named. The expression dates from the early years of the 20th century. *See also* GO THROUGH THE ROOF.

Hit the deck, To. To get out of bed; to throw oneself to the ground.

Hit the ground running, To. To proceed with energy and enthusiasm. The imagery is military, of a person who has jumped from a landing craft or helicopter or even landed by parachute and who instantly springs into action. The expression dates from the 1960s.

> The Marx Brothers' movie career began almost at its peak. They hit the ground running, and fast ran out of hits because by 1929 ... the brothers were already middle-aged.
> *Sunday Times* (14 November 1999)

Hit the hay or **sack, To.** To go to bed. The image is of a weary wanderer in a hay barn or granary.

Hit the headlines, To. To receive prominent attention in the newspapers or the news media generally. The phrase dates from the 1930s. *See also* MAKE THE FRONT PAGE.

Hit the jackpot, To. To win any great prize or un-expected 'bonanza'. The expression dates from the 1930s and comes from a form of poker in which the pool or pot accumulated until a player could open the bidding with at least a pair of jacks or higher.

> Denis, the host for the evening, excitedly informed me that I had hit the jackpot: a large hen party and an all-female 21st birthday party had booked.
> *Sunday Times* (13 November 1994)

Hit the panic button, To. *See* PANIC BUTTON.

Hit the roof, To. *See* HIT THE CEILING.

Hit the sack, To. *See* HIT THE HAY.

Hit the silk, To. *See* TAKE THE SILK.

Hit the wall, To. In marathon running to reach the point of extreme fatigue at which the body's stores of energy are virtually exhausted. The 'wall' is thus the barrier that one runs into and that must be surmounted if the course is to be completed. The expression dates from the 1970s.

Hitty, Her First Hundred Years. A novel (1929) by the American writer Rachel Field (1894–1942), recounting the adventures over a hundred years of a wooden doll named Hitty from its manufacture in New England in the early 19th century to a New York antiques shop. It was published in Britain in 1932 as *Hitty, the Life and Adventures of a Wooden Doll*.

HIV-positive. A term used of a person who has had a positive result in a test to determine whether they are infected with the AIDS virus HIV (human immuno-deficiency virus). The expression dates from the Aids-anxious 1980s and loosely means simply 'liable to develop Aids'. 'HIV-negative' also exists, but like 'germ-free' is less attention-worthy.

HMS Ulysses. The first novel (1955) by Alistair Maclean (1922–88) reflects his own experience as a leading torpedo operator in a destroyer on the terrifying convoys of supplies to Murmansk during the Second World War. It is a record of just such a convoy and of the endurance of the officers and crew of the ship most involved. The screen rights to the novel were sold but no film has so far resulted.

HMV. The music stores so called take their name from the abbreviation of 'His Master's Voice', registered as an official trademark in 1911 but in use on a record label two years earlier. The name itself is properly the title of a picture of a dog listening to an old-fashioned phonograph, an early type of American wind-up gramophone. The picture was painted in 1898 by the photographer and artist Francis Barraud, and the dog himself, named Nipper, belonged to his brother. In 1899 Barraud visited the Gramophone Company, formed in London in 1897 as an offshoot of the American Berliner Gramophone Company, and left a photograph of his painting. The company bought the picture on condition that Barraud paint out the phonograph and replace it with a gramophone. The picture was duly altered and assigned to the Gramophone Company on 31 January 1900 together with its title, 'His Master's Voice', to be adopted for commercial use in due course.

Hobbit. One of an imaginary race of benevolent, half-size people, the creation of Professor J.R.R. Tolkien. They feature in his two works, *The Hobbit* (1937) and *The* LORD OF THE RINGS (1954–5). The name was their own for themselves, and according to them meant 'hole-dweller'. *See also* BAGGINS, BILBO; FIRST LINES OF NOVELS; FRODO; GOLLUM; SHIRE.

> In a hole in the ground there lived a hobbit.
> J.R.R. TOLKIEN: *The Hobbit* (1937)

Hobble skirt. A long skirt with a wide band below the knees and above the ankles, in fashion just before the First World War. The style impeded the wearer in walking, much as a horse is hobbled.

Hobson's Choice. A play (1916) by the British playwright Harold Brighouse (1882–1958) about a tyrannical shoe-shop owner who is eventually obliged to succumb to the wishes of his equally strong-willed daughter after she takes up with his gormless apprentice, Willie Mossop. The title refers to the proverbial 'Hobson's choice' available to those who have no choice at all. The play was filmed in 1955, with Charles Laughton as the patriarch.

The original Hobson was the Cambridge liveryman Thomas Hobson (*c*.1544–1631) who always offered his customers the horse nearest the door of the stable, and no other.

Ho Chi Minh Trail. A route from North Vietnam through neighbouring Laos and Cambodia used by the communists in the VIETNAM War (1964–75) to supply the VIET CONG guerrillas fighting in South Vietnam. The US attacks on Cambodia (1970) and Laos (1971) were principally aimed at the trail, which had started as a network of jungle paths and had developed into an elaborate and efficient supply system. It was named after the North Vietnamese leader Ho Chi Minh (1890–1969). After the North Vietnamese victory and the unification of Vietnam in 1975, Saigon, the former capital of the South, was renamed Ho Chi Minh City.

Hogs Norton. A village in Oxfordshire, now long called Hook Norton, 8km (5 miles) northeast of Chipping Norton. The name owes its more recent fame to Gillie Potter, the English comedian and radio broadcaster, who in the 1930s described in mock erudite fashion a long series of unlikely events taking place in this village.

> The humorous corruption to Hogs Norton, recently employed by Mr Gillie Potter, goes back to at least the 16th century, when the village had become proverbial for rusticity and boorishness. ... There was evidently a jingle about Hogs Norton, where pigs play on the organ.
>
> MARGARET GELLING: *The Place-Names of Oxfordshire*, ii (1954)

Hog the limelight, To. To keep the focus of attention on oneself. The limelight is the theatrical spotlight, so called because its intense white light was originally produced by directing an oxyhydrogen flame against a block of lime. The hog or pig is a famously gluttonous animal.

Hokey-cokey. A light-hearted Cockney dance, popular during the 1940s, with a song and tune of this name to go with it. It is also known as the 'Cokey-Cokey', especially in the version written by Jimmy Kennedy in 1945 and recorded by Billy Cotton and His Band, among others.

Hokey-pokey. An early form of cheap ice cream, sold by street vendors until the 1920s with the cry 'Hokey-pokey penny a lump'. The name is derived from hocus pocus, although mistakenly said by some to be from the Italian *Ecco un poco* ('Here is a little') or *O che poco* ('Oh how little'), Italian street vendors being associated with ice cream. Hokey-pokey is also used to mean nonsense.

Hold on to your hat! *See* HANG ON TO YOUR HAT!

Hold someone's hand, To. To give them moral support; to comfort them. The expression dates from the 1930s.

Hold the fort, To. To look after something in a person's temporary absence. The phrase became current from the 1930s and has been traced to an order given by General William T. Sherman in 1864: 'Hold the fort [against the enemy at Allatoona] at all costs, for I am

coming.' These words were subsequently familiar as the first line of a popular hymn:

> 'Hold the fort, for I am coming',
> Jesus signals still,
> Wave the answer back to heaven,
> 'By Thy grace we will'.
>
> PHILIP BLISS: *Sacred Songs and Solos sung by Ira D. Sankey*, 'Hold the Fort' (1874)

Hole in one. A perfect achievement. The reference is to a stroke in golf in which the ball is driven straight from the tee into the hole with a single stroke.

Hole in the wall. A colloquial term for a cash machine in the wall of a bank. The phrase has several prior applications. In the 19th century it was an American term for an illicit liquor store, then more generally came to be used for any small or cramped place, such as a tiny apartment. As a proper name, the Hole in the Wall is now found for several restaurants and pubs. In some of these there may be a reference to a particular spy-hole or similar site, but the name also has overtones of the earliest American sense, agreeably combining a notion of cosiness with one of covert drinking.

> If I couldn't get cash from a hole in the wall ... I would cash a cheque at one of those foreign exchange shops.
>
> *The Times* (15 September 1999)

Holiday of a lifetime. A travel company's lure that in most cases promises more than it actually delivers. 'Win the holiday of a lifetime' is a typical promotional enticement.

Holier than thou. Having the appearance of being morally superior. The phrase is first recorded only in the early years of the 20th century but its origin is biblical: 'Stand by thyself, come not near to me; for I am holier than thou' (Isaiah 65:5).

> 'He and I have decided that I'm going to work out. It sounds holier than thou.'
>
> *The Times* (28 December 1999)

Holism (Greek *holos*, 'whole'). A term coined by General J.C. Smuts in the 1920s when defining his philosophical belief that the fundamental principle of the cosmos is the creation of self-contained systems or 'wholes'. In current usage holism tends to refer more to an attitude than to a philosophical principle and 'holistic' relates to the consideration of a system in its entirety rather than focusing on individual parts of it. Holism has a recognized application in medicine, the idea being that the doctor considers the whole person, both as a 'whole' of body, mind and spirit and as a 'whole' within the systems of family, community, culture and environment. To some extent all general practitioners would probably regard themselves as holistic.

Hollywood. The internationally famous byname of the American film industry and of the glamorous actors and actresses who are its vital exponents. Geographically it is the suburb of Los Angeles where a number of independent producers set up their studios in 1912 and to the casual visitor looks far from glamorous. The location's actual name is said to have been given by Horace Wilcox, who laid it out in 1886. *See also* SODOM BY THE SEA; TINSELTOWN.

Hollywood Bowl. A huge natural amphitheatre in HOLLYWOOD, noted for its remarkable acoustics. It has seating for 25,000 and was purchased in 1919. Since 1922 it has staged the so-called 'Symphonies Under the Stars' in the form of concerts given over nine weeks every summer by the Los Angeles Philharmonic Orchestra.

Hollywood East. *See* GREAT COMMUNICATOR.

Hollywood 10. The 10 American screenwriters, film producers and directors who in 1947 refused to tell the Un-American Activities Committee whether or not they were communists. They were Alvah Bessie (1904–85), Herbert Biberman (1900–71), Lester Cole (1905–85), Edward Dmytryk (1908–99), Ring Lardner Jr (b.1915), John Howard Lawson (1894–1977), Albert Maltz (1908–85), Samuel Ornitz (1891–1957), Adrian Scott (1912–73) and Dalton Trumbo (1905–76). All served prison sentences and for several years had difficulty obtaining work in HOLLYWOOD.

Holmes, Sherlock. *See* HOUND OF THE BASKERVILLES.

Holocaust. The name given to the murder of some 6 million Jews by Hitler in the Second World War. The terror began within a month of Hitler's becoming German chancellor in January 1933. The Nuremberg Laws of 1935 deprived Jews of German citizenship, and the night of 9–10 November 1938 saw the *Kristallnacht*, a night of violence against Jewish persons and property, so called ironically from the litter of broken glass left in the aftermath. Discussion of the *Endlösung* or FINAL SOLUTION was held on 20 January 1942, when it was agreed that the Jews of central and western Europe would be deported and sent to camps in eastern Poland, where they would be exterminated or made to work as slave labourers until they perished.

The word holocaust literally means 'burned whole', from the Greek, and originally applied to a sacrifice wholly consumed by fire. This is the 'burned offering' of the Old Testament, when slaughtered sacrificial animals or birds were burned on the altar, the skin being given to the priest who performed the ritual. The current use of the word was introduced by historians in the 1950s as an equivalent of the Hebrew *Shoah* ('Catastrophe') or *Hurban* ('Destruction'). This particular word was probably suggested by the crematoria in which the bodies of the victims were burned. *See also* AUSCHWITZ; EINSATZGRUPPEN.

Holy cow! An exclamation of surprise of American origin, dating from the 1920s. The words presumably pun on the 'sacred cow' of the Hindus while rhyming on 'Wow!' The phrase is a variant of such earlier exclamations as 'Holy mackerel!' or 'Holy smoke!'

Holy Fox. A punning nickname given by the Churchill family to Edward Frederick Lindley Wood, 1st earl of Halifax (1881–1959), viceroy of India (1925–31) and Conservative foreign secretary (1938–40). Halifax's father had been a leader of the Anglo-Catholic movement, and Halifax was himself a devout high churchman. While viceroy of India his profound religious faith helped him to get on well with the nationalist leader, MAHATMA Gandhi. His reputation was later tarnished when, as foreign secretary, he supported Neville Chamberlain's policy of appeasement, and advocated that Britain should seek to make peace with Germany in 1940. In December of that year he was sent to Washington, D.C. as the British ambassador.

Homburg. A soft felt hat popularized by Edward VII (reigned 1901–10). It was originally made at Homburg in Prussia where the king 'took the waters'.

Home alone. Said of a child left at home unsupervised while the parents are out or away. The expression was popularized by the American film *Home Alone* (1990), in which a young boy is inadvertently left behind when his parents go on holiday. The phrase can be extended to anyone left after family members have departed, such as EMPTY NESTERS. *See also* LATCHKEY CHILD.

> One of the paradoxes of being 'home alone' is that no sooner have parents got used to it than students come home for a weekend.
> *The Times* (20 September 1999)

Home and dry. Safe and successful, having satisfactorily completed some endeavour. The allusion is to a horse race home, when the winning rider has such a good lead that he can rub down his mount before the rest of the field arrive. The expression dates from the 1930s.

Homeboy. A person from one's own home town or region, or a member of one's own peer group. The term is of black American origin and became associated in the 1980s with the HIP-HOP subculture. The female equivalent is a homegirl, although here the word may also apply to a shy or domesticated girl or young woman, one who likes to 'stay home'.

Home economics. A school subject usually studied by girls rather than boys and including diet management, budgeting, child care and other aspects of running a home. It was formerly familiar as domestic science.

Home Guard. In Britain the force of volunteers raised early in the Second World War and trained for defence against the threat of invasion. It was originally known as the Local Defence Volunteers but was renamed the Home Guard at Winston Churchill's suggestion. It soon came to be affectionately known as DAD'S ARMY and at its peak, in about June 1943, consisted of around 2 million men. The Home Guard was officially disbanded in 1957.

Home, James! A light-hearted instruction to a driver to set off for home. A fuller version is 'Home, James, and don't spare the horses', as the title of a popular song of 1934 by Fred Hillebrand.

Home page. In computing the document on the WORLD WIDE WEB that serves either as a point of introduction to a person or organization or that is a focus of information on a particular topic. It usually contains links to other related documents.

Home Rule. The name given by Isaac Butt (1813–79), its first leader, to the movement for securing governmental independence for Ireland under the British crown. The Home Government Association was founded in 1870 (renamed the Home Rule Association in 1873), and when Charles Stewart Parnell (1846–91) became leader in 1879 its policy of obstruction in Parliament became a thorn in the flesh of British governments. A Home Rule Bill was eventually passed in 1914, but its implementation was postponed by the First World War. The EASTER RISING in 1916, the activities of SINN FÉIN and resistance in Ulster, led to the establishment of the Irish Free State in 1921, but Northern Ireland continues to be represented in the British Parliament. See also CURRAGH MUTINY; DEVOLUTION; DIRECT RULE; FREE-STATERS.

Home Service. The main BBC broadcast service from September 1939, when it was formed by a merger of the National Programme and the Regional Programme. On 30 September 1967 it was renamed Radio 4. See also LIGHT PROGRAMME; THIRD PROGRAMME.

Home shopping. Shopping carried out from home by means of mail order catalogues, satellite television channels, the INTERNET and the like. Although having apparent advantages, the procedure can nevertheless be frustrating and unsatisfactory, as the purchaser cannot see or handle the goods directly and can incur inconvenience and expense when returning unsuitable items.

Homicide Hank. The nickname of the US boxer Henry Armstrong (1912–88), who simultaneously held the world featherweight (1937), welterweight (1938) and lightweight (1938) titles.

Homme moyen sensuel (French, 'average sensual man'). The average man, the man in the street. The expression implies a person with normal appetites and desires, neither an intellectual on the one hand nor an idiot on the other. The expression dates from the early 20th century.

Honeypot. A nickname for a person or thing regarded as attractive or in some way 'sweet'. This sense does not apply, however, to the 'honeypot' that is a children's term, dating from the 1940s, for a jump into a swimming pool with one's knees drawn up and one's hands clasped round them. The name alludes to the posture, resembling the shape of a honeypot. The term itself apparently comes from a children's game of 19th-century origin:

> One of the players, called a honey-pot, sits with his hands locked under his hams, while the 'honey-merchants' lift him by the arm-pits as handles, pretend to carry him to market, and shake him, with the aim of making him let go his hold.
>
> *Oxford English Dictionary* (1933)

Honey trap. A scheme to lure a person into a compromising sexual situation in order to blackmail them. The scenario typically involves a seductive woman as the 'honey' and a senior civil servant as the victim.

> High-flyers in the Ministry of Defence no longer have to fear the 'honey traps' set by foreign spymasters. They can now confess their sexual peccadilloes without their careers being ruined.
>
> *Sunday Times* (3 January 1999)

Hong Kong dog. See MONTEZUMA'S REVENGE.

Honkers. A nickname for Hong Kong current among British expatriates from the 1920s. The *-ers* is similar to that in HARRY STARKERS and similar concoctions.

Honky-tonk. A disreputable nightclub or low road-house; a place of cheap entertainment. A honky-tonk piano is one from which the felts of the hammers have been removed, thus making the instrument more percussive and giving its notes a tinny quality. Such pianos are often used for playing ragtime and popular melodies in public houses.

Hooked on. Addicted to. An American expression dating from the 1920s, originally referring to drugs. An addict has been 'caught' and finds it hard to escape.

Hooray Henry. A loud and lively but 'wet' upper-class young man, whose bray is better than his brain. A female equivalent is a 'Hooray Henrietta'. The term dates from the 1930s and rather unexpectedly for a peculiarly British phenomenon is of American origin. It appears, for example, though in a slightly different form, in Damon Runyon's story *Tight Shoes* (1936), in which a young man called Calvin Colby is described as 'without doubt strictly a Hoorah Henry'.

Hooter. A slang term for the nose in British slang but in American slang (in the plural) for the female breasts. The former refers to the sound of a nose being blown or 'trumpeted'. The latter alludes to the supposed resemblance to an old-fashioned car horn with its bulbous end.

Hoover. The tradename of a firm of vacuum cleaner makers, which, to the company's displeasure, has come to be used as a noun and a verb relating to vacuum cleaners and vacuuming in general. The name was patented by the company in 1927, although this cannot legally stop people using it in a generic sense. The name is that of William H. Hoover (1849–1932), a saddler of North Canton, Ohio, who saw the potential of an 'electric suction cleaner' invented in 1907 by Murray Spangler, a department store guard.

Hooverville. A nickname for a shanty town in the United States built by the unemployed and destitute during the GREAT DEPRESSION of the 1930s during the presidency of Herbert Hoover (1874–1964).

Hopalong Cassidy. The black-garbed hero of the Old West was created by the American writer Clarence E. Mulford for his novel named after him (1910). Sequels followed, and he then re-emerged on the cinema screen in the 1930s in a series of 60 cheaply made movies, in which he was played by William Boyd. Many Western fans regard his film persona as an improvement on the original.

Hop in, To. To get into a car, especially when being given a lift, as: 'Come on, hop in.'

Hop it! Clear off! A phrase dating from the early 20th century.

Horlicks. To make a Horlicks of a thing is to make a mess of it. The word uses the proprietary name of the malted milk drink as a pun on 'bollocks', itself a (related) synonym of 'balls'. The use of the name in this sense dates from the 1980s. *See also* NIGHT STARVATION.

> They made a Horlicks of the casting: the plain sister was far better-looking than the pretty one.
> *Sunday Times* (12 September 1999)

Hormones. Internal secretions that stimulate a specific physiological action on reaching a particular part of the body. Their existence was discovered by the British researchers William Bayliss and Ernest Starling in 1902 and they coined the word from Greek *horman*, 'to stir up'. A comment such as 'It's her hormones' to explain a person's mood or uncharacteristic behaviour is taken to refer to their sex hormones. Hormone replacement therapy (HRT) involves the use of oestrogen hormones to alleviate menopausal symptoms such as HOT FLUSHES.

Hornblower, Horatio. The naval officer hero of a series of eleven books by C.S. Forester, beginning with *The Happy Return* (1937). The novels chart his career from midshipman to admiral at the time of the Napoleonic Wars, and throughout he is calm, taciturn, intelligent, a first-class seaman and an excellent strategist. He was portrayed by Gregory Peck in a film based on the books, *Captain Horatio Hornblower RN* (1951), and in a radio series of the early 1950s was played by Michael Redgrave. *See also* HAPPY WARRIOR.

Horror movie. A film made to shock or scare its audience by means of a fearful or gruesome subject treated in such a way as to emphasize its unpleasant or macabre aspects. The genre was initiated in the early 20th century by the Germans and was only slowly taken up by HOLLYWOOD. Early classic examples are *The Cabinet of Dr* CALIGARI (1919), *Dracula* (1931) and *The Mummy* (1932), while in more recent times a notorious box-office hit was *The* EXORCIST (1973). After 1950 many of the story lines were influenced by SCIENCE FICTION. *See also* DISASTER MOVIE; HAMMER FILMS; SLASHER MOVIE.

Horsefeathers. An American colloquialism for nonsense. The notion of a horse having feathers is ridiculous. Hence *Horse Feathers* (1932), the title of one of the MARX BROTHERS' wildest films.

Horse opera. A WESTERN film or television series, in which horses play a prominent role. The expression dates from the 1920s. *See also* SOAP OPERA.

Horse's Mouth, The. The third (1944) in a trilogy of novels by Joyce Cary (1888–1957) about artistic expression, each of which is told from the point of view of a different protagonist. The painter Gulley Jimson, based on an amalgam of William Blake and Stanley Spencer, verges violently between rage and creative expression as he tries to wheedle some of his early canvases out of his one-time mistress, while engaged in illicitly covering walls with ambitious murals. According to Cary, the title refers to the 'voice that commands Gulley to be an artist, and makes him struggle to realize his imagination in spite of all discouragement'. This itself echoes the title of the second novel in the trilogy, *To Be a Pilgrim*, which comes from the famous song in John Bunyan's *The Pilgrim's Progress* (1684): 'There's no discouragement/Shall make him once relent/His first avow'd intent/To be a pilgrim.' The first novel in the series was *Herself Surprised* (1940). An amusing film version of *The Horse's Mouth* (1958) with a screenplay by Alec Guinness, who also starred as Jimson, and with paintings by John Bratby, was directed by Ronald Neame.

Horst Wessel Song. *Die Fahne Hoch* ('Raise the flag'), the party anthem of the NAZIS. It was written by a student, Horst Wessel (1907–30), killed in the communist quarter of Berlin where he lived as commander of an SA section. The tune was a music-hall song popular at the German Front in 1914.

Hospice. A hospice was originally a medieval house of rest and entertainment for pilgrims, travellers and strangers run by a religious order, as those set up by the monks of St Bernard and St Gotthard in the Alps. In its modern sense as a home for the terminally ill the word dates from the late 19th century. The modern hospice movement, however, was founded by Dame Cicely Saunders in 1967 in response to her concern that many terminally ill people have no choice but to spend their last days in a noisy hospital surrounded by strangers. There are now more than 200 hospices in Britain admitting some 60,000 patients a year and offering them peace, privacy and care as they approach death. The word is directly related to host, hostel, hospital and hotel.

Hot button. A crucial issue, especially one that is highly charged emotionally or politically. The 'button' is the one that must be identified and pressed in each individual if their favourable response is to be obtained, so that they back the contentious cause or give the politician their vote. The image is perhaps that of a PANIC BUTTON rather than a starter button, 'hot' implying urgency. The expression dates from the 1970s. *See also* HOTLINE.

Hot dog. A sausage, especially a frankfurter, served in a hot roll split lengthways. The following story is told to account for the name. A Bavarian sausage seller, Anton Ludwig Feuchtwanger, began selling hot wieners at the World's Columbian Exposition, Chicago, in 1893, giving his customers white gloves to keep them from burning their fingers as they devoured the tasty meat. When the gloves started disappearing as handy souvenirs, Feuchtwanger substituted elongated bread rolls to hold the frankfurters. The fashion caught on at baseball stadiums, where vendors hawked 'dachshund sausages red hot', a cumbersome description soon streamlined to 'hot dogs'. The name was popularized further by the US cartoonist and sportswriter Tad Dorgan (*see* CAT'S PYJAMAS), who included a dachshund inside a frankfurter among his many animal inventions.

Hotel California. The title of a song and album by the American West Coast country rock group the Eagles, released in 1976. The album's theme is the hedonistic lifestyle of southern California, of which the hotel is a symbol.

Hotel du Lac. A novel (1984) by Anita Brookner (b.1928), which won the BOOKER PRIZE for fiction. Brookner began writing fiction in 1981, when she embarked on a range of subtly observed stories of blighted female lives. *Hotel du Lac*, her fourth novel, is set in a fashionable hotel in Switzerland, the place of retreat of a young woman in disgrace with her family for having a mind of her own about marriage.

Hot flushes. A sudden sensation of heat in the skin, especially in the face, neck and upper trunk, experienced by many women at the time of the menopause. The cause is decreased oestrogen hormone production by the ovaries. The term dates from the early 20th century, and the American equivalent is 'hot flashes'. *See also* HORMONES.

Hot from or **off the press.** Just printed. The phrase dates from the turn of the 20th century, a time when hot (i.e. molten) metal was used for printing. Hence 'hot news' as the latest news.

Hotline. A special direct telephone line, for use in emergencies. In commercial use, the term is applied to an ordinary line over which a customer can place an order.

Hot off the press. *See* HOT FROM THE PRESS.

Hot on. Strict on, as in the phrase: 'The boss is very hot on punctuality.'

Hot pants. Very brief, skin-tight shorts, as worn by young women in the early 1970s as a sort of development of the MINISKIRT, although even more revealing. They were first so called by the American periodical *Women's Wear Daily*. The name evokes the 'hot pants' of a sexually aroused person. The first flush of fashion soon passed but the style is subject to revival, as at the close of the 1990s, and has been fairly consistently preserved by prostitutes and American CHEER-LEADERS.

Hot potato. A delicate or tricky situation, which, as the term suggests, has to be handled with great care. The expression dates from the 1950s.

> The maternity subject is such a hot potato that once you know you have a problem, legal advice from an employment specialist is a must.
> *The Times* (12 August 1998)

Hot rod. An old car stripped and tuned for speed and, by transference, the owner of such a vehicle. The expression dates from the 1940s and has an implied sexual imagery.

Hot seat. A difficult or precarious position. The hot seat is also American slang for the electric chair.

Hot spot. A region of potential violence or danger, as a war zone.

Hotspur. An adventure paper for boys published by D.C. Thomson from 1933 until the early 1980s. It featured the heroic Wilson, the Wonder Athlete, who is 128 years old but, thanks to his healthy lifestyle and diet of 'gruel, nuts and berries', does not appear even to have reached middle age.

Hot stuff. A thing or person that is outstandingly good or, specifically, sexually exciting.

Hot ticket. A person or thing that is very fashionable or in great demand. The American term dates from the 1940s and originally applied to a successful theatre show or performer.

> Proust and Shakespeare are box-office dynamite and Elizabeth Gaskell and Jane Austen are TV hot tickets.
> *The Times* (25 February 2000)

Houdini, Harry. The stage name of Ehrich Weiss (1874–1926), the most celebrated illusionist and escapologist to date. Born in Budapest to Jewish parents, who emigrated to New York, he began his career as a magician in 1890, but world fame began with his appearance at London in 1900. No lock could hold him, not even that of the condemned cell at Washington jail. He escaped from handcuffs, ropes, safes and similar restraints and was nicknamed the 'King of Handcuffs'. In 1907 he introduced an escape in under three minutes from a sealed milk can filled with liquid, and in 1912 got out of a locked, roped packing case submerged in New York Harbour. In 1915 he freed himself from a straitjacket while dangling head first from a skyscraper. He repeated these feats often and the straitjacket escape drew outdoor crowds of up to 100,000. He took his professional name from the French illusionist Jean-Eugène Robert-Houdin (1805–71), with Ehrich anglicized as Harry. He died from a punch in the stomach, delivered before he had tensed his muscles. A biopic, directed by George Marshall and starring Tony Curtis as Houdini, was released in 1953.

Hound Dog. A song, released in 1953, written by Jerry Leiber and Mike Stoller for the black lesbian rhythm-and-blues singer Willie Mae 'Big Mama' Thornton (1926–84). The song was later recorded by Elvis Presley, THE KING, who turned the sexually ambiguous flavour of Thornton's original performance into a bright and breezy number that became a worldwide hit.

Hound of the Baskervilles, The. A novel (1902) by Arthur Conan Doyle (1859–1930), featuring his intellectual detective, Sherlock Holmes, Holmes's worthy henchman, Dr Watson, and mysterious activities around the isolated Devonshire mansion of the Baskerville family, which seem to be connected to the appearances of a fearsome black dog. The stories of Sherlock Holmes were serialized in the *Strand Magazine* from July 1891 until December 1893, when Doyle killed off Holmes and his arch-enemy, Professor Moriarty. Public pressure prevailed, and Holmes was miraculously resurrected in the magazine in October 1903. In the meantime Doyle had written *The Hound of the Baskervilles* as a longer story, serialized from

August 1901 to April 1902. There have been several film versions, but the first and best is that of 1939, with Basil Rathbone as Holmes and Nigel Bruce as Watson.

House. An electronic development of disco music, first emerging in Chicago in the mid-1980s and characterized by electronic drum machines, synthesized bass lines, sparse vocals and a fast beat. The term is short for Warehouse, the name of the Chicago nightclub where it was first played.

House church. A term used either for a group meeting for Christian worship in a private house or for a church within the CHARISMATIC MOVEMENT that is independent of traditional denominations. In the latter case services were originally held in private houses although subsequently many congregations acquired their own buildings.

House for Mr Biswas, A. A tragi-comic novel (1961) by the Trinidadian novelist V.S. Naipaul (b.1932). Set in the Indian community of Trinidad, it covers three generations and features the convergent (and mixed) fortunes of two families. At the centre of much of the action is Mohan Biswas's obsession with having a house of his own. His difficulties, and the corruption and ingenuous incompetence that he encounters on the way, are symptomatic of the colonial culture in which Naipaul was brought up.

House husband. A married man who carries out house hold duties traditionally undertaken by a housewife, including the care of children. The term originated in the United States in the 1950s. *See also* NEW MAN.

> Nor was either of us keen on Bruce becoming – the dread phrase – a househusband. The answer for him was a part-time academic job. He would earn less but be able to do more around the house.
> *The Times* (11 December 1998)

House of the Rising Sun. A traditional folk song arranged by Alan Price, the keyboard player with the Animals, and released by the group in 1964. The 'House of the Rising Sun' is a brothel that has 'been the ruin of many a poor boy'. The song originated in Jacobean England, later crossing the Atlantic to America with emigrants to become an Appalachian folk song. A earlier version of 'House of Rising Sun' had been sung on Bob Dylan's first album in 1962. *See also* ROCK GROUP NAMES.

Housewives' choice or **favourite.** A male radio or television personality admired by older women, who are largely home- and family-centred. The phrase owes much to the popular radio programme *Housewives' Choice* (1946–67), a record request show aimed at women at home.

> Robert Kilroy-Silk, daytime TV star and housewives' favourite, is poised to make a political comeback.
> *Sunday Express* (27 February 2000)

Hove into view, To. A fairly common journalistic variant of the correctly nautical 'to heave into view', meaning to come into view. 'Hove' is really the past tense or past participle of this verb, which is also subject to other irregularities.

> As the solar surface hoves into view, the daylight quickly resumes.
> *The Times* (21 July 1999)

> Because he can live by his wit, a more attractive set of options hoved into view for McCoist.
> *The Times Magazine* (27 November 1999)

Hovercraft. The first air-cushion vehicle so named 'took off' in 1955 as the invention of the engineer Christopher Cockerell (1910–99). It was only a balsa wood model powered by a model-aircraft petrol engine, but it worked, and Cockerell filed his patent the same year. The following year he founded Hovercraft Ltd, using a name that he and his wife devised. The first hovercraft proper successfully crossed the English Channel in 1959 with the inventor on board.

Howards End. A novel (1910) by E.M. Forster (1879–1970). Howards End is a country house, based on Forster's early home in Hertfordshire. The question of who will inherit it underlies the basic conflict, which is between culture and commerce. The germ of the idea seems to have occurred to Forster in 1906, as a result of visiting a newly wed couple who lived in rural isolation. The wife was pretty, pleasant, clever and cultured; the husband boorish and philistine. A noted MERCHANT IVORY FILM (1991) was made of the novel.

How did you feel? A crass and clichéd question put by a television journalist to a person who has suffered a devastating loss or other personal blow, from the death of a loved one to an unposted winning pools coupon. News editors frequently claim that the question is legitimate and of real interest to the public, although some accept that the response alone should be broadcast. When the civil rights lawyer Thurgood Marshall (1908–93) retired from the US Supreme

Court in 1991 he was asked at a press conference, 'How do you feel?' His reply was, 'With my hands'.

How Far Can You Go? A novel (1980; in USA as *Souls and Bodies*) by David Lodge (b.1935), which, to quote his own description, has a prominent 'metafictional' thread running through it. It follows the lives of a group of Catholic students from the early 1950s to the late 1970s, recording social changes but particularly centring on attitudes to contraception.

How Green Was My Valley. A novel (1939) by Richard Llewellyn (pen-name of Dafydd Vivian Llewellyn Lloyd; 1906–83). It is a first-person narrative of a Welsh mining community, for whom coal has destroyed the rural environment but brought employment, at a cost. The rhythm and structure of the language corresponds to the English spoken in Wales. The film version (1941), an effective TEARJERKER, was directed by John Ford.

Howler. A glaring and unintentionally amusing mistake, as typically perpetrated by a school student in written work. The error may simply be the result of sloppy expression, such as the definition of a gynaecologist as 'a specialist in women and other diseases'. But it may equally come from a misuse of words, or by confusion between similar words, such as: 'The whole story was a virago of lies' (for 'farrago'). Translators and interpreters fear howlers like the plague, as do copywriters employed by companies marketing products overseas. One food company promoted its *burrito* (a type of tortilla) in Spanish-speaking countries as a *burrada*. This was something of a *faux pas*, because *burrada* is Spanish for 'big mistake'. Even the slip of a single letter can produce a howler, as that of the American motor company which advertised two new models with the words, 'Cars that break tradition, now your bank account' (instead of 'not'). Collections of genuine howlers like these make enjoyable but salutary reading.

How old is Ann? Who knows? An American catchphrase current in the early years of the 20th century and deriving from a 'brain-twister' published in the *New York Press* of 16 October 1903: 'Mary is 24 years old. She is twice as old as Ann was when Mary was as old as Ann is now. How old is Ann?' (Answer: Ann is 18.)

How's your father? A purely rhetorical question that originated as a humorous catchphrase in the music-halls before the First World War. It later came to be a synonym for 'nonsense' or meaningless ritual, so that the Northern Ireland MP Bernadette Devlin was reported in the *Daily Mail* of 23 April 1969, following her maiden speech, as saying: 'All this stand up, sit down, kneel down and how's-your-father was so funny.' Later still, the phrase acquired a sexual connotation on the lines of hanky-panky, as 'a bit of the old how's-your-father'.

How to ... . The stock opening words of the title of a book offering practical help or advice. Two famous titles of this type are Dale Carnegie's HOW TO WIN FRIENDS AND INFLUENCE PEOPLE (1936) and Shepherd Mead's *How to Succeed in Business Without Really Trying* (1953), the latter turned into a musical by Frank Loesser in 1961. On the fictional front there is also Erica Jong's novel *How To Save Your Own Life* (1978), a tale of the personal pilgrimage of a pornographic writer. More recently there have been such humorous compilations as *How to Become Ridiculously Well-Read in One Evening* (1985), *How to Become Absurdly Well-Informed about the Famous and Infamous* (1987), *How to Be Tremendously Tuned-in to Opera* (1989) and the like.

How to Win Friends and Influence People. The title of a self-help book published in 1936 by Dale Carnegie (1888–1955), a US lecturer and writer who specialized in teaching public speaking. The book, which sought to show how anybody could make a success of their lives, became an immense bestseller, and its title a hardy perennial of catchphrases and clichés. *See also* HOW TO ...

Hoxne treasure. In November 1992 an extensive hoard of Roman coins, jewellery and tableware was dug up in a field at Hoxne near Eye in Suffolk and was found to contain the largest collection of Roman coins yet discovered in Britain, originally buried in the 5th century. The find was declared treasure trove in September 1993 and bought by the British Museum in April 1994.

HP Sauce. A commercial brand of sauce first made in the 1870s. The initials that form its name are traditionally supposed to stand for 'Houses of Parliament', a picture of which appears on the label. However, the name was adopted by the Midland Vinegar Company, its original manufacturers, from that of another firm's product, 'Garton's H.P. Sauce', and it was thus ready-made, whatever the letters themselves might have actually meant. The name was registered as a trademark in 1912.

HTML. Hypertext Markup Language, in computing a specification for generating WORLD WIDE WEB pages that enables the viewing software to display text, images and other resources and to execute links to other such pages. It also allows the user to create and print out documents. *See also* HYPERTEXT.

Hughligans. See HEDGERS AND DITCHERS.

Hugh the Drover. The hero of Ralph Vaughan Williams's opera that bears his name, first performed in 1924 with a libretto by Harold Child. The scene is set in the early 19th century in a small Cotswold town where Hugh the Drover and John the Butcher are rivals for the hand of Mary, the constable's daughter. She loves Hugh, but her father wants her to marry the wealthy John. A boxing match is held by way of a duel. Hugh wins, but is accused by John of being a Napoleonic spy and is placed in the village stocks by Mary's father. He is released by the sergeant, who turns out to be an old friend, and Hugh and Mary leave together. The composer used the work as a vehicle for a variety of English folk songs, some of them set to his own music.

Hugo award. One of several awards made annually from 1955 by the World Science Fiction Convention for the best new SCIENCE FICTION novel, short story or the like. The name is that of the American editor and publisher Hugo Gernsback (1884–1967), founder of the first science fiction magazine, *Amazing Stories*, in 1926. The names of winning authors and titles are mainly unfamiliar to those to whom the genre is a closed book.

Hula hoop. The large hoop spun round the body by gyrating the hips, whether for pleasure or exercise, became all the rage in 1958. It was the brainchild of the Wham-O Manufacturing company, creator of the FRISBEE, who copied it from a hoop used by Australian children in gym class. The simplicity and cheapness of the hoop assured it instant international fame. The first word alludes to the hula, the Hawaiian women's dance, which involves undulation of the hips.

Hulot, Monsieur. The comic hero of films by the French film director and actor Jacques Tati (1908–82). He made his first appearance in *Les Vacances de Monsieur Hulot* (1953), bringing Tati instant fame, and set forth on a second outing in *Mon Oncle* (1958), a film that made his creator rich. The gawky, accident-prone character, eagerly apologetic in soft hat and triangular raincoat, with pipe, furled umbrella and striped socks, became one of cinema's most enduring creations.

Human shield. A person or group of people held near a potential target to deter an attack. The term became prominent in the second GULF WAR when the Iraqi government forcibly deployed Western citizens in military and other installations that were expected to be targets.

> More than 30 people who died in Nato's attack on Belgrade television were sacrificed as 'human shields' by the Yugoslav authorities, who knew that the bombing was imminent.
>
> *The Times* (6 May 1999)

Hun. An uncivilized brute, from the barbarian tribe of Huns who invaded the East Roman Empire in the 4th and 5th centuries. In the First World War it became a colloquial name for the Germans. Ironically, it was a speech by Wilhelm II that promoted the latter sense. On 27 July 1900 the German emperor addressed troops at Bremerhaven about to set sail for China. As reported in the English press, the speech contained the following passage:

> No quarter will be given, no prisoners will be taken. Let all who fall into your hands be at your mercy. Just as the Huns a thousand years ago, under the leadership of Etzel [Attila] gained a reputation in virtue of which they still live in historical tradition, so may the name of Germany become known in such a manner in China that no Chinaman will ever again even dare to look askance at a German.
>
> *The Times* (30 July 1900)

Hundertwasser, Fritz. The eccentric and blatantly self-promoting Austrian artist of this name was born in Vienna in 1928 as Friedrich Stowasser. After studying briefly at the Academy in 1948, he adopted the name Hundertwasser, translating the initial 'Sto-', the Czech word for 'hundred', to German *Hundert*. From about 1969 he signed his work 'Friedensreich Hundertwasser', the extended first name, German for 'kingdom of peace', being his boast that through his painting he would introduce the viewer to a new life of peace and happiness. He often subsequently added 'Regenstag', German for 'rainy day', so that his full name was now Friedensreich Hundertwasser Regenstag. This further expansion symbolized his happy mood on rainy days because colours then have an extra sparkle. Hundertwasser has been an outspoken critic of modern architecture but has made his own contribution in the fantastic, polychromatic Hundertwasser House in Vienna, completed in 1986.

Hundred and One Dalmatians, The. A fantasy (1956)

for children by 'Dodie' (Dorothy Gladys) Smith (1896–1990), in which the villainous Cruella DE VIL kidnaps Dalmatian puppies for their fur. It was made into a successful cartoon film, *One Hundred and One Dalmatians* (1961), by the Walt Disney studios. Dalmatians were the author's passion.

Hundred days. A term used by supporters of President Franklin Roosevelt to refer to his first three months in office in 1933, during which he pushed through an avalanche of legislation to establish the NEW DEAL. The phrase echoes Napoleon's 'hundred days', between his escape from Elba and his defeat at Waterloo (1815). *See also* FDR; THOUSAND DAYS.

Hundred Flowers campaign. A campaign initiated by Mao Zedong in China in May 1956 to encourage constructive criticism of government and the Communist Party, following the classical Chinese slogan: 'Let a hundred flowers bloom, and a hundred schools of thought contend.' Mao was inspired by the recent 'thaw' in the Soviet Union that had followed Nikita Khrushchev's denunciation of STALIN in February 1956. By April 1957, however, intellectuals were voicing such strong criticisms that Mao called off the campaign, replacing it with an 'anti-rightist' campaign against the critics.

Hungerford massacre. The shooting of 28 people, of whom 13 died, by an unbalanced gunman, Michael Ryan. The massacre took place at Hungerford, a small town in Berkshire, on 20 August 1987. Ryan, whose victims included his own mother, ended his killing spree by shooting himself. *See also* DUNBLANE MASSACRE.

Hunger march. A march of the unemployed to call attention to their grievances, as that of 1932, the year in which Wal Hannington, the leader of the communist-backed National Union of Unemployed Workers, led a march on London. The biggest of the marches organized by the union was the Jarrow Crusade of 1936, led by the local MP, 'Red Ellen' Wilkinson, when 200 men from the unemployment blackspot of Jarrow on the Tyne marched to London to seek aid for their town. The march received much sympathetic publicity, and a petition was presented to Parliament, but little practical help was forthcoming.

Hunt, Laura. The *femme fatale* in Vera Caspary's mystery novel *Laura* (1943). She is presumed dead at the outset of the story and the policeman assigned to investigate her murder gradually falls in love with her image. The film of the novel (1944) is a highly ingenious FILM NOIR, with Gene Tierney in the title role.

Hunting, shooting and fishing. The traditional sporting trinity of the British landed gentry, centring on the capturing, wounding and killing of animals. The phrase is sometimes written 'huntin', shootin' and fishin'' to convey the clipped accent of some of the more venerable practitioners. *See also* GREEN WELLIES.

> Mr [Alan] Clark, a vegetarian, sided with the hunting, shooting and fishing set and declared: 'I could not countenance legislation to block hunting.'
> *The Times* (8 September 1998)

Hunt the Shunt. A nickname of the world champion racing driver James Hunt (1947–93), so called early in his career from his propensity to propel his vehicle into the path of others.

Hurricane names. The modern custom of assigning names to hurricanes originated with the Australian meteorologist Clement Wragge (1852–1922), who gave women's names to tropical storms and men's to non-tropical. The practice was officially adopted by US meteorologists in 1953, when an alphabet of women's names was created for the purpose: Alice, Barbara, Carol, Dolly, Edna, Florence, Gilda, Hazel, Irene, Jill, Katherine, Lucy, Mabel, Norma, Orpha, Patsy, Queen, Rachel, Susie, Tina, Una, Vickie and Wallis. These names were also used in 1954, when the severity of hurricanes Carol, Edna and Hazel prompted some to suggest that men's names would have been more suitable. Women's names remained, however, until the 1970s, when feminist pressure led to the adoption of alternate men's and women's names in 1977.

Hurry Upkins. A nickname given in Britain to the US special envoy to Britain Harry Hopkins (1890–1946) before America's entry into the Second World War. The name referred to both Hopkins's whistle-stop visits to London and the British desire that the USA 'hurry up' and enter the war. Hopkins had been a NEW DEAL administrator, and throughout the Second World War was FDR's closest personal adviser, heading the LEND-LEASE programme from 1941.

Hush-hush. A term that came into use in the First World War to describe very secret operations, designs, or inventions, from the exclamation 'hush' demanding silence.

Hush money. Money given as a bribe for silence or hushing a matter up.

Hush puppy. An American aliment of deep-fried corn meal batter, often served with fried fish in the Southern states. Pieces thrown to hungry barking dogs with the injunction 'Hush, Puppy!' were said to effect an instant silence. 'Hush Puppies' were familiar in the 1960s as the trade name of a type of soft shoe. The allusion is to shoes that comfort 'barking dogs', slang for tired or sore feet.

Hustle. A dance devised by black American youths in East Harlem in the early 1970s. It had a lively and strenuous style, in which the male would spin his partner and toss her in the air. Its steps were akin to those of the foxtrot. It was brought before the public at large by the hit instrumental song 'The Hustle' released in 1975 by Van McCoy and the Soul City Symphony.

Hustler. The title of a popular US porn magazine founded by Larry Flynt in the early 1970s. The magazine pushed the boundaries of what was acceptable: its second issue published photographs of Jacqueline Onassis (JACKIE O) sunbathing naked on a Greek beach, after which sales soared. Flynt was soon surrounded by a rising and hostile tide of puritanism from the US religious right, and was sued by the Reverend Jerry Falwell over a *Hustler* satire on the TV evangelist's first sexual experience. The case went all the way to the Supreme Court, which upheld Flynt's right to free speech. Flynt's career was the subject of the 1996 film *The People vs. Larry Flynt*.

In US slang 'hustler' has several meanings, but 'successful womanizer' is presumably what Flynt had in mind (following the model of PLAYBOY, but with appropriately raunchier overtones). Other meanings include: (1) a prostitute of either sex (as in Andy Warhol's 1965 film *My Hustler*); (2) a person who pursues life and business aggressively and successfully; (3) a gambler or pool player or similar who makes a living beating less talented players (as in the 1961 Paul Newman film, *The Hustler*).

Hutber's Law. Improvement means deterioration, a cynical construct proposed by Patrick Hutber (1928–80), originator of the 'Questor' column in the *Daily Telegraph* and City Editor of the *Sunday Telegraph* from 1966 to 1979.

> Ask [British Telecom] for the telephone number of someone who has moved house and you will be told that it is not listed. ... 'It takes at least three weeks to get on to the computer'. With computers, Hutber's law doubles in force.
> *Daily Telegraph* (2 May 1992)

Hype. Extravagant publicity; exaggerated promotion, especially in flowery, convoluted or even ungrammatical language. The word, perhaps a shortening of 'hyperbole', is of American origin and initially meant a swindle. It began to gain its present sense in the 1920s. The following, quoted in *The Times* of 24 January 2000, is a sample, as part of a press release by the firm Procter & Gamble promoting its new site on the INTERNET.

> This site is a great opportunity for P&G to further increase the relevance of our brands to the teenage audience. The internet gives us a unique platform to leverage the scale of our portfolio to better meet the needs of specific target groups.

Hypertext. A term coined in 1974 by the American computer expert Theodor Nelson to describe electronic texts embedded with links to other texts. It now denotes a software system that allows cross-referencing between such texts and associated graphic material. It is the 'h' of 'http' (hypertext transport protocol), providing file access on the WORLD WIDE WEB, and of HTML.

Hyphenate. A person who combines two or more roles, so called because these are often joined with a hyphen, as 'writer-director'. Similarly, a hyphenated American is one who can trace their ancestry to another part of the world, such as an African-American or Irish-American.

> [Dominic] Anciano and [Ray] Burdis ... are the ultimate multi-hyphenates: they are writer-producer-directors who also act in their work.
> *The Times* (25 September 1999)

I

I am the Walrus. A bizarre, anarchically anti-establishment song by the BEATLES, credited to John Lennon and Paul McCartney and released in Britain in November 1967. The song and its title reflect Lennon's love of schoolboy nonsense lyrics (witness 'yellow matter custard dripping from a dead dog's eye'), but also includes grotesque and scurrilous invective targeted against conventional institutions and morality. Edgar Allan Poe (1809-49), the enigmatic American poet, short-story writer, part-time alcoholic and hero of the 1960s counter-culture, is 'kicked' at one point in the song's lyrics. The song featured in the film of MAGICAL MYSTERY TOUR.

ICBM. The abbreviation for intercontinental ballistic missile. Nuclear-armed ICBMs threatening Armageddon have hung over the world like the sword of Damocles since the 1950s, although with the ending of the COLD WAR the threat has receded. With ranges up to 12,000 km (8000 miles) or more, they were designed to hit targets in the Soviet Union if launched from the USA and vice versa. They can also be launched from submarines, although in such cases they are usually referred to as SLBMs (submarine-launched ballistic missiles). *See also* ABM; MAD; POLARIS; SALT; STAR WARS; TRIDENT.

Ice beer. A type of strong lager. 'Ice' refers to the brewing process, in which the beer is cooled to sub-zero temperatures so that ice crystals form. These are then filtered out. Breweries claim that the process produces a smoother taste as well a higher alcoholic content. Beer of this type was originally introduced in the early 1990s as a marketing gimmick.

Iceberg. A nickname of the US film star Grace Kelly (1929–82), famed for her performances in such films as *High Noon* (1952), *Rear Window* (1954) and *High Society* (1956). She abandoned her screen career to marry Prince Rainier III of Monaco in 1956. The name derives from her blond hair and cool demeanour. The director Alfred Hitchcock, who directed her in three films, spoke of her 'sexual elegance'. She died following a driving accident.

Ice Break, The. A characteristically off-beat opera by Michael Tippett (1905–98) with a libretto by the composer. It was first performed in 1977. The theme of the opera is imprisonment, both physical and emotional, and the need for people to break out of their stereotypes. At the end one character, Yuri, who has been badly injured in a riot, is released from his cracking plaster and is reconciled with his father, who at the beginning of the opera had spent 20 years in prison camps.

Ice cream pants. An American term of the early 20th century for white flannel trousers, especially when worn with a blue blazer as a standard 'uniform' for a young man going out on a date.

Ice-Cream War, An. A novel (1982) by William Boyd (b.1952), set largely in East Africa during the First World War. Accidents and misunderstandings abound, death is a common feature, and irony is employed to the full. The title refers obliquely to the torrid heat endured by those fighting in the British campaign against the Germans in East Africa. As one character remarks: 'It is far too hot for sustained fighting … we will all melt like ice-cream in the sun!'

Ice maiden or **queen.** A 'cold' and apparently emotionless woman. The expressions became current from the 1950s but evoke folkloric figures such as the Russian 'Snow Maiden' (Snegurochka). *The Ice Maiden*

(1927), a ballet choreographed by Fydor Lopokov based on Grieg's *Peer Gynt* suite, tells the story of the Ice Maiden, who disguises herself as a beautiful girl to attract young men and bring them death.

> *Second Voice*: Sinbad Sailors watches her [Gossamer Beynon] go by, demure and proud and schoolmarm in her crisp flower dress and sun-defying hat, ... the butcher's unmelting icemaiden daughter veiled for ever from the hungry hug of his eyes.
> DYLAN THOMAS: *Under Milk Wood* (1954)

Iceman Cometh, The. A play (1946) by the US playwright Eugene O'Neill (1888–1953) in which a disparate group of characters gather in Harry Hole's saloon to lament the death of their collective illusions. The play was inspired by the down-at-heel characters O'Neill encountered in the bars of lower Manhattan during his own early years of disillusion and depression. The mysterious 'iceman' of the title (the man bringing ice to the saloon) is referred to several times in the script and comes to represent death. The choice of the word 'cometh' suggests biblical overtones, and Hickey the cheery salesman is commonly interpreted as a Christ figure.

Ice queen. *See* ICE MAIDEN.

Icing on the cake. An attractive but inessential addition to something already good. An American equivalent is 'frosting on the cake'. The expression dates from the 1960s.

I, Claudius. A historical novel (1934) by Robert Graves (1895–1985) about the emperor Claudius (10 BC– AD 54), who in AD 41 succeeded his nephew Caligula in unlikely fashion as ruler of the Roman empire. It begins: 'I, Tiberius Claudius Drusus Nero Germanicus This-that-and-the-other (for I shall not trouble you yet with all my titles) ... .' *Claudius the God and His Wife Messalina* (1934) is a sequel. Their timely appearance in 1976 as a television drama series, directed by Herbert Wise and written by Jack Pulman, saved the author from financial embarrassment. The stammering but wily Claudius was memorably played by Derek Jacobi.

Icon. Apart from its original use to denote a painting of a holy figure, by the early 1990s 'icon' had acquired two new meanings: first, and generally, as a word for a famous person regarded as a cult figure (as if worshipped, like the holy icon); second, and specifically, as a term for a small symbolic figure on a computer screen that represents a particular facility and that can be activated to provide it. By the end of the 1990s the word in the former sense had itself become an 'icon'.

> It's something of an overused word, icon. There are film icons, fashion icons, gay icons, and the original religious icon, Jesus – those deemed to have changed us for ever. But that doesn't mean the term is exhausted.
> *Sunday Times Magazine* (15 August 1999)

I couldn't care less. I am quite indifferent. The cliché may in fact mean the opposite, since the speaker has reacted with some passion to a situation. The expression dates from the 1940s. An American variant of the 1960s was 'I could care less', perhaps influenced by 'I should care'.

> Never say 'I couldn't care less'. It's rude, common, and usually untrue.
> GUY EGMONT: *The Art of Egmontese*, ch vi (1961)

Ideal Home Exhibition. An annual exhibition of the latest home comforts at Earl's Court, London. The popular show, famous for its spectacular displays, including a full-size house of the future, evolved from the exhibition first held in 1908 by the *Daily Mail* as an advertising gimmick.

Identikit. A method of identifying criminals from composite photographs based on an assemblage of individual features selected by witnesses from a wide variety of drawings. The method was developed by Hugh C. McDonald and first used at Los Angeles in 1959.

Identity cards. While identity cards have long been a regular fact of life in many countries, they were first issued in Britain only in the early days of the Second World War. They were abolished in 1952 but the introduction of a voluntary identity card was under discussion in the 1990s.

Idlewild. The former popular name of the New York International Airport, situated at Idlewild on the northeast shore of Jamaica Bay, Long Island. In 1963 it was renamed the John F. Kennedy International Airport, popularly referred to as JFK.

Idiot savant (French, 'knowledgeable idiot'). A psychological term current in English from the 1920s for a person with a mental disability who nevertheless displays a remarkable talent in some respect, typically memorizing or rapid calculation. The expression also gained a more general sense to apply to an otherwise unworldly person who displays natural wisdom and insight.

Idiot zone. An Americanism for a time or place devoid of worthwhile activity; a 'silly season'.

> Summer is more traditionally the 'idiot zone' in American cinemas when all the big popcorn movies clog up thousands of air-conditioned theatres.
>
> *heat* (14–20 October 1999)

I don't believe this! How could this have happened? An exclamation of disbelief that such a situation could have arisen (and been caused by my or someone else's action).

I Don't Like Mondays. A song by the PUNK ROCK group the Boomtown Rats, released in 1979. The title of the song derives from the explanation given by the American schoolgirl Brenda Spencer for her shooting dead several of her classmates on 29 January 1979. When asked why she had carried out the shootings she replied 'I don't like Mondays'. A number one hit in Britain, the song unsurprisingly fared less well in America, where many radio stations chose not to play the single on grounds of taste. *See also* ROCK GROUP NAMES.

I don't think so. Certainly not. A catchphrase current in the 1990s to denote that in the speaker's view the statement just made, the question just asked or the situation described is patently untrue. In spoken form the phrase is usually stressed on the 'I'.

> I am sure she [Jade Jagger] is as sweet as she is pretty, but a role model for grown-up women? I don't think so.
>
> *Sunday Times* (9 January 2000)

If. 'If —', the title of a famous moralistic poem by Rudyard Kipling, originally appeared in *Rewards and Fairies* (1910). It enumerates 12 conditions, the successful fulfilment of which will bring the doer 'the Earth and everything that's in it, / And – which is more – you'll be a Man, my son!' The poem gave the ironic title of the highly praised film IF ... .

If ... The film (1968), written by David Sherwin and John Howlett, is an allegory about the violent rebellion of pupils at an English public school against the authority of their masters. Directed by Lindsay Anderson and starring Malcolm McDowell, the script was originally titled *The Crusaders* but acquired its final title in ironic reference to Rudyard Kipling's celebrated poem 'If —' (*see* IF). *If ...* is also the name of a satirical cartoon strip by the illustrator Steve Bell, which first appeared in the *Guardian* newspaper in 1981.

If on a Winter's Night a Traveller. An avant-garde novel (1981; published in Italian as *Se una notte d'inverno un viaggiatore*, 1979) by Italo Calvino (1923–85). It concerns the narrator's quest, which begins in a railway station, for the elusive Ludmilla. The quest chapters are interspersed with episodes in which Calvino plays games with the reader. At one point sections of *If on a Winter's Night a Traveller* are said to have been bound up with those from another novel, *Outside the Town of Malbork*. This particular exercise continues through the book, with consecutive chapter headings finally making a complete sentence, beginning, 'If on a winter's night a traveller, outside the town of Malbork ...'.

If you ask me. If you want to know my opinion (whether you actually ask for it or not).

Ike. The nickname of Dwight D. Eisenhower (1890–1972), US general and 34th president of the USA (1953–61). The name, originally a school tag based on Eisenhower's surname, was in regular use throughout his military career and formed the basis of his winning slogan, 'I like Ike', first appearing on buttons as early as 1947. It seemed irrelevant that 'ike' was 19th-century US slang for an ignorant rustic, or that 'Ikey' is a derogatory name for a Jew. *See also* MONTY.

IKEA. The brand of self-assembly furniture, giving a semblance of stability and style at a reasonable cost, was first produced in 1947 by the Swedish manufacturer Ingvar Kamprad. The name is a blend of his initials and those of the farm where he was born, Elmtaryd, and his village, Agunnaryd. The acronym is interpreted by cynical Germans as *Idioten kaufen eben alles*, 'Some fools will buy anything'.

I kid you not. I am perfectly serious. The jocular expression, of US origin and current from the 1950s, has been attributed to the entertainer and talk show host Jack Paar (b.1918).

> David Boreanaz and (I kid you not) Charisma Carpenter head the good-looking young cast.
>
> *The Times* (7 January 2000)

I Know Where I'm Going. A film (1945) co-written and directed by Michael Powell (1905–90) and Emeric Pressburger (1902–88) about a headstrong young woman's plan to marry her wealthy elderly employer. The scheme is thrown awry when she falls for a young naval officer while on her way to be married in the Hebrides. Starring Wendy Hiller and Roger Livesey, it took its title from an Irish song that Powell's wife sang to him as they travelled on a London bus to Piccadilly Circus:

I know where I'm going
And I know who goes with me
I know whom I love
But the dear Lord (or Devil) knows whom I'll marry.

On Powell's instructions, music from the film was played at his funeral.

Illywhacker. An Australian slang word of 1940s provenance for a confidence trickster, especially one who follows fairs around the country. *Illywhacker* (1985) by the Australian novelist Peter Carey (b.1943), is the epic fictional autobiography of a 109-year-old boaster, aviator and conman.

Imagism. A school of poetry founded by Ezra Pound (1885–1972), derived from the ideas of the philosopher T.E. Hulme (1883–1917). The imagist poets were in revolt against excessive romanticism and proclaimed that poetry should use the language of common speech, create new rhythms, be uninhibited in choice of subject and present a precise image. Imagism was a key influence on MODERNISM in English-language verse.

I'm All Right Jack. A film (1959) adapted by John Boulting and Frank Harvey from Alan Hackney's novel *Private Life* about the comical clashes between a communist trade unionist and factory management during a strike. Starring Peter Sellers as the shop steward in question and Ian Carmichael as a management representative caught in the middle of the dispute, the film was retitled in reference to the traditional English saying 'I'm all right, Jack', denoting the selfishness of a man who does not care what happens to those around him as long as his own interests have been taken care of. A nautical equivalent of the phrase is 'Pull up the ladder, Jack, I'm inboard.'

IMAX. A proprietary name for a technique of cinematography developed in Canada which produces an image approximately 10 times larger than that from standard 35mm film. The name is a blend of 'image' and 'maximum' and the system was first introduced in 1970. To watch a film made by this method, viewers sit on a series of elevated rows angled 30 to 45 degrees in such a way that they feel fully involved in the picture, which is on a screen 10 times the normal size and up to 8 storeys high. At the close of the 20th century Britain had three IMAX cinemas, two in London and one at the National Museum of Photography, Film and Television in Bradford, West Yorkshire. A new version of Walt Disney's cartoon classic FANTASIA (1940) opened on IMAX screens worldwide on 1 January 2000.

I may be some time. The last recorded words of the English explorer Captain Lawrence Edward Oates (1880–1912), spoken just before he walked to his death on the Antarctic expedition of Captain Robert Falcon Scott on March 16, 1912. Oates, who had decided that his illness was slowing down his companions, walked calmly out into a blizzard with the remark 'I am just going outside, and I may be some time.' The words were recorded by Scott and appeared in his journals, published as *Scott's Last Expedition* in 1913. Oates's statement, interpreted by succeeding generations as the essense of stiff-upper-lipped British courage, has since become widely disseminated as a catchphrase used when someone absents themselves from a gathering for any reason. *See also* BIRTHDAY BOYS; SOUTH POLE.

IMF. The abbreviation for the International Monetary Fund, a specialized agency of the United Nations set up at the BRETTON WOODS Conference in 1944. The purpose of the IMF is to promote trade expansion, the stabilization of currencies and international monetary cooperation. Along with its sister organization, the WORLD BANK, it has been criticized for policies unfavourable towards the environment and the THIRD WORLD and for undermining national sovereignty by dictating economic policies to governments as a condition for making loans.

Imperial Conference. The name given to the conferences held in London between the prime ministers of the various dominions of the British Empire between 1907 and 1946 inclusive. These conferences had their origin in the first Colonial Conference, which met in 1887 on the occasion of Queen Victoria's Jubilee. Since 1948 the Commonwealth Prime Ministers' Conference has replaced the Imperial Conference.

Imperial presidency. A term for the office of the president of the United States viewed as exceeding in power and authority the executive role provided by the Constitution. The term derives from the book *The Imperial Presidency* (1973) by the American historian Arthur M. Schlesinger Jr.

One area in which the imperial presidency is as regal as ever is the matter of international airline routes: by law the President can bestow on any airline of his choice the right to fly between any American city and any foreign one and he need not bother to state a reason.

Time (16 January 1978)

Impulse buyer. A person who buys something on a whim or the spur of the moment, especially when doing so without consideration of cost, quality or usefulness. Most supermarkets place confectionery and other attractive or useful items at the entrance to a checkout in the hope of tempting such shoppers to make a purchase.

A new range of McVitie and Price cake packages … will be on display in supermarkets this week, designed to attract the 'impulse' buyer.

The Times (11 March 1970)

I'm Sorry, I'll Read That Again. A chaotically cheerful and crudely comic radio programme broadcast from 1964 to 1973, its title based on the stock apology of a stumbling or stuttering newsreader. Billed as 'a radio custard pie', it was full of groan-inducing puns and mildly smutty sketches and helped to launch the career of many of its participants, including John Cleese of FAWLTY TOWERS and the three comedians who later cast themselves as the GOODIES.

In a bad way. Suffering; in difficulties. There is no contrary 'in a good way'.

Inch war. Dieting; the 'fight against flab', when the struggle is to lose inches round the waistline. The term can also apply to any gradual campaign. The *Evening Standard* of 8 June 1994 had a sub-heading 'Battle of the inch war' that referred to a plan by airlines to provide more passenger accommodation by dropping first-class seating.

In Cold Blood. Subtitled *A True Account of a Multiple Murder and Its Consequences*, this book (1966) by the US author Truman Capote (1924–84) has been described both as 'a non-fiction novel' and 'creative reporting'. Capote worked from 1959 to 1965 on his investigation into the motiveless murder of a Kansas family and accompanied the two perpetrators on their way to the gallows several years after they had been convicted. An action carried out 'in cold blood' is performed in a cool and calculated manner, not in the heat of passion. A complex and brutal film version (1967), directed by Richard Brooks, was remade as a television mini-series (1990) directed by Jonathan Kaplan and starring Anthony Edwards and Eric Roberts.

Incredible Hulk. The huge green humanoid into which the humble scientist, Dr David Bruce Banner, meta-morphoses whenever he is possessed by anger. The creature was the brainchild of the US writer Stan Lee and first featured in Marvel Comics in 1962. It (he) later appeared in a television version screened from 1978 to 1982, with Lou Ferrigno in the role of the man-beast.

Suddenly, bursting out of her skimpy tennis tops, we have a pair of arms like Boris Becker's thighs. It is like the Incredible Hulk in drag and slow motion.

The Times (5 May 1999)

Indie. An abbreviation of 'independent' used for a pop group or record label that does not belong to a major record company and whose music in many cases is intentionally unpolished. Indie rock is strictly speaking rock music released on such labels, but the term has come to apply more generally to the noisy guitar bands that descended from the PUNK groups of the 1970s and, by extension, to the youth subculture coalescing around such bands from the late 1980s.

Industrial action. A strike or stoppage. The expression seems curiously contradictory, since what is involved is a ceasing of work, otherwise inaction. On 14 May 1980 the Trades Union Congress even called a 'Day of Action' for such a tactic. But those resorting to the strategy see it as a positive move rather than a negative stance. The term itself dates from the 1970s.

Strikes or 'days of action' are planned for later this month … Renault, Bull, and Thomson CSF are also threatened with further industrial action.

Independent (10 May 1995)

Indy 500. The popular name of the Indianapolis 500 motor race, held annually with the exception of war years from 1911 at the Indianapolis Motor Speedway, near Indianapolis, Indiana. It was originally held on Memorial Day, 30 May, but later took place on the preceding Saturday or Sunday. It is 805km (500 miles) in length, which means that drivers of the 33 participating cars need to circuit the near-oblong 4km (2½ mile) track 200 times, starting three abreast from the initial line-up. The Indy 500 draws more spectators than any other US sporting event, and an attendance of 300,000 is not unusual.

Inferiority complex. A psychiatric term for a complex resulting from a sense of inferiority dating from childhood. Attempts to compensate for the sense of worthlessness may take an aggressive or violent form, or manifest themselves in an overzealous involvement in activities. The term dates from the 1920s.

In good nick. In good condition. A phrase of dialect origin, with 'nick' here the same word as that for a notch or cut, and as in other phrases, as 'in the nick of time'. The converse, 'in bad nick', is not often encountered.

> He looked the woman up and down. She was a little older, perhaps in her forties, but still in good nick, he noticed.
> DERMOT BOLGER (ed.): *Finbar's Hotel*, 'No Pets Please' (1997)

In-joke. A joke shared exclusively by a small group of people. 'In' here has rather the sense of 'fashionable' than simply meaning within the group. The expression dates from the mid-1960s.

Inkatha. The Zulu political organization of this name was originally founded in 1928 but was revived by Chief Buthelezi in 1973. It claims an aim of racial equality and universal franchise in South Africa, but has been subject to clashes both with the rival African National Congress (ANC) and among factions within the party itself. Its name is a Zulu word for a crown of woven grass, a tribal emblem representing the force that unites the Zulu nation.

Inklings. A group of Oxford friends, centring on the literary scholar and critic C.S. Lewis (1898–1963), who met from the 1930s to the 1960s to talk and to read their compositions aloud to one another. Other members were the philologist and writer J.R.R. Tolkien (1892–1973), the poet and theological writer Charles Williams (1886–1945), the medieval literary scholar Nevill Coghill (1899–1980) and the academic H.V.D. Dyson (1896–1975). Many of their meetings were held at the Eagle and Child inn in St Giles'. The group name puns rather obviously on 'ink'. Humphrey Carpenter's *The Inklings* (1977) is a study of the circle.

In My Life. A reflective and affectionate song by the BEATLES, credited to John Lennon and Paul McCartney and released in Britain in December 1965 on the album RUBBER SOUL. The 'Life' in question is John Lennon's, the roots of the song lying in a previously attempted lyric in which Lennon proposed to describe the sights and sounds he saw during the course of a bus journey from his home into Liverpool city centre. 'In My Life' represents a leaner and less ambitious version of this original idea. A curious feature of the song is the appearance halfway through it of a witty piece of baroque pastiche played on the electric piano by George Martin, the Beatles' producer (*see* FIFTH BEATLE).

Inner Cabinet. A name dating from the turn of the 20th century for a decision-making group of ministers within the regular Cabinet, or for a similar group within another body, such as a council.

Inner city. A central or innermost area of a city regarded as having social problems such as inadequate housing and high levels of crime and unemployment. Many inner cities have seen scenes of violence and rioting and their troubles have been associated with a racial element. Examples of such locations are Brixton in London, Toxteth in Liverpool, Handsworth in Birmingham and the St Paul's district of Bristol.

Responses by the government to deal with the problem have included the establishment of so called 'enterprise zones' in 1981 designed to encourage new commercial and industrial enterprises and the setting up of an Urban Regeneration Agency in 1993 with the aim of reclaiming derelict land in decayed inner cities. The term is of US origin and dates from the 1960s.

Inner space. A term introduced in the late 1950s for the part of the human mind that is not normally accessible to consciousness. Attempts have been made to explore this region, in ancient times through meditation and in the psychedelic 1960s and 1970s through drugs, but results have remained unsatisfactory or at best inconclusive. The term itself was probably prompted by the then current interest in the exploration of outer space.

Innit. A representation of a casual pronunciation of 'isn't it', usually as a tag question rather like the French *n'est-ce pas*. An example might thus be 'Cold, innit?' The form dates from the 1950s.

Innocent bystander. A bystander who is not responsible for or directly involved in an event or incident yet suffers as a result of it. An innocent victim is similar. The terms evolved in the 1950s.

In no uncertain terms. Very clearly; emphatically. A meiotic turn of phrase that seems to have become popular only from the 1950s.

> When I asked her to calm down, she informed me, in no uncertain terms, of my place in the scheme of things.
> *Today* (15 February 1995)

In orbit. In a state of great excitement; exhilarated; 'high'. The phrase dates from the 1960s and ultimately alludes to the launch of the first Soviet SPUTNIK in 1957. *See also* GO INTO ORBIT.

I have recently found the man of my dreams. … I'm in orbit and feel as if all my Christmases have come at once.

TARA PALMER-TOMKINSON in *Sunday Times* (8 August 1999)

Inside job. A crime committed by someone familiar with the layout and routine of the place where it happened. *See also* OUTSIDE JOB.

Police investigating the theft of personal items belonging to the Princess Royal in Buckingham Palace believe it to be an 'inside job'.

The Times (4 October 1999)

Insider dealing. A Stock Exchange term for the buying or selling of shares when in possession of 'inside' information that will affect the price. The practice was made illegal by the Company Securities (Insider Dealing) Act of 1985 and the first person to be prosecuted under it, in 1987, was Geoffrey Collier, joint manager of Morgan Grenfell Securities, who was fined £25,000.

Inspector Appleby. *See* APPLEBY, INSPECTOR.

Inspector Calls, An. A play (1946) by J.B. Priestley (1894–1984) in which a complacent Yorkshire industrialist and his family are quizzed about their individual involvement in the suicide of a poor young woman. The inspector of the title is merciless in his exposure of each person's guilt, but towards the end of the play his own identity comes into a question as it is revealed he is not an official inspector at all. A film version (1954) was directed by Guy Hamilton.

Inspector Clouseau. *See* CLOUSEAU, INSPECTOR.

Inspector Gadget. A nickname for a mechanical expert or 'techno-whiz'. The name is that of an American animated cartoon character of the late 1980s who is the first 'gadgetized' and bionic inspector to work for INTERPOL.

Peter Snow, in charge of maps and gadgets for the BBC, was hero of the hour. … To call him Inspector Gadget would be making light of his talent. He is Deputy Assistant Commissioner Gadget.

Sunday Times (2 January 2000)

Inspector Ghote. *See* GHOTE, INSPECTOR.

Inspector Morse. An elegantly filmed television crime series, screened from 1987, centring on the investigations of Chief Inspector Morse of Thames Valley Police, a complex character originally created in novels by Colin Dexter. Accompanied by his Geordie sidekick, Lewis, the irascible, crossword-solving,

REAL ALE-drinking, music-loving Morse pursues plots that bridge the gap between a regular WHODUNNIT and a sophisticated allegory. One episode, 'Promised Land', was not only a murder mystery but a parody on Mozart's opera *The Magic Flute*. The series was filmed in and around Oxford, which added to the nostalgic feel and cerebral charm of the whole.

Intelligence quotient or **IQ.** The ratio, expressed as a percentage, of a person's mental age to his or her actual age, the former being the level of test performance that is median for that age tested by the Binet type scale or some similar system. Thus if a 10-year-old has a mental age of nine years, the IQ is 90. 100 indicates average intelligence. The term was introduced by the German educationist Wilhelm Stern as *Intelligenz-Quotient* in 1912 and popularized by the work of Cyril Burt (1883–1971), Lewis M. Terman (1877–1956) and others.

InterCity train. A brandname introduced by British Railways in the mid-1950s for what was formerly known as an express train. The word 'intercity' meaning 'linking cities' is not new, nor was its application to the BR trains original, as the North British Railway was running 'inter-city expresses' between Edinburgh and Aberdeen as early as 1906.

International Brigades. The units of foreigners who volunteered to fight on the Republican side in the Spanish Civil War (1936–9). Most of the volunteers, who came from around 50 countries, were communists, and the International Brigades were organized by the COMINTERN, the Soviet-led Communist (or Third) International. In all, some 37,000 men and women volunteered, and each of the seven brigades were organized into battalions according to nationality: for example, many Americans were in the Abraham Lincoln Battalion, and there was also a John Brown Battery, named after two heroes of the anti-slavery movement in the USA. The International Brigades were withdrawn in 1938 as the USSR slimmed down its support for the Republic. Not all anti-fascist foreign volunteers joined the International Brigades: George ORWELL, for example, joined the militia of the Marxist but anti-Stalinist POUM (Partido Obrero de Unificación Marxista) in 1936, and ended up fighting the Soviet-controlled communists who set out to destroy the POUM and other ideological opponents within the Republican camp.

International Standard Book Number. *See* ISBN.

International Monetary Fund. *See* IMF.

International Women's Day. The day so named was proclaimed in 1910 at the Second International Socialist Women's Conference in Copenhagen on the suggestion of the German communist leader Clara Zetkin (1857–1933). It was first observed the following year by comrades in Germany, Austria-Hungary, Switzerland and Denmark and subsequently other countries. At first the date varied but from 1914 it settled as 8 March. It was fully celebrated in the Soviet Union, where the Presidium of the Supreme Soviet, in a decree of 8 May (VE DAY) 1965, declared it a public holiday 'in honour of the outstanding services of Soviet women in the building of communism and the defence of the Motherland during the GREAT PATRIOTIC WAR, and of their heroism and selflessness at the front and in the rear, and also to mark the great contribution of women to the cementing of friendship between nations and the struggle for peace'. Satellite states took a similar line, but the demise of communism in eastern Europe in the early 1990s allowed the day to be taken up more openly in the United States and elsewhere.

Internaut. An expert or habitual user of the INTERNET. The term hints at ASTRONAUT or COSMONAUT, since such a person 'visits' the site on the WORLD WIDE WEB as a space traveller 'visits' a celestial region. There is also an implied suggestion of CYBERSPACE.

> [The Bibliothèque nationale of France] has now set up a website for the public on which books amounting to two million pages can be read by the 'internauts', as the French call them.
> *The Times* (8 April 1999)

Internet. An international computer network that provides E-MAIL and information from computers in educational establishments, government agencies and industry. It is accessible to the general public and had its origins in the COLD WAR, when in 1969 the US Defense Department built an experimental computer network designed to withstand a nuclear attack. The expansion of this network eventually came to provide information in the form of HYPERTEXT on the WORLD WIDE WEB. Concern has been expressed regarding the ease with which children can gain access to pornography on the Net, either through a website devoted to the subject or via a CHAT ROOM ostensibly treating an innocent topic but in fact having a sexual basis.

> Previously the domain of techie anoraks and boffins in lab coats, the Internet is now part of everyday life.
> *The Times* (25 September 1999)

Interpol. The short name of the International Criminal Police Organization, set up in Vienna in 1923 to facilitate the cooperation of the police forces of different countries in the international fight against crime. In 1938 NAZI Germany seized Austria and Interpol with it and took all its records to Berlin. It was reorganized immediately after the Second World War and is now based in Paris.

In the bag. Settled; made certain. The allusion is to game that has been shot and placed in the game bag. The expression is of US origin and dates from the 1920s.

In the club. Pregnant. The expression is short for 'in the pudding club', the 'pudding' being the foetus in the womb. *See also* BUN IN THE OVEN; UP THE DUFF.

In the doghouse. In trouble or disgrace, as a dog is confined to its kennel after misbehaving. The phrase is traditionally applied to an errant husband. In J.M. Barrie's PETER PAN (1904) Mr Darling lived in the dog kennel until his children returned as a penance for his treatment of NANA. The term dates from the 1930s.

In the frame. Eligible. The allusion is either to the racetrack, where the names of the winning horses are displayed in a frame, or to snooker, where the balls ready for play are positioned in a frame. The phrase is often expanded as 'names in the frame' to refer to particular eligible individuals.

> England need a [rugby] coach with the mental dexterity of a chess master, the calmness and surety of a surgeon, the communication skills of a television presenter and the passion and flair of a flamenco dancer. So who is in the frame?
> *The Times* (16 November 1999)

In the front row. In the best seats; in the place of privilege. The term applies specifically to the front row at a fashion show. A political equivalent exists in the House of Commons as the front bench, i.e. the foremost seats, occupied by members of the Cabinet and Shadow Cabinet. Either term has potential for figurative use.

> 'You're either in the front row, or you're just at the show.' A friend at Vogue said the very same thing to me recently. ... And make no mistake, the front row it has to be. Fighting it out for a second- or third-row seat is pointless.
> *Sunday Times Magazine* (19 September 1999)

In the Heat of the Night. A film (1967) adapted by Stirling Silliphant from a novel by John Ball about the conflict that develops between a bigoted Mississippi sheriff and the black detective with whom he has to collaborate while investigating a racial murder. Directed by Norman Jewison and starring Rod Steiger and Sidney Poitier, the film was set in a sweltering cotton town, hence the title. Such was the political 'heat' involved in racist issues in Mississippi in the 1960s, it was felt necessary to make the film some distance away, in Illinois.

In the loop. Belonging to the circle of people who are influential or well informed. To be 'out of the loop' is conversely to be excluded from the circle of those in the know. The expression arose as US political jargon of the 1990s but can apply to a social, business or any other circle.

> [Conservative leader William] Hague will need to fasten [Michael] Portillo's seatbelt. Word in the loop is that he might get the party chairman's job.
>
> *Sunday Times* (28 November 1999)

In the Night Kitchen. A picture book (1970) by the US illustrator Maurice Sendak (b.1928). A boy called Michael is mixed into a batter by three identical fat bakers (drawn to resemble the comedian Oliver Hardy) after he falls from his bed into a Night Kitchen. He manages to escape on a flying-machine made of dough and returns to his bed. The inspiration for the book's title came from Sendak's childhood memory of a New York bakery that displayed the slogan 'We bake while you sleep!'

In the pipeline. Forthcoming; about to happen; in the process of being prepared. The phrase dates from the 1950s and perhaps alludes to oil or gas that is processed and about to be to be delivered.

> We hope that similar coverage will be given to other initiatives in the pipeline.
>
> *The Times* (Letter to the Editor) (31 July 1999)

In the right ballpark. Approximately accurate; within reasonable bounds. A US phrase of the 1960s referring to a baseball stadium. *See also* BALLPARK FIGURE.

In the sticks. In a remote rural location; in the 'back of beyond'. 'The sticks' are the world of trees and nature. More specifically, in US theatrical jargon, 'the sticks' are a town outside the regular touring circuit, far removed from New York. A headline in *Variety* for 17 July 1935 ran: 'Sticks nix hick pix', meaning that rural residents gave the thumbs-down to films about farms.

In this day and age. Now. A more or less meaningless piece of journalistic padding that apparently dates

from the early 20th century and that has the merit of seeming more sonorous and dignified than it actually is. Cecil B. de Mille's film *This Day and Age* (1933) describes how, during an American youth week, boys put a gangster on trial and by his own methods force him to confess to murder. The movie was condemned by some at the time as an incitement to FASCISM.

> 'We knew drug-dealing was going on ... but I thought that, in this day and age, you just had to learn to accept that sort of thing.'
>
> *People* (4 December 1994)

Intifada (Arabic, 'a jumping up'). This term for an Arab uprising or revolt, as a 'jumping up' in reaction to something, became familiar in the West from 1987, when the PLO began its campaign of sustained unrest in the Israeli-occupied WEST BANK and GAZA STRIP.

Intranet. A communications network belonging to a particular organization and employing the same technology as that of the INTERNET.

In your face. Bold and aggressive; blatant and provocative. The image is of a thing thrown or thrust directly into a person's face. The phrase originated partly among American blacks and partly from basketball jargon, in which a defensive player closely marking an attacker is said to be 'in the face of' that player. A spelling reflecting a colloquial pronunciation is 'in-yer-face'. *See also* GET OUT OF SOMEONE'S FACE.

> David Thomson ... a parish councillor, is appalled. 'The [road] signs are what they call "In yer face". They shout and hit you when you are driving down a country lane,' he said.
>
> *The Times* (15 June 1999)

Ipcress File, The. A film (1965) based on a spy thriller (1962) of the same title by the novelist Len Deighton (b.1929) about a reluctant counter-intelligence agent who finds himself caught up in a convoluted spy plot involving the kidnap of top scientists. Starring Michael Caine as the antihero Harry Palmer (who is not named in the books), the film spawned two sequels, *Funeral in Berlin* (1966) and *Billion Dollar Brain* (1967). The Ipcress File of the title is a mysterious tape simply labelled 'Ipcress' that Palmer turns up during his investigations.

IQ. *See* INTELLIGENCE QUOTIENT.

IRA. The Irish Republican Army, a guerrilla force largely reorganized by Michael Collins (1890–1922; *see* BIG FELLA) from the former Irish Volunteers, which confronted the Royal Irish Constabulary and the BLACK AND TANS from 1919 to 1921. After the Irish Civil War (1922–3) extremists kept it in being as a secret organization, and although it was proscribed in 1936, the IRA continued to make occasional raids into Northern Ireland, in pursuit of its aim of establishing a united Irish republic. After a period of quiescence, violence steadily increased from the mid-1950s. From 1969 to 1994, when it announced a ceasefire, its commission of acts of terrorism in Northern Ireland, mainland Britain and elsewhere made a settlement of Northern Ireland's TROUBLES increasingly difficult. It ended the ceasefire in 1996, when a bomb in London's DOCKLANDS killed 2 and injured 100, but announced its restoration in 1997. The GOOD FRIDAY AGREEMENT of 1998 seemed to bring a peace settlement nearer, but the disarmament of the IRA remained a sticking point and the deadlock was not broken by further discussions in the summer of 1999, despite the creation in December that year of Northern Ireland's first devolved government since 1974. The power-sharing assembly was suspended in February 2000 and DIRECT RULE reimposed when the IRA and other paramilitary groups failed to 'decommission' their weapons by a deadline set by the British government. However, the IRA's decision to open their arms dumps to inspection by a team of international observers allowed the assembly to recommence its functions in the early summer of 2000

In the aftermath of the Good Friday Agreement there emerged two dissident Republican groups opposed to the Accord: the 'Real IRA' and the 'Continuity IRA', the former responsible for the Omagh bombing of 1998. The names of both groups reflect their claims to be the true inheritors of Irish Republican tradition. The Real IRA broke away from the Provisional IRA, while the Continuity IRA is associated with Republican Sinn Féin, a faction that broke away from Provisional SINN FÉIN in the 1980s. The 'continuity' implied is that of strict Republican orthodoxy in keeping with the aims and methods of the instigators of the 1916 EASTER RISING. See also DECOMMISSIONING; HILLSBOROUGH DECLARATION; PROVOS; STICKIES.

Iran-Contra Affair. A more formal name for Irangate. See GATE.

Irascibles. A group of American artists who in 1950 protested against the exhibition policy of the Metropolitan Museum, New York, demanding the setting up of a department to show modern American art. Their number included many leading lights of ABSTRACT EXPRESSIONISM such as de Kooning, Newman, Pollock, Rothko and Still, and a subsequently much reproduced photograph of 15 of the original 18 members appeared in Life magazine on 15 January 1951.

Irgun. In full, Irgun Zvai Leumi (Hebrew, 'national military organization'), an underground anti-socialist Zionist military organization established by right-wing Jewish settlers in Palestine in 1931 as a rival organization to the HAGANAH. Its aim was to establish a Jewish state in Palestine, and to this end it carried out acts of terrorism against both Arabs and the British, who were administrators of the League of Nations mandate. Its leader from 1943 to 1948 was Menachem Begin (1913–92) the future prime minister of Israel (1977–83). The Irgun was responsible for the bomb attack on the King David Hotel in Jerusalem in 1946, which resulted in the deaths of 91 military and civilian personnel, including Britons, Arabs and Jews. The following year its commandos killed all 254 inhabitants of an Arab village (see DEIR YASSIN). The Irgun disbanded on the establishment of the state of Israel in 1948, and Begin founded the Herut ('freedom') Party. The STERN GANG was a splinter group of the Irgun.

Irish Free State. See FREE-STATERS.

Irish Republican Army. See IRA.

Irish R.M., The. A compendium (1956) of stories by E.O. Somerville (1858–1949) and her cousin Martin Ross (pen name of Violet Martin; 1862–1915), consisting of Some Experiences of an Irish R.M. (1899), Further Experiences of an Irish R.M. (1908) and In Mr Knox's Country (1915). The R.M. (resident magistrate) is Major Sinclair Yeates, appointed to Skebawn, Co. Cork, where he meets robust and ingenious opposition to his application of the law, while occasionally turning the tables on his tormentors.

I, Robot. The first volume of short stories (1950) by Isaac Asimov (1920–92), in which he promulgated his three 'laws of robotics', presaging the science of artificial intelligence.

Iron Brew. A patent carbonated soft drink popular in Scotland and said to have curative properties with regard to a hangover. It originated in the early part of the 20th century under the impetus of the temperance movement and derived some of its inspiration from the tradition of tonics and health drinks prepared by herbalists. The name is something of a misnomer, since it often contained no iron and was hardly a 'brew' in the traditional manner. A commercial brand, dubbed 'Scotland's other drink' (the prime being Scotch), is now sold under the registered name of Irn Bru. The first word of this represents 'eye-rin' as a local pronunciation of 'iron'.

Iron Butterfly. (1) The nickname of the US singer and actress Jeanette MacDonald (1901–65), who teamed up with Nelson Eddy (1901–67) in a string of successful if high-camp screen musicals in the 1930s. The two were referred to as America's Sweethearts, or, less charitably, as the Iron Butterfly and the Singing Capon. In the 1960s a US rock group took the name Iron Butterfly, and the nickname has sometimes also been applied to the straight-laced UK actress and singer Julie Andrews (b.1935).

(2) It is also the nickname of Imelda Marcos (b.1930), wife of President Ferdinand Marcos (1917–89) of the Philippines. As a young woman she had been a singer, and she was notorious for her vanity and greed. She was accused of benefiting from her husband's corrupt rule, for example by accumulating an astonishingly large collection of shoes. When her husband was ousted from power in 1986 she went into exile with him but subsequently returned to the Philippines, where she unsuccessfully ran for the presidency in 1992. In 1995 she was elected to the Philippines House of Representatives. *See also* FILM STAR NICKNAMES.

Iron Chancellor. Originally the name given to Prince Otto von Bismarck (1815–98), the creator of the German empire. A century later, Gordon Brown (b.1951), Chancellor of the Exchequer in the Labour government elected in 1997, was also so dubbed for his proverbial frugality with the nation's resources.

> Maybe the Iron Chancellor should read carefully what his boss [Prime Minister Tony Blair] said in Davos. The more money the state takes, the less there is for the private sector to invest.
> *Sunday Times* (30 January 2000)

Iron Curtain. The phrase denoting the barrier of secrecy created by the former USSR and its satellites along the Stettin–Trieste line, the communist countries east of this line having cut themselves off from western Europe after the Second World War. The name was popularized by Winston Churchill in his Fulton Speech (5 March 1946), but it was used previously in Germany by Josef Goebbels in *Das Reich* (25 February 1945) and by Churchill himself in a cable to President Truman (4 June 1945). It has earlier antecedents: Ethel Snowden used it in 1920 with reference to BOLSHEVIK Russia; Lord D'Abernon used it in 1925 with regard to the proposed Locarno Treaties; and in 1914 Elisabeth, queen of the Belgians, spoke of a 'bloody iron curtain', between her and the Germans. The phrase occurs in the Earl of Munster's journal as far back as 1819.

> From Stettin, in the Baltic, to Trieste, in the Adriatic, an iron curtain has descended across the Continent.
> WINSTON CHURCHILL: Fulton Speech

Iron Guard (Romanian *Garda de fier*). A Romanian fascist organization that constituted a major social and political force between 1930 and 1941. It evolved from the Legion of the Archangel Michael founded in 1927 by Corneliu Zela Codreanu, was committed to the 'Christian and radical' renovation of Romania, and fed on anti-Semitism and mystical nationalism. Repeated attempts to suppress it were unsuccessful until its final discreditation in 1941.

Iron Lady. The name bestowed on Margaret Thatcher (b.1925), when leader of the Conservative opposition in the House of Commons, by the Soviet Defence Ministry newspaper *Red Star* (24 January 1976). After she had warned the Commons of the increasing Russian threat to the West, the *Red Star* accused the 'Iron Lady' of trying to revive the COLD WAR, referring to her 'viciously anti-Soviet speech', and to 'the peace-loving policy of the Soviet Union'. Her speech (made on 19 January) had included the words: 'The Russians are bent on world dominance ... the Russians put guns before butter.' *See also* GUNS OR BUTTER.

Iron lung. An airtight metal cylinder that encloses a person's body and that provides artificial respiration in cases where the patient's respiratory muscles are paralysed, as in poliomyelitis. The artificial respirator, as it is more formally known, was the invention in 1927 of the brothers Cecil and Philip Drinker of Harvard University, USA.

Ironside. The chief of detectives in the San Francisco police force, with full name Robert Ironside. He was the creation of scriptwriter Collier Young and was played by Raymond Burr in the long-running television series named after him (1967–75). Although confined to a wheelchair, Ironside always gets his man. *See also* MASON, PERRY.

I Saw in Louisiana a Live-Oak Growing. An early painting, dating from 1963, by David Hockney (b.1937). Like WE TWO BOYS TOGETHER CLINGING, the title comes from Walt Whitman. Hockney explains: '[The painting] is from the Whitman poem about the tree that's "uttering joyous leaves of dark green" all its life without a friend or lover near. I thought, what marvellous lines about a man looking at a tree. The tree is painted upside down to make it look more alone; it was just as simple as that, really.'

ISBN. The abbreviation of International Standard Book Number, a 10-digit number assigned to every book before publication. The system, necessitated by computerization, was introduced to Britain in 1967 as the SBN and in 1970 became the ISBN. The main part of an ISBN consists of three groups of digits identifying the geographic, language or other area of the work in question together with its publisher, title, edition and volume number. A single 'check digit' in the form of a final figure or letter is then added to this, as for a BARCODE.

Ish kabbible. An exclamation of indifference, nonchalance or the like, the equivalent of 'I should worry.' It is presumably of Yiddish origin, although the precise sense is obscure. Possibly none was ever intended, although the 'ish' is certainly 'I'. It was apparently introduced, and perhaps even invented, by the American Jewish comedienne Fanny Brice (1891–1951) in the 1930s.

Ishmaelia. The fictional African country featuring in Evelyn Waugh's novel *Scoop* (1938). It is a mountainous, isolated land to the south of Sudan, and its capital, a shoddy place, is Jacksonville. There is another town, Laku, shown prominently on the map, but it cannot be visited as it does not exist. The Ishmaelites are Christians, but polygamy is still practised. The people themselves are fond of oratory in all forms, whether sermons, lectures or even charity appeals. *See also* FIRST LINES OF NOVELS.

Islington Man. A middle-class socially aware person of left-wing views, regarded as typical of the north London borough of Islington.

> Just as Essex Man ... represented the 1980s, Islington Man – more properly Islington Person – may turn out to be the most potent composite of the late 1990s.
> *Independent on Sunday* (17 July 1994)

ISP. In computing the abbreviation of 'internet service provider', as a company that provides access to the INTERNET, either free or for a monthly fee. The connection is made through a telephone line, with calls usually charged at local rates. Examples of well-known ISPs are AOL (America Online), BT Click, Freeserve and LineOne.

Istanbul. Turkey's former capital received its present name in 1930. Until then it was Constantinople, after Constantine the Great, who rebuilt ancient Byzantium and made it his capital in AD 330. The European part of Istanbul contains the old city of Stamboul. All three names are in fact identical, although Istanbul and Stamboul have lost the first syllable of Constantine's name.

Is your journey really necessary? An official anti-travel slogan in the Second World War, originally issued in 1939 to dissuade evacuated civil servants from going home for Christmas. The question was put to civilians generally from 1941, when the government decided against the introduction of any positive measure, such as a ban on travel without a permit over more than 50 miles (80km), but instead relied on voluntary compliance. To encourage this, it took to making travel uncomfortable by reducing the number of trains.

IT. Information technology, as the study or use of computer and telecommunications systems for storing, receiving and sending information. It is also known as ICT (information and communications technology) and was introduced as a school subject in Britain in the 1990s with the aim of producing an efficient and computer literate workforce. The expense of purchasing and maintaining computers in schools has so far restricted any realization of the objective.

It Ain't Half Hot Mum. A television SITCOM screened in eight series from 1974 to 1981 and depicting the exploits of a Royal Artillery Concert Party based in India in the Second World War. The focus was the antagonistic relationship between Sergeant-Major Williams, played by Windsor Davies, and his charges, who included the somewhat feminine 'Gloria' Beaumont, played by Melvyn Hayes, the intellectual pianist Graham, played by John Clegg, the diminutive lead singer 'Lofty' Sugden, acted by Don Estelle, and Christopher Mitchell's dense Parkins, whose use of the phrase 'It ain't half hot mum' in his letters home gave the title of the series.

Italia irredenta (Italian, 'unredeemed Italy'). Those parts of Italy remaining under foreign domination after the war of 1866. The phrase gave the name of the Irredentists, the Italian patriots who sought to deliver Italian lands from foreign rule in the late 19th and early 20th centuries. Many areas at that time were still controlled by Austria. The phrase dates from the early years of the 20th century.

Itchy feet. To have or get itchy feet is to be restless and to have a desire to travel.

> When I'm on the road for any length of time, I start to look forward to the odd day in the office. Then, as soon as I've been cooped up for more than two days, I get itchy feet.
>
> *The Times* (14 February 2000)

Item. A colloquialism for a couple, who if famous will provide more than one item of gossip for the media. The term dates from the 1980s.

> Natalie [Appleton] was quoted in the *Sun* as saying: 'We want to remain friends but we are no longer an item.'
>
> *heat* (13–19 January 2000)

'It' Girl. The American film actress Clara Bow (1905–65), an embodiment of the FLAPPER. She was so promoted following her appearance in the film *It* (1927), based on Elinor Glyn's novel titled by this word, itself already in use as a euphemism for sex appeal. The term has since been applied by the media to other PARTY GIRLS and supposed sex symbols. *See also* OOMPH.

> The tattlers called Tara [Palmer-Tomkinson] an It Girl, meaning a professional partygoer, a member of a privileged, hedonistic sub-cult among Thatcher's children.
>
> *The Times* (17 June 1999)

It had to happen. A more or less meaningless journalistic phrase used to introduce a news item or piece of gossip. The implication is that it was an inevitable consequence of something.

> It had to happen. New York's 24/7 approach to work has finally hit London's beauty salons.
>
> *The Times* (28 June 1999)

I, the Jury. A crime novel (1947) by 'Mickey' (Frank Morrison) Spillane (b.1918), in which he introduced his hardboiled detective Mike HAMMER. At the denouement Hammer addresses the murderess, unmasked and also naked: 'I'm the jury, now, and the judge, and I have a promise to keep. Beautiful as you are, as much as I almost loved you, I sentence you to death.' There were two tough film versions, directed respectively by Harry Essex (1953) and Richard T. Heffron (1982), the latter more in line with the tone of the original.

-itis. A suffix of Greek origin properly used to form the name of an inflammatory disease, the first part of the word naming the organ affected. Thus hepatitis is inflammation of the liver, arthritis of the joints and appendicitis of the appendix. In the 20th century the suffix came to be appended to any word or phrase regarded as causing a figurative 'disease', so that politicians are periodically prone to 'electionitis' and schoolchildren become feverish with 'end-of-term-itis'.

> When in 1997 Mr Ashdown attacked Labour's spending plans, Peter Mandelson savaged him for 'oppositionitis' and he shut up.
>
> *The Times* (22 September 1999)

It is not. A phrase common in an idiosyncratic linguistic inversion popular in the 1990s, the preceding word usually being a noun or adjective and the whole designed for emphasis, often by way of a comparison. Thus a run-down resort might be described as 'Tuscany it is not' or a poor landscape painter derided as 'Constable he is not'. The verb is invariably some form of 'to be', and when a contrast is involved an affirmative statement may precede the negative.

> A virgin home buyer I may be. Stupid I am not.
>
> *The Times* (14 August 1999)

It'll Be Alright On The Night. A popular long-running television series consisting of a series of amusing or embarrassing 'outtakes' from the cutting room floor, first shown in 1977 and always good-humouredly presented by Denis Norden. The title is an old theatrical catchphrase, as an optimistic reassurance that however dire the dress rehearsal, all will go well when it comes to the first performance. The populist spelling of 'Alright' has concerned some pedants.

ITMA (initials of *It's That Man Again*). This highly popular radio comedy series did much to brighten the dreariness of the BLACKOUT years in Britain during the Second World War. It was devised and maintained by the comedian Tommy Handley (1896–1949), the script being written by Ted Kavanagh, and ran from 1939 until Handley's death. Among the characters were the char MRS MOPP, Funf the spy, Claude and Cecil the polite handymen, Ali Oop the saucy SEASIDE POSTCARD seller, the bibulous Colonel Chinstrap, Signor Soso the FUNNY FOREIGNER and the lugubrious laundress Mona Lott. Each character had a memorable catch phrase. Mrs Mopp's was 'Can I do yer now, sir?', Colonel Chinstrap's was 'I don't mind if I do', Mona Lott's was 'It's being so cheerful as keeps me going', Funf's was 'Ziss iss Funf speakink'. Mrs Mopp's farewell was 'Ta-ta for now', abbreviated as 'TTFN'. 'That man' was Handley. Kavanagh took the full title from a *Daily Express* headline of 2 May 1939 referring to Hitler.

> It is sometimes forgotten that the full title of the opening broadcast, It's That Man Again, was merely the use of a catchphrase already established. Hitler might not yet, on July 12, 1939, have made one territorial grab too many. But he had long exceeded what even the patient British thought was any reasonable speech ration.
>
> *The Times* (18 September 1958)

It's a Knockout. A series of televised open-air comic team games screened from 1966 to 1982 and set in towns competing for the right to represent Britain in the European finals of *Jeux sans frontières*. The title puns on the two senses of 'knockout', as a sporting elimination on the one hand and a 'hit' on the other. The series was revived in 1999 in a pale imitation of the original.

It's a Wonderful Life. A film (1946) based on the story 'The Greatest Gift' by Philip Van Doren Stern about a suicide who is dissuaded from killing himself by an angel who shows him what the world would have been like without him. Directed by Frank Capra and starring James Stewart, it was hailed as one of the most life-affirming movies ever made. Philip Van Doren Stern's original story was penned to send to his friends as a Christmas card.

It takes two to tango. Both parties in a situation are equally responsible for it. The reference may be to anything from a simple agreement to an act of adulterous sexual intercourse. The tango is usually regarded as a sexually charged dance, perhaps partly from the suggestion of 'tangle'. The phrase became popular from the 1950s.

> There are lots of things you can do alone!
> But, takes two to tango.
> AL HOFFMAN and DICK MANNING: 'Takes Two to Tango' (song) (1952)

Ivanikha. A fictional village in the former USSR that is the setting of Yevgeny Zamyatin's 'Two Tales for Adult Children' (1922). All the peasants are called Ivan, but they are distinguished by their nicknames, as Ivan Self-Eater, who chewed his own ear off in his sleep, Ivan the Bald, Ivan Nose-Poker and Ivan Spit-Farthest. The Ivans are famous for having visited new lands in the belief that the soil and water there were better than in their own country. They were not, and they returned home disappointed.

Ivory tower. To live in an ivory tower is to live in seclusion, divorced from everyday life, and wilfully or unwittingly excluding the harsh realities of the outside world. The phrase is first recorded in English in 1911 as a translation of French *tour d'ivoire*, a term used by the critic and poet Charles Sainte-Beuve to refer to his fellow poet Alfred de Vigny. The English phrase was then used by Henry James for the title of his novel *The Ivory Tower* (1916) and was popularized by the writings of Hart Crane, Ezra Pound, H.G. Wells, Aldous Huxley and others.

> Et Vigny plus secret,
> Comme en sa tour d'ivoire, avant midi rentrait.
> (And Vigny more discreet, as if in his ivory tower, retired before noon.)
> CHARLES SAINTE-BEUVE: *Les Pensées d'Août, à M. Villemain* (1837)

Ivy League. The eight US universities that have a similar academic and social reputation to Oxford and Cambridge in England. They are all in the northeastern states and are, with year of foundation: Harvard (1636), Yale (1701), Pennsylvania (1740), Princeton (1746), Columbia (1754), Brown (1764), Dartmouth (1769) and Cornell (1853). The Ivy League is also the name of the athletic conference for intercollegiate (American) football and other sports to which they belong. Various explanations have been offered to account for the name, such as a derivation in the Roman numeral IV for an early sports league formed by four of them, but it seems likely that the allusion is simply to the ivy-clad walls that the buildings of some of them have or had. The term is first recorded in the 1930s. *See also* SEVEN SISTERS.

> The fates which govern [football] play among the ivy colleges and academic boiler-factories alike seem to be going around the circuit.
> *New York Herald Tribune* (16 October 1933)

IWW. *See* WOBBLIES.

Izvestia (Russian, 'news'). The official newspaper of the government of the former Soviet Union, founded in 1917 as the organ of the revolution. In 1991, when the Soviet Union collapsed, *Izvestia* became an independent newspaper. *See also* PRAVDA.

J

Jackal, The. A journalistic name for the Venezuelan-born assassin Illich Ramirez Sanchez (b. 1949), who himself used the nom de guerre Carlos. He has worked with various terrorist gangs in different countries. In the 1970s he was involved in various acts of international terrorism in the cause of Palestinian liberation, including the 1972 massacre at Tel Aviv airport and the 1975 kidnapping of oil ministers at the OPEC meeting in Vienna. The nickname is drawn from Frederick Forsyth's thriller The DAY OF THE JACKAL (1971), whose central character is a professional assassin hired to kill President de Gaulle.

Jackanory. A long-running series of stories for young children read on television from 1965 by various famous actors and actresses. The title represents modern rhyming slang for 'story'.

Jackie O. A nickname of Jacqueline Bouvier Kennedy Onassis (1929–94), the glamorous widow of President J.F. Kennedy. She married Greek shipping magnate Aristotle Onassis (1906–75) in 1968, he having cast off his long-term mistress, opera diva Maria Callas. See also CAMELOT; JACK THE ZIPPER; JFK.

Jack the Lad. A self-assured and carefree young man, especially when bold and brash. The nickname is said to have been that of the thief Jack Sheppard (1702–24), the subject of numerous ballads and popular plays. He was imprisoned four times and on each occasion effected a spectacular escape, even when manacled to the floor of his cell in solitary confinement. After his fifth arrest he was hanged, reputedly before a gathering of some 200,000 people. The popular hornpipe in Sir Henry Wood's *Fantasia on British Sea Songs* (1905), which is traditionally performed at the LAST NIGHT OF THE PROMS, is known as *Jack's the Lad*, but here Jack is a 'tar'.

This [Don] Giovanni … is a 20th-century Jack-the-lad, all designer stubble, shy smiles and off-the-shoulder shifts – an expert at pulling the birds.
The Times (11 October 1999)

Jack the Zipper. A posthumous nickname given to President John ('Jack') Fitzgerald Kennedy (1917–63) after it emerged that during his period of office (1961–3), despite being married to a beautiful wife (the future JACKIE O), he had had frequent sexual liaisons in the White House with a succession of young women visitors, including, it has been rumoured, Marilyn MONROE. The name puns on the nickname of the unidentified Victorian serial killer Jack the Ripper, who murdered and mutilated at least seven women prostitutes in the East End of London in 1888. *See also* JFK.

Jacob's Pillow. A farm near Lee, Massachusetts, that was bought in 1930 by the American dancer Ted Shawn as a summer residence and theatre for his all-male dancers. It later became an internationally important centre where many European dancers and dance companies made their debut, and the Jacob's Pillow Dance Festival is now one of the top summer dance attractions in the United States. The name of the farm derives from a nearby rock formation suggesting the biblical story telling how Jacob has a vision of a ladder while sleeping at a place where he 'took of the stones … and put them for pillows' (Genesis 28:11). *See also* DENISHAWN SCHOOL OF DANCING.

Jacuzzi. The 'whirlpool' bath takes its name from its Italian-born American inventor, Candido Jacuzzi (1903–86), who devised it in 1949 for his seven-year-old son, a victim of rheumatoid arthritis. He subsequently patented his invention and began to market the finished product in the early 1950s as a hydromassage unit for bathtubs of conventional size. The whirlpool pump system that evolved was subsequently incorporated into specially large baths, known as 'hot tubs'.

Jaffa cake. A small sponge cake coated in chocolate and with a jelly-type filling made from Jaffa oranges. Jaffa, on the Mediterranean coast of Israel, is the biblical Joppa.

Jai alai. A game like pelota played with hard ball and a basket-like racket strapped to the arm. It is of Basque origin, in which language its name means 'jolly feast', and it was introduced to the United States at the World's Fair in St Louis in 1904. The name is pronounced 'high-a-lie'.

Jailbait. A young girl below the AGE OF CONSENT, sexual intercourse with whom would constitute statutory rape and in most cases result in the jailing of the perpetrator.

Jailhouse Rock. The title of a rock 'n' roll film and its title song, sung by Elvis Presley, the KING, and released in 1957. The song was written by Jerry Leiber (b.1933) and Mike Stoller (b.1933). The possibly homosexual implication of the words appears to have been lost on Elvis himself.

Jalopy. A dilapidated old car. The word is American in origin and dates from the 1920s. Its derivation is unknown but it could be partly imitative of the car's unsteady progress while also suggesting a blend of 'jolt' and 'lollop'.

> We got a ride from a couple of young fellows – wranglers, teenagers, country boys in a put-together jalopy.
>
> JACK KEROUAC: *On the Road*, Pt I, ch iii (1957)

Jamaica Inn. A historical adventure (1936) by Daphne du Maurier (1907–89). The Cornish inn of the title is the centre of the activities of a gang of smugglers, while divided loyalties inform the romantic aspects of the plot. A stilted film version (1939) was directed by Alfred Hitchcock.

Jam and Jerusalem. A traditional epithet of the Women's Institutes. The movement originated in Canada in 1897 and was introduced to Britain in 1915 by a Canadian, Mrs Alfred Watt (1868–1948), who founded a branch in Anglesey. The aim of the first WI members was to help the war effort, and an early lecture was on jam-making. A competition was held in the 1920s to find a theme song. No decision was made, but Hubert Parry's *Jerusalem* (1916), a setting of

William Blake's poem, was sung at the 1924 annual WI meeting and has been associated with the movement ever since. WI stalls selling homemade jam are still a feature at weekly markets.

Jamdung. A Jamaican nickname for the island of Jamaica, punning on a local pronunciation of 'jam down' and alluding to the oppression of ordinary Jamaicans by their political masters.

Jammy dodger. A type of small cake with a jam filling. 'Dodger' was originally an American term for a hard-baked corncake but in the early 20th century came to apply to other kinds of bread and cake. The origin is probably in a dialect word 'dodge' meaning 'piece', 'lump'.

Jane. A strip cartoon heroine popular in the Second World War. She was created by the artist Norman Pett in 1932 for a strip in the *Daily Mirror*. She began as a reasonably recognizable BRIGHT YOUNG THING but in the war years progressed to more exotic roles, in many of which she managed to lose most of her clothes. The newspaper strip ran until 1959, but she was revived in 1982 for a semi-animated television series, in which she was played by Glynis Barber. The comic strip was also the inspiration for the 1988 film *Jane and the Lost City*.

Janet and John. The stereotypical two children of a (middle-class) British family. They take their names from the *Janet and John* graded readers for small children first published in 1949 and described at the time by their publishers as 'true to the best in the life of modern children'. The series was widely adopted in British primary schools.

> I am not for a minute suggesting that there is anything wrong with the Janet and John model of a model family. … It's just that I don't know any such families.
>
> *Sunday Times* (8 August 1999)

Jankers. A military nickname for a punishment. The term dates from the First World War but is of uncertain origin. A possible source is 'jangle' referring to the locking of a prisoner in a cell.

Janus word. A word that has two opposite meanings, such as 'cleave' (both 'stick' and 'split') and CHUFFED. The allusion is to Janus, the Roman god of doorways and gates, who was represented with two faces, one looking forwards, the other back.

Jargonaut. A punning term for someone who uses an excessive amount of jargon, a 'jargon argonaut'. The word also plays in sound and to some degree sense on juggernaut, since such a person can crush or overwhelm with their GOBBLEDYGOOK.

Jarrow Crusade. *See* HUNGER MARCH.

Java. The proprietary name of a computer programming language used to create networking applications, especially interactive elements within WORLD WIDE WEB pages. The name alludes to Java coffee, a favourite drink of many American computer programmers, and was chosen to suggest the richness and strength of the language.

Javal, Camille. A name stated by many reference works to be the original name of the French film actress Brigitte Bardot (b.1934). The misinformation is given in such otherwise reputable authorities as David Thomson's *A Biographical Dictionary of Film* (1994) and *The Penguin Biographical Dictionary of Women* (1998) and even appeared in earlier editions of Leslie Halliwell's famous *Halliwell's Who's Who in the Movies* (1999). In reality the name is that of the character Bardot played in *Le Mépris* (1963), a film based on Alberto Moravia's novel *Il Disprezzo* (1954), but cinema historians seized on it and chose to promote it as her 'real' name. The facts of the matter are given in Jeffrey Robinson's *Bardot: An Intimate Portrait* (1994).

Jaw-dropping. Amazing. A person struck with amazement or other strong emotion may well drop their jaw and gape open-mouthed. An extreme reaction of this kind is sometimes expressed in a kind of cartoon imagery by saying 'their jaw hit the ground'.

> 'There was genuine shock at the amount of venom dripping from the page. It is not an exaggeration to say jaws hit the ground and eyes were out on stalks.'
> *The Times* (13 December 1999)

Jaw-jaw. To talk; to discuss; to negotiate. The slang term comes from a speech made by British prime minister Harold Macmillan (SUPERMAC) at Canberra, Australia, on 30 January 1958: 'Jaw-jaw is better than war-war.' Macmillan was echoing Winston Churchill, who had uttered the phrase 'To jaw-jaw is always better than to war-war' at the White House on 26 June 1954. The slang term 'jaw' on its own (meaning much the same thing) dates from the mid-18th century.

Jaws. A film (1975) based on a novel of the same title by Peter Benchley (the grandson of the humorist Robert Benchley) about a man-eating great white shark that terrorizes a small seaside resort on the western seaboard of the United States. The title of Benchley's book was a last-minute inspiration that neither author nor publisher was immediately very happy with. Previous suggestions had included *Great White*, *The Shark*, *Leviathan Rising*, *The Jaws of Death*, *A Silence in the Water* and the rather less seriously intended *What's That Noshin' on My Laig?* Superfluous sequels were *Jaws 2* (1978), *Jaws 3-D* (1983) and *Jaws: The Revenge* (1987).

> Just when you thought it was safe to go back in the water.
> Publicity slogan for the sequels to *Jaws*

Jaws of Life. An American proprietary name for a hydraulic device shaped like a pair of scissors in which the jaws are used to prise apart the wreckage of crashed vehicles to rescue people trapped inside. The name is probably based on KISS OF LIFE. The device dates from the 1970s.

Jaywalker. A person who crosses or walks in a street thoughtlessly, regardless of passing traffic. The word alludes both to the bird, which hops in an erratic fashion, and to the jay that is a foolish person. The term is of American origin and dates from the early 20th century. A periodic series of half-hour television documentaries on social and religious matters presented by Susan Jay in the 1970s was inevitably titled *Jaywalking* in the punning manner beloved of television producers.

Jazz (of unknown origin). A type of dance music originating in the folk music of the black American of the cotton fields. It first developed in New Orleans and reached Chicago by 1914 where it gained its name. It is characterized by syncopation and the noisy use of percussion instruments, together with the trombone, trumpet and saxophone. Its impact grew steadily and it has had many notable exponents. The name has been somewhat loosely appropriated by popular dance orchestras playing their own conception of the jazz idiom. *See also* BLUES; BOOGIE-WOOGIE; SWING; JAZZ AGE.

Jazz Age. The era, especially in the USA, between the end of the First World War in 1918 and the WALL STREET CRASH in 1929 that marked the onset of the GREAT DEPRESSION. The term, popularized by F. Scott Fitzgerald (1896–1940) in the title of a short-story collection, *Tales of the Jazz Age* (1922), reflected the growing popularity of JAZZ in the 1920s. The period was one of relative prosperity, and, for the middle-class young at least, of liberation from earlier social and sexual mores, for this was the era of the emancipated young woman, the FLAPPER. *See also* ROARING TWENTIES.

Jeep. The registered name of a small all-purpose car first developed by the United States during the Second World War and known as GP, i.e. General Purpose, the US Army designation for this type of car. The name probably derives from this, although was influenced by 'Eugene the Jeep', a versatile cartoon character that had a cry of 'Jeep'. It was introduced in the comic strip 'Thimble Theater' (the forerunner of POPEYE) by the cartoonist Elzie C. Segar in 1936 and used briefly for the name of a commercial vehicle the following year. According to another account, the name came from the exclamation, 'Jeepers creepers!', made by Major General George Lynch, US Army chief of infantry, when he first rode in a prototype of the vehicle at Fort Myer, Virginia, in 1939, and accordingly adopted then by the vehicle's designer, Charles H. Payne. The experimental models were also called Beeps, Peeps and Blitz Buggies, but the name Jeep arrived to stay in 1941.

Jeeves. Bertie WOOSTER's dignified and loyal butler in the books by P.G. Wodehouse. He is as intelligent as his master is vacuous, and as soberly resourceful as he is cheerfully inept. Wodehouse took his name from a Gloucestershire county cricketer, Percy Jeeves (1888–1916), killed in the First World War. The name is generally applied to any loyal manservant or faithful personal attendant. Jeeves has appeared in a number of films and television series, the latter including *The World of Wooster* (1965–8), in which he was played by the urbane Dennis Price, and *Jeeves and Wooster* (1990–3), in which Jeeves is portrayed by Stephen Fry and Bertie Wooster by Hugh Laurie.

Jeffrey Bernard is Unwell. A play (1991) by Keith Waterhouse (b.1929) in which an alcoholic journalist recalls his past career in Fleet Street. Jeffrey Bernard (1932–97) was a real Fleet Street journalist famed for his ill-health as much for the dissolute ways that so grievously affected his health. The title refers to the announcement that regularly appeared in the place of his *Spectator* column when he was 'indisposed'.

Jemima Shore. *See* SHORE, JEMIMA.

Jennings. The spirited schoolboy hero of a long series of books by Anthony Buckeridge (b.1912), starting with *Jennings Goes to School* (1950). He attends Linbury Court preparatory school, where he gets into a number of comic scrapes, and his best friend is Darbishire, a staid, bespectacled foil to his unruly persona. His full name is John Christopher Timothy Jennings, and he first appeared in the radio play *Jennings Learns the Ropes*, broadcast on 16 October 1948 in CHILDREN'S HOUR. The books containing his adventures and antics have been translated into a number of languages, and in French he is known as Bennett, in German as Fredy, and in Norwegian as Stompa.

Jerry (from 'German'). Since the First World War a nickname for a German or Germans collectively. Also an old colloquialism for a chamber pot, said by some to allude to the shape of an upturned German helmet although the word may actually be a shortening of jeroboam. *See also* FRITZ.

Jerrycan. A 20.5-litre (4½-gallon) petrol or water container, which would stand rough handling and stack easily, developed by the Germans for the AFRIKA KORPS in the Second World War. It was borrowed by the British in Libya and became the standard unit of fuel replenishment throughout the Allied armies. The name is an allusion to its origin.

Jersey, Beast of. *See* BEAST OF JERSEY.

Jersey Lily. The nickname of the British actress and famous beauty, Lillie Langtry (1853–1929), who was born as Emilie Charlotte le Breton on the island of Jersey in the Channel Islands. Her nickname comes from the title of a portrait of her by John Everett Millais (1829–1896), in which she is holding a Jersey lily. In 1874 she married Edward Langtry, and two years after his death in 1897 she married Hugo de Bathe, who became a baronet in 1907, making her Lady de Bathe. There was a sensation in 1881 when she made her stage debut – the first society lady to embark on a stage career. Among her admirers was the Prince of Wales, the future Edward VII.

Jerusalem Bible. A modern Roman Catholic translation of the Bible, published in 1966 as the English version of the French *La Bible de Jérusalem*, so called as the work of the faculty of the *École Biblique* in Jerusalem, a Dominican biblical and archaeological graduate school founded in 1890. The *New Jerusalem Bible*, based on the revised French edition of 1973, appeared in 1985, with some books extensively retranslated to give a more readable style.

Jesus boots, shoes or **slippers.** Simple sandals, of the kind that Jesus is popularly portrayed as wearing. The terms are of American origin and date from the 1940s.

> He [rock singer Mick Hucknall] wears Jesus sandals, incontinence trousers and a scruffy white shirt. Oddly, he doesn't look like a vagrant.
>
> *heat* (7–13 October 1999)

Jesus Christ Superstar. *See* ROCK OPERA.

Jesus freak. A fervent Christian evangelist, especially one adopting a lifestyle similar to that of a HIPPIE. The term originated in the United States and dates from the 1970s.

> On leaving ... she [Victoria Adams, of the SPICE GIRLS] was accosted by a proud Jesus Freak in the car park, telling her that she needed God in her life.
> *heat* (20–26 January 2000)

Jesus movement or **revolution.** A Protestant FUNDA-MENTALIST movement in the United States in the 1960s. It consisted mainly of young people who spread the Christian message independently of any established churches of organizations and had a peculiarly American flavour. *See also* CHILDREN OF GOD.

Jesus shoes or **slippers.** *See* JESUS BOOTS.

Jesus wept! A general and blasphemous oath, current from the 1920s. The words are those of the shortest verse in the Bible (John 11:35) in a passage describing the raising of Lazarus.

Je t'aime ... moi non plus. A notorious pop song written in 1967 by the dissolute, chain-smoking French singer Serge Gainsbourg (1928–91). The song was originally written as a duet for Gainsbourg and Brigitte Bardot, but the latter's husband refused to allow its release because of the sounds of sexual groaning it contained. Gainsbourg then re-recorded the song with his girlfriend Jane Birkin. The resulting record, with background noises of orgasm, was banned by the BBC and condemned by the Vatican. The song's French title means 'I love you ... nor do I'.

Jet lag. The lassitude and sense of temporal disorientation experienced after a long flight across different time zones. The sufferer's BIOLOGICAL CLOCK does not adjust to the new time for some days but lags behind it. The phenomenon arose with the development of long-distance flights by passenger jet in the 1960s. Opinions vary regarding the best remedy for the disturbance.

Jet set. Wealthy and fashionable people who travel widely for business or pleasure, typically by jet. The expression dates from the 1950 and generally superseded the earlier 'smart set'.

Jewel in the Crown, The. The first (1966) in the Raj Quartet of novels by Paul Scott (1920–78), set in the five years leading up to the independence of India in 1947. 'The Jewel in Her Crown' is a painting of Queen Victoria with some of her Indian subjects, owned by the elderly mission schools' supervisor in Mayapore, who commits suicide after her house is ransacked by a mob. Events in Mayapore are a microcosm of what will happen nationally during the next few years. The remaining three novels are *The Day of the Scorpion* (1968), *The Towers of Silence* (1971) and *A Division of Spoils* (1975). A stunningly scenic televised version (1985), with star performances by Peggy Ashcroft, Susan Wooldridge, Art Malik, Tim Piggott-Smith, Geraldine James, Charles Dance and Rachel Kempson, rightly won an International EMMY for 'Best Drama'. *See also* FIRST LINES OF NOVELS.

Jewish princess. An American nickname dating from the 1970s for a rich or spoiled Jewish girl or woman. An alternative form of the nickname is JAP, standing for Jewish American princess.

> To add the necessary dramatic tension, he's lower class and a bit of a slob while she's rich and Jewish-princess chic.
> *Maclean's* (16 March 1981)

Jew Süss. The English title of *Jud Süss*, a historical novel (1925) by Lion Feuchtwanger (1884–1958). Feuchtwanger was a German novelist and playwright, born of a Jewish family, known for his historical romances. He went into exile in France in 1933, and in 1940, after spending some time in a concentration camp, he escaped to the USA. Set in 18th-century Württemberg, *Jud Süss* tells the story of Josef Süss Oppenheimer, a Jew who rises to a position of power to help his people but is destroyed by his enemies. In the process he finds he is a Gentile, and the novel points up the meaninglessness of racial distinctions. The book was made into a play and a British film (1934). It became notorious when the Nazi propaganda minister, Josef Goebbels, revised the script for an anti-Semitic film version (1940) directed by Veit Harlan. In this version, 'to serve the politics of the state', the Jew is depicted as entirely evil, ravishing Aryan girls.

JFK. The commonest nickname of John Fitzgerald Kennedy (1917–63), Democratic president of the USA from 1961 until his assassination on 22 November 1963. The use of the initials was modelled on FDR, the nickname of President Franklin Delano Roosevelt. The style was also taken up by Kennedy's successor, LBJ. JFK has also become the popular name for the John F. Kennedy International Airport, New York

City's main airport (formerly known as IDLEWILD). *JFK* is also the title of a much-excoriated film (1991) based on the book *On the Trail of the Assassins* by New Orleans district attorney Jim Garrison. The film is based on Garrison's interpretation of the events surrounding Kennedy's assassination, which rejects the findings of the WARREN COMMISSION. It was directed by Oliver Stone and starred Kevin Costner as Garrison. *See also* GRASSY KNOLL; JACKIE O; JACK THE ZIPPER; KENNEDY CURSE.

Jigger. *See* SHOT GLASS.

Jihad. *See* MUJAHEDIN.

Jim Crow. A name coined by Winston Churchill in 1940 for a roof-top spotter of enemy aircraft, punning on 'crow' as thieves' slang for a person who keeps watch while another steals and 'crow's nest' for a lookout's platform at a ship's masthead, but ultimately deriving from Jim Crow as a former nickname for a black person. Jim Crow was also a shorthand for the systematized discrimination against blacks in the American South from the 1870s.

Jim'll fix it. The catchphrase of a children's television series of the same title, screened from 1975 to 1978, in which Jimmy Savile arranged for the pipe dreams of his young viewers to be realized.

Jimmy. A name used by the Scots increasingly commonly from the 1980s as an address to a stranger, and to some extent replacing the time-honoured 'Jock'.

Jitterbug. Originally a SWING enthusiast in the late 1930s, with the name probably coming from Cab Calloway's song 'Jitter bug' (1934), in which a 'jitter bug' was a person who drank regularly and so 'has the jitters ev'ry morning'. The name passed to a person who danced the jitterbug, a fast, twirling, whirling American dance to a JAZZ accompaniment, popular in the 1940s. Hence also more generally, a nervous person, one who 'has the jitters'.

Jive. A type of fast, lively JAZZ, or the jerky dancing to it, popular in the 1920s and revived, to ROCK 'N' ROLL, in the 1940s and 1950s. Hand jive, with synchronized movement of the hands and forearms, was a British development, as seen, for example, in the popular television series *Rock Follies* (1976–7). Jive talk is the specialized vocabulary of its adepts.

Jix. The nickname of Sir William Joynson-Hicks, 1st viscount Brentford (1865–1932), noted puritan and tactless speaker. He was home secretary (1924–9) and was prominent in defeating the adoption of the Revised Prayer Book of 1928. A short-lived term for a type of two-seater taxicab licensed in 1926 during his secretaryship was 'Jixie'.

> We mean to tread the Primrose Path,
> In spite of Mr Joynson-Hicks.
> We're People of the Aftermath
> We're girls of 1926.
>
> JACQUES REVAL: *The Woman of 1926*, 'Mother's Advice on Father's Fears' (1926)

Job satisfaction. The factor in one's work that brings fulfilment to one's hopes and desires.

Jobseeker. A euphemism for an unemployed person, whether actively seeking a job or not.

> When we began calling the unemployed 'jobseekers', it was clear we were forgetting the English tradition of saying what you mean.
>
> JOHN MORTIMER in *Sunday Times* (10 May 1998)

Jobs for the boys. A form of favouritism giving jobs and appointments to friends and acquaintances or through the OLD BOY NETWORK, regardless of their qualifications or ability and not by fair and open competition.

Jobsworth. A minor official or underling who insists on the letter of the law being applied in all cases, however unreasonable or unsympathetic this may seem. He dare not deviate or accommodate, because 'It's more than my job's worth'.

> I sat myself at the bar and asked for a menu. When I realized that there are different bar and restaurant menus I wondered if I could have the latter at the bar. The jobsworth's initial response was no. Then he charmlessly relented.
>
> *The Times Magazine* (29 January 2000)

Jockey for position, To. To manoeuvre or manipulate for one's own benefit. The reference is to a horse race, in which a jockey will aim to manoeuvre his horse into a better position for winning. The figurative sense of the phrase dates from the 1950s.

Joe Bloggs. A nickname for an average man, frequently used as a random name in examples of form-filling and the like. Despite its somewhat disparaging overtones, the name was seized on by an immigrant Manchester businessman, Shami Ahmed, to found the highly successful Joe Bloggs Clothing Company.

Joe Blow. An American equivalent of JOE BLOGGS, perhaps so called because originally an 'oompah man' or supporting player in a wind band.

Joe Public. A member of the general public, and specifically a member of an audience. Performers will usually be keen to see what 'Joe Public' thinks of their act.

Joe Six-pack. An American nickname for an ordinary beer-drinking man, so called from the popularity of SIX-PACKS of beer among working males.

> To bring all these new people into its ranks, however, the G.O.P. [Grand Old Party, i.e. Republican Party] is going to have to modify its country club image: Joe Sixpack does not belong to a country club.
> *Time* (21 July 1980)

Joe Soap. A foolish or gullible person, who is easily swayed by smooth talk or 'soft soap'.

Joe Who? A nickname of the Canadian politician Joe (Charles Joseph) Clark (b.1939), who became leader of the Progressive Conservatives in 1976 and in June 1979 became Canada's youngest ever prime minister. His minority government lasted only until March 1980, however. Clark, regarded as well meaning but ineffective, continued as party leader until 1983.

Joffrey Ballet. The origins of this ballet company go back to the Robert Joffrey Ballet Concert, which gave its first New York performance in 1954, its dancers coming mostly from the American Ballet Center, directed by Robert Joffrey (born Abdulla Jaffa Anver Bey Khan) (1930–88) and Gerald Arpino. In 1956 it toured for the first time as Robert Joffrey's Theater Dancers and after further tours became the Robert Joffrey Ballet in 1960. At this time it was funded by Rebekah Harkness, founder of the HARKNESS BALLET, but following a disagreement between Joffrey and Harkness most of the dancers left to join her company. Joffrey built up a new company, which first performed in 1965 at the JACOB'S PILLOW festival. Its success was now ensured. It became the resident ballet company at the New York City Center in 1966, with Joffrey as artistic director and Arpino as chief choreographer, and in 1976 adopted its present shorter name.

Jogger's nipple. Soreness of the nipple caused by the rubbing of clothing against it while jogging or long-distance running. It can affect men as well as women and can be prevented by applying petroleum jelly to the nipple before setting out. The term dates from the 1970s, when jogging itself was already becoming established as a popular sport in its own right.

John Birch Society. A reactionary American organization founded in 1958 to combat communism. It was named after John Birch (1918–45), a Baptist missionary and US intelligence officer killed by Chinese communists and regarded by the Society as the 'first casualty' of the COLD WAR.

John Macnab. A novel (1925) by John Buchan (1875–1940), inspired by the exploit of Captain James Brander Dunbar in 1897, when he caught a salmon or killed a stag on three separate Scottish estates without being apprehended. Three bored, respectable, middle-aged men concoct a bet on similar lines, with the twist that each landowner is to be warned of what is to happen in a note signed 'John Macnab'.

Johnny Foreigner. A not unfriendly nickname for someone from another country, even if speaking the same language, as an American from the point of view of a Briton, or vice versa.

> We ask a lot of our politicians. We want them to be entirely honest – except when we ask them to lie on our behalf as they negotiate with Johnny Foreigner.
> *Sunday Times* (28 November 1999)

John o'London's Weekly. A magazine of literary articles and book reviews founded in 1919. It was aimed at a popular readership who normally steered clear of the weightier literary press and took its title from the pen-name of its editor, Wilfred Whitten (d.1942). It ceased publication in 1936.

Johnson, Pussyfoot. William E. Johnson (1862–1945), the temperance advocate, gained his nickname from his 'cat-like' policies in pursuing law breakers in gambling saloons and elsewhere in Indian territory when serving as Chief Special Officer of the US Indian Service (1908–11). After this he devoted his energies to the cause of PROHIBITION and gave many lectures on temperance.

Joined at the hip. Inseparable. Said of two intimate friends or close colleagues who see eye-to-eye on everything. The allusion is to Siamese twins, who are typically joined at the waist.

> Michael Portillo's presence at his leader's [William Hague's] right shoulder also gave rise to mockery. The two men were certainly not joined at the hip.
> *Sunday Times* (20 February 2000)

Joined-up writing. Literacy; coherent written expression. The phrase alludes to a child's early efforts to write, when letters at first formed separately in a word progress to the cursive stage. The expression has variants in other fields.

> There will be an excellent opportunity in the House of

Commons ... for some joined-up thinking to be translated into legislation.

The Times (Letter to the Editor) (16 April 1999)

Join up the dots, To. To complete the picture; to fill in the details; to recall in entirety. The allusion is to the child's (or adult's) diversion of drawing a line through a succession of numbered dots that form an outline picture on completion.

He [SKIFFLE player Lonnie Donegan] ... hardly expects his collaboration with [Van] Morrison to bring pop stardom all over again. But he does hope the record will join up the dots for some of today's record buyers.

The Times (11 January 2000)

Jokari. The proprietary name of a type of bat and ball game in which the ball is attached to the bat with a long length of rubber cord. The name dates from the 1960s and presumably derives from Italian *giocare*, 'to play', or its source, Latin *jocari*, 'to jest'.

Jolly d. Jolly decent (of you). A middle-class slang term of the mid-20th century. 'Oh, jolly d!' was a catchphrase popularized by Maurice Denham as Dudley Davenport in the radio comedy series MUCH-BINDING-IN-THE-MARSH.

Jolly hockeysticks. Said of a woman who is (often) public-school educated and who is brightly enthusiastic and optimistic in her approach to the world and 'sporty' in her interests and code of moral decency and fair play. The catchphrase 'Jolly hockey sticks!', epitomizing such a person, was first heard in the late 1940s in the radio comedy series *Educating Archie*, in which it was uttered by Monica, Archie's schoolgirl friend. *See also* DIMSIE.

The painstakingly put-together facsimile of project leader Heather's diary, allowing you to trace her descent from early jolly hockeysticks-style excitement to later demented hysteria.

heat (18–24 November 1999)

Jolly Jack. An ironic nickname for the Yorkshire writer and actor J.B. Priestley (1894–1984), who was notoriously grumpy.

Joltin' Joe. The nickname of the legendary baseball player Joe Dimaggio (1914–99), whose feats with the New York Yankees made him the hero of a generation. His fame is reflected in references to him in contexts as diverse as Hemingway's *The Old Man and the Sea* (1952) and the Simon and Garfunkel lyric 'Mrs Robinson' for the soundtrack of the film *The*

GRADUATE (1968). Dimaggio was also known as 'The Yankee Clipper'. His younger brother Dom Dimaggio (b.1917), a successful player with the Boston Red Sox, was known as the 'Little Professor'.

What's that you say, Mrs Robinson?
Joltin' Joe has left and gone away.

SIMON and GARFUNKEL: 'Mrs Robinson' (song) (1968)

Jonah word. A colloquial term for a word that a chronic stutterer finds difficult to utter in ordinary conversation. The allusion is to the biblical Jonah, who brought bad luck (and who was thus thrown overboard to be swallowed by a whale). A notorious Jonah word is 'mother', whose initial 'm' can be a fearsome obstacle since it involves sealed lips that must be opened.

Jones, Bridget. The independent, unattached woman in her 30s who recounts the ups and (mostly) downs of her life in the humorous fictional *Bridget Jones's Diary* (1996) by Helen Fielding, in which she counts her calories, cigarettes, glasses of Chardonnay, weight and other obsessions. She is shallow and neurotic, but also endearingly amusing in her manic enthusiasms and petulant disappointments. The name became a synonym for any real female relationship-obsessed THIRTYSOMETHING of this type. A sequel, *Bridget Jones: The Edge of Reason* (1999), was a further affectionate portrayal of the original comic creation.

Jonestown. The site in northwestern Guyana of a mass suicide on 18 November 1978 of 913 members of the People's Temple cult led by Jim Jones (1931–78). Jones set up his cult in northern California in the 1960s, but, after allegations that he was appropriating the income of his members, he and his followers left the USA to set up a commune at Jonestown in 1977. After further allegations of appropriation of funds and tyrannical behaviour on the part of Jones, US Representative Leo Ryan arrived in Guyana, accompanied by journalists and relatives of cult members, to carry out an investigation. Four days later, as they were about to leave Jonestown, cult members attacked the visiting group, killing five of them, including Ryan, although the others managed to escape. At this point Jones ordered his members to drink a punch laced with cyanide, which most of them, including 276 children, duly did. Jones himself was found dead, having been shot in the head.

Journey's End. A play (1929) by R.C. Sherriff (1896–1975) depicting the horror of trench warfare during the First World War. The central character, Captain

Stanhope, is on the verge of mental collapse after three years at the front, while 18-year-old 2nd Lieutenant Raleigh actually reaches 'journey's end' at the end of the play when he is mortally wounded. The play drew on Sherriff's own experiences as a captain in the trenches, although he wrote the piece only in order to raise money for his rowing club. He planned originally to call the play *Suspense*, but changed his mind when he admitted it did not have any, then considered *Waiting* before settling on the final title after coming across the following line in a book he was reading: 'It was late in the evening when we came at last to our Journey's End.'

Joy. The first word of various book titles alluding to a specific that presumably gave the writer pleasure and that he or she wishes to share with readers. The vogue was apparently launched with *The Joy of Cooking* (1931) by the American cookery expert Irma S. Rombauer. Forty years on Alex Comfort rejuvenated the formula with *The Joy of Sex* (1972), following it with a companion volume, *More Joy of Sex* (1974), and at the age of 70 finally updating it as *The New Joy of Sex* (1991). Titles listed in *British Books in Print* (1982) include *Joy of a Home Fruit Garden*, *Joy of Beauty*, *Joy of Building*, *Joy of Flying*, *Joy of Hand-Weaving*, Leonard Bernstein's *Joy of Music* and Margaret Allan's *Joy of Slimming*. In 1984 Nigel Rees published the ironically titled *Joy of Clichés* and soon after came Fritz Spiegl's *The Joy of Words* (1986). A book that is a joy to write is not necessarily, however, a joy to read.

Joyriding. Driving and riding in a car for pleasure, especially a stolen one. Joyriding gained notoriety in the early 1990s when teenage blacks in Newark, New Jersey, took to racing and crashing model sports cars taken from the white suburbs. The 'sport' was soon overshadowed by CARJACKING.

Joystick. The control column of an aircraft, which is linked to the elevators and ailerons. It is so nicknamed from the great pleasure and 'kicks' it gives to the pilot who operates it. The term was later extended to the control lever used to play computer games.

> Lewis sat on the pilot's right, trying to make sense of all the dials and gauges.
> 'And this one?' he ventured. 'Joystick, I suppose?'
> The plane was a trainer and had dual controls. Alex corrected him: 'We call it the control column nowadays. One for me and one for you if I faint.'
> BRUCE CHATWIN: *On the Black Hill*, ch xlviii (1982)

Judge a book by its cover, To. To assess the nature of a person or thing by outward appearances alone. The expression often appears in the proverbial form, 'You can't judge a book by its cover.' Most publishers are aware that potential readers often do illogically judge a book in this way.

> I thought we would get married and have children. I'm afraid it's a case of never judge a book by its cover.
> *The Times* (16 November 1999)

Judges' rules. Rules that concern the questioning of suspects by the police and the taking of statements. They were first formulated in 1912, revised in 1918 and reformulated in 1964. They were superseded by the provisions regarding the detention, treatment and questioning of persons by the police contained in the Police and Criminal Evidence Act of 1984, Part V, and the Secretary of State's Code of Practice.

Jud Süss. *See* JEW SÜSS.

Juggernaut. A word for a large lorry, especially one that travels throughout Europe. Such lorries or HGVs (heavy goods vehicles) have become increasingly common in Britain with the expansion of the EUROPEAN UNION, and 'juggernaut' for this reason has become a dirty word with environmentalists. The word itself has become popularly associated with -naut in its application to long-distance voyagers such as the Argonauts or an Astronaut, while jugger- is in some cases misapprehended as a form of 'judder'. The name derives from that of a Hindu god, whose name is an alteration of Hindi *Jagannath*, from Sanskrit *Jagannā tha*, 'lord of the world'. The name is a title of Vishnu, chief of the Hindu gods. Juggernaut is also sometimes used to denote a regime or institution beneath which people are ruthlessly crushed.

Juke box. A kind of large automatic record player, usually in a public place such as a public house or bar, in which coins are inserted and buttons pressed to select the relevant tunes. 'Juke' was a black American slang term of the 1930s, denoting an establishment offering food, drink, music, dancing and perhaps baser pleasures as well. It ultimately derives from the word *juke* or *joog* in the Gullah language of West Africa, meaning 'disorderly', 'wicked'.

Juliet Bravo. A television crime drama series screened from 1980 to 1985 with a central character in the policewoman Jean Darblay, who although a victim of sexism from her male colleagues at the (fictional)

Hartley station in Lancashire manages to solve a number of realistic cases. The title represents the letters JB as her police call sign. *See also* ROGER.

July Bomb Plot. The attempted assassination of Adolf Hitler on 20 July 1944 by senior German officers. The conspirators were alarmed at the deteriorating military situation and sought to take power in Germany and seek favourable peace terms with the Allies. The plot, which was first hatched towards the end of 1943 and code-named *Walküre* ('Valkyrie'), is also referred to as the Stauffenberg Plot or the Rastenburg Assassination Plot. The conspirators included General Ludwig Beck (formerly chief of the general staff), Colonel Claus Philipp Schenk (usually referred to by his title, Graf von Stauffenberg) and Field Marshal Erwin Rommel (*see* DESERT FOX). Rommel, however, had been seriously wounded three days before and was unable to take a direct part. It was Stauffenberg who prepared and carried out the plan, depositing a briefcase containing a bomb in a conference room at Hitler's 'Wolf's Lair' headquarters at Rastenburg in East Prussia. An aide moved the briefcase away from where Hitler sat, however, so that when it went off Hitler received only minor injuries, although four other people in the room died. Meanwhile Stauffenberg had flown to Berlin to meet up with the other conspirators. However, they were betrayed by one of their number, General Friedrich Fromm, and over the next few months some 200 plotters (including Fromm) were arrested, tortured and executed in a variety of gruesome ways. Beck and Rommel were forced to commit suicide. Apparently Hitler watched films of some of the executions.

Jumbo jet. Although now applied generally to any large airliner, the nickname was originally bestowed on the Boeing 747, developed in the 1960s and making its maiden flight on 9 February 1969. The early version accommodated 350–490 passengers, but later types could take up to 650 people. Jumbo was the name of an elephant at the London Zoo from 1865 to 1882.

Jumpers. A play (1972) by Tom Stoppard (b.1937) in which a professor of ethics struggles to cope with a variety of misfortunes, from the body of a dead politician to the death of his pet hare. The jumpers of the title are the gymnasts of the play's opening scene, who are subsequently revealed to be professional philosophers, leaping under the direction of the distinguished Sir Archibald Jumper.

Jumpin' Jack Flash. A song by the ROLLING STONES, released in 1968 and credited to Mick Jagger and Keith Richards. The name Jumpin' Jack Flash evinces a number of verbal influences, from JACK THE LAD (a roguish and adventurous youth), to jumping jack (a type of firework). It also reflects the almost demonic energy of Mick Jagger as a vocalist. The song dates from the same period as SYMPATHY FOR THE DEVIL, and its lyrics have much of the latter's darkly aggressive nature:

> I was raised by a toothless, bearded hag
> I was schooled with a strap right across my back
> But it's all right now, in fact it's a gas
> But it's all right, I'm Jumpin' Jack Flash
> It's a gas, gas, gas.

A comedy film of the same title was released in 1986, starring Whoopi Goldberg. Jack Flash is also an Australian slang term for the drug hashish.

Jump in the lake! Go away! GET LOST! The expression dates from the early 20th century and is frequently preceded by 'Go'. A person who jumps in a lake will disappear from sight.

Jump into bed with someone, To. To have sexual intercourse readily with them.

Jump jet. A nickname for a VTOL (vertical take-off and landing) aircraft, and specifically for the Harrier fighter that in 1969 became the first fixed-wing VTOL type in service with the RAF. The latter's own sobriquet for it was the 'Leaping Heap'.

Jump jockey. Racing parlance for a jockey in a steeplechase. The term dates from the 1970s.

> Graham Thorner, that most determined of jump jockeys, rode his heart out three times over fences in stamina sapping conditions at Worcester yesterday.
> *The Times* (25 January 1977)

Jump leads. A pair of cables fitted with crocodile clips that are used to start a motor vehicle when the battery is flat by connecting the battery to another battery.

Jump start. A method of starting a car when the engine cannot be started by the ignition in the normal way. The car is pushed along or allowed to freewheel downhill and the gears are suddenly engaged. The term is also used for a similar start using JUMP LEADS.

Jumpsuit. A one-piece garment of trousers and a sleeved top, worn as a fashion garment or as protective clothing or uniform. The name was originally given to the garment worn by American parachutists in the Second World War. Hence 'jump'.

Jump the gun, To. To act prematurely. The allusion is

to a false start in a race, when a runner sets off before the starting pistol has been fired. The phrase dates from the 1930s.

Jump through hoops, To. To go through an elaborate procedure in order to achieve an objective; to go to great lengths to please someone. The allusion is to circus animals trained to jump through hoops. The expression dates from the early 20th century.

Jump up and down, To. To bring oneself into notice by one's movements or actions; to be busy or physically active.

> 'Shooting a comedy is such a tonic. It's nice to jump up and down and have a laugh.'
> *The Times* (4 December 1999)

June War. *See* SIX-DAY WAR.

Jungle Book, The. The Disney cartoon (1967), based on Rudyard Kipling's *The Jungle Book* (1894), was the last animated film to be personally supervised by Walt Disney. The similarities between the movie and Kipling's book are few, but the film brought Kipling's books and characters of Mowgli, Shere Khan (the tiger), Bagheera (the panther), Kaa (the snake) and Baloo (the bear) to a wider audience.

Jungle bunny. A derogatory nickname for a dark-skinned person, especially one of African origin.

Jungle gym. A type of climbing frame for young children, originating in America in the 1920s. It was originally a proprietary name and in turn gave the name of the comic strip character Jungle Jim, created by Alex Raymond in the 1930s.

Jungle juice. Strong, rough alcoholic drink. The term arose among the armed forces in the Second World War to apply to various homemade alcoholic drinks, but originally to a kind made of jungle-grown fruits and plants.

Jungle music. A style of dance music popular in Britain from the early 1990s, also known simply as 'jungle'. It incorporates elements of RAGGA, HIP-HOP and hard core and mainly consists of very fast electronic drum tracks and slower synthesized bass lines. It is presumably named from its drumming and chanting, sounds associated with the jungle, although there could also be a more subtle reference to the CONCRETE JUNGLE.

> 'Warning,' a jungle night at The Junction, was the last thing I went to, and although I flaked far too early, it really kicked.
> *The Times* (11 September 1999)

Junk bond. A high-yielding, high-risk security, typically issued to raise capital speedily in order to finance a takeover. Such bonds first emerged on Wall Street in the 1970s and were so called because of doubts whether the issuing company would be able to pay the promised interest. If it could not, the bonds would be worthess, or 'junk'. The American financier Michael Milken (b.1947) was known as the 'junk bond king' from his ability to raise millions in minutes by selling junk bonds that came with his personal commendation and interest rates that older hands would have considered usurious. All ended in tears when he was filed for bankruptcy in 1990.

Junk food. Food of low nutritional value, such as potato crisps, sugar-coated cereals and the like, or as typically sold by FAST FOOD outlets such as McDONALD'S. According to an article in *The Times* of 23 October 1999 the following are the 12 most popular junk foods worldwide: meat pie, pizza, chips, popcorn, BIG MAC, doughnut, samosa, kebab, felafel, HOT DOG, ice cream and KFC. Most Westerners will at some time have consumed one or more of these. Junk food is usually irresistible to children, who are thus the consumers mainly targeted by the manufacturers. *See also* E-NUMBERS.

Junkie. An impressionistic novel (1953) by William Lee (pen-name of William Burroughs; 1914–97). Subtitled *Confessions of an Unrepented Drug Addict*, it reflects the progress of his own addiction to HEROIN ('junk') from 1944. He was finally cured of the habit in London in 1957. *See also* BEAT GENERATION.

Juno. A Canadian award presented annually for outstanding achievements in music, on the lines of the American GRAMMY. The name is probably that of the Roman goddess in its special use as the code name of the beach in Normandy on which Canadian forces landed in Operation OVERLORD. *See* JUNO BEACH.

Juno and the Paycock. A play (1924) by the Irish playwright Sean O'Casey (1880–1964), first performed at the ABBEY THEATRE, Dublin. It concerns the fate of a Dublin family, the Boyles, during the Irish Civil War (1922–3). 'Juno' is Juno Boyle, the long-suffering but resilient wife of the workshy 'Captain' Boyle, who spends his time 'strutting about the town like a paycock' (peacock).

Juno Beach. The Allied code name for the stretch of beach on the Normandy coast between GOLD BEACH to the west and SWORD BEACH to the east. On D-DAY Juno Beach was where the 3rd Canadian Division and the 2nd Canadian Armoured Brigade came ashore. In Roman mythology Juno was the wife of Jupiter, ruler of the gods.

Jurassic Park. A film (1993) based on a novel by Michael Crichton about the chaos that overtakes an ambitious island THEME PARK in which the main attractions are dinosaurs from the Jurassic era (208–146 million years ago) recreated by scientists using fossilized DNA (*see* DOUBLE HELIX). The novel idea that a Jurassic Park could be created in real life provoked much discussion among audiences at the time of the film's release, although the suggestion was panned by scientists. It was noted, however, that the scientists had also criticized the fact that the bloodthirsty velociraptors that featured in the film were (on the instructions of director Steven Spielberg) twice as large as fossil records suggested they had been, until a new fossil was identified as a variety of velociraptor much larger than any known hitherto.

Jury is out. A decision has yet to be made; the general opinion of the public is unknown. The implication is that the subject is controversial. A fuller form of the phrase is 'The jury is still out.' The reference is to a jury debating their verdict before returning to the courtroom.

> Six months after the official launch of the individual savings account (Isa), the jury is still out.
> *The Times* (2 October 1999)

Just deserts. Deserved reward; 'comeuppance'. A quasi-biblical phrase that caught on as a 20th-century cliché.

> The father thumps the yob, pulls out his warrant card to reveal he's a policeman, and arrests him. Just deserts for the yob and cheers for the PC?
> ANDREW NEIL in *Daily Mail* (9 March 1995)

Just So Stories. Animal fables for children (1902) by Rudyard Kipling (1865–1936). These amusing beast-myths explain, for instance, how the leopard got his spots, the camel his hump and how the rhinoceros his folded skin and bad temper. They are accompanied by uplifting verses:

> The Camel's hump is an ugly lump
> Which well you may see at the Zoo;
> But uglier yet is the hump we get
> From having too little to do.

The 'Best Beloved' to whom each story is addressed was Kipling's eldest child Josephine, to whom he read the stories aloud. She died in 1899 at the age of six. *See also* JUNGLE BOOK.

Just What Is It that Makes Today's Homes So Different, So Appealing? The satirical and influential collage by Richard Hamilton (b.1922) was a pioneering work of British POP ART. Dating from 1956, the picture includes photographs of a muscleman, a woman with impossible breasts, a tape recorder and other consumer durables, various brand labels and so on. The title is in the style of an article heading from a home-interiors magazine. *See also* $HE.

Just what the doctor ordered. Just right; exactly what is needed, like the precise prescription made by a doctor for a specific treatment or cure. The catchphrase dates from the early 20th century. *See also* YOU'RE THE DOCTOR.

Just William. *See* WILLIAM.

Jutland. The battle of Jutland was one of the major naval events of the First World War. It took place on 31 May 1916 when the British Grand Fleet under Admiral Jellicoe engaged the German High Seas Fleet in the North Sea west of Jutland. The outcome was a tactical victory for the Germans but a strategic victory for the British, and the German fleet never again sought a full-scale engagement with the British.

K

Kafkaesque. An adjective used to describe a work of literature, drama or film, or a real situation, in which an ordinary, innocent individual is at the mercy of anonymous, bizarre and frightening forces, usually in the form of a malevolent or indifferent state bureaucracy. The word derives from the Czech writer Franz Kafka (1883–1924), whose posthumously published novels and stories embody such situations. In *The* TRIAL (1925), for example, Joseph K. is arrested and brought before a court, but the charges against him are never stated. He is driven to find out what he is supposed to have done wrong, and to seek acquittal, which he never succeeds in doing, but is taken to the edge of the city and killed 'like a dog'. Kafka himself is supposed to have said: 'In the fight between you and the world, back the world.'

Kai Lung. The Chinese sage and tale-teller who is the central character of an entertaining series of short stories by Ernest Bramah (real name Ernest Bramah Smith). They abound in mock-Chinese aphorisms of the kind popularized by Charlie CHAN and are collected in five volumes: *The Wallet of Kai Lung* (1900), *Kai Lung's Golden Hours* (1922), *Kai Lung Unrolls His Mat* (1928), *The Moon of Much Gladness* (1932) and *Kai Lung Beneath the Mulberry Tree* (1940).

Kaiser, The. The nickname accorded to Franz Beckenbauer (b.1945), a gifted football player for Bayern Munich and West Germany in the 1960s and 1970s. The German word *Kaiser* ('emperor') is, like the Russian 'tsar', derived from the Latin word *Caesar*. The nickname reflects Beckenbauer's imperious skills as a player and the respect in which he was held.

Kaiser Bill. A British nickname for Wilhelm II (1859–1941), king of Prussia, emperor (*Kaiser*) of Germany (1888–1918) and nephew of Queen Victoria. Like many German military figures and their conservative supporters he believed that a short victorious European war would solve Germany's problems. As the First World War dragged on, however, he was sidelined by the right-wing military-industrial complex and the virtual dictatorship of Generals Hindenburg and Ludendorff that controlled Germany from 1916. He abdicated and went into exile in the Netherlands on the defeat of Germany in November 1918. *See also* LAUGHING MURDERER OF VERDUN.

Kalashnikov. The popular name for the AK-47, a Soviet make of assault rifle designed by Mikhail Timofeyevich Kalashnikov (b.1919), who ended up as a major general in the Red Army. AK stands for *Avtomat Kalashnikova* ('automatic Kalashnikov'), and 47 for 1947, the year in which the weapon was adopted by Soviet forces. It went on to be manufactured in many communist countries and was the standard infantry weapon in communist armies for some four decades. It has also been widely used by nationalist, guerrilla and terrorist groups, including the IRA.

Kamerad (German, 'comrade'). A word used by the Germans in the First World War as an appeal for mercy. For a while it was taken up in English to mean 'I surrender'.

> 'Kamerad, Bull! I'll come in,' said Loftie. Vaughan's hands had gone up first.
> RUDYARD KIPLING: *Limits and Renewals* (1930)

Kamikaze. A Japanese word meaning 'divine wind', referring to the providential typhoon that on a night in August 1281 balked a Mongol invasion. In the Second World War it was applied to the 'suicide' aircraft attacks organized under Vice-Admiral Onishi in the Philippines between October 1944 and January

1945. Some 5000 young pilots gave their lives when their bomb-loaded fighters crashed into their targets.

Kampuchea. The official name of Cambodia for international purposes between 1976 and 1989. Kampuchea is the traditional Khmer name of the country, of which Cambodia (and the French *Cambodge*) are transliterations. The name Democratic Kampuchea was given to the country by the KHMER ROUGE, who had taken power the previous year. After the Vietnamese invaded the country in 1978 and set up a puppet regime, the country was renamed the People's Republic of Kampuchea. When the Vietnamese withdrew in 1989 the official name was changed again to State of Cambodia (Khmer *Roat Kampuchea*).

Kanga. A media nickname for Lady Tryon (b.1948), at one time an 'adviser' to Prince Charles, so called from her Australian background. The name may have been coined by the prince himself.

Kangaroo. In British parliamentary procedure the process by which the Speaker, on the report stage of a bill, selects the amendments to be debated, rather than having all the amendments discussed. The procedure was first used on the discussion of the Financial Bill of 1909. It is so named because the debate leaps from clause to clause. The word is also applied when the chairperson of a parliamentary committee selects some amendments for discussion but not others.

Kangaroo court. A term applied to an irregular court or tribunal that is conducted in disregard of proper legal procedure, as, for example, a mock court held among prisoners in a jail. 'To kangaroo' means to convict a person on false evidence. The term, which probably arose from some resemblance of the 'jumps' of the kangaroo to the progress of 'justice' in such courts, was common in the USA during the 19th century. It obtained wide currency in Britain in 1966 when it was applied to the irregular punitive measures taken by certain trade unions against their members who were regarded as strike-breakers.

Kangaroo Valley. A nickname given in the 1960s to the Earls Court area of West London, the allusion being to the large number of temporary or permanent Australian immigrants living there.

Kangol. The proprietary name of a range of headwear, safety harnesses and seat belts traces its origins back to the Polish-born British beret manufacturer Jacques Spreiregen and his nephew, Jo Meisner, who in 1937 set up a factory at Cleator, near Whitehaven, Cumbria,

to make berets for schoolwear, GIRL GUIDES uniforms and fashion wear. They devised the name from the three original raw materials used for the headgear, sil*k*, *ang*ora and woo*l*, and after the Second World War extended the range to military berets and subsequently to related fabric-based items.

Kansas Coolidge or **Kansas Sunflower.** A nickname of the US politician Alf (Alfred Mossman) Landon (1887–1987), governor of Kansas (1933–7). As the Republican candidate in the 1936 presidential election he was annihilated by Franklin D. Roosevelt, winning only eight votes in the electoral college. One of the Democrats' slogans in the election was 'Sunflowers wilt in November'. The charismatically challenged Calvin Coolidge, SILENT CAL, had been Republican president of the USA (1923–9).

Kapp Putsch. *See* FREIKORPS.

Karaoke. A popular feature of the British pub and club from the early 1980s, in the form of a pre-recorded track of popular music without the vocal part, enabling a person to sing along with it and, as desired, record the resulting performance on tape or video. The system derives from Japan (the word means literally 'empty orchestra') and caught on among business people in that country visiting bars and clubs on their way home from work.

> The idea of the karaoke bar is very simple. You get roaring drunk, chat up the bar girls and sing maudlin popular songs, dreadfully out of tune.
> *Daily Telegraph* (19 May 1989)

Karloff, Doris. A nickname of Conservative politician Anne Widdecombe (b.1947), shadow home secretary from 1997. The name puns on the name of Boris Karloff (1887–1969), star of HORROR MOVIES in the 1930s and 1940s, and reflects both the supposed frumpiness and fierceness of her appearance ('Doris' is generally regarded as an old-fashioned and faintly comic name) and her forthright and uncompromising manner. She achieved particular notoriety as a junior Home Office minister (1995–7) in John Major's government, when she ordered that a woman prisoner be shackled while giving birth. *See also* SOMETHING OF THE NIGHT.

Katanga. A mineral-rich Congolese province whose secession from the newly independent Congo in 1960 precipitated the so-called Congo Crisis (1960–65). Katanga was reintegrated into the Congo, with the assistance of UNITED NATIONS forces, in 1962, but bloody chaos still reigned elsewhere. Central authority was finally imposed in 1965 by the iron fist of Colonel Mobutu, who was to rule the Congo (as Zaire) in an increasingly corrupt manner until 1997.

Kat stitch. A stitch in lace-making that forms a star-shaped ground net. The name dates from the early 20th century, but the reference is historically much earlier. 'Kat' is Catherine of Aragon (1485–1536), the first wife of Henry VIII, who is said to have invented the stitch.

Katyn Massacre. On 12 April 1943 German radio announced that the bodies of 4143 Polish officers had been found in eight communal graves in the Katyn Forest near Smolensk in western Russia. The Soviet authorities long maintained that the Germans had killed the Poles during Operation BARBAROSSA and only in 1989 began to admit that the murders had, in fact, been carried out in the spring of 1940 by the NKVD (*see* KGB). The reason for the pogrom is still not clear. Some claim it was ordered by STALIN simply through his hatred of Poles. Others hold that the NKVD was evacuating prison camps to make way for deportees from the Baltic States. The massacre left a deep scar on Polish–Soviet relations during the remainder of the Second World War and afterwards.

Katyusha. A Soviet 130-millimetre rocket used in the Second World War and installed in batches of 14 to 48 on a box-like launcher known as a Stalin Organ, mounted on a gun carriage. Its name is one of the many affectionate diminutives of the Russian girl's name Yekaterina (Catherine).

Kay Harker. *See* HARKER, KAY.

Keedoozle. *See* PIGGLY WIGGLY.

Keep ahead of the game, To. To maintain an advantage over others in a competitive situation. The 'game' here is literally sporting but is usually understood as meaning a business or interest, as in 'What's your game?' The verb may vary but the basic phrase dates from the 1970s.

Keep Britain tidy. This simple anti-litter slogan was first promoted in 1952 through the Central Office of Information by means of a sticker produced for the Ministry of Housing and Local Government. Litter louts have largely ignored the plea, despite the plentiful provision of litter bins.

Keeping Up Appearances. A television SITCOM first broadcast on BBC1 in 1990 and centring on the outrageously snobbish Hyacinth Bucket (pronounced 'bouquet'), played by Patricia Routledge, and her hen-pecked husband Richard, played by Clive Swift. Much of the programme's mostly rather unsubtle humour lay in Hyacinth's barnstorming efforts to order the lives of others.

Keep one's chin up, To. To remain cheerful in difficult circumstances. To raise one's chin is to tilt the head back in an attitude of bravery or defiance. The expression dates from the 1930s and is often found in the simple exhortation 'Chin up!'

Keep one's eye on the ball, To. To remain alert and attentive. In most sports it is important to follow the path of the ball to plan or make one's next move.

Keep one's fingers crossed, To. To hope for success. The expression dates from the 1920s, but the ultimate allusion is to making the sign of the cross in order to banish evil and invite good. Many people actually cross their index finger and forefinger when saying 'Keep your fingers crossed', meaning 'Wish me luck', and children cross their fingers in some games to mean they are 'safe'.

Keep one's head down, To. To remain inconspicuous in difficult times; to concentrate on one's work.

Keep on trucking. Keep going; don't give up. A general term of encouragement, from 'to truck' in the sense 'to move', 'to travel'.

Keep up with the Joneses, To. To endeavour to maintain one's social level; to keep up appearances with one's neighbours. The phrase was invented by the cartoonist Arthur R. Momand ('Pop') for a comic-strip series ('Keeping up with the Joneses – by Pop'), which began in the New York *Globe* on 1 April 1913 and ran for 28 years. He based it on his own experiences as a newly married young artist living in an affluent New York suburb on a limited salary.

Keller plan or **course.** An American method of college instruction in which the subject matter of a course is divided into study units that students are allowed to master at their own pace. The name is that of the US psychologist Fred S. Keller, who proposed the plan in 1968.

Kelly, Ned. The hero of Australian folklore became a favourite subject of the great Australian painter Sidney Nolan (1917–92). Kelly (1855–80) was a notorious bushranger, who wore homemade armour for his armed escapades. He was hanged after being captured following a shoot-out in 1880. Nolan started his series of paintings of Kelly in 1946. In most of these paintings Kelly is part of what Nolan described as 'the great purity and implacability' of the Australian landscape.

Kelvinside. A wealthy residential area of west Glasgow that has given its name to the affected and over-refined form of Scottish English spoken by its gen-teel, upper-class inhabitants. A characteristic is the pronunciation of 'a' as 'e' in such words as 'fancy' ('fency') and 'actually' ('ectually'). The area takes its name from nearby Kelvingrove Park. *See also* MORNINGSIDE.

Kennedy curse. The American Kennedy dynasty, whose brightest star was President John F. Kennedy, suffered an extraordinary series of tragedies during the 20th century. The dynasty began with Joseph Patrick Kennedy (1888–1969) and Rose Elizabeth Fitzgerald (1890–1995), who had nine children. In 1944 their son Joseph Kennedy Jr was killed in an air crash while flying a secret wartime mission. In 1948 Joseph's sister, Kathleen Agnes Kennedy, was killed in a plane crash in France. In 1963 Patrick Bouvier Kennedy, son of John and Jacqueline Kennedy, died days after his premature birth. On 22 November 1963 President John Fitzgerald Kennedy (1917–63) was assassinated in Dallas. On 6 June 1968 his brother, Robert Francis Kennedy (1925–68), was assassinated in Los Angeles. In 1969 Senator Edward M. Kennedy was involved in a car accident on the island of CHAPPA-QUIDDICK, killing his passenger. In 1973 his son, Edward Kennedy Jr, had his right leg amputated in a (successful) bid to halt the spread of cancer. In 1984 one of Robert's 11 children, David Kennedy, died of a HEROIN overdose. In 1997 Robert's son Michael was killed while playing ski football in Colorado. In 1999 President John F. Kennedy's only son, John F. Kennedy Jr (1960–99), died in an air crash off the Massachusetts coast. His wife, Carolyn Bessette Kennedy, and her sister, Lauren Bessette, perished with him. It was Edward M. Kennedy who first voiced the suspicion that the Kennedys seemed to be living in the shadow of a curse. *See also* JFK.

Kenwood. The well-known make of electric food mixer takes its name from Kenneth Wood (1916–97), who launched its prototype in 1948, basing it on existing models. His most popular model, the Kenwood Chef, made him a millionaire at the age of 42, although a misguided foray into refrigerators in the early 1960s was the cause of a notable financial setback. His company was taken over by Thorn Electrical Industries in 1968.

Kerb-crawling. The action of driving slowly close to the kerb in order to pick up a prostitute or indeed any woman on the pavement or by the roadside. The term dates from the early 1970s in this sense, although it existed earlier in spoken slang and police jargon as an expression for walking along the pavement for this same purpose.

Kermit. The garrulous, green-garbed puppet frog was the mainstay of Muppets, created by Jim Henson. He first appeared on US television in 1957, but did not become generally familiar until 1969, when he featured in the children's educational programme *Sesame Street*. This in turn led to The MUPPET SHOW, running from 1976 to 1981, in which Kermit pranced and parleyed with his equally esoteric friends, among them Miss Piggy and Fozzie Bear. His name is not uncommon as an American first name, and is familiar as that of the businessman and explorer Kermit Roosevelt (1889–1943), the son of Theodore Roosevelt, 26th president of the United States.

Kerr's cur. A description of Australian Liberal polit-ician Malcolm Fraser (b.1930) by Gough Whitlam (b.1916). The occasion was on 11 November 1975 when the governor general of Australia, Sir John Kerr (1914–91), dismissed Whitlam and his Labor adminis-tration and appointed Fraser as caretaker prime min-ister. As leader of the opposition Fraser had blocked Whitlam's money bills, and the crisis came when Whitlam refused to call a general election. Fraser won the election that followed Whitlam's dismissal and remained in that post until 1983.

Kestrel for a Knave, A. A novel (1968) by Barry Hines (b.1939). The only consolation for a boy from a council estate in northeast England, whose family back-ground and environment are responsible for the trouble into which he gets, is the hawk that he caught and has raised. The film version (1969), one of the key British movies of the period, was directed by Ken Loach with the title *Kes,* which was subsequently used for new editions of the book.

Kewpie doll. The American celluloid doll, designed by Joseph Kallus and made by George Borgfeldt, evolved from Rose O'Neill's drawings of chubby, top-knotted cherubs, first appearing in the *Ladies' Home Journal* (1909). By 1913 the dolls had become a commercial phenomenon, decorating soaps, fabrics and station-ery. The name comes from Cupid, with perhaps a dash of 'cute'. The dolls' latter-day descendants were the TELETUBBIES.

Keyhole Kate. The nosy schoolgirl whose insatiable curiosity leads to a host of comic disasters in the DANDY comic, in which she appeared from 1937 to 1955. She was the creation of the artist Allan Morley and in 1965 was revived by other hands for the new paper *Sparky*.

Keyhole surgery. The colloquial term for a surgical technique that involves operations being performed with minimal external incision through a small opening (the 'keyhole') and monitored via fibre optics on a screen. The formal term for the technique is minimally invasive surgery. The procedure was introduced in the late 1980s.

Keynesianism. The economic doctrine named after the British economist John Maynard Keynes (1883–1946). Broadly, Keynesian theories argue that high unemployment can be avoided by government intervention in the free-market economy, for example by manipulating demand through the use of fiscal and monetary policies. Keynesianism dominated the economic policies of many Western governments in the decades after the Second World War, but was later challenged by FRIEDMANISM.

Keystone Kops. A troupe of slapstick film comedians led by Ford Sterling and including Charlie Chaplin (1889–1977), Fatty Arbuckle (1887–1933) and Chester Conklin (1888–1971) who, from 1912 to 1920 under the inspiration of Mack Sennett (1880–1960), made a number of action-packed comedies at the Keystone Studios, HOLLYWOOD, complete with crazy chases and trick effects. The 35 Keystone films starring Charlie Chaplin are particularly significant, especially *Tilly's Punctured Romance* (1914), regarded as the first feature-length comedy. Sennett's Bathing Beauties were added in 1915 to complement the Kops and introduce a note of glamour.

KFC. The registered abbreviation of Kentucky Fried Chicken, a style of batter-dipped chicken sold by the company of this name. It was founded by 'Colonel Sanders', otherwise Harland D. Sanders (1890–1980), an American farmer's son from Indiana whose catering career began in 1930 when he opened Sanders' Café behind a petrol station at North Corbin, Kentucky, and who five years later was awarded his honorary colonel's title from the governor of Kentucky.

KGB. The secret police of the USSR, the initials standing for *Komitet gosudarstvennoy bezopasnosti* ('Committee of State Security'). Russia's original secret police was set up in 1917 as the Cheka, *Chrezvychaynaya komissiya* ('Extraordinary Commission' i.e. to combat counter-revolution). In 1922 this became the GPU, *Gosudarstvennoe politicheskoe upravlenie* ('State Political Directorate'), and the following year Ogpu, adding *Ob"edinënnoe* ('United') to the previous title. In 1934 it was renamed the NKVD, *Narodnyy komissariat vnutrennykh del* ('People's Commissariat for Internal Affairs'). In 1946 this was superseded by the MGB, *Ministerstvo gosudarstvennoy bezopasnosti* ('Ministry of State Security'), which in 1953 was renamed the MVD, *Ministerstvo vnutrennykh del* ('Ministry of Internal Affairs'). The KGB was formed in 1954 but ceased to exist in 1991 on the demise of the Soviet Union. It was succeeded by the FSK, *Federal'naya sluzhba kontrrazvedki* ('Federal Counter-Intelligence Service'). In 1995 this was renamed the FSB, *Federal'naya sluzhba bezopasnosti* ('Federal Security Service').

Khaki Cup Final. A nickname for the 1915 FA Cup Final at Old Trafford, which Sheffield United won 3–1 against Chelsea. The name alludes to the large number of servicemen in the crowd, a year after the outbreak of the First World War. On presenting the trophy, Lord Derby said that it was 'now the duty of everyone to join with each other and play a sterner game for England'.

Khaki Election. The name given to the general election of 1900 (28 September to 24 October) by which the Conservatives sought to profit from the recent military victories in the Second BOER WAR (1899–1902), when khaki was first generally familiar as the colour of active service uniforms. It was promoted by Joseph Chamberlain (1836–1914), and the Conservatives won, although their gain in seats was very slight.

Khmer Rouge. A communist movement in Cambodia, initially backed by North VIETNAM. It opposed the Cambodian government in the 1960s and waged civil war from 1970 to 1975, when it gained total power. For the next four years it exercised a regime of terror under Pol Pot (1926–98), resulting in the deaths of at least 2 million. It was overthrown by the Vietnamese in 1979 and became a guerrilla movement until 1991, when it declared itself 'reformed'. Since then it has maintained its guerrilla activities from bases in Thailand. The Khmer are the indigenous people of Cambodia. These particular ones were *rouge* (French, 'red') because communist. Cambodia was a French protectorate until 1955. *See also* KAMPUCHEA; KILLING FIELD.

Kibbutz (Modern Hebrew *qibbūṣ*, 'gathering'). A Jewish communal settlement in Israel organized on socialist lines by which land and property are shared. Work and meals are arranged collectively. Adults have private quarters but children are housed together. Kibbutzim were originally agricultural only, but various factories and industries later developed. The first kibbutz was set up in the Jordan Valley in 1909 by Jewish immigrants from Europe. They have played a considerable part in defending Israeli territory.

Kick ass, To. To act roughly or aggressively; to be impressive or assertive. The expression is of US origin and evolved in the 1980s from the earlier literal sense of beating or defeating someone by booting their backside.

> Her aim … is to give Londoners a taste of New York verve. 'These dancers are phenomenal, they really know how to kick ass as performers.'
> *The Times* (30 July 1999)

Kickback. An American slang term dating from the 1950s, denoting a bribe or other illicit payment. An earlier sense was of a negative reaction, or repercussion.

Kick in, To. To begin to start working or take effect. The 'kick' was originally the sharp stimulus afforded by a drug. To kick in with a payment, on the other hand, is to make a contribution. The distinction in sense is usually clear from the context.

> Many people may have heard that the thing to do when a panic attack kicks in is to breathe into a paper bag.
> *The Times* (3 August 1999)

Kick someone when they are down, To. To cause further misfortune to someone who is already in an unfortunate or disadvantageous situation. The image is of a person knocked down in a fight who is then kicked by the victor.

> Despite [Lord] Archer facing the prospect of a criminal prosecution … the loyalty he engendered among friends remains. Even some of the most senior Tories still refuse to kick him while he is down.
> *Sunday Times* (28 November 1999)

Kick something into touch, To. To remove it from the centre of attention; to 'sideline' it. The metaphor dates from the 1980s and is from football. If a ball is kicked over the touchline (at the side of the field) it goes out of play. 'To kick something into the long grass' is similar in sense and origin.

> Kicking the europoll into the long grass – 2003 or further – is viewed as too risky.
> *Sunday Times* (30 January 2000)

Kick up one's heels, To. An expression that together with variants such as 'to turn up one's heels' or 'to turn up one's toes' originally meant to die. In the 20th century a virtually converse sense emerged of to enjoy oneself, to 'have a fling'. The later imagery is of a horse freed from its harness or of an exuberant dancer.

Kid brother or **sister.** One's younger brother or sister. A 20th-century Americanism.

Kids and cars. A stock succinctness to describe a council housing estate, where children are everywhere and where cars and vehicles of various kinds are parked on most grass verges.

Kid sister. *See* KID BROTHER.

Kids' stuff. Anything very simple, such as child could handle. The expression dates from the 1920s.

Kiki of Montparnasse. The most famous artists' model of the 20th century was born in 1901 as Marie Prin, a French farmer's daughter who settled in Paris at the end of the First World War. Her original intention was to find work in a shoe factory, but she was discovered by the painter Moïse Kisling and began a career posing for him and other artists. The most notable of these was Man Ray (1890–1977), with whom she lived for six years, and he immortalized her in a photograph entitled *Le Violon d'Ingres* (1924) in which he painted a violin's two *f*-holes on her naked back. The title was a pun on the French phrase VIOLON D'INGRES. From 1926 Kiki exhibited her own paintings and made a name for herself as a nightclub singer. She latterly lost her looks and died in drunken poverty in 1953. The name Montparnasse, that of the famous artists' quarter of Paris, remains as a reminder of her youthful fame and beauty.

Kildare, Dr. The young doctor originally created by the US pulp-magazine writer Max Brand (real name Frederick Schiller Faust) for a series of stories with titles such as *The Secret of Dr Kildare* or *Calling Dr Kildare*, from which MGM produced seven films (1938–41). Dr James Kildare works at Blair General Hospital under the supervision of the tetchy Dr Gillespie, who is confined to a wheelchair. A popular television series bearing his name followed (1961–6) with Richard Chamberlain as Kildare and Raymond Massey as his boss.

Killer instinct. A ruthless determination to succeed or win. The phrase dates from the 1920s, and was in particular applied by the press to the American world heavyweight champion Jack Dempsey (1895–1983). The allusion is to a predatory animal that lives by killing.

Killer submarine. A small submarine designed for searching out and sinking enemy submarines. The analogy is with a predatory animal, such as a shark or killer whale, which hunts down and kills its prey.

Killing field. A place of mass slaughter. The term originally applied to Cambodia under the KHMER ROUGE regime in the mid-1970s, when thousands of so-called 'bourgeois elements' were deported from the cities to the countryside and executed in what became known as the 'killing fields'. The phrase passed generally into the language following the film on this grim subject, *The* KILLING FIELDS (1984). The term later came to apply to any large-scale killing, whether in the countryside or not.

Killing Fields, The. A film (1984) based on the real-life relationship between US journalist Sidney Schanberg and his Cambodian translator Dith Pran following the US withdrawal from Phnom Penh in 1975. The plot recounts Schanberg's attempts to locate Pran after the latter is seized for 're-education' by the KHMER ROUGE. The 'killing fields' of the title were the paddy fields around Phnom Penh in which the Khmer Rouge executed their opponents. The part of Dith Pran was played by Haing S. Ngor, a doctor who had himself fled from the Khmer Rouge. In reality Dith Pran saw the killing fields himself for the first time only when he visited them as mayor of his home town, long after the Khmer Rouge had been thrown out. *See also* KILLING FIELD.

Kilroy. During the Second World War the phrase 'Kilroy was here' was found written up wherever the Americans (particularly Air Transport Command) had been. Its origin is a matter of conjecture. One suggestion is that a certain shipyard inspector at Quincy, Massachusetts, chalked up the words on material he had inspected. Pictorially Kilroy was a wide-eyed, bald-headed face peering over a fence, something like Mr CHAD. The outrageousness of the GRAFFITI was not so much what it said but its ubiquity, and Kilroy's presence was marked in such sacred sites as the torch of the Statue of Liberty in New York Harbour and the walls of the Arc de Triomphe in Paris.

Kim. The orphan boy, Kimball O'Hara, who is the hero of the novel by Rudyard Kipling that bears his name (1901), regarded by many as the writer's finest. He passes as a native Indian boy nicknamed 'Little Friend of All the World', takes up with a wise old Tibetan lama, and eventually becomes a secret agent on behalf of the British government. The British spy Kim Philby (*see* CAMBRIDGE SPY RING) was nicknamed after him, his original forenames being Harold Adrian Russell.

Kim's game. A memory-testing game introduced to BOY SCOUTS by their founder, Robert Baden-Powell, as a development of the 'Jewel Game' described in Rudyard Kipling's KIM, ch ix (1901). As explained in *Scouting for Boys* (1908), it consists in placing a number of small articles on a tray, covering them up, then uncovering them for one minute, at the end of which they are covered again. Whoever recalls the greatest number of articles wins the game. The principle lies behind more recent games and contests, such as the prize-winning procedure in *The* GENERATION GAME on television.

Kinder, Kirche, Küche (German, 'children, church, kitchen'). A traditional slogan, dating from the early years of the 20th century, regarding the place of women in Germany. The phrase was adopted by the NAZIS, who emphasized the role of women as homemakers and breeders of little Aryans. From 1933 German women were actively discouraged from going to university or taking employment, and during the Second World War women were not mobilized on anything like the same scale as they were in Britain or the Soviet Union, an ideological reservation that certainly put constraints on industrial output.

Kindertotenlieder. A moving cycle of five songs with orchestral accompaniment, composed in 1901–4 by Gustav Mahler (1860–1911) with words by Friedrich Rückert. The title means 'songs on the death of children'. The work was sadly prophetic, for in 1907 Mahler's adored eldest daughter died at the age of four, one of a number of tragedies to beset his family.

Kind Hearts and Coronets. A celebrated British film comedy (1949), loosely based by Robert Hamer and John Dighton on the turn-of-the-century novel *Israel Rank* by Roy Horniman, about a lowly relation of the aristocratic D'Ascoyne family who murders his way to the dukedom he believes is rightfully his. Starring Dennis Price as Louis Mazzini, the amoral murderer, and Alec Guinness as eight of his blueblooded victims, the film owes its title to a poem by Tennyson:

Trust me, Clara Vere de Vere,

From yon blue heavens above us bent

The grand old gardener and his wife

Smile at the claims of long descent.

Howe'er it be, it seems to me,

'Tis only noble to be good.

Kind hearts are more than coronets,

And simple faith than Norman blood.

'Lady Clara Vere de Vere' (1842)

King, The. The nickname of Elvis Presley (1935–77), regarded by many people as the first and greatest ever rock 'n' roll star. It is also the nickname of the Welsh rugby union international Barry John (b.1945), a fly-half of regal skill. *See also* KING KENNY.

King and I, The. A musical play (1951) with a score by Richard Rodgers (1902–79) and book by Oscar Hammerstein II (1895–1960) about the experiences of an English governess who is engaged to care for the children of the King of Siam. Filmed with Yul Brynner and Deborah Kerr in 1956, the play was based on the biographical book *Anna and the King of Siam* by Margaret Landon, in which she related the experiences of Anna Leonowens as governess to the king of Siam's 67 children. The story was filmed for the first time in 1946, with the same title as Landon's book. It was the actress Gertrude Lawrence, who played Anna in the first stage production, who first suggested the book would make a good musical. Among the memorable numbers are 'Hello, Young Lovers' and 'Shall We Dance?'

King Arthur. A hostile nickname given to Arthur Scargill (b.1938), militant president of the National Union of Mineworkers from 1981. Margaret Thatcher described the miners as 'the enemy within' during their bitter and protracted 1984–5 strike, which ended in the closure of most of Britain's pits. *See also* PLUTONIUM BLONDE.

King David Hotel. *See* IRGUN.

Kingfish. A nickname of populist and charismatic US politician Huey Long (1893–1935). He was governor of Louisiana from 1928, and a US senator from 1931, and became virtual dictator of the state. The nickname was drawn from the popular radio show AMOS 'N' ANDY. He was also known as the Prince of Piffle. Long proposed to run against Franklin D. Roosevelt in the 1936 presidential election on the 'Share-our-Wealth' platform, an alternative to Roosevelt's NEW DEAL. One of his own slogans was 'Every man a king, but no man wears a crown.' He was so confident of victory that he published a book entitled *My First Days in the White House* (1935). However, Long was assassinated by a New Orleans doctor, Carl Austin Weiss, on 10 September 1935. His life was fictionalized by Robert Penn Warren (1905–89) in his PULITZER PRIZE-winning novel, *All the King's Men* (1946), which was adapted as a stage play and as an Oscar-winning film (1949) in which the Long character was named Willie Stark.

King Kenny. The nickname of the Scottish footballer and football club manager Kenny Dalglish (b.1951). His successes as a player and as a manager are probably without parallel in British football. Quite apart from winning 102 caps for Scotland and a Scottish league and cup double with Glasgow Celtic, during his time at Liverpool as a player (from 1977) and a manager (from 1985), Liverpool won the league championship nine times, the European Cup four times, the League Cup four times and the FA Cup twice. Small wonder that a Liverpool supporter's banner in the 1970s was seen to carry the punning message 'Kenny's from heaven'.

King Kong. The giant ape who is the fearsome yet curiously touching star of the HORROR MOVIE (1933) that bears his name. He is discovered on a Pacific island and brought to America as a circus attraction. He breaks loose there, runs riot in New York and climbs the Empire State Building. He is finally gunned down by fighter planes, but not before he has gently carried a young woman (played by Fay Wray) in his hairy hand to the top of the skyscraper. Both parts of his name suggest that he is a king (Danish *Kong*). The story was written by Merian Cooper and Edgar Wallace. Jessica Lange played Wray's part in the 1976 remake.

Kingledon. A name for the Wimbledon tennis courts coined in 1972 by the *Daily Mirror* as a tribute to the US player Billie Jean King (b.1943) when she won the women's singles title there for the fourth time.

King of Calypso. A nickname for the US singer Harry Belafonte (b.1927). A calypso is a type of West Indian ballad, often satirical. As a child Belafonte spent five years in Jamaica, and subsequently had a great popular success with calypsos, such as 'Banana Boat Song' ('Day-O, day-O, daylight come an' I wanna go home').

King of Hollywood. A title awarded in the 1930s to the US film star Clark Gable (1901–60), whose most famous role was as Rhett Butler in GONE WITH THE WIND (1939). It was the columnist Ed Sullivan who polled his readers as to who was the 'King of Hollywood', and Gable won by an enormous margin. However, Gable did not have an auspicious start: after a screen test in the 1920s the MGM producer Irving Thalberg had exclaimed, 'It's awful – take it away!', and Howard Hughes, Darryl F. Zanuck and Jack L. Warner had all been put off by the famous Gable ears.

King of Rock 'n' Roll. *See* KING.

King of Swing. A nickname of Benny Goodman (1909–86), the US clarinettist and band leader, who made his name playing swing, a style of jazz popular in the 1930s and 1940s.

King-sized. Extra large. The term arose in the 1940s to refer to extra-long cigarettes but subsequently came to apply to anything specially grand, as a very big bed or a huge hamburger. The idea is that the size is fit for a king. A queen-sized bed is similar, but slightly less large.

> She found herself pondering the word king-sized. What did it mean, really? A king could be any size, when it came down to it. Richard III, for example, was almost a midget, whereas Henry VIII was six foot tall and could have worn his stomach as a kilt.
> DERMOT BOLGER (ed.): *Finbar's Hotel*, 'The Test' (1997)

King Street. A name for the executive committee of the Communist Party of Great Britain, from its former location in the London street of this name leading to the present Covent Garden Market.

Kingston bypass. One of Britain's earliest urban bypasses, south of Kingston-upon-Thames, and now part of the A3. Planning of the bypass began in the 1920s and the name came to encapsulate the mixed pleasures and frustrations of motoring in and around London.

> Give me the Kingston By-Pass
> And a thoroughly 'posh' machine
> Like a Healey three-litre
> All complete with heater
> Or a shiny grey Chevrolet Limousine.
> NOËL COWARD: *The Globe Revue*, 'Give Me the Kingston By-Pass' (1952)

Kinnockio. A hostile nickname given to Neil Kinnock (b.1942), leader of the Labour Party (1983–92), and subsequently a European Union commissioner. The nickname was modelled on Pinocchio, the childlike puppet hero of a children's story by the Italian writer C. Collodi (pseudonym of Carlo Lorenzini; 1826–90). Pinocchio, whose nose grows whenever he tells a lie, was also the subject of a 1940 Walt Disney cartoon film. *See also* WELSH WINDBAG.

Kinsey Report. When the US zoologist Dr Alfred C. Kinsey (1894–1956) found himself short of answers to his students' questions about human sexual behaviour he set out to compile the sexual life history of the human species. The result in 1948, after 10 years of research and thousands of interviews, was his landmark study, *Sexual Behaviour in the Human Male*, otherwise the *Kinsey Report*. What shocked its readers was not the varieties of sexual experience it detailed but the explicit nature of the research. A second volume on female sexuality followed in 1953.

Kipper tie. A very wide and brightly coloured tie popular in the 1960s, so named punningly because it was promoted by the London menswear designer Michael Fish.

> On stage [Paul] Scofield would tease [Barry] Cryer, sotto voce, about his garish taste in kipper ties.
> *The Times* (10 September 1999)

Kir. A drink made from dry white wine and crème de cassis, named after and perhaps even devised by Canon Félix Kir (1876–1968), the resistance hero and mayor of Dijon during the Second World War. It was first sampled in Britain in the mid-1960s.

Kirlian photography. A technique said to record directly on photographic film the field radiation of electricity emitted by an object to which an electric charge has been applied. It was developed in the 1930s by the Russian technicians Semyon D. and Valentina K. Kirlian and continues to attract both claims and counterclaims regarding its efficacy, especially as a tool in psychotherapy.

Kirov Ballet. The famous Russian ballet company is a descendant of the Bolshoi Theatre of St Petersburg, which housed the city's opera and ballet company from 1783 to 1860, and the Maryinsky Theatre, which opened in 1860. After the October Revolution of 1917 it became the State Academic Theatre for Opera and Ballet, and in 1935 received its present name, in honour of the Russian revolutionary Sergei Kirov (1886–1934), head of the Leningrad Communist Party, assassinated the previous year. It has retained the name, even after the demise of the Soviet Union in 1991, since this is the one by which it won renown worldwide as one of the supreme classic ballet troupes. Its reputation suffered in the 1960s when its repertory became sterile, resulting in the mass defection to the West of some of its top dancers, including the finest, Rudolf Nureyev (1938–93).

Kismet. A musical play (1953) based on a play (1911) by Edward Knoblock about a poet turned beggar who has a series of adventures reminiscent of *The Arabian Nights*. The music of Alexander Borodin was arranged by Robert Wright and George Forrest, and the show's most popular numbers include 'Baubles, Bangles and Beads', 'Stranger in Paradise' and 'This is My Beloved'. The title came from the Turkish *kismet* ('portion' or 'lot') and is now commonly understood to mean 'fate'.

Kiss and make up, To. To become reconciled. The image is of two children resuming a friendship after a quarrel or fight, or two lovers resuming their attachment after a tiff. The expression emerged in the 1940s as an alternative to the much older and still current 'to kiss and be friends'.

> [Foreign Secretary] Robin Cook has kissed and made up with Sir David Gore-Booth, the retired diplomat who publicly savaged Cook's handling of the Foreign Office.
> *The Times* (11 October 1999)

Kiss goodbye to something, To. To accept its loss or non-realization, as: 'When the children went down with flu we had to kiss goodbye to our holiday.' The expression dates from the early years of the 20th century and relates to a genuine kiss on parting. The ironic touch was probably intensified by the First World War, in which a farewell kiss may well have been a final one.

> Wretched Derby can surely kiss the play-offs goodbye after being outgunned by Burnley, going down 3–1.
> *People* (16 April 1995)

Kissing garden. A garden designed for private use by its owner's family and friends. It typically consists of a small enclosed paved area with seats and potted plants or shrubs arranged semi-formally around a rectangular pond and takes its name from the title of Charlotte Bingham's romantic novel *The Kissing Garden* (1999), set in the English countryside in the years following the First World War. The sentimental analogy is an old one. *See also* HEARTS AND FLOWERS.

> We've known about cloister gardens, knot gardens, walled gardens, even secret gardens. But kissing

gardens? I turn to my *Oxford Companion to Gardening* … Nope, not a mention.
> *The Times* (18 December 1999)

Kiss Me Deadly. A crime novel (1953) by 'Mickey' (Frank Morrison) Spillane (b.1918). Detective Mike HAMMER, having destroyed a crime syndicate and killed its boss, now finds himself up against a blonde armed with a gun and wearing just a robe after her bath. She says, 'You're going to die now … but first you can do it. Deadly … deadly … kiss me.' Instead Hammer ignites her with his cigarette lighter. An exuberant film version (1955), with brutal close-ups and unusual camera angles, was directed by Robert Aldrich with Ralph Meeker as Hammer.

Kiss Me Kate. A musical comedy (1948) with a score by Cole Porter (1892–1964) loosely based on William Shakespeare's *The Taming of the Shrew*. The show interweaves elements of the original play with the backstage goings-on of a company supposedly rehearsing it. The title was based on a line in Shakespeare's play:

> *Katharina*: Husband, let's follow, to see the end of this ado.
> *Petruchio*: First kiss me, Kate, and we will.
> *Katharina*: What! in the midst of the street?
> WILLIAM SHAKESPEARE: *The Taming of the Shrew*, V i.

Kiss-me-quick. A type of small hat sold at the seaside and perhaps even bearing the words of the invitation or some similar device. In the 19th century the name was in use for a small bonnet worn on the back of the head. The implication is that the hat leaves the face open for the desired action, unlike more ornate or veiled articles of millinery.

> For more than fifty years [theatre organist] Douglas Reeve was as much a part of the town of Brighton as the Palace Pier, candy-floss and kiss-me-quick hats.
> *The Times* (28 July 1999)

Kiss my arse or **ass.** A crude challenge or rejection, inviting a person to perform the stated obsequious and degrading act. *See also* POGUES *under* ROCK GROUP NAMES.

Kiss of death. Anything certain to cause the end of an enterprise, as: 'The new regulation was the kiss of death for our farming experiment.' The phrase dates from the 1940s. The original 'kiss of death' must have been that given treacherously by Judas to Jesus (Matthew 26:49).

> *American Psycho* … attracted the dreaded NC–17 rating from the Motion Picture Association of

America, normally the kiss of death at the box office because it bars the crucial teen audience.

The Times (22 January 2000)

Kiss of life. A name originally used in the 1960s for mouth-to-mouth resuscitation. Sleeping Beauty was awakened from her deathlike sleep by the Prince's kiss. The expression is also used metaphorically for anything that revives or reinvigorates. *See also* KISS OF DEATH.

Kiss of peace. A mutual greeting between members of the congregation in the Eucharist. It is not an actual kiss, but a shaking of hands, usually accompanied by words such as 'Peace be with you'. It is a revival of a custom in the primitive church and is not welcomed by some of the faithful, who claim that it is artificial and disrupts the progression of the service.

Kiss of the Spider Woman. A film (1985) based on a novel *El beso de la mujer araña* (1976) by the Argentinian writer Manuel Puig. It is about the unlikely friendship that develops between a gay man and a political prisoner when they are thrown into the same cell in a South American prison. The title refers to a B-MOVIE about 'Spider Woman' that the two discuss between sessions of torture at the hands of their captors.

Kissogram. A greetings service for a party or celebration, in which a person, typically a provocatively dressed young woman, is hired to come and kiss the celebrator. The word is a blend of 'kiss' and 'telegram'. *See also* STRIPPERGRAM.

Kitchener's Army. A nickname given to the mass volunteer army recruited in Britain by Field Marshal Earl Kitchener (1850–1916) in the First World War. The recruits were also referred to as the New Army or New Armies. Kitchener, who had become a British national hero after his campaigns in the Sudan and the Boer War, was appointed war minister on the outbreak of the First World War. Between 1914 and the introduction of conscription in January 1916 some 2.6 million men had volunteered. Kitchener's enormously successful campaign was aided by the famous poster with his uniformed and moustachioed portrait pointing towards the viewer, accompanied by the slogan 'Your Country Needs You'. However, this success created problems of training and equipping so many men and in filling the gaps in the labour force that they left behind. Kitchener himself died when the cruiser *Hampshire*, on which he was sailing on a diplomatic mission to Russia, struck a mine off the Orkneys.

Kitchen sink drama. A type of drama popular in the 1950s, in which the plot centres on the more sordid aspects of working-class or lower-middle-class domestic life, much of which is spent at the kitchen sink. Examples of the genre include John Osborne's LOOK BACK IN ANGER (1956), set in a cluttered bedsitter, Shelagh Delaney's A TASTE OF HONEY (1958), set in a cheerless flat in Salford, and Arnold Wesker's *The Kitchen* (1959), set in the chaotic kitchen of a busy restaurant. *See also* ANGRY YOUNG MAN; KITCHEN SINK SCHOOL.

Kitchen Sink School. A group of artists active in the 1950s who specialized in drab working-class subjects, especially interiors and still-lifes of domestic clutter. The main artists covered by the term were John Bratby (1928–92), Derrick Greaves (b.1927), Edward Middleditch (1923–87) and Jack Smith (b.1928). The name was coined by the critic David Sylvester in the December 1954 number of *Encounter*. *See also* KITCHEN SINK DRAMA.

Kitemark. The label on a manufactured product that says it meets with the approval of the British Standards Institution. It consists of a kite-shaped monogram of the letters BSI, the Institution's initials. The BSI was founded in 1901, and the Kitemark was already in use in 1903 on tram rails.

Kiteworld. A SCIENCE FICTION novel (1985) by Keith Roberts (b.1935). Britain has been taken over by religious fanatics, which makes difficulties for the crews of the giant kites that protect the borders against demonic beings. *See also* PAVANNE.

Kitsch. A term first recorded in English in the 1920s for any art, object or design that is considered to be lacking in taste because of its garishness or sentimentality but that, because of these attributes, may well have gained a value in its own right. The word is German for 'vulgar trash', and derives from *verkitschen*, 'to cheapen', 'to sentimentalize'. It was originally applied to sentimental German novels and novelettes but was then extended to cover other forms of expression.

> Whether it be a crinolined-lady loo-roll-holder, a 'dress your own [Princess] Diana' doll or a recording of [13-year-old] Charlotte Church singing *Ave Maria*, kitsch is easy to recognize, but far harder to define.
> *The Times* (11 December 1999)

Kitten heel. A type of low heel on a woman's shoe, or a shoe with such a heel. The heel is so called because it supposedly suggests that its wearer is a SEX KITTEN.

Such heels were in fashion in the early 1960s, and again in the 1990s.

> Kitten heels are still very much in evidence, although many seem to have grown well past the kitten stage into teetering columns that are more Marilyn Monroe than Audrey Hepburn.
>
> *The Times* (20 October 1999)

Kitty Hawk. A town in North Carolina, situated on a sandy stretch of Atlantic coast. It was just south of the town, in the Kill Devil Hills, on 17 December 1903 that Orville (1871–1948) and Wilbur Wright (1867–1912) made the first sustained, manned, powered and controllable flight in a heavier-than-air aircraft. Their aeroplane was named *The Flyer*. The name Kitty Hawk, which has become almost synonymous with that first flight, probably derives from the Algonkian name Chickahauk, the meaning of which is unknown.

Kiwanis. An organization founded in Detroit in 1915 aiming to improve business ethics and provide leadership for raising the level of business and professional ideals. There are many Kiwanis clubs in the United States and Canada, and also several in Britain. The name is said to come from a Native American language and to mean 'to make oneself known'.

Kiwi. A native of New Zealand, especially a soldier or member of a sports team, from the indigenous Maori name of the flightless bird that is the country's symbol or mascot.

> Nearly six years ago, as a 19-year-old New Zealander, I first set foot on English soil. And although I will always be a Kiwi at heart, England is starting to feel more like my home.
>
> *The Times* (13 October 1999)

KKK. *See* KU KLUX KLAN.

Kleenex. The trade name of a type of soft paper tissue, used for paper handkerchiefs. Kleenex (originally known as Celluwipes) were the world's first paper handkerchiefs (1924), and were manufactured by Kimberly-Clark in the USA. The task of selling the concept to the public was entrusted to the advertising guru Albert Lasker (1880–1952), who, with his 1921 Kotex campaign, had already introduced the world at large to the sanitary towel.

Kneecapping. A form of punishment used by paramilitary groups in Northern Ireland, especially the IRA. Used against informers, defectors or minor criminals, kneecapping involves shooting or drilling through the victim's kneecaps, so crippling them. Such punishments have continued in the late 1990s, even though a cease-fire has been in force. In Italy, kneecappings were carried out by left-wing terror groups in the 1970s against businessmen and judges, along with kidnappings and shootings.

Knee-jerk reaction. An automatic and unthinking response. The allusion is to the test of the nervous system known as the knee-jerk reflex. A tap with a rubber hammer just below the kneecap stretches a tendon of one of the thigh muscles, causing it to contract and jerk the lower leg up.

> Divorce specialist Vanessa Lloyd Platt advises: 'Many people see a solicitor before they're psychologically ready to deal with it [divorce] – it's a knee-jerk reaction.'
>
> *Independent on Sunday* (3 October 1999)

Kneesies. Amorous play with the knees, usually covertly under the table. *See also* FOOTSIE.

Knee-slapper. An uproarious joke, of the kind that makes the listener slap their knee with delight. The American expression dates from the 1960s.

Knees-up. A boisterous and energetic dance, in which the dancers raise alternate knees. Hence any lively party or celebration. The dance gets its name from 'Knees up, Mother Brown!', the song to which it is traditionally performed. Both date back to at least 1918, and the dance was widely performed in squares, streets and pubs on Armistice Night (11 November) that year, but the first published version of the song would seem to be as below. It was widely popularized by the Cockney duo GERT AND DAISY.

> Ooh! Knees up Mother Brown!
> Well! Knees up Mother Brown!
> … knees up, knees up!
> Don't get the breeze up
> Knees up Mother Brown.
>
> HARRIS WESTON, BERT LEE and IRVING TAYLOR:
> 'Knees up, Mother Brown!' (1938)

Knickerbocker Glory. A dessert consisting of ice cream served with fruit, cream and other ingredients in a tall glass. It is uncertain what relationship it has, if any, with knickerbockers. The name first became familiar in the 1930s.

> 'Have a *parfait* … They do a very good Maiden's Dream. Not to speak of Alpine Glow. Or the Knickerbocker Glory.'
>
> GRAHAME GREENE: *Gun for Sale*, ch i (1936)

Knievel, Evel. The adopted name of the American motorcycle stunt performer Robert C. Knievel (b.1938). He began to perform stunts as a teenager and after a succession of varied jobs, from hockey player to safecracker, formed Evel Knievel's Motorcyle Devils in 1965. He soon gained fame for his spectacular and dangerous performances, one of which resulted in spinal injuries when in May 1975 his car failed to clear 13 buses. His son, Robbie Knievel, followed him in his hazardous career.

Knight in shining armour. An idealized chivalrous man who comes to the aid of a DAMSEL IN DISTRESS. The image of a dashing knight in glittering armour on a white charger is an old one, but the expression dates only from the 1960s. *See also* WHITE KNIGHT.

Knight of the shire. A Conservative MP for a country consistency who has been knighted for political services. The designation derives from the term for a gentleman representing a shire or county in parliament in medieval times, originally one of two of the rank of knight.

Knightsbridge. The nickname given by British forces to a crossroads in the desert south of Tobruk, during the North African campaign in the Second World War. There were fierce tank battles here in May–June 1942 prior to the German advance to ALAMEIN. The name comes from an affluent area of London that includes the department store Harrods.

Knock or **hit for six, To.** To demolish utterly an argument or to defeat completely an opponent, figuratively or literally. In cricket the ball is 'knocked for six' when the batsman, by hitting it full pitch over the boundary of the field, scores six runs, so 'punishing' the bowler. The expression dates from the early 20th century and a hit over the boundary scored only four runs until 1910, when six runs were allotted to such a stroke. In the quotation below, the expression is applied punningly to England's 6–0 football win over Luxembourg in 1999.

> A hat-trick for [England's captain Alan] Shearer, as England knock Luxembourg for six.
>
> *BBC1 Television News* (headline) (4 September 1999)

Knock, knock! An invitation to respond to a riddle punning on a personal name. An old example is: 'Knock, knock!' 'Who's there?' 'Roland.' 'Roland who?' 'Roland mow the lawn.' More sophisticated examples may be allusive: 'Knock, knock!' 'Who's

there?' 'Sam and Janet.' 'Sam and Janet who?' 'Sam and Janet evening.' A restriction to personal names is not essential: 'Knock, knock!' 'Who's there?' 'A little old lady.' 'A little old lady who?' 'I didn't know you could yodel.'

Knock-on effect. A secondary or indirect effect; a consequence of an earlier action. The image is of a 'pile-up', in which one vehicle runs into another, which in turn strikes a third.

> [Actress Sandra] Bullock exudes so much charisma that her co-stars can only benefit from an inevitable knock-on effect.
>
> *The Times* (6 May 1999)

Knock someone's block off, To. To hit them hard on the head. The expression is mostly used in general threats that are not implemented, as: 'If he does that again I'll knock his block off.'

Knock or **blow someone's socks off, To.** To impress them. The image is of a stunning or explosive effect that causes the socks to fly from the feet.

> The top-of-the-range digital tuner that has knocked my socks off ... costs £750.
>
> *The Times* (26 November 1999)

Knole sofa or **settee.** A type of sofa designed in the style of an early 17th-century model, with adjustable sides that can be lowered to make it into a 'day bed'. It was first fashionable in the 1940s and takes its name from the prototype at Knole House, Kent.

Knot Garden, The. A semi-mystical opera by Michael Tippett (1905–98) with a libretto by the composer. It was first performed in 1974. The symbolic knot garden of the title is a revolving stage device, in which the various characters work out their relationships. The characters include a benevolent analyst, Mangus (a variant of 'magus'?), who sets up an elaborate charade based on Shakespeare's *The Tempest* to help the others work through their problems.

Know all the answers, To. To be knowledgeable or expert on something. The expression dates from the 1930s and is often sarcastically used of a 'know-all': 'You know all the answers, don't you?'

Knowledge, The. The test that drivers of London BLACK CABS must pass to show that they know the name and location of every street and the shortest or quickest route to it. Drivers have typically prepared for the test by riding a moped around the streets while memorizing routes from a plan clipped to the handlebars. This particular method formed the subject of Jack Rosenthal's enjoyable television play *The Knowledge* (1979), with Nigel Hawthorne as the sadistic examiner.

Know one's onions, To. To be knowledgeable in a particular field. The expression dates from the 1920s and is sometimes said to refer to the lexicographer C.T. Onions (1873–1965), co-editor of the *Oxford English Dictionary* and author of books on English. This seems unlikely, however, because its earliest record is in American usage. Also unlikely is a proposed source in rhyming slang, with 'onions' short for 'onion rings', meaning 'things'. It may well be simply a whimsical variant on 'to know one's stuff', perhaps with an implied pun on 'stuffing', of which (sage and) onions were by the 1920s a stock ingredient.

Know the score, To. To understand the situation; to appreciate what is happening. The expression dates from the 1930s and alludes to someone who keeps up with the score in a particular sport.

Knuckle-duster. A loop of heavy metal, gripped in the hand and fitting over the knuckles, used as an offensive weapon. Its origin goes back to the days of Roman pugilism.

Knuckle sandwich. A punch in the mouth.

Kojak. The tough New York policeman played by Telly Savalas in the popular television series that bore his name (1973–8). He was the creation of the writer Abby Mann, and his 'trademarks' were his bald head, his habit of sucking lollipops and his catchphrase, 'Who loves ya, baby?'

Kon-Tiki expedition. The unique voyage made by the Norwegian Thor Heyerdahl (b.1914) with five companions in 1947, who sailed a balsa raft from Callao in Peru to Tuamotu Island in the South Pacific. Their object was to support the theory that the Polynesian race reached the Pacific islands in this fashion and were descendants of the Incas of Peru. Their raft was called *Kon-Tiki* after the Inca sun-god.

> The original name of the sun-god Virakocha, which seems to have been more used in Peru in old times, was Kon-Tiki or Illa-Tiki, which means Sun-Tiki or Illa-Tiki. Kon-Tiki was a high priest and sun-king of the Incas' legendary 'white men' who had left the enormous ruins on the shores of Lake Titicaca.
> THOR HEYERDAHL: *The Kon-Tiki Expedition* (1950)

Kop, The. The former terrace at the south end of the Anfield stadium, the home ground of Liverpool football club, was opened on 1 September 1906 and within weeks dubbed the Spion Kop, or simply the Kop, after the BOER WAR battle of 24 January 1900 at Spion Kop ('Lookout Hill') that arose from repeated British attempts to relieve the siege of Ladysmith. The battle resulted in some 250 British casualties, including many Merseysiders. The Kop was roofed in 1928 and became the largest covered terrace in Britain, with room for 28,000 people. It was demolished following the club's final home match of the 1993–4 season on 30 April 1994 against Norwich City and a concert on 1 May featuring Merseybeat bands of the 1960s, such as Gerry and the Pacemakers and the Searchers. It was replaced by a new stand seating 12,000 and housing a club shop and a branch of McDONALD'S, the first at a sports stadium in Britain. The initiator of the original nickname is said to have been Ernest Edwards, sports editor of the *Liverpool Daily Post*. The name was also in use elsewhere, as at Arsenal's Plumstead ground and Birmingham's Tilton Road. Bradford City's Valley Parade ground had a 'Nunn's Kop', named after one of the club's founders.

Korean War. A conflict between North and South Korea. In 1950 the communist North, supported by the USSR, invaded the South, but a counterattack by mainly US forces sent by the UNITED NATIONS Security Council pushed the communists back over the 38th parallel of latitude (the original dividing-line between the two Koreas, established in 1945), and pressed as far north as North Korea's border with China. Chinese intervention on the North Korean side then drove the UN forces as far south as the South Korean capital, Seoul, in early 1951. After two more years of fighting, an armistice was signed in 1953, restoring the territorial status quo. The threats to bomb China uttered by Gen. Douglas MacArthur, commander of the UN forces, at times seemed likely to start a THIRD WORLD WAR, and led to his sacking by President Harry S. Truman. *See also* COLD WAR.

Korfball (Dutch *korfbal*, literally 'basket ball'). A combination of NETBALL and basketball invented in 1901 by an Amsterdam schoolmaster, Nico Broekhuysen, and soon after adopted in Britain and elsewhere. It is played out of doors by two teams of six, usually women against men, and goals are scored by throwing the ball into an open-ended basket at the top of a goalpost. Action consists almost entirely in passing the ball from hand to hand, and kicking or punching the ball, or running with it, are illegal. Correct play is courteous and considerate, and the fact that the game was devised for both sexes has caused it to be both gentlemanly and even at times ladylike.

Kraken Wakes, The. A SCIENCE FICTION novel (1953) by John Wyndham (pen-name of John Wyndham Parkes Lucas Beynon Harris; 1903–69). As a result of a global disaster, interstellar invaders settle on the seabed and flood Britain. The title was inspired by Tennyson's poem 'The Kraken' (1830):

> Below the thunders of the upper deep;
> Far, far beneath in the abysmal sea,
> His ancient, dreamless, uninvaded sleep
> The Kraken sleepeth.

Krankies, The. A Scottish comic double act consisting of the husband-and-wife team Ian and Janette Tough, the latter in the role of 'wee Jimmy', a naughty school-boy. The pair were established as regulars on the children's television programme CRACKERJACK and then had their own television show in *The Krankies Klub* (1982–4). Their humour consisted largely of juvenile 'anti-authoritarian' routines with raucously delivered quips and the inevitable slapstick.

K ration. An emergency food ration consisting of a single prepared meal, supplied to US soldiers in com-bat in the Second World War. It was named after the American physiologist who instigated it, Ancel B. Keys (b.1904).

Kray twins. The murderers Ronnie (1933–95) and Reggie (b.1933) Kray were born in the East End of London, where they ran a criminal Mafia-style opera-tion in the 1960s. Their 'firm' collected protection money, organized illegal gambling and drinking clubs, and participated in gang warfare. The dom-inant twin was Ronnie, who modelled himself on Chicago gangsters. In the late 1960s he entered the Blind Beggar, a pub on Mile End Road, and shot dead George Cornell, a member of a rival gang, while Reggie lured another, Jack 'The Hat' McVitie, to a flat and stabbed him to death. The twins were tried at the Old Bailey in 1969 and given prison sentences of not less than 30 years. A campaign to free them failed, and Ronnie died in prison. In 1999 a further campaign to free Reggie was mounted on the grounds that he had now served the full prison term.

Krazy Kat. The comic-strip alley cat so known was invented by the cartoonist George Herriman in 1910, and his adventures with his friend Ignatz Mouse were syndicated in US newspapers until the artist's death in 1944. The mad moggy has also led a long life in animated films.

Kremlin. The walled palace complex of the tsars of Russia in Moscow, mostly dating from the 15th to the 18th centuries. The Kremlin subsequently became the centre of government of the Soviet Union (and since 1991 of the Russian Federation). 'The Kremlin' thus became synonymous with the Soviet government, and Western analysts of Soviet affairs became known as Kremlinologists or Kremlin-watchers.

Kriegspiel (German, 'war play'). A word adopted in English for a game introduced in the British army after the Franco-Prussian War of 1870. It arose in Switzerland earlier in the 19th century and was played by moving blocks representing parts of armies, guns and the like about on maps. As such it provided useful strategical and tactical training for military students. In *c*.1900 the word was applied by H.M. Temple to a form of chess in which two players at separate boards play without seeing each other or even being told each other's moves. They may, how-ever, put a restricted number of questions to an umpire, who sits at a third board. The variant on the traditional form of the game is, however, hardly a 'war game'.

Kristallnacht. *See* HOLOCAUST.

Kronstadt Mutiny. A revolt in 1921 by the Soviet garrison of the naval base at Kronstadt in northwest Russia. Kronstadt is situated on Kotlin Island in the Gulf of Finland. The mutineers demanded greater democratic freedom, a free market for peasants to sell their produce and an end to the requisitioning of grain. Although the mutiny was put down, this and other disturbances encouraged LENIN to change direc-tion and adopt the NEW ECONOMIC POLICY.

Krypton Factor, The. A popular television programme in the form of a combined quiz and physical en-durance test, screened from 1976 to 1995. Competitors were tested for brawn on a military assault course and for brain in a series of IQ, observational and general knowledge questions. The prize was a trophy. The title had nothing to do with the gas so called but was taken from the name of the home planet of the comic-book hero SUPERMAN.

Ku Klux Klan. A secret US society of white suprem-acists, noted for acts of violence against blacks. It is often referred to as the KKK or the Klan. The name possibly derives from the Greek *kuklos* ('circle') with

Klan ('clan') spelt thus for the sake of orthographic alliteration, although another theory is that the name echoes the sound of a rifle bolt being drawn back ready for firing. The Klan was originally formed in Tennessee in 1866 to resist the introduction of civil rights for blacks in the South in the wake of the American Civil War. A combination of anti-Klan federal legislation and the fact that it had managed to achieve most of its objectives led to its virtual disappearance by the late 1870s. However, the Klan was revived in 1915 by Colonel William J. Simmons (1880–1945), and added anti-socialism, anti-Semitism, anti-Catholicism and general xenophobia to its portfolio of hatreds. It received a further boost from the white backlash against the black civil rights movement and federal civil rights legislation introduced in the 1950s and 1960s, but it has subsequently declined and fragmented. Some members are thought to be associated with neo-NAZI groups. When in action, Klan members light fiery crosses and dress up in long white robes and long pointed caps that also cover their faces. The top Klansman is traditionally known as the grand wizard, and other officers in the hierarchy go by such titles as grand dragon, grand titan and grand cyclops. *See also* BIRTH OF A NATION.

Kulaks. Those wealthier peasant farmers in Russia who owned their own land and who were important figures in the social structure of village life. The word *kulak* derives from the Russian for 'fist', and means 'a tight-fisted person'. After the Bolshevik Revolution of 1917 the kulaks' position was eroded, but the introduction of the NEW ECONOMIC POLICY in 1921 favoured them. They opposed the drive to collectivize agriculture from 1929, and as a result were 'liquidated' as a class on STALIN's orders (the process was called 'dekulakization'). By 1934 most kulaks had been arrested, exiled to remote parts of the Soviet Union or executed, and their property taken over by the state.

Kultur (German, 'culture'). A word taken up in English in a derogatory sense for the German view of civilization in the First and Second World Wars, the latter necessarily from a darker NAZI angle. It involved notions of racial and cultural superiority, militarism and imperialism and became popularly associated with the remark attributed to Hermann Goering: 'Whenever I heard the word culture, I reach for my pistol.' The words correctly belong to the dramatist Hanns Johst: *Wenn ich Kultur höre entsichere ich meine Browning* ('When I hear the word "culture" I release the safety-catch of my Browning') (*Schlageter*, 1933).

Kumbayah. The title and key word of a Gullah spiritual, originating some time in the 1920s or even earlier and first published in the 1930s. It was then redisovered in Angola, where it may have been taken by missionaries, and was revived in the folk-singing boom of the 1950s and 1960s. It has since been recorded by various singers, such as the American folk trio Peter, Paul and Mary, who included it in their album *Around the Camp Fire* (1998). The word itself is Creole for 'come by here'. It ends every line of the song, one version of which runs as follows:

> Someone's crying, Lord, kumbayah,
> Someone's singing, Lord, kumbayah,
> Someone's praying, Lord, kumbayah,
> Sinners need you, Lord, kumbayah,
> Someone's sleeping, Lord, kumbayah,
> Come by here, my Lord, kumbayah.

Kuomintang (Chinese, 'National People's Party'). A Chinese political party formed by Sun Yat-sen (1867–1925) in 1912, which, after his death, passed to the control of General Chiang Kai-shek (1887–1975). From 1927 to 1949 the Kuomintang was in power in China when it was driven out by the Communist Party under Mao Zedong (1893–1976). The Nationalists still maintain themselves in Taiwan (formerly Formosa). *See also* CASH-MY-CHEQUE, GENERAL.

Kwok's disease. *See* CHINESE RESTAURANT SYNDROME.

L

Labanotation. A system of recording human movement, invented by the Hungarian dance theorist Rudolf Laban (1879–1958) and first published in 1928. The basic symbol is the rectangle, which is modified in shape to show direction of movement, in length to show duration of movement, and in shade to show level. It is written on a vertical, three-line stave, with the centre line representing the division of the body into left and right and the two columns used as symbols to indicate means of support and left and right leg gestures. Additional columns of symbols show positions for the body, arms, hands and head. The stave is read from top to bottom and written from the performer's point of view. The most frequent application of Labanotation is for recording dance choreographies.

Labour Party. One of the major political parties of Britain, established with the aim of promoting socialism. It has been so called since 1906 but was originally formed as the Labour Representation Committee in 1900 from such elements as the Independent Labour Party, the trade unions, and the Fabian Society. The first Labour government was that of Ramsay MacDonald in 1924; the second lasted from 1929 to 1931, when the party split over the cuts in unemployment benefit. It was not returned to power again until 1945 and was replaced by the Conservatives in 1951. It was again in office from 1964 to 1970, 1974 to 1979, and from 1997 when, as NEW LABOUR, it was reborn in the image of its leader, Tony Blair, ridding itself of its commitment to state socialism and generally making itself more appealing to that part of the electorate that had previously voted for the Conservative Party.

Ladette. The female equivalent of the NEW LAD of the late 1990s, as an embodiment of the type of up-front feminism displayed by RIOT GRRLS. The term became particularly attached to the television presenter Zoë Ball (b.1970).

> 'I [television presenter Denise Van Outen (b.1974)] don't drink pints and I'm not a ladette. People say I'm a ladette just because I'm an outspoken girl. But I don't down pints and go to pubs and snooker halls'.
> *The Times Magazine* (11 September 1999)

Ladies who lunch. A term for the wealthy set of dowagers, countesses, heiresses and TROPHY WIVES who inhabit Manhattan's fashionable Upper East Side, one of whose staple pleasures is to meet up for lunch and gossip at expensive restaurants. The term is also used for such women generally, and less critically for those who raise money for charity by organizing lunches.

> A toast to that invincible bunch
> The dinosaurs surviving the crunch
> Let's hear it for the ladies who lunch.
> STEPHEN SONDHEIM: *Company*, 'The Ladies who Lunch' (song) (1970)

Lady Bird. A name given to Claudia Johnson (b.1912), wife of President Lyndon Johnson, by her childhood nurse. The name stuck, and when she married Johnson both had the initials LBJ. The 1965 Highway Beautification Act restricting billboard advertising was prompted by her, and became known as the Lady Bird Act. She also pioneered the planting of native wild flowers along the highways of her native Texas. The name Lady Bird does not have the connotations that it would have in Britain, as in North America a ladybird is called a 'ladybug'.

Ladybird Books. A series of small-format children's books published from 1964 from Loughborough. Starting as a series of graded readers featuring the lives of two JANET AND JOHN-like, middle-class children, Peter and Jane, the Ladybird series expanded to embrace a wide range of subject matter, including fairy tales, history and natural history books.

Ladyboy. A euphemism for a young male transvestite, especially an oriental one.

> Once inside, there were gyrating Thai ladyboys.
>
> *heat* (17–23 February 2000)

Lady Chatterley's Lover. A novel (1960; privately printed 1928) by D.H. Lawrence (1885–1930). Written in Italy after Lawrence had been diagnosed as having terminal cancer, it is an intense study of human relationships and sexuality. Lady CHATTERLEY's husband, after they have had only one month together, is wounded in the First World War and paralyzed from the waist down. After one unsatisfactory affair with an outsider, she responds to the advances of Mellors, the gamekeeper, who has an intriguing background. There is much steamy sex, but a moral ending. On 2 November 1960, after a six-day trial, a jury of nine men and three women found PENGUIN BOOKS not guilty of publishing 'an obscene article' (*see* LADY CHATTERLEY TRIAL). *See also* FIRST LINES OF NOVELS.

Lady Chatterley trial. The trial in 1960 of PENGUIN BOOKS on a charge of obscenity for publishing LADY CHATTERLEY'S LOVER, written by D.H. Lawrence in 1928. The book, which contains detailed descriptions of sex acts and makes liberal use of FOUR-LETTER WORDS, had been published privately in 1928. In 1960 Penguin deliberately published the book in an uncut version to test the English law of obscenity, and called a number of distinguished expert witnesses, including Richard Hoggart, to testify on its behalf as to the literary merits of the work. The defence team, Gerald Gardiner, Jeremy Hutchinson and Edward du Cann, might have believed that the case was lost on the first day when Mervyn Griffith-Jones, counsel for the prosecution, uttered the words, much derided since: 'Is it a book that you would have lying around in your own house? Is it a book that you would even wish your wife or your servants to read?'

The jury found that the work was neither obscene nor corrupting. A similar verdict had been returned by a US court the previous year. Penguin went on to sell more than 3.5 million copies, and the verdict opened the way to a much greater freedom in the treatment of sex in literature. *See also* CHATTERLEY, LADY.

Lady Di. A popular name for Diana, Princess of Wales, who before her marriage to Prince Charles in 1981 was Lady Diana Spencer. *See also* PEOPLE'S PRINCESS.

Lady Forkbender. A nickname given by *Private Eye* to Marcia Falkender, née Williams (b.1932), who was Harold Wilson's private and political secretary from 1956 to 1983. She became Baroness Falkender in 1974, and was said to have influenced Wilson's notorious 1976 resignation honours list, nicknamed the LAVENDER LIST because it was typed on Lady Falkender's lavender-coloured note paper. The nickname, which first appeared in 'Mrs Wilson's Diary' in *Private Eye* in 1975, was presumably inspired by the widespread publicity given to the supposedly magical ability of Israeli showman Uri Geller to bend forks and spoons by gently manipulating them. *See also* GANNEX.

Ladykillers, The. A sublime and enduring EALING COMEDY (1955) about a criminal gang, which hides up after a big robbery in the quiet house of a little old lady, pretending for her benefit to be amateur classical musicians. The irony in the title lies in the fact that none of the criminals (Alec Guinness, Peter Sellers, Cecil Parker, Herbert Lom and Danny Green) turns out to be prepared to murder the old lady (Katie Johnson) after she discovers what they have really been up to, and they are instead obliged to kill each other.

Lady Macbeth of the Mtsensk District. A formerly controversial opera by Dmitri Shostakovich (1906–75), with a libretto by the composer and A. Preys, after an 1865 story by Nikolai Leskov (1831–95) about a woman who, somewhat in the manner of the wife of Shakespeare's Macbeth, lives and dies by violence. It was first performed in 1934 and proved popular until the Soviet authorities started to show their disapproval of MODERNISM in 1936. In that year *Pravda* sinisterly commented: 'It is a leftist bedlam instead of human music. The inspiring quality of good music is sacrificed in favour of petty-bourgeois clowning. This game may end badly.' The work was not revived in the Soviet Union until 1963, when it was staged under the title *Katerina Izmailova*. It was, however, performed in the United States in 1935. One American critic described the music as 'pornophony'.

Lady Muck. A nickname for a pompous or self-opinionated woman. *See also* LORD MUCK.

Lady of the night. A euphemism for a prostitute.

> I doubt that the *Daily Star* … would dare print a story today about a senior Labourite and a lady of the night.
>
> *The Times* (29 November 1999)

Lady's Not For Burning, The. An historical play (1948) by Christopher Fry (b.1907) about a beautiful alchemist who finds herself accused of witchcraft and is threatened with death by burning. The play is perhaps now best remembered for having furnished Margaret Thatcher, then prime minister, with her most famous quote (*see* LADY'S NOT FOR TURNING).

Lady's not for turning. A declaration by Margaret Thatcher, the IRON LADY, to the 1980 Conservative Party Conference, asserting her determination not to perform a U-turn in her economic policies, which were inflicting so much discomfort. The phrase, coined by speechwriter Sir Ronald Millar, plays on the title of a poetic drama, *The* LADY'S NOT FOR BURNING (1948), by Christopher Fry (b.1907). It is said that Mrs Thatcher was unaware of its source. *See also* TINA.

> To those waiting with bated breath for that favourite media catchphrase, the U-turn, I have only one thing to say. You turn if you want to The lady is not for turning.

Lady Vanishes, The. A film thriller (1938) adapted by Sidney Gilliat from a novel *The Wheel Spins* by Ethel Lina White about the mystery surrounding the apparent disappearance of an elderly lady on board a trans-European train. Directed by Alfred Hitchcock, the film concentrates on the efforts of the hero and heroine to unravel the truth behind the woman's disappearance. The title of the film refers to a traditional magician's trick in which a woman is apparently made to disappear before the audience's very eyes. Anthony Page directed a dire remake (1979).

Lady with the Blowlamp. A description of Margaret Thatcher, the IRON LADY, by Denis Healey, the GROMYKO OF THE LABOUR PARTY, giving a sinister twist to the by-name of Florence Nightingale (1820–1910), 'the Lady with the Lamp', who nursed wounded British soldiers during the Crimean War (1853–6). The ever-imaginative Healey also called Thatcher Miss Floggie, Rhoda the Rhino and a Pétain in petticoats (*see* PÉTAINISTS).

Laff. A source or occasion of amusement. The word is a jocular or journalistic respelling of 'laugh', as in 'a bit of a laff', and pronounced to rhyme with 'caff' rather than 'calf'. Another respelling of the same word, but with a pronunciation closer to the norm, is 'larf', as in the title of Len Deighton's novel about three confidence tricksters, *Only When I Larf* (1968).

> 'She's got a wicked sense of humour and laffs outrageously'. (You have to write 'laff' instead of 'laugh' – that is what [comedian Jimmy] Tarbuck says and it

means something different from 'laugh': it is its own word.)
> *Sunday Times* (22 August 1999)

Lager lout. A term in use from the late 1980s and applied to a young hooligan who creates disturbances, damages property and the like after drinking too much lager or beer. The phrase may owe something to the earlier 'litter lout'. *See also* ESSEX MAN.

Laid-back. Relaxed; unconcerned; peacefully passive. The expression arose in the SWINGING SIXTIES and came to be particularly associated with HIPPIES.

Lake Wobegon. An imaginary small town in Minnesota that first appeared in *Lake Wobegon Days* (1985), a bestselling collection of gently humorous but acutely observed short stories about the lives of the town's inhabitants by Garrison Keillor (b.1942). His later *Wobegon Boy* (1997) tells the story of John Tollefson, an unmarried man in his forties, first encountered in *Lake Wobegon Days*, who leaves his family behind in Minnesota for a job as a public radio station manager in upstate New York. A radio broadcaster also famed for his public readings of his fictional works, Keillor has hosted the hugely popular nationally syndicated radio show *A Prairie Home Companion* since 1974.

La-La land. A nickname for Los Angeles (known as L.A.) or HOLLYWOOD, evoking the alleged eccentricities of the people who live and work there. The name puns on 'la-la-land' as a term for a person's fantasy world or dreamworld, especially one brought on by drink or drugs.

Lambada. A fast erotic dance of Brazilian origin which couples perform with their stomachs touching. It was a logical development of DIRTY DANCING in the late 1980s and takes its name from the Brazilian Portuguese word meaning 'beating', 'lashing'.

Lambeth Walk. A thoroughfare in Lambeth leading from Black Prince Road to the Lambeth Road. It gave its name to the popular Cockney dance featured by Lupino Lane (from 1937) in the musical show *Me and My Gal* at the Victoria Palace. The dance has couples strutting forward, arms linked, then strutting back and jerking their thumbs in the air to the exclamation 'Oi!' Many council housing estates now have a Lambeth Walk as a memento.

> Any time you're Lambeth way,
> Any evening, any day,

You'll find us all
Doin' the Lambeth walk.

DOUGLAS FURBER and ARTHUR ROSE: 'Doin' the Lambeth Walk' (1937)

Lambretta. A type of motor scooter made by the Italian firm Innocenti from the 1950s, which, along with the VESPA, became the standard transport of Britain's Mods. The name 'Lambretta' derives from the Lambrate district of Milan, where the motor scooter was manufactured. *See also* MODS AND ROCKERS.

Lamington. A confection more familiar in Australia and New Zealand then elsewhere in the English-speaking world, in the form of a small cake covered with chocolate icing and rolled in coconut. Its name, first recorded in the early 20th century, is believed to come from Lord Lamington, governor of Queensland from 1896 to 1901, or else from his wife, in whose kitchen it may have been created. Fund-raising Lamington drives still thrive in Australia and testify to the popularity of the cake.

Lanark. The first novel (1981) by Alasdair Gray (b.1934) was begun when he was 18 years old. It is subtitled *A Life in Four Books*, Book Three preceding the Prologue and Book One. Set in the disintegrating city of Unthank, which represents Glasgow, it interweaves both fantastically and naturalistically episodes from the lives of Duncan Thaw and of Lanark, Thaw's alter ego, the early experiences of both of whom echo those of Gray himself.

Lance the boil, To. To make a bold stroke with the aim of solving a problem or ending an undesirable situation such as an occurrence of corruption. The allusion is to the cutting open of a boil to release the purulent matter inside.

The Treasury rules should be changed to close this loophole and lance the nasty little boil of councillors awarding themselves poll tax payers' cash without having to account.

Sunday Times (20 August 1989)

Land camera. The proprietary name of a camera that can produce a near instant picture. It takes its name from the US scientist Edwin H. Land (1909–91), the inventor in 1936 of Polaroid, as a material which in the form of thin sheets produces a high degree of plane polarization in light passing through it. The camera evolved as the result of a holiday trip in 1943 to New Mexico, when Land's three-year-old daughter asked why she could not immediately see a photograph he had taken of her. The first public demonstration of a sepia-and-white Polaroid camera was in 1947. Black-and-white cameras followed in 1950 and a popular low-price colour camera, the Swinger, was launched in 1965.

Land girls. Young women recruited for agricultural work during the two world wars. The first land girls were the members of the Women's Land Army, first established in 1917. In June 1939 the organization was re-formed, and more than 10,000 young women volunteered to do what had previously been regarded as exclusively male jobs. Their duties included driving tractors, milking cows, planting, harvesting, cleaning pigsties and cowsheds and reclaiming land. It was not unusual to work a 14-hour day. At the end of the war they were demobbed on a 'first-come-first-leave' basis. They were obliged to return their uniforms but were allowed to keep their shoes and greatcoat so long as they dyed the latter from brown to navy blue. Each woman was allocated six clothing coupons, enough to buy a hat, a tie and some knickers. The WLA was disbanded in 1951. A sentimental film *The Land Girls*, based on a novel (1995) of the same name by Angela Huth, was released in 1998.

Land of a thousand contrasts. A travel agent's overblown lure to attract the potential tourist to a foreign country, especially one regarded as 'exotic'. An advertisement in Austin Reed's spring and summer catalogue for 1995 described Morocco as 'this beautiful land of a thousand contrasts'. More factually, Finland is sometimes promoted as the 'land of a thousand lakes'.

Land of Hope and Glory. Great Britain was so portrayed in the heyday of imperialism in Sir Edward Elgar's famous melody with words by A.C. Benson. It was sung by Dame Clara Butt in 1902 and widely used at EMPIRE DAY celebrations and other occasions. It is now a traditional item at the LAST NIGHT OF THE PROMS. The tune was taken from Elgar's POMP AND CIRCUMSTANCE march, No. 1 (1901). The words were originally written to be sung as the finale to Elgar's *Coronation Ode* of 1902.

Land of Hope and Glory, Mother of the Free,
How shall we extol thee who are born of thee?
Wider still and wider shall thy bounds be set;
God who made thee mighty, make thee mightier yet.

Land of the Long White Cloud. A nickname for New Zealand, as a translation of the country's Maori name, Aotearoa, from *ao*, 'cloud', *tea*, 'white', and *roa*, 'long'. The native name itself now has a certain official status, appearing in the New Zealand passport and on some postage stamps. The reference is to the cloud that hangs over many of the mountains of North Island. The country's highest peak, Mt Cook, has the Maori name of Aorangi, 'cloud piercer'.

Landslide Lyndon. *See* LBJ.

La Niña. The weather system that is the counterpart of EL NIÑO. Whereas El Niño is characterized by unusually warm ocean temperatures in the Equatorial Pacific, La Niña causes cold temperatures. Its name, Spanish for 'the little girl', indicates its contradistinction from El Niño, 'the little boy'. There is some confusion about the nomenclature, especially as La Niña is also known as El Viejo, 'the old one', the contrast in this case being between an old man (who is cold) and a young boy (who is warm).

> La Niña has brought months of abnormally low rainfall that have left the Everglades dangerously dry.
> *The Times* (20 April 1999)

Lap dancer. A woman who performs an erotic dance or striptease close to, or actually sitting on, the lap of a paying customer in a club or bar. The dance itself is of US origin.

> Last week a judge ruled that 'lap dancers' working in a London club must wear a G-string while dancing at tables, rather than performing nude.
> *Sunday Times* (8 November 1998)

Lap of honour. A celebratory circuit of a racetrack or sports field by a winner or winning team to receive applause. The expression and practice date from the 1950s and originated among cyclists.

Lara Croft. *See* CROFT, LARA.

Lark Ascending, The. A popular and lyrical 'romance' for violin and orchestra by Ralph Vaughan Williams (1872–1958), composed in 1914 and revised in 1920. It was inspired by a poem of the same name by George Meredith (1828–1909). In 1931 Aaron Copland wrote of Vaughan Williams: 'His is the music of a gentleman-farmer, noble in inspiration, but dull.' Those who generally agree with Copland's verdict might make an exception for *The Lark Ascending*.

Larkin family. Pop and Ma Larkin are a happy-go-lucky farming couple who appear in a series of comically rustic novels by H.E. Bates, beginning with *The* DARLING BUDS OF MAY (1958). They live on a ramshackle farm deep in the Kent countryside and have a brood of six children with horticultural sounding names such as Zinnia, Petunia and Primrose.

Surprisingly, the stories were not brought to the television screen until 1991, when they appeared to popular acclaim under the title of the first novel, with David Jason playing Pop Larkin, Pam Ferris as Ma and Catherine Zeta-Jones as their eldest daughter, Mariette.

Larks and owls. Someone who works best early in the day is frequently known as a 'lark' or 'morning person', while one who does not begin functioning fully until the afternoon or early evening is an 'owl' or 'evening person'. Psychologists claim that there is a real difference between the two types, but medical evidence is largely lacking for the supposed distinction. *See also* DAY PERSON.

Larry Parnes's Stable of Stars. Larry Parnes (1930–89), regarded by many as the pre-eminent manager and impresario of British ROCK 'N' ROLL, was responsible for promoting and in many cases rechristening a string of pop and rock successes, beginning with Tommy Steele (b.1936), whose real name was Thomas Hicks. Steele devised his own stage name, but among those renamed by Parnes were Marty Wilde (b.1936), born Reginald Smith, Billy Fury (1941–83), born Ronald Wycherley, Johnny Gentle (b.1941), formerly John Askew, Dickie Pride (c.1940–c.1970), earlier Richard Knellar, Vince Eager (b.c.1940), originally Roy Taylor, and Georgie Fame (b.1943), born Clive Powell. The Cockney guitarist Joe Brown (b.1941), however, refused to become Almer Twitch. Parnes's business approach and financial acuity earned him his own nickname of 'Parnes, Shillings and Pence'. His supremacy as kingmaker was ended by the BEATLES, whose potential he had seriously underestimated some time before.

Larry the Lamb. The wooden toy lamb that first appeared in 1925 in a series of story books for young children by S.G. Hulme Beaman. From 1929, together with his friends, Dennis the Dachshund and Ernest the Policeman, Larry appeared regularly on BBC radio's CHILDREN'S HOUR, his voice bleatingly rendered by 'Uncle Mac' (Derek McCulloch). *See also* TOYTOWN.

Lascaux caves. On a day in September 1940 four French schoolboys were hunting rabbits near the village of Montignac in the Dordogne when their dog disappeared down a hole. Climbing down to retrieve him, they found themselves in a grotto filled with delicate paintings of animals. An examination by archaeologists revealed a magnificently decorated main cavern, dubbed *la grande salle des taureaux* (Great Hall of Bulls), connected by passageways to side galleries. They dated the paintings to about 18,000 BC and declared the cave one of the richest treasure troves of Palaeolithic art ever discovered. The find rapidly became a tourist attraction, but by 1963 the colours were fading and fungus beginning to spot the frescoes, necessitating its closure to the public. A replica cave has since been built nearby for tourists to visit.

Laser. The device generating an intense beam of light of a very pure single colour was first constructed in the United States in 1960 by Theodore H. Maiman, using a rod of ruby. The name is an acronym of 'light amplification by stimulated emission of radiation'. A forerunner, operating on the same basic principle, was the maser, the first letter standing for 'microwave'. The application of lasers is wide, and ranges from supermarket BARCODE scanners to compact disc players. They are also used in surgery, fibre optics, laser printers and weapons guidance systems.

Lassa fever. This acute and often fatal viral disease, occurring chiefly in West Africa, takes its name from the village of Lassa, near Mubi in northeast Nigeria, where it was first reported in 1969. It is usually acquired from infected rats.

Lasseter's Lost Reef. In 1929 the Australian writer and explorer Lewis Hubert 'Harold Bell' Lasseter (1880–1931) claimed that in about 1911 he had discovered 'a vast gold-bearing reef in Central Australia'. The government of the day were not interested in his story, but when he repeated it in 1930 he interested one John Bailey, of the Australian Workers' Union, and a small expeditionary party, led by Fred Blakeley and guided by Lasseter, set off to find it. In September 1930 the expedition abandoned the search but Lasseter went on alone, only to meet his death in the Petermann Ranges in the centre of the continent. The key to one of Australia's greatest enigmas continued to be sought, and versions of Lasseter's story were retold in such popular books as Ion Idriess's *Lasseter's Last Ride* (1931) and Fred Blakeley's *Dream Millions* (1972). The true facts about Lasseter and his reef seem to have been finally settled by the research of Gerald Walsh for the *Australian Dictionary of Biography* (1983) but the mystery of the reef has never been solved.

Lassie. One of the most popular dogs in the cinema. The first film starring her (played by a male dog called Pal) was in 1943, and was itself based on Eric Knight's children's novel *Lassie Come Home* (1940). Lassie is an intelligent collie who is sold by her owners when they cannot afford to keep her, much to the distress of their young son. She promptly runs away from her new home in Scotland until, after travelling hundreds of miles, she 'comes home', and is reunited with the family she loves. *See also* RIN TIN TIN.

Last chance saloon. A legendary bar where one has a last chance to drink before meeting one's fate. Many US casinos bear the name, such as the one in Deadwood, South Dakota, the town that gave the name of the dime novel hero 'Deadwood Dick'. In the famous Western DESTRY RIDES AGAIN (1939) Marlene Dietrich stands on a bar in the Last Chance Saloon to sing 'See What the Boys in the Back Room Will Have' (*see* BACKROOM BOYS). The phrase now alludes to any final opportunity or seemingly irrevocable annihilation.

> This is … a critical week for the Conservatives. It is almost closing time in their last chance saloon.
> *The Times* (2 October 1999)

Last Exit to Brooklyn. A bleak novel (1964) by Hubert Selby Jr (b.1928). The British publisher was found guilty of issuing an obscene publication in 1967, but a successful appeal against the judgement, led by John Mortimer QC, was made the following year. The book consists of a series of loosely connected episodes, in which some characters recur, reflecting the life and activities in New York's Brooklyn of crooks, queers, fairies, tarts, thugs and bystanders. There are some moments of tenderness among descriptions of violence and heterosexual and homosexual sex. The title is a road sign on the motorway giving drivers a final chance to turn off for Brooklyn. An equally gloomy film version (1989) was directed by Uli Edel.

Last hurrah. The final act in a politician's career or, more generally, any final performance or flourish. The phrase comes from the title of Edwin O'Connor's bestselling novel of 1956 about the political boss of an eastern city in the United States. It was filmed in 1958.

> In 1911 Elgar and England could still reach out and touch the hope and the glory. That is why the Second Symphony is so potent and poignant a document. It is the last hurrah of a civilization which had smelt death in the air.
> *The Times* (17 September 1999)

Last in, first out. A method of accounting in which all goods of the same kind are valued at the price paid for those most recently acquired. In business the phrase can also apply to a redundancy scheme whereby those who have most recently joined as employees are the first to leave, the theory being that their youth or inexperience makes them more readily 'expendable'.

Last Night of the Proms. The final evening of the annual Promenade Concerts at the Royal Albert Hall, London, in September, popularly regarded as the apotheosis of the series. The audience is mainly made up of young promenaders who enthusiastically join in the traditional choruses of LAND OF HOPE AND GLORY and 'Rule, Britannia' while waving Union Jacks, bursting balloons, throwing streamers, and displaying other signs of patriotic fervour and good humour. The FIRST NIGHT OF THE PROMS may also be something of an occasion, if only as a prelude to this rousing finale.

> Little, it seems, is ever going to change at the Last Night of the Proms. So there is no point in worrying about the hopefully good-natured jingoism of those who believe that, once a year at least, Britannia still Rules the Waves.
>
> *The Times* (14 September 1998)

Last of the Summer Wine. The longest running SITCOM on British television, first screened in 1973 and still running a quarter of a century on. It is set in the Yorkshire Pennines and centres on three old school friends who, now elderly and unemployed, set about enjoying a second childhood in a series of mischievous escapades. The trio consists of the ex-army man Foggy Dewhurst, played by Brian Wilde, the unobtrusive and wary Norman Clegg, played by Peter Sallis, and the small and fearless Compo, played by Bill Owen, who usually comes down to earth with a bump or ends up to his neck in water. A fourth character is the daunting, wrinkled-stocking housewife Nora Batty, played by Kathy Staff. The title is almost too lyrical for its purpose.

Last taboo. A subject or condition regarded as so sordid, shameful or otherwise offensive that it is still not openly discussed or written about. The term is traditionally applied to drug abuse, although it may also be used of a deviant sexual practice such as incest, bestiality or paedophilia.

Last Tango in Paris. A film (1972) co-written and directed by Italian director Bernardo Bertolucci (b.1940) about the sexual relationship that develops between Paul, a recently widowed American (played by Marlon Brando), and Jeanne, a young French woman (played by Maria Schneider), who is engaged to a NOUVELLE VAGUE film-maker, after they meet while flat-hunting in Paris. The affair ends with Paul's suicide. The title of the film, evoking the potent sexuality of the tango, underlines the passion of the couple's affair. The appearance of a pat of butter as an aid to sodomy was for many their abiding memory of a film described in *Halliwell's Film Guide* as a 'pretentious sex melodrama mainly notable for being banned'.

Last Year at Marienbad. A film (1961) written by Alain Robbe-Grillet (b.1922) and directed by Alain Resnais (b.1922) in which a man apparently tries to persuade a woman that they know each other and may have had an affair. The truth of their relationship is left obscure: the suggestion is that they met 'last year in Marienbad' and planned to run away together. One critic described the film as 'elaborate, ponderous and meaningless'. *See also* NOUVELLE VAGUE.

Latchkey child. A child left at home without adult supervision for some of the day. The term dates from the 1960s and originated in the United States in the 1940s with reference to children who let themselves into their home after school because the parents were still out at work. The US source explains the use of 'latchkey' instead of the more usual British front door key. *See also* HOME ALONE.

Lateral thinking. The solving of problems by an indirect or creative approach, typically by viewing the problem in a new light or approaching it from a different angle. The term was coined by Professor Edward de Bono in his account of the method, *The Use of Lateral Thinking* (1967). His term for the conventional, direct method of reasoning was 'vertical thinking'.

Lateran Treaty. A treaty concluded between the Holy See and the kingdom of Italy on 11 February 1929, settling the 'Roman Question', which had resulted from the fall of the city of Rome as the last territory of the Papal States. The Holy See was financially compensated for the loss of property, the Vatican City State was established as a political entity independent of Italy, and a concordat was agreed upon that guaranteed and regulated the role of the Roman Catholic Church in the life of Italy, making it the official religion of the country. The concordat was renegotiated and formally ratified on 3 June 1985. Catholic instruction is no longer mandatory in state schools, and the clergy are no longer paid salaries by the state.

Laugh all the way to the bank, To. To be so fortunate or wealthy that one can afford to ignore criticism. The image is of someone happily hastening to deposit a large sum of money in the bank. The US pianist and entertainer Liberace (1919–87) joked in the 1950s that bad reviews made him 'cry all the way to the bank'.

> Frank McCourt is entitled to his memoir. Not only is he laughing all the way to the bank but he has joined the long and distinguished list of Irish literati whose books were banned or vilified in [Richard] Harris's old-fashioned Ireland.
>
> *Sunday Times* (Letter to the Editor) (30 January 2000)

Laughing, To be. To be in a fortunate or successful position, especially by comparison with others. A typical use of the expression might be, 'Once I get that contract I'll be laughing'. No actual laughter is normally involved although a smile of satisfaction may be evidenced. The phrase dates from the 1930s.

Laughing Murderer of Verdun. A nickname given to Crown Prince Wilhelm of Germany (1882–1951), who held various commands on the WESTERN FRONT throughout the First World War, and was associated with the most militaristic sectors of German society. The nickname was earned from his command of the hugely costly German offensive at VERDUN from February 1916. British troops also referred to him as LITTLE WILLIE, in contrast to his father, Kaiser Wilhelm II, KAISER BILL, whom he joined in exile after the armistice in 1918.

Laugh like a drain, To. To laugh heartily; to chuckle inordinately. The sound of a guffaw can suggest that of water gurgling down a drain.

Laughter lines. A name dating from the 1930s for the small lines or wrinkles at the corners of the eyes that are supposed to have been produced by years of intermittent laughter. An older and less flattering term for the feature, going back to the time of Chaucer, is crow's feet.

> Once, discussing the deep wrinkles on his face with fellow horn-player Jack Sheldon, [Chet] Baker jokingly described them as laughter lines.
>
> *Sunday Times* (27 February 2000)

Lavender and old lace. Old-fashioned gentility. The phrase comes from the title of a novel by Myrtle Reed published in 1902. A dramatized version by Rose Warner appeared in 1938. This was given a new twist as a black comedy by Joseph Kesselring under the title ARSENIC AND OLD LACE (1941), and an enjoyable film version was screened in 1942.

Lavender Hill Mob, The. A sparkling EALING COMEDY (1951), written by T.E.B. Clarke and directed by Charles Crichton, about a mild-mannered civil servant who decides to use his inside knowledge of bullion transport to steal a million pounds' worth of gold and then spirit it out of the country after melting it down into miniature Eiffel Towers. The ludicrous notion that such a retiring, dull individual could pull off this breathtaking crime is underlined by the film's title, which cheekily conveys the unlikelihood of hardened criminals hailing from such a respectable part of London as Lavender Hill. The film stars Alec Guinness as the criminal mastermind, and Stanley Holloway as his right-hand man.

Lavender list. The dissolution honours awarded by Harold Wilson (1916–95) after his resignation as Labour prime minister in 1976. The name is said to stem from the fact that the list was written on lavender-coloured paper by Marcia Williams (later Lady Falkender; b.1932), Wilson's private and political secretary, with only a few corrections added by Wilson himself. The implication was thus that the choice had been hers. *See also* LADY FORKBENDER.

Laverstock Panda. Many of the figures cut out of the chalk hillside in central and southern England are ancient. The white horses of Wiltshire, however, were joined by a newcomer to the county in the early hours of Sunday 26 January 1970 when a group of students from the University College of North Wales, Bangor, delineated the figure of a panda in a hillside to the left of the A30 road to Exeter, 1.6km (1 mile) north of Salisbury, just before the turn to Laverstock. The operation was executed by removing the topsoil and filling the resultant shallow excavation with chalk dug from nearby pits. When discovered, it was at first supposed that the cutting celebrated the meeting of the two pandas Chi-Chi and An-An in the London Zoo. In fact it was a rag week stunt, the panda being Bangor's rag symbol, while the particular location was chosen because one of the instigators lived nearby and knew the site would be suitable. The outlines of the artwork are still faintly visible.

Law of Martinis. A rule of thumb among scuba divers, based on the fact that the deeper one goes beneath the surface of the water, the greater the sense of euphoria, similar to drunkenness. In roughly equivalent terms, a descent of one atmosphere (a unit of pressure equal to mean atmospheric pressure at sea level), reached at approximately 10m (33ft), has an effect similar to that of imbibing a single Martini cocktail. Two atmospheres thus equals two Martinis and so on. The deeper one goes, however, the greater the danger of vertigo (through disorientation) and 'the bends', which in some cases can lead to death, as can an equivalent excessive intake of Martinis.

Law of the jungle. Ruthless competition, especially when motivated by self-interest. The phrase became current from the 1920s and derives from Rudyard Kipling's JUNGLE BOOK (1894):

> The Law of the Jungle, which never orders anything without a reason, forbids every beast to eat Man except when he is killing to show his children how to kill.
>
> 'Mowgli's Brothers'

Lawrence of Arabia. The name by which the British soldier, archaeologist, Arabist, classical scholar and writer T(homas) E(dward) Lawrence (1888–1935) is popularly known. During the First World War Lawrence went to Arabia (October 1916) to assess the chances of success of the revolt of the Arabs against their Turkish Ottoman rulers. Judging the outcome to be promising, he became a key military commander in the revolt and conducted an innovative and successful guerrilla campaign against the Turks. His success in commanding the respect of the Arabs was partially due to a deliberate cultivation of his own image as a legendary hero. The Arabs themselves had their own name for their extraordinary leader, calling him 'El Aurens' and coming to treat him very much as one of their own. After the war Lawrence found his celebrity back home difficult to deal with, and public fascination was increased by the obvious psychological complexity of his character. He was also disillusioned by the failure of the Western powers to grant Arab independence. In 1922, to escape the limelight, he enlisted in the RAF as Aircraftsman Ross (having assumed the name John Hume Ross), but he was found out by journalists and had to leave shortly afterwards. He then enlisted in the Royal Tank Corps as Private T.E. Shaw (borrowing the surname from his friend George Bernard Shaw) but was later transferred back to the RAF. He recounted his wartime adventures in *The Seven Pillars of Wisdom* (1926), which served to increase his mythic status. Within three months of retiring from the RAF in 1935 he was killed while riding his motorcycle BOANERGES.

A play by Terence Rattigan (1911–77) entitled *Ross* (1960) deals with Lawrence's life. The epic historical film *Lawrence of Arabia* (1962), adapted by Robert Bolt (1924–95) from Lawrence's *The Seven Pillars of Wisdom* (1926), follows Lawrence's maverick career as a commander of the Arab revolt. Directed by David Lean and starring Peter O'Toole as Lawrence, the film would probably not have met with its subject's approval had he been still alive as he developed a pathological dislike of the fame his exploits brought him.

Laxton's Superb. This popular variety of late-ripening eating apple takes its name from Messrs Laxton of Bedford, sons of the horticulturist William Laxton (1830–90), who introduced it in 1921. The brothers produced thousands of cross-bred apples, other well-known varieties including 'Laxton's Pearmain', 'Laxton's Fortune' and 'Laxton's Exquisite'.

Lay an egg, To. To fail absolutely, especially in a variety performance. The implication is presumably that one has laid a bad egg. The origin is not likely to be in the 'duck's egg' or zero score in cricket, as sometimes explained.

Layer cut. A style first in fashion in the 1960s in which the hair is cut in overlapping layers.

Layered look. A fashion in clothes of the 1970s in which garments of various types and lengths are worn on top of one another. The term 'layering' to describe this mode of dressing was coined in 1950 by the US fashion designer Bonnie Cashin.

Lay it on the line, To. To speak frankly and directly. The image is of setting one's words on a line, where all can see their true value, as when placing a bet. The expression dates from the 1940s.

Layla. An anguished love song by Derek and the Dominos (the guitarist Eric Clapton accompanied by an ad hoc group of instrumentalists), released in 1972 and featuring one of the best known guitar 'riffs' in pop music. The title comes from a story by the 12th-century Persian poet Nizami, entitled *The Story of Layla and Majnun*, concerning an ill-starred love affair. It reflects Clapton's feelings for Patti Harrison, the wife of his friend, the Beatle George Harrison. Clapton eventually married Patti Harrison, but the couple divorced in 1988, although not before Clapton had written another decidedly uxorious love song for her, entitled 'Wonderful Tonight'.

Lazy daisy stitch. An embroidery stitch used in making flower patterns, and consisting of a long chain stitch. It first caught on in the 1920s.

Lazy dog. In US military jargon a fragmentation bomb that detonates in mid-air and scatters steel pellets over a wide target area.

Lazy eight. An aerobatic manoeuvre in which the aircraft executes an S-shaped path which, when viewed laterally, resembles a figure 8 lying on its side.

Lazy eye. An ambiguous term dating from the 1930s for an eye that has poor vision and so is little used, with the result that its sight deteriorates even further. It is most commonly the unused eye in a squint.

Lazy susan. A type of revolving stand or tray on a table for holding condiments and the like. The device is of US origin and dates from the early 20th century. Susan is taken as a typical maidservant's name.

LBJ. A nickname of Lyndon Baines Johnson (1908–73), Democratic president of the USA (1963–69). The use of initials as a nickname was by then well established by Democratic presidents (*see* JFK; FDR). One of Johnson's slogans during the 1964 presidential election was 'All the way with LBJ'. Subsequently, demonstrators opposed to his pursuance of the VIETNAM War chanted: 'Hey, hey, LBJ, / How many kids did you kill today?' Johnson's earlier nickname was Landslide Lyndon, earned after his narrow win in the US Senate election of 1948. *See also* LADY BIRD.

L-committee. A short form of legislative committee, as a committee formed annually from members of the British Cabinet to decide which legislation should be introduced in the following session (beginning in November). The workings and composition of this committee are secret, but it is known that it includes the leaders of both Houses and the Government whips of both Houses.

Leaderene. A media nickname for Margaret Thatcher both as leader of the opposition and as prime minister (1979–90). The term is a jocular (or ironic) feminine form of 'leader', perhaps partly based on French *speakerine*, a female radio or television announcer. It has also been suggested that the nickname refers to the Gadarene swine, into whom Christ cast the devils possessing a 'man with an unclean spirit' (Mark 5). The swine subsequently 'ran violently down a steep place into the sea … and were choked in the sea'. The word can also be applied to any female leader. *See also* ATTILA THE HEN; IRON LADY.

Lead in one's pencil. Male sexual vigour. To put lead in someone's pencil is thus to boost or bolster them. A pencil is useless without lead. The resemblance of

'pencil' to 'penis' is etymologically justified, since the words are related, both ultimately deriving from Latin *penis*, 'tail'.

Lead someone up the aisle, To. To marry them. The bride in fact goes up the nave of a church, not one of the aisles which run parallel to it. The use of the word in this sense perhaps springs from an association with 'alley'.

Lead with one's chin, To. To act incautiously. The reference is to a boxer who leaves his chin unprotected, thus rendering him dangerously vulnerable. The expression dates from the 1940s.

Leaf-peeping. The pastime of touring to see the colours of the trees change in autumn, a popular activity in New England. Those who travel for this pleasant purpose are known as leaf-peepers.

League of Nations. A league, having at one time about 60 member nations with headquarters at Geneva, with the essential aim of preventing war as well as promoting other forms of international cooperation. It was formed on 10 January 1920 as a consequence of the TREATY OF VERSAILLES but was weakened from the outset by the refusal of the United States to participate (although President Woodrow Wilson of the United States had played a major part in its foundation) and the exclusion of Russia. Its achievements were considerable in many fields, but it failed in its primary purpose. It last met on 18 April 1946, being replaced by the UNITED NATIONS Organization, which had been established on 24 October 1945. *See also* MANDATE.

Lean over backwards, To. *See* BEND OVER BACKWARDS.

Learjet. The small passenger jet aircraft, popular among the rich and famous, takes its name from its designer, the US electrical engineer William Lear (1902–78), the first of the fleet being launched from his base at Wichita, Kansas, in 1962. It has since come to be regarded as one of the most glamorous aircraft, its name entering the language as a symbol of affluence and power.

> This perk [tax-free earnings] has seen at least one desperately ill superstar rushed on a stretcher to a waiting Learjet, rather than have him outstay his permitted number of days in this country.
> *The Times* (11 May 1999)

Learner's dictionary. A monolingual dictionary for foreign learners of a language. A pioneer in the field was A.S. Hornby's *A Learner's Dictionary of Current English* (1948), followed by the same author's *Advanced Learner's Dictionary of Current English* (1963).

Learning curve. The rate of a person's progress in learning a new skill. The literal reference is to a curve on a graph indicating an animal's or human's rate of learning, as of a rat in a maze or an unskilled worker in a new job. The term dates from the 1920s and arose as psychological jargon.

> Even her allies expected her to go through a steep learning curve. Now they say that within three days she was acting as if she had been in newspapers all her life.
> *The Times* (30 July 1999)

Lease-Lend. *See* LEND-LEASE.

Leave it out! Stop it! Cut it out! A request dating from the 1960s directed at someone who talks nonsense or behaves undesirably.

Lebensraum (German, 'living space'). A term used in NAZI ideology for vast areas of eastern Europe, particularly the 'breadbasket' of the Ukraine, earmarked for German settlement. This 'living space' would allow the German population to expand and dominate the world. This use of the term originated in Adolf Hitler's MEIN KAMPF, and the area targeted was considered suitable by Hitler as its Slavic inhabitants were deemed UNTERMENSCHEN (sub-humans), ruled by BOLSHEVIKS, themselves the puppets of a world Jewish conspiracy. The achievement of *Lebensraum* lay behind German military and foreign policy through the 1930s, and the invasions of Poland (1939) and the Soviet Union (1941). The origin of the term *Lebensraum*, is however, rather different. It was the German geographer and ethnologist Friedrich Ratzel (1844–1904) who first developed the concept, which he used as a way of relating groups of humans to the geographical location where they develop; his essay *Lebensraum* (1901) is regarded as a seminal work in geopolitics. The Nazi idea was based on the reinterpretation of Ratzel's concept by the Swedish political scientist Rudolf Kjellén (1864–1922), whose *The State as a Life Form* (1916) was influential in Germany.

Leboyer birth. A manner of childbirth involving as little pain and disturbance to the baby as possible. Forceps are not used, a quiet, softly lit room is provided for the delivery, and the infant is placed in a warm bath upon birth. The technique was recommended by the French obstetrician Frédéric Leboyer (b.1915) in his book *Birth Without Violence* (1975).

Lecter, Hannibal. *See* SILENCE OF THE LAMB.

Lee, Lorelei. An archetypal GOLD-DIGGER of the FLAPPER era in Anita Loos's comic novels GENTLEMEN PREFER BLONDES (1925) and *But Gentlemen Marry Brunettes* (1928). The first of these became a stage play (1925), a silent film (1928), a stage musical (1949) and a musical movie (1953), in the last of which Marilyn MONROE starred as Lorelei. A high spot was her rendering of the song 'Diamonds Are a Girl's Best Friend'.

Lee, Terry. The young blond hero of the popular US comic strip *Terry and the Pirates*, created in 1934 by Milton Caniff. Terry goes treasure-hunting in China and falls foul of a band of pirates led by the infamous DRAGON LADY. His chief ally is the manly, pipe-smoking Pat Ryan, while another friend is the brassy blonde known as Burma. Connoisseurs of comic strips rate *Terry and the Pirates*, which ran until 1973, as one of the finest ever.

Left Book Club. A publishing venture launched in 1936 by Victor GOLLANCZ in association with John Strachey and Harold Laski. It was modelled on commercial book club lines and aimed to counter the rise of FASCISM and Nazism by providing politically educative left-wing literature. Early titles included André Malraux's *Days of Contempt* (1936), Stephen Spender's *Forward from Liberalism* (1937) and J.B.S. Haldane's *A.R.P.* (1938). By 1939 it had over 56,000 subscribers and more than a thousand 'left discussion groups' in Britain, with major rallies held at the Albert Hall. The outbreak of the Second World War that year initiated a sharp decline in membership and it closed in 1948 with the publication of G.D.H. Cole's *The Meaning of Marxism*. Few of the orange cloth-bound books have survived, with the exception of George ORWELL's *The* ROAD TO WIGAN PIER (1937), a title about which, ironically, Gollancz had profound misgivings.

Left-field. Unorthodox; experimental; out of the ordinary. A US jazz jargon term picked up by British journalists and musicians in the 1970s. It derives from the phrase 'out of left field', relating to baseball, in which the left field is the area to the batter's left, beyond third base, which rarely sees any action and from which the ball rarely arrives.

Left-footer. A nickname for a Roman Catholic, current from the 1930s. The allusion seems to be to an Irish turf-cutter who uses a special left-footed spade, many Irish being Catholics.

Left-footers also favour rightwingers, hence the battle for the soul of [MP] Alan Clark, who felt the Ten Commandments were à la carte.

The Times (19 October 1999)

Legal eagle. A keen and astute lawyer. The phrase dates from the 1940s.

Legend in one's lifetime. A person so famous that they are the subject of popular repeated stories in their lifetime. The expression derives from Lytton Strachey's *Eminent Victorians* (1918), in which he applied it to Florence Nightingale (1820–1910): 'She was a legend in her lifetime, and she knew it.' Veteran journalists of a certain type are sometimes punningly known as 'a legend in their lunchtime'. *See also* EMINENT VICTORIAN.

Leading libel lawyer Peter Carter-Ruck once said of him [Lord Goodman]: 'He became a legend in his lifetime.'

Sunday Express (14 May 1995)

Legionnaires' disease. A form of pneumonia that was first identified in 1976 as being caused by a previously unknown bacillus, *Legionella pneumophila*, which thrives in contaminated air-conditioning units. The name comes from a convention held that year at a Philadelphia hotel by members of the American Legion, an organization of retired US servicemen. A total of 192 Legionnaires contracted the disease, 29 of them fatally.

Lego. The construction toy consisting of interlocking plastic building blocks arose from a business set up in 1932 at Billund, Denmark, by Ole Kirk Christiansen, a master carpenter and joiner, who originally made and sold stepladders, ironing boards and wooden toys. In 1934 he named the latter Lego, from Danish *leg godt*, 'play well', a name that it was later realized was also Latin for 'I study'. The business introduced plastic toys in 1947, and began to perfect what were at first known as 'Automatic Binding Bricks'. The firm's products grew in variety and in 1958 the coupling system for the blocks was patented. In 1960 the company opened Legoland, an entire village made of Lego at Billund. It remained the sole Lego Mecca until 1996 when a second Legoland opened at Windsor, close to London. A third was added in 1999 at Carlsbad, California. The company's products now range from Disney characters to working models of all kinds.

Legs. If a product or idea is said to have legs it is successful and popular, enjoying a long run. The expres-

sion typically applies to television programmes or books and particularly to films that are 'good box office' at a single cinema.

Leg show. A now dated term first current at the turn of the 20th century for a theatrical production in which dancing girls displayed their legs.

Leg warmers. A pair of tubular knitted garments designed to cover the leg from ankle to knee or thigh. They are typically worn by dancers during rehearsal but in the 1970s also became generally fashionable.

Le Mans. A town in northwest France famous for its motor-racing circuit, on which an annual 24-hour endurance race, *les Vingt-Quatre Heures du Mans*, has from 1923 been the high spot.

Lemmy Caution. *See* CAUTION, LEMMY.

Lemon, Answer's a. *See* ANSWER'S A LEMON.

Lender of last resort. In the world of finance an institution that will lend to a borrower when no one else will. More generally a lender of last resort is a central bank that will lend to other banks when they run low on funds because of heavy withdrawals.

Lend-Lease or **Lease-Lend.** Reciprocal agreements made by the United States with Britain and the Allied nations in the Second World War to foster the pooling of resources. The policy began with the destroyers sent to Britain in return for naval and air bases in parts of the British Commonwealth and was formalized by the Lend-Lease Act of March 1941. When Lend-Lease ended in 1945 the United States had received somewhat less than one-sixth, in monetary terms, of what they had expended in aid to their allies, over 60 per cent of which went to the British Commonwealth.

Lenin. The assumed name of Vladimir Ilyich Ulyanov (1870–1924), founder of the Soviet Union and propagator of its guiding doctrine of Marxism-Leninism. The origin of his pseudonym remains uncertain. It is popularly said to derive from the Siberian River Lena, but although he had been exiled to Siberia, it was not to this river. He first used the name in 1901.

Leningrad. The name given in 1924 on the death of LENIN to Petrograd which, until 1914, was known as St Petersburg, the former capital of Tsarist Russia founded by Peter the Great in 1703. In 1991 it reverted to its original name of St Petersburg. The siege of Leningrad in the Second World War (August 1941–January 1944) caused more than one million deaths from cold and famine. It was the inspiration for

Shostakovich's 7th Symphony, whose march theme may evoke the brutality of Stalinism as much as it does that of the besieging Nazis.

Leopard, The. A novel (1960; in Italian as *Il Gattopardo*, 1958) by Giuseppe di Lampedusa (1896–1957), Duke of Palma and Prince of Lampedusa. It is set in Sicily, to which in May 1860 Giuseppe Garibaldi (1807–82) sailed with 1000 volunteers to win the island from the Bourbons. The narrative describes the reactions to historical events of Fabrizio, Prince of Salina, and the Salina family between 1860 and 1910. The leopard is the family motif, which appears as the centrepiece of a vaulted ceiling in the family convent and, at the book's end, 'in red thread' on the border of a towel. The author died of cancer a week after the manuscript had been rejected by the house of Mondadori. He left instructions that his family should pursue publication. It appeared under the imprint of Feltrinelli, to become the highest selling and most widely translated 20th-century Italian novel.

Leotard. The close fitting garment so called, worn by acrobats and dancers, takes its name from the French trapeze artist Jules Léotard (1839–70), who wore something similar. The costume is first recorded in the United States in the 1920s, its design presumably based on the particular original. It subsequently became a fashion garment.

Less is more. Restraint or moderation is more effective than overemphasis or exaggeration. The aphorism was a favourite of the German-born American architect Ludwig Mies van der Rohe (1886–1969) but the words come from Browning.

> Yet do much less, so much less, Someone says,
> (I know his name, no matter) – so much less!
> Well, less is more, Lucrezia: I am judged.
>
> ROBERT BROWNING: *Andrea del Sarto* (1855)

Let George do it. Let someone else do the work or take the responsibility. The expression is of US origin and dates from the turn of the 20th century. The source of the phrase is uncertain but it is possibly a learned adoption of the French *Laissez faire à Georges* in the same sense, where the reference is to Cardinal Georges d'Amboise (1460–1510), a church and government official under Louis XII responsible for major tax and judicial reforms. It was the English phrase that gave 'George' as the colloquial term for an automatic pilot in an aircraft.

Let it all hang out, To. To do just what one wants; to be quite uninhibited. The allusion is probably to a naked or 'unbuttoned' person. The expression gained popularity in the counterculture of the 1960s and originated with American blacks.

> It's a fellow with hair curling over his neck shrieking: 'Up-tight–outasight! What you gonna doo–boogaloo! Let it all hang out!'
>
> RICHARD GILBERT in *Anatomy of Pop* (1970)

Let It Be. The thirteenth and last album by the BEATLES, released in Britain in May 1970. It included the tracks 'Across the Universe', 'Let It Be', MAGGIE MAY, 'The Long and Winding Road' and 'Get Back', the last having been the original title of a project that was cancelled in favour of *Let It Be*. The Beatles' final album has a markedly spiritual and reflective flavour, exemplified by the overtly religious stamp of its title song. A film of the same title was released in the same month as the album. The similarity of its title to that of the Rolling Stones' song and album LET IT BLEED (released the previous year) appears to be coincidental.

Let it Bleed. A song and album by the ROLLING STONES, released in 1969. The album includes such tracks as 'Gimme Shelter', 'Let It Bleed', 'Midnight Rambler', 'Monkey Man' and 'You Can't Always Get What You Want'. *See also* LET IT BE.

Let's be having you. A stock order to respond by a sergeant to his men or a police officer to a suspect or criminal. A street outside the police station at Sheffield Airport is called 'Letsby Avenue', the outcome of a prank perpetrated on the Ordnance Survey by an anonymous policeman.

Let's face it. Let's face the facts. The hackneyed phrase does not normally imply any challenge.

Letter from America. One of the BBC's longest running programmes, in the form of a weekly talk on an American topic by the British-born broadcaster Alistair Cooke (b.1908), who took US citizenship in 1941. The first talk was broadcast in 1946 in what was originally commissioned as a series of 13. Cooke's weekly address was still going out in his measured tones at the end of the 20th century, recorded by the programme's producers in his New York apartment.

Level playing field. An area of activity that offers no advantage to any particular side. In real terms, a field that is not level may serve to favour a home team, who will be familiar with it. The metaphorical use of the expression is chiefly found in the worlds of business and politics.

Levittown. The name applied to a type of pioneering postwar suburban housing tract in the USA constructed by the building firm William Levitt and Sons. The first Levittown was built in Hempstead, New York, between 1947 and 1951. It eventually provided more than 17,000 private homes. Although the houses were extremely basic, the privacy they offered was greatly valued, and the company subsequently built a second Levittown on the outskirts of Philadelphia and a third in southern New Jersey. The name came to be applied to similar housing developments all over the USA, and not just those built by Levitt and Sons.

Lewinsky, Monica. *See* MONICA.

Ley lines. Imaginary mystic lines running across Britain, said to connect places of power such as churches and different types of ANCIENT MONUMENT and so to form 'power grids'. Stonehenge is one of several monuments said to lie at the intersection of at least two ley lines. The idea of such lines was introduced to the public by Alfred Watkins in his *Early British Trackways* (1922). His original theory 'that mounds, moats, beacons and mark stones fall into straight lines throughout Britain' was firmly rejected by archaeologists and historians but in more recent times has generated a lively NEW AGE cult. The longest ley line is the St Michael Line, extending from Cornwall to East Anglia, and running past many churches dedicated to St Michael, including St Michael's Mount itself and those at Brentor in Devon, Trull, Othery and Stoke St Michael in Somerset, Clifton Hampden in Oxfordshire and Hopton in Suffolk. 'Ley' is a variant of 'lea', meaning 'field', 'meadow'.

LG. A nickname for David Lloyd George, the WELSH WIZARD.

LHOOQ. The letters inscribed beneath a reproduction of the *Mona Lisa*, on whose upper lip a moustache has been drawn, on the front cover of a 1920 Dada manifesto by Marcel Duchamp (1887–1968) and Francis Picabia (1879–1953). If the letters are read in French, they sound like *elle a chaud au cul*, which means 'she's got a hot arse'.

Lib Dems. A short name, favoured by the news media, for the LIBERAL DEMOCRATS.

Liberal Democrats. Britain's third main political party, after the LABOUR PARTY and the Conservatives. It was formed from the old Liberal Party in May 1988 as a merger between that party and the Social Democrats and was at first known as the Liberal and Social Democrats. In 1989 the cumbersome title was shortened to the Liberal Democrats or, colloquially, the Lib Dems. Its first leader (to 1999) was Paddy Ashdown (b.1941). In the political spectrum it is mainly left of centre, and it came to support several of the measures introduced by NEW LABOUR under Tony Blair.

> By-elections are what the Lib-Dems are good at.
> *Sunday Express* (27 February 2000)

Liberation Day. The annual holiday (9 May) in the Channel Islands to mark the liberation of the islands in 1945 from the Second World War German occupation. The Channel Islands were the only part of the British Isles to be conquered by the NAZIS, being occupied unopposed following the fall of France in 1940. The German garrison surrendered as part of the overall surrender of German forces at the end of the European war.

Liberation theology. The theory originating among Roman Catholic theologians in South America that liberation from social, political, and economic oppression is a vital constituent of the Christian message. The term translates Spanish *teología de la liberación*, coined by the Peruvian Gustavo Guttierez in 1968 and used for the title of his book published in 1971. 'Liberation' expresses a dislike of 'development', meaning an imposed solution to South America's problems, determined by the industrialized nations and involving little initiative on the part of the people.

Liberty bodice. A type of sleeveless vest formerly worn by young children. The name was a commercial one given to suggest a greater freedom of movement than that provided by the conventional bodice. It was first manufactured in the early 20th century by the firm of R. & W.H. Symington, of Market Harborough, Leicestershire, but ceased to be produced in the 1960s.

Liberty Bonds. Between 24 April 1917 and 2 March 1919 the US government authorized five issues of gold bonds in aid of the war effort. The sales of these Liberty Bonds, as they were known, peaked in 1918, their appeal enhanced by endorsements from such HOLLYWOOD stars as Charlie Chaplin, Mary Pickford and Douglas Fairbanks. A patriotic poster for the 3rd Liberty Loan bore the words: 'Remember the Flag of Liberty! Support It! Buy U.S. Government Bonds.'

Lib-Lab Pact. The agreement in 1977–8 between the Liberals led by David Steel (the BOY DAVID) and the Labour government of James Callaghan (SUNNY JIM).

The government, to shore up its slim majority, agreed to follow moderate policies and to consult the Liberals on important issues in return for their support. The Liberals ended the pact in the autumn of 1978, and in March 1979 the government lost a vote of no confidence and was obliged to call a general election.

Librium. The proprietary name of a white crystalline compound used as a tranquillizer. Together with VALIUM it was a prime resort of the stressed and superanxious in the 1960s. The name may derive from Latin *libra*, 'balance'.

Lidice. This village of about 450 inhabitants near Prague was 'liquidated' by the Germans on 10 June 1942 as part of a massive reprisal for the assassination by Czech underground fighters of Reinhard Heydrich (1904–42), deputy leader of the SS. The 172 men were shot and the women were transported to the Ravensbrück concentration camp. The 90 children, after being screened and found to be 'racially pure', were dispersed throughout Germany to be renamed and brought up as Germans. When the massacre and deportation were complete, the SS burned the village, dynamited anything that was left standing and levelled the rubble. In 1947 a new village site was designated nearby, while a museum, with a monument and rose garden, marks the original site. *See also* HANGMAN, ORADOUR-SUR-GLANE.

Lie back and think of England, To. To submit to unavoidable sexual intercourse. The phrase seems to blend two different expressions: 'to close one's eyes and think of England' and 'to lie back and enjoy it'. The former is usually attributed to Alice, Lady Hillingdon's *Journal* of 1912: 'I am happy now that Charles calls on my bedchamber less frequently than of old. As it is, I now endure but two calls a week and when I hear his steps outside my door I lie down on my bed, close my eyes, open my legs and think of England.' Alice, Lady Hillingdon (1857–1940) married the 2nd Baron Hillingdon in 1886, but the whereabouts or even existence of her *Journal* is unknown. The latter expression is of more uncertain origin. In his novel *The* JEWEL IN THE CROWN (1966), Paul Scott refers to it as 'that old, disreputable saying', but quite how ancient it is remains a mystery.

Lie detector. An informal name for the polygraph, a US invention that records the physiological changes of a person under questioning. It is based on the assumption that a human being cannot tell a lie without changes in breathing, blood pressure, pulse

rate and palm perspiration, and the knowledge that these can be recorded. The rare instances when individuals have succeeded in duping a lie detector point to the fact that automatic physiological responses can with practice be brought under conscious control. US courts have consistently ruled against lie detector evidence. In the intelligence community, however, security officials have just as consistently upheld its use.

Lie down in a darkened room, To. Metaphorically to recover one's composure or regain one's sanity. The described action is often recommended to someone expressing an eccentric notion.

> I feel a strange urge to rush to the defence of ... Sir Cliff Richard. Probably if I lie down in a darkened room it will pass.
> *The Times* (21 December 1999)

Lied von der Erde, Das. The posthumously performed 'song-symphony' by Gustav Mahler (1860–1911), composed in 1908 and featuring German translations of six Chinese poems from the 8th century. The title means 'Song of the Earth', and the final song is entitled '*Der Abschied*', the farewell. Although Mahler called the work a symphony he did not give it a number as it would have been his ninth, and he was superstitiously aware that Beethoven, Schubert and other composers had died after completing their ninth symphonies. Nevertheless, he appears to have overcome his anxieties, and went on to write a ninth and parts of a tenth symphony; the latter lay uncompleted at his death. In his memory, Bruno Walter gave the first performance of *Das Lied von der Erde* in 1911.

Life after death. This phrase typically found in the form of a question, 'Is there life after death?', has become a catchphrase in the 20th century. As such it was memorably caricatured in an episode of the television comedy MONTY PYTHON'S FLYING CIRCUS on 21 December 1972: 'Tonight on "Is There" we examine the question, "Is there life after death?" And here to discuss it are three dead people.' Film titles such as *Is There Sex After Death?* (1971) and *Is There Sex After Marriage?* (1973) vary the formula, while a graffito seen in Ballymurphy, Ireland, in the early 1970s was recorded as, 'Is there life *before* death?' Seamus Heaney quotes this in his poem 'Whatever You Say You Say Nothing' in *North* (1975).

> Is there life after redundancy?
> *Sunday Times Magazine* (headline) (14 October 1984)

Life and Death of Colonel Blimp, The. A film (1943) written and directed by Michael Powell (1905–90) and Emeric Pressburger (1902–88) about the life of a British colonel from his early army days in the Boer War through to 1943 and the Second World War. Starring Roger Livesey as Colonel Blimp, the film was controversial in sending up the pomposity of a certain type of elderly senior officer and consequently incurred the wrath of Prime Minister Winston Churchill, who feared it would damage wartime morale: he had its exportation banned and only relented two years later, by which time the film had enjoyed huge success with British audiences. The 'Colonel Blimp' character was not original to the film but was derived from the cartoons of David Low in the *London Evening Standard*. *See also* BLIMP.

Life and Loves of a She-Devil, The. A blackly comic novel (1983) by Fay Weldon (b.1931), in which the macabre and ugly Ruth Patchett takes her revenge on bestselling author Mary Fisher, who she feels has stolen her husband, Bobbo. In the triumphant televised version (1986), directed by Philip Saville, Julie T. Wallace played Ruth in a physically and emotionally memorable performance.

Life and Times of Michael K. A novel (1983) by J.M. Coetzee (b.1940), which won the BOOKER PRIZE for fiction. A political fable, it concerns Michael's journey with his mother to the farm of her birth. When she dies on the way, he carries on, tries to live in isolation, but is overtaken by a civil war, captured and imprisoned as a guerrilla. The name of the central character echoes that of Josef K., the protagonist of Franz Kafka's *The* TRIAL (1925).

Life begins at 40. A view held generally by optimists and an increasing number of realists, whereas pessimists are inclined to opine that at this age one is OVER THE HILL. The words come from the book *Life Begins at Forty* (1932) by the US writer Walter B. Pitkin.

Life of Riley. The good life; a comfortable existence. Riley or Reilly, a common Irish surname, is said to be a character in a 19th-century song. Two possible candidates are Pat Rooney's 'Are You the O'Reilly?', originally 'Is That Mr Reilly?' (1883), and Charles B. Lawlor's 'The Best Man in the House' (1898). The first certain use of the name is in Harry Pease's 'My Name is Kelly' (1919), which has two lines as follows:

Faith and my name is Kelly, Michael Kelly,
But I'm living the life of Reilly just the same.

Life sentence. A sentence of imprisonment for life, awarded in Britain as the mandatory sentence for murder and the maximum penalty for a number of serious offences such as robbery, rape, arson and manslaughter. Since 1997 courts in England and Wales have been required to impose life sentences also on those convicted for a second time on a serious violent or sexual offence. Unless 'life means life', people serving life sentences are normally detained for at least 20 years. They are then released but remain on licence for the rest of their lives and are subject to recall if their behaviour suggests that they could again be a danger to the public.

Light at the end of the tunnel. A long-awaited indication that a period of hardship or lengthy endeavour is nearing an end. The allusion is to the distant light at the exit of a railway tunnel, which is all that is seen while the train travels in darkness. The expression apparently dates no earlier than the 1920s and is chiefly used by politicians or journalists with reference to a slight upturn in an economic or other situation. It is on record as having been resorted to by Stanley Baldwin in 1929 and by Neville Chamberlain in 1937 and is said to have been exploited by Winston Churchill in 1941. At some point in the 1960s a jocular variant emerged: 'If we see the light at the end of the tunnel, it's the light of the oncoming train.' This is quoted by Robert Lowell in his poem 'Since 1939' (1977) and was repeated as 'Rowe's Rule' by Paul Dickson in an article in the *Washingtonian* of November 1978: 'The odds are five to six that the light at the end of the tunnel is the headlight of an oncoming train.' *See also* GREEN SHOOTS.

Light of one's life. A dearly loved person. The expression has now mostly superseded, at first ironically or semi-seriously, the much older 'light of one's eye'.

Lolita, light of my life, fire of my loins.
VLADIMIR NABOKOV: *Lolita*, Pt I, ch i (1955)

Light Programme. The BBC radio service inaugurated in 1945 as the peacetime successor to the Forces Programme. It continued the same mixture of broad comedy and light music that had made it so popular in the Second World War and the essential ingredients were maintained when it changed its name to Radio 2 on 30 September 1967. *See also* HOME SERVICE; THIRD PROGRAMME.

Like a bat out of hell. Very fast. The expression is said to have originated among US fighter pilots in the First World War. An alternative image is of bats fleeing the glare of the fires of hell. The expression dates from the 1920s.

Like a bomb. Very successfully. The phrase is often used ironically.

Like a fish needs a bicycle. Not in the least; the exact opposite. A fish does not need a bicycle. The colourful simile derives from the comment attributed in *c.*1970 to the US feminist Gloria Steinem (b.1934) that 'a woman without a man is like a fish without a bicycle'. The expression can take various forms.

> Buying a sports-related item was like a fish buying a bicycle.
>
> *The Times* (25 August 1999)

Likely lad. An able or smart youth. 'Likely' in this sense goes back to the 15th century but the particular alliterative combination dates from the 20th century as a friendly north of England phrase for a young man of promise or enterprise. It was popularized by the title of the television SITCOM *The Likely Lads* (1965–9) about the friendship between two working-class young men in northeast England, Terry Collier, played by James Bowlam, and Bob Ferris, played by Rodney Bewes. A sequel was *Whatever Happened to the Likely Lads* (1973–4).

> The likely lads of Manchester United failed to win friends and influence people during the first week of the Club World Championship in Rio.
>
> *Sunday Times* (9 January 2000)

Like nobody's business. To an extraordinary extent; like mad, as: 'She was pedalling along like nobody's business.' An unusual phrase dating from the 1930s.

Like the clappers. Very fast; very hard. The phrase dates from the 1940s and is a shortening of 'like the clappers of hell', meaning those of HELL'S BELLS.

Li'l Abner. The handsome HILLBILLY created by the US newspaper cartoonist Al Capp in 1934. He comes from the dead-end town of Dogpatch and has a DUMB BLONDE girlfriend, Daisy Mae. His adventures have been represented in both stage and screen versions. *See also* SADIE HAWKINS DAY.

Lili Marlene. A German song of the Second World War. It was based on a poem written in 1917 by a German soldier, Hans Leip (1894–1983), and was composed by Norbert Schultze in 1938. The German singer Lale Andersen initially made it known in 1939. It became increasingly popular, especially with the AFRIKA

KORPS, and the recorded version was played nightly by Radio Belgrade from the late summer of 1941 virtually until the end of hostilities. Other German stations relayed it, and it was picked up and adopted by the EIGHTH ARMY, the English version of the lyric being by Tommy Connor (who deleted an implication in the original that Lili Marlene was a prostitute). There were French, Italian and other renderings of what became the classic song of the war, and it was one of the theme songs of its namesake, the German-born actress Marlene Dietrich. A recording of the song by Ann Shelton in 1944 sold a million copies. Leip subsequently said he had based Lili Marlene on two girls, Lili and Marlene, whom he had known in Berlin when on leave.

> Bei der Kaserne
> Vor dem grossen Tor,
> Stand eine Laterne
> Und steht sie noch davor …
> Mit dir, Lili Marlene,
> Mit dir, Lili Marlen'.
> (Underneath the lantern
> By the barrack gate,
> Darling, I remember
> The way you used to wait …
> My Lili of the lamplight,
> My own Lili Marlene.)

Limbo dancing. A dance of West Indian origin popular from the 1950s in which the dancer bends backwards to pass under a horizontal bar, which is progressively lowered until it is barely off the ground. The word derives from 'limber' in the sense lithe, supple.

> One question the Wiltshire bobbies should ask is how to escape looking ludicrous as they place their helmets on the heads of gyrating limbo dancers.
>
> *The Times* (14 April 1999)

Lime, Harry. The intriguing villain who runs a drugs racket in postwar Vienna in the film *The* THIRD MAN (1949), scripted by Graham Greene. He was played by Orson Welles, and although he does not appear until halfway through the film, all Welles's obituary notices mentioned his memorable portrayal of the role. The radio series *The Lives of Harry Lime* (from 1951) also starred Orson Welles. An authentic Harry Lime is depicted in David Thomson's book *Suspects* (1985), in which he is shown as a South London WIDE BOY who makes a killing from a crooked salvage business during the BLITZ before going to Vienna to meet a literally dirty end in the city's sewers.

In his role as Harry Lime in Carol Reed's *The Third Man*, Welles gave perhaps the definitive Wellesian performance. Though on-screen for only about ten minutes, Welles/Lime *defines* this film.

The Annual Obituary 1985 (1988)

Limousine liberal. A US term for a wealthy person who professes sympathy for the deprived. The term's conflicting image of a person who drives an expensive car while pitying the poor is intended to imply the hypocrisy of the stance. The British equivalent is a CHAMPAGNE SOCIALIST.

Limp-wristed. Effeminate; affected; CAMP. The phrase dates from the 1950s and refers to the supposedly typical gestures or poses of male homosexuals.

Lindbergh, Charles Augustus. The US aviator (1902–74), nicknamed 'The Lone Eagle', who was the first to make a solo nonstop flight across the Atlantic (New York to Paris), in his monoplane SPIRIT OF ST LOUIS. The flight, on 20–21 May 1927, took 33½ hours, made Lindbergh into an instant hero and earned him his nickname. The waist-length aviation jacket he wore inspired a fashion, and the so-called Lindbergh jacket was popular in the 1930s. In 1932 Lindbergh's two-year-old son was kidnapped and murdered, and the Lindbergh baby case became one of the most notorious of the decade. In 1936 Bruno Richard Hauptmann was executed for the murder. Lindbergh's speeches in favour of US isolationism in 1940–41 led to criticism from President Franklin D. Roosevelt, and Lindbergh resigned his commission in the Air Corps Reserve in April 1941. However, once the USA entered the war, Lindbergh was active in the Allied cause. *See also* LINDY HOP.

Lindsey. The name of a remarkable Australian family who played a leading role in Australian art throughout the 20th century. Chief among them were the five children of R.C. Lindsey of Creswick, Victoria: painter and graphic artist Percy Lindsey (1870–1952), art critic, painter and graphic artist Sir Lionel Lindsey (1874–1961), painter, critic and novelist Norman Lindsey (1879–1969), graphic artist Ruby Lindsey (1887–1919) and painter Sir Daryl Lindsey (1889–1976), who in 1942 was appointed director of the National Gallery of Victoria. Norman's son Raymond (1904–60) and Daryl's wife Joan (1896–1984) were also painters. Norman Lindsey is generally regarded as the most forceful personality of all, although his emphasis on sex as the mainspring of life and art led to the labelling of much of his work as pornographic.

Lindy hop. The frenzied dance of this name originated in the Savoy Ballroom, Harlem, New York, in the late 1920s and was inspired by Charles LINDBERGH's pioneering solo transatlantic flight of 1927, reported in the news headline 'Lindy hops the Atlantic'. The dance re-enacted the flight, with the couple standing face to face and the man tossing the woman in a whirl of solo turns and supported leaps. After a 'landing', she was ready for the next 'flight'. According to legend, the dance began with a group of men and women leaping and yelling, 'Look, I'm flying like Lindy!'

Lindy's. A restaurant opened by Leo Lindemann on Broadway, New York, in 1921 and frequented by many celebrities from the world of sport and entertainment. Lindemann opened a second Lindy's on Broadway in 1930 and both restaurants became known for their sandwiches, sturgeon, herring and cheesecake. As 'Mindy's' they were immortalized in the short stories of Damon Runyon. The original restaurant closed in 1949 and the second in 1957.

Linear B. The bald academic designation of a form of Bronze Age writing discovered on clay tablets in Crete and deciphered as an early form of Greek by Michael Ventris in 1952. It proved to be a syllabic script composed of linear signs dating from c.1400 to c.1200 BC and is believed by some scholars to have developed from the earlier, undeciphered Linear A. Ventris's tragically early death in a car accident at the age of 34 deprived the world of a possible key to the riddle.

Line dancing. A dance craze of the 1990s similar to COUNTRY AND WESTERN dancing. Dancers line up without partners and follow a fixed pattern of steps to music. The sight of the dancers kicking and turning in unison is almost as satisfying to the viewer as the actions themselves are to the dancers.

Line dancing, giant leek growing, Koi carp breeding, even 2CV owning. These are eccentric but popular hobbies ... and to the financial services industry they offer endless, seductive marketing opportunities.

The Times (10 April 1999)

Link trainer. A flight simulator, as a device enabling pilots to learn and practise flying techniques while still on the ground. It was the invention in 1929 of the US pilot Edward A. Link (1904–81). Hence the name, which also happens to suggest a link between ground and air.

Lion of Judah. The title of Hailie Selassie (1892–1975), emperor of Ethiopia from 1930 until his overthrow in 1974. Before becoming emperor he was known as Ras (Prince) Tafari Makonnen, the origin of the name of the RASTAFARIAN cult, which worships him as the Messiah.

Lions Clubs. Civilian service clubs that comprise the International Association of Lions Clubs, founded in Dallas, Texas, in 1917 to foster a spirit of 'generous consideration' among the peoples of the world and to promote good government, good citizenship and active interest in social and moral welfare. Lions Clubs activities include general community welfare projects, aid to the blind and support of the UNITED NATIONS. There are now Lions Clubs in over 150 countries and the headquarters of the association is in Oakbrook, Illinois.

Lions led by donkeys. A metaphor traditionally associated with British soldiers in the First World War, with reference to their complaints about their generals. Alan Clark in *The Donkeys* (1961) attributes the saying to Max Hoffman (1869–1927) but the phrase was already known by the 1870s.

Lion, the Witch and the Wardrobe, The. A fantasy (1950) for children by C.S. Lewis (1898–1963), the first to be published of seven books about the mythical land of NARNIA. The lion, known as ASLAN, is a Christ-like figure. The witch has held Narnia in thrall for a hundred years. The wardrobe is the means through which four children enter Narnia. The series upholds Lewis's dictum that 'a book which is enjoyed only by children is a bad children's book'. A faithful televised version was made in 1963, to be followed by a less satisfactory re-creation, full of technical wizardry, in the series *Chronicles of Narnia* (1988–90). *See also* FIRST LINES OF NOVELS.

Liquid lunch. A midday meal in which the consumption of alcoholic liquor is greater than that of solid food.

LISP. *See* PROGRAMMING LANGUAGES.

Listen with Mother. A popular radio programme for very young children, broadcast from 1950 to 1982. It consisted of 15 minutes of stories, songs and nursery rhymes and the opening words were always the same: 'Are you sitting comfortably? Then I'll begin.' *See also* WATCH WITH MOTHER.

Lite. A respelling of 'light', especially with reference to a low-calorie light beer. The first such beer, Miller Lite, was marketed in the United States in 1975.

Literary type. A derisory term for one seen as claiming a superior or specialized literary interest.

> Historical novels: everyone's at it these days. ... But I sometimes wonder if an imagined future or an alternative present isn't a greater challenge: though fiction so set is usually herded into the ghetto of science fiction or fantasy and ignored by Literary Types.
>
> *The Times* (7 September 1999)

Litmus test. Figuratively, a decisively indicative test. This sense of the phrase dates from the 1950s and derives from the physical litmus test, in which a piece of blue litmus paper turns red under acid conditions and back to blue again under alkaline ones.

> Opposition to Section 28 has become a litmus test of worthy opinion, an entry requirement to the Communion of the Correct.
>
> *The Times* (3 November 1999)

Little Black Banda. A highly offensive nickname bestowed on Dr Hastings Kamuzu Banda (1905–97), the autocratic leader of Malawi from 1963 to 1994. The nickname, based on the now-frowned-upon children's story LITTLE BLACK SAMBO, was coined by David Frost on THAT WAS THE WEEK THAT WAS.

Little black book. A notebook in which men supposedly keep a list of potential dates.

Little black dress. A woman's short or medium-length black dress, deemed to be suitable for almost any social engagement. It was created in the 1920s by the French dress designer Coco Chanel (1883–1971) who made it out of jersey wool, then an unfashionable material associated with maids' uniforms, and adorned it with lavish costume jewellery. Amy Holman Edelman's book *The Little Black Dress* (1998) is a study of the style.

> The great, old-fashioned, little black dress is going to make a resurgence. Championed on the catwalk and Gucci, this ever practical number is back.
>
> *The Times* (8 January 2000)

Little Black Sambo. The now controversial tale of a little black boy, written and illustrated by Helen Bannerman (1862–1946) and first published in 1899 by the publishers Grant Richards of London. Little Black Sambo encounters a group of menacing tigers in the jungle, but bribes them by offering them his clothes, shoes and umbrella. The tigers argue among themselves for possession of the objects and, racing round a tree, are turned into a pool of melted butter, which is later used by Sambo's mother to cook delicious pancakes. In the 1970s *Little Black Sambo* was criticized for its apparent racism in Britain by, among others, Teachers against Racism and in the United States by the National Association for the Advancement of Colored People. It nevertheless continued to sell in significant numbers. The book popularized the use of the word 'Sambo', which had been used as a term for a black person as early as the 18th century, but the term, like the book, has long ceased to be acceptable.

Little Boy. *See* ENOLA GAY.

Little boys' room. A coy euphemism for a men's lavatory, dating from the 1930s.

Little Caesar. A gangster film (1930) based on the novel (1929) by W.R. Burnett about the career and ultimate demise of the ambitious mobster Rico Bandello (played by Edward G. Robinson). It was the first 'talkie' gangster film. Rico's vicious and unrepentant campaign to establish himself as a latterday Caesar in the underworld caused considerable controversy at the time of the film's release, not least because of the clear parallels that could be made with the career of the real-life gangster Al CAPONE.

> Mother of God, is this the end of Rico?
> EDWARD G. ROBINSON as Rico Bandello (his last words)

Little Entente. The name given to the political alliance formed between Czechoslovakia, Yugoslavia and Romania (1920–22). It was originally designed to prevent the restoration of Habsburg power but became broader in scope. It was brought to an end by the destruction of Czechoslovakia after the MUNICH Agreement (1938).

Little Foxes, The. A play (1939) by the US playwright Lillian Hellman (1907–84) about the machinations of the ambitious Regina Hubbard, who is prepared to sacrifice all those around her in the pursuit of material gain. The biblical title comes from the Song of Solomon 2:15: 'Take us the foxes, the little foxes, that spoil the vines; for our vines have tender grapes.'

Little Gidding. The last part of *Four Quartets* (1942), a poetical work by the Anglo-American poet T.S. Eliot (1888–1965) exploring the theme of 'time past and time present'. Following 'Burnt Norton', 'East Coker' and 'The Dry Salvages', 'Little Gidding' took as its subject the religious community established at Little Gidding in 1625 by Nicholas Ferrar (1592–1637) and finally broken up by the Puritans in 1646. Little Gidding is a hamlet in Cambridgeshire, a few miles northwest of Huntingdon.

> You are here to kneel
> Where prayer has been valid.
> T.S. ELIOT: 'Little Gidding'

Little girls' room. A coy euphemism for a women's lavatory, dating from the 1940s and based on the LITTLE BOYS' ROOM that is its male counterpart.

Little green men. Imaginary people of peculiar appearance, supposedly landed from outer space. The description derives from cartoons of such creatures emerging from FLYING SAUCERS. *See also* ALIENS.

Little Grey Men, The. A Carnegie Medal-winning fantasy novel (1942) by B.B. It is the tale of three Warwickshire gnomes named Sneezewort, Baldermoney and Dodder who search for a missing brother.

Little Grey Rabbit. The name of the main character in a series of more than 30 illustrated books for young children by Alison Uttley (1884–1976), which began with *The Squirrel, the Hare and the Little Grey Rabbit* (1929), illustrated by Margaret Tempest. The last book in the series was *Hare and the Rainbow* (1975). The Little Grey Rabbit works tirelessly for the lazy Hare and Squirrel, who remain unappreciative of her efforts.

Little House in the Big Woods. The first (1932) of eight autobiographical studies by the US writer Laura Ingalls Wilder (1867–1957) of her pioneering family. Told in the third person, the sequence covers her life from the age of four to her marriage at 18, as the family moves westward from Wisconsin, through Minnesota to South Dakota. The best known title in the series is *Little House on the Prairie* (1935), which was also the title of the popular television series (1974–82) based on Wilder's books.

Little local difficulty. A euphemism for a major problem. The expression was popularized by Harold Macmillan's statement at London Airport on 7 January 1958. The prime minister was about to leave for a Commonwealth tour following the resignation of the Chancellor of the Exchequer, among others.

> I thought the best thing to do was to settle up these little local difficulties and then turn to the wider vision of the Commonwealth.
> HAROLD MACMILLAN: quoted in *The Times* (8 January 1958)

Little man. An insignificant man. The expression is also used of a local handyman who operates on a small scale.

Little Mary. A former euphemism for the stomach, from the play of that name by J.M. Barrie (1903).

> And what is the subject of the piece? Who is Little Mary? It is nobody; it is simply a nursery name that the child-doctor invents as a kind of polite equivalent to what children ordinarily allude to as their 'tum-tum'.
>
> *Punch* (14 October 1903)

Little Mo. The US tennis star Maureen Connolly (1934–69) was so dubbed by the media, 'Mo' being a pet form of her first name and 'Little' alluding to her small size and slight figure. The name also punned on 'Big Mo', the US battleship *Missouri*, flagship of the US Pacific Fleet in the Second World War and scene of the Japanese surrender in 1945, four years before 'Little Mo' became the youngest female to win the National Junior Championships. She went on to win nine 'grand slam' titles between 1951 and 1954, when injury ended her meteoric career.

Little old ladies in tennis shoes. A nickname for conservative Republican women voters in US elections, said to be typified by an elderly resident in the western states who does not care about her appearance and who 'votes for values'. Their support did much to boost the position of the conservative Republican Senator Barry Goldwater in the late 1950s and 1960s. *See also* BLUE-RINSE BRIGADE.

> 'Burt Reynolds has done more for little old ladies in tennis shoes than anyone else in the history of the world,' said Dinah Shore at the annual Friars Club roast, where Reynolds was the guest of honor.
>
> *Newsweek* (1 June 1981)

Little Orphan Annie. The archetypal American waif in Harold Gray's comic strip in the *New York Daily News* from 1924. She is adopted by a billionaire businessman, Daddy Warbucks, and has many adventures during his regular absences from home. Her name if not her persona appears to have been adopted from a poem of 1885 by James W. Riley entitled 'Little Orphant Annie'. She has subsequently appeared in films and on the radio and she was the subject of Charles Strouse's musical *Annie* (1977), itself filmed in 1982 with Aileen Quinn in the name part.

Little Red Book. The popular name of *Quotations from Chairman Mao*, Lin Biao's simplified and dogmatized version of the thoughts of Mao Zedong, a vademecum of the RED GUARD during the CULTURAL REVOLUTION. One 'thought' included in Section 2 but originally written in 1927 was: 'A revolution is not a dinner party.' The name simply described the work's physical form. Some 800 million copies of the booklet were said to have been sold or distributed from 1966 to 1971, when possession became virtually mandatory. A European equivalent but with an educational agenda was the Danish *Den lille røde bog for skoleelever* by Søren Hansen and Jesper Jensen, published in 1969 and appearing in English translation in 1971 as *The Little Red Schoolbook*. It gave frank advice to schoolchildren on sex and drugs as well as routine matters such as lessons and homework and was condemned as obscene or at best subversive in its day.

Little Red Engine, The. A series of picture books, recounting the adventures of an anthropomorphized railway engine, by the British writer Diana Ross (b.1910), of which the first to be published was *The Little Red Engine Gets a Name* (1942).

Little Shop of Horrors. A very funny cult HORROR MOVIE (1960) directed by Roger Corman (b.1926) about a carnivorous talking plant that quickly outgrows the flower shop of its dimwitted owner and becomes a voracious man-eating monster. Corman's film was dreamed up and filmed in just two days and three nights after he was offered the chance to make a low-budget movie on the street set used for another film in the two days remaining before it was due to be torn down. The film includes one of Jack Nicholson's earliest performances, as a masochistic dental patient. The success of Corman's original inspired a stage musical with the same title in the 1980s and an inferior film remake in 1986, in which the fully grown plant was over 3.5m (12ft) tall and required almost 20km (12 miles) of cable.

Little Venice. A London beauty spot centring on the western end of the Regent's Canal and famous for its artists. It is hardly like Venice, although it was romantically compared to that city in the 19th century by Lord Byron and Robert Browning. The present name appears not to have become established until after the Second World War, although Margery Allingham, in *Death of a Ghost* (1934), mentions 'Little Venice in 1930'.

Little Willie. A nickname of Crown Prince Wilhelm of Germany and Prussia (1882–1951), later applied disparagingly to various people and by army personnel to a range of weapons. In the 1990s it was used tongue-in-cheek by Baroness Thatcher to refer to John Major's successor as Conservative leader, William Hague. *See also* LAUGHING MURDERER OF VERDUN.

Live Aid. *See* BAND AID.

Live high on the hog, To. To have a luxurious lifestyle. An expression of US origin alluding to the best part of a pig to provide a cut of rich and succulent pork.

His reckless determination to live high on the hog was his undoing, and he had to resign from the Cabinet after barely five months.
The Times (6 May 1999)

Live in each other's pockets, To. To live in close dependence on someone or be closely involved with them. The expression dates from the 1950s.

Though we meet with regularity, we don't live in each other's pockets.
The Times (6 December 1999)

Liver bird. A nickname for a young woman from Liverpool, especially when working-class or lower-middle-class. The name puns on 'Liver', rhyming with 'fiver', the fanciful bird appearing in Liverpool's coat of arms (and on the twin towers of the Royal Liver Exchange Building), and 'bird' as a colloquialism for a young woman. The term was popularized by Carla Lane's television SITCOM *The Liver Birds* (1969–78) about the exploits of two young female friends in Liverpool, Sandra Hutchinson, played by Nerys Hughes, and Beryl Hennessey, played by Polly James.

Liverpool Poets. A group of Liverpool writers prominent in the 1960s whose poetry was in the same self-ironizing spirit as the lyrics of the BEATLES and like them intended for public performance, often with a musical accompaniment. They were also known as the Merseyside Poets. Core exponents were Brian Patten (b.1946), Roger McGough (b.1937) and Adrian Henri (b.1932). *See also* MERSEY.

Living Theatre. A US avant-garde theatre company founded in 1947 by Judith Malina and her husband Julian Beck. Its original commitment was to poetic drama and modernist plays that had little chance of commercial success, such as T.S. Eliot's *Sweeney Agonistes* (1932), but it later progressed to subversive social politics and to the promotion of street performances as a way of dissociating itself from the traditional elitism of the conventional theatre. It subsequently modified its political extremism and effectively ceased to exist when Beck left the company in the mid-1980s.

Living will. A document drawn up by a person giving instructions that they are not to be kept alive by artificial means in the event of becoming severely disabled or terminally ill. The concept is of a will that defines acceptable living conditions. The idea was originally mooted in the United States in the 1960s, and the first living will was drawn up by a Chicago lawyer in 1969. Such wills were regarded as legally binding in most US States by 1990, but have yet to be tested in British courts. Their use has, however, been endorsed by the British Medical Association. *See also* EXIT.

Lizard of Oz. A nickname given by the *Sun* newspaper to the Australian Labour politician Paul Keating (b.1944), prime minister from 1991 to 1996. The name is a play on the children's story *The* WIZARD OF OZ (1900) by L. Frank Baum, the basis of the perennially popular 1939 film. Keating had incurred the tabloid's wrath through his forthright anti-British republicanism. He particularly incensed royalists when he touched the Queen's arm during a visit to Australia.

Llareggub. The little town by the sea that is the fictional setting for Dylan Thomas's 'play for voices', UNDER MILK WOOD (1954). The original title of the work was *Llareggub* (*A Piece for Radio Perhaps*), but the spelling of the town's palingrammatic name was altered after the author's death to the more delicate Llaregyb. The play was written in Thomas's home town of Laugharne, and its own name may have been the initial inspiration for the literary invention. Both places, real and fictional, are harbour towns at the mouth of a river on the Welsh coast.

Loaded question. One charged with an underlying meaning or hidden implication, as: 'Have you quite finished?' The expression dates from the 1940s.

Loadsamoney. A nickname for person flaunting excessive wealth, or for vulgar consumption in general. The character of this name created by Harry Enfield for the television comedy show *Friday Night Live* (1988) was based on observation of philistine skilled and semi-skilled working-class young people from southeast England who used their relative wealth to taunt and provoke those worse off than themselves. The catchphrase 'Loadsamoney!' was seized on by journalists and taken up by the Labour leader Neil Kinnock, who in May 1988 accused Margaret Thatcher's Conservative administration of fostering an uncaring 'loadsamoney mentality'. *See also* ESSEX MAN.

Lobby. The most general meaning of 'lobby' is an entrance hall, but in politics it has come to have a number of related meanings. In the Houses of Parliament and various other legislatures, the 'division lobbies' are corridors on either side of the two chambers, through which members pass to record their votes. Backbenchers who always vote unthinkingly for their own party are collectively known as 'lobby fodder' (on the model of 'cannon fodder', infantry who are sacrificed in an attack). At Westminster, the lobby is an informal group of journalists ('lobby correspondents') who are given briefings by politicians on a non-attributable basis (on 'lobby terms'); the name derives from the Members' Lobby at the entrance to the Commons chamber, where only MPs, officers of the House and lobby correspondents are allowed. More generally, a lobby can be a hall in a legislative building where the public can meet politicians, hence the verb 'to lobby', meaning to try to influence legislators over a particular policy; those who do this professionally are known as 'lobbyists'.

Local Defence Volunteers. *See* HOME GUARD.

Local talent. The attractive women in a region. The colloquialism dates from the Second World War.

Local yokel. A local resident, especially in a rural locality. The potentially belittling term dates from the 1950s.

Loch Ness Monster. On 22 July 1933 a grey monster some 1.8m (6ft) long was spotted crossing a road near Loch Ness, Scotland, and subsequent 'sightings' reported a strange object some distance out in the water. Descriptions of it varied, so that two years later its length was said to be nearer 6m (20ft) and its appearance a cross between a seal and a plesiosaur, with a snake-like head at the end of a long neck and two flippers near the middle of its body. From then on it became a continual object of media attention. Investigations showed no substantial evidence of the existence of the supposed monster but more recent observations have increased the belief in the presence of 'Nessie', and in 1987 a sonar scan of the loch revealed a moving object some 181kg (400lb) in weight which scientists could not identify. The ornithologist Sir Peter Scott dubbed the creature *Nessiteras rhombopteryx*, after its appearance on a photograph taken by some Americans. The name was taken to mean 'Ness monster with the diamond-shaped fin', but crossword fans soon pointed out that it was in fact an anagram of 'monster hoax by Sir Peter S'.

Lockerbie air disaster. On 21 December 1988 a Boeing 727 aircraft, PanAm flight PA 103, *en route* from London to New York, was blown up by a terrorist bomb as it passed over Lockerbie, southwest Scotland, killing all 259 passengers on board and 11 on the ground. Two Libyan suspects were named in 1991 and brought to Europe in 1999 for trial by a Scottish court at Camp Zeist in the Netherlands in 2000.

Logic bomb. A set of instructions secretly incorporated into a computer program so that when a particular set of conditions occurs the instructions will cause the system to break down. The term evolved in the 1980s in connection with the type of computer sabotage that was then becoming prevalent. Some logic bombs were inserted by disgruntled employees, who were well away by the time the fault was triggered off. Others were planted in an attempt to blackmail or to suppress evidence of fraud. The expression itself is based on 'time bomb', with 'logic' the technical term for the principles that underlie the arrangements of elements in a computer system.

Log in or **on, To.** To go through the appropriate procedures to start using a computer system. The operation in particular involves establishing one's identity. The converse, on completion of a session, is 'to log off' or 'to log out'. *See also* CLOCK IN.

> Millions of workers have already logged out and clocked off for a Christmas exodus that is expected to cost British industry more than £5 billion.
> *The Times* (23 December 1999)

Loiner. A colloquial name for a resident or native of the city of Leeds. The word dates from the 1950s and is of uncertain origin, although the Venerable Bede recorded the place-name as *Loidis* in the 8th century.

Loins of Longleat. A lubriciously punning nickname for the Marquess of Bath (b.1932), from his residence, famous for its SAFARI PARK of lions, and his many WIFELETS.

Lolita. The 12-year-old NYMPHET who is the beloved of Humbert Humbert in Vladimir Nabokov's brilliant but controversial novel that bears her name, a name subsequently used for any underage sexpot. Her full name is Dolores Haze. The book was filmed by Stanley Kubrick (1962) and Adrian Lyne (1997) but neither picture did proper justice to the original, partly because the actresses in the name part, respectively Sue Lyon and Dominique Swain, were necessarily some years older than the prototype.

> She was Lo, plain Lo, in the morning … She was Lola in slacks. She was Dolly at school. She was Dolores on

the dotted line. But in my arms she was always Lolita.

VLADIMIR NABOKOV: *Lolita*, Pt I, ch i (1955)

See also FIRST LINES OF NOVELS.

Lollipop lady or **man.** A friendly name for a school crossing patrol, so called from the pole with a red warning disc on top to halt the traffic, suggesting the lollipop confection of youthful delight. The term dates from the 1960s.

The spread of road rage has forced lollipop ladies to take protective action against angry motorists.

The Times (28 October 1999)

London Bridge. The present bridge of three spans over the Thames was built in 1967–72 and replaced the earlier five-arched one, completed in 1831. This was dismantled and in 1968 sold for $1.8 million to the McCulloch Oil Corporation, USA, who re-erected it to span an inlet on the Colorado at Lake Havasu City, Arizona. It was long rumoured that the Americans thought they were buying Tower Bridge, a canard hotly denied by the company chairman, George Mc-Culloch. The first London Bridge was probably made of wood and built during the Roman occupation.

London Eye. *See* MILLENNIUM.

London Group. A society of artists founded in 1913 by an amalgamation of the CAMDEN TOWN GROUP with various small groups and individuals. The first president was Harold Gilman (1876–1919) and apart from other former Camden Town Group artists there were those who would subsequently be associated with VORTICISM, including David Bomberg (1890–1957), Sir Jacob Epstein (1880–1959), C.R.W. Nevinson (1889–1946) and Edward Wadsworth (1889–1949). Its aim was to break away from academic tradition and to draw inspiration from French post-impressionism.

London's Burning. A SOAP OPERA about the firefighters of Blue Watch B25, Blackwall, London, first screened in 1988. The series dwelt as much on the fighters' heroics in the many spectacular conflagrations as on their domestic problems. The title comes from the old round about the Great Fire of London (1666): 'London's burning,/Look yonder,/Fire, fire,/And we have no water'.

Lone Eagle. *See* LINDBERGH, CHARLES AUGUSTUS.

Loneliness of the Long-Distance Runner, The. A novella (1959) by Alan Sillitoe (b.1928), published as the title piece of his first collection of stories. The long-distance runner is the protagonist and narrator, a lad in BORSTAL because of a 'bakery job', carrying on a running battle of wits with the governor, who sees him purely as a means to win the inter-institution cross-country race. Smith, as he is called, enters the sports ground for the final lap far ahead of his nearest rival, and then runs on the spot until he is overtaken. A compelling film version (1962) was directed by Tony Richardson and starred Tom Courtenay and Michael Redgrave.

Lonely Passion of Judith Hearne, The. A novel (1955; originally published as *Judith Hearne*), set in Belfast in the 1950s, by Brian (pronounced Bree-an) Moore (1921–99). A middle-aged Catholic spinster is let down in love and also, as she feels, by God and the Church. An intelligent film version (1987), sensitively directed by Jack Clayton, had Maggie Smith in the title role.

Lone Piners. The group of teenagers who feature in many of the children's adventure novels by the British writer Malcolm Saville (1902–82), the first being *Mystery at Witchend* (1943). The name reflects the wild settings, including rural Shropshire and the English Lake District, of many of Saville's novels.

Lonely Planet. The guidebooks of this name had their genesis in the early 1970s, when Tony Wheeler and his wife Maureen travelled as backpackers from London across Europe, the Middle East and Asia to Australia. They were soon being asked for advice from other would-be travellers, so sat down at their kitchen table in Sydney, Australia, to write an account of their trip, publishing it in 1973 as a guide to backpacking on the cheap. By the end of the century more than 400 Lonely Planet travel books had won repute for their well-researched, up-to-date information and were regarded as indispensable vade mecums by many independent travellers. The name arose by way of a mistake. Wheeler had liked a line in Joe Cocker's song 'Space Captain', 'Once while travelling across the sky this lovely planet caught my eye', but had misheard 'lovely' as 'lonely'.

Lone Ranger, The. The masked adventurer of the American west, whose 'real' name was John Reid, was the creation of George W. Trendle and Fran Striker for a US radio series that began in 1933. The Lone Ranger is an ex-Texas Ranger who has become an enforcer of law. He is honest, upright and well-spoken, and shoots only to wound, using special silver bullets. He has an Indian friend, Tonto, and a horse, Silver, whom he urges off with a cry of 'Hi-ho, Silver, awaaaaay!'

The Lone Ranger was also a nickname of the Democratic US senator Wayne Morse (1900–74), because he so often voted on the minority side. *See also* SLOANE RANGER.

Lone wolf. A person who prefers to do without the company or assistance of others. Wolves usually live in packs but some species tend to hunt alone. The term is of US origin and at the turn of the 20th century originally applied to a criminal operating alone. In the novels by Louis Joseph Vance, The Lone Wolf is a gentleman thief. His real name is Michael Lanyard, and he first appears in *The Lone Wolf* (1914). Several films followed, in which he was played by various actors including Francis Lederer, Warren William, Gerald Mohr and Ron Randell.

Long Day's Journey into Night. A PULITZER PRIZE-winning play (1956) by the US playwright Eugene O'Neill (1888–1953) depicting the four self-destructive members of the Tyrone family, who variously seek salvation in drugs and drink. The partly autobiographical work was written by O'Neill in the early 1940s but not produced until after his death. Its title reflects the time sequence within the play, which begins at 8.30 in the morning and ends around midnight on the same hot August day in 1912.

> A play of old sorrow, written in tears and blood.
> EUGENE O'NEILL: of *Long Day's Journey into Night*

Longest Day, The. A film (1962) based on the novel of the same title by Cornelius Ryan about the Allied invasion of occupied France during the Second World War. The day in question is D–DAY, 6 June 1944, when a huge Allied force landed on the beaches of Normandy and began the liberation of Europe. In an effort to ensure authenticity filming only took place when weather conditions matched those that prevailed during the actual invasion. *See also* OVERLORD.

Long Fellow. *See* DEV.

Long Good Friday, The. A highly regarded film (1980), written by Barrie Keeffe, about a London gangster boss who embarks on a mission to find out who is murdering his henchmen. Starring Bob Hoskins as crime boss Harold and Helen Mirren as his wife, Victoria, the film follows what happens in the course of a Good Friday in the early 1980s after Harold is given just 24 hours by his Mafia contacts to solve the mystery or risk a major deal with them falling through.

Long hot summer. A period of civil unrest, as that in the summer of 1967 in the United States, when riots erupted among underprivileged blacks in several cities. *The Long Hot Summer* was the title of a film of 1958 based on William Faulkner's story *The Hamlet* (1928), in which one of the chapters is headed 'The Long Summer'. The expression later evolved to denote any difficult period or enterprise, especially if it actually takes in summer. *See also* SUMMER OF LOVE.

> It looks as if it will be a long hot summer for the dons of Christ's College, Cambridge, who are once again faced with the tricky business of electing a Master.
> LADY OLGA MAITLAND in *Sunday Express* (11 July 1982)

Long johns. A US colloquialism of Second World War vintage for long woollen underpants. Half a century later *The Long Johns* was the title of a series of satirical sketches by John Bird and John Fortune in the form of face-to-face television interviews. The two took it in turn to be interviewer and interviewee, the former putting a number of forthright questions on a topical business or political issue, the latter, usually called George Parr, either evading the answer or responding shamelessly in a way that revealed startling hypocrisy, greed or inefficiency. The sketches first appeared in the 1990s in the satirical shows of the impressionist Rory Bremner.

Long March. The journey of about 9650km (6000 miles) made in 1934–5 by about 100,000 Chinese communists when they were forced out of their base at Kiangsi in southeastern China. They made their way to Shensi in northwestern China, with only some 8000 surviving the ordeal.

Longstocking, Pippi. The gawky, red-headed, athletic young girl who first appeared in the Swedish children's novel by Astrid Lindgren that bears her name (1945). (In the original she is known as Pippi Langstrump.) Pippi is an orphan who believes that her father is a South Sea cannibal king. She is so strong that she can lift policemen and horses, is very untidy and, as her name suggests, wears mismatched stockings. In a word, she is the ideal children's fantasy figure, entirely free of adult constraints or restraints and with superhuman strength. A number of sequels followed, as did four Swedish films (1969–71), in which she is played by Inger Nilsson. One of these was dubbed in English as *Pippi in the South Seas* (1974) but is so poorly made and badly dubbed that it is virtually unwatchable.

Long time no see. A mock traditional greeting to a person one has not seen for a long time. It is a form of pidgin English based on Chinese *hǎo jiǔ méi jiàn*. *See also* NO CAN DO.

> Phil, faced by Janet – Claire's friend – trembles: 'Hi, Jan, long time no see!'
> VIKRAM SETH: *The Golden Gate*, 4.9 (1986)

Lonrho. A multinational company run for many years by Tiny Rowland (born Roland Fuhrhop; 1917–98). The name of the company derives from the London and Rhodesian Mining and Land Company, with which Rowland merged his own business interests in 1961, becoming co-chief executive and managing director of the firm. In 1973 a corruption scandal involving Lonrho attracted the observation from the Conservative prime minister, Edward Heath, that this was the UNACCEPTABLE FACE OF CAPITALISM. From 1981 to 1993 Rowland owned the *Observer* Sunday newspaper and was criticized for attempting to influence editorial policy to protect his business interests in Africa. He also became involved in a vitriolic feud with the Al Fayed brothers, his successful rivals in a bid to buy Harrods. He ceased being managing director of Lonrho in 1994, following a long-running row within the company.

Loo. This common euphemism for a lavatory or toilet dates from the 1940s but is of much disputed origin. One theory is that the word puns on *Waterloo* as the trade name of a make of iron water cistern in the early years of the 20th century. Professor A.S.C. Ross appears to favour this origin in his examination of possible sources in *Blackwood's Magazine* for October 1974. Other proposals, which should almost all be taken with a grain of salt, include the following:

1. From French *lieu*, 'place', as in the now dated euphemism, *lieux d'aisances*, 'places of ease'

2. From French *l'eau*, 'water'

3. From *gardyloo*, from French *gardez l'eau*, 'beware of the water', a cry in old Edinburgh when emptying the contents of a chamber pot from a high window into the street below

4. From *bordalou*, a type of 18th-century portable commode carried by ladies in their muff when travelling, supposedly from the name of Louis Bourdaloue (1632–1704), a fashionable but prolix Jesuit preacher

5. From the name of Lady Louise Hamilton, said to have been fixed to a lavatory door in Dublin in 1870

6. From *louvre*, referring to the slatted doors of some lavatories

7. From *leeward*, as the side of a boat (downwind) from which one would logically urinate

8. From an abbreviated form of the word 'lavatory' itself

Yet one more ingenious explanation is offered by Peter Lyon, writer of a letter to William and Mary Morris, authors of the *Morris Dictionary of Word and Phrase Origins* (1977), and reproduced in their second edition (1988):

> When I was in England researching a biography of Eisenhower, I spent a day with Brigadier Sir James Gault [(1902–77)], who had been Eisenhower's British aide during the war. When I mentioned that I had researched *loo* in the British Museum and found your theories and a couple of others, Lady Gault said they were all wrong. She explained that after the first Great War, when the Bright Young People began to cross the Channel again to France, they naturally stopped at French hotels. The French numbered the rooms from 1, say, to 12 on the first floor, picking up with 13 through 25 on the second, then on to 26 through 40 on the third. On each floor would be one room marked 00, which, of course, was the bathroom. Now, said Lady Gault, the British visitors simply prefaced that 00 with the appropriate French *l*, and so fetched up with *l*'00 or *loo*. That certainly is a more elegant explanation.

Lookalike. A person who looks like another, especially when the other is a celebrity. A surprising number of people aspire to be convincing impersonators of the famous and may be seen in pubs and clubs and on stage and television as the *alter ego* of their idol. Some manage a convincing evocation in more than just appearance. In 1979 Susan Scott Lookalikes was set up to exploit the commercial potential of the concept, engaging Jeanette Charles to impersonate the queen, Vicki Scott to incarnate Marilyn Monroe and Kenny Whymark to pose as Humphrey Bogart. Other agencies followed and celebrity lookalikes were soon a standard feature at corporate functions, their fee being a mere tithe of that demanded by their eponym for a personal appearance.

> The *New Woman* party shoot is in full swing in the basement. A Daryl Hannah lookalike poses in a sequinned miniskirt and bikini top.
> *The Times* (21 September 1999)

Look and lick brigade. A nickname for tourists in the mass, especially the British, who look cursorily about them in some sightworthy place while licking an ice cream.

They call them the Look and Lick brigade, the day-trippers who swamp Cambridge every summer, buy an ice cream, wander around King's College Chapel, then disappear.
The Times (31 July 1999)

Look away now. A light-hearted request for someone to avert their eyes, from the catchphrase used by television sports reporters – in full, 'Look away now if you don't want to know the score' – when about to show the result of a match yet to be broadcast, so as not to spoil the anticipation of intending viewers. The phrase is sometimes humorously adopted by journalists and columnists.

He saw *The Beach*, a story of in-fighting among a tribe of young idealists. At the climax – look away now if you don't want to know – the gang leader tries to kill the rebellious hero.
Evening Standard (21 February 2000)

Look Back In Anger. A play (1956) by John Osborne (1929–94) about a young man's dissatisfaction with his marriage, his life and the world in general, in particular the hidebound conventions of the older generation. Jimmy Porter, the play's protagonist, represented the restless, frustrated youth of the immediate postwar generation, and the controversial play helped to establish Osborne as the archetypal ANGRY YOUNG MAN. The title of the play resurfaced in 1996 in 'Don't Look Back in Anger', a hit song by the British rock band Oasis.

I doubt if I could love anyone who did not wish to see *Look Back in Anger*. It is the best play of its decade.
KENNETH TYNAN

Look like death warmed up, To. *See* FEEL LIKE DEATH WARMED UP.

Look over someone's shoulder, To. To be uninterested in them or in what they are saying or doing; to have one's mind on something else. The image is of a bored lover in an embrace.

Supermodels refused to sleep with him. Even the bog-standard girl about town looked over his shoulder at parties.
The Times (4 February 2000)

Look who's talking! You're a fine one to say that! A phrase implying that the original speaker is in no position to judge the other. The expression became current in the 1940s.

Looney Tunes. The title under which WARNER BROTHERS released their many cartoon shorts from the 1930s, featuring such characters as BUGS BUNNY, Daffy Duck, Porky the Pig and Tweetie Pie.

We are especially not going to tolerate these attacks from outlaw states run by the strangest collection of misfits, Looney Tunes, and squalid criminals since the advent of the Third Reich.
RONALD REAGAN: speech following the hijack of a US plane (8 July 1985)

Loon pants. Close-fitting flared trousers, popular in the 1970s. The name derives either from the slang verb 'to loon', to fool around, to act irresponsibly, itself perhaps from 'loony', or from 'pantaloon'.

Loony Benn. *See* LOONY LEFT; WEDGIE.

Loony left. A term coined by the popular press in the late 1970s to describe the more hard-line activists of the LABOUR PARTY, whether MPs or trade union activists. Notable among them were Tony Benn (b.1925), Ken Livingstone (b.1945) and Bernie Grant (1944–2000). Their influence had largely evaporated by the general election of 1992. 'Loony' is 'lunatic'. *See also* RED KEN.

Loop the loop, To. The air pilot's term for the manoeuvre that consists of describing a perpendicular circle in the air. At the top of the circle, or loop, the pilot is upside down. The term is from a kind of switchback once popular at fairs in which a moving car or bicycle performed a similar revolution on a perpendicular circular track.

Loose cannon. An unpredictable or uncontrolled person who may unintentionally cause damage. The phrase dates only from the 1970s but alludes to an unsecured cannon on a warship, which is liable to career unpredictably across the deck with the rolling or pitching of the ship. The expression is of US origin and is frequently applied to military personnel. It was used of General Alexander Haig (*see* HAIGSPEAK) in the Reagan administration and of Colonel Oliver North (b.1943), implicated in the Irangate scandal (*see* GATE), under the same administration.

In the upper echelons of The Parachute Regiment, Colonel Wilford is regarded as a loose cannon and out of control.
The Times (7 July 1999)

Loose lips sink ships. A US government security slogan in the Second World War. *See also* BE LIKE DAD, KEEP MUM.

Lord Emsworth. *See* EMSWORTH, LORD.

Lord Haw-Haw. *See* HAW-HAW, LORD.

Lord Jim. A novel (1900) by Joseph Conrad (1857–1924). Jim (we never know his second name) is a young ship's officer who leaps overboard in a crisis to save himself. In order to expiate his guilt, he wanders from place to place in the East, finally settling in a remote part of Malaya, where his integrity earns him the respect he has craved. A visitor asks:

> 'What's his name? Jim! Jim! That's not enough for a man's name.'
>
> 'They call him,' said Cornelius, scornfully, 'Tuan Jim here. As you may say Lord Jim.'

A worthy film version (1964) of the novel was directed by Richard Brooks.

Lord love a duck! Good Lord! A mild expression of surprise dating from the early years of the 20th century. The words are an elaboration of 'Lord lumme' ('Lord love me').

Lord Love-a-Duck of Limehouse. The title that Clement Attlee (1883–1967), Labour prime minister (1945–51), said he would take should he ever be elevated to the peerage. LORD LOVE A DUCK is a Cockney expression of disbelief, and Limehouse is an area in the Cockney East End of London. When Attlee resigned as LABOUR PARTY leader in 1955 he actually became 1st earl Attlee of Walthamstow, Viscount Prestwood.

Lord Lucan. *See* LUCAN, LORD.

Lord Muck. A pompous or self-opinionated man. He assumes the air of a lord but is 'as common as muck'. The expression is a variant of the earlier 'Lord High Muck-a-Muck', where the name probably represents Chinook *hiyu muckamuck*, 'plenty of food'. *See also* LADY MUCK.

Lord of the Flies. A novel (1954) by William Golding (1911–93), illustrating how internal and external pressures can cause a society to disintegrate, exemplified in this case by a group of schoolboys marooned on an island. The title represents one interpretation of the Hebrew term for Beelzebub, who appears in 2 Kings 1:2 as Baal-zebub, a Caananite god whose shrine is at Ekron, and in the New Testament as 'prince of the devils' (Matthew 12:24). In the story itself, the name 'Lord of the Flies' is applied to the fly-infested pig's head that the boys impale on a stick. A rather crude film version (1963) was directed by Peter Brook, and a US remake (1990) was little better. *See also* FIRST LINES OF NOVELS.

Lord of the Rings, The. The title of J.R.R. Tolkien's sequel (1954–5) to *The* HOBBIT (1937). It is also the title of SAURON the Great, the ruler of MIDDLE-EARTH, whose power depended on the possession of certain rings, especially the One Ring, the Ruling Ring, the Master Ring, which he had lost many years ago and which he now sought to regain to give him strength to cover the land in a second darkness. This ring had eventually come into the hands of the hobbit Bilbo BAGGINS, who passed it on to FRODO Baggins, his adopted heir. If Sauron recovered it, the Hobbits would be doomed, and the only way to destroy the ring was to find the Cracks of Doom and cast it into the volcano Orodruin, the 'Fire-mountain'. The saga essentially concerns Frodo's struggles, trials and adventures to achieve this. *See also* FIRST LINES OF NOVELS; GONDOR; MINAS MORGUL; MORDOR; SHIRE.

Lord Peter Wimsey. *See* WIMSEY, LORD PETER.

Lord Porn. A media nickname for Frank Pakenham, 7th earl of Longford (b.1905). The name derived from his campaigns against pornography and other aspects of the PERMISSIVE SOCIETY, which took him on a 'fact-finding' mission to investigate the sex industry in Scandinavia, accompanied by a mob of gleeful journalists.

Lord's Taverners. An amateur cricket team founded in 1950 by a group of actors with the aim of raising money for charitable causes. It was named after the Tavern at Lord's cricket ground in London. The group now includes many show business personalities and professional cricketers and conducts a wide range of fund-raising events to raise money to encourage cricket at a grass-roots level, particularly among the young. It also raises money for disabled children, and those with special needs.

Lord Suit. *Private Eye*'s nickname for the successful businessman David Ivor Young (b.1932), one of the MEN IN SUITS, on whom Margaret Thatcher bestowed the title Lord Young of Graffham in 1984 in order to bring him into her government. He was initially minister without portfolio (1984–5) and subsequently served as secretary of state for employment (1985–7), and then for trade and industry (1987–9). He was deputy chairman of the Conservative Party(1989–90) before returning to the private sector.

Lorelei Lee. *See* LEE, LORELEI.

Lose it, To. To lose one's temper or self-control momentarily, 'it' being either of these. The expression dates from the 1970s. *See also* LOSE ONE'S COOL.

Dale told police there had been ill feeling between the two girls dating from this year's Mid Lent Fair. 'She said the girl was laughing at her and she just lost it,' Mr Grys said.

Stamford Mercury (28 May 1999)

Lose one's cherry, To. To lose one's virginity. The image is of ripeness rather than any physical resemblance. The expression dates from the 1930s. To take someone's cherry is thus the converse. The metaphor has led some modern academics to reach a purely sexual construal for J.E. Millais' well-known painting *Cherry Ripe* (1879), a portrait of a small girl seated next to a bunch of cherries, not merely on the basis of the title but also from certain supposedly sexually significant details in the picture itself (Pamela Tamarkin Reis and Laurel Bailey in *Victorian Studies*, vol 24, no. 2, Winter 1991). More directly, however, the title could simply derive from Robert Herrick's poem *Cherry-Ripe* (1648), beginning "Cherry-ripe, ripe, ripe, I cry," itself the call of a street vendor. The visual imagery is even so familiar enough to many and has been drawn upon in modern times by cartoonists, advertisers and others to impart a salacious gloss to their work.

A jump cut [in a television commercial] takes us to a nunnery, where 'Brother Damian' is offered a basket of cherries by a beautiful nun. The Devil takes the nun's cherry. Fnaar! Fnaar!

The Times (17 December 1999)

Lose one's cool, To. To lose one's temper or self-control. 'Cool' here means 'composure', 'poise', and originated as a term used in the 1960s among US street gangs for a temporary armistice between rival gangs, who were thus for a time no longer heated. *See also* COOL IT; LOSE IT.

Lose one's gills, To. To mature; to gain experience and wisdom as one grows older. The analogy is with a tadpole, which loses its gills soon after hatching as it grows into a frog.

Miss India said that if she won she hoped 'to evolve as a person'. She did win and is losing her gills even as you read this.

The Times (6 December 1999)

Lose one's marbles, To. To become mentally unhinged. The origin of the phrase is uncertain. One suggestion is that it derives from a story about a boy whose marbles were carried off by a monkey. An unlikely derivation is in rhyming slang, as if 'marbles and conkers', two popular children's games, represented BONKERS. The expression dates from the 1920s.

At a time when the Prime Minister seems to be losing his marbles, a Hague–Portillo alliance could be as effective and formidable as was the Blair–Brown alliance before 1997.

The Times (2 November 1999)

Lose one's rag, To. To lose one's temper. The allusion is to the 'red rag' or tongue, which is unbridled when one is in a rage.

Lose the plot, To. To lose one's way in a situation; to miss the meaning. The expression dates from the 1980s and may allude to a film director who, after an auspicious debut, lost his sense of direction.

As the elite of America gorge on an unprecedented run of spectacular stock market flotations, one question begs to be asked. Have Wall Street bankers lost the plot?

The Times (20 December 1999)

Loss leaders. A term of US origin dating from the 1920s for articles offered for sale below normal prices, usually in department stores and supermarkets, with the aim of attracting customers, who will then be drawn to make other purchases at unreduced prices. The theory is that the losses incurred will be more than made up by the greater number of sales at normal prices.

Lost Gardens of Heligan. In early 1990 a group of entrepreneurs looking for land near St Austell, Cornwall, to start a rare breeds farm stumbled across the remains of an extensive area of gardens and woodland, neglected for half a century. The gardens, occupying some 63ha (157 acres), were created by the Tremayne family over the years from 1780 to 1914, but the First World War brought ruin following the death of many estate workers and new tenants after the war could not afford to maintain the grounds. Painstaking restoration and reconstruction began following the discovery, and by the end of the century the gardens were open in all their re-created glory to the public.

Lost Generation. A name sometimes applied to the young men, especially of the cultivated upper and middle classes, who lost their lives in the First World War. According to James R. Mellow's *Charmed Circle* (1974) the phrase originated with Gertrude Stein (1874–1946), who on one occasion in the south of France heard a French garage owner address his incompetent mechanics as *une génération perdue*. She herself applied the term to the disillusioned US writers, such as F. Scott Fitzgerald, Ezra Pound and

Ernest Hemingway, who went to live in Paris in the 1920s, and Hemingway himself used the words 'You are all a lost generation' to preface *The Sun Also Rises* (1924). *See also* BARNES, JAKE.

Lost in the shuffle. Overlooked or missed in the mêlée or multitude. The reference is to a card missed in a shuffle of the pack. The expression is of US origin and dates from the 1930s.

Lost weekend. One spent in dissolute living or drunkenness. The expression was popularized by Charles Jackson's bestselling novel *The* LOST WEEKEND (1944).

> The legends of [actor Robbie] Coltrane's dissolution in the old days, the three-day benders and lost weekends, suggest both a lust for life and profound contempt of it.
> *Sunday Times Magazine* (28 November 1999)

Lost Weekend, The. A film (1945) adapted by director Billy Wilder and Charles Brackett from a novel (1944) by Charles R. Jackson about a struggling writer who surrenders to alcoholism one weekend after he falls victim to writer's block. Starring Ray Milland, the film caused a considerable stir: representatives of the liquor industry offered $5 million for the negative, so that it could be destroyed, fearing the effect it would have upon sales of alcohol, and members of the temperance movement also tried to have the film banned, suspecting that it might actually encourage people to drink.

Lost World. *See* MAPLE WHITE LAND.

LOTS. The acronym of Left On The Shelf, a campaign group formed by Tottenham Hotspur football club supporters in 1988 to prevent the club from replacing the middle terrace area of the East Stand, known as 'The Shelf', at their home ground, White Hart Lane, with seating and executive boxes. The campaign delayed the work and meant that Tottenham were unable to play their opening fixture of the 1988–9 season against Coventry City. As a result they had two points deducted, although this penalty was later commuted to a £15,000 fine. LOTS and the club eventually reached a compromise, albeit a short-lived one, whereby some of the area would be retained for standing spectators. In 1994 the area was finally converted to seating.

Lotus position. In yoga a sitting position with the legs folded and intertwined and the hands resting on the knees. The expression translates Sanskrit *padmasana*, from *padma*, 'lotus', and *asana*, 'posture'. The allusion is to the lotus leaf, which rests on water without becoming wet, so giving an impression of detachment.

Lounge lizard. A popular phrase in the 1920s to describe a young man, a gigolo, who spends his time dancing and waiting upon rich women, typically in the lounge of a grand hotel. A lizard is colourful, reptilian, and 'suns' itself as if lazily lounging. The term has been attributed by some to the US cartoonist Tad Dorgan (*see* CAT'S PYJAMAS).

Lovat green. A muted green colour found mainly in tweed and woollen garments. The name is that of the hamlet of Lovat on the River Beauly west of Inverness, Scotland, where the cloth was made at the turn of the 20th century.

♥ Pictorial shorthand for 'love' in such slogans as 'I ♥ DOGS', using the playing-card 'heart' symbol. It was originally popularized as 'I ♥ New York', a slogan promoted in 1977 by the New York State Department of Commerce.

> 'I ♣ winos', 'I ♥ L.A.'
> Or 'Have you hugged your whale today?'
> VIKRAM SETH: *The Golden Gate*, 2.12 (1986)

Loveable rogue. A wrongdoer or even criminal whom one admires for their attractive qualities or enterprise, which to some extent redeem them from their transgressions.

> The voters always love a man of energy and wit, he [Jeffrey Archer] calculated, just as the readers of fiction cannot help admiring a loveable rogue.
> *Sunday Times* (21 November 1999)

Love-bombing. A style of recruitment practised by some religious cults, notably in the United States. Potential members are saturated with expressions of love, care and beguiling idealism. The term expresses the intensive CHARM OFFENSIVE used to bring about a capitulation. The strategy is also known as FLIRTY FISHING.

Love for or **of Three Oranges, The.** The comic opera by Sergei Prokofiev (1891–1953) with a text by the composer was based on a 1761 comedy by Carlo Gozzi (1720–1806). The oranges of the title are taken into the desert by a prince; each contains a princess, two of whom die of thirst, but the third survives and is united with the prince. The work was first performed in 1921.

Love handles. Bunches of excess fat at the waist, which one's lover can grasp. The term dates from the 1970s. *See also* SADDLEBAGS.

Eating chocolate, so far from melting away the pounds, will give you unattractive love handles.
New Statesman (10 May 1999)

Love–hate relationship. A relationship characterized by ambivalent feelings of love and hate by one or both of two people. It frequently exists between a child and a parent and is typically found between a daughter and her father. The term originated as psychoanalysts' jargon in the 1920s. The two words form one of the commonest pairs of antonyms. Certain macho males have 'LOVE' tattooed on the knuckles of one hand and 'HATE' on the other, the idea presumably being that one can stroke with the one and strike with the other. The concept itself is an ancient one, as expressed in the 1st century BC by Catullus: *Odi et amo* ('I hate and I love') (*Carmina* No. 85). *See also* MAN YOU LOVE TO HATE.

My relationship with him [the writer's father] is complicated. It's love-hate – but with far more emphasis on the love. We've had flaming rows, but always make it up with tears and hugs.
Sunday Times Magazine (19 September 1999)

Love in a Cold Climate. A light novel (1949) by Nancy Mitford (1904–1973), whose narrative takes place at about the same time as that of her first novel, *The Pursuit of Love* (1945) and which concerns some of the same characters. The environment is that of the eccentric, impoverished, aristocratic society in which she was brought up. The novel was originally to have been called 'Diversion'. The final title recalls the remark made by the poet Robert Southey (1774–1843) in a letter to his brother about Mary Wollstonecraft's letters from Sweden and Norway: 'She has made me in love with a cold climate, and frost and snow, with a northern moonlight' (28 April 1797).

Love Is a Many-Splendored Thing. A film (1955) based on a novel (1952) by Han Suyin depicting the doomed relationship between a US journalist (played in the film by William Holden) and a Eurasian doctor (Jennifer Jones). Han Suyin disliked the film, as did most of the critics, which is remembered mainly for the OSCAR-winning theme song. The title came originally from a poem by Francis Thompson:

The angels keep their ancient places;
Turn but a stone and start a wing!
'Tis ye, 'tis your estrangèd faces,
That miss the many-splendoured thing.
FRANCIS THOMPSON: 'The Kingdom of God' (1913)

Lovejoy. An antiques dealer who doubles as an amateur detective in the comic mystery novels by Jonathan Gash (real name John Grant). He narrates his own adventures but does not reveal his first name. Titles in the series include *The Judas Pair* (1977), *Gold from Gemini* (1978), *The Grail Tree* (1979), *Spend Game* (1980), *The Vatican Rip* (1981), *Firefly Gadroon* (1982), *The Sleepers of Erin* (1983), *The Gondola Scam* (1984) and *The Tartan Ringers* (1986). A somewhat sanitized version of the raunchy original stories was screened as a television series from 1986 to 1994 with Ian McShane in the name part.

Lovely jubbly. Good! Excellent! In the 1990s a general term of approval, popularized by the character 'Del Boy' in the television SITCOM ONLY FOOLS AND HORSES. The phrase is more narrowly used as a slang term for money or wealth, and has its roots in an advertising slogan of the 1950s for an orange drink called 'Jubbly' (presumably a blend of 'juice' and 'bubbly'). The second word is not thus simply a meaningless rhyme on the first.

Lovely Rita. A jolly song that appears on the BEATLES album SERGEANT PEPPER'S LONELY HEARTS CLUB BAND, credited to John Lennon and Paul McCartney. The Rita (METER MAID) of the title is based on a real-life encounter McCartney had with a traffic warden called Meta Davis in St John's Wood, London.

Love of Three Oranges. *See* LOVE FOR THREE ORANGES.

Love on the Dole. The first novel (1933) by Walter Greenwood (1903–74), set in the industrial town of Salford, where he was brought up. For one man, an apprenticeship leads only to the dole queue and a life of poverty when his girlfriend becomes pregnant. For another, marriage is on the cards when he is made redundant, and he dies after being beaten up while participating in a mass protest. His fiancée, who has to support an out-of-work brother and father, chooses to be the mistress of a local businessman rather than plumb the depths of poverty. A depressing film version (1941) was directed by John Baxter.

Love rat. A condemnatory nickname for a man who abandons his wife or girlfriend for another.

The handsome captain of the England rugby team [Will Carling] went from being a likeable lad to a loathsome 'love rat' for walking out on his girlfriend Ali Cockayne and their 21-month-old baby Henry.
Sunday Times (26 September 1999)

Lover boy. A lover; an attractive man or boy; a woman-chaser. The phrase is frequently used as a term of address to one who is this last.

Lovers' acronyms. Love letters between couples or spouses have long carried coded messages of passion, in particular when the man is away from home on military service. The following are some of the more modern examples, mostly based on names of countries:

> BOLTOP: Better on lips than on paper (of a kiss)
>
> BURMA: Be undressed ready, my angel
>
> EGYPT: Eager to grab your pretty tits
>
> HOLLAND: Hope our love lasts and never dies
>
> ITALY: I trust and love you
>
> MALAYA: My anxious lips await your arrival
>
> NORWICH: (K)nickers off ready when I come home
>
> POLAND: Please open lovingly and never destroy

Love Song of J. Alfred Prufrock, The. A poem by the Anglo-American poet T.S. Eliot (1888–1965), first published in the United States in 1915 in the magazine *Poetry* and in Britain in 1917 in the collection *Prufrock and Other Observations*. It depicts the doubts and sexual inhibitions of a shy Bostonian by the name of J. Alfred Prufrock. Eliot took the name of his celebrated central character from that of a St Louis furniture company.

> I grow old ... I grow old ...
> I shall wear the bottoms of my trousers rolled ...
> I have heard the mermaids singing, each to each.
> I do not think that they will sing to me
> T.S. ELIOT: 'The Love Song of J. Alfred Prufrock'

Love Story. A tear-jerking film (1970) based on the novel of the same title by Erich Segal about the romance that blossoms between a young man and woman but that ends prematurely with her death. Starring Ryan O'Neal as Oliver and Ali MacGraw as Jenny, the film was publicized as the ultimate 'weepie', and stories were told of boxes of tissues being sold in cinema foyers for the use of distraught audiences. A sequel, *Oliver's Story* (1979), failed to excite much interest. *See also* TEAR JERKER.

> Love means never having to say you're sorry.
> ERICH SEGAL: *Love Story* (Oliver speaking)

Love that dares not speak its name. Homosexual love. The expression originated in the poem 'Two Loves' (1896) by Lord Alfred Douglas, intimate of Oscar Wilde: 'I am the Love that dare [*sic*] not speak its

name.' The phrase was later adopted to apply to any 'secret' love or loyalty.

> Why nationalist sentiments should be seen as a threat rather than simple patriotism is hard to explain. At a recent conference on national identities, held in Edinburgh, one speaker called it 'the love that dares not speak its name'.
> *The Times* (21 October 1999)

Love Thy Neighbour. A television SITCOM screened from 1972 to 1976 and centring on the relationships that develop between Eddie Booth, a jingoistic, beer-swilling socialist, played by Jack Smethurst, and his wife Joan, played by Kate Williams, and their newly arrived next-door neighbours, the West Indian couple Bill and Barbie Reynolds, played by Rudolph Walker and Nina Baden-Semper. The script's blatantly racist content, although intended comically, would never have been tolerated in the climate of POLITICAL COR-RECTNESS that prevailed a decade later, despite the title's biblical adjuration (Mark 12:31).

Love you! A more or less meaningless 'sign-off' on parting or at the end of a telephone conversation.

Lower 48. A name for the 48 states of the continental United States excluding Alaska, so called as all lying south of or below the latter.

> People arrive steadily. And people go. They go from Anchorage and Fairbanks [in Alaska] ... Some, of course, are interested only in a year or two's work, then to return with saved high wages to the Lower Forty-eight.
> *New Yorker* (20 June 1977)

Lowest form of animal life. Literally the simplest form of biological life, generally taken to be protozoa. In the 20th century the phrase came to apply figuratively to any despised person or group of people, 'the lowest of the low'. In the film *Mutiny on the Bounty* (1935) a midshipman is described as the 'lowest form of animal life in the navy'.

LSD. Lysergic acid diethylamide, a powerful hallucinogenic drug, colloquially known as acid. It was formulated in 1943 by the Swiss biochemist Albert Hoffman, who notoriously experienced its disorientating effect when riding his bicycle through the streets of Basle. It was the favoured PSYCHEDELIC drug among the young in the latter half of the 1960s.

L7. SQUARE. If the thumb and forefinger of the left hand form a letter L and the thumb and forefinger of the right hand form a figure 7, the two joined together will form a square. The expression arose as black or teenage American slang in the 1950s. A RIOT GRRLS rock band of this name was formed in Los Angeles in 1985.

Lubbock's Law. In literature the principle that the point of view of a novel's heroine must be such that a female reader can readily identify with it. The concept was formulated by the critic and biographer Percy Lubbock (1879–1965), author of *The Craft of Fiction* (1921). The narratives of most MILLS & BOON novels obey Lubbock's Law at a popular level.

Lubyanka. The building off Dzerzhinsky Square, Moscow, that was the headquarters of the KGB and other Russian-Soviet state security organs. It also served as a prison and execution centre. Before the 1917 Revolution the building housed two insurance companies, 'Anchor' and 'Russia'. After 1917 these were taken over by the Soviet insurance company *Gosstrakh*, short for *gosudarstvennoye strakhovaniye*, 'state insurance'. In Russian the second half of the acronym, *strakh*, happens to mean 'terror', and with typical wry humour Soviet citizens would pun, 'It used to be *Gosstrakh* but now it's *Gosuzhas*', i.e. 'It used to be state terror but now it's state horror.'

Lucan, Lord. Richard John Bingham, 7th Earl of Lucan (b.1934), nicknamed 'Lucky' for his success at the gaming table, allegedly murdered the family nanny, Sandra Rivett, following an attack on his estranged wife in 1974. He then disappeared, and was long sought without success. In 1999 his family was granted probate by the High Court and he was officially declared dead in a document stating: 'Be it known that the Right Honourable Richard John Bingham, Seventh Earl of Lucan, of 72a Elizabeth Street, London SW1, died on or since the 8th day of November 1974.'

Luck of the draw. The outcome of chance rather than of design. The allusion is to the random drawing of a playing card. The expression dates from the 1950s.

Lucky Country. A nickname for Australia, originating from the title of Donald Horne's *The Lucky Country* (1964), a critique of contemporary Australian society and a considered definition of the 'Australian dream'. The name was originally intended ironically, and Horne saw Australia as 'a lucky country run mainly by second-rate people who share its luck'.

Lucky Jim. The first novel (1954) by Kingsley Amis (1922–95), recording the tribulations of Jim Dixon, a lecturer in history at a new university. 'Lucky' is in turn a justifiable and an ironic description of his

fortunes. Although it was not the first of the wave of novels that gave their authors the sobriquet ANGRY YOUNG MAN, it was the one that did most to suggest the existence of such a movement. The title comes from a US song by Frederick Bowen and Charles Horwitz, which tells how a man waited for his childhood friend to die so that he could marry the girl they both wanted. Unhappily married, however, he wishes he were also dead: 'Oh, lucky Jim, how I envy him.' A film version (1957) was directed by John Boulting, with Ian Carmichael in the title role. *See also* FIRST LINES OF NOVELS.

Lucy in the Sky with Diamonds. A dreamily PSYCHEDELIC song that appears on the BEATLES album SERGEANT PEPPER'S LONELY HEARTS CLUB BAND, and is credited to John Lennon and Paul McCartney. The title comes from a drawing by Lennon's four-year-old son Julian. Despite the patently psychedelic nature of the lyric and its musical ambience, and the coincidence of the song's initials with those of the hallucinogenic drug LSD, it seems that no allusion to LSD was intended by the Beatles. This notwithstanding, the song was banned by the BBC for the alleged reference. The song also reflects Lennon's obsession with the hallucinatory world of Lewis Carroll in *Through the Looking-Glass* (1872), the latter being a favourite text of the counterculture of the 1960s.

Lucy Stoner. A woman who declines to adopt her husband's surname when she marries. The exemplar for this action was the US feminist Lucy Stone (1818–93), who continued to use her own name on marrying Henry Blackwell in 1855. In 1879, when women in Massachusetts were allowed to vote in school district elections, Lucy Stone registered in her own name, but the Board of Registrars removed her name from the voting list. The Lucy Stone League was subsequently founded by Ruth Hale, who similarly refused to change her name after marrying Heywood Broun in 1917. The term Lucy Stoner appears in some pre-1960 American dictionaries.

Luftwaffe (German, 'air weapon'). The German Air Force, first officially mentioned in a proclamation by Goering in May 1935, although it had in fact existed since 1933. It was configured primarily to fly in support of ground forces, and its Ju–87 STUKA dive-bomber was its principal ground-attack aircraft in the Spanish Civil War (1936–9) and the opening years of the Second World War. The postwar Luftwaffe was formed in 1956. *See also* BATTLE OF BRITAIN.

Luke Skywalker. *See* STAR WARS.

Lulu. The central character in a duet of plays, *The Earth Spirit*, originally *Erdgeist* (1895), and *Pandora's Box*, originally *Die Büchse der Pandora* (1903), by the German playwright Frank Wedekind (1864–1918). The plays are about the sexual career of Lulu, a dancer, and although her uninhibited enjoyment of sex is essentially innocent, her character has gone down as a symbol of feminine guile and eroticism, whose licentiousness proves fatal to the men who fall for her. At the close of the second play she is reduced to working as a prostitute in London and meets her end at the hands of Jack the Ripper. The character was suggested to Wedekind by the women he met while he was working on a ballet for the Folies Bergère in Paris around the turn of the century. Her name was probably intended to recall that of the biblical Lilith, Adam's rebellious first wife.

The opera, also named *Lulu*, by Alban Berg (1885–1935) was based on Wedekind's two plays, and it was first performed in Zurich in 1937 in the original two-act form in which the composer had left it at the time of his death. The missing third act was supplied by the Viennese composer Friedrich Cerha (b.1926), and the full work finally emerged in Paris in 1979 under the baton of the French composer and conductor Pierre Boulez.

Lumpectomy. A surgical operation to remove a tumour ('lump') from the breast, typically when cancer is present but has not yet spread. The procedure, employed since the early 1970s, is obviously an improvement on the traditional mastectomy, which entails the amputation of the entire breast. The term is an ugly combination of English 'lump' and classical Greek '-ectomy', from the root word meaning 'excision' (literally 'cutting out'). Most medical terms with this element have a Greek specific, as 'mastectomy' itself (Greek *mastos*, 'breast'). Although *phuma* exists as Greek for 'tumour', presumably the English word was preferred as less intimidating.

Lumps or bumps. A medical euphemism for growths or swellings on or in the human body. 'Lumps and bumps' is also a colloquialism for a woman's breasts and the natural curves of the female figure, especially when regarded as disproportionate.

> It's for the rest of the gender, those of us who are an average size 14–16 and have lumps and bumps that can be disguised only with the help of clever clothing.
> *Sunday Times* (7 November 1999)

Luna Park. An amusement centre opened on Coney Island, New York, in 1903. It presented a world of fantasy in which, as the name implies, the moon played a key role. In 1904 a highly popular show 'Trip to the Moon' opened, in which visitors in a darkened theatre watched passengers embarking on an imaginary trip through outer space. The park burned down in 1944 but meanwhile the name had been adopted for amusement centres elsewhere, such as a fun parlour that opened in Sydney, Australia, in 1935, and that in its day was regarded as a classic example of fairground art.

Lunar landscape. An alliterative cliché for any bleak or barren-looking region, the imagery being that of the Moon during its close-up photographic observation in the 1960s.

Lunatic fringe. The small section of the community who follow and originate extremist ideas and whose behaviour is sometimes eccentric by conventional standards but whose influence on the majority is mostly minimal. The expression is attributed to President Theodore Roosevelt, who in a letter of 1913 to Henry Cabot Lodge commenting on the defeat of the Bull Moose Party, a faction of the Republican Party, in the previous year's election, wrote: 'There is apt to be a lunatic fringe among the votaries of any forward movement.' *See also* LOONY LEFT; MONSTER RAVING LOONY PARTY.

Lunchbox. A mildly amusing term for the male genitals, especially when prominently outlined beneath tight trousers or shorts. The word is an elaboration of 'box' as a term for a light shield to protect a sports player's genitals and was applied by the *Sun* in various headlines of the mid-1990s to the athlete Linford Christie (b.1960). The alliteration with his first name afforded an added attraction.

> He pranced around the stage with co-host Jenna Elfman but, unlike Elfman, who had a modest and tiny skirt-effect covering her, David [Hyde Pierce] bravely exposed his lunchbox area.
> *heat* (23–29 September 1999)

Lupin, Arsène. The gentleman thief turned gentleman detective in the stories and novels of Maurice Leblanc, beginning with *Arsène Lupin, gentleman cambrioleur* (1908). He is a French blend of E.W. Hornung's Raffles and Arthur Conan Doyle's Sherlock Holmes and the latter actually appears in some of the stories under the name 'Herlock Sholmès'. Many of the books have been translated into English and there have been movie versions of Lupin's exploits, beginning with five German films of 1910–11. A French television series duly followed in the 1970s.

Lusitania. The Cunard liner made its last voyage on 1 May 1915, carrying 1959 passengers from Liverpool to New York, its regular run since 1907. Approaching the Irish coast the vessel was struck by two German torpedoes and sank in 18 minutes with the tragic loss of 1198 lives. Both the *Lusitania* and the TITANIC became unforgettable symbols of maritime disaster.

Luv. A colloquial written form of 'love' adopted from the 1950s to indicate casual or local speech ('There you are, luv') or to sign off a private note or letter ('Luv, Nick'). *See also* LUVVY.

Luvvy. A humorous or with some speakers even derogatory term for an actor or actress, as a form of the affectionate vocative 'lovey'. The word first began to appear in print in the early 1990s. It encapsulates the supposed demonstrativeness or flamboyance of theatre folk and the frequent terms of endearment used by and between them. The film director Sir Richard Attenborough (b.1923) is sometimes cited as a prime example of the type, with his regular recourse to 'darling' as a stock form of address to males and females alike.

> Sir Ian McKellen, the revered thespian, has caused uproar among luvvies for refusing to assist a Cambridge theatre company that helped to launch his career.
>
> *The Times* (2 November 1999)

Luxe, calme et volupté. The hedonistic painting of nude bathers on a beach by Henri Matisse (1869–1954) was painted with a free pointillist technique in St Tropez in 1904–5. The title comes from the refrain of the poem *L'Invitation au Voyage* by Charles Baudelaire (1821–67): *Là, tout n'est qu'ordre et beauté,/ Luxe, calme et volupté* ('There, all is simply order and beauty,/Luxury, calm and delight'). The painting was

bought in 1905 by the painter Paul Signac (1863–1935), one of the originators of the pointillist technique. Another painter, Raoul Dufy (1877–1953), wrote in 1925: 'On looking at that picture I grasped all the new reasons for painting; the realism of the impressionists lost its charm for me as I contemplated the miracle of the imagination introduced into draughtsmanship and colour.' Matisse returned to the theme in 1907–8. *Le Luxe* is still quite painterly, but *Le Luxe II* is characterized by flat planes of colour and hard outlines.

Lycra. This lightweight stretchy polyurethane fibre or fabric, patented in the US by E.I. du Pont de Nemours and Co. in 1958, was originally used for underwear and swimming costumes but later gave rise to the body-hugging designs of the sportswear worn in the fitness fetish of the 1980s. The name seems to suggest a partial anagram of 'acrylic'.

Lyin' and testifyin'. Misleading talk; persuasive badinage. The expression originated in the 1990s in black street talk and was included in so-called EBONICS. 'Lyin'' is positive, not negative, and denotes skilful story-telling.

> It was precisely the danger that lyin' and testifyin' homeys (smooth-talking blacks) would be classified as stupid that Oakland wanted federal funds for its teachers to learn Ebonics.
>
> *Sunday Times* (29 December 1996)

Lyme disease. A form of arthritis caused by bacteria that are transmitted by deer ticks. It takes its name from Lyme, Connecticut, where an outbreak occurred in 1975.

Lymeswold. A British make of blue creamy cheese, on sale for 10 years from 1982. Its name, suggesting 'slime' and 'mould', may have contributed to its uncertain reception, although it was apparently intended to evoke 'limes' and 'wold', as words of rural imagery. It may have been suggested by Wymeswold, a village near Loughborough in Leicestershire, a county noted for its cheese. It was actually produced at Aston in Cheshire, similarly famed.

M

Maastricht Treaty. The agreement reached between the heads of government of the 12 members of the European Community (*see* EUROPEAN UNION) at Maastricht in the Netherlands in 1991. It was designed to prepare the way for economic, monetary and political union within the EC and contained a protocol regarding social and employment policy in member states. Ratification of the treaty was hampered by various factors, one being Britain's reluctance to accept certain directives set out in the SOCIAL CHAPTER. The treaty was regarded by some as a threat to national sovereignty. It was eventually ratified in 1993.

McCarthyism. Political witch-hunting, such as the hounding of communist suspects to secure their removal from office and public affairs. The name is that of US Republican Senator Joseph McCarthy (1908–57), who declared in the early 1950s, at the height of the COLD WAR, that there existed an orchestrated communist campaign to infiltrate the US government at all levels, and embarked on a campaign to root out 'un-American' activity in all walks of life. *See also* HISS AFFAIR.

McDonald's. The chain of fast-food outlets grew from a germ planted in April 1955 when Ray A. Kroc (1902–84), a former jazz pianist, opened a franchise in the Chicago suburb of Des Plaines. He joined Richard and Maurice McDonald to set up assembly-line production of HAMBURGERS, French fries and milk shakes and in 1961 bought out the brothers, by which time his business had grown to a chain of over 200 branches. The company's trademark letter M and golden arches are now a worldwide symbol of American consumerism, and in 1990 East met West in a clash of vultures rather than culture when McDonald's opened in Moscow. *See also* BIG MAC; MAC OUT.

Macfarlane. A type of overcoat incorporating a shoulder cape and with slits at the waist to allow access to pockets in clothing worn beneath. The name is presumably that of its original Scottish designer or manufacturer. The word is first recorded in English in 1920 but is found in French much earlier, in an issue of *Le Monde illustré* for 1859.

McGee, Fibber. The compulsive liar who lives with his wife Molly at 79 Wistful Vista somewhere in the United States in the radio comedy series *Fibber McGee and Molly* (1935–7) and the television series of the same title (1959–60), starring Bob Sweeney and Cathy Lewis. The characters also appeared in various films, among them *Look Who's Laughing* (1941) and *Here We Go Again* (1942), in which they were played by Bob and Marian Jordan. Every time Fibber opened his built-in wardrobe its contents debouched in deafening disarray. To say, 'It's like Fibber McGee's closet in here' is to comment on a state of spectacular untidiness.

McGuffin. A name devised by the film director Alfred Hitchcock (1899–1980) for an object or event, of little interest in itself, such as secret plans or stolen papers, that serves to trigger the action. The term was later extended to a similar device in fiction. The origin of the name is uncertain, but it purportedly comes from a Scotsman who appeared in a story about two men in a train. On the other hand 'guff', as a word for anything trivial or worthless, may lie at the root.

Machismo (Spanish *macho*, 'male'). A usage of American origin denoting assertive masculinity that emphasizes such features as bravery, virility and the domination of the opposite sex.

Mach number. An expression of the ratio of flight speed to the speed of sound, devised by the Austrian physicist and psychologist Ernst Mach (1838–1916).

An aircraft that is flying at Mach 2 is travelling at twice the speed of sound.

Macintosh. *See* APPLE MACINTOSH.

McJob. A low-paid or menial job with few prospects and little job satisfaction. The expression, combining the name of MCDONALD'S with 'job', was coined by Douglas Coupland in his book GENERATION X (1991) and alludes both to the type of job available in the named fast-food chain and to the JUNK FOOD it sells.

> The customer is no longer always right. Stroppy service from surly shop assistants has returned to haunt the high street, thanks to the economic boom and 'McJob' working methods.
> *Sunday Times* (26 September 1999)

McKenzie friend. A person who attends a court of law to help a party to a case by making notes, quietly giving advice and the like. The name is that of the litigants in the case of McKenzie v. McKenzie (1970), in which the Court of Appeal ruled that such a helper had a right to attend a trial to assist a person who did not wish to use the services of a lawyer.

McLuhanism. The ideas of the influential Canadian media and communications theorist Marshall McLuhan (1911–80). In books such as *The Gutenberg Galaxy* (1962) he predicted the death of the book as the world became a GLOBAL VILLAGE linked by instant electronic media such as TV and computers. He also held that these new media would dominate and shape the content that they carried, summed up in his aphorism 'The medium is the message.'

Mac out, To. To overeat. American teenage slang of the 1980s, implying that one has over-indulged in BIG MACS and other forms of fast food at McDONALD'S.

Mac the Knife. A nickname of Harold Macmillan (1894–1986), prime minister from 1957 to 1963, following his sacking in 1962 of seven cabinet ministers, including the Chancellor of the Exchequer, in the NIGHT OF THE LONG KNIVES. Mack the Knife is a character in Kurt Weill's *The* THREEPENNY OPERA (1928), and its jazzy song so titled was familiar at the time from a staging of the work in New York and from Bobby Darin's number one hit recording of it in 1959. *See also* SUPERMAC; WIND OF CHANGE.

MAD. The appropriate acronym for 'mutually assured destruction', the doctrine that ensured the deterrent effect of nuclear weapons throughout much of the COLD WAR. If one side were to launch a nuclear attack, it could be confident that it would be wiped out in retaliation. See also ABM; ICBM; STAR WARS.

Madam Cyn. The self-styled nickname of Cynthia Payne (b.1933), a London brothel-keeper who was revealed in the 1970s as selling £25 luncheon vouchers to her clients by way of an entitlement to food, drink, a STRIPTEASE and a spell upstairs with a girl of their choice. In 1987 she was cleared by an Old Bailey jury of technically running a brothel in the so-called 'sex on the stairs' case.

Madame Butterfly. The central character of Giacomo Puccini's opera *Madama Butterfly*, first performed at La Scala, Milan, in 1903, with a libretto by Giuseppe Giacosa and Luigi Illica based on David Belasco's play *Madame Butterfly* (1900), in turn taken from John Luther Long's short story so titled (1898), itself inspired by an actual event. The scene is set in Nagasaki in the early 20th century. The young and pretty geisha Cio-Cio-San (Madame Butterfly) marries Lieutenant Pinkerton of the US Navy, an arrangement that he treats lightly despite the warnings of the American consul, Sharpless. Deserted by her husband soon after the wedding, Butterfly awaits his return. She now has a son, 'Trouble'. She remains insistent that Pinkerton will return, and Sharpless hesitates to read her a letter from her husband saying that he now has an American wife. She refuses to listen, however, and undertakes an all-night vigil with her loyal servant, Suzuki. The next day, when Pinkerton returns with his new wife, Kate, Butterfly is obliged to face reality. Giving her young child an American flag to play with, she commits hara-kiri.

Mad cow disease. The colloquial name of bovine spongiform encephalopathy (BSE), a disease of cattle that affects the central nervous system, causing staggering and usually resulting in death. It is believed to be caused by prions (protein particles) and to be related to Creutzfeldt-Jakob disease (CJD), a fatal degenerative disease affecting nerve cells in the human brain. Both BSE and CJD became major concerns in the 1990s.

> Scientists are creating a genetically engineered cow that is immune to BSE. ... The revelation comes as official figures show that 'mad cow' disease ... is still infecting British cattle.
> *Sunday Times* (7 June 1998)

Maddermarket Theatre. An unusual theatre in Norwich, built in 1921 as a replica of an Elizabethan playhouse. Its amateur company puts on a new production every month for just nine performances and the actors are always anonymous. It takes its name from the former medieval market there, itself so called from the locally growing madder, a plant whose root yields a red dye or pigment.

Mademoiselle from Armenteers. In the First World War Armentières in northern France was held by the British until the great German offensive of 1918. The popular army song 'Mademoiselle from Armenteers' originated *c*.1915 as a modification of the much earlier song 'The Landlady's Little Daughter', otherwise known as 'Three Prussian Officers Crossed the Rhine', with words by Ludwig Uhland set to a traditional air. It readily lent itself to improvisation, especially of a scurrilous nature. One version ran:

O Madam, have you any good wine?
Parlez-vous;
O Madam, have you any good wine?
Parlez-vous.
O Madam, have you any good wine?
Fit for a soldier of the line?
Hinky-dinky, parlez-vous.

Madison Avenue. A street in New York that was formerly the centre of the American advertising and public relations business. The name is still used allusively in this connection and first came into use in this sense in 1944 when an article on the contribution of advertising to the war effort appeared in the *New Republic* magazine by a writer signing himself 'Madison Avenue'.

Britain's Madison Avenue widely predicted that after a decent interval, *Ad Weekly* would also attempt something spectacular.
The Times (24 August 1970)

Mad Max. The violent hero, played by Mel Gibson, of the futuristic Australian film *Mad Max* (1979) and its sequels, *Mad Max 2* (1981) and *Mad Max beyond Thunderdome* (1985), depicting violently anarchic combat between motorcycle gangs and the police. The character's name has in some cases come to be applied to people and objects, such as vehicles or clothing, similar to those in the films.

Mad money. In the 1920s money kept by a woman for use in an emergency, in particular when abandoned far from home by a boyfriend. 'Mad' denotes more the anger of the man than that of the woman. The phrase was subsequently adopted to mean money set aside for some frivolous or self-indulgent purpose. Here 'mad' indicates the crazy spending.

Both uses of this American phrase are now dated but not quite obsolete.

Mad Monk. A nickname of the Conservative politician Sir Keith Joseph (1918–94), regarded as the *éminence grise* behind THATCHERITE ideology. The name, first applied to RASPUTIN, was awarded to Joseph because of his generally crazed look, his inability to communicate with the public and the extremity of his free-market beliefs.

Mad Mullah. A nickname given to Mohammed bin Abdullah, a mullah who caused great problems for the British in Somaliland at various times between 1899 and 1920. He claimed to be the Mahdi and made extensive raids on tribes friendly to the British. The dervish power was not finally broken until 1920 when the Mad Mullah escaped to Ethiopia, where he died in 1921.

Madness of George III, The. A play (1991) by Alan Bennett (b.1934) depicting the political and personal turmoil arising from one of King George III's periodic bouts of insanity (believed by modern doctors to have been caused by porphyria). The play was subsequently filmed as *The Madness of King George*. A possibly apocryphal anecdote ascribes the alteration of the title to the concerns of the film's US backers who feared that US audiences would assume the film was the third in a series of 'King George' movies.

Mae West. The name given by RAF personnel early in the Second World War to the inflatable life jacket worn when there was danger of being forced into the sea. The allusion was to the full figure of the American film actress of this name (1892–1980), who apparently approved the adoption.

I've been in *Who's Who*, and I know what's what, but it'll be the first time I ever made the dictionary.
MAE WEST: letter to the RAF, early 1940s; quoted in Fergus Cashin, *Mae West*, ch ix (1981)

Mafeking Night. 18 May 1900, when news reached London that Mafeking in South Africa, now Mafikeng in Bophuthatswana, had been relieved after a seven-month siege by the Boers during the South African War (Second BOER WAR). The resultant jubilation led to the coining of the word 'maffick' meaning 'to indulge in extravagant demonstrations of exultation on occasions of national rejoicing' (*Oxford English Dictionary*). The usage was chiefly confined to journalism and was virtually extinct by the end of the First World War.

Maggie. An affectionate nickname given to Margaret Thatcher, the IRON LADY, by her supporters. It was also taken up by her opponents, and many anti-Thatcher demonstrations rang to the cry of 'Maggie, Maggie, Maggie – Out, out, out!'

Maggie Mae. A rendition of a traditional sailors' song about a Liverpool prostitute that appeared on the BEATLES album LET IT BE, released in Britain in May 1970. The Beatles version is credited as 'trad. arr. John Lennon, Paul McCartney, George Harrison and Richard Starkey' (Ringo Starr).

Magical Mystery Tour. A television film and song by the BEATLES, credited to John Lennon and Paul McCartney and released in the UK in December 1967, and based on the idea of a PSYCHEDELIC roadshow in a brightly coloured coach.

Magic bullet. A medicine or other remedy with highly specific properties that can serve as a simple cure for a particular disease. The fact that in some cases one particular drug does knock out a disease, as penicillin can syphilis, has lent disproportionate support to the theory that a similar remedy can be found for any disease, whether treated by conventional or ALTERNATIVE medicine. As a result, many sufferers either look to the doctor for a single prescribed 'quick fix' that will clear up their condition or attribute undue efficacy to a supposed 'tried and trusted' home remedy, as adherents of herbal medicine, for example, may do with evening primrose oil.

Magic Circle. (1) The British society of magicians was founded in 1905 with the famous David Devant (real name David Wighton; 1868–1941) and Nevil Maskelyne (1839–1917) as its earliest presidents. Its journal, *The Magic Circular*, was started the following year. Members meet once a week at the society's headquarters near Gower Street, London, where there are libraries, a small theatre and a museum of historic conjuring apparatus. The highest distinction is to be a member of the Inner Magic Circle. The motto of the Circle is *Indocilis privata loqui*, 'Not apt to disclose secrets', and its symbol the circular sign of the zodiac, which appears on the floor of the club room. The name ultimately puns on the magic circle invented by Benjamin Franklin in 1749 as an arrangement of numbers in radially divided concentric circles with arithmetical properties similar to those of a magic square.

(2) In politics the 'magic circle' is a term for the inner group of Conservative politicians viewed as choosing the party leader in the days before this was an electoral matter. The name was coined by Iain Macleod in a critical article in the *Spectator* of 17 January 1964 on the 'emergence' of Alec Douglas-Home in succession to Harold Macmillan in 1963.

Magic Mountain, The. A novel (1927; in German as *Der Zauberberg*, 1924) by Thomas Mann (1875–1955). The densely symbolic story of the young Hans Castorp's search for self-knowledge while undergoing treatment for tuberculosis in a sanatorium in the Swiss Alps is ultimately a study of the uneasy situation in Europe before the outbreak of the First World War. The theme is the application of art and philosophy (the mountain) to the crisis of contemporary existence below. *See also* FIRST LINES OF NOVELS.

Magic Pudding, The. A comic book for children by the Australian cartoonist and writer Norman Lindsay (1879–1969). It concerns the adventures of a koala bear, Bunyip Bluegum, who leaves home to travel the world. Characters he encounters include the sailor Bill Barnacle, a penguin called Sam Sawnoff and a steak and kidney pudding that magically becomes whole again when eaten.

Magic realism. A style of fiction writing in which the realistic and everyday are blended with the unexpected or inexplicable. The term was adopted in this sense in the 1970s by a number of young British writers, such as Emma Tennant (b.1937), Angela Carter (1940–92) and Salman Rushdie (b.1947). The latter's MIDNIGHT'S CHILDREN (1981) and *Shame* (1983) are regarded as typical of the genre.

The exact origin of the term is uncertain, but it may have lain in the question posed by the Cuban novelist Alejo Carpentier: 'What is the story of Latin America if it is not a chronicle of the marvellous in the real?' It was first employed as a literary definition by the American critic Alastair Reid with reference to the large body of fantastic fiction produced in South American countries after the Second World War. Gabriel García Márquez' novel *Cien años de soledad* (1967), familiar in Gregory Rabassa's translation from the Spanish as *One Hundred Years of Solitude* (1970), is generally regarded as the paradigm.

Magic Roundabout, The. A popular children's television puppet series that became cult viewing for many adults. It was written by Eric Thompson (1929–82), who based it on a French programme of the same title by Serge Danot. It ran from 1965 to 1977, and its characters included Dougal the dog, BRIAN the snail, Ermintrude the cow, Dylan the rabbit, Zebedee the spring-man and Florence, a little girl.

Magic sponge. A footballer's term for the wet sponge traditionally wielded by the trainer when administering first aid to an injured player. It has now been outlawed following concern regarding the risk of blood-borne infections and has been mostly replaced by ice packs, 'deep-heat' treatment and muscle sprays.

Maginot line. A zone of fortifications built along the eastern frontier of France between 1929 and 1934 and named after André Maginot (1877–1932), minister of war, who sponsored its construction. The line, essentially to cover the returned territories of Alsace-Lorraine, extended from the Swiss border to that of Belgium and lulled the French into a belief that they were secure from any German threat of invasion. In the event, Hitler's troops entered France through Belgium in 1940. *See also* SIEGFRIED LINE.

Magnificent Seven, The. A WESTERN (1960) that was inspired by Akira Kurosawa's film *The Seven Samurai* (1954) and its theme of a small band of rough-hewn heroes defending a village against hordes of blood-thirsty bandits. The success with which director John Sturges transposed the story to the Wild West inspired numerous imitations, not least four lesser sequels featuring survivors of the original seven. The title itself has since been aped not only by subsequent movies (*The Seven Deadly Magnificent Sins*, starring Spike Milligan and others, or *The Magnificent Two*, starring Eric Morecambe and Ernie Wise, for instance) but in many other spheres of human activity, including international espionage (the 'Magnificent Five' were, to the Soviets, the notorious British spies involved in the BURGESS AND MACLEAN spy scandal that erupted in the early 1960s).

Magoo, Mr. The incompetent, myopic cartoon character was the creation of animators John Hubley and Robert Cannon. He first appeared in the late 1940s, and 'played' various famous fictional characters, such as Dr Jekyll and Long John Silver, in a television series of the 1960s.

Mahatma (Sanskrit, 'great soul'). The title bestowed by his followers on the Indian nationalist leader Mohandas Karamchand Gandhi (1869–1948), owing to his great spirituality and emphasis on non-violence. A hagiographic film version of the life of Gandhi,

directed by Richard Attenborough and starring Ben Kingsley as Gandhi, was released in 1982.

Mah-jongg. A Chinese game played with 'tiles' like dominoes, made of ivory and bamboo, with usually four players. The tiles, 136 or 144 in all, are made up of numbered bamboo, circle and character suits, honours (red, green and white dragons), winds (north, east, south and west) and, additionally, numbered flowers and seasons.

The game itself is probably of 19th-century origin but was brought from Shanghai to the United States after the First World War by an American missionary, Joseph P. Babcock, under the tradename Mah-jongg, which he coined. It is Chinese dialect for 'sparrows', referring to the 'bird of a hundred intelligences' that appears on one of the tiles. At the peak of the fad, in 1923, some 10 million American women were meeting regularly for mah-jongg parties as an escape from housework.

Maiden's prayer, Answer to a. *See* ANSWER TO A MAIDEN'S PRAYER.

Maigret, Inspector. The pipe-smoking police detective who features in a long list of novels and stories by the Belgian writer Georges Simenon, who conceived him in 1929. His full name is Jules Maigret, and he solves mysteries by analyzing character rather than by examining physical clues. He first appeared in *Pietr le Letton* ('Peter the Latvian') (1930). The first Maigret titles to be published in Britain were *Introducing Inspector Maigret* (1933), *Inspector Maigret Investigates* (1933) and *The Triumph of Inspector Maigret* (1934). Each book contained two short novels, a scheme that continued until the 1950s, when the stories began to appear singly. Maigret has appeared in many European films and was played by Rupert Davies in the BBC television series *Maigret* (1960–3).

Main squeeze. An American colloquialism for a boyfriend or girlfriend, the allusion being to a tight hug or embrace, representing a close or intimate relationship. The term dates from the 1970s.

Main Street. The principal thoroughfare in many of the smaller towns and cities of the United States. Sinclair Lewis's novel of this name (1920) epitomized the social and cultural life of these towns, and the term came to denote the mediocrity, parochialism and materialism of small-town existence.

Major Barbara. A play (1905) by the Irish playwright George Bernard Shaw (1856–1950) about a Salvation

Army officer who debates the role that capitalism plays in supporting charity. Major Barbara is Barbara Undershaft, the daughter of an arms manufacturer who struggles with the idea that her charitable efforts are underwritten by the capitalism her father represents.

> *Bill Walker*: Wot prawce selvytion nah?
>
> GEORGE BERNARD SHAW: *Major Barbara*, II

Majors, The. Golfing jargon for the four most important tournaments: the Open, played annually in Britain since 1860, the US Open, first held in 1895, the US PGA (Professional Golfers' Association), dating from 1916, and the US Masters, first played in 1934.

Make all the right noises, To. To talk in generally positive terms but without any real indication of action. The expression, which sometimes omits 'all', dates from the 1950s.

> There is another group of parents ... that makes all the right noises but lacks enthusiasm. Why bother?
>
> *Sunday Times* (19 December 1999)

Make a meal of something, To. To treat it with greater attention to detail than is necessary. A retort to an elaborate description of some exploit might thus be: 'There's no need to make a meal of it.' But the phrase may also apply to a pleasant experience that one savours to the full.

> It was August, a punishingly hot month. ... I made a meal out of crossing the river below the farm, drenching myself from head to foot in cool water before climbing towards the house.
>
> *Sunday Times* (30 May 1999)

Make an issue of something, To. To turn it into a subject of contention; to make a fuss about it. The expression dates from the 1920s.

Make a pass at someone, To. To make an amorous advance to them. The expression dates from the 1920s.

> Men seldom make passes
> At girls who wear glasses.
>
> DOROTHY PARKER: 'News Item' (1937)

Make a pig of oneself, To. To overeat; to be extremely greedy. The pig has long symbolized gluttony, more for its manner of eating than for the amount it consumes. The phrase is of US origin and dates from the 1940s. *See also* PIG OUT.

Make babies, To. To engage in sexual intercourse. A coy euphemism dating from the 1960s.

Make it snappy! Hurry up! Get on with it! An American phrase dating from the 1920s.

Make it up as one goes along, To. To improvise or 'ham'; to present information in an idiosyncratic or informal manner. The phrase need not imply that one is fabricating the facts.

> 'A lot of the time on *Neighbours* we were making it up as we went along, a lot of young actors do, but you are gaining an incredible amount of experience.'
>
> *The Times* (6 September 1999)

Make like a tree and leave, To. To leave; to depart. The punning phrase is of US origin and has a number of equivalents, such as 'to make like a drum and beat it', 'to make like a banana and split'. These all date from the 1950s.

Make music together, To. To engage in sexual intercourse. The adjective 'beautiful' is sometimes added. The expression implies a sweet harmony.

Make my day. Do what you threaten to do so that I have the satisfaction of doing what I have to do. The catchphrase is of US origin and is particularly associated with a scene in the film *Sudden Impact* (1983) in which Clint Eastwood, as the tough San Francisco police detective Harry Callahan, known as DIRTY HARRY, points his gun at a criminal and says, 'Go ahead, make my day.' If the criminal proceeds with the crime, Callahan will have the justification for shooting him. More straightforwardly, to say of a person or thing that they 'made my day' is to say that they made it a success. Even here, however, the usage may be ironic. A variation on the familiar 'Beware of the dog' notice is a picture of a guard dog with the words: 'Break in. Make my day.'

Make out with someone, To. To engage in sexual activity with them.

Make the cut, To. To do well; to come up to standard. The expression dates from the 1990s and was adopted from golfing jargon, in which the sense is to equal or better a required score, thus avoiding elimination from the last two rounds of a four-round tournament.

> This ... Modern Library decided that *The Charterhouse of Parma* no longer made the cut, and deleted the novel from its list of the world's great literature in reprint.
>
> *Times Literary Supplement* (22 October 1999)

Make the front page, To. To be important enough to appear on a newspaper's front page. *See also* HIT THE HEADLINES.

Make the grade, To. To rise to the occasion; to reach the required standard or level; to overcome obstacles. The allusion is to climbing a hill or gradient. The expression is of US origin and dates from the early 20th century.

Make the weather, To. To be influential and authoritative. The image is of a person so powerful that they can create or control the weather conditions.

> He [John Major] has not been the kind of party leader or prime minister who 'makes the weather'.
>
> ROBIN OAKLEY in *The BBC News General Election Guide* (1997)

Make waves, To. To cause trouble by 'rocking the boat' (*see* ROCK THE BOAT). A phrase of US origin that became current in the 1970s.

> The revelations from [KGB defector] Vasili Mitrokhin's smuggled papers is [*sic*] making waves in Germany.
> *The Times* (14 September 1999)

Make with, To. To proceed to use or supply, as: 'Come on, make with the drinks.' The phrase is an adoption of Yiddish *machen mit*, 'to brandish something'.

Making Cocoa for Kingsley Amis. The engaging title of a poem by Wendy Cope (b.1945) and of the collection of light verse in which it appears (1986). *See also* LUCKY JIM.

> It was a dream I had last week
> And some kind of record seemed vital.
> I knew it wouldn't be much of a poem
> But I love the title.
>
> WENDY COPE: 'Making Cocoa for Kingsley Amis'

Malarkey. This US term for meaningless talk or nonsense is first recorded in the 1920s in J.P. McEvoy's novel *Hollywood Girl*: 'It's a wonder you notice me, I told him. There's a lot of malarky [*sic*], says he' (ch vii). The origin of the word is uncertain, but Irish *mullachán*, 'large-headed person', hence 'fathead', 'idiot', has been suggested.

Malcolm X. The name adopted by the US black activist Malcolm Little (1925–65), who in 1952 joined the NATION OF ISLAM while in prison for burglary, and disowned his original surname as a 'slave name'. Malcolm X rejected the Civil Rights Movement's aim of integration, which he described as cultural suicide, and was suspicious of the cult of personality that he saw growing up around the movement's leader, Martin Luther King (1929–68). He also rejected the movement's emphasis on non-violence, asserting the right of blacks to defend themselves. Malcolm X broke with the Nation of Islam in the winter of 1963–4 and set up the Organization of Afro-American Unity. He also converted to orthodox Islam, took the name Malik El-Shabazz and initiated a dialogue with Martin Luther King with the aim of creating a broader front in the struggle for equality between the races. On 21 February 1965 he was assassinated at a rally in New York by Nation of Islam loyalists. A film starring Denzel Washington as Malcolm X and directed by Spike Lee was released in 1992.

Male chauvinist pig. A man who believes in and actively proclaims the supposed superiority of men over women. The phrase, frequently abbreviated to MCP, arose in the American women's liberation movement of the 1970s.

'Pig' has long been established as a derogatory term for a male member of some unpopular group and the police were already known as 'pigs' in the early 19th century. In addition feminists regard such a man as not 'kosher'.

Male menopause. A stage in a middle-aged man's life supposedly corresponding to the menopause of a woman. It is generally accompanied by, or even caused by, a loss of potency and typically manifests itself in a crisis of confidence and identity. The term dates from the late 1940s but is not in strict medical use.

> J.M. Coetzee's [novel] *Disgrace*, a bleak but gripping story of sex, love, the male menopause and race in South Africa after Apartheid.
> *The Times* (3 December 1999)

Malice Aforethought. A crime novel (1931) by Francis Iles (pen-name of Anthony Berkeley Cox; 1893–1971). It is a forerunner of the psychological murder story. The murderer is named on the first page but suspense derives from following his thoughts before, during and after the crime and from his ultimate fate. 'Malice aforethought' is criminal law jargon for the determination to perform an unlawful act.

Malice in Wonderland. A detective novel (1940) by Nicholas Blake (pen-name of Cecil Day-Lewis; 1904–72). Day-Lewis wrote poetry and criticism as C. Day Lewis and was appointed Poet Laureate in 1968. He took to writing detective stories in 1934 to earn a living, with most of his tales featuring his amateur detective, Nigel Strangeways. The title *Malice in Wonderland* is a play on *Alice in Wonderland*, the more usual title of *Alice's Adventures in Wonderland* by Lewis Carroll (1832–98). Wordplay informs the titles of other Blake novels, such as *There's Trouble Brewing* (1937) and *The Widow's Cruise* (1959).

Maltese Falcon, The. A thriller (1930) by Dashiell Hammett (1894–1961), an early example of the 'hard-boiled' genre of US detective novels. A complex story of deception and self-deception, it features the PRIVATE EYE Sam Spade. The Maltese falcon is, or purports to be, an ancient artefact in the form of a jewel-encrusted falcon, emanating from Malta. The film of 1941, directed by John Huston as a remake of the 1931 version, was a triumph in every respect. It was Huston's first film as director, and it starred Humphrey Bogart as Sam Spade and Peter Lorre as Joel Cairo. A 1936 film version of the story was entitled *Satan Met a Lady*.

Mambo. A Latin American dance similar in rhythm to the rumba. It emerged in North America in the 1940s and became a craze of the 1950s, its appeal enhanced by such popular songs as 'Mambo Italiano' and 'Papa Loves Mambo'. A spin-off was CHA-CHA, and like all such dances it has enjoyed periods of revival. 'Mambo' itself is a word of Yoruba origin meaning literally 'to talk'.

> Merger mania is threatening to take over the big City law firms just as the mambo dance craze is threatening to take over our pop charts. Both are products of the 'feel-good' factor.
>
> *The Times* (14 September 1999)

Mamelles de Tirésias, Les. A surrealistic *opéra burlesque* by Francis Poulenc (1899–1963) with texts by the modernist poet Guillaume Apollinaire (1880–1918). It was first performed in 1947. The title means 'the breasts of Tiresias'. The story tells of a couple who each change their sex, the woman getting rid of her breasts while her husband gives birth to 40,000 children. In Greek mythology Tiresias was a Theban man who had spent seven years of his life as a woman. Zeus and Hera consulted him to resolve the argument as to whether men or women get more pleasure out of sex. Tiresias declared in favour of women and was struck blind by Hera. Tiresias became a seer and informed Oedipus of his true parentage. Tiresias also makes an appearance in Part III of T.S. Eliot's *The* WASTE LAND (1926):

> I Tiresias, though blind, throbbing between two lives,
> Old man with wrinkled female breasts, can see ...

Management buyout. The purchase of a company by its own managers, usually with financial assistance from a bank or other institution and almost always when the company concerned is experiencing financial difficulties. The term is of US origin and dates from the late 1970s.

Man and Superman. A play (1903) by the Irish playwright George Bernard Shaw (1856–1950) in which the author discusses the notion of the Nietzschean SUPERMAN, a superior race who represent the future of mankind. The superman of the title is John Tanner, an intelligent but haughty man, who resists, but finally succumbs to, the primacy of women (in Shavian terms, the victory of instinct over intellect).

Manchester School. A collective name for the playwrights who wrote for Annie Horniman's company at the Gaiety Theatre, Manchester, between 1907 and 1921. Chief among them were Stanley Houghton (1881–1913), author of *Hindle Wakes* (1912), and Harold Brighouse (1882–1958), writer of the acclaimed comedy HOBSON'S CHOICE (1916).

Manchukuo. A state set up in Manchuria in 1932 by the Japanese, who seized the territory from China in 1931–2 following the MUKDEN INCIDENT. Henry Pu-Yi (1906–67), who had been deposed as the last emperor of China in 1912 while still a child, was made the puppet ruler. A LEAGUE OF NATIONS Commission condemned the Japanese occupation, leading to Japan's withdrawal from the League in 1933. Manchukuo ceased to exist after the Japanese surrender in 1945, and the area came once again under Chinese rule.

Manchurian candidate. A term for a person who has been brainwashed by some organization or foreign power and programmed to carry out its orders automatically. The allusion is to Richard Condon's novel *The Manchurian Candidate* (1959) and the memorable film based on it (1962), telling the story of a KOREAN WAR 'hero' who returns as a brainwashed zombie triggered to kill a liberal politician, his 'control' being his ambitious mother.

Mandate. The authority conferred on certain nations by the LEAGUE OF NATIONS after the First World War to administer the former German colonies and Ottoman Turkish dependencies outside Europe. By the treaty of Sèvres (August 1920) France received 'Greater Syria' (modern Syria and Lebanon) while Britain gained Palestine, Transjordan (now Jordan) and Iraq.

Mandy. A nickname of Peter Mandelson (b.1953), widely regarded as the *éminence grise* and presentational enforcer of Tony Blair's Labour government, whose election he did much to ensure in 1997. The nickname Mandy (usually a girl's name) alludes to Mandelson's homosexuality, which was revealed to the world at large by former Tory MP, Matthew Parris, himself gay, during the course of a TV discussion. Subsequently the BBC decreed that no mention of Mandelson's sexuality should be made on its programmes. Among Mandelson's government responsibilities was the construction of the MILLENNIUM DOME in Greenwich, earning him the title of Dome Secretary. Mandelson resigned as secretary of state for trade and industry in 1998 following revelations that he had obtained a loan to purchase a house from fellow minister Geoffrey Robinson, into whose business affairs his department was carrying out an investigation. In 1999 he was back in government as secretary of state for Northern Ireland. *See also* PRINCE OF DARKNESS.

Maneater. A sexually predatory woman. The analogy is with a man-eating tiger.

> Ali McGregor, who has by far the best voice in the cast, plays Polly as a slender, luscious, doe-eyed man-eater.
> *Sunday Times* (5 December 1999)

Man For All Seasons, A. A play (1960), later a film (1967), by Robert Bolt (1924–95) about the Tudor statesman Sir Thomas More and his opposition to Henry VIII's divorce from Catherine of Aragon. The title was derived by Bolt from a description of More by his contemporary Robert Whittington (*c*.1480–*c*.1530), who wrote:

> More is a man of angel's wit and singular learning; I know not his fellow. For where is the man of that gentleness, lowliness and affability? And as time requireth, a man of marvellous mirth and pastimes; and sometimes of as sad a gravity: as who say: a man for all seasons.
> *Vulgaria* (1521)

Whittington in turn borrowed the tag from Erasmus, a friend of More's, who had described More in his preface to *In Praise of Folly* (1509) with the words *omnium horarum hominem* ('a man of all hours'). The construction caught on after the success of Bolt's play and film, and many leading personalities of the day have since been eulogized as 'men (or women) for all seasons'.

Man from Missouri. *See* GIVE-'EM-HELL HARRY.

Man from the ministry. A tag dating from the 1960s for a government official or bureaucrat, especially of the officious kind. The phrase was adopted from the title of a radio SITCOM, *The Men from the Ministry* (1962–77), about two timorous and incompetent civil servants, played by Richard Murdoch and Deryck Guyler, forever trying to placate their irritable boss, Sir Gregory.

Manga. A Japanese genre of comic book, usually with a SCIENCE FICTION or fantasy theme, and often containing violent or sexually explicit material. Typical titles (in translation) are *Battle Angel Alita*, *Oh My Goddess!* and *You're Under Arrest!* The word literally means 'indiscriminate picture'. *See also* ANIME.

Manhattan. A cocktail made from whisky and vermouth, with a dash of Angostura bitters and Curaçao or Maraschino. It is named from Manhattan Island, New York.

Manhattan Project. The US government research project of 1942 to 1945 that produced the first atomic bomb, so named because it was undertaken by the Manhattan District of the US Army Corps of Engineers. It was headed by Brigadier General Leslie R. Groves, and 'Manhattan Project' subsequently became the code name for similar research work right across the country. The first atomic bomb was exploded at 5.30 a.m. on 16 July 1945 at a site on the Alamogordo air base south of Albuquerque, New Mexico.

Man in black. A nickname for a football referee, who generally wears black to be distinguished from the shirts of the two teams. Where a team's strip is itself black he will naturally wear a different colour. Referees originally wore a jacket top and PLUS FOURS but this was replaced by a blazer and shorts, then by a tunic top, which ultimately evolved into the all-black outfit of today.

> There is a widespread sentiment that the transformation of football as an industry demands an increase in professionalism among the men (and the occasional woman) in black who officiate it.
> *The Times* (10 January 2000)

Man mountain. A fat man, who seems mountainous by comparison with most other men.

Mannerheim Line. *See* WINTER WAR.

Manny. A nickname of Emanuel Shinwell (1884–1986), the astonishingly long-lived and sharp-tongued Labour politician. He started his political career as a militant agitator (in 1919 he was jailed for five months for incitement to riot during a dockers' strike) and ended it as Baron Shinwell of Easington in the House of Lords, where from 1982 he sat with the independents in protest against 'left-wing militancy' in the Labour Party. *See also* CLYDESIDERS.

Man of the match. The player adjudged to have played the best in a particular game.

Man of the moment. A person who is currently popular or in the news. The phrase is sometimes misused to mean a person who acts spontaneously (on the spur of the moment) or instantly (in the same moment that the need for action is apparent.) The first word may vary according to gender.

> 'Someone told me two seasons ago that I was the girl of the moment,' she [model Gisele Bundchen] says, 'and now I still am.'
> *The Times* (2 October 1999)

Man o' War. The most famous thoroughbred racehorse in the United States and the greatest horse of the first half of the 20th century was foaled in 1917. In a brief career of only two seasons (1919–20), the chestnut colt, nicknamed 'Big Red', won 20 out of 21 races. His sole loss was to Upset on 13 August 1919 at Saratoga, New York, and occurred only because he was facing the wrong way when the race started. He was retired to stud in 1930 and died in 1947.

Manson murders. A series of gruesome murders in California in 1969 that saw the HIPPIE dream turn to nightmare. The murders were perpetrated by a mini-cult called 'The Family', led by Charles Manson (b.1934), an unbalanced ex-convict who encouraged his followers into sexual excess and experimentation with LSD. Their first victims were Leno LaBianca (the millionaire owner of a supermarket chain) and his wife. They then raided the mansion of the film director Roman Polanski in BEVERLY HILLS and in a frenzied attack killed five people, including Polanski's wife, the actress Sharon Tate, who was eight months pregnant. During their subsequent trial the four accused members of the Family claimed that they had been inspired by listening to the BEATLES song, HELTER-SKELTER. Also during the trial President Nixon (*see* TRICKY DICKY) attracted criticism for breaking *sub judice* rules by declaring Manson's guilt prior to the verdict, which turned out to be 'guilty' anyway, and

the defendants ended up serving indefinite sentences. *See also* ALTAMONT.

Man the lifeboats, To. To prepare to extricate oneself from a difficult situation.

> I did ask, but everybody pretends they don't know, a sure sign they are manning the lifeboats.
> *Sunday Times* (5 December 1999)

Man Upstairs. A euphemism or nickname for God, dating from the 1960s. Its level of mild humour is similar to that of 'the big round shiny thing in the sky' for the sun and similar conceits.

Man Who Came to Dinner, The. A film comedy (1941) adapted by Julius and Philip Epstein from a successful stage play by George S. Kaufman (1889–1961) and Moss Hart (1904–61) about an opinionated radio host, called Sheridan Whiteside, who is obliged by injury to outstay his welcome at the home of a suburban family. The original 'man who came to dinner' was the real-life US theatre critic Alexander Woollcott (1887–1943), who was renowned for his eccentric, domineering character. Far from being offended by his portrayal, Woollcott enjoyed the notoriety (he had long pleaded with Hart to be preserved for posterity in one of his plays) and ultimately played the part of Whiteside himself when the play went on tour.

> I'm perfect for the part. I'm the only man you know who can strut sitting down.
> ALEXANDER WOOLLCOTT: lobbying Hart for the role of Sheridan Whiteside

Man Who Mistook His Wife for a Hat, The. A collection of case studies (1985) by Oliver Sacks (b.1933), a clinical neurologist. The title piece concerns a musician suffering from visual agnosia:

> He reached out his hand, and took hold of his wife's head, tried to lift it off, to put it on. He had apparently mistaken his wife for a hat! His wife looked as if she was used to such things.

Man Who Would Be King, The. A film (1975) adapted by its director John Huston and Gladys Hill from a short story by Rudyard Kipling (1865–1936) about two British adventurers who set themselves up as rulers of a remote region of Afghanistan. A pet project of John Huston (he first planned the film in the 1940s, with Clark Gable and Humphrey Bogart in mind), it was eventually filmed with Sean Connery and Michael Caine in the lead roles. The film had to be shot on location in Morocco rather than Afghanistan because of violent unrest in the area.

Man with No Name. The mysterious avenger of the American West played by Clint Eastwood in a series of SPAGHETTI WESTERNS, beginning with *A FISTFUL OF DOLLARS* (1964) and continuing with *For a Few Dollars More* (1965) and *The Good, the Bad and the Ugly* (1966). He wears a poncho, smokes a cheroot and says very little. Eastwood played essentially the same character in *Hang 'Em High* (1968) and *High Plains Drifter* (1973). The credits of *A Fistful of Dollars* reveal that the drifter's name is Joe.

Man with the Golden Arm, The. A novel (1949) by Nelson Algren (born Nelson Algren Abraham; 1909–81), set in the Polish slums of Chicago. Francis Majcinek (known as Frankie Machine), a dealer in a gambling den, is said to have a 'golden arm', so sure is his handling of the cards, his cue when playing pool, the dice and his drumsticks. He is unable, however, to break out of his social environment, and this and his heroin addiction lead to his suicide. A rather muddled film version (1956) was directed by Otto Preminger, with Frank Sinatra in the title role.

Man you love to hate. A nickname for any villainous or unpleasant type whom one nevertheless finds attractive or alluring, as in a LOVE–HATE RELATIONSHIP. The description was specifically associated with the Austrian actor Erich von Stroheim (1885–1957) following his appearance in the First World War propaganda film *The Heart of Humanity* (1918), in which he not only attempts to rape the leading lady but casually tosses a baby out of the window.

Mao suit. A suit of the type worn by China's communist leader Mao Zedong (1893–1976). He usually appeared in a cotton suit of loose trousers and a straight jacket with a close-fitting, upright collar, a style indistinguishable from the clothing commonly worn in China at the time (1949–76). Mao's name was given to the so-called mandarin collar style taken up in Paris in 1967 and in later years applied to other items, including the distinctive peaked cap. *See also* NEHRU JACKET.

> Out, apparently, are Mao caps, Guevara beards, Maharishi gowns and Zapata moustaches.
> *Punch* (24 July 1968)

Maple White Land. A fictional volcanic plateau north of the Amazon in Brazil. It is the subject of Arthur Conan Doyle's novel *The Lost World* (1912), as which it is also commonly known, and it is named after its discoverer, an artist and poet from Detroit, Michigan. It was first explored by Professor CHALLENGER, who gave his name to Fort Challenger, now ruined.

Mapp and Lucia. The comic novel (1935) by E. F. Benson (1867–1940) in which the scheming Elizabeth Mapp, who first appeared in *Miss Mapp* (1922), and the formidable Emmeline Lucas (Lucia), of *Queen Lucia* (1920) and sequels, come together in Mapp's home town of Tilling. Mapp's home is modelled on Benson's house, previously owned by the novelist Henry James (1843–1916), and Tilling on the town of Rye, Sussex, where the house is. A television series (1985–6) based on the stories had Prunella Scales as the dowdy Mapp and Geraldine McEwan as Lucia.

Maquis. The name by which the French Resistance in the Second World War came to be known. *Maquis* is the thick, impenetrable shrubby vegetation found in southern France which formed useful cover for resistance fighters. After the fall of France in 1940 resistance was at first haphazard, but gradually became more organized, partially through the efforts of the British SOE. The French Resistance became involved in helping Allied airmen to escape, in sheltering Jews and in carrying out acts of sabotage.

Three distinct resistance groups emerged. The supporters of General de Gaulle, who had formed a government-in-exile in London, formed L'Armée secrète (the Secret Army). The French communists formed the National Liberation Front, whose military wing was called the Francs-Tireurs et Partisans Français (*francs-tireurs* had been the name given to civilian snipers who had resisted the German invasions of 1870 and 1914). A third group, the Organisation de Résistance de l'Armée (ORA, Army Resistance Organization), rallied round General Henri Giraud, who became the leader of the Free French (FFL) in North Africa in 1942, and who was favoured by the USA and Britain over de Gaulle, who was regarded as 'difficult'. The three groups formed the Conseil National de la Résistance (National Council of the Resistance) and declared de Gaulle to be their overall leader in 1943. Early in 1944, with the prospect of an Allied invasion, the groups merged their military resources into the FFI (French Forces of the Interior), which played an important role in disrupting German communications before and during the Normandy landings. The symbol of the French Resistance was the Cross of Lorraine, the two-barred cross that was the emblem of Joan of Arc. Such crosses mark memorials to the Resistance all over France.

Maradona of the Carpathians. The Romanian footballer Gheorghe Hagi (b.1965), a talented midfield player. The flawed but brilliant Argentinian Diego Maradona (b.1960) was probably the best player of the 1980s (*see* HAND OF GOD), while the Carpathians are a Central European mountain system that form a semi-circle through Slovakia, Poland, Ukraine, Moldova and Romania.

Marchioness disaster. A fatal accident on the River Thames in London on 20 August 1989 involving a pleasure boat, the *Marchioness*. On the night in question the boat had been hired for a birthday party by a young City businessman. In the early hours of the morning a Thames dredger, the *Bowbelle*, collided with the *Marchioness*, which rapidly sank, resulting in the deaths of 51 people.

March on Rome. The means by which Mussolini (the DUCE) came to power in Italy. With many in Italy disappointed by the country's meagre gains in the First World War and with the middle classes fearful of a communist revolution, Mussolini's fascists received increasing support. In the summer of 1922 a general strike was threatened, and Mussolini declared that either the government should stop it or the fascists would. On 24 October 1922, with the country on the verge of civil war, Mussolini ordered his BLACKSHIRTS to take control of various key localities throughout Italy and to converge on the capital. On 28 October the government declared Rome to be under siege, but King Victor Emmanuel III refused to sign the order that would have obliged the army to resist the fascists. The king's motives have been the subject of debate and controversy, but on 29 October he invited Mussolini to form a cabinet. Mussolini arrived in Rome from Milan the following day. Although the March on Rome was subsequently portrayed by the fascists as a seizure of power by force, the transition of power was entirely within the constitution, and it was not until 1925 that Mussolini suspended democratic rights and began to establish a dictatorship.

Marciano, Rocky. The US heavyweight boxer, born Rocco Francis Marchegiano (1923–69), helped to popularize ROCKY as a nickname for boxers. Marciano served in Britain in the Second World War, and it was during this period that he took up boxing. When he retired from the ring in 1956 he was undefeated and had 49 victories out of 49 bouts to his name, including 43 knockouts. He died in an aircraft. *See also* BROCKTON BOMBER; GRAZIANO, ROCKY.

Marconi scandal. A scandal involving the Liberal politician David Lloyd George that broke in 1913 and almost ended the WELSH WIZARD's career. In April 1912 Lloyd George, then chancellor of the exchequer, together with the attorney general Rufus Isaacs, had purchased shares in the US Marconi company at a price below that available to the public. The deal was made via Isaacs's brother, who was managing director of the company. The British Marconi company, closely connected with the US company, had just received the go-ahead from the British government for the construction of a relay of radio stations throughout the British empire, and its share price leapt upwards. The affair came before a Commons select committee. Lloyd George and Isaacs denied speculating in 'the Marconi company', which technically referred to the British company, and were cleared of charges of corruption by the Liberal-dominated committee. The prime minister, H.H. Asquith, refused to accept Lloyd George's proffered resignation. *See also* OLD SQUIFFY.

Mardi Gra. The code name of Edgar Pearce, a 61-year-old former advertising employee, who for five years from 1994 waged a campaign across London and the Home Counties in an attempt to extort millions of pounds from Barclays Bank and Sainsbury's supermarkets. He planted some 36 explosive devices, injuring six, and took his name because he began his campaign on a Tuesday, alluding to the French *Mardi Gras* or Shrove Tuesday festival. He omitted the final 's' so that the police would recognize the bombs as his work. He was finally arrested in April 1999 moments after withdrawing £700 in cash from a bank machine in southwest London. In some respects he was a paler version of the American UNABOMBER.

Marianne. The female figure who symbolizes the French republic. She first appeared in 1792 during the French Revolution, the name then being that of a secret republican society formed to overturn the Second Empire (1852–70). The name was at first derisory but soon lost its pejorative sense. The lightly clothed figure wears a Phrygian cap, a symbol of liberty at the time of the Revolution, and appears on French coins and stamps. Her bust similarly has a place in every French town hall. The models for the figure were at first anonymous but in 1969 the authorities decided that Marianne would henceforth be based on the film star Brigitte Bardot (b.1934). Her successor in this role in 1984 was another actress, Catherine Deneuve (b.1943), and in 1999 she in turn handed on the torch to Laetitia Casta, a 21-year-old Corsican model. Marianne's transatlantic counterpart exists in the figure of the Statue of Liberty at the entrance to New York harbour, dedicated in 1886. It was the work of the French sculptor Frédéric-Auguste Bartholdi and commemorates the friendship of the peoples of the United States and France.

The reason for the choice of this particular name is uncertain. It may have been intended to honour the Spanish Jesuit historian Juan de Mariana (1532–1624), a campaigner for the assassination of tyrant monarchs. Other sources claim it to be a mystical representation of the French words *République démocratique et sociale*. From a religious viewpoint the name can be seen as a twofold tribute to the Virgin Mary and her mother, St Anne.

Marie Celeste. To say that a place is 'like the Marie Celeste' is to say that it gives the appearance of having been suddenly and inexplicably deserted. The expression dates from the 1930s and refers to the US cargo ship, properly named *Mary Celeste*, that in December 1872 was found mysteriously abandoned with sails set in the North Atlantic.

Marketese. The abbreviated names of fruit, flowers and vegetables, used not only on the price labels of market stalls and in the shops of fruiterers, florists, greengrocers, etc, but also on domestic shopping lists. Examples are 'strawbs' for strawberries, 'toms' for tomatoes, 'pots' for potatoes and 'mums' or 'xanths' for chrysanthemums. This last is a linguistic curiosity, since although 'xanth' represents an abbreviated pronunciation, based on the second syllable, the full name means 'golden flower', from the Greek, yet Greek *xanthos* means 'yellow', which is equally appropriate.

Mark of Zorro, The. A film (1940) based on 'The Curse of Capistrano' by Johnston McCulley about a masked swordsman who rights wrongs and combats evil in 19th-century Los Angeles. Starring Tyrone Power as ZORRO, this was just one of several cinematic treatments of the same story, others starring the likes of Douglas Fairbanks, Yakima Canutt, Frank Langella, George Hamilton and, in the 1990s, Antonio Banderas. The 'mark of Zorro' is the slashed Z he habitually slices into his victims.

Marks and Sparks. A colloquial jingling name for the Marks & Spencer clothes and food stores, current from about the 1940s.

In their Marks and Sparks' woollies and living in what looks like a remarkably nice housing estate, Topsy and Tim clearly stand in for classless society.
Sunday Times (5 April 1964)

Mark someone's card, To. To provide them with information; to tip them off; to put them right. The expression dates from the 1960s and derives from horse racing, in which the 'card' is the programme of events that the punter or tipster will annotate ('mark') to indicate possible winners.

After *The Mail on Sunday* article [favouring support for an alleged murderer] I orchestrated local coverage and spoke to columnists on national papers. I call it marking people's cards.
MAX CLIFFORD in *The Times* (17 September 1999)

Marlowe, Philip. The Californian PRIVATE EYE in the stories and novels of Raymond Chandler. He is probably the most famous of all fictional private eyes, an oddly noble figure who moves incorruptibly through the 'mean streets' of America's West Coast underworld. He first appears in *The* BIG SLEEP (1939), and continues in FAREWELL, MY LOVELY (1940), *The High Window* (1942), *The Lady in the Lake* (1943), *The Little Sister* (1949), *The Long Goodbye* (1953) and *Playback* (1959). He has been played by various actors in different films, ranging from Dick Powell in *Murder My Sweet* (1944) to Robert Mitchum in *The Big Sleep* (1977), and in 1984 Powers Boothe portrayed him in the British television series *Marlowe – Private Eye*.

Marmalize, To. To thrash or crush; to defeat decisively. The slang word, first recorded in the 1960s, may be a blend of 'marmalade' and 'pulverize', and although there is no English verb 'to marmalade' the sense of crushing is clear, as in the pseudo-English words of the Wedgwood Teapot to the Chinese Cup in Colette's French libretto for Ravel's opera *l'Enfant et les Sortilèges* (1925): 'I boxe you, I marm'lad' you.' French *marmelade* does not in fact mean marmalade but a mixture of fruits cooked in sugar. The image is even so equally valid. *See also* FAUX AMIS.

Marmite. The proprietary name for a tangy yeast spread, usually eaten on bread or toast. It is made from brewers' yeast and was first produced in 1902 in the brewery town of Burton-upon-Trent, Staffordshire. Its name is represented pictorially on its label, as the French word for a cooking pot. *See also* VEGEMITE.

Marple, Miss. The elderly spinster detective, full name Jane Marple, who is the heroine of a number of crime novels by Agatha Christie (1890–1976), beginning with *Murder at the Vicarage* (1930), in which she is 74 years old. She bases her methods on the belief that 'human nature is much the same everywhere' and regards her village, St Mary Mead, as a microcosm of the world. She has been played by various well-known actresses in film and television versions of the stories, including Margaret Rutherford in the former medium and Joan Hickson in the latter. *See also* 4.50 FROM PADDINGTON.

Married ... With Children. A US television SITCOM first screened in its homeland in 1987 and shown in Britain from 1989. It centred on the bickering 'white trash' Bundy household, shoe shop salesman Al, his COUCH POTATO wife, Peggy, and their two teenage children, sexually promiscuous Kelly and sexually frustrated Bud, and derived its humour from an amazingly indiscriminate range of gags and puns. Its raunchy content led to its condemnation by moral watchdogs, as a result of which many viewers first became aware of its actual existence.

Mars Bar. The chocolate bar ultimately takes its name from the company set up in 1911 by the US candy maker Frank C. Mars. Its predecessors were the Mar-O-Bar, launched by Mars in 1922 but only tepidly received by the public, and the much more successful Milky Way, first on the market in 1924. Frank's son Forrest Mars (1904–99) was a partner in the business, but in 1932 the two fell out and Forrest, armed with the foreign rights to the Milky Way, moved to Europe, at first working for Nestlé in Switzerland. He then moved to England, where he started his own confectionery business in Slough and, in 1933, launched his father's product as the Mars Bar.

Marshall Plan. The popular name for the European Recovery Programme sponsored by US Secretary of State George C. Marshall (1880–1959), to bring economic aid to stricken Europe after the Second World War. It was inaugurated in June 1947. Most states, apart from the Soviet Union and its satellites, participated. Britain ceased to receive Marshall Aid in 1950. The name has subsequently been applied allusively to any scheme in which countries group together to aid a stricken state. *See also* LEND-LEASE.

The idea of a new Marshall Plan as part of the peace deal with Serbia [after its confrontation with ethnic Albanians in Kosovo in 1999] is music to the ear of Balkan countries.
The World Today (July 1999)

Marteau sans maître, Le. The musical gauntlet thrown down by the one-time *enfant terrible* of the musical avant-garde, Pierre Boulez (b.1925). The work

was first performed in 1955 and established Boulez's reputation as a fiercely cerebral modernist. The title means 'the hammer without a master'. Scored for contralto and instruments, Boulez's piece is a setting of René Char's surrealist poems of the same title (1934). One critic described the work as 'Webern sounding like Debussy'.

Martha Stewart syndrome. A wry name for a housewife's state of awareness that her household falls short of the standard exemplified by the US millionaire homemaker Martha Stewart (b.1941). The latter's very name suggests her perfection in this respect, Martha being the eager and attentive biblical hostess who was 'cumbered about with much serving' (Luke 10:38) and Stewart meaning 'steward'.

I still have a month to worry about Christmas decorations, but Olive's festive display has brought on an attack of Martha Stewart syndrome.
The Times (26 November 1999)

Martial arts. The ancient Japanese sports of judo and ju-jitsu as forms of unarmed combat have been familiar in the west since the 19th century. More recently other martial arts have been added to the western armoury, and include the following:

aikido (Japanese, 'way of adapting the spirit'): uses locks, holds and throws

hapkido (Korean, 'art of coordinated power'): uses locks, throws and high kicks

karate (Japanese, 'empty hand'): uses hands and feet to deliver and block blows

kendo (Japanese, 'way of the sword'): a form of fencing with two-handed bamboo swords

kung fu (Chinese, 'master of merit'): similar to *karate*

ninjutsu (Japanese, 'art of stealth'): a method of espionage using stealth and camouflage

qigong (Chinese, 'energy exercise'): *see* FALUN GONG

tae kwon do (Korean, 'art of hand and foot fighting'): similar to *karate*

t'ai chi ch'uan (Chinese, 'great ultimate boxing'): uses very slow controlled movements

Martian poetry. A term introduced by the poet James Fenton for a mode of writing that uses strikingly original metaphors and similes produced by transposing visual information. The style sprang from the publication in 1979 of Craig Raine's poem 'A Martian sends a Postcard Home', its title serving as key example of the idiom and giving the name of the genre itself. The matching of an image and its origin can involve the reader in a task as complex as the solving of a crossword puzzle, as in the following from this same poem:

In homes, a haunted apparatus sleeps,
that snores when you pick it up.

If the ghost cries, they carry it
to their lips and soothe it to sleep

with sounds. And yet, they wake it up
deliberately, but tickling it with a finger.

Martini shot. In film production a nickname for the last shot of the day, after which one goes home and has a Martini. *See also* ABBY SINGER SHOT.

Marvel. An adventure paper for boys published from 1893 until 1922. It included the adventures of the fictional detective Sexton BLAKE.

Marvel, Captain. *See* CAPTAIN MARVEL.

Marx Brothers. The four brothers who formed one of the finest comic teams in the history of the cinema: Leonard Marx, known as Chico (1886–1961), Adolph Marx, otherwise Harpo (1888–1964), Julius Marx, familiar as Groucho (1890–1977), and Herbert Marx, otherwise Zeppo (1901–79), who left the act in due course. A fifth brother, Milton Marx, known as Gummo (1897–1977), left the team early. Their names mostly grew out of their characters. Chico was always chasing the 'chicks', Harpo played the harp, Groucho had a GROUCH BAG, Zeppo was born about the time the first ZEPPELIN was built, and Gummo had holes in his shoes so wore gum shoes over them. The least madcap and most human of the four was Groucho, memorable for his wisecracks. Their first film was *The Cocoanuts* (1929); their best perhaps *A* NIGHT AT THE OPERA (1935). *See also* ANIMAL CRACKERS; DUCK SOUP; HORSE FEATHERS; NIGHT IN CASABLANCA.

Mary Poppins. *See* POPPINS, MARY.

Mary Whitehouse Experience, The. A television series of irreverent sketches shown in 1991 and 1992 and involving four young comedians, Steve Punt, Hugh Dennis, Rob Newman and David Baddiel. Its humour was sometimes tasteless and juvenile, making it predictably popular with younger viewers. Its title was a flippant reference to the famous 'clean-up TV' campaigner Mary Whitehouse (b.1910), leading some viewers to switch on in the hope of seeing a salutary series on the watchdog in question.

MASH. A US acronym for a mobile army surgical hospital, the word gruesomely evoking some of the casualties treated. The term became familiar to the British from the television comedy series *M*A*S*H* (1973–84) centring on events in such a hospital. It was essentially a dark, anti-war satire developed from Robert Altman's award-winning film of the same name (1970) about the weary surgeons and staff of the 4077th mobile hospital during the Korean War. This was itself based on a book by Richard Hooker, who disowned the televised version because of its liberalism.

Mason, Perry. The investigating lawyer in a series of 89 crime novels by Erle Stanley Gardner, starting with *The Case of the Velvet Claws* (1933). Much of the action takes place in the courtroom, and Mason is assisted in his work by his legman Paul Drake and secretary Della Street. A Perry Mason series was broadcast on US radio from 1943 to 1955 and he successfully transferred to television, where from 1957 to 1966 (1961 to 1967 in Britain) he was played by Raymond Burr, who later portrayed IRONSIDE.

Masquerade. A bestselling children's picture book (1979) by the British illustrator Kit Williams (b.1946). Masquerade is a treasure-hunt, the pictures in the book being clues to the discovery of a golden hare made and actually buried by the author himself. The mystery was solved (by an unnamed reader) and the hare dug up in 1982.

Massage parlour. Strictly, commercial premises providing massage. Since many such establishments also offered various types of sexual services, the term was tacitly understood from the first as a euphemism for a brothel. The name dates from the early years of the 20th century.

Mass hysteria. In July 1982 at an annual jazz festival at Hollinwell, Nottinghamshire, there was a sudden unexplained outbreak of nausea, vomiting, stomach pains, burning eyes and a metallic taste in the mouth among children. Food poisoning was ruled out as there had been no communal meal. Crop-spraying was considered, but there had been none. The only explanation was mass hysteria, a manifestation of psychologically produced symptoms that passes from person to person. It usually occurs in schools or institutions of young women in an emotionally charged atmosphere, and in this case arose in a parade of young females marching and blowing musical instruments with a risk of hyperventilation. Some 500 people were treated either at the site or in hospital and several victims were still unconscious two hours after the onset of the attack.

Massive. Black teenage slang dating from the 1980s for a group of people who share social interests such as music. The word is usually prefixed by a name that geographically identifies the group or by that of the cult object, such as a dance or pop group.

What will the Steps massive think in the playground?
heat (16 December 1999–5 January 2000)

Mass Observation. A British tradename for a system of obtaining information as to popular opinion, similar to the GALLUP POLL. It grew out of a voluntary organization started by Charles Madge and Tom Harrison in 1937 and lasted until the late 1940s. The enterprise was revived in 1981 under the auspices of the University of Sussex.

Master, The. The nickname of the magisterial Surrey and England batsman Jack Hobbs (Sir John Berry Hobbs; 1882–1963). The most skilful and prolific of all English batsmen, he scored more first-class runs (61,237) and centuries (197) than anyone else, and continued playing into his 50s.

The Master: records prove the title good:
Yet figures fail you, for they cannot say
How many men whose names you never knew
Are proud to tell their sons they saw you play.
JOHN ARLOTT: 'To John Berry Hobbs on his Seventieth Birthday' (16 December 1952)

Master and Margarita, The. A philosophical fantasy (written 1928–40, serialized 1966–7 in Russian as *Master i Margarita*) by Mikhail Bulgakov (1891–1940). Combining an account of how the Devil visited Moscow in the 1930s with the appearance of Jesus before Pontius Pilate in Jerusalem, it was translated into English in 1967. The second of the three planes of which it is composed is a contemporary narrative set in Moscow, where the Master, who has written a novel about Pilate, and Margarita live.

Master bedroom. An estate agent's name for the main bedroom in a house, usually containing a double bed. The implication is that the master of the house sleeps here with his mistress. The term dates from the 1920s.

Mastermind. A television quiz for individual contestants who sat on a spotlit black chair and answered two rounds of questions, the first on a specialized subject of their own choice, the second on general knowledge. It ran from 1972 to 1997 and always had the same question-master, Icelandic-born Magnus Magnusson (b.1929). His routine formula when caught in mid-question by the timeout buzzer, 'I've started, so I'll finish', became a familiar catchphrase. Since contestants were required to regurgitate facts and figures rather than respond with original reasoning, it has been suggested that a more appropriate title might have been *Master Memory*.

Mata Hari. The assumed name of the Dutch dancer and courtesan Margaretha Gertruida MacLeod, née Zelle (1876–1917), from a Malay expression for the sun, meaning 'eye of the day'. She was shot by the French on charges of spying for the Germans in the First World War, although precise details of her espionage activities remain rather obscure. Her own story was that she had agreed to act as a French spy in occupied Belgium without telling the French intelligence authorities of her agreement with the Germans. Her physical allure and glamorous role meant that her stage name was afterwards used for any seductive female spy. She first danced in Paris in 1905, billed as the 'Hindu dancer', in the library of the Musée Guimet, a repository of Asiatic art refitted as an Indian temple for the occasion. Parisians later recalled that they had never seen anything like it.

Matchstick men. Simple human figures drawn with short, thin, straight lines, like matchsticks. Such figures are associated with the works of the painter L.S. Lowry (1887–1976), to whom the pop duo Brian and Michael dedicated their number 1 hit 'Matchstalk Men [*sic*] and Matchstalk Cats and Dogs' (1978).

Mathis der Mahler. The title of an opera and a symphony by Paul Hindemith (1895–1963) meaning 'Mathis the painter'. The work is based on the life of the great German painter Matthias Grünewald (d.1528) and his startlingly expressionistic depiction of the Crucifixion on the *Isenheim Altarpiece* in Colmar, Alsace. In real life Grünewald was thought to be sympathetic to the Peasants' Revolt of 1524–5. In Hindemith's libretto he actually leads the peasants against the church, but then renounces worldly things and devotes himself to his art. The opera was due to be premiered in 1934, but, despite protests by (and ultimately the resignation of) the great conductor Wilhelm Furtwängler, the work was banned by the NAZIS. Hindemith, who had to leave Germany, extracted music from the opera to make the symphony, which was performed that year. However, the première of the opera did not take place until 1938, in Zurich.

Matthew effect. A term introduced in 1968 by the US sociologist Robert K. Merton for the tendency whereby more is given to those who already have, and in particular whereby established individuals and institutions receive continued or even excessive recognition to the detriment of their less well-established counterparts. The allusion is to the words in St Matthew's Gospel: 'Unto every one that hath shall be given, and he shall have abundance; but from him that hath not shall be taken away even that which he hath' (25:29).

Matinée idol. A handsome actor of the type supposed to be attractive to women attending a matinée performance. The term dates from the turn of the 20th century, and soon became associated with the cinema as well as the stage. It can also be used ironically of any theatrically handsome man.

Matryoshka. The native name for the well-known type of wooden Russian doll that is actually a nest of hollow dolls, each doll containing a smaller inside it. The word is one of the many diminutives of the Russian woman's name Matrona, itself directly related to English 'matron'.

Mau Mau. This African secret society, originating among the Kikuyu, came to the fore in the 1950s when it used violence and terror in the cause of expelling European settlers and ending British rule in Kenya. In 1952 Jomo Kenyatta (c.1891–1978), Kenya's future president, was sentenced to life imprisonment for leading the Mau Mau and by 1957 the movement was crushed by the British. Kenyatta was released in 1961 and Kenya gained independence two years later. The origin of the name Mau Mau is uncertain.

Mauve Decade. A now little heard or used nickname for the 1890s, deriving from Thomas Beer's 1926 book of the same title, in which he views it as a peaceful and prosperous but decadent decade. Mauve, like purple, suggests idle self-indulgence. *See also* NAUGHTY NINETIES.

Max Factor. The cosmetics of this name owe their origin to the Polish-born entrepreneur Max Faktor (c.1872–1938), who after four years in the Russian army opened a small shop in Ryazan, near Moscow, making and selling his own creams, fragrances and wigs. In 1904 he and his family emigrated to New York, where he adjusted his name to Factor and opened a barber's shop. In 1909 he founded Max Factor and Company, producing his own line of theatre make-up products, and his cosmetics empire grew from there, much of its wealth coming from his work for HOLLYWOOD.

Maximum John. A nickname for the US federal judge John J. Sirica (1904–92), famous from his participation in the WATERGATE prosecutions of the 1970s. The allusion was to his reputation for awarding the stiffest penalties.

Maxwell's Silver Hammer. A blackly comic BEATLES song about a homicidal maniac, credited to John Lennon and Paul McCartney and appearing on the album ABBEY ROAD, released in September 1969. The song includes a reference to 'pataphysical science', the latter being a 'science of imaginary solutions' devised by the French writer Alfred Jarry (1873–1907), author of the grotesque avant-garde drama *Ubu Roi* (1896).

Maze. The Maze Prison, a high-security prison for the internment of Republican and Loyalist terrorists, near Belfast, Northern Ireland. The Maze was originally known as Long Kesh, and is still referred to by that name by former internees. It owed much of its notoriety to its H-Blocks, eight H-shaped internment blocks opened in 1977, at the height of the TROUBLES, to house some of Northern Ireland's most dangerous paramilitaries. The H-Blocks became familiar to the world at large as the location of the BLANKET PROTEST, which later evolved into the Republican hunger strike of 1981. Most of its remaining inmates left the Maze in the summer of 2000 in accordance with the early release scheme agreed as part of the GOOD FRIDAY AGREEMENT.

MBE. *See* MEMBER OF THE ORDER OF THE BRITISH EMPIRE.

Mean machine. A sports team of high ability. The term, sometimes extended to 'lean, mean machine', is of US origin and arose in the 1970s. In the mid-1980s it was specifically applied to the Australian men's 4 × 100m freestyle relay swimming team. It is also used of a fast or stylish car. 'Mean' here has its black American sense of attractive or fashionable.

Mean Mr Mustard. A short BEATLES song credited to John Lennon and Paul McCartney, part of the 'Long Medley' that appears on the second side of the album ABBEY ROAD, released in September 1969. 'Mean Mr Mustard' was recorded in a single sequence with 'Sun King', whose languorous Mediterranean flavour contrasts with the cheerful vulgarity of 'Mean Mr Mustard'. The latter is immediately followed on the album by POLYTHENE PAM.

Means test. The principle of supplying evidence of need before qualifying for relief from public funds, i.e. a test of one's means. Such a test was introduced by the NATIONAL GOVERNMENT in 1931 when a person's unemployment benefit was exhausted, and the resulting inquisition was much resented by those concerned. It took note of any earnings by members of the household and all monetary assets, and penalized the provident. The regulations governing public assistance were modified after the Second World War.

Mean Streets. A film (1973) written and directed by Martin Scorsese (b.1942) about the violence of New York's criminal underworld. Starring Robert De Niro and Harvey Keitel, it took its title from a much-quoted line in 'The Simple Art of Murder' (1944) by US crime thriller writer Raymond Chandler (1888–1959):

> Down these mean streets a man must go who is not himself mean; who is neither tarnished nor afraid.

Meat and potatoes. The ordinary but fundamental part or parts of something; the essential ingredients, as: 'These two clauses are the meat and potatoes of the contract.' Meat and potatoes are or were the basic ingredients of a cooked meal, and 'meat' has long been synonymous for the essence or chief part of something.

> Their detractors refer to them as a meat and potatoes band – in other words, doggedly ordinary.
> *heat* (18–24 November 1999)

Mebyon Kernow (Cornish, 'Sons of Cornwall'). The society of Cornish nationalists, established in 1951. Their flag is the emblem of St Piran: a white cross, which symbolizes tin, on a black field, which represents the ground rock from which it is extracted.

Meccano. The familiar construction set evolved from a toy kit of perforated metal strips devised by Frank Hornby (1863–1936) for his children at the turn of the 20th century. After failing to interest manufacturers, Hornby set up his own business together with a partner, D.H. Elliott, who provided financial support. The earliest kits were sold under the name of Mechanics Made Easy, but by 1907 the name Meccano had been registered and the business grew rapidly at its Liverpool base. Despite legal wrangles over patents, particularly in the United States, Meccano soon outstripped all competitors to become widely acknowledged as 'The World's Most Famous Toy'. Hornby introduced the clockwork trains named after him in 1920. These were known as gauge '0', but later the smaller gauge '00', or Hornby Dublo, was the one that took the fancy of most fanatics. *See also* DINKY TOYS.

Med, The. A nickname for the Mediterranean, dating from the Second World War.

Medallion man. A man, or type of man, who wears a neck chain and a large gold medallion, often with his shirt opened by several buttons to reveal this display on an extravagantly hirsute chest. The exhibition is or was intended to signify style, wealth and of course virility. The phenomenon was a macho manifestation of the 1970s and mercifully began to fade from the late 1980s.

> While it is easy to mock him [popular singer Tom Jones] as a Medallion Man ... his longevity has now brought him 'elder statesman' status.
> *heat* (23–29 September 1999)

Medical abbreviations. Doctors in their surgeries and surgeons in their hospitals have evolved a host of abbreviations and acronyms for use in the world of medicine. The following examples typify some of the laconicism and wry humour of the profession. *See also* TIB AND FIB; TLC.

> BIBA: brought in by ambulance
> BID: brought in dead
> DNA: did not attend
> DOA: dead on arrival
> FLK: funny-looking kid
> FOOH: fell on outstretched hand
> GOMER: get out of my emergency room
> HBD: has been drinking
> HPC: history of presenting complaint
> I-PSS: international prostate symptoms score (for measuring ease of urination)
> LOLNAD: little old lady with no actual disease
> NFN: normal for Norwich (a supposedly typical provincial city)
> NLM: nice-looking mother (used by paediatricians)
> OAP: over-anxious parent
> OD'd: took an overdose of a drug (and died)
> O-sign: the rounded open mouth of a dead person (pictorial); (*see also* Q-sign *below*)
> PAFO: pissed and fell over
> PP: plumbum pendulans (sham Latin for 'swinging the lead')
> PVN: patient very nervous
> Q-sign: the rounded open mouth of a dead person with the tongue lolling out (pictorial)
> RICE: rest, ice, compression, elevation (treatment for soft tissue injury, typically in sport)
> SIG: stroppy ignorant git
> T&E: TIRED AND EMOTIONAL

TEETH: tried everything else, try homeopathy

TUBE: totally unnecessary breast examination (*see also* BOOB TUBE)

UQ: useless quack

Medjugorje. On 24 June 1981 four teenage girls and two boys in this Croatian village claimed to have seen a vision of the Virgin Mary. Various apparitions have been reported since then, although the local bishop, Pavao Zanic, dismissed them as a case of 'collective hallucination' and accused the Franciscans of exploiting the situation for self-interest. Medjugorje soon became a popular place of pilgrimage and in 1986 Pope John Paul II approved travel there for prayer, fasting and conversion.

Meeja. A humorous respelling of 'media', meant to represent a colloquial pronunciation of the word, which arose in the 1980s as a term for the print and electronic media seen as a social group.

A lot of locals are unaccustomed to the sight of black polo-neck sophisticates making a weekend pilgrimage to this country home-from-home [Babington House, Somerset] for London's 'meeja' set.

The Times (19 August 1999)

Meeter and greeter. A person employed to greet and deal with customers or clients, as at the entrance to a club or store. A commissionaire at the entrance to a hotel or theatre performs a somewhat similar function but more formally. The term dates from the 1980s.

Meeting of minds. An agreement or understanding; a 'seeing eye to eye'. The expression has been current from at least the 1960s.

Meet one's maker, To. To die. One's maker is God. The expression, which dates from the 1930s, is also used frivolously of the destruction of something, as: 'It's time this old toaster met its maker.'

Megan's Law. A US law requiring that communities should be notified if a convicted sex offender becomes resident locally. It takes its name from Megan Kanka, a seven-year-old girl raped and murdered in New Jersey in 1994 by a convicted paedophile who had moved into the street where she lived. The principle was subsequently taken up in Britain, where it was more usually known as 'community notification'.

Me generation. The young generation of the 1980s and its concomitant creed of THATCHERISM, widely perceived as a period of selfishness and materialistic greed. The expression arose as a broadening of the 'me decade' identified by the US writer Tom Wolfe in the 1970s as an age of narcissism among the young, manifested in a cult of therapy, health clubs and the like and an almost pathological obsession with self-improvement.

We are now in the Me Decade – seeing the upward roll of ... the third great religious wave in American history ... and this one has the mightiest, holiest roll of all, the beat that goes ... *Me* ... *Me* ... *Me* ... *Me*.

TOM WOLFE: *Mauve Gloves and Madmen*, 'The Me Decade and the Third Great Awakening' (1976)

Meibion Glyndŵr (Welsh, 'sons of Glyndŵr'). A clandestine Welsh nationalist organization which since 1980 has claimed responsibility for waging a campaign of arson against holiday homes owned by English people in Welsh-speaking districts of north and west Wales. They take their name from Owain Glyndŵr (Owen Glendower; *c*.1354–*c*.1417), the Welsh chief who proclaimed himself Prince of Wales and who led a national uprising against Henry IV of England. Communiqués issued by the organization are usually signed 'Rhys Gethin', the name of one of Glyndŵr's captains.

Mein Kampf (German, 'My Struggle'). The title adopted by Adolf Hitler (1889–1945) for the book embodying his political and racial theories and misreadings of history, which in due course became the NAZI 'bible'. The first part was written when he was in prison after the abortive BEER HALL PUTSCH of 1923. It was published in two parts (1925 and 1927). *See also* HITLERISM.

Der breite Masse eines Volkes ... fällt einer grossen Lüge leichter zum Opfer als einer kleinen.

(The broad mass of a nation ... will more easily fall victim to a big lie than to a small one.)

ADOLF HITLER: *Mein Kampf*, I, x (1925)

Mekon. The deadly foe of DAN DARE in the comic strip by Frank Hampson in the EAGLE. The Mekon is a 'Treen' from the planet Venus. He is green-skinned and slitty-eyed, with a small body and a huge head, and generally resembles, perhaps intentionally, a monstrous human foetus. In the late 1970s the Conservative politician Angus Maude (b.1912) was dubbed 'The Mekon' by his junior parliamentary colleagues, from a supposed physical similarity to the creature.

Melancholy. An atmospheric early 'metaphysical' painting by Giorgio de Chirico (1888–1978). The picture, painted in 1912, features an almost empty classical townscape, in which the lengthened shadows emphasize the perspective. Two silhouetted figures lurk in the background, while in the foreground square is a statue of a reclining Roman lady, leaning her head on her hand. Both the title and the composition suggest a number of cultural references.

The posture of the statue recalls that of the figure in Albrecht Dürer's famous engraving *Melancholia* (1514), while Giorgio Vasari in his *Lives of the Painters* (1568 edition) seems to have voiced a common belief when he claimed that any painter who pays excessive attention to perspective 'becomes solitary, eccentric, melancholy and poor'.

Melissa virus. A computer virus that caused chaos in a number of company E-MAIL systems in 1999. It worked through Word 97 and Word 2000 and derived its designation, in full W97M/Melissa.A, from that of the class module that contained the virus. The name Melissa is said to have been taken by its creator, 30-year-old hacker David L. Smith, from that of a topless dancer in Florida. *See also* WORM.

Melvin. A forename that for some reason has gained 'nerdish' overtones. Hence its adoption in the 1950s for a studious or stupid person and in the 1980s for a state in which someone's clothing rides up high between their buttocks. It is assumed that anyone called Melvin would be so unaware that he would be happy with this arrangement. 'To give someone a melvin' is thus to tug a person's underwear up suddenly with the aim of jerking them off the ground. The prank originated on US campuses. *See also* NERD.

Member of the Order of the British Empire. The lowest of the five classes of the ORDER OF THE BRITISH EMPIRE and similarly awarded for service in a wide range of fields. The BEATLES were invested with the MBE on 26 October 1965 but on 26 November 1969 John Lennon notoriously returned his award to the Queen with the following note:

> Your Majesty, I am returning this in protest against Britain's involvement in the Nigeria-Biafra thing, against our support of America in Vietnam, and against *Cold Turkey* slipping down the charts. With love. John Lennon of Bag.

Memoirs of a Midget. A fantasy (1921) by Walter de la Mare (1873–1956), which microscopically explores the world of the minute Miss M, who is scarcely taller than a book, and the dark depths of feeling that are generated. The ending is ambivalent, when Miss M vanishes with an unidentified visitor.

Men Behaving Badly. A television SITCOM first shown in 1991 and conceived as a slap in the face to POLITICAL CORRECTNESS in general and to the cult of the NEW MAN in particular, and thus as an encomium to the NEW LAD in all his bawdy glory. The story centres on the antics of Gary Strang, played by Martin Clunes, and Dermot, played by Harry Enfield (later Tony, played by Neil Morrissey), who share a chaotic London flat. They swig beer, talk out their fantasies and try to avoid work by opening another tin or heading off to their private room for the pleasures of *Playboy*. Two 'girls', Deborah, played by Leslie Ash, and Dorothy, played by Caroline Quentin, are embroiled in the goings-on. The episode screened as a 'Christmas special' in 1998 drew criticism for its explicit sexual content.

Menin Gate. A massive arched war memorial built in 1927 near the Belgian town of Ypres (WIPERS; Flemish *Ieper*), site of three great battles (1914, 1915 and 1917) in the First World War. The third battle of Ypres is also called PASSCHENDAELE. The memorial is covered with the names of 55,000 British soldiers whose bodies were never found, and is surrounded by the graves of those who were identified. Running eastwards from Ypres to the town of Menin (Flemish *Menen*) is the Menin Road, scene of some of the heaviest fighting involving British forces on the WESTERN FRONT. To the British it became a symbol of national sacrifice. Its stark, shattered landscape was the subject of a number of paintings by the official war artist Paul Nash (1889–1946), such as *The Menin Road* (1918), now in the Imperial War Museum. *See also* THIEPVAL MEMORIAL; WIPERS.

Men in suits. High-ranking executives in a business or organization, especially when influential in some way. The term, describing their efficient, conformist dress, is sometimes contracted to 'the suits' or expanded to include 'grey' as the typical 'faceless' colour of a business suit. *See also* LORD SUIT.

> If Mr Hague had been truly tough he would have … sent the men in grey suits round to sort him out.
> *The Times* (25 November 1999)

Men in white coats. Psychiatrists or psychiatric workers, who are traditionally regarded as wearing such coats. The phrase is usually found in a light-hearted statement about a person's mental state.

> People who claim that the Earth is flat can expect men in white coats to come and take them away.
> *The Times* (1 December 1999)

Mensa. The society of this name was founded in Oxford in 1946 by Roland Berrill, a barrister, and Dr Lance Ware, a scientist and lawyer, with the aim of providing a social organization for the mentally gifted. Accordingly membership is restricted to those with an IQ equal to the top 2 per cent of the population. The name seeks to play down any implied elitism by representing the Latin word for 'table', the allusion being to a round table at which all have equal status. The founders may further have meant Latin *mens*, 'mind', to be apprehended as a secondary sense. The society grew rapidly from the 1960s in the United States and in the 1990s had about 100,000 members worldwide.

Mensheviks. A Russian word for a minority party (Russian *men'she*, 'less'). The name was applied to the moderate Russian social democrats who opposed the BOLSHEVIKS in the Russian Revolution of 1917.

Merchant Ivory film. A so called 'heritage film' that is typically a rich visual dramatization of an Edwardian novel but that replaces its original irony with a lovingly nostalgic re-creation of the past. The name is that of the Indian producer Ismail Merchant (b.1936) and the American director James Ivory (b.1928), who became Indian on marriage to the novelist and screenwriter Ruth Prawer Jhabvala (b.1927). The first Merchant Ivory film was *Shakespeare Wallah* (1965). Adaptations of novels include Henry James's *The Bostonians* (1984), E.M. Forster's *A ROOM WITH A VIEW* (1986) and HOWARDS END (1991) and Kazuo Ishiguro's *The Remains of the Day* (1993). *See also* EDWARDIAN ERA.

Mermaid Theatre. The theatre at Puddle Dock by the Thames developed from that created in 1951 by Sir Bernard Miles and his wife in the garden of their house in St John's Wood. They named it after the historic Mermaid Tavern, famous for its literary connections.

Merry widow. An amorous or designing widow. The phrase comes from the English title of Franz Lehár's operetta *Die Lustige Witwe* (1905), in which the widow is Hanna Glawari.

Mers-el-Kébir. A former French naval base on the Mediterranean coast of Algeria, near Oran. It was here that much of the French fleet concentrated after the fall of France in June 1940. The British, fearing that the fleet would fall into German hands, sent a powerful naval force to demand that the French fleet surrender or scuttle itself, otherwise the Royal Navy would

attack. On 3 July, after hours of unsuccessful negotiations, the British opened fire, sinking one battleship and seriously damaging two others, with the loss of 1147 French sailors. Three days later British aircraft from the *Ark Royal* finished off one of the damaged battleships and strafed the survivors, killing a further 150 men. The controversial engagement seriously damaged Anglo-French relations.

Mersey. A river synonymous with Liverpool, and giving its name not only in 1974 to the new county of Merseyside but some 10 years earlier to the Mersey beat and Mersey sound, the English type of rhythm 'n' blues music associated with the BEATLES and with such groups as Gerry and the Pacemakers (*see* FERRY ACROSS THE MERSEY), the Searchers, and the Swinging Blue Jeans. The river name itself derives from the Old English words for 'boundary river'. The Mersey formed the boundary between the counties of Cheshire and Lancashire, and before that, between the Anglo-Saxon kingdoms of Mercia and Northumbria. This long historic link was broken overnight when the new county was created. It has in its turn now been deconstructed into five 'unitary authorities' as administrative divisions of local government.

Merseyside Poets. *See* LIVERPOOL POETS.

Merz. A generic term (tantamount to 'trash') applied by the German DADA poet and artist Kurt Schwitters (1887–1948) to his elaborate constructions of bits and pieces he picked up from dustbins and gutters. 'I am a painter and I nail my pictures together,' said Schwitters. The term forms part of the title of many of Schwitters' works, for example, *Merzbild Einunddreissig* (1920).

Mess of plottage. A theatre critic's punning term for a play with a poorly constructed plot. The phrase dates from the 1940s and alludes to the 'mess of pottage' as the price for which the biblical Esau sold his birthright to his brother Jacob (Genesis 25:29–34).

Metamorphosen. The mournful and dense piece of music by Richard Strauss (1864–1949) is scored for 23 solo strings. The work was composed in 1945 and first performed in 1946. The title is German for 'metamorphoses', and the piece is inscribed 'In Memoriam'. Strauss's activities during the NAZI era were the subject of controversy: his opera *Friedenstag* (1938) was enjoyed by Hitler, and he stayed in Germany throughout the Second World War. On the other hand, Strauss was supportive of his Jewish librettist Stefan Zweig. Many saw *Metamorphosen* as a lament for Hitler (it was even banned in the Netherlands after the war), but others have seen it more sympathetically as a threnody for the destruction of German culture.

Meter maid. A nickname of American origin for a female traffic warden, originating in the 1950s.

> When I caught a glimpse of Rita,
> Filling in a ticket in her little white book.
> In a cap she looked much older,
> And the bag across her shoulder
> Made her look a little like a milit'ry man.
> Lovely Rita, Meter Maid.
> JOHN LENNON and PAUL MCCARTNEY:
> 'Lovely Rita' (1967)

See also LOVELY RITA.

Method acting. A technique of acting in which the actor aims to lose himself in the part he is playing and identify completely with the character being played. It is based on the system evolved by Stanislavsky, propounded by him in *An Actor Prepares* (1926), and first became prominent in the United States in the 1930s. The technique was fostered by such institutions as the Actors' Studio, New York, especially by Elia Kazan (b.1909) and Lee Strasberg (1901–81), and it became particularly associated with the actors Marlon Brando (b.1924) and Dustin Hoffman (b.1937).

Metroland. An early 20th-century term for the region around a metropolis. As a proper name, Metroland is the region northwest of London served by the Metropolitan Railway, lovingly evoked in John Betjeman's poem 'The Metropolitan Railway' (1954) and further explored in his television programme *Metro-land* (1973). The name was adopted by the railway in 1915 as a term for the districts through which it ran, and *Metro-Land* was the title of its guidebook, issued annually from that year to 1932, the last full year of its existence as an independent company. Lady Metroland, née Margot Beste-Chetwynde, is the wife of Lord Metroland, né Sir Humphrey Maltravers, Minister of Transportation, in Evelyn Waugh's *Decline and Fall* (1928), while in his first novel, *Metroland* (1980), Julian Barnes drew on memories of his suburban childhood.

> Metro-Land is a country with elastic borders which every visitor can draw for himself, as Stevenson drew his map of Treasure Island.
> *Metro-Land* (1932)

Mexican overdrive. Coasting or freewheeling a motor vehicle downhill to save petrol. An American expression of the 1960s. Mexicans have a generally negative or risible image in the United States. Hence other phrases with the word, such as a 'Mexican breakfast' as a cigarette and a glass of water and 'Mexican rig' as anything poorly constructed.

Mexican wave. A stunt periodically indulged in by spectators at a sporting event such as an athletics contest or football match. Successive sections of the crowd stand up with their arms raised then sit down with them lowered, causing a rising-and-falling 'wave' effect. The procedure was repeatedly carried out at the World Cup football competition at Mexico City in 1986 but was practised before this by American football crowds. *See also* WALLY.

Mezzanine level. An intermediary post or position, midway between the 'ground floor', where a new employee usually begins, and the 'first floor', as a more senior post. A mezzanine, from Italian *mezzano*, 'middle', is properly a low storey between two others in a building.

> 'She didn't want to go straight into mainstream from children's TV. We can offer her a mezzanine level of television.'
> *The Times* (4 June 1999)

MGM. Metro-Goldwyn-Mayer, HOLLYWOOD's biggest film studio, was founded in 1924 when the struggling companies started by Samuel Goldwyn (1882–1974) and Louis B. Mayer (1885–1957) merged with the theatre chain owned by Marcus Loew (1870–1927), themselves owners of Metro Pictures. The new studio promptly released one of the most important films in the history of cinematic realism, Erich von Stroheim's *Greed* (1925), a drama of human degradation.

Michelin guide. The series of guidebooks was launched in 1900 as the French *Guide Michelin*, the first systematic survey of European restaurants. It was published by the Michelin Tyre Company, founded in 1888 by the brothers André (1853–1931) and Édouard (1858–1940) Michelin.

Michelin man. A nickname for an obese person, from the rotund figure made of motor tyres so named as an advertising 'mascot' for the Michelin Tyre Company. *See also* MICHELIN GUIDE.

Michurinism. A genetic theory, named after the Soviet horticulturist I.V. Michurin (1855–1935), repudiating the laws of Mendel and essentially claiming that acquired characteristics can be inherited. It is alternatively called Lysenkoism, after T.D. Lysenko (1898–1976), the Soviet agriculturist, whose pamphlet *Heredity and its Variability* attempted to discredit orthodox genetics. Its revolutionary character was more due to Marxist wishful thinking than scientific proof, and the acceptability of such teaching to the Soviet government. Lysenkoism replaced orthodox genetics in the USSR in 1948 but after 1952 lost ground. Lysenko was dismissed from his key position in 1965.

Mickey Finn. A surreptitiously doctored or drugged drink, used to render someone insensible. The name dates from the 1920s and according to one theory is that of a notorious Chicago saloon-keeper active at the turn of the 20th century.

Mickey Mouse. One of the best known cartoon characters of all time. He is the hero of Walt Disney films and first appeared in the short silent movie *Plane Crazy* (1928), followed soon after the same year by a sound cartoon, *Steamboat Willie*. His main friends are Minnie Mouse and the clumsy dog Pluto. They were joined in the 1930s by another dog, Goofy, and by Mickey's closest rival in popularity, DONALD DUCK. He is represented 'live' by a costumed human at DISNEY-LAND and elsewhere and has a whole host of toys, games and artefacts bearing his cheery image worldwide, including in France where he is known as *Michel Souris*, Germany where he is *Mickey-Maus*, Italy where he is *Topolino* and Japan where he is *Miki Mausu*. The term 'Mickey Mouse' is also used for anything of inferior quality, such as a 'Mickey Mouse radio' or a 'Mickey Mouse business agreement'.

Mick the Miller. One of the most successful of all racing greyhounds. He was bred by a parish priest in Ireland and won 15 out of 20 races before going to England in 1929, where he became the first dog to win the Greyhound Derby twice, in 1929 and 1930. In this same golden two-year period he also won 46 of his 61 races in Britain, 19 of them consecutively. His fame resulted in his appearance as the star in the film of his life, *Wild Boy* (1935), and when he died in 1939 his body was embalmed and sent for display to the Natural History Museum in London.

Middle-age spread. A name dating from the 1930s for the paunchiness that can appear in a middle-aged person, especially one leading a sedentary lifestyle. Since the interpretation of 'middle-aged' is variable (*see* CHAMBERSISMS) and 'spread' hardly specific, the term is really a euphemism designed to hide the reality of an undesirable development.

Middle America. The central and western states of the United States, which are generally regarded as typifying the 'model' American citizen, with his conservative political views and an unadventurous way of life. *See also* FLYOVER ZONE; MIDDLE BRITAIN; MIDDLE ENGLAND.

> Laid out like a sheet of rolled steel on the Great Miami River, a major industrial center plopped down on the placid, undulating farmland of southwestern Ohio, Dayton is about as Middle America as you can get.
> *The Atlantic* (September 1971)

Middle Britain. A more broadly representative equivalent of MIDDLE ENGLAND.

> 'Middle Britain' is easy to make fun of, but it constitutes most of the nation, does most of the work, pays most of the taxes, and mans the organizations … which knit the country together.
> *The Times* (21 September 1999)

Middle-earth. The fantasy world that is the setting of J.R.R. Tolkien's trilogy *The* LORD OF THE RINGS (1954–5). It is ruled over by SAURON the Great and in the canon the name is said to translate *Endorë* or *Ennor*, meaning 'Mortal Lands'. Middle Earth is also an old Anglo-Saxon name for the world, regarded as situated midway between heaven and hell. The name is a corruption of Old English *middangeard*, from words related to modern 'mid' and 'yard', and as such is directly related to the Midgard of Scandinavian mythology. *See also* GONDOR; HOBBIT; MORDOR; SHIRE.

Middle East. A geographical name dating from the turn of the 20th century for an area approximating to southwestern Asia and northern Africa, extending from the Mediterranean to Pakistan and including the Arabian peninsula. A designation was necessary for this region owing to its increasing importance as a source of oil for Western countries. It is the 'Middle' East because it was originally regarded as lying between the Near East, at a time when that designation applied to the Balkan states of southeastern Europe, and the Far East, or the countries of eastern Asia such as China and Japan. Confusingly, the Middle East and Near East are now synonymous.

Geographical names are rarely open to dispute at law, though I once waited all day in Court on the chance of being called to make a discouraging statement on the names Near, Middle, and Far East.

M. AUROUSSEAU: *The Rendering of Geographical Names,* ch vi (1957)

Middle eight. A short section, typically of eight bars, in the middle of a conventionally structured popular song. As such, it is generally of a different character from the rest of the song. The term dates from the 1960s.

These were the days of the new pop, when Boy George, Simon Le Bon and Spandau Ballet paid as much attention to their trousers as they did to the middle eights.

Sunday Times Magazine (19 September 1999)

Middle England. The middle classes in England outside London, regarded as representing a conservative political viewpoint. They are self-reliant in their outlook, hold national values higher than international, dislike change and aspire to self-improvement. It was essentially Middle England that brought NEW LABOUR into power in the 1997 general election. The concept is thus not a geographical one, despite the analogy with MIDDLE AMERICA. *See also* HEART OF ENGLAND; MIDDLE BRITAIN.

While Middle England is in vogue with politicians, research suggests that the traditional values it is seen as espousing may be under threat.

Sunday Times (4 October 1998)

Middle name. A personal name following the first name and preceding the surname, as typically found for Americans, where it is often represented by an initial. The middle name of Dwight D. Eisenhower (1890–1956) was thus David. *See also* NMI.

The expression is also used to denote a person's most characteristic quality, as: 'Caution is my middle name.' The quality or attribute may actually serve as a sobriquet in the manner of a middle name, as typically with gangsters. George 'Machine Gun' Kelly (1895–1954) is an example.

Middle of nowhere. A remote and isolated place. The expression dates from the early 20th century.

Hydro-Quebec is starting to move far up the Manicouagan, in the middle of nowhere.

The Times (Canada Supplement) (21 November 1960)

Middle-of-the-road. Moderate; not extreme; especially in political views.

Much could depend on the men Reagan chooses to help form the policies, and on whether he moves closer to the middle of the road once he assumes office.

Newsweek (17 November 1980)

Middlesex Twins. The nickname of the Middlesex and England batsmen Denis Compton (*see* BRYLCREEM BOY) and Bill Edrich (W.J. Edrich; 1916–86), who enjoyed record-breaking success in the 1947 English season, both men scoring over 3000 runs and often batting together. They gave every sign of enjoying life to the full.

Midinettes. Young French female shop assistants, especially in the Paris fashion or millinery business, are so known, from their thronging of the parks and cafés at midday. The word is a blend of *midi*, 'midday' and *dînette*, 'snack'.

The midinettes are working girls who appear (for their lunch hour) at noon. The place to see them in crowds is in the Jardin de la Trinité, about half-past twelve.

E.I. ROBSON: *A Guide to French Fêtes*, ch iv (1930)

Midlife crisis. An emotional rather than a physical crisis that can occur in one's late 40s or early 50s, especially among men. Its cause is the realization that life may be passing one by. The psychologist who coined the term in 1965, Elliott Jaques, referred to the typical age of crisis as 35, but this biblical mean hardly matches the popular conception of 'midlife'.

Suddenly all the talk is of how great it is to be on the Viagra side of your midlife crisis.

The Times (23 July 1999)

Midnight, Captain. *See* CAPTAIN MIDNIGHT.

Midnight Express. A film (1978) adapted by Oliver Stone from a book by Billy Hayes and William Hoffer based on Hayes's experiences in a Turkish prison after he was found guilty of smuggling hashish out of the country. Directed by Alan Parker and starring Brad Davis as Billy Hayes, the film owed its title to prison slang, 'taking the midnight express' meaning simply 'to escape'.

Midnight feast. A secret snack eaten late at night by children, usually neither at midnight nor in the ritualized manner of a feast. It was a frequent feature in school stories of the 1930s and later, when it was typically held in a dormitory after lights-out. The thrill was the risk run as much as the unusual hour and the concealed comestibles. It is now often held openly in a child's home when a friend comes to stay, as in a SLEEPOVER.

> Alexander is taking a more practical view. There is to be a midnight feast, he announces. So I am to put fizzy orange and marshmallows on my list. Also prawn cocktail-flavour crisps.
>
> *The Times* (3 September 1999)

Midnight Folk, The. A fantasy novel (1927) by John Masefield (1898–1967). The 'Midnight Folk' are a collection of animals and toys with whom the orphan Kay HARKER searches nightly for a hoard of treasure hidden by his great-grandfather. *See also* BOX OF DELIGHTS.

Midnight's Children. A novel (1981) by Salman Rushdie (b.1947), which won the BOOKER PRIZE for fiction. The midnight is 15 August 1947, when India became independent. The children are the 581 born at that midnight. The narrator, who is one of them, is, like Rushdie himself, on the borderline between cultures. The book, which has been read as history and as fantasy, encompasses the post-independence of the nation. *See also* FIRST LINES OF NOVELS; MAGIC REALISM.

Midsummer Marriage, The. A mystical 'quest' opera by Michael Tippett (1905–98) with a libretto by the composer. The work, which was first performed in 1955, is consciously modelled on Mozart's *The Magic Flute*. The parts of Tamino and Pamina are taken by Mark and Jennifer, who quarrel on their wedding day and are obliged to undergo a series of trials, after which they are reunited. This also has echoes of the lovers' tiffs, transmutations and reconciliations in Shakespeare's *A Midsummer Night's Dream*. Another couple in Tippett's opera, Jack and Bella, take the parts of Mozart's Papageno and Papagena.

Midwich Cuckoos, The. A SCIENCE FICTION novel (1957) by John Wyndham (pen-name of John Wyndham Parkes Lucas Beynon Harris; 1903–69). All the women in the English village of Midwich are impregnated at the same time by an astral force, resulting in the births of a breed of children with frightening powers. They are 'cuckoos' in the sense that they are alien, like the chicks that hatch from eggs laid by cuckoos in the nests of other birds. A memorable film version appeared as *Village of the Damned* (1960). A remake (1995) was entirely forgettable.

MI5. The British intelligence service was organized by Captain Vernon Kell (1873–1942) when, in 1909, the Admiralty established the Secret Service Bureau to counter the threat posed by the expanding German fleet. Kell became responsible for counter-espionage within the British Isles, and in 1915 his service was incorporated in the Directorate of Military Intelligence as MI5. The number originally indicated Europe as its area of operations, as distinct from MI1, MI2, MI3 and MI4, which covered the other continents. MI5 played a major role in both world wars and in countering the subsequent communist threat. *See also* MI6.

MiG. A type of Russian fighter aircraft first familiar in the Second World War. It takes its name from its designers, Artyom Mikoyan (M) and Mikhail Gurevich (G), with *i* the Russian for 'and'. The wartime MiGs were all propeller-driven, but the MiG–9 of 1946 was a jet. Appropriately for a fast plane, Russian *mig* means 'instant', 'moment', while *migom* means 'in a flash'.

Mighty Wurlitzer. The majestic electric theatre organ takes its name from its manufacturers, the Rudolf Wurlitzer Company of Cincinnati, Ohio. Rudolf Wurlitzer (1831–1924), a German instrument-maker, went to America in 1853 and founded the company that bears his name in 1890. In 1910 it acquired the Hope-Jones Organ Company of Elmira, New York, and moved its operations to North Tonawanda, New York. It was there where the organ originally known as the 'Unit Orchestra' and now familiar as the 'Mighty Wurlitzer' was developed to become, in the 1920s and 1930s, almost as great an attraction in a cinema auditorium as the film on the screen.

Mikrokosmos. A challengingly modernist collection of 153 piano pieces by Béla Bartók (1881–1945), intended as an instructional course in piano technique. The pieces were written between 1926 and 1939. The title is German for 'microcosm', a concept reflected in the titles of some of the pieces, such as 'From the Diary of a Fly'.

Mildenhall treasure. In 1944 a hoard of Roman silver tableware was discovered in a field near the remains of a 4th-century Roman building northwest of Mildenhall, Suffolk. It included a great dish showing Bacchus and Hercules and was presumably buried for safety by the building's occupants during the troubled days of the Anglo-Saxon invasions. It is now in the British Museum.

Mile a minute. Very fast or rapidly, as: 'He talks a mile a minute.' The expression dates from the 1950s when

British Railways took to advertising trips at this speed, although trains had been travelling at 60mph (97kph) long before this.

Mile-high club. A notional 'club' evolving in the 1970s of those who have coupled sexually while in an aeroplane. The first recorded incident of this type is said to have taken place in 1916, when Lawrence Sperry, an aircraft designer flying a biplane over New York, lost control and crashed, although he and his lover lived to tell the tale. A more recent equivalent is the 'mile-deep club', whose members have followed their example while travelling through the CHANNEL TUNNEL.

> The Mile High Club has had a bad press over the past couple of days. The arrest of married strangers Amanda Holt and David Machin, following their brief encounter in the business-class section of an American Airlines aircraft, was an unromantic ending to their sky-high liaison.
> *The Times* (6 October 1999)

Miles away. Lost in thought; inattentive. The expression dates from the 1940s and is typically used of a person whose thoughts wander while waiting or with others: 'Sorry, I was miles away.'

Militant Tendency. This left-wing grouping, Trotskyite in its policies but aiming to work within the LABOUR PARTY, was formed in the early 1960s as the Revolutionary Socialist League but came to be known by the shorter name, based on that of its newspaper, *Militant*. Considerable damage was done to the image of the Labour Party when evidence emerged in 1980 that Militant had worked to gain control of Labour constituency and regional organizations, as well as trade union branches and trade councils. It was subsequently judged by Labour to be a distinct party, making its adherents ineligible for Labour Party membership. Neil Kinnock, on becoming Labour leader in 1983, undertook the task of rooting out Militant, beginning with the expulsion of five leading members. The peak of Militant's power was its control of Liverpool City Council in the 1980s, with Derek Hatton as deputy council leader. He was expelled from Labour in 1986. *See also* HATTONISTAS; TROT.

Milk Race. The popular name of the Tour of Britain, the country's leading long-distance cycle race, so called because originally sponsored by the Milk Marketing Board in 1958. It had actually been launched seven years earlier, on the basis of the TOUR DE FRANCE, with sponsorship from the *Daily Express*. It takes place over

12 days with distances that have varied from 1475km (922 miles) to 2424km (1515 miles). As in its French equivalent, the yellow jersey is awarded to the daily race leader. The red jersey is the 'King of the Mountain' trophy, awarded to the rider who makes the fastest ascent of the hill peaks.

Milk round. An expression dating from the 1970s for the annual tour of universities and college made by recruiting staff from large companies. A milk round is normally the milkman's daily delivery of milk, but here the idea is presumably to 'milk' the best talent from the universities or to find the 'cream' of business potential.

> For many undergraduates, the milk round appears to be the only hope of a career, rather than just a job.
> *The Times* (28 February 2000)

Milk run. An RAF expression of the Second World War for any sortie flown regularly day after day, or a sortie against an easy target on which inexperienced pilots could be used with impunity. It was as safe and simple as a milkman's early morning round.

Milk Snatcher. A nickname given to Margaret Thatcher, the IRON LADY, while she was secretary of state for education and science (1970–74) in Edward Heath's government (*see* GROCER). In this capacity she ended the provision of free milk to schoolchildren, hence the playground rhyme, 'Thatcher, Thatcher,/ Milk Snatcher.'

Millennium. The arrival of the year 2000 (strictly speaking a bimillennium) fired the imagination of many countries, and special ceremonies were devised to mark the event. In Britain the focus was on the Millennium Experience exhibition by the Thames in London, where the two talking points were the MILLENNIUM DOME and, at the western end of the SOUTH BANK, a huge Millennium Wheel officially called the London Eye. Many events for the millennium weekend itself were held throughout the country, millennial postage stamps were issued, and special grants were made to a whole host of organizations and enterprises. *See also* MILLENNIUM BUG.

Millennium bug. The name given to the nightmare that threatened the correct operation of computer systems in the first second after midnight on 31 December 1999, the opening moment of the year 2000 and of the new MILLENNIUM. The problem arose because most computers manufactured before 1993 used only two digits instead of four to represent the year portion of the date. The danger was thus that as the new era dawned, the untreated computer chips would register the year as 1900, not 2000. In consequence the closing years of the 20th century witnessed a sort of MASS HYSTERIA, with companies racing against the clock to debug their 'non-compliant' systems in order to avert widespread chaos. The measures were either successful or unnecessary in the first place, and there was little or no disruption to business or inconvenience to the public.

Millennium Dome. The showpiece and centrepiece of the Millennium Experience exhibition in London marking the new MILLENNIUM. It was erected on a tract of previously derelict land on the Greenwich peninsula as the largest structure of its kind ever built and was divided into 14 exhibition zones, each sponsored by a well-known company: Body, Faith, Home Planet, Journey, Talk, Learning, Living Island, Mind, Money, Work, Play, Rest, Self Portrait and Shared Ground. The Dome was opened by Queen Elizabeth II on 31 December 1999 but initially disappointed many visitors, who endured long waits to see poorly explained or even malfunctioning exhibits.

Millennium Island. On 11 August 1997 the Republic of Kiribati, in the southwest Pacific, declared the International Date Line to pass east of Caroline Island, instead of west, at the same time renaming it 'Millennium Island' so that it would be the first place in the world to see in the MILLENNIUM. The uninhabited island gained brief fame in consequence and featured worldwide on television.

Millennium Wheel. *See* MILLENNIUM.

Mills, Bertram. A name synonymous with circuses. Bertram Mills (1873–1938) was the son of a coach proprietor, and originally helped his father with coaches. After the First World War, when there was little call for coaches, he entered the circus world, setting up his own first circus at Olympia, London, in 1920. The circus continued after his death but closed in 1967.

Mills & Boon. The byname for accessible, affordable romantic fiction had its origin in the publishing partnership in 1908 of Gerald Mills (1877–1928) and Charles Boon (1877–1943). They began with editions of standard popular authors such as P.G. Wodehouse, Jack London and Hugh Walpole. Later, during the depressed 1930s, when people took to reading as a form of escapism, they decided that the genre to cultivate was romantic fiction. Their combined name is now generic for a GIRL MEETS BOY love story or even a real-life 'love match'. All Mills & Boons are written to a formula, described in a manual for the authors called *Behind the Hearts and Flowers*. *See also* HARLEQUIN ROMANCES; LUBBOCK'S LAW.

> Girl meets boy, momentous events force separation, girl meets second boy, what happens next? If you have read much Mills & Boon – and it's surprising the people who have – you may also recognize the style.
> *Sunday Times* (23 August 1998)

Mills bomb. A type of hand grenade used by the British army for several decades. It was designed in 1915 by William Mills (1856–1932) and entered service in the First World War as Grenade No. 5. Later models (designated Grenade No. 23 and No. 36) could be fired from a rifle. It continued in use until the 1960s. Mills bombs were also popularly referred to as 'pineapples', from their shape.

Milly-Molly-Mandy. A character created by the British writer and artist Joyce Lankester Brisley (1896–1978). Milly-Molly-Mandy, a little girl who lives in a cottage with her parents, grandparents, aunt and uncle, first appeared in *Milly-Molly-Mandy Stories* (1928) and many other titles followed.

Milner's Kindergarten. A nickname given to a group of young men associated with Sir Alfred Milner (Viscount Milner from 1902) in the period after the Boer War. Milner (1854–1925) was the aggressively imperialist British high commissioner in South Africa (1897–1905), who had done much to precipitate the war. His 'Kindergarten', which included the future novelist John Buchan, was involved with him in the task of postwar reconstruction, employing policies aimed at encouraging British immigration and creating a British majority in South Africa. The group went on to become ardent advocates of the British imperial idea.

Minas Morgul. A sinister fortress-city in J.R.R. Tolkien's epic *The* LORD OF THE RINGS (1954–5), situated on the borders of MORDOR. Formerly known as Minas Ithil (the Tower of the Moon), it was renamed Minas Morgul (the Tower of Sorcery) after its capture by SAURON, the Dark Lord. *See also* GONDOR.

Mind-boggling. Overwhelming; startling. The literal sense of the term, which dates from the 1960s, is 'causing the mind to boggle', i.e. to be alarmed or scared, from a word related to 'bogey'. The catchphrase 'The mind boggles' is used to describe a reaction to anything unusual or unlikely.

> Barry Cryer singing in a West End musical? The mind boggles.
>
> *The Times* (10 September 1999)

Minder. A television comedy series of 1979–94 about a well-meaning bodyguard or 'minder', Terry McCann, played by Dennis Waterman, and his boss, a shady second-hand car dealer, Arthur Daley, played by George Cole. The series began as a thriller but low ratings and critical disfavour caused a reduction in its violence and an increase in its humour, to the benefit of all concerned. It was Daley who popularized the catchphrases HER INDOORS and NICE LITTLE EARNER.

Ming. A nickname of Australian politician Sir Robert Menzies (1894–1978), Liberal prime minister of Australia (1939–41, 1949–66), the Scottish pronunciation of name Menzies being 'Mingis'. The evil Emperor Ming was a character in the US space opera FLASH GORDON. Menzies's long tenure of office became known as the Ming dynasty (the original Ming dynasty ruled China from 1368 to 1644).

Mini. The popular British car was an instant success when launched by the British Motor Corporation in 1959. It cost just under £500, achieved maximum room for its small size by placing its engine sideways under the bonnet, and owed its good road-holding property to its front-wheel drive and independent suspension. It was originally marketed under the Morris and Austin labels, the former marked by straight lines on its radiator grille, the latter by wavy. A speedier version, designed by John Cooper, was available from 1961 as the Mini-Cooper. Forty years on the Mini was still regarded with nostalgic affection and was still seen on the road.

Miniature for Sport. A nickname given to the diminutive Conservative politician Colin Moynihan (b.1955) when he became minister for sport in 1987.

Minimalism. A trend in abstract art, and especially sculpture, of the 1960s, involving an emphasis on simple geometric shapes, the use of primary colours and a minimum of meaning, emotion or illusion. In the next decade minimalism emerged as an avant-garde movement in music, where it is characterized by the repetition of very short phrases which gradually change, producing a hypnotic effect. Leading minimalist sculptors include Carl Andre (b.1935), Donald Judd (1928–94) and Tony Smith (1912–80), while Philip Glass (b.1937), Steve Reich (b.1936) and Terry Riley (b.1935) may be named as major minimalist composers. All six are American.

Miniskirt. The skirt with the daringly high hemline, at its peak reaching heights of up to 9in (23cm) above the knee, was created in 1965 by the Parisian couturier André Courrèges, popularized by British designers such as Mary Quant, and publicized by the model Jean Shrimpton, the SHRIMP. Moral watchdogs condemned the rising hem, which often revealed more than a flash of thigh, as a sign of falling standards, but many young women, and some older ones, saw it as the epitome of the new freedoms, particularly since the advent of the PILL. The maxiskirt, reaching to the ankles, soon followed as if in reaction, and the midiskirt, reaching to midcalf, evolved soon after to balance the two extremes.

Minister of Fun. A nickname given to the Conservative politician David Mellor (b.1949) when appointed in 1992 as the first 'secretary of state for the national heritage', whose portfolio included sport and the arts. It was then revealed that Mellor, an avid football fan, had had an affair with a young actress and had allegedly made love to her wearing a Chelsea strip. Just as Mellor seemed to be riding this scandal, it emerged that he had accepted a holiday from the daughter of a senior figure in the PLO, and he was obliged to resign. Earlier in his career, while a junior Foreign Office minister, he had publicly criticized Israeli brutality in dealing with the Palestinian INTIFADA. Mellor lost his seat in the 1997 general election and later described himself as a 'broadcaster and international business adviser'. *See also* MINISTRY OF ... .

Ministry of ... . A nickname for an organization or authority of some kind, its nature indicated by the appropriate word or phrase, such as the Ministry of Silly Walks in the comedy series MONTY PYTHON'S FLYING CIRCUS or the Ministry of Sound nightclub in southeast London. The formula is based on political titles such as the Ministry of Transport or Ministry of Agriculture. The usage is facetious or decorative rather than satirical.

> The Ministry of Silly Names has been at it again. Corus, the moniker for merged British Steel and Koninklijke Hoogovens, is not the worst of its ilk. But like most of these rebranding exercises Corus brings the usual, inexplicable, neo-classical pretensions.
>
> *The Times* (1 October 1999)

Minor public school. A somewhat demeaning term dating from the 1930s for an English public school that is not one of the ancient foundations, such as Eton, Harrow, Rugby or Winchester.

> [Conservative MP] Jeffrey Archer has been telling little fibs since he went to a minor public school [Wellington School].
>
> *Sunday Times* (28 November 1999)

Mint condition. Perfect condition; new or good as new. The expression derives from philately, in which a stamp in mint condition is one 'retaining all the freshness and perfection with which it was endowed at the time it left the manufacturers' (B.W.H. Poole and Willard O. Wylie, *The Standard Philatelic Dictionary*, 1922). Philatelists in turn adopted the term from numismatists. The phrase was subsequently taken up by used-car salesmen and second-hand dealers, not always with the greatest degree of veracity.

Mir (Russian, 'peace', 'world'). The core module of the Soviet space station so named was launched on 19 February 1986 and was first occupied a month later by the cosmonauts Leonid Kizim and Vladimir Solovyev, who spent 53 days adjusting equipment and bringing the complex into working order. In March 1987 the module Kvant ('Quantum') 1 was added for work in astrophysics, and Kvant 2 and 3 followed in February and March 1990 respectively. *Mir* was designed to last five years but survived until 1999 when it was abandoned after more than 77,000 orbits and 1600 breakdowns, marking the end of a heroic episode in Russian space exploration.

Miracle in the Gorbals. A justly neglected ballet by Arthur Bliss (1891–1975) with choreography by Robert Helpmann (1909–86). The work was first performed in 1944. The Gorbals is an area of Glasgow, to the south of the river Clyde, and was then a notoriously rough slum district, hence the expression a 'Gorbals kiss' for a head butt.

Miracle Mile. A nickname applied by the developer A.W. Ross in the 1930s to a stretch of Wilshire Boulevard, Los Angeles, extending about 1.5km (1 mile) from La Brea Avenue to Fairfax Avenue. The aim was to promote the Boulevard's commercial potential.

Miracle on 34th Street. A film (1947) adapted by George Seaton from a story by Valentine Davies about the extraordinary events that follow after a kindly old man calling himself 'Kris Kringle' is recruited as Macy's Santa Claus during New York's Christmas rush. The 'miracle' that takes place in the film is the influence this latter-day Santa Claus (played by Edmund Gwenn) has in reminding busy shoppers of the true meaning of Christmas. There was an unnecessary remake in 1994.

Miramax. A film company based in New York that has done much to raise the profile of American independent cinema. It was founded in 1979 by brothers Bob and Harvey Weinstein and has prospered by distributing and marketing a number of highbrow films, among them *The Thin Blue Line* (1988), SEX, LIES AND VIDEOTAPE (1989), *My Left Foot* (1989), *Reservoir Dogs* (1991) and *The Piano* (1993). In 1989 it began to make its own films, such as the SLASHER MOVIE *Scream* (1996), *Good Will Hunting* (1997) and *Sliding Doors* (1998).

Miranda Rights. In US law the rights of an arrested person to have access to legal counsel and to remain silent under questioning. The rights resulted from the four cases of 1966 known collectively as Miranda v. State of Arizona. Ernesto Miranda, a 23-year-old dropout arrested for rape and kidnap, had signed a written confession without being aware of his rights and had not been informed of them by the arresting officers. The US Supreme Court thus ruled that the explicit statement of the rights must become a required part of the arrest procedure.

> You have a right to remain silent, the Constitution requires that I so inform you of this right and you need not talk to me if you do not wish to do so. You do not have to answer any of my questions.
>
> *Miranda Rights* (Clause 1) (1966)

Misérables, Les. A musical tragedy (1980) with a score by Claude-Michel Schönberg (b.1944), lyrics by Herbert Kretzmer and libretto by Alain Boublil about the life of Jean Valjean, a former prisoner who rises to become the leader of a revolutionary movement in France. The show was based on Victor Hugo's novel of the same name (1862), the title referring to the oppressed people whom Valjean represents. The show became familiarly known as *Les Miz* as it established itself as one of the West End's longest running entertainments.

Misery Line. A former nickname for the railway line from Fenchurch Street, London, to Southend, given by commuters for its crowded, dirty and frequently late trains. The Northern Line of the London Underground was also so known before the introduction of new rolling stock.

Prism, which operates four rail franchises, including the London, Tilbury and Southend service once dubbed the 'misery line', said the fall in profits was due to a sharp drop in government subsidy.

Daily Telegraph (9 December 1998)

No more Misery Line, guys! I couldn't believe it, the Northern Lights have finally reached south London! Brand new trains, automatic doors, sexy blondes, beautiful brunettes, attractive Afro-Cubans, spicy Latinos are all here to invite you to the new Millennium trip from High Barnet to Morden.

The Smoke (London Newsletter), Issue 6 (1999)

Misfits, The. A film (1961) based on a screenplay by US playwright Arthur Miller (b.1915) about a small group of lonely souls whose lives become intertwined through their mutual sympathy. Starring Clark Gable and Montgomery Clift as drifting rodeo riders and Marilyn MONROE as a recently divorced former stripper, the film entered movie legend if only on the strength of the fact that all three stars died not long after. The title, which clearly reflects upon the main characters themselves, also refers to the 'misfit' horses Gable is often hired to round up, 'misfits' being wild mustangs considered too small to be used for rodeo or ranch work and suitable only as an ingredient in dog food.

MI6. The British secret service, also known as the Secret Intelligence Service (SIS). In its modern form it dates from 1909 when Captain Mansfield Cumming (1859–1923) was put in charge of overseas intelligence operations. *See also* 'C'; FIFTH MAN; MI5.

Misper. Police slang for a missing person. The term was publicized in 1994 following the horrific discovery of the bodies of several young women in Gloucester, killed and buried over a number of years. Concern was expressed that many of the victims had become 'mispers' without their disappearance being registered by family or friends. The word has become familiar by its frequent use in the television drama series *The* BILL and was even the title of a 1997 opera.

Mispronounced words. Many words in English are regularly mispronounced. In some cases the cause is confusion with a similar-sounding word of quite different meaning; in others it is ignorance of the word's composition. The following, based on Professor J.C. Wells's *Longman Pronunciation Dictionary* (1990), is a selection of 50 common corruptions, the words

so garbled being annexed in brackets. Incorrect or disputed syllable stresses, as *con*troversy/con*tro*versy, are not included. *See also* MISSPELLED WORDS.

anenome (anemone)
anythink (anything)
artheritis (arthritis)
athelete (athlete)
Bolzac (Balzac)
bought (brought)
cerstificate (certificate)
dash-hound (dachshund)
deterorate (deteriorate)
dimunution (diminution)
ecsetera (etcetera)
everythink (everything)
Febury (February)
fith (fifth)
funery (funerary)
geneologist (genealogist)
grievious (grievous)
haitch (aitch, the letter H)
hari-kari (hara-kiri)
height-th (height)
hyperbowl (hyperbole)
intregal (integral)
itinary (itinerary)
libary (library)
loathe (loath or loth)
macco (macho)
maintainance (maintenance)
meterologist (meteorologist)
mischievious (mischievous)
nucular (nuclear)
obsequous (obsequious)
pacifically (specifically)
particly (particularly)
perculate (percolate)
portentious (portentous)
pronounciation (pronunciation)
protruberance (protuberance)
reconize (recognize)
revelant (relevant)
reverent (reverend)
sacrosant (sacrosanct)

secetry (secretary)

sikth (sixth)

somethink (something)

stipendary (stipendiary)

suffrajan (suffragan)

supernumary (supernumerary)

tempory (temporary)

tenderhooks (tenterhooks)

Westminister (Westminster)

Miss America. The first beauty pageant of this name was held in Atlantic City, New Jersey, in 1921, mainly as a publicity stunt to extend the tourist season beyond Labor Day (the first Monday in September). There were only eight contestants representing towns rather than states and in 1928 the annual event was discontinued, only to be revived in 1935. In 1954 the pageant was first televised and since then has known both fame and shame. In 1984 Vanessa Williams, the first black Miss America, was deprived of her crown when explicit photographs of her appeared in *Penthouse* magazine. *See also* MISS WORLD.

Miss a trick, To. To fail to see an opportunity; to be unaware of a potential advantage. The expression is mostly found in the negative, as: 'He never misses a trick.' The allusion is to a card game such as whist or bridge, in which a trick is a group of cards played in a given round and either won ('taken') or lost ('missed'). The phrase dates from the 1920s.

Miss Frigidaire. A media nickname for the American tennis champion Chris Evert (b.1954), given on account of her cool and unsmiling style. The derivation is in the refrigerator so named, itself suggesting 'frigid air'. Hillary Clinton (b.1947), wife of US President Bill Clinton, has similarly been dubbed 'Sister Frigidaire' by the media for her cold exterior. *See also* ICE MAIDEN.

Missionary position. The usual position for sexual intercourse, in which the woman lies underneath the man. Early missionaries are said to have recommended this position as the 'proper' one to Polynesian people, to whom the practice was unknown. The term dates from the 1960s.

Mission impossible. Any impossible or seemingly impossible task. The catchphrase was popularized by the title of an American television spy thriller broadcast from 1966 to 1972 (in Britain from 1967 to 1974). Each week's instalment opened with the following words spoken on a tape recorder that self-destructed five seconds later: 'Your mission, Jim, should you decide to accept it ... .' Jim was Jim Phelps, played by Peter Graves, head of the elite espionage agency Impossible Missions Force (IMF).

> She said there was no fish on the menu. So Brogan took out a fiver and discreetly approached the porter who said he would look into it. Mission Impossible.
> DERMOT BOLGER (ed.): *Finbar's Hotel*, 'No Pets Please' (1997)

Mission statement. A formal summary of the policy and objectives of a business firm, government organization or the like. The expression is of American origin and was first taken up in Britain in the early 1990s. 'Mission' here carries deliberate associations of vocation or even a religious calling, as well as simply denoting an intention. Some mission statements are brief and pithy, while others are rambling and repetitive, such as the following, that of the Football League:

> The role of the Football League is to provide a nationwide membership organization and structure for professional football through which the Football League can facilitate financial success, stability and development of professional football clubs, administer and regulate the professional game and promote the values and contribution of the professional game to our national life.

Miss Marple. *See* MARPLE, MISS.

Misspelled words. The varieties and vagaries of English spelling are notorious, and it is perhaps understandable if not forgivable that many people, even the 'great and good', err in the correct spelling of quite common words. In 1992 the *Sunday Times* commissioned a leading British examination board to test a sample of 1500 secretaries, clerks, administrative and office trainees for their ability to spell everyday words. Four words were misspelled by more than half the sample, and many could not differentiate words in pairs of similar spelling. The top 20 misspellings were as follows, with (in brackets) the percentage of errors.

practice/practise (54%)

withhold (52%)

occurred (52%)

innovate (52%)

benefited (48%)

principal/principle (45%)

incur (44%)

grievance (40%)

concede (40%)

transferred (39%)

competent (37%)

calendar (35%)

warranty (35%

acquire (34%)

liaise (34%)

truly (34%)

expedite (33%)

discrete/discreet (33)

affect/effect (32%)

accommodation (32%)

Miss Smilla's Feeling for Snow. A novel (1993; in USA as *Smilla's Sense of Snow*; in Danish as *Frøken Smillas Fornemmelse for Sne*, 1992) by Peter Høeg (b.1957). Part mystery story on land and part adventure thriller at sea, it is told in the first person by a personable Inuit academic whose special study is snow.

Miss World. The annual beauty contest was inaugurated by Eric Morley in 1951 as a British equivalent of the American Miss Universe. It was regularly televised until 1988, when mounting feminist protests resulted in its transfer from Britain to Asia and Latin America. It reverted to London in 1999. A Mr World competition was introduced in 1996. *See also* MISS AMERICA.

Mitty, Walter. *See* WALTER MITTY.

Mix and match. A term for the selection and combination of any different but complementary items, such as clothing or pieces of equipment. A social gathering of supposedly compatible individuals may also be so described.

> At an experimental mix'n'match do the other day, an Old Etonian friend of mine, when asked where the loos were, replied: 'They don't have any loos here. Only toilets'.
> *Sunday Times* (13 June 1999)

Miz Lillian. The nickname of the much-respected Lillian Carter (1898–1983), wife of a Georgia peanut warehouser and mother of Jimmy Carter, Democratic president of the USA (1977–81). Her other son, Billy Carter, was a hard-drinking Southern redneck and ongoing embarrassment for his brother.

Miznerisms. The American dramatist Wilson Mizner (1876–1933) is best remembered for his philosophical maxims, many of which are included in Alva

Johnston's *The Legendary Mizners* (1953). The following three are probably the best known: 'Be nice to people on your way up because you'll meet 'em on your way down', 'Treat a whore like a lady and a lady like a whore', and 'If you steal from one author, it's plagiarism; if you steal from many, it's research'.

Moaning Minnie. A Second World War term for a six-barrelled German mortar. The first word alludes to the rising shriek when it was fired; the second was based on the German word for 'mortar', *Minenwerfer* (literally 'mine thrower'). The name was also given to the air-raid warning siren from its repetitive wail, and it is colloquially applied to any constant moaner or habitual 'whinger' or complainer.

> Although I am not overly fond of moaning minnies, I have decided that complaining is no bad thing. In fact, we all should complain more.
> *Sunday Times* (5 September 1999)

Mob, The. A nickname for the US Mafia, dating from the 1920s.

> The award-winning Channel 4 Mafia drama, *The Sopranos*, has attracted the kind of critical review that far outstrips any praise from mere critics. The show is a hit with the Mob.
> *The Times* (18 December 1999)

Mobile phone. A type of telephone with access to a cellular radio system, enabling it to be used over a wide area without being physically connected to a network. It is less commonly known as a cellphone. A 'cell' is a particular local area covered by a short-range transmitter, and calls are automatically switched from one transmitter to the next as the caller enters an adjoining cell. The mobile is particularly popular with teenagers, and by the beginning of the 21st century five out of ten Britons owned such a phone.

Mockney. An affected imitation of Cockney speech or vocabulary, or a person who adopts such speech, often with the aim of winning STREET CRED. The name is a felicitous blend of 'mock' and 'Cockney'.

> With her large, inquisitive eyes, tousled Brit-girl hair, well-behaved Mockney accent and the twenty-something uniform of black sporty clothes, she [fashion designer Stella McCartney] looks like someone who can't wait to get back to her own quarters.
> *The Times* (26 October 1998)

Mock-up. A phrase originating in the Second World War for a trial model or full-size working model. In the US Air Force, a panel mounted with models of aircraft parts and used for instructional purposes was so called.

Modelizer. A term of the late 1990s for a man who dates models or SUPERMODELS. It is based on 'womanizer' and arose in New York bars frequented by models, such as Lot 61 and the Bowery, but caught on worldwide when the television series *Sex and the City* (1998), starring Sarah Jessica Parker, devoted an entire episode to men who compete to date models. Nor are modelizers confined to the American social scene, since they are equally active in Britain, especially in clubs such as ANNABEL'S and TRAMP. Examples are the photo gallery owner Tim Jeffries, who has dated Elle Macpherson, Claudia Schiffer and Koo Stark, and the investment banker Robert Hanson, who has 'conquered' Normandie Keith, Sophie Anderton and Brenda Schad. The phenomenon thus saw the supermodel shifting her emphasis from the furtherance of her career to the desirable social cachet of public recognition in the company of a rich but relatively unknown 'nice young man'.

Modern classic. A modern literary work that is seen as, or promoted as, one that will be come to be regarded as of high or lasting quality. The phrase was popularized by the 'PENGUIN Modern Classics' of the 1960s, which complemented the 'Penguin Classics' of the 1940s. *See also* FIRST LINES OF NOVELS.

Modernism. An umbrella term for the various movements in the arts developing in the 20th century that were characterized by a rejection of traditional subjects, attitudes and techniques. In literature it is associated with the STREAM OF CONSCIOUSNESS style, in music with SERIALISM and in the visual arts with the various movements of non-representational or abstract art (*see* CUBISM; DADAISM; FUTURISM). *See also* POSTMODERNISM.

The term also denotes a movement in the Roman Catholic Church that sought to interpret the ancient teachings of the church with due regard to the current teachings of science, modern philosophy and history. It arose in the late 19th century and was formally condemned by Pope Pius X in 1907 in the encyclical *Pascendi*, which stigmatized it as the 'synthesis of all heresies'.

Modesty Blaise. *See* BLAISE, MODESTY.

Mods and rockers. The mods (from 'modern') developed as a teenage cult in London in the early 1960s, initially putting their emphasis on fastidiousness

and extravagance in dress and fashion. The rise of CARNABY STREET as their dress centre was a consequence. Mainly devoid of social conscience, they had some association with homosexuality and drugs, and their mode of life reflected the less desirable results of the AFFLUENT SOCIETY. With the rise of the rival gangs of leather-jacketed rockers (from ROCK 'N' ROLL), akin to the TEDDY BOYS of the 1950s and modelling themselves on the American HELL'S ANGELS, trouble began. Bank holiday clashes between mods and rockers, who arrived in their hordes on scooters and motorcycles, made some seaside resorts, notably Brighton, hazardous places.

Mogadon Man. A nickname for the politician Sir Geoffrey Howe, Baron Howe of Aberavon (b.1926), chancellor of the exchequer (1979–83) and foreign secretary (1983–9), from his measured manner and somnolent appearance. Mogadon is the name of a proprietary soporific. The Labour politician Denis Healey, when criticized by him, said it was 'like being savaged by a DEAD SHEEP' (House of Commons, 14 June 1978). Howe held his cabinet posts under Margaret Thatcher, the IRON LADY, with whom he eventually fell out over Europe. His resignation speech in 1990 criticizing her leadership style led to her downfall.

Mohican. A style of haircut current from the early 1980s in which the head is shaved except for a brushlike strip of hair over the top of the head to the back of the neck. It derives its name from its supposed resemblance to that worn by the Mohican Indians.

Mole, Adrian. The intellectually ambitious schoolboy in Sue Townsend's humorous novel *The Secret Diary of Adrian Mole Aged 13¾* (1982) and its sequels *The Growing Pains of Adrian Mole* (1984), *True Confessions of Adrian Albert Mole* (1989), *Adrian Mole from Minor to Major* (1991), *Adrian Mole: The Wilderness Years* (1993) and *Adrian Mole: The Cappuccino Years* (1999). In the first of these he is faced with a precarious family life and beset by various emotional problems and fantasies, the latter mainly involving the beautiful Pandora Braithwaite.

Molesworth, Nigel. The inky schoolboy who is 'the curse of St Custard's'. He was the creation of the writer Geoffrey Willans and the artist Ronald Searle and his adventures and misadventures are recounted in *Down with Skool!* (1953) and *How To Be Topp* (1954). One of his distinctive attributes is his quirky, quasi-phonetic spelling in phrases such as 'as any fule kno'.

Still xmas is a good time with all those presents and good food and i hope it will never die out or at any rate not until i am grown up and hav to pay for it all.
How To Be Topp, ch xi

Molotov. The alias (meaning 'hammer') of the Soviet statesman Vyacheslav Mikhailovich Skryabin (1890–1986), commissar (later minister) for foreign affairs (1939–49). In the Second World War the name became associated with the MOLOTOV BREADBASKET and MOLOTOV COCKTAIL.

Molotov breadbasket. A canister of incendiary bombs which, on being launched from a plane, opened and showered the bombs over a wide area. It took its name from V.M. MOLOTOV.

Molotov cocktail. A homemade anti-tank bomb, invented and first used by the Finns against the Russians in 1940 and developed in Britain as one of the weapons of the HOME GUARD. It consisted of a bottle filled with inflammable and glutinous liquid, with a slow match protruding from the top. When thrown at a tank, the bottle burst, the liquid ignited and spread over the plating of the tank. V.M. MOLOTOV organized the production of similar grenades.

Moment of truth. The time when a person is put to the test or a decision must be made. The expression translates Spanish *el momento de la verdad* and refers to the time of the final sword-thrust in a bullfight. The English equivalent is first found in Ernest Hemingway's *Death in the Afternoon* (1932) with reference to the literal meaning:

> The whole end of the bullfight was the final sword thrust, the actual encounter between the man and the animal, what the Spanish call the moment of truth.
> ch vii

Monday Club. A club of right-wing Conservatives founded in 1961, so named because they originally met regularly for lunch on a Monday. They chose this day to mourn BLACK MONDAY, the day of Harold Macmillan's WIND OF CHANGE speech, which to them was anathema. They are regarded, or regard themselves, as the proper guardians of true Conservatism.

Monday morning blues or **feeling.** Disinclination to start work after the weekend. The perception that one feels unhappier on Mondays than on other days of the week is a myth. It is simply that the day follows directly after the weekend, when one is usually more cheerful and relaxed. *See also* I DON'T LIKE MONDAYS.

Monday morning quarterback. A person who criti-

cizes with the benefit of hindsight. The term derives from American football and originated in the 1930s when the game as a SPECTATOR SPORT was mostly watched at weekends. Office discussions of the past weekend's game would take place on Mondays and be dominated by various 'experts' who would revise the quarterback's instructions to his team in such a way as to optimize the results.

Mondo (Italian, 'world'). A word used as an intensive when coupled with another word, the latter given the Italian-style ending -*o*. Examples are 'mondo-weirdo' for something very unusual, 'mondo-cheapo' for something impressively cheap. The linguistic quirk arose among American students in the 1960s and specifically derives from the title of the Italian documentary film *Mondo Cane* (1961), literally 'Dog's World', depicting eccentric human behaviour.

Monica. A female first name tarnished in the latter half of the 20th century from its association with prostitutes and illicit sexual relationships, as notably by Monica Coghlan, a prostitute with whom the Conservative politician Jeffrey Archer was alleged to have been involved in 1986, and by Monica Lewinsky, an American White House employee with whom President Clinton was similarly associated in 1998. The sleazy overtones were increased by the media's regular use of the name in connection with such contexts. *See also* ORAL OFFICE.

> We live in an age of sexual hype, in which every journalist knows that 'Monica' stories sell newspapers.
> *The Times* (22 November 1999)

Monkey see, monkey do. A comment to or about a person who is imitating another's action or whose action might itself be imitated. It is mostly used as a criticism or admonition and arose in the United States in the 1920s, probably from a children's game.

Monkey suit. A uniform or formal suit; a man's evening dress. The allusion is probably to performing monkeys, who were dressed or rigged out in such suits.

Monkey Trial. The highly publicized trial from 10 to 21 June 1925 of John T. Scopes, a high school teacher in Dayton, Tennessee, charged with violating state law by teaching the theory of evolution. The nickname alludes to the Darwinians' belief that human beings were descended from monkeys. Scopes was convicted and fined $100 but subsequently acquitted on the technicality that the fine was excessive.

Monocled Mutineer, The. The nickname of Private Percy Toplis (c.1897–1920), who deserted from the British Army in 1917 and was alleged to have come out of hiding to join the mutiny at the training camp at Étaples, France, that year. He is said to have passed as an officer wearing a monocle. He was shot dead in the Lake District after a police hunt when wanted on charges of shooting two police officers and a taxi driver in Andover, Hampshire. He had a long criminal record but was glorified by a television drama of 1986, titled with his nickname, in which he was dashingly portrayed by Paul McGann. The play drew official condemnation for its suggestion that British soldiers had been executed for desertion, although this is known to have been the case.

Monopoly. The well-known board game, based on the acquisition of real estate, was patented in 1933 as the brainchild of Charles B. Darrow, an American heating equipment engineer from Germantown, Pennsylvania. Its origins, however, date back to the late 19th century, when property games began to become popular, and it in fact bears a close similarity to 'The Landlord's Game', invented by Elizabeth Magie in 1904. Magie had developed her game as a piece of anti-capitalistic propaganda, with the aim of showing how unscrupulous landlords could charge exorbitant rents. It is thus somewhat ironic that Monopoly evolved to became one of the great symbols of capitalism. It sells in over 20 languages around the world, and the properties on the board are named after the streets of a city in the appropriate country. This is usually the capital, so that the British version has London streets, the French those of Paris and so on. The American game has streets in Atlantic City, New Jersey, as this was where the Darrows spent their holidays.

Monroe, Marilyn. The American actress who became a symbol of HOLLYWOOD's ruthless exploitation of beauty and youth, born Norma Jean Mortensen in Los Angeles in 1926. She had a disturbed childhood spent for the most part in foster homes as the result of the mental illness suffered by her mother. She was married for the first time at 16, to James Dougherty, partly to prevent her return to an orphanage. They were divorced four years later, and that same year, 1946, she had her first screen test, adopting the name Marilyn Monroe. It has been suggested that she became a prostitute to support herself. After several small film parts she starred as a sexy DUMB BLONDE in

How to Marry a Millionaire and GENTLEMEN PREFER BLONDES (both 1953). Wanting more serious roles she studied at Lee Strasberg's Actors' Studio and appeared to critical acclaim in *Bus Stop* (1956) and *The* MISFITS (1961). The latter was her last film, written for her by the playwright Arthur Miller, whom she had married in 1956. She had a close relationship with John F. Kennedy and Robert F. Kennedy (*see* KENNEDY CURSE) and famously sang 'Happy Birthday, Mr President'. She was divorced from Miller in 1961 and the following year died of an overdose of sleeping pills. *See also* CANDLE IN THE WIND; SOME LIKE IT HOT.

> Marilyn Monroe was a legend. In her own lifetime she created a myth of what a poor girl from a deprived background could attain. For the entire world she became a symbol of the eternal feminine.
>
> LEE STRASBERG (at her funeral), quoted in EPHRAIM KATZ: *The Macmillan International Film Encyclopedia* (1994)

Monroe effect. A term for any sudden gust of wind or draught that lifts women's skirts. It derives from the famous publicity photograph of the actress Marilyn MONROE (1926–62) from the film *The* SEVEN YEAR ITCH (1955), in which she is shown standing on a subway (underground railway) grating just as a train passes underneath, blowing her skirt high in the air.

Mons, Angels of. *See* ANGELS OF MONS.

Monsieur Hulot. *See* HULOT, MONSIEUR.

Monster Raving Loony Party. The best known British FRINGE PARTY was the brain child of David 'Screaming Lord' Sutch (1942–99), a former pop musician and eccentric stage artist who on a whim in 1963, when the PROFUMO AFFAIR caused a by-election in Stratford-upon-Avon, decided to enter the political fray and set himself up as the National Teenage party candidate. The one-man band was the germ of the Official Monster Raving Loony Party, Sutch himself being by implication the 'raving loony'. The party regularly met the challenge of subsequent elections, and its absurd policies injected a note of welcome zaniness and levity into the traditionally po-faced proceedings. They included the abolition of all work before lunchtime, the decimalization of time, with 100 minutes to the hour, 10 hours to the day, and 10 days to the week, and the turning upside down of Battersea Power Station to make a snooker table. At first, inevitably, Sutch polled minimal votes, but in the 1990s did rather better, reaching a peak of 1114 at Rotherham in 1994.

Beset by personal problems that few knew about, Sutch took his own life at the age of 58, but his loyal supporters appointed a new leader and the party has continued its colourful existence.

Monte Cassino. *See* GUSTAV LINE.

Montessori method. A system of training and educating young children evolved by the Italian educationist, Dr Maria Montessori (1870–1952). Based on 'free discipline' and the use of specially devised 'educational apparatus' and 'didactic material', it has exercised considerable influence on work with young children. In 1907 Dr Montessori opened the first *Casa dei Bambini* ('Children's House'), a school for young children from the San Lorenzo slum district of Rome, and in 1909 set forth her theories in *Il metodo della pedagogica scientifica* (1909), a work appearing in English translation as *The Montessori Method* (1912).

Montezuma's revenge. One of several colourful euphemisms for diarrhoea suffered by visitors to Mexico or abroad in general, in allusion to the Aztec emperor's supposed reprisal after his defeat. Others of similar local reference are Aztec two-step, Cairo crud, Delhi belly, gippy (i.e. Egyptian) tummy, Hong Kong dog and Rangoon runs.

Montoneros. A left-wing urban guerrilla group active in Argentina in the 1970s. The group was founded by Juan Perón (1895–1974), populist president of Argentina, before his overthrow and exile in 1955. In 1970 the Montoneros set about eliminating the moderate Perónista union leadership, and when Perón returned to power as president in 1973 he condemned the Montoneros, who embarked on a wider campaign of political violence. Under the right-wing military junta that overthrew Perón in 1976, the Montoneros became the target of the 'Dirty War', and many joined the DISAPPEARED. In South American Spanish *montonero* is a generic term for a guerrilla fighter.

Mont Sainte-Victoire. The small rocky mountain in Provence became the favourite subject of the painter Paul Cézanne (1839–1906). He started painting it in the 1880s, and his last version was completed in 1902. In this late period, the fruits of which were to dictate the course of art in the 20th century, Cézanne described how: 'The landscape becomes human, becomes a thinking, living being within me. I become one with my picture … We merge in an iridescent chaos.' However, he was not always so effusive: on being asked what he was going to paint for his next submission to the Salon he replied, 'A pot of shit.'

Monty. The affectionate nickname of the British public's favourite Second World War commander, Field Marshal Bernard Law Montgomery (1887–1976), who was created 1st viscount Montgomery of Alamein in 1946. He first came to prominence as commander of the 8th Army at the third battle of ALAMEIN (23 October–4 November 1942), Britain's first significant victory of the war. After the successful conclusion of the North African campaign, Montgomery went on to serve (somewhat irritably) under General Eisenhower in Operation OVERLORD and the subsequent campaign in northwest Europe. Although Montgomery's relations with other senior commanders (including Eisenhower) were poor, his attention to the morale of his men made him popular with the troops. He is also known for the respect he showed to his enemies: in the caravan that served as his HQ in the Western Desert he placed on the wall a portrait of the German commander of the AFRIKA KORPS, Erwin Rommel. *See also* DESERT FOX; FULL MONTY; IKE.

Monty Python's Flying Circus. A cult television comedy series screened in three series from 1969 to 1974. Each programme consisted of a succession of finely honed sketches with situations and settings of an imaginative or often surreal nature, yet involving characters whose odd credibility made them memorable. By their subtle juxtaposition of real and unreal, lifelike and dreamlike, the programmes stood the traditional tenets of television comedy on their head, and soon won a wide following. The title was suggestive rather than significant. The series spawned a number of catchphrases, the most familiar being the link line: 'And now for something completely different.' *See also* BRIAN; FLYING CIRCUS.

Moog synthesizer. The synthesizer, as an electronic musical instrument, and so called because it originally 'synthesized' or combined different items of equipment, was at first a large and cumbersome device based on valve technology. In 1966 two American engineers, Robert Moog (b.1934) and Donald Buchla, formed separate companies to manufacture a more compact instrument, and the former gave his name to the model that prevailed.

Moominland. A region on the coast of the Gulf of Finland that is the fictional setting of the 'Moomintroll' books for children by the Finnish writer Tove Jansson (b.1914), beginning with *The Magician's Hat* (1949) To the north lies Daddy Jones's Kingdom, while to the south is Moominpapa's Island. The Moomins or

Moomintrolls themselves are small, white, hibernating animals with large snouts, short tails, and smooth, hairless skin. They walk on their hind legs and communicate by whistling.

Moonies. A religious sect, properly called the Unification Church, founded by Sun Myung Moon (b.1920) in South Korea in 1954. It spread to the United States in the 1960s and subsequently to Great Britain, Australia and elsewhere. Moon claims that he is the Second Messiah and that his devotees will save mankind from Satan. Funds built up by his followers by selling artificial flowers and other items were used by Moon to create a large property and business organization in America where he has lived since 1973. Tax avoidance led to his prosecution and imprisonment (1984–5). In 1995 he conducted a wedding service in South Korea in which he simultaneously married 35,000 couples present in the stadium before him and another 325,000 couples linked in by satellite.

Mooning. The displaying of one's bare buttocks as a taunt or insult or simply to amuse. The practice seems to have originated among American women students in the mid-1950s as some sort of sexual statement, although it would be ingenuous to adduce an allusion to the Moon and its traditional femininity. When done by men the act is typically associated with football teams travelling on coaches. The word refers to the round shape and pale hue of the exposed anatomy. *See also* BARE-FACED CHEEK.

Moonlight and roses. A situation or atmosphere characterized by sentimentality or romance. The phrase comes from the title of a 1925 song by Neil Moret and Ben Black.

Moonlighter. A person who takes up a second job, especially one undeclared for tax purposes and notionally carried on in the evening or at night by moonlight. This usage of the word dates from the 1950s and derives from an original 19th-century sense for a thief who operates at night.

Moon of Gomrath, The. A fantasy (1963) for children by Alan Garner (b.1934), the sequel to *The* WEIRDSTONE OF BRISINGAMEN. The bracelet containing the weirdstone is again the pivot of a plot with Arthurian undertones. The children unwittingly release the forces of the Old Magic by lighting a fire on a hill while they wait for the moon to rise on the eve of Gomrath.

Moonraker. The name by which Detective-Inspector George Smith (1906–70), a noted spycatcher, was regularly known inside Scotland Yard. *The Times* obituary of him states that 'none of his senior contemporaries … is able to remember how he got the name' (27 October 1970), although the answer is straightforward. Smith lived at Edington, Wiltshire, and native or long-established residents of that county are called 'Moonrakers' with reference to a legend telling how local yokels, when raking a pond to retrieve kegs of smuggled brandy, pretended to be raking for the moon when surprised by excisemen.

Moors murders. A particularly horrifying series of crimes between 1963 and 1965 in which Ian Brady (b.1938) and his mistress Myra Hindley (b.1942) collaborated on five child murders. The children, among them 12-year-old John Kilbride and ten-year-old Lesley Ann Downey, were raped and tortured, in some cases being tape-recorded and photographed in their final moments, and then buried on Saddleworth Moor near Oldham, northeast of Manchester. Brady and Hindley were convicted of the crimes in 1966 and sentenced to life imprisonment. Campaigners for the release of Hindley on compassionate grounds have consistently had their case repudiated.

Mopp, Mrs. *See* MRS MOPP.

Moral high ground. A position of advantage or superiority in a moral debate or issue. The phrase 'high ground' was first used figuratively in this sense but the fuller form dates from the 1980s. The literal 'high ground' was originally elevated terrain in a military campaign that afforded an important strategic advantage to those who occupied it.

> This Government chooses its moral high ground with curious selectivity.
>
> *The Times* (Letter to the Editor) (18 August 1999)

Moral Majority. In the United States an association of FUNDAMENTALIST Christians founded in 1979 in Lynchburg, Virginia, by the Baptist minister Jerry Falwell with the aim of promoting 'traditional values' and reversing what he saw as the godless advance of liberal political and social attitudes.

> The Moral Majority, an organization that once struck fear into the hearts of liberals and inspired bumper stickers like 'The Moral Majority is Neither', has been laid to rest. It came in like a lion in March 1979 and went out like a lamb. Jerry Falwell, who proclaimed its creation, announced its demise in Las Vegas, Nevada,

a city that shows off many sins he tried to fight. The Moral Majority never lived up to its supporters' highest expectations or its detractors' worst fears.

International Herald Tribune (15 June 1989)

Moral Rearmament. A movement, known as MRA, which was founded in 1938 by the American evangelist Frank Buchman (1878–1961). Its purpose was to counter the materialism of present-day society by persuading people to live according to the highest standards of morality and love, to obey God, and to unite in a worldwide association according to these principles.

Mordor. The mountain-ringed land of darkness in J.R.R. Tolkien's *The* LORD OF THE RINGS (1954–5), ruled over by SAURON, the Dark Lord, and contrasting with the realm of GONDOR to the west. Mordor is a barren land with the volcano Orodruin (Mount Doom) at its centre. The casting of the One Ring into the volcano, which successfully concludes the quest of FRODO the ring-bearer, causes Orodruin to erupt, laying Mordor to waste. *See also* MINAS MORGUL.

Morecambe and Wise Show, The. A series of memorable television comedy shows broadcast first by ITV from 1961 to 1968, then by the BBC from 1968 to 1977, and finally again by ITV from 1978 to 1983. Its core was the long-standing double act perfected by Eric Morecambe (real name Eric Bartholomew) (1926–85) and Ernie Wise (real name Ernest Wiseman) (1925–99), Morecambe assuming the role of a droll, pipe-smoking sceptic and Wise that of his pompous foil. The humour lay in the wit of their lines and the insouciance of their delivery, as well as in the classic contrast between the tall, imposing Morecambe and the shorter, unassuming Wise. The close rapport between the two in their respective personae made every sketch and stand-up routine a delight.

More dash than cash. A catchphrase of the fashion world popularized by *Vogue* in the 1950s. It refers to clothes that are stylish but cheap and was subsequently taken up by the media generally.

The march of Waterstone's bookshops through the 1980s high streets owed more to dash than cash.

Observer (4 September 1994)

More Pricks than Kicks. A collection of short stories (1934), the first prose work by Samuel Beckett (1906–89). They all concern a student called Belacqua Shuah, whose first name is that of a Florentine musical instrument maker and friend of the Italian poet and philosopher Dante Alighieri (1265–1321), who used him in his *Divina Commedia* as a symbol of indolence. The title reflects the answer given by Jesus to Paul: 'I am Jesus whom thou persecutest: it is hard for thee to kick against the pricks' (Acts 9:5). *See also* FIRST LINES OF NOVELS.

Morning-after pill. A contraceptive PILL that is effective if taken within 72 hours after intercourse (assumed to have taken place at night) but preferably much sooner to ensure its effectiveness.

The morning after pill is an increasingly popular form of contraception despite unpleasant side-effects and concern that it encourages unprotected sex.

Daily Mail (27 February 1999)

Morning breath. A euphemism for bad breath experienced and probably sensed by others 'the morning after the night before', i.e. typically after drinking and smoking the previous evening.

The film's [teenage] leads happily reveal their foibles and worries about morning breath, sexual performance, what their friends will think, etc.

The Times (31 January 2000)

Morningside. A prosperous residential area of south Edinburgh that has given its name to the widely mocked upper-middle-class Scottish accent supposedly spoken by its inhabitants. A characteristic is the pronunciation of 'a' as 'e' in such words as 'back' ('beck') and 'marry' ('merry'), much as in KELVINSIDE, its Glasgow equivalent. The name is also used generally in allusion to the strait-laced, conservative attitudes traditionally attributed to the upper middle class in Edinburgh. Both accent and attitude are nicely reflected in Muriel Spark's novel *The* PRIME OF MISS JEAN BRODIE (1961), about a schoolmistress who tries to mould her select group of girls, the 'Brodie set', into proper young ladies. The televised version of the novel (1978) conveyed the speech and style much more effectively than the film version (1969). The name of the area itself dates no earlier than the 17th century and appears to mean what it says, 'morning side'.

Moron. Now a colloquial word for a stupid person, 'moron' was originally a specific medical term for an adult with a mental age of about eight to 12. It was proposed in 1910 by the American psychologist Henry H. Goddard (1866–1957) and was formally adopted by the American Association for the Study of the Feeble-Minded in May that year. The word itself is the neuter form of Greek *moros*, 'foolish'.

Morrison shelter. Whereas the Second World War ANDERSON SHELTER was erected outdoors and was more or less permanent, the Morrison shelter was a transportable indoor refuge against bombs and falling masonry. It was made of steel and table-shaped, so that it could actually be used as a table when people were not sheltering under it. It took its name from Herbert S. Morrison (1888–1965), home secretary during the war.

Morse, Inspector. *See* INSPECTOR MORSE.

Moses basket. A portable cot for babies in the form of a basket with handles. The name alludes to the 'ark of bulrushes' in which the baby Moses was left by the Nile (Exodus 2:3).

> Christopher's sudden death while he lay in his Moses basket was initially attributed to a respiratory tract infection.
>
> *The Times* (10 November 1999)

Moshing. A type of frenzied dancing that gained a vogue in the 1990s. It chiefly involves jumping up and down and colliding deliberately with other dancers. As part of the activity, dancers pack together to support a person 'surfing' overhead on raised arms. Diving off a platform or stage onto such a crowd is another variant, but one that has caused injury in some cases and even death. At rock concerts a special moshpit by the stage may be available for this mostly male indulgence. The word perhaps evolved from 'mash' or 'mush' with a further suggestion of 'mass'.

> She [singer Courtney Love] ... threw herself into the moshpit and claimed that it was the British who had taught her how to be badly behaved.
>
> *The Times* (28 June 1999)

Mosleyites. The supporters of Sir Oswald Mosley (1896–1980), who founded (1932) and led the British Union of Fascists (BUF). His followers, also known as BLACKSHIRTS, numbered some 20,000, and became involved in violent demonstrations, often directed at Jews. Among Mosley's supporters was the newspaper proprietor Viscount Rothermere. The BUF was banned in 1940, and Mosley was interned from 1940 to 1943. In 1948 Mosley became the leader of the Union Movement, the successor of the BUF.

Mosquito Coast. A novel (1981) by the US-born Paul Theroux (b.1941) in which a mentally unbalanced inventor abandons civilization in protest against modern culture and takes his family to Honduras, which has a coastal region called Mosquitia. Habitually leaving chaos behind him, he travels inland in an attempt to find an environment untouched by humans, where he can work unhampered by outside influences. Bungling to the last, he meets his death, and the family struggle back to civilization. A visually striking film version (1986), starring Harrison Ford and Helen Mirren, was directed by Peter Weir.

Mosquito State. A nickname for New Jersey, USA, apparently alluding to an abundance of the troublesome insects. The name dates from the 1920s.

Mossad. The principal secret intelligence service of Israel, established in 1951, three years after the creation of the Jewish state itself. The name is Hebrew for 'institute', as the first word of the organization's full name, *Mosad 'Elyon le-Modi'in u-Bitahon*, Supreme Institute for Intelligence and Security. The name was earlier in use for an underground organization formed in 1938 for the purpose of bringing Jews from Europe to Palestine. Here the full name was *Mosad le-'Aliyah Bet*, Institute for the Second Immigration.

Motel. The roadside hotel for motorists, its name an obvious blend of 'motor' and 'hotel', originated with the 'Mo-tel Inn', San Luis Obispo, California, which opened in 1925. Initially a motel was simply an administration building with a small group of cottages or chalets, each with its garage. Later it became a more regular hotel with ample parking space, so that a modern hotel, which usually also caters for motorists, is a 'motel' in all but name. A development of the 1950s was the 'botel' or 'boatel', a waterside hotel with facilities for mooring boats.

> To any other type of tourist accommodation I soon grew to prefer the Functional Motel – clean, neat, safe nooks, ideal places for sleep, argument, reconciliation, insatiable illicit love.
>
> VLADIMIR NABOKOV: *Lolita*, Pt II, ch i (1955)

Mother. An affectionate if somewhat fearful nickname given to Margaret Thatcher, the IRON LADY, by her loyalists, who referred to those Conservatives who engineered her downfall in 1990 as 'matricides'.

Mother Courage and her Children. A play (1961) by the German playwright Bertolt Brecht (1898–1956), in German as *Mutter Courage und ihre Kinder* (1941) and first staged in Zurich. It is about an indomitable woman who fights to protect her family at the time of the Thirty Years' War (1618–48). Mother Courage is the nickname of a canteen-woman called Anna Fierling. Her courage avails her little, however, as she declines to become politically involved in the events that threaten her family and is thus doomed to lose them all. Brecht based his play loosely on *Trutz Simplex* (1670), by the German author Hans Jacob Christoffel von Grimmelshausen (*c*.1622–76), who had served in the Thirty Years' War before writing his account of the sufferings of the German peasants during that conflict. *See also* EPIC THEATRE.

Mother of … . The biggest of; the most extreme example of. The expression originated during the second GULF WAR as a translation of Iraqi leader Saddam Hussein's phrase *umm al-ma'arik*, 'mother of all battles', made in a speech in the Iraqi capital city of Baghdad on 6 January 1991 in which he declared that Iraq had no intention of relinquishing Kuwait and was prepared for a major conflict. The phrase was popularly rendered by the media as 'mother of battles' and came to apply to other examples of extremes, as: 'They treated us to the mother of all dinners.' Arabic *umm*, 'mother (of)', is a figurative term for 'the best', 'the biggest', as if meaning one that had engendered all others.

> The mother of all floating gin palaces hits the high seas in December 2001.
> *heat* (18–24 November 1999)

Mothers and fathers. A young children's game in which the roles of mothers and fathers are acted out, not perhaps without some unconscious or subconscious sexual role-playing.

Mother's Day. The modern and secular equivalent of Mothering Sunday. The campaign for such a day was led in the United States by Anna May Jarvis (1864–1948), a Philadelphia suffragist and temperance worker, who was troubled by the fact that she had neglected her mother in her youth. Its origin is dated to 1908, when she observed the anniversary of her mother's death (9 May 1906) at the Andrews Methodist Church in Grafton, West Virginia. In 1914 the second Sunday in May was officially designated Mother's Day by President Woodrow Wilson. *See also* FATHER'S DAY.

Mother's ruin. Gin. The nickname dates from the 1930s.

Motormouth. A mostly derogatory colloquialism originating in black American slang of the 1960s for anyone who talks rapidly and incessantly. A running motor cannot turn itself off.

> She [television director Janet Street-Porter] cultivated the image of a Cockney motormouth to provide a burst of colour at the monochrome BBC.
> *The Times* (1 July 1999)

Motorway madness. Irresponsible or reckless driving on a motorway, especially in bad weather. The expression dates from the 1960s, when motorways first experienced behaviour of this kind.

> [Transport minister] John Prescott believes in a new concept of motorway madness, doing his best to madden all motorists [by clearing cars from one lane on a three-mile section of the M4 between Heathrow and west London in order to reserve it for buses, taxis and coaches].
> *The Times* (Letter to the Editor) (1 July 1999)

Motown. A shortening of 'Motor Town' as a nickname for Detroit, Michigan, a city that thanks to the enterprise of Henry Ford became the 'automobile capital of the world'. Detroit has a high black population. Hence TAMLA MOTOWN as the name of the first black-owned record company in the United States.

Moulton bicycle. An unusual type of 'foldaway' bicycle invented in the 1960s by the engineer Alex Moulton (b.1920), who had earlier designed the suspension for the MINI. The bicycles were portable, easy to store and, thanks to the innovative rubber suspension on both front and back wheels, easy to handle and comfortable to ride. A popular model was the 'Stowaway' of 1965.

Mountain bike. A sturdy type of bicycle with light frame, broad, deep-treaded tyres, straight handlebars and multiple gears. It was developed in California by Charlie Kelly and Gary Fisher during the 1970s for use on rough cross-country or mountain tracks. Hence its name, which belies its subsequent adoption by the fashion-conscious for general town use during the late 1980s.

Mourning Becomes Electra. A play (1931) by Eugene O'Neill (1888–1953) consisting of a trilogy of plays set in New England during the US Civil War. The central character, Lavinia, wears mourning black in the first two plays, then in the third appears in bright colours until her lover Peter shoots himself and she dons black once again. Deliberately evoking links with the ancient Greek legend of Agamemnon's daughter Electra, whose life is similarly beset with tragedy and death, the title did not initially find favour with O'Neill's publishers, Harper and Brothers, who complained that it was 'meaningless', failing to understand that here O'Neill used the word 'becomes' in its rather old-fashioned sense of 'flatters'.

Mouse potato. A person who spends an inordinate amount of time at a computer (using its mouse). The term arose in the mid-1990s as a pun on the earlier COUCH POTATO.

Mousetrap. Ordinary cheese, such as is used to bait a mousetrap. The term dates from the 1940s, when more refined varieties of cheese were in short supply. Cheddar cheese is sometimes dismissed as 'mousetrap'.

Mousetrap, The. A murder mystery by Agatha Christie that holds the record for the world's longest running play. It opened in London on 25 November 1952 at the Ambassador's Theatre and in 1974 moved next door to St Martin's. The evening of its 40th anniversary, in 1992, was the 16,648th performance. The audience, typically composed of tourists, is asked not to reveal the identity of the murderer, but a few have unsportingly divulged the secret. The title comes from the 'play-within-a-play' in *Hamlet*.

> *King*: What do you call the play?
> *Hamlet*: The Mouse-trap. Marry, how? Tropically. This play is the image of a murder done in Vienna.
> WILLIAM SHAKESPEARE: *Hamlet*, III, ii (1601)

Movers and shakers. Powerful people who initiate events and influence people. The phrase in this sense dates from the early 1970s, yet derives from the poem 'Music and Moonlight' (1874) by the minor English poet Arthur O'Shaughnessy (1844–81), where it specifically refers to poets. The adoption of the words a whole century later is curious. The rather fine lines are as follows:

> We are the music-makers
> And we are the dreamers of dreams.
> Wandering by lone sea-breakers,
> And sitting by desolate streams;
> World-losers and world-forsakers,
> On whom the pale moon gleams:
> Yet we are the movers and shakers
> Of the world forever, it seems.

Move the goalposts, To. To alter the basis of a procedure, especially in order to accommodate unfavourable developments. The idea is of a fixed aim or goal whose agreed parameters are changed after action has begun. The more vivid image is of a football goal whose posts have been shifted nearer each other, so narrowing the goal mouth to the disadvantage of the opposing side.

> If Mr Grant and the Strategic Rail Authority have decided to move the goalposts, who is going to shout foul?
> *The Times* (19 October 1999)

Moving Church. In 1951 Major the Rev. Vivian Symonds was appointed to the living of St Mark's, BIGGIN HILL, the church then being a 50-year-old iron building that had never been consecrated. In order to rebuild it he obtained permission to use material from a war-damaged church, All Saints, Peckham, 27km (17 miles) away. Standing on a lorry facing the latter, he is said to have commanded in a loud voice, 'In the name of Jesus Christ be thou removed to Biggin Hill.' Working with volunteer labour, but often quite alone, he rebuilt St Mark's, the 'Moving Church', over a period of three years.

MRA. *See* MORAL REARMAMENT.

Mr and Mrs Clark and Percy. One of the best known post-Pop, 'cool', naturalistic portraits by David Hockney (b.1937), painted in 1970–71. It is one of a series of double portraits of Hockney's friends and features the British fashion designer Ossie Clark (1942–96) and his wife, the fabric designer Celia Birtwell, together with Percy, the cat. Hockney painted the work from photographs and drawings and simplified the interior of the Clarks' sitting room in Bayswater. Of the positions of the sitters Hockney has commented: 'It's odd that Ossie is sitting down; it should really be the lady who's sitting down, but Celia's standing up. That alone causes a slight disturbance, because you know it should be reversed.' Hockney made the portrait as a wedding present, but the marriage ended in 1974. Clark was murdered by his Italian lover, Diego Cogolato.

Mr Bean. The first of a series of television comedies starring Rowan Atkinson (b.1955) in the name part and running from 1990 to 1996. Mr Bean is essentially a NERD in a sports jacket with leather elbow patches and owns a small temperamental car. His involvement with the highs and lows of life either ends in chaos or progresses to a point of acute embarrassment. Each of the episodes is virtually dialogue-free and thus reminiscent of the comedy classics of the silent cinema. Atkinson wanted the character to be named after a vegetable. Mr Cauliflower and Mr Cabbage were considered but Mr Bean eventually won the day. The final episode, *Goodnight Mr Bean*, was shown in 1995 whereupon Mr Bean moved to the big screen as the hero of *Bean – The Ultimate Disaster Movie* (1997), a worldwide box-office hit.

Mr Big. The head of an organization of criminals; any important person.

> It is less obvious that Tom Parker Bowles or the now former England rugby captain Lawrence Dallaglio … are quite the Mr Bigs of the drug world that would justify such sophisticated forms of entrapment.
> *The Times* (28 May 1999)

Mr Blobby. A grotesque, egg-shaped figure in the form of a pink plastic dummy with leering lips, lascivious lashes and yellow spots, introduced by the BBC in 1992 as a source of amusement in the knock-about television comedy series NOEL'S HOUSE PARTY (1991), compèred by Noel Edmonds. The figure was operated by a human inside the costume and went on to record a hit pop song, with lines, 'Blobby, oh Mr Blobby, / You're the guy who put the 'do' in 'do or die'. / Blobby, oh Mr Blobby, / Your deeds are guaranteed to stupefy', lyrics so inane that Radio 1 refused to broadcast them. The figure must even so have touched something of a chord in the critical media, since he was the subject of an open letter by John Lyttle in the *Independent*, an article by Bryan Appleyard in the *Mail on Sunday*'s 'Day and Night' section and a piece by Cosmo Landesman in *The Sunday Times*. In theological student circles the nickname 'Mr Blobby' has also been applied, purely from a supposed facial resemblance, to George Carey (b.1935), Archbishop of Canterbury from 1991.

> What *is* it about the English? What *is* Mr Blobby – just a gormless colossus or something of far grander import? I don't know. As someone said on the wireless just the other day, 'It's just far too big to get your intellectual hands around'.
> *Q* (February 1994)

Mr Chad. *See* CHAD.

Mr Chips. *See* CHIPS, MR; GOODBYE, MR CHIPS.

Mr Clean. An honourable or incorruptible politician, with a clean reputation. The name has specifically been applied to John Lindsay, mayor of New York from 1965 to 1973, and the US Attorney General Elliot Richardson, who resigned in 1973 rather than agree to the restrictions then being imposed by President Nixon on investigations into the WATERGATE affair.

The term dates from the early 1970s and derives from the brandname of an American cleanser.

Mr Five Per Cent. A name applied shortly before the First World War to the Turkish-born oil millionaire and philanthropist Calouste Gulbenkian (1869–1955) when his share of the Turkish Petroleum Company was reduced from 40 per cent to 5 per cent following an Anglo-German agreement. He claimed, however, it was better to have a small slice of a big cake than a big slice of a small cake.

Mr Fixit. Literally a person who fixes things by repairing them, otherwise a handyman, but metaphorically a TROUBLESHOOTER or someone who arranges deals by underhand methods. The term is of American origin and dates from the 1960s.

> [Sidney] Stanley was a Mr Fixit, a product of the austerity world of coupons, licences and regulations. … Not to put too fine a point on it, he was also a 'conman'.
> *The Times* (22 January 2000)

Mr Nice Guy. An amiable and pleasant person. The nickname is often found in a negative context, especially when a 'nice' person becomes 'nasty'. Hence the catch phrase, sometimes bearing an ironic implication, 'no more Mr Nice Guy', first applied in 1972 by his aides to Senator Muskie as challenger for the presidency and more recently popularized as the title of Howard Jacobson's novel, *No More Mister Nice Guy* (1998).

Mr Norris Changes Trains. A novel (1935; in USA as *The Last of Mr Norris*) by Christopher Isherwood (1904–86), reflecting the uneasy political situation in the early 1930s in Germany, where Isherwood taught English in Berlin from 1930 to 1933. The observer and narrator William Bradshaw (who is Isherwood himself, under his second and third names) meets Arthur Norris, a suspicious character, on a train, and through him is involved in sinister activities.

Mr Patel. A stock derogatory nickname for an immigrant Indian or Pakistani, often implying the owner of a corner shop. The name is as common as Smith is in England, and it is found in large numbers in cities such as Leicester and Bradford where Ugandan Asians have settled from the early 1970s. The name itself is the Hindi word for the headman of a village.

Mr Perfecto. A nickname for a handsome film star, popular singer or the like, especially when of the 'Latin lover' type. *Perfecto* is Spanish for 'perfect'.

Today, Mr Perfecto sports a light stubble, a black baseball cap concealing his unkempt, highlighted hair.

The Times (9 July 1999)

Mr Plastic Fantastic. The nickname of Walter Cavanagh (b.1943) of Santa Clara, California, owner of the world's biggest collection of credit cards. His total in 1999 was recorded at 1397. *See also* PLASTIC.

Mr Rising Price. *See* DESICCATED CALCULATING MACHINE.

Mrs Dale's Diary. A radio SOAP OPERA broadcast from 1948 to 1969 depicting the placid, middle-class life of Mary Dale and her husband Jim, a doctor, in the fictional south London suburb of Parkwood Hill. The title was changed to *The Dales* in 1962 when the family moved to the expanding new town of Exton somewhere in the Home Counties. Despite the blandness of the action and paleness of the characters, the programme was generally regarded with affection and attracted many regular listeners.

Mrs Dalloway. A novel (1925) by Virginia Woolf (1882–1941), with which she introduced the STREAM OF CONSCIOUSNESS technique into her *oeuvre*. The action takes place on a single day, on which Clarissa Dalloway, the fashionable wife of a member of parliament, is due to hold a party. A sub-plot tells of the shell-shocked Septimus Smith, and at the end of the day he commits suicide. A gripping film version (1997) was directed by Marleen Gorris, with Vanessa Redgrave in the title role.

Mrs Miniver. A film (1942) that aimed to celebrate the patient heroism of British women during the Second World War. Mrs Miniver, played by Greer Garson, was the archetypal middle-class English gentlewoman, who presided over the home front while her husband (Walter Pidgeon) went off to help rescue the British army at DUNKIRK. Briefly fêted as a fitting tribute to England's wartime resilience, the film's HOLLYWOOD origins hit a false note with postwar audiences and a sequel, *The Miniver Story* (1950), in which Mrs Miniver fought terminal cancer, failed to win approval. Mrs Miniver herself was originally conceived by the writer Joyce Anstruther, who (using the pen-name Jan Struther) published what purported to be Mrs Miniver's diary recollections of the war years as *Mrs Miniver*. Winston Churchill claimed the film did more to win the war than the efforts of six divisions.

Mrs Mopp. A charwoman or 'daily'. The name dates from the 1940s and was adopted from that of a character in the radio comedy show ITMA.

Mr Standfast. A thriller (1919) by John Buchan (1875–1940), the third in which Richard Hannay appears. German spies are still the problem, and the action ranges from London to Skye, Switzerland to the South Tyrol, and a French chateau to the battlefields of the First World War. One of the novel's themes is the significance of fortitude, loyalty and moral strength, represented, in *The Pilgrim's Progress* (1678) by John Bunyan (1628–88), by Mr Standfast, and in *Mr Standfast* by Peter Pienaar, who is reading Bunyan's book, references to which recur throughout the novel. *See also* GREENMANTLE; THIRTY-NINE STEPS.

Mr Tambourine Man. A infectiously good-humoured, folksy song with a catchy chorus by Bob Dylan, released in 1965 on the album *Bringing It All Back Home*. Mr Tambourine Man is a kind of HIPPIE minstrel, and the song's lyrics accordingly contain much hallucinatory imagery ('Take me on a trip upon your magic swirling ship') and intriguing wordplay. The song became a hit for the Byrds (*see* ROCK GROUP NAMES), who recorded a shortened version of the song and released an album of the same name.

> Hey! Mr Tambourine Man, play a song for me,
> I'm not sleepy and there is no place I'm going to.
> Hey! Mr Tambourine Man, play a song for me,
> In the jingle jangle morning
> I'll come followin' you.

Mr Teasie Weasie. The byname of the hairdresser Raymond (1911–92), whose original name was Raymond Pierre Carlo Bessone. He earned his sobriquet as a result of his appearances on the television programme *Quite Contrary* (1953), in which he would demonstrate his art by holding up a lock of hair and saying, 'A teasie-weasie here, and a teasie-weasie there'. He later commented, 'Teasie Weasie may be a rotten name but the man behind it is not what he is purported to be' (*Daily Telegraph*, Obituary, 2 April 1992).

Mr Tough. A nickname for an uncompromising or demanding person, especially one readily facing criticism or challenges: 'Five minutes with Norman Davies and you know you have met the Mr Tough of the history world.'

Mr Weston's Good Wine. A light-hearted parable of wickedness and virtue (1927) by T.F. Powys (1875–1953). God comes to Folly Down, Dorset, in the form of Mr Weston who, after miraculously restoring a small girl he has inadvertently run over in his motor car, causes an advertisement for 'Mr Weston's Good Wine' to appear in the sky. After quaffing it, the inhabitants of the village receive their respective just rewards or punishments.

Ms. An abbreviation, pronounced 'Miz', of either Mrs or Miss, designed to avoid distinguishing between married and unmarried women. The title first arose in the United States in the 1950s. The feminist magazine *Ms.*, founded by Gloria Steinem 'for the liberated female human being', first appeared in January 1972.

> As an old-fashioned man, the President [Richard Nixon] prefers the old conventions, such as addressing a woman as 'Miss' or 'Mrs' rather than the new, liberated, statusless 'Ms' – not pronounced 'Muss' or 'Mess' as certain fastidious male chauvinists have suggested. No, for reasons that elude me, 'Ms' is pronounced 'Miz'.
> *New York Post* (3 January 1972)

MTV. Music Television, the first 24-hour music channel, introduced in 1981 by the Warner Amex Satellite Entertainment Company, America's largest cable entertainment programmers. It proved hugely popular, tripling its subscribership in just over a year, but was initially criticized for its neglect of black performers and the sexist nature of its videos, in which male artistes were usually surrounded by scantily clad females. It was MTV that launched the careers of such superstars as Madonna and Michael Jackson.

Much-Binding-in-the-Marsh. A radio comedy series that ran from 1947 to 1953. It was written by and starred Kenneth Horne (1907–69) and Richard Murdoch (1907–90), who had met in the Air Ministry during the Second World War, and was supposedly set in an RAF station doubling as a country club. Each programme ended with the whole cast singing a humorous ditty about the location that gave the title, a mock rural place-name that itself puns on 'binding' in the sense of complaining, an activity associated with service life on a remote RAF base.

Muck and magic. A derisory nickname in the 1990s for organic farming, especially among practitioners of scientifically based farming, with its use of industrial feedstuffs and antibiotics. Public support for the organic lobby was boosted at this time following several incidents of MAD COW DISEASE and media reports of contaminated beef imports.

> Such people [organic farmers] got used to being jeered at, dubbed muck-and-magic merchants, suspected of plotting to grow stringy beards, and patronisingly assured that 'scientific' farming was the future.
> *The Times* (26 October 1999)

Muck in, To. To share tasks or accommodation without expecting any privileges; to DO ONE'S BIT. The expression dates from the First World War and originally applied specifically to sharing one's army rations with a comrade-in-arms. Hence 'mucker' as a slang term for a friend or companion.

> During the build-up to the show I answered the phone, dealt with exhibition queries and mucked in where I was needed.
> *The Times* (2 February 2000)

Muckraking. In 1903 *McClure's* magazine in the United States began to publish a series of articles that exposed corruption and greed in business and politics, pricking the consciences of their middle-class readers in the process. President Theodore Roosevelt dubbed them 'muckrakers' after the man with the muckrake in John Bunyan's *Pilgrim's Progress* (1684), who pursues worldly gain at the expense of celestial rewards by raking filth from the ground and not looking up to see the celestial crown he was being offered for the muckrake he was using. The publication planted the seeds of investigative journalism.

Mudiad Amddiffyn Cymru (Welsh, 'Movement for the Defence of Wales'). A Welsh nationalist group responsible for explosions in various parts of Wales in the late 1960s, mainly as a protest against the investiture of the Prince of Wales in 1969. Buildings damaged included the Temple of Peace in Cathays Park, Cardiff. *See also* ABERGELE MARTYRS.

Muesli belt. A general nickname for a middle-class district where people are or were likely to eat muesli and other health foods. The term arose in the late 1970s. Children who are undernourished as a result of the health food diet imposed on them by their well-meaning parents are sometimes said to suffer from 'muesli-belt malnutrition'. The debilitation is caused not by the diet itself but by the fact that the food takes longer to chew, so that the children do not eat enough.

Mug's game. An activity in which it is unwise to engage oneself as it is likely to be unsuccessful or dangerous. The term dates from the early years of the 20th century, with 'mug' in its already existing sense of a foolish person.

> *Nicobar*: I am going out of politics. Politics is a mug's game.
>
> GEORGE BERNARD SHAW: *The Apple Cart*, II (1929)

Mugshot. A photograph of a person's face ('mug'), especially for official purposes.

Mujahedin. These Islamic guerrilla fighters became prominent in Afghanistan in the 1970s and were primarily responsible for overthrowing the Marxist regime there in 1992. The name is a plural form of Arabic *mujahid*, a person who fights a *jihad*, a holy Muslim war against unbelievers.

Mukden incident. An incident in Manchuria in 1931, engineered by right-wing Japanese officers as an excuse for the Japanese occupation of the region, which they renamed MANCHUKUO. Since the end of the Russo-Japanese War in 1905 the Japanese had exercised certain rights in Manchuria, including the right to station troops there to protect the South Manchurian Railway. When an explosion occurred on the railway near the city of Mukden (now called Shenyang) on 18 September 1931 the Japanese military in Manchuria blamed the Chinese army, and, without reference to the civilian government in Japan, occupied Mukden, and then the rest of Manchuria. The Tokyo government fell, and its successor retrospectively authorized the military's actions.

Mulberry. In the Second World War this was the code name given to the prefabricated ports towed across to the Normandy coast to make possible the supply of the Allied armies in France in 1944 consequent upon the D-DAY landings. Submersible sections of concrete formed a breakwater and quay alongside which the transports were unloaded. The name was chosen at the time because it was the next in rotation on the British Admiralty's list of names available for warships. Two such Mulberries were set up, but the one serving the US beaches was wrecked by a storm (19 June). That serving the British beaches was kept in service until Antwerp was available.

Mulligan. An extra stroke in golf awarded after a poor shot and not counted on the score card. The name dates from the 1940s and according to one account derives from a bottle called a 'Mulligan' kept on the bar in American family-type saloons. It contained a concoction of pepper seeds and water that could be added to 'spice up' one's beer, the effect being a shock to the system similar to the humiliating blow of being granted an extra shot at one's ball.

Mummerset. A mock West Country accent as adopted by actors or by speakers in real life. The essence is to burr the letter 'r' ('barrrn'), sound 'f' as 'v' and 's' as 'z' ('varm', 'Zummerzet') and pronounce 'i' in 'bite' or 'y' in 'my' as 'oi' ('Oi be boidin' moi toim'). Liberties are also taken with verbs and pronouns ('Er be allus after we'). The word itself blends 'mumble' and 'Somerset'. *See also* OO-AR!

Mummy's boy. A young male who is excessively influenced by or attached to his mother. The phrase is a variant on the earlier 'mother's boy' in this sense.

> I was very family oriented and my family were there all the time, they probably thought, 'He's a mummy's boy, daddy's boy – we won't offer it [marijuana] to him.'
>
> *heat* (9–15 December 1999)

Munchausen's syndrome. A type of mental disorder in which a person repeatedly feigns illness so as to obtain hospital treatment. It was first recognized in the 1950s among people who had travelled a good deal, like Baron Munchausen, the hero of a book of fantastic travellers' tales written in 1785 by Baron Raspe. Munchausen's syndrome by proxy is identical but caused by parents in their children.

Munchkin. An American colloquialism for a young child, from the Munchkins, the race of small childlike creatures who help Dorothy in her quest for the city of OZ in L. Frank Baum's children's fantasy *The WIZARD OF OZ* (1900). Public awareness of these grew as a result of the 1939 film of the book, in which the Munchkins are played by midgets.

> [Pop singer] Britney [Spears], a 17-year-old munchkin turned Madonna-lookalike.
>
> *heat* (18–24 November 1999)

Munich. A common shorthand for the Munich Agreement, signed in 30 September 1938 on behalf of Germany, Britain and France by Hitler, Neville Chamberlain and Edouard Daladier. The Italians were also present at the conference. The agreement, which has come to be seen as the low point of Britain and France's appeasement of Nazi Germany, ceded to Germany the right to the Czechoslovak territory of the SUDETENLAND, which contained a large German-speaking population. Chamberlain returned to Britain claiming he had achieved PEACE FOR OUR TIME, while Churchill commented: 'We have sustained a defeat without a war.' The following year the Nazis occupied the rest of Czechoslovakia. Since then, the phrase 'another Munich' has been used for any potentially disastrous, humiliating or dishonourable act of appeasement or surrender.

Munich air crash. *See* BUSBY'S BABES.

Munich Putsch. *See* BEER HALL PUTSCH.

Munro. A Scottish mountain over 914m (3000ft) in height. The name is that of Hugh T. Munro (1856–1919), who published a list of them in the *Journal of the Scottish Mountaineering Club* for 1891. There are 277 such peaks, eight of them over 1220m (4000ft) and the highest of all Ben Nevis (1343m/4406ft). A climber who attempts to ascend all 277 is known disparagingly among hillwalkers and mountaineers as a 'Munro-bagger', a term implying an emphasis purely on the height of the hill rather than on the activity itself. There are also Corbetts, between 762 and 914m (2500–3000ft), listed by J.R. Corbett, and Donalds, over 610m (2000ft), by Percy Donald.

> Geography students were once outdoor hearties. … They played rugby, went potholing, climbed mountains. It wasn't the *nouvelle vague* and Monica Vitti's legs they talked about; it was Shap and Striding Edge and 'bagging' Monroes [*sic*].
> *The Times* (17 August 1999)

Muppet Show, The. A television comedy series screened from 1976 to 1981 and featuring puppets of all shapes and sizes. They were the creation of the American puppeteer Jim Henson (1936–90) and originally appeared on the American children's programme *Sesame Street*, first screened in 1969. They were then adapted in Britain to adult entertainment. Each show was ostensibly put on by the puppets in a theatre, the compere being KERMIT, a garrulous green-garbed frog. Other characters were the cosy Fozzie Bear and the impossibly vain Miss Piggy. A human was usually introduced as a victim of their pranks. The name 'Muppet' seems to be a blend of 'marionette' and 'puppet', although Henson himself said it was 'simply a word that sounded good to him' (*Time*, 25 December 1978).

Murder, Inc. A name given by President Ronald Reagan to Iran under the AYATOLLAHS, referring to that state's involvement in anti-US terrorism. Like so much of the GREAT COMMUNICATOR's phraseology, the term derives from the movies: *Murder, Incorporated* was a 1960 Hollywood film about 1930s gangsters. *See also* IRAN-CONTRA AFFAIR.

Murder on the Orient Express. A detective novel (1934; as *Murder on the Calais Coach*, 1934) by Agatha Christie (1890–1976), involving her retired Belgian policeman Hercule POIROT, who first appears in *The Mysterious Affair at Styles* (1920). The original Orient Express ran from Paris via Vienna to Istanbul and other Balkan cities between 1883 and 1961. A film version (1974) directed by Sidney Lumet was disappointing, despite the cast, which included Albert Finney (as Poirot), Ingrid Bergman, Lauren Bacall, Sean Connery and Vanessa Redgrave.

Murphy bed. The type of folding bed so known from the 1920s takes its name from the American manufacturer William L. Murphy (1876–1959), its original designer. In its earliest form the bed folded or swung into a cupboard when not needed and was thus mainly found in small apartments, where space was at a premium.

Murphy's law. 'If anything can go wrong, it will.' If a slice of bread and jam is dropped on the floor, it is bound to land jam side down. The expression is said to derive from a remark made in 1949 by Captain E. Murphy of the Wright Field-Aircraft Laboratory. More likely, it is simply a use of the common Irish surname, in allusion to the alleged illogicality of the Irish. *See also* SOD'S LAW.

Museumland. A nickname for South Kensington, London, and in particular for the area south of the Royal Albert Hall where the Victoria and Albert Museum, Science Museum and Natural History Museum are located.

Museum piece. An old-fashioned or decrepit person or thing. The term passed early in the 20th century from a genuine description of an item of value or rarity to this pejorative sense.

Music to one's ears. Something that is very pleasant to hear, typically good news.

Music While You Work. A radio programme first broadcast in 1940. It consisted of a medley of popular tunes, played by a different band each day, and was introduced in the dark days at the beginning of the Second World War to keep factory workers contented and so productive. It continued in the happier years of peacetime until 1967.

Though 'Music while you work' is now our wont,
It's not so nice as 'Music while you don't'.
JOHN BETJEMAN: *A Few Late Chrysanthemums*, 'The Dear
Old Village' (1958)

Musso's Lake. A Second World War nickname for the Mediterranean, 'Musso' being the Italian dictator Benito Mussolini (1883–1945), who entered the war on Germany's side in 1940. His attempt to chase the British out of the Mediterranean that year proved fruitless.

Mutt and Jeff. A nickname for a stupid pair of men, especially one tall and one short. The names are those of two such characters in American comic strips drawn by Bud Fisher from 1907 and soon after appearing in short cartoon films. Mutt was tall and lanky; Jeff was short and bald.

Muzak. The proprietary name of a system of recorded light background music played through speakers in public places such as supermarkets, restaurants, factories and the like. It is objected to by some but providers of the service claim it relaxes people and so encourages the customer to buy more, the diner to order more and the worker to produce more. The name, based on 'music', was registered as a trademark by Rediffusion Ltd in 1938.

We shall have muzak wherever we go.
Listener (16 June 1965)

Mwah. A representation dating from the mid-1990s of the sound made by someone giving an air kiss, i.e. a social kiss made without lip contact but often with cheek contact, typically once on each cheek. The utterance is most common among media people and LUVVIES. When first encountered in print it was mistaken by some as a respelling of French *moi*, as in 'Snobbish, *moi*?'

Not all the post is depressing. I've also been sent the [television gardener] Charlie Dimmock calendar, personally signed to me by her. Thank you, mwah, mwah. What a way to see in the new century.
Sunday Times (19 September 1999)

My Dog Tulip. An autobiographical study (1965) by J.R. Ackerley (1896–1967), author and literary editor, focusing on the activities and habits of his Alsatian bitch, Queenie, and his intimate relationship with her. He shared a small flat in Putney with her, his elderly aunt and his emotionally disturbed sister. After Queenie's death in 1961 Ackerley lapsed further into depression. Christopher Isherwood described the

novel (perhaps ironically) as 'one of the greatest masterpieces of animal literature'.

My Fair Lady. A film musical (1964) based on a stage musical by Alan Lerner (1918–86) and Frederick Loewe (1901–88) depicting the transformation of roughly spoken cockney FLOWER GIRL Eliza DOOLITTLE into a well-groomed society lady through the efforts of the arrogant linguist Professor Henry Higgins. Starring Audrey Hepburn and Rex Harrison, the film was derived ultimately from the play PYGMALION (1913) by George Bernard Shaw (1856–1950). Shaw had reservations about the film and the musical was given a different title partly to differentiate it from the original play. The new title was extracted from a traditional rhyme:

London Bridge is falling down, falling down, falling
    down,
London Bridge is falling down, my fair lady.
'London Bridge is falling down'.

My Family and Other Animals. An autobiographical study (1956) by the zoologist Gerald Durrell (1925–95) of the unorthodox household in Corfu in the 1930s, of which his brother Lawrence Durrell (1912–90), the poet and novelist, was also a member.

My feet are killing me. My shoes are uncomfortably tight. A complaint mostly voiced by women, for whom fashion frequently takes precedence over fit in matters of footwear.

It's hard enough to concentrate at a party when your feet are killing you, but at the office it's downright handicapping.
The Times (22 May 1999)

My foot! I don't believe it! You can't be serious! The phrase dates from the 1920s, as does its variant, 'My left foot!' *My Left Foot* (1954) was the title of the autobiography of the Irish writer Christy Brown (1932–81), a cerebral palsy victim who was able to write only by using his left foot to operate a specially adapted typewriter.

My Generation. A frenziedly anti-establishment song by The Who, released in 1965 and described by its writer Pete Townshend as 'anti-middle age, anti-boss class, and anti-young marrieds'. Its title comes from a line in a Bob Dylan song, 'Talkin' New York, Talkin' 'bout my generation'. A sort of PUNK anthem *avant la lettre*, the song includes the nihilistic wish 'Hope I die before I get old' and the near-expletive of the line 'why don't you all f-fade away'.

People try to put us d-down (Talkin' 'bout my
  generation)
Just because we get around (Talkin' 'bout my
  generation)
Things they do look awful c-c-cold (Talkin' 'bout my
  generation)
I hope I die before I get old (Talkin' 'bout my
  generation)

My Lai Massacre. A more than shameful incident
during the VIETNAM War (1964–75), when on 16 March
1968 American troops killed 109 civilians in My Lai, a
small village in South Vietnam. An investigation into
the atrocity in 1969 produced enough evidence to
charge 30 soldiers with war crimes, but the only one
to be convicted was Lieutenant William Calley, the unintelligent and inexperienced platoon commander.
He was sentenced to life imprisonment but was
released after only three years, thanks to the intervention of President Nixon.

Myra Breckenridge. *See* BRECKENRIDGE, MYRA.

Mystic Marquess. A nickname of Spencer Compton,
7th Marquess of Northampton (b.1946), given for his
interest in spiritualism.

N

NAAFI. The popular acronym for the Navy, Army, and Air Force Institutes, set up in 1921 to provide canteens for servicemen and later developing to run shops and recreational facilities for service personnel wherever they are posted.

> The NAAFI is a sort of caafi
> Where soldiers are rude
> About the food.
> *Spectator* (23 January 1959)

Nab. A nickname for Conservative backbencher Sir Gerald Nabarro (1913–73), best remembered for his handlebar moustache and his Rolls Royce, registration number NAB 1. Nabarro in fact owned not just NAB 1 but the series NAB 1 to NAB 8, and also NAB 10, NAB 99 and NAB 555. *See also* CHERISHED NUMBER.

Nadsat. The jargon spoken by 15-year-old Alex and his teenage friends in Anthony Burgess's black comedy *A* CLOCKWORK ORANGE (1962). The words are based on Russian, as is *nadsat* itself, representing the equivalent of '-teen', and some of them have entered youth slang generally. Examples are *droog*, 'friend', *horrowshow*, 'good' and *gloopy*, 'stupid'. Burgess often adds the English equivalent in the narrative, but even where he does not the sense is usually perceptible. *See also* COPYCAT KILLING.

> Then we slooshied the sirens and knew the millicents were coming with pooshkas pushing out of the police-auto-windows at the ready. That little weepy devotchka had told them, no doubt.
> ch ii

Naff. Lacking taste or style. The slang word surfaced in the 1950s but its origin remains uncertain. It is not likely to derive from NAAFI, as sometimes suggested, and may be a euphemistic formation. It appears not to be related to 'naff off' meaning 'go away', which is probably based on the 'F-word' (*see* FOUR-LETTER WORD). In 1982 Princess Anne famously lost her temper with pestering PAPARAZZI and told them to 'naff off'.

> Davina McCall … gets away with presenting programmes that are the naffest of the naff.
> *heat* (6–12 January 2000)

Naked and the Dead, The. The first novel (1948) by Norman Mailer (b.1923). Mailer enlisted in the US Army in the Second World War with the idea of writing 'a short novel about a long patrol'. *The Naked and the Dead* is a long novel about a long patrol during the US assault on the Philippines, whose 14 members represent a microcosm of American society. The term 'naked' in the title is referred to in the text: 'A shell sighed overhead, and unconsciously [Sergeant] Martinez drew back against a gunhousing. He felt naked.' It also recalls the cry of Cardinal Wolsey in Shakespeare's *King Henry VIII*:

> O Cromwell, Cromwell!
> Had I but serv'd my God with half the zeal
> I serv'd my king, he would not in mine age
> Have left me naked to my enemies.
> III.ii

A film version (1958) directed by Raoul Walsh was shorn of the FOUR-LETTER WORDS that made the novel notorious. *See also* FIRST LINES OF NOVELS.

Naked ape. A human being. The term was introduced by the ethologist Desmond Morris (b.1928):

> There are one hundred and ninety-three living species of monkeys and apes. One hundred and ninety-two of them are covered with hair. The exception is a naked ape self-named *Homo sapiens*.
> DESMOND MORRIS: *The Naked Ape*, Introduction (1967)

Naked as nature intended. Nude; unclothed. The phrase was popularized as the title of a British nudist film of 1961, originally to have been entitled *Cornish Holiday*. The equation of nakedness with naturalness is an old one, and Rudyard Kipling has a passage in *Stalky & Co.* (1899) in which he described a group of schoolboys 'stripping as they ran, till, when they touched the sands, they were naked as God had made them, and as happy as He intended them to be'.

> He [Prince Charles] must have felt like he was caught in one of those terrible nightmares – you know, the ones where you find yourself in the High Street as naked as unforgiving Mother Nature intended.
>
> *Daily Mirror* (8 September 1994)

Naked Lunch, The. A surrealist novel (1959, Paris; in USA as *Naked Lunch*, 1962) by William Burroughs (1914–97), which was the last book to be censored by the US authorities. It was created by a form of linguistic collage from thousands of pages of notes he made while addicted to HEROIN. The Nobel prize-winning author Samuel Beckett (1906–89) commented on the technique: 'That's not writing, it's plumbing.' The title was suggested to Burroughs by the BEAT GENERATION author Jack Kerouac (1922–69), who helped with the manuscript, and implies, according to Burroughs, 'that frozen moment when everyone sees what is on the end of every fork'. David Cronenberg's film of the same title (1991) explored the creation of the novel through the hallucinatory experiences of a writer. *See also* FIRST LINES OF NOVELS.

Nam or **'Nam.** The regular short name for VIETNAM as used by US armed forces during the Vietnam War (1964–75).

Name and shame, To. To make a public disclosure of a person's or group of people's perceived or actual wrongdoing. The phrase arose in the United States in the climate of moral reformativism of the early 1990s.

> A dentist became the first health professional to be 'named and shamed' by the Health Service Ombudsman for bad treatment of a patient yesterday.
>
> *The Times* (25 November 1999)

Name of the game. What matters most; the way things are supposed to be. The phrase became current from the 1960s and is of American origin, perhaps arising from sports journalism. It was popularized by an American television melodrama, *Fame is the Name of the Game* (1966), and by a series of films following from this, *The Name of the Game* (1968–70). 'The Name of the Game', by the Scandinavian pop group Abba, was a catchy chart-topping number of the late 1970s. Lovers of apt personal names like to play 'the game of the name', finding doctors called C. Fitt and dentists named I. Pulham.

> Anything that interrupts the vital flow of e-mails is fuddy-duddy. Instant communication is the name of the game.
>
> *Sunday Times* (26 December 1999)

Name of the Rose, The. An historical novel (1983; in Italian as *Il nome della rosa*, 1980) by Umberto Eco (b.1932), Professor of Semiotics at the University of Bologna. It is a metaphysical quest for truth and meaning in the form of a whodunnit set in a medieval Benedictine monastery in a mountain castle, in which a learned English Franciscan, William of Baskerville, seeks the serial murderer of several monks. According to Eco, the cryptic Latin hexameter, with which the book closes, implies that 'departed things leave (only, or at least) pure names behind them'. The title 'came to me virtually by chance, and I liked it because the rose is a symbolic figure so rich in meanings that now it hardly has any meaning left'. A curiously muted film version (1986) was directed by Jean-Jacques Annaud, with Sean Connery in the role of Baskerville, and Christian Slater in the role of Adso of Melk, the tale's youthful narrator.

Nana. In the story of PETER PAN, the gentle and faithful old dog who always looked after the children of the Darling family. (Hence her name, as 'nana' is a children's word for 'nurse'.) When Mr Darling played a trick on Nana by giving her unpleasant medicine, which he himself had promised to drink, the family did not appreciate his humour. This put him out of temper, and Nana was chained up in the yard before he went out for the evening. As a consequence Peter Pan effected an entry into the children's bedroom. *See also* IN THE DOGHOUSE.

Nancy boy. A derogatory nickname for an effeminate man or male homosexual, dating from the early 20th century and evolving from the earlier 'Miss Nancy'. It is also common as 'nancy', which in turn is shortened to 'nance'.

Nanny state. A nickname for the government and government institutions, seen as authoritarian and paternalistic, and as imposing on people what is good for them, for 'nanny knows best'. The term is first recorded in a *Spectator* article of 1965 by the Conservative politician Ian Macleod, and the 'nanny' herself was epitomized for many by Margaret Thatcher when prime minister (1979–90).

> The nanny state has found its way into the mother of parliaments. Pint drinkers in the bars of the House of Commons now find a stark message staring at them from the bottom of the glass – 'Don't drink and drive'.
> *Sunday Times* (20 February 2000)

Nansen passport. An identification document issued after the First World War to a stateless person ineligible for a formal passport. It took its name from the Norwegian diplomat and explorer Fridtjof Nansen (1861–1930), who was responsible for the issue of these papers.

Napalm. The highly inflammable sticky jelly of this name, used in incendiary bombs and flame-throwers and consisting of petrol thickened with special soaps, takes its name from a combination of *na*phthenic acid and *palm*itic acid. It is so called because the aluminium salts of these acids are used in the manufacture of the chemical that thickens petroleum. It was invented in 1942 and first gained notoriety in 1966 when 20 US soldiers died in South VIETNAM as a result of one of their own aircraft bombarding them with napalm. One of the most haunting images of the Vietnam War is a widely reproduced photograph of 1972 showing children fleeing from their burning homes, one girl with her clothes burned off her back, after an American napalm attack, supposedly targeted at a VIET CONG village, instead devastated the 'friendly' South Vietnamese village of Trang Bang. Napalm was also used with destructive effect by Iraq in the Iran–Iraq War (*see* GULF WAR).

Napoo. Soldier slang of the First World War for something that is of no use or does not exist. It represents the French phrase *il n'y en a plus* ('there is no more of it'). It occurs in a popular song in which the returning British soldier bids a fond farewell to his French mam'zelle:

> Good-bye-ee! good-bye-ee!
> Wipe the tear, baby dear, from your eye-ee.
> Tho' it's hard to part, I know,
> I'll be tickled to death to go.
> Don't cry-ee! – don't sigh-ee! –
> There's a silver lining in the sky-ee! –
> Bonsoir, old thing! cheerio! chin-chin!
> Nahpoo! Toodle-oo! Good-bye-ee!
> ROBERT P. WESTON and BERT LEE: 'Good-Bye-Ee' (1917)

See also FIRST WORLD WAR SLANG.

Nappy brain. A colloquial term for a mother's besottedness with her newborn child.

> It is ten weeks since Caroline Quentin gave birth to her first baby … and her mind appears to remain totally addled by nappy brain. 'She is gorgeous. I know everyone says that about their baby, but she is just so *lovely,*' she says, scrunching up her face in adoration.
> *The Times* (17 November 1999)

Narnia. The fictional land in which are set the seven children's books by C.S. Lewis, beginning with *The* LION, THE WITCH AND THE WARDROBE (1950). It is visited only by select children, and peopled by talking beasts, giants, witches and other characters of myth and legend. To the north lie Ettinsmoor and the Wild Lands of the North; to the south, Archenland and Calormen. It seems that Lewis chose the name simply because liked the sound, although as a classicist he may well have come across the various Roman places so called, the best known of which is the Narnia (now Narni in Italy) that was formerly the Umbrian hill town of Nequinum. *See also* ASLAN.

Narziss und Goldmund. A novel (1930; translated from German as *Death and the Lover*, 1932, and as *Narcissus and Goldmund*, 1968) by Hermann Hesse (1877–1962). It is a medieval allegory of an artist and an intellectual on their way to self-discovery.

NASA. The National Aeronautics and Space Administration, an independent American government agency founded in 1958 to research and develop vehicles and activities for the exploration of space. It was created largely in response to the Soviet launch of the first SPUTNIK in 1957 and accepted President John F. Kennedy's challenge to put a man on the Moon by the end of the 1960s. It designed the APOLLO programme to that end, and achieved its aim when the US astronaut Neil Armstrong became the first man on the Moon in 1969.

Nasty bit or **piece of work.** An unpleasant person. The expression dates from the 1920s.

National Forest. A planned forest of some 520 square km (200 square miles) in central England, covering parts of Staffordshire, Derbyshire and Leicestershire, on the site of old coal tips and other damaged land. Trees were first planted in 1998, and about 70 per cent of the new planting is expected to have been achieved by 2005.

National Front. An extremist organization formed in 1967 from various small right-wing groups. It came to prominence in the 1970s in the wake of concern about the increasing number of immigrants to Britain, a fear fanned by Enoch Powell and other Conservative politicians. It had strong support in various parts of London, the Midlands and some northern cities. This support declined after 1977, however, and in the 1979 General Election the National Front received only 1.3 per cent of the vote. In 1982 its chairman, John Tyndall, left to form the British National Party, and this has since supplanted the National Front on the extreme right-wing edge of British politics.

National governments. As a result of the financial crises and the collapse of the Labour government in 1931, a COALITION GOVERNMENT was formed under J. Ramsay MacDonald (1931–5), the first of a series of governments called 'National' that held office in succession until 1940, under MacDonald, then Stanley Baldwin (1935–7) and lastly Neville Chamberlain (1937–40). Those Liberal and Labour MPs who supported these governments called themselves National Liberal candidates and National Labour candidates. The administrations became increasingly Conservative in character.

National Service. Until the First World War Britain relied on volunteer forces to fight its wars. The carnage on the WESTERN FRONT caused a severe shortage of fighting men, however, and in February 1916 the government introduced conscription for men aged between 18 and 40 (later 50). Compulsory military service ended in 1918 but as war again threatened in 1939 it was reintroduced under the National Service Act for men aged between 18 and 41 (later 51). From 1942 unmarried women were also made available for service. The call-up continued after the Second World War until 1960 for men of 18, who served a period of 18 to 24 months' service. *See also* KITCHENER'S ARMY.

National treasure. A nickname for any respected or admired celebrity, such as an actor, writer or sportsman or woman, especially one who is 'getting on'.

> Not so long ago, [Anita] Brookner was being roundly mocked for being dull, old fashioned and overrated. This summer, the wind has changed and with her 19th novel … she is once more a national treasure.
> *Sunday Times* (8 August 1999)

National Trust. The short name of the National Trust for Places of Historic Interest or Natural Beauty, Britain's foremost conservation body. It began as a private venture, founded by the housing reform pioneer Octavia Hill and others in 1895. Its first two properties came through the gift of a small scenic coastal area in North Wales and the purchase for £10 of a 14th-century timber-frame clergy house in Alfriston, East Sussex. Open spaces and small houses remained the key interest until the 1930s, when it became evident that the country's stately homes must have priority. The first to be given was Blickling Hall in Norfolk, together with its contents, gardens and estate. By the close of the 20th century the Trust had come to own some 300 houses open to the public, as well as complete villages, such as Lacock, Wiltshire, given in 1944 by Matilda Talbot (a descendant of the photographic pioneer William Fox Talbot), and extensive areas of countryside.

National Velvet. A novel (1935) by Enid Bagnold (1889–1981). Velvet, a butcher's daughter, wins a piebald horse in a raffle. Disguised as a boy, she rides it in the Grand National, Britain's premier steeplechase, and is first past the winning post but is disqualified for dismounting before the weighing-in. A popular film version (1945), directed by Clarence Brown, starred the 14-year-old Elizabeth Taylor.

Nation of Islam. A black nationalist religion, also known as Black Muslims, that evolved in the United States in the 20th century. The movement proper was founded by Wallace Fard, who established a temple in Detroit in 1931. The chief developer of the movement, however, was Elijah Muhammad (1897–1975), who founded a second temple in Chicago. Although the Nation has never actually joined Islam, its creed urges blacks to drop the 'slave religion' of Christianity and return to their native Islamic faith. *See also* FIVE PERCENTERS; MALCOLM X.

Nation shall speak peace unto nation. The motto of the BBC, suggested by Dr Montague Rendall, one of the first five governors, when the original company was incorporated in 1927. It is based on a phrase in a biblical verse: 'They shall beat their swords into plowshares, and their spears into pruninghooks: nation shall not lift up sword against nation, neither shall they learn war any more' (Isaiah 2:4).

Native American. A term for the indigenous peoples of North America, favoured by many from the early 1970s for the formerly familiar Red Indians, whose skin is not uniformly copper-coloured and who are not Indians, although dubbed as such following Christopher Columbus's mistaken assumption that he had discovered the East Indies. An intermediate variant, 'American Indian' or 'Amerindian', was also at one time a preferred designation.

NATO. The North Atlantic Treaty Organization, set up in 1950 at the time of the COLD WAR for the defence of Europe and the North Atlantic against the perceived threat of Soviet aggression. Its signatories were those of the North Atlantic Treaty of 1949 between Britain, Canada, the United States, France, Belgium, the Netherlands, Luxembourg, Norway, Denmark, Iceland, Italy and Portugal. Greece and Turkey joined NATO in 1952, West Germany in 1955 (reunited Germany in 1990) and Spain in 1982. In response the Soviet Union and its allies signed the WARSAW PACT. The number of NATO members grew to 19 in 1999 with the accession of the Czech Republic, Hungary and Poland.

Natural Law Party. A body of TRANSCENDENTAL MEDITATION practitioners who came into the public eye in Britain in 1992 when they contested every seat in the general election and lost every one. They have their base at Mentmore Towers, Buckinghamshire, where they practise yogic flying, and their avowed aim is 'for everyone to enjoy Heaven on Earth through the implementation of Maharishi's Master Plan to Create Heaven on Earth'.

Nature of the Beast, The. A novel (1985) for young adults by Janni Howker (b.1957), set on the edge of a northern industrial town. Unemployment is one beast that is ravaging the community. The other, the Haverstock Beast, which may or may not exist, spreads fear through the countryside. Anger and frustration cause the narrator to exclaim, 'I'm going to take over where the Beast left off.' The title recalls the biblical reference: 'And that no man might buy or sell, save that he had the mark, or the name of the beast, or the number of his name' (Revelation 13:17).

Nature ramble. A leisurely but purposeful stroll in the country, especially one made with children to observe and discuss the wildlife. The term is first recorded only in the 1940s but the exercise existed long before this.

> The nature rambles of 'Romany' … were familiar to listeners in the north of England long before he made his national debut on Children's Hour in 1938.
> *Sunday Times* (13 February 2000)

Naturism. Nudism, as practised for health, quasi-mystic or hedonistic reasons in holiday camps or other centres, typically by the seaside. The term dates from the 1930s and implies both a 'state of nature' and an identity of the unclothed human body with the rightly unadorned world of nature. The word is felt to have a respectability clearly not present in 'nudism', a word itself dating from the previous decade, and in 1961 members of the British Sun Bathing Association voted to substitute 'naturism' for 'nudism' in their official literature. *See also* NAKED AS NATURE INTENDED.

Naughty bits. A jocular euphemism for the male or female genitals or female breasts, popularized and possibly even coined by the creators of MONTY PYTHON'S FLYING CIRCUS. *See also* WOBBLY BITS.

> The fact that Middle England has made this woman [television gardener Charlie Dimmock] a sex symbol says all we need to know about our sexual maturity as a nation. … And all because you can sometimes almost see her naughty bits on telly.
> *The Times* (21 July 1999)

Naughty but nice. Disobedient or forbidden (which is bad) but delectable (which is good). The phrase was the title of an American film of 1939 but was later familiar as an advertising slogan for various tasty products, such as cream cakes in the late 1970s (the novelist Salman Rushdie once claimed to have coined the phrase at this time as a slogan to promote fresh cream in cakes for the National Dairy Council). The ultimate source is undoubtedly the fuller phrase 'It's naughty but it's nice', found as the title of a song of 1873 by Arthur Lloyd. The words are sexually suggestive.

Naughty Nineties. The 1890s, when the puritanical Victorian code of behaviour and conduct gave way in certain wealthy and fashionable circles to growing laxity in sexual morals, a cult of hedonism, and a more light-hearted approach to life generally. The expression is first recorded only in the 1920s. A nickname for the 1990s has yet to be established. *See also* MAUVE DECADE; NOUGHTIES.

Nausea. A modernistic novel (1949, also known as *The Diary of Antoine Roquentin*; in French as *La Nausée*, 1938) by the Existentialist philosopher Jean-Paul Sartre (1905–80). 'Nausea' in this context signifies a sense of disgust at the fact that people and things cannot help existing, yet there is no reason for their existence. Roquentin's former mistress leaves him but returns. When she leaves him again, he discovers that because there is no more reason for him to live, he is nevertheless free. His conclusion is that in the act of creation lies an escape from the oppression of the accident of existence, and he considers writing a book.

Nautilus, USS. A US submarine, the world's first nuclear-powered vessel (launched in 1954), which in 1958 sailed across the Arctic Ocean, under the polar ice cap and directly beneath the North Pole. *Nautilus* had also been the name of one of the first-ever submersible craft, designed by the American Robert Fulton in 1800. It was also the name of Captain Nemo's submarine in Jules Verne's *Twenty Thousand Leagues Under the Sea* (1870). The name derives from the nautilus, a kind of marine mollusc related to squids and cuttlefish; this in turn owes its etymology to the Greek *nautilos*, 'sailor', from *naus*, 'ship'.

Navel-gazing. Complacent self-absorption; concentration on a single issue at the expense of a wider view. The allusion is to mystic religions such as Buddhism, in which the navel is venerated as the source of birth and being. To contemplate one's own navel, in the sense of spending time complacently considering one's own interests, is a similar concept. Such figurative expressions date from the turn of the 20th century.

> Working in television ... you become accustomed to the charge that you are a self-indulgent navel-gazer. When the accusation is levelled at me, I usually reply that it is other people's navels, not my own, that I am eager to examine.
>
> *The Times* (23 July 1999)

Nazi. A shortened form for a member of the National-sozialistische Deutsche Arbeiterpartei or NSDAP (National Socialist German Workers' Party), founded in 1919 and led by Adolf Hitler from 1921 to 1945. The term is now used colloquially to describe any person of extreme right-wing views. *See also* MEIN KAMPF; NIGHT OF THE LONG KNIVES; SA; SS.

Near miss. A narrowly avoided mishap; an attempt that almost succeeds. The expression is first recorded in the Second World War with reference to a bomb exploding in the water near enough to a ship to cause damage but not to sink it. It could have been a hit, but was fortunately a miss, and 'a miss is a good as a mile'. The phrase was probably based on the earlier 'near thing'.

Neasden. A district of the London borough of Brent that in the mid-20th century came to be regarded as a typical London suburb, faceless and formless. It was satirically pictured as such by *Private Eye*, no doubt partly on account of its name, which though actually

meaning 'nose-shaped hill' suggests 'Nilsdon' or in American terms 'Nowheresville'.

Neddy. The popular name for the National Economic Development Council set up by the British government in 1962 and functioning until 1992. The numerous Economic Development Committees for particular industries that appeared were called 'Little Neddies'.

Need no introduction, To. To be known to all concerned. The expression is popular with those who introduce a speaker to a meeting, although some negate its import by following it with a potted biography of the individual in question.

Need something like a hole in the head, To. Not to need it at all. The expression dates from the 1940s and renders the Yiddish phrase *ich darf es vi a loch in kop*, 'I need it like a hole in the head'.

Nehru jacket. A type of lapel-less jacket that buttoned down the front, popular in the 1960s. It was based on that worn by Jawaharlal Nehru (1889–1964), the first prime minister of independent India, and was promoted in modified form by the French couturier Pierre Cardin. *See also* MAO SUIT.

Neighbourhood Watch. As a result of increasing crime, especially burglary, residents in particular areas began organizing Neighbourhood Watch groups from the early 1980s with police cooperation. Suspicious activities and circumstances are reported to the police, and some worthwhile effect on burglary has resulted. The idea was copied from similar schemes in the United States.

NEP. See NEW ECONOMIC POLICY.

Nepman. A term applied in the former Soviet Union to a person allowed to engage in private enterprise business under the NEW ECONOMIC POLICY (NEP) begun in 1921.

Nerd. This term for a studious but tedious person dates from the 1950s but only fully came into its own in the 1980s, when a T-shirt reading 'I'm a Nerd, and I'm Proud' was popular. A typical nerd wore a white shirt, baggy trousers and black-rimmed glasses and carried a pack of pens in his shirt pocket. The term itself apparently derives from Californian surfers' jargon. *See also* ANORAK; GEEK; MELVIN.

> And the jock shall dwell with the nerd and the cheerleader lie down with the wimp and there will be peace upon the campus.
>
> *Observer* (29 May 1988)

Nervous Nelly. A nickname for a foolish or timid person. It was originally used of Frank B. Kellogg (1856–1937), American secretary of state from 1925 to 1929. He was so dubbed by isolationists when he negotiated the Kellogg–Briand Pact (1928) to outlaw war.

> He called her 'flibbertigibbet' and 'nervous Nellie', according to the not-always-accurate *National Enquirer*.
>
> *heat* (13–19 January 2000)

Nervous wreck. A person suffering from stress or emotional exhaustion. The phrase dates from the early 20th century with 'nervous' qualifying 'wreck' in the sense of a physically or mentally broken person.

Nesbitt, Rab C. The string-vested Scottish philosopher of this name, created by Ian Pattison, was wonderfully embodied by the actor Gregor Fisher, who first assumed his persona in the television sketch series *Naked Video* (1986–91). He burgeoned to his full foul-mouthed, beer-boozing self in the series that bore his name, first screened in 1990, where he appears with his wife, Mary, his teenage sons, Gash and Burney, his devious drinking pal, Jamesie, and the latter's baby-craving wife, Ella. Beneath his crude exterior he is patently a vulnerable individual and at the very least a LOVABLE ROGUE. He soon endeared himself to viewers, even if they could make little of his slang-ridden speech and his almost impenetrable musings, delivered in a strong Glasgow accent.

Netball. The sport of this name originated at a physical training college for girls in Hampstead, where in 1895 a visiting American introduced a version of basketball which the girls played with wastepaper baskets at each end of the hall. The rules were at first imprecise, but were codified in 1901. Netball's association with girls' schools stems entirely from this particular place of origin. In modern times the game has become familiar to Londoners and visitors to London from the lunchtime games played by office staff in Lincoln's Inn Fields. *See also* KORFBALL.

Net Book Agreement. The agreement set up in Britain in 1900 between booksellers and publishers, by which with a few exceptions the former undertook not to sell books at less than the price marked on or inside the cover. The agreement effectively collapsed in 1995 when three major publishers, HarperCollins, Random Century and PENGUIN BOOKS, withdrew their support.

Net-head. A nickname for an enthusiastic or compulsive user of the computer INTERNET. The term originated in the early 1990s as American jargon. *See also* INTERNAUT; NETIQUETTE.

Nether regions. A genteel euphemism for the genital and excretory area, adopted from an earlier term for the underworld or hell. *See also* DOWN THERE.

> Running, climbing and sprawling are all recognizable teenage desires and all of them are less easily achieved if you are in danger of exposing your nether regions to all and sundry.
>
> *The Times* (Letter to the Editor) (11 September 1999)

Netiquette. A punning semi-serious coinage of the 1990s for the largely unwritten rules of behaviour on the INTERNET.

Neue Sachlichkeit (German, 'New Objectivity'). A movement in German art in the 1920s and 1930s that reflected the resignation and cynicism of the postwar period. It had no unified style or group affiliation but its main trend involved the use of meticulous detail and violent satire to portray the face of evil. Its leading exponents were Otto Dix (1891–1969) and George Grosz (1893–1959). The name of the movement, which dissipated in the 1930s with the rise of the NAZIS, was coined in 1923 by Gustav Hartlaub, director of the Kunsthalle, Mannheim, and was used by him as the title of an exhibition he staged there in 1925.

Never a dull moment. A phrase used positively to indicate the constant variety of a full life but also negatively or ironically in allusion to something difficult or dangerous. The expression apparently arose in the Royal Navy in the 1930s and from there spread to civilian use.

Never Give a Sucker an Even Break. A film comedy (1941) written by and starring the US comedian W.C. Fields (1879–1946). Its absurd plot, which begins with Fields falling out of an aeroplane in pursuit of his bottle of whisky, was allegedly jotted down by Fields ON THE BACK OF AN ENVELOPE and sold to Universal Studios for $25,000. Released in the UK under the less memorable title *What a Man!*, the film is now known chiefly for its title, which has long been quoted as a quintessentially Fieldsian piece of advice. Fields himself suggested shortening it to *Fields: Sucker*, thinking the longer version might be a trifle unwieldy.

Never had it so good. Earlier current in the United States, the phrase became popular in Britain after its use by Harold Macmillan, Conservative prime minister (1957–63), in a speech at Bedford (20 July 1957).

Referring to the overall prosperity and general improvement of living standards, he said: 'Most of our people have never had it so good.'

Never Mind the Bollocks, Here's the Sex Pistols. The title of an infamous PUNK album by the Sex Pistols released in 1977, including the songs 'Anarchy in the UK', GOD SAVE THE QUEEN, 'Pretty Vacant' and 'Holidays in the Sun'. A (possibly apocryphal) story tells that Malcolm McLaren, the manager of the Sex Pistols, was in a pub with the guitarist Steve Jones and was anxious because Virgin, the company to which they had just signed, were demanding a title for the album and they didn't have one. Jones commented, 'Never mind all that bollocks', and thus a title was found. Jamie Read, who designed the album's cover, gives a different account, claiming that he and Jones were discussing possible titles with John Varnom of Virgin, one possibility being 'God Save the Sex Pistols', when Jones, unimpressed, said 'Never mind the bollocks'. *See also* ROCK GROUP NAMES.

Never Mind the Quality, Feel the Width. A television SITCOM broadcast from 1967 to 1971, centring on the unlikely business partnership formed in the East End of London between Patrick Kelly, an Irish Catholic trousermaker, played by Joe Lynch (initially by Frank Finlay), and Emmanuel Cohen, a Jewish jacketmaker, played by John Bluthal. The humour largely devolves on the inability of each to understand the other's religious beliefs, patriotic loyalties or philosophy of life. But although apparently incompatible, the two need each other to succeed in their enterprise, just as a jacket needs trousers. The title is said to have derived from a phrase that one of the scriptwriters, Vince Powell, had heard an Irish tailor use, but it may have been a deliberate inversion of a general cloth trade saying: 'Never mind the width, feel the quality.'

Never-never. To get or buy something on the never-never is to obtain it on hire purchase, a system of deferred payment.

Never Never Land. The land (originally 'the Never Land') where the Lost Boys and Red Indians lived, and where Pirates sailed up the lake in J.M. Barrie's PETER PAN (1904). The phrase was also applied to the whole of the Australian outback, but since the publication of Jeannie Gunn's *We of the Never-Never* (1908), an affectionate portrait of life in the back of beyond at the turn of the 20th century, it has been restricted to northwest Queensland and the Northern Territory.

Never Say Never Again. A film (1983) starring Sean Connery as secret agent James BOND, based on the spy novels of Ian Fleming (1908–64). The title was an in-joke between the movie producers and Connery himself, who had sworn that his appearance in the earlier Bond movie, DIAMONDS ARE FOREVER (1971), would be his last.

New Age. A philosophy of the late 1980s centring on ALTERNATIVE medicine, astrology, spiritualism, animism and the like. Two notable phenomena of the period were New Age music, as a type of gentle melodic music combining elements of jazz, folk and classical music, played largely on electronic instruments, and New Age travellers, as groups of latter-day HIPPIES, who lead a nomadic existence, travelling the country with their children and animals in ancient vehicles to set up camp at such spiritually significant sites as Stonehenge and Glastonbury (*see* GLASTONBURY FESTIVAL). The name itself evokes the AGE OF AQUARIUS.

New Boots and Panties!! A characterful pop album by Ian Dury (1942–2000), released in 1977. The album contains a series of witty musical portraits of characters such as 'Plaistow Patricia', 'Billericay Dickie' and 'Clevor Trever', the last two being a pair of ESSEX MEN *avant la lettre*. Blending music-hall vulgarity with elements of PUNK, the songs owe much of their impact to Dury's playfully sinister cockney voice and his imaginatively crude lyrics. 'Plaistow Patricia' is a seedy East End drug-addict, killing herself through a life of excess; 'Billericay Dickie' tells the sordid tale of the conquests of an Essex WIDE BOY; while 'Clevor Trever' (the misspellings are intentional), represents the sorry attempts at self-expression of the hopelessly inarticulate Trevor of the title.

> Had a love-affair with Nina in the back of my
> 　Cortina,
> A seasoned-up hyena could not have been more
> 　obscener.
> 　IAN DURY: 'Billericay Dickie'

New Criticism. A school of literary critical theory that emerged after the First World War. It insisted on the intrinsic value of a work of art and concentrated attention on the individual work as an independent unit of meaning. The technique employed in the approach, involving a close, analytical reading of the text, is the subject of I.A. Richards' *The Principles of Literary Criticism* (1924) and William Empson's *Seven Types of Ambiguity* (1930). The movement did not have a name, however, until it was further treated in John Crowe Ransom's *The New Criticism* (1941).

New Deal. The name given to US President Franklin D. Roosevelt's policy of economic reconstruction to tackle the effects of the GREAT DEPRESSION, announced in his first presidential campaign (1932). 'I pledge you, I pledge myself, to a new deal for the American people.' A relief and recovery programme known as the 'First New Deal' was inaugurated in March 1933, and a 'Second New Deal', which was concerned with social reform, in January 1935. The 'Third New Deal' of 1938 sought to preserve such gains made by its predecessors. In Britain in the late 1990s NEW LABOUR introduced a number of 'New Deals' as special initiatives to improve the country's social, economic and educational status.

New Economic Policy. A policy introduced in the USSR by LENIN in 1921, to replace the 'war communism' that had been official policy since the 1917 OCTOBER REVOLUTION. The NEP was introduced in the wake of economic difficulties and disturbances such as the KRONSTADT MUTINY. It allowed a degree of private enterprise and internal trade, and established state banks. It was replaced under STALIN in 1929 by the first of the FIVE-YEAR PLANS. *See also* KULAKS.

New kids on the block. Newcomers to a particular place or activity, especially those that have yet to prove themselves. The American phrase was popularized by New Kids on the Block, a pop group of five New England teenagers who enjoyed a brilliant but brief career in the first half of the 1990s. 'Block' here is an urban area centring on a block of buildings. Variants naturally exist.

> Having opened their markets to global trade in the 1990s, the new boys on the international currency trading block ... were the innocent victims of a brutal mugging.
>
> *The World Today* (October 1999)

New Labour. The LABOUR PARTY as restyled under Tony Blair, its leader from 1994. While paying lip service to the party's traditional socialist values, it stressed the importance of the individual in society and indicated its receptiveness to new ideals and aspirations and its willingness to modernize. Its acceptance of many aspects of market-based economics overturned the old Labour policy of nationalization. *See also* BLAIRISM; COOL BRITANNIA; EDUCATION, EDUCATION, EDUCATION.

> Everybody should have a taste of the good life. A decade ago it was the Tories; now it is new Labour.
>
> *Sunday Times* (10 October 1999)

New lad. A young man who embraces sexist attitudes and who pointedly eschews POLITICAL CORRECTNESS and the apparent effeteness of the NEW MAN. The concept of the new lad evolved in the early 1990s and later came to be associated with young rock bands and BRITPOP. The use of 'lad' evokes such phrases as 'a bit of a lad' and 'one of the lads'. *See also* LADETTE.

New Look. The name given to the long-skirted women's dress of 1947 that was launched as the DIOR LOOK. The style was reminiscent of the EDWARDIAN ERA and was short lived. The phrase is also used generally for a redesigned periodical or restructured radio or television programme. An annual 'makeover' of this kind usually takes place in the autumn.

> Next week, your New Statesman will have a new look. Alongside a brighter, easier-to-read design, we shall bring you an extended arts, culture and books section.
>
> *New Statesman* (11 September 1998)

New Machiavelli, The. A political novel (1911) by H.G. Wells (1866–1946). A British Liberal member of parliament, disaffected with his party, becomes a Tory, as which he is re-elected. His affair with a much younger woman who had worked in his office when he was campaigning as a Liberal becomes public knowledge. Unwilling to face the political and marital implications and unable to keep away from each other, they run away to the Continent. The original Niccolò Machiavelli (1469–1527) was an Italian political philosopher whose realistic view of government and trenchant precepts gave him a reputation for guile.

New man. In modern terms a man who actively expresses his latent caring nature by helping with domestic work and young children in the home. *See also* HOUSE HUSBAND; NEW WOMAN.

> Laddish [television chef] Jamie Oliver may be, but he's New Man enough to offer to cook for his sister's hen night and offer his utterly cool Central London apartment for the occasion.
>
> *The Times* (21 April 1999)

New morality. A popular term of the 1960s implying that the hitherto publicly accepted canons of morality were no longer relevant to contemporary society, owing to the rapid spread of social and technical change, the advent of the PILL, and more 'enlightened' attitudes generally. Such thinking was induced by the growth of the AFFLUENT SOCIETY, the diminishing of individual responsibility occasioned by the WELFARE STATE, the declining influence of Christian standards and 'middle-class morality', and the championship of hedonism and self-indulgence by certain writers and theorists. *See also* NEW WOMAN.

New rock 'n' roll. Something new, highly fashionable and, potentially, profitable. The term draws on the impact made by ROCK 'N' ROLL in the 1950s, when the new style of music was seen as the quintessence of all that was modish and exciting.

New Romantic. A style of popular music and fashion in vogue in the early 1980s in which both men and women wore make-up and dressed in flamboyant clothes. Androgyny was a key feature, and groups such as Culture Club and Soft Cell were typical of the genre, while Boy George (b.1961) embodied its archetype.

News of the Screws. A frivolous nickname for the *News of the World*, as a Sunday newspaper specializing in sensational stories of sexual shenanigans.

Newsom Report. The report *Half Our Future* (1963) by Sir John Newsom (1910–71) considered the education of 13- to 16-year-olds of average and less than average ability attending full-time courses at school or in further education establishments. It recommended a raising of the school age to 16 for all pupils entering secondary schools from 1965 and certain other measures, ranging from the replacement of slum secondary schools by new schools to positive guidance on sexual behaviour. The report was compassionate and practical and the policies it advocated were taken up again in the PLOWDEN REPORT, when Newsom served as chairman.

Newspeak. A language in which words change their meaning to accord with the official views of the state. The word was coined by George ORWELL in his novel *Nineteen Eighty-Four* (*see* 1984).

New Statesman, The. (1) A moderate left-wing weekly magazine founded in 1913 by the social reformers and Fabian Society founders Sidney (1859–1947) and Beatrice Webb (1858–1943).

(2) A television SITCOM, screened on ITV from 1987 to 1992, centring on the blatant machinations and depravities of the newly elected Conservative MP Alan B'Stard, played by Rik Mayall. Despite the outrageous travesty of political life, the series nevertheless reflected some truths of 1980s Britain.

The story owed much of its success to Mayall's full engagement with his obnoxious persona, allowing his character's latent boyish charm to shine through the sleaze.

News to me. Something I was not aware of. The expression dates from the turn of the 20th century, typically in the phrase 'That's news to me.' One may similarly apprise a person of a fact by saying 'I have news for you', especially when one believes they are misinformed or mistaken. *See also* HAVE I GOT NEWS FOR YOU.

New town. A town established as a new settlement with the aim of relocating populations away from large cities. The first new towns in Britain were inspired by the GARDEN CITY concept formulated at the end of the 19th century. They were proposed in the New Towns Act of 1946, and 12 were designated in England and Wales over the next four years, with a further 2 in Scotland. Each had its own development corporation financed by the government. Further new towns were set up in the 1960s. Many new towns are based on existing towns or villages. The general tally is:

ENGLAND: Basildon, Bracknell, Crawley, Harlow, Hatfield, Hemel Hempstead, Stevenage, Welwyn Garden City, Newton Aycliffe, Corby, Milton Keynes, Northampton, Peterborough, Peterlee, Redditch, Runcorn, Skelmersdale, Telford, Warrington, Washington

WALES: Cwmbran, Newtown

SCOTLAND: Cumbernauld, East Kilbride, Glenrothes, Irvine, Livingston

New wave. A type of rock music in vogue in the late 1970s. It derived from PUNK ROCK but was generally more melodious in sound and less aggressive in performance. 'New Wave' is also used as the English equivalent of NOUVELLE VAGUE.

New woman. A type of 'liberated', independently minded and self-motivated woman who emerged in the late 19th century as a successor to the feminist crusaders of the 1860s. Her successors in the 20th century include the 'career girl' or 'career woman' of the 1950s and, in the backlash against the open promiscuity and AIDS scares of the 1980s, the NEW MORALITY 'virgin' or sexual abstainer of the 1990s. The term has largely been a creation of the media. *See also* NEW MAN.

New World Order. A state of affairs held by some commentators to have arrived with the ending of the COLD WAR and the collapse of the Soviet Union in 1991. In this New World Order there was only one superpower, the USA, which would act as 'the world's policeman'. The apparent unity of so many countries in following the US lead in condemning Iraq's invasion of Kuwait in 1990, and in the GULF WAR of 1991, seemed to confirm this view. In a much-discussed book, the US academic Francis Fukuyama proclaimed *The End of History* (1992) and the final victory of Western-style capitalism and liberal democracy. Subsequent events have cast a shadow over this triumphalism, and the USA has been criticized for acting as 'the world's policeman' only where US interests are affected. The term has unfortunate echoes of Hitler's plans for a 'New Order' in Europe, and the 'New Order in East Asia' declared by the Japanese government in 1938.

New Year's resolution. A decision made on New Year's Eve to abandon a bad habit or adopt a good one in the New Year. A survey in 1997 showed that two people out of three make such resolutions but that most soon break them. The most popular resolutions are to give up smoking and to diet.

New Yorker. An influential weekly American magazine launched in February 1925 by Harold Ross and Jane Grant with funds from the family that owned the Fleischmann Yeast Company. It is aimed at an urbane and literate readership and became famous for certain regular features, such as its 'Profiles', or biographical sketches on prominent living men and women. Cartoons and comic drawings in the magazine have also had a widespread influence on artists and editors elsewhere. It underwent significant changes in style and editorial practice in the late 1980s and early 1990s but on the whole retained its high-profile image and the loyalty of its long-standing readers.

Nice little earner. Money earned easily or effortlessly, possibly but not necessarily illicitly. The colloquialism was popularized by the main character, Arthur Daley, in the television series MINDER. *See also* HER INDOORS.

> For private investors, thinking in terms of thousands rather than millions or even billions of pounds, Pibs [Permanent Interest-Bearing Shares] can be a nice little earner.
>
> *Sunday Times* (7 November 1999)

Nice Nellyism. Excessive prudishness. An American expression emerging in the 1930s and based on 'nice Nelly' as a conventional nickname for an ultra-respectable woman.

Nice one. A general term of approval, popularized in the 1970s by 'Nice one, Cyril', originally used in a television commercial of 1972 for Wonderloaf bread, and subsequently taken up by football fans in a chant dedicated to the Tottenham Hotspur player Cyril Knowles. The Spurs team went on to record, under the name Cockerel Chorus, a song based on the phrase:

> Nice one, Cyril.
> Nice one, son!
> Nice one, Cyril.
> Let's have another one.
> SPIRO and CLARKE: 'Nice One, Cyril' (1973)

Nice work if you can get it. An envious reaction to what is seen as someone's more favourable situation, especially one easily obtained. The words quote the title of a song by Ira Gershwin:

> Holding hands at midnight
> 'Neath a starry sky,
> Nice work if you can get it,
> And you can get it if you try.
> IRA GERSHWIN: *Damsel in Distress*, 'Nice Work If You Can Get It' (1937)

Niche marketing. The selling of a product or service in a profitable corner of a commercial market. The concept evolved from the 1960s, and the art of identifying and exploiting this type of market became known as nichemanship.

Nickelodeon. The first cinema theatre called a 'Nickelodeon' (i.e. 'Nickel Odeon', because the admission price was only five cents), was that opened by John P. Harris and Harry Davis at McKeesport, near Pittsburgh, Pennsylvania, in 1905. The picture shown was *The Great Train Robbery*. It was the first real motion-picture theatre and thousands more nickelodeons soon sprang up throughout the United States. Hence, a cheap entertainment, and also its application to a JUKEBOX.

> Put another nickel in,
> In the nickelodeon,
> All I want is loving you
> And music, music, music.
> STEPHEN WEISS and BERNIE BAUM: 'Music, music, music' (1950)

Nicknames. *See* DRUG NICKNAMES; FILM STAR NICKNAMES; SPORTING NICKNAMES.

Nicorette. A proprietary name familiar from the 1980s for a type of nicotine-flavoured chewing-gum used to reduce dependency on tobacco. The name is apparently a blend of 'nicotine' and 'cigarette', thus seemingly delivering the very objects of desire that the taker seeks to abandon.

Nigel. A male forename that for some reason gained a pejorative patina in the 1960s. It came to be regarded as typical of the British upper-middle-class or upper-class male, and was seen as epitomizing young men who drive sports cars and wear flat caps and tweed jackets. It has since acquired NERD overtones.

> I am proud of never quite managing to live up to the awfulness of being Nigel. I think that was one of the reasons I wrote my first situation comedy under a false name.
> NIGEL WILLIAMS in *Sunday Times* (7 November 1999)

Nigel Molesworth. *See* MOLESWORTH, NIGEL.

Night at the Opera, A. A film comedy (1935) written by George S. Kaufman and Morrie Ryskind and starring the MARX BROTHERS. As the title suggests, the film has an operatic setting and culminates in the hilarious sabotaging of a performance of Verdi's opera *Il Trovatore*. The title enjoyed a new lease of life in the 1970s as the title of a bestselling album released by the British rock group Queen.

Night in Casablanca, A. A film comedy (1946) featuring the MARX BROTHERS. Starring Groucho Marx as the manager of a hotel in Casablanca much frequented by spies, it clearly owed a great deal to the Bogart classic CASABLANCA. Warner Brothers, which had released *Casablanca*, threatened to sue over the use of the word 'Casablanca' in the title, only for Groucho to retort that if they did then he would sue them in return over their use of the word 'Brothers'.

Nightmare on Elm Street. *See* ELM STREET.

Night of the Barricades. The name given to the night of 10 May 1968, when students of the Sorbonne in Paris, locked out of their campus, fought the tear gas of the riot police with barricades, bricks, paving stones and MOLOTOV COCKTAILS. The unrest was the climax of a nationwide movement of protest against the authoritarianism of the GAULLIST regime and its pursuit of purely political prestige over progressive social policies. The name recalls earlier occasions of Parisian unrest, notably the three-day 'war of the barricades' during the Revolution of July 1830.

Night of the Long Knives. A descriptive phrase applied to the night of 30 June 1934, when Hitler, assisted by Himmler's SS, secured the murder of

the leaders of the SA. The shootings (mainly at Munich and Berlin) actually began on the Friday night of the 29th and continued through the Sunday. The estimates of those killed vary between 60 and 400, and Ernst Röhm and Kurt von Schleicher were among them. Hitler had decided to rely on the *Reichswehr* rather than risk dependence on Röhm and the SA. Himmler presented the assassins with 'daggers of honour' inscribed with his name.

In British politics the term is used of 13 July 1962, when Harold Macmillan sacked a third of his cabinet following a disastrous by-election (*see also* MAC THE KNIFE). When on 14 August 1981 Margaret Thatcher dismissed some WETS from her own cabinet, some commentators referred to the cull as 'the night of the long hatpin'.

The term, now applied to any treacherous massacre or betrayal, has its antecedents. George Borrow, referring to a treacherous murder of South British chieftains by Hengist in 472, wrote:

> This infernal carnage the Welsh have appropriately denominated the treachery of the long knives. It will be as well to observe that the Saxons derived their name from the saxes, or long knives, which they wore at their sides, and at the use of which they were terribly proficient.
> *Wild Wales*, ch lii (1862)

Night starvation. A phrase created and promoted in the early 1930s by the manufacturers of HORLICKS malted milk powder drink, the theory being that a cup of their product just before bedtime would maintain blood and sugar levels throughout the night and so give restful sleep. A healthy person does not, of course, normally starve or go hungry in the night, although the suggestion of abstinence of food is present in the word 'breakfast', meaning the meal with which one breaks one's fast. Horlicks itself takes its name from William A. Horlick (1846–1936), a saddler's son from Gloucestershire who emigrated to the United States in 1869 and together with his brother James, a chemist, began to manufacture baby food in Chicago in 1873.

Night to Remember, A. A DISASTER MOVIE (1958) adapted by Eric Ambler from a book by Walter Lord about the sinking of the TITANIC on the night of 14 April 1912. The *Titanic* had by then already sunk once, in a film simply entitled *Titanic* in 1953 and went down once more, under the same title, in 1997, with Leonardo DiCaprio and Kate Winslet on board. In

1980 Lew Grade attempted to reverse the process in his film *Raise the Titanic*, the financial cost of which prompted Grade himself to observe that it would have been cheaper to have lowered the Atlantic.

Nightwatchman. In cricket a term for an inferior batsman sent in to bat when a wicket falls just before the end of the day. The aim is to avoid the dismissal of a better batsman, who thus remains 'protected' for the following day's play, just as a nightwatchman guards a building overnight.

Nike. A make of training shoes, first on sale in 1972 and soon becoming a fashionable item of footwear, even among non-sporting fans. The name is that of the goddess of victory in Greek mythology, who on vases of the classical period is depicted striding, running or flying. The name is pronounced to rhyme with 'spiky', not 'spike'.

Nikkei index. The figure indicating the the price of shares on the Tokyo Stock Exchange. The name is an abbreviation of Japanese *Nihon Keizai Shimbun*, 'Japanese Economic Journal', the newspaper that has calculated the index since 1974. It was earlier calculated by the Tokyo Stock Exchange itself.

Nimby. An acronym of 'not in my back yard', expressing the stance adopted by someone who objects to a development perceived as undesirable or hazardous in their own neighbourhood, while not raising the same objection about a similar development elsewhere. The expression often relates to environmental issues, such as the proposed location of a nuclear waste disposal site or the construction of a new bypass. The term dates from the 1980s and the use of 'yard' betrays its American origin. A Briton would be more likely to say 'not in my back garden'.

> Arthur Scargill and the Archbishop of York are manning the front line in a country-wide Nimby battle. Scargill has joined the Archbishop ... in protesting against plans to erect 50 miles of spindly metallic pylons across the majestic Vale of York.
> *The Times* (21 September 1999)

Nine-nine-nine. In Britain the telephone number for summoning emergency services such as police, ambulance or fire brigade. It was introduced in London in July 1937. The number is popularly said to have been chosen because on the old dial telephones the fingerhole for the number 9 was easy to find in the dark or in smoke. The real reason was more practical. The number 0 was already in use to call the operator free of charge from public call boxes, and it was relatively simple to modify the mechanism so as to extend coin-free dialling to 9, the dial number next to it.

Nine Tailors, The. A detective novel (1934) by Dorothy Sayers (1893–1957). The Nine Tailors, perhaps standing for 'nine tellers', is a peal performed on the eight bells of the church of Fenchurch St Paul, where Lord Peter WIMSEY is stranded and where he investigates two deaths.

1984. A year of the 20th century long regarded as apocalyptic and as such even entered in the *Oxford English Dictionary*. It derives from the title of George ORWELL's novel of 1949, a prophecy of the totalitarian future of mankind, portraying a society in which government propaganda and terrorism destroy the human awareness of reality. It is generally thought that Orwell named the novel by reversing the last two figures of the year in which it was written, 1948, but an article by Sally Coniam in the *Times Literary Supplement* of 31 December 1999 proposed another theory. In 1934 Orwell's first wife, Eileen O'Shaughnessy, published a poem, 'End of the Century 1984', in *The Chronicle*, the school magazine of Sunderland Church High School, where she had been a pupil in the 1920s. The poem was written to mark the school's 50th anniversary, looking back then forward to the future and to the school's centenary in 1984. It seems likely that Orwell could have adopted the year accordingly, although for him it was a random date. Support for this theory lies in the poem's mention of 'telesalesmanship' and 'Telepathic Station 9', terms strangely modern for their time, which seem to prefigure Orwell's own NEWSPEAK, 'teleprogrammes' and 'telescreen'. *See also* BIG BROTHER; DOUBLETHINK.

Nineteenth hole. The bar in the club house of a golf club, to which players resort after playing the 18 holes of the course. There is an implied pun on 'sink', since after sinking a putt one sinks a drink.

> Thousands of male golfers retreat to the 19th hole every weekend and quietly toast their continuing ability to exclude women from the bar, the fairways and the committee room.
> *The Times* (2 November 1999)

1922 Committee. A term for the entire body of backbenchers in the Conservative Party. It takes its name from a meeting of Conservative MPs in the Carlton Club in October 1922, when those present voted against Austen Chamberlain's policy of remaining in Lloyd George's COALITION GOVERNMENT, even though the meeting was chaired by Chamberlain himself. The decision caused his downfall as party leader, and the sudden taste of power suggested the need for a body through which backbenchers might exert influence. The executive of the Committee now meets weekly when the Commons are sitting and the chairman has direct access to the Conservative Party leader.

Nine-to-five job. A standard working day of eight hours, from 9 a.m. to 5 p.m., with one hour off for lunch.

Ninety-nine. An ice cream with a chocolate flake in it. The '99' was originally so called because the flake it carried was 99mm long. Such flakes were specially made for the ice cream trade and were sturdier than the traditional crumbly flake chocolate.

Ninety-seven-pound weakling. A physically or morally puny person. The term comes from one of the many striking pronouncements made by the American bodybuilder Charles Atlas, real name Angelo Siciliano (1893–1972), who boasted, 'I was once a 97-pound weakling'. The stated weight equals 7st 13lb, and the phrase is sometimes adjusted to '98-pound weakling' to make 8st exactly.

> It is possible to continue in daily life to talk of pints of milk, and half pounds of butter, and seven league boots, and broad acres, and 98lb weaklings ... without budging an inch on the principle that the metric system is of greater utility ... than imperial units.
> *The Times* (Letter to the Editor) (20 December 1999)

Ninety-two Club. A loose association of football fans who have visited every one of the 92 Premier League and Football League grounds in Britain. It was formed in 1978.

Nintendo. *See* GAME BOY.

Nip and tuck. A 19th-century phrase of American origin meaning neck and neck, as in a close-run race, that was adopted in the 20th century for a cosmetic surgical operation to reduce an area of sagging skin. The latter sense is perhaps closer than the former to the source of the expression, which is probably in a process of sewing or tailoring.

> Hillary Rodham Clinton, we have been unreliably told, sneaked into the surgery of a Manhattan plastic surgeon sometime this summer for a bit of nip and tuck.
> *Independent on Sunday* (28 November 1999)

Nippies. Waitresses in teashops run by J. Lyons & Co. Ltd of London were so known from the 1920s to the 1950s from their nimbleness and adroitness as they sped from table to table. The name was registered by Lyons in 1924.

Nisei (Japanese, 'second generation'). An American whose parents were immigrants from Japan, especially one interned during the Second World War, following Japan's attack on PEARL HARBOR. A famous example was TOKYO ROSE.

Nissen hut. A type of semi-cylindrical, corrugated-iron hut, named after its inventor, Colonel Peter N. Nissen (1831–1930). *See also* QUONSET HUT.

Nitty-gritty. The realities or practical details of a situation; 'brass tacks'. The origin of the phrase is uncertain, although nits are tiny and grit is composed of minute particles. There may have originally been a specific reference to grooming.

Nixon in China. A 'post-minimalist' political opera by John Adams (b.1947), first performed in 1987. The opera concerns the visit that US President Richard Nixon made to China in 1972 as part of his strategy of DÉTENTE and that led to the establishment of diplomatic relations between the United States and the People's Republic. One critic has commented of the opera that it 'proved to some listeners that there is more to minimalism than at first meets the ears'.

NKVD. *See* KGB.

NMI. An American abbreviation for 'no middle initial', thus breaking the norm, since most Americans have three names, the middle one often simply appearing as an initial, as Franklin D. Roosevelt, John F. Kennedy. Some Americans choose to be known by first and last name alone, however, in the British tradition. Very rarely an American's middle name is IO (initial only). This was famously the case with President Harry S. Truman (1884-1972), where the letter alone was a compromise designed to appease his maternal grandfather, Solomon Young, and his paternal grandfather, Anderson Shippe Truman. 'Although it could be said to stand for nothing, Truman customarily placed a period after it, thus tacitly recognizing it as the dual-purpose abbreviation his parents had intended' (*American National Biography*, 1999).

Nobel prize. One of six international prizes awarded annually for outstanding work in physics, chemistry, physiology or medicine, literature, economics and the promotion of peace. They were endowed by

Alfred Nobel (1833-96), the Swedish inventor of dynamite, and were first awarded in 1901. Public interest centres mostly on the winners of the literature and peace prizes. The former have included Eugene O'Neill (1936), T.S. Eliot (1948), Sir Winston Churchill (1953), Ernest Hemingway (1954), Samuel Beckett (1969), Alexander Solzhenitsyn (1970) and Seamus Heaney (1995). It was declined by Boris Pasternak in 1958. The peace prize has been awarded to Albert Schweitzer (1952), Martin Luther King Jr (1964), Mother Teresa of Calcutta (1979), the Dalai Lama (1989) and Mikhail Gorbachev (1990), among others, and to the International Red Cross Committee three times (1917, 1944, 1963), but in some years it has not been awarded at all.

No big deal. Nothing much; not worth bothering about. A phrase originating in American teenage slang of the 1960s. *See also* BIG DEAL.

> The headmaster of an independent school is said to have dismissed as 'no big deal' the discovery of four boys with cannabis.
>
> *The Times* (6 August 1999)

No can do. I am unable to do that. A pidgin-English-style phrase of American origin and mostly with apologetic overtones. It became familiar as the title of a popular song by Charles Tobias and Nat Simon, first performed in 1945. *See also* LONG TIME NO SEE.

No comment. A conventional statement of refusal to comment on a situation, especially in response to questions from a reporter or interviewer. The phrase dates from the 1950s.

Nodding donkey. A type of pump for pumping oil from land-based oil-wells, as typically in America. The shape and up-and-down motion of the pump gave its colloquial name.

Noddy. The wooden figure of a small boy whose head nods when he speaks, the creation of Enid Blyton (1897–1968). He lives in Toyland, drives a bright red motor car, and has friends who include Big Ears, a bearded gnome, and Mr Plod, a policeman. Noddy first appeared in *Little Noddy Goes to Toyland* (1949). He and his friends have subsequently been criticized by teachers, librarians and others as infantile stereotypes, and the stories in which they appear as undesirable and patronizing. They remain popular with their young readers, however.

Noddy bike. In the days before the PANDA CAR a lightweight motorcycle used by police officers on patrol

duty. The name is nothing to do with NODDY but came about because an officer riding such a bike could not safely salute but had to nod his head instead.

No dice. Nothing doing; out of the question. An expression of American origin dating from the 1930s and presumably referring to the refusal of a gambling-house proprietor to allow a player to start or continue playing.

Noel's House Party. A live television show hosted by a constantly genial Noel Edmonds and first screened in 1991. It was set in a mock manor house in the (obviously fictional) village of Crinkley Bottom and subjected its guests, both famous and unknown, to a variety of pranks and performances for the delectation of the delirious audience. A regular feature was a tank that poured a torrent of gaudy 'gunge' over guests. A later addition was a pink plastic dummy with yellow spots called MR BLOBBY.

No-fly zone. An area over which military aircraft are forbidden to fly, mainly during and even for some time after an armed conflict. The United States maintained its no-fly zone in southern Iraq for some years after the GULF WAR.

No-go area. An area which is dangerous or impossible to enter, or to which entry is restricted or forbidden. The term came to the fore in the early 1970s to apply to parts of Northern Ireland that were dominated by the IRA. *See also* BANDIT COUNTRY; BOGSIDE.

NoHo. A nickname given to a neighbourhood in lower Manhattan, New York, so called as it is 'north of Houston Street'. The name puns on SOHO. The area became fashionable in the 1970s after artists such as Robert Rauschenberg and Frank Stella moved into converted loft buildings here.

No holds barred. With all restrictions relaxed; anything goes. The American expression is first recorded in the 1940s and derives from wrestling terminology.

> *Media Watch*, a no-holds-barred version of the old *What the Papers Say*.
>
> *The Times* (30 July 1999)

Nomenklatura. A Russian term (from the Latin *nomenclatura*, 'summoning of names') applied in the former Soviet Union and its satellites in the Eastern bloc to those who played key roles in the state and Communist Party machines. The term became synonymous with the privileged ruling class. The term was also used for the system, controlled by Communist Party committees, by which people were appointed to such key roles.

No names, no pack drill. The identity in question will not be revealed. The allusion is to military punishment. Offenders may be sent on a forced march in full kit, but if the drill sergeant does not have the names of the miscreants, he is unable to impose this ordeal on them.

> I once entertained ... a visiting British bishop (no names, no pack-drill) to the Finnish social habit of a sauna, where episcopal robes would not have been appropriate.
> *The Times* (Letter to the Editor) (14 August 1999)

None but the Lonely Heart. A film (1944) adapted by US playwright Clifford Odets from a novel of the same title by the Welsh writer Richard Llewellyn (1906–83). It tells the story of a shiftless young cockney who drifts into a life of crime. Starring Cary Grant and Ethel Barrymore, it took its title from a song of 1869 written by the Russian composer Tchaikovsky, which was itself based on 'Mignon's Song' in the novel *Wilhelm Meisters Lehrjahre* (1795–6) by Johann Wolfgang von Goethe. In Tchaikovsky's song the relevant lyric is usually translated as:

> None but the weary heart can understand how I have suffered and how I am tormented.

Nonesuch Press. A distinctive and distinguished private press founded in 1923 by Francis Meynell (1891–1975) with the aim of demonstrating that machine-produced books could be as good as those hitherto hand-produced by private presses and yet be sold for a fraction of the price. It relied on the best commercially available type and issued both limited and 'unlimited' editions. Its first production, John Donne's *Love Poems*, issued on 3 May 1923, appeared in an edition of 1250 copies. One of its most popular productions was *The Week-End Book* (1924), an anthology edited by Meynell and his wife Vera, and it went on to produce works by writers such as Wycherley, Rochester, Otway, Vanbrugh, Farquhar and Dryden as well as illustrated books. It is now an imprint of Reinhardt Books Ltd, a firm acquired by Max Reinhardt in 1947.

Non-event. A disappointing or insignificant occurrence or occasion, especially one that was expected to be important or original. The expression dates from the early 1960s.

No-no. A thing that is NOT ON or impossible, as:

'Mowing the lawn was a no-no after the night's rain.' The expression dates from the 1940s.

> A big no-no is liquid eyeliner. 'Avoid it at all costs, one drop of rain will send it running down your face,' cautions the make-up artist Adam De Cruz.
> *The Times* (23 August 1999)

No pain, no gain. A motto of bodybuilders, perhaps deriving from Adlai Stevenson's slogan, 'There are no gains without pain,' first voiced when accepting the Democratic nomination for the US presidency in 1952. The words can apply to any situation to indicate that no progress is possible without effort.

No problem. It's all right; that is easily done. A catchphrase of the latter half of the 20th century, often used as a stock response to 'Thank you'. There is usually no question of a problem existing in the first place. *See also* NO SWEAT.

No pun intended. A phrase said when one realizes that a word or phrase just spoken could be understood in a punning sense, as: 'Boys essentially differ from girls in their make-up.' The converse, 'Pun intended', is sometimes similarly used to draw attention to a play on words that might otherwise have been missed.

> This biopic of trash novelist Jacqueline Susann is played for loud, broad comedy (pun intended).
> *The Times* (31 January 2000)

No purchase necessary. A phrase familiar in the text of promotional competitions. It indicates that the promotion is not legally a competition since it is not based on skill and does not require, for example, the writing of a slogan. The wording arose in order to avoid falling foul of the Lotteries and Amusement Act 1976 which prohibits games of chance. Potential entrants are thus offered a way of participating without purchasing. The usual method is to enter the draw by sending one's name and address on a plain piece of paper or by writing in to request a person in a handling house to open an actual product to see if the required symbol or notice is inside. Such promotions are successful because most people cannot be bothered with such a rigmarole but instead buy the product to discover instantly if they have won.

No questions asked. I suspect that what you are doing may be illegal but I shall say nothing since I am interested myself. A phrase that might apply to certain street traders, for example.

Nora. A female forename evoking a dull or unattractive woman. The sense was current in the 1990s and may have specifically evolved from Nora Batty, the untidy housewife in the popular television SITCOM *The* LAST OF THE SUMMER WINE.

Noraid. The acronym of *Northern Irish Aid* Committee, an American organization whose principal objective is to raise funds for the Republican cause in Northern Ireland, and in particular the IRA. It first came into public notice in the early 1970s, at the height of the TROUBLES. Its forerunner was Northern Irish Aid (NIA), an outfit to which it subsequently emerged that John Lennon, of the BEATLES, had donated the royalties from his song 'The Luck of the Irish', one of the tracks on the album *Sometime in New York City* (1972).

Norman. A male forename that is supposedly characteristic of a dull and typically bourgeois or even petit bourgeois person. An evocation of 'normal' is strong, and 'Norman Normal' is a nickname dating from the 1960s for a notably conventional or conformist person.

North by Northwest. A classic film thriller (1959), directed by Alfred Hitchcock and written by Ernest Lehman, about an advertising executive who becomes confused with another man and consequently finds himself pursued across the United States by people trying to kill him. Starring Cary Grant as the businessman driven to the point of madness by his experiences, the film derived its title from Shakespeare's *Hamlet*, specifically the passage in which the 'gloomy prince' denies the fact that he is actually mad:

> I am but mad north-northwest; when the wind is southerly I know a hawk from a handsaw.
>
> II.ii

North of Watford. *See* WATFORD.

North Pole. The pole was first reached on 6 April 1909 by the American explorer Robert Edwin Peary (1856–1920). In May 1933 it was claimed by the Russians and four years later they established a polar station there under Professor Otto Schmidt. *See also* SOUTH POLE.

North–south divide. The division of England into regions north or south of a line running approximately between the Severn and the Wash. A severe economic recession with consequent depression of house prices above the line in the 1980s, especially in the northeast, made the residents of that region the effective poor relations of those below it, where the recession was less marked and where property prices were booming. In the early 1990s much of the dis-

tinction between north and south dissolved, but later in the decade the former differences re-emerged, with a reduction in industrial output in the north and a growing economy in London and the southeast. A social and political distinction between the 'hard' north and 'soft' south has long been popularly implicit, and Elizabeth Gaskell drew on the concept for her novel *North and South* (1854), contrasting the 'satanic mills' of Manchester with the easy country life of Hampshire. The notion of such a divide can be taken back to Roman times, when the construction of Hadrian's Wall in the 2nd century AD separated colonized and settled Britannia from the wilder provinces north of the border. The same duality was later present in the Scandinavian Danelaw of northern and eastern England and the settled Saxon kingdom of Mercia in the centre of the country. *See also* FORTNUM–MASON LINE.

> The North-South divide is so stubborn a pattern in the British economy that it seems to have become a geographical feature snaking across the Midlands ... with boom to the south and bust to the north.
>
> *Independent on Sunday* (10 October 1999)

Norway spruce. A long-coned European spruce widely grown for timber and pulp and often used in Britain as a Christmas tree. A giant specimen is donated every year by Norway to London as a mark of the country's appreciation for the role Britain played in defeating the NAZIS in the Second World War. The tree is erected in Trafalgar Square in December and the annual ceremony in which the Norwegian ambassador turns on the lights is one of the most popular in the Christmas calendar.

Norwegian Wood (This Bird has Flown). A folk-influenced song by the BEATLES, credited to John Lennon and Paul McCartney and released in Britain in December 1965. 'Norwegian Wood' concerns an affair that John Lennon was conducting with a female journalist and features the first use of a sitar in a pop single. The true meaning of the song's title (and its lyrics) is nonetheless obscure and may simply reflect the contemporary predilection for teasingly elusive lyrics *à la* Bob Dylan. The subtitle was originally intended to be the song's actual title.

Norwegian Wood was also a nickname given to the US Democratic politician Walter Mondale (b.1928) on account of his expressionless delivery and Scandinavian origins. Mondale was vice-president (1977–81) under Jimmy Carter (*see* GRITS AND FRITZ) and was trounced in the 1980 presidential elections by the GREAT COMMUNICATOR, Ronald Reagan.

Nosey Parker. A prying person. The name is popularly said to allude to Matthew Parker, archbishop of Canterbury (1504–75), who was noted for the detailed articles of inquiry concerning ecclesiastical affairs generally and the conduct of the clergy, which he issued for the visitations of his province and diocese. However, the term is first recorded only in the early 20th century, so such a reference seems highly unlikely. According to one account, it was the nickname given to a man who spied on courting couples in Hyde Park, London. An alteration of 'nose-poker' is another possibility.

No skin off one's nose. Said of something that has no adverse effect on oneself. The allusion may be to a fight, in which one has scratched one's adversary while remaining unscathed oneself. The expression dates from the 1920s.

> Possibly by the time this appears someone will have actually won a million pounds. That would be no skin off the production company's nose.
> *The Times* (11 September 1999)

No strings attached. Said of an offer that carries no special conditions or restrictions. The reference is to a puppet that is free to move of its own volition when not manipulated by strings.

> 'We're entering a float for the Carnival. Needs someone to be in charge – what's wrong with you?'
> 'No, thank you,' said Natalie.
> 'No strings attached,' he pleaded.
> FAY WELDON: *The Heart of the Country* (1987)

No such animal. 'There ain't no such animal' is often said to mean that something does not exist. The catchphrase originated as the caption of a cartoon in *Life* magazine of 7 November 1907 showing a farmer at the circus looking at a dromedary.

No such thing as a free lunch. To say that there's no such thing as a free lunch is to repeat the popular truism that one cannot get something for nothing. A lunch involves preparation and expense, otherwise time and money. The words were particularly associated with the American economist Milton Friedman (b.1912) and have been recorded since 1938.

> 'Oh, "tanstaafl". Means "There ain't no such thing as a free lunch". And isn't,' I added, pointing to a FREE LUNCH sign across room, 'or these drinks would cost half as much. Was reminding her that anything free

costs twice as much in the long run or turns out worthless.'
> ROBERT A. HEINLEIN: *The Moon is a Harsh Mistress,* ch xi (1966)

No sweat. No trouble; no bother; NO PROBLEM. A phrase from the 1950s. The implication is that there is no need to make an effort that would produce perspiration.

> Think you have a tough time getting your boyfriend or girlfriend to hurry up when you're late for a social event? Try doing it when you've got a posse of about 30 people to cope with. No sweat.
> *Sunday Times* (19 September 1999)

Not! A word added at the end of a statement to negate it, the statement itself often being ironic. An example might be: 'He's one of the smartest people I know – not!' The usage appears to have stemmed from VALSPEAK but was popularized by the American film *Wayne's World* (1992) about a chaotic cable TV show devised by two girl-mad, rock-crazed teenagers.

Not a happy man. Displeased, especially as a reaction to a piece of news or a situation. A more evocative variant is 'not a happy bunny'.

> The father of Roland Rat ... is not a happy bunny. Greg Dyke, the BBC chief-in-waiting, spent New Year's Eve ... in the renowned dome queue and had an anxiety attack.
> *Sunday Times* (9 January 2000)

Not a hope in hell. No chance whatsoever. A phrase from the early years of the 20th century. The implication is that one is so deeply damned that one has no chance for heavenly salvation.

Not a pretty sight. Unpleasant to look at. The ironic phrase, current from the 1980s, was at first used to describe the body of a person who had met a sudden death. It was later applied to any particularly unprepossessing person.

> Mr Eclipse is heading for Cornwall and he isn't a pretty sight. He wears baggy shorts, Clarks sports sandals and ... a wide-brimmed hat.
> *The Times* (6 August 1999)

Not give a monkey's, To. To be completely indifferent or unconcerned; NOT TO GIVE A STUFF. The missing word is the 'F-word' (*see* FOUR-LETTER WORD) or alternatively 'toss'. The expression dates from the 1960s.

Not give a stuff, To. To be completely indifferent or unconcerned; NOT TO GIVE A MONKEY'S. 'Stuff' is a euphemism for the 'F-word' (*see* FOUR-LETTER WORD). The expression dates from the 1970s.

> To be honest, there was also the problem that the [television] ads weren't very good and nobody gave a stuff what happened to their principals [*sic*].
> *The Times* (3 September 1999)

Not give someone the time of day, To. To have no time for them; to refuse even to exchange civilities with them. The expression emerged in the 1950s, although in its now rare positive form to give someone the time of day dates from the time of Shakespeare. The modern negative phrase is typically found in a statement such as 'I wouldn't give him time of day'.

Not have a clue, To. To have absolutely no idea. The expression dates from the 1920s.

> 'Are you a belted earl?' I ask him [Alex Uxbridge, Earl of Uxbridge], wondering what exactly that means and whether all earls are belted. 'Haven't a clue,' he replies.
> *The Times* (26 January 2000)

Nothing to write home about. Unremarkable or insignificant, despite reports or rumours to the contrary, as: 'The hotel was nothing to write home about.' The expression arose at the turn of the 20th century and probably originated among troops stationed overseas.

Not just a pretty face. Intelligent as well as attractive. The expression, which dates from the 1950s, is often used humorously by someone who has achieved something praiseworthy: 'I'm not just a pretty face, you know!'

Not know one's arse from one's elbow, To. To be ignorant or stupid; to be quite incompetent. The two parts of the anatomy are unmistakably distinctive, but the comparison seems random.

Not know shit from Shinola, To. To be ignorant or innocent. The expression dates from the early 20th century, with Shinola (based on 'shine') the proprietary name of an American brand of boot polish. Similar is 'neither shit nor Shinola', with the sense 'neither one thing nor the other'.

Not know what has hit one, To. To be taken entirely unawares by an event; to be dealt an unexpected blow or awarded an unexpected benefit.

> The workers at Maldon Sea Salt do not know what is about to hit them. For they … are about to become

beneficiaries of the 'Delia effect'. … Ms Smith puts it [their product] at the top of her list of store cupboard essentials.
> *The Times* (27 December 1999)

Not me guv. It's nothing to do with me. A representation of a response from an employee when charged with avoiding responsibility for a duty or the like, 'guv' (for 'governor') being a working man's supposedly stock form of address to a superior.

> Last week it was 'Steady on, not me guv.' First the Live Group was blamed for not posting those dome tickets. Then it turned out to have been the fault of [Lord] Falconer's own quango.
> *Sunday Times* (9 January 2000)

Not much chop. Not very satisfactory; not up to much. The phrase dates from the turn of the 20th century, with 'chop' here in the sense 'seal', 'stamp'. The word is of Hindi origin and subsequently passed to China, whence it came into Australian and New Zealand usage.

Not my cup of tea. Not to my taste; of no interest to me. This negative phrase evolved in the 1930s from the positive '(just) my cup of tea', referring to a person or thing that is right or suitable.

Not on. Socially or otherwise unacceptable; impossible. The allusion is perhaps to a military operation that was first 'on' then cancelled because of unforeseen circumstances.

Not one's day. A day when one has a succession of misfortunes. The possessive is obviously variable, as 'not my day', 'not your day', etc. The expression dates from the 1920s.

> [Golfer Jarmo] Sandelin must have known it was not going to be his day when a marshal greeted him cheerfully: 'How are you doing, Jeremy?'
> *The Times* (28 September 1999)

Not Only… But Also… . A revue-style television comedy series screened from 1965 to 1966 and 1970 to 1973. Its absurdist skits won it instant cult status, and its regular high spot was a routine in which Peter Cook and Dudley Moore as 'Pete and Dud', a pair of cloth-capped proletarian philosophers, discussed the vanity of the world in a sequence of nicely inconsequential musings. 'Pete and Dud' also spawned the characters of 'Derek and Clive', two ageing perverts whose lavatorial exploits are recorded in three obscenity-laden albums, *Derek And Clive (Live)* (1976), *Derek and Clive Come Again* (1977) and *Derek and Clive* *ad Nauseam* (1978), the first of which included the 'tracks' 'In The Lav' and 'Winkie Wanky Woo'.

Not on your nelly. Certainly not. A variant of 'not on your life'. The phrase gained popularity in the 1940s as a shortening of 'not on your Nelly Duff', a name used as rhyming slang for 'puff', i.e. breath of life.

Not Pygmalion likely! A somewhat dated euphemism for 'not bloody likely!' In Shaw's play PYGMALION (1913) the Cockney flower girl Eliza Doolittle simultaneously shocked and delighted the audiences of her day by uttering the then taboo emphatic negative.

> *Freddy* [*opening the door for her*]: Are you walking across the Park, Miss Doolittle? If so –
> *Liza*: Walk! Not bloody likely. [*Sensation*]. I am going in a taxi. [*She goes out*].
> GEORGE BERNARD SHAW: *Pygmalion*, III (1913)

Not So Much a Programme More a Way of Life. A television comedy programme of the mid-1960s that packed the same satirical punch as its predecessor, THAT WAS THE WEEK THAT WAS. Its most contentious sketch, featuring John Bird as President Jomo Kenyatta of Kenya, drew an official complaint from that country's High Commission.

Not the Nine O'Clock News. A topically satirical television sketch series running from 1979 to 1982 and scheduled on BBC2 at the same time as the *Nine O'Clock News* on BBC1. The series launched the careers of the comedians Rowan Atkinson (*see* MR BEAN), Mel Smith, Griff Rhys Jones (*see* ALAS SMITH AND JONES) and Pamela Stephenson. The latter's impressions of women newsreaders were an enjoyably irreverent ingredient.

Not the only pebble on the beach. Not unique or irreplaceable. The expression originally referred to an eligible young man or woman and became popular at the turn of the 20th century following its occurrence in Harry Braisted's song 'You're Not the Only Pebble on the Beach' (1896):

> If you want to win her hand,
> Let the maiden understand
> That she's not the only pebble on the beach!

Notting Hill. A film (1999) written by Richard Curtis about a celebrated US film actress who falls for a humble British bookshop manager while on a visit to London. Starring Julia Roberts and Hugh Grant as the hesitant lovers, the pair first meet in Grant's bookshop in Notting Hill, the area where most of the action takes place (with the consequence that the district eagerly looked forward to a flood of tourists inspecting the locations used in the film).

Notting Hill Carnival. Europe's largest street festival, held annually in the district of Notting Hill, northwest central London, on the last (bank holiday) weekend of August as a celebration of the West Indian way of life. It had its origins in a street party held in 1964 for the children of Trinidadian immigrants who had settled in the area. Two years later the party evolved into a regular event, with steel bands providing the music and food and drink donated by local traders. In due course the colour and extravagance of costume, volume and variety of music, and originality and ingenuity of the floats rivalled the panache of New Orleans or Rio de Janeiro and a huge amount of trade was generated. The carnival was dogged by violence and disorder for many years, notably in 1976, when black youths clashed with police, but in the 1990s was mostly peaceful.

Not to worry. Don't worry. The implication is that the difficulty can be easily resolved. A phrase dating from the 1950s.

Not want to know, To. To be uninterested; to prefer not to be told. The phrase frequently applies in a situation where one person does not wish to hear what another says or does, either because it is irrelevant and irksome, or because it is illegal and 'ignorance is bliss'.

> Don't bother telling your boss that you have got in early all week and that your prediction about the Boots share price was right. He won't want to know.
> *The Times* (4 October 1999)

Not waving but drowning. A phrase describing a situation in which a gesture may be misinterpreted. It derives from a poem of this name by Stevie (Florence Margaret) Smith (1901–71), written in 1953 when its author was suffering from clinical depression. Much of Smith's verse was characterized by an eccentric directness. In a poll conducted in 1995 'Not Waving But Drowning' emerged as Britain's fourth favourite poem. *See also* NOVEL ON YELLOW PAPER.

> Nobody heard him, the dead man,
> But he still lay moaning:
> He was much further out than you thought
> And not waving but drowning.

Noughties, The. A nickname for the first decade of the 21st century, from 2000 to 2009, so called from the prominent noughts (zeros) in the dates. The suggestion of 'naughties' may have promoted the popularity of the name. *See also* NAUGHTY NINETIES.

> If the 90s will be remembered as the decade when everyone stopped worrying about nuclear war and began to care about the environment, the 'noughties' are the decade that will see people going into space for recreation.
> *heat* (6–12 January 2000)

Nouveau roman (French, 'new novel'). An alternative term for the French ANTINOVEL, adopted in Britain in the early 1960s.

Nouvelle cuisine (French, 'new cookery'). A style of French cooking that was developed by French chefs in the 1970s. It involves the use of fresh and healthy ingredients, light sauces, quick cooking to retain the colour and texture of the ingredients, and artistic presentation. This last feature was initially a cause of some derision, since it apparently involved the arrangement of minute portions of brightly coloured items on the plate for purposes of admiration rather than actual consumption. The style was subsequently modified, with the preparation of more sustaining portions and the reintroduction of some traditional elements of French cooking.

Nouvelle vague (French, 'new wave'). A movement in French cinema beginning in the late 1950s that sought innovation in subject matter and technique as a reaction to the moribund French film industry. Exponents included the former film critics François Truffaut, Claude Chabrol, Jean-Luc Godard, Eric Rohmer and Alain Resnais. The first film of the type is generally reckoned to be Chabrol's *Le Beau Serge* (1958), although the true rise of the movement was marked by Truffaut's *Les Quatre Cents Coups* (1959), an unsentimental autobiographical portrait of an alienated youth, Resnais's *Hiroshima Mon Amour* (1959), centring on a love affair between a Japanese man and a Frenchwoman ravaged by memories of the Second World War, and Godard's *À Bout de Souffle* (1959), known in English as BREATHLESS, paying homage to the American gangster film. *See also* LAST YEAR AT MARIENBAD.

Novel on Yellow Paper. A novel (1936) by Stevie (Florence Margaret) Smith (1902–71). After trying to get some of her poems published and being advised instead to 'go away and write a novel', Smith did just that, typing it in the firm's time (she worked for a

publisher) on the firm's 'very yellow' carbon-copy paper. The book itself is an autobiographical exercise in the free association of ideas and experience.

No way. It is impossible or NOT ON. There is no way in which it can be done or I will not do it. The expression became current in the late 1960s. An extended form is 'in no way, shape or form' and a stock rhyming variant is 'No way, José'.

> No panto for me this New Year, thank God. I do it every year, but this year, I just thought, no way.
> *The Times* (20 November 1999)

Nowhere Man. An introspective and mildly nihilistic song by the BEATLES, credited to John Lennon and Paul McCartney and released in Britain in December 1965. The title and lyrics ('He's a real nowhere man, sitting in his nowhere land, making all his nowhere plans for nobody') reflect John Lennon's sense of aimlessness and inadequacy during a time of personal difficulty.

No-win situation. One in which one loses whatever one does. The phrase dates from the 1960s and perhaps originally had a military relevance. *See also* YOU CAN'T WIN.

Now, Voyager. A film (1942) based on a novel (1941) of the same title by Olive Higgins Prouty about a repressed New England spinster who finds love with a married man while on a recuperative cruise. Prouty derived her title from the poetry collection *Leaves of Grass* (1855) by the US poet Walt Whitman:

> Now voyager, sail thou forth to seek and find.

Nubile. Sexually attractive. This popular sense of the word evolved in the 1970s from the original 17th-century meaning 'available for marriage', itself from Latin *nubilis*. The passports of single Italian girls and women are annotated *nubile* as an official record of their marital status.

Nuclear winter. A term describing the conjectured period of extreme cold and environmental devastation that would follow a nuclear war, caused by the blocking out of the sun's rays by smoke and dust particles in the upper atmosphere. It was coined by the scientist Richard Turco in December 1983 and was popularized by the science writer Carl Sagan in an article in the *Washington Post*.

Nude Descending a Staircase, No. 2. The remarkably kinetic painting (1912) by the DADAIST Marcel Duchamp (1887–1968) has become as much an icon of early MODERNISM as Picasso's *Les* DEMOISELLES

D'AVIGNON. In a CUBIST style, the picture evokes a sense of motion by repeating fragments of the same figure down a diagonal. Duchamp himself later remarked: 'When the vision of the *Nude* flashed upon me, I knew that it would break for ever the enslaving chains of Naturalism.' The poet X.J. Kennedy wrote of the painting:

> One-woman waterfall, she wears
> Her slow descent like a long cape
> And pausing, on the final stair
> Collects her motions into shape.

Nudge nudge, wink wink. A phrase used to draw attention to a sexual innuendo. It arose as a catch-phrase from a 1969 episode of the television comedy series MONTY PYTHON'S FLYING CIRCUS: 'Your wife interesting in … *photographs*? Eh? Know what I mean – *photographs*? He asked him knowingly … nudge nudge, snap snap, grin grin, wink wink, say no more.'

> Andrew Wallace-Hadrill … said there was nothing obscene about the collection, every item of which was a masterpiece. 'The Vatican's stand just fuels the widespread "nudge-nudge, wink-wink" approach to sex in ancient times,' he said.
> *Sunday Times* (13 February 2000)

Number cruncher. A nickname for any powerful computer that can handle large numerical calculations, especially when the machine itself is large or operates ponderously. The term dates from the 1970s and has also come to apply to a human calculator or manipulator of such numbers.

Nuremberg laws. The infamous NAZI laws promulgated in September 1935. Jews, and all those of Jewish extraction, were deprived of all rights of German citizenship, and regulations were made against those of partial Jewish ancestry. Marriage between Jew and 'German' was forbidden. Nuremberg (Nürnberg) was the centre of the annual Nazi Party convention.

Nuremberg Rally. The name of any of the massive NAZI rallies held in 1923, 1927, 1929 and from 1933 to 1938 in Nuremberg (Nürnberg), mainly as propaganda events, carefully staged to reinforce party enthusiasm and to showcase the might of Nazism to Germany and the world. The first major rally was that of 1929, which included most of the overblown ingredients that featured in future rallies, such as blaring brass-band music, goose-step marches, human swastika formations, torchlight processions, bonfires and dazzling fireworks displays. Hitler and other Nazi leaders delivered ranting orations, and buildings were festooned with giant flags and Nazi insignia. The events of the 1934 rally were captured in Leni Riefenstahl's classic film *Triumph of the Will* (1936), its opening sequence showing the FÜHRER descending by plane from the skies. A planned peace rally for 1939 was cancelled because of preparations for war with Poland. The Germans themselves knew the rallies as the *Nürnberger Parteitage*, 'Nuremberg Party Days'. *See also* CATHEDRAL OF LIGHT.

Nuremberg trials. The trial of 22 NAZI leaders conducted by an international military tribunal at Nuremberg (Nürnberg) after the Second World War (November 1945 to October 1946). Three were acquitted; Goering, Ribbentrop and ten others were condemned to death; three, including Rudolf Hess, were sentenced to life imprisonment; and four, including Speer, were sentenced to terms ranging from 10 to 20 years. Goering avoided retribution by committing suicide. *See also* SPANDAU.

Nutmeg. In football a ball played between an opponent's legs. The term is sometimes shortened to 'nuts' or 'megs' but ultimately derives from 'nutmegs' as a former slang word for the testicles. The mascot of the 1999 Women's World Cup football tournament in the United States was a figure of a fox named Nutmeg.

Nutopia. The fictional country that is the setting of John Lennon's album *Mind Games* (1973). It has no land, no boundaries and no passports but only people. It also has no laws other than cosmic laws. Its international anthem is *Bring on the Lucie*. Further information can be obtained from the Nutopian Embassy, 1 White Street, New York, New York 10013, USA.

Nuts! An expression of defiance or contempt; a statement of refusal or negation. A story of the Second World War tells how General Anthony C. McAuliffe, acting commander of the American 101st Airborne Division at Bastogne in the Ardennes at the time of the BATTLE OF THE BULGE (December 1944), when surrounded by enemy forces, was informed by the Germans that they would accept a surrender. His terse response to this proposal was 'Nuts!', a message that the Germans initially interpreted to mean 'crazy'. Agence France Presse later reported the incident, translating the General's retort more expansively but not altogether accurately as, *Vous n'êtes que de vieilles* *noix* ('You're just old fogeys'). A British officer in the same situation might well have said 'Balls!', the actual sense of McAuliffe's retort.

Nuts and bolts. The essentials of a situation. Nuts screwed onto bolts can serve to hold a basic structure together. The expression dates from the 1960s.

Nuts and sluts. Eccentric men and promiscuous women, regarded as typically making up the most provocative type of guests or audience in a television talk show.

> Poor Vanessa Feltz was crucified for having spoof guests on her nuts 'n' sluts show. But what did it matter? They were seen, they performed, they were as real as anything else in the 1990s.
>
> *Sunday Times* (26 December 1999)

Nutty as a fruitcake. Completely crazy; quite mad. A fruitcake contains nuts as well as fruit. 'Nutty' meaning 'insane' dates from the early 19th century, but the elaborated expression from the 1930s.

Nye. The nickname of the left-wing Labour politician and noted orator Aneurin Bevan (1897–1960), who resigned from Clement Attlee's postwar government over prescription charges in 1951, having established free medical care in the form of the National Health Service three years earlier.

Nylon. The synthetic polymer, originally known as superpolymer 66, was first produced by the Du Pont Company in the United States in the 1930s. Nylon stockings were displayed in 1939 at the New York World's Fair and San Francisco Golden Gate International Exposition and were in instant demand, even though 'nylons' cost twice as much as silk stockings. Their great attraction was that they were shrinkproof, mothproof and resistant to mildew, whereas silk stockings were subject to all three hazards. When nylon was taken up in the Second World War for the manufacture of parachutes, nylon stockings could be had only on the black market. The word itself is popularly said to derive from the initials of New York but it was actually patterned on 'cotton' and 'rayon'.

Nymphet. A sexually attractive young girl. Although already existing as a word for a young or small (classical) nymph, the term was first used in the current sense by Vladimir Nabokov in his novel LOLITA (1955). A spelling 'nymphette' is sometimes found, as if to emphasize the bearer's diminutiveness or femininity.

> At 16, Una is a striking heroine: a teenage nymphette, who could out-flirt Lolita, living a life that is moviestar glamorous in a garret in Paris.
>
> *The Times* (16 October 1999)

O

OAS. An abbreviation for l'Organisation de l'Armée Secrète (French, 'the secret army organization'), a right-wing organization of French settlers in Algeria opposed to Algerian independence. It was formed in 1961 and led by General Raoul Salan (1899–1984). He and other high-ranking French officers who had assisted President de Gaulle's return to power in 1958 now felt betrayed by de Gaulle's apparent willingness to consider Algerian independence. They staged an attempted coup in Algiers in 1961 and then mounted a terrorist campaign in both Algeria and France, including a number of attempts on de Gaulle's life. However, with Algerian independence granted in 1962 and Salan's imprisonment in the same year (he was released in 1968), the OAS campaign fizzled out.

OAS is also an abbreviation for the Organization of American States, an international body of North American, South American and Caribbean countries, founded in 1948 to foster cooperation in the social, economic and security fields.

OBE. *See* ORDER OF THE BRITISH EMPIRE.

Obedience test. A competition designed to test a dog's obedience to particular commands. The term dates from the 1930s and came to be applied figuratively to any real or supposed test of a person's loyalty or willingness to 'toe the party line'.

> A sharp contrast to … the London Labour Party, where the Prime Minister insists that each candidate submit to an obedience test before their names will be allowed to go forward.
>
> *The Times* (Letter to the Editor) (4 January 2000)

Objective correlative. A somewhat obfuscatory term introduced by T.S. Eliot in a famous essay on *Hamlet* to denote the literary and artistic technique of representing a particular emotion by means of symbols, which then indicate the emotion and become associated with it.

> The only way of expressing emotion in the form of art is by finding an 'objective correlative'; in other words, a set of objects, a situation, a chain of events which shall be the formula of that *particular* emotion; such that when the external facts, which must terminate in sensory experience, are given, the emotion is immediately evoked.
>
> T.S. ELIOT in *Atheneum* (26 September 1919)

Obolensky's try. The classic try scored for England by Prince Alexander Obolensky (1916–40) in a rugby international against New Zealand in 1936.

Ocker. A boorish or aggressive Australian. The term dates from the early 1970s and derives from an alteration of Oscar used for a character devised and played by Ron Frazer in an Australian television series, *The Mavis Bramston Show* (1965–8).

O'clock. Apart from its regular use for naming an hour, this term has been employed in military parlance since the turn of the 20th century to denote a bearing corresponding to the position of the hands on a clock-face, from the standpoint of a person facing twelve o'clock. Thus three o'clock will be due east and nine o'clock due west. The usage is most familiar in naming a target to be fired at, so that a shot ending up below the bull will be at six o'clock and one to its right at three o'clock. In the Second World War the term became more widely familiar from the radio communications of fighter pilots, with 'six o'clock' indicating a location under the speaker, so that 'Bandits at six o'clock' meant 'Enemy aircraft below me'. *See also* TEN TO TWO.

October Revolution. In Russian history the BOLSHEVIK revolution of October 1917 (November in the Western calendar), which led to the overthrow of Kerensky and the MENSHEVIKS and the triumph of LENIN.

Octobrists. A 'constitutionalist' centre party in Russia supported by the landlords and wealthy mercantile interests, prominent in the *dumas* between 1907 and 1914, after the Tsar's liberal manifesto published in October 1905.

Octopush. A game resembling underwater hockey, first played in the early 1970s. The name combines 'octopus' and 'push' and the game itself consists in propelling a lead puck, or 'squid', along the bottom of a swimming pool and trying to push it into the opposing goal, or 'gulley'.

Octopus's Garden. A song by the BEATLES credited to Richard Starkey (Ringo Starr) and appearing on the album ABBEY ROAD, released in September 1969. Starkey's inspiration for the song came from a holiday he spent in Sardinia during which he learned that octopuses roam the seabed, picking up stones and shiny objects with which they build gardens. Like the earlier YELLOW SUBMARINE, the song includes various underwater sound effects created in the recording studio.

Odds and sods. Miscellaneous people or things; odds and ends. The expression originated as services' slang in the 1930s.

Odeon. The British cinemas so called arose in the 1930s as a chain owned by the film distributor Oscar Deutsch (1893–1941), who named them partly after the odeon or odeum of ancient Greece and Rome, as a building used for musical performances, and partly after his own initials. The first cinema to bear the name opened in Perry Barr, Birmingham, in 1930. *See also* ROXY.

Oder-Neisse Line. The frontier between Poland and East Germany (initially the Soviet zone of occupation of Germany) established at the Potsdam Conference of the victorious Allies in 1945, after the end of the Second World War in Europe. The frontier, which now forms the border between the reunified Germany and Poland, follows the course of the River Oder south to its junction with the River Neisse, which it then follows to the Czech border. As the new border awarded substantial areas of what had been Germany to Poland, West Germany did not recognize it until 1970. The change of policy was part of the OSTPOLITIK pursued by Chancellor Willy Brandt.

Odessa or **ODESSA.** An acronym for Organisation der Ehemaligen SS-Angehörigen (German, 'organization of former SS members'), the best known of a number of secret organizations that sought to smuggle Nazis out of Germany to safety after the Second World War. It was founded in 1947, and among those it helped to escape was Adolf Eichmann. Favoured destinations were Franco's Spain, Arab countries of the Middle East, and South American countries such as Argentina and Paraguay. Odessa, which inspired Frederick Forsyth's 1972 thriller *The Odessa File*, was wound up in 1952 and replaced by the Kameradenwerke ('comrade workshop'). *See also* SS.

Odessa Steps. One of the most famous sequences in the history of cinema, from the silent classic BATTLE-SHIP POTEMKIN (1925), directed by Sergei Eisenstein (1898–1948). The film is a partly fictionalized account of the mutiny of the Russian Black Sea fleet at the Crimean port of Odessa during the failed 1905 Revolution. In the sequence, which features much cross-cutting, innocent civilians are slaughtered by Tsarist forces. A particularly celebrated image is that of a baby in a pram, bouncing unattended down the steps.

Oedipus complex. The psychoanalytical term introduced by Sigmund Freud for the sexual desire (usually unrecognized by himself) of a son for his mother and conversely an equally unrecognized jealous hatred of his father. The situation may lead to repression, feelings of guilt, and an inability to form normal emotional or sexual relationships. The allusion is to Oedipus in Greek tragedy, who unknowingly killed his father, King Laius, and married his mother, Jocasta. *See also* ELECTRA COMPLEX.

Off-Broadway. In the American theatre, a term relating to productions that are experimental, low budget or not commercially viable, as against the mainstream productions of Broadway. They are, in turn, contrasted with off-off-Broadway productions, which are highly experimental and often staged in small halls, cafés, churches and the like. *See also* FRINGE.

> For proof that the theme of sexual diversion can be honestly and yet dramatically treated, one has to go, not to off-Broadway but to what is called off-off-Broadway. Actually the distinction between the two is quite real.
> *Manchester Guardian Weekly* (17 October 1968)

Office party. A party for members of the staff of an office or the employees of a company, especially one held just before Christmas. The office party became an established feature from the 1950s and soon came to be regarded as an occasion when the usual hierarchy of authority was set aside and traditional social constraints abandoned. The norm instead became an overindulgence in alcohol, a careless indiscretion of speech, and an eager exploitation of amorous opportunities.

> An office party is not, as is sometimes supposed, the Managing Director's chance to kiss the tea-girl. It is the tea-girl's chance to kiss the Managing Director.
> KATHARINE WHITEHORN: *Roundabout*, 'The Office Party' (1962)

Official Secrets Act. The legislation that controls access to confidential information important for national security in Britain originated as the Official Secrets Act of 1911. There have been several amended versions since. Apart from its general prohibition on spying the essence of the act is contained in section 2, which makes it a criminal offence for government employees to divulge certain categories of information. It was under this act that the civil service 'moles' Sarah Tisdall and Clive Ponting were charged in 1983. Tisdall, working in the Foreign Office, was jailed for six months for passing secret papers to the *Guardian* relating to the arrival in Britain of cruise missiles. Ponting, employed by the Ministry of Defence, leaked documents about the sinking of the GENERAL BELGRANO in the FALKLANDS WAR. He was eventually acquitted.

Off-message. Departing from the official party line. The term is chiefly used of politicians who stray in this way, and who are thus more newsworthy than those who remain 'on-message'. The 'message' is the party line itself. *See also* GET THE MESSAGE.

> Some reporters were even called after midnight yesterday to be told they would not be given access [to the speeches], having dared to write copy which was deemed 'off-message'.
> *The Times* (15 October 1999)

Off-roading. The sport of driving or racing a vehicle over rough terrain or along unmade roads, i.e. off the main road. An off-roader is a vehicle, usually having a four-wheel drive, used in such a pursuit. The sport originated in the United States in the late 1960s but has existed in Britain from the late 1970s as an organized activity. *See also* 4×4.

Offshore. A term used of a financial account, such as building society savings account, based abroad, where tax arrangements are more advantageous than in one's own country. In Britain 'offshore' in this sense applies to the Channel Islands and Isle of Man as well as further afield.

Off the cuff. Without previous preparation. The phrase, of American origin and dating from the 1930s, refers to the habit of some after-dinner speakers of making jottings on their stiff shirt cuffs as ideas occurred to them during the meal.

Off the hook. When a telephone is off the hook the receiver is not on the rest and no incoming calls can be received. This expedient is commonly resorted to by those who do not wish to be disturbed or to hear from a particular caller, although these days it is equally possible to switch off the ringer. There is now no actual hook as such but in the early days of telephony, when it was not in use, the receiver hung from a hook next to the mouthpiece.

Off the record. Unofficially; confidentially. A term originating in the United States in the 1930s and taken up by spokesmen for public bodies when giving the media information that is not for publication. The phrase may have a legal origin and refer to evidence that the judge has ordered to be struck off the court record as irrelevant or improper and thus to be ignored by the jury.

Off the top of one's head. Spontaneously; impromptu. An American phrase dating from the 1930s. Anything said or done spontaneously will not have been considered inside one's head but allowed to emerge uncontrolled.

Off the wall. Unorthodox; bizarre. The allusion may be to the unpredictable angle of return of a ball rebounding from a wall, as in baseball or squash. The phrase dates from the 1950s.

Of Human Bondage. A semi-autobiographical novel (1915) by W. Somerset Maugham (1874–1965). The action is held together by the character of Philip CAREY, who has a club foot. His is a largely tragic, isolated life, with two disastrous affairs, one without feeling and the other without sex, until Philip, with the encouragement of a friend, takes up his medical studies again, marries his friend's daughter and becomes a country general practitioner. The title is that of one of the five parts of *Ethics* by the Dutch philosopher and theologian Benedict de Spinoza (1632–77), issued posthumously by his friends in 1677 in an anonymous volume.

Of Mice and Men. A novella (1937) by John Steinbeck (1902–68). It centres on two casual labourers, Lennie, a simple, sentimental giant who loves small animals but does not know his own strength, and his friend George. In a tragic ending, George's efforts are not enough to keep Lennie out of the trouble that he has unwittingly brought upon himself. The title is from 'To a Mouse' (1786) by Robert Burns (1759–96):

> The best laid schemes o' mice an' men
>   Gang aft a-gley,
> An' lea'e us nought but grief an' pain,
>   For promis'd joy.

A persuasive film version (1939) was directed by Lewis Milestone.

Ofsted. The Office for Standards in Education, a government body set up in 1992 to monitor standards in schools by means of regular inspections. It answers directly to the secretary of state for education. The name aligns with those of similar bodies emerging in Britain from the 1980s, including Offer, the Office of Electricity Regulation, Ofgas, the Office of Gas Supply, Ofrail, the Office of the Railway Regulator, Oftel, the Office of Telecommunications, and Ofwat, the Office of Water Services. The fact that the last four titles suggest 'off' and thus negation or disruption does not seem to have occurred to their creators.

> The reliability of education watchdog Ofsted was thrown into doubt today after a primary school inspected by two different teams in the same month received startlingly different reports.
> *Evening Standard* (9 June 1998)

Of the essence. Vital; indispensable. The implication is that whatever is so described should contain or display its most important quality or constituent element.

> 'To most people fishing is all maggots and creepy-crawlies, whereas the reality is your mind is working overtime and body constantly moving,' she said. 'Speed is of the essence, especially in competition.'
> *The Times* (14 June 1999)

Ogopogo. A water monster supposedly inhabiting Okanagan Lake, British Columbia, Canada. The name is said to come from a music-hall song of the 1920s sung by Davy Burnaby (1881–1949), with lines as follows, quoted in Peter Costello, *In Search of Lake Monsters*, ch x (1974):

> His mother was an earwig,
> His father was a whale,

> A little bit of head,
> And hardly any tail,
> And Ogopogo was his name.

Ogpu. *See under* KGB.

Oh, Calcutta! A stage revue (1969) devised by the British theatre critic Kenneth Tynan (1927–80), which caused a considerable furore for its sexual explicitness. The title was suggested to Tynan by his wife, Kathleen Tynan, who was writing an article about a painting of a nude by the French surrealist Clovis Trouille entitled 'Oh! Calcutta! Calcutta!' (1946). Unbeknown to the Tynans at the time, the French title was a pun on *oh, quel cul t'as* (meaning 'oh, what a lovely arse you've got').

Oh-so. An intensive phrase prefixed to an adjective or adverb, the 'oh' representing a hesitation while searching for an appropriate word or else simply an expression of emotion before the 'so'. Thus the statement 'he is oh-so-ordinary' would have originated as 'he is, oh, so ordinary!' The phrase is recorded from the 1920s.

> Julian Sands … saunters in for his fitting and is incredibly laid back and oh-so-ca-su-al compared to my oh-so-strung-up state.
> RICHARD E. GRANT: *With Nails* (1996)

Oh, What a Lovely War! A musical (1963) created by Joan Littlewood's Theatre Workshop at the Theatre Royal, Stratford East, London, as a satirical commentary on the huge losses suffered in the First World War. The show featured lampoons of popular songs of the day, as sung by soldiers in the trenches.

> Oh, oh, oh, it's a lovely war,
> Who wouldn't be a soldier, eh?
> Oh, it's a shame to take the pay;
> As soon as reveille is gone,
> We feel just as heavy as lead,
> But we never get up till the sergeant
> Brings our breakfast up to bed …
> 'Oh, What a Lovely War!'

Oil and water. Said of two incompatible people or things. Oil is insoluble in water. An earlier equivalent, dating from the 17th century and still sometimes found, was 'oil and vinegar'.

> *Living with the Enemy* A new [television] series of the oil-and-water encounters, in which people with opposing views share lives for a week.
> *The Times* (11 September 1999)

Okies. A derogatory term for American migrant workers, and especially those from Oklahoma who were forced off their farms in the 1930s during the GREAT DEPRESSION and who sought a new life in a hostile California. They are the subject of John Steinbeck's novel The GRAPES OF WRATH (1939) and of John Ford's powerful film based on it (1940). Ford said that the subject of the book reminded him of the famine years of his ancestral Ireland.

Oklahoma! A musical (1943) by Richard Rodgers (1902–79) and Oscar Hammerstein (1895–1960) set among the cowboys and farmers of the rural American west. Based on Lynn Rigg's play Green Grow the Lilacs (1931), it was originally to be titled Oklahoma and Away We Go! It was of Oklahoma! that one dismissive critic commented of its prospects: 'No legs, no jokes, no chance.'

Okun's Law. A law devised in 1962 by the American economist Arthur M. Okun (1928–80). It states that as the gross national product of a country declines because of recession, debt or inefficiency, there is a proportional rise in unemployment, statistically calculable according to specific indices.

Olbers' Paradox. The paradox propounded by the German astronomer Heinrich Olbers (1758–1840) that if stars were distributed evenly in sufficient numbers throughout an infinite static universe, the sky ought to be as bright at night as in the daytime, since although the apparent brightness of a star decreases with distance, the actual number of stars increases in the same proportion. The anomaly is first recorded under this name in the 1950s. The paradox can be resolved by identifying its incorrect assumptions, the chief of which is that as shown by the BIG BANG theory the universe is not infinite.

Ol' Blue Eyes. A publicity oriented nickname for the popular American singer Frank Sinatra (1915–98), a teenage idol in his twenties. He announced his retirement in 1971 but two years later returned with the slogan, 'Ol' Blue Eyes is back', adopted as the title of a television special.

Old bag. A term dating from the 1940s for an elderly and unattractive or slovenly woman or for a 'lady of easy virtue'.

> Ah reckon you must have fired that old bag you had in the kitchen and got yourself a hundred per cent American cook.
>
> PAUL GALLICO: Mrs Harris goes to New York, ch xvi (1960)

Old bean. A familiar form of address to a man, dating from the First World War. See also OLD FRUIT.

Old Bill. A nickname for the police force, or a member of it. See BETTER 'OLE.

Old boy network. To arrange something on the old boy network is to fix it through a social contact (properly someone from one's old school) instead of through the usual channels. The expression dates from the late 1950s although the system obviously goes back further than that. See also OLD SCHOOL TIE.

Old Boys, The. A novel (1964) by the Anglo-Irish writer William Trevor (pen-name of (William) Trevor Cox; b.1927), concerning the infighting between members of the committee of the old boys' association of a minor English public (i.e. private) school.

Old codger. An old or eccentric person who is, even so, regarded with affection and even respected for his worldly wisdom. From 1936 to 1990 the Daily Mirror ran a 'Live Letters' column in which a couple of supposed 'Old Codgers' answered readers' questions on a variety of subjects in an entertaining and anecdotal way. 'Codger' is perhaps a variant of 'cadger'.

> This sprightly old codger [Prince Philip] has one major regret: that the Queen has never named him 'Prince Consort'.
>
> COMPTON MILLER: Who's REALLY! Who (1997)

Old Contemptibles. Members of the British Expeditionary Force of 160,000 men that left Britain in 1914 to join the French and Belgians against Germany. The soldiers are said to have given themselves this name from an army order (almost certainly apocryphal) issued by the German Kaiser (see KAISER BILL) at Aix on 19 August and published in an annexe to BEF Routine Orders of 24 September 1914:

> It is my royal and imperial command that you exterminate the treacherous English, and walk over General French's contemptible little army.

He may have actually called the BEF 'a contemptibly little army', which is not nearly so disparaging.

The surviving veterans held their last parade at the garrison church of All Saints, Aldershot, on Sunday, 4 August 1974 in the presence of Elizabeth II, who took tea with them before their final dispersal.

Old Dun Cow. A derisive nickname given by the troops to the steamer River Clyde beached at GALLIPOLI in 1915 during the First World War. It was probably a reference to the song of this name, popularized by

Harry Champion, that contained the words, 'The Old Dun Cow she's done for now', the Old Dun Cow in question being a public house that had run dry.

Oldest Living Confederate Widow Tells All. A novel (1989) by Allan Gurganus (b.1947) in which the 99-year-old widow of a Confederate veteran remembers the American South from the times of Robert E. Lee (1807–70) and Abraham Lincoln (1809–65) to Martin Luther King (1920–68) and the CHALLENGER space shuttle disaster (1986). The inspiration was a story in the *New York Times* about widows of Confederate soldiers being still alive and receiving pensions from the government. It contained the phrase, 'oldest living Confederate widow', from which developed first a story, then a novella and finally a 736-page novel.

Olde worlde. Old-fashioned in style; quaintly attractive. A pseudo-archaic phrase that is supposedly suggestive of 'the good old days'. It dates from the 1920s and is typically applied to a tea shop. *See also* OLD-TIME DANCE.

> Dymchurch is full of olde-worlde seaside charm – lovely.
> *Sunday Times* (26 December 1999)

Old fogy. An old-fashioned person; a 'stick-in-the-mud'. *See also* YOUNG FOGY.

Old fruit. A familiar form of address to a man, dating from the 1920s. It is now as dated or mannered as OLD BEAN.

Old grey whistle test. In New York's 'Tin Pan Alley', where popular music was at one time published, songwriters used to play their compositions to the 'old greys', the elderly doorkeepers and other employees in the publishing houses. If the 'old greys' were still whistling the tunes after a week or so, they were likely to be worth publishing. The phrase was adopted for the title of a weekly television pop music programme broadcast from 1971 to 1983 on BBC2 as a 'serious' partner to *Top of the Pops* on BBC1.

Old Groaner. A nickname of the popular American singer Bing Crosby (1904–77), a pioneer of CROONING.

Old Man and the Sea, The. A novella (1952) by Ernest Hemingway (1899–1961), which won the PULITZER PRIZE for fiction and was instrumental in Hemingway being awarded the NOBEL PRIZE for Literature in 1954. It tells of an elderly fisherman who, after 84 days going out in his skiff without a catch, and 44 without his boy assistant, who has abandoned him, hooks an enormous marlin. The battle with the fish and the struggle to get it back to land in the face of the predations of sharks, have been interpreted as an allegory of the contribution of courage and endurance to survival in the natural world. A rather disappointing film version (1958), starring Spencer Tracy, was directed by John Sturges.

Old Man River. A nickname for the Mississippi, originating in the song of this name by Oscar Hammerstein II for the musical *Showboat* (1927) and subsequently popularized by Paul Robeson. The name is not inappropriate, for the river's Native American name means 'great water', similarly suggesting seniority and implying veneration. The title could apply equally or even more aptly to other major rivers. The name of Ireland's longest river, the Shannon, is thus related to Irish *sean*, 'old', and probably refers to the ancient water god, or 'old man', who was at one time believed to inhabit it.

> Ol' man river, dat ol' man river,
> He must know sumpin', but don't say nothin',
> He jus' keeps rollin',
> He jus' keeps rollin' along.
> OSCAR HAMMERSTEIN II: 'Ol' Man River' (song)

Old Mother Riley. The garrulous old washerwoman was the creation and persona of the music-hall comedian Arthur Lucan (born Arthur Towle; 1887–1954), whose Irish wife, Kitty McShane (1897–1964), stood in as her daughter. Her heyday was the 1930s, when she appeared on the stage of the London Palladium. She then transferred to the cinema and a number of radio series.

Old school tie. Literally, a distinguishing neck-tie worn by the former pupils of a particular school. Such ties being essentially associated with the public schools and the older grammar schools led to 'old school tie' being given a pejorative use as a symbol of class distinction, e.g. 'the old school tie brigade', meaning the members of a privileged class. The phrase is first recorded in Rudyard Kipling's *Limits and Renewals* (1932) but would have already then been current. A suggestion of 'tie' in the sense 'bond', 'association' is also perhaps present. *See also* OLD BOY NETWORK.

> If you are entitled to wear what is generically known as an Old School Tie, whether it represents your public school, university, regiment, golf club, rowing club, or any other sporting or social associations, wear it sparingly.
> GUY EGMONT: *The Art of Egmontese*, ch i (1961)

Old Smoky or **Sparky.** A grimly humorous nickname for the electric chair, from the effects caused when operated.

> Davis perished in a chair that replaced 'Old Sparky', which killed 200 people from 1923.
> *The Times* (30 October 1999)

Old Spanish custom. A long-standing but unauthorized practice. The phrase dates from at least the 1930s and in the 1980s came to describe the irregular behaviour of newspaper production workers, especially with regard to cheating over pay packets. The reason for the particular national attribution is uncertain, although the Spanish have come to be associated with casual working practices and what might be called the '*mañana* syndrome'.

Old Squiffy. A nickname given to H.H. Asquith (1852–1928), British Liberal prime minister (1908–16), by Lord Alfred Douglas on account of Asquith's tippling skills, 'squiffy' being an informal term for 'tipsy'. However, the Conservative politician Andrew Bonar Law (1858–1923), who helped to engineer the downfall of Asquith's wartime coalition, observed that 'Asquith, when drunk, could make a better speech than any of us sober.' *See also* SQUIFFITES.

Old sweat. An experienced soldier of long service, or even any old soldier. The expression dates from the First World War.

Old thing. A formerly familiar mode of address between friends. Preceded by a descriptive, as 'funny old thing', 'poor old thing', it is still current. In Britain the phrase has become especially associated with the fruity-voiced cricket commentator Henry Blofeld, an old Etonian, who uses it to address his fellow-commentators on BBC radio's *Test Match Special*. *See also* NAPOO.

Old Timber. A punning nickname of the English conductor Sir Henry Wood (1869–1944), who founded the London Promenade Concerts ('the Proms') in 1895 and continued to conduct them until his death. He was knighted in 1911.

Old-time dance. A formal or formation dance of the kind danced in the 19th century or the early years of the 20th. To indicate its nostalgic nature the term is sometime spelled 'olde-tyme dance'.

Old Vic. The London theatre opened in 1818 as the Royal Coburg Theatre, taking its name from its chief patrons, Prince Leopold of Saxe-Coburg (1790–1865), the future King Leopold I of Belgium and uncle of Queen Victoria, and his wife Princess Charlotte (d.1817). In 1833 it was renamed the Royal Victoria Theatre in honour of 14-year-old Princess Victoria, later Queen Victoria. It was soon popularly known as the 'Vic' but by the turn of the 20th century this name had been expanded to 'Old Vic', partly in reference to Victoria's age and reign (she died aged 81 after 54 years on the throne, longer than any other British monarch), but mainly as a token of affection. The name later became effectively official and in 1970 the 'Young Vic' was founded as a counterpart to provide good theatre for young people at cheap prices.

Olympic Games. The modern games, as a revival of the ancient Greek festival held every four years at Olympia, were organized in 1896 as international sporting contests. The first Summer Olympics were held at Athens, and subsequently at Paris (1900), St Louis (1904), London (1908), Stockholm (1912), Antwerp (1920), Paris (1924), Amsterdam (1928), Los Angeles (1932), Berlin (1936), London (1948), Helsinki (1952), Melbourne (1956), Rome (1960), Tokyo (1964), Mexico City (1968), Munich (1972), Montreal (1976), Moscow (1980), Los Angeles (1984), Seoul (1988), Barcelona (1992), Atlanta (1996), Sydney (2000), Athens (2004).

Winter Olympic Games were inaugurated in 1924 at Chamonix, with subsequent sites at St Moritz (1928), Lake Placid (1932), Garmisch-Partenkirchen (1936), St Moritz (1948), Oslo (1952), Cortina d'Ampezzo (1956), Squaw Valley (1960), Innsbruck (1964), Grenoble (1968), Sapporo (1972), Innsbruck (1976), Lake Placid (1980), Sarajevo (1984), Calgary (1988), Albertville (1992), Lillehammer (1994), Nagano (1998), Salt Lake City (2002), Turin (2006).

Omaha Beach. The Allied code name for the stretch of beach on the Normandy coast between the Vire River and Port-en-Bressin, where the US 5th Corps landed on D-DAY. The beach became known as 'Bloody Omaha' for the stiff German opposition there. The Allied army also landed on four other Normandy beaches, code-named UTAH, GOLD, JUNO and SWORD.

Ombudsman (Swedish, 'legal representative'). In Scandinavian countries an official appointed by the legislature whose duty it is to protect the rights of the citizen against infringement by the government. Sweden has had one since 1809, Denmark since 1955, and Norway since 1962. New Zealand was the first Commonwealth country to appoint such a commissioner (1962) and Britain appointed a Parliamentary Commissioner for Administration in 1967, commonly known as the 'Ombudsman'. Local Commissioners, or local government ombudsmen, were later appointed to investigate complaints from the public against local authorities, and independent ombudsmen schemes were similarly set up for banks, building societies, insurance companies, financial institutions and independent financial advisers.

OMOV. An acronym, rhyming with 'home of', of 'one member, one vote', as a principle of democratic election within an organization. It was achieved in the LABOUR PARTY in 1993, so ending the block vote of the trade unions, and was first used in 1994 for the election of Tony Blair as leader. The term ultimately derives from 'one man, one vote' as a principle of universal suffrage dating from the mid-19th century.

On a collision course. Adopting an approach or following a line that is bound to lead to conflict with another person or group of people. The expression dates from the Second World War and originally applied literally to two ships on converging courses. The figurative sense was current from the 1960s.

> The great powers are now headed on a collision course over Berlin.
>
> *New Statesman* (21 July 1961)

On a roll. Experiencing luck; enjoying success; doing well. The American expression originates from gambling (specifically crapshooting), and dates from the 1970s. The roll is that of the dice, which keep falling favourably.

> Gardening is on a roll, that much is clear. But the fascinating thing is the direction in which it seems to be rolling.
>
> *The Times* (13 August 1999)

On a wing and a prayer. With only a small hope or chance of success. The phrase comes from a Second World War song based on the words that the pilot of a damaged aircraft radioed to ground control as he prepared to come in to land:

> Tho' there's one motor gone, we can still carry on
> Comin' in on a wing and a pray'r.
>
> HAROLD ADAMSON: 'Comin' in on a wing and a Pray'r' (1943)

Once and Future King, The. A tetralogy (1958) by T.H. White (1906–64), consisting of *The Sword in the Stone* (1938), *The Witch in the Wood* (1939), *The Ill-Made Knight* (1940) and *The Candle in the Wind* (1958). It is a reworking of the Arthurian legend, beginning with Arthur's childhood, and offering with wit and pathos a parable for modern times and a commentary on the *Morte D'Arthur* of Thomas Malory (*c.*1410–71), which has the following passage: 'And many men say that there is written on his tomb this verse: *Hic iacet Arthurus, rex quondam, rexque futurus*' ('Here lies Arthur, once a king and a future king') (Bk 21, ch vii). *The Sword in the Stone* was turned into a unsubtle cartoon film (1982) directed by Albert Pyun.

Ondes Martenot (French, 'Martenot waves'). This unusual electronic instrument, originally known as *ondes musicales*, 'musical waves', was developed by the French musician Maurice Martenot (1898-1980) and first demonstrated by him at the Paris Opéra on 20 April 1928. It somewhat resembles a spinet, with a keyboard of five octaves, but can produce only one note at a time. It is operated by a wire across the keyboard, which the player manipulates to produce the desired pitch. The signal is then amplified through a loudspeaker. Tone colour and timbre are obtained by pressing a button and volume is controlled by a key. The instrument may be heard in Olivier Messiaen's TURANGALÎLA SYMPHONY (1949) and Arthur Honegger's dramatic oratorio *Jeanne d'Arc au bûcher* (1935).

One-armed bandit. A FRUIT MACHINE operated by the insertion of coins and the pulling of an arm or lever and so called because it 'robs' one of change. It has now mostly been superseded by electronic machines.

One Day in the Life of Ivan Denisovich. A novella (1963; in Russian as *Odin den' Ivana Denisovicha*, 1962) by Alexander Solzhenitsyn (b.1918), first published outside the USSR. Life in one of STALIN's labour camps is seen through the eyes of an inmate. The author was himself in such a camp from 1950 to 1953. A film version (1971) directed by Caspar Wrede was a fairly faithful adaptation of the original, with all its harrowing detail.

Onedin Line, The. A television drama of the sea, running from 1971 to 1980. The story concerned the ruses devised by James Onedin, a 19th-century ship's master, to own a fleet of sailing vessels. The combination of salt-sprayed action, romantic intrigue and costume drama made the series required regular Sunday evening viewing.

One Flew Over the Cuckoo's Nest. A novel (1962) by Ken Kesey (b.1935). The narrator is the Chief, whose father was the last chief of his tribe. He is a patient in a mental hospital (the 'cuckoo's nest', also a reference to a nursery rhyme), in which authority is represented by 'Big Nurse'. The admission of McMurphy from prison precipitates a struggle between 'good' (the patients) and 'evil' (Big Nurse), with the 'liberation' of the patients from institutional restrictions as the stake. The film version (1975), directed by Milos Forman, was amusing and horrifying in equal parts and an unexpected commercial success.

One Foot in the Grave. A television SITCOM running from 1990 to 1993. The story centres on the cantankerous Scotsman Victor Meldrew, forced into early retirement and trying to adjust to his final years of leisure with his wife Margaret. His well-meaning attempts to take on odd jobs, help with good causes and generally offer help to others invariably end in disaster or at best misunderstanding and confusion. Embroiled in the muddles of his own making, Meldrew's already simmering temper usually explodes into a violent 'I don't be-*lieve* it!' The series elevated the comic bit-part actor Richard Wilson, as Meldrew, to star status almost overnight.

One for the book. Anything noteworthy or remarkable. The expression, of American origin and dating from the early 20th century, originally referred to record books kept for sports.

One for the road. A final drink before departure to fortify one for the journey ahead. The expression fell victim to the increasing enforcement of DRINK-DRIVING legislation from the 1980s and also to subsequent POLITICAL CORRECTNESS. A similar enticement exists in the phrase 'Afore ye go', found (as a registered trademark) on bottles of Bell's whisky.

One Hundred Years of Solitude. *See* MAGIC REALISM.

One-liner. A short joke or witty remark. The term is of American origin and dates from the turn of the 20th century.

> [President] Reagan's substitute for strong emotions seems to be humor, both memorized and spontaneous. He is a walking repertory theater of show-biz anecdotes, one-liners, elaborate routines.
> *Time* (20 October 1980)

One-man band. Properly, a street entertainer who plays several instruments at the same time. Metaphor-ically a one-man band is a person who runs a business alone. The phrase dates from the 1920s and was made familiar by the title of Ted Weems's bestselling record hit 'The One-Man Band' (1931).

One Million Years B.C. A film (1939) depicting the lives of a band of cave-dwellers in prehistoric times. Based on an earlier silent movie called *Man's Genesis*, directed by D.W. Griffith in 1912, and also known by the alternative titles *The Cave Dwellers*, *Cave Man* and *Man and His Mate*, this version of human existence in prehistoric times diverged wildly from scientific fact, with men pitting themselves against dinosaurs that were extinct millions of years before. This did not prevent a remake of the film, complete with dinosaurs, appearing in 1966, starring Raquel Welch (in a fur bikini) and John Richardson in the roles originally taken by Carole Landis and Victor Mature.

One-night stand. A single performance by a touring theatrical company or the like at a town that will probably provide an audience for only one night. Also, a sexual liaison lasting only one night. The latter sense evolved from the former in the 1930s.

> I've never had a one-night stand. It will look like I'm trying to seem like a modern, caring man but I've never been able to go out on the pull.
> *The Times* (12 June 1999)

One-off. An unusual or unique person, especially positively so. The expression dates from the 1930s and originally applied to a single manufactured object of some kind, often produced as a sample or specimen.

> [Conservative MP Alan] Clark was a one-off. In a political party where 'sound' is the strongest expression of approval … Clark was his own man, and very unsound indeed.
> *The Times* (Obituary of Alan Clark) (8 September 1999)

One of Our Aircraft is Missing. A film (1941) co-written and directed by Michael Powell (1905–90) and Emeric Pressburger (1902–88) about the crew of a Wellington bomber during the Second World War who are shot down but make their way back to England with the help of the Dutch underground. The title was inspired by a stock formula of wartime broadcasts about recent raids on enemy territory. The original title was *One of Our Aircraft Failed to Return*. In 1975 Walt Disney released a comedy adventure entitled *One of Our Dinosaurs is Missing*, apparently under the influence of the Powell/Pressburger film.

One of the boys. One who mixes well socially; an equal member of a team or group. The phrase dates from the turn of the 20th century and frequently applies to a 'woman in a man's world'.

> In those days war reporting was very much a man's world. It seemed important to blend in and the only way to do that was to be 'one of the boys'.
>
> *Sunday Times* (10 October 1999)

One picture is worth a thousand words. This supposed traditional maxim was the creation of Fred R. Barnard of the American magazine *Printer's Ink*. He first published it in the issue for 8 December 1921 but with 'look', not 'picture'. He changed the phrase to its present form for the edition of 10 March 1927, calling it 'a Chinese proverb, so that people would take it seriously'. The story behind the familiar saying is given in Burton Stevenson's *The Home Book of Proverbs, Maxims, and Familiar Phrases* (1948).

One-stop shop. A shop providing a wide range of goods, so that a customer can make various purchases in a single visit. Such shops arose in the United States in the 1930s and are now found in British suburban streets and as village stores.

One that got away. The prize that one only just missed and that was better than all the others. The metaphor is from fishing mythology, according to which it is always the biggest fish that just manages to elude capture: 'You should have seen the one that got away!'

One-track mind. A mind with one dominant preoccupation, which constantly reverts to the one subject, as a single-track railway allows traffic in only one direction at a time. The expression is first recorded in D.H. Lawrence's LADY CHATTERLEY'S LOVER (1928) but must date from before this.

> That's the only way to solve the industrial problem: train the people to be able to live and live in handsomeness, without needing to spend. But you can't do it. They're all one-track minds nowadays.
>
> D.H. LAWRENCE: *Lady Chatterley's Lover*, ch xix (1928)

One-upmanship. The art or knack of being 'one up', or gaining an advantage over other people. The term was popularized by Stephen Potter in his book of this title (1952). *See also* GAMESMANSHIP.

On Hearing the First Cuckoo in Spring. The orchestral piece by Frederick Delius (1862–1934) is not as English as one might think, in that it makes use of a Norwegian folk song that had previously been drawn on by Edvard Grieg (1843–1907) in his *Nineteen Norwegian Folk Tunes*. The work was first performed in 1913, and the cuckoo itself is played by the clarinet. It was this sort of thing that made Debussy characterize Delius's output as 'music to rock the convalescents of the rich neighbourhoods'. Bernard Levin called it 'the musical equivalent of blancmange'.

Only Fools and Horses. A long-running television SITCOM first screened in 1981. It centres on the comic adventures of WHEELER-DEALER Derek ('Del Boy') Trotter and his put-upon brother Rodney, played by David Jason and Nicholas Lyndhurst, as they eke out a living in the streets of London. The title derives from the Cockney saying 'Only fools and horses work'. The series is memorable for its colourful writing, and the dialogues of the two are peppered with slang words such as 'dipstick' and 'plonker' for an idiot and LOVELY JUBBLY as a term of approval.

Only joking. I didn't mean it. A phrase said after one has cracked a joke or made a (supposedly) witty remark which might be taken seriously by some.

> One of the band went into an Irish pub and was called a 'faggot' and I swear I saw someone knitting at the front of our gig. Only joking!
>
> BOY GEORGE in *Sunday Express* (27 February 2000)

On one's own time and own dime. Entirely at one's own expense. The American expression is often shortened to 'on one's own dime'. 'Dime', properly a 10-cent coin, here simply means 'money'.

> 'I live in Los Angeles, and Kimberly [Peirce] was conducting interviews in New York,' she [actress Hilary Swank] says. 'I got over there on my own dime, put myself up and read for her.'
>
> *Sunday Times* (27 February 2000)

On one's tod. On one's own. The origin of the expression, which dates from the 1930s, is in rhyming slang, with 'own' from the name of the American jockey Tod Sloan (1874–1933), who came to England in 1897 and was the leading winner of 1900. He was as much noted for his gambling and social climbing as his innovative racing style and success on the course itself.

On one's toes. Alert; ready for any eventuality. The image is of a runner set to race or of a dancer poised to perform. The expression was popularized by the Rodgers and Hart musical *On Your Toes* (1936).

On the back burner. Having low priority; available in

reserve. The allusion is to the back burners (hotplates, rings) of a stove, which cook more slowly than the front ones. The phrase dates from the 1960s. *See also* COOK ON THE FRONT BURNER.

> From Monday, thousands of people will be putting burgers on the back burner, giving chicken the bird, and scaling down their fish intake for the next seven days. Why? It's National Vegetarian Week!
> *The Times* (12 June 1999)

On the back of. Resulting from; following as a consequence. An expression often associated with the business world.

> Share prices rallied in London on the back of the overnight rebound on Wall Street. But it was a half-hearted affair, lacking conviction.
> *The Times* (3 September 1998)

On the back of an envelope. The traditional location for an initial calculation or sketch that may well evolve into a major feat or invention.

> The chairman asked Major Bill Tillman, the notorious lightweight explorer and mountaineer, if he would like to say a few words. 'Yes,' said Bill, 'in my experience, any worthwhile expedition can be organized on the back of an envelope.'
> *The Times* (10 June 1999)

On the ball. Alert; well informed. The expression is American in origin and dates from the early 20th century. The reference is to baseball, in which to put something on the ball is to pitch with extra speed or a special spin in order to strike out more batters.

On the Black Hill. The second novel (1982) by the travel writer Bruce Chatwin (1940–89). It is an evocation of the intertwined lives of two brothers on a hill farm in the Welsh border country, set in the early years of the 20th century. An unsentimental film version (1988) was directed by Andrew Grieve.

On the buroo. Receiving unemployment benefit. A Scottish phrase dating from the 1930s, in which 'buroo' is a pronunciation of 'bureau', meaning the Labour Bureau or social security office..

On the button. Exactly right; precisely correct. The expression derives from boxing slang in which 'button' is the chin, the part of the body a boxer aims to punch to score a knockout blow.

On the club. Off work sick, especially when receiving sickness benefit.

On the dot. Precisely on time. The reference is to the minute hand of the clock being exactly over the dot marking the hour (or one of the five-minute intervals) on the dial of a clock or watch.

On the job. Actively at work; engaged in sexual intercourse.

On the lam. On the run from prison; in flight from the police. The phrase originated as American underworld slang in the 1920s. 'Lam' is probably from the more familiar verb meaning 'to beat'. There may thus be a pun on 'beat it'.

On the pull. Seeking a sexual liaison. The 'pull' is the endeavour to attract or draw to oneself. The expression dates from the 1960s.

> 'I've never been able to go out on the pull. I'm not clever enough with the old banter. I'm terrible at small talk.'
> *The Times* (12 June 1999)

On the Q.T. Secretly; unofficially. 'Q.T.' stands for 'quiet'.

On the receiving end. Bearing the brunt; 'taking the rap'. The allusion is to being the recipient of a blow or punishment, and by implication unjustly so. The expression dates from the 1930s.

On the Road. A novel (1957) by Jack Kerouac (1922–69), based on several wild trips across the United States with Neal Cassady (1926–68). In it he used the term BEAT GENERATION 'to describe guys who run around the country in cars looking for odd jobs, girlfriends, and kicks'. The book became the prose manifesto of the culture it evokes. *See also* FIRST LINES OF NOVELS.

On the same wavelength. In complete agreement; in full rapport. The expression alludes to radio waves carrying a broadcast.

On the wagon. Voluntarily abstaining from alcohol. Such a person is 'on the water wagon' as distinct from the wine bottle.

> She has no difficulty in drinking in moderation. She's not on the wagon, but she hasn't fallen off it either. She's poised.
> *The Times* (5 August 1999)

On the Waterfront. A film (1954) with a screenplay by Budd Schulberg from his own novel, which was based on a series of articles by Malcolm Johnson about corruption in New York's docklands (hence the title). Starring Marlon Brando, Rod Steiger and Lee J. Cobb, the film depicted Brando's character, Terry, a former boxer, as a stool pigeon who nonetheless achieves heroic status in the struggle against the waterfront mafiosi. Many critics interpreted this approach as a defence on behalf of Schulberg and director Elia Kazan, who had both controversially testified before the McCARTHYITE House Un-American Activities Committee and had thus caused problems for many left-wing colleagues in the film business.

> *Terry*: See! You don't understand! I could've been a contender. I could've had class and been somebody.

On top of the world. Happy and elated. The allusion is to a peak of happiness or success. The expression dates from the 1920s.

On your bike! Go away! Clear off! The phrase dates from the 1960s but later gained the implication that one should go and look for work. This sense was popularized in a speech at the Conservative Party Conference in 1981 by Norman Tebbit, then Employment Secretary, when he said that his father had not rioted in the 1930s when unemployed but 'got on his bike and looked for work'. *See* CHINGFORD SKINHEAD.

> The gut instinct of this Government is no different from the last. It yearns to support the cause of the motorist, the shopping mall, the rural housing estate, the enterprise ideology of 'on your bike'.
> *The Times* (22 September 1999)

Oo-ar! A representation of a stock MUMMERSET equivalent of 'oh yes!'.

> Oo-arr! There's nothing *Blue Peter* new boy Matt Baker likes better than getting down on the farm.
> *The Times* (11 September 1999)

Oo-er! An exclamation of surprise or alarm, representing an 'ooh' of surprise followed by an 'er' of hesitation.

> 'Oo-er!' cried Jenny. 'We aren't going to sleep in the dark?'
> COMPTON MACKENZIE: *Carnival*, ch ix (1912)

Ooh-la-la or **oh-la-la.** A phrase intended to evoke a French-style 'naughtiness'. It dates from the 1940s and represents French *ô là! là!*, literally 'Oh there, there!'

> Those two great standbys of French fashion, quality and a little bit of ooh-la-la.
> *The Times* (10 April 1973)

Oomph. Sex appeal; attractiveness; energy or 'go'. The word is imitative of something that has 'punch'. The American film star Ann Sheridan (1915–67) was promoted by WARNER BROTHERS as the 'Oomph Girl' for her sex appeal, just as Clara Bow before her was the 'IT' GIRL.

Oor Wullie. 'Our Willie', the shock-headed little boy whose strip-cartoon adventures appear in the Scottish *Sunday Post*. He wears dungarees and sits on an up-turned bucket and his speech is scripted in broad Scots dialect. He was the creation in 1936 of Dudley D. Watkins, and he has become part of Scotland's popular mythology.

Op art. A form of abstract art that evolved in the 1960s. It gives an illusion of movement by the precise use of pattern and colour or by creating conflicting patterns that emerge and overlap. The name, while patterned on POP ART, is intended as an abbreviation of 'optical art' and was first used in print in the American magazine *Time* in October 1964. The term was popularized by the exhibition 'The Responsive Eye' held in 1965 at the Museum of Modern Art, New York as the first international exhibition with a predominance of Op art paintings. Leading exponents are Victor Vasarely (1908–97) and Bridget Riley (b.1931). Op art became something of a fad in the world of fashion and in 1965 Riley unsuccessfully tried to sue an American clothing company that had used one of her paintings as a fabric design.

Op-Ed. The abbreviation of 'opposite editorial', as an American term for a page in a newspaper opposite the editorial page and devoted to personal comment, feature articles and the like. It was the creation of the US newspaper editor Herbert B. Swope, who introduced it to the *New York World* soon after becoming that paper's executive editor in 1920.

Open All Hours. An enjoyable television SITCOM running from 1976 to 1985 and starring Ronnie Barker as the stuttering, miserly, lustful shopkeeper Arkwright. The humour was as much physical as verbal, and Barker was supported by strongly drawn contrasting characters, the chief being Arkwright's dreamy nephew, Granville, played by David Jason.

Open diplomacy. The opposite of secret diplomacy, as defined in the first of US President Woodrow Wilson's FOURTEEN POINTS, 'open covenants of peace openly arrived at, after which there shall be no private international understandings of any kind'. It is perhaps significant that the TREATY OF VERSAILLES was an 'open treaty' negotiated in secret.

Open Skies Treaty. The treaty signed in March 1992 between the United States, Russia, Britain and France and a number of former republics of the USSR. It sanctioned each country's right to fly reconnaissance aircraft over the territory of the others in order to photograph military installations. Former WARSAW PACT members later joined the accord, and by 1996 42 nations had signed.

Opportunity Knocks. A long-running television talent show screened by ITV from 1956 to 1978, when it was hosted by a genial Hughie Greene, and by the BBC from 1987 to 1990, when the host was Bob Monkhouse. A popular feature of the first series was Greene's 'clapometer', which registered the volume of applause from the audience. The show launched the careers of many celebrities, among them the comedians Freddie Starr and Little and Large and the singers Mary Hopkin and Bonnie Langford. 'Opportunity knocks' itself is a catchphrase of American origin dating from the 1940s. It was earlier common in the fuller form, 'Opportunity knocks but once'.

Opposite number. A person's equivalent in an organization or system, their 'number' being the same in the hierarchy. The expression dates from the early 20th century and later gave 'oppo' as a colloquialism for a best friend or 'mate'.

Opus Dei (Latin, 'God's work'). An international Roman Catholic organization of lay people and priests founded in Spain in 1928 by Monsignor Josemaría Escrivá de Balaguer (1902–75) with the aim of spreading Christian principles. The activity of the organization is shaped by Escrivá's work *The Way* (1935), a series of 999 spiritual maxims. Opus Dei members have at times been controversial in the Church.

Oradour-sur-Glane. A village in south central France, northwest of Limoges, destroyed by the Germans on 10 June 1944, exactly two years after a similar fate had befallen the Czechoslovakian village of LIDICE. All 652 inhabitants were routed from their homes and into the village square. The men were then herded into barns, and the women and children into the church. German troops barred the doors and set fire to the whole village. The death toll was 642, with 10 somehow managing to survive the fire and feign death until the SS had departed. After the war the gutted church and its cemetery were left as a memorial and a new village was built nearby.

Oral Office. The OVAL OFFICE in the White House, as renamed by wags in the wake of the MONICA Lew-insky affair. The quip was suggested by the acts of fellatio performed on President Clinton by the love-struck intern. *See also* COMEBACK KID; SLICK WILLIE.

Oranges Are Not the Only Fruit. A semi-auto-biographical first novel (1985) by Jeanette Winterson (b.1959) about the childhood and growing up of a fictional Jeanette against the background of the religious fanaticism of her Pentecostal mother. The oranges of the title represent her mother's attitude to life, in which 'everything in the natural world was a symbol of the Great Struggle between good and evil'. The crunch comes when she abandons the forces of good, which she was destined to promote as a missionary, in favour of those of evil, having been discovered *in flagrante delicto* in bed with an-other girl. In a memorable televised version (1990), adapted by Winterson from her own novel, the central character, Jess, was played as a teenager by Charlotte Coleman.

Orcs. The name used to refer to goblins in J.R.R. Tolkien's epic *The* LORD OF THE RINGS (1954–5), in which they are employed as soldiers by SAURON. They are first encountered as 'goblins' beneath the Misty Mountains by Bilbo BAGGINS in *The* HOBBIT (1937), but in Tolkien's later works they are referred to as Orcs. Brutal, dirty and grotesquely ugly, with long arms, bow legs and long fangs, the Orcs present a stark contrast to the home-loving and gentle hobbits.

Order of Lenin. The highest award in the former Soviet Union, named after V.I. LENIN, the leader of the 1917 OCTOBER REVOLUTION. It was established in 1930 and awarded to individuals or institutions that had made outstanding contributions to science and tech-nology, medicine, the arts or economics, or to the service of the state. It was also awarded to foreigners for the promotion of good relations with the USSR. Notable recipients included Yuri Gagarin, the first man in space (*see* VOSTOK), and Marshal Zhukhov, the victorious RED ARMY commander in the Second World War.

Order of Merit. An order for distinguished achieve-ment in all callings founded by Edward VII in 1902, with two classes, civil and military. It is limited to 24 men and women and confers no precedence. The badge is a red and blue cross with a blue medallion in the centre surrounded by a laurel wreath, and it bears the words 'For Merit'. The ribbon is blue and crimson. Crossed swords are added to the badge for military members. *See also* COMPANION OF HONOUR.

Order of the boot. A rejection or dismissal. 'I was given the order of the boot' could thus mean that I was rejected by a lover or sacked from a job. To reject or dismiss someone is to boot them out. The phrase puns on genuine orders of honour, such as Order of the Bath, Order of the Garter.

Order of the British Empire. The OBE was instituted by George V on 4 June 1917, in the darkest days of the First World War, as a way of rewarding British and Allied subjects who had rendered conspicuous service at home, in India, and in the Dominions and Colonies other than that rendered by the Navy or Army. It was divided into civil and military divisions in 1918 and was subsequently used to reward service in every field. For the first time it enabled a large number of women to be admitted to honours but in some years was so generously granted that to remain undecorated seemed almost a greater distinction. There are also those who feel that the name is increasingly anachronistic, the British Empire having effectively ceased to exist in the aftermath of the Second World War, when the process of decolonization began. *See also* MEMBER OF THE ORDER OF THE BRITISH EMPIRE.

Oreo. A black person despised by other blacks for seeking to integrate with whites. The nickname comes from the commercially marketed Oreo biscuit, which consists of two chocolate wafers containing a white sugar cream filling. An 'Oreo' is thus 'brown outside but white inside' (Alan Dundes, *Mother Wit from the Laughing Barrel*, 1973).

Origin of the Brunists, The. A POSTMODERNIST novel (1966) by the US writer Robert Coover (b.1932). Giovanni Bruno believes himself to have been saved in a mine collapse by divine intervention. This 'miracle' is cynically used by a newspaper editor as justification for the survivor to establish a religious movement, the Brunists. The novel explores man's need to extract explanatory myths from catastrophic events.

Orlando. A novel (1928), subtitled *A Biography*, by Virginia Woolf (1882–1941). It is a literary fantasy whose central character 'was a man till the age of thirty; when he became a woman and has remained so ever since'. The book is dedicated to Vita Sackville-West (1892–1962), who has been identified as the original of Orlando. A visually striking film version (1992) was directed by Sally Potter.

Orphan Island. The imaginary island that is the setting of Rose Macaulay's novel of the same name (1924). It is so known after a group of orphans shipwrecked here in 1855 on their journey from London to California. It was formerly called Smith Island, after Miss Charlotte Smith, the orphans' teacher, who was cast ashore with them and who laid down the laws of the land.

Orphism. A movement in painting started by Robert Delaunay (1885–1941) as a development from CUBISM and characterized by patches and swirls of intense and contrasting colours. The name, given by the poet Guillaume Apollinaire in 1912, alludes to the poetry of the mythological Greek poet Orpheus. Artists associated with the movement apart from Delaunay include Marcel Duchamp (1887–1968), František Kupka (1871–1957), Fernand Léger (1881–1955) and Francis Picabia (1879–1953). *See also* CUBISM; DADAISM; FAUVISM; FUTURISM; RURALISM; SURREALISM; SYNCHROMISM; VORTICISM.

Orpington man. A term that enjoyed a currency in the 1960s following the victory of the Liberal candidate in the Orpington by-election of 1962. Orpington, in Kent, is an outer London suburb, and 'Orpington man' was the typical home-county commuter who abandoned the habits of a lifetime to vote Liberal rather than Conservative. *See also* ESSEX MAN; ISLINGTON MAN; SELSDON MAN; WORCESTER WOMAN.

Or three. A semi-humorous substitution for 'or two', in such contexts as 'a glass or two', to denote an even greater quantity.

> Whenever football is discussed in pubs or clubs over a beer or three, the question is nearly always raised as to how the standard of football has improved (or otherwise) over the years.
>
> PETER OSGOOD: Foreword to MICHAEL HEATLEY and IAN WELCH: *History of Football* (1997)

Orwell, George. The pen-name adopted by Eric Arthur Blair (1903–50), Old Etonian and socialist, author of *The* ROAD TO WIGAN PIER (1937), ANIMAL FARM (1945) and *Nineteen Eighty-Four* (1949) (*see* 1984), among other works. His derived his pen-name from St George, patron saint of England, and the River Orwell in Suffolk, on whose banks he had once lived. *See also* DOUBLETHINK; DOWN AND OUT IN PARIS AND LONDON; BIG BROTHER; NEWSPEAK.

Oscar. A gold-plated figurine awarded annually by the American Academy of Motion Picture Arts and

Sciences for the best film acting, writing, production and so on of the year. There are two claims for the origin of this name. One is that in 1931 the future executive secretary of the Academy, Mrs Margaret Herrick, joined as librarian, and on seeing the then nameless gold statue for the first time, exclaimed, 'It reminds me of my Uncle Oscar.' The other is that it derives indirectly from Oscar Wilde (1854–1900). When on a lecture tour of the United States he was asked if he had won the Newdigate Prize for Poetry, and he replied, 'Yes, but while many people have won the Newdigate, it is seldom that the Newdigate gets an Oscar.' When Helen Hayes was presented with the award, her husband Charles MacArthur, a noted wit and playwright, said, 'Ah, I see you've got an Oscar,' and the name stuck. *See also* BAFTA AWARD; EMMY.

Oscar and Lucinda. A period novel (1988), with elements of MAGIC REALISM, by Peter Carey (b.1943), which won the BOOKER PRIZE for fiction. Oscar sees in gambling a way of providing the essentials of education and family background, having rejected those provided by his father, a figure based on the father in FATHER AND SON (1907) by Edmund Gosse (1849–1928). Oscar's compulsion is shared by Lucinda, whose ambition is to run a successful glass-works in Sydney. The result is a mad wager to transport a glass church into the Australian bush, which ends in violence. A film version (1997), directed by Gillian Armstrong, did not quite catch the spirit of the original. *See also* FIRST LINES OF NOVELS.

Ossi. A nickname in Germany for a citizen of the former German Democratic Republic, as an abbreviation of *Ostdeutsch*, 'East German'. East and West Germany were reunified in 1990.

Ostpolitik (German, 'east politics'). The foreign policy of DÉTENTE among Western countries in the 1960s with regard to the former Soviet Union and communist bloc. It was implemented by Willy Brandt, socialist chancellor of West Germany, in 1970, when his government signed a 'renunciation-of-force' treaty with the USSR. *See also* ODER-NEISSE LINE.

Othello. The proprietary name of a sweet tartlet filled with chocolate cream custard. The allusion is to Shakespeare's hero, who was a Moor and thus chocolate-coloured. Related confections from the same galley are the Desdemona, filled with white vanilla custard, and the Iago, with coffee custard. *See also* OREO.

Other Club. A dining club founded in 1911 by Sir Winston Churchill and F.E. Smith (Lord Birkenhead) and said to be so called because they were not wanted at an existing fraternity known as The Club. It still meets at the Savoy, and membership is not confined to Tories or politicians.

Other guy. One's opponent or rival. The expression belittles him by not naming him and by trivializing his status as simply 'guy'.

> Autobiography offers the chance to draw across the past a warm duvet, or knee the other guy in the stomach.
> *The Times* (12 October 1999)

Other Place. A studio theatre in Stratford-upon-Avon, opened in 1974 and owned by the Royal Shakespeare Company. It showcases modern and experimental works, as well as revivals of rarely performed plays, and has a name based on that of its forerunner, The Place, a small London theatre where the RSC staged plays for three seasons from 1971 to 1973. *See also* SWAN.

OTT. *See* OVER THE TOP.

'Our Gang'. A group of American child film actors first appearing in the 1920s in short slapstick comedies produced by Hal Roach. Their personnel changed over the years but the originals included 'Fat' Joe Cobb, Jackie Condon, Mickey Daniels, Mary Kornman and Ernie 'Sunshine Sammy' Morrison. In the 1930s the gang was led by Spanky McFarland. Production continued until 1944, after which many of the shorts appeared on television and were released on video, with the gang renamed in the latter medium as 'The Little Rascals'.

Our Gracie. An affectionate nickname for the popular singer Gracie Fields (1898–1979). 'Our' is a typical North of England possessive for a family member, as 'Our Jack', and it came to be applied to various personalities, especially in show business or sport, or as a bantering term in the media. Others are 'Our Marie' for the music-hall entertainer Marie Lloyd (1870–1922), 'Our Shirl' as a *Private Eye* name for the Labour politician Shirley Williams (b.1930), and 'Our Ginnie' as a nickname for the tennis player Virginia Wade (b.1945).

Our Island Story. An enormously popular children's history book (1910), subtitled *A Child's History of England*, by H.E. Marshall, who retold stories from English history (including some, such as that of King Arthur, that properly belong in the domain of legend), to two Australian children. The title reflects without embarrassment the untroubled Anglocentric mindset of the period, for the book deals almost exclusively with tales from English history.

Not once or twice in our rough island-story,
The path of duty was the way to glory.

ALFRED, LORD TENNYSON: *Ode on the Death of the Duke of Wellington* (1852)

Outing. In its modern sense, the word denotes the act of making it publicly known that a particular well-known person is homosexual, i.e. when they have not themselves chosen to 'come out'. The verb for this action is thus 'to out'. There was a small spate of political outings in the late 1990s.

Chris Smith, Labour's national heritage spokesman, who is homosexual, said: 'I don't believe that outing is either just or sensible. More is gained by gay people coming out voluntarily.'

Sunday Times (4 December 1994)

Out like a light. Instantly asleep or unconscious, as if a light had been extinguished or turned off. Switching off the bedside light is usually the last conscious act of the day before falling asleep. The metaphor dates from the 1930s.

Out of Africa. An autobiographical memoir (1937) by Karen Blixen (1885–1962), who also wrote novels in her native language, Danish, as Isak Dinesen. Rejected by a cousin with whom she had fallen in love, in 1914 she married instead his twin brother, Baron Bror Blixen-Finecke. They settled on a farm near Nairobi, in what is now Kenya, but after a year she returned to Denmark for treatment for syphilis, which she had contracted from him. They were divorced in 1921. *Out of Africa* is the story of her struggle to keep the farm going and of her love for Denys Finch-Hatton, a safari conductor, who died when his plane crashed in 1931, just after she had been forced to sell up. She subsequently left Africa for good. The title is based on a line from Pliny's *Historia Naturalis* (1st century AD): *Semper aliquid novi Africam adferre* ('Africa always brings [us] something new'), often quoted as *Ex Africa semper aliquid novi* ('Always something new out of Africa'). Blixen's own Afrikaans title for her book was *Den afrikanske farm* ('The African Farm'). A critically acclaimed film version (1985) was directed by Sydney Pollack.

Out of one's skull. Extremely bored; intoxicated by drink or drugs; crazy. The expression dates from the 1960s.

Since my teens I have wondered why people use alcohol or drugs to get out of their skulls. ... For the trip of a lifetime, get 'right' outside your skull. ... The best-known OOBE [out-of-body experience] is the near-death experience.

URI GELLER in *The Times* (6 October 1999)

Out of one's tiny mind. Mentally unbalanced; completely crazy. The phrase evolved in the 1960s as an elaboration of 'out of one's mind'. The implication is that one's mind was inadequate or deficient to begin with.

Out of order. Apart from its everyday senses of not working or not according to the rules this phrase has a colloquial meaning 'unacceptable', 'in bad taste'. The new sense evolved in the 1980s.

'I think you're well out of order,' he said. Apparently he had been waiting for seven years to see Grace [Jones] again, and was peeved about the extra four hours standing around.

Independent (30 March 1990)

Out of this world. Fantastic; amazing; wonderful. The implication is of something too good for this world. The phrase dates from the 1920s.

Out on one's ear. Ejected unceremoniously; summarily dismissed. The image is of being thrown out head first. The expression dates from the 1920s.

Outside job. A crime committed by someone not associated with the place where it occurred. The opposite, which is generally more effective, is an INSIDE JOB.

Outsider. A person who is not a member of a particular circle or group, or one who is not considered a socially desirable companion; also a horse or person not thought to be in the running. The usage comes from coaching days when the humbler passengers travelled outside (other than on the box next to the coachman). In more recent times the word has been specifically applied to a person who in some way is alienated from society, and *The Outsider* in this sense is the title of a novel (1953) by the black American writer Richard Wright, of a study (1956) by Colin Wilson of the alienation of a man of genius, and as the English rendering (1946) of the title of Albert Camus' novel *L'Étranger* (1942), about a rebel or misfit who is out of tune with the times.

Out to lunch. Crazy; eccentric; absent-minded. The implication is that one is temporarily 'out of one's mind' in the same way that a person who is out to lunch is temporarily absent from work. The phrase arose as US campus slang in the 1950s.

Oval Office. The official office of the President of the United States, in the White House, and so named for its shape. It was added to the West Wing of the building in 1909, during the presidency of Theodore Roosevelt, and is the place where key meetings are held, interviews granted, and important policy decisions made. See also ORAL OFFICE.

> With the convention still in progress, an aide to the President's media man, Gerald Rafshoon, plastered a hotel-room wall with ideas for negative T.V. spots – 'Empty Oval Office', 'Places He Would Attack' and 'He Is Not Active, He Means It'.
> *Newsweek* (25 August 1980)

Ovaltine. The food drink so named was launched by Dr George Wander in Berne, Switzerland in the 19th century and was originally called 'Ovomaltine', alluding to two of its main ingredients, eggs (Latin *ovum*, 'egg') and malt. The name was then shortened as now and was registered in Britain in 1906. The drink itself became the archetypal soothing nightcap and its popularity was enhanced by *The Ovaltineys*, a children's radio show sponsored by the manufacturers and first broadcast on RADIO LUXEMBOURG in 1935. It was complemented by a club, the League of Ovaltineys, which had its own secret codes and Seven Rules. By 1939 some 5 million children had joined and Ovaltiney comics were included free with *Chuckler* and *Dazzler*.

> He gives his Ovaltine a stir
> And nibbles at a 'petit beurre'.
> JOHN BETJEMAN: *Mount Zion*, 'The Wykehamist' (1932)

Over a barrel. In a helpless position; at someone's mercy. The allusion is said to be to the practice of draping over a barrel someone who has been rescued from the water when close to drowning, so encouraging the ejection of water from the lungs. A more likely reference may be to a form of punishment in which the victim is bent over a barrel and beaten. The expression is of American origin and dates from the 1930s.

Over easy. Of a fried egg, turned over carefully without breaking the yolk, as distinct from 'sunny side up', with the yolk left uppermost. An Americanism. *See also* DINERESE.

Overlord. The code name given to the Allied operation for the invasion of German-occupied Normandy,

which began on D-DAY 1944. It was so named as it was regarded as the over-riding operation of the day. *See also* SECOND WORLD WAR OPERATIONAL CODENAMES.

Over my dead body. Not if I can help it. The implication is that you cannot do what you propose as long as I am alive to prevent it.

Overpaid, overfed, oversexed and over here. A humorous description of American troops in Britain in the Second World War. The words are attributed to the comedian Tommy Trinder (1909–89) but are probably not original. The phrase lends itself to variants applicable to other Americans.

> The San Francisco Ballet: overdue, overtalented and over here.
> *Sunday Times* (31 October 1999)

Over the hill. Escaped from custody; middle-aged. In the former sense the escapee has vanished over the hill. In the latter the person has passed life's high point and is beginning to go downhill. See also LIFE BEGINS AT 40.

> Why do television channels pay huge amounts of money for long-in-the-tooth, over-the-hill presenters?
> *Sunday Times* (8 August 1999)

Over the moon. Very happy. An expression that came to be a standard expression of delight and satisfaction among sports players after a win or a promotion. It comes from the phrase 'to jump over the moon', in turn from the familiar nursery rhyme about the cow that jumped over the moon, dating from at least the 18th century. *See also* SICK AS A PARROT.

> A hospital spokeswoman yesterday said Martin was in a 'stable but serious condition'. Mrs Hunisett said: 'I am over the moon. I never thought I would see my son alive again.'
> *Independent* (21 June 1995)

Over the top. Excessive; gross. The expression is often shortened to OTT, an abbreviation popularized as the title of a short series of comic sketches on television (1982). The allusion is probably to troops going 'over the top' of the trenches in battle. OTT was the name of an 'adult' version of TISWAS, shown on ITV in 1982.

> Tony Blair always feels he has to justify himself to a Labour conference. Yesterday his performance went over the top. Ten minutes of emotional self-indulgence … marred what was otherwise a powerful statement of where the Government stands and where it is going.
> *The Times* (29 September 1999)

OVRA. The acronym for Opera di vigilanza e repressione antifascista (Italian, 'organization of vigilance and repression of antifascism'). OVRA was the secret police of Fascist Italy, set up in 1927 and modelled on Lenin's Cheka (*see* KGB) in the USSR, which had shown how effective state terror could be in suppressing dissent.

Owl Service, The. A fantasy (1967) for children by Alan Garner (b.1934), in which dialogue predominates. The moving force behind this story of passions and possession, with a violent climax, is a tale from the medieval Welsh storehouse of folklore, *The Mabinogion*. It is reflected in modern times by a set of dinner plates bearing a floral pattern which resembles the form of owls.

Own goal. An act that unintentionally harms one own interests or puts one at a disadvantage. The term is from football, in which a goal scored when a player inadvertently strikes or deflects the ball into his own team's goal is awarded to the other side. In practice own goals are attributed only if a genuine error has been made and not, for instance, if a player merely makes contact with a shot towards the goal. A diverting collection of blunders, gaffes and 'goofs' of the metaphorical type of own goal is to be found in Graham Jones' *Own Goals* (1985).

> In an embarrassing own goal, the makers of Britain's most expensive stretch of rural bypass have achieved what green protesters could only dream about: parts of the road will be closed only ten months after it opened.
>
> *The Times* (18 August 1999)

Oxfam. The Oxford Committee for Famine Relief was founded in Oxford in 1942 to raise funds for the feeding of hungry children in Greece. After the Second World War it concentrated on providing aid to refugees and in the 1960s broadened its scope to help improve agriculture and food production in THIRD WORLD countries. More generally it provides emergency aid for areas stricken by natural disasters such as droughts, floods and earthquakes.

Oxford accent. A term in use from the early 20th century to denote a supposedly educated English accent, although the phrase has long also implied the affected tones of Oxford undergraduates. The accent now regarded as that of standard southern English is usually known as Received Pronunciation.

Oxford bags. Wide baggy trousers, as typically worn by Oxford undergraduates in the interwar years.

Oxford comma. A comma before the 'and' in a listing, as 'bread, butter, cakes, and jam', so called as the house style of Oxford University Press. It is also the standard North American style, but mostly not the British, who would normally write 'bread, butter, cakes and jam'.

Oxford English. English spoken with an OXFORD ACCENT.

Oxford Group. The name until about 1938 of the MORAL REARMAMENT movement, so called because it was first popularized in Oxford in the 1920s.

Oxfordianism. The literary conceit that the works of William Shakespeare were in fact written by Edward de Vere, 17th earl of Oxford (1550–1604). The theory was propounded in 1920 by J. Thomas Looney, a schoolmaster, on the basis of four main tenets: (1) that the few facts known about Shakespeare's life give little indication of poetic or literary activity (despite the fact that to Ben Jonson he was the 'Sweet Swan of Avon'); (2) that the many details of Oxford's life show him to have been a poet, a playwright and a patron of writers and actors; (3) that the works themselves are full of references to exclusively aristocratic pastimes and sports, with 36 of the 37 plays set in courtly or wealthy society; (4) that the noble sentiments expressed in the works could only have proceeded from a nobleman's heart. The popularity of Oxfordianism lay in its romantic and nostalgic appeal to a war-disoriented generation who longed for a return to the class-based hedonism of the EDWARDIAN ERA.

Oxford marmalade. A type of thick-cut marmalade originally made in the 1870s at 84 High Street, Oxford. The name, registered as a trademark in 1908 and 1931 by the manufacturers, Frank Cooper, is redolent of the archetypal genteel English breakfast.

Oz. (1) A colloquialism for Australia, as a phonetic rendering of 'Aus', an abbreviation frequently used for that country. *See also* STRINE.

(2) The name of the magical country inhabited by the WIZARD OF OZ, with the Emerald City as its capital and the seat of its ruler, Princess Ozma. The Land of Oz is surrounded by four small countries: MUNCHKIN Country, Winkie Country, Quadling Country and Gillikin Country. These in turn are flanked by four deserts: Shifting Sands, the Great Sandy Waste, the Deadly Desert and the Impassable Desert. To the north lies the Kingdom of Ix, to the northeast Merryland, to the southwest the Land of the Mangaboos,

and to the northwest Nomeland. These last two are underground.

(3) *Oz* was also the title of a HIPPIE-style 'underground' magazine of the late 1960s, so named as it was founded by an Australian, Richard Neville. It gained notoriety through a court case in 1971, when it was charged with 'conspiracy to corrupt the morals of liege subjects of Her Majesty the Queen by raising in their minds inordinate and lustful desires'. The offending issue had not, in fact, been edited by Neville and his two co-editors but by schoolchildren, and this so called 'schoolkids' issue' caused particular offence by dealing with the sex life of RUPERT BEAR. The editors were convicted and given prison sentences, but these were quashed on appeal.

Ozark country. A popular tourist region in the south central United States, in Missouri, Arkansas and Oklahoma, taking its name from the Ozark Mountains there. It has its local folklore, expressed in sayings such as: 'An Ozarkian's wealth is mostly dogs.' The tourist trade was boosted by Harold Bell Wright's novel *The Shepherd of the Hills* (1907), which romanticized the Missouri mountains. The name itself is said to be a corruption of 'Aux Arcs', a French trading post set up in the region in the early 18th century. *See also* WHITEWATER AFFAIR.

Ozone Man. A nickname given during the 1992 presidential election by sitting president and Republican presidential candidate George Bush to Al Gore (b.1948), the Democratic vice-presidential candidate, on account of the latter's airing of environmental concerns. Gore and his presidential running mate Bill Clinton, the COMEBACK KID, went on to win the election.

P

Pacific Rim. A name for the nations of Asia that border on the Pacific Ocean, including the island nations actually located in the ocean and, in the fullest sense of the term, the shorelines of Central and South America. The name dates from the 1960s, when the nations in question began to form an increasingly important and interconnected economic region.

> Winds of Change … The first of a week-long series shot within the Pacific Rim countries.
>
> *Sunday Times* (24 October 1999)

Pacific 231. The 'symphonic movement' by Arthur Honegger (1892–1955) evokes the 'visual impression and physical enjoyment' produced by a steam locomotive (*Pacific 231* being the name of a US engine). The piece dates from 1923. Honegger seems to have felt a particular affinity with locomotives. In his book *I am a Composer* (1951) he wrote: 'I am like a steam engine: I need to be stoked up, it takes me a long time to get ready for genuine work.'

Package deal. A settlement including a number of conditions that must be accepted in its entirety by the parties concerned. The allusion is to a parcel or package containing in one wrapping a number of different items. Similarly, a package tour or holiday includes provision for meals, entertainment, gratuities, lodging and the like for a single payment. These and similar terms date from the 1950s and are of American origin.

Pack a punch, To. To deliver a skilful or forceful blow; to have a powerful effect. The expression is of American origin and dates from the 1920s.

Packet of Woodbines. The nickname given to the Russian cruiser *Askold* from its five long thin funnels, Woodbine cigarettes being thin and sold in packets of five. The ship was taken from the BOLSHEVIKS after the OCTOBER REVOLUTION of 1917 and used by the Royal Navy against the revolutionaries in the White Sea. *See also* WOODBINE WILLIE.

Pack it in, To. To stop doing something. The expression, dating from the 1920s, is usually heard as a command, as: 'Stop that! Pack it in, will you?' The notion is of 'putting away' one's action.

Pack up your troubles in your old kit-bag. The opening line of one of the most memorable choruses of the First World War. It was written by George Asaf, whose real name was George Powell, and composed by his brother, Felix Powell, in 1915. Ironically, Felix committed suicide in 1942, despairing at the world's apparent commitment to fight a war to end all wars.

> Pack up your troubles in your old kit-bag,
> And smile, smile, smile.
> While you've a lucifer to light your fag,
> Smile, boys, that's the style.
> What's the use of worrying?
> It never was worth while,
> So, pack up your troubles in your old kit-bag,
> And smile, smile, smile.

Pac-Man. A video game popular in the early 1980s, in which Pac-Man is a voracious 'munching menace', devouring enemies who attack him. He was based on a Japanese folk hero and his name apparently relates to the way he 'packed away' his opponents. In American business parlance a 'Pac-Man defence' is a tactic in which a company threatened by a hostile takeover bid launches its own takeover bid for the company that threatens it. The allusion is obvious if one is familiar with the game.

Pact of Steel. *See* AXIS.

Paddington Bear. The small, ursine hero of numerous children's books by Michael Bond (b.1926). He wears a sou'wester, wellington boots and a duffle coat and is so called because he was found by the Brown family at Paddington Station, London, with a label saying 'Please look after this bear'. He first appeared in *A Bear Called Paddington* (1958). The name is apt for an animal that 'pads'. In 1999 the original story was published in a Latin version by Michael Needham under the title *Ursus Nomine Paddington*, following the example of Dr Alexander Lennard's more ambitious rendering of the first WINNIE-THE-POOH book as *Winnie Ille Pu* (1961).

Paddy Clarke Ha Ha Ha. A novel (1993) by Roddy Doyle (b.1958), which won the BOOKER PRIZE for fiction. It records the day-to-day life in a Dublin suburb of a 10-year-old boy, with his reactions to the break-up of his parents' marriage, reflected in the chant of boys at his school:

> Paddy Clarke
> Has no da.
> Ha ha ha!

Paddy Pantsdown. A nickname given in 1992 by a *Sun* headline writer to Paddy Ashdown (b.1941), leader of the Liberal Democrats (1988–99), after Ashdown revealed a long-dead affair with a former secretary. The revelation resulted in a significant boost in the Liberal Democrats' poll rating.

Pageboy. A woman's hairstyle consisting of a shoulder-length bob curling slightly under at the ends and with a fringe at the front. The style was adopted from historical depictions of court pages.

> In tight trousers and tails, with her page-boy fringe flopping down to her eyes, [Chrissie] Hynde was an enduring study in female machismo.
> *The Times* (1 October 1999)

Page Three girl. A euphemistic term for a nude female model, so called from the daily photo of a topless young woman that first appeared on page 3 of the *Sun* newspaper on 17 November 1970. The feature was so popular that other tabloids copied it. The publishers of the *Sun* have now registered the term as a trademark. Hence the capitals in the heading above and the passage below.

> Selling advertising time was about as difficult as persuading a Page Three model to take her top off. They had no competition.
> *The Times* (15 October 1999)

Page-turner. A gripping novel such as a thriller that encourages the reader to turn its pages. The expression dates from the 1970s.

> One of the best page-turners of the year is *Red Gold*, a sequel to Alan Furst's acclaimed Second World War thriller noir, *The World at Night*.
> *The Times* (7 August 1999)

Pain in the neck. A difficult or annoying person. The expression, dating from the 1930s, is probably a euphemism for 'pain in the arse' (or 'ass'). Anyone or anything annoying or tiresome can similarly be called simply 'a pain', and the word is typically applied to an unwelcome task or bore, as: 'It's a pain having to wash the floor each time'.

> Frankly, it's a pain reading about anyone's holiday. They are out there in the sun ... while you sit at a bus stop in the rain wondering if you will ever go on holiday again.
> *The Times* (11 August 1999)

Paintball. A war game of American origin that first became popular in the 1980s. Participants use weapons that fire capsules of brightly coloured paint which burst on impact, and a player marked in this way is immediately eliminated from the game.

The game has become particularly associated with the team-building exercises beloved of contemporary management theorists, in which corporate executives spend time together outside the workplace engaged in outdoor activities intended to foster cooperation and a sense of collective identity.

Paint oneself into a corner, To. To end up in a situation from which it is difficult to escape or in which one has little room to manoeuvre. If one paints a floor to finish in a corner, one will find it hard to extricate oneself.

> Why are we still dropping bombs on power stations and bridges? As punishment for the atrocities or because Nato has painted itself into a corner from which it can only bomb?
> *Observer* (30 May 1999)

Paint the Forth Bridge, To. To carry out an apparently endless task that has to be started again as soon as it is finished. The reference is to the railway bridge over the Firth of Forth in southeast Scotland, built in 1890 and legendary for its continuous painting process, each session of which traditionally takes four years to complete. The procedure is likely to end in 2001, however, with the application of a new coat designed to last ten years.

Paisleyites. Supporters of the Rev. Ian Paisley (b.1926), Northern Ireland Free Presbyterian minister and Unionist politician, since 1970 MP for North Antrim and co-founder in 1971 of the Democratic Unionist Party as a hardline rival to the dominant ULSTER UNIONIST PARTY. He has long been a vociferous and outspoken defender of the Protestant Unionist position in Northern Ireland and his party has taken a more intransigent stance than the Ulster Unionists on sectarian issues and on relationships with the Republic of Ireland. Paisley's dire warnings of the supposedly imminent betrayal of Ulster's Protestants (by perfidious British politicians and Unionists of lesser mettle than he) are expressed in language of a distinctly biblical hue and have been a constant factor in Northern Irish politics since the start of the TROUBLES. He was particularly hostile to the Anglo-Irish Agreement of 1985 and the GOOD FRIDAY AGREEMENT of 1998. In Northern Ireland he is sometimes known as the 'Big Man', for his considerable physical presence and stentorian voice.

Pakistan. The name of this state formed in 1947 was coined in 1933 by a Cambridge Muslim student, Chaudhari Rahmat Ali, to represent the units that should be included when the time came: P for Punjab, A for the Afghan border states, K for Kashmir, S for Sind and 'stan' for Baluchistan. At the same time the name can be understood to mean 'land of the pure', from Iranian or Afghani *pāk*, 'pure', and Old Persian *stān*, 'land' (as in Afghanistan itself).

Pak pai. A term for a car illegally used as a taxi in Hong Kong. The words are Chinese for 'white licence', referring to the white registration plates bearing black numerals, like those on private cars. The nickname was taken up in English from the 1970s.

Palais glide. A type of ballroom dance that came into being in the 1930s. It was not exactly a dance in the accepted sense but something like the gallop popular at hunt balls. It was usually performed to the foxtrot. 'Palais' is short for French *palais de danse*, a grand-sounding designation adopted in English for any type of dance hall, however unpalatial.

Pale Fire. A novel (1962) by Vladimir Nabokov (1899–1977) in the form of a 999-line poem ('Pale Fire'), purporting to be by a recently murdered academic, John Shade, with foreword, notes, commentary and index by an exiled European who was his neighbour. The title of both the novel and the poem comes from Shakespeare's *Timon of Athens*:

> The moon's an arrant thief,
> And her pale fire she snatches from the sun.
> IV.iii

Palestine Liberation Organization. *See* PLO.

Palm Court. From the early years of the 20th century many fashionable hotels had a courtyard or tea room decorated with potted palms, where a string ensemble played to provide light background music for guests. Such players gave the name to the various palm court orchestras that evolved, one of them broadcasting regularly even in the years after the Second World War.

> David Galliver sings with the Palm Court Orchestra in Grand Hotel at 9.0 tonight.
> *Radio Times* (22 April 1955)

Palmer, Laura. *See* TWIN PEAKS.

Palookaville. An imaginary town or community of idiots or incompetents. The name arose in the 1990s from American slang 'palooka' as a term for a stupid person, or more precisely a slow and stupid boxer. It was itself coined in the 1920s by Jack Conway of *Variety* magazine, and popularized by Ham Fisher's comic strip 'Joe Palooka', launched on 19 April 1930, and brought before a wider audience in the 1934 film *Palooka*. In the film *Joe Palooka, Champ* (1946), a boxing promoter grooms a young dope for the ring.

Panda car. A small police patrol car. Such cars, generally blue or black in colour, originally bore a broad white stripe, evoking the markings of the giant panda. The name dates from the 1960s and may have been suggested by the former panda pedestrian crossing, which was marked with black and white chevrons. The term, often shortened to 'panda', is now rarely used.

> It was felt that panda drivers should be warned that the vehicles were not meant to be pursuit cars.
> *Daily Telegraph* (19 May 1971)

Panic attack. A sudden spell of acute anxiety. The laconic phrase belies the unpleasantness of the experience and its real physical symptoms, which can include sweating, a feeling of choking, a pounding heart, and a terror of losing control or even one's reason. The cause of such attacks is unknown but they may be associated with particular phobias.

Panic button. A button to be pressed in the event of an emergency, as in an office or bank, a hospital ward or a private home, usually by means of a telephone-linked emergency response service. Figuratively to push, press or hit the panic button is to call for or take emergency action, often over-hastily and even unnecessarily. *See also* HOT BUTTON.

> It may all look uncomfortably like a rerun of Wall Street in the Thirties, but don't hit the panic button yet.
> *The Times* (27 September 1999)

Panic stations. A state of alarm of emergency. The colloquialism dates from the 1960s and puns on ACTION STATIONS.

> While getting our makeup done and costumes donned, we hear that the Art Department has been fired and it's PANIC STATIONS.
> RICHARD E. GRANT: *With Nails* (1996)

Panorama. The flagship current affairs programme of BBC television, first screened in 1957 and presenting each week a documentary on a matter of topical concern. Its edition of 10 May 1982 notoriously presented opposing views on the FALKLANDS WAR from both Labour and Conservative politicians. *See also* DIMBLEDOM.

Pansy. A derogatory nickname for a male homosexual or effeminate man, dating from the 1920s. An association with the flower is uncertain, and it is possible that the word is a variant of the earlier 'nancy' (from the girl's name) in the same sense. *See also* NANCY BOY.

Panzer divisions. This term entered the English language in the Second World War as a part-translation of German *Panzerdivisionen*, referring in particular to Rommel's tanks and armoured troop-carriers in the North African desert. The first three panzer divisions were created in October 1935, and by the outbreak of the war in 1939 there were six. In the campaign against France there were ten panzer divisions incorporating all the German tanks in that campaign, 2474 out of the 3400 tanks that Germany possessed. Soon after, in 1941, 17 panzer divisions, grouped in four panzer armies, spearheaded the German invasion of the Soviet Union (*see* BARBAROSSA). 'Panzer' came to be regarded as a name of some kind to English speakers, perhaps meaning 'panther', but it is simply the German word for 'armour', deriving from Latin *pantex*, 'paunch', and in turn related to English 'paunch' itself.

> Germany is out to conquer the world once more – not with Panzers but sex aids, porno books and exotic lingerie that you cannot find in Marks & Spencer.
> *The Times* (26 February 2000)

Papa Doc. The nickname given to François Duvalier (1907–71), the brutal dictator of Haiti from 1957 until

his death. He was succeeded by his son Jean-Claude Duvalier (b.1951), known as Baby Doc, who was overthrown in 1986.

Papa Dop. A nickname, by analogy with the brutal Haitian dictator PAPA DOC, given to Georgios Papadopoulos (1919–96), leader of the GREEK COLONELS who seized power in 1967.

Paparazzi. The Italian term for press photographers who pester celebrities is not related to any form of the word 'paper'. The word, in the singular *paparazzo*, comes from the name of such a photographer in Federico Fellini's famous film *La Dolce Vita* (1960), a cynical evocation of modern Roman high life. It was supplied by Fellini's scenarist, Ennio Flaiano, who himself took the 'prestigious' name, as he called it, from *Sulle rive dello Ionio* (1957), Margherita Guidacci's translation of George Gissing's travel narrative *By the Ionian Sea* (1901). In this, Gissing devotes two paragraphs to the worthy proprietor of the Albergo Centrale, Catanzaro, where he spent a few days in 1897. He noted that the owner, Coriolano Paparazzo, had put up a notice on the door of each room expressing his regret that some of his clients chose to dine in other establishments.

Paperback Writer. A humorous song about ambition by the BEATLES, credited to John Lennon and Paul McCartney and released in Britain in June 1966. The 'paperback writer' of the title is a naively aspiring writer who wishes to tempt a publisher into accepting his novel ('Dear sir or madam, will you read my book/ It took me years to write, will you take a look?'). The allusion in the fourth line of the lyric ('It's based on a novel by a man named Lear') is to the nonsense writer Edward Lear (1812–88).

Paper over the cracks, To. To resort to a temporary expedient; to create a mere semblance of order or arrangement. The shorter form 'to paper over' subsequently evolved in the sense of disguising problems rather than solving them. The original expression translated a phrase by the German Chancellor, Otto von Bismarck, in a letter of 14 August 1865 at a time when he was attempting to unite Germany under Prussian leadership shortly before the Convention of Gastein, which provided for Schleswig to be administered by Prussia and Holstein by Austria: *Wir arbeiten eifrig an Erhaltung des Friedens und Verklebung der Risse im Bau*, 'We are working keenly for the preservation of peace and the papering over of the cracks in the building.'

Paper tiger. A person or thing that seems strong, forceful or powerful, but that is, in fact, feeble or ineffective; a balloon when pricked. The expression arose from a Chinese saying applied by Chairman Mao in the 1940s to the USA (in the original, zhǐ lǎohǔ).

> The atom bomb is a paper tiger which the United States reactionaries use to scare people. It looks terrible, but in fact it isn't ... All reactionaries are paper tigers.
>
> MAO ZEDONG: interview (1946) in *Selected Works*, IV (1961)

Pap test. A diagnostic test made on a cervical smear to detect cancer of the cervix or womb. The procedure was set out by the Greek-born American anatomist and oncologist George N. Papanicolaou (1883–1962) in a book written jointly with Herbert F. Traut, *The Diagnosis of Uterine Cancer by the Vaginal Smear* (1943). The test has resulted in a marked decrease in the death rate from the disease.

Paradise. An evocative word increasingly associated in the 20th century with an exotic foreign holiday, as 'A stunning island paradise' (Bermuda Tourism advertisement in *The Times*, 25 September 1999). The religious overtone of the word is significant, and is found equally in the converse, a ruined holiday that is 'hell'. In his novel *Paradise News* (1991), set in Hawaii, David Lodge describes an anthropologist who is carrying out research for an academic study of the tourist industry. The thesis of his book is that 'tourism is the new world religion'. Sightseeing is a substitute religious ritual, souvenirs are relics and guidebooks are devotional aids. The holiday itself is thus both pilgrimage and paradise, with the beach holiday resort a place where the subject 'strives to get back to a state of nature, or prelapsarian innocence', otherwise the Garden of Eden. The simile is extended in the ultimate origin of the word in Persian *pairidaeza*, 'enclosed park', 'pleasure ground', a description equally appropriate for a 20th-century THEME PARK.

Para Handy. This modern Scottish folk hero, skipper of the 'puffer' or small cargo boat *The Vital Spark*, with real name Peter McFarlane, first appeared in the *Glasgow Evening News* on 16 January 1905 as the creation of the writer Neil Munro. He eventually progressed to a weekly column in which his anecdotal tales of seafaring life were a regular delight to his readers. Munro considered him lightweight fare compared to his main literary contributions, however, and when his columns were published in book form masked his identity as 'Hugh Foulis'. Para Handy's gentle drollery was seen as suitable fare for television and he duly made an appearance in that medium in 1959, with *Para Handy – Master Mariner* set in the very locations that Munro had used in his original stories and shot on a 'puffer' of a similar vintage to the one described. The hero was played by Duncan Macrae in this first series, and subsequently by Roddy McMillan in *The Vital Spark* (1965–74) and Gregor Fisher in *The Tales of Para Handy* (1994–5).

Paralympics. An international athletic competition for disabled athletes, modelled on the OLYMPIC GAMES. The name is short for Paraplegic Olympics, and the contest evolved from that originally held for paraplegic athletes at Stoke Mandeville hospital, Buckinghamshire, in the early 1950s. The element 'para-' in the name could also be appropriately interpreted as 'beside', referring to a person or thing distinct from, but analogous to, what is named. Thus the Paralympics are analogous to the Olympics in the same way that paramedics are analogous to qualified doctors. The latter, however, should not be confused with the paramedics who are parachuted in to give emergency aid. *See also* PARAMILITARY.

Paramilitary. A term in use from the 1970s to refer to an armed force that has a military structure but not a professional personnel and that in many cases operates outside the law. The word has become generally familiar as a result of the TROUBLES in Northern Ireland, and the IRA together with various armed Protestant groups may be properly described as paramilitary. *See also* ULSTER VOLUNTEER FORCE.

Pardon me for breathing! An ironic exclamation countering some minor or annoying criticism. The phrase dates from the 1940s.

Pardon my French. Excuse my swearing or FOUR-LETTER WORDS. Real French is unlikely to be involved. The French are unfairly associated with anything 'naughty' in the British mind. *Pardon My French!* (1998) is the title of a pocket French slang dictionary published by Harrap.

> 'If you really want to get married and have children and cook, well, you better get a move on, little sister. ... You should shit or get off the pot, pardon my French.'
>
> 'Beautiful French,' said Suzanne. 'Is that some Berlitz thing I'm not aware of?'
>
> CARRIE FISHER: *Postcards from the Edge* (1987)

Parent Trap, The. A film (1961) based on the novel *Das Doppelte Lottchen* by Erich Kästner (better known as the author of EMIL AND THE DETECTIVES (1928)) about identical twins who plot to reunite their divorced parents. Starring Hayley Mills in the dual starring role, the film was unnecessarily remade in 1998 with Lindsay Lohan as the twins.

Par for the course. As expected or predicted, given the circumstances, as: 'He's half an hour late but that's par for the course, knowing him.' The phrase dates from the 1940s and alludes to a golf player's expected score for a particular course.

> Some midnight assignations, a bit of bonking and a good deal of philosophizing are obviously par for the course.
> *Venue* (26 April 1985)

Parfumée, La (French, 'the perfumed one'). A nickname of Edith Cresson (b.1934), unpopular Socialist prime minister of France (1991–2). She subsequently became a European Union commissioner, and allegations of corruption against her and other commissioners led to the resignation of the entire commission in 1999.

Parkinson's Law. As satirically promulgated by C. Northcote Parkinson (1909–93) in his book with this title (1958), the proposition states that 'work expands so as to fill the time available for its completion'. The 'law' is mainly directed at public administration, but it is also aimed at inefficient business administration.

> As Parkinson's Law observes, work expands to fill the time available for doing it. With twice as much time at its disposal, Congress created twice as much work, which meant twice as much governing.
> *New York Times Magazine* (9 July 1978)

Parkway. As part of a railway station name, such as Didcot Parkway, this word denotes a mainline station with a large car park. The station itself is close to the named town or city, which is either within easy driving distance or easily reached by bus or taxi. It may also serve an important catchment area of some kind. The term was coined by British Railways and first applied to Bristol Parkway in 1972.

Part of the furniture. As familiar as a piece of furniture that one takes for granted in one's home. The expression dates from the early years of the 20th century.

> Consider Yourself at home,
> Consider Yourself one of the family. …

> Consider Yourself well in:
> Consider Yourself part of the furniture.
> LIONEL BART: *Oliver!*, 'Consider Yourself' (song) (1960)

Party animal. A regular partygoer; a frequenter of the social scene.

> 'You say I have a reputation for being a party animal?' he shrugs and smirks. 'Well, if you ask me, that ain't a bad reputation to have.'
> *Sunday Times* (19 September 1999)

Party girl. A young woman who regularly attends parties, especially as a celebrity or star who is already a frequenter of the social scene and in the public eye. The expression dates from the early 1930s, the age of the BRIGHT YOUNG THINGS.

> Serious party girls such as Elizabeth Hurley, Donatella Versace and Victoria Beckham can still be spotted nipping out in nothing but small scraps of very expensive cloth.
> *Sunday Times* (2 January 2000)

Party pooper. A person whose behaviour or attitude spoils other people's enjoyment; a 'wet blanket'. An antidote to a party pooper might be a PARTY POPPER.

> My husband and I will be spending New Year's Eve with a good book … and then having an early night. We are not party-poopers, but we will have spent Christmas with our families.
> *The Times* (Letter to the Editor) (18 December 1999)

Party popper. An amusing device which throws forth a paper streamer with a strident wail, used at parties as a diversion and as a corrective to a PARTY POOPER.

Party's over, The. The good times have come to an end. The phrase was popularized by the 1956 song of the same title by Betty Comden and Adolph Green with the line: 'The party's over, it's time to call it a day.' The words were famously repeated by the Labour Environment Secretary Anthony Crosland when cutting back central government's support for housing rates in the 1970s.

PASCAL. *See* PROGRAMMING LANGUAGES.

Pas devant les enfants (French, 'not in front of the children'). A phrase used with reference to a remark or action that is regarded as inappropriate for children (or other present company) to hear. The warning is expressed in French so as not to be understood by the person(s) in question. It is often shortened to *pas devant*.

Passage to India, A. A novel (1924) by E.M. Forster (1879–1970) whose three parts represent respectively the Muslim, Western and Hindu approaches to truth, rationality and spirituality. Forster visited India in 1912–13, when he saw the Barabar Hills, which became in his novel the Marabar Caves, where the fateful encounter takes place that is at the heart of the book. He returned to India for six months in 1921, to act as secretary to the Maharaja of Dewas, after which he went back to writing the novel, which he had begun in 1913. The title comes from the poem of the same name by Walt Whitman (1819–92), of whom Forster wrote that there was 'no-one who can so suddenly ravish us into communion with all humanity or with death' (*Two Cheers for Democracy*). An intelligent film version (1984) of the novel was directed by David Lean. *See also* AZIZ, DR; FIRST LINES OF NOVELS.

Passchendaele. A village in western Belgium whose name became synonymous with the appalling loss of life inflicted by the First World War. From July to November 1917 British, Canadian and Australian troops fought an unsuccessful offensive battle, also known as the Third Battle of Ypres, resulting in more than 350,000 casualties. Much of the fighting took place in appalling weather conditions, and the battle achieved only minimal territorial gains. The poignancy of the name is increased by its coincidental evocation of 'passion'. *See also* WESTERN FRONT; WIPERS.

> It is high time the Conservative leadership recovered its collective nerve. Two years after our election defeat they are still behaving like shell-shocked subalterns at Passchendaele.
>
> *The Times* (Letter to the Editor) (5 May 1999)

Passive smoking. The involuntary inhalation by non-smokers of smoke from the cigarettes, cigars and pipes that others are smoking. Passive smoking has been shown to increase the risk of lung cancer and those in the vicinity of smokers can at the least also suffer considerable immediate discomfort in the form of coughing, wheezing and watering eyes. The term dates from the 1970s.

Pass Laws. A notorious and much-resented aspect of APARTHEID-era South Africa. The laws, introduced in 1948, strengthened existing regulations by imposing stringent restrictions on the movements of non-white people and demanded that non-whites in 'white' areas had to carry an appropriate 'pass' authorizing them to be there. It was a demonstration against the Pass Laws that resulted in the SHARPEVILLE MASSACRE in 1960. The Pass Laws were among the institutions of apartheid that began to be dismantled in the later 1980s.

Passport to Pimlico. A delightful film comedy (1948) about a district of London that declares itself to be an independent state after the discovery of an ancient charter identifying the area as part of Burgundy. Starring Stanley Holloway and Margaret Rutherford among the citizens of the breakaway republic, it was the first of the EALING COMEDIES, and its title is still commonly quoted whenever a British village, town or city threatens to exert political independence in some form or other.

Past one's sell-by date. *See* SELL-BY DATE.

Pastry, Mr. The much loved alter ego of the comedian Richard Hearne (1908–79), as a bumbling, accident-prone old man forever involved in slapstick and physical comedy in a host of films and television sketches. His name, based on a character Hearne had played in *Big Boy* (1945), a stage comedy by Fred Emney, was reflected in his appearance, with his GRANNY GLASSES, white moustache and flour-sprinkled hair.

Pathé. The name of a popular cinema newsreel, founded in France in 1909 as *Pathé Gazette* by Charles Pathé (1863–1957). Pathé newsreels were introduced in the USA in 1910, and in Britain in 1911, and continued until 1956.

Pathological liar. An inveterate or habitual one. The implication is that such a person lies as the result of a mental abnormality. The term dates from the 1940s.

> The former wife of a Labour MP was a 'pathological liar' with a drink problem … a court was told yesterday.
>
> *The Times* (11 February 2000)

Patience and Fortitude. The names of the two marble lions lying before the New York Public Library at Fifth Avenue and 42nd Street. They were so named by the mayor of New York, Fiorello La Guardia, who always ended his Sunday radio broadcasts in the 1940s with the exhortation, 'Patience and fortitude'. They were originally named Leo Astor and Leo Lenox, after the Astor and Lenox libraries on which the new library was based. They had also been known as Lord Lenox and Lady Astor, or Leo and Leonora, despite the fact that they are obviously males, as indicated by their manes. They were set on their pedestals a few days before the building was dedicated by President Taft on 25 May 1911 but were disliked by the public who called them 'absurd' or 'squash-faced'. They have since become a popular landmark, especially at Christmas, when each sports a big red bow. Their presence also enables library users to joke punningly about 'reading between the lions'.

Patrial. This rare 17th-century word, from Latin *patria*, 'fatherland', was reintroduced by the Immigration Bill of 1971 to refer to a person who has the right to live in Britain through the British birth of a parent or grandparent. The term became a subject of controversy, as it was seen as a thin disguise for 'white person'. It is now chiefly used in the context of immigration control.

Patron saints for the 20th century. There have been patron saints for particular groups of people, things or occupations for centuries, such as St Dunstan for the blind, St Nicholas for children, St Andrew for fishermen or St Valentine for lovers. The categories listed below all arose or became established in the 20th century and duly acquired their individual patron saints. The list is necessarily only a selection of the many that exist and not all are official.

Advertisers and advertising: St Bernardino of Siena (1380–1444), named patron saint by Pope Pius XII in 1956 because of the powers of his sermons, which he enlivened with anecdotes and mimicry

Aircraft pilots and crews: the Virgin Mary, depictions of whose Assumption (celebrated 15 August) often show her ascending through the clouds. Declared a patron by France in 1952

Air hostesses and flight attendants: St Bona of Pisa (1156–1207), so named by Pope John XXIII in 1962 for her pilgrimages to Jerusalem, Santiago de Compostela and Rome

Astronauts: St Joseph of Cupertino (1602–63) is popularly so named, from his ability to levitate

Blood banks: St Januarius (3rd century), for the miraculous liquefaction of his blood, first reported in 1389; his relics were translated to Naples in the 5th century

BOY SCOUTS: St George, patron saint of England, where the movement was founded

Cavers: St Benedict of Nursia (6th century), declared patron of Italian cavers by Pope Pius XII in 1954 for the three days the saint spent in an inaccessible cave

Ecologists and ecology: St Francis of Assisi (1181–1226), so named by Pope John Paul II in 1979

Motorists: St Frances of Rome (1384–1440), who was named the patron saint of Roman motorists by Pope Pius XI (reigned 1922–39) from her continuous vision of her guardian angel, which enabled her to see at night; the decree was confirmed in 1951

Motorways: St John the Baptist, who proclaimed, 'Make straight the way of the Lord' (John 1:23); the patronage has so far been only provisionally proposed

Petrol-station attendants: St Eligius (7th century), earlier the patron of blacksmiths and farriers

Telecommunications: St Gabriel the Archangel, so named by Pope Benedict XV in 1921; 'archangel' literally means 'chief messenger'

Television writers: St Clare of Assisi (1193–1253), so named by Pope Pius XII in 1958 from the vision that she had of a matins service, complete with singers and organ, which she was too ill to attend; SOAP OPERA fans often claim their addiction stems from watching television while off work sick

YUPPIES: St Bathild (7th century), an Anglo-Saxon saint who is portrayed as ascending a ladder; the patronage has been provisionally proposed for those who are 'upwardly mobile'

Patter of tiny feet. A sentimental or ironic poeticism for the forthcoming birth of a child. An earlier form was 'the patter of little feet', made popular by Longfellow:

> I hear in the chamber above me
> The patter of little feet,
> The sound of a door that is opened,
> And voices soft and sweet.
>
> H.W. LONGFELLOW: *Birds of Passage*, 'The Children's Hour' (1860)

Patterson, Sir Les. An Australian 'attaché for cultural affairs' created by the comedian Barry Humphries (b.1934), the begetter of Dame Edna EVERAGE. He is a literally filthy figure of fun, forever swilling alcohol and spilling food down his front, and appeared regularly on television in the 1970s and 1980s. He has supposedly written a book, *The Traveller's Tool* (1985), and has released an LP of songs, *Twelve Inches of Sir Les* (1985).

Paul Jones. A dance popular in Britain in the 1920s, in which the ladies formed an outward-facing circle moving in the opposite direction to the men, who faced inwards. The couples facing each other when the music stopped became partners for the next part of the dance, this pattern being repeated several times. It was earlier one of the 'sets' in American barn-dancing, and is said to be named after John Paul Jones (1747–92), a Scottish-born naval officer noted for his victories for the Americans during the War of Independence (1775–83).

Pavane pour une infante défunte (French, 'Pavan for a Dead Infanta'). A solo piano composition (1899) by Maurice Ravel (1875–1937) the name of which recalls the Spanish court custom of performing solemn dances at periods of royal mourning.

The *infanta* is an eldest daughter of a ruling monarch of Spain who is not the heir to the throne. A pavan or pavin is a stately dance of the 16th and 17th centuries. The origin of the name is uncertain. One theory has it originating in Spain and so called because in it the dancers stalk like peacocks (Latin *pavones*). Another traces its derivation to the Italian town of *Padova* (Padua). The pavan was especially popular with English composers of the late 16th and early 17th centuries, and in the compositions of Byrd, Bull, Gibbons, Dowland and others was generally followed by a faster dance, the galliard.

Pavanne. A collection of linked stories (1968) by Keith Roberts (b.1935), in the form of an alternative history. Elizabeth I has been assassinated; the Spanish Armada has defeated the English fleet; and a militant Catholic Church rules a technologically retarded England. The pavan or pavin was a stately dance of Spanish or Italian origin, which was highly popular in 16th-century England. *See also* PAVANE POUR UNE INFANTE DÉFUNTE.

Pavlova. A dessert consisting of a meringue base or shell filled with whipped cream and fruit. It was created as a compliment to the Russian ballerina Anna Pavlova (*see* DYING SWAN) during her visit to Australia and New Zealand in 1926. It is uncertain which of the two countries has the true right to the honour. Australians claim that the dessert was invented in 1935 by Herbert Sachse, an Australian chef, and named by Harry Nairn of the Esplanade Hotel, Perth. The built-up sides of the pavlova are said to suggest the shape of a tutu. New Zealanders, however, claim that the name was being used as early as 1927, a date supported by the *Oxford English Dictionary*, but this use apparently relates to a different dessert.

Pavlovian response. Ivan Petrovich Pavlov (1849–1936) pioneered the study of the conditioned reflex in animals. In his classic experiment, he first rang a bell when feeding a hungry dog, then trained the dog to salivate on hearing the bell even when there was no sight of food. A Pavlovian response is now generally regarded as any automatic or 'knee-jerk' reaction.

> The report does not hesitate to name names, a procedure that will inevitably touch off a Pavlovian response from Leftist circles to deride it as a 'Reds under the Beds' scare.
> *Daily Telegraph* (8 February 1974)

Pax Americana (Latin, 'American peace'). A term based on *Pax Britannica*, denoting the peace formerly imposed by Britain in her colonial empire. The latter phrase is in turn modelled on the Latin *Pax Romana*, the peace existing between the different parts of the Roman Empire. The phrase *Pax Americana* came into vogue from the 1960s, a time when the USA was increasingly taking over Britain's former role.

> Never in the history of the world had any single nation dominated the international system as fully as the United States did for almost a quarter of a century after the Second World War. But the logic of Pax Americana led to the war in Vietnam, and the American people have learned their lesson.
> *Newsweek* (28 November 1983)

Payola. A bribe given to gain a special favour, such as a payment made to a disc jockey to 'plug' certain records or tapes, or to promote a particular commercial product. The word arose in the 1930s as a blend of 'pay' and either 'Pianola' or 'Victrola', the latter being an American make of gramophone.

PC 49. A rather dated nickname for a policeman, especially a 'bobby on the beat'. It derives from the central character of a radio series of over 100 adventures broadcast from 1947 to 1953, in which the improbably upper-class constable so numbered was actually named Archibald Berkeley-Willoughby. 'P.C. 49' was earlier the title of a popular song of 1913 by William Hargreaves, author of 'Burlington Bertie from Bow'. *See* BURLINGTON BERTIE.

PC Plod. A nickname for a policeman, from Mr Plod in Enid Blyton's NODDY books for children. The name is also shortened to simply 'plod', the ultimate reference being to the policeman's measured walk along his beat.

Peace Corps. The US government agency of volunteers so named was set up in 1961 by President John F. Kennedy to assist other countries in their development efforts by providing skilled workers in a wide range of fields. Once abroad, the volunteer is expected to remain as a good neighbour in the host country for at least two years, speaking its language and living on a level comparable to that of his or her counterparts in the USA. The initial intake of 900 volunteers served in 16 countries, but the latter number was nearer 90 by the 1990s.

Peace for our time. The unfortunate phrase used by Neville Chamberlain on 30 September 1938 after his meeting with Hitler in MUNICH and his agreement to the latter's annexation of the German-speaking SUDETENLAND. The agreement was part of the policy of appeasement that originated as a way of compensating Germany economically for the vindictive terms of the TREATY OF VERSAILLES (1919) which brought a formal end to the First World War. The phrase was based on words in the Order of Morning Prayer: 'Give peace in our time, O Lord.'

Peacehaven. This tranquilly named East Sussex town, a near neighbour of Newhaven, is a relatively recent creation. It arose in the First World War as a PLOTLAND development, as happened elsewhere along the south coast, and was originally called New Anzac-on-Sea, a name resulting from a competition: '£2,600 in prizes for a Name of a New South Coast Resort' (*The Times*, 10 January 1916). The name was intended as a tribute to the ANZAC troops who were stationed locally. In 1917, however, the original planner of the plotland, Charles Neville, announced a new name, Peacehaven, both denoting a 'haven of peace' and expressing the common desire for peace to end the war. The name also matched that of nearby Newhaven.

Peaceniks. A derisive term applied by the American right to those who opposed US policy and campaigned for peace during the COLD WAR. The coinage is on the model of BEATNIK, with the '-nik' suffix suggesting a Russian connection (as in SPUTNIK, for example). Those peaceniks who opposed US involvement in the VIETNAM War were sometimes disparagingly referred to as Vietniks. *See also* BETTER RED THAN DEAD; REFUSENIK.

Peace Pledge Union. A body pledged to renounce war, organized by Canon Dick Sheppard of St Martin-in-the-Fields in 1936.

Peace sign. *See* V FOR VICTORY.

Peaches and cream complexion. A fair complexion with delicately white skin and pink cheeks. The phrase also implies a sweetness and 'lusciousness', as of the dessert itself.

Peak District. Britain's first national park, over half of which lies in northern Derbyshire. It opened in 1951 and includes a highly popular tourist area, with the moors of the so-called 'dark peak' and vales of the 'white peak'.

Pearl Harbor. The American naval base at this harbour on Oahu Island, Hawaii, was the object of a surprise air attack by the Japanese on 7 December 1941. Much of the US Pacific Fleet was damaged or destroyed, including the USS *Arizona*, which sank with the loss of more than 1100 men. Overall casualties totalled more than 3400, with over 2300 killed. The action brought the USA into the Second World War on the Allied side. *See also* TORA! TORA! TORA!

Pearly king. The so called pearly kings and queens, princes and princesses of the London boroughs are named from their glittering attire studded with innumerable pearl buttons. There has been a pearly king of London since the FESTIVAL OF BRITAIN. They were originally elected by the street traders of London to safeguard their rights from interlopers and bullies, but they now devote their efforts to collecting and working for charities. Their tradition is said to have stemmed from an incident in the 1880s when a boat spilled its cargo of Japanese pearl buttons after foundering in the Thames. Henry Croft, a local roadsweeper, decorated his suit, hat and stick with his share of the salvage, thus becoming the first 'pearly king'. On his death in 1930 some 400 'pearlies' followed his coffin to St Pancras cemetery.

Pecking order. A term translating German *Hackliste*, literally 'peck list', applied in the 1920s by animal psychologists to a pattern of behaviour originally observed in hens whereby those of high rank within the group are able to attack (peck) those of lower rank without provoking an attack in return. The phenomenon was later recognized in other groups of social animals. In the 1950s the term was adopted to apply to any form of human hierarchy based on rank or status. The concept is sometimes popularly misunderstood to refer to pecking at food, as if those at the top were able to pick the choicest morsels while the underlings had to wait their turn and take what was left.

Social mobility has not extinguished class, nor has Britain a monopoly of social pecking orders.
The Times (19 July 1999)

Pedal-pushers. Women's tight trousers or jeans similar to CAPRI PANTS, so called as suitable for wear when riding a bicycle.

> Supermodel-cum-soap star Jerry Hall talks about dating, glamour and white pedal-pushers.
> *The Times* (sub-heading) (14 June 1999)

Peekaboo. Apart from the hiding game played with young children the word in the 1940s came to apply to a woman's hairstyle in which the hair, worn long, is allowed to fall over one eye. The style was popularized by the American film star Veronica Lake (1919–73), who first wore it during the Busby Berkeley film *Forty Little Mothers* (1940). Its introduction created a national fashion trend and established her as Hollywood's newest sex symbol.

Pelican crossing. A type of road crossing that can be controlled by pedestrians. Hence its name, from '*pe*destrian *li*ght *con*trolled crossing', with the acronym assimilated to 'pelican'. *See also* GREEN MAN; PUFFIN CROSSING; ZEBRA CROSSING.

> It is safer to cross at subways, footbridges, islands, Zebra, Pelican and Puffin crossings, traffic lights or where there is a police officer, school crossing patrol or traffic warden.
> *The Highway Code*, The Green Cross Code, 7a (1996)

Pellucidar. The fictional underground continent that is the setting of several novels by Edgar Rice Burroughs, beginning with *At the Earth's Core* (1922). It is lit by its own fixed sun which bathes it in a perpetual bright light. Hence its name. The sun has a small satellite, however, which casts a permanent darkness over the area known as the Land of the Awful Shadow. Most of the inhabitants dwell in caves in the cliffs, living by hunting and gathering fruit. Travellers need not expect a land of paradise, for there are many dangerous animals on the land and in the waters.

Pelmanism. A system of mind and memory training. It takes its name from Christopher Louis Pelman, who in 1899 founded the Pelman Institute for the Scientific Development of Mind, Memory and Personality in London. Owing to its extensive advertising, the verb 'to pelmanize', meaning to obtain good results by training the memory, was coined. It also gave its name to a card game, popular with children, which largely depends on mental concentration and memory.

The game is also known as 'Pairs' or 'Concentration' and is played as follows. The cards are shuffled and placed face down on a table or the floor, preferably at random rather than in rows. The first player turns over any two cards. If they make a pair, as two 7s, the player wins them. The same player then turns up another two cards, and continues until the cards are different. Having thus given the other players time to see which cards have been turned face-up, the player then turns the two odd cards face down again, in exactly the same position as they were in before. The next player to the left then has a turn. The player who has the most pairs when all the cards have been picked up wins the game.

Pelvis, The. *See* ELVIS THE PELVIS.

PEN Club. The international organization of writers takes its apt acronymic name from the poets, playwrights, editors, essayists and novelists who form its members. It was founded in 1921 by the novelist John Galsworthy and has since grown to include writers worldwide. The club promotes international intellectual exchanges among writers and is particularly active in defending and supporting writers who are being harassed, persecuted or oppressed by their government.

Penfriend or **pen pal.** The notion of a friend with whom one keeps in touch by correspondence evolved in the 1930s. Many such correspondents never meet, although cases are known of happy marriages resulting from a sharing of news and views in this manner. 'Penfriend' is the commoner term in England, and 'pen pal' in America.

Penguin Books. The paperbacks so called take their name from the publishing firm founded in 1935 by Allen Lane, the name itself being one suggested by his secretary, Joan Coles. According to Sir Allen, the logo appealed because it 'had an air of dignified flippancy and was easy to draw in black and white'. Earlier considered names were 'Dolphin' and 'Porpoise', but another publisher, Faber and Faber, already owned the latter. Among the first ten Penguins to be published, priced at sixpence each, were Ernest Hemingway's *A Farewell to Arms*, Dorothy L. Sayers' *The Unpleasantness at the Bellona Club*, André Maurois's *Ariel* and Eric Linklater's *Poet's Pub*. In 1960 Penguin was prosecuted for publishing an uncut version of D.H. Lawrence's sexually explicit LADY CHATTERLEY'S LOVER, but after intense publicity won a historic victory against censorship. The novel sold 2 million copies in six weeks, overtaking Penguin's previous bestseller, E.V. Rieu's translation of Homer's *Odyssey* (1946), the first of the 'Penguin Classics'. *See also* MODERN CLASSIC; PEVSNER GUIDES.

Penguin suit. A man's evening dress, so nicknamed from its black and white colours and because it makes the wearer look stiff and formal, like a strutting penguin.

Penicillin. One of the first and still one of the most widely used antibiotic drugs, derived from the *Penicillium* mould in 1928 by Sir Alexander Fleming, who had observed that colonies of the pus-producing bacterium *Staphylococcus aureus* failed to grow in those areas of a culture that had been accidentally contaminated by the green mould *Penicillium notatum*. He isolated the mould, grew it in a fluid medium, and found it capable of producing a substance that killed many of the common bacteria that infect humans. The mould derives its name from Latin *penicillum*, 'paint-brush', since the penicillium cells resemble small brushes.

Pennies and pence. Whereas 'p' is now the standard abbreviation for 'pence' in stating amounts under £1, such as 10p, 25p, 80p and so on, before decimalization in 1971 the written abbreviation was 'd', for Latin *denarius*, 'penny', and the spoken word 'pence'. The latter invariably formed a single word with the amount, so that one had twopence (pronounced 'tuppence' and written thus colloquially), threepence (similarly 'thruppence'), fourpence, fivepence, sixpence and so on up to elevenpence. The same held for adjectival twopenny ('tuppenny'), threepenny ('thruppenny'), fourpenny, etc. Although now historical in their literal sense, these words survive in phrases such as 'twopenny-halfpenny' for anything worthless, 'fourpenny one' for a blow, 'right as ninepence' meaning in perfect condition etc. *See also* TURN ON A SIXPENCE; TWOPENNY TUBE.

> I've got sixpence, jolly, jolly sixpence,
> I've got sixpence to last me all my life:
> I've got twopence to spend, and twopence to lend,
> And twopence to send home to my wife.
>
> DESMOND COX: 'I've Got Sixpence' (song) (1941)

Pennies from heaven. Unexpected financial benefits; a windfall. The expression seems to have originated from the song of this title popularized by Bing Crosby, who first sang it in the film of the same name (1936).

> Every time it rains, it rains
> Pennies from heaven.
> Don't you know each cloud contains
> Pennies from heaven?
>
> JOHNNY BURKE: 'Pennies from Heaven' (1936)

Pennies from Heaven was also the title of a critically lauded television drama (1978) by Dennis Potter. It starred Bob Hoskins and featured a number of popular songs of the 1920s and 1930s.

Penny dropped, The. It became clear. The phrase indicating a person's final realization of something alludes to the old penny-in-a-slot machine, as on the door of a public lavatory. The expression dates from the 1940s. *See also* SPEND A PENNY.

Penny Lane. A song of charm, vigour and no little musical sophistication by the BEATLES, credited to John Lennon and Paul McCartney and released in February 1967. Inspired by the Beatles' Liverpool childhood and incorporating motifs as diverse as a fireman's handbell and a reference to the Second *Brandenburg Concerto* by J.S. Bach, 'Penny Lane' evokes a kaleidoscope of images of the city, from the banker 'waiting for a trim' in a barber's shop to the rhapsodic celebration of its 'blue suburban skies'. The reference to 'fish and finger pie' at one point in the song is a smuttily nostalgic allusion to adolescent sexual experimentation. Penny Lane is both a Liverpool street name and an area of the city. *See also* STRAWBERRY FIELDS FOREVER.

Pen pal. *See* PENFRIEND.

Pentagon. A vast five-sided building erected in Washington, D.C., in 1943 to house government officials. It now houses the US Department of Defense, and Pentagon is a synonym for the official American line in military matters. *See also* PUZZLE PALACE.

Pentagon Papers. Official documents detailing a history of the US role in Indochina from the Second World War until 1968. They were commissioned in 1967 by Robert S. McNamara, the US Secretary of Defense, and were leaked to the press by Daniel Ellsberg, a government official, in 1971. They revealed, among other things, that the Harry S. Truman administration had given military aid to France in its colonial war against the Viet Minh, thus directly involving the USA in VIETNAM. The *New York Times* began publishing the papers on 13 June 1971 and they were subsequently commercially issued in book form in four volumes. Their release stirred controversy not only throughout America but also internationally.

People carrier or **mover.** A form of transport for several people. The two terms are sometimes used indifferently but are not properly synonymous. A people carrier is a vehicle with (usually) three rows of seats, affording greater accommodation than the average car, while a people mover is an automated transport system, such as a moving pavement or driverless car. Both types of transport were to the fore in the 1990s and, confusingly, are each also known as a multipurpose vehicle.

> So that's it. High summer is over, the last caravans and people-carriers have crawled back up the dual carriageway for the new term.
> The Times (31 August 1999)

People person. A person who interacts well with others and enjoys doing so. The expression has a positive application in business circles as well as socially.

> Friendly & informal yet highly professional Nanny agency based in South Kensington require a dynamic and organized 'people person' to run own department in a busy and often hectic office.
> The Times (advertisement) (16 September 1999)

People power. Political or other pressure exerted by ordinary people, as distinct from politicians and other influential individuals. The term arose in the mid-1970s and originally applied to physical effort exercised by people rather than machines. The present sense dates from the early 1980s.

People's Budget. The radical budget brought before Parliament in 1909 by David Lloyd George (see WELSH WIZARD), chancellor of the exchequer in Asquith's Liberal government. To fund social reform measures, such as the proposed old-age pensions, and also to raise money for more battleships to challenge the German naval expansion programme, Lloyd George proposed taxes on land sales and land values, higher death duties and a supertax on higher incomes. All this was anathema to the Conservative landed interests which dominated the House of Lords, which refused to pass the budget, so breaking with constitutional convention. Asquith retaliated by introducing the Parliament Act (1911), which put severe restrictions on the powers of the Lords. The Lords agreed to pass the act only when Asquith threatened to swamp the Lords with new Liberal peers. See also DIEHARDS; HEDGERS AND DITCHERS; OLD SQUIFFY.

People's Princess. A media nickname for Diana, Princess of Wales (1961–97), noted for her charity work and her special interest in children and the sick, in particular AIDS victims. The term was popularized by the Labour prime minister, Tony Blair, after Diana's death in a car crash in Paris.

> Two years after the death of The People's Princess, it's high time that Tony Blair and the Queen honoured her with a fitting memorial.
> Mirror (headline) (3 August 1999)

People's Republic. A title assumed by various socialist or communist states from the late 1940s. The most familiar example is the People's Republic of China, formed in 1949, when Hungary also adopted the title. Despite the decline of communism from the late 1980s, People's Republic remained a designation at the close of the 20th century, sometimes together with a political 'Socialist' or a tautological 'Democratic', for Bangladesh, China, North Korea, Laos and Libya.

Peoria. See PLAY IN PEORIA.

PEP. The Personal Equity Plan was introduced in Britain in 1987 as a type of investment scheme that allowed relatively small investors to own shares in British companies free from income tax and capital gains tax. The PEP had its enthusiasts, but was replaced in 1999 by the less enterprising ISA (Individual Savings Account). See also TESSA.

Pepsi-Cola. The familiar cola drink was the invention of a North Carolina pharmacist, Caleb D. Bradham, who named it in 1898 and who incorporated the Pepsi-Cola Company in 1902. He based the name on that of COCA-COLA, with 'Pepsi-' implying that his concoction could relieve dyspepsia. The real founder of modern Pepsi-Cola, however, was Charles G. Guth, who established a new company under the same name in 1931, got a chemist to formulate a better drink, and set up bottling operations. His 12-ounce bottle of Pepsi-Cola, costing 5 cents, realized spectacular sales.

Pep talk. An inspirational address aimed at boosting morale. The phrase dates from the 1920s and is based on the 20th-century word 'pep' meaning 'energy', as a shortened form of 'pepper'.

Per ardua ad astra (Latin, 'through difficulties to the stars'). The motto of the Royal Air Force. The phrase, originally the motto of the Mulvany family, was adopted as the motto of the RAF (then the Royal Flying Corps) in 1914. The headquarters of the former Air Ministry (now part of the Ministry of Defence) was set up at Adastral House, London, in 1955.

Percy. Like CUTHBERT, a nickname in the First World War for a CONSCIENTIOUS OBJECTOR. The name was apparently chosen for its suggestion of effeteness, perhaps from some sort of folk memory of the noble North of England Percy family, many of whom fell in battle or were executed. *See also* FIRST WORLD WAR SLANG.

Perestroika (Russian, 'restructuring'). The policy of restructuring or reforming the economic and political system of the former Soviet Union was first proposed by Leonid Brezhnev in 1979 and actively promoted by Mikhail Gorbachev. The original concept was of increased automation and labour efficiency but the term subsequently came to denote a greater awareness of economic markets and the phasing out of central planning. *See also* GLASNOST; GORBY.

Performance art. An art form combining elements of theatre and music with the visual arts. It dates from the late 1960s and has involved a wide range of expression, from self-inflicted discomfort and humiliation to surreal whimsicality. An example of the latter was staged in 1975 when the three-man Ddart Performance Group walked around East Anglia in a 240km (150 mile) circle with a pole attached to their heads. The style has also been linked to rock music, a field in which Laurie Anderson (b.1947) is the most noted exponent. Other artists in this variable arena are Joseph Beuys (1921–86), Gilbert and George (b.1943 and 1942) and Bruce Nauman (b.1941).

Perm. A shortening of permanent wave, as a method of setting the hair in waves or curls and then treating it with chemicals so that the style lasts for several months, although hardly 'permanently'. The procedure was introduced in 1906 and initially took between 8 and 12 hours.

Permissive society. A term widely used in Britain in the 1960s to denote the increasingly tolerant and liberal attitudes in society that tend to blur the distinctions between right and wrong. Gambling clubs, strip clubs, the legalizing of homosexual practices between 'consenting adults', and the growing use of 'bad language' and obscenities in publications, in the theatre and on television, were typical manifestations. *See also* NEW MORALITY; SWINGING SIXTIES.

Perpetua. *See* GILL SANS.

Perrin, Reginald. The frustrated businessman who attempts to remake his life by faking suicide and starting afresh in the comic novels by David Nobbs, beginning with *The Death of Reginald Perrin* (1975). He made a memorable translation to television in the talented hands of Leonard Rossiter in *The Fall and Rise of Reginald Perrin* (1976–9), a SITCOM unusually cerebral for its time.

Perry Mason. *See* MASON, PERRY.

Pershing missile. A type of US intermediate-range ballistic missile (IRBM), first developed in the 1960s. Pershing II missiles were controversially deployed in Western Europe in 1984, during a particularly chilly period of the COLD WAR, to face the Soviet equivalent, the SS-20. The Pershing II had a range of 1760km (1100 miles) and could carry a 15-kiloton warhead. They were withdrawn following the INF (intermediate nuclear forces) treaty of December 1987. The Pershing missile, like the US Pershing heavy tank of the Second World War, was named after General John J. Pershing (1860–1948), commander of the American Expeditionary Force in Europe in the First World War, who in 1919 became the USA's first General of the Armies (*see also* BLACK JACK).

Persistence of Memory, The. The famous 'soft watches' painting by Salvador Dalí (1904–89) was executed in 1931. As Dalí helpfully explained in *Conquest of the Irrational* (1969): 'The famous soft watches are nothing else than the tender, extravagant, solitary, paranoic-critical camembert of time and space.'

Pester power. A nickname for the persistent pressure that children put on parents or other adults to buy them an object of desire seen in a shop, television commercial or elsewhere. The mania is particularly rife at Christmas, when commercial HYPE is at its height.

Pétainists. The supporters of Marshal Pétain, head of the VICHY regime in France (1940–44), which collaborated with the Nazis after the fall of France. Philippe Pétain (1856–1951) had been a French hero in the First World War, leading the defence of VERDUN. Having become a military figurehead of enormous prestige, he was summoned to join the French cabinet as the German armies poured through Belgium in 1940. When France fell in June 1940, Pétain persuaded his colleagues to reject the proffered military union with Britain and to seek an armistice with the Germans. The prime minister, Paul Reynaud, resigned, and Pétain took his place, agreeing to the German terms at COMPIÈGNE on 22 June. Pétain attempted a reactionary National Revolution to establish a quasi-fascist state, with the slogan 'work, family and fatherland' replacing the French Republican 'liberty, equality, fraternity'. Pétain attempted to maintain a semblance of independence and rejected calls for France to join Germany in its war against Britain. However, he found his position steadily eroded by more ardent collaborationists and by the Germans, who eventually arrested him in August 1944. He returned to France in 1945 and was sentenced to death, although General de Gaulle commuted the sentence to life imprisonment.

Peter and the Wolf. The charming musical tale for children by Sergei Prokofiev (1891–1953) was first performed in 1936. The narration is interspersed with orchestral interludes, in which each character is portrayed by a different solo instrument, the duck by the oboe, for example, making the piece a perennially popular way of teaching the sounds of different orchestral instruments. Needless to say, the boy Peter triumphs over the fierce wolf, who is taken to a zoo.

Peter Grimes. The moody and gloomy opera by Benjamin Britten (1913–76) with a libretto by Montagu Slater was first performed in London in 1945 and was Britten's first major success. The story is based on one of the dark verse tales from *The Borough* (1810) by George Crabbe (1754–1832), set in his native Aldeburgh, Suffolk, which was also to become Britten's home. Grimes is a fisherman and a loner. Suspected by the townspeople of murdering a boy, he escapes to sea in fog and sinks his boat.

Peter Pan. The little boy who never grew up, the central character of J.M. Barrie's famous play of this name (1904). The story begins when Peter entered the nursery window of the house of the Darling family to recover his shadow. He flew back to NEVER NEVER LAND accompanied by the Darling children, to rejoin the Lost Boys. Eventually all were captured by the pirates, except Peter, who secured their release and the defeat of the pirates. The children, by now homesick, flew back to the nursery with their new friends, but Peter refused to stay as he did not wish to grow up. In their absence Mr Darling lived in the dog kennel as penance for having taken NANA away, thus making possible the children's disappearance in the first place.

The name of Barrie's hero resulted from the combination of those of the Greek god Pan and of Peter Llewelyn Davies, one of the five young sons of Barrie's friends Arthur and Sylvia Llewelyn Davies (who became Mr and Mrs Darling in the play). Barrie explained to the boys that he made Peter Pan 'by rubbing the five of you violently together, as savages with two sticks produce a flame', but it was Peter Llewelyn Davies who came to be most closely associated with the character. He was named Peter after the title character in his grandfather George Du Maurier's novel

Peter Ibbetson (1891). The five brothers generally met unhappy fates: one (George) died fighting in the First World War; another (Michael) drowned while at Oxford; and Peter himself (by then a publisher) committed suicide in 1960 by throwing himself under a train in the London Underground. Sir George Frampton's statue of Peter Pan in Kensington Gardens was not, incidentally, modelled on Peter Llewelyn Davies, but on his brother, Michael. The name of WENDY, the little girl who befriended Peter, was invented by Barrie and soon caught on as a new girl's name.

In 1929 Barrie donated the lucrative royalty rights to the play to the Great Ormond Street Hospital for Sick Children. *See also* FIRST LINES OF NOVELS; IN THE DOGHOUSE; WENDY HOUSE.

> To die will be an awfully big adventure.
> J.M. BARRIE: *Peter Pan*, III

Peter Pan collar. A flat collar with rounded points, as traditionally worn by PETER PAN in the play that bears his name and in illustrations to the book based on it. The style was popularized in the 1930s by the child film star Shirley Temple (b.1928), whose dresses had collars of this type.

Peter Principle. The theory, usually taken not too seriously, that all members of a hierarchy rise to their own levels of incompetence. It is named after the Canadian-born American educationist Dr Laurence J. Peter (1919–90), who, with Raymond Hull, first propounded it in *The Peter Principle* (1969).

Peter Rabbit. The most familiar of the animal characters created by Beatrix Potter (1866–1943) for her nursery tales. He is small and harmless, and first appears in *The* TALE OF PETER RABBIT (1901).

Petit Prince, Le. An allegorical story for children (1943; in English as *The Little Prince*, 1944) by Antoine de Saint-Exupéry (1900–44), in which he explores his personal philosophical convictions about values. A film version (1974), directed by Stanley Donen, turned the charming original into an arch musical. *See also* PILOTE DE GUERRE.

Petrified Forest, The. A play (1935) by the US playwright Robert Sherwood (1896–1955) about a group of gangsters who hide up in a rundown desert roadhouse. Filmed in 1936 with Leslie Howard, Bette Davis and Humphrey Bogart, the play owed its title to a roadmap, which Sherwood found in the otherwise bare office that he occupied while writing the text. It was while looking at the map that Sherwood decided to set his story in the Arizona desert, and when one of the characters subsequently referred to his destination up the road, the author automatically checked the map to see where it led in reality: it led straight to a place identified as the Petrified Forest.

Petrushka. The ballet of this name, with an innovative MODERNIST score by Igor Stravinsky (1882–1971) and choreography by Michel Fokine (1880–1942), was first performed by Diaghilev's BALLETS RUSSES in 1911 in Paris. The ballet tells of the fate of Petrushka, a puppet who comes to life. Stravinksy's music makes much use of the chord of C against F sharp, which has become known as 'the Petrushka chord'.

Petting zoo. An American term dating from the 1970s for a zoo where children are allowed to handle and feed the animals.

Pevsner guides. The magisterial series *The Buildings of England*, published by PENGUIN BOOKS, was inaugurated in 1951. Its author was Nikolaus Pevsner (1902–83), a German-born art historian who fled to Britain when the NAZIS came to power in 1933. The series of 46 volumes, of which 32 were written single-handedly by Pevsner, ran until 1974 and covered a wide range of buildings of architectural interest throughout England, with at least one volume to a county. Later authors have revised Pevsner's text, adding newer buildings, but respecting the personally authoritative, and often censorious, tone of the originals.

Phalange. *See* FALANGE

Phantom goal. In football a goal awarded although not actually scored. In a Division One match against Ipswich Town on 26 September 1970 Alan Hudson of Chelsea was awarded such a goal although the ball in fact hit the metal stanchion outside the net and bounced back into play. The referee, Roy Capey, awarded a goal rather than a goal kick to Ipswich in the belief that the ball had struck the stanchion inside the goal. Although BBC television cameras showed that it was not a goal, the Football League ruled that a replay could not be ordered, as Ipswich demanded, because the laws of football state categorically that the referee's decision is final.

Perhaps the most hotly debated of all goals, with the possible exception of the HAND OF GOD, was the second goal of Geoff Hurst's hat-trick for England against West Germany in the 1966 World Cup final. Hurst's shot hit the underside of the bar and dropped straight down. After consultation with a Russian linesman, the referee allowed the goal, giving England a 3–2 lead. Photographs and archive films fail to prove conclusively whether the goal was valid. *See also* THEY THINK IT'S ALL OVER.

Phantom Major. The nickname of Major (later Colonel) James Stirling (1915–90), who founded the Special Air Service (SAS) in 1941 to conduct sabotage missions behind enemy lines during the North Africa campaign in the Second World War. The nickname was given to Stirling by the German AFRIKA KORPS, who were amazed by the ability of his force to appear out of the desert and disappear again. In 1943 Stirling was captured in Tunisia, escaped four times and was finally imprisoned in COLDITZ. He was knighted in 1990.

Phantom of the Opera, The. The central character of Gaston Leroux's novel of the same name (1911). His real name is Erik, and he is a man with a hideous skull-like face who lives in seclusion beneath a Paris opera house. He falls in love with a singer, masking his deformity and committing a number of murders to achieve his desire, but in the end fails to get the girl. The unusual story was made into a film of 1925 with Lon Chaney, 'the man of a thousand faces', in the name part, and following further cinematic versions was given a new lease of life in Andrew Lloyd Webber's identically titled hit musical (1986), still running in 2000.

Phantom pregnancy. An uncommon psychological disorder, also known as false pregnancy and medically as pseudocyesis, in which there are all the usual physical signs of pregnancy without any foetus being present. Many women experiencing the condition are childless or approaching the menopause, and an intense desire to have children is a concomitant. Treatment usually consists of counselling or psychotherapy.

Philadelphia Story, The. A film (1940) based on a play by Philip Barry (1896–1949) about a spoiled Philadelphia heiress, Tracy Lord, who begins to have doubts about her forthcoming marriage to a dull company executive in the face of the taunts of her ex-husband and the growing interest of a magazine reporter, Mike Conner. Starring Katharine Hepburn (in a role specially written for her) alongside Cary Grant and James Stewart, the film was remade as the musical *High Society* (1956), with Bing Crosby, Frank Sinatra and Grace Kelly.

Philosophy in the Boudoir. The disturbing painting by the Belgian Surrealist René Magritte (1898–1967) was executed in 1947. The picture features a night-dress with breasts and a pair of high-heeled shoes with human toes. The title presumably refers to the notorious *La Philosophie dans le boudoir* (1793) by the Marquis de Sade.

Phoneday. 16 April 1995, when the British telephone system was extensively renumbered to cater for the growing demand for telecommunications services. The term was promotionally also spelled *PhONEday*, as a reminder of the added figure 1 in most exchange numbers. Thus London's 071 became 0171.

Phoney. Fraudulent, bogus or insincere. The word is an American colloquialism and slang term that became anglicized about 1920. It is said to derive from 'fawney', an obsolete underworld cant word meaning the imitation gold ring used by confidence tricksters, itself from Irish *fáinne*, 'ring'. The period of comparative inactivity at the beginning of the Second World War, from the outbreak to the invasion of Norway and Denmark, was characterized by American journalists as the Phoney War. The French knew this period as *la drôle de guerre*.

Phoney Quid. An ingenious nickname for Admiral of the Fleet Sir Dudley Pound (1877–1943), First Sea Lord in the Second World War. 'Quid' is a general naval nickname for anyone called Pound, while 'Phoney' derives from the admiral's first name, which is popularly shortened as 'Dud'.

Photo opportunity. A staged opportunity for the press to take photographs of famous people. The expression originated in the USA as media jargon in the 1970s but did not became generally familiar until the 1980s, when it was used of newsworthy pictures of President Reagan and Mrs Thatcher by public relations advisers who realized the advantages of giving press photographers what they wanted instead of simply leaving matters to chance. A negative aspect of the photo opportunity is its trivialization of politics by treating it almost as an offshoot of show business.

Phwoar! An exclamation dating from the 1980s, found mostly in the media, to express male sexual desire. The suggestion is of a blend of 'phew!' and 'wow!' There are variant spellings. *See also* WOLF WHISTLE.

Physical Impossibility of Death in the Mind of Someone Living, The. The notorious shark in formaldehyde by Damien Hirst (b.1965) dates from 1991. Hirst said of the work: 'I wanted the real thing, I wanted people to think "that could … eat me".' The

same could not be said of *Away From the Flock*, Hirst's 1994 sheep in formaldehyde. When exhibited at the Serpentine Gallery in London, someone poured ink into the sheep's tank; Hirst was not unduly upset.

Pick-and-mix or **pick'n'mix.** Assembled or collected by choosing different items from an overall variety. The term can apply to a method of selecting confectionery or other goods from a store's display to a blending of elements in an undertaking such as the compilation of an educational course or the drafting of a political programme.

> Whereas once the Book of Common Prayer meant that every church … [was] using a similar liturgy Sunday by Sunday, now there seemed to be an increasing 'pick'n'mix', especially at both ends of the [Church of England] spectrum.
> *The Times* (24 January 2000)

Pick up the tab, To. To pay the bill; to meet the cost. 'Tab' is perhaps a shortening of 'tabulation'. The phrase is of American origin and dates from the 1950s.

Pick your own. A marketing arrangement whereby customers purchase fruit or vegetables by picking or digging them at the site where they are commercially grown. The system is ingenious, since the customer exercises quality control and therefore cannot subsequently complain. The term is often abbreviated to PYO.

Picture window. A large window consisting of a single pane of glass, through which the view appears like a picture in a frame. The term is of American origin and dates from the 1930s.

> If you have a large picture window, we suggest sill-length casement drawn curtains.
> *American Home* (20 November 1938)

Piece of cake. Something easy, or easily obtained. The allusion is to the ease with which a slice of cake is taken and eaten. The RAF appropriated the expression in the Second World War, and a cartoon at the time of the Berlin airlift in 1948 depicted a pilot saying, 'Piece of Gatow, old boy'. (Gatow was a strategic Berlin airfield used for this operation.)

Piece of the action. Involvement in a profitable activity, or one that promises to be so. The expression is associated with the criminal or gambling world and dates from the 1950s.

Pie in the sky. A 'reward in heaven' (Matthew 5:12), here taken to mean the good time or good things promised that will never come. The term comes from a rallying song of the WOBBLIES attributed to their martyred organizer, Joe Hill (c.1872–1915).

> You will eat, bye and bye,
> In the glorious land above the sky;
> Work and pray, live on hay,
> You'll get pie in the sky when you die.
>
> JOE HILL: *Songs of the Workers*, 'The Preacher and the Slave' (1911)

Pierrot Lunaire. A landmark MODERNIST musical 'melodrama' by Arnold Schoenberg (1874–1951). It was written in 1912 for solo female voice and a small instrumental group. The title means 'Moonstruck Pierrot', and the work consists of settings of 21 poems by Albert Giraud, translated into German by Otto Erich Hartleben. The vocal part features *Sprechgesang*, a technique between singing and speaking. In a letter in 1931 Schoenberg wrote: '*Pierrot Lunaire* is not to be sung! Song melodies must be balanced and shaped in quite a different way from spoken melodies.'

Piggly Wiggly. The proprietary name of a chain of American self-service stores founded in Memphis, Tennessee, in 1916 by Clarence Saunders (1881–1953) and a forerunner of the modern supermarket. When asked by a business associate why he had chosen the name, Saunders replied, 'So people would ask me what you just did' (*New Yorker*, 6 June 1959). He later devised the Keedoozle, from 'key does all', a type of automated grocery store in which the customer selected merchandise by placing a 'key' into a slot beside the desired item and pushing a button. This perforated a tape inside the key. On completing the trip, the customer handed the tape to a clerk who ran it through a machine that added up the bill. This in turn was thus an early equivalent of the modern EFTPOS and 'card swipe'.

Piggy bank. A child's money box, especially one in the shape of a pig. In a transferred sense 'piggy bank' is used for one's savings, as: 'I'll have to draw on my piggy bank.'

Pig Island. A nickname for New Zealand dating from the early 20th century. The reference is to the pigs introduced by Captain Cook when he surveyed the islands in 1769. They later went wild.

Pig out, To. To overeat; to MAKE A PIG OF ONESELF. An expression evolving in the 1970s.

Popcorn, ice-cream, chocolate and cappuccino or Coke to drink. If you're going to sit on the sofa and pig out, do it properly!
The Times (25 September 1999)

Pig's ear or **breakfast.** A mess; an inept handling. 'You've made a right pig's ear of that' means you have made a complete muddle of it or have indeed failed to do it at all. It is possible 'ear' may be a euphemistic form of 'arse'. The phrases date from the 1930s. *See also* DOG'S DINNER.

The in-text variants … make a pig's breakfast of some of the finest prose Ralegh wrote.
Times Literary Supplement (22 October 1999)

Pigs might fly. The concept of pigs flying as an unlikely occurrence dates from the 16th century but in the 19th century settled to proverbial form as 'Pigs may fly, but they are very unlikely birds'. The current shorter and modified form of this is a 20th-century creation.

It would be nice to think that John Major, with his proclaimed belief in 'a classless society', might turn it [a knighthood] down anyway. Pigs might fly and cows jump over the moon.
The Times (8 September 1999)

Pilates. A system of gentle exercises performed lying down that stretches and lengthens the muscles, making the body long, lean, supple and strong. It came into vogue on both sides of the Atlantic in the 1990s and was invented in the 1920s by Joseph Pilates (1880–1967), a German entrepreneur who studied different exercise routines to strengthen his body after a sickly childhood. The name is pronounced 'Pi-lah-teez'.

Pile it high, sell it cheap. The byword of Sir John ('Jack') Cohen (1898–1979), founder of the Tesco supermarket chain in 1931. The '-co' of the store name derives from his surname, while the 'Tes-' represents the initials of T.E. Stockwell, of Messrs Torring & Stockwell, his original tea suppliers.

Pilgrim Trust. The American philanthropist Edward S. Harkness (1874–1940) set up the $10-million trust of this name in 1930. It was inspired by his interest in Britain and the British and supports such projects as the preservation of historic sites and training for the unemployed.

Pill, the. Since the introduction of the oral contraceptive in the early 1960s, its impact has caused it to be known as *the* pill, to the exclusion of all others, for whatever ailment or condition. *See also* MORNING-AFTER PILL.

Pillbox. A name given to the small concrete outposts erected in Britain at the start of the Second World War in case of a German invasion. Some of them still survive, mainly by canals.

Pillbox hat. A woman's hat something like the cylindrical box formerly used for medicinal pills. It first came into fashion in the 1930s but was given social cachet when worn by Jackie Kennedy (*see* JACKIE O) at the presidential inauguration of John F. Kennedy in 1961. She was wearing it again when sitting next to her husband in the open-top car in which he was assassinated in Dallas in 1963.

Pilote de Guerre. An autobiographical study (1942; in English as *Flight to Arras*, 1942) by Antoine de Saint-Exupéry (1900–44) about the role of the pilot in the Second World War. In 1944 he managed to get permission from the US authorities to make five reconnaissance flights from Sardinia. He disappeared without trace on the tenth. *See also* PETIT PRINCE.

Piltdown man. *See under* FAKES.

Piña colada (Spanish, 'strained pineapple'). A type of long drink popular in the latter half of the 1970s and made with pineapple juice, rum and coconut. Its name is as exotic as its content.

Pincher Martin. A philosophical novel (1956) by William Golding (1911–93), set on a rock in the Atlantic. Realistic flashbacks are combined with the surrealistic efforts of Martin's dead persona to survive; a 'pincher' in this context can be read as an identity-preserver. In the British armed forces and elsewhere, 'Pincher' has been a nickname for anyone surnamed Martin since the mid-19th century, when Admiral Sir William F. Martin was notorious for 'pinching' (arresting) sailors even for trivial offences. In the United States Golding's novel was published as *The Two Deaths of Christopher Martin*. It is possible that his choice of title was influenced by that of *Pincher Martin, O.D.* (1915), an early volume of stories and sketches of life in the Royal Navy by the naval officer and writer 'Taffrail' (Captain Henry Taprell Dorling) (1883–1968). Golding himself served in the Royal Navy in the Second World War.

Pinch oneself, To. To be incredulous; to be unable to appreciate the reality of a situation. The image is of someone pinching their own body to be reassured that they actually exist.

I learnt to listen, sitting in on book conferences, then off to the BBC to meet story editors. Me at the BBC! I had to keep pinching myself.
The Times (13 October 1999)

Pindown. A practice in some children's homes in the 1980s, whereby 'difficult' children were kept in solitary confinement, often dressed in just their nightclothes or underwear. The reference was supposedly not to physically 'pinning down' the children but to pinning down the problem they caused by means of so called 'behaviour modification therapy'. The treatment as used in Staffordshire was halted by High Court order in 1989 and came to light in a report published in 1991, achieving instant notoriety.

Pineapple. *See* MILLS BOMB.

Pinewood Studios. The film studios near Iver, Buckinghamshire, date from 1934 when Charles Boot, a wealthy local builder, bought Heatherden Hall and named what he hoped would become the most advanced film studio in the world after the tall pines in the grounds. The name also compliments (and complements) that of HOLLYWOOD, which Boot saw his enterprise as rivalling. He formed a partnership with J. Arthur Rank and the studios went on to achieve several blockbuster successes, among them *The Red Shoes* and *Oliver Twist*, both made in 1948. American production companies were attracted to Pinewood from the 1960s and the CARRY ON FILMS and James BOND films were made there, as were television series such as MINDER.

Ping-pong. The game of table tennis took its popular name at the turn of the 20th century, 'ping' representing the sound made when the bat strikes the ball and 'pong' the sound when the ball hits the table. According to the *Daily Chronicle* of 2 May 1901 the inventor of Ping-Pong was one James Gibb, a former Cambridge athlete. The game was originally sold under various names, such as 'Gossima', 'Whiff Whaff' and 'Flim Flam', and like these 'Ping Pong' was a proprietary name, registered in Britain in 1900 and in the USA in 1901. The American rights to the name were sold to Parker Brothers of Salem, Massachusetts, soon after and it is still a trademark there.

'Ping-pong diplomacy' is a former term for the establishment of trade and other relations between the USA and China, begun when an American table tennis team went to China in 1971. *See also* AERIAL PING-PONG.

Pink. A colour associated with homosexuals from the time of the Second World War, when NAZI concentration camp prisoners identified as such were obliged to wear a pink triangle. The colour is readily accepted by the gay community, and *The Pink Paper* is a weekly national newspaper for lesbians and gay men founded in 1987. The adoption of this particular colour probably comes from its traditional feminine associations, as distinct from 'masculine' blue. *See also* PINKO.

Pink-collar worker. An American term for a working woman, especially one in a job where women predominate, such as teaching, clerical and retail sales. The expression dates from the 1970s and arose by contrast with the WHITE-COLLAR WORKER, BLUE-COLLAR WORKER and GREY-COLLAR WORKER.

Pink elephants. The hallucinatory creatures supposedly seen by those in the throes of delirium tremens. 'Pink spiders' are an earlier variant manifestation. The phrase dates from the 1930s.

Pinko. A socialist sympathizer, tending to the red of communism but holding moderate or liberal views that merit a paler tone than the full-blown colour. The colloquialism dates from the 1930s.

> Down here in the West Country they wouldn't understand why. ... No one but puffy pale pinkos in sight down here, and racism's rampant.
>
> FAY WELDON: *The Heart of the Country* (1987)

Pink Panther, The. A film comedy (1963) starring Peter Sellers as the incompetent Inspector CLOUSEAU, a French policeman on the trail of a notorious diamond thief (played by David Niven). The 'Pink Panther' of the title is, in fact, the name of the famous diamond that Niven's character plots to steal, although audiences quickly came to identify the name instead with the pink-hued cartoon panther which appeared in the animated title credits and which quickly became a hugely successful film and television character in his own right. No mention was made of the 'Pink Panther' diamond in the various sequels that followed in the *Pink Panther* series, although most included the words 'Pink Panther' in their titles.

Pink pound. A term arising in the 1990s for the combined purchasing power of homosexuals considered as a consumer group. *See* PINK.

> The pink pound has never been more fiercely chased. The spending power and brand loyalty of gay consumers are not to be ignored lightly.
>
> *Independent on Sunday* (6 February 1994)

Pink slip. In the USA a notice of dismissal, printed on pink paper. Hence a term for the dismissal itself. In some US states a pink slip is also a learner's permit for driving a car.

Pin one's ears back, To. To listen attentively. The expression dates from the 1940s and in its imperative form is often heard in the light-hearted form 'Pin back your lugholes'. This became a catchphrase of the comic broadcaster Cyril Fletcher (b.1913) who used it to preface one of his humorous poems or 'Odd Odes'.

Pin-up. In the Second World War servicemen used to pin up in their quarters pictures of film stars and actresses (often scantily clad) or their own particular girlfriends. These were called 'pin-up girls'. The most popular pin-up picture among American forces was a photograph of the actress Betty Grable (1916–73) turning towards the camera with a smile and a wink in high heels and a white swimsuit, a pose that earned her $300,000 in one year. The term 'pin-up girl' itself first appeared in the armed forces newspaper *Yank* on 30 April 1943 and was reinforced by the film *Pin-Up Girl* (1944), in which Grable was the central character. The art form was subsequently taken up in such specialized publications as PLAYBOY and the PIRELLI CALENDAR. *See also* PAGE THREE GIRL.

Pinyin. A system for transliterating Chinese into Roman characters, introduced in China in 1958 as a teaching aid but not utilized to communicate with foreigners until 1979. Until then, the most widespread romanized system had been the Wade-Giles system, devised by Sir Thomas Wade (1818–95) and modified by Herbert Giles (1845–1935). In the Pinyin system the name of Chairman Mao Tse-tung is rendered Mao Zedong, and that of Premier Chou En-lai as Zhou Enlai. The system is most readily observed in Chinese place-names, so that Canton become Guangzhou, Nanking is Nanjing, Peking is Beijing and Tientsin is Tianjin. The term is Chinese for 'transcription', literally 'spell-sound'.

Pip emma. Signalese for p.m. (post meridiem) in the First World War. The equivalent for a.m. was ack emma. Emma was replaced by Monkey in 1921. *See also* ACK-ACK GUN; ROGER.

Pippi Longstocking. *See* LONGSTOCKING, PIPPI.

Pip-pip. Dated slang for 'goodbye', representing a toot on a motor horn from a departing guest.

Pips. The term for the time signal on BBC radio, consisting of five short pips and one longer one on the hour, the exact hour beginning at the start of the latter. The pips were first broadcast in 1924 and until 1990 were officially known as the Greenwich Time Signal.

Pipsqueak. A nickname for an insignificant person, especially when small or young (or both). The term dates from the early 20th century and each half of the word represents its respective sound.

Pip, Squeak and Wilfrid. A term for any group of three things or people, such as the three First World War medals 1914–15 Star, War Medal and VICTORY MEDAL. The names are those of three animal characters, a dog, a penguin and a baby rabbit, in a *Daily Mirror* children's comic strip that ran from 1919 to 1953. Wilfrid, the baby, could only say 'Gug' and 'Nunc' (for 'Uncle') and a fan club was formed with members known as 'Gugnuncs'. *See also* PIPSQUEAK; SQUEEZE SOMEONE UNTIL THE PIPS SQUEAK.

Pirate radio. A term for the radio stations that in the 1960s began broadcasting without official authorization from offshore sites. Many such stations were located on ships or boats anchored in international waters in the North Sea, an area chosen because the low-lying coast of eastern England offered no hindrance to radio signals. They broadcast pop music, eagerly lapped up by a young audience who were not yet catered for by the BBC. They attracted rewarding advertising until this development was banned by Harold Wilson's Labour government under the Marine Etc Broadcasting (Offences) Act 1967, whereupon many of the ships gave up. The most famous and persistent of these pioneers was RADIO CAROLINE. Pirate radio stations later surfaced on the mainland, such as those run by black reggae enthusiasts from council tower blocks in the mid-1980s, but again the government moved in and ordered all pirates to close in 1988. Most obeyed, but a third generation of pirates emerged in the 1990s, transmitting HOUSE and other types of music.

Pirelli calendar. A famous annual PIN-UP calendar published by the tyre manufacturers Pirelli from 1964. The original intention was to enhance the mostly sleazy photographs found on greasy garage walls to a proper art form. Professional photographers were employed for the purpose and were so successful that the calendars became better known than the firm itself. Only a limited number were issued to favoured clients each year and as a result became collectors' items.

Piss. A number of figurative phrases based on this FOUR-LETTER WORD have evolved in the 20th century.

They include 'piss artist', a despised person; 'piss-elegant', extremely elegant; 'piss in the wind', a waste of time; 'to piss oneself', to be utterly terrified; 'to piss off', to go away; and 'piss poor', very poor. More recondite is a 'pissing contest' as a term of American origin for any form of rivalry in which the participants are keener to assert their individual superiority than to achieve the best overall result. The image is of small boys seeing who can 'do it' farthest or highest.

Pit lizard. An American colloquialism for a female fan or follower of racing drivers. The term dates from the 1970s and arose on an analogy with the LOUNGE LIZARD, the pit here being the area beside a racetrack where cars are serviced and fuelled and where the drivers are thus obliged to stop and can be fleetingly admired.

> 'Pit lizards', camp followers, or dedicated racing fans, whatever you choose to call them, they are part of the scene and their presence is pleasing to racing men.
> *Atlantic* (June 1973)

Pits, the. Anyone or anything that is the worst of its kind or absolutely unbearable. The Americanism was brought before a wide British public by the tennis player John McEnroe (b.1959) in 1981, the year in which he first won the Wimbledon men's singles title, when he characterized a Wimbledon umpire as 'the pits of the world'. The allusion is to something hellish or 'dark and deep' rather than to the armpits, as sometimes explained. *See also* BRAT.

Pittura colta (Italian, 'cultured painting'). A movement in Italian painting dating from the 1980s, in which artists imitate certain stylistic features of the Old Masters in an ironic manner regarded as characteristic of POSTMODERNISM. A leading exponent is Carlo Maria Mariani (b.1931), while others associated with the genre are Alberto Abate (b.1946), Bruno d'Arcevia (b.1946), Antonella Cappuccio (b.1946) and Vittio Scialoja (b.1942), all of whom paint mythological or pseudo-mythological subjects in a gaudy and stagy reworking of the historical conventions. The name was coined by the Italian critic Italo Mussa for the title of his book *La Pittura colta* (1983).

Pixilation. A film-making technique whereby the movements of real people are filmed in such a way that they appear to move like animated characters. The method involves taking the shots one frame at a time with the person moving slightly between each shot. Special effects such as flying can be achieved in this way, and pixilation was used to good effect in *The Secret Adventures of Tom Thumb* (1993), a film that combined animated and human figures. The term itself derives from 'pixilated' in the sense 'crazy', 'confused'.

Plaid Cymru (Welsh, 'Party of Wales'). The Welsh nationalist party, set up in 1925 by six men in Pwllheli with the object of achieving self-government for Wales. Support grew from the 1960s and the party gained three seats in the House of Commons in 1974, two in 1979 and 1983, three in 1987 and four in 1992 and 1997. Plaid Cymru reaped the first fruits of its objectives when a National Assembly for Wales was set up in 1999 following a referendum on DEVOLUTION. *See also* SNP.

Plan B. An alternative strategy; another option. The expression derives from military jargon. 'Plan A' is usually implicit as the prime intention or scheme, although not always designated as such, even when there is a declared 'Plan B'.

> As the Hour of the Abyss approaches, Tony Blair claims that there is no Plan B for Ulster. As far as he is concerned, it is Plan A or Armageddon.
> *The Times* (30 June 1999)

Planet Japan. A name used by Western salesmen and businessmen for the potential market in Japan, as a distant and exotic 'world' waiting to be explored and exploited.

> The Boots ambassador to 'planet Japan' is Bill Spence … who has been in Tokyo since Boots sent him on an exploratory mission four years ago.
> *The Times* (15 October 1999)

Planets, The. A much-played orchestral suite by Gustav Holst (1874–1934). The seven movements are: 'Mars, the Bringer of War', 'Venus, the Bringer of Peace', 'Mercury, the Winged Messenger', 'Jupiter, the Bringer of Jollity', 'Saturn, the Bringer of Old Age', 'Uranus, the Magician' and 'Neptune, the Mystic' (which also features a wordless female chorus). Astronomers will note the unastronomical order of the first three and the absence of Earth and Pluto. The work had its first full public performance in 1920. The theme from 'Jupiter' provided the music for the hymn 'I vow to thee, my country'.

Planet X. Originally the provisional name for an as yet undiscovered planet predicted in 1902 by the American astronomer Percival Lowell (1855–1916). He began searching for it in 1905 but it was not discovered until 1930, some years after his death, when it was named PLUTO. In 1972 the name was revived for a supposed tenth planet in the solar system, the 'X' standing for both 'ten' and 'unknown'. Several long-term searches have failed to find a body of the appropriate size, however, and there is now no reason to invoke a Planet X.

Planned obsolescence. The policy of deliberately giving manufactured goods a short usage life by introducing changes in design, ceasing to supply spare parts, using materials of poor quality or the like, so encouraging consumers to purchase a replacement. The practice dates from the 1970s.

Plastic. A colloquialism for a payment made by plastic card, as distinct from cash, cheque or credit. By the end of the 20th century the proliferation of various types of plastic card such as credit card, bank card, debit card, charge card, store card and the like made it relatively easy for the routine shopper to say 'I prefer to pay with plastic'. *See also* FLEXIBLE FRIEND.

Plastic bag moment. A whimsical term for the moment when one suddenly glimpses a touch of beauty in a normally utilitarian object. The reference is to an empty plastic bag such as a dustbin liner lying in the street that suddenly fills and floats up in a gust of wind. The concept may seem pretentious but the experience is not unusual and other examples readily suggest themselves.

Plasticine. Commercial production of this modelling material was begun in 1900 by William Harbutt (1844–1921), an art teacher, in an old flour mill at Bathampton, near Bath. Its name indicates its nature as a plastic substitute for modelling clay, intended for creative educational and recreational purposes. At first it was available only in grey, but a three-colour pack of red, blue and yellow Plasticine called 'The Complete Modeller' soon followed.

Plate glass universities. The universities of East Anglia, Essex, Kent, Lancaster, Sussex, Warwick and York, built in the 1960s with plate-glass windows, in marked contrast to the earlier REDBRICK Universities.

> The collective academic phenomenon now known as the Plateglass universities coincides with a break in the great graduate bull market of the 1950s and 1960s.
> *Manchester Guardian Weekly* (22 May 1971)

Platform shoes. Shoes with thick raised soles, first in vogue in the 1970s and favoured by both sexes. They were the forerunner of the 'clumpy' shoes popular among young women in the 1990s. Entertainers such as Elton John (*see under* PSEUDONYMS) took the platform shoe to ludicrous and dangerous heights.

Platinum blonde. A woman with silvery-blonde hair. The vogue for hair of this colour was at its height in the 1930s and the English actress Binnie Barnes appeared as a platinum blonde in Noël Coward's musical *Cavalcade* (1931) although her natural hair colour was auburn. The epithet was primarily associated, however, with the American film actress Jean Harlow (1911–37), who was so dubbed by Columbia Pictures for a film originally to have been called *Gallagher* but retitled in her image as *Platinum Blonde* (1931). The result was a craze of 'peroxide blondes' among the public in general that was also taken up by such actresses as Joan Crawford (1908–73) and Alice Faye (1912–98). *See also* PLUTONIUM BLONDE.

Play at soldiers, To. To serve as a volunteer or new recruit in the army. A derisive term originating from the children's game of 'soldiers' in which one child 'drills' the others or leads them in a march.

Play ball with, To. To cooperate with; to respect the requirements of another. The phrase implies a mutual understanding: 'You play ball with me and I'll play ball with you.'

Playboy. A monthly magazine famous for its 'girly' pictures. It was launched by the American publisher Hugh Hefner (b.1926) in December 1953, the first issue depicting Marilyn MONROE posing nude. The combination of high-quality photographs of nude or semi-nude models, practical advice on sexual problems, men's talk and articles of high literary standard soon made Hefner a millionaire and the magazine itself a conspicuous success. The *Playboy* empire subsequently extended into real estate, clubs with BUNNY GIRL hostesses, and sundry related products. The magazine did much to pioneer the CENTREFOLD, calling its subject 'Playmate of the Month'.

Playboy of the Western World, The. A play by the Irish playwright J.M. Synge (1871–1909), which provoked demonstrations when it was first staged at the ABBEY THEATRE, Dublin, in January 1907. It is about the disruption that follows when a feckless young man, Christy Mahon, arrives in a country pub in Mayo in the west of Ireland boasting that he is on the run after killing his own father. Although it is subsequently learned that he has done no such thing, he retains the spurious glamour he has acquired in the eyes of

Pegeen Mike, the daughter of the landlord, and after he is driven out of the village she laments:

> Oh, my grief, I've lost him surely. I've lost the only Playboy of the Western World.

Playgroup. A group of pre-school children or RISING FIVES, organized to provide basic care and an opportunity to socialize before compulsory schooling begins. Playgroups are run mainly by volunteers and usually operate in rented accommodation such as the local town hall. The movement grew in the 1960s out of the acute shortage of nursery school places.

Play hardball, To. To be ruthless in the pursuit of one's goal, especially in politics. The allusion is to baseball, alternatively called hardball to be distinguished from softball, a variant form of the game. The American phrase dates from the 1960s.

Play hard to get, To. To appear aloof and dispassionate in order to make oneself more attractive or desirable. The expression, traditionally but by no means exclusively used of women, dates from the 1920s. The conceit is: 'The harder the chase, the greater the catch.'

> [Film director Sam] Mendes … has, apparently, been saying that he wants to make only the occasional film and is looking for more theatre work. 'He may just be playing hard to get,' one producer acquaintance of Mendes speculated.
>
> *The Times* (4 December 1999)

Play in Peoria, To. To be acceptable to the average consumer. The expression originated in the 1930s among touring theatre companies keen to ensure that their productions would find favour in MIDDLE AMERICA, represented by the small town of Peoria, Illinois. 'It'll play in Peoria' subsequently became a catchphrase of the Nixon administration (1969–74).

Play It Again Sam. A film comedy (1972), based on a stage play (1969), written by and starring US comedian Woody Allen (b.1935). Allen plays a film critic who receives advice about his love life from the ghost of Humphrey Bogart, complete with trench coat. The title comes from a line in the classic Bogart movie CASABLANCA (1942), although it does not appear exactly in that form in the original film. The closest anyone gets to it is: 'Play it, Sam. Play "As Time Goes By",' as directed to the pianist Sam, played by Dooley Wilson. The song was nearly left out of the film at the request of its composer, Max Steiner, who begged Warner Brothers to drop it, fearing it would not work.

Play one's cards close to one's chest, To. To be secretive or cautious about one's intentions. The metaphor derives from card-playing, in which a player may hold his cards close to his chest so that others cannot see his hand. The phrase dates from the 1950s.

Play one's cards right, To. To make the best use of one's assets or knowledge. The metaphor is obviously from card games. An earlier form of the expression was 'to play one's cards well'.

Play the field, To. To indulge in a number of sexual relationships without committing oneself to any single one of them. The expression dates from the 1930s and takes its image from horse racing, where it means to bet on all the horses with the exception of the favourite.

Plc. The abbreviation of 'public limited company', replacing 'Ltd' ('Limited') as the official designation of a British limited-liability company under the terms of the 1980 Companies Act. All British companies are registered with the Registrar of Companies and most corporate businesses are 'limited liability' companies, meaning that their liability is restricted to contributing an amount related to their shareholding. Companies may be public or private. Before a company becomes a plc it must be limited by shares and have a share capital, state in its memorandum of association that it is to be a plc, meet specified minimum capital requirements, and add 'plc' to its name. All other British companies are private companies which are generally prohibited from offering their shares to the public. *See also* BRITAIN PLC.

Please, Sir! One of the top television SITCOMS of its day (1968–71), centring on the experiences of a newly qualified teacher at a tough south London secondary modern school. His lofty idealism is predictably blunted, not least by the ineducable Class 5C, whose form teacher he is. The hapless hero, Bernard Hedges, nicknamed 'Privet' by his pupils, was played by John Alderton.

Pleidiol wyf I'm gwlad (Welsh, 'loyal am I to my country'). These words from the Welsh national anthem *Hen Wlad Fy Nhadau* ('Land of my Fathers') have appeared on the milled edge of the Welsh one-pound coin since 1985. 'Land of my Fathers' was written by Evan James, a weaver from Mid Glamorgan, in 1856, and the song was adopted as the Welsh national anthem in the late 19th century.

Plenty. A play (1978) by the British playwright David Hare (b.1947) about a former Resistance heroine whose life descends into disillusion and madness after the war. Filmed in 1986 with Meryl Streep in the central role, the title reflects the main theme of despair implicit in living in a society that is materially rich but spiritually impoverished.

Plinge, Walter. A fictitious name used on English playbills for an actor who is 'doubling' or playing two parts. There are two stories to account for the name. The first derives it from the landlord of a public house near the stage door of the Lyceum Theatre, London, in c.1900. The second takes it from a phrase 'Mr Plinge is waiting', used by an actor for a supposedly convivial acquaintance who has invited him out for a drink. The first to use the name on a playbill may have been the actor and producer Oscar Asche (1871–1936), who took over the management of His Majesty's Theatre in 1907. The American equivalent of Walter Plinge is George Spelvin, a name first found in New York in 1886 in the cast list of Charles A. Gardiner's *Karl the Peddler*.

PLO. The Palestine Liberation Organization, formed in 1964 from AL FATAH to unite various Palestinian Arab groups and ultimately bring about an independent state of Palestine. Yasser Arafat (b.1929) became its leader in 1969. In the early 1970s it made its base in Lebanon but when PLO forces were expelled from that country in 1982 it set up its headquarters in Tunisia. Frustration at Israel's continued occupation of its claimed territory led to the start of the INTIFADA in 1987 but since then it has recognized Israel's rights to exist in secure borders. Israel, for its part, has in turn recognized the PLO as the legitimate representative of the Palestinian people. An accord with Israel in 1994 enabled the GAZA STRIP to become self-governing and a similar agreement in 1995 gained autonomy for the WEST BANK. *See also* BEIRUT.

PL/1. *See* PROGRAMMING LANGUAGES.

Plonk. An Australian term for cheap red wine fortified by methylated spirit. It is also popularly applied to any cheap red wine. Despite this, the origin of the word may be in French *vin blanc*, 'white wine'.

> Toby Brocklehurst ... dealt with the kitchen staff and ferried bottles of plonk to and fro.
> *Sunday Times* (10 May 1998)

Plotlands. A name given in the 1920s to the settlements that sprang up along the south and southeast coasts of England after the First World War. Houses in such places were at first little more than shacks or shanties, in some cases built out of old buses or railway carriages or based on deserted army camps, while the plots of land themselves could be obtained at little cost or even free if occupied by squatters. Despite the initial primitive conditions, as well as tussles with the local authorities, the settlers themselves were delighted with their enterprise, which offered them fresh air, a sea view, tranquillity and a sense of freedom. They were criticized in many quarters for their desecration of the countryside, much as the NEW AGE travellers have been in more recent times. But while some of the settlements have remained rudimentary, others, such as PEACEHAVEN, have grown into respectable, thriving townships.

Plough and the Stars, The. A play (1926) by the Irish playwright Sean O'Casey (1880–1964), first produced at the ABBEY THEATRE, Dublin, when its depiction of the sufferings of Dublin slum-dwellers during the EASTER RISING of 1916 caused a riot. The title refers to the designs on the flag of the Irish Citizen Army, the working-class organization behind the Rising, but was also intended by the author to suggest the contrast between the real and the ideal in life.

Ploughman's lunch. A meal of bread and cheese, typically served with pickle and salad and consumed in or outside a pub as a bar snack. The name arose as a marketing ploy of the English Country Cheese Council in the early 1970s. The lauded film *The Ploughman's Lunch* (1983) tells of the deepening cynicism experienced by members of the media as a result of the FALKLANDS WAR.

Plowden Report. The report *Children and the Primary Schools* (1967) by Lady Bridget Plowden (b.1907) marked a watershed in the development of English primary education. It considered such education in all its aspects, including the transition to secondary schools, and recommended that schools, local education authorities and the Department of Education should encourage parents to become more actively involved in their children's education and that increased resources be made available for nursery education and 'educational priority areas', or areas starved of new investment. Child-centred approaches should be taken to their logical limits and the teaching-learning process should be completely individualized. *See also* NEWSOM REPORT.

Plum. An inevitable nickname for a person whose first name is Pelham, as the cricketer Pelham Francis Warner (1873–1963) or the novelist P.G. (Pelham Grenville) Wodehouse (1881–1975), creator of JEEVES and Bertie WOOSTER.

Plunging neckline. A very deep-cut neckline on a woman's garment, so called as it 'dives' into the cleavage. The term is first recorded in the 1940s but the style itself dates from much earlier, and the craze for plunging necklines in 1910 caused concern that the female population could be decimated as a result of pneumonia.

> Victoria Beckham wasn't to be outdone. Her necklines plunged with the temperature as she gamely flitted from one party to the next.
> *Sunday Times* (2 January 2000)

Plus fours. Loose knickerbockers overlapping the knee and thereby giving added freedom for active outdoor sports. They were particularly popular with golfers in the 1920s. The name derives from the 4 extra inches (about 10cm) of cloth required below the knee in tailoring. Plus twos also exist as a shorter variant, and are favoured by some current golfers. *See also* MAN IN BLACK.

> [Payne] Stewart, one of the most recognizable players in the game because of his trademark plus-twos and tam-o'-shanter hat, has won 18 tournaments around the world.
> *The Times* (26 October 1999)

Pluto. The ninth planet in the solar system was discovered only in 1930 by the American astronomer Clyde W. Tombaugh during a systematic search for a planet beyond Neptune, itself discovered in 1846. Tombaugh recognized the new planet in a series of photographs he had taken at the Lowell Observatory at Flagstaff, Arizona. Continuing the tradition of naming planets after Roman gods, Vesto M. Slipher, the director of the observatory, chose the name Pluto, god of the regions of darkness. The name also embodies the initials of Tombaugh's fellow astronomer, Percival Lowell, who had long sought his PLANET X, and Pluto's planetary symbol is a superimposed 'P' and 'L'.

PLUTO. Pipe Line Under the Ocean, a project essential to the Normandy invasion in the Second World War. In its original version pipelines from out at sea ran to the beachheads, so enabling ships to deliver fuel without docking. Later undersea pipelines were laid to carry petrol the full distance from Dungeness to Boulogne and from the Isle of Wight to Cherbourg. The acronym has an appropriate reference to Pluto, the Greek god of the underworld, whose name means 'wealth'. *See also* D-DAY; OVERLORD.

Plutonium Blonde. A nickname given to Margaret Thatcher (the IRON LADY) by Arthur Scargill (KING ARTHUR), the left-wing leader of the bitter 1984–5 miners' strike. Thatcher successfully crushed the strike, and subsequently closed down most of Britain's pits. The nickname, a play on PLATINUM BLONDE, refers both to Thatcher's liking for nuclear energy in preference to coal and to her partiality for nuclear weapons.

Poet's day. The weary worker's acronymic name for Friday: 'Push off early, tomorrow's Saturday.'

Po-faced. Solemn and humourless; serious where one might have expected a show of amusement. The term probably derives from 'poker-faced', referring to the expressionless face of a poker player, but with a suggestion of 'po', a chamber pot.

Pogo stick. A toy for jumping about on, consisting of a long, spring-loaded pole with a handle at the top and a rest at the bottom for the feet. The name may be a blend of 'pole' and 'go'. The device itself is first recorded in 1919.

Poictesme. The small fictional kingdom that is the setting of James Branch Cabell's fantasy novel *Jurgen* (1919). It is a pleasant land, lying to the west of Provence in southern France, and its first great hero was Count Manuel, the Redeemer. Its second was Jurgen, who rescued Guenevere of Cameliard from the troll king who lived beneath the Amneran Heath in the centre of the country.

Point of no return. The point in an aircraft's flight at which it has not enough fuel to return to its point of departure and must continue. Hence the figurative application of the expression to a point or situation from which there is no going back. The phrase originated among pilots in the Second World War.

Points. A term from the Second World War relating to the system of rationing food, clothing and other commodities. Apart from direct rationing of meat, bacon, sugar, fats and tea, miscellaneous groceries were given 'points' values and each ration-book holder was given a certain number of points to spend in an allotted period. Hence 'it's on points' was a common reference to many commodities.

Point someone in the direction of something, To. To show them where it is. An expression apparently arising as a facetious military or civil service circumlocution.

Points system. A system used by a local authority for granting a council house to a tenant. Points are awarded according to the person's status, depending on such factors as length of residence in the area, number of children in the family and so on.

Pointy head. A nickname for an intellectual, on an analogy with an EGGHEAD. The term 'pointy-headed' is said to have been coined in 1968 by the anti-integrationist US politician George C. Wallace (1919–98), following his first term of four as Governor of Alabama.

Poirot, Hercule. The small and unassuming Belgian detective, with his waxed moustache and comically fastidious manner, was the creation of Agatha Christie (1890–1976) and appeared in her first detective novel, *The Mysterious Affair at Styles* (1920). He went on to play a key role in some 40 further novels, including the famous MURDER ON THE ORIENT EXPRESS (1934). He has since appeared in the cinema and on television in a number of popular adaptations of the stories, being played by such disparate actors as Austin Trevor, Albert Finney, Peter Ustinov, Ian Holm and David Suchet. *See also* DEATH ON THE NILE.

> 'This affair must all be unravelled from within.' He tapped his forehead. 'These little grey cells. It is "up to them" – as you say over here.'
> AGATHA CHRISTIE: *The Mysterious Affair at Styles*, ch x (1920)

Poison pen letter. An anonymous letter that is abusive, libellous or malicious. The suggestion is that the pen to write the letter has been dipped in poisonous ink, and will wound or kill the recipient in the manner of a poison-tipped arrow. The expression dates from the early 20th century. *See also* HATE MAIL.

Poison pill. A pill containing a fast-acting poison such as cyanide, a traditional resort by captives in some countries as a means of suicide when defeat in combat is inevitable. In financial jargon a poison pill is a ploy used by a company to deter a bidder when faced with an unwelcome take-over bid. The term is said to have been first used in the latter sense by an American lawyer in 1982.

NatWest was strangely mute yesterday, saying little other than that it rejected the bid. By lunchtime, the market was awash with rumours that the bank was preparing some poison pill.

The Times (25 September 1999)

Pokémons. These toy monsters so named were launched worldwide by the Japanese in 1999 as the annual children's Christmas fetish. The object was to collect every one of the 150 named models to become 'Pokémon Master'. Pokémon is also a multimedia toy and exists as a card game, a television series and a video game. In this last, played on a GAME BOY or the equivalent, the player takes the role of Ash, a Pokémon trainer. With the aid of Pikachu, a helpful Pokémon, Ash moves around Pokémon Island fighting other Pokémons, disabling them with his trusty ball so that they lose their energy. When a Pokémon is captured, its powers can be used to fight other Pokémons, although some Pokémons turn into others when captured. By early 2000 there were three games, the Blue, the Red and the Yellow, the twist being that no game contains all 150 Pokémons. The name itself, pronounced 'po-kay-moan', is pidgin Japanese for 'Pocket Monster'.

Polaris. A type of US nuclear-armed SLBM (submarine-launched ballistic missile) with a range of 4800km (3000 miles) that entered service with the US Navy in 1960. By the 1962 Nassau Agreement the USA agreed to supply Britain with the missiles. (This led President de Gaulle of France to veto Britain's application to join the COMMON MARKET in 1963, on the grounds that the UK was not sufficiently oriented towards Europe.) In the USA Polaris was replaced by Poseidon missiles in 1969, which in turn were replaced by TRIDENT missiles in the 1980s. In the UK Polaris was replaced by Trident in the 1990s. Polaris is the astronomers' name for the North or Pole Star.

Polaroid. *See* LAND CAMERA.

Poldark. *See* ROSS POLDARK.

Pole position. In motor racing the starting position in the front row and on the inside of the first bend, usually regarded as the best and most advantageous. The reference is to the pole as the term for the inside fence on a racecourse and also the starting position closest to it. A horse was said to 'have the pole' if the jockey had drawn this position. Hence 'to be in pole position', meaning to have the advantage generally.

Ipswich relinquished their hold on the pole position to champions Liverpool.

News of the World (17 April 1977)

Poles apart. In complete opposition; having nothing in common. The poles here are the earth's geographical extremities, the North and South poles. The expression dates from the early 20th century.

Policy wonk. Someone who takes an excessive interest in the minor details of political policy. The expression dates from the 1980s, using 'wonk' as an existing derogatory term for a studious person or NERD.

New Labour's fashionable policy wonks sniff that their deputy PM [John Prescott] is not chic.

Sunday Times (5 December 1999)

Polish Corridor. The territory given to Poland by the TREATY OF VERSAILLES (1919) to give access to the Baltic Sea west of Danzig. The Corridor cut off East Prussia from the rest of Germany and proved to be a bone of contention from the outset. It followed roughly the line of the River Vistula.

Polish the apple, To. To curry favour; to seek to flatter. The allusion is to the bright and shiny apple that a schoolchild traditionally gives a teacher in the hope of winning approval.

Politburo. Formerly, the chief policy-making body of the Communist Party in the USSR, first formed in 1917. It examined matters before they were submitted to the government and consisted of five members. It was superseded by the PRESIDIUM of the Central Committee of the Communist Party in 1952. The word is a typical Soviet abbreviation, here for *Politicheskoye byuro* ('political bureau').

Political correctness. A philosophy of the 1990s, of American origin, that promoted the avoidance of expressions or actions that could be understood to denigrate groups or minorities traditionally regarded as disadvantaged in some way, as by race, gender, class, disability, religious or political leanings, or sexual orientation. Propagandists of this new morality recommended particular expressions that can and should be substituted for the traditional ones, such as 'the common citizen' for 'the common man' and 'childcare worker' for 'nursemaid'.

Dictionaries of such terms have been published, such as Henry Beard and Christopher Cerf's *The Official Politically Correct Dictionary and Handbook* (1992). Such revisionism extended even to the rewriting of established religious texts, such as the Bible, one version of which, published in 1994, not only avoided most 'gender-specific' words but substituted

'God's mighty hand' for 'God's right hand' for fear of offending the left-handed.

According to Nigel Rees's *The Politically Correct Phrasebook* (1993), the following '-isms' are politically *in*correct:

ableism: discrimination in favour of able-bodied people

ageism: discrimination on grounds of age, especially against the middle-aged and elderly

alphabetism: discrimination according to the alphabetical position of a person's surname

animalism: discrimination against animals on the grounds that they are inferior to humans

classism: discrimination on grounds of social status

disableism: discrimination against the disabled

diseaseism: discrimination against the sick

fattism: discrimination against fat or overweight people

hairism: discrimination on the grounds of hair colour or length

handism: discrimination against the left-handed

heightism: discrimination against tall women or short men

heterosexism: discrimination against homosexuals

lookism: discrimination on the grounds of (supposed) unpleasant looks

racism: discrimination on grounds of race

sexism: discrimination against a person's sex (usually male against female)

sightism: discrimination against the blind

sizeism: discrimination on the grounds of size, i.e. weight and/or height

smellism: discrimination on the grounds of body odour

smokeism: discrimination against smokers (by non-smokers)

uglyism: discrimination on the grounds of (supposed) unfavourable appearance

weightism: discrimination on the grounds of (excessive) weight

Pollyanna. The cheerfully optimistic young heroine of the novel named after her (1913) by Eleanor H. Porter (1868–1920). Her full name is Pollyanna Whittier, and she is known as the 'glad girl' for her determination to remain cheerful whatever happens. She is orphaned at the age of 11, and sent to live with a grim spinster aunt, but melts the hearts of everyone she meets, however sour and dour. Her name has entered the language to describe anyone who is unduly optimistic or who is able to remain happy through self-delusion.

I feel like an embarrassingly unfashionable Pollyanna when I admit that our family grinned our way through Central London and then had a wholly wonderful time.
LIBBY PURVES in *The Times* (4 January 2000)

Polytechnics. The former institutions of higher education originated from the Polytechnic Institution founded in London in 1838 for the exhibition of objects connected with the industrial arts, the name itself deriving from the Greek for 'many arts'. In 1989 the British 'polys' gained autonomy from local education authorities and in 1992 were able to call themselves universities. This led to a number of name changes, especially where there was an existing university, as at Birmingham, Leicester, Liverpool, Nottingham, Oxford and Sheffield. Some of the new names are noted below, the earlier name given in brackets.

De Montfort University (Leicester Polytechnic)

Liverpool John Moores University (Liverpool Polytechnic)

Nottingham Trent University (Nottingham Polytechnic)

Oxford Brookes University (Oxford Polytechnic)

Sheffield Hallam University (Sheffield Polytechnic)

Thames Valley University (Polytechnic of West London)

University of Central England in Birmingham (Birmingham Polytechnic)

University of Glamorgan (Polytechnic of Wales)

University of Greenwich (Thames Polytechnic)

University of Hertfordshire (Hatfield Polytechnic)

University of Northumbria at Newcastle (Newcastle Polytechnic)

University of Plymouth (Polytechnic South West, earlier Plymouth Polytechnic)

University of the West of England, Bristol (Bristol Polytechnic)

University of Westminster (Polytechnic of Central London)

Polythene Pam. A song by the BEATLES credited to John Lennon and Paul McCartney, part of the 'Long Medley' that originally appeared on the second side of the album ABBEY ROAD, released in September 1969. The 'Polythene Pam' of the title is one of the Beatles' original fans at the CAVERN CLUB in Liverpool who was apparently known for eating thermoplastic. In the song she is turned into a grotesque fetishist. On the album the song immediately follows MEAN MR MUSTARD and runs directly into 'She Came In Through The Bathroom Window'.

Pommy or **Pommie.** An Australian and New Zealand term for an Englishman, used both affectionately and disparagingly. The name is of uncertain origin. Evidence suggests that it arose as a blend of 'pomegranate' and 'immigrant', the former word referring to the ruddy complexions of the English. A less convincing explanation is that it was formed from the initials POME, 'Prisoner of Mother England', alluding to the transportation of English convicts to Australia. Expansions of the name are 'Pommy Bastard' and 'Whingeing Pom', the latter with reference to the supposed British national pastime of 'grousing'. The name first gained currency in the First World War.

Pomp and Circumstance. The collective title given by Edward Elgar (1857–1934) to five marches for orchestra, first performed separately between 1901 and 1930. The title comes from Shakespeare's *Othello* III.iii:

> Farewell the neighing steed and the shrill trump,
> The spirit-stirring drum, the ear-piercing fife,
> The royal banner, and all quality,
> Pride, pomp, and circumstance of glorious war!

With slight alterations, the trio section of the first march became the finale of Elgar's *Coronation Ode* (1902), with words by A.C. Benson beginning LAND OF HOPE AND GLORY. This was later published as a separate song under that title. The song is traditionally performed with audience participation at the LAST NIGHT OF THE PROMS and has also become associated with right-wing English nationalism.

Pontin's. The main rival to BUTLIN'S in the holiday camp business takes its name from its founder, Fred Pontin, who opened his first centre in 1946 on a former army training site at Brean Sands near Weston-super-Mare, Somerset. The staff are known as Bluecoats, as distinct from the Butlin's REDCOATS.

Pony car. An American term dating from the 1970s for a medium-sized car. The name originally applied specifically to certain small and sporty cars that were modelled on the Ford Mustang, the latter word of which suggested 'pony'.

Ponzi scheme. A type of investment fraud in which initial investors are paid off with funds taken from subsequent investors attracted by the prospect of sizeable profits. The term arose in the 1970s and takes its name from the American swindler Charles Ponzi, who devised such a scheme in 1919 and within six months had defrauded investors of more than $10 million.

Poo. Children's slang for excrement, dating from the 1950s and deriving from the involuntary exclamation on reacting to an unpleasant smell. From the 1980s 'poo' was also American student slang for champagne. Here the origin is in a shortening of 'shampoo', as an extension of 'sham', itself a 19th-century abbreviation of the name.

> Yes, I admit it, me, the ultimate party girl, was never a big fan of 'poo'. Indeed, in my experience, it always gave me the most frightful headache.
> TARA PALMER-TOMKINSON in *Sunday Times* (2 January 2000)

Poodle-faker. A term current at the turn of the 20th century for a man who cultivates female society, especially for purposes of personal advancement. The image is of one who poses like a poodle, a fashionable pet. The expression originated as army slang.

Poohsticks. A game originating from A.A. Milne's stories about WINNIE-THE-POOH. Players simultaneously drop sticks into the upstream side of a bridge over a stream or river. The winner is the player whose stick emerges first on the downstream side. Pooh originally played the game alone with two fir cones, one large and one small, but later switched to sticks because they were easier to mark. The sport has gained something of a cult status, especially among college students, and 'virtual' Poohsticks can be played on the INTERNET.

> Cambridge University's sports federation has been asked to recognize Poohsticks. ... Students want quarter Blue status and matches against Oxford.
> *The Times* (7 May 1999)

Poontang. Sexual activity, or a woman or women regarded solely in terms of this. The Americanism dates from the 1920s and is a corruption of French *putain*, 'prostitute'. The French word itself is ultimately related to English 'putrid'.

Pooper scooper. An implement for clearing up dog excrement, as a 'scoop' for its 'poop'. The expression is of American origin and dates from the 1970s.

Poor but honest. Penniless but principled; modest but moral. The words are familiar from the song 'She Was Poor But She Was Honest' popular among troops in the First World War. Its provenance and date are uncertain and its verses variable, but one version of the chorus is given below. The phrase itself is found much earlier, and in Shakespeare's *All's Well That Ends Well* (1602) Helena says, 'My friends were poor, but honest; so's my love' (I, iii).

It's the same the whole world over,
It's the poor wot gets the blame,
It's the rich wot gets the pleasure,
Ain't it all a bloomin' shame?

Poor little rich girl. A wealthy young woman whose fortune brings her no contentment. The phrase was famously applied by the press to the heiress Barbara Hutton (1912–79), whose life was a series of misfortunes after she inherited $10 million at the age of 21. It was already familiar, however, as the title of a film of 1917 starring Mary Pickford, and was later brought before the public by a film of 1936 based on it, starring Shirley Temple. Noël Coward also popularized the term:

Poor little rich girl,
You're a bewitched girl,
Better beware!
Laughing at danger,
Virtue a stranger,
Better take care!

NOËL COWARD: *On With the Dance*, 'Poor Little Rich Girl' (1925)

Pop art. A movement in painting and sculpture which began independently in Britain and the USA in the 1950s. It was largely a reaction against the self-centred seriousness of 'high art' and the remoteness of abstract art. The images were gaudy and vulgar, owing much to contemporary advertising and commercial packaging. 'Pop' refers as much to an explosiveness as to 'popular', and the first recorded use of the word in art is in a collage by Eduardo Paolozzi (b.1924) entitled *I Was a Rich Man's Plaything* (1947) which shows a gun firing 'POP!' at the sexy plaything in question. Other leading exponents are David Hockney (b.1937), Jasper Johns (b.1930), Robert Rauschenberg (b.1925), Roy Lichtenstein (1923–97) and, famously, Andy Warhol (1928–87). *See also* OP ART.

Popcorn movie. An undemanding film watched purely for amusement or diversion by a popcorn-eating audience, this confection being as transitorily satisfying or nutritious as the entertainment itself. The attribute can be attached to other media areas, such as 'popcorn television', 'popcorn press' or

'popcorn music'. The word itself has appropriate overtones of 'pop' or 'popular'.

Summer is more traditionally the 'idiot zone' in American cinemas when all the big popcorn movies clog up thousands of air-conditioned theatres.
heat (14–20 October 1999)

Popemobile. The special vehicle used by the pope on official visits. The first Popemobile was a white Toyota off-roader (*see* OFF-ROADING), introduced by Pope Paul VI in 1976. Pope John Paul II acquired a customized Mercedes 500 in 1997 and in 1999 used an open-top Cadillac DeVille while visiting St Louis in the United States. This last had escalator-type steps at the back, an elevated platform to raise the pontiff while waving to the crowds, and a revolving white leather papal throne. Later the same year the increasingly frail John Paul added a 'Pope-Kart' in the form of an adapted golf buggy to his range of Popemobiles for use both inside and outside the Vatican.

Popeye. The muscle-bound sailor man came into the cartoon world in 1919 when the American comic strip artist Elzie C. Segar created him for his classic *Thimble Theatre* strip. He was at first known as Ham Gravy, but was renamed with his familiar sobriquet in 1929. He gains his muscular might from the can of spinach that he carries with him. His girlfriend is the stick-like Olive Oyl. Popeye's first appearance in a film was in the Betty BOOP cartoon, *Popeye the Sailor* (1933). He has a unique, strangulated delivery, with catch lines such as 'Blow me down' or 'I eats my spinach', and his jaws are constantly clamped jauntily on his pipe, even when eating or speaking.

Pop group names. *See* ROCK GROUP NAMES.

Popmobility. One of many keep-fit fads of the late 20th century, in this case fashionable in the late 1970s and consisting of the performance of movements to pop music.

Pop one's clogs, To. To die. The incongruous euphemism is particularly favoured in the media and is typically used in light-hearted fashion by television presenters and disc jockeys. The image seems to be that of 'popping' (pawning) a person's clogs after their death. The expression itself is first recorded in the 1970s but probably dates from some time before this.

Poppins, Mary. The children's nanny who possesses magical powers in the stories by P.L. Travers, beginning with the one named after her (1934). She can not only slide *up* the banisters but walk into a picture, understand what dogs are saying and travel round the world in seconds. She was played by Julie Andrews in the film of 1964, also named after her. *See also* SUPERCALIFRAGILISTICEXPIALIDOCIOUS.

Poppy Day. After the First World War the Allies adopted the poppy as a symbol of sacrifice, both from its blood red colour and from its prominence on the fields of Flanders where many soldiers lost their lives. Poppy Day for this reason became a popular name for REMEMBRANCE DAY, when artificial poppies are worn. *See also* ARMISTICE DAY; BRITISH LEGION.

Popski's Private Army. A British raiding and reconnaissance force of about 120 men formed in October 1942 under Lieutenant Colonel Vladimir Peniakoff (1897–1951), who had previously worked with the Libyan Arab Force. He was familiarly known as 'Popski', and his men wore the initials PPA on their shoulders. He was born in Belgium of Russian parents, educated at Cambridge and resident in Egypt from 1924. Popski and a small element of his force, together with the Long Range Desert Group, reconnoitred the route by which Montgomery conducted his surprise attack around the Mareth Line, and subsequently operated in Italy and Austria.

Popsocks. Women's short stockings reaching up to the knee, fashionable in the 1990s and popularized by the actress Alicia Silverstone, who wore them in the film *Clueless* (1995). They are usually worn under trousers and are so called as they are easy to pop on and off, unlike full-length stockings.

> Perched precariously between the fishnet and bobby-sox camps comes the … pop sock, shown at Vivienne Westwood in unprepossessing turquoise.
> *The Times* (25 February 2000)

Popular Front. A political alliance of left-wing parties (communists, socialists, liberals, radicals and so on) against reactionary government, especially dictatorship. The idea of an anti-Fascist Popular Front was proposed by the Communist International in 1935 (*see* COMINTERN). Such a government was set up in Spain in 1936, but the Civil War (1936–9) soon followed. The French Popular Front government, set up by Léon Blum in 1936, ended in 1938.

Porgy and Bess. The pioneering work by George Gershwin (1898–1937) was the first opera written for an all-black cast. The libretto was by Du Bose Heyward and Ira Gershwin, and the numbers include the immortal 'Summertime'. The disabled Porgy competes with Crown for the favours of Bess, who, however, goes off to New York with Sportin' Life. Porgy kills Crown and pursues Bess. The work was first performed in 1935, and in 1955 it became the first American opera to be staged at La Scala, Milan. It has also been staged in Russia in 1955 and at Glyndebourne, Sussex, in 1988. It was filmed in 1959. Gershwin's will requires that all stage performances be given with an all-black cast.

Porkies. Lies, as rhyming slang from 'pork pies'. The London working-class expression suddenly became popular from the 1970s, when policemen in television programmes always seemed to be questioning suspects with lines such as, 'You wouldn't be telling me porkies, would you, son?'

> It's a pity, really, Lord Archer didn't go into show-business. He would have made a good luvvie and no one would have minded that he tells porkies.
> *The Times* (4 December 1999)

Porridge. A colloquial term for imprisonment, punning on earlier 'stir' as a slang word of Romany origin for prison while also referring to a supposedly typical prison breakfast. The expression, dating from the 1940s, was brought before a wider public as the title of a television SITCOM series of 1973–7 starring Ronnie Barker as the wily old London lag Norman Stanley Fletcher.

Portage scheme. A scheme designed to help children of pre-school age with learning or developmental difficulties. It involves parents and teachers working together to support the child in the home and takes its name from Portage, Wisconsin, where it originally evolved in 1978.

Porterhouse Blue. A satirical novel (1974) by Tom Sharpe (b.1928), set in the imaginary Cambridge college of Porterhouse, based (if only in name) on Peterhouse. The main plot concerns the political infighting between rival factions of academics over proposed changes to the running of the college, culminating in a furore over the succession to the position of head of the college. The irascible college porter, Skullion, stops at nothing to preserve tradition but is dismissed after 45 years' loyal service. Another strand of the plot charts the grotesque sexual efforts of Zipser, a frustrated postgraduate, which culminate in his seduction by his bedder and their subsequent incineration in an explosion caused by gas-filled condoms becoming stuck in a college chimney. The novel generally is a satire on Oxbridge rituals, with its paraphernalia of dons, porters, bedders (gyps), high-table dining and the like. A 'Porterhouse blue' is a cerebral stroke, such as is suffered by one of the principal characters at a critical moment, leading to a bizarre denouement. A television version (1987) by Malcolm Bradbury featured David Jason, who played Skullion to the hilt. *See also* BLOT ON THE LANDSCAPE.

Portillistas. A nickname given to supporters of the Conservative politician Michael Portillo (b.1953), modelled on Spanish terms such as Peronistas, supporters of Juan Perón, populist president of Argentina (1946–55, 1973–4), and SANDINISTAS, the left-wing guerrillas who took power in Nicaragua in 1979. Portillo's father was Spanish and fought on the Republican side in the Spanish Civil War. In contrast, Portillo is on the right of his party and was regarded as a dangerous threat to the leadership of John Major, in whose cabinet he served from 1992 until he lost his Enfield and Southgate seat in the 1997 general election. Portillo has subsequently attempted to present a more caring image and has admitted to homosexual experiences while a student at Cambridge. He returned to Parliament in November 1999, winning the seat of Kensington and Chelsea in a by-election, and became shadow chancellor in 2000. He is widely regarded as aiming to replace William Hague as leader of the Conservative Party. *See also* HATTONISTAS.

Portmeirion. This remarkable Italianate village near Porthmadog in northwest Wales, described variously as 'the last nobleman's folly', 'a Welsh Xanadu' and 'a home for fallen buildings', was the creation in the 1920s of the inspired Welsh architect Clough William-Ellis (1883–1978), a campaigner against the ever-encroaching spoliation of the natural landscape. He purchased the old mansion of Aber Ia here, added Castell Deudraeth and its grounds to the property, then began the transformation of the site into something on the lines of Portofino in northwest Italy. The locality is one of the showplaces of North Wales and its eccentricity made it an ideal setting for the cult television spy series *The Prisoner* (1967–8). The name of the village partly reflects that of Portofino itself, as well as of nearby Porthmadog, but also geographically identifies it as a port in the former county of Merioneth, Welsh *Meirionnydd*, now an administrative district in the county of Gwynedd.

Portnoy's Complaint. A novel (1969) by Philip Roth (b.1935). It is prefaced with a spoof definition of Portnoy's Complaint: 'A disorder in which strongly felt ethical and altruistic impulses are perpetually warring with extreme sexual longings, often of a perverse nature.' The main thrust of Alexander Portnoy's argument, outlined as a confession to his psychiatrist, concerns the repressive attitude of his mother, with whom he carried on into manhood a war of attrition (his main 'complaint'). His condition manifested itself in his compulsive masturbation as a boy (another 'complaint') and his subsequent obsession with having sex with Gentile women. With this novel, Roth claims that he finally managed to absorb his 'ideas about sex, guilt, childhood, about Jewish men and their Gentile women' into 'an overall fictional strategy'. A lacklustre and ill-judged film version (1972), starring Richard Benjamin, was directed by Ernest Lehman. *See also* HAND-REARED BOY.

Porton Down. The site on Salisbury Plain of the Ministry of Defence's Chemical and Biological Defence Establishment, which was set up in 1916 to develop and manufacture chemical weapons (including poison gas) for use by the British army in the First World War. Porton Down is now part of the MOD's Defence Evaluation and Research Agency.

Portrait of the Artist as a Young Man, A. An autobiographical novel (1916) by James Joyce (1882–1941), extracted from a long work called *Stephen Hero*, a fragment of which was published in 1944. Stephen Dedalus, the protagonist, is not Joyce, but his consciousness is the means through which the author filters the relationship between imagination and reality. The five chapters cover events from infancy to 1902, when Joyce made his first visit to Paris. The beginning is in the third person in what corresponds to the language of childhood. The narrative ends with diary entries of the artist, whose soul has been 'born' through experience. The title suggested that of Dylan Thomas's *A Portrait of the Artist as a Young Dog* (1940), a collection of autobiographical short stories. *See also* FIRST LINES OF NOVELS; ULYSSES.

Portsmouth Point. The rumbustious concert overture by William Walton (1902–83) was first performed in 1926. The work is based on a print by Thomas Rowlandson (1756–1827) depicting a crowded scene at the quayside.

Posh. This colloquial word meaning stylish or elegant is first recorded in *Punch* of 25 September 1918: 'Oh, yes, Mater, we had a posh time of it down there.' It is popularly said to be an acronym of 'port out, starboard home', referring to cabins on the north-facing, cooler side of ships on voyages between England and India, but this origin lacks substantiation. The source in an identical but now obsolete word for a dandy is a more plausible possibility and a contraction of 'polished' has also been proposed. The word is sometimes humorously pronounced to rhyme with 'gauche'.

Posh is also the nickname of Peterborough United football club, founded in 1934 from the remnants of Peterborough & Fletton United. There are various accounts purportedly explaining the name. The most widely accepted claims that supporters referred to the team as looking 'posh' when they kicked off in the Southern League against Gainsborough on 1 September 1934 wearing a new strip. According to another account, in 1921 the manager of Fletton United said that he wanted 'posh players for a posh new team' and the name stuck when Peterborough & Fletton United was established in 1923. But on its formal founding in 1934 Peterborough United gained professional status and 'posh' may thus actually derive from 'professional'.

Position paper. A written statement of views, attitudes or intentions. The American term originated in the 1960s and has its chief application in business and politics.

Positive thinking. The expedient of concentrating one's mind on the good and positive aspects of a matter in order to eliminate destructive attitudes and emotions. The expression comes from the title of Norman Vincent Peale's book *The Power of Positive Thinking* (1952).

Posslq. An acronym, pronounced 'possle-kew', of '*person of the opposite sex sharing living quarters*', as a euphemism for one half of an unmarried couple living together. The term was coined in 1979 by the US Census Bureau and despite its artificiality gained currency for a time.

Possum. The proprietary name of an electronic device that enables a disabled person to telephone or operate a keyboard. It was introduced in the early 1960s and was officially known as a patient-operated selector mechanism, the initial letters of which, POSM, were reinterpreted as Latin *possum*, 'I am able'.

Postcode. The British postal addressing system, consisting of a combination of letters and numbers, dates back to the division of London into postal districts in

the mid-19th century. These were denoted by letters representing compass points, as N for Northern, E for Eastern, and WC for West Central. Numerical suffixes were then added as a labour-saving device in the First World War to denote sub-districts, so that the Eastern District became E1, Bethnal Green Sub-District became E2 and Bow became E3. This system prevailed until after the Second World War, when a more sophisticated method was needed. Experiments based on Norwich from 1959 led to the decision to use an alphanumeric postcode. Despite considerable publicity, however, mail senders in the areas concerned proved reluctant to adopt the device. A revised system was accordingly introduced in Croydon in 1966 and proved more successful, so that by 1974 the whole of the UK had been allocated postcodes and Norwich had been recoded.

The postcode itself is now divided into two halves, the first being the inward code and the second the outward. In the postcode AL6 9QA, used for a small group of houses in New Place, Welwyn, Hertfordshire, AL indicates the postal area (St Albans), 6 indicates the postcode district within that area, 9 is the postcode sector within the district, and QA is the postman's 'walk'. *See also* ZIP CODE.

Post-It Notes. The handy adhesive notes of this name were the invention in 1975 of the American chemical engineer Art Fry, an employee of the company 3M. Annoyed by the fact that the scrap of paper he used to mark his hymn book kept falling out, he saw a solution in a bookmark with a light adhesive that would stay in place but that could be easily removed and reapplied. His 'Press and Peel Pads', as they were originally called, did not immediately catch on because people did not know what to do with them, but with the backing of his employers, who gave away sheets of the notes with instructions how to use them, his innovation was at last successfully launched in 1979.

Postman Always Rings Twice, The. A film thriller (1946) based on the book (1934) by James M. Cain (1892–1977) about the liaison between a hobo and a bored waitress, which culminates in the murder of the latter's husband. Also made into a play and an opera, the film version starred Lana Turner and John Garfield. It was remade in 1981, with a screenplay by David Mamet and starring Jessica Lange and Jack Nicholson. Cain offered two explanations for the title of this, his first novel. The first was that while he was writing the book the postman always rang his doorbell twice if he was bringing bills, but only once if he had personal mail. The second was that the postman would ring the bell twice if he was delivering one of Cain's manuscripts after it had been rejected by a publisher: this happened so often that when the postman finally rang just once, to signify that the work had been accepted, the author gratefully altered the title to celebrate the fact.

Postmodernism. A style and concept in the arts, architecture and criticism of the late 20th century, representing a departure from MODERNISM and having at its root a general distrust of grand theories and ideologies as well as suspicion of anything smacking of 'art'. The style is best seen in architecture, and one famous example is the Lloyd's Building in London, designed by Richard Rogers. Another is the AT&T skyscraper in New York, completed in 1984. Whereas the predominant style of modern architecture was formerly geometrical, functional and unornamented, postmodernist architecture borrows from many styles, especially the Classical, with playful, colourful and even intentionally vulgar use of decoration.

Post-traumatic stress disorder. A psychological disorder suffered by a person who has experienced a traumatic event such as a major disaster. The term was invented by American psychologists dealing with casualties of the VIETNAM War in the early 1970s. Disturbance of sleep and a constant vivid recall of the experience are typical symptoms, resulting in a dulled response to others and the outside world generally. The term is ponderous but more precise than the equivalent 'shell shock' of the First World War.

Potatohead. One of many terms for an idiot, in this case one whose head is as 'thick' as a potato.

Potato Jones. Captain D.J. Jones, who died in 1962 aged 92. In 1937, with his steamer *Marie Llewellyn* loaded with potatoes, he tried to run General Franco's blockade off Spain, but was prevented by a British warship. Two other blockade-running captains were called 'Ham-and-Egg' Jones and 'Corncob' Jones.

Potato Pete. A human figure in the form of a potato publicized in posters by the Ministry of Food in the Second World War with the aim of encouraging people to make the most of available vegetables. He had a fellow in Doctor Carrot. The London department store John Lewis held a 'Potato Christmas Fair' sponsored by Potato Pete in their bombed-out

premises in Oxford Street. Children received hot baked potatoes as they pledged, 'I promise as my Christmas gift to the sailors who have to bring us our bread that I will do all I can to eat home-grown potatoes instead'.

Pot Noodles. A proprietary name for a fast-food dish consisting of a plastic tub of flavoured noodles, which can be prepared for eating by adding hot water. The product dates from the late 1980s and was regarded as a step up from the existing ubiquitous but barely nutritious JUNK FOOD.

POTUS. *See* FDR.

Poujadistes. The supporters, chiefly shopkeepers and peasants, of Pierre Poujade (b.1920), a French bookseller who in the 1950s led a right-wing populist movement that campaigned against high taxes. He founded the Union de Défense des Commerçants et des Artisans (Union for the Defence of Traders and Artisans), and in the 1956 elections Poujadistes won 52 of the 595 seats in the National Assembly. In the 1958 elections, however, Poujadistes won no seats, and Poujadisme was a spent force.

Pound for a pound. 1lb for £1. A familiar cry of market traders for much of the 20th century, usually relating to the sale of fruit or vegetables. With the gradual dominance of decimal values in the last two decades, however, the euphonious enticement became ever rarer.

Pound the pavement, To. To walk the streets in search of work. An expression of American origin dating from the 1950s.

Pour on the coal, To. To speed up. The phrase is of American origin and alludes to the coal-burning fireboxes of railway engines. The application of the phrase can be figurative as well as literal.

Poverty trap. A situation arising when a person's increase in income is offset by a resultant loss in state benefits, so that they are no better off.

> Robert Carlyle stars as Gaz, the enterprising leader of a group of former steelworkers who aim to become Sheffield's answer to the Chippendales and escape the poverty trap.
> *The Times* (24 December 1999)

Powder one's nose, To. To go to the lavatory, one of many euphemistic phrases for the action, here (usually) applicable to a woman, who might well literally powder her nose among other cosmetic adjustments while in the place in question. The expression, dating from the 1920s, is now rather old-fashioned but 'powder room' is still sometimes found as a term for a women's lavatory.

Powellism. The political and economic policies advocated by the controversial Conservative politician Enoch Powell (1912–98), especially that of restricting or terminating the immigration of people into Britain. In 1968 Powell lost his Conservative shadow cabinet post as a result of his infamous 'Rivers of Blood' speech, in which he argued that Britain was building 'its own funeral pyre' by allowing such people to claim British citizenship through their Commonwealth status.

Power dressing. A style of dressing for work and business in such a way that an impression of efficiency and self-assurance is conveyed. The term is applied more to women than to men, and can further the intention of breaking through the GLASS CEILING. *See also* POWER SUIT.

> Power dressing is definitely out, open shirts and chinos in. This has filtered through to many organisations where Friday is now casual day.
> *Sunday Express* (27 February 2000)

Power lunch. A working lunch at which top-level business or political discussions are held. The devoting of one's meal or leisure hours to business came to be regarded by many Americans in the 1980s as a symbol of commercial or political success. A 'power nap', as a brief daytime sleep in the working day, bestows a similar status, and the high-flying lifestyle also involves POWER DRESSING.

> The power lunch we all know about, and very passé it is too. These days any Manhattan style maven worth her expense account is probably spending her lunch hours having a power peel.
> *The Times* (20 September 1999)

Power Ranger. The proprietary name of a plastic toy figure resembling a character from the American children's television series *Mighty Morphin Power Rangers* (1993–6), about five teenagers able to 'morph' (transmute) into kung-fu superheroes to do battle with evil ALIENS.

Power-sharing. A key term in the political lexicon of Northern Ireland's TROUBLES, denoting the sharing of power between the province's Unionist and Nationalist communities and referring specifically to attempts to create a devolved government for Northern Ireland

in the early 1970s. The SUNNINGDALE AGREEMENT of December 1973 included provisions for a power-sharing executive, and the Northern Ireland Executive Council, a coalition of Protestants and Catholics including representatives from all Northern Ireland's political parties and led by the Ulster Unionist leader Brian Faulkner, took office in 1974. However, it was rejected soon afterwards by the ULSTER UNIONIST PARTY and was eventually brought down six months later after a strike by the Protestant Ulster Workers' Council (organized with the connivance of hardline PAISLEYITES and Loyalist PARAMILITARIES) had paralyzed Northern Ireland. DIRECT RULE from Westminster was then reimposed.

Power suit. A woman's tailored business suit, conventionally with shoulder pads and a knee-length skirt, the former intended to give the outfit a more masculine outline. Such suits were in favour in the 1980s and early 1990s and were an essential part of the fashion for POWER DRESSING.

> The key points of the futuristic look ... all look great in the office and have become as much a sartorial code for the 'successful and self-assured business woman' as the red power suit ever was.
> *The Times* (9 October 1999)

Power to the people. The slogan of the BLACK PANTHERS from 1969, subsequently adopted by other groups. It echoes the call of the Petrograd workers in the months before the Russian Revolution, 'All power to the Soviets!'

Prague Spring. The brief period of liberalizing and democratizing reform in Czechoslovakia in 1968 after Alexander Dubček (1921–92) became first secretary of the Communist Party (January 1968). The reforms were dismantled following the invasion of Soviet-led WARSAW PACT forces on the night of 20–21 August 1968. Prague was the capital of Czechoslovakia (and is now the capital of the Czech Republic), while 'spring' suggests an ending of COLD WAR oppression and echoes the short-lived liberalizing 'thaw' in the USSR under Nikita Khrushchev in the late 1950s.

Praise the Lord and pass the ammunition. A phrase from the Second World War, said to have been used by an American naval chaplain during the Japanese attack on PEARL HARBOR, although the actual identity of the chaplain has since been in dispute. One candidate is Lieutenant Howell M. Forgy; another is Captain William H. Maguire. It was made the subject of a popular song by Frank Loesser in 1942. It is said to date from the American Civil War (1861–5).·

Prang. RAF slang in the Second World War meaning to bomb a target with evident success, to shoot down another or to crash one's own aircraft, and generally to collide with, or bump into, any vehicle. Hence, also, 'wizard prang', for an accurate hit or other successful strike. According to Eric Partridge in *A Dictionary of RAF Slang* (1945), the word may be a blend of 'paste' and 'bang', but it is more likely to be simply imitative.

Pravda. A play (1985) by the British playwrights Howard Brenton (b.1942) and David Hare (b.1947) depicting the unprincipled behaviour of Lambert Leroux, a South African newspaper magnate, after he buys up two daily British newspapers. The play profited from the parallels that could be drawn with the media empires of Robert Maxwell and Rupert Murdoch, and it offered a bleak picture of how the truth can be manipulated by egocentric press barons. The title *Pravda* is an ironic reference to the Russian newspaper of the same name (meaning 'truth' in Russian), in which the propagandist influence over what was printed during the Soviet era was obvious even to the casual reader.

Precious Bane. A rural novel (1924) by Mary Webb (1881–1927), featuring a heroine, Prudence Sarn, who is disfigured by a hare-lip, as was the author herself. The plot abounds with romance and melodrama. The title, from John Milton's *Paradise Lost* (1667), has a rustic ring:

> Let none admire
> That riches grow in hell; that soil may best
> Deserve the precious bane.
> Bk I

The book received posthumous publicity when the then prime minister, Stanley Baldwin, praised it at a Royal Literary Society dinner in 1928. Stella Gibbons wrote a parody of it, COLD COMFORT FARM.

Premonition of Civil War. One of the more repellent paintings of Salvador Dalí (1904–89), this bears the alternative title *Soft Construction with Boiled Beans*. It was painted in 1936, the year that the Spanish Civil War broke out. The composition largely consists of two humanoid constructions made of various limbs and other body parts. The lower figure is fiercely squeezing the breast of the grimacing upper figure, while various pieces of soft offal lie around, along

with the eponymous beans. Dalí's support for Franco in the Civil War led to his expulsion from the SUR-REALIST movement in 1938. As Herbert Read commented 30 years later: '[His] theatricality … is now at the service of those reactionary forces in Spain whose triumph had been the greatest affront to humanism which, in spite of all its extravagance, had been the consistent concern of the surrealist movement.'

Preppy. Stylish in dress or appearance, like the aspirational students at an American prep school, the equivalent of a British public school. The vogue reached its height in the early 1980s, its connotations promoted by Lisa Birnbach's *The Preppy Handbook* (1981). *See also* SLOANE RANGER.

> He is variously described as 'Ivy League' or 'preppy' and he is instantly recognized by his blue button-down Oxford cloth shirt, navy blazer, club tie and penny loafers. He might be viewed as an American Hooray Henry, except that he is quietly-spoken, excessively polite and never throws muffins.
> *Independent* (12 March 1988)

Presidium. In the former USSR the Presidium of the Supreme Soviet was a body elected by the Supreme Soviet to fulfil the role of constitutional head of the state. Its chairman was its representative in ceremonial affairs and it issued ordinances when the Supreme Soviet was not in session. Apart from its chairman, it consisted of 15 deputies (one for each of the republics), a secretary and 20 members. The term itself was adopted from Latin *praesidium*, 'garrison'. *See also* POLITBURO.

Press the flesh, To. To shake hands, especially formally or repeatedly.

> Donald Trump, a self-confessed 'germ freak' who once wrote of his loathing for handshakes, will have to press a lot of flesh in the coming months.
> *The Times* (21 October 1999)

Press the panic button, To. *See* PANIC BUTTON.

Prestel. The proprietary name of a computerized visual information system introduced in the late 1970s as a form of teletext. It was pioneered by BT (British Telecommunications) and enabled data selected from one or more databases to appear on a television screen by dialling the appropriate telephone number. The word presumably combined 'press', or perhaps 'presto', with 'telephone' or 'television'.

Pretty as a picture. Very pretty. A pretty person or thing will often be depicted with an idealized prettiness in a painting. The expression is American and dates from the turn of the 20th century.

Pretty please. An intensified form of 'please', implying a request made deliberately decorously or even decoratively, as if 'gift-wrapped'. The somewhat cloying phrase dates from the 1950s.

Price is right, The. The price is reasonable; whatever is being sold is good value. The phrase was the title of a popular television GAME SHOW screened from 1984 to 1988, in which members of the public had to guess the retail price of various consumer goods. Whoever came closest to the correct amount won the object in question.

Pricksongs and Descants. A collection of fictions (1969) by Robert Coover (b.1932). It contains ten of his earlier stories, tellings from new perspectives of traditional tales and pieces exploring the multiple possibilities of fiction. A pricksong is an archaic term for a piece of music written down or 'pricked'.

Primal scene. A term for the first time that a young child is emotionally aware of his parents having sexual intercourse. The expression originated with Sigmund Freud and became familiar in English from James Strachey's translation of Freud's work (1925).

Primal scream therapy. A type of psychotherapy in which patients, often in groups, are encouraged to scream and behave violently to relive birth and the sufferings of infancy and to express aggressive emotions about their parents. The treatment was developed by the American psychologist Arthur Janov and named by him in his book *The Primal Scream* (1970).

Prime Minister of Mirth. The billboard byname of the music-hall entertainer George Robey (originally George Edward Wade) (1869–1954), given when he was well established in his career. The analogy is perhaps not so much with a political prime minister as with a person supremely skilled in ministering (i.e. providing) laughter.

> He was billed later on as 'The Prime Minister of Mirth', but prime ministers are the dominant figures of democracies, ruling by persuasion. Robey could more accurately have been called the dictator of laughter, so firmly did he grip and subdue his audiences.
>
> IVOR BROWN in *Twentieth-Century Dictionary of National Biography*, Vol 6 (1951–60)

Prime of Miss Jean Brodie, The. A novel (1961) by Muriel Spark (b.1918), set, and reflecting her upbringing, in Edinburgh. It recounts the long-term influence on five impressionable schoolgirls of Jean Brodie, their stylish teacher in the junior department of the Marcia Blane School during the 1930s. There have been both film (1969) and television versions. *See also* MORNINGSIDE.

> 'Next year,' she said, 'you will have the specialists to teach you history and mathematics and languages, a teacher for this and a teacher for that, a period of forty-five minutes for this and another for that. But in this your last year with me you will receive the fruits of my prime. They will remain with you all your days.'
>
> ch i

Prime Suspect. A gripping television thriller series by Lynda La Plante first screened in 1991. The plot focused on the sexism that cramped the career of the ambitious CID officer DCI Jane Tennison in her pursuit of high-profile crimes, among them a serial prostitute murderer and a case of paedophilia. The series owed much of its success to the genius of Helen Mirren as Tennison.

Prime time. The time of day when a radio or television audience is expected to be at its greatest. For television this is usually mid-evening. The concept is American and dates from the 1960s.

Primordial soup. A scientific name dating from the 1950s for the solution rich in organic compounds which is thought to have formerly made up the oceans or lakes of the Earth and to have been the environment in which cellular life originated.

> We can't say why the elements in the primordial soup knitted themselves into DNA any more than the ancient Egyptians could say where the Sun went at night.
>
> *The Times* (24 December 1999)

Prince of Darkness. A nickname for any dubious or 'shady' character, especially if dark haired or swarthy. The source is ultimately biblical, with a reference to Satan: 'For we wrestle … against principalities, against powers, against the rulers of the darkness of this world' (Ephesians 6:21). The precise phrase occurs in Shakespeare: 'The black prince, sir; *alias*, the prince of darkness; *alias*, the devil' (*All's Well That Ends Well*, IV.v, 1601). In modern times it has been applied, among others, to Douglas Haig (1861–1928), commander-in-chief of British forces in France in the First World War, for his strategy that led to the loss of so many men's lives (the slaughter on the SOMME led to his being dubbed 'the Butcher'); to Richard N. Perle (b.1941) assistant secretary of defence from 1981 to 1987 in the Reagan administration, for his hostility to the Soviet Union; and, a shade more lightly, to the Labour politician Peter Mandelson (b.1953), trade and industry minister under Tony Blair in 1998, a post from which he resigned when a loan from the paymaster-general was disclosed (*see* MANDY). More trivially, the name has also been used of the American television chat-show host Johnny Carson (b.1925), simply because his programme went out at night.

Princess Diana. *See* PEOPLE'S PRINCESS.

Princeton Plan. In the USA a plan to give college students a recess, usually of two weeks, in an election year in order to enable them to work for the election candidate of their choice. It was first implemented in the early 1970s at Princeton University, New Jersey. This same university had pioneered another Princeton Plan in the 1960s, as a scheme to achieve racial balance in public schools by pairing a school of mainly white students with one of black students, so that all students in certain grades attended the same school.

Prisoner of conscience. A person imprisoned or detained because of their political or religious beliefs, where these run counter to the official line of the state in which they live. The term was made familiar following its adoption by AMNESTY INTERNATIONAL in the early 1960s.

> Burmese officials freed a three-year-old girl described as the world's youngest prisoner of conscience, Amnesty International said. ... She was held for five days.
> *The Times* (30 July 1999)

Private eye. A private detective. 'Eye' as a term for a detective dates from the 19th century, and an all-seeing eye was adopted as the badge of Pinkerton's National Detective Agency, founded in 1855. The British satirical magazine *Private Eye*, founded in 1961, gave the phrase further familiarity.

Private Lives. A play (1930) by the British playwright Noël Coward (1899–1973) about two divorcés, Elyot and Amanda, who find themselves staying in the same hotel on their honeymoons following their marriages to new partners. The film version (1931), which was somewhat lifeless, starred Robert Montgomery and Norma Shearer. The title occurs early in the first act when Amanda reflects upon the nature of normality:

> I think very few people are completely normal really,

deep down in their private lives. It all depends upon a combination of circumstances. If all the various cosmic thingummys fuse at the same moment, and the right spark is struck, there's no telling what one mightn't do.

Prix Goncourt. The most prestigious French literary prize, awarded by the *Académie des Goncourt*, founded in 1902 under the will of the novelist Edmond de Goncourt (1822–96). The annual prize, first awarded in 1903, is given to what is judged to be the best imaginative prose work of the year, a verdict not always justified by posterity but nevertheless usually generating good sales. Winners have included Marcel Proust, *À l'ombre des jeunes filles en fleurs* (1919), André Malraux, *La Condition humaine* (1933), Marguerite Duras, *L'Amant* (1984) and Pascale Roze, *Le Chasseur Zéro* (1996). The award was declined by Julien Gracq for *Le Rivage des Syrtes* (1951) and by Vintila Horia for *Dieu est né en exil* (1960).

Proactive. 'Making things happen'. This BUZZWORD of the 1990s, typically in a management or business context, originated in the 1930s as the converse of 'reactive', as applied to someone who, instead of reacting to a situation, anticipates it (Greek *pro*, 'before') and takes action to create or control it.

> Elle Macpherson takes a proactive approach to protecting her privacy. Spotting a shoal of photographers on her Ibizan beach, the model started hurling stones until they left.
> *The Times* (9 August 1999)

Product placement. A practice whereby firms use films or photo sessions to promote their products or services, either visually or, in the case of films, by inclusion in the dialogue. The ploy arose in the 1980s, an early classic example being the promotion of Reese's Pieces in *E.T.* (1982), resulting in a tripling of sales for these sweets, produced by the makers of the HERSHEY BAR. (Universal Studios had originally suggested to the makers of the MARS BAR that a trail of their M&M chocolate buttons lead the alien out of the brush, but the company had turned down the proposal.) Later 'plugs' were for the American 'Taco Bell' restaurant chain in *Demolition Man* (1993) and 'Red Stripe' beer in *The Firm* (1993). *See also* SOAP OPERA.

> A close-up of my face, a hand entering the frame to slip on a pair of black Ray-Bans (an instance of well-paid product placement).
> BRET EASTON ELLIS: *Glamorama*, Pt 4, ch xxxii (1998)

Professional foul. In football a deliberate foul committed, usually as a last resort, to prevent an opponent from scoring. The euphemism was greeted with widespread derision when it first became public in the 1970s. The term can also be applied to a similar tactic in business or politics. Tom Stoppard's television play *Professional Foul* (1977) tells what happens when an academic attending a conference in Prague is asked by a former student to smuggle a manuscript out to the free world. The metaphor of the play, as well as its title, came specifically from the football international that was being played in the city.

Professor Challenger. *See* CHALLENGER, PROFESSOR.

Profumo Affair. The most extensive political scandal in Britain in the postwar years takes its name from the Conservative politician John Profumo (b.1915), secretary of state for war under Harold Macmillan (*see* MAC THE KNIFE). Rumours began circulating that he was consorting with a teenage prostitute, Christine Keeler (b.1942), mistress of the Soviet assistant naval attaché, Yevgeny Ivanov (1926–94). In March 1963 Profumo assured the House of Commons that there was no truth in the allegation, but three months later he confessed that he had lied and resigned his seat. The doubts cast upon the efficiency of the security service almost resulted in the downfall of the government. *See also* MONSTER RAVING LOONY PARTY.

Programming languages. Even the non-computerate will be familiar with many of the names of languages used for writing computer programs. FORTRAN was the first, invented in 1956. It appears below together with a selection of more recent names, most of them acronyms.

Ada: from Ada Augusta King, Countess of Lovelace (1815–52), daughter of the poet Lord Byron, who became assistant to the machine computing pioneer Charles Babbage (1791–1871) and worked with him on his early mechanical model

ALGOL: acronym of *algo*rithmic *l*anguage or *alge*braic *o*riented *l*anguage

BASIC: acronym of *b*eginners' *a*ll-purpose *s*ymbolic *i*nstruction *c*ode, punning on 'basic'

C: developed from *B*, short for *BCPL*, abbreviation of *b*asic *c*omputer *p*rogramming *l*anguage

COBOL: acronym of *c*ommon *b*usiness-*o*riented *l*anguage

FORTRAN: acronym of *for*mula *tran*slation

LISP: acronym of *lis*t *p*rocessing

PASCAL: acronym of French *p*rogramme *a*ppliqué à la *s*élection et la *c*ompilation *au*tomatique de la *litt*érature ('program for the selection and automatic compilation of literature'), but also from the name of the French mathematician and physicist Blaise Pascal (1623–62)

PL/1: abbreviation of *p*rogram *l*anguage 1

PROLOG: acronym of *pro*gramming in *log*ic, punning on 'prologue'

Prohibition. The prevention by law of the manufacture and sale of alcohol in the United States from 1919 to 1933. The legislation ultimately arose out of the intense religious revivalism of the 1820s and 1830s but was more immediately aimed at improving efficiency in the workplace and reducing the level of corruption in saloons. Prohibition brought the bootlegger into being as a new kind of criminal, epitomized by the career of the notorious Al CAPONE.

> This is the time to acquire your Wines and Liquors. Prices are advancing daily and will continue to advance whether Prohibition becomes effective July 1, 1919, or January 20, 1920.
> *New York Times* (advertisement) (4 May 1919)

PROLOG. *See* PROGRAMMING LANGUAGES.

Prom queen. The most outstanding girl or young woman at a prom, a dance held by a high school class at the end of the academic year in American schools. Stephen King's first novel *Carrie* (1974) concerns a gawky 16-year-old girl who is elected prom queen as a malicious prank but who uses her supernatural powers to exact her revenge on her tormentors.

Propeller-head. A person with an obsessive interest in computers or technology. The reference is to a BEANIE hat with a propeller on top, as popularized by SCIENCE FICTION enthusiasts and as actually worn by some children. The propeller suggests that the wearer has some sort of cerebral 'lift-off' or specialized technical knowledge. The term became current in the 1990s.

> They call them propeller-heads – that small band of flight simulator fanatics who sit night after night with the eerie glow of screens on their faces, flying their computers to goodness knows where from goodness knows where.
> *The Times* (24 February 1999)

Prop up the bar, To. To drink alone at the bar of a public house. 'Prop' refers to the bar as supporting the drinker, rather than the drinker the bar.

Protocols of the Elders of Zion. *See under* FAKES.

Provos. A nickname for members of the Provisional IRA, a faction favouring terrorist action that broke away from the 'Official' IRA in 1969. The name was probably patterned on *provo*, from French *provocateur*, as a term for a member of a group of young Dutch activists in the 1960s. The name 'Provisional IRA' derives from the Dublin EASTER RISING of 1916, when Irish Republicans rose against the British and proclaimed a 'provisional government'. For Irish Republicans, therefore, the name created a link between the present-day IRA and their 'heroes' of 1916. The Provisionals are also referred to as Provies (this has a slightly softer nuance than Provos) or occasionally as 'pinheads'. *See also* STICKIES.

Prozac. A trade name for fluoxetine, a drug used to treat depression by inhibiting the uptake of serotonin in the brain. It first went on the market in 1987 and rapidly became the 'wonder drug' of the decade. Its proponents believe that its ability to enhance confidence, self-image and energy levels outweigh its known side-effects, which include nausea, diarrhoea and sexual dysfunction.

Psammead, The. The sand fairy created by E. Nesbit for her children's books *Five Children and It* (1902), 'It' being the fairy, and *The Story of the Amulet* (1906). The Psammead is an unattractive creature, with a fat furry body, bat-like ears and eyes on stalks. It is also bad-tempered, but it can at least grant wishes. In the former book, this creates chaos, while in the latter the Psammead's powers permit the children to travel back in time to ancient Egypt and Babylon. The Psammead's name comes from Greek *psammos*, 'sand'.

Pseud. A pretentious person or poseur. The term, an abbreviation of 'pseudo', became a BUZZWORD in the 1960s, partly because of its use by the magazine *Private Eye*, whose long-running column *Pseud's Corner* reprints instances of pretentiousness. This latter phrase is also used as a general label for anything regarded as absurdly exaggerated or overwrought.

> Occasionally out of nowhere comes a band bursting at the seams with great songs. A band that prompts the average critic to make a determined bid for a place in Pseud's Corner.
> *The Times* (16 October 1999)

Pseudonyms. The 20th century can with some justification be called the Age of the Pseudonym, especially in the worlds of popular fiction, the cinema, the theatre and pop music. The crime novelist John Creasey (1908–73) generously exemplifies the phenomenon, with two dozen pen-names for different novels and genres: Gordon Ashe, Margaret Cooke, M.E. Cooke, Norman Deane, Elise Fecamps, Robert Caine Frazer, Patrick Gill, Michael Halliday, Charles Hogarth, Brian Hope, Colin Hughes, Kyle Hunt, Abel Mann, Peter Manton, J.J. Marric, James Marsden, Richard Martin, Rodney Mattheson, Antony Morton, Ken Ranger, William K. Reilly, Tex Riley, Henry St John and Jeremy York. Pseudonyms can be counted in thousands but the following is a selection of just 100 of the most familiar of the century, together with their (usually less well-known) originals. *See also* LARRY PARNES'S STABLE OF STARS.

Woody Allen, US actor (b.1935): Allan Stewart Konigsberg

Julie Andrews, English actress (b.1935): Julia Elizabeth Wells

Fred Astaire, US dancer and actor (1899–1987): Frederick Austerlitz

Charles Atlas, US bodybuilder (1893–1972): Angelo Siciliano

Lauren Bacall, US actress (b.1924): Betty Joan Perske

Anne Bancroft, US actress (b.1931): Anna Maria Luisa Italiano

Jack Benny, US comedian (1894–1974): Benjamin Kubelsky

Cilla Black, English television presenter (b.1943): Priscilla Maria Veronica White

Dirk Bogarde, British actor and writer (1921–99): Derek Gentron Gaspart Ulric van den Bogaerde

Mark Bolan, British pop musician (1947–77): Mark Feld

Bourvil, French comic actor (1917–70): André Raimbourg

David Bowie, English rock musician (b.1947): David Robert Hayward-Jones

Boy George, English pop singer (b.1961): George Alan O'Dowd

Bricktop, US cabaret singer (1894–1984): Ada Beatrice Queen Victoria Louise Virginia Smith

Elkie Brooks, English popular singer (b.1946): Elaine Bookbinder

Anthony Burgess, English novelist (1917–93): John Burgess Wilson

Richard Burton, Welsh actor (1925–84): Richard Walter Jenkins

Red Buttons, US comic actor (b.1918): Aaron Schwatt

Marti Caine, English singer and entertainer (1945–95): Lynda Denise Ives, née Crapper

Michael Caine, English actor (b.1933): Maurice Joseph Micklewhite

Cantinflas, Mexican clown, bullfighter, comic actor (1911–93): Mario Moreno Reyes

Diahann Carroll, US singer and actress (b.1935): Carol Diann Johnson

Jasper Carrott, English comedian (b.1945): Robert Davies

Christopher Caudwell, English writer (1907–37): Christopher St John Sprigg

Blaise Cendrars, French writer (1887–1961): Frédéric Louis Sauser

Cyd Charisse, US actress (b.1921): Tula Ellice Finklea

Chubby Checker, US pop musician (b.1941): Ernest Evans

Judy Chicago, US artist (b.1939): Judy Cohen

Upton Close, US journalist and writer (1894–1960): Josef Washington Hall

Nat 'King' Cole, US jazz musician (1919–65): Nathaniel Adams Coles

Robbie Coltrane, Scottish television actor (b.1950): Anthony Robert McMillan

Russ Conway, English popular pianist (b.1927): Trevor Herbert Stanford

Alice Cooper, US rock singer (b.1945): Vincent Damon Furnier

Truman Capote, US writer (1924–84): Truman Streckfus Persons

Elvis Costello, British rock singer (b.1954): Declan MacManus

Joan Crawford, US actress (1904–77): Lucille Fay Le Sueur

Tony Curtis, US actor (b.1925): Bernard Schwartz

Clemence Dane, English writer (1888–1965): Winifred Ashton

Skeeter Davis, US country singer (b.1931): Mary Frances Penick

Doris Day, US actress and singer (b.1924): Doris von Kappelhoff

Chris De Burgh, Irish-born British popular singer (b.1948): Christopher John Davidson

Bo Diddley, US jazz musician (b.1928): Otha Ellas Bates, later McDaniel

Marlene Dietrich, German-born US actress (1901–92): Maria Magdalene Dietrich von Losch

Diana Dors, English actress (1931–84): Diana Mary Fluck

Fifi D'Orsay, Canadian-born US actress (1904–83): Angelina Yvonne Cecil Lussier D'Sablon

Kirk Douglas, US actor (b.1916): originally Issur Danielovitch, then Isidore Demsky

O. Douglas, Scottish writer (1875–1940): Anna Buchan

Fabia Drake, British actress (1904–90): Ethel McGlinchy

Bob Dylan, US rock musician (b.1941): Robert Allen Zimmerman

Adam Faith, English pop singer and actor (b.1940): Terence Nelhams

Georgie Fame, English pop singer (b.1943): Clive Powell

M.J. Farrell, Irish writer (1904–96): Mary ('Molly') Nesta Keane, née Skrine

Fernandel, French comic actor (1903–71): Fernand-Joseph-Désiré Contandin

Stepin Fetchit, US actor (1902–85): Lincoln Theodore Monroe Andrew Perry

Gracie Fields, English popular singer (1898–1979): Grace Stansfield (*see also* OUR GRACIE)

W.C. Fields, US comic actor (1879–1946): William Claude Dukinfield

Margot Fonteyn, English ballerina (1919–91): Margaret Hookham

Greta Garbo, Swedish-born US actress (1905–90): Greta Lovisa Gustafsson

Cary Grant, English actor (1904–86): Alexander Archibald Leach

David Hamilton, English radio and television compère (b.1939): David Pilditch

Jean Harlow, US actress (1911–37): Harlean Carpentier

James Herriot, English writer (1916–95): James Alfred Wight

Jack Higgins, English writer (b.1929): Henry Patterson

Billie Holiday, US jazz singer (1915–59): Eleanora Gough McKay, née Fagan

Buddy Holly, US rock musician (1936–59): Charles Hardin Holley (*see also* AMERICAN PIE)

Rock Hudson, US actor (1925–85): Roy Harold Fitzgerald, originally Roy Scherer

Engelbert Humperdinck, English pop singer (b.1936): Arnold George Dorsey

Elton John, English pop musician (b.1947): Reginald Kenneth Dwight

Tom Jones, Welsh popular singer (b.1940): Thomas Jones Woodward

Boris Karloff, English actor (1887–1969): William Henry Pratt

Penelope Keith, English actress (b.1940): Penelope Timson, née Hatfield

Alexander Korda, Hungarian-born British film producer (1893–1956): Sándor László Kellner

Veronica Lake, US actress (1919–73): Constance Frances Marie Ockleman

Dorothy Lamour, US actress (1914–96): Dorothy Mary Leta Lambour, earlier Slaton

Lupino Lane, British comic actor (1892–1959): Henry Lane George Lupino

Mario Lanza, Italian-born US opera singer (1921–59): Alfredo Cocozza

John Le Carré, English writer (b.1931): David John Moore Cornwell

Vanessa Lee, English actress and singer (1920–92): Winifred Ruby Moule

Sophia Loren, Italian actress (b.1934): Sofia Scicolone

Lulu, Scottish popular singer, television presenter (b.1948): Marie McDonald McLaughlin Lawrie

Vera Lynn, English popular singer (b.1917): Vera Margaret Welch

Hugh MacDiarmid, Scottish poet (1892–1978): Christopher Murray Grieve

Marilyn MONROE, US actress (1926–62): Norma Jeane Dougherty, née Mortensen, later Baker

Ivor Novello, Welsh actor and playwright (1893–1951): David Ivor Davies

Maureen O'Hara, Irish-born US actress (b.1920): Maureen FitzSimons

Patti Page, US pop singer (b.1927): Clara Ann Fowler

Nicola Pagett, English actress (b.1945): Nicola Mary Scott

Jean Plaidy, British novelist (1906–93): Eleanor Alice Hibbert, née Burford

Ted Ray, English comedian (1905–77): Charles Olden

Miss Read, English writer (b.1913): Dora Jessie Saint, née Shafe

Mary Renault, British writer (1905–83): Eileen Mary Challans

Frank Richards, English writer (1875–1961): Charles Hamilton (*see also* BUNTER, BILLY)

Roy Rogers, US actor (1912–98): Leonard Franklin Slye

Sax Rohmer, English writer (1886–1959): Arthur Sarsfield Ward

Omar Sharif, Egyptian actor (b.1932): Michael Shalhoub

Alvin Stardust, English rock singer (b.1942): Bernard William Jewry

Sophie Tucker, US actress (1884–1966): Sophia Abuza, originally Kalish

Arthur M. Winfield, US writer (1863–1930): Edward L. Stratemeyer

John Wyndham, English writer (1903–69): John Wyndham Parkes Lucas Beynon Harris

Ximenes, English crossword compiler (1902–71): Derrick Somerset Macnutt

See also BARA, THEDA; JAVAL, CAMILLE; LENIN; ORWELL, GEORGE; SAKI.

Psion. The proprietary name of a make of palmtop computer, as an acronym of Potter Scientific Instruments plus '-on' as a flourish, the company set up in 1980 by David Potter, originally a designer of computer games. 'Psion' itself happens also to be a scientific term for a psi particle.

Psmith. The eccentric young snob created by P.G. Wodehouse for a series of stories, and first appearing in a boys' paper, the *Captain*, in 1908. His full name is Rupert (or Ronald) Eustace Smith, and the initial P is an affectation, as is the monocle he sports. Although educated at Eton, he claims to be a socialist and calls everyone 'Comrade'. He is the leading character in three novels, *Psmith in the City* (1910), *Psmith Journalist* (1910) and *Leave it to Psmith* (1923), in the last of which he visits Blandings Castle and makes the acquaintance of Lord EMSWORTH. Wodehouse based Psmith on Rupert D'Oyly Carte (1876–1948), son of Richard D'Oyly Carte, the impresario and producer of Gilbert and Sullivan operas.

Psychedelic. The term relating to hallucinogenic drugs such as LSD was on the lips of many in the 1960s but was coined in 1956 in a letter to Aldous Huxley by Humphry Osmond, a British research scientist, then living in Canada. It represents Greek *psukhé*, 'mind', and *dēlos*, 'clear', since he regarded such drugs as 'enriching the mind and enlarging the vision'. Purists argued that 'psychodelic' would have been a better formation. The BEATLES album SERGEANT PEPPER'S LONELY HEARTS CLUB BAND (1967) was described at the time as 'psychedelic' music but the word came to be mostly used as a general term for anything perceived as remotely avant-garde.

Psycho. A suspenseful film (1960) adapted by Joseph Stefano from a novel by Robert Bloch about the deranged Norman BATES, a psychopath (hence the title) who murders visitors to the Bates Motel that he runs. Arguably the most famous of all Alfred Hitchcock's thrillers, it is best remembered for the much-imitated scene in which Janet Leigh is knifed to death in a shower. It spawned two lesser sequels, both starring Anthony Perkins, who played Norman in Hitchcock's original.

> Alfred Hitchcock: Don't give away the ending – it's the only one we have!

Psychobabble. A derogatory term for the jargon of popular psychology, especially as used by lay people with regard to their own personality or relationships. The word dates from the 1970s and was popularized by the title of R.D. Rosen's book *Psychobabble: Fast Talk and Quick Cure in the Era of Feeling* (1977).

> 'Borderline personality disorder', a term of American psychobabble that embraces a multitude of miseries.
> *Sunday Times* (19 September 1999)

Psych oneself up, To. To gird up one's mental loins for an important or challenging enterprise. The phrase originated in the USA in the 1960s in the context of self-expression or GROUP THERAPY.

Psych someone out, To. To intimidate them by out-manoeuvring them. The implication is that one is using psychology to seek out one's opponent's weak points.

Pub bore. A solitary drinker in a pub who importunes others with lengthy reminiscences or other tedious monologues. He has come for the company, but usually succeeds in alienating it. The type has long provided good material for comedians and has been portrayed in various shows and programmes, such as television's FAST SHOW, in which he is played by Paul Whitehouse.

Pub crawl. To go on a pub crawl is to partake in a drinking session in which one progresses, after suitable refreshment, from one public house to another, the number of such visited obviously depending on the length of stay at each and the capacity of the 'crawler' to stay the course.

Pub grub. Commercial jargon for food served in a pub. For many years the British public house was simply a dedicated beer bar and 'boozer', but by the end of the 1970s had become a place of civilized refreshment. The use of 'grub' rather than 'food' is an earnest of a friendly welcome.

Public enemy number one. Literally the first named in a list of criminals, but more generally anyone regarded as a threat to the community. The expression is of American origin and dates from the early 1930s, when the gangster Al CAPONE was sometimes so referred to by the media. The black American activist

Angela Davis (b.1944) was also so named by the FBI for her championship of black prisoners and in particular for her association with the revolutionary George Jackson, one of the so-called Soledad (Prison) Brothers. She was arrested in 1970 to face charges of kidnapping, murder and conspiracy but was subsequently acquitted.

Pub quiz. This peculiarly British and predominantly male pastime has become an essential weekly ritual in many pubs. It evolved in the 1980s with the introduction of the board game TRIVIAL PURSUIT and quiz machines in pubs, the quiz itself having its roots in American GAME SHOWS. Typical pub quiz questions are: 'What colour is the flight recorder in aeroplanes?' or 'Which way did Dickens always face when writing?' (The respective answers are 'Orange' and 'North'.) The real point of such quizzes is for participants to show how intelligent they are, although it is normally a limited sort of intelligence that is expected, as these examples illustrate.

Puckoon. A comic novella (1963) by Spike Milligan (b.1918). 'Several and a half metric miles North East of Sligo, split by a cascading stream, her body on earth, her feet in water, dwells the microcephalic community of Puckoon.'

Pudding bowl or **basin.** A term used for a hairstyle in which the hair is cut, or looks as if it has been cut, by inverting a pudding bowl on the person's head and trimming off the hair that protrudes underneath. The style is popularly or pictorially associated with holy or saintly individuals.

> After years of civil strife, she [St Joan] arrived at the dauphin's court in boys' clothes with a pudding-bowl haircut and declared herself ready to fight.
> *Sunday Times* (11 July 1999)

Puffin crossing. A pedestrian crossing with traffic lights that revert to showing green only when infrared detectors and mats on the crossing detect that no pedestrians are present. The name derives from 'pedestrian user-friendly intelligent', assimilated to 'puffin' in the manner of the earlier PELICAN CROSSING.

Pugwash, Captain. *See* CAPTAIN PUGWASH.

Puleeze. Don't give me that! An emphatic respelling of 'please' to denote one's objection to a remark or action.

> Alix embarrassed? Vulnerable? Oh, puleeeze, Mr Connery, do *not* be so patronizing!
> *The Times Magazine* (20 November 1999)

Pulitzer prizes. Prizes for literary work, journalism, drama and music, which are awarded annually from funds left for the purpose by the Hungarian-born American newspaper magnate Joseph Pulitzer (1847–1911). The prizes are administered by the trustees of Columbia University and were first awarded in 1917.

Pull a fast one, To. To obtain an advantage by trickery or deception. The phrase is generally said to have its origin in cricket matches of the 1930s, when the English captain, Douglas Jardine, instructed his fast bowlers, Larwood and Voce, to abandon gentlemanly deliveries and bowl fast and short at the batsman's body. Such BODYLINE BOWLING produced the desired results, and the intimidated batsmen were speedily dismissed. The expression is recorded in American texts of the 1920s, however, and may in fact allude to a fast shuffle of the cards in gambling.

Pull one's punches, To. To restrain oneself. A phrase of the 1930s that originated in the boxing ring. When a boxer 'pulls his punches' he pulls back during a punch just before the full force of the blow is felt, so landing a lighter blow than usual on his opponent. The usage is mainly negative, as: 'He didn't pull his punches when it came to saying what he thought.'

Pull rank, To. To use one's senior status within a hierarchy to unfair advantage. The expression is of American military origin and dates from the 1920s.

> No one at *The Spectator* pulls rank at work.
> *The Times* (4 February 2000)

Pull the plug on, To. To terminate; to cancel. The image is now usually of an electric plug being pulled from its socket but the reference is in fact to an early type of lavatory flush which involved the pulling out of a plug to empty the pan into the soil pipe. 'To pull the plug' is also to commit suicide, as if disconnecting oneself from a life-support machine.

> Earlier this year Mirror Group pulled the plug on its accident-prone plan to relaunch *The Sporting Life* as a daily sports newspaper.
> *The Times* (13 August 1999)

Pull the rug from under someone, To. To abruptly withdraw one's support for them. The image is similar to the childish trick of pulling away a person's chair as they are about to sit down on it. The expression dates from the 1940s.

Pulp Fiction. A violent but entertaining film thriller (1994) written and directed by Quentin Tarantino (b.1963) in which four tales about the underworld are cleverly interwoven in circular fashion. The title deliberately evokes the kind of trashy, violent crime fiction, published in PULP MAGAZINES.

Pulp magazines. A genre of popular American magazines at their height in the 1920s and 1930s. They contained sensationalist crime writing, often highly erotic in nature, and helped create the character of the laconic 'tough guy'. The most influential of the kind was *Black Mask*, founded in 1930 and publishing Raymond Chandler's first short story, 'Blackmailers Don't Shoot' (1933). Others were *Popular Detective* and *Dime Detective Magazine*. The magazines were so called as they were originally printed on rough paper made of cheap wood pulp.

Pump iron, To. To exercise with weights in fitness training or for purposes of body-building. 'Pump' refers to the up-and-down movements of the exerciser's arms, and 'iron' to the weights. The term is of American origin and dates from the early 1970s.

Punch-drunk. Stupefied, like a boxer who has sustained brain damage from repeated blows to the head and who thus resembles a drunkard. The expression dates from the early years of the 20th century and is usually applied literally to any state of physical confusion or disorientation.

Punk. An old word for a harlot, a worthless person or thing. From the 1970s it came to be applied to certain young people wearing bizarre clothes and hairstyles, and to the PUNK ROCK music they favoured. *See also* HELL'S ANGELS; MODS AND ROCKERS; RIOT GRRLS; SKINHEAD.

> *Lucio*: My lord, she may be a punk; for many of them are neither maid, widow, nor wife.
> WILLIAM SHAKESPEARE: *Measure for Measure*, V, i (1603)

Punk rock. A form of pop music of a coarse and cacophonous nature, as typified by the Sex Pistols. The heyday of British punk was the late 1970s, and when this group disbanded in 1978, the punk revolution was to all intents and purposes over. Punk rock itself was then succeeded by a rather more melodious 'post-punk' idiom, notably NEW WAVE. *See also* NEVER MIND THE BOLLOCKS, HERE'S THE SEX PISTOLS; ROCK GROUP NAMES.

Puppy fat. Chubbiness in young child, which usually disappears at adolescence. The phrase dates from the 1930s and can also be used generally of any young person's plumpness. Nutritionists claim that the amount of puppy fat on an 11-year-old gives the best indication of the size of subsequent MIDDLE-AGE SPREAD.

Victoria [Adams of the SPICE GIRLS] may now have the teen fragility of a cartoon heroine but her diminishing weight is more than compensated for by … Emma Bunton's gloriously persistent puppy fat.
The Times (6 December 1999)

Purple Heart. The original US military decoration of this name was instituted by George Washington in 1782 and awarded for bravery in action. It was simply a purple heart-shaped piece of cloth edged with silver braid and sewn onto the coat. Records show that only three men received it during the War of American Independence (1775–83), after which it was forgotten about for some 150 years. It was revived on 22 February 1932, the bicentenary of Washington's birth, this time as a medal in the form of a purple heart-shaped badge with bronze edges and a relief bust of Washington in military uniform. The reverse side has the inscription 'For Military Merit' and the recipient's name. Purple hearts was also a 1960s slang term for amphetamines.

Purple prose. Over-elaborate prose. The term is based on 'purple patch' or 'purple passage' for an excessively ornate passage in a literary composition. This in turn derives from Horace's reference to *purpureus pannus*, 'purple patch', in his *Ars Poetica* (1st century BC), as the purple piece of cloth which is an irrelevant insertion of a grandiloquent passage into a work.

'What came out bore no relation to what I told them,' muttered one graduate, whose face appeared next to some purple prose extolling the benefits of her employer.
The Times (6 December 1999)

Pusher. A supplier of illicit drugs. The expression, dating from the 1930s, takes 'push' as verb meaning 'to promote', 'to attempt to sell'. The term is only rarely used by pushers or dealers themselves.

Push one's luck, To. To act rashly on the assumption that one will continue to be successful; to seek to gain greater favour than one has already been granted. The expression is frequently found in a negative warning: 'Don't push your luck.'

Push paper about, To. To engage in paperwork; to do petty office jobs.

Push someone around, To. To treat them roughly or inconsiderately; to browbeat or dominate them. The expression dates from the 1920s.

Push the boat out, To. To be lavish in one's spending, especially when entertaining others. The reference is to a shore party setting off to the mother ship, an operation in which one member of the group is usually soaked while freeing the boat from the beach. The expression dates from the 1930s.

Ministers … can still push the boat out for one set of cronies: their backbench colleagues.
The Times (10 July 1999)

Push the envelope, To. To go beyond normal limits; to pioneer. The phrase comes from aviation, in which an 'envelope' is the known limit of an aircraft's range and powers, so called from their appearance on a graph. 'Pushing' such an envelope could thus mean flying fast enough to break the sound barrier.

The start of a second [television] series for Alexander and Ben, who are staying faithful to the sketch-show format while pushing the envelope in an appealing manner.
The Times (7 August 1999)

Push the panic button, To. *See* PANIC BUTTON.

Push tin, To. To work as an air traffic controller, the 'tin' being the aircraft. The American colloquialism was popularized by the film *Pushing Tin* (1999), about the stresses and strains in the professional and private life of an operator at New York's Terminal Radar Approach Control.

Push up the daisies, To. To be dead and buried. The idea is that the dead body fertilizes the soil, so stimulating the growth of the daisies in the churchyard. The expression is first recorded in a poem by Wilfred Owen written in the First World War. Keats had earlier written of 'daisies growing over me' in a letter of 1821, the year of his death.

Put a sock in it, To. To be quiet; to shut up. The mouth can be gagged with a sock. The expression dates from the First World War.

Put down roots, To. To settle in a locality; to make a place one's home. The expression dates from the 1920s and likens human settlement to the rooting of a plant.

Put lead in one's pencil, To. *See* LEAD IN ONE'S PENCIL.

Put oneself about, To. To be socially active or, depending on context, sexually promiscuous. The expression dates from the 1970s.

As people tend to do when their autobiographies are published, [actor and singer] Michael Crawford is putting himself about.
Sunday Times (3 October 1999)

Put one's foot down, To. Apart from the established sense to adopt a firm position a more recent meaning of the phrase is to speed up a motor vehicle by pressing on the accelerator. *See also* STEP ON IT.

> I put my foot down and the Zephyr gathered speed up the slope.
> JOHN BRAINE: *Life at the Top*, ch ii (1962)

Put one's foot in one's mouth, To. To make a verbal gaffe; to say something that embarrasses oneself as much as the hearer. The expression is an elaboration of the older 'to put one's foot in it'. *See also* FOOT-IN-MOUTH DISEASE.

> He [deputy prime minister John Prescott] ... has an ability to put his foot in his mouth unmatched since the days of [gymnast] Olga Korbut.
> *Sunday Times* (19 December 1999)

Put one's hand or **hands up, To.** To confess. An underworld expression originating in the 1950s from the classroom, as a child's response to a question such as 'Who knows?' or 'Whose is this?'

Put one's hands together, To. To applaud; to clap. A stock phrase with a master of ceremonies, as: 'I now ask you to put your hands together for [the person announced].'

Put or **raise one's head above the parapet, To.** To speak out and make one's views heard, especially with regard to a controversial issue about which one might otherwise have stayed silent. The image is of raising one's head above the protective wall of a trench, so exposing oneself to possible enemy fire.

> Any woman who puts her head above the parapet in public life still tends to find that she attracts a degree of hatred, suspicion and antagonism that would be thought remarkable for a man.
> AMANDA CRAIG in *Sunday Times* (26 December 1999)

Put one's money where one's mouth is, To. To support one's statements or opinions with suitable action. The expression relates to gambling in the general context of 'deeds, not words'.

Putsch. *See* BEER HALL PUTSCH; FREIKORPS.

Put someone down, To. To belittle them by criticizing or deriding them before others. Hence 'put-down' as a term for such criticism or derision.

Put someone in the picture, To. To inform them what is happening; to include them as an active participant in an undertaking. The idea is that one can add a person to the existing scenario. The expression dates from the turn of the 20th century.

Put someone off their stroke, To. To disconcert them; to disrupt the pattern of their work. The expression

dates from the early 20th century and alludes to a player's stroke in a game of golf.

Put someone through the wringer, To. To pressurize them; to subject them to severe interrogation. The wringer here is the old-fashioned mangle used to wring water from rinsed clothes after washing. The expression dates from the 1940s.

> 'I find it extraordinary that somebody who can put people through the wringer every day on his radio show cannot come to answer a few simple questions.'
> *The Times* (7 July 1999)

Put something on hold, To. To postpone or defer it. The term dates from the 1960s and alludes to the period in which one waits for a connection during a telephone call. *See also* CALL-WAITING.

Put the arm on someone, To. To attempt to force them to do something, especially to hand over money. The reference is to an attack from the rear by a robber who hooks his arm around his victim's throat. The expression dates from the 1930s.

Put the boot in, To. Literally, to kick hard and brutally. Metaphorically, to treat someone harshly, especially when they are vulnerable. The phrase dates from the First World War but was taken up by SKINHEADS in the 1960s.

> One can't help sympathizing with the man [prospective mayor of London Ken Livingstone] when his former fellow 'loony left' council leaders queue to put the brotherly boot in.
> *Sunday Times* (20 February 2000)

Put the cat among the pigeons, To. To say or do something that causes trouble or alarm. The allusion is obvious.

> Professor Stephen Hawking put the cat among the pigeons last week with his cheery remarks about comet Machholz-2, which some astronomers believe could be heading our way.
> *The Times* (19 September 1994)

Put the finger on, To. To betray; to inform; to identify a target or possible victim. The image is of pointing one's finger at the person concerned. The phrase originated in American underworld slang and dates from the 1920s.

Put the frighteners on, To. To intimidate; to menace. An underworld expression of the 1960s. The frighteners are any threatening things or people that will scare a person into complying.

> A key-jangling oaf in tanned acrylic and a brown peak

cap might put the frighteners on the bumbling British shoplifter but in Rio de Janeiro ... protecting your property requires a little more attention to detail.
Maxim (April 2000)

Put the mockers on, To. To put a stop to; to put a jinx on. The expression was in Australian use in the early years of the 20th century but may have originally come from the language of English market traders and be based on Yiddish *makkes*, ultimately from Hebrew *makot*, 'plagues', 'visitations'. It is hard to see 'the mockers' as 'the people who mock' for no such regular class exists.

Put the screws on, To. To pressure. The screws are the thumbscrews, formerly used in tortures to extract information.

Put the squeeze on, To. To put the pressure on; to coerce. The phrase dates from the 1940s.

'No one knows if she put the squeeze on him, but he's certainly going to quit his job and come and live in London to be close to Christiane,' says a friend.
The Times (21 December 1999)

Putty in someone's hands. Easily swayed or manipulated by them. An expression dating from the 1920s that transfers the malleable quality of putty to human behaviour.

Puzzle Palace. An American nickname dating from the 1950s for any place of decision-making and in particular the White House and the PENTAGON. The term was used for the title of James Bamford's book *The Puzzle Palace* (1982), a definitive and revealing account of the work of the National Security Agency, the principal US signals intelligence organization.

Pygmalion. A play (1913) by George Bernard Shaw (1856–1950) about a phonetician's campaign to transform a roughly spoken cockney FLOWER GIRL into a sophisticated society lady. The play was the basis of the popular musical MY FAIR LADY (1956; film 1964). The title refers to Ovid's story of Pygmalion, the sculptor whose statue of a beautiful woman comes to life so that he can marry her. The inclusion of the word 'bloody' in the script, the first time it had been heard on the English stage, caused a sensation and for some years later the title of the play itself entered use as a euphemism for 'bloody' (*see* NOT PYGMALION LIKELY!).

Pyjama party. A party at which the guests wear pyjamas, as if prepared for the nocturnal fun to come.

The expression and activity date from the early years of the 20th century.

A government minister dished out the sort of big-sisterly advice more suited to a pyjama party than an official appointment yesterday. Teenage girls ... asked Tessa Jowell for practical advice on the emotional side of relationships.
The Times (22 July 1999)

Pylon school. A name applied to various poets of the 1930s whose writing contained imagery reflecting the impact of industry and technology on Britain's countryside and culture. Pylons themselves feature in several works of the period, with Stephen Spender's 'The Pylons' (1933) being typical of the genre and providing its name:

Now over these small hills, they have built the concrete
That trails black wire;
Pylons, those pillars
Bare like nude, giant girls that have no secret.

PYO. *See* PICK YOUR OWN.

Pyramid selling. A system of selling goods whereby distributors recruit other distributors and sell them the goods at a profit. The second batch of distributors does the same, and the process proceeds similarly, as if down the side of a pyramid. The inevitable consequence is that the final distributors, at the lowest level, are likely to find themselves with stock that is too expensive to sell. The system is illegal in Britain. The term itself dates from the mid-1970s.

Pyrex. The heat-resistant glass ovenware of this name was first manufactured in 1915 by the Corning Glass Works, established in Corning, New York, in 1868. The name itself is popularly explained as blending Greek *pur*, 'fire', with Latin *rex*, 'king', but the company has a different explanation:

The assistant secretary of the [Corning Glass] company wrote me as follows: The word *pyrex* is a purely arbitrary word which was devised in 1915 as a trademark for products manufactured and sold by Corning Glass Works. ... We had a number of prior trademarks ending in the letters *ex*. One of the first commercial products to be sold under the new mark was a pie plate and in the interests of euphonism the letter *r* was inserted between *pie* and *ex* and the whole thing condensed to *pyrex*.
American Speech, XXXII (1957)

Q

QALY. The acronym of *quality-adjusted life year*, a term invented by economists at the Centre for Health Economics at the University of York as a way of assigning a numerical value to the quality of extra years of life which a particular person's medical treatment will yield if successful. The procedure enables administrators to decide who to treat by dividing the expected cost of the treatment by the number of QALYs. Although not yet used as an official yardstick by the NHS, it was taken seriously enough to be the subject of a BMA seminar in 1986.

Q. B. VII. A novel (1970) by the US writer Leon Uris (b.1924). The title stands for the name of the court, Queen's Bench number seven, in which a libel trial is played out between an American novelist and a Polish surgeon who has supposedly performed experimental sterilizations on Jews in a concentration camp.

QE2. The short name of the *Queen Elizabeth 2*, the passenger liner launched in 1967 that made its maiden voyage in 1969. The ship was launched by Queen Elizabeth II but is not named after her. Its name commemorates its predecessor, the *Queen Elizabeth*, launched in 1938 and named after the wife of George VI, i.e. the future Queen Elizabeth the Queen Mother. While being built the *QE2* was actually known as the 'Q3', as the third of the 'Queens', the first being the *Queen Mary*.

Q fever. An infectious disease caused by rickettsiae and transmitted to humans from cattle, sheep and goats by unpasteurized milk. It was first recorded in 1935 in Queensland, Australia, among slaughtermen, cattle ranchers and dairy farmers, when its causative organism was unknown. Hence the name, with Q standing for 'query'.

Q ships. In the First World War the name given to warships camouflaged as tramp steamers. These 'mystery ships' were used to lure U-BOATS to their destruction. 'Q' represents 'query'.

Quality circle. A group of employers who meet to discuss ways of improving production, resolving problems and so on, within their organization, especially in factories. The concept evolved in Japan and was adopted in Britain from the early 1980s, partly as a result of Japanese ownership of some businesses and the consequent introduction of certain Japanese management techniques.

Quality of life. A more or less meaningless BUZZWORD or watchword that has surfaced at various times and in various contexts from the 1970s. It seems to imply that life is not rewarding or properly realized unless it is in some way 'lived to the full'. The chances of achieving such a goal are said to be constantly improving thanks to innovations in science and technology, whereas the truth is that 'quality of life', however one interprets it, is not dependent on material enhancements but either remains untouched by them or even weakens and worsens under their influence.

Quality Street. The confectionery assortment of this name was introduced in 1936 by John Mackintosh & Sons Ltd (*see* ROWNTREE MACKINTOSH). The name was adopted from the title of J.M. Barrie's play *Quality Street* (1902), set in *c*.1805, and the product's identity was based on the play's main characters, a soldier and his young lady. Early advertisements depicted the couple, renamed 'Miss Sweetly' and 'Major Quality', dressed in period costume, with Miss Sweetly opening a tin of the assortment to show to the Major and with dialogue beginning as follows:

Major Quality: Sweets to the Sweet, Miss Sweetly.

Miss Sweetly: Spare my blushes, Major Quality. Feast your eyes rather on this sumptuous array of Toffees and Chocolates.

Major Q.: A feast, indeed. What is this wonderful confection?

Miss S.: 'Tis the most momentous thing that has yet happened in the world of sweetness. It is a box of Mackintosh's 'Quality Street' Assortment.

Major Q.: The fame of Mackintosh for Quality I know well.

Miss S.: And that, dear Major, is just why they have called this, their very latest and greatest achievement – 'Quality Street' – for Quality is its keynote through and through.

Daily Mail (advertisement) (2 May 1936)

Quality time. An American phrase and concept of the 1970s, meaning time spent productively or profitably, either with a partner or especially by parents with their children. The expression subsequently gained a euphemistic veneer for the limited time available for this. Many working parents are too tired at the end of the day to spend much time, 'quality' or otherwise, with their children.

> As Nathan tells Emily: 'People with girlfriends tend to get non-productive. They spend a lot of "quality time" together.'
>
> *The Times* (19 May 1994)

Quango. An acronym for quasi (or quasi-autonomous) non-governmental organization, as a cumbersome term for a type of semi-administrative body that is outside the civil service but that is financially supported by the government, which also appoints its members. Quangos originated in the USA in 1967 and first emerged in Britain in 1973. They multiplied rapidly, so that by the end of the 1970s they numbered over 3000. Despite government promises to review the proliferation, there were still more than 2000 quangos in the mid-1990s. Examples of such bodies are British Waterways and the Police Complaints Authority. The name has gained a derogatory taint.

> Public opinion ... is unlikely to be swayed by the announcement last week of new quangos to monitor developments.
>
> *Sunday Times* (23 May 1999)

Quantum leap. A sudden large advance; a spectacular leap forward. The term evolved in the 1970s as a variant of the older 'quantum jump', which properly and originally described the abrupt transition of an electron, atom or molecule from one energy state to another. Such a 'leap' is not of course large in the traditional sense, however spectacular it may have seemed to physicists. The present sense may have come about through a wrong association of 'quantum' with 'quantity'.

> The imperial Presidency did not begin with Richard Nixon although under him abuses of the offices took a quantum leap.
>
> *New Yorker* (13 June 1977)

Quare Fellow, The. A play (1954) by the Irish playwright Brendan Behan (1923–64) about events in a Dublin prison on the eve of an execution. The 'quare fellow' of the title is the man due to be hanged, a pork butcher who butchered his own brother with a meat cleaver.

Quark. A term in physics for any of a group of subatomic particles, originally three in number, believed to be among the fundamental constituents of matter. Quarks have not been directly observed but theoretical predictions based on their existence have been confirmed experimentally. There are six types or 'flavours': up, down, top, bottom, strange and charm, each of which has three varieties or 'colours': red, yellow and blue. To each quark there is an antiparticle, called an antiquark. The name of the particle was coined in 1964 by the American physicist Murray Gell-Mann and based on the line 'Three quarks for Muster Mark' in James Joyce's novel FINNEGANS WAKE (1939), words that are said to be a whimsical perversion of 'Three quarts for Mr Mark'.

Quarry Men. The SKIFFLE group founded by John Lennon that was to metamorphose into the Beatals in 1960 and eventually into the BEATLES.

Quartet for the End of Time. A presumably eschatological chamber work for violin, clarinet, cello and piano by Olivier Messiaen (1908–92). The work was written in 1941 while Messiaen was a prisoner of war of the Germans in Silesia, which explains the unusual combination of instruments and perhaps also the title.

Quatermass. A pioneering SCIENCE FICTION television series screened live from 1953 to 1959. It concerned a professional scientist of the name whose experimental spaceship returns to Earth with its sole occupant contaminated by an alien virus that subsequently transmutes him into a vast vegetable. The series owed its impact both to Nigel Kneale's unsettling script and to Rudolph Cartier's inspired production and direction. There were two subsequent serials, and all three stories were subsequently filmed: *The Quatermass Experiment* (1955), *Quatermass II* (1957) and *Quatermass and the Pit* (1967).

Queen Elizabeth. *See* QE2.

Queen Mary. A former nickname for a long, low-loading road trailer, comparing it to the huge passenger liner of this name, launched in 1938 but in 1967 turned into a floating hotel.

Queen Mary hat. A type of toque popularized by Queen Mary (1867–1953), wife of George V, and favoured by her because it enabled the public to have a clear view of her face.

Queen of Crime. A promotional nickname given to the crime novelist Agatha Christie (1891–1976), and subsequently to her successor in this role, P.D. James (b.1920).

Queen of the Air. A nickname given by journalists to the pioneer British aviator Amy Johnson (1903–41). She came into the public eye in 1930 when she flew solo from Britain to Darwin in Australia, although she failed to beat the record by three days. Her flights to Tokyo (1931) and to Cape Town (1932) did break records, however. In the Second World War she served with the Air Transport Auxiliary and disappeared while on a mission somewhere over the Thames estuary.

Queen of the Halls. A nickname of the music-hall singer and comedienne Marie Lloyd (originally Matilda Alice Victoria Wood; 1870–1922). She made her debut in 1885 and collapsed on stage in 1922, dying a few days later. Her brand of risqué Cockney comedy was highly popular, and her songs included 'Oh, Mr Porter', 'I'm One of the Ruins that Cromwell Knocked About a Bit' and 'A Little of What You Fancy Does You Good'.

Queer. The sense 'homosexual' for this word emerged only in the 1920s, its origin perhaps not so much in the established English sense of 'strange', 'unusual', but closer to the possible source in German *quer*, 'oblique', 'perverse'. Homosexuals long found the word offensive, but later came to adopt it as an alternative for GAY, and it was readily promoted in the 1990s by the homosexual liberation movement Queer Nation, their motto being: 'We're here, we're queer. Get used to it.'

Queer Hardie. A nickname of Keir Hardie (1856–1915), the former coalminer who in 1892 became the first socialist member of Parliament, founding the Independent Labour Party the following year. He lost his seat in 1895 but was re-elected in 1900, holding his seat until his death. The nickname refers to his quirks of manner and dress, such as attending Parliament in a cloth cap rather than the conventional top hat and dress coat. *See also* GUMMIDGE, WORZEL.

Question mark. To say that a question mark hangs or is over something is to express doubt or uncertainty about it. The phrase dates from the 1920s.

> All four [pop singers] agree that there was a big question mark over the future of the band.
> *Sunday Times* (26 December 1999)

Quick and dirty. Makeshift; done or produced hastily. The term arose in the 1960s as an American colloquialism for a cheap café, where food preparation is perfunctory and hygiene deficient.

Quick buck. *See* FAST BUCK.

Quick fix. A quick but probably none too permanent or satisfactory solution to a problem. The expression dates from the 1960s.

Quick on the draw. Quick to act or react. The allusion is to the gunslinger of the American West who was adept at drawing his gun instantly from its holster when necessary. An earlier variant was 'quick on the trigger'.

Quids in. In luck or money; in profit; up on a deal. The phrase dates from the First World War.

Quiet American. A nickname for a person suspected of being an undercover agent or spy. The name comes from the title of Graham Greene's novel *The Quiet American* (1955), in which Alden Pyle, an idealistic graduate who becomes involved in political terrorism, is the 'quiet American'.

Quiller Memorandum, The. A mystery thriller (1964) by Adam Hall (pen-name of Elleston Trevor; 1920–95). It is the first in a series of 19 books, told in the first person, about Quiller, a peripatetic executive for an ultra-secret international agency in London.

Quincunx, The. A wilfully complicated and extremely lengthy novel (1989) by Charles Palliser (b.1947), following the conventions of the Victorian mystery novel as exemplified by Wilkie Collins (1824–89). A document that is discovered determines the fates of five families and sets the pattern of the protagonist's own life. Many aspects of the narrative centre on the quincunx, the mystical symbol of five.

Quisling. A traitor or fifth columnist, from Vidkun Quisling (1887–1945), the Norwegian admirer of Mussolini and Hitler, who acted as advance agent for the German invasion of Norway in 1940. He duly became puppet minister-president. He surrendered (9 May 1945) after the German defeat and was tried and shot (24 October). Quisling is now popularly regarded as one of the 'five famous Norwegians' (*see* FAMOUS FIVE).

Quonset hut. The American equivalent of a NISSEN HUT as a type of military shelter. It takes its name from Quonset Point, Rhode Island, where such huts were first erected at a US Air Force base in the Second World War.

Quorn. A type of textured vegetable protein made from an edible fungus and used as a meat substitute. It was launched on the market in Britain in 1984 and takes its name from its original manufacturers, Quorn Specialities Ltd, located in the Leicestershire village of Quorn or Quorndon, best known as the home of a famous hunt. The provenance of a meatless product from a place associated precisely with the pursuit of live flesh has a somewhat unpalatable irony.

Quote, unquote. A parenthetical expression said before a word or phrase to indicate that if written the latter would be in quotation marks, as: 'I gave him a little quote, unquote talking-to.' A variant is to say 'quote' before and 'unquote' after. An alternative is to mime quotation marks by twitching one's raised forefingers as one says the word or phrase. The expression dates from the 1930s and has its origin in the oral formula for quotation marks in a dictation.

Quo Vadis? A biblical film epic (1951) based on the book (1896) of the same title by Henryk Sienkiewicz about the martyrdom of St Peter during the reign of the Emperor Nero. Starring Robert Taylor, Deborah Kerr and Peter Ustinov, the film followed two earlier versions (1912 and 1924). The title was derived from the word *Domine, quo vadis?* ('Master, whither goest thou?') reputedly uttered by St Peter when he encountered Christ on the Appian Way during his flight from Nero's Rome. Christ replied that he was on his way to Rome 'to be crucified again', on which the shamefaced Peter turned around and went back to Rome to meet his death. According to tradition he asked to be crucified head downwards and related his meeting with Christ as he was nailed to the cross.

QWERTY. The standard layout on English-language typewriter keyboards, representing the first six letters from the left on the top row. The layout, still found even on modern computer keyboards, was originally designed to slow down typing and so prevent jamming of the keys on the early manual machines. This was effected by having the typebars come up from opposite directions and so not clashing together. It so happens that all the letters needed to type the word 'typewriter' are in the top line of the layout (QWERTYUIOP), but the theory that this was intended to help non-skilled sales staff demonstrate the machine is an old secretaries' tale. The French equivalent is AZERTY. In 1986 Anthony Burgess published a collection of his reviews under the title *Homage to QWERTYUIOP. See also* DSK.

R

Rab. The popular initialism of R.A. Butler (1902–82), Conservative minister of education (1941–5) in the Second World War, when he introduced the radical Education Act of 1944. His political career then progressed to chancellor of the exchequer (1951) and Lord Privy Seal (1955). He was widely expected to succeed Anthony Eden as prime minister in 1957 after the SUEZ CRISIS, but Harold Macmillan was chosen and Butler instead became home secretary. He again narrowly lost the premiership to Alec Douglas-Home in 1963 and was appointed foreign secretary. Butler was epitomized in political circles as 'both irreproachable and unapproachable'.

Rabbit. The nickname of Harry Angstrom, the hero of a series of four novels by John Updike: *Rabbit, Run* (1960), *Rabbit, Redux* (1971), *Rabbit Is Rich* (1981) and *Rabbit at Rest* (1990). His byname comes from his former glory days as a high school basketball champion. He subsequently becomes the owner of a car sales agency, but is generally limited and complacent in his attitudes, as a sort of latter-day BABBIT. (The resemblance between the names is presumably coincidental.) He finally dies of a heart attack during a playground game of basketball.

Rabbit on, To. To talk at length; to chatter away. 'Rabbit' here represents rhyming slang for 'rabbit and pork', i.e. 'talk', although happening to suggest similar words relating to talking such as 'babble', 'gabble', 'ramble' and the like. The expression dates from the Second World War.

Rabbit punch. A sharp chop with the edge of the hand to the back of the neck, like that traditionally given by a gamekeeper to put a rabbit out of its misery. The term dates from the early 20th century.

Rabbits. A charm-word traditionally said by children on the first day of the month. An alternative is or was 'white rabbits', and the ritual is sometimes extended by saying 'hares' on the last day of the month. No response to the utterance is now normally expected, although it apparently once was, when first recorded in the early 20th century.

> On the first day of the month you have to say 'Rabbits'. If you say it to me first, I have to give you a present, and if I say it to you first, you have to give me a present.
> DORNFORD YATES: *The Courts of Idleness*, Pt II, ch ii (1920)

Race to the sea. In the First World War, following the First Battle of the Aisne (13–28 September 1914), both the French and German sides realized that they lacked the manpower for frontal assaults and that the only alternative was for each side to try and overlap and envelop the flank of the other, in this case the one on the side pointing towards the North Sea and the English Channel. The developing trench networks of both sides were thus extended in a north-westerly direction as a 'Race to the sea' until they reached the coast at a point just inside Belgium, west of Ostend, creating the WESTERN FRONT.

Rachel Papers, The. The first novel (1973) by Martin Amis (b.1949). The protagonist is a bright young man on the way up, who uses literature as a tool of seduction and does not care how he achieves his aims. Rachel, whose 'character was about as high-powered as her syntax', finally walks out 'without telling me a thing or two about myself, without asking if I knew what my trouble was, without providing any come-uppance at all'. The title echoes that of *The Aspern Papers* (1888) by Henry James (1843–1916), in which the chief character is also a literary critic. A forgettable film version (1989) was directed by Damian Harris.

Rachmanism. The exploitation of and intimidation of tenants by unscrupulous landlords. The name comes from that of Peter Rachman (1919–62), a Polish immigrant whose undesirable activities of this kind in the Paddington area of London were brought to light in the early 1960s. His name was brought to public attention from a former connection with the women in the PROFUMO AFFAIR.

Rack something up, To. To achieve it, typically as a score or amount. The expression probably alludes to the accumulation of points in pool-playing. At the beginning of the game the balls are placed in a triangular wooden frame called a rack. When the frame is removed, the balls themselves are also known as the rack. Players are then in a position to start playing and so accumulate points. The phrase dates from the 1950s and is distinct from the more recent 'to ratchet up', meaning to make something rise in a step that is part of an irreversible progress.

> In just the last six years … the UK has racked up a current account deficit with the rest of the EU of £47 billion.
>
> *The Times* (Letter to the Editor) (30 July 1999)

RADA. The Royal Academy of Dramatic Art, Britain's leading drama school. It was founded in 1904 by the actor Sir Herbert Beerbohm Tree in the dome of His Majesty's Theatre in the Haymarket, London, but later that year was transferred to the Georgian house in Gower Street that it has occupied ever since. It was granted a royal charter by George V in 1920 and for many years was run by Sir Kenneth Barnes (1878–1957), under whom its theatre, the Vanburgh, named after his sisters, the actresses Irene (1872–1949) and Violet (1867–1942) Vanburgh, was built to replace an earlier one, destroyed in the BLITZ of 1941.

Radar. A term formed from *radio detection and ranging*, as a means of detecting the direction and range of aircraft, ships and the like by the reflection of radio waves. It is particularly valuable at night or in fog when the eye is of no avail. It was first developed effectively for the purposes by Sir Robert Watson-Watt in 1934–5 (and independently in the United States, France and Germany) and was of great importance during the Second World War, especially during the BATTLE OF BRITAIN.

Radical chic. The fashionable affectation of radical left-wing views. The expression was coined by the American writer Tom Wolfe in 1970 to denote high society's adoption of radicals and radical issues as fashion accessories. The term subsequently came to apply to anything left-wing that seemed to be embraced on grounds of being fashionable rather than through personal conviction. *See also* SHABBY CHIC.

> Radical Chic … is only radical in Style; in its heart it is part of Society and its tradition – Politics, like Rock, Pop, and Camp, has its uses.
>
> TOM WOLFE in *New York* (8 June 1970)

Radiocarbon dating. A scientific method of estimating the age of organic materials. Carbon dioxide from the atmosphere, which contains the radioactive isotope Carbon-14, is taken up by all living matter. After the organism has died, the amount of Carbon-14 diminishes at a known rate, thus permitting the age of the material to be dated approximately. The method was devised in 1946 by the American chemist Willard F. Libby (1908–80).

Radio Caroline. The first and most famous of Britain's North Sea PIRATE RADIO stations went on the air on Easter Day, 29 March 1964 with the following welcome from its disc jockey, Simon Dee: 'Good morning, ladies and gentlemen. This is Radio Caroline broadcasting on 199, your all-day music station.' Its initiator was a young Irishman, Ronan O'Rahilly, who claimed that he named the station after Caroline Kennedy, daughter of President John F. Kennedy, assassinated the previous October. Cynics, however, suggested he hoped to curry favour with the then chancellor of the exchequer, Reginald Maudling, who also had a daughter named Caroline. The station soon attracted millions of fans, who saw it as a symbol of freedom and rebellion, and although it later ran into troubled waters, sometimes literally so, it survived several setbacks until it finally fell silent in 1990.

Radio City Music Hall. The largest and most prestigious theatre in the United States, at Rockefeller Center, New York, was conceived by Samuel Rothafel (*see* ROXY) as a palatial entertainment centre affordable to the general public and opened on 27 December 1931 with a gala performance by Martha Graham, Ray Bolger and Gertrude Niesen. The ceiling of the auditorium gives the impression of a giant sunset, and the opulence of the foyer stunned theatregoers during the GREAT DEPRESSION, with its ceiling 18m (60ft) high, ornate mirrors and slender chandeliers. Soon after its opening the theatre presented programmes combining feature films with stage shows, a format that remained popular for almost 50 years. It subsequently became a principal venue for live spectacles and television events, and the GRAMMY awards were staged there from the 1980s. The theatre's best known institution are the ROCKETTES.

Radio Doctor. The by-name of Dr Charles Hill (1904–89), who was the BBC's 'Radio Doctor' from 1942 to 1950. He went on to became a Conservative health minister in the 1950s, then chairman of the Independent Television Authority and finally chairman of the BBC.

Radio Luxembourg. This famous commercial radio station helped to train some of the best known disc jockeys (DJs) in British broadcasting, among them David Jacobs, Pete Murray, Jimmy Savile, Jimmy Young, Noel Edmonds, Mike Read and Peter Powell. It began its nightly English-language service in 1933, when its first DJ was Stephen Williams. The station took the lead in developing sponsored programmes with shows such as The Ovaltineys (see OVALTINE) and its entertainers and singers included such famous names as George Formby and Gracie Fields (see OUR GRACIE). During the Second World War the NAZIS used Radio Luxembourg as a propaganda outlet, employing such stooges as Lord HAW-HAW, but after the war it entered its golden age, delighting pop music fans who were not catered for by the BBC until the advent of Radio 1 in 1967. Its audience shrank when PIRATE RADIO lured listeners away from its wavelength of 208 metres on medium wave, and its last English-language broadcast went out in 1992.

Radio Priest. The by-name of the US priest Father Charles Edward Coughlin (1891–1979), whose regular radio show in the 1930s became notorious for his increasingly extreme denunciations of Franklin Roosevelt (FDR) and the NEW DEAL as a conspiracy of communists and Jewish bankers. He was disowned by Catholic leaders in 1937, and in 1942 his broadcasts were suppressed for opposing American's entry into the Second World War.

Raft of the Medusa, The. A controversial oratorio by Hans Werner Henze (b.1926). Its title in German is Das Floss der Medusa, and it was described by the composer as an oratorio volgare e militare. It was commissioned by Hamburg Radio, and its first performance in 1968 was disrupted by demonstrators and police intervention. The work certainly had a radical agenda: it was dedicated to Che Guevara and commemorated a shocking episode in French naval history, when in 1816 the officers of the wrecked Medusa abandoned their men to float on a raft, leading to the deaths of 139 of the 154 originally set adrift. The story is also the subject of a famous painting (1818–19) by Théodore Géricault.

Ragga. A style of music similar to dance hall in which a DJ improvises lyrics over an electronic backing track. It arose in the 1990s as a fusion of REGGAE and urban HIP-HOP and takes its name from 'ragamuffin', alluding to the casual dress of its followers.

Ragged-Trousered Philanthropists, The. A fable (1914, in full 1955) by Robert Tressell (pen-name of Robert Noonan; 1870–1911). Subtitled Being the story of twelve months in Hell, told by one of the damned, and written down by Robert Tressell, it was written between 1907 and 1910 to give his only daughter some financial security. It takes the form of an account of the lives of a band of men who work for an unscrupulous decorating firm, and it reflects the attitudes of the philanthropists (the working class) towards their capitalist exploiters.

Raging Bull. A film (1980) based on the autobiography of US middleweight boxer Jake LaMotta. Directed by Martin Scorsese and starring Robert De Niro as LaMotta, the film's title indicates its theme of uncompromisingly violent masculinity and male values. De Niro reputedly put on more than 20kg (50lb) in order to play the bloated LaMotta later in his career.

Rags to riches. From poverty to wealth; from nonentity to fame. The phrase, often found as an adjectival phrase, became current in the Second World War. The allusion is to the heroine of a fairy tale who makes such a transition, such as Cinderella, who met and married Prince Charming.

> The story of Carl Cushnie, the 49-year-old son of a Jamaican engineer, read ... like the ultimate tale of rags to riches.
>
> The Times (10 December 1999)

Rah-rah skirt. See RA-RA SKIRT.

Raiders of the Lost Ark. A film (1981) adapted by Lawrence Kasdan from a story by George Lucas and Philip Kaufman about the adventures of an archaeologist, Indiana Jones, as he struggles to locate the biblical Ark of the Covenant, allegedly still containing the Ten Commandments, before the Nazis do in 1936. The film was inspired by the cliffhanger adventure series shown in cinemas in the 1930s and starred

Harrison Ford as 'Indy' (although Tom Selleck was director Steven Spielberg's first choice). Its success led to two sequels, *Indiana Jones and the Temple of Doom* (1984) and *Indiana Jones and the Last Crusade* (1989).

Railway Children, The. A much-loved children's novel (1906) by E. Nesbit (1858–1924). It tells of three siblings who move to a country cottage with their mother when their father is mysteriously taken away. Their adventures centre on the railway line that runs close to their new home. It emerges that their father has been wrongly imprisoned for passing secrets to the enemy, but he is released when the true culprit is identified. The novel's enduring popularity is reflected in a number of film and television versions. A nostalgically textured film version (1970), directed by Lionel Jeffries, had many memorable moments, not least that of 17-year-old Jenny Agutter whipping off her petticoat to avert tragedy on the railway line. A remake (2000), directed by Charles Elton, was a more measured version of the original, with 18-year-old Jemima Rooper in Agutter's role as Roberta and Agutter herself as the mother of the three children. *See also* FIRST LINES OF NOVELS.

Rainbow coalition. A term arising in the United States for a political grouping of minority peoples and other disadvantaged elements, especially in order to elect a candidate. The allusion is both to the diversity of political shades, 'all the colours of the rainbow', and to the connotations of hope associated with a rainbow ('where the rainbow ends', 'somewhere over the rainbow'). The concept was embraced by the politician Jesse Jackson (*see* HIS SHADOWSHIP) when running for the Democratic 1984 presidential nomination, the first black American to mount a serious campaign for this office.

> When I look out at this convention, I see the face of America, red, yellow, brown, black and white. We are all precious in God's sight – the real rainbow coalition.
> JESSE JACKSON: Speech at Democratic National Convention, Atlanta, (19 July 1988)

Rainbow Corner. In the Second World War Messrs Lyons' Corner House in Shaftesbury Avenue, London, was taken over and turned into a large café and lounge for American servicemen under this name, and it became a general meeting place for Americans in London. The name was in reference to the 42nd Infantry Division of the US Army, nicknamed the Rainbow, and the rainbow in the insignia of

SHAEF (Supreme Headquarters Allied Expeditionary Forces). The division itself was so called because it was composed of military groups from the District of Columbia and 25 states, representing several sections, nationalities, religions and viewpoints. They blended themselves into a single harmonious unit and a First World War major, noting its various origins, said: 'This division will stretch over the land like a rainbow.'

Rainbow Nation. A nickname for South Africa, alluding to its multiracial population. The term was coined by Nelson Mandela, South African president (1994–99), following the end of APARTHEID in 1991. *See also* RAINBOW COALITION.

> The Rainbow Nation had a surprise for the folks at Birmingham ... South Africa won the critical doubles rubber in the Davis Cup promotion decider.
> *Sunday Times* (26 September 1999)

Rainbow Warrior. *See* GREENPEACE.

Rain on someone's parade, To. To prevent them from enjoying an occasion; to spoil their plans. The expression is of American origin and dates from the turn of the 20th century.

> Would we Conservative wets please now shut up and stop raining on William Hague's parade?
> *The Times* (23 October 1999)

Rain or shine. No matter what happens. A figurative use, dating from the turn of the 20th century, of the much older phrase meaning 'whatever the weather'.

Raise one's eyebrows, To. To show surprise, disbelief or mild disapproval by the described movement of the features. 'Raised eyebrows' are thus a general expression of this kind. The phrase dates from the early years of the 20th century.

> There have been raised eyebrows over the news that Nick Pisani will become the new editor of the BBC's *Question Time*.
> *The Times* (10 December 1999)

Raise one's head above the parapet, To. *See* PUT ONE'S HEAD ABOVE THE PARAPET.

Raise one's sights, To. To become more ambitious; to increase one's expectations. The sights are those on a gun through which one takes aim after raising the gun to one's shoulder. The converse, literally and figuratively, is 'to lower one's sights'.

Rake's Progress, The. The 'neoclassical' opera by Igor Stravinsky (1882–1971) has a libretto by W.H. Auden and Chester Kallmann, loosely based on the 'moral narrative' of William Hogarth (1697–1764), painted in 1733–5 and subsequently made into popular engravings. The story concerns the decline and fall of one Tom Rakewell, who deserts Anne Trulove for the delights of London in the company of Nick Shadow, who turns out to be the Devil. Tom ends up in Bedlam, and the moral of the tale is: 'For idle hearts and hands and minds the Devil finds a work to do.' The opera was first performed in 1951. For the 1975 Glyndebourne revival, striking sets and costumes were designed by David Hockney (b.1937).

Rambert Dance Company. The oldest British existing ballet company arose from the dance studio opened in London in 1920 by Marie Rambert (1888–1982), a Polish-born dancer whose original name was Cyvia Rambam. By 1931 regular Saturday matinée performances were being given under the name of the Ballet Club, and in 1934 this became the Ballet Rambert. Its base was the minute Mercury Theatre in Notting Hill, a former Victorian school building, and this remained its home until the 1960s. Early choreographers were Frederick Ashton (1904–88) and Antony Tudor (1908–87). Rambert herself remained director until 1966. The company adopted its present name in 1987, after Richard Alston became director. Of all established London dance companies, the Rambert has consistently enjoyed a progressive and young-minded public.

Ramblers. The word is generally used for anyone who enjoys walking for pleasure in the countryside or even through city streets. More specifically it is associated with the Ramblers' Association, a pressure group formed in 1935 with the twin aims of encouraging people to enjoy the countryside, as they had always done, and ensuring that there is public access to it, as there has not always been (*see* RIGHT TO ROAM). It has thus campaigned to prevent the closure of footpaths and rights of way, in some cases trespassing on private land in order to do so. Many landowners and farmers are ambivalent about the Association: it shares their rural interests but seeks to deprive them of their traditional proprietorial rights, or what they hold to be such.

Rambo. The tough VIETNAM War veteran first appeared in David Morrell's violent thriller, *First Blood* (1971), in which he runs into trouble with a local sheriff, takes to the hills and finally massacres an entire unit of the National Guard single-handed. He was brought before a wide public by the film of the same title

(1982), in which he is played by Sylvester Stallone, and by its unashamedly melodramatic sequels, *Rambo First Blood Part II* (1985) and *Rambo III* (1988). His name became a household word when President Reagan praised the second film in one of his speeches, as a result of which 'Rambo' became a nickname for Reagan himself, especially with regard to his policy of foreign military intervention.

> Given the bomb-'em-kill-'em suggestions pulsing from the typewriters of 100 literate Rambos, a boycott of the airport was the most reasonable act suggested.
> *Washington Post* (6 July 1985)

Ram raid. A robbery carried out by ramming a vehicle into the wall or window of the building to be robbed, typically commercial premises.

Ramsay Mac. A nickname of (James) Ramsay MacDonald (1866–1937), Britain's first Labour prime minister (1924). He became prime minister of a second Labour government in 1929, then in 1931 broadened it into a National Government coalition, which was increasingly dominated by Conservatives, resulting in his condemnation as a traitor by most socialists. *See also* BONELESS WONDER; COALITION GOVERNMENT.

Random Harvest. A film (1942) based on a novel (1941) by the British writer James Hilton (1900–54) about a First World War veteran who has lost his memory in battle but later regains it after being hit by a car, only to find he has forgotten all that happened in the intervening period. The title was derived from wartime German propaganda claims that German planes had successfully dropped bombs on the English town of Random (a claim based on misinterpretation of a British communiqué that German bombs had been 'dropped at random').

Random House. This noted US publishing firm was founded in New York in 1927 by Bennett Cerf (1898–1971) and Donald S. Klopfer (1902–86), owners of the Modern Library, to publish their own luxury editions 'at random'. It soon developed into a trade publisher and gained a reputation for its substantial and highly profitable children's department and for its commitment to publishing dramatic works. Its authors have included such disparate writers as William Faulkner, Robert Penn Warren, Eugene O'Neill, Lillian Hellman and Gertrude Stein.

Rangoon runs. *See* MONTEZUMA'S REVENGE.

Ranji. The Indian-born Sussex and England batsman His Highness the Maharajah Jam Sahib of Nawangar (Kumar Shri Ranjitsinhji; 1872–1933). The Ranji

Trophy competition in India is named after him. Ranjitsinhji's is one of a number of cricketers' names that appear in punning versions in the cricket-loving James Joyce's esoteric novel FINNEGANS WAKE:

> At half-past quick in the morning. And her lamp was all askew and trumbly-wick-in-her, ringeysingey.

R and R. Rest and recreation, an abbreviation of US military origin dating from the 1990s. The reference is to off-duty time as a positive and integral ingredient of regular military routine.

Rap music. A style of music, originally dating from the 1970s when it was established by black musicians in New York, in which the often improvised lyrics are sung or chanted against a heavy bass line (the latter being often created by a drum machine or synthesizer). The use of the word 'rap' in this context is probably a 1960s usage meaning to indulge in repartee or street talk. *See also* GANGSTA RAP; HIP-HOP.

Ra-ra or **rah-rah skirt.** A short skirt with multiple layered flounces, of the kind worn by American CHEERLEADERS, who are colloquially known as 'ra-ra girls', from their cries of 'ra-ra' (from 'hurrah'). The heyday of the ra-ra as a fashion fetish was the early 1980s, when they were popularized by such all-girl pop groups as the Belle Stars and Bananarama. One reason for their early demise was their impracticality.

Rarin' to go. Keen to get started. The verb is an American dialect form of 'rearing', alluding to a horse that rears up when anxious to be off. The expression dates from the early 20th century.

Rasputin. Grigoriy Yefimovich Novykh (*c.*1871–1916), the Siberian monk notorious for his baneful influence over the Russian monarchy in its last years, was apparently so called by his fellow villagers. Rasputin means 'dissolute' and he lived up to his nickname until the end. His easy conquests over women were helped by his assertion that physical contact with him was itself a purification. His gross indecencies and disgusting coarseness did not prevent his excessive familiarity with the Empress Alexandra and Tsar Nicholas II, which arose from his undoubted success in healing and sustaining the Tsarevich Alexis, a victim of haemophilia. Rasputin was first called to the palace in 1905, and his power increased steadily, until his murder by Prince Yusupov and his associates.

The method of dispatch was a sorry saga. On the night of 29 December 1916 Rasputin was invited to Yusupov's home in St Petersburg and there given poisoned wine and tea cakes. When he did not die, the desperate Yusupov shot him. Rasputin collapsed but managed to run into the courtyard, where he was shot again by Vladimir Purishkevich, a member of the Duma. The conspirators then bound Rasputin and bundled him through a hole in the ice into the River Neva, where he at last drowned.

Rastafarians. Members of the Ras Tafari, a black political and religious group originating in the 1920s in Jamaica, recognizing Haile Selassie (1892–1975), emperor of Ethiopia, as a god. They consider that blacks are superior to whites, that Ethiopia is heaven and that Haile Selassie would arrange that all of African origin will find a homeland in Ethiopia. *Ras* means 'duke' and *Tafari* was a family name of Haile Selassie ('Might of the Trinity'). There are now Rastafarians in the West Indies, the United States, Canada and Europe, conspicuous by their DREADLOCKS. *See also* LION OF JUDAH.

Rat fink. An unpleasant person, especially one suspected of being an informer ('rat'). 'Fink' probably derives from the identical German word meaning 'finch', in the sense of someone who 'sings' or informs. The term dates from the 1960s.

Rationing. *See* POINTS.

Rat pack. A juvenile gang. The best known such group, although not of juveniles, was the Holmby Hills Rat Pack of HOLLYWOOD, as the drinking friends of Humphrey Bogart. Its successor was the Rat Pack, a name given by *Time* magazine to the showbiz entourage of Frank Sinatra, earlier known as The Clan. A later development was the BRAT PACK.

Rat race. The relentless struggle to get ahead of one's rivals, particularly in professional and commercial occupations.

Rat run. A residential street used by drivers as a short cut or to avoid a congested main road, especially during the rush hour. A rat run is a maze of small passages used by rats when running about their territory.

> The rat-run has become the front line in the war between people and cars. As the number of vehicles rises and traffic calming measures proliferate, more roads are being used as short cuts.
> *Sunday Times* (6 December 1998)

Rattle someone's cage, To. To irritate or annoy them. The image is of a caged bird or animal being provoked in this manner. The expression dates from the 1970s and is mostly found in the form of a rhetorical question, as: 'Who rattled his cage?'

Rave. The word passed from its use to mean an enthusiastic recommendation for someone or something (a 'rave review') before gaining the more specific sense of a party attended by large numbers of young people, typically one with energetic dancing fuelled by drugs such as ECSTASY.

Raw and rude. Unsparingly revealing; bleak and unflattering. A phrase mostly used of a literary or artistic style.

> Fans of Gilbert and Sullivan must have received the news that the director Mike Leigh was making a film about their heroes with some trepidation. After all, what has Leigh's raw'n'rude realism got in common with their genteel, topsy-turvy surrealism?
> *Sunday Times* (20 February 2000)

Raw deal. A transaction that is harsh or unfair to a person, perhaps from the idea that it leaves them feeling 'raw' or hurt. The expression is American in origin.

Reader's Digest. An American-based monthly magazine with one of the largest circulations of any periodical in the world. It was first published in February 1922 as a digest of condensed articles of topical interest and entertainment value taken from other periodicals. The founders, working on a low budget, were DeWitt Wallace (1889–1981) and his wife, Lila Acheson, who had at first failed to interest publishers in their plan. The pocket format appealed to many, however, and sales gradually rose. The magazine began publishing condensed versions of current books in 1934. It then took to commissioning articles which it would offer to other publications only to reprint them in due course, offering the other magazine a fee for reprint rights. It has been criticized by some for its unadventurous content and conservative point of view but its circulation has rarely faltered.

Ready, steady, go! A formula for starting a race, especially among children. At the word 'ready' the runner prepares himself, at 'steady' he braces himself, at 'go!' he starts to run. In professional athletics, when contestants are UNDER STARTER'S ORDERS, the formula is usually 'On your marks, get set, go!', or simply 'Marks, set', with 'go!' replaced by the firing of the starter's pistol. The *Oxford English Dictionary* records the former phrase no earlier than the 1960s, and the latter first in the 1930s. An earlier equivalent, still in use, was simply 'One, two, three, go!'

Reaganauts. The nickname of a clique of right-wing ideologues who strongly influenced the policies in office of President Ronald Reagan, the GREAT COMMUNICATOR. The name comes by analogy with 'astronaut', with a suggestion both of bold, pioneering spirit and of being not of this world.

Reagan Democrats. A name given to those former Democrat voters in the USA, mostly white, male, blue-collar workers, who voted for the Republican presidential candidate Ronald Reagan in 1980.

Reaganomics. The economic policies of Ronald Reagan, the GREAT COMMUNICATOR, during his presidency (1981–9). Cuts in taxes and social services budgets were their centrepiece, and they led to a record rise in the national budget deficit. The name, originally intended derisively, was a variation on 'Reaganism', coined during an earlier phase of the president's career to denote his politics in general.

Real ale. Cask-conditioned beer that is served traditionally, not from metal kegs under gas pressure. The term implies that beer produced by mass-production methods is not 'real', whereas 'ale' has agreeable historical or 'heritage' associations. The Campaign for Real Ale (CAMRA), founded in 1972, has done a great deal to preserve and promote the original kind of beer, to the extent that many pubs came to advertise it as a lure to potential customers. *See also* GUEST BEER.

Real Madrid. The leading Spanish football club was founded by students in 1902 as the *Madrid Club de Fútbol*. In 1920 it was given its royal (Spanish, *real*) blessing by King Alfonso XIII and turned professional in 1929 when the Spanish national league began. Real's rise to prominence began in earnest after the Spanish Civil War (1936–9) and in the late 1950s it achieved European dominance, winning five European Cups between 1956 and 1960. The ultimate accolade came when General Franco let it be known that Real Madrid was his favourite team.

Real Spain. The Spain that is far removed from the artificiality of the popular tourist resorts. The phrase is travel journalistic jargon and an enticement to visitors to explore those parts of Spain that do not form part of the usual holidaymaker's 'paella-and-chips' destination.

> The Costa Brava … is also known as 'The Gateway to Spain,' but those who treat it as such, hurtling down

the A17 autopista in search of 'the real Spain' further south, miss out on the best bit of all.
Sunday Telegraph (10 July 1994)

Real Thing, The. A play (1982) by Tom Stoppard (b.1937) in which a married playwright debates whether his love for an actress (also married) is the 'real thing' or not. The phrase has been used with relation to 'genuine' love as distinct from mere infatuation or sexual desire for many years, with records of its appearance going back as far as 1857. Since 1942, however, it has also become well known as an advertising slogan for COCA-COLA, an association that Stoppard almost certainly had in mind when he was selecting the title for his play.

Real world. The reality of everyday life and routine, as distinct from the world of one's imagination, innocence or ignorance. *See also* GET OUT MORE.

> At the end of a working day I [novelist Rose Tremain] do 45 minutes of yoga. Then I switch off and return to the real world. I go to the kitchen, pour myself a drink and cook.
> *The Times* (11 September 1999)

Rearrange someone's face, To. To hit or punch it so that its features are unrecognizable.

> Journalist Ian Stafford trains with Flamengo, is bounced out by the Aussie test team ... and has his face rearranged by boxer Roy Jones Jr.
> *The Times* (4 December 1999)

Rear Window. A claustrophobic suspense film (1954) directed by Alfred Hitchccok and starring James Stewart and Grace Kelly. The rear window is a window through which a photographer, recuperating after breaking his leg, sees a murder committed. The film is based on a short story by Cornell Woolrich entitled *It Had to be Murder* (1942).

Rebecca. A novel (1938) by Daphne du Maurier (1907–89). Although the unnamed Mrs de Winter is at the centre of this study of psychological jealousy, it is Rebecca, her husband's first and dead wife, who dominates the action. The book grew out of the author's jealousy of an ex-fiancée of her husband, Lieutenant-General Frederick Browning (1896–1965), whom she married in 1932. It has been adapted for screen, stage and television, but the classic version remains the 1940 film, directed by Alfred Hitchcock, in which key roles were played by Laurence Olivier, Joan Fontaine, George Sanders, Judith Anderson, Nigel Bruce and Gladys Cooper. *See also* FIRST LINES OF NOVELS.

Rebel Without a Cause. A film (1955) adapted by Stewart Stern and Irving Shulman from the story 'Blind Run' by Robert M. Lindner about a rebellious teenager whose unruly behaviour culminates in a death-defying challenge in which he and a rival drive their cars full speed towards the edge of a cliff. Starring James Dean, Natalie Wood and Sal Mineo, the film acquired iconic status among the restless young of the 1950s, Dean in particular often being referred to as the 'rebel without a cause'. The tragedy of the characters in the film was reflected in the premature deaths of all three stars: Dean died in a car crash eerily reminiscent of the climax of the film in 1955, Mineo was murdered in West Hollywood in 1976, and Wood drowned in obscure circumstances in 1981.

Rebirthing. A form of ALTERNATIVE therapy using yogic breathing techniques to release the trauma that, according to specialists, can manifest itself as physical pain or negative behaviour. It was developed in San Francisco in the 1970s and involves talking to a therapist about the circumstances of one's birth, as far as one can recall them, then lying in a darkened room and breathing in a particular way, inhaling and exhaling through the mouth. Tingling in areas where trauma is stored should then be felt. The technique has gained some credence in scientific circles.

Received Pronunciation. *See* OXFORD ACCENT.

Recharge one's batteries, To. To regain one's strength and energy by resting and relaxing for a time. The fairly obvious allusion is to the restoring of an electric charge to a battery. The expression dates from the 1920s.

> After the excesses of the festive season, relax and recharge your batteries with a short stay at the luxurious GLENEAGLES hotel.
> *The Times* (advertisement) (5 January 2000)

Recipe for disaster. A plan or course of action that could lead to injury or collapse.

> 'I'm not happy about the incorporation of three regulation fences including an open ditch,' said Nicholson. 'I think they should stick to cross-country fences, otherwise it could be a recipe for disaster.'
> *Guardian* (24 November 1994)

Reclaim the night. The slogan of an annual march by women first made on 23 November 1977 in Leeds, Manchester, Newcastle and other English cities to protest against men's control of the streets at night. Similar marches were held in the United States under the slogan TAKE BACK THE NIGHT and the organized protests developed in some cases into political campaigns such as 'Women Against Violence Against Women'.

Recreational drug. A drug taken for pleasure rather than for medical reasons. The implication is that drug use (or abuse) is optional, and not the consequence of addiction. The expression became current from the early 1970s. *See also* ECSTASY; HEROIN; LSD.

Red alert. A warning of danger; an instruction to be prepared for an emergency. The term dates from the 1950s and chiefly finds application in military establishments and hospitals. In the latter it is an instruction that emergency cases only are to be admitted.

> Facing a flu epidemic, some hospitals have been placed on red alert. Non-urgent operations have been cancelled.
>
> *The Times* (10 January 2000)

Red Army. The combined Soviet army and air force were officially so named from 1918 to 1946, when the forces were renamed the Soviet Army. The original name was long preferred by the Western media, however. *See also* WHITE ARMY.

Red Army Faction. *See* BAADER-MEINHOF GANG.

Red Arrows. The aerobatic display team of the RAF, formed in 1965. They are familiar from the nine red aircraft with which they perform complex coordinated manoeuvres at high speed and from the trails of coloured vapour that they release to add to the already breathtaking spectacle.

Red Badge of Courage, The. The novel (1895) by Stephen Crane (1871–1900), about the experiences of a naive young recruit in the Union forces during the US Civil War, was adapted as a film (1951) by director John Huston and Albert Band. Although Crane had no personal experience of war, the star of the film, Audie Murphy, was the most decorated US soldier of the Second World War. The making of the film, which was cut to ribbons by studio executives after Huston abandoned it to start work on *The African Queen*, has long been the subject of legend, as related in Lillian Ross's book *Picture*. The 'red badge' of the title refers to the bloody wounds of soldiers hurt in battle.

Red Baron. The First World War German fighter pilot Manfred Freiherr von Richthofen (1892–1918) was so known from his red Fokker aircraft. He led what became known as Richthofen's Circus, creating havoc

and destroying some 80 planes. When eventually shot down over Allied lines he was given a military funeral, with a firing party provided by the Australian Flying Corps. Germans know him as *der rote Kampfflieger*, 'the red fighter pilot', rather than the Red Baron.

Redbrick. A term that came to be loosely applied to all English universities of a late 19th or early 20th century foundation. The name was introduced by 'Bruce Truscot' (Professor E. Allison Peers) in his book *Redbrick University* (1943). He was primarily dealing with the universities of Birmingham, Bristol, Leeds, Liverpool, Manchester, Reading and Sheffield, and expressly excluded London. In his Introduction he says: 'Though red brick, rather than dingy stone, has been chosen as the symbol of the new foundations, it must be categorically stated that no one university alone has been in the author's mind.' *See also* PLATE GLASS UNIVERSITIES.

Red Brigades (Italian *Brigate rosse*). The group of URBAN GUERRILLAS who in 1978 kidnapped and murdered the former Italian prime minister Aldo Moro. Their reputed founder was Renato Curcio (b.1945), who set up a left-wing group at the University of Trento in 1967, married a fellow radical, Margherita Cagol, in 1969, and moved with her to Milan. They proclaimed the existence of the Red Brigades in 1970, fire-bombing factories and warehouses, then began kidnappings in 1971 and murders in 1974. By the late 1980s they had ceased to be a major force.

Redcap. A name for a military policeman, who wears such a cap as part of his uniform.

Red card. In football a card shown by the referee to a player who is to be sent off the field for a repeated or serious infringement. Red cards were introduced to English football on 2 October 1976. That same day the first red card in the English league was shown to David Wagstaffe of Blackburn Rovers in their match against Leyton Orient, and also to George Best, for foul and abusive language, when playing for Fulham in their game at Southampton. *See also* YELLOW CARD.

Red carpet. A ceremonial carpet unrolled for the arrival or departure of an important visitor. In British tradition red is used to signify importance and dignity. Hence its use for so called 'red books' such as court guides, peerage lists, official regulations and the like, or for a government minister's 'red box' in which official papers are held. To roll out the red carpet for someone is thus to lavish hospitality on them, to give them a 'right royal welcome'.

> In 1985 we celebrated the 300th anniversary of J.S. Bach's birth. This year, the red carpet is being rolled out for the 250th anniversary of his death.
> *The Times* (11 January 2000)

Red Clydeside. *See* CLYDESIDERS.

Redcoats. The former entertainers and organizers at BUTLIN'S holiday camps, so named from their red jackets. Redcoats were also British soldiers of the 16th century and later, similarly so dubbed from their uniform.

> Her beach house at Middleton-on-Sea was ridiculed as 'Bognor', where she was supposedly woken by Butlin's redcoats shouting wakey-wakey every morning.
> *Sunday Times Magazine* (29 August 1999)

Red Dean. Dr Hewlett Johnson (1874–1966), Dean of Canterbury from 1931 to 1963. The name alludes to his left-wing views and his genuine belief that the communist ideal was compatible with Christian ethics. He visited Russia in 1938 and launched his public lauding of Sovietism in *The Socialist Sixth of the World* (1939). In 1951 he was awarded the Stalin Peace Prize. His sobriquet was a self-bestowed title when, during the Spanish Civil War, he said: 'I saw red – you can call me red.'

Red Devils. The freefall display team of the Parachute Regiment, formed in 1963. Dressed in red jumpsuits and trailing plumes of coloured smoke, they 'swim' into a succession of formations as they fall, passing through hoops that they hold for one another and landing on or near a narrowly defined target area in front of the public.

Red Duster. A nickname for the Red Ensign, the flag flown by British merchant ships.

Red Dwarf. A long-running SCIENCE FICTION space SITCOM, first screened in 1988 and soon developing a keen international cult following. The premise is that the crew of a 21st-century spaceship, the *Red Dwarf*, have all, with one exception, been wiped out following a radiation leak. The sole survivor is David Lister, who after remaining in suspended animation for 3 million years is joined by a motley assortment of characters, including 'Ace', a hologram of Arnold Rimmer, his former shift leader, Holly, the now senile shipboard computer, and 'Cat', a strange humanoid creature. The story devolves on their adventures as they roam the universe.

Red-eye. A colloquialism dating from the 1960s for a plane flight that deprives passengers of proper sleep as a result of take-off or arrival times or because of differences in time zones.

> 'Gosh, you're so lucky!' they cry, fresh off the Friday night red-eye from Heathrow as they stock up on jeans at The Gap.
> *The Times* (24 January 2000)

Red flag. A sign generally used to indicate danger or as a stop signal. It is also the symbol of international socialism and *The Red Flag* is a socialist anthem still used, somewhat incongruously, by the the British LABOUR PARTY. It is not the same as the *Internationale* (French *chanson internationale*, 'international song'), the official international socialist anthem, and the Soviet national anthem until 1944, whose words were written in 1871 by Eugène Pottier, a Parisian transport worker, and set to music by Pierre Degeyter, a woodworker of Lille (1848–1932).

> Then raise the scarlet standard high!
> Within its shade we'll live or die.
> Tho' cowards flinch and traitors sneer,
> We'll keep the red flag flying here.
> JAMES CONNELL: 'The Red Flag' (1889)

Red Friday. Friday, 31 July 1925, when a stoppage in the coal industry, planned to meet the threat of wage cuts, was averted by promise of government subsidies to support wages. It was so called by the Labour press to distinguish it from BLACK FRIDAY of 1921.

Red gold. Payment made by the KGB in the former Soviet Union to Western spies and informants.

> In his resignation letter ... [he] admitted taking 'red gold' in the form of expenses for foreign trips paid for by the KGB, but not cash for information.
> *Sunday Times* (11 December 1994)

Red Guard. A movement of armed workers in Russia prior to the October Revolution of 1917. A militant youth movement of the name also existed in China from 1966 to 1976 (*see* CULTURAL REVOLUTION). Its members wore red armbands and carried a copy of Chairman Mao's LITTLE RED BOOK. Their name was probably a conscious copying of the Russian original (*Krasnaya gvardiya*).

Red Harvest. The first novel (1929) by Dashiell Hammett (1894–1961), who submitted it to the publishing house of Knopf as 'an action-packed detective story' under the title of *Poisonville*. When a change of title was demanded, Hammett eventually came up with *Red Harvest*, suggestive of left-wing radicalism and a profusion of blood. The book is about the malign influence that capitalism has on the town of Poisonville.

Red-hot momma or **mama.** A name for an 'earthy' female jazz singer, especially when black or coloured. The vaudeville singer Sophie Tucker (1884–1966) was known as 'The Last of the Red-Hot Mamas' and in her latter years billed herself as such.

> The week before sailing for London [in 1930] I played the Palace in New York again. I was billed as 'SOPHIE TUCKER, THE LAST OF THE RED-HOT MAMAS!' This was the first time I carried this billing, which was to become so closely associated with me that it has persisted through all the years since that season when I introduced Jack Yellen's song hit, 'I'm the Last of the Red-hot Mamas' [1929].
> SOPHIE TUCKER: *Some of These Days: An Autobiography,* ch xxiii (1948)

Red Ken. A fairly obvious media nickname for Ken Livingstone (b.1945), Labour leader of the Greater London Council (GLC) from 1981 to its dissolution in 1986. He transformed the GLC from a mainly administrative body into an instrument of left-wing policies and a key tool in Labour's consistent criticism of the Conservative national programme. The right-wing press, in conjunction with Margaret Thatcher's government, launched a concerted campaign against him, portraying him and his policies as the epitome of the LOONY LEFT. However, Thatcher's decision to abolish the GLC in 1983 (implemented in 1986), together with Livingstone's self-deprecatory wit and GLC policies such as cutting fares on London Transport, made him popular with Londoners, even with Tory voters. In 1987 Livingstone became Labour MP for Brent. In 2000 he stood in Labour's contest to select its candidate for mayor of London but narrowly lost to Frank Dobson, then secretary of state for health. He then stood as an independent, easily defeating his (official) Labour, Conservative and Liberal Democrat rivals to become London's first elected mayor.

Red light. A children's game of US origin in which one player turns his back on the others and counts rapidly to 10. While he is doing so the others try to sneak up to him without being seen moving. When he reaches 10 he calls out 'red light!', whereupon each advancer must stop in his tracks and hold the position in which

he was caught. The allusion is to the red light that halts a railway train. *See also* GRANDMOTHER'S STEPS.

Red-light district. The district of a town or city where prostitution or other commercialized sexual activities are concentrated. The allusion is to a red light as a sign of a brothel.

Red mafia. A name current in the 1990s for the organized criminal gangs of Russia and eastern Europe, who after siphoning millions of dollars from the former Soviet Union through fraud, extortion and smuggling invested heavily in London stocks and shares. The gangs were linked to the murder in 1999 of the billionaire banker Edmond Safra, one of the world's richest men.

Red menace. A term arising in the 1920s for the political or military threat apprehended as emanating from the Soviet Union. An alternative was 'red peril', based on the earlier YELLOW PERIL.

Red Nose Day. A day once a year when people wear a small red nose or sport a large one on the front of their car. A red nose is a badge of the clown, and in this instance it is a symbol of the charitable enterprise COMIC RELIEF that the nose-buyers have supported.

Red Robbo. A nickname given by the right-wing tabloid press to Derek Robinson (b.1937), hard-left union convenor at British Leyland's Longbridge plant in Birmingham. Robinson was sacked in 1976 following a succession of unofficial strikes.

Red Rum. The bay gelding who won the Grand National an unprecedented three times, in 1973, 1974 and 1977, was foaled in 1965 and bought in 1972 when crippled with a form of equine arthritis, a condition eased by being trotted in the sea along Southport beach. He was to have been entered for the 1978 National but was withdrawn because of injury less than 24 hours before the start. He was retired from racing that year but continued to earn money until 1994, when he retired altogether from public life. He died the following year.

Red spotted handkerchief. The gaudy item of clothing which a runaway or rover traditionally uses as a bundle to carry his scant belongings.

> 'Sharon's brother, Trevor, couldn't stand the strain of it: he packed his red spotted handkerchief and moved out.'
> *The Times* (26 February 2000)

Reds under the bed. Undisclosed communist sympathizers. The phrase was current in the COLD WAR with mocking reference to those obsessed with hunting down supposed communists (*see* McCARTHYISM). A person hiding under a bed may overhear the most intimate or closely guarded secrets.

Red-tops. Media jargon for the TABLOID press, referring to the red-coloured mastheads of newspapers such as the *Mirror* and the *Sun*. The term became current in the late 1990s.

> A tabloid paper had a story about his private life. 'I can't talk about it,' said the 50-year-old Labour peer ... But the redtops could – and did.
>
> *Sunday Times* (24 October 1999)

Reeperbahn. 'Ropewalk', a street in Hamburg's RED-LIGHT DISTRICT. The name is sometimes used of similar districts elsewhere.

> The Reeperbahn or 42nd Street of Sydney is King's Cross.
>
> JAN MORRIS: *Journeys* (1985)

Reese's Pieces. *See* PRODUCT PLACEMENT.

Refained. A respelling of 'refined' intended to evoke an affected pronunciation of this word to denote the type of accent adopted by a certain class of 'refined' people.

> The proprietress informed me – with the kind of pained smile and 'refained' accent that would normally make me snort with laughter – that we would be 'more comfortable' in the teashop next door.
>
> *Sunday Times* (26 September 1999)

Referendum Party. A single-issue party founded in 1994 by the billionaire Anglo-French financier Sir James Goldsmith (1933–97). His aim was to force the government to hold a plebiscite on the issue of whether Britain should be part of a federal Europe or a bloc of independent trading nations. The party attracted several high-profile defectors from the right wing of the Conservative Party, such as Alan Walters (b.1926), a former economics adviser to Margaret Thatcher, and for a brief spell the MP Sir George Gardiner (b.1935). Despite extensive media advertising, however, funded by Goldsmith with £20 million from his personal fortune, the party's support in national opinion polls failed to rise above 1 per cent. After the 1997 general election, in which it failed to win a single seat, it suffered a humiliating demise. *See also* GOLDENBALLS.

Reflexology. A technique for relief of tension by massaging the feet, popular as an ALTERNATIVE therapy in the 1980s. The premise is that pressure points on the feet are linked to various parts of the body, so that action on a pressure point has a reflex ('reflected') action on some other organs.

Refusenik. A term in the 1970s for a Jew in the Soviet Union who was refused permission to emigrate to Israel, the *-nik* being as in BEATNIK. The word is now used more generally for anyone who refuses to obey orders, especially as a protest.

> A dwindling breed of rock authenticists still object to such events on the old sell-out principle, and won't turn up no matter what. Richard Ashcroft ... is a notable refusenik.
>
> *Sunday Times* (27 February 2000)

Reggae. A style of popular music with a strongly accented subsidiary beat, originating in Jamaica. It evolved in the late 1960s from ska and other local variations on the calypso and rhythm and blues, and was widely popularized in the 1970s by Bob Marley and the Wailers. The word itself perhaps derives from Jamaican English *rege-rege*, meaning 'row', 'quarrel', literally 'ragged clothes', from the casual dress of its performers. *See also* RAGGA.

Reinvent oneself, To. To take on a new or radically different character or guise, often as a result of altered circumstances. In the case of a public figure, the move might be made in order to refresh and refurbish one's public image. The term dates from the late 1980s.

> As Archibald Delaney, the son of a Sussex doctor who reinvented himself in the Thirties as a campaigning American Indian, [Pierce] Brosnan's prospects weren't aided by his pony-tail.
>
> *Sunday Express* (27 February 2000)

Reinvent the wheel, To. To waste time or effort in creating something that already exists. The wheel is one of mankind's earliest and most radical inventions, dating from at least 3500 BC.

> 'It used to be you almost had to reinvent the wheel to get funding,' said Daniel Cobb, dean of the faculty at the small liberal arts college in West Virginia.
>
> *Washington Post* (16 July 1984)

Reith Lectures. An annual series of radio lectures broadcast by the BBC and named after its first director-general, John Reith (1889–1971), a Scottish Presbyterian minister's son famous for his championing of the moral and intellectual role of broadcasting. The series was inaugurated in 1948, when the philosopher Bertrand Russell spoke on 'Authority and the Individual'. Each series consists of six lectures, the speakers being mostly white English male academics.

For many years the subjects were lofty, but have latterly tended towards the banal and unoriginal.

> The Reith lectures have become a kind of scrapyard for used ideas. Any second-hand trendy theory with a bent chassis and bald tyres is likely to end up in this peculiar corner of the BBC, waiting to be flogged off as nearly new.
> *Sunday Times* (9 May 1999)

Relais routier (French, 'transport café'). The roadside restaurants so known in France were originally designed for lorry drivers, like the old British 'pull-ups', but from the 1960s have been sought out by tourists and travellers for their high-class food at reasonable prices.

Reliant Robin. A well known make of three-wheeled car, regarded with amused disdain by many 'real' car drivers but with loyalty and affection by their owners. The Reliant Motor Company had its beginnings in the workshop set up in 1935 by T.L. Williams in his garden at Tamworth, Staffordshire, to make three-wheeled delivery vehicles. The first passenger tricar was the Regal, launched in 1953. The Robin superseded it in 1972 and soon found favour for its cheap road tax and the fact that it could be driven on a motorcycle licence. The use of Reliant Robins by repair and delivery staff in the television comedy ONLY FOOLS AND HORSES enhanced rather than diminished their cult status.

Remembrance Day. After the First World War ARMISTICE DAY, or Remembrance Day, commemorating the fallen, was observed on 11 November. From 1945 to 1956 it was observed on the first or second Sunday of November, now commemorating the fallen of both world wars. In 1956 Remembrance Day was fixed on the second Sunday of November. *See also* POPPY DAY; TWO-MINUTE SILENCE; VETERAN'S DAY.

Remembrance of Things Past. The title of a sequence of seven novels (1922–31; in French as *À la recherche du temps perdu*, 1913–27) by Marcel Proust (1871–1922). Together, they constitute a deeply significant, quasi-autobiographical study of people and the society in which they moved, in the course of which the protagonist, Marcel, assumes a variety of roles before ultimately regaining his lost vocation as a writer. When G.K. Scott-Moncrieff started publishing the first famous English translation of the work in 1922, the year of Proust's death, he gave it an evocative but not entirely accurate title taken from Shakespeare: 'When to the sessions of sweet silent thought / I

summon up remembrance of things past' (Sonnet 30). The title was well in keeping with the florid tone of his translation, and its poetic resonance doubtless helped to sell his work. Proust, however, was not writing about idle remembrance but about arduous research (*recherche*), as he himself exemplified in the 12 years of illness and solitude that he spent writing the sequence. When, therefore, a freshly revised translation of the work was published in 1992, it was given a title much closer to the intention of the original: *In Search of Lost Time*. *See also* FIRST LINES OF NOVELS.

Renaissance man. A man with many talents and interests, especially in the humanities, and so to some degree evoking the Renaissance itself, as the revival of art and literature in the 14th century.

> The Renaissance man may now be no more than an historic ideal, but in our lifetimes one historian could lay a languid, yet secure, claim to that title. Alan Clark, whose death we mourn today, was more than a politician of remarkable qualities who helped to define an age.
> *The Times* (8 September 1999)

Renamo. *See* FRELIMO.

Rent-a-crowd or **mob.** A crowd of demonstrators. The implication is that they have been paid to demonstrate and that they will happily do so for or against any cause, simply for the financial reward. The term derives from the American car hire company *Rentacar*, established in 1921.

> The day that rent-a-mob came to the City of London did have its comical side. The thuggish anarchists and Trotskyists who were intent on causing violent confrontation with the police were accompanied by such unlikely groups as the Association of Autonomous Astronauts and the Biotic Baking Brigade.
> *Sunday Times* (20 June 1999)

Rentaquote. A term applied by the press to those backbench MPs (mostly Tories) who always seem to be willing to sound off to journalists on any subject that is required, particularly on days when there is little 'real' news.

Rent boy. A young male prostitute, a 'boy' available for 'rent'. The term, but not the phenomenon, dates from the 1960s.

Repetitive strain injury. A rather grand term for a medical condition in which injury to muscles or tendons is caused by the repeated use of particular muscles, as when operating a keyboard. Some insurance companies refuse to recognize the condition as validating a compensation claim, although many employers are now aware of it as an occupational health hazard.

Repo man. A repossession man, employed by finance companies to repossess goods whose buyer has defaulted on payments. In American parlance a repo man is usually associated with cars. The term dates from the 1960s. Alex Cox's FILM NOIR, *Repo Man*, was made in 1984.

Resistible Rise of Arturo Ui, The. A play, originally entitled *Der aufhaltsame Aufstieg des Arturo Ui* (1958), by the German playwright Bertolt Brecht (1898–1956) about the career of a small-time Chicago gangster as he seeks to establish a stranglehold over the city's cauliflower business. Arturo Ui himself is a thinly disguised portrait of the NAZI dictator Adolf Hitler, although the character was first suggested to Brecht when he read newspaper reports in New York about the killing of a real-life gangster called Dutch Schulz. These he combined with details culled from his reading of a biography of Al CAPONE and his viewing of numerous American gangster movies.

Rest is history, The. You know what happened later. A stock formula for breaking off a biographical anecdote, either because the outcome is generally familiar or because the speaker cannot be bothered to repeat it. When describing his transition from Oxford history don to Broadway revue artist the writer Alan Bennett, speaking at a seminar at Nuffield College, Oxford, in 1986, said: 'The rest, one might say pompously, is history. Except that in my case the opposite was true. What it had been was history. What it was to be was not history at all.'

> There across all the papers was the photograph of me presenting the Queen Mother with her chart, under the caption 'Astrologer Royal'. Well, the rest, as they say, is history.
> RUSSELL GRANT in *TV Times* (15 October 1983)

Retro. A vogue word of the 1980s and 1990s, indicating little more than a nostalgic harking back to the past, a sentimental retrospection. The term particularly caught on in the worlds of popular music and fashion, and was prefixed to other words to form impressive-looking compounds such as 'retro-chic' or 'retro-culture'.

> Black patent Grace Kelly handbags, long black gloves and high-heeled slingbacks are retro accessories to the elegant look.
> *The Times* (1 July 1986)

Reuben sandwich. A type of sandwich popular in the United States in the 1960s, containing a combination of corned beef, Swiss cheese and sauerkraut served hot. It is said to take its name from Arnold Reuben (1883–1970), a restaurant owner.

Revised Standard Version. A modern translation of the Bible produced in the United States and published between 1946 and 1957. It was in the tradition of the Authorized (King James) Version of 1611 but aimed to eliminate excessively archaic language. It became the standard text in many churches and communities and remained in widespread use until 1990, when a further revision, the New Revised Standard Version, was published, with the text presented in a more contemporary idiom. An anglicized edition was published in 1995.

Revolver. A critically acclaimed album by the BEATLES, released in the UK in August 1966 and favoured by some over its better known successor SERGEANT PEPPER'S LONELY HEARTS CLUB BAND. The title of the album refers to the revolutions of an LP on a record turntable, rather than to a gun, and was chosen over such earlier candidate names as 'Freewheelin' Beatles', 'Bubble and Squeak' and 'Four Sides to the Circle'. *Revolver* includes the tracks ELEANOR RIGBY, 'Tomorrow Never Knows', I'm Only Sleeping', 'Here, There and Everywhere' and DOCTOR ROBERT and confirms the creative progress of the Beatles, which had begun with RUBBER SOUL, from pop group to PSYCHEDELIC rock band.

Rexists. A group of Belgian fascists who collaborated with the Nazis during the German occupation in the Second World War. The Rexist Movement was founded in 1930 by Léon Degrelle (1906–94) as a branch of the Catholic Party, with the aim of purging politics from the Catholic Church. The name derives from *Christus Rex* (Latin, 'Christ the King'), the slogan of the Catholic Young People's Action Society, which had been established in 1925. The Rexists went on to establish their own political party, which, subsidized by Mussolini, became a fascist organization. During the German occupation Rexists took control of local government and the press and also organized Belgian units to fight for the Germans on the Eastern Front. After the liberation Degrelle fled to Franco's Spain, where he remained for the rest of his life.

Rhinoceros. A play (1959), characteristic of the THEATRE OF THE ABSURD, by the Romanian-born French playwright Eugène Ionesco (1912–94) depicting how an ordinary man in a small French town discovers that everyone he knows is gradually turning into a rhinoceros. In Ionesco's hands the disease 'rhinoceritis' became an allegory for the spread of FASCISM through the populations of Europe in the years before the Second World War.

Rhubarb. A word conventionally repeated by actors to represent the murmur of conversation in a crowd scene. The practice, dating from the 1930s, is not unknown in Shakespeare productions, especially at an amateur level. Other languages have similar dodges, and Russian actors repeat *govoryu, ne govoryu,* 'I speak, I don't speak'.

> And in the next-door room is heard the tramp
> And 'rhubarb, rhubarb' as the crowd rehearse
> A one-act play in verse.
> JOHN BETJEMAN: *Summoned by Bells,* ch ix (1960)

Riallaro. The fictional archipelago in the southeast Pacific that is the subject of Godfrey Sweven's fantasy novel of the same name, in full *Riallaro, the Archipelago of Exiles* (1901). Its name means 'ring of mist', referring to the ring of fog that surrounds it, and ships that have sailed into it have never reappeared. The islands that form the archipelago are Aleofane, Broolyi, Coxuria, Fanattia, Feneralia, Figlefia, Haciocram, Kloriole, Limanora, Loonarie, Meskeeta, Spectralia, Swoonarie, Thanasia and Torralaria. Their names in many cases give a clue to their distinctiveness. Thus Figlefia is an 'Island of Love', Loonarie houses the archipelago's lunatic asylum, and the inhabitants of Spectralia all believe in ghosts.

Rich bitch. A derogatory nickname of American origin for a wealthy woman, especially one who dresses or deports herself ostentatiously.

> Nowhere does the rich bitch and her acolyte, the would-be rich bitch, feel more spiritually at home than in that mega-boutique that is Italian fashion.
> *The Times* (28 February 2000)

Richter scale. The numerical scale for expressing the magnitude of an earthquake on the basis of seismograph oscillations takes its name from the US geologist Charles F. Richter (1900–85). The scale is logarithmic, and the numerical value assigned to an earthquake measures its overall size, not its intensity at a given point. Richter's own name for his invention, created in 1927 and perfected in 1935, was 'the magnitude scale', and he regretted that the new name did not reflect the contribution to his work made by his fellow seismologist Beno Gutenberg (1889–1960).

Earthquakes had previously been measured in subjective terms, by recording the damage sustained by structures of different types. The scale itself begins at 1, detected only by seismographs, and has no theoretical upper limit although the largest earthquakes have not exceeded a scale value of 9.

Riddle of the Sands, The. A thriller (1903) by Erskine Childers (1870–1922), set against the background of the Anglo-German Great Naval Race of the early 20th century. The 'sands' are the mudflats and sandbanks of the Friesian Islands, and the 'riddle' is to resolve the mystery that lies there. Ultimately two Englishmen thwart the traitorous aim of a former British naval officer who is preparing for a German invasion of Britain. An ardent Irish nationalist, Childers became a minister in the self-constituted Irish parliament (DÁIL Éireann) in 1921. He was captured, courtmartialled and shot on the orders of the Irish Free State government for the illegal possession of a revolver. This, his only novel, is memorable as much for its descriptive passages on sailing as for its gripping story line. A rather tame film version (1978) was directed by Tony Maylam. *See also* FIRST LINES OF NOVELS.

Riddley Walker. A novel (1980) by the US writer Russell Hoban (b.1925), set in a brutal environment 2000 years after a universal nuclear holocaust. When a father is crushed under a piece of ancient machinery, his 12-year-old son takes over his role as 'Riddley Walker', whose function is to walk around asking riddles, the answers to which will reveal the relationship between mankind and the universe. The dialogue is a phonetically spelled, stylized dialect resembling English.

Ride a tiger, To. To embark on a course of action that turns out to be unexpectedly difficult but that cannot be safely abandoned. The expression comes from the modern proverb, 'He who rides a tiger is afraid to dismount,' itself of Chinese origin. A tiger is a dangerous beast. One may ride it in an attempt to capture it, but it may turn on one at any moment and one cannot readily dismount.

> 'Hugh was such an intelligent boy. ... He thought he could ride a tiger. He thought he could be a free spirit – and he was. But it was the tiger that captured Hugh – not Hugh the tiger,' said Mr McCartney, who concluded by patting Hugh's coffin.
> *The Times* (1 October 1999)

Ride off into the sunset, To. To conclude an episode or experience with a happy resolution. The reference is to the classic final scene of certain Western films of the 1930s in which the cowboy hero, having vanquished the 'baddies', literally rides off into the sunset.

Riders to the Sea. A play (1904) by the Irish playwright J.M. Synge (1871–1909) about the grieving of an old peasant woman, Maurya, for her husband and five of her six sons, lost at sea. It is realized that the last son has been claimed by the sea when the old woman reports having seen his image riding a grey horse by the sea, the grey horse recalling the 'pale horse' of the Apocalypse: 'his name that sat on him was Death'.

Ride shotgun, To. To guard a person or thing in transit. The American expression alludes to the armed assistant on a stagecoach who sat beside the coachman to protect him from marauding Indians, bandits and the like. The term was later used of any person riding in the front passenger seat of a motor vehicle.

Ride the clutch, To. In driving a motor vehicle to keep one's foot too long on the clutch pedal, depressing it slightly. If persisted in the tactic will soon wear out the friction lining.

Ride the cushions, To. To travel luxuriously by public transport, as by train with a first-class ticket. An American expression dating from the early 20th century. *See also* RIDE THE RAILS.

Ride the gain, To. In broadcasting to reduce or increase the gain when the input signal becomes too large or too small. The manoeuvre is necessary in order to keep the gain within the proper limits for the equipment in question. The expression is of American origin and dates from the 1920s.

Ride the lightning, To. To be executed in the electric chair. A vivid American metaphor dating from the 1940s.

Ride the rails, To. To travel by train, and especially on a freight train without paying. A mostly Canadian expression dating from the 1940s. *See also* RIDE THE CUSHIONS.

Right on. Modern; fashionable; politically sound; ideologically correct. The expression dates from the 1950s and originated from a black American shortening of 'right on time'. The transference of sense was thus from temporality to topicality.

Right to roam. Although there has long been no automatic right of public access to open country in England and Wales, in 1999 the government announced its intention to introduce laws giving walkers a new right to explore the countryside. This 'right to roam' would apply to mountain, moor, heath, down and registered common land and could be extended to other types of open country such as some woodland. At the same time walkers would have a clear responsibility to respect the rights of landowners and managers. *See also* RAMBLERS.

> Right-to-roam legislation poses problems for river and waterside life, but the biggest concern is over changes in public attitude to animals.
> *The Times* (3 January 2000)

Rillington Place. A cul-de-sac in Notting Hill, west London, where No. 10, a shabby terraced house, was the location of the murders of at least eight women over the period 1943–53. John Christie had moved in to the ground-floor flat with his wife in 1938 and 10 years later Timothy Evans moved in to the second-floor flat with his pregnant wife. In 1949 Evans, who was mentally retarded, confessed to the murder of his wife and baby girl and was hanged. In 1953 the mouldering bodies of three young women were found in Christie's kitchen cupboard. His wife's body was then discovered under the kitchen floorboards and the skeletons of two women buried some 10 years earlier in the garden. Christie, a necrophiliac, confessed to these murders and to that of Mrs Evans and was also hanged. Evans was granted a posthumous pardon in 1966. The house has now been demolished and the street renamed. The film *Ten Rillington Place* (1971), based on a book by Ludovic Kennedy, offered a realistically sordid reconstruction of the *cause célèbre* with Richard Attenborough in the role of the murderers and John Hurt as Evans.

Ring a bell, To. To jog one's memory; to sound familiar, as: 'That name rings a bell.' The expression dates from the 1930s and may have derived from the fairground 'try-your-strength' machine, in which a bell on top of a tall column could be struck by hammering a pivot at the base and sending a projectile upwards. Alternatively the reference may be to a summoning of the memory in the same way that a ring at the door or the ring of a telephone summons one to answer. *See also* CLOSE, BUT NO CIGAR.

Ring of steel. A surrounding armed defence, especially one preventing escape. In a speech on the Italian armistice in 1943 Adolf Hitler said, 'Tactical necessity may compel us ... to give up something on some front in this gigantic fateful struggle, but it will never break the ring of steel that protects the Reich' (translated from Gordon W. Prange, ed., *Hitler's Words*, 1944).

Ring of steel round [Falkland] islands.
The Times (headline) (30 April 1982)

Rinky-dink. Cheap and shoddy; outdated and unfashionable. The American term dates from the early years of the 20th century but is of uncertain origin. It perhaps represents the repetitive percussive sounds of an uninspired musical group.

The range of discontinued old rockets with chipped paint, spare parts from Skylab and rusting moonbuggies brought one (American) phrase to mind: rinky dink.
The Times Magazine (5 June 1999)

Rin Tin Tin. The talented German shepherd (Alsatian) dog who became a star of HOLLYWOOD movies in the 1920s. The original dog that bore the name was real, not fictional, and was one of a litter that American airmen rescued from an abandoned German dugout in France in September 1918. Corporal Lee Duncan named the pup after a tiny doll that the French soldiers carried for luck, and took him home to California. At first trained for dog shows, 'Rinty' was so successful in his first film, *Where the North Begins* (1923), that over the next nine years he made more than 40 movies, earned over £1 million and kept WARNER BROTHERS solvent. After he died in 1932 his son, Rin Tin Tin Jr, starred in Westerns until 1938, and another descendant appeared in *The Return of Rin Tin Tin* (1947). *See also* LASSIE.

Riot grrls. A loose-knit grouping of feminist PUNKS formed in Washington, D.C., in the early 1990s. Their rallying cry was 'Revolution Girl Style Now!' and a chief aim was to combat the male dominance of the punk scene. Their overall platform was that of GIRL POWER. The term subsequently became attached to any aggressive or overtly sexual female rock group.

Rip-off. A fraud or swindle, in which something is stolen from or 'ripped off' the victim.

Always a joke and a smile, always an attempt to rip you off with the scales or the change.
The Times (31 May 1999)

Ripping Yarns. A series of television comedies broadcast in 1977 and 1979 as a spoof of the type of stirring adventure stories found in boys' publications such as the BOY'S OWN PAPER. The nine episodes were created by members of the MONTY PYTHON'S FLYING CIRCUS team and their surreal humour is evident throughout.

Two of the episodes, *The Testing of Eric Olthwaite* and *Golden Gordon*, are virtually without peer in the realm of British comedy half-hours.

Rise and Fall of the City of Mahagonny. A ferocious political satire of an opera, *Aufstieg und Fall der Stadt Mahagonny*, by Kurt Weill (1900–50), with a libretto by Bertolt Brecht (1898–1956). It was first produced in 1930, following an earlier, simpler version of 1927. Mahagonny is an imaginary city of material pleasure, with a capitalist morality: when the hero, Jimmy Mahoney, is arrested and brought to trial, he is sentenced to two days' imprisonment for indirect murder, four years for seduction by means of money and is condemned to die for failing to pay his whisky bill.

Rise and shine, To. To get smartly out of bed. The phrase was originally a military command at the turn of the 20th century. The rather obvious analogy is with the sun.

Rising Damp. The television SITCOM of this name, screened from 1974 to 1978, owed its success to the wonderful acting of Leonard Rossiter in the role of its central character, Rupert Rigsby, the landlord of a run-down boarding-house in a northern university town. Rigsby is racist, lecherous, interfering and generally obnoxious, but in Rossiter's talented hands he is almost lovable. His tenants include the lovelorn spinster Ruth Jones, played by Frances de la Tour, the immature medical student Alan Moore, played by Richard Beckinsale, and the wise black student Philip Smith, played by Don Warrington.

Rising fives. Educational jargon for young children just below the compulsory school age of five. At the close of the 20th century many such children were attending nursery schools and classes or reception classes in primary schools, or else received pre-school education at private day nurseries and pre-school PLAYGROUPS, largely organized by parents. From 1998 the government provided free nursery education in England and Wales for all four-year-olds whose parents wanted it.

Rite of passage. A ceremony or event marking an important stage in someone's life, such as birth, initiation, marriage or death. The term translates French *rite de passage*, coined by the French ethnographer Arnold van Gennep in his major work *Les Rites de passage* (1909), in which he considered such ceremonies. The title of William Golding's prize-winning novel *Rites of Passage* (1980), the first of a trilogy, puns on 'passage' in the sense of sea journey, and all three books are set in the 18th century on a ship travelling to Australia.

Rite of Spring, The. The throbbingly rhythmic ballet with music by Igor Stravinsky (1882–1971) and choreography by Vaslav Nijinsky (1890–1950), was first performed by Diaghilev's BALLETS RUSSES in 1913 at the Théâtre des Champs-Elysées, Paris. It is often referred to by its French title, *Le Sacre du printemps*. The subtitle of the work is 'pictures from pagan Russia', and its two parts are titled 'The Adoration of the Earth' and 'The Sacrifice'. The hitherto unknown ferocity of the music's grinding discords and rhythms caused a riot at the first performance. One contemporary critic commented that it was 'rather a *Massacre du printemps*'; Diaghilev himself called it 'the 20th-century's Ninth Symphony'.

Ritzy. In colloquial usage, fashionable and luxurious; ostentatiously smart. The allusion is to one or other of the Ritz-Carlton Hotel, New York, the Ritz Hotel, Paris, or the Ritz Hotel, London, which became identified with wealth. The last of these was established in 1906 by the Swiss hotelier César Ritz (1850–1918). Hence 'to put on the Ritz', meaning to make a display of riches or luxury. The phrase was popularized by Irving Berlin's song 'Puttin' on the Ritz' (1929):

> If you're blue and you don't know what to do
> Why don't you go where Harlem sits
> Puttin' On The Ritz.

RNVR. *See* WAVY NAVY.

Road movie. A type of film in which the main character takes to the road or travels, usually in a car, either as an escape from something or in a search for something, typically in a journey of self-discovery. The form was best defined in Jack Kerouac's novel *On the Road* (1957), in which the characters seek fulfilment as they travel. Road movies had an instant appeal to American youth, and to some extent replaced the Western as entertainment. Male bonding was an integral feature until the 1990s, when feminism found its voice in *Thelma and Louise* (1991) and later films.

Road numbers. The roads in England are numbered by the Department of Transport according to a system, introduced in 1919, which divides the country into sectors. The six major routes leaving London are numbered A1 to A6 and the same number, 1 to 6, is given to the sector of country adjacent to each route, going clockwise. The A1 thus runs north to Berwick-

upon-Tweed, the A2 southeast to Dover, the A3 southwest to Portsmouth, and the A4 west to Bristol. All main roads in sector 1 have 1 as the first digit of their number, with A or B as a prefix depending on their greater or lesser importance. Thus in sector 1 the A12 runs northeast to Great Yarmouth and in sector 4 the A40 runs northwest to Cheltenham and Wales. The subsequent digits are random, a new road being given the next unallocated number in its own sector. A road originating in one sector but passing through others keeps its original number for its entire length. The same system applies in Scotland, where the sectors are defined by the routes A7 to A9 radiating from Edinburgh. Motorway numbers are organized similarly, with the prefix M.

Road rage. A driver's uncontrolled aggressive behaviour towards other road users. It is supposedly caused by the stress of modern driving, and can range from the brandishing of a fist or the mouthing of a curse to a full-scale beating-up or even, in a few cases, to an actual killing. The term has been evoked by some drivers in mitigation of their behaviour, as if a medical condition. See also WHITE VAN MAN.

Road to Wigan Pier, The. A sociological investigation (1937) by George ORWELL into the conditions of the unemployed in the towns of Wigan, Sheffield and Barnsley in the north of England. In the second half, he took a revolutionary stance that opposed Marxism, embarrassing members of the LEFT BOOK CLUB, of which it was a choice. The title is ironic, as Wigan is more than 30km (20 miles) from the sea. *See also* WIGAN PIER.

Roaring Twenties. The 1920s, a time of liberation and buoyancy after the First World War. The decade was characterized in the United States by the BRIGHT YOUNG THINGS and their flamboyant fashions, by PROHIBITION, with its SPEAKEASIES and gangsters, and by its financial boom that continued until the GREAT DEPRESSION.

Robot (Czech *robota*, 'forced labour'). An automaton with semi-human powers and intelligence. From this the term is often extended to mean a person who works automatically without employing initiative. The name comes from the mechanical creatures in Karel Čapek's play R.U.R. (*Rossum's Universal Robots*), which was successfully produced in London in 1923.

Rock Around the Clock. The song usually (though not necessarily correctly) identified as the first ROCK

'N' ROLL record, first released in 1954 by Bill Haley and his Comets. The song's title derived from an earlier song written by Bill Haley's manager Jimmy Myers entitled 'Dance Around the Clock', the title of which was changed for the new song to the happily rhyming 'Rock Around the Clock'. The song first appeared as the B-side of a song called 'Thirteen Women'. It later appeared in the teenage rebellion film *The* BLACK-BOARD JUNGLE and when reissued reached the top of the charts in both America and Britain. 'Rock Around the Clock' was associated by the conservative-minded with what they saw as a rising tide of juvenile delinquency. *The Blackboard Jungle* provoked the following reaction from the Scottish Conversative politician Lord Boothby:

> What worries me is that a fourth-rate film with fifth-rate music can pierce the shell of a civilization. The sooner this ridiculous film is banned the better.

Rock Drill, The. The aggressively mechanistic sculpture of a robot-like figure by Jacob Epstein (1880–1959) is one of the most famous works of early British MODERNISM (sculpted in 1913–14). The figure has certain drill-like qualities and was originally displayed on a real drill. Epstein himself commented: 'Here is the armed, sinister figure of today and tomorrow. No humanity, only the terrible Frankenstein's monster we have made ourselves into.'

Rocket science or **rocket scientist.** Terms generally used in negative constructions expressing the extreme simplicity of a task, such as 'It's hardly rocket science' or 'You don't have to be a rocket scientist to understand how the internal combustion engine works.' The implication is that, in contrast with the intellectually unchallenging nature of the matter alluded to, understanding the workings of rockets demands a great deal of specialist knowledge and mental prowess.

Rockettes. A team of 36 high-kicking, bejewelled dancers who first appeared at the RADIO CITY MUSIC HALL in 1933 and soon became icons of New York and 'showbiz' generally. They originated as a 16-member troupe from St Louis called the Missouri Rockets. They then became the Rockets and, when appearing at the ROXY Theatre, New York, the Roxyettes. This name was modified as now in 1934, since when a highlight has been the dancers' performance of their 'Parade of the Wooden Soldiers' routine at the annual Christmas show.

Rock group names. No one living in the second half of the 20th century can have failed to be struck by the many distinctive names of pop and rock groups, ranging from the apparently meaningless to the seemingly surreal. Like the covers of their albums, they have become almost an art form in themselves, although with an appeal that is verbal rather than visual. The following are the origins of the names of some of the most familiar groups, based on information in Mark Beech's *The A–Z of Names in Rock* (1998). Each group name is followed by the dates of its existence (still ongoing in many cases, if only notionally so), as given in the *Guinness Rockopedia* (1998).

Abba (1972–83): a palindromic acronym of the names of its four Swedish members: *Agnetha Fältskog, Björn Ulvaeus, Benny Andersson, Anni-Frid Lyngstad*

AC/DC (from 1973): from the standard abbreviation meaning 'alternating current/direct current', referring to a musical instrument that can be switched to either in any country

Aerosmith (from 1970): a blend of 'aerospace' and 'songsmith'

a-ha (from 1982): an exclamation of satisfaction

Animals (1962–83): from 'Animal' Hogg, the nickname of a friend of the lead singer Eric Burden. The name was appropriate for the group's wild stage act

Anthrax (from 1981): a word adopted by the heavy metal group for its unpleasant associations

Aztec Camera (from 1980): a combination of 'Aztec', adopted simply for its surreal sound and appearance, and 'Camera', a *Teardrop Explodes* single (*see below*)

Bananarama (from 1981): a blend of 'banana', a fruit with sexual associations, and the *Roxy Music* single 'Pyjamarama'

Bay City Rollers (from 1967): from *Bay City*, Oregon, Texas (or Rochester, Michigan), and 'roller', for its association with surf and ROCK 'N' ROLL

Beach Boys (from 1961): for the California group's surfing associations

BEATLES

Bee Gees (from 1955): from the initials of the *Brothers Gibb*, its three members, or those of its lead singer, *Barry Gibb*, or of the group's promoter, *Bill Gates*

B-52s (from 1976): for the beehive hairstyle of two of its members, Kate Pierson and Cindy Wilson, the style in turn being named after the American Air Force B–52 bomber

Black Sabbath (from 1969): from one of the group's own songs, based on bass player Terry 'Geezer' Butler's interest in black magic

BLONDIE

Blue Öyster Cult (from 1969): for bluepoint oysters (from Blue Point, Long Island, New York), the subject of a song by the group's manager Sandy Pearlman, with an umlaut added to enhance the name's mystery

Blur (from 1988): a name chose for its suggestion of the effect of alcohol, drugs or simply the passage of time, as well as vagueness of vision or memory

Boomtown Rats (1975–86): from the name of a gang in Woody Guthrie's autobiographical novel *Bound for Glory* (1943), read by the group's lead singer, Bob Geldof

Boo Radleys (from 1988): from the village idiot, Boo Radley, in Harper Lee's novel *To Kill a Mockingbird* (1960)

Boyzone (from 1993): from the boys' magazine BOY'S OWN PAPER, with a presumed pun on 'boy zone'

Bread (from 1968): for the money ('bread') that the group hoped to make; *see also* BREAD

Byrds (1964–73): for the group's 'lofty' ambition, coupled with the interest in aeronautics of its founder, Roger McGuinn

Canned Heat (from 1966): for Tommy Johnson's song 'Canned Heat Blues', itself punning on 'canned' in the sense 'drunk'

Chemical Brothers (from 1989): said to allude to the 'chemical bond' of the group's music, although its two members are not brothers

Chicago (from 1966): for the group's city of origin

Clannad (from 1970): from Irish *clan na Dobhair*, 'family of Dore', referring to Gweedore, Co. Donegal, the Irish group's place of origin

Clash (1976–86): a general word to evoke the PUNK group's music and its members' aggressive view of life

Cranberries (from 1990): from 'cranberry sauce' via the puerile pun 'the cranberry saw us'

Cream (1966–8): for the group's exalted view of themselves as an elite band

Creedence Clearwater Revival (1967–72): from a mutual friend, Creedence Nuball, coupled with

'Clearwater' in an advertisement about the use of pure drinking water in a brand of beer, and a 'revival' of the group's original musical direction

Cult (1982–95): originally the Southern Death Cult, from the title of an anthropological study of Native Americans from Mississippi

Culture Club (1981–6): for the group's love of night-clubbing and its mixed background or 'culture'

Cure (from 1976): a shortening of Easy Cure, from a song by the group's original drummer Laurence Tolhurst, who (like others before him) thought love a cure for all ills

Deep Purple (from 1968): a 'colour' name on the lines of *Black Sabbath* and *Pink Floyd*

Def Leppard (from 1977): an allusion to deafness as an occupational hazard of heavy metal fans combined with 'leopard' as a fashionable animal name, both words being phonetically respelled

Depeche Mode (from 1980): apparently an adoption of *Dépêche Mode*, 'Dispatch Mode', the title of a French trade and general interest fashion magazine

Dire Straits (from 1977): an allusion to the group's initial impecunious status

Doors (1965–73): ultimately from William Blake's *The Marriage of Heaven and Hell* (1790): 'If the doors of perception were cleansed everything would appear to man as it is, infinite.' Aldous Huxley borrowed the words for the title of *The Doors of Perception* (1954), an essay on experiments with mescaline and LSD, and this is a more immediate source for the group name

Duran Duran (from 1978): from the mad scientist Durand Durand played by Milo O'Shea in the cult film BARBARELLA (1967)

East 17 (from 1990): from the postal district, E17, of the group's London homes

Echobelly (from 1993): according to the band's lead singer, Sonya Aurora Madan, a name was chosen that was 'quite female and organic and voluptuous' and that suggested a hunger for something

Electric Light Orchestra (from 1971): a reference to the group's electric instruments playing light music in combination with the stringed instruments normally associated with a classical orchestra

Everything But the Girl (from 1984): said to derive from a notice in a second-hand furniture shop in Hull reading: 'For your bedroom needs we sell everything but the girl'

Fairport Convention (from 1966): from a house

named Fairport in Muswell Hill, London, where the group originally rehearsed as a 'convention' of musicians

Fine Young Cannibals (1985–92): from the title of the film *All the Fine Young Cannibals* (1960)

Fleetwood Mac (from 1967): from the names of two of the group's members, drummer Mick Fleetwood and bass player John McVie

Foo Fighters (from 1994): US military slang for fighter pilots called out to investigate 'foos', i.e. UFOs

Frankie Goes to Hollywood (1982–7): from a *New Yorker* headline about Frank Sinatra's move from Las Vegas to Los Angeles: 'Frankie Goes to Hollywood'

Fugees (from 1987): an abbreviation of 'refugees'

Genesis (from 1967): an allusion to the first book of the Bible to denote the group's debut

Grateful Dead (1965–95): said to derive from the old legend telling of those who return from the dead to help those still living who had helped them while they were alive

Hawkwind (from 1969): not a mystic or esoteric reference but simply a nickname given singer Nik Turner for his aquiline features and troublesome flatulence

Heaven 17 (1980): from a fictional pop group in Anthony Burgess's novel A CLOCKWORK ORANGE (1962): 'The Heaven Seventeen? Luke Sterne? Goggly Gogol?' (Pt I, ch iv)

Hootie and the Blowfish (from 1986): the nicknames of two of the band's friends, Ervin 'Hootie' Harris and Donald 'Blowfish' Feaster

Hot Chocolate (1969–87): for the group's 'hot' music and its Jamaican lead singer, Errol Brown

Human League (from 1977): the name of one of two rival empires in a SCIENCE FICTION computer game

Hüsker Dü (1979–88): the name of a Swedish children's board game meaning 'Do you remember?'

INXS (1977–97): a representation of 'in excess'

Iron Butterfly (from 1967): based on the name of the Aztec god Izpapaloti, literally 'stone butterfly'

Iron Maiden (from 1976): from the instrument of torture, a coffin-shaped box lined with iron spikes

Jam (1976–82): from the 'jam sessions' that the band's members held when at school

Japan (1974–83): a name chosen simply for its orientally exotic associations

Jefferson Airplane (from 1965): from the Jefferson Airplane Company. From 1970 to 1989 the group was known as Jefferson Starship, the latter word a reference to the SCIENCE FICTION cult of the day

Jethro Tull (from 1967): from the English farmer Jethro Tull (1674–1741), inventor of the seed drill

Kinks (from 1963): said to allude to the 'kinky boots' worn by Honor Blackman in the television series *The* AVENGERS

Kiss (from 1972): a basic amatory or sexual reference

Kraftwerk (from 1970): the German band produced music that reflected their industrial environment. Hence the name, meaning 'power plant'

Kula Shaker (from 1995): from a Krishna mystic named Kula Sekhara

Led Zeppelin (1968–80): said to derive from a prediction by Keith Moon, drummer of the *Who*, that the group would GO DOWN LIKE A LEAD BALLOON; *see also* ZEPPELIN

Level 42 (1980–94): from '42', the answer to the question 'What is the meaning of life, the universe and everything' posed in Douglas Adams's novel *The* HITCH-HIKER'S GUIDE TO THE GALAXY (1979)

Lindisfarne (from 1969): the group was founded in Newcastle and took its name from the island off the coast to the north, also known as Holy Island

Lovin' Spoonful (1965–8): from the words 'I love my baby by the lovin' spoonful' in Mississippi John Hurt's song 'Coffee Blues'

Lynyrd Skynyrd (from 1965): a corruption of Leonard Skinner, the name of the unpopular gym coach at the high school in Jacksonville, Florida, that most of the group's members originally attended

Madness (from 1979): from the Prince Buster song of the same name (1964)

Mamas and the Papas (1965–8): a San Francisco colloquialism for men and women, with specific reference to the band's two couples

Manic Street Preachers (from 1988): allegedly a term for a fanatical evangelist, a 'manic street preacher', perhaps with reference to the band's enthusiastic guitarist, James Dean Bradfield

Marillion (from 1979): from the title of J.R.R. Tolkien's posthumous cult novel *The* SILMARILLION (1977)

Monkees (from 1966): a respelling of 'Monkeys', with particular allusion to the group's drummer

Mickey Dolenz, who had earlier 'monkeyed about' in roles as a juvenile film actor

Mötley Crüe (from 1981): a respelling of 'motley crew' as an allusion to the heavy metal band's mixed background and musical style

Motörhead (from 1975): from the American slang term for an amphetamine user or 'speed freak'

Mott the Hoople (1969–76): from the title of an obscure novel by Willard Manus

Nazareth (from 1968): from the song 'The Weight' by The Band, about the trials and tribulations of Joseph and Mary, whose home town according to the biblical account was Nazareth

Nirvana (1987–94): from the transcendent state of being that is the final goal of Buddhism, with an implication of the word's literal meaning of 'extinction' as a form of total self-absorption

Oasis (from 1991): allegedly from a club named the Swindon Oasis where the group's lead guitarist, Noel Gallagher, once performed

Orchestral Manoeuvres in the Dark (from 1978): from an early act in which a tape recorder played sound effects in the form of tank noises and battlefield explosions

Pearl Jam (from 1990): apparently from Pearl, the Native American great-grandmother of the lead singer, Eddie Vedder, and the supposedly hallucinogenic jam that she made

Pet Shop Boys (from 1981): said to derive from a suggestion by the group's lead singer, Neil Tennant, that three young men working in an Ealing pet shop should start their own band

Pink Floyd (from 1964): usually said to compliment two of the group's musical heroes, Pink Anderson (1900–74) and Floyd Council (1911–76), but perhaps in fact from two cats, Pink and Floyd

Pogues (1982–96): originally Pogue Mahone, representing Irish *póg mo thón*, 'kiss my arse', an intentionally irreverent name chosen by the group's Irish lead singer, Shane MacGowan

Police (1977–86): a reference to the fact that the group's American drummer, Stewart Copeland, was the son of a former senior CIA officer

Prefab Sprout (from 1982): from a mishearing by the group's lead singer, Paddy MacAloon, of the words 'pepper sprout' in Nancy Sinatra and Lee Hazlewood's song 'Jackson', in which the two sing

that their love for each other is stronger than the plant in question

Pretenders (from 1978): from The Platters' hit song 'The Great Pretender' (1956), admired by the group's lead singer, Chrissie Hynde

Pretty Things (from 1962): from the Bo Diddley hit 'Pretty Thing' (1963). The name was intended as an ironic reference to the group's unprepossessing appearance, with long, unkempt hair

Procol Harum (from 1967): said to derive from the name of a friend's cat, although classicists posit an (ungrammatical) origin in a Latin phrase supposedly meaning 'far from these things'

Psychedelic Furs (1977–92): from the *Velvet Underground* song 'Venus in Furs', itself the English title of the pornographic novel *Venus im Pelz* (1870) by the Austrian writer Leopold von Sacher-Masoch (who gave his name to masochism)

Queen (from 1970): a name chosen by the group's flamboyant gay lead singer, Freddie Mercury, for its evocation of royal grandeur and as a tongue-in-cheek allusion to his own sexuality

R.E.M. (from 1980): an allegedly random name but popularly interpreted as the standard abbreviation for 'rapid eye movement', a term for the movement of a person's eyes when asleep and dreaming

REO Speedwagon (from 1968): from a make of American truck manufactured in the 1920s by Ransom E. Olds, father of the Oldsmobile, the letters being his initials

ROLLING STONES

Rose Royce (from 1976): from ROLLS-ROYCE, with the name appropriately given by the group's MOTOWN producer, Norman Whitfield

Roxy Music (1970–82): given by the group's lead singer, Bryan Ferry, as a blend of the ROXY cinema name and 'rock music'

Run D.M.C. (from 1982): from the nicknames of two of the group's singers, 'Run' being Joseph Simmons and 'DMC' Darryl McDaniels

Runrig (from 1973): a Scots dialect word for the Scottish band's name, 'runrig' being (historically) a ridge ('rig') of land running among others held by joint tenure but now a ridge between furrows

Santana (from 1966): the name of the group's Mexican-born lead singer, Carlos Santana

Scritti Politti (from 1977): from Italian *scritti politichi*, 'political writing', a phrase used in a work by the Italian communist and political theorist Antonio Gramsci (1891–1937)

Searchers (from 1963): from the title of the John Wayne Western *The Searchers* (1956)

Sex Pistols (1975–8): from Sex, the Chelsea clothes store run by the group's manager, Malcolm McLaren, and a perversion of 'pistil', the term for a flower's female reproductive organs

Shakespear's Sister (from 1989): from the Smiths' song, 'Shakespeare's Sister' (1985), itself named after Virginia Woolf's fictional character Judith Shakespeare in her feminist essay so titled (1929), in which she ponders the possible consequences of Shakespeare being a woman

Shalamar (from 1978): from a travel brochure describing the Shalamar garden in Lahore, India

Shangri-Las (1963–9): from the SHANGRI LA of James Hilton's novel *Lost Horizon* (1933)

Simple Minds (from 1978): a jocularly self deprecatory name for the group, taken from David Bowie's song 'The Jean Genie' about an astronaut 'so simple-minded' that he cannot operate his module

Simply Red (from 1984): for the band's red-haired lead singer, Mick Hucknall, and a pun on 'simply read'

Skunk Anansie (from 1994): from the skunk and spider characters in Jamaican folk tales

Slade (from 1966): originally Ambrose Slade, the latter word deriving from Slade Heath, north of Wolverhampton, the group's town of origin

Smiths (1982–7): a name chosen for its commonness to counter the pretentious portentousness of names such as *Orchestral Manoeuvres in the Dark*. There were no actual Smiths in the group

Soft Cell (1979–84): a blend of 'soft sell' and 'padded cell'

Soft Machine (1966–76): from the title of William Burroughs's novel (1961), a sequel to *The* NAKED LUNCH (1959)

Spandau Ballet (from 1979): from a graffito seen on a wall in Berlin, the location of SPANDAU prison, the place of confinement of the Nazi leader Rudolf Hess until his death in 1987

SPICE GIRLS

Status Quo (from 1962): from the standard Latin phrase meaning 'the existing state of affairs'

Stone Roses (1984–96): from the Jam song 'English Rose' (1978) and the ROLLING STONES

Suede (from 1990): a 'fabric' name in the mould of the Chiffons, Felt etc, with perhaps a punning reference to the slightly 'swayed' appearance of the group's lead singer, Brett Anderson

Supertramp (from 1969): ostensibly from the title of W.H. Davies's *The Autobiography of a Super-Tramp* (1910) but more directly a reference to the group's initial 'super-scruffy' appearance

Sweet (1968–81): for the group's aim to attract young fans through its BUBBLEGUM MUSIC

Take That (1991–6): a phrase implying a sexual invitation to the group's young female fans

Talking Heads (1975–91): from the term for a television speaker; *see* TALKING HEAD

Tangerine Dream (from 1967): a surreal creation suggested by the titles of paintings by Salvador Dalí, one of the more extravagant being *Dream Caused by the Flight of a Bee around a Pomegranate One Second before Waking Up* (1944)

Teardrop Explodes (1978–83): from the caption to a cartoon in a D.C. Marvel comic: 'Filling the wintered glades of Central Park with an unearthly whine ... painting the leaf-bare branches with golden fire ... THE TEARDROP EXPLODES!! ... for echoing seconds the sky is filled with silver webs of lightning – and, with the glow's fading, a new menace is revealed!' (*Prince Namor*, No 77, June 1971). The PSYCHEDELIC name was chosen by the group's lead singer, Julian Cope

Tears for Fears (from 1981): a term from the jargon of PRIMAL SCREAM THERAPY for a method of releasing emotion ('tears') to relieve depression ('fears')

10cc (1972): a random name, as if 'ten cubic centimetres', given the group by Jonathan King, the entrepreneur who signed the group up

The The (from 1979): a name chosen purely for its memorability, but also serving as an ironic allusion to the trend for names beginning with a definite article as if to imply uniqueness

Thin Lizzy (1969–83): *see* TIN LIZZIE

Thompson Twins (from 1977): from the twins, Thompson and Thomson, in Hergé's comic strips about the adventures of the cub reporter TINTIN (from 1930). No members of the group had the name

TLC (from 1991): partly from the familiar abbreviation (*see* TLC) but more specifically from the initials of the nicknames of the group's three female members, Tionne 'T-Boz' Watkins, Lisa 'Left-Eye' Lopes and Rozonda 'Chilli' Thomas

T Rex (1969–77): a shortening of the group's original name, Tyrannosaurus Rex, from the scientific name of the species of dinosaur

Troggs (from 1964): from 'trog', a nickname for a contemptible person, as an abbreviation of 'troglodyte', properly a primitive cave-dweller

UB40 (from 1978): from the designation of the British unemployment benefit form

Ultravox (from 1976): from Latin *ultra*, 'beyond', and *vox*, 'voice', the intended meaning being 'the ultimate voice' or more precisely 'the voice from beyond'

U2 (from 1978): allegedly a pun on 'you too' or 'you two', implying that all fans could share the Irish band's music, whether individually or as couples

Velvet Underground (1965–73): from Michael Leigh's book about sadomasochism so titled. The name was chosen because it seemed to imply an involvement with the underground film scene

Wet Wet Wet (from 1982): from the words 'his face is wet, wet with tears' in the *Scritti Politti* song 'Gettin', Havin' and Holdin'' (1982)

Wham! (1981–6): from the line WHAM, BAM, THANK YOU MA'AM in a song by the group's lead singer, George Michael

Who (from 1964): a name chosen for its potential to bemuse and amuse, especially in a verbal exchange such as: 'Have you heard The Who?' 'The Who?' 'The Who'

XTC (from 1975): a representation of 'ecstasy', meaning happiness rather than the drug ECSTASY

Yardbirds (from 1963): a tribute to the American saxophonist Charlie 'Bird' Parker (1920–55), himself so nicknamed for his fondness for chicken (a 'yardbird')

Yes (from 1968): a word chosen for its positive quality and its brevity on posters

Rockhampton Rocket. The nickname of the great Australian tennis player Rod Laver (b.1938), who was born in Rockhampton, Queensland. The nickname reflects his speed around the tennis court. Laver won the GRAND SLAM of tennis tournaments twice in his career, in 1962 and 1969.

Rock 'n' roll. Rock and roll, or just rock, was *the* pop music of the latter half of the 1950s, characterized by its swing or rhythm and the style of dancing that went with it. Its fans were called rockers and they belonged to the days of the TEDDY BOYS, before the advent of the mods (*see* MODS AND ROCKERS). Famous practitioners included Elvis Presley (1935–77) and Bill Haley (1925–81) and the Comets, and the latter's hit ROCK AROUND THE CLOCK (1954) was the first to popularize the style. The term itself probably alludes to the vigorous movements of the dancers, swaying the body backwards and forwards ('rocking') and from side to side ('rolling'). *See also* HIT PARADE; ROCK GROUP NAMES.

Rock opera. A somewhat pretentious term for a drama set to rock music. The first successful examples of the genre were *Hair* (1969) and *Jesus Christ Superstar* (1970). Later compositions have mostly been simply known as musicals rather than 'operas'.

Rock the boat, To. To disturb a stable situation, especially when it is potentially to one's advantage. A small craft such as a canoe can be capsized by moving carelessly about. The phrase is commonly found in the negative advice, 'Don't rock the boat'. The song 'Sit Down, You're Rocking the Boat' sung by Stubby Kaye in Frank Loesser's musical *Guys and Dolls* (1950) further popularized the phrase, which dates from the early years of the 20th century. *See also* MAKE WAVES.

Rocky. (1) The professional boxer created by Sylvester Stallone as the hero of the film named for him (1976) and of its three sequels: *Rocky II* (1976), *Rocky III* (1982) and *Rocky IV* (1985). His full name is Rocky Balboa, and although he is not very intelligent his physical prowess and grim determination to win brought him many fans. The first of the series was directed by John G. Avildsen and the remainder by Stallone himself, who also played him.

(2) Rocky was also a nickname of the moderate Republican politician Nelson Rockefeller (1908–79), governor of New York (1959–73) and vice-president of the USA under Gerald Ford (1974–7). He unsuccessfully sought his party's nomination as presidential candidate in 1960, 1964 and 1968.

Rocky Graziano. *See* GRAZIANO, ROCKY.

Rocky Horror Picture Show, The. A film (1975) based on the successful stage rock musical *The Rocky Horror Show* (1973), written by Richard O'Brien. The title reflects the show's anarchic mixture of ROCK 'N' ROLL music and horror film clichés, all delivered in a high CAMP style. The show quickly attracted a cult following and both live performances and showings of the film (often at midnight) were commonly attended by audiences wearing the outlandish costumes of such favourite characters as Dr Frank N. Furter and Riff Raff the hunchbacked butler.

Rocky Marciano. *See* MARCIANO, ROCKY.

Rocky Mountains and Tired Indians. One of the most frequently reproduced earlier paintings of David Hockney (b.1937), this dates from 1965, when Hockney was teaching at Boulder, Colorado. Hockney recalls: 'I was given a studio that had no window, no windows to view the Rocky Mountains ... So ... the whole picture is an invention from geological magazines and romantic ideas (the nearest Indians are at least three hundred miles from Boulder). The chair was put in just for compositional purposes, and to explain its being there I called the Indians "tired".'

Rodney. A foolish or stupid person. The male first name was adopted by schoolchildren in the 1980s from the character Rodney Trotter, played by Nicholas Lyndhurst, in the television comedy ONLY FOOLS AND HORSES.

Rogallo. A mainly American alternative term for a hang-glider, a type of one-man aircraft that evolved from the kite-like device used to slow down the re-entry of a space probe, the invention in *c.*1962 of Francis M. Rogallo, an engineer working for NASA.

Roger. In radio communications, a term meaning 'message received and understood'. It represents a former telephonic name for the letter R, the initial of 'received'. The signalling alphabet current in the period 1921–41, based on that used in the First World War, was:

A = Ack, B = Beer, C = Charlie, D = Don, E = Edward, F = Freddie, G = George, H = Harry, I = Ink, J = Johnnie, K = King, L = London, M = Monkey, N = Nuts, O = Orange, P = Pip, Q = Queen, R = Roger, S = Sugar, T = Toc, U = Uncle, V = Vic, W = William, X = X-ray, Y = Yellow, Z = Zebra

In 1942 the following was introduced:

A = Able, B = Baker, C = Charlie, D = Dog, E = Easy, F = Fox, G = George, H = How, I = Item, J = Jig, K = King, L = Love, M = Mike, N = Nan, O = Oboe, P = Peter, Q = Queen, R = Roger, S = Sugar, T = Tare, U = Uncle, V = Victor, W = William, X = X-ray, Y = Yoke, Z = Zebra

In 1956 the NATO alphabet was generally adopted (although Roger was kept for 'received'):

A = Alpha, B = Bravo, C = Charlie, D = Delta, E = Echo, F = Foxtrot, G = Golf, H = Hotel, I = India, J = Juliet, K = Kilo, L = Lima, M = Mike, N = November, O = Oscar, P = Papa, Q = Quebec, R = Romeo, S = Sierra, T = Tango, U = Uniform, V = Victor, W = Whiskey, X = X-ray, Y = Yankee, Z = Zulu

Rogers, Buck. *See* BUCK ROGERS.

Rogue Male. A thriller (1939) by Geoffrey Household (1900–88). Published in the very month in which the Second World War was declared, this topical story begins with an unsuccessful attempt by the narrator to assassinate an unnamed dictator, who has affinities with Adolf Hitler. The rest of the story concerns his attempts to avoid being killed by a secret agent of the dictator or being arrested by the British police after he has had to kill an accomplice of the agent at Aldwych Underground station in London. The title is a reference to beasts who, through pain or having lost their mate, isolate themselves from their fellows and act with increased cunning and ferocity, as is the case with the narrator.

Roland Rat. A rodent puppet 'superstar' on British breakfast television in the 1980s. He was credited with saving the commercial breakfast television company TV-am by boosting its falling ratings and was promoted in this role by Greg Dyke, subsequently Director-General of the BBC.

Role model. A person regarded by others as an example to be followed, as a teacher by a pupil or an officer by his men. The term emerged from sociological jargon in the 1950s.

Is [Tony Blair's wife] Cherie Booth a celebrity? Some people certainly think so. Others say she is a role model.

The Times (1 October 1999)

Role-playing game. A form of game in which players act out the part of imaginary characters in an imaginary setting. The exercise as a technique in psychiatry dates back to the 1940s, but in its modern form evolved in the 1970s when a number of new games, notably 'Dungeons and Dragons', were devised to involve the participants as characters in a particular setting. Computer games in similar style came on the market in the 1980s and are also known as role-playing games.

Rolfing. A massage technique aimed at the vertical realignment of the body and deep enough to release muscular tension at skeletal level. It was developed by the Swiss-born American biochemist Dr Ida Rolf (1896–1979) and adopted from the 1950s. A typical Rolfer devotes 10 one-hour sessions to a client to achieve this alignment and various emotional and psychological insights may be achieved during the course. The release of emotional pain may also be involved.

Rollerblading. A roller-skating fad of the late 1980s and early 1990s in which the old 'quad' wheel design was replaced by 'in-line' wheels to give the acceleration and manoeuvrability of ice skates. In-line skates first appeared on the highways of America in 1980.

Roller coaster. The THEME PARK attraction originated in the late 19th century but reached its apogee in the late 20th, with at least a dozen of the devices vying to provide the greatest thrills. The most intense experience in Britain is by general agreement offered by Nemesis at Alton Towers, while its neighbour there, Oblivion, is notorious for its awesome drop. In BLACKPOOL the Pepsi Max Big One is one of the highest, while the Grand National is an exhilarating wooden racing coaster built in 1935. The Traumatizer at Southport and the Millennium Roller Coaster near Skegness also pull the public, but the wooden Megafobia at Narberth, Pembrokeshire, has been generally judged to give the best 'shake, rattle and roll' ride in the country.

Rolling Stones. The rock group so named was formed in 1962 with Mick Jagger (b.1943) as lead singer and Keith Richards (b.1943) as guitarist. The other original members were Brian Jones (1942–69), Charlie Watts (b.1941) and Bill Wyman (b.1941). Their music was derivative but distinctive, and their raunchy style won them many fans. The group took their name from Muddy Waters's song 'Rollin' Stone' (1950), and their format was initially influenced by the American blues musician's electrically amplified band. *See also* ALTAMONT; BROWN SUGAR; JUMPIN' JACK FLASH; LET IT BLEED; (I CAN'T GET NO) SATISFACTION; STICKY FINGERS; SYMPATHY FOR THE DEVIL.

Roll one's own, To. To make one's own cigarettes (by rolling loose tobacco in cigarette papers). Hence the subsequent figurative sense, 'to do something without assistance'.

Rolls-Royce. The automobile name first came before the public in 1906 when the motoring and aviation pioneer Charles S. Rolls (1877–1910) and the electrical engineer Henry Royce (1863–1933) formed a company to produce a high-quality car. Models such as the Silver Ghost and Silver Shadow became equal names of excellence, and the car's bonnet figure, Charles Sykes's 'Spirit of Ecstasy', was part of the prestigious image. Rolls, the first Englishman to fly across the Channel, lost his life in an air crash and when Royce died in 1933 the colour of the monogram RR on the car's bonnet was changed from red to black. The name came to be used allusively to describe a person or thing that is the best of their kind.

> It [*Animal Fair*] is the Rolls-Royce of dog magazines which will focus on the pashmina-wrapped lifestyles of celebrities and their beloved pets.
> *The Times* (9 October 1999)

Roll something out, To. In the language of politicians, to present the first stage of a plan or policy, the rest of which is to be introduced subsequently, often at some unspecified date. The reference is to the first public showing of the prototype of a new aircraft, which is rolled out of its hangar but which has yet to fly or even to make its first test flight. The phrase was current in the late 1990s.

Roll up one's sleeves, To. To get down to work; to tackle the matter in hand. One rolls up one's sleeves both to free one's hands and arms for action and to keep the sleeves themselves clean.

> You'll see me on TV, getting on and off planes, meeting Presidents and Prime Ministers, Kings and Queens. It's all part of the job. But the part that matters most to me is getting my sleeves rolled up and pushing through the changes to our country that will give to others, by right, what I achieved by good fortune.
> TONY BLAIR: Speech at Labour Party conference (28 September 1999)

Roll with the punches, To. To adapt to adversity; to deal with events and problems as they come. The image is from boxing, in which a contestant will bend (roll) his body to one side when deflecting the full force of his opponent's blow. The expression dates from the 1950s.

> You have to roll with the punches of the culture that surrounds you.
> *The Times* (4 February 2000)

Rom-com. A romantic comedy, as a film or, less often, play or novel. A colloquialism of the 1990s.

> The fringe (his), the sweet smile (hers), the laughter (ours), the tears (everybody's): it's all here in the rom-

com [*Notting Hill*] that outgrossed *Four Weddings And a Funeral*.

heat (3–9 February 2000)

Romper room. A place for lively meetings or gatherings. The term arose as US campus slang in the 1980s, the allusion being to young children in rompers playing and brawling.

> Dress is polos, chinos and loafers, and office colours are bright and stimulating. There's a romper room for meetings and break-out space for chats.
>
> *The Times* (27 September 1999)

Ronde, La. A play (1903) by the Austrian playwright Arthur Schnitzler (1862–1931) in which the action traces a series of ten interlinked sexual liaisons. The title reflects the play's circular structure: it begins with a prostitute having sex with a soldier and ends with a count picking up the same prostitute. The play has been filmed twice, once in 1950 and once, with a screenplay by Jean Anouilh, in 1964.

R 101. The world's biggest airship was commissioned by the British government in 1924 and made its maiden flight in 1929, taking off from Cardington, Bedfordshire, with 52 people on board, and circling over London and the southeast of England. On 1 October 1930, following a successful maiden transatlantic flight earlier that year, it set off for India, the official party now including Lord Thomson, secretary of state for air. At 2 a.m. the following morning it touched the ground on its approach to Beauvais, France, caught fire and exploded. A total of 44 people died, including the minister. The cause of the tragedy was heavy rain, which forced the dirigible to lose height. The disaster put an end to the use of airships in Britain.

Ronnie Scott's. Club Eleven, the first club set up in 1958 by the saxophonist Ronnie Scott (original name Ronald Schatt; 1927–97), closed after a few months following a drugs raid. In 1959 Scott opened a second club in Gerrard Street, Soho, where he and his fellow jazz musicians could play. It attracted major figures from the world of jazz, and its heyday was in the latter half of the 1960s, following its move to larger premises in Frith Street. It remains a centre of British jazz today.

Room at the Top. The first novel (1957) by John Braine (1922–86) was an iconoclastic story of an opportunist, amoral, working-class young man, Joe Lampton, who achieves social acceptance and material prosperity. Braine returned to this formula and to his original characters in *Life at the Top* (1962). The words 'There is always room at the top' are attributed to the US politician Daniel Webster (1782–1852), said when he was advised against joining the overcrowded legal profession. Simone Signoret won an Oscar for her part in the film (1958), when she played the married woman with whom Lampton has a brief affair. *See also* FIRST LINES OF NOVELS.

Room 40. A euphemistic nickname for the codebreaking work undertaken by the Royal Navy in the First World War, originating as the number of the room in the Old Admiralty Building, Whitehall, that was assigned to cryptanalysts for the purpose. After the war Room 40 evolved into the Government Code and Cypher School (GC&CS) that was itself the forerunner of GCHQ.

Room with a View, A. A novel (1908) by E.M. Forster (1879–1970). It is a domestic comedy, set in Florence and England, and explores the differences between Italian and English temperaments. It opens with a contretemps in a pension largely occupied by English visitors to Italy about the rooms with a view that had been promised, instead of which they have 'north rooms, looking into a courtyard, and a long way apart'. The model for Mrs Honeychurch, the mother of Lucy, who is the book's female protagonist, was Forster's maternal grandmother, Louisa Whichelo, who died in 1912. The novel was the subject of a MERCHANT IVORY FILM in 1985.

Roots. A sociological study (1976), with fictional interpolations, by Alex Haley (1921–92). It purports to be a chronicle of his family through seven generations, beginning with the African, Kunte Kinte, who was brought as a slave from Gambia to Annapolis in 1767. The bestseller won a PULITZER PRIZE and had an even greater impact when it was made into a gripping television mini-series (1977).

Rope-a-dope. In boxing the tactic of feigning to be trapped against the ropes, so goading an opponent (the 'dope') into throwing tiring, ineffectual punches. The phrase was coined in the 1970s by the American heavyweight Muhammad Ali with reference to his use of the dodge in a match with his great rival, George Foreman.

Roping and doping. Taking drugs, 'rope' being a slang term for marijuana, from the use of hemp in ropemaking, and also a word for a vein, so called from its appearance when 'shooting up'.

Rorschach test. A type of psychological personality test in which the subject looks at a series of ink-blots and describes what they suggest or resemble. The test was devised by the Swiss psychologist Hermann Rorschach, who introduced it in 1921. The ink-blots in the test are usually symmetrical, which to some extent restricts the degree of subjectivity of their interpretation.

Roseanne. The central character of the top-rank American television SITCOM running from 1988 (in Britain from 1989) to 1997. Roseanne Conner is the smart, wisecracking and overweight wife of the equally well-rounded Dan, her high-school sweetheart, and mother of David Jacob ('DJ'), Darlene and Becky. The family's involvements and relationships were remarkable for their social realism, with Roseanne played by the talented stand-up comic Roseanne Barr as a variation of a character she developed for the stage.

Rose Bowl. The annual American college football contest, held on New Year's Day at Pasadena, California. The contest and name derive from the Battle of the Flowers, first held on New Year's Day in 1890, in which local residents decorated their buggies and carriages with flowers and drove round a planned route. The parade was followed by amateur athletic events. In 1902 the first Tournament of Roses American football game was held, and in 1922 the Rose Bowl stadium opened for this annual contest. The morning parade still takes place with many decorated floats. *See also* SUPER BOWL.

Rosemary's Baby. A horror film (1968) based on a novel by Ira Levin about a young New York couple whose happiness about the forthcoming birth of their first child is undermined by the wife's growing conviction that she is carrying the Devil's child. Directed by Roman Polanski and starring Mia Farrow as the expectant mother, the movie did much to revitalize the HORROR MOVIE genre in the modern cinema.

Rosenberg case. The case of Julius (1918–53) and Ethel (1915–53) Rosenberg, the first American civilians to be executed for espionage. Julius Rosenberg, originally named Greenglass, became an engineer with the US Army Signal Corps in 1940 and from this point of vantage together with his wife aimed to turn over to the Soviet Union military secrets that came into their possession. Ethel's brother, assigned to the atomic bomb project at Los Alamos, New Mexico, gave the couple data on nuclear weapons. This information was passed on to Harry Gold, a courier for the US espionage ring, and by him to the Soviet vice-consul in New York. The Rosenbergs were brought to trial in New York on 6 March 1951, found guilty under the Espionage Act of 1917, and despite several appeals and a worldwide campaign for mercy, executed at Sing Sing on 19 June. The case fuelled McCARTHYITE paranoias in the USA during a tense period of the COLD WAR. It formed the subject-matter of a novel by E.L. Doctorow, *The Book of Daniel* (1971), in which the Rosenberg's story is told by their fictional son.

Rosencrantz and Guildenstern are Dead. A play (1966) by Tom Stoppard (b.1937) focusing on the fate of two minor characters from William Shakespeare's *Hamlet* (1601). Rosencrantz and Guildenstern are the two 'attendant lords' who accompany Hamlet to England, while secretly carrying letters asking the English king to execute their master but end up being executed themselves after Hamlet inserts their own names in the fatal document. The names Rosencrantz and Guildenstern were fairly common in Denmark in Shakespeare's time and the full title is a straight quotation from the last scene of the original play, in which news of their demise is perfunctorily reported by the First Ambassador in the aftermath of Hamlet's own death and that of the king, Claudius:

> The sight is dismal;
> And our affairs from England come too late:
> The ears are senseless that should give us hearing,
> To tell him his commandment is fulfill'd,
> That Rosencrantz and Guildenstern are dead.

Rosenkavalier, Der. The lushly romantic and highly popular opera by Richard Strauss (1864–1949) has a libretto by Hugo von Hofmannsthal. It was first performed in 1911. The title is German for 'the knight of the rose'. Old Baron Ochs, looking for a messenger to take a silver rose as a betrothal token to the young Sophie, visits his cousin the Marschallin. The Marschallin's husband is away, and she is entertaining her young lover, Oktavian. Aware that she is growing too old for him, the Marschallin gives Oktavian the rose to take to the young Sophie. The two fall in love, and, following various complications, the Marshallin persuades Sophie's father to bless the pair.

Rose Tattoo, The. A play (1951) by Tennessee Williams (1911–83) about a Sicilian widow's quest for love. The title of the play refers most obviously to the rose tattoo that is described as adorning the chest of the widow's

dead husband, but it also relates to the name of the
widow, Serafina Delle Rose, and that of her spouse,
Rosario. The prevalence of rose imagery in the play
reflected the author's preoccupation with his sister
Rose, who was troubled by mental illness throughout
her life. Other 'rose' titles that he considered included
*Novena to a Rose, A Candle to a Rose, A Rose for Our Lady,
A Rose from the Hand of Our Lady* and *Perpetual Novena
to a Rose.* However, the play began its life under the
alternative titles *The Eclipse of May 29, 1919* and
Stornella.

Rosie the Riveter. While GI JOE was on the battlefront
in the Second World War his other half was busy on
the home front in the weapons industry. The American women engaged in such work were embodied
by the fictional Rosie the Riveter, a young woman
wearing slacks and armed with a rivet gun. She was
commemorated in song and depicted by Norman
Rockwell on the cover of the *Saturday Evening Post,*
where she rolled up her sleeves beneath the words,
'We Can Do It!'

Ross Poldark. A novel (1945; in USA as *The Renegade,*
1951) by Winston Graham (b.1912). Subtitled *A Novel
of Cornwall 1783–1787,* it is the first of a sequence of ten
historical adventure novels featuring members of the
Poldark family, of which the last is *The Loving Cup: a
Novel of Cornwall 1813–1815* (1984). A television series,
Poldark (1976–7), was based on the novels as a popular
Sunday evening BODICE-RIPPER, with Robin Ellis as
Ross Poldark and Angharad Rees as the urchin
servant girl, Demelza, for whom he has a passion.

Rotary Club. A movement among business men, which
takes for its motto 'Service above Self'. The idea originated with Paul Harris, a Chicago lawyer, in 1905. In
1911 it took root in Britain and there are now clubs in
most towns, membership being limited to one member each of any trade, calling or profession. Lectures
are delivered at weekly meetings by guest speakers.
The name derives from the early practice of holding
meetings in rotation at the offices or business premises
of its members. The Rotary Clubs are now members of
one association called Rotary International.

Rough Guides. A series of 'user-friendly' travel guides
to all parts of the world. The first guide was published
in 1982, when Mark Ellingham, a graduate just out
of university, was travelling in Greece. Although he
had brought with him many of the popular guides of
the day, he found that they were all deficient in some
way. Their priority was the visitor's standard Mecca

of ruins and museums, and they said little about the
country's contemporary world, its politics, culture
and people. He therefore set about writing his own
book, aiming to give the sort of practical information
that the traveller really wanted. By the end of the 1990s
there were 100 such titles.

Rough trade. Male homosexuality or prostitution,
especially when involving brutality or sadism. The
expression dates from the 1930s. Hence related 'a bit of
rough', originally applied to a female sexual partner
but subsequently to a male whose attraction lies in his
lack of sophistication.

Round House. The London theatre so named evolved
from Arnold Wesker's CENTRE 42, set up in 1961. The
building was originally a 'roundhouse', a locomotive
shed with tracks radiating from a central turntable.
Hence the name, which was further appropriate for
the THEATRE-IN-THE-ROUND productions subsequently staged here, such as Peter Brook's experimental
version of Shakespeare's *The Tempest* in 1968.

Round the bend or **twist.** Crazy; eccentric. The implication is that one is not 'straight'.

Route One. In football a long pass upfield as an attacking tactic, usually by way of exploiting the heading
skills of tall attackers. The name comes from a television football quiz show of the 1960s, *Quiz Ball,* in
which questions, graded in difficulty, led to scoring a
goal, Route One being the direct path.

Route 66. The major highway that runs for some
3540km (2200 miles) across America from Chicago to
Los Angeles, a symbol of romance and adventure. Its
name, familiar from Bobby Troup's song of 1946 so
titled, has become metaphorical for any road with
similar associations.

> Winding through a grim, polluted landscape of new
> wrecks, new graffiti, new drug dealers and new
> prostitutes, Europastrasse-55 is the Route 66 of the
> lands that communism betrayed.
> *Independent on Sunday* (21 June 1992)

Rowan and Martin's Laugh-In. An American television comedy series running from 1968 to 1973 (1971
in the UK) and hosted by the gifted comedians Dan
Rowan and Dick Martin. The programme presented a
kaleidoscope of sketches and skits, with many recurring characters, and popularized a number of catchphrases, such as SOCK IT TO ME, 'You bet your bippy'
and 'Look that up in your Funk and Wagnalls'. The
second of these is a euphemistic form of 'You bet your
ass', the final word of which was 'bipped' or 'bleeped'

on television. Funk and Wagnalls, despite their suggestive name, are the publishers of *A New Standard Dictionary of the English Language*, sales of which are said to have soared as a result of this unusual PRODUCT PLACEMENT.

Rowntree Mackintosh. The confectionery company of this name was formed in 1969 following a merger of Rowntree & Co. Ltd, founded in 1869 by Henry Isaac Rowntree, a York tea dealer and chocolate manufacturer, and John Mackintosh & Sons Ltd, founded in 1890 by John Mackintosh, a Halifax confectioner. Rowntree introduced a number of popular brands of confectionery to the public, all of them still selling today. The following is a list of the best known, with year of introduction. *See also* QUALITY STREET.

> Rowntree's Fruit Gums (1893)
> Black Magic (1933)
> Kit Kat (originally Chocolate Crisp) (1935)
> Aero (1935)
> Dairy Box (1936)
> Smarties (1937)
> Polo (1948)
> After Eight (1962)

Roxy. The chain of cinemas so called took their name from the American radio host and movie theatre impresario Samuel L. Rothafel (1881–1936), known as 'Roxy'. (His original surname was Rothapfel, but the family dropped the 'p' at the end of the First World War when Germanic names were in disfavour.) The name was originally that of the sumptuous Roxy Theater, New York, constructed by Rothafel in 1927 as a 'cathedral of the motion picture'. *See also* ODEON; ROCKETTES.

Royal Borough. A name sometimes applied to the London borough of Kensington and Chelsea. Royal status was granted to Kensington in 1901 by Edward VII in honour of Queen Victoria, who died that year and who had been born at Kensington Palace, and when the boroughs of Kensington and Chelsea merged in 1965 the honorific title passed to them jointly.

Royal Hunt of the Sun, The. A play (1964) by Peter Shaffer (b.1926) about the conquest of the Inca nation by the Spanish conquistadors. The Spaniards, led by Pizarro, come on a hunt for gold, but during the course of the play it becomes clear Pizarro is obsessed by the hunt for a god-figure, as personified by the sun-god Ahahuallpa (hence the title of the play).

> *Pizarro*: I've gone god-hunting and caught one.
> PETER SHAFFER: *The Royal Hunt of the Sun*

Royal Mile. A name for the road in Edinburgh that runs from Edinburgh Castle down to the royal palace of Holyrood House. It is first recorded in W.M. Gilbert's *Edinburgh in the Nineteenth Century* (1901), in which it appears in inverted commas, and was further popularized as the title of a 1920 guidebook by Robert T. Skinner. The name is not only historically meaningless but also falsely implies that the road was created as a royal route between the castle and the palace. It is in fact a modern translation of medieval Latin *via regia*, 'king's street', as a term for any public highway and in this case for the Canongate and the High Street that now form part of the route.

Royal Ulster Constabulary. The police force for Northern Ireland, created in 1922 and patterned on the Royal Irish Constabulary. The initial establishment was 3000 men, and although it was intended that one-third of the total be allocated to Roman Catholics, the quota was never filled. The RUC lost just under 200 men and over 100 reserves during the TROUBLES, and circumstances at this time brought radical changes to its structure, one consequence being an increase in members to almost 8500 by 1991. In 1999 further changes were recommended, including a change of name to the Northern Ireland Police Service, a new oath to uphold human rights and the removal of portraits of the Queen from police stations in Northern Ireland. *See also* BATTLE OF THE BOGSIDE; B SPECIALS.

Royle Family, The. An acclaimed television SITCOM first screened in 1998, and intended as a subtle parody on the British royal family, as the punningly ironic title indicates. There is little in the way of action and the story concentrates on the gentle chattering and bickering between members of a working-class Manchester family as they sit slumped in their living room idly watching television. The programme is remarkable for its observational detail and for the naturalistic performances of the cast, headed by Ricky Tomlinson as the jaded, beer-bellied paterfamilias and Caroline Aherne as his starry-eyed, bride-to-be daughter.

Rozelle rule. In American football the provision in a contract between a free agent and a professional team that requires the team to give the free agent's former team either a negotiated compensation or a compensation set by the commissioner of the National Football League. The name is that of Alvin Ray ('Pete') Rozelle (1926–96), league commissioner from 1960, who established the rule in 1974.

Rubber cheque. A cheque drawn on an account without the funds to pay it, and so one that 'bounces'. The punning expression dates from the 1920s.

Rubber chicken circuit. The circuit followed by professional speakers. The American expression dates from the 1950s and alludes to the supposedly customary dish of tough chicken in the meal that precedes the speech.

> The wealthy and successful … desperately need party funding. In between the powdered soup and rubber-chicken circuit their lavish hospitality cheers MPs up.
> *Sunday Times* (26 December 1999)

Rubber Soul. An album by the BEATLES released in December 1965, hailed at the time as their most substantial collection of songs to date. The title, invented by Paul McCartney, is a humorous allusion to white musicians who attempt to perform in a soul idiom and also puns on 'rubber sole' in the sense of the underside of a shoe. The album includes the tracks NORWEGIAN WOOD, NOWHERE MAN, 'Michelle', 'Girl' and IN MY LIFE. *See also* REVOLVER.

Rube Goldberg. An American name used from the early 20th century for any complicated machine or arrangement, especially one devised for the accomplishing of a simple task. It is that of the cartoonist Rube Goldberg (1883–1970), whose drawings and characters were soon familiar to many. His absurdly complicated devices, however, were designed not only to amuse but also to satirize the American mania for gadgets. A typical device was a 'simple' alarm clock, operated as follows: a bird on a bedroom windowsill catches a worm, a string attached to the worm pulls the trigger of a pistol, the pistol fires a bullet that bursts a balloon, the balloon drops a brick on an atomizer, the atomizer squirts liquid onto a sponge, the weighted sponge pulls a string, the string tilts a board, and a cannon ball rolls off the board to fall on the chest of a sleeper and by an attached string pull the cork off a vacuum flask filled with iced water, which falls on the sleeper's face to aid the wake-up blow delivered by the cannon ball. The whole is in the style of the British HEATH ROBINSON.

Rubik's Cube. A teasing puzzle invented by the Hungarian Ernö Rubik (b.1944) in 1974. A cube, apparently composed of 27 cubelets, initially has each of its six faces made up of nine cubelets of the same colour. An interior system of pivots allows any layer of nine cubelets to be rotated with respect to the rest, so that repeated rotations cause the cubelet faces to become scrambled. The challenge is to restore a scrambled cube to its initial configuration. With millions of combinations, there is only one possible way of achieving the desired solution. There was a brief but intense craze for the puzzle in the early 1980s.

Rub salt into someone's wounds, To. To make a painful experience even more painful. Salt will sting an open wound, although it may also help to heal it. The expression dates from the 1940s.

> Steven Norris has had salt rubbed into his wounds at the Tory conference. After Lord Archer … beat him to become the Tories' official London mayoral candidate, Norris's autobiography *Changing Trains* has been cut from £15.99 to £5.99 at the Politico's conference bookstall.
> *The Times* (7 October 1999)

Rub someone's nose in it, To. To draw their attention to an embarrassing or painful fact by constantly or repeatedly drawing attention to it. The allusion is to the practice of rubbing a puppy's or kitten's nose in its misplaced excreta ('it') in an attempt to house-train it. The expression dates from the 1960s and variants are frequently found.

> To run off with someone else … is one thing. But publicly to rub poor Della's face in the ruins of her shattered life is cruel.
> *The Times* (13 October 1999)

RU 18. A mock car number plate displayed in some pubs as a reminder that alcoholic drinks cannot be served to minors. Before the age of majority was lowered to 18 in 1970 the sign was RU 21.

Rufty-tufty. A person involved in any basic fieldwork or groundwork, especially when it is both physically and mentally demanding. The phrase, unrecorded in many dictionaries, combines 'rough' with 'tough'.

> The pool boys are known among the rest of the hacks as 'the rufty tufties' because they are supposed to travel with their army units and have, therefore, to resort to sleeping in odd places on occasions, including out in the open.
> *The Times* (18 June 1999)

Rug rat. A small child, especially one who cannot walk yet but crawls on the carpet. The nickname dates from the 1970s. The children's television cartoon series *Rugrats*, first screened in 1996, depicts life and adults as seen through the eyes of a gang of children and animals.

Rule 43. A prison regulation whereby prisoners, especially sex offenders, can be isolated for their own protection.

Rules or **rule, OK?** A stock formula in graffiti slogans from the 1970s, preceded by whoever or whatever the writer wishes to promote, as: 'Big Mal rules, OK?', 'Three-wheelers rule, OK?' As with much graffiti, the wording is subject to punning variation and corruption, as 'Queen Elizabeth rules UK', 'Rodgers and Hammerstein rule OK, lahoma' and 'Dyslexia rules, KO?' In 1981 Virginian rubbed tobacco was advertised with the slogan 'Virginian Rolls OK' and a well-known brand of French cigarette with *Gauloises à rouler, OK*.

> Gold rules OK?
>
> *Observer* (headline) (13 November 1983)

Rum. The name of this island of the Inner Hebrides is still spelled Rhum in many sources, including the Post Office's *Postal Addresses and Index to Postcode Directories* (1987). The name is not a optional alternative but a pseudo-classical invention introduced either by John Bullough, a Lancashire textile millionaire who bought the island in 1888, or his son Sir George Bullough (1870–1939), who inherited it in 1891, to take account of Victorian sensibilities over strong liquor. The name itself is properly pronounced 'Room' and derives from Gaelic *rùim*, 'wide', alluding to the island's relative spaciousness by comparison with neighbouring Eigg and Muck.

Rumble in the Jungle. A near-rhyming nickname given to the epic heavyweight boxing bout fought on 30 October 1974 in Kinshasa, Zaïre (now Democratic Republic of the Congo) between George Foreman and Muhammad Ali and won by the latter. *See also* THRILLER IN MANILA.

Rumpole of the Bailey. A television drama series running from 1975 to 1992 and centring on defence lawyer Horace Rumpole and the cases in which he is involved. The series owed its success in equal measure to the bibulously Dickensian performance of Leo McKern as Rumpole, henpecked by Hilda, 'she who must be obeyed', and to John Mortimer's richly ironic script.

Rumpy-pumpy. Surreptitious sexual intercourse. The semi-humorous euphemism is an elaboration of 'rump', alluding to the male backside, and 'pump', alluding to the action.

> Miss Mandy Rice Davies, told that Lord Astor denied all knowledge of her allegations of rumpy pumpy and good times at Cliveden, replied: 'Well, he would, wouldn't he?'
>
> *The Times* (30 October 1999)

Rum, sodomy and the lash. Winston Churchill's characterization of the Royal Navy, in response to an argumentative naval officer: 'Don't talk to me about naval tradition. It's nothing but rum, sodomy and the lash.' The remark has been reported as dating from 1911 and from the Second World War. The version quoted above comes from Peter Gretton, *Former Naval Person* (1968), while Harold Nicolson in his diary entry for 17 August 1950 has: 'Naval tradition? Monstrous! Nothing but rum, sodomy, prayers and the lash.' The version 'rum, buggery and the lash' may predate Churchill altogether.

In 1884 the US politician Samuel Dickinson Burchard (1812–91) had said in a speech: 'We are Republicans and don't propose to leave our party and identify ourselves with the party whose antecedents are rum, Romanism and rebellion.' *Rum, Sodomy and the Lash* was the title of an album by the Irish punk-folk band the Pogues in the 1980s. The jazz musician and writer George Melly used *Rum, Bum, and Concertina* as the title of his autobiography (1977).

Run around in circles, To. To be fussily busy with little result. A phrase of American origin.

Runaway success. A journalistic and promotional cliché for anything selling well, or showing promise of doing so. The phrase is typically applied to a novel that is a 'runaway bestseller'. The term dates from the 1950s and was adopted to apply to anything regarded as giving good results, as: 'His plan was a runaway success.'

Running on empty. At the end of one's resources. The reference is to a car that is about to run out of petrol. The phrase was popularized by Jackson Browne's award-winning 'road' album *Running on Empty* (1978).

> Back at the hotel [comedian] Eddie [Izzard] is sitting in my room … He is clearly running on empty and still rather down about his performance, disappointed with himself for losing it on a couple of occasions.
>
> *The Times* (10 December 1999)

Running start. An initial advantage. The allusion is to an athletic event such as the long jump, in which the person runs up to the point of take-off, so having an advantage over anyone who attempts the jump from a standing position. The expression dates from the 1920s.

Run of the mill. Ordinary or undistinguished. The allusion is to materials or fabrics as they emerge from the production process in a mill and before they have been sorted or inspected for quality. The expression dates from the turn of the 20th century.

Run out of road, To. Of a motor vehicle, to fail to negotiate a bend and to skid off the road. The expression dates from the 1960s and gave a figurative sense along the lines of 'to go off the rails'.

Run out of steam, To. To lose energy; to tire. Although steam engines were a 19th-century invention the phrase dates from the 1960s.

Run someone ragged, To. To exhaust them or wear them out. The image is of working so hard that one is reduced to rags. The expression is American in origin and dates from the 1920s.

Run something past someone, To. To present it to them for their opinion or reaction, as: 'I'd like to run these figures past you.'

Rupert Bear. The distinctive strip cartoon bear, with his check trousers, red jersey and scarf, was the creation of the illustrator Mary Tourtel, who introduced him in the pages of the *Daily Express* in 1920. The picture books with his adventures in rhyme began to appear in the mid-1920s, and the famous Rupert Annuals in 1936, the latter illustrated by Alfred Bestall. Rupert's world centres on his village of Nutwood, but he travels far and wide and has companions in the form of Bill Badger, Algy Pug, Edward Trunk, Bingo the Brainy Pup and others. *See also* OZ.

R.U.R. A play (1920) by the Czech playwright Karel Čapek (1890–1938) about a rebellion by robots against their human masters. Standing for 'Rossum's Universal Robots', *R.U.R.* inaugurated a new genre in SCIENCE FICTION and incidentally introduced a new word to the English language: ROBOT (derived by Karel's brother Josef from the Czech *robota*, meaning 'drudgery').

Ruralism. The Brotherhood of Ruralists arose in 1975 as a group of seven British painters then living in the rural West of England: Ann and Graham Arnold (b.1936 and 1932), Peter Blake (b.1931) and his former American-born wife Jann Haworth (b.1942), David Inshaw (b.1943) and Annie and Graham Ovenden (b.1945 and 1943). They held that the country offered a potent source of inspiration and imagery that artists

could not ignore and sought to bring to it their experience and subjective perception of poetry, literature, music, history and myth. Their name and to some extent their concepts echo those of the Pre-Raphaelite Brotherhood, founded in 1848. *See also* CUBISM; DADAISM; FAUVISM; FUTURISM; ORPHISM; SURREALISM; SYNCHROMISM; TACHISM; VORTICISM.

Rushed off one's feet. Extremely busy. The expression dates from the 1930s and derives from the slightly earlier phrase 'to rush someone off their feet', meaning to hurry or pressure them.

> Dear Dorothy, I give you back your word. I have been prepared for this. It has all been a mistake. It was my fault for having rushed you off your feet.
> ARNOLD VILLIERS: *Everybody's Letter Writer*, 'Love Letters' (c.1930)

Russell Flint. The name of the artist Sir William Russell Flint (1880–1969), a byword in his own lifetime for his mildly erotic nudes and Spanish gypsy scenes, painted in a distinctive but rather garish style. John Betjeman's poem 'A Russell Flint' in *High and Low* (1966) is an evocation of a beautiful woman with grey-green eyes that he had met at the Garrick Club in London.

Russian roulette. A potentially fatal game of chance in which a 'player' loads a bullet into one chamber of a revolver, spins the cylinder, puts the gun to his head and pulls the trigger. The practice was popularized by Russian officers at the Tsar's court in the months before and during the 1917 Revolution, when the term is first recorded. It subsequently gained a figurative sense to apply to any potentially dangerous activity.

Rust Belt. A nickname in the 1980s for the declining steel-producing and other industrial areas of the American Midwest and northeastern states. The cause of the decline was recession on the one hand and foreign competition on the other. The name, patterned on SUN BELT, alludes to the decaying steel industry.

Rust bucket. A jocular term for a rusty old car, and earlier for a dilapidated ship or aeroplane. The original sense dates from the 1940s.

Ruth, 'Babe'. *See* BABE.

Rutland. England's smallest county, which although still a historic entity was removed from the political map when it was absorbed by Leicestershire in the local government county boundary changes of 1974, much to the annoyance of the local people. The name itself means 'Rōta's land', referring to an Anglo-Saxon landowner, and the county motto is *Multum in parvo*, 'Much in little'. The county was reinstated as a unitary authority in 1997.

Rutland Panther. A mysterious large animal with black fur and a long tail glimpsed on several occasions in different parts of RUTLAND from 1994. It is probably a big cat released into the wild either because it grew too large to be kept as a pet or as a consequence of the Dangerous Animals Act 1976, which ruled that animals such as lynxes, panthers and pumas must not be kept as pets. *See also* BEAST OF BODMIN MOOR.

Ryder Cup. The golfing trophy so named was presented by the English seed merchant Samuel Ryder (1856–1936) and first competed for by British and US teams in 1927. The contest is held every two years and until 1979 was dominated by the Americans. The opposing team then became Europe, whereupon the balance began to be redressed. *See also* SOLHEIM CUP.

S

SA (German *Sturmabteilung*, 'assault division'). Hitler's NAZI paramilitary organization, founded in 1921 and drawing its early members chiefly from the FREIKORPS ('Free Corps'), armed freebooter groups consisting mainly of former soldiers. It was kitted out in brown uniforms after the fashion of Mussolini's BLACKSHIRTS and accordingly became known as the Brownshirts. It was notorious for its methods of violent intimidation, both before and after its reorganization in 1925. Its leadership was purged in the NIGHT OF THE LONG KNIVES. *See also* SS.

Sabotage. Wilful and malicious destruction of machinery or plant by strikers, rebels, fifth columnists and the like. The term came into use after the great French railway strike in 1912. The word is traditionally said to have referred to the action of the strikers, who threw sabots into the machinery to damage it. This explanation cannot be sustained, however, and the allusion is probably to the noise made by the wooden shoes in walking, evoking a clumsy or bungling action.

Sabra and Chatila. *See* BEIRUT.

Sabre-rattling. A display or threat of military force, alluding to the sabres brandished by the Hungarian cavalry in the 18th century before an armed conflict. The term was much in evidence in the COLD WAR and in one form or another entered the languages of the countries concerned, as French *bruits de sabre*, German *Säbelrasseln* and Russian *bryatsanie oruzhiem*.

Sabrina neckline. A neckline with ties at the shoulders, as that of the dress worn by Audrey Hepburn (1929–93) in the film *Sabrina* (1954) (in the UK titled *Sabrina Fair*).

Sacco–Vanzetti case. A highly controversial American legal case that culminated in the execution of two Italian-born anarchists, Nicola Sacco and Bartolomeo Vanzetti, for the murder during an armed robbery of two employees of the firm of Slater & Morrill in Braintree, Massachusetts, on 15 April 1920. Controversy arose from the fact that the evidence on which the two men were condemned was largely circumstantial and from the patent intolerance of the men's radical politics displayed by the legal system. The trial judge, Webster Thayer, apparently referred to the men as 'dagos' and 'anarchist bastards'. The men remained on death row for six years and, despite pleas for clemency from Albert Einstein and George Bernard Shaw, were executed by electric chair on 23 August 1927. In 1977 the state of Massachusetts declared that the two men had been improperly tried.

Sack dress. A woman's short, loose, unwaisted dress, somewhat resembling a sack, fashionable in the 1950s.

Sacred cow. A term dating from the early years of the 20th century for a person or thing held to be above criticism. The cow is venerated by the Hindus from its association with certain deities, and verses of the Rig Veda refer to the animal as Devi (goddess).

> Green belts should no longer be regarded as sacred cows in a rural pasture in which no development is allowed.
>
> *The Times* (Letter to the Editor) (10 January 2000)

Sacred mushroom. A name given to various hallucinogenic mushrooms, especially species of *Psilocybe* and *Amanita*, which have been ritually eaten in different parts of the world. John Allegro, author of books on the DEAD SEA SCROLLS, aimed to prove in *The Sacred Mushroom and the Cross* (1970) that an intrinsic interrelationship exists between the mushroom as cause and catalyst of heightened spiritual awareness and the essentially mystic mainspring of Christianity.

SAD. An appropriate acronym for the depressive state known officially as seasonal affective disorder. It is associated with the autumn and winter seasons and is believed to be caused by a lack of light. The condition was first identified in the 1980s.

Saddlebags. A euphemism dating from the 1960s for folds of excess flesh round the stomach. *See also* LOVE HANDLES.

> I do a 10-minute workout with a Cindy Crawford video every other day and am pleased with the results. Which video would have exercises to get rid of saddlebags?
>
> *Sunday Times* (3 October 1999)

Sadie Hawkins Day. 9 November, in the United States a day corresponding to the English Leap Day (29 February) on which according to a 'tradition' begun by the cartoon series L'IL ABNER in 1938, women can propose marriage to men. In modern times the custom usually centres on a college dance, with the girls issuing invitations to the boys. Sadie Hawkins herself is a character in the cartoon, in which on the day named after her the unmarried women of Dogpatch chase the unmarried men across the countryside like hounds after a hare, marrying those whom they catch.

Sad sack. A colloquialism for an incompetent person who is well-intentioned but cannot help making mistakes. The name was originally that of an American cartoon character, a lugubrious little GI, created by the artist George Baker in the Second World War for the US Army magazine *Yank*. The implied full expression is 'sad sack of shit', a demeaning description of a human being as simply a container of excrement.

Safari park. As an imitation of an African game park, where lions and other large wild animals are kept in open spaces for public viewing, the safari park in Britain was the brainchild of the circus owner Jimmy Chipperfield (1912–90). The first such park opened at Longleat in 1966 and was soon copied elsewhere. Safari itself is a Swahili word deriving from Arabic *safara*, 'to travel'.

Safari suit. A lightweight suit, typically with short sleeves and four pleated pockets in the jacket, as originally worn by quasi-colonials or military men on safari. The safari jacket was particularly associated with the writer Ernest Hemingway (1899–1961), and he is depicted wearing one in many of his photographs. The garment was still fashionable at the close of the 20th century.

Safe haven. A place of refuge or security, especially for members of a religious or ethnic minority. The apparently tautological term gained prominence in the aftermath of the second GULF WAR when protected zones were set up in northern Iraq for the Kurds, many of whom had fled to Turkey and Iran after coming under attack by Saddam Hussein's troops. Similar zones were later set up by the United Nations in the former Yugoslavia following the implementation of ETHNIC CLEANSING. The expression is not limited to this specific sense, however.

> Dioceses such as Chichester are seen as safe havens by those most virulently opposed to the growing acceptance of women priests.
>
> *The Times* (Letter to the Editor) (9 July 1999)

Sailor Who Fell from Grace with the Sea, The. A novel (1965; in Japanese as *Gogo no eiko*, 1963) by Mishima Yukio (1925–70) in which a group of boys rejects the adult world. When the mother of one of them begins an affair with a naval officer, at first the boy reacts with hero-worship. Subsequently, after spying on them in bed, he turns vindictive and castrates his former hero. Mishima, having mounted an unsuccessful coup in favour of the Emperor against the prevailing administration, disembowelled himself with his sword. A film version (1976) of the novel, directed by Lewis John Carlino, was set in Dartmouth and described by the critic Benny Green in *Punch* as an 'everyday tale of torture, scopophilia, copulation, masturbation, dismemberment and antique dealing'.

Saint, The. The 'Robin Hood of modern crime' created by the Anglo-Chinese thriller writer Leslie Charteris. 'The Saint' is his crime name, his real name being Simon Templar. His symbol is a haloed stick-figure. He lives beyond the law, but he is otherwise a perfect English gentleman, a rescuer of damsels in distress and a jolly joker. He first appeared in the novel *Meet the Tiger* (1928), and went on to star in a long series of stories and books, as well as in film and television versions, the latter running from 1963 to 1968 and starring Roger Moore in the title role.

St Clair, Amber. The beautiful but promiscuous heroine of Kathleen Winsor's bestselling novel *Forever Amber* (1944), She has various adventures among the royalty and aristocracy of Restoration England and in the film of the novel (1947) was played by Linda Darnell. Her name created a certain vogue for the female first name Amber.

The novel was not called *Forever Amber* when first

offered to us. ... One of the publicity staff was discussing the manuscript one day. She said, in effect, 'I get a little tired of Amber – it's forever Amber, forever Amber, forever Amber ... ' 'Wait a minute', one of her listeners exclaimed, 'we've been wanting a title. You've given it to us – *Forever Amber'*.

HAROLD S. LATHAM: *My Life in Publishing*, II (1965)

St Ives School. A loosely structured group of artists who flourished in the Cornish fishing port of St Ives from the late 1940s to the early 1960s. The town had long been popular with artists, as had the fishing village of Newlyn near Penzance, but St Ives remained only of local artistic importance until the sculptor Barbara Hepworth (1903–75) and painter Ben Nicholson (1894–1982) moved there in 1939, just before the Second World War. Hepworth lived in St Ives for the rest of her life, and Nicholson stayed there until 1958. The two formed a nucleus of avant garde artists who made St Ives an internationally recognized centre of abstract art, and in 1993 the Tate Gallery opened a branch museum there housing displays of 20th-century artists associated with the town.

St Mugg. A nickname of the writer and broadcaster Malcolm Muggeridge (1903–90), who became a fervent Roman Catholic in 1982.

St Trinian's. An outrageous girls' school, the exact converse of a genteel and well-ordered 'seminary for young ladies', in the cartoons by Ronald Searle (b.1920), first collected in *Hurrah for St Trinian's* (1948). The riotous scenarios were subsequently transferred to the screen in a series of films, the best of which was *The Belles of St Trinian's* (1954), with Alastair Sim in the role of the headmistress. Searle's own daughters attended St Trinnean's School, Edinburgh, and this probably inspired the name of the fictional establishment, which subsequently became a byword for any lawless behaviour on the part of uniformed schoolgirls, real or imaginary.

Nina, Beth and Lou are three latter-day belles of St Trinians. Bosom chums at a girls' boarding school in the late Eighties, they flout the rules, smoking, ... bamboozling off-licences into selling them bottles of cider and licking Hula Hoops off their fingers in the dormitory.

Sunday Times (review of Kate Bingham, *Slipstream*) (15 January 2000)

St Valentine's Day Massacre. The mass murder of a group of bootlegging gangsters in Chicago on 14 February 1929. Disguising themselves as policemen, members of the Al CAPONE gang entered a garage on North Street run by members of the George 'Bugs' Moran gang, lined their opponents up against the wall, and gunned the seven men down. Moran himself was not there, and neither was Capone, who had gone to Florida. The bloody incident dramatized the intense rivalry for control of the illegal liquor traffic during the PROHIBITION era in the United States. The massacre features in a number of movies and is the starting point for the classic cross-dressing comedy SOME LIKE IT HOT (1959).

Saki. The pseudonym of Hector Hugh Munro (1870–1916), the author of many short stories, such as the collections *Reginald* (1904), *The Chronicles of Clovis* (1911), *Beasts and Super-Beasts* (1914) and *The Toys of Peace* (1919), and three novels, of which the best is *The* UNBEARABLE BASSINGTON (1912). He took his pen-name either from a line in Edward FitzGerald's *The Rubáiyát of Omar Khayyám* (1859) ('And when like her, O Saki, you shall pass') or as a contraction of Sakya Muni, one of the names of the Buddha. He was killed in the First World War in France, shot in the head while resting in a crater. His style is often wickedly but wittily satirical. His stories frequently involve animals who take their revenge on humans and children who display their superiority of spirit over feckless adults. Much of the enjoyment comes from the names of his characters, as in story titles such as 'The Jesting of Arlington Stringham', 'Filboid Studge, the Story of a Mouse That Helped', 'The Secret Sin of Septimus Brope' and 'The Remoulding of Groby Lington'.

Salami technique. A method of carrying out a plan by means of a series of small or imperceptible steps, and specifically a type of computer fraud in which small amounts of money are transferred from several accounts into an account under a false name. The term dates from the 1970s and refers to the gradual steps of the operation, like successive thin slices of salami.

Salop. An abbreviated name of the county of Shropshire, representing a contraction of *Salopescira*, a Norman form of the original Old English name, recorded in the Domesday Book as *Sciropescire*. The name was officially adopted for the county in 1974 but was disliked by many local people and was particularly unpopular with the Euro-MP for Salop and Staffordshire, who discovered when attending conferences in continental Europe that *Salop* was uncomfortably close to French *salope*, meaning 'slut'. The original name was thus readopted in 1980. Despite these objections, the adjective Salopian continues in use to describe the county's inhabitants and remains the name for past and present members of Shrewsbury School. It was Shrewsbury, the county town, that gave the name of the county in the first place, so that it is effectively 'Shrewsburyshire'.

SALT. The Strategic Arms Limitation Talks, organized from 1968 as a series of negotiations between the United States and the Soviet Union with the aim of reducing, or at any rate limiting, nuclear armaments. They resulted in two treaties, signed respectively in 1972 and 1979, although the second was never ratified by the US Senate. They were superseded by START.

Saltash luck. An unwelcome task that involves getting soaked through. The phrase dates from the early years of the 20th century and supposedly alludes to the poor catches of the fishermen of Saltash in Cornwall, a port that is now essentially a suburb of Plymouth.

Samaritans. An organization founded in 1953 by the Rev. Chad Varah (b.1911) of St Stephen Walbrook, London, to help the despairing and suicidal. By the early 1990s there were more than 180 centres in the British Isles as well as some overseas. Trained volunteers give their help at any hour to those who make their needs known, mostly by telephone. The name alludes to the New Testament parable of the Good Samaritan, who tended the victim of a robbery (in modern terms, a mugging) where others 'passed by on the other side' (Luke 10:30–37).

Same difference. Essentially the same; not different despite appearances. The expression dates from the 1940s.

Same old story. The latest bad situation is monotonously familiar. The expression was popularized in the Second World War by its occurrence in Herman Hupfeld's song 'As Time Goes By' (1931), performed by Dooley Wilson in the film CASABLANCA (1942):

It's still the same old story,
A fight for love and glory,
A case of do or die!
The world will always welcome lovers,
As time goes by.

Samizdat. Banned dissident literature in the former Soviet bloc or the system by which it was printed and distributed. Printing was often in the form of photocopying. The term is Russian, and literally means 'self-publishing house'.

Samson and Delilah. A biblical film epic (1949) depicting the doomed liaison between Samson, who was famed for his great strength, and the beautiful but treacherous Delilah. Starring Victor Mature and Hedy Lamarr, it was the impressive expanse of Mature's chest that prompted one of Groucho Marx's most famous observations:

You can't expect the public to get excited about a film where the leading man's bust is bigger than the leading lady's.

Sandbagger. A term of American origin dating from the 1960s for a person who deliberately under-performs in a sport in order to gain an unfair handicap or other advantage.

Sanpaku. The name for a condition of the eye when the white is visible below the iris as well as on both sides. It is said to result from a failure to follow a macrobiotic diet, with its organically grown sugar, fruit and vegetables, in favour of a traditional diet of meat, eggs and the like. The term derives from Japanese *san*, 'three', and *haku*, 'white', and was adopted in English in the 1960s.

The publicist introduces a girl of about twenty who is very sanpaku – in fact, an inordinate amount of veinless white shows beneath the lampblack pupils – and almost intimidatingly beautiful.
Esquire (January 1972)

Sandinistas. Members of a left-wing Nicaraguan political organization, the Sandinista National Liberation Front (SNLS), which came to power in 1979 after overthrowing the dictator Anastasio Somoza (1925–80). They were opposed during much of their rule by the US-backed CONTRAS and were voted out of office in 1990. They took their name from Augusto César Sandino (1893–1934), the nationalist leader of a similar earlier organization. *See also* PORTILLISTAS.

Sarajevo. The capital of Bosnia–Herzegovina has twice gained particular notoriety during the course of the 20th century.

(1) On 28 June 1914 the Archduke Franz Ferdinand, heir of the Austro-Hungarian empire, and his wife were assassinated in Sarajevo by Gavrilo Princip, a Bosnian Serb student and member of the secret Serbian nationalist organization, the BLACK HAND. The shooting lit the 'powder-keg' of a system of national alliances that had developed during the last decades of the 19th century and has thus been described as 'the shot heard round the world'. Austria-Hungary, which had long perceived Serbia to be a sponsor of

nationalist unrest in its Balkan provinces, used the assassination as a pretext to make unreasonable demands on Serbia. When Serbia, acting on the advice of its Slav ally, Russia, refused to comply with these demands, the Austrian army was mobilized and the Serbian capital city, Belgrade, bombarded. When Russia mobilized in response, Germany, fearing the disintegration of its Austro-Hungarian ally, demanded that Russian mobilization cease and asked France, Russia's ally, to guarantee that it would remain neutral in the event of a Russo-German war. The stage was now set for the outbreak of a coalition war. Germany put into action the SCHLIEFFEN PLAN and declared war on Russia and France. When the German army crossed into neutral Belgium as a preliminary to its attack on France, Britain, guarantor of Belgian neutrality since 1831, declared war on Germany and the WAR TO END WAR was under way. See also CENTRAL POWERS; ENTENTE CORDIALE; SCRAP OF PAPER; TRIPLE ENTENTE.

> We come to Sarajevo, Herr Burgomeister, and have a bomb thrown at us.
>
> ARCHDUKE FRANZ FERDINAND, last words before he was assassinated (28 June 1914)

(2) From 1992 to 1994 Sarajevo was subjected to a hellish siege during the Bosnian civil war that followed the break up of the former Yugoslavia. Sarajevo was besieged and bombarded from high points overlooking the city by the Bosnian Serb army (with the effective backing of the Serbian army), as part of its efforts to carve up in its favour the newly independent, multi-ethnic republic of Bosnia-Herzegovina. However, a United Nations ultimatum, allied to a threat of bombing by NATO, led to a ceasefire in February 1994, and the Bosnian Serb artillery withdrew.

Sardines. A party game dating from the 1920s and played mainly by children. One person hides somewhere in the house and is looked for by everyone else. When someone finds the hider, they join him, so that ultimately all except the final searcher are packed tight, like sardines, in a single hiding place. The last finder then becomes the next seeker. The game is also played by adults, since it provides a legitimate excuse for close physical contact. The American version is generally known more fully as 'sardines-in-the-box' or alternatively as 'hide-and-go-seek'.

SAS. The British Special Air Service traces its origins to the Second World War, when it was formed to operate behind enemy lines, conducting raids, sabotaging aircraft and disrupting communications and lines of supply. It was disbanded in 1945 but reborn four years later as the Malayan Scouts. In 1951 it officially became 22 Special Air Service. It was in action in Malaya, Oman, Borneo and Aden in the 1950s and 1960s, and was first sent to Northern Ireland in 1969. In 1980 the normally clandestine force was on public view when television cameras filmed an SAS team storming the besieged Iranian Embassy. Five of the six terrorists were killed. See also WHO DARES WINS.

Satanic Verses, The. A novel (1988) by Salman Rushdie (b.1947). Questions of faith and doubt underlie this panoramic vision of Britain during the Thatcherite era, India, and the mystical landscape in which the Prophet Mahound does battle, through which Rushdie explores the clash of cultures between East and West. The satanic verses are whispered by Shaitan in the ear of Mahound, who then repudiates them: 'The Devil came to him in the guise of the archangel, so that the verses he memorized ... were not the real thing but its diabolical opposite, not godly, but satanic.' The novel caused offence among Muslims for certain remarks put into the mouths of its characters. As a result, a Muslim FATWA (legal ruling) was issued by Iran's AYATOLLAH Khomeini, declaring Rushdie an apostate who should be killed for insulting the Prophet Muhammad. On 24 September 1998, after Rushdie had spent the intervening time in hiding, the government of the Islamic Republic of Iran announced that it had no intention, nor would it take any action, to threaten Rushdie's life or anybody associated with his work, or encourage or assist anybody to do so. See also FIRST LINES OF NOVELS.

(I Can't Get No) Satisfaction. A blues-influenced anti-establishment song by the ROLLING STONES, released in 1965. The satisfaction that eludes the singer is both sexual and existential, the lyrics railing against society in general, the claims of advertising ('some man comes on and tells me how white my shirts could be / but he can't be a man 'cos he doesn't smoke the same cigarettes as me') and problems with girls ('I can't get no girl reaction'). Its message of adolescent protest captured the mood of the 1960s in a similar manner to the Who's MY GENERATION. The phrase 'trying to make some girl' was bleeped when the group made an appearance on the *Ed Sullivan Show* in the United States.

Saturday girl. A girl or young woman who helps out in a shop or store on Saturdays, one of the busiest shopping days of the week.

Saturday Night and Sunday Morning. The first novel (1958) by Alan Sillitoe (b.1928) was a gritty story of working-class Nottingham, based on his own background. Arthur ('Don't let the bastards grind you down') Seaton makes the most of what life has to offer, including the wives of his workmates, though ultimately he settles for marriage. The title refers to the period spent with a married woman while her husband is away. The award-winning film version (1960), starring Albert Finney and Rachel Roberts, was imaginatively directed by Karel Reisz.

Saturday Night Fever. The title of a film and its soundtrack album, both released in 1978, and featuring music by the Bee Gees, the Tavares and Kool and the Gang. The album and its songs, including 'Stayin' Alive', 'How Deep is Your Love', 'Jive Talkin'' and 'Night Fever', is seen as the essence of the sound of 1970s disco music. The film starred John Travolta, whose dance routine was much imitated.

Saturday night special. A cheap pistol or revolver, as used by petty criminals in the United States. The allusion is to the use of the weapon in barroom and street fights at the weekend.

Saturday, Sunday, Monday. A play, originally entitled *Sabato, domenica e lunedì* (1959), by the Italian playwright Eduardo De Filippo (1900–92) about a warring Neapolitan family presided over by the matriarchal Rosa, who eventually restores peace. The play, which was translated into English by Keith Waterhouse and Willis Hall, derives its title from the structure of the play, the first act taking place on a Saturday, the second over Sunday lunch, and the third on Monday.

Saudi Arabia. The kingdom in southwestern Asia was founded in 1932 by the Muslim leader Ibn Saud (1880–1953), and named after him. His name derives from the Arabic word meaning 'good fortune', 'happiness', but it is purely a coincidence that the main part of the Arabian peninsula was known to the Romans as Arabia Felix, 'Arabia the fortunate'.

Sauron. The Lord of Darkness in J.R.R. Tolkien's *The* LORD OF THE RINGS (1954–5). Sauron is ruler of the land of MORDOR and dwells at Barad-dûr, the Dark Tower. The deep sense of evil and menace with which Tolkien invests him is heightened by his never actually appearing in physical form in the novel. Sauron's efforts to regain the One Ring from FRODO, the ring-bearer, are the motor of the plot, and the Ring's destruction leads to the shattering of his power. The name Sauron, coincidentally or otherwise, is reminiscent of the Greek word *sauros* ('lizard').

Saved by the bell. Extricated from an unpleasant or undesirable situation by the intervention of someone or something. The reference is to the sounding of a bell at the end of a round in a boxing match, rescuing the loser from further punishment. Schoolchildren are sometimes similarly saved from answering an awkward question in class by the sounding of the bell at the end of a lesson.

Save the Children Fund. A charity founded in Britain in 1919 by a Shropshire woman, Eglantyne Jebb (1875–1928), in response to the famine among children in Europe caused by the First World War. It now operates to improve the lives of children in 70 countries.

Save the whale. An environmental slogan of the early 1980s alerting the public to the rapid decline of the whale population. It was instrumental in bringing about the moratorium on commercial whaling introduced in 1985.

Savoy Hill. The site of the first studios of the British Broadcasting Company (1922) and until 1932 the headquarters of the British Broadcasting Corporation, the original BBC call sign being 2LO (i.e. No. 2, London).

Savrola. A political satire (1900) by Winston Churchill (1874–1965), set in the imaginary country of Laurania. Savrola, who resembles the politician Benjamin Disraeli (1804–81), leads the people against a military dictator, who uses his beautiful wife, Lucille, to divert the young man's attentions. Lucile and Savrola fall in love, and there are complications.

Say cheese! A traditional injunction from a photographer to a group of people about to be photographed, in order to make them smile (by saying the word 'cheese').

Say it ain't so, Joe. The attributed words of a young fan to the American baseball star 'Shoeless Joe' Jackson of the Chicago White Sox as he emerged from a grand jury session at the time of the BLACK SOX SCANDAL of 1919. Jackson always maintained his innocence, but he and seven others were barred from baseball for life.

Scamperdale. A type of Pelham bit for horses, thus with combined snaffle and bit but angled back to prevent chafing. It was invented in the 1930s and takes its name from Lord Scamperdale in R.S. Surtees's *Mr Sponge's Sporting Tour* (1853).

Scapa Flow. This sea basin in the Orkneys was the main base of the British fleet in the First World War. The surrendered German fleet scuttled itself here in 1919 but most of the ships were salvaged over the following 20 years. It was again a fleet base in the Second World War. On 14 October 1939 a U-BOAT penetrated the anchorage and sank the battleship *Royal Oak* with the loss of 810 lives.

Scare the living daylights out of someone, To. *See* BEAT THE LIVING DAYLIGHTS OUT OF SOMEONE.

Scarface. A nickname of the gangster Al CAPONE (1899–1947), from the scar on his left cheek, caused by a razor slash sustained in a Brooklyn gang fight in his younger days.

Scarlet Pimpernel. The fictional spy hero created by Baroness Orczy for her bestselling novel *The Scarlet Pimpernel* (1905). His real name is Sir Percy Blakeney and he is the head of the League of the Scarlet Pimpernel, a band of young Englishmen pledged to rescue the aristocratic victims of the Reign of Terror that followed the French Revolution. He outwits his French opponents through his courage and ingenious disguises, identifying himself in his secret rescue missions by a signet ring with the image of a scarlet pimpernel flower. The verse with which Blakeney mocks his chief enemy, Citizen Chauvelin, one of Robespierre's most cunning agents, is well known:

> We seek him here, we seek him there,
> Those Frenchies seek him everywhere.
> Is he in heaven? – Is he in hell?
> That demmed, elusive Pimpernel?
> ch xii

A first-class period film version (1934), starring Leslie Howard, Merle Oberon and Raymond Massey, was directed by Harold Young.

Scat singing. In JAZZ a form of singing without words, using the voice as a musical instrument. It is said to have been started by Louis Armstrong in the 1920s when he forgot the words or accidentally dropped the paper on which they were written while singing a number. Jelly Roll Morton, on the other hand, claimed to have sung scat as early as 1906. The word itself is presumably imitative.

Schicklgruber, Herr. A contemptuous nickname that was applied occasionally by Winston Churchill to

Adolf Hitler (1889–1945), the Nazi FÜHRER. Hitler's father, Alois Schicklgruber (1837–1903), used his mother's surname until the later 1870s, when he started to use the surname Hitler, based on a local priest's mistranscription of his father's name, Johann Georg Heidler, who had fathered him five years before marrying his mother. The Schicklgruber connection was discovered by Hitler's opponents in Germany and Austria in the 1930s. *See also* AUSTRIAN CORPORAL.

Schindler's Ark. A novel with historical interpolations (1982; in USA as *Schindler's List*) by the Australian novelist Thomas Keneally (b.1935), which won the BOOKER PRIZE for fiction. It describes the life and times of Oskar Schindler (1908–74), an ethnic German born into a Catholic family living in Moravia (incorporated in the new republic of Czechoslovakia in 1918 and now part of the Czech Republic). During the Second World War Schindler, playboy industrialist and 'discoverer of unprocurables', saved some 1100 Polish Jews by the device of setting up at his own expense a personal 'labour camp' within the forced labour camp of Plaszów, near Cracow, and passing the men and women off as 'skilled workers'. The film version (1993), entitled *Schindler's List* and directed by Steven Spielberg, was acclaimed by Terrence Rafferty of the *New Yorker* as the finest film ever made about the HOLOCAUST.

Schindler's List. *See* SCHINDLER'S ARK.

Schlieffen Plan. The German military's strategic plan for achieving victory in a war against France and Russia, developed between 1899 and 1905 by Count Alfred von Schlieffen (1833–1913), chief of the general staff (1891–1905). The plan was devised in response to the 1892 alliance between France and Russia, and it was based on the premise that Russia would be much slower to mobilize than either France or Germany. Germany would make its main attack on France through neutral Belgium, while smaller German forces withdrew along France's eastern frontier, drawing after them the bulk of the French army, which would then be attacked in the rear by the main German force. Having surrounded and destroyed the French army, German forces would be transferred to the east, to defeat Russia. The whole plan was to follow a detailed timetable, but when it came to it a number of unpredicted events, such as determined Belgian resistance, a quick British intervention and a rapid Russian offensive, served to thwart the outcome. The successful German offensive on the Low Countries and France in 1940 followed a variant of the Schlieffen Plan. *See also* SARAJEVO.

Schlock. Cheap or inferior; trashy. The term is one of several words of Yiddish origin that came to denote a shoddy or defective object or a stupid or boorish person. Examples of the latter include schlemiel, schlep, shlub, schlump, schmo, schmuck and schnook. *See also* SCHM-.

Schm-. This initial element of various words of Yiddish origin, such as schmaltz, schmooze and schmuck, can be prefixed to any word to express one's disparagement, dismissal or derision of the word in question, which is quoted before it, as in the old joke about the psychiatrist and the fond Jewish mother: 'I have to tell you, madam, that your son is suffering from an Oedipus complex.' 'Oedipus, Schmoedipus! What does it matter so long as he loves his mother?'

> To consider in what particulars they [prime ministers] were wise or unwise ... is so much trickier than to chin-wag about 'honour' and 'personal integrity'. Honour, schmhonour; integrity be damned.
>
> *The Times* (4 September 1999)

Schneider Trophy. An international trophy for aviation, presented in 1913 by Jacques Schneider, a French patron of aviation. It was open to seaplanes of all nations and was won outright by Britain in 1931, when contests ceased.

Schoolgirl complexion. Beautiful skin and colouring, without any wrinkles, lines or signs of ageing. The expression derives from an American advertising slogan for Palmolive soap from 1917, more fully: 'Keep that schoolgirl complexion'. The slogan was coined by Charles S. Pearce, a Palmolive executive. The healthy image of a young person's clear skin and radiant features has long been traditional, as for example in Shakespeare's 'schoolboy, with ... shining morning face' (*As You Like It*, II, vii). *See also* PEACHES AND CREAM COMPLEXION.

Schoolgirl French. Fragmentary French, such as might at one time have been learned by a schoolgirl as a social grace rather than a standard subject.

> 'With extras?' asked the Mock Turtle, a little anxiously.
> 'Yes', said Alice: 'we learned French and music.'
> LEWIS CARROLL: *Alice in Wonderland*, ch ix (1865)

School of hard knocks. The painful or difficult experiences that are regarded as providing a salutary lesson

on the realities of life. The American expression dates from the early 20th century.

Schweppes. The manufacturers of the mineral waters and soft drinks of this name used its sibilance to create a number of amusing neologisms in the 20th century, such as 'Schweppervescence', introduced in 1946. The company produced its own newspaper, the *Schweppshire Post*, published in 'Cirenschwepster' and costing 'Schweppence', to report such incidents as 'Councillor collides with cow' (in 'Schwepton Mallet'), 'Streetcar kidnapped in Hove, Pa.', and to print its own weather forecast, promising a 'Schweppitome of dullness' in the Midlands. The name itself, for all its onomatopoeic evocation, derives from German entrepreneur Jacob Schweppe (1740–1821), who moved to Britain in 1792.

Science fiction. A fiction based on imagined future developments in science, especially with regard to space or time travel, life on other planets, visits to Earth from ALIENS and the like. Much science fiction is sophisticated and fires the imagination, but the worst types of the genre are mostly risible and fit only for crude comic strips or picture stories. The term first gained general currency in the 1920s.

Scientology. A religious system, in full the Church of Scientology, based on the seeking of self-knowledge and spiritual fulfilment by means of special courses and training. It was founded in 1955 by the American SCIENCE FICTION writer L. Ron Hubbard, developer of DIANETICS. It been the subject of considerable criticism, to which it has responded with vigorous lawsuits.

Scofflaw. An American term for a person who flouts ('scoffs at') the law, especially one who fails to comply with a law that is difficult to enforce. The origin of the word dates from 1923, when many law-enforcement officers were concerned at the increasing disrespect shown for the newly enacted Eighteenth Amendment, the PROHIBITION law, on the grounds that an attitude of defiance to one federal law could lead to gradual loss of respect for the whole body of laws. They therefore sought a word to describe people who derided the National Prohibition Act. A Massachusetts millionaire, Delcevare King, announced a prize contest for the most appropriate word. The prize was a mere $200 but it attracted 25,000 entries. In January 1924 King announced that the winning entry, 'scofflaw', had been submitted independently by Henry Irving

Shaw and Kate Butler, both residents of Massachusetts. The neologism was soon entered in the dictionaries.

Scooby Doo. The cowardly Great Dane created in 1969 by Hanna-Barbera Productions for television cartoons. He helps four teenage detectives tour the country in their 'Mystery Machine' mobile van in search of the supernatural and gained his name from the meaningless phrase 'scooby-dooby-doo' in Bert Kaempfert's song 'Strangers in the Night' (1966), made into a hit by Frank Sinatra.

Scorched earth policy. A policy of burning and destroying crops and anything that may be of use to an invading force. The term arose in the late 1930s and apparently translates Chinese *shāotǔ zhèngcè*, from *shāo*, 'to burn', *tǔ*, 'earth' and *zhèngcè*, 'policy'.

Score, To. A verb that has acquired various colloquial meanings in the 20th century, among them to commit a crime, to steal, to obtain an illegal drug and, of a man, to find a sexual partner.

Scorpion kick. A style of kick in football pioneered by the Colombian goalkeeper Rene Higuita. His technique has been to wait for a high, goal-bound ball then dive forward and kick the ball away with his heels, in the process adopting a scorpion shape. He used the trick effectively at Wembley in Colombia's 0–0 draw with England in the autumn of 1995.

Scotch tape. In 1930 the Minnesota Mining and Manufacturing Company of St Paul, Missouri, now known as 3M, introduced a specialized new product in the form of a transparent, adhesive cellulose tape. As 'a little went a long way' when it came to sealing packages, they gave it a name that complimented the reputed thriftiness of the Scots. By 1935, when a dispenser was added, the tape was already an institution and its name as familiar as that of its British rival, SELLOTAPE.

Scotland the Brave. A traditional tune to which new words were written in the 1950s by a Scottish journalist, Cliff Hanley. For several years it was the unofficial Scottish national anthem, sung by sports spectators, but was subsequently replaced in popularity by FLOWER OF SCOTLAND.

Scottish Colourists. A term used for four Scottish painters who in the years before the First World War each spent some time in France, where they were influenced by the rich colours and bold handling of recent French painting, especially FAUVISM. They were

F.C.B. Cadell (1883–1937), J.D. Fergusson (1874–1961), Leslie Hunter (1877–1931) and S.J. Peploe (1871–1935). The name was popularized by T.J. Honeyman's book *Three Scottish Colourists* (1950), dealing with Cadell, Hunter and Peploe. The four did not form a group but knew one another individually.

Scottish National Party. *See* SNP.

Scottish Renaissance. A term coined in 1924 by the French literary critic Denis Saurat to describe the interwar revival of consciousness and culture in Scotland. The name became loosely associated with such writers as Hugh MacDiarmid (1892–1978), Lewis Grassic Gibbon (1901–35), Edwin Muir (1887–1959) and Neil M. Gunn (1891–1973). The resurgence itself was prompted partly by the growth of national awareness in Scotland after the First World War, partly as a reaction against the sentimental trend in 19th-century Scottish writing. The first major work of the genre was MacDiarmid's STREAM OF CONSCIOUSNESS poem *A Drunk Man Looks at the Thistle* (1926).

Scott of the Antarctic. *See* SOUTH POLE.

Scouse or **Scouser.** A nickname for an inhabitant of Liverpool, so called from the lobscouse, or sailor's meat stew, formerly popular as a local dish. The name also serves for the form of English spoken in Liverpool. Characteristics of this are the pronunciation of words such as 'fair' and 'spare' as 'fur' and 'spur', the separate sounding of the 'g' in 'long' (as normally in 'longer'), and the sounding of 't' as 'r' in words such as 'matter', giving 'marrer'. In a publicity drive for the Liverpool clean streets campaign litter was described as 'norra lorra fun'. The voice quality of the Scouse speaker is markedly adenoidal, a feature that has puzzled phoneticians.

Scouting for Boys. A book, published in fortnightly parts in 1908, by Robert Baden-Powell (1857–1941), the founder of the Scout Movement. It includes advice on healthy living (particularly camping in the wild), and a number of 'camp fire yarns'. *See also* BOY SCOUTS.

Scouts. *See* BOY SCOUTS.

Scout's honour. I am telling the truth; trust me. The allusion is to the honour on which BOY SCOUTS promise to obey the Scout Law, as originally defined by Robert Baden-Powell in SCOUTING FOR BOYS (1908): 'A Scout's Honour is to be trusted.' The phrase is now used as an asseveration that what one says is true, as: 'I won't tell anyone, scout's honour.'

Scrabble. The well-known game, in which players compete in forming words with lettered tiles on a board of 225 squares, was invented in 1931 by a New York architect, Alfred M. Butts (1900–93), who called it 'Criss Cross' with reference to the way the words interlock on the board, as in a crossword puzzle. It was redesigned and renamed Scrabble by Jim Brunot, a social worker, in 1948, and he and his wife began to manufacture sets by hand the following year. They failed to make a profit, however, and it was only when Jack Strauss, chairman of Macy's, the New York department store, became interested in 1952 that the Brunots finally achieved a breakthrough. Each lettered tile is worth a given number of points, the commonest letters having the lowest value and the rarest the highest. Words are scored by adding up the values of their letters, multiplied by any of the 'premium' squares that may be covered, such as double letter, triple letter, double word or triple word. The player who scores the most points is the winner. The game has gained a serious enough status to be played in official tournaments.

Scrambled egg. Services' slang dating from the Second World War for the gold braid on an officer's cap, hence for an officer himself.

Scrape the barrel or **the bottom of the barrel, To.** To be reduced to using the most mediocre things or people simply because there are none other available. The expression dates, significantly, from the Second World War.

> So scraped is the barrel of BBC sport that unkind souls may wonder whether competitive ballet is now to be their secret weapon.
> *Sunday Times* (8 August 1999)

Scrap of paper. A treaty of pledge that one does not intend to honour. The phrase is said to have been used by the German Chancellor, Theobald von Bethmann Hollweg, in connection with the German violation of Belgian neutrality in August 1914 (*see* SARAJEVO).

> The Chancellor said that … just for a word – 'neutrality', – just for a scrap of paper Great Britain was going to – make war on a kindred nation.
> EDWARD GOSCHEN: letter of 8 August 1914 in *Collected Diplomatic Documents relating to the Outbreak of the European War* (1915)

Scratch at the wall, To. To be keen to participate in an activity. The image is of a prisoner who seeks to escape from his cell into the 'real world' where he can resume a normal life.

What does he [Ivan Massow, Tory candidate for Mayor of London] offer London Conservatives? 'Apart from being fresh, entrepreneurial etc, I am instinctively metropolitan in my outlook. I'm scratching at the wall to get back there on Sunday evening.'
The Times (4 December 1999)

Scratch card. A card with a section (or sections) covered in a silver waxy coating which can be scratched off, usually with a coin, to reveal a possible winning symbol. Scratch cards were introduced in the United States in the 1980s and the flutterer's delight (or downfall) soon spread to Britain, where they could either be bought or were given free as a consumer incentive. Some of the most popular purchasable cards were the so called *Instants*, linked to the National Lottery.

Scratch one's head, To. To think hard in order to find a solution; to express puzzlement. The gesture is traditionally regarded as accompanying these mental processes, presumably as it symbolizes a 'stirring of the brain'.

Scratch the surface, To. To deal with or investigate only superficially. The implication is that one must dig deeper to resolve the matter properly or fully.

Screaming habdabs. A fit of great anxiety; the 'heebie-jeebies'. The origin of the latter word is uncertain – it may represent a stuttering or gulping – but the phrase dates from the 1940s.

Screaming Lord Sutch. *See* MONSTER RAVING LOONY PARTY.

Screaming Popes, The. A series of paintings executed between 1949 and the mid-1950s by Francis Bacon (1909–92). They were inspired by the portrait of Pope Innocent X by Velázquez (1599–1660), a painting described by Sir Joshua Reynolds in the 18th century as 'the most beautiful picture in Rome'. Sir Joshua would not have appreciated Bacon's reworkings, which are nightmarish depictions of hysterical terror, sometimes accompanied by hunks of meat. As one critic put it: 'The major influence on Bacon has been his own surname.'

Scream queen. A term for an actress who plays a part in a HORROR MOVIE, in which she will be invariably required to scream. The colloquialism became particularly attached to Jamie Lee Curtis (b.1958), who appeared in such films as *Prom Night*, *Terror Train* and *The Fog* (all 1980).

Screw around, To. To be sexually promiscuous; to fool about. The former term dates from the 1930s; the latter from the 1950s.

Screw up, To. To mess up; to ruin; to blunder, as: 'I really screwed it up that time.' The phrase is of American origin and dates from the 1920s.

Scrumpy. Rough cider made from 'scrumps', withered or stunted apples, and a drink particularly associated with the West Country. The word itself is of dialect origin and first recorded in the early 20th century.

Scrunchy. A circular band of fabric-covered elastic used for holding a bunch of hair, especially a pony tail, and so called from its crumpled ('scrunched') appearance. 'Scrunchies' is also sometimes used for 'crunches', gymnastic exercises used to strengthen the abdominal muscles by means of 'sit-ups'.

> He did go to the same gym as Mel [C of the SPICE GIRLS], he was on the exercise bike while she did scrunchies.
>
> *heat* (23–29 September 1999)

Scud. The NATO code name for a type of long-range surface-to-surface guided missile developed in the Soviet Union. They came into the news in 1991 during the second GULF WAR when they were launched against Allied forces in Saudi Arabia. The name is not an acronym but a conventional word beginning with *S* used for a type of Soviet surface-to-surface missile. Other types were *Savage*, *Scapegoat* and *Scrooge*. Names beginning with *G* were chosen for surface-to-air missiles (SAMs), with *K* for air-to-surface missiles, and with *A* for air-to-air missiles.

Sea and sangria. An encapsulation of the pleasures of a holiday in Spain for the British tourist. The latter word, as the name of a drink of red wine mixed with lemonade and fruit, became familiar in English only in the 1960s. A similar earlier drink was known as 'sangaree', and the origin of both is apparently in Spanish *sangría*, 'bleeding'. *See also* SUN, SEA AND SAND.

> Claiming to have blown their £1,800 sponsorship on the 'sun and sangria' trip, they later admitted that their tans were from a sunbed.
>
> *The Times* (10 June 1999)

Sealed Knot. An organization founded in 1971 to re-enact battles of the English Civil War between Charles I and his parliamentary opponents (1642–9). The enterprise is enacted both for pleasure and for charitable purposes, and the name derives from a Royalist secret society active during the Protectorate (1654–9) and dedicated to the restoration of the Stuart line. Its modern namesake cuts more of a dash than the original.

Sea Lion. On 2 August 1940 Hermann Goering, head of the German LUFTWAFFE, issued a directive laying down a plan of attack in which a few massive blows from the air would destroy British air power and so open the way for an amphibious invasion, termed Operation Sea Lion (German, *Seelöwe*). Victory by RAF Fighter Command in the BATTLE OF BRITAIN blocked this possibility, however, and essentially created the conditions for Britain's survival, for the extension of the Second World War and for the eventual defeat of NAZI Germany.

Sean Connery *is* James Bond. A promotional device identifying an actor with his screen role, in this case for the James BOND film YOU ONLY LIVE TWICE (1967). The somewhat misleading formula was repeated with 'Paul Hogan *is* Crocodile Dundee' (1987) and is not restricted to actors. 'The Sunday Times *is* the Sunday papers' is one still carried regularly by the newspaper in question.

Searchlight tattoo. A military entertainment, carried out at night in the open air with illuminations, military exercises and martial music. The best known is that at Edinburgh Castle, staged during the Edinburgh Festival on the Castle Esplanade, with the floodlit castle as a dramatic backdrop.

Search me! I've no idea! Don't ask me! The expression dates from the early years of the 20th century and is of American origin. The suggestion is that one may search the speaker for the answer but it will not be found there.

Seaside postcards. The collecting of picture postcards while on holiday by the sea has been a British hobby since the EDWARDIAN ERA. A particular development has been the gaudily coloured comic postcard with a caption involving a mildly ribald *double entendre*. Such cards owe much to the talents of Donald McGill, an English artist whose original name was Fraser Gould (1875–1962). Outsize women in bathing costumes paddling alongside weedy husbands are typical of his subjects, while salacious girls and cheeky children also feature. An example of the music-hall humour is a scenario in which a big-bosomed customer buying a brassiere is asked by the assistant 'What bust,

Madam?' only to receive the rejoinder 'Ee luv, nothing bust, it just wore out.'

> Benny Hill, whose oh-so-British, seaside postcard humour became a cult in America, has a new website.
> *The Times* (1 September 1999)

Sea, the Sea, The. A visionary novel (1978) by Iris Murdoch (1919–99), which won the BOOKER PRIZE for fiction. It is set in and around an isolated house by the sea to which a theatrical director, Charles Arrowby, retires in order to write his autobiography. He is beset by welcome and unwelcome people from his past. There are parallels with Shakespeare's play, *The Tempest*, and always the influence of the sea and its changing moods. The title comes from the *Anabasis* of the Greek historian Xenophon (*c*.430–*c*.355 BC), recounting his epic march to bring the defeated army of Greek mercenaries from Babylon to the sea in 401 BC. It is their cry as they reach their objective. *See also* FIRST LINES OF NOVELS.

Secondary picketing. Picketing by strikers of the premises of a firm that trades with their employer but that is not otherwise involved in the dispute in question.

Second banana. A supporting comedian, the leading performer being a TOP BANANA.

Second front. In the Second World War a front in NAZI-occupied Europe additional to the Russian sector of fighting, and as such a reality much desired by the Soviet Union, to disburden it of what it saw as its unfair share of the land war against Germany. Despite various schemes proposed by Winston Churchill and others, it did not begin to achieve realization until D-DAY.

Second honeymoon. A holiday, something like a honeymoon, that a couple take after they have been married for some years. The aim, if possible, is to 'recapture that first fine careless rapture'.

Second World War operational code names. The following is a list of the military code names of some of the most significant military operations of the Second World War.

A: the Japanese counter-offensive in June 1944 following the US capture of the Marshall Islands. The plan ended disastrously for the Japanese in the Battle of the Philippine Sea, 'the Great Marianas Turkey Shoot'.

Adlerangriff ('eagle attack'): the German air offensive against RAF bases in Britain during August–September 1940. The air battles that followed became known as the BATTLE OF BRITAIN.

Anvil: the planning stage of Operation Dragoon (*see* below).

Archery: the British commando raid on the Lofoten and other Norwegian islands in December 1941–January 1942 (*see also* Claymore *below*).

Avalanche: the first Allied landings in mainland Italy, near Salerno, on 9 September 1943.

Bagration: the major and successful Soviet offensive in June–August 1944 through Belarus and into Poland.

BARBAROSSA: the German invasion of the Soviet Union, launched on 22 June 1941.

Battleaxe: the unsuccessful British offensive in the Western Desert in June 1941.

Big Scheme: the Polish resistance plan for a rising in the summer of 1944 that resulted in Operation Burza (*see* below).

Blau I–III ('blue'): the German offensive in the Soviet Union in the summer of 1942.

Burza: the ill-fated WARSAW RISING of the Polish resistance in August–October 1944.

Catapult: the controversial British naval attack on the French fleet at MERS-EL-KÉBIR in Algeria on 3 July 1940, to prevent the fleet falling into German hands.

Catchpole: the US capture of Eniwetok Atoll in the Marshall Islands during February 1944.

Chariot: the 'St Nazaire raid' of 28 March 1942 by British commandos and naval forces, which succeeded in destroying a strategic dry dock.

Claymore: the successful British commando attack on the Norwegian Lofoten Islands in March 1941, the first major commando operation of the war.

Cobra: the Allied break-out from the hedgerows of Normandy in July 1944, following the D-DAY landings.

Compass: the successful British and Commonwealth offensive in December 1940–February 1941 against the Italians in Egypt and Libya, which prompted the arrival of German forces in North Africa.

Coronet: the planned follow-up to Operation Olympic (*see* below), aimed at ending all Japanese resistance in the home islands.

Crusader: the British and Commonwealth offensive in the Western Desert in November 1941–January 1942. It achieved limited success.

Demon: the British withdrawal from Greece in April 1941.

Dragoon: the Allied invasion of southern France in August 1944. Planning for the operation was under the code name Anvil.

Dynamo: the British withdrawal from DUNKIRK and the adjacent coast in May–June 1940.

Eiche ('oak'): the daring raid by German commandos in September 1943 to rescue Mussolini (*see* DUCE) from imprisonment on the Gran Sasso in the high Apennines.

Elkton: the overall code name for Allied operations in the southwest Pacific in 1943–4, involving offensives in the Bismarck Archipelago, the Solomon Islands and New Guinea.

Extended Capital: the major and successful British offensive in central Burma in November 1944–March 1945.

Fischreiher ('heron'): the strategically disastrous German offensive to capture STALINGRAD, launched in July 1942.

Flintlock: the US capture of the southern Marshall Islands in January–February 1944.

Forager: the US capture of the Marianas Islands in June–August 1944, bringing the Japanese home islands within range of Allied bombers.

Freshman: the British commando raid in November 1942 that succeeded in destroying a crucial German HEAVY WATER plant in Norway.

Frühlingserwachen ('spring awakening'): the optimistically chosen code name for the last German offensive on the Eastern Front in March 1945. It failed to stem the Soviet advance.

Frühlingswind ('spring breeze'): the German offensive in North Africa in February 1943. Although temporarily successful, in the end it failed to prevent AXIS forces from being trapped between Allied armies advancing from both east and west.

Georg: the German siege of Leningrad (St Petersburg), which began in September 1941 and was not ended until January 1944.

Granite: the US Admiral Chester Nimitz's 1944 strategic plan for defeating Japan by cutting its empire in two. It was abandoned in favour of General Douglas MacArthur's plan for a direct offensive towards the Japanese home islands.

Grapefruit: the final, successful Allied offensive in northern Italy in April–May 1945.

Herbstnebel ('autumn mist'): the German offensive in the Ardennes in December 1944–February 1945, resulting in the BATTLE OF THE BULGE.

Himmler: the German operation involving the staging of a hoaxed Polish raid against a German radio station, providing the immediate pretext for the German invasion of Poland on 31 August 1939.

Husky: the Allied invasion of Sicily on 9 July 1943.

Iceberg: the US invasion of Okinawa, launched on 1 April 1945. However, it was not until 21 June that organized resistance ended.

Impact: the British and Commonwealth offensive across Lake Comacchio in northern Italy in April 1945.

Ironclad: the British capture of the port of Diego Suarez in the VICHY-held island of Madagascar in May 1942 to prevent the port from falling into Japanese hands. The whole island was under Allied control by November.

Jubilee: the controversial Canadian and British raid on Dieppe in August 1942, carried out as an experiment in landing techniques. The raid resulted in two-thirds of the attackers being killed, wounded or taken prisoner.

Judgement: the attack by 21 Fleet Air Arm Fairey Swordfish on the Italian naval base at Taranto on 11 November 1940. It was the world's first carrier-based air attack and resulted in three Italian battleships being disabled.

KETSU: the Japanese plan for defending the home islands from the expected US assault.

Kikushi ('floating chrysanthemum'): the Japanese kamikaze campaign against US naval forces off Okinawa in April–May 1945.

King II: the US invasion of Leyte Island in October–December 1944, the first step in the reconquest of the Philippines.

Koltso ('ring'): the successful Soviet operation to wipe out the encircled German army in STALINGRAD in January–February 1943.

Kugelblitz ('ball lightning'): the temporarily successful German campaign against the Yugoslav partisans in December 1943–February 1944.

Lightfoot and **Supercharge:** the two phases of the British and Commonwealth offensive during the Second Battle of El ALAMEIN in October–November 1942.

Loincloth: the first CHINDIT expedition behind Japanese lines in Burma, February–April 1943.

Love III: the US recapture of Mindanao in the Philippines, December 1944–January 1945.

Lumberjack: the Allied offensive towards the Rhine in March 1945, which resulted in the establishment of a bridgehead on the far side at Remagen.

Madison: the Allied offensive in eastern France in November–December 1944, which took US forces to the SIEGFRIED LINE.

Margarethe I: the German occupation of Hungary on 9 March 1944.

Margarethe II: the planned German occupation of Romania should it go over to the Allied side. When it did, in August 1944, it was too late, as Soviet forces were sweeping through the country.

Marita: the German conquest of Yugoslavia and Greece in April 1941.

Market Garden: the unsuccessful Allied campaign at Arnhem in September 1944, aimed at securing a bridgehead over the lower Rhine. The airborne component was Operation Market, while the advance by ground forces to relieve the airborne forces was called Operation Garden. It was a BRIDGE TOO FAR.

Menace: the unsuccessful attempt by the British and Free French to capture the VICHY-held naval base at Dakar in French West Africa, August–September 1940.

Merkur ('Mercury'): the German conquest of Crete in May 1941, including a notable early use of airborne troops, perhaps the reason the operation was named after the winged messenger of the gods.

MI: the Japanese naval offensive against the US base at Midway Island that led to the Battle of Midway (May–June 1942), the turning point in the war in the Pacific.

Micki Maus ('Mickey Mouse'): the German abduction of the regent of Hungary, Admiral Horthy, on 15 October 1944, after he went over to the Allies.

Mike I–VII: the US recapture of Luzon in the Philippines, January–April 1945.

Millennium: the first RAF THOUSAND-BOMBER RAID, against Cologne, on 30 May 1942.

Mincemeat: the Allied plan to deceive the Germans that the invasion of southern Europe would take place in Sardinia and Greece, rather than in Sicily (Operation Husky; *see* above). The plan, carried out in May 1943, involved planting phoney secret documents on the body of a drowned man, and was the subject of the classic film *The Man Who Never Was* (1955).

MO: the Japanese plan to capture Tulagi in the Solomon Islands, Port Moresby in New Guinea and the Louisiade Islands. The operation was thwarted at the Battle of the Coral Sea in May 1942.

Montclair: the operation in which US forces retook Mindanao and the Visayas (Panay, Cebu, Negros and Bohol) in the Philippines and Australian forces retook Borneo, in April–July 1945.

Morgenluft ('morning air'): the German operation in Tunisia in February 1943, to complement Operation Frühlingswind (*see* above).

Morgenrote ('dawn'): the German counter-offensive against the Allied landings at Anzio in February 1944.

Neptune: the code name for all the naval operations within Operation OVERLORD, the Allied invasion of Normandy in June 1944.

Noball: the Allied air operations against V-1 launching sites in northwest Europe in 1944.

Nordwind ('north wind'): the fruitless German counter-offensive in Alsace in December 1944–January 1945.

Oboe I–III: the three phases of the Australian recapture of Borneo (part of Operation Montclair; *see* above) in May–July 1945. (*see* HIROSHIMA).

Ochsenkopf ('ox head'): the ineffective German offensive in North Africa in February–March 1943.

Olive: successful Allied assault in August–September 1944 on the GOTHIC LINE, the line of German defences stretching across Italy north of Florence.

Olympic: the plan for the Allied invasion of the Japanese home islands, due to start on 1 November 1945 but abandoned following the dropping of the atomic bombs in August 1945 (*see* HIROSHIMA).

Orkan: the successful German operation to take the Crimea in May–July 1942.

OVERLORD: the Allied invasion of northwest Europe via the Normandy beaches in June 1944.

Pedestal: perhaps the best known of several heroic convoys to Malta. Pedestal took place in August 1942 and brought the first significant supplies to get through that year. Perhaps its most important delivery was the 10,000 tonnes of oil on board the tanker *Ohio*. *See also* GEORGE CROSS ISLAND.

Persecution: the US landings in northern New Guinea in April 1944, which, in combination with the Australian advance up the coast, succeeded in encircling the Japanese forces on the island.

Plans X, Y and Z: the Allied plans for the recapture of three main sectors of Burma, hatched in 1943 but not carried out until 1944–5.

Plunder: the massive British offensive across the Rhine north of the Ruhr in March 1945 (*see also* Varsity below).

Pointblank: the overall code name for the strategy of bombing German military, economic, industrial and civilian targets after January 1943.

Postern: the US-Australian attack on the Huon peninsula of New Guinea in September 1943–April 1944.

Princeton: the overall US strategic plan for the recapture of parts of the Philippines, Borneo and Indonesia in 1943–4.

Providence: the operation in which the Allies recaptured part of the northern coast of Papua in November 1942–January 1944.

Pugilist-Gallop: the British advance that broke through the German Mareth Line in Tunisia in March 1943.

Queen: the Allied offensive from eastern Belgium towards the Rhine across the plain of the River Ruhr. Launched in November 1944, the advance ground to a standstill in December.

Quick Anger: the Canadian offensive through the Netherlands and into Germany in April 1945.

R: the capture by the Japanese of the strategically important Australian base at Rabaul in New Britain, along with Kavieng in New Ireland, in January 1942.

Rainbow: the Chinese offensive through southern China into Burma in May–August 1944.

Raincoat: the only partially successful Allied offensive towards the GUSTAV LINE and the Anzio beach-head in southern Italy in December 1943.

Raubtier ('beast of prey'): the successful German counter-offensive between Novgorod and Leningrad (St Petersburg) in March 1942.

Regenbogen ('rainbow'): the German naval operation against Arctic convoys heading for the Soviet Union, in which the battle cruiser *Scharnhorst* was sunk by the Royal Navy on 31 December 1943.

Reno: the strategic plan for US forces in the Pacific in 1942–4, involving advances through the Bismarck Archipelago, New Guinea and eastern Indonesia, culminating in the invasion of the Philippines.

Rheinübung ('Rhine exercise'): the commerce-raiding sortie into the Atlantic by the German battleship BISMARCK and the heavy cruiser *Prinz Eugen* in May 1941, during which the *Bismarck* was sunk by the Royal Navy.

RI: the Japanese landings in Papua in July 1942 before the offensive against Port Moresby.

Rösselsprung ('knight's move'): the German attack by air and sea in July 1942 on the Arctic convoy PQ17, resulting in only 13 of the 34 Allied ships reaching northern Russia.

Rot ('red'): the second part of the German conquest of France in June 1940 (part one being entitled Tiger; *see below*).

Rupert: the seizure by British and French forces of the strategic port of Narvik in northern Norway in May 1940. However, the crisis in France led to the Allied withdrawal in June.

Saturn: the major Soviet offensive in southern Russia, including the STALINGRAD front, in December 1942.

Schwarz ('black'): the German plan for the military take-over of Italy in the event of Italian capitulation. It was duly put into effect, with some modification, in 1943.

Scipio: the successful British and Commonwealth offensive in southern Tunisia in April 1943. The name was particularly appropriate, as it was in Tunisia that the Roman general Scipio Africanus won his decisive victory over the Carthaginians, at Zama in 202 BC.

SEA LION (German 'Seelöwe'): the German plan for the invasion of Britain in 1940.

Setting Sun: the US bombing campaign against Japan in 1944. The name played on Japan as 'the land of the rising sun', as depicted on its wartime flag.

Shingle: the Allied landings at Anzio in central Italy in January 1944, which failed in their strategic objective.

SHO: the Japanese defensive strategy from mid-1944, including SHO-1 for the Philippines, SHO-2 for Taiwan and the Ryukyu Islands, SHO-3 for Kyushu and Honshu and SHO-4 for the Kurile Islands and Hokkaido.

Sonnenblume ('sunflower'): the commitment of German troops to North Africa in January–February 1941 following the failures of the Italians in the Western Desert.

Source: the attack by British midget submarines on the *Tirpitz* in northern Norway on 22 September 1943, which succeeded in seriously damaging the German battleship.

Star: the major Soviet offensive in February–March 1943 that succeeded in taking Kharkov only to lose it again to the Germans.

Steinbock ('ibex'): the German bombing campaign in January–May 1944 against London and various British ports, also known as the 'baby BLITZ'.

Strike: the final Allied offensive against AXIS forces in Tunisia in May 1943, ending the campaign in North Africa.

Sunrise: the secret negotiations between the Allies and the SS commander in Italy leading to the surrender of German forces there on 2 May 1945.

Supercharge: *see* Lightfoot *above*.

Taifun ('typhoon'): the German offensive against Moscow, which began on 2 November 1941 and was abandoned on 5 December.

Talon: the British and Indian offensive in central Burma in early 1945.

Thunderclap: the Allied strategic plan to bring about a German surrender by the all-out bombing of Berlin, Chemnitz, Leipzig, Dresden and other German cities in 1945. Only DRESDEN had been completely destroyed by the time of the German surrender.

Thursday: the second CHINDIT expedition behind Japanese lines in Burma, March–August 1944.

Tidal Wave: the costly and ineffective attack on the Ploeşti oilfields in Romania by US bombers on 1 August 1943.

Tiger: the first part of the German conquest of France in June 1940. It struck through the MAGINOT LINE from the north and was complemented by Operation Bär ('Bear') through Alsace further south to make a pincer movement. It was followed by Operation Rot (*see above*).

Toenails: the US invasion of the central Solomon Islands in June–October 1943.

Torch: the Allied landings in French North Africa on 8 November 1942.

U: the attempted Japanese invasion of India via Imphal and Kohima in Assam in March–June 1944.

Undertone: the US offensive south of the Mosel as part of the drive to the Rhine in March 1945.

Uranus: the Soviet offensive that trapped the German 6th Army in STALINGRAD in November 1942.

Varsity: the airborne operation to cross the Rhine on 24 March 1945, in conjuction with the ground-based Operation Plunder (*see* above).

Veritable: the British and Canadian offensive between the Maas and the Rhine in February 1945.

Vert ('green'): the disruption of rail traffic by French railway workers at the time of the D-DAY landings.

Vesuvius: the recapture of Corsica by Free French forces in September–October 1943.

Victor I–V: the US recapture of the southern and central Philippines in February–July 1945.

Violet: the disruption of communications by French telephone workers at the time of the D-DAY landings.

Watchtower: the US operation to recapture the southeastern Solomon Islands, including Guadalcanal, in August 1942. The battle for Guadalcanal did not end till February 1943.

Weiss ('white'): the German invasion and conquest of Poland in September–October 1939.

Weserübung ('Weser exercise'): the German invasion and conquest of Denmark and Norway in April–June 1940.

Wintergewitter ('winter storm'): the failed German attempt to relieve STALINGRAD in December 1942.

Z: the Japanese attack on PEARL HARBOR on 7 December 1941.

Zitadelle ('citadel'): the German offensive in the Soviet Union that ended in devastating defeat at the Battle of Kursk in July 1943.

Secret Garden, The. A much-loved children's novel (1911) by Frances Hodgson Burnett (1849–1924). It charts the gradual transformation of the character of Mary Lennox, the daughter of a British civil servant in India, who is sent to Misselthwaite Manor, the Yorkshire home of her reclusive uncle. Mary discovers a secret garden, neglected for ten years, and starts gardening there. She also effects a miraculous cure of Colin, her uncle's invalid-hypochondriac son, and their friendship blossoms as the garden itself starts to bloom. The fictional garden is based on the Rose Garden at Maytham Hall in Kent, where Burnett spent the years 1898–1907.

Secret Seven. A series of 15 novels by Enid Blyton (1897–1968), beginning with *The Secret Seven* (1949). The novels recount the adventures of seven children and their dog, Scamper, and are aimed at a younger age group than the books about the FAMOUS FIVE.

Secret weapon. A weapon officially classified as secret, especially one with the power to end a conflict by a decisive strike. The term emerged in the 1930s during the build-up to the Second World War, during which Winston Churchill described the magnetic mine as Germany's 'secret weapon'. Figuratively the term can allude to any person or thing potentially available to achieve a result.

> Women are the secret weapon for [political] recovery.
> *Independent on Sunday* (headline) (28 November 1999)

Section 28. A controversial law banning the 'promotion' of homosexuality in British schools. It was introduced by the Conservative government in 1988 as an amendment to its Local Government Bill following a sexual error committed by a Tory backbencher and was passed in the midst of a political storm surrounding a book, *Jenny Lives with Eric and Martin*, that the then Inner London Education Authority had decided to put into a reference library for teachers.

In 2000 the Labour government sought to repeal the legislation (although the Shadow Cabinet chose to defend it), and in the same year the newly devolved Scottish parliament voted to abolish it.

Securicor. The ubiquitous security services company began its career in 1935 as a small private guard business called Night Watch Services. Contracts were at first hard to come by, and at the outbreak of the Second World War it had just 12 patrol guards. After the war its luck changed following a move into industrial security and the return into the jobs market of hundreds of soldiers. It changed its name to Securicor, a contraction of Security Corps, in the early 1950s, by which time it employed nearly 200 guards. It subsequently entered the 'cash-in-transit' business, as well as parcels delivery and detective work, and later added mobile communications to its portfolio.

Securitate. The secret police of communist Romania. The Securitate became the main support of the tyrannical rule of Nicolae Ceauşescu (1918–89), who by the 1980s had turned Romania into a police state. The downfall of Ceauşescu within a week in December 1989 resulted from a combination of popular unrest and a conspiracy by dissident party members and Securitate and army personnel. Even after Ceauşescu's execution on 25 December, however, loyalist Securitate forces continued to mount a short-lived but violent resistance, leading to many civilian and military deaths.

Security blanket. Something that dispels anxiety, such an appointment diary carried on the person. The expression evolved in the 1960s from the blanket or piece of cloth held by a young child to reduce anxiety. An entirely different security blanket is an official sanction imposed on information to maintain secrecy on a particular matter.

See a man about a dog, To. To excuse oneself abruptly from a meeting, party or the like in order to visit the lavatory. The fiction is that one is going to place a bet on a dog in a race. The expression dates from the 1930s.

Seeing Eye. An American organization that provides GUIDE DOGS, corresponding to the Guide Dogs for the Blind Association in Britain. It was founded in January 1929 by Mrs Dorothy Harrison Eustis, a dog breeder. The first Seeing Eye dog was a German shepherd (Alsatian) bitch named Buddy, assigned to guide Morris Frank, a young blind man in Tennessee. *See also* HEARING DOG.

The hearing ear, and the seeing eye, the Lord hath made even both of them.
Proverbs 20:12

See red, To. To become suddenly angry. The phrase is popularly said to allude to a bull's angry reaction to a red cape waved by a matador. A more likely association is with the reddened face and heated blood of anger, as one similarly speaks of a fiery temper.

See stars, To. To see what seem to be flashes or darts of light as a result of a blow on the head.

See things, To. To experience hallucinations. The phrase is usually found in participial form, as: 'I thought I was seeing things.'

See where someone is coming from, To. To understand or appreciate their meaning or motives. The expression originated in black American slang in the 1960s.

Clearly, as with all relationships, areas open themselves up for abuse – but I suddenly see where [actress] Patsy Kensit is coming from. And it doesn't seem quite as deep a pit as it once did.
Ms London (27 September 1999)

See you later, alligator. A stock pleasantry current from the 1950s when taking one's leave. The one left conventionally replied: 'In a while, crocodile'. The popularity of the expression stemmed from a hit song performed by Bill Haley and the Comets, but 'alligator' was already a term in the 1930s for a jazz or swing fan, as someone who 'swallowed up' everything on offer.

See you later, alligator,
After 'while, crocodile, –
Can't you see you're in my way, now,
Don't you know you cramp my style?
R.C. GUIDRY: 'See You Later Alligator' (song) (1957)

Sega. The coin-operated computer games so named are made by the company founded in 1951 as Service Game Inc. with the aim of producing and managing amusement arcade machines. The name was shortened to Sega in 1965. Business long brought in steady revenue but began to be adversely affected in the 1990s by competition from home-gaming systems.

Seinfeld. The American television SITCOM of this name, first shown in 1990 (in the UK from 1993) and based on the stage act of the standup comic Jerry Seinfeld (b.1955), is essentially a series of episodes about the minutiae of daily living, as experienced by four single New Yorkers who are obsessed about such minor matters as queuing for the theatre, getting caught in traffic jams, meeting friends and the like. The quartet are Seinfeld as himself, Julia Louis-Dreyfus as the feisty Elaine Benes, Jason Alexander as the intense, nervy George Costanza and Michael Richards as the eternally optimistic Cosmo Kramer. The series came to be billed as 'the show about nothing', and its unique observational style soon won it a cult following on both sides of the Atlantic.

Selfish gene. In genetics a gene that exploits the organism in which it occurs as a vehicle for its own self-perpetuation. A gene of this type was posited by the biologist Richard Dawkins in his book *The Selfish Gene* (1976). His theory overturned the traditional concept of the gene as a vehicle of inheritance for the organism and did much to popularize the study of sociobiology.

Selfridges. The London store of this name was opened on 15 March 1909 as the creation of the American entrepreneur Harry Gordon Selfridge (1858–1947), the son of the owner of a dry-goods business. The grandiose emporium on the north side of Oxford Street originally had 130 departments and a wide range of facilities for its customers, including its own library, a post office, rooms for foreign visitors, an American soda room, a department for the clergy and a 'silence room' with a notice reading 'Ladies Will Refrain From Conversation'. 'Miss Selfridge', providing for teenage fashions, opened as a spin-off in 1966.

Self-starter. Originally a term for the electric motor that started the engine of a motor vehicle, a self-starter in business jargon was later a term for a well-motivated person capable of exercising initiative. The latter sense arose in the 1960s in the vocabulary of job advertisements.

Sell-by date. The date by which a perishable item, such as a food product, must be sold if it is to be consumed in a fresh or fit state. It is not the same as a use-by or best-before date, which is usually a day or two later. The expression has gained a facetious figurative sense to refer to a person who is 'getting on', so that if one is 'past one's sell-by date' one is past one's prime. *See also* BEST-BEFORE DATE.

> Once described by an over-enthusiastic newspaper as 'one of London's most eligible bachelors', Stacpoole is now grey, portly and, at 55, looking rather past his sell-by date.
> *Today* (1 September 1994)

Sell off the family silver, To. To dispose of valuable assets that, once gone, cannot be retrieved. The phrase is said to have been popularized by Sir Harold Macmillan's speech of 8 November 1985 to the Tory Reform Group attacking the Thatcher government's programme of privatization of nationalized industries, although his actual words were: 'First of all the Georgian silver goes, and then all that nice furniture that used to be in the saloon. Then the Canalettos go.'

Sellotape. A name sometimes used for any 'sticky tape' but one that properly belongs to the British company who first marketed it in 1937. The name is based on Cellophane, but with the initial C changed to S for purposes of trademark registration. A famous American rival is SCOTCH TAPE.

Sell someone short, To. To fail to recognize or state their true value. To sell oneself short is thus to underrate oneself, to be silent or unduly modest about one's achievements or abilities.

> Mr Blair sells himself short. He is emerging as a far more remarkable Prime Minister than he displays.
> *The Times* (29 September 1999)

Selsdon man. A nickname given to a supposed supporter of the proto-THATCHERITE policies outlined at a conference of Conservative Party leaders at the Selsdon Park Hotel near Croydon in 1970. They included support for a market economy as opposed to state intervention, rejection of compulsory wage control and a refusal to rescue industrial 'lame ducks'. The coinage is based on PILTDOWN MAN (*see under* FAKES).

Seminal work. A written work that may or may not be original but that strongly influences later developments. The use of the adjective in this sense dates from the 1960s and it can equally apply to anything similarly influential, such as an article, a piece of research or even a person, as a 'seminal pianist'. The literal sense is 'sowing seed', from Latin *semen*, 'seed'.

> Though this dish has a long history in Burgundy, it was not really introduced to Britain until 1960, by Elizabeth David in her seminal work, *French Provincial Cooking.*
> *Independent on Sunday Magazine* (14 May 1995)

Semtex. A type of plastic explosive originally manufactured near the village of Semtín in the Czech Republic and familiar from its use by terrorists in the mid-1980s, in some cases in letter bombs. In 1991 Czechoslovakia announced that Semtex was no longer being made, but it was estimated that stocks worldwide could last for several decades.

Senderista. *See* SHINING PATH.

Send someone up the wall, To. *See* DRIVE SOMEONE UP THE WALL.

Senior citizen. A somewhat patronizing euphemism for a retired person or pensioner. The term arose in the US in the 1930s but did not reach Britain until the 1960s. It is now commonly found in notices relating to admission charges, concessionary rates and the like. The use of 'citizen' betrays the US origin, as a word found only in formal British English.

Sensory deprivation. A process developed by Dr John Lilly in the 1950s by which a person floats in a special isolation tank, naked, enclosed and completely cut off from all external stimuli. Without stimulation the brain eventually begins to hallucinate. Initially Lilly used the method to investigate altered states of consciousness but a later purpose was to reduce stress and tension through relaxation. Meditation can achieve the same end by mental control rather than mechanical means.

Sensurround. The tradename of a system of special effects which are used to enhance the physical impact of a DISASTER MOVIE or similar 'action' film. It was developed by the Universal film company in 1974 to magnify the tremor scenes in *Earthquake* (1974) by adding air vibrations to the sound track during the dubbing process. The vibrations then 'blast' the body and ears of members of the audience to create the illusion of participation in the scene on the screen. Subsequent episodes using Sensurround (a combination of 'sense' and 'surround') include a battle scene in *Midway* (1976) and a roller coaster ride in *Rollercoaster* (1977).

Separate Tables. A pair of plays (1954) by Terence Rattigan (1911–77) about the hidden lives of a variety of guests in a Bournemouth hotel. The plays are separately entitled *Table by the Window* and *Table Number 7*, after the tables in the dining-room where the characters concerned sit. A film version (1958) starred Burt Lancaster and David Niven, who won an OSCAR for his portrayal of the ersatz hero Major Pollack. An unnecessary remake (1983) starred Alan Bates and Julie Christie.

Separate or **sort out the men from the boys, To.** To distinguish those who are brave, mature, professional, etc from those who are weak, immature, amateur, etc. The expression dates from the 1930s and is always used figuratively.

Sequel numbers in film titles. The practice of titling a film sequel with the name of the original followed by a number appears to have originated with *Quatermass II* (1957), a simplified version of the television series QUATERMASS. It did not become fashionable until the 1970s, however, which saw, among others, *French Connection II* (1975) following *The* FRENCH CONNECTION (1971) and *Jaws 2* (1978) following JAWS (1975), in turn followed by *Jaws 3-D* (1983). Some spawnings are prolific, as with ROCKY (1976), which produced *Rocky II* (1979), *Rocky III* (1982), *Rocky IV* (1985) and *Rocky V* (1990), although none of these was up to the standard of the original. The procedure was nicely guyed by *Naked Gun 2½: The Smell of Fear* (1991) and *Naked Gun 33⅓: The Final Insult* (1994) in the wake of *The Naked Gun: From the Files of Police Squad* (1988). *See also* MADNESS OF GEORGE III.

Sergeant Pepper's Lonely Hearts Club Band. The title track of a celebrated BEATLES album, one of the most fêted in the history of popular music, which was released in June 1967. The name 'Sergeant Pepper's Lonely Hearts Club Band' (a mythical band that forms a kind of *alter ego* for the Beatles), was influenced by the often vaudeville-tinged names of contemporary American West Coast groups. The album's 13 tracks include LUCY IN THE SKY WITH DIAMONDS, WITH A LITTLE HELP FROM MY FRIENDS, BEING FOR THE BENEFIT OF MR KITE!, 'When I'm Sixty-Four', LOVELY RITA and DAY IN THE LIFE. The title song, credited to John Lennon and Paul McCartney, combines a 'big band' sound with thunderous electric guitar textures that were to be an influence on the development of HEAVY METAL music.

The album is a milestone in the history of 20th-century popular music and a seminal popular cultural document of the SWINGING SIXTIES. It was the first album to have a gatefold sleeve, the first to offer a set of printed lyrics and is also sometimes described as the first CONCEPT ALBUM.

The much-imitated cover of the album was designed by the pop artist Peter Blake (*see* RURALISM). It focuses on period fashion, and features an array of celebrities past and present (not all of them recognizable) including Mae West, W.C. Fields, Edgar Allan Poe (*see also* I AM THE WALRUS), Sir Robert Peel, Stuart Sutcliffe (the original FIFTH BEATLE), Marilyn MONROE, Dr David Livingstone, LAWRENCE OF ARABIA and Diana Dors. The cover includes a number of waxworks lent by Madame Tussaud's museum in London. *See also* SUMMER OF LOVE.

> A decisive moment in the history of Western Civilization.
>
> KENNETH TYNAN: quoted in Howard Elson, *McCartney* (1986)

Serialism. A technique of musical MODERNISM, in which the traditional rules of melody, harmony and rhythm are replaced by a structural 'series' of notes which dictate the development of a piece. The series or 'tone row' consists of the twelve notes of the chromatic scale arranged in a fixed order and used by the composer to generate melodies and harmonies. The first fully realized works of serialism were composed by Arnold Schoenberg (1874–1951) in 1923. The technique is also known as the twelve-tone or twelve-note system. The melodic strangeness of music composed in this vein can make for uncomfortable listening, but serialism has nonetheless influenced most 20th-century composers.

Serial killer. A term arising in the 1970s for what until then had been known as a mass murderer (or multiple murderer). It implies that the murderer used a similar weapon or method for killing each of his individual victims, and was prompted by crimes of this type in the 1960s and early 1970s. The term itself is said to have been coined at the FBI's behavioural unit at Quantico, Virginia. *See also* DR DEATH.

Serious. Meaningful or important; not trivial or ephemeral. A BUZZWORD of the 1990s to denote someone or something running counter to the hedonistic superficiality and self-centredness of the decade and that is precisely what it claims to be, such as a 'serious' boyfriend or a 'serious' hobby.

Serjeant Musgrave's Dance. A play (1959) by John Arden (b.1930) about a group of soldiers who arrive in a mining town in northern England apparently on a recruiting drive, but who are subsequently revealed to be deserters traumatized by their involvement in an atrocity while on service overseas. Serjeant Musgrave, the leader of the soldiers, dances a wild dance in front of the skeleton of a former comrade before threatening to kill 25 people of the town when they fail to rally to his cause. Following Musgrave's arrest, the miners join in their own celebratory dance. The play shows the influence of the EPIC THEATRE of Bertolt Brecht.

Servant problem. A fly in the golden ointment of the EDWARDIAN ERA, caused by the increasing number of people unwilling to enter domestic service. The problem was subsequently exacerbated by the First World War, after which those who had been in service, or who at one time might have entered it, saw the alternatives available and sought employment elsewhere.

Set alarm bells ringing, To. To alert to a problem or danger. The bells in question are presumably those set off by a fire or a break-in.

> The decision early this summer to cut the price from £1.5m to £750,000, however, sent [*sic*] alarm bells ringing through the business. Is English wine facing a crisis?
>
> *Independent on Sunday* (14 August 1994)

Set one's sights on something, To. To aim at achieving it. The sights are those of a gun or rifle through which one looks when aiming.

Set one's watch by someone, To. To note their unfailing punctuality. The expression may be approbatory, in admiration of such correctness and orderliness, or derisory, in contempt of such calculated and possibly unfeeling lack of flexibility.

> 'Where's Daddy?' Ben asked, at seven o'clock. 'He said he'd be back at six-thirty. He's always punctual. I set my watch by him.' He didn't, of course, but he liked the ring of the phrase.
>
> FAY WELDON: *The Heart of the Country* (1987)

Set someone up, To. To lead them on in order to cheat or incriminate them; to frame them. Hence a set-up as a scheme or trick to incriminate or deceive someone.

Seuss, Dr. The pseudonym of the US writer and illustrator Theodor Seuss Geisel (1904–91), a prolific and successful author of children's picture books, such as *The Cat in the Hat* (1947), aimed at the early reading market. Geisel invented the doctorate for himself but his alma mater, Dartmouth College, conferred an authentic doctorate on him in 1955.

Seven and Five Society. An association of progressive British artists formed in 1919 and originally consisting of seven painters and five sculptors. Ivon Hitchens (1893–1979) was a leading member and by the 1930s the society was the most important avant-garde group of artists in Britain. It disbanded in 1935.

Seven Dwarfs. The dwarfs who try to protect Snow White in the Walt Disney film *Snow White and the Seven Dwarfs* (1937). They whistle while they work and individually are Happy, Sleepy, Doc, Bashful, Sneezy, Grumpy and Dopey.

Seven-session slide. A stock market tongue-twisting

term for a fall in the value of leading company shares on seven consecutive trading days, regarded as a possible portent of further collapse.

> Leading London shares finally halted their seven-session slide as a flurry of corporate deals and a resurgent Wall Street coaxed buyers back into the market.
>
> *The Times* (28 July 1999)

Seven Sisters. The alliterative term has long been used for a grouping of seven things or people. In the 20th century it has notably applied to the seven international oil companies (Exxon, Mobil, Gulf, Standard Oil of California, Texaco, British Petroleum and Royal Dutch Shell) who had a dominant influence on the production and marketing of petroleum in the 1960s, and to the long-established group of women's colleges (Barnard, Bryn Mawr, Mount Holyoke, Radcliffe, Smith, Vassar and Wellesley) regarded as being the most prestigious in the United States. *See also* IVY LEAGUE.

Seventh art. The art of the cinema. The phrase was coined in 1916 by the Italian poet and film critic Ricciotto Canudo (1879–1923).

Seventh Seal, The. A highly regarded film (1957) directed by the Swedish director Ingmar Bergman (b.1918). A vision of a medieval land ravaged by the Black Death, the film impressed and mystified audiences around the world. The title refers to a verse which appears in the Bible:

> And when he had opened the seventh seal, there was silence in heaven about the space of half an hour
>
> Revelation 8:1

Seven-year itch. A tendency towards infidelity, said to set in after about seven years of marriage. The expression was popularized by George Axelrod's comedy of this name (1952), made into a film (1955), in which a married man has a fling with the girl upstairs.

Severed Head, A. A novel (1961) by Iris Murdoch (1919–99). In spite of its macabre title and solemn themes, which include adultery, incest, castration, violence and suicide, this is also a comedy about valuing relationships. The narrator is told by Honor Klein, with whom he is in love: 'I am a severed head such as primitive tribes and old alchemists used to use, anointing it with oil and putting a morsel of gold upon its tongue to make it utter prophecies.' A stage version of the novel by J.B. Priestley, written in collaboration with Murdoch, was produced in 1963, and an unduly

boisterous film version, written by Frederic Raphael and directed by Dick Clement, followed in 1970.

Sew something up, To. To bring it to a satisfactory conclusion; to gain exclusive control over it. In both cases the image is of completing a garment or other item of needlework or embroidery.

Sex and drugs and rock and roll. An encapsulation of the late SWINGING SIXTIES and early 1970s as a song title of 1977 by the British rock musician Ian Dury (1942–2000).

Sex and shopping. A type of popular fiction in which the characters enjoy the pleasure of fashionable consumer goods and frequent explicit sexual encounters. Within the world of literary criticism the genre is also known by the crude abbreviation S & F, putting the shopping first and the FOUR-LETTER WORD activity second. Mark Ravenhill's play of the latter title in its spelled-out form, about five misfits in an uncertain drug society, was published to some acclaim in 1996. *See also* BONKBUSTER.

> This trivial sex-and-shopping confection flaunts superior pretensions on every page. The sex, of which there is a lot, comes gift-wrapped in cultural allusions ... But more often it is a matter of brandnames.
>
> *Sunday Times* (review of Jonathan Keates, *Smile Please*) (20 February 2000)

Sex and the Single Girl. A feminist study (1962) by Helen Gurley Brown (b.1922). She was brought up to believe that: 'I would have to make do on whatever brains I had, because I was told I would never be pretty enough to get a rich husband and succeed that way.' The book was written after her marriage to a film producer when she was 36: 'I knew I wanted to write a book about sex being okay for single women.' In 1965 she was appointed editor-in-chief of *Cosmopolitan*, a popular magazine appealing to career women and those looking for personal emancipation. She held the post until 1996, when she retired, at the age of 73. On the eve of her 78th birthday she was photographed lying on a sofa with a cushion embroidered with the legend: 'Good girls go to heaven, bad girls go everywhere.'

Sex bomb. An 'explosively' attractive woman. The expression dates from the 1960s. *See also* BIKINI; BLONDE BOMBSHELL.

> The girl [Brazilian model Gisele Bundchen] is a goddess, a knockout of the sort we haven't seen since Cindy Crawford. 'She's a straightforward sex bomb,'

says British Vogue editor Alexandra Shulman. ... 'She's got perfect looks and an absolutely incredible figure.'

Sunday Times (23 January 2000)

Sex kitten. A young woman who asserts her sex appeal. The appellation came to be particularly associated with the film actress Brigitte Bardot (b.1934), who established her reputation as an international sex symbol by posing and pouting in sun-tanned nudity in *Et Dieu créa la femme* (*And God Created Woman*) (1956). *See also* JAVAL, CAMILLE.

sex, lies, and videotape. A film (1989) written and directed by Steven Soderbergh about an impotent film-maker who becomes emotionally involved in the marital discord that has developed between an old college friend and his wife. The catalyst for trouble is his collection of videotapes he has made of his interviews of women about their sex lives. Critical acclaim at the Cannes film festival was matched by commercial success, which was much promoted by the prurient interest evoked by its title (although relatively little sex is actually portrayed on screen). The film starred James Spader and Audie MacDowell.

Sex on legs. A colloquialism for an sexually attractive person, the latter part of the phrase denoting that they are 'walking sex', i.e. personify it wherever they go, just as a 'walking dictionary' is a person with an impressive store of words or a 'walking encyclopedia' one with a mine of facts. There is probably also an implicit allusion to the location of the sex organs themselves. The term is more often used by women of men than the converse.

The concert was out of this world. I come every time he [popular singer Barry Manilow] comes here. He is brilliant. I am a devoted fan. ... He is sex on legs.

heat (20–26 January 2000)

Sexton Blake. *See* BLAKE, SEXTON.

Sexual politics. The principles determining the relationship of the sexes and the role of gender in society, especially with regard to feminism, gay rights, sexual discrimination and the like. The term originated as the title of a classic study (1970) by the American feminist Kate Millett.

Sexual politics, after technology and widespread prosperity, have been one of the most important catalysts in bringing forth many of the new manners.

The Times (8 January 2000)

Sez you. That's what you say (but I don't believe it or think much of it). The phrase and spelling are of American origin.

Sfogliatella. A type of rich cheese puff of Italian origin. Its name derives from Italian *sfogliare*, 'to strip the leaves from', literally 'to defoliate', referring to the appearance of its pastry casing.

I seek one thing only: a *sfogliatelle* [*sic*], an expensive piece of heavy, edible sculpture whose cool heart of sweetened ricotta is enclosed in crisp, crusty scallops of parchment pastry, exquisitely folded like a golden Botticellian shell. Even to pronounce that tongue-twisting name is a ticket to instant approbation in South Philadelphia.

CAMILLE PAGLIA in *Times Literary Supplement* (16 July 1999)

Shabby chic. A type of stylishness derived through being old and worn. The term alludes chiefly to dress but can also apply to anything untidy or neglected or to an object such as a dilapidated building or run-down residential area. The style came into vogue in the late 20th century, partly in reaction to the smart and 'trendy' fashions of earlier years. *See also* HEROIN CHIC; RADICAL CHIC.

In what may be the country's most expensive example of shabby chic, English Heritage has spent £1 million to preserve a romantic hilltop ruin exactly as it stands.

The Times (13 October 1999)

Shack up with someone, To. To make one's home or cohabit with them, as if sharing a shack.

Shadow cabinet. A group of members of an opposition party nominated as counterparts of the government cabinet. The expression dates from the turn of the 20th century but was not widely in use until after the Second World War, by which time 'shadow' had also come to apply to an individual counterpart, as the 'Shadow Chancellor' or 'Shadow Transport Minister'.

Shaggy dog story. A supposedly funny story told laboriously and at great length with an unexpected twist at the end. It is usually more amusing to the teller than the hearer and is so called from the shaggy dog that featured in many stories of this genre in the 1940s. The following classic shaggy dog story is recounted by Eric Partridge:

Travelling by train to London from one of its outer dormitories, a businessman got into a compartment and was amazed to see a middle-aged passenger playing chess with a handsome Newfoundland. The players moved the pieces swiftly and surely. Just before the train pulled in at the London terminus, the game ended, with the dog victorious. 'That's an extraordinary dog, beating you like that – and obviously you're pretty good yourself.' – 'Oh, I don't think he's so hot; I beat him in the two games before that.'

ERIC PARTRIDGE: *A Charm of Words*, 'The Shaggy Dog' (1960)

Shangri La. The hidden Buddhist lama paradise described in James Hilton's novel *Lost Horizon* (1933). In 1942 the name was adopted as a code name for the US aircraft carrier *Hornet*, from which the great air raid on Tokyo was launched on 18 April. In 1945 it was further applied by President Franklin D. Roosevelt to CAMP DAVID in order to avoid identifying its location. The name is now used similarly for any imagined earthly 'paradise' or utopia.

Shangri is an invented name, but *la* is the Tibetan word for a mountain pass. In real geographical terms the Indian state of Sikkim, between Nepal, Tibet and Bhutan, has been so dubbed and when in 1963, before its annexation by India, Palden Thondup Namgyal, the crown prince, announced his marriage to Hope Cooke, a 23-year-old American debutante, the match was described in the foreign press as 'The Fairy-Tale Wedding in Shangri-La'.

Shankill Butchers. The grimly appropriate name given to a Loyalist gang responsible for a series of grisly sectarian murders of Catholics in the SHANKILL ROAD area of west Belfast at the height of the TROUBLES in the mid-1970s. In 1979 11 members of the gang were given life sentences for the murders by a Belfast court. The gang was led by 'Lenny' Murphy, a renegade member of the ULSTER VOLUNTEER FORCE. He was shot dead outside his home in 1983, probably by the Provisional IRA. The gang's activities were meticulously chronicled by Martin Dillon in his book *The Shankill Butchers* (1990). *Resurrection Man* (1995), a novel by Eoin McNamee, was based on Murphy's murderous exploits, and a film version of the novel, directed by Marc Evans and starring Stuart Townsend, was released in 1998.

Shankill Road. An exclusively Protestant working-class street of industrial west Belfast, Northern Ireland. During the TROUBLES 'the Shankill', the road and its adjacent streets, became synonymous with hard-line Loyalism. In the same way 'the Falls' around

the nearby Catholic FALLS ROAD became synonymous with hard-line nationalism.

Shape of things to come. The way the future is likely to develop. The phrase derives from the title of a novel of 1933 by H.G. Wells chillingly predicting war in 1939 followed by plague, rebellion, a new glass-based society, the first rocketship to the moon and the establishment of a world government in 2059. The work formed the basis of Alexander Korda's acclaimed film *Things to Come* (1935).

Shape up, To. To improve; to reform; to develop satisfactory. The sense is of gaining a full satisfactory shape. The expression dates from the 1930s.

Shape up or ship out, To. To do properly what one is supposed to do or, if one cannot manage this, stop doing it altogether. The expression originated in the American armed forces in the Second World War, when any soldier, sailor or marine judged to be unworthy of the name was liable to be sent overseas to a combat zone.

As he stumbled around the world in 1997, losing in the first round to people he had never heard of, he [tennis player André Agassi] decided that he had to shape up or ship out.

The Times (14 September 1999)

Shapwick Hoard. The largest hoard of early Roman coins ever discovered in Britain came to light in a field at Shapwick, Somerset, in 1999 when Kevin Elliott, a dairy farmer's son, tried out a metal detector lent him by his cousin, Martin Elliott, a self-employed welder. The 9000 or so silver *denarii* date from between the time of Mark Antony (31 BC) and the emperor Severus Maximus (AD 222–235) and are calculated to have been buried in about AD 230 and to be the equivalent of 10 years' pay for a legionary soldier in the Roman army. The find is now in the British Museum.

Sharon. A female forename of biblical origin: 'I am the rose of Sharon, and the lily of the valley' (Song of Solomon 2:1). The name was adopted by the attraction of the rose that here accompanies it, although Sharon itself is not a person but a plain in the north of Palestine. The forename had became very popular by the 1970s but subsequently came to gain a pejorative patina, especially when coupled with the name TRACY. To say, for example, that a club was full of Sharons and Tracys is to say that it was full of ESSEX GIRL types. In the 1990s television comedy series

BIRDS OF A FEATHER the two main characters, Sharon and Tracey, are sisters of this kind.

> There was a forest of spindly tables carrying drinks, populated by Sharon and Tracy.
>
> *Financial Times* (4–5 December 1999)

Sharpeville massacre. The shooting of unarmed civilian demonstrators by South African police on 21 March 1960, resulting in the deaths of 67 blacks and the wounding of a further 186, including women and children. The demonstration, organized by the Pan-African Congress (PAC, an offshoot of the ANC), was held in the Transvaal township of Sharpeville, and was to protest against the hated PASS LAWS. Following the incident, both the ANC and the PAC were banned; the ANC went underground and turned to armed struggle. The incident drew international attention to the iniquities of APARTHEID and provoked worldwide condemnation of the South African government.

She. The picture of a toaster and a fridge with a woman styled to match by Richard Hamilton (b.1922) was executed in 1958–61, and the work had a major influence on POP ART in Britain. Presumably the punning title refers to the commodification of human beings in the consumer society. *See also* JUST WHAT IS IT THAT MAKES TODAY'S HOMES SO DIFFERENT, SO APPEALING?

Sheena. Essentially the female counterpart of TARZAN, the jungle girl of American comic books has the real name Janet Ames. She is a white foundling raised by an African tribe who teach her MARTIAL ARTS and shamanistic skills. She was the creation of Will Eisner and S.M. Iger for *Jumbo Comics*, and made her debut in 1938. She subsequently appeared in a television series and in a film of 1984, named after her, in which she is played by Tanya Roberts.

Shell suit. A casual and typically garish outfit consisting of a loose jacket and trousers with an elasticated waist, or else cut all-in-one. It was a fashion garment of the late 1980s and early 1990s at a time when sportswear was popular as general leisurewear and was so called from its shiny polyester outer shell. It was worn mainly but not exclusively by males of the ESSEX MAN type.

Shergar. The three-year-old bay colt, by Val de Loir out of Sharmeen, that won the Derby by a record 10 lengths in 1981, ridden by Walter Swinburn. After winning several other races, he retired to stud in Co. Kildare, Ireland, but was abducted there in February

1983 by armed and masked men, never to be seen again. The melancholy conclusion was that he had been taken by members of the IRA and probably killed soon afterwards.

She who must be obeyed. A description of Margaret Thatcher, the IRON LADY, by Julian Critchley (b.1930). The name derives from the heroine of the novel *She* (1887) by Sir Henry Rider Haggard (1856–1925), the long-lived white queen Ayesha (properly 'She-Who-Must-Be-Obeyed'). Critchley was a Conservative backbencher from 1970 to 1997.

Shiatsu. A form of ALTERNATIVE therapy of Japanese origin in vogue from the 1960s and based on the same principles as ACUPUNCTURE but without the use of needles. The word is Japanese for 'finger pressure'. Central to the technique is *qi*, a Chinese word meaning literally 'air', 'breath', representing the circulating life force which each person possesses and which, according to oriental medicine, can be lightly replenished or heavily taxed. Shiatsu practitioners thus begin a subject's first session by assessing the two most extreme meridians in their body in terms of *qi*.

Shin Bet. The principal security service of Israel, which was established on 30 June 1948, only six weeks after Israeli independence. Its successes, unlike those of MOSSAD, have been rarely publicized. It is so called from the Hebrew letters that begin the first two words of its full name, *Sherut Bittahon Kelali*, General Security Service.

Shine On Harvey Moon. A television comedy serial running from 1982 to 1985 and created by Laurence Marks and Maurice Gran as a humorous evocation of one family's life. The story, set just after the Second World War, opens when Corporal Harvey Moon, newly demobilized, returns home to Hackney, east London, where everyone believes him to have been killed in action. The part of Moon was taken by Kenneth Cranham, then Nicky Henson, while Elizabeth Spriggs was his wife, Nan. The title puns on Jack Norworth's song 'Shine On Harvest Moon' (1908), and one episode was titled 'Goodnight, Sweetheart', after Ray Noble's song of 1931. This in turn was adopted as the title of Marks and Gran's subsequent sitcom, GOODNIGHT SWEETHEART.

Shining Path. A translation of Spanish *Sendero Luminoso*, as the name of a neo-Maoist Peruvian revolutionary movement. It was founded in 1970 following a split in the Communist Party of Peru and subsequently became a secret guerrilla organization involved in terrorist activities. Its name refers to the maxim of José Carlos Mariátegui, founder of Peru's original Communist Party in 1928: *El Marxismo-Leninismo abrirá el sendero luminoso hacia la revolución*, 'Marxism-Leninism will open the shining path to revolution.' Members are known as Senderistas.

Ship in a bottle. A model ship inside a bottle whose neck is smaller than the ship. The expression can be used allusively for a thing that can be managed or organized so long as one knows how.

Shipping forecast. A regular feature of BBC radio, as information provided four times a day by the Meteorological Office on wind conditions and visibility at sea, given individually for each of the 31 forecasting areas around the British Isles. The mesmeric names of the latter are mostly based on geographical features, such as rivers (Tyne, Humber), bays (Biscay, German Bight), islands (Hebrides, Rockall) or underwater sandbanks (Dogger, Forties).

> This nightly recitation of troublesome wind in Dogger and Fisher has all the calming qualities of a repeated mantra or, for traditionalists, a favourite part of the Book of Common Prayer.
>
> KEN BRUCE in PAUL DONOVAN: *The Radio Companion* (1991)

Shipping News, The. A tragi-comic novel (1993) by the US writer E. Annie Proulx (b.1935), which won the PULITZER PRIZE for fiction. Quoyle, a newspaper reporter in Mockingbird, New York, takes refuge in Newfoundland with his aunt and his two small delinquent daughters after his wife, having sold the daughters to a pornographer, is killed in a car crash while absconding with her lover. The aunt opens a shop, and Quoyle gets a job on the local paper. 'I want you to cover local car wrecks. ... We run a front-page photo of a car-wreck every week, whether we have a wreck or not. ... And the shipping news.'

Shire, The. A region of MIDDLE-EARTH in J.R.R Tolkien's *The* HOBBIT (1937) and *The* LORD OF THE RINGS (1954–5). The Shire is the home of the hobbits. Bilbo BAGGINS and later his nephew FRODO live at Bag End in the village of Hobbiton. As is implied by its name, the Shire bears many of the characteristics of a long-gone rural England, its gentle landscapes and rustic homeliness contrasting with the epic landscapes found elsewhere in Middle Earth. Many place-names in the Shire,

coincidentally or otherwise, seem to echo English village-names. Buckland, the home of the Brandybuck family of hobbits, is actually the name of a village in western Oxfordshire.

Shit. This FOUR-LETTER WORD in its basic sense of 'to void excrement' goes back to medieval times. Its figurative applications mostly date from the 20th century, however, and include 'in the shit' (in trouble), 'up shit creek' (in difficulties), 'shit-scared' (very frightened) and 'when the shit hits the fan' (when the disastrous consequences become known). As an exclamation, 'shit' can express anything from a keen annoyance to a mild deprecation. In this role it has a variant form, 'shite', a stylized American representation, 'she-ite', and a euphemistic equivalent, 'sugar'. In slang usage (from the 1940s), 'shit' denotes both drugs in general and HEROIN and cannabis in particular.

Shock, horror or **Shock! Horror!** An ironic exclamation made in response to something that supposedly shocks. 'Shock-horror' headlines are sensationalistic banner headlines, as typically found in the TABLOID press. The expression dates from the 1970s.

> Recently there has been a lot of fuss about ten-year-old girls wearing make-up and even having – shock, horror – facials.
>
> *The Times* (14 August 1999)

Shocking pink. A vibrant shade of pink, introduced by the Italian-born French fashion designer Elsa Schiaparelli (1890–1973) in February 1937. 'Shocking' here means little more than 'vivid', but the word derives its impact from its use to describe a colour normally regarded as soft and gentle.

Shock jock. A radio disc-jockey who is intentionally offensive or provocative. The phenomenon arose in the United States in the latter half of the 1980s, but was less well tolerated when it crossed to Britain in the 1990s.

> Forget shock-jock Howard Stern: America's most controversial talk-show host is Art Bell, the right-wing crusader for the Home of the Weird, Land of the Bizarre.
>
> *The Times* (7 July 1999)

Shoestring. The unusual British PRIVATE EYE, with full name Eddie Shoestring, who is the central character of the television series named after him (1979–80). He is somewhat dishevelled, drives a Cortina estate car and his regular employment is with Radio West, a local commercial radio station, where listeners call on him to solve their mysteries. He was played to the letter by Trevor Eve, for whom he served as a break-through career role.

Shogun. A historical novel (1975) by James Clavell (1924–94). There is a clash of cultures in medieval Japan when a shipwrecked Englishman is compelled, in return for his survival, to serve as secretary to a war lord (*shogun*) and has to reconsider his personal principles. A mini-series, starring Richard Chamberlain, was shown on BBC1 in 1982.

Shoo-fly pie. A rich tart of treacle baked in a pastry case with a crumble topping, so called because of the (real or imagined) need to shoo flies away from the sweet treacle. American 'pie' here equates to British 'tart', and the confection as a whole is thus a modern equivalent of the much older British treacle tart. The name dates from the 1930s.

Shoo-in. A person or thing that is sure to succeed, especially to win a contest. The expression dates from the 1930s and originally referred to a horse in a rigged horse race that one metaphorically merely needed to 'shoo in' to win. The term is often misspelled 'shoe-in' by writers unaware of the origin, presumably from an image of being kicked in, like a successful shot at goal: 'Muhammad Ali … who was a shoe-in for sportsman of the last millennium' (*The Times*, 1 January 2000); 'With these names, I'd have thought lottery cash was a shoe-in' (*Sunday Times*, 9 January 2000).

> Politics directly intervened in literature with the appointment of [Ted] Hughes's successor as poet laureate … Once [Seamus] Heaney had declared himself Irish … Andrew Motion was a shoo-in.
>
> *Independent on Sunday* (28 November 1999)

Shoot from the hip, To. To react hastily or inconsiderately; to respond aggressively. The imagery derives from Western films, in which a rider faced with a challenge would respond with a shot from a gun drawn quickly from the holster on his hip.

> He [film actor Guy Pearce] is, he tells me, prone to shooting from the hip when perhaps he should consider things a little more.
>
> *The Times* (6 September 1999)

Shoot oneself in the foot, To. To harm one's own cause inadvertently; to damage one's chances. The allusion is to an accidental shooting of this type as distinct from the deliberate shooting of oneself in the foot in order to avoid military service, a ruse entered in various army records.

> 'I got past 30 and I'd had relationships with men. … But I was the one shooting myself in the foot. I picked people who weren't emotionally available, or only up to a certain point.'
>
> *The Times* (2 October 1999)

Shoot someone or **something down, To.** To crush a person or reject their opinions by means of forceful criticism or argument. The metaphor derives from aerial combat in the First World War. An emphatic form is 'to shoot down in flames', as: 'I was shot down in flames for my trouble.'

Shoot the breeze or **the bull, To.** To chat idly; to gossip. A 'breeze' is a rumour, which is wafted from one person to another, as when one 'gets wind of' something. 'Bull' is short for 'bullshit'. The phrases are of American origin and date from the early 20th century.

Shop around, To. Literally to go from shop to shop searching out where prices are lowest or the best bargains to be had. More generally to shop around is to compare any products or services with such an aim. A slang sense of the phrase, which dates from the 1920s, is to engage in a number of sexual relationships before selecting the one that will serve for a longer term or even marriage.

> Which bank is best? Sweeteners today can come at a price later. It definitely pays to shop around.
>
> *The Times* (26 August 1999)

Shopping days to Christmas. Preceded by a figure, such as fifty, the phrase is an irritating reminder of the decreasing opportunities to buy Christmas presents. The commercial countdown was first promoted by SELFRIDGE's department store in London, and its American founder, Gordon Selfridge, when still in his native Chicago, is said to have sent out an instruction to Marshall Field's heads of departments and assistants reading: 'The Christmas season has begun and but twenty-three more shopping days remain in which to make our holiday sales record.' As virtually every day of the week is now a shopping day, the figure is essentially the number of days to 25 December. The countdown usually begins in earnest from October, and there are 85 shopping days from the 1st of that month.

Shop till one drops, To. To indulge in a shopping spree, especially after coming into money. A phrase that epitomized the hedonistic commercialism of the 1980s and 1990s.

> What is the golden rule of retail? Is it 'Sell, sell, sell?'

Is it 'Shop till you drop' or is it 'Smile, sell, sell?' That is how Asda opens its quiz for aspirant graduate employees.

The Times (10 January 2000)

Shore, Jemima. The high-flying television reporter who investigates various mysteries in the series of novels by the historian Antonia Fraser, beginning with *Quiet as a Nun* (1977). She subsequently appeared as the central character in the television series *Jemina Shore Investigates* (1983), in which she was played by Patricia Hodge.

Short sharp shock. A punitive regime intended to deter by the instant impact of its severity. It has been particularly associated with young offenders, who in the 1980s were in some cases subjected to military-style treatment when under detention. Doubts have been raised regarding its efficacy. The phrase gained popular currency from the 1950s but in fact has a Gilbertian genesis.

> Awaiting the sensation of a short, sharp shock,
> From a cheap and chippy chopper on a big black
> block.
> W.S. GILBERT: *The Mikado*, I (1885)

Shot glass. A small glass for serving spirits, traditionally one containing a 'shot' of 1½ US fluid oz (44.5ml). Such a glass is also known as a 'jigger', probably so called because it goes up and down ('jigs') between the bottle and the customer's glass.

> Proof of a successful party, empty glasses, beer bottles and shot glasses littered every available space.
> *heat* (17–23 February 2000)

Shotgun wedding. One forced upon the couple, usually by the bride's parents, when the bride is pregnant. The image is of the bride's father threatening the groom with a shotgun, itself perhaps serving as a symbol of the act that caused her condition. The expression dates from the 1920s.

Shot in the arm. An encouraging stimulus. The allusion is to the injection of a stimulant. The expression dates from the 1920s.

> 'Hopefully it will bring Ilfracombe out of the Sixties. It needs a shot in the arm, something to bring it into the real world,' said restaurateur John Clemence.
> *Evening Standard* (27 September 1999)

Shoulder to cry on. A person who listens sympathetically to one's problems. The phrase evokes both the resting of a weeping person's head on the shoulder of

another and also the shoulder itself as a traditional source of strength and support. Hence the pleasant dedication of Claire Rayner's novel *Long Acre* (1978): 'For Joan Chapman, with gratitude for her ever-patient rusty shoulder'.

Showa. The auspicious name or reign title given to the period of rule (1926–89) of the Japanese emperor Hirohito (1901–89). It means 'Enlightened Peace' and became the emperor's name after his death. He was succeeded by his son, Akihito (b.1933), whose reign was designated Heisei, meaning 'Achieving Peace'.

Show and tell. An elaborate public presentation or display, as of a couple's photographs of their round-the-world cruise. The expression arose in the 1940s from the American teaching method for young children, in which each child brings some object to class to show and describe to the others.

Show must go on, The. The activity in progress must continue; we must keep going. The expression appears to have originally applied to a circus, which despite difficulties, such as sick animals or absent performers, must continue to hold its performances in order not to disappoint the public. A film of 1937, *The Show Goes On*, tells how a mill-girl becomes a star singer with the help of a dying composer, and 'The Show Must Go On' is a song by Ira Gershwin in Jerome Kern's musical *Cover Girl* (1944).

> Why must the show go on?
> Why not announce the closing night of it?
> The public seem to hate the sight of it.
> NOËL COWARD: 'Why Must the Show Go On?' (1950s)

Show, carry, fly or **wave the flag, To.** To demonstrate support for one's country or organization, especially when abroad. A ship of the Royal Navy literally 'flies the flag' of the White Ensign when in a foreign port. A reluctant but dutiful attender of a social function may also be said to 'show the flag'.

> Hugh Grant led the Brit-pack to the Brooklyn Museum [in New York] to wave the flag at the gala opening of the controversial exhibition 'Sensation'.
> *The Times* (2 October 1999)

Show trial. A judicial trial attended by great publicity. The term usually relates to the prejudged trial of political dissidents by a totalitarian government. The Stalinist show trials of the 1930s, with the sinister Andrei Vyshinsky (1883–1954) as prosecutor (1936–8), are a well-known example. The expression itself dates from the 1930s. *See also* U–2.

Shrimp, The. A media nickname for the petite model Jean Shrimpton (b.1943), who introduced the MINI-SKIRT to a delighted or dismayed public. She was one of the first SUPERMODELS and at the centre of the London scene that shook the world in the SWINGING SIXTIES. Her boyfriends included the photographer David Bailey, the man who made her, and the actor Terence Stamp. She retired from modelling at the age of 28 and became a virtual recluse, telling one interviewer, 'The trouble is I really hate clothes.'

Shrink. A psychiatrist. The word is a shortening of 'headshrinker' in the same sense, adopting the term used historically for a headhunter who preserved and shrank the heads of his dead enemies. The term sheds interesting light on the extent to which people feel diminished as individuals by the process of psycho-analysis and psychotherapy.

> I wonder if my shrink (sorry, psychiatrist) was a woman not a man I'd be in a better or worse state, after three months in this place?
>
> FAY WELDON: *The Heart of the Country* (1987)

Shrinking violet. A unduly shy or modest person. The violet, although nobly coloured and sweetly scented, grows in secluded spots, as if anxious to hide these two attributes. The expression, dating from the early years of the 20th century, is often found in the negative, as: 'She's no shrinking violet.' In a positive sense it can imply a reluctance to face one's responsibilities.

> In his 24 years in the post [of Master of the Queen's Music, Malcolm] Williamson has not overtaxed his talents. But surely this shrinking violet should now be prodded into collaborating with our new Poet Laureate, Andrew Motion.
>
> *The Times* (31 August 1999)

Shuttle diplomacy. Diplomatic negotiations conducted by a mediator who travels between two or more parties that are themselves reluctant to meet for direct discussions. Henry Kissinger, US Secretary of State in the 1970s, was a master of the method. *See also* FLYING PEACEMAKER.

Sick as a parrot. Very disappointed. The expression arose in the 1970s and came to be regarded as the stock response of a football player or team manager after losing a match. The reason for the particular attribution is uncertain. According to some, the full phrase is 'sick as a parrot with a broken beak'. *See also* OVER THE MOON.

Sick building syndrome. A condition affecting office workers, typically manifesting itself in headaches and respiratory problems. Its cause is attributed to unhealthy or stressful factors in the working environment, such as poor ventilation, passive exposure to tobacco smoke, absence of natural light, and a frustration at being unable to control the ambient physical conditions. A 'sick' building is one that is not functioning properly. The expression dates from the 1980s.

Sick joke. An insensitive, morbid or sadistic joke, not amusing in the normal way but the product of warped wit. An example is the following:

> What's a thousand metres long and eats vegetables? A Moscow meat queue.
>
> 'NORMA P. LAMONT': *The Official Ministry of Fun Joke Book* (1992)

Sid. A name selected for the average small investor when encouraged to take part in the share issue of British Gas on its privatization in 1986. The full form of the lure then posted everywhere was 'If you see Sid, tell him.' The name was taken up in the media for any typical small-scale share-buyer or shareholder and was itself presumably chosen for its 'plebeian' associations.

> House of Fraser stores groups will be embarking on a 'Sid-style' marketing campaign to woo private investors and shoppers.
>
> *Sunday Telegraph* (30 January 1994)

Sidney Street siege. An incident on 3 January 1911 when police and soldiers, on the orders of the home secretary Winston Churchill, who personally attended the siege, surrounded 100 Sidney Street in London's East End. Inside the house were three Latvian anarchists who had killed three policemen during a raid on a jeweller a few weeks earlier. Two of the gang were killed in the siege, but the leader, 'Peter the Painter' (a sign painter by trade), escaped.

Siegfried Line. The defences built by the Germans on their western frontier before and after 1939 as a reply to France's MAGINOT LINE. The British song, popular in 1939, 'We're gonna hang out the washing on the Siegfried Line' was somewhat premature. When Canadian troops penetrated the Line in 1945 they hung up a number of sheets with a large notice on which was written 'The Washing'. The name is that of the hero of Wagner's *Ring* cycle and of the medieval epic on which that work is based, the *Nibelungenlied*, and many Germans will have been aware of its literal significance, from *Sieg*, 'victory', and *Fried*, 'peace'.

The Germans had already used the name in the First World War for what other countries knew as the HINDENBURG LINE.

Sieg Heil. A German phrase with the literal meaning 'hail victory', from the German *Sieg* ('victory') and *Heil* ('hail'), used as a victory salute at NAZI political rallies. The phrase became familiar from films about the Second World War. *See also* HEIL HITLER.

Signature tune. A musical theme played regularly as a means of identification to introduce a particular artist or regularly broadcast programme. One of the best known signature tunes in the days of STEAM RADIO was 'Here's To the Next Time', played in the 1930s at the close of every broadcast by Henry Hall and the BBC Dance Orchestra. *See also* THEME MUSIC.

> If one wished to be facetious, one could say that the *leitmotiv* of characters in Wagner's *Ring* are their 'signature tunes'.
> MICHAEL KENNEDY: *The Oxford Dictionary of Music* (1994)

Significant other. A person with whom one has a romantic or sexual relationship; a boyfriend or girlfriend. The expression is of American origin, dating from the 1970s, and was adopted from the jargon of sociology as a term for a person who directly influences an individual's self-evaluation and behaviour, as a parent does a child or an employer an employee. *See also* ROLE MODEL.

Significant Others. A volume (1988) in a series of novels by the US writer Armistead Maupin (b.1944), chronicling, through a wide range of characters and rapid changes of plot, life in San Francisco in the 1980s. *Significant Others* introduces three new characters to Maupin's regular cast of characters, known to television audiences through the television serialization of his *Tales of the City* (1978): Wren Douglas, 'the world's most beautiful fat woman', Polly Berendt, a lesbian, and Thack Sweeney, a restorer of old houses. *See also* SIGNIFICANT OTHER.

Sign one's own death warrant, To. To bring about one's own downfall; to do oneself irreparable harm. In 1921 the Irish nationalist leader Michael Collins, after signing the treaty establishing the Irish Free State, wrote in a letter: 'I tell you – early this morning I signed my death warrant.' The following year he was ambushed and assassinated by anti-treaty Republicans. *See also* BÉAL NA MBLÁTH; BIG FELLA; FREE-STATERS.

Sign on the dotted line, To. To indicate one's acceptance of the terms agreed, literally by writing one's signature on the line allotted for it in a contract. The term dates from the early 20th century.

Silence of the Lambs, The. A horror novel (1989) by Thomas Harris (b.1940) about a homicidal genius and cannibal, Hannibal Lecter, on the loose. The title refers to a childhood experience of his potential victim, a female trainee investigator, who recalls the lambs on the farm where she was brought up being rounded up and taken away for slaughter. At the book's enigmatic ending, 'she sleeps deeply, sweetly in the silence of the lambs'. A tense and sometimes gruesome film version (1990) was directed by Jonathan Demme.

> *Hannibal*: A census taker once tried to test me. I ate his liver with some fava beans and a nice chianti.

Silent Cal. A nickname of Republican politician Calvin Coolidge (1872–1933), president of the USA (1923–9). Noted for his taciturnity, Coolidge was once approached by a guest at the White House who informed him that she had just made a bet that she could elicit more than three words from the great conversationalist. Coolidge replied: 'You lose.' Dorothy Parker famously responded to the news that the former president was dead with the words: 'How could they tell?' Coolidge himself admitted, 'I always figured the American public wanted a solemn ass for President, so I went along with them.'

Silent majority. The majority of people, who hold moderate opinions but rarely express them. President Richard Nixon gave the expression a political emphasis when using it in speeches of 1969–70 appealing for support from MIDDLE AMERICA. The implication was that such people did not bother to make their opinions known but should do so.

Silicon Fen. England's answer to America's SILICON VALLEY, as the Fenland city of Cambridge with its many electronics companies. The name puns on that of SILICON GLEN.

> For more than a decade, the Cambridge phenomenon has been illuminating Silicon Fen by spawning a legion of biotechnology and electronics groups originating in the university's laboratories and lecture theatres.
> *Sunday Times* (6 June 1999)

Silicon Glen. Scotland's answer to America's SILICON VALLEY, as the region of central Scotland around the

NEW TOWN of Glenrothes where there are many electronics companies.

> The project aims to raise the level of expertise in Silicon Glen and push the industry forward from its current manufacturing base to a more knowledge-led, R & D-based industry.
>
> *Scotsman* (12 January 1999)

Silicon Prairie. A nickname for a region near Dallas, Texas, that is the site of many high-technology and computer companies. *See also* SILICON FEN; SILICON GLEN; SILICON VALLEY.

Silicon Valley. A name given to the Santa Clara Valley, south of San Francisco, California, where a number of electronics and computing industries are located. The name, alluding to the use of silicon in the manufacture of microchips, was subsequently extended to similar sites elsewhere, both in the United States and in other countries. *See also* SILICON FEN; SILICON GLEN; SILICON PRAIRIE.

> Silicon Valley's 'computer cops' are using the latest high-tech tools to track down the growing number of criminals who plan to kidnap children.
>
> *Sunday Correspondent* (22 April 1990)

Silly ass. A stupid person. The ass or donkey is traditionally regarded as a stupid animal. The expression is first recorded only at the turn of the 20th century, in G.B. Shaw's *Captain Brassbound's Conversion* (1899). A 'silly ass' was later established as the stereotype of the effete, upper-class, braying Englishman, nicely described by George Orwell as 'the silly-ass Englishman with his spats and monocle' (*The Windmill*, II, 1945).

Silly me. A facetiously ironic or gently self-deprecating rebuke following a slip or error, as: 'Silly old me, I thought today was Tuesday.'

Silly Putty. An American plaything first marketed in 1949 as a form of 'putty' that could be stretched, shattered and bounced if appropriately manipulated. A later British equivalent was 'Potty Putty'.

Silly Symphonies. A series of animated character cartoons produced by Walt Disney from 1928, their aim being to evoke settings, seasons and events in the style of Aesop's *Fables*. Animals thus regularly featured (though not MICKEY MOUSE or DONALD DUCK), as in *Birds of a Feather* (1931), *Three Little Pigs* (1933), *The Tortoise and the Hare* (1935) and *The Country Cousin* (1936). The overall title refers to the humorously appropriate musical accompaniment.

Silmarillion, The. A posthumously published collection (1977), edited by his son, of imaginative tales by J.R.R. Tolkien (1892–1973). They constitute the storehouse of materials from which he developed his children's novel, *The* HOBBIT (1937), and the saga *The* LORD OF THE RINGS (1954–5). The Silmarils are 'the three jewels made by Fëanor before the destruction of the Two Trees of Valinor, and filled with their light'.

Silver Bodgie. A nickname of Australian politician Bob (Robert) Hawke (b.1929), Labour prime minister (1983–91). A 'bodgie' is Australian slang for a TEDDY BOY, and Hawke earned the name from his mane of silver hair, which the novelist Patrick White described as 'his cockatoo hairdo'.

Silver screen. The cinema, whose screen was originally covered with metallic paint to produce a highly reflective silver-coloured surface. It is now usually made of white opaque plastic, although glass-beaded screens and platinum screens are used for special daylight presentations.

Silver Sword, The. A novel (1956) by Ian Serraillier (1912–94) relating the efforts of three Polish refugee children to reunite themselves with their parents after their family is broken up by the NAZI invasion of Poland. The sword of the title refers to a sword-shaped silver penknife, which was given by the children's father to another child, named Jan, and which he knows will be recognized by his own children.

Silver Tassie, The. A play (1928) by the Irish playwright Sean O'Casey (1880–1964) in which the author laments the loss of life in the First World War. The 'silver tassie' of the title is a silver cup brought home in victory by Dublin footballer Harry Heegan in the first act.

Simpson, Bart. The brash, spiky-haired, school-hating 'bad boy' hero of the television cartoon series *The Simpsons*, created in 1987 by the American cartoonist Matt Groening. Each episode opens with 10-year-old Bart (an anagram of 'brat') at a school blackboard writing as punishment such lines as 'I will not drive the principal's car' or 'I did not see Elvis'. The show's humour is primarily aimed at adults, but Bart himself has a direct appeal for younger viewers, who delight in his catchphrases such as 'Aye, caramba' and 'Eat my shorts'. Other members of the Simpson family are Homer, the thick-headed, beer-swilling father, Marge, his sensible, down-to-earth wife, Lisa, their young hyper-intelligent daughter, and Maggie, their perpetually dummy-sucking infant.

Sinatra doctrine. A phrase coined on 25 October 1989 by the Soviet foreign ministry spokesman, Gennadi Gerasimov, to describe the policy of the reforming Soviet leader Mikhail Gorbachev (*see* GORBY) towards the USSR's allies in Eastern Europe. These countries would now be free to pursue their own destinies, 'to do it their way', after the song 'My Way' popularized by the US singer Frank Sinatra (1915–98). The Sinatra doctrine was in contrast to the earlier BREZHNEV DOCTRINE. According to early-1970s graffitists, Sinatra was also responsible for a significant contribution to philosophy.

> 'To do is to be – Rousseau. To be is to do – Sartre. Doobedoobedoobedoo – Sinatra.'
> Quoted by Ronald Fletcher in BBC radio programme
> *Quote ... Unquote* (5 April 1978)

See also OL' BLUE EYES.

Sin bin. In ice hockey an enclosure where offending players have to sit out for a stated time. Hence a term for a centre where offenders are sent for detention or rehabilitation.

Since when? Since when has that been so? A phrase casting doubt on the veracity of a statement.

> *Broadbent* [*very solemnly*]: No: I am a teetotaller.
> *Aunt Judy* [*incredulously*]: Arra since when?
> *Broadbent*: Since this morning, Miss Doyle.
> G.B. SHAW: *John Bull's Other Island*, IV (1904)

Since you ask. A phrase preceding an answer to a spoken or unspoken question, in the latter case often to pre-empt an actual inquiry. The question itself usually seeks clarification regarding a possibly dubious or devious aspect of the matter, and the implication is that if the question had not been put or presumed, the information would not have been given.

> Did we hear rumours, before his appointment, that the outcome had been decided in advance of the interviews? Yes, since you're asking, but it can only have been a coincidence.
> *Times Literary Supplement* (30 July 1999)

Sinfonia Antartica. The atmospheric seventh symphony of Ralph Vaughan Williams (1872–1958). The title is Italian for 'Antarctic symphony'. The piece was adapted from Vaughan Williams' music for the film *Scott of the Antarctic* (1948) (*see* SOUTH POLE), starring John Mills, James Robertson Justice and Kenneth More. The symphony, which was first performed in Manchester in 1953, includes parts for wind machine, vibraphone, wordless soprano solo and women's chorus. At a rehearsal of the piece the conductor

Sir John Barbirolli instructed the chorus: 'I want you to sound like twenty-two women having babies *without* chloroform.'

Sing from the same hymn sheet, To. To present a united front in public by not disagreeing with one another. The image is of people of different religious groups or even faiths joined in worship.

> Why ... are the Treasury and the DTI [Department of Trade and Industry] not singing from the same hymn sheet over details of the Cat standard?
> *The Times* (6 January 2000)

Singin' in the Rain. A film musical (1952) written by Adolph Green and Betty Comden about the struggles of a top Hollywood production team to adapt from silent movies to talkies in the late 1920s. Starring Gene Kelly, Donald O'Connor, Debbie Reynolds and Jean Hagen, the idea for the film grew out of the song 'Singin' in the Rain', which remains the highlight of the movie, with Kelly dancing with joy in the puddles (despite the fact that he made much of the movie while suffering from a heavy cold).

Single currency. A unified currency proposed for all member states of the EUROPEAN UNION, the currency itself being the EURO. More generally the term symbolizes the relationship between national sovereignty and economic and monetary union. *See also* WAIT AND SEE.

Sinister Street. A novel (1913–14) by Compton Mackenzie (born Edward Montague Compton; 1883–1972), originally published in two volumes. It is divided into four books: 'The Prison House' (Michael's childhood), 'Classical Education' (school), 'Dreaming Spires' (Oxford) and 'Romantic Education'. The last book largely concerns Michael's ultimately fruitless efforts to find and redeem a former girlfriend who has become a prostitute, in the course of which he takes lodgings in London and traverses streets that are the haunts of the city's lowest life. In a dedication, the author states: '*Sinister Street* is a symbolic title which bears no reference to an heraldic euphemism.'

Sink one's teeth into something, To. *See* GET ONE'S TEETH INTO SOMETHING.

Sink without trace, To. To disappear and not be seen or heard of again. The expression dates from the 1920s and translates German *spurlos versenkt*, 'sunk without trace'. This phrase became widely known during the First World War following the publication in September 1917 of a secret telegram sent to Berlin in

May that year by Count Luxburg, the German minister in Buenos Aires, advising that Argentine shipping should be either turned back or sunk without trace.

Sinn Féin (Irish, 'ourselves alone'). A political party formed in 1905 with the aim of establishing a united Irish republic. After winning a majority of Irish seats in the 1918 British general election, it set up a secessionist Irish Republic (1919) under Éamon de Valera (see DEV). It carried on guerrilla warfare (see BLACK AND TANS) against British forces until the Anglo-Irish Treaty of 1921 which created the Irish Free State and partitioned Ireland. Led by de Valera, a section of Sinn Féin refused to accept the treaty, triggering armed conflict between anti-treaty Republicans and FREE-STATERS. De Valera's resignation of the presidency of Sinn Féin in 1926 and his creation of a new party, FIANNA FÁIL, began a period of marginalization for the party, but it returned to prominence with the outbreak of Northern Ireland's TROUBLES. Sinn Féin's links with the IRA prompted the British government in 1988 to ban the broadcasting of speeches by its members, including its leader, Gerry Adams. In return for a ceasefire in 1993, however, it was allowed to take part in talks on the future of Northern Ireland and in 1999 became part of the province's first devolved government since 1974. See also ARMALITE; GOOD FRIDAY AGREEMENT.

Siren suit. A one-piece lined and warm garment on the lines of a boiler suit, sometimes worn in London in air-raid shelters during the bombing raids of the Second World War. It was famously worn by Winston Churchill, who referred to his blue siren suit as his 'rompers', and was so named from its being slipped on over nightclothes at the first wail of the air-raid siren.

Sister Frigidaire. See MISS FRIGIDAIRE.

Sitcom. A situation comedy in the form of a radio or television series in which the same characters are involved in various amusing situations. Classic British examples of the latter are PORRIDGE and The GOOD LIFE. The first television sitcom is generally held to be CBS's The Goldbergs, first shown in 1949.

Sit next to Nellie, To. To learn an occupation by watching an experienced worker.

Sit on one's hands, To. To withhold one's approval; to take no action. The expression arose in the 1920s and originally applied to members of an audience who withheld their applause.

Sitting duck. An easy target. A duck that is sitting is much easier to hit than one in flight. The phrase dates from the 1940s.

Sitting pretty. Doing very nicely; enjoying the material comforts of life. The image is of being handsomely placed. The phrase dates from the 1920s and was popularized as the title of two musicals, one of 1924 with lyrics by Jerome Kern, the other of 1933.

Sit-up-and-beg bike. An old-fashioned bicycle on which the rider sits upright, like a dog begging.

Sitzkrieg (pseudo-German). The 'sitting war', the descriptive term applied (in contrast to BLITZKRIEG) to the period of comparative quiet and seeming military inactivity at the outset of the Second World War (September 1939 to April 1940), the period also known as the PHONEY war.

Six, The. The six countries Belgium, France, Germany, Italy, the Netherlands and Luxembourg, as the original participants in three economic communities: the European Coal and Steel Community (ECSC) (1952), the European Economic Community (EEC) (1957), and the European Atomic Energy Community or Euratom (1957). In 1967 these combined to form the European Community (EC), but until 1987 the grouping was commonly known as the EEC. See also EUROPEAN UNION.

Six, Les. A group of French composers formed at Paris in 1918 under the aegis of Jean Cocteau and Erik Satie to further their innovative ideas and those of modern music generally. Its members were Arthur Honegger (1892–1955), Darius Milhaud (1892–1974), Francis Poulenc (1899–1963), Louis Durey (1888–1979), Georges Auric (1899–1983) and Germaine Tailleferre (1892–1983). The name was given in 1920 by the French music critic Henri Collet, but the group lost cohesion soon after.

Six Characters in Search of an Author. A play, originally titled Sei personaggi in cerca d'autore, by the Italian playwright Luigi Pirandello (1867–1936), first performed in 1921, in which the actors in a theatre act out the destiny of a family of six strangers who have interrupted their rehearsal. When they first appear the family believe they are merely characters in a play and are in search of the author to find out what is to become of them. After the actors show them their fate they are appalled, despite the actors' insistence that their fate is not real.

Six Counties. A term mainly used by Republicans for Northern Ireland, which consists of six of the nine counties of the ancient province and kingdom of Ulster. The remaining three counties are part of the Republic of Ireland, often referred to by Republicans as the Twenty-six Counties. The use of these terms reflects the commitment of Irish Republicans to a 32-county Irish Republic, and their reluctance to accept the legitimacy of any state structures that fall short of their ideal. *See also* FREE-STATERS; SINN FÉIN.

Six-Day War. The war of 5–10 June 1967 in which Israel occupied the Sinai peninsula, Old Jerusalem, the WEST BANK and the GOLAN HEIGHTS, and defeated the alliance formed between Egypt, Lebanon, Jordan, Syria and Iraq. The conflict is also known as the June War.

Six feet under. Dead and buried. A phrase of American origin dating from the 1930s. *See also* DEEP SIX.

Six of the best. Six strokes of the cane, as a once regular ration of corporal punishment in schools. They are 'the best' since they are or were of the best quality.

> 'You'll get six of the very best, over the back of a chair,' said one.
> 'They'll draw a chalk line across you, of course, you know,' said another.
> 'A chalk line?'
> 'Rather. So that every cut can be aimed exactly at the same spot. It hurts much more that way.'
> 'SAKI' (H.H. MUNRO): *The Unbearable Bassington*, ch ii (1912)

Six-pack. A colloquial term for pack of six cans of beer. Hence also, from their resemblance to such cans, a set of well-developed abdominal muscles ('abs').

> 'If there's a gaggle of inebriated girls, then I actually get sexually harassed. I've been prodded, had my bum pinched and my T-shirt pulled up so that they could look at my six pack.'
> *The Times* (24 April 1999)

Sixty-four or **sixty-four thousand dollar question.** The last and most difficult question; the crux of the problem. The allusion is to a prize awarded in an American GAME SHOW for answering the final question, the stake having doubled seven times. The expression dates from the 1950s.

> Did that mean the whole area had extractable tin underneath it? 'That's the 64,000 dollar question.'
> *Sunday Telegraph* (5 August 1979)

Skateboarding. A sport in which a person 'skates' along pavements or other asphalt surfaces on a narrow wheeled board, propulsion being effected by occasionally pushing one foot against the ground, as in riding a scooter. It was a popular teenage activity in the 1970s, but fell foul of the law and the public for the accidents it caused and the damage it did to walls, benches and passers-by.

Skegness is so bracing. The wording on a famous railway poster first issued by the Great Northern Railway in 1908. It depicts a jolly, pipe-smoking fisherman bounding along the beach at Skegness, the Lincolnshire resort that later became the home of the first BUTLIN'S holiday camp.

Skid row. An American expression applied to a district abounding in vicious characters and down-and-outs. In the lumber industry a skid row was a skidway or grass track down which felled timber was hauled to the river that would carry it down to the sawmill. Early on, Tacoma, near Seattle, flourished on its lumber production and in due course liquor (in taverns) and women (in brothels) became available for loggers descending the skid row. In time the part of a town where loggers lived or spent their free time came to be known generally as Skid Road. In the mid-20th century this name reverted to 'skid row' and was applied to any area of cheap bar-rooms and seedy hotels frequented by vagrants and alcoholics.

Skiffle. A name given to a style of JAZZ of the 1920s, and subsequently to a type of jazz folk music current in Britain in the late 1950s played by a skiffle group, consisting of guitar, drums, kazoo, washboard and other improvised instruments. The word is perhaps of imitative origin. *See also* QUARRY MEN.

Skin flick. A pornographic film, featuring (usually female) nudity ('skin'). 'Flick' derives from the FLICKS as an old term for the cinema.

Skinhead. A young person with closely cropped or shaved head, typically the member of an aggressive or racist gang and prevalent in the latter half of the 1960s. The term was originally applied in the United States to an army recruit with an extreme CREW CUT. *See also* BOVVER BOY; MODS AND ROCKERS; PUNK.

> It is at these shows that Rosko the brash, shrieking voice, becomes flesh and blood to his different fans – reggae-loving skin-heads, draped and winkle-pickered rockers, tumescent girls.
> RICHARD GILBERT in *Anatomy of Pop* (1970)

Skinny-dipping. Swimming in the nude, when all one has on is one's skin.

Skin of Our Teeth, The. A play (1942) by the US playwright Thornton Wilder (1897–1975) in which the characters jump about almost at whim through the whole range of human history. The title appears in the text when one of the characters describes how they came through the Napoleonic Wars 'by the skin of our teeth' (in other words, very narrowly indeed), but it also expresses the aggressive stance the author was taking in the play against the conventional middle-class drawing-room drama that he himself had already rejected. The saying is an old one, appearing in Job 19:20: 'My bone cleaveth to my skin and to my flesh, and I am escaped with the skin of my teeth.'

Skin on skin. A term in the fashion industry for leather garments such as jeans worn next to the skin.

Skirt-chaser. A man who compulsively pursues women; a dedicated ladies' man. The term dates from the 1940s.

Sky art. A term coined in 1969 by the German artist Otto Piene (b.1928) to describe works of art that are viewed in or from the sky. The tag has been used to embrace kite-flying and fireworks displays as well as works using advanced technology. Two noted examples are Piene's own *Olympic Rainbow* (1972), consisting of five helium-filled polythene tubes each 600m long, produced for the Munich Olympic Games, and Charlotte Moorman's *Sky Kiss* (1981–6), in which the artist played her cello while suspended from helium-filled tubes. A high technology work is Tom Van Sant's *Desert Sun* (1986), in which a series of mirrors reflected sunlight to the sensors of a satellite orbiting the earth.

Skyhook. An imaginary device by which something could be suspended in the air.

Skyjacker. A criminal who secures passage on an airliner with the intent to terrorize the crew into flying him to a particular destination. Skyjackers are often terrorists but robbers and deranged individuals are also among them. *See also* CARJACKER; HIJACKER.

Skylab. The USA's first space station, launched into orbit round the Earth on 14 May 1973. Three successive teams of astronauts conducted experiments on board in the period to February 1974, and its orbit was then adjusted to an altitude which was judged to be sufficient to keep it in space until 1983. It wandered from its orbit in 1978, however, and on 11 July 1979 burned up and disintegrated as it plunged back into the Earth's atmosphere.

Skytrain. The name of a service of cheap-rate 'no-frills' transatlantic flights with unreserved single-class seating operated in the 1970s by Laker Airways Ltd, the enterprise of Freddie Laker (b.1922). His career suffered following the failure of the project in 1982 but in 1995 he founded Laker Airways Inc and started a service of daily transatlantic flights from Gatwick to Miami.

Slag someone off, To. To criticize them abusively. The sense is that one is calling them a slag, a term for a contemptible person dating from the 18th century and ultimately deriving from 'slag' in its common sense of refuse or waste material. The current sense dates from the 1970s.

> The following day, Johnny's back on the phone, checking he hadn't got carried away and slagged anybody off.
> *heat* (6–12 January 2000)

Slam dancing. A type of dancing to rock music in vogue in the 1980s in which participants deliberately collide with ('slam into') one another. The violent variant arose at PUNK ROCK concerts.

Slam dunk. Something reliable or certain; a foregone conclusion. The imagery is from baseball, in which a slam dunk is a forceful shot ('dunk') in which the player thrusts ('slams') the ball down through the basket with both hands from above the rim.

Slap and tickle. Amorous play or sexual foreplay. The expression dates from the 1920s.

Slap or **smack on the wrist.** A reprimand, as administered to a naughty child. An adult who has made some slip may make the gesture to their own wrist by way of self-rebuke. The expression dates from the early 20th century.

> Richard Branson has reportedly delivered the ginger-haired one [Chris Evans] a smack on the wrist through his solicitors, warning him not to associate himself and his company, Virgin Radio, too closely with its weighty, corporate namesake.
> *The Times* (21 August 1999)

Slapsie Maxie. The nickname of Maxie Rosenbloom (1904–76), the US boxer and actor in boxing and gangster films. The name was given him by the New York journalist and sportswriter Damon Runyon for his unorthodox style, which consisted in slapping his opponents with open gloves rather than punching them. The use of such blows was subsequently banned by New York's State Athletic Commission.

Slash. A slang word of opposite meanings: on the one hand an alcoholic drink; on the other an act of urination. The former is more common in American than British usage. Both date from the 1930s.

Slasher movie. A sadistic genre of HORROR MOVIE in which victims, typically women or teenage girls, are slashed with knives or razors. A famous example is MIRAMAX's *Scream* (1996), about a psychopathic killer who targets high school students. *See also* ELM STREET; SPLATTER MOVIE.

Slaughterhouse-Five. A novel (1969) by the US writer Kurt Vonnegut Jr (b.1922), drawing on his experience of witnessing, as a prisoner of war, the Allied destruction of DRESDEN by fire bombs during the Second World War. The framework of the book concerns Billy Pilgrim, who is transported by ALIENS through a TIME WARP, enabling him to witness events in the past of which he has foreknowledge. So it is that, with other US prisoners, he finds himself shut up in a slaughter house (Slaughterhouse-Five) in Dresden when the city is bombed. A film version (1972) was directed by George Roy Hill.

Sleaze factor. The sleazy or sordid aspect of a situation, especially in politics. The term originated in the United States and in Britain became associated with various scandals and alleged malpractices in the 1980s and 1990s, one of which was the CASH FOR QUESTIONS affair. 'Sleaze' as an alternative form of 'sleaziness' is a relatively recent linguistic development, first recorded in the 1960s.

> Fairly or not ... this was the [Conservative] parliament which added the word 'sleaze' to the lexicon of political scribes, and the 'sleaze factor' to the textbooks of political pundits.
>
> JOHN PIENAAR in *The BBC News General Election Guide* (1997)

Sleep around, To. To have a number of casual sexual partners. The expression is American in origin and dates from the 1920s. 'To sleep' implying to engage in sexual intercourse dates from Anglo-Saxon times and occurs thus in Chaucer and Shakespeare.

> People in London are far more concerned with safe sex; if you sleep around you get a reputation for being a slut.
>
> *Sunday Times Magazine* (2 January 2000)

Sleeping elephant. Stock market slang for a vast but spectacularly unenterprising company that avoids risks, offers security and never falls into financial disaster. A notable example is that of Great Universal Stores, familiarly known as GUS, which until a

disastrous slump in its profits in 1999 simply counted the cash generated from its mail order catalogues and did little else.

Sleeping policeman. A slight bump built across a road in order to slow the speed of traffic. The image is of a recumbent but law-enforcing police officer, and for this reason other names are now mostly used, such as (unofficially) speed bump or (officially) TRAFFIC CALMING measure. The device was introduced in the 1970s and the name is said to derive from Caribbean English.

Sleepover. A night spent away from home, especially by a child or young person at a friend's house. The practice took a commercial turn when in the late 1990s the Science Museum, London, organized a 'Science Sleepover' for groups of young visitors, who after attending a series of workshops and lectures were allowed to sleep in the museum following a picnic feast.

Slick Willie. A nickname given to Bill Clinton, also known as COMEBACK KID, by George Bush (b.1924), his unsuccessful Republican rival in the 1992 US presidential election. Since then, Clinton has proved himself as slick as TEFLON.

Slingback. A type of woman's shoe fashionable from the 1940s, so called because it is held in place by a strap ('sling') around the ankle above the heel.

> [Actress Jennifer] Aniston swept the glam stakes in a multi-petticoated, black satin dress, black-and-white pointed sling-backs and an over-the-arm granny bag.
>
> *heat* (20–26 January 2000)

Slipped disc. An anatomical misnomer dating from the 1950s for a disorder of the spine properly known as disc prolapse, in which an intervertebral disc ruptures and part of its pulpy core protrudes, causing pressure on a nerve and pain in the back. The condition, most frequently experienced in the lumbar region, became almost fashionable for a time.

Slippery slope. A risky course of action. The image is of traversing a slithery hillside, where one is in danger of losing one's footing and sliding to the bottom. The expression dates from the 1950s. The two words are often associated in sense but quite unrelated in origin.

Sloane Ranger. A young upper class or upper-middle class person who is disciplined, well mannered and speaks educated English. Sloanes (or Sloanies) are conservative in dress, the women having no freakish hair styles and the men being clean-shaven. The women wear expensive but informal country clothes and the men the attire of a city gentleman or country squire, those in town living around Sloane Square, Holland Park and Kensington. The term was coined in October 1975 by Martina Margetts, a sub-editor on *Harpers and Queen*, and was taken up by the magazine's style editor Peter York (real name Peter Wallis). The name puns on LONE RANGER. The *Official Sloane Ranger Handbook* (1982) by Ann Barr and Peter York elaborated the theme. *See also* PREPPY.

Sloppy Joe. An American colloquialism dating from the 1940s for three different objects: (1) a long, loose sweater or pullover worn by women; (2) a dish made from minced meat cooked in a barbecue sauce and spread on an open bun; (3) a multi-layer sandwich filled with meats, cheeses and mayonnaise. The two lavish comestibles are difficult to eat without getting the fingers and face messy, so essentially justify their name.

Slow burn. An American term dating from the 1930s for gradually increasing anger, as distinct from a sudden outburst of rage. It was associated with the 'Slow Burn Man', the comedian Edward 'Killer' Kennedy.

Slow learner. One of a number of euphemisms for a school pupil of below-average intelligence. This one dates from the 1930s.

Smack on the wrist. *See* SLAP ON THE WRIST.

Small Back Room, The. A suspense novel (1943) by Nigel Balchin (1908–70) about a disabled bomb-disposal expert in the Second World War whose efficiency and nerve are eroded by drink, emotional problems and bureaucracy. It draws on Balchin's experience as a psychologist in the War Office, and as deputy scientific adviser to the Army Council, with the rank of brigadier. The title echoes Lord Beaverbrook's famous speech about BACKROOM BOYS. A film version (1949) was directed by Michael Powell and Emeric Pressburger.

Small but perfectly formed. Said of someone or something noticeably small but compensating for this by a perfection of quality. The phrase occurs in a letter written in October 1914 by the Conservative MP and diplomat Duff Cooper to Lady Diana Manners, later his wife, and quoted in Artemis Cooper's *Durable Fire* (1983): 'Your two stout lovers frowning at one another across the hearth rug, while your small, but perfectly

formed one kept the party in a roar.' The expression was probably not original to Cooper but drawn from the fashionable talk of the period. The usage is often tongue-in-cheek or journalistically formulaic for anything small.

> Small but perfectly formed, a miniature fruit fly has been created by Swiss scientists.
>
> *The Times* (25 September 1999)

Small is beautiful. A phrase popularized by the German-born British economist E.F. Schumacher in the title of his book subtitled 'A Study of Economics as if People Mattered' (1973). The concept is of opposition to large-scale institutions, bureaucratic centralization, expansionist businesses and all that is blind to the human scale. It does not necessarily follow that small is always beautiful. *See also* BLACK IS BEAUTIFUL; SMALL BUT PERFECTLY FORMED.

Small print. *See* FINE PRINT.

Smart bomb. A type of radio- or laser-guided bomb that can accurately home on a target. It is 'smart' because it is seemingly intelligent. The general public awareness of such weapons arose from media descriptions of their deployment in the second GULF WAR, although the bomb itself dates from the 1970s. *See also* BRILLIANT PEBBLES; SMART CARD.

Smart card. A plastic card (*see* PLASTIC) with a built-in microprocessor, holding personal data or financial information and thus able to serve as an IDENTITY CARD. It dates from the 1980s.

Smash-and-grab raid. A directly descriptive phrase of the 1920s for a robbery in which the thief smashes a shop window and grabs some of the objects on display. A later development, evolving partly as a result of the deterrent presented by toughened glass, was the RAM RAID.

Smear campaign. An attempt to ruin a person's reputation by slander or vilification. The expression dates from the 1930s, with 'smear' in the sense of a unpleasant mark that 'sticks'.

Smersh. The popular name for the Soviet counter-espionage organization responsible for maintaining security within the Soviet armed and intelligence services during the Second World War. It was created in 1941 by Lavrenty Beria as an agency of the NKVD (*see* KGB) and from 1943 to 1946 functioned as a separate agency directly under STALIN. An organization known as Smersh also features as the 'baddies' in some of Ian Fleming's novels about James BOND. The name is a shortening of Russian *smert' shpionam*, 'death to spies'.

Smiley, George. The British intelligence chief who features in various novels by John Le Carré, beginning with *Call for the Dead* (1961) and *A Murder of Quality* (1962). He plays a relatively small part in Le Carré's early spy stories, *The Spy Who Came in From the Cold* (1963) and *The Looking Glass War* (1965) but comes to the fore in TINKER, TAILOR, SOLDIER, SPY (1974) and its immediate sequels, *The Honourable Schoolboy* (1977) and *Smiley's People* (1980), in the last of which his deadly enemy is a Russian master-spy known as Karla. The novels raised Smiley to a cult figure appropriate to the age of the CAMBRIDGE SPY RING. In the television version of *Tinker, Tailor, Soldier, Spy* (1979) Smiley was played with great subtlety by Alec Guinness, who again took the role in *Smiley's People* (1982).

> Smiley is his [Le Carré's] best known and best loved character because he is a still point in the turn-around world, a figure of stability amid so much that is confused and provisional.
> BLAKE MORRISON in *Times Literary Supplement* (11 April 1986)

Smiley face. A circular smiling yellow face, with a curve for the smile and two dots for the eyes, and originating in the youth culture of the 1970s as an international symbol of hope, peace or solidarity. The face can also be created on a computer keyboard using punctuation marks, and is used in this form in E-MAIL, when it appears sideways. Its basic form is :-), denoting that the writer is pleased or joking. There are many variants, such as ;-) to denote lasciviousness and 0:-) for innocence. The symbol is also known as an emoticon (from 'emotion' and 'icon').

Smith Square. A name for the leadership of the Conservative Party, and formerly also for that of the LABOUR PARTY. It is that of the square in Westminster, London, where the Conservative Party has had its headquarters since 1958 and where the Labour Party was also based from 1928 to 1980, when it moved to Walworth Road. *See also* TRANSPORT HOUSE.

Smog. A linguistic and literal blend of smoke and fog, as an insidious form of polluted air. The word appears to have been first used in 1905 by H.A. des Vœux of the Coal Smoke Abatement Society to describe atmospheric conditions over British towns. It was

popularized by his report to the Manchester conference of the Society in 1911 on the many deaths caused by the pall that paralyzed Glasgow and Edinburgh during the autumn of 1909. The dense smoke-laden fogs that afflicted London and other major cities in the 1950s and 1960s are now a thing of the past, but they have been succeeded by the so called 'summertime smogs' and 'wintertime smogs' periodically produced by emissions from the growing number of motor vehicles. Measures to control pollution of this type as well as that resulting from industrial processes have had some success but the nuisance has still not been reduced to acceptable levels, let alone abolished.

Smoke and mirrors. An explanation or evincement that is essentially misleading. The allusion is to the smoke and mirrors used by conjurors in order to create an illusion.

> When confronted with the sort of fiscal numbers that [Chancellor of the Exchequer] Gordon Brown laid out last week, professional cynics are bound to search high and low for the catch. Has it been done with smoke and mirrors?
> *The Times* (15 November 1999)

Smoke-filled room. A room filled with tobacco smoke from which political leaders emerge with a decision after long hours of discussion or bargaining. The original smoke-filled room was a suite in the Blackstone Hotel, Chicago, in which Warren Harding was selected as the Republican presidential candidate in June 1920. The phrase itself appears to have come from a comment by Harding's chief supporter, Harry Daugherty, that the meeting would not be able to decide between the two obvious candidates and that a group of bleary-eyed senators would 'sit down about two o'clock in the morning around a table in a smoke-filled room in some hotel and decide the nomination'. That was what actually happened, and Warren Harding was duly selected. The smoke in this instance was probably emitted by cigars. *See also* BEER AND SANDWICHES.

> The House of Lords, that last redoubt of smoke-filled rooms and political incorrectness, has rejected demands for a smoking ban throughout its precincts.
> *The Times* (11 May 1999)

Smokestack industries. An American term dating from the 1970s for the heavy manufacturing industries, especially when coal-powered and associated with high levels of pollution and old-fashioned technology.

Smokey Bear. An American nickname for a policeman, especially a state highway patrol officer. The allusion is to the broad-brimmed ranger's hat worn by such officers, resembling that worn by Smokey Bear, an animal character used in American fire-prevention campaigns. The familiar poster figure, with ranger hat, blue jeans and shovel, was created in 1944 by the US Forest Service. There was also a real bear of this name, found in 1950 as a badly burned cub in the Lincoln National Forest, New Mexico, after a five-day fire. He was nursed back to health, adopted by the Forest Service, and taken to Washington, D.C., where he became one of the most popular inhabitants of the National Zoo. He died in 1976 and was buried in the Smokey Bear National Park at Capitan, New Mexico, near the site where he had been originally found.

Smoking gun. A piece of incontrovertible incriminating evidence. The allusion is to a gun that has obviously only just been fired after being used to commit a crime. The expression is particularly applied to the incriminating tape of 23 June 1973 in the WATERGATE affair, on which President Nixon can be heard approving a plan to direct the CIA to request that the FBI halt its investigation into the source of the cash possessed by the Watergate burglars and into the 'silence' money promised them by the administration. Nixon would almost certainly not have been threatened with impeachment if the tape had remained undiscovered.

Smokin' Joe. A nickname for the heavyweight boxer Joe Frazier (b.1944), winner of the 'fight of the century' against Muhammad Ali in 1971 (when he became the first boxer to defeat Ali in a professional fight) and possessor of a ferociously powerful punch. The name has sometimes been applied to the great West Indian batsman Viv Richards (Isaac Alexander Vivian Richards; b.1952), because of his brooding demeanour and powerful batting style. *See also* THRILLER IN MANILA.

Smorgasbord (Swedish, 'bread and butter table'). A Swedish-style range of open sandwiches and delicacies served as hors d'oeuvres or a buffet. The term dates from the 1920s and gained a figurative sense for any wide range or variety, whether of things or people.

> But what really stands out are the women, a smorgasbord of international female talent.
> *heat* (23–29 September 1999)

Smurfs. These blue pixies with white stocking caps were created by the Belgian illustrator Pierre 'Peyo' Culliford and first appeared in the comic *Le Journal de Spirou* in 1958. They came before a wider public in the late 1970s, when they featured in a series of promotions by British Petroleum, and the peak of their popularity was in 1982. Their name varied in different countries. To the French they were *les Schtroumpfs*, to the Germans *die Schlümpfe*, to the Dutch *de smurfen*, to the Spanish *los Pitufos*, to the Italians *i Puffi*, to the Czechs *Šmoulové* and to the Finns *Smurffit*.

Snail mail. A jocular term for conventional mail, which is by its very nature slower than E-MAIL.

Snake. A former nickname for the European Monetary System (EMS), inaugurated in 1979, under which the exchange rates of the currencies of member nations fluctuate within certain limits. The name derived from the earlier 'snake in the tunnel', or narrow fluctuation in rates of exchange agreed by the SIX and countries awaiting EEC membership, so called by contrast with the wider range of fluctuation in the foreign exchange markets.

Snake eyes. A throw of two at dice, regarded as unlucky. The two white dots suggest the eyes of a snake about to strike.

Snakes and ladders. A favourite board game among children, evolving at the turn of the 20th century from an Indian game called *moksha patamu* ('heaven and hell', literally 'salvation by flight'), used as a means of religious instruction. The board is divided into 100 numbered squares and decorated with snakes and ladders running respectively from a higher number to a lower and vice versa. A counter landing at the foot of a ladder thus takes the player nearer to the finish, while one landing on the head of snake is a setback or reversal. The symbolism is vaguely biblical, the ladder going up to heaven and the snake representing a 'fall'.

Snap out of it! Pull yourself together! Cheer up! An exhortation to a person to quit their mood of depression or despair and revert to normal. The expression dates from the 1920s.

Snatch squad. A group of personnel trained to operate as a unit in riot control by identifying ringleaders and arresting ('snatching') them. The technique was first used by the army in Northern Ireland in the early 1970s (*see* TROUBLES) and was later adopted by the police generally.

Sneak preview. The screening of a film in advance of its general release to test audience reaction. More generally a sneak preview is an advance sighting of any forthcoming work or event, as the viewing of a new car model before it is officially revealed.

> For a sneak preview of Barbie's big break, watch out for the behind-the-scenes special *Andi Meets Toy Story 2 ...* on Channel 4.
>
> *The Times* (4 December 1999)

Snettisham treasure. A ploughman working near this Norfolk village in 1948 turned up a metal object that his foreman pronounced to be a bit of brass bedstead. It turned out to be a gold torque and the beginning of the discovery of the richest Iron Age hoard in Britain. Further finds were made over the years, that in 1991 yielding a treasure trove of 1st-century BC Celtic coins. The location of the hoard is a mystery, as there is no sign of any contemporary settlement.

Snoopy. The day-dreaming beagle first appeared in Charles M. Schulz's comic strip *Peanuts* in 1950. He is Charlie Brown's dog, and although he never speaks, he makes up for it by his endless dreams of glory, enacting in his imagination roles that will make him world famous. *See also* HAPPINESS IS A WARM PUPPY.

Snowball's chance in hell. No chance at all. The phrase is usually found in the negative, as: 'He doesn't have a snowball's chance in hell of passing.' The expression dates from the 1950s. *See also* TILL HELL FREEZES OVER.

Snow bunny. Skiers' slang for an inexperienced female skier or alternatively for an attractive young woman who frequents ski slopes.

Snow Goose, The. A novella (1941) by the US writer Paul Gallico (1897–1976). It is a love story, in which a goose flies over the rescue craft at the evacuation of the Allied troops from DUNKIRK in 1940.

Snow job. A deception or concealment of one's real motive in an attempt to flatter or persuade. The image is of an object concealed under innocent-looking snow. The expression arose among American GIs in the Second World War, when it was typically applied to an elaborate fiction presented to a superior officer with the aim of excusing some misdemeanour.

SNP. The Scottish National Party, a left-of-centre political party that evolved from the National Party of Scotland formed in 1928 by Hugh MacDiarmid and others. The name was changed in 1934 when it merged with the Scottish Party, a rival nationalist party foun-

ded two years earlier. It has had mixed fortunes in elections but has consistently campaigned for the establishment of an independent Scottish parliament, a goal finally achieved in 1999. *See also* PLAID CYMRU; TARTAN TORIES.

Snuff movie. A pornographic film supposedly recording the actual death of one of the participants. The genuineness of such films remains in doubt. 'To snuff it' is a 19th-century colloquialism meaning 'to die', in allusion to the sudden extinction of life, like a snuffed candle.

Soames, Enoch. The would-be decadent poet who is the hero of a short story in Max Beerbohm's *Seven Men* (1919), set in the 1890s. He is the author of *Negations*, of which the first line runs, 'Lean near to life. Lean very near – nearer', of a second book of poems called *Fungoids*, and of a third, whose title Beerbohm forgets. Soames is depressed by the failure of people to recognize his genius but consoles himself with the thought that he will be appreciated by posterity. He enters into a pact with the Devil that he will travel ahead in time to visit the Reading Room of the British Museum on 3 June 1997 and look up the sources on him there. On visiting the Museum, however, he finds nothing but a reference in a literary history by one T.K. Nupton, in a reformed spelling, to a story in which Beerbohm 'pautraid an immajnary karrakter kauld "Enoch Soames"'. He surrenders to the Devil with a final cry of despair to Beerbohm, 'Try, *try* to make them know that I did exist!' The arrival of the actual day was awaited with interest. Beerbohm's story was dramatized by the BBC, Soames's haunts were revisited, and an actor impersonating him was sent to the British Library, although it was now in the process of abandoning its Reading Room. An Enoch Soames Society was founded and 3 June was declared Enoch Soames Day.

Soap opera. A term for a sentimental type of play, usually in serial form, as originally used by commercial radio and television in advertising soap and other commodities. Such programmes were sponsored by soap manufacturers as an early form of PRODUCT PLACEMENT, perhaps because they were obviously 'clean'. Radio producers then nicknamed the plays 'soaps', and when they were taken up by television, 'opera' was added as a humorous allusion to their increasingly 'heavy' content.

Noted British soap operas of the 1990s apart from CORONATION STREET and the high-rating EASTENDERS are *Brookside* (first screened 1982), set on a private housing estate in Liverpool, and *Emmerdale* (1972), centring on a Yorkshire Dales farm. Australian soaps include *Home and Away* (1988), set in a fictional seaside town, and *Neighbours* (1985), located in Ramsay Street in the fictional Melbourne suburb of Erinsborough, the latter's name being a near anagram of the title. *See also* ANGELS.

Sob sister. A now dated nickname for a female journalist who writes the answers to readers' personal problems, so called because of the tear-provoking sentimentality involved. The expression dates from the early years of the 20th century.

Sob story. An explanation, especially an excuse, that plays on the emotions. The phrase dates from the early 20th century and presumably represents a reaction to Victorian sentimentality. *See also* USHER IN VIOLINS.

Sob stuff. A phrase describing newspaper, film or other stories of a highly sentimental kind, otherwise cheap or tear-jerking pathos.

Socceroos. The nickname of the Australian international soccer team, as a blend of 'soccer' and ''roo', the colloquial abbreviation of 'kangaroo'.

Social chapter. The part of the MAASTRICHT TREATY that dealt with social policy, and in particular workers' rights and welfare, and that among other points recommended a minimum wage. Its basis was the so called social charter, signed in December 1989 by 11 EUROPEAN UNION member states.

Social Credit. An economic theory introduced by the Scottish engineer Clifford Douglas (1879–1952), according to which consumer spending power should be increased either by subsiding producers so that they can lower prices or by distributing the profits of industry to consumers. Most economists doubted the efficacy of such a system, but a Social Credit Party in Alberta, Canada, won state elections there in 1935 and subsequently.

Socialist realism. A term used to describe the official artistic doctrine adopted by the Congress of Soviet Writers in 1924 and approved by STALIN, Gorky, Bukharin and Zhdanov. It required the creative artist to serve the Revolution by presenting images of socialist possibility and enterprise, and condemned the bourgeois artist, together with all forms of experimentalism and formalism, as degenerate and pessimistic. The works of James Joyce (*see* ULYSSES) were singled out for particular denigration.

Socionyms. Such may be called the acronyms, mainly of American origin, devised by marketing men from the 1980s to designate particular social groups, especially from the point of view of age, income, marital status and professional placing. The designations were originally those of aspirational young people, the so-called YUPPIES, climbing the ladder of fame and fortune, but the emphasis then shifted to the older groups, who at the end of the 1990s in Britain were the fastest growing and potentially most profitable categories. The acronyms themselves were often evocative, and ranged from the factual to the facetious, the latter punningly devised for the purpose. A selection of some of the better known is given below.

DING: double income, no girlfriend (typically a professional sportsman with a regular job)

DINK: double income, no kids

DINKY: double income, no kids – yet

DUMP: downwardly mobile urban middle-class professional

GLAM: grey, leisured, affluent middle class

PIPPY: person inheriting parents' property

SINBAD: single income, no boyfriend and desperate

SITCOM: single income, two children, oppressive mortgage

TRIFFID: three recent infants, falling further into debt

WOOP: well-off older person

YUMP: young upwardly mobile manual person

In the 1980s there were yuppies. In the 1990s, downshifters. Now, there are yetties ... This new American acronym stands for young, entrepreneurial, technology-based. Also dubbed 'entreprenerds' or the 'digerati', yetties are those irritating bright young things who are making a killing on the internet – or trying to.

Sunday Times (20 February 2000)

Sock it to me! Amaze me! Surprise me! Let's hear it! To 'sock' (not related to the garment) is to hit forcefully. The catchphrase was popularized by the American television comedy series ROWAN AND MARTIN'S LAUGH-IN.

Sodom by the Sea. A nickname given to HOLLYWOOD by those who regard it as a den of sexual depravity. The allusion is to Sodom and Gomorrah, the 'cities of the plain' destroyed by God with fire and brimstone 'because their sin is very grievous' (Genesis 18–19).

Sod's law. Essentially the same as MURPHY'S LAW but dating later, from the 1970s. 'Sod' here is simply a name for an awkward or frustrating situation that provokes one to think or say 'Sod it!' Some linguistic legalists discern a fine distinction between the two laws. If a piece of bread lands buttered side down when dropped, they say, that is Sod's law. Murphy's law, on the other hand, dictates that as a piece of bread can land this way, sooner or later it will. Viewed thus, Sod's law can be seen as a corollary of Murphy's law.

> Sod's law is quite specific on the issue. If there is some crisis in 2015, one [aircraft] carrier will be undergoing major refit and the other will be unavailable due to some unplanned eventuality.
>
> *The Times* (Letter to the Editor) (1 December 1999)

Sod this for a game of soldiers. An expression of irritation or exasperation at a situation, especially one that seems pointless or a waste of time. One common variant is: 'Blow this for a lark.'

SOE. The Special Operations Executive, a branch of the British intelligence services in the Second World War that specialized in sending agents to foster and support resistance movements in occupied Europe. SOE was set up in July 1940, and disbanded in 1946. One of its major successes was in helping Tito's communist partisans in Yugoslavia, but its most important theatre was France, where SOE agents worked with the MAQUIS. One of the many SOE agents who died in France was Violette Szabo, whose story is the subject of the 1958 film CARVE HER NAME WITH PRIDE.

Sofa sitcom. A disparaging term for a mild, middle-class, domestic television SITCOM in which the characters mostly exchange banter and humour while sitting around on sofas. Such sitcoms were particularly common from the late 1960s, such as *Father Dear Father* (1968–1973) and *Terry and June* (1979–87), but the term was turned on its head overnight with the screening in the late 1990s of *The* ROYLE FAMILY, in which the sofas essentially epitomize the characters seated on them.

Soft art. A term for sculpture that uses non-rigid materials, such as rope, cloth, leather, paper or canvas. Such works were in vogue in the 1960s and 1970s and an early and influential exponent was the Swedish-born American sculptor Claes Oldenburg (b.1929), famous for giant replicas of foodstuffs such as hamburgers made from stuffed vinyl and canvas.

Soft focus. A slight and deliberate blurring of the focus in a photograph, often used for advertising effect or to tone down an otherwise pornographic image. In a film it may be used to photograph an actress who may not stand up to sharper definition, or to enhance an exotic shot in a musical number. In F.W. Murnau's silent film *Sunrise* (1927) soft focus is used to create a romantic mood, while it evokes nostalgia and idealism in the picnic scene in Arthur Penn's BONNIE AND CLYDE (1967).

Softly-softly. Said of any action that is cautious and patient. The term comes from the quasi-proverb, 'Softly, softly, catchee monkey', recorded in the early years of the 20th century. The present phrase was popularized by the television series *Softly, Softly* (1966–76), about the work of a fictional Midlands crime squad. 'Softly, Softly' is the motto of the Lancashire police. *See also* Z-CARS.

Soft-shoe dance. A form of tap dance performed in soft-soled shoes instead of shoes with metal taps. It first became popular in the United States in the 1920s and one of its most watchable practitioners was the American actor and dancer Ray Bolger (1904–87).

Soft touch. A person who is easily imposed upon, especially to give or lend money. The expression is of American origin and gained currency in the GREAT DEPRESSION.

SoHo. An American acronym of the 1990s for 'small office, home office', meaning the small-business sector of the economy, especially the part of it that is home-based. The spelling with capital 'S' and 'H' derives from SoHo, the nickname of an area in Manhattan, New York City, itself an abbreviation of 'south of Houston Street' and in turn evoking London's Soho.

Soldiers. Strips of bread or toast dipped into a soft-boiled egg, so called as the yolk gives them a yellow 'coat' or uniform. The colloquial term, popular with children, like the breakfast *bonne bouche* itself, dates from the 1960s.

> What better ... than a glorious boiled egg with soldier dipped in yolk, which if started from boiling water will take only four minutes to prepare (toast included).
>
> *The Times* (Letter to the Editor) (28 December 1999)

Solheim Cup. The women's golfing trophy corresponding to the RYDER CUP, awarded to the winners of a biennial match between European professionals and those of the United States. It takes its name from the Norwegian-born American inventor of the Ping putter, Karsten Solheim (1911–2000), who together with his wife Louise first presented it in 1990.

Solidarity. An independent trade union in Poland which evolved into a mass campaign for political change and which lit the touchpaper for sweeping opposition to communist regimes right across central and eastern Europe. It was formed in 1980 under Lech Walesa (b.1943), banned in 1981 following the imposition of martial law, but legalized again in 1989, when it won a majority in elections. Its name translates the Polish original.

Solomon Gursky Was Here. A novel (1989) by the Canadian novelist Mordecai Richler (b.1931). It takes the form of a labyrinthine Jewish family saga through five generations, in which Canadian history (and some notable Canadians) and the innate Jewish ability to stir things up are inventively combined. The title refers to Solomon's apparent death when a Gypsy Moth plane disappears in 1934, during the trial of his two brothers for bootlegging. Or, as Gursky himself says, in a remark prefaced to the narrative: 'Gerald Murphy got it wrong. Living twice, maybe three times, is the best revenge.'

Somebody up there loves me. I am having a good run of luck at the moment. 'Somebody' is God; 'up there' is heaven. The expression is of American origin and dates from the 1960s. *Somebody Up There Likes Me* (1956), starring Paul Newman and Pier Angeli, is a sentimental film based on the life of the boxer Rocky MARCIANO.

Some Like It Hot. A sparkling film comedy (1959), written by Billy Wilder (b.1906) and I.A.L. Diamond (1920–88). Jack Lemmon and Tony Curtis star as two jazz musicians who disguise themselves as women and join an all-girl band in Miami in order to escape the murderous attentions of some gangsters after they accidentally witness the ST VALENTINE'S DAY MASSACRE. The title of the film related as much to the heat of the situation in which the two heroes find themselves as to the 'hot' jazz they like to play. In retrospect, it also came to symbolize aspects of the film that caused it to receive a heated reception in conservative quarters, especially the sensual performance of Marilyn MONROE and the dubious relationship that develops between the disguised Lemmon and a besotted millionaire, played by Joe E. Brown. Brown's character delivers the film's celebrated closing lines,

'Nobody's perfect', on discovering that his fiancée is in fact a man.

There may be a link between the film's title and the 18th-century nursery rhyme 'Pease porridge hot':

Some like it hot
Some like it cold
Some like it in the pot
Nine days old.

Some Mothers Do 'Ave 'Em. A television SITCOM broadcast from 1973 to 1978 and starring Michael Crawford as the well-meaning but disastrously accident-prone wimp Frank Spencer, typically wearing mac and beret. His long-suffering, sympathetic wife, Betty, was played by Michelle Dotrice. Crawford's interpretation of his role as Spencer imbued him with a nature that was as childlike as it was comical, earning him an affectionate place in the public psyche. The title adopted a 1920s catchphrase implying that some mothers seem to have a simpleton for a son.

Some Tame Gazelle. The first novel (1950) by Barbara Pym (1913–80). It is a *roman-à-clef* in that Harriet and Belinda, two spinster sisters, are based on Pym's sister and herself, and other characters on people she knew as an undergraduate at Oxford, represented now in middle age. Both sisters turn down offers of marriage, preferring their known routine to the uncertainties of the married state: 'Some tame gazelle or some gentle dove or even a poodle dog – something to love, that was the point.' The title and the reference are from a song by Thomas Haynes Bayly (1797–1839):

Some tame gazelle, or some gentle dove:
Something to love, oh, something to love!

They also recall the parody by Charles Dickens of lines of Thomas Moore (1779–1852), put into the mouth of Dick Swiveller: 'I never loved a tree or flower, but 'twas the first to fade away; I never nursed a dear Gazelle, to glad me with its soft black eye, but when it came to know me well, and love me, it was sure to marry a market-gardener' (*The Old Curiosity Shop*, ch lvi).

Something else. An exceptional person or thing. The variant 'something else again' is used when a comparison is made with what is already noteworthy.

Getting out of a car is always an ordeal for women in the public eye. When you're heavily pregnant it's something else again.
Sunday Times (6 June 1999)

Something for the weekend. 'Something for the weekend, Sir?' was a supposedly stock question put to a male customer by a barber after a haircut, the 'something' implicitly being a packet of condoms. The euphemistic catchphrase still exists in various contexts and was the title of a spectacularly NAFF television series of 1999 in which members of the public were interviewed about their sex lives and participated in a range of suggestive games and stunts.

> The days when a Friday night visit to the barber's shop ended with the whispered enquiry: 'Anything for the weekend, Sir?' are long past.
> *The Times* (11 August 1999)

Something in the water. 'It must be something in the water' is a humorous way of accounting for the unusual fecundity of a place's population or for any eccentric human or animal behaviour.

> Teachers at High Crags Nursery, West Yorkshire, have to deal daily with five sets of twins in the same class. … Joanne Light, a nursery nurse, said: 'There must be something in the water round here.'
> *The Times* (29 November 1999)

Something nasty in the woodshed. Something shocking or distasteful in a person's past that has been kept secret. The phrase comes from Stella Gibbons's novel COLD COMFORT FARM (1932), in which Aunt Ada Doom's repeated assertion that she had seen 'something nasty in the woodshed' ensures that her family continually attend her. There is a curious echo of the 19th-century 'nigger in the woodpile' although the sense there is of a hidden snag or drawback.

Something of the night. A description of Conservative politician Michael Howard (b.1941) by Anne Widdecombe, who had served under him when he was home secretary (1993–7) in John Major's government. The actual phrase she used, quoted in the *Sunday Times* of 11 May 1997 after the Tory defeat in the 1997 general election, was: 'He has something of the night in him.' *See also* KARLOFF, DORIS.

Something Wicked This Way Comes. A SCIENCE FICTION fantasy (1962) by Ray Bradbury (b.1920). When a circus comes to town, two boys watch an old woman becoming young again and a man's severed leg being put back. The transformations are a deep mystery to them. The title quotes the words of the Second Witch about Macbeth in Shakespeare's *Macbeth*:

> By the pricking of my thumbs
> Something wicked this way comes.
> IV.i

A film version (1983) directed by Jack Clayton presented the original as a grim fairy tale.

Somewhere in X. In the First World War a reference to a locality in the theatre of war could not name it directly for security reasons. It was thus said to be 'somewhere in' a larger region, such as 'somewhere in Flanders', 'somewhere in France'. In the Second World War 'Somewhere in England' was similarly current, and the expression is still in use for any undivulged location.

Somewhere to the right of Genghis Khan. Said of right-wing views of the most extreme kind. Genghis Khan (1162–1227), the founder of the Mongol empire, is generally regarded as the archetype of a repressive and tyrannical ruler.

> Of course, in those days, the union leaders were well to the right of Genghis Khan.
> ARTHUR SCARGILL quoted by John Mortimer in *Sunday Times* (10 January 1982)

Somme. The name of a river and *département* in northern France, notorious in British folk memory as the location of an extended and costly Allied offensive on the WESTERN FRONT in the First World War. Launched on 1 July 1916, the battle dragged on until 18 November. Initially the plan called for the involvement of large numbers of French troops, but with the French army being 'bled white' at VERDUN, the burden fell largely on their British allies, commanded by Sir Douglas Haig (1861–1928). By the time it was launched the operation had become a large-scale diversion, intended not only to gain territory but to drain German manpower.

The offensive took place along a 30-km (18-mile) front running more or less northwards from the River Somme between Amiens and Péronne. Despite a massive preliminary bombardment lasting eight days, the deeply entrenched German defences were left largely intact, as was the barbed wire. On the first day of the attack the British lost 58,000 casualties, a third of them killed, making this the worst day in the history of the British army. By the end of the day nearly all the attackers had been forced back to their own trenches. However, the Allies continued to attack throughout the summer and autumn, and by the time operations were suspended owing to the winter weather, they had gained a maximum of 12km (7 miles).

Total British casualties were 420,000, while the French total was nearly 200,000. The Germans suffered an estimated 500,000, and never really recovered the loss of junior officers and NCOs, in some ways justifying Haig's unimaginative war of attrition. However, the Somme has subsequently become synonymous with senseless slaughter. *See also* THIEP-VAL MEMORIAL; ULSTER VOLUNTEER FORCE.

Son et lumière (French, 'sound and light'). Pageantry and dramatic spectacles presented after dark in an appropriate natural or historic setting, in vogue in Britain during the 1960s, and adopted from enactments of this type at French châteaux such as Chambord. They are accompanied by, and dependent on, lighting effects, suitable music and narrative.

Song in one's heart, A. A feeling of joy or pleasure. The phrase comes from a song by Lorenz Hart in the musical *Spring is Here* (1929).

> With a song in my heart, –
> I behold your adorable face.
> LORENZ HART: 'With a Song in My Heart' (song)

Sonny Jim. *See* SUNNY JIM.

Sony. The consumer electronics company of this name was founded in Tokyo in 1946 by Ibuka Masaru, whose Japan Precision Instruments Company had supplied electronic devices in the Second World War, and Akio Morita, an applied sciences instructor. Their company was called the Tokyo Tsushin Kogyo Kabushiki Kaisha, or Tokyo Telecommunications Engineering Corporation, and clearly a shorter name was desirable. They thought of Latin *sonus*, 'sound', and at first considered adapting this as 'Sonny' or 'Sonny Boy', for homeliness. But 'Sonny' in Japanese would suggest *son-ni*, 'at a loss', so they instead adjusted the spelling to 'Sony', rhyming with 'bony' rather than 'bunny'. *See also* WALKMAN.

Sooner State. A nickname for Oklahoma, which became the 46th state of the USA in 1907. 'Sooners' was already a name for those who endeavoured to get into Government territory in the West before (sooner than) the time appointed for the settlement. This was particularly common in the area now known as Oklahoma before its official opening to settlers on 22 April 1889.

Sooty. A TEDDY BEAR with black ears, manipulated as a glove puppet on children's television by his creator in the 1950s, Harry Corbett, and inherited by his inventor's son, Matthew. Sooty's sidekick was Sweep, a grey spaniel, and the two took a succession of roles in a range of adult locations such as hospitals, law courts,

workshops and gymnasiums. Corbett helped them resolve their problems in these grown-up situations. The mute Sooty whispered 'confidentially' in his ear, while Sweep 'spoke' in staccato yelps. Corbett's endless patience was rewarded by being pelted with various messy missiles and his invariable 'Bye-bye, everybody' was delivered with mournful resignation.

Sophie's Choice. A novel (1979) by the US novelist William Styron (b.1925), a dark story of love and loss. Sophie's choice is not so much between the two men in her life, with one of whom she chooses to commit suicide, but the agonizing experience of having been forced, by a Nazi officer in AUSCHWITZ, to select which of her two children will be taken from her. An honourable film version (1982) was directed by Alan J. Pakula.

Sophie's World. A novel (1995; in Norwegian as *Sofies verden*, 1991), subtitled *A Novel about the History of Philosophy*, by Jostein Gaarder (b.1952). A philosopher guides 14-year-old Sophie Amundsen through a tour of Western philosophy after leaving two questions in her letterbox: 'Who are you?' and 'Where does the world come from?'.

Soroptimists. Members of an international service club for professional and business women, founded in California in 1921 on lines similar to those of the ROTARY CLUB. The name comes from Latin *soror*, 'sister', and the earlier Optimist Club, founded in Buffalo, New York in 1911.

Sort out the men from the boys, To. *See* SEPARATE THE MEN FROM THE BOYS.

SOS. The Morse code signal (3 dots, 3 dashes, 3 dots, · · · – – – · · ·) used by shipping and the like in distress to summon immediate aid, hence any urgent appeal for help. The signal was recommended at the Radio Telegraph Conference in 1906 and officially adopted two years later. It replaced the call 'CQD', standing for 'call to quarters' or 'come quickly', or representing 'seek you' and the initial of 'distress'. The letters are simply a convenient and readily recognizable combination and are not an abbreviation, although they have been held to stand for 'save our souls' or 'save our ship'.

Sosban Fach (Welsh, 'Little Saucepan'). The Welsh rugby song of this name is usually associated with the town of Llanelli, whose civic emblem is a saucepan. The first verse was originally written in 1873 by Richard Davies (1833–77), known by the bardic name of Mynyddog ('Man of the Mountain'), as part of a poem. It was later altered by Talog Williams, an accountant from Dowlais, who added four verses and the chorus, the whole forming a sort of parody of a nursery rhyme or even a nonsense song. Characters mentioned include Meri Ann, Dafydd the servant, Joni Bach and Dai Bach the soldier, although it is not clear what relevance they have, if any, to the story, which involves a boiling saucepan and a crying baby. The tune to which the song is sung, reminiscent of a Welsh hymn, is one of those most frequently heard at rugby matches.

> Lionel Jospin's socialism is popular in Wales: in Llanelli they sing Jospin Fach.
>
> RHODRI MORGAN (Welsh Labour leader) quoted in *The Times* (11 February 2000)

Sot-Weed Factor, The. A novel (1960; revised edition 1967) by John Barth (b.1930). The starting point is Ebenezer Cook's *The Sot-Weed Factor: or, A Voyage to Maryland* (1708), a satirical poem purporting to describe the exploits of an Englishman who comes to America to work as an agent (or factor) for a dealer in sot-weed (tobacco). The novel, which is written in an 18th-century style, reconstructs the activities of the factor and comments on aspects of the poem, with historical and critical digressions.

Soul food. A term dating from the 1960s for food which is traditionally associated with black people in the American South. Typical examples of soul food are hominy, corn breads, black-eyed peas and chitterlings.

Sound and the Fury, The. A novel (1929) by William Faulkner (1897–1962). A tragic family situation, stemming originally from a brother's obsession with his sister, is told from four different points of view, employing STREAM OF CONSCIOUSNESS techniques. The brother's own account suggests:

> a tale
> Told by an idiot, full of sound and fury,
> Signifying nothing.
>
> SHAKESPEARE: *Macbeth* (V.v)

An unimaginative film version (1959) was directed by Martin Ritt.

Sound bite. A short, succinct extract from a recorded interview or speech, used to summarize a stance or policy as part of a news or party political broadcast. Politicians and others now make frequent use of the device to capture the attention of a public too inattentive to respond to anything longer. An example is, 'One million more patients treated annually since NHS reforms,' a (Conservative) government claim of 1994. The expression itself dates from the 1980s.

Sound of Music, The. A musical (1959), with a score by Richard Rodgers (1902–79) and Oscar Hammerstein II (1895–1960) and book by Howard Lindsay (1889–1968) and Russel Crouse (1893–1966), about a postulant nun who becomes governess to the aristocratic Von Trapp family in Austria at the time of the NAZI take-over. Filmed in 1965 with Julie Andrews as Maria, the show was based on *The Trapp Family Singers*, the memoirs of the real Maria Von Trapp, who left Austria in similar circumstances. The title refers not only to Maria's love of music but to the fame of the Trapp family singing troupe she organized with her youthful charges. Such was the success of the show, both on stage and in the cinema, that it acquired cult status, and in the 1990s 'singalong' presentations of the film, with the audience dressing up as members of the cast, proved highly popular.

Sound of silence. A pseudo-poetic term for the stillness and peace found in an isolated or sheltered place, increasingly sought after in the frenetic bustle and stress of the 20th century. The phrase comes from Paul Simon's song 'Sound of Silence' (1964).

Souped-up. Of a car, modified by its owner to produce a higher power or acceleration than it had when it left the manufacturer. The phrase probably derives from 'supercharged', perhaps reinforced by 'soup' as colloquialism for fuel for a powerful motor or for a substance injected into a horse to change its speed or temperament. The expression dates from the 1930s.

Soup run. A periodical delivery of soup or other sustenance to homeless 'street people', undertaken by a members of a charitable organization.

> The Government's new authority on homelessness is to call for an end to soup runs and handouts, arguing that such help encourages people to sleep rough rather than find a permanent home and job.
>
> *The Times* (15 November 1999)

South Bank. A stretch of the Thames in London across the river from the Victoria Embankment, from Westminster Bridge to London Bridge. It was the site of the FESTIVAL OF BRITAIN, held on derelict land here in 1951, and now extends eastwards from the South Bank Centre, a composite of venues devoted to the arts, including the Royal Festival Hall, Queen Elizabeth Hall, Purcell Room, Hayward Gallery, National

Theatre and National Film Theatre. More recent buildings are the Tate Modern Gallery in the disused Bankside power station, the new Globe Theatre and, at the western end, south of COUNTY HALL, the London Aquarium. In the 1980s the South Bank gained notoriety as a 'home for the homeless' in CARDBOARD CITY. *See also* BRUTALISM.

South Bank religion. A journalistic label for the religious activities in the diocese of Southwark in London, south of the Thames. It was associated with Mervyn Stockwood, bishop of Southwark (1959–80), John Robinson, Suffragan Bishop of Woolwich (1959–69), author of *Honest to God* (1963), and some of their diocesan clergy. Characterized by outspokenness on moral and political issues, often from a socialist angle, and energetic attempts to bring the Church into closer relation with contemporary society and its problems, South Bank religion was not without its critics and the label was often applied disparagingly by opponents. *See also* SOUTH BANK.

> That is rather the new idea inside the Church. I should definitely say you were a South Banker.
> AUBERON WAUGH: *Consider the Lilies*, ch ix (1968)

South Ken. A familiar name of South Kensington, London, famous on the one hand as MUSEUMLAND and on the other for its fashionable shops and residences.

South Pacific. A musical (1949), with a score by Richard Rodgers (1902–79) and Oscar Hammerstein II (1895–1960) and book by Hammerstein and Joshua Logan (1908–88), about a US Navy nurse who falls in love with a French planter while stationed on a South Pacific island. The plot was based on 'Fo' Dolla', a story from James A. Michener's *Tales of the South Pacific* (1947), combined with 'Our Heroine', another story from the same collection, about a US lieutenant's love for a Polynesian girl.

South Park. A scatological and surreal American television cartoon series first screened in 1998 and featuring four anything-but-cute kids from South Park, Colorado: Waspy Stan, a permanently hooded and regularly killed Kenny, a fiendish fat boy Eric Cartman, and a mixed-up Jew, Kyle. The vivid language ensured a late-night scheduling on most networks but did not prevent the series from becoming a predictable playground hit.

South Pole. The South Pole was first reached by a Norwegian expedition under Roald Amundsen (1872–1928) on 14 December 1911. A party led by Captain Robert Falcon Scott ('Scott of the Antarctic'; 1868–1912) reached the Pole on 17 January 1912, only to discover that Amundsen had beaten them to it. All members of Scott's party perished in appalling weather conditions on the return journey to their ship, the *Terra Nova*. The deaths of Scott and his companions were quickly mythologized as the epitome of selfless heroism, and extracts from Scott's journals (published in 1913) cited as matchless statements of British pluck in adversity: 'Had we lived, I should have a tale to tell of the hardihood, endurance and courage of my companions which would have stirred the hearts of every Englishman. These rough notes and our dead bodies must tell the tale.' Scott is now generally seen as having made errors of planning that made the demise of his expedition inevitable, notably his reliance on horses rather than teams of dogs.

A 1948 film, *Scott of the Antarctic* (starring John Mills as Captain Scott), in what was clearly a piece of propagandist fable-making tailored to the austerity of postwar Britain, reinvents the expedition as a moving tale of the integration of different social classes. A television adaptation of Roland Huntsford's *Scott and Amundsen* (1979) depicted Scott as an Edwardian amateur and representative of a class-ridden British 'Establishment', defeated in the race for the South Pole by a group of efficient, 'classless' Norwegians. *See also* BIRTHDAY BOYS; I MAY BE SOME TIME; NORTH POLE.

South Riding. A regional novel (1936) by Winifred Holtby (1898–1935), finished a month before its author's death from kidney cancer, which had been diagnosed in 1932. The complexities and conflicts of local government are explored, and the characters of those involved in the decision-making revealed. South Riding is a fictional creation, but has affinities with the East Riding of Yorkshire, where Holtby was born and brought up. A satisfying film version (1937) was directed by Victor Saville.

Soviet calendar. Somewhat on the lines of the French Republican calendar of 1793–1806, a rationalized, secular calendar was introduced in the Soviet Union on 1 October 1929. Each month was allocated 30 days, with five extra days as national holidays: LENIN Day following 30 January, two Workers' First of May days after 30 April, and two Industry Days after 7 November (the day of the 1917 Revolution in the New Style calendar). In a leap year 30 February was to be followed by Leap Day. The seven-day week was replaced by a five-day cycle from Monday to Friday, and each day was a rest day for one-fifth of the population, symbolized by a slip in one of five colours, yellow, pink, red, purple and green, given to each citizen. The national holidays remained outside the cycle. The aim was not only to combine personal leisure with continuous industrial production but also to disrupt religious observance. The Western months were restored from 1 December 1931 but with a six-day week of five working days followed by a rest day on the 6th, 12th, 18th, 24th and (except in February) 30th of the month. The 31st was outside the cycle. This system was in turn abandoned on 26 June 1940, supposedly to increase production but in fact because the peasantry had sabotaged the new system by taking Sundays off as well as the new free days. The old weekdays had meanwhile never really been forgotten, even in official documents.

Soviet sayings. As one of the world's major geographical and political systems to rise, flourish and fall within the historical parameters of the 20th century (1918–91), the Soviet Union saw the creation of a number of catchphrases, slogans, Leninisms and propagandistic precepts that became familiar to most Russians. They are less familiar in the West, however, and by way of preserving their memory, but not necessarily endorsing their message, a selection is offered below.

Attacking class: a metaphor for the ideal revolutionary class in its spearhead role in bourgeois society, from Vladimir Mayakovsky's poem *Vladimir Ilyich Lenin* (1924).

At the top of one's voice: a phrase to emphasize the force, rightness or frankness of a saying or action, from the title of a poem of 1930 by Vladimir Mayakovsky.

Broad is my native land: the first line of the chorus of the 'Song of the Motherland' from the film *The Circus* (1936), alluding to the vastness of the Soviet Union. The musical notes accompanying the words were used by Moscow Radio as a call sign for its foreign broadcasts.

Communism is Soviet power plus the electrification of the whole country: LENIN's famous practical definition of communism, from his report to the 8th party congress of 1920.

Dr Ouch-It-Hurts: a children's nickname for a doctor, from Korney Chukovsky's children's verses of 1929, in the original Russian *Aybolit*, from *ay*, 'ouch!', and *bolit*, 'it hurts'.

Dress rehearsal for the October Revolution: LENIN's term in his *'Left Wing' Communism: An Infantile Disorder* (1920) for the First Russian Revolution (1905–6), which opened with BLOODY SUNDAY (1).

Great initiative: a name for the enterprise of the communist *subbotniki* (*see* Red Saturday *below*), from the title of a tract by Lenin published in 1919.

How the steel was tempered: a metaphor for the moulding of the ideal Soviet citizen, from the title of Nikolay Ostrovsky's novel of 1932–4, telling how the young worker Pavel Korchagin fights for his country in the Civil War and becomes a Komsomol (Communist Youth League) leader.

In the name of man, for the good of man: a phrase encapsulating communist aims for Soviet society. A phrase from the Communist Party Programme of 1961.

My universities: the title of Maxim Gorky's autobiographical novel of 1923, telling of the SCHOOL OF HARD KNOCKS that in his youth shaped him as an adult.

Nobody is forgotten and nothing is forgotten: a tribute to the fallen of the Second World War, or in Soviet terms, the GREAT PATRIOTIC WAR (1941–5). The words, by Olga Berggoltz, are engraved on the main memorial at the Piskarev Cemetery, St Petersburg, the burial place of Leningraders who lost their lives in the blockade of 1941–3 and of troops killed on the Leningrad front during the war, some 470,000 in all.

Path to life, A: the title of Nikolay Ekk's highly praised film of 1931 about the communal re-education of homeless orphans left after the OCTOBER REVOLUTION and the Civil War (1917–21). The term was adopted for any 'gateway' to a person's career or future generally.

Red Saturday: A specified Saturday when young workers known as *subbotniki* (from *subbota*, 'Saturday') undertook voluntary unpaid work as part of the Great Initiative (*see above*).

Road through purgatory: a metaphor for the difficulties of life, sometimes used jocularly for difficulties that are really negligible. The words form the title of Aleksey Tolstoy's trilogy of 1920–42, a study of Russian intellectuals converting to the BOLSHEVIK cause in the Civil War. The title itself derives from the old religious story of the Virgin Mary's visit to Hell.

Scarlet sails: an expression of the romantic and ambitious dreams of youth, from the title of a novel of 1923 by Alexander Grin.

State is us, The: a term from LENIN's report of the Communist Party Congress of 1922, as a reminder that ultimately the effectiveness and authority of the state depend on each of its individual members. The statement paraphrases Louis XIV's famous *L'état, c'est moi* (1651).

Story of a real man, The: the title of a novel of 1946 by Boris Polevoy about the exploits of a Soviet airforce pilot in the Second World War. The words came to be used for any story of heroic deeds.

Study, study and study: *see* EDUCATION, EDUCATION, EDUCATION.

Tempest-born, The: the title of a novel of 1934–6 by Nikolay Ostrovsky about young revolutionaries battling to establish Soviet rule in the Ukraine in the 1920s. The phrase was used for members of the Komsomol (Communist Youth League) born then and for the YOUNG GUARD subsequently.

What is good and what is bad: the title of a poem of 1925 for children by Vladimir Mayakovsky, as applied to a situation where the positive must be distinguished from the negative. The words were often applied humorously or trivially, since their source in a children's poem was well known.

Your mother country calls you!: a patriotic slogan on a poster of 1941, at the start of the GREAT PATRIOTIC WAR, calling Soviet citizens to fight for their homeland against the enemy.

SP. In racing terminology, starting price, meaning the final odds at the start of a horse race. Hence from the 1950s the more general sense 'information', 'facts'.

'So I'm showin' this Pakistani all the catalogues and givin' him the full SP and he's noddin' away at me.'
DERMOT BOLGER (ed.): *Finbar's Hotel*, 'The Test' (1997)

Space age. The age of space exploration, generally regarded as beginning on 4 October 1957 with the launch of SPUTNIK 1, the world's first artificial satellite, but foreseen by scientists and visualized by fantasists long before this.

Space cadet. An eccentric person, especially one who seems permanently 'high' on drugs. The phrase dates from the 1970s and may have its origin in the 1950s US television programme *Tom Corbett, Space Cadet*, which showed the adventures of a group of teenage cadets at a futuristic space academy, regarded as

being 'far out'. The term is also used for a real drug addict. *See also* GOVERNOR MOONBEAM.

Spaced out. 'High' on drugs. The imagery is of one 'flying' in space, or perhaps of a person whose regular chain of existence has been broken by blanks and 'spaces'. The expression arose in the HIPPIE counter-culture of the SWINGING SIXTIES. *See also* SPACE CADET.

Space Invaders. An animated computer game of the late 1970s, in which players attempt to defend themselves against a fleet of enemy spaceships. No pun appears to be intended on the expression 'to invade someone's space', meaning to encroach on their personal way of life.

Space Oddity. The title of an album and song by David Bowie first released in 1969. The song concerns an astronaut who is so disillusioned by what he sees on earth that he decides to stay in space. The title puns on Stanley Kubrick's film 2001: A SPACE ODYSSEY, which also concerns an astronaut lost in space. The song was re-released in 1975, when it reached number one in the charts in Britain.

Space opera. A genre of unsophisticated science-fiction adventure stories, films and TV series involving spacemen, rockets and LITTLE GREEN MEN. FLASH GORDON is a classic of the genre. The term is modelled on SOAP OPERA and HORSE OPERA.

Spaceship Earth. A name for the planet Earth and its inhabitants regarded as a spacecraft and its passengers, who depend on its resources to survive. The concept dates from the 1970s and was popularized by the US inventor and environmentalist R. Buckminster Fuller (1895–1983) in his book *Operating Manual for Spaceship Earth* (1969).

We also demonstrate our respect for 'spaceship earth', the concept of accepting that there are limitations on the world's resources and that their use is a matter of common international concern. The more enlightened oil exporters, by the way, endorse 'spaceship earth' themselves.
Manchester Guardian Weekly (8 May 1977)

Spaghetti Junction. The nickname of the Gravelly Hill Interchange, the junction between the M1 and M6 motorways near Birmingham, where the many winding and intersecting roads, underpasses and overpasses bear a fanciful resemblance to spaghetti. It was opened in 1971.

Spaghetti western. A dismissive name for the Italian imitations of American WESTERN films that became popular in the 1960s, using such actors as Lee Van Cleef and Clint Eastwood. They gained an international repute, and in the process made Eastwood a star through the work of Sergio Leone, beginning with his *A* FISTFUL OF DOLLARS (1964), in which the actor plays an avenging stranger who cleans up a Mexican border town. The genre had lost much of its impact by the early 1970s. The name alludes to the Italian fondness for spaghetti. *See also* MAN WITH NO NAME.

Spam. (1) The tradename of a tinned meat product, first marketed in the United States by George A. Hormel & Co. in 1937. A competition was held for a neat name for the new product and the $100 prize was won by the entry 'Spam', standing for 'spiced ham'.

(2) More recently spam has become computer jargon for inappropriate or unwanted messages sent by E-MAIL on the INTERNET, the equivalent of 'junk mail' in standard postal terms. The term apparently derives from a sketch in the television comedy series MONTY PYTHON'S FLYING CIRCUS in which every item on the menu in a café is Spam. The nuisance grew steadily in the 1990s.

> Spam leaves nasty taste for Net users.
> *The Times* (headline) (22 April 1999)

Spandau. A prison in the Spandau district of Berlin that after 1946 was used to incarcerate Nazi war criminals. Among the prisoners was Albert Speer (1905–81), Hitler's architect (*see* CATHEDRAL OF LIGHT), who was released in 1966. After 1966 the sole inmate was Rudolf Hess (1894–1987), Hitler's deputy, who died in the prison, according to some in suspicious circumstances. Spandau Ballet was the name of a 1980s pop group. *See under* ROCK GROUP NAMES.

Spanish flu. A misnomer for the influenza pandemic of 1918, the worst in history, in which some 21 million people died. The outbreak did not begin in Spain but received its name simply because a news agency in Madrid issued the first uncensored wartime report of its existence. The epicentre was in fact probably South China, as it was for the Asian flu epidemic of 1957, the Hong Kong influenza epidemic of 1968, and the outbreak in 1997 of a strain of avian influenza among the human population of Hong Kong.

Spanner in the works. Something that prevents the successful implementation of a task; a 'spoke in one's wheel'. The suggestion is of a person who deliberately throws a spanner into smooth-running machinery in order to stall it. John Lennon's *A Spaniard in the*

Works (1965) was a bestselling collection of stories and drawings.

Spare someone's blushes, To. To avoid embarrassing them by praise.

Spare tyre. A roll of fat round the midriff, especially as a consequence of MIDDLE-AGE SPREAD. It is 'spare' because it is additional to the body, like the extra tyre carried around by a car in case of a puncture.

Sparrow units or **squads.** Small guerrilla squads in the Philippines. They arose in the 1980s as militant communist activists, conducting attacks on policemen, government ministers and other persons in authority. Their name alludes to their rapid 'in-and-out' tactics.

Spartacists. An extreme socialist group in Germany that flourished between 1916 and 1919. It was founded by Karl Liebknecht (1871–1919) who, with Rosa Luxemburg (1871–1919), led an attempted revolution in January of the latter year, in the suppression of which they were both killed. The movement was finally crushed by Friedrich Ebert's government in April. It took its name from the Thracian gladiator, Spartacus, who in 73 BC led a slave rebellion against Rome, which was not suppressed until 71 BC. During the uprising he defeated five Roman armies and devastated whole tracts of Italy.

Speakeasy. A place where alcoholic liquors are sold illegally. A US term widely current in the years of PROHIBITION. 'Easy' here means 'softly', and the name refers either to the fact that such places were spoken about quietly or that people spoke quietly in them, to avoid attracting the attention of police or neighbours. *See also* CAPONE, AL.

Speakers' Corner. A small area near Marble Arch in the northeast corner of Hyde Park, London, where a motley band of speakers holds forth every Sunday. The name is relatively recent but the practice dates from 1855, when a large crowd gathered here to protest against Lord Robert Grosvenor's Sunday Trading Bill. There was no right of assembly then but it was granted in 1872 and anyone may now indulge in soapbox oratory on any subject they choose, so long as it is not obscene or blasphemous, or does not constitute an incitement to a breach of the peace. By the end of the 20th century most of the speakers were religious extremists. In 1999 the Home Secretary, Jack Straw, announced his intention to set up 'speakers' corners' in more than 250 British towns. Straw himself became something of an outdoor orator, frequently setting up his soapbox outside Marks & Spencer in his Blackburn constituency. *See also* BUGHOUSE SQUARE.

> Speakers' Corner is a mixed grill of apostles and propagators, of oddities and crudities, of fanatics and eccentrics.
>
> J.C. GOODWIN: *One of the Crowd*, ch xix (1936)

Spear-carrier. An actor with a walk-on part. Hence any minor participant in a group effort.

Speccy-built. Said of a house built as a speculative investment, chiefly through its favourable siting.

> The green belt is being encroached upon by 'speccy-built' houses.
>
> *Sunday Times* (Letter to the Editor) (24 October 1999)

Special needs. An educational euphemism for children who have particular requirements at school because they are physically disabled, emotionally disturbed or have 'learning difficulties'. The phrase can also be taken as implying that such children are 'special'. *See also* STATEMENTED.

> I realized she'd picked up on the phrase 'special needs' and she liked that. So, we've gone from the word 'mongol' to 'mentally handicapped' to 'special' – and I think that's about right.
>
> *Sunday Times Magazine* (30 May 1999)

Special Operations Executive. *See* SOE.

Special relationship. The relationship between Britain and the United States, regarded as particularly close in terms of common origin and language. The term is associated with Winston Churchill, who in the House of Commons on 7 November 1945 declared that 'we should not abandon our special relationship with the United States and Canada'.

Spectator sport. A sport such as football that provides as much entertainment and excitement for the spectators as it does for the players. The phrase is of US origin and dates from the 1940s.

> The reduction of politics to a spectator sport ... has been one of the more malign accomplishments of television.
>
> J.K. GALBRAITH: *A Life in Our Times* (1981)

Speed merchant. Anyone who moves fast, as a driver, runner, bowler, pitcher, swimmer or the like.

Spelvin, George. *See* PLINGE, WALTER.

Spencer, Frank. *See* SOME MOTHERS DO 'AVE 'EM.

Spend a penny, To. To urinate. The allusion is to the door lock on a cubicle in a public lavatory, which in the pre-decimal era was opened by inserting a penny (1d). *See also* PENNY DROPPED.

Spice Girls. A phenomenally popular British pop group of the late 1990s. Taking their name from an early song 'Sugar and Spice', the five young women released their first single in 1996 and were instantly nicknamed. Emma Bunton was 'Baby Spice' for her innocent air and youth, Victoria Adams was 'Posh Spice' for her aloof demeanour and designer clothes, Melanie Brown ('Mel B') was 'Scary Spice' for her spiky hair and BODY PIERCING, Melanie Chisholm ('Mel C') was 'Sporty Spice' for her keep-fit interests and sports gear, and Geraldine Halliwell ('Geri') was 'Ginger Spice' for her hair colour. The lives and loves of the women were long a titillating topic of interest to the media, and Adams's marriage to the glamorous footballer David Beckham in 1999 was a gaudy social event.

> The nickname 'Scary', of course, is an oblique way of saying 'black'. She is no more 'scary' than Victoria Adams is 'posh'.
>
> *The Times* (12 June 1999)

Spiderman. A comic strip hero of the 1960s, the creation of scriptwriter Stan Lee and artist Steve Ditko. His real name is Peter Parker, who as a youth had been bitten by a mutant spider and acquired its characteristics. He has great strength, can climb almost anything, especially New York skyscrapers, and pursues villains with a 'webshooter'. His costume, which extends to a face mask, is a red and blue uniform decorated with black webbing.

Spill the beans, To. To divulge information, especially under pressure or unintentionally. The allusion is to vomiting, as when one is urged to 'cough it up' or 'spit it out'. The expression is of US origin and dates from the early 20th century.

Spin, To. To give a news story a particular slant, in the manner of a SPIN DOCTOR. The past tense of this verb is normally 'spun' but the archaic form 'span' is frequently found in the media.

> They span she was exhausted, they span she'd no eye for detail. ... She span back.
>
> *The Times* (28 July 1999)

Spin doctor. An expression originating in the United States in the mid-1980s to refer to a politician or public relations expert employed to give a favourable interpretation of events to the media. Its origin is in baseball, from the spin put on the ball by a pitcher to make it go in the desired direction. The idiom later passed into British usage.

> The spin doctors, the PR [public relations] generals, argued after Reykjavik talks that Reagan still stands by Star Wars and within reach. The White House's primary target was opinion-makers in Washington and New York, but a special spin patrol will descend on 15 other cities this week.
>
> *Newsweek* (27 October 1986)

Spion Kop. *See* KOP.

Spirit of St Louis. The aeroplane in which Charles A. LINDBERGH made the first nonstop solo flight from New York to Paris on 20–21 May 1927, taking 33 hours 33 minutes. The plane was a single-engine high-wing monoplane, adapted by Lindbergh so that the space normally used for four passengers was occupied by fuel tanks, and was named in tribute to the St Louis businessmen who had financed its construction. The plane is now in the Smithsonian Institution in Washington, D.C.

Spit-and-sawdust. Said of a run-down or dirty pub or bar. The allusion is to the sawdust formerly strewn on the floor of the general bar of a public house and to the spitting of drinkers onto it.

Spitting Image. A satirical television series screened from 1984 to 1996, in which famous people in British and international life were re-created in the form of latex puppets which, in the manner of political cartoons, exaggerated the particular person's most obvious physical features or personality characteristics. Each programme consisted of a series of witty topical sketches, the voices of the unseen actors often providing uncannily convincing versions of those portrayed. The series specifically lampooned politicians, foreign heads of state and media personalities, and even the British royal family were not spared. The creators of the puppets were the model-makers Peter Fluck and Roger Law, whose effigies of politicians had earlier appeared in the press.

The title puns on 'spitting image' as a term for an exact likeness (as if one person is 'spit' by another), the 'spitting' being the satire and the 'image' the programme itself.

Spiv. A man, typically flashily dressed, who makes his living by disreputable dealings. The slang term came to the fore in the Second World War with reference to black market negotiations, but it undoubtedly dates from much earlier. Its origin is problematic, but it may

be related in some way to 'spiffing'. Popular theories derive it from a reversal of 'VIPs' (very important persons) or from a police abbreviation for 'suspected person and itinerant vagrant'. *See also* WIDE BOY.

Splash out, To. To spend money extravagantly or ostentatiously. The image is of emptying a bucket of water in a single throw. The expression dates from the 1930s.

> If you really want to indulge yourself, why not splash out and buy a copy of Marilyn Monroe's autopsy report … from Fraser's Autographs?
>
> *The Times* (5 January 2000)

Splatter movie. A genre of film in which characters die in a violent or gruesome manner. The allusion is to the physical disintegration of bodies, which appear to be splattered across the screen. The first film to earn the title was *The* TEXAS CHAINSAW MASSACRE (1974). Aspects of the genre were parodied in Quentin Tarantino's highly lauded PULP FICTION (1994). *See also* SLASHER MOVIE.

Spock, Dr. The popular name of the US paediatrician Benjamin Spock (1903–98), author of the influential bestseller *The Common Sense Book of Baby and Child Care* (1946), which challenged traditional methods of child-rearing by telling parents to follow their instincts instead of imposing set routines and rigorous discipline. His name became a literal household word in the art of parenting. *See also* SPOCK-MARKED.

> A single woman, even if she is a file clerk, moves in the world of men. … Her world is a far more colorful world than the one of P.T.A., Dr Spock and the jammed clothes dryer.
>
> HELEN GURLEY BROWN: *Sex and the Single Girl* (1962)

Spock, Mr. The impassive, pointed-eared member of the Starship *Enterprise* played by Leonard Nimoy in the cult US television series STAR TREK. He became the most famous character of the series, and featured prominently in the books that were based on it.

Spock-marked. A punning colloquialism, based on 'pock-marked', for a baby felt to be hampered rather than helped by an upbringing based on the recommendations of Dr SPOCK.

Spoiler. In journalism a news story or other newspaper item published to spoil the impact of a related item published in another paper. The usual way of doing this is to present it 'bigger and better', and if possible sooner, with a more detailed text coverage and a greater number of photos.

Spoonerism. A form of metathesis that consists of transposing the initial sounds of words so as to form some ludicrous combination, often the accidental result of mental tiredness or absentmindedness. It is so called from the Rev. W.A. Spooner (1844–1930), Warden of New College, Oxford. Some of the best (but possibly apocryphal) attributed to him are: 'We all know what it is to have a half-warmed fish within us' (for 'half-formed wish'). 'Yes, indeed; the Lord is a shoving leopard', and 'Kinkering Kongs their titles take'. Sometimes the term is applied to the accidental transposition of whole words, as when the teashop waitress was asked for 'a glass bun and a bath of milk'. This sort of spoonerism can lend itself to deliberate word play, as when Oscar Wilde said, 'Work is the curse of the drinking classes' (quoted in Hesketh Pearson, *Life of Oscar Wilde*, ch xii; 1946). The word itself is first recorded in 1900 but was colloquially current at Oxford for some years before this.

Sporting nicknames. Many sportsmen and women have acquired nicknames, some more flattering than others. A selection is included here.

Air Jordan: the basketball player Michael Jordan (b.1963), reflecting his legendary jumping ability

AMBLING ALP

Anfield Iron: the footballer Tommy Smith (b.1945), a 'hard man' in the Liverpool sides of the 1960s and 1970s

BABE

Baby-faced Assassin: the Norwegian and Manchester United footballer Ole Gunnar Soljskaer (b.1973), in recognition of his youthful appearance and goal-scoring ability

BANDITO

BARNACLE BAILEY

BEEFY

Big Bill: the tall and imposing US tennis player Bill Tilden (1893–1953), a leading player of the 1920s; *see also* LITTLE BILL

Big Bird: the Barbados, West Indies and Somerset cricketer Joel Garner (b.1952), a towering fast bowler who stood 2m (6ft 9in) tall

BIG MAN

BIG O

BIG TRAIN

Bites Yer Legs: the Leeds United and England footballer Norman Hunter (b.1943), so called for his fearsome tackling

BLACK BRADMAN

Black Diamond: the Brazilian footballer Leonidas (Leonidas da Silva; b.1913); *see also* BRAZILIAN FOOTBALLERS

Black Octopus or **Black Spider:** the footballer Lev Yashin (1929–90), a mobile-limbed goalkeeper for Moscow Dynamo and the Soviet Union in the 1950s and 1960s

Black Panther: *see* EUROPEAN PELÉ

BLACK PEARL

Blockbuster: *see* BROCKTON BOMBER

BOUNDING BASQUE

BROCKTON BOMBER

BROWN BOMBER

BRYLCREEM BOY

CANNIBAL

Cannonball Kid: the US tennis player Roscoe Tanner (b.1951), famous for his fast serves

CAPTAIN MARVEL

CAT

CHARIOTS OFFIAH

Chin: the English footballer, club manager and commentator Jimmy Hill (b.1928), so called for his very prominent lower jaw

Chopper: the hard-tackling Chelsea footballer Ron Harris (b.1944), a much-feared member of the successful Chelsea sides of the 1960s and 1970s

Clones Cyclone: the fast-punching Irish boxer Barry McGuigan (b.1961), born in Clones, Co. Monaghan, in the Republic of Ireland

Crafty Cockney: Eric Bristow (b.1957), a London-born darts player who was the most skilful and successful exponent of the sport during its high noon of popularity in the 1980s

CROUCHER

DEADLY DEREK

DIVINO

DON

DR J

Durable Dane: the Copenhagen-born US lightweight boxer Oscar Nelson (born Oscar Nielsen; 1882–1954), famed for his ability to take punches

Electric Eel or **Electric Heel:** the Blackpool, Hull City, Southampton and England footballer Stan Mortensen (1922–91), a forward of slippery skill

EUROPEAN PELÉ

FEARSOME FOURSOME

FIERY FRED

Flo-Jo: the flamboyant US sprinter Florence Griffith Joyner (née Delorez Florence Griffith; 1959–98), winner of the 100m and 200m at the 1988 Olympics and famous for her colourful attire and long, painted fingernails

FLYING FINN

FOUR MUSKETEERS

Galloping Major: the Hungarian footballer Ferenc Puskás (b.1927), a fast-paced inside-forward, so named for the rank he held in the Hungarian army

GAZZA

GENERAL

GENTLE GIANT

GODFATHER

GORGEOUS GUSSIE

Governor General: the cricketer Charles Macartney (1886–1958), an authoritative strokemaking batsman for New South Wales and Australia

Great One: the Canadian ice hockey player Wayne Gretzky (b.1961), Canada's greatest ever goal scorer

Great White Shark: the Australian golfer Greg Norman (b.1955), one of the best players of the 1980s and 1990s, so named for his striking blonde hair

HIT MAN

HOMICIDE HANK

HUNT THE SHUNT

Hurricane: the Northern Irish snooker player Alex Higgins (b.1949), so called because of the phenomenal speed of his potting

Iron Gloves: an unflattering nickname applied to the record-breaking Australian wicketkeeper Rodney Marsh (b.1947) during the early part of his career, when catches often seemed to bounce straight out of his gloves

Iron Mike: the US heavyweight boxer Mike Tyson (b.1966), a brutally powerful puncher and the youngest ever world heavyweight champion, notorious as much for his activities outside the boxing ring, including a prison term for rape, as for his boxing prowess

JOLTIN' JOE

J.P.R.: the Welsh rugby union fullback J.P.R. Williams (John Peter Rhys Williams; b.1949)

KAISER

KING

KING KENNY

King of East Anglia: the football club manager Bobby Robson (b.1933), so called for his successful period as manager of Ipswich during which the team won the FA Cup (1978) and the UEFA Cup (1981)

Little Bill: the US tennis player William Johnson (1894–1946), who lost six times to BIG BILL Tilden in US championship finals

Little Miss Poker Face: the US tennis player Helen Wills Moody (1905–98), so called for her lack of any display of emotion on court

LITTLE MO

Livermore Larruper: the US heavyweight boxer Max Bauer (1909–59), who was known as much for his fast-paced lifestyle as for his powerful punching; 'larrup' is a slang term meaning to beat or thrash

Lloyd George of Welsh Football: *see* WELSH WIZARD

Lord Ted: the Sussex and England cricketer Ted Dexter (b.1935), a powerful stroke-making batsman of aristocratic bearing at the wicket

Magic Johnson: the US basketball player born Earvin Johnson (b.1959), one of the greatest all-round players in history

Manster: the US football player Randy White (b.1953), a strong defensive tackler; the name is a portmanteau word combining 'man' and 'monster'

MARADONA OF THE CARPATHIANS

MASTER

Marvelous Marvin: the US middleweight boxer Marvin Hagler (b.1952) who was so enamoured of this nickname that he had his name legally changed to 'Marvelous Marvin Hagler'

MIDDLESEX TWINS

Michigan Assassin: the US middleweight boxer Stanley Ketchel (born Stanislaus Kiecal; 1886–1910), who was born in Grand Rapids, Michigan

Mighty Mouse: the English footballer Kevin Keegan (b.1951), the leading forward of his generation and so called for the power and energy of his game, which belied his relatively small size

Multiple Mac: the US field athlete Mac Wilkins (b.1950), who threw the discus, javelin and hammer, as well as throwing the shot

Nugget: the Australian cricketer Keith Miller (b.1919), a dynamic all-rounder who formed a fearsome new-ball partnership with Ray Lindwall (1921–96)

Orchid Man: the French light-heavyweight boxer Georges Carpentier (1894–1975), so called because of his debonair appearance

Pistol Pete: (1) the US basketball player Pete Maravich (1947–88); (2) the US tennis player Pete Sampras (b.1971)

Preston Plumber: the footballer Tom Finney (b.1922), a fleet-footed winger for Preston North End and England, who ran a plumbing business both during and after his career as a professional footballer

Psycho: the footballer Stuart Pearce (b.1962), a 'hard man' in defence for Nottingham Forest and England

RANJI

ROCKHAMPTON ROCKET

ROCKY

Rumble of Thunder: the Italian footballer Luigi Riva (b.1944), a prolific goalscorer with Legnano, Cagliari and Italy

Shoeless Joe: the US baseball star Joe Jackson (1887–1951); *see also* BLACK SOX SCANDAL; SAY IT AIN'T SO, JOE

Sicknote: the Tottenham Hotspur and England footballer Darren Anderton (b.1972), who has the reputation of missing games through injury

SMOKIN' JOE

SUGAR RAY ROBINSON

TARMAC

THOMMO

THREE WS

Tich Freeman: the Kent and England leg-spinner Alfred Freeman (1888–1965), who stood just 1.57m (5ft 2in) tall

Tiger O'Reilly: the Australian cricketer Bill O'Reilly (1905–92), an aggressive bowler of leg-breaks and googlies in the 1930s and 1940s

Toey Tayfield: the South African cricketer Hugh Tayfield (1929–94), an off-spin bowler who earned his nickname from his habit of grinding his toe into the ground before each ball that he bowled

Tylerstown Terror: the Welsh flyweight boxer Jimmy Wilde (1892–1969), who was born in Tylerstown, Wales, and the power of whose punching belied his diminutive size

Typhoon Tyson: the Northamptonshire and England cricketer Frank Tyson (b.1930), a fast bowler of lightning pace

Vaulting Vicar: the US pole vaulter Bob Richards (b.1926), who was ordained as a minister in 1948

WELSH WIZARD

W.G.

WHISPERING DEATH

WHITE PELÉ

Wor Jackie: the footballer Jackie Milburn (1924–88), a star with Newcastle United and England in the 1940s and 1950s; Wor Jackie is a Geordie rendition of 'Our Jackie'

Yifter the Shifter: the Ethiopian middle-distance runner Miruts Yifter (b.1944), winner of the 5000m and 10,000m at the 1980 Olympic Games

See also BEAUTIFUL GAME.

Spot the ball. A type of weekly competition run by some newspapers and FOOTBALL POOLS companies. For a small fee, the competitor is given a photograph of a football game from which the ball has been erased and places a cross where he judges or guesses its original position to have been. The winner is the entrant who places the cross closest to the centre of the ball. In 1975 a levy was placed on spot-the-ball competitions operated by pools companies in order to finance the Football Grounds Improvement Trust and later the Football Trust.

Spotting. A technique among ballet dancers to prevent giddiness while turning. It consists in fixing one's eyes on a spot in the auditorium or the wings for as long as possible to ensure one's sense of orientation. Hence the frequent frozen look on the face of a twirling dancer.

Spratt, Sir Lancelot. The senior surgeon at St Swithin's general hospital in the series of humorous novels by Richard Gordon, beginning with *Doctor in the House* (1952). He is a 'surgeon of the grand old school' referred to behind his back as 'that bloody old butcher'. He is said to have earned his knighthood by performing 'a small but essential operation on a cabinet minister that allowed him to take his seat in the House with greater ease'. He does not feature in the second novel of the series, *Doctor at Sea* (1953), but reappears in the later volumes. He was played with extrovert panache by the red-bearded actor James Robertson Justice in the films based on the books, starting with *Doctor in the House* (1954).

Spread betting. A form of betting popular in the 1990s in which the amount of money won or lost depends on the degree to which a score or result in a sporting contest exceeds or falls short of a level decided by the gambler. Such betting is particularly suited to football. If the bookmakers thus offer the time of Manchester United scoring their first goal against Sheffield Wednesday as between 14 minutes and 20 minutes, and the gambler thinks they will score before 14 minutes, he will 'buy' the spread. If he puts £10 on this, and the first goal is in fact scored in the ninth minute, he will win £50. But if he 'sells' the spread, betting that the goal will be later, he will lose £50.

Spreadsheet. In computer jargon a program used chiefly for accounting, in which figures arranged in the rows and columns of a grid can be manipulated and used in calculations. The term dates from the early 1980s.

Spring chicken. A young person. The phrase is usually found in the negative, as: 'She's no spring chicken.' The implication is that she has reached an age when she is no longer a chick. A spring chicken is a young fowl ready for eating, which was originally in the spring. The expression is of US origin and dates from the early years of the 20th century.

Spud-bashing. Potato-peeling, especially when done in a lengthy session. The term dates from the Second World War and is associated with army routine and JANKERS. *See also* SQUARE-BASHING.

Sputnik (Russian, 'fellow traveller'). The Soviet artificial satellite, Sputnik 1, was launched on 4 October 1957 as the first of its kind to be projected successfully into orbit around the earth. Achieving an apogee of 942km (548 miles) and a perigee of 230km (143 miles), it circled the earth every 96 minutes and remained in orbit until early 1958. Sputnik 2, launched on 3 November 1957, carried the dog Laika ('Barker'), the first living creature to be shot into space and orbit the earth. *See also* FELLOW TRAVELLER; SPACE AGE.

Spycatcher trial. A legal case of 1986 in which the British government sought to suppress publication of the book *Spycatcher*, an account by Peter Wright (1916–95), then living in Australia, of his experiences as a senior MI5 officer. The course of justice hardly ran smoothly. The Cabinet Secretary, Sir Robert Armstrong, was obliged to apologize to the Australian court for unintentionally giving misleading evidence (*see* ECONOMICAL WITH THE TRUTH), while in 1987 contempt proceedings were brought against the *Sunday Times* for publishing extracts from the book. The bid to ban Wright's memoirs ended ignominiously in 1988.

Spy in the cab. A term for a tachograph, as an instrument that makes a record of engine speed over a period in a commercial road vehicle. The device has been resented by many lorry drivers, even though in recording their driving hours it is designed to enhance their productivity and efficiency.

Spy in the sky. A nickname dating from the COLD WAR for a satellite or aircraft used to gather military intelligence.

Squander bug. A symbol of reckless extravagance and waste, familiar in Britain in the Second World War from a series of publicity campaigns promoted by the National Savings Committee to encourage economy. It was graphically portrayed as an evil-looking insect.

Square. A slang term for a person who is not in with current trends or fashions and is hence old-fashioned. There are several suggestions for the origin of the term, none of which is particularly convincing. One explanation derives the word from a JAZZ musician's and standard conductor's hand gesture that beats out a regular rhythm, the hand describing a square figure in the air. The term originated in black American slang and has been current from the 1940s. *See also* L7.

> [Actor] Joseph Fiennes was voted Britain's most stylish man. He laughs when I bring this up. 'Actually, I'm a bit of a square,' he says. This is not false modesty. He *is* a bit of a square. The look he's wearing today ... is more 80s than new millennium man.
> *heat* (20–26 January 2000)

Square-bashing. Army drill on a parade ground, when one bashes the ground with one's boots. The term dates from the Second World War.

Square Deal. Theodore Roosevelt succeeded to the US presidency in 1901 and the following year used this term for his personal approach to current social problems and the individual. At its core was the ideal of peaceful coexistence between big business and labour unions. The concept was subsequently incorporated into the platform of the Progressive Party when Roosevelt was its presidential candidate in 1912.

Square-eyed. Affected by or given to watching too much television, as if to make one's eyes the same shape as the screen. A light-hearted phrase dating from the 1960s.

Squarial. A square dish aerial for receiving satellite television broadcasts. They enjoyed a brief moment of fame at the end of the 1980s but production ceased in 1990 when the company that manufactured them, British Satellite Broadcasting, merged with Sky Television.

Squeaky clean. Above criticism; beyond reproach. The suggestion is of the squeaking of one's shoes when walking over a newly washed floor or of one's finger when rubbed over a clean glass. Army sergeant majors sometimes demand that boots be highly polished so that they squeak when worn.

> The Labour Party insisted that the dinner was a legitimate event. A spokesman said: 'We have been at pains to make sure these functions are all open and above board. We are squeaky clean.'
> *The Times* (29 September 1999)

Squeegee merchant. A person with a squeegee (a rubber-edged blade on a handle) who willy-nilly cleans the windscreen of a car stopped in traffic and demands payment from the driver. The ploy arose in American downtown streets in the 1980s. The second word can vary and the importuners are often simply referred to as 'squeegees'.

> This one-time left-wing student radical [Jack Straw] was now calling for the streets to be reclaimed from aggressive 'winos, addicts, and squeegee merchants' (September 1995).
> JANE PEEL in *The BBC News General Election Guide* (1997)

Squeeze play. A US term dating from the early 20th century for a situation in which one must apply force or pressure to get what one wants. The allusion is to a baseball tactic in which the runner on third base breaks for home plate (dashes to the base by the batter) while the batter himself bunts (helps him by tapping the ball gently so that it does not roll beyond the infield).

Squeeze someone until the pips squeak, To. To exact the maximum payment from them. The expression originated in a speech on 10 December 1918 at the Beaconsfield Club, Cambridge, by Sir Eric Geddes, First Lord of the Admiralty and Unionist MP for Cambridge, with reference to Germany's indemnity after the First World War.

> Sir Eric said: The Germans, if this Government is returned, are going to pay every penny; they are going to be squeezed as a lemon is squeezed – until the pips squeak. My only doubt is not whether we can squeeze hard enough, but whether there is enough juice.
> *Cambridge Daily News* (11 December 1918)

Squiffites. The supporters of the Liberal politician H.H. Asquith, OLD SQUIFFY, after he had been ousted from the premiership by fellow Liberal David Lloyd George, the WELSH WIZARD, in December 1916. The Squiffites were at odds with the rest of the Liberal Party until Asquith resigned as party leader in 1926. The split marked the terminal decline of the Liberal Party's fortunes.

Squillions. A very large number. The word emerged in the 1940s as a fanciful form of 'millions', 'billions', 'trillions' and the like, perhaps with the idea of one of these 'squared'. *See also* ZILLIONS.

> Squillions of steaming wet people squeeze into a space the size of my kitchen.
> *Evening Standard* (27 September 1999)

SS (German *Schutzstaffel*, 'protection squad'). An armed force that originated as part of Hitler's bodyguard in 1925, two years after the formation of the SA, to which it was initially subordinate. In 1929 Heinrich Himmler took on the SS and defining its duties as 'to find out, to fight and to destroy all open and secret enemies of the FÜHRER, the National Socialist Movement, and our racial resurrection', raised it to a position of power and great numerical strength. During the Second World War, SS divisions fought with fanatical zeal. The sleek black uniforms of the SS men earned them the name BLACKSHIRTS and made them feel superior to the Brownshirts (*see* SA). *See also* ABWEHR; NIGHT OF THE LONG KNIVES; WAFFEN SS.

Stab in the back. A treacherous act. The expression dates only from the early years of the 20th century but the image is ancient and popularly applies to the conspiratorial assassination of Julius Caesar on 15 March (the Ides of March) 44 BC.

> Not for him [John Major] the swagger of some other prime ministerial memoirs; nor the stab-in-the-back beloved of Sunday newspaper serializations.
> *The Times* (12 October 1999)

Stack up, To. To measure up; to compare; to make sense. The allusion is to piling up one's chips in a game of poker.

Stadium of Light. The impressive home ground of Sunderland Football Club, built in 1997 on the site of the former Wearmouth Colliery, which closed in 1993, as the largest all-seater stadium in Britain since the Second World War. Its name was not adopted from Benfica's ESTÁDIO DA LUZ but reflects both the Davy lamps worn by the miners of old and the desire of the club to be in the limelight and to serve as a beacon in the world of football. The ground is also close to the National Glass Centre, suggesting a further association with light. There is also a practical realization, for the whole stadium is illuminated every evening from twilight to midnight as a symbol of the regeneration of Sunderland itself. The name remained a secret until it was unveiled by the club's directors at a midnight news conference on 29 July 1997. The new stadium has provided STATE-OF-THE-ART pre-match entertainment for its spectators, and before the home side's Division One match against Portsmouth on 21 March 1998 the Northern Symphony Orchestra played music from Prokofiev's ballet *Romeo and Juliet* complete with a troupe of dancers.

Stagecoach. A WESTERN film (1939) directed by John Ford and starring John Wayne, set in a stagecoach making its way through hostile American Indian territory. The film rises above the conventional Western thanks to the excellence of the characterization of the seven individuals brought together in the stagecoach. The scenery of Arizona's Monument Valley adds much to the visual excitement of the film, which is based on a short story, 'Stage to Lordsburg', by Ernest Haycox.

> The basic western, a template for everything that followed.
>
> JOHN BAXTER (1968), quoted in *Halliwell's Film & Video Guide* (1999)

Stage-door Johnny. A man who hangs around stage doors to waylay actresses as they leave.

Stag night. A festive gathering of men only, especially on the eve of a wedding, the guest of honour then being the groom. *See also* HEN NIGHT.

Stairway to Heaven. An eight-minute acoustic-meets-HEAVY METAL anthem by the rock group Led Zeppelin. It appeared on the album *Led Zeppelin IV*, released in 1971. The song's obscurely Tolkienesque and metaphor-laden lyrics are, according to one's viewpoint, insufferably pretentious or excitingly and allusively ambiguous ('Sometimes words have two meanings', sings Robert Plant).

Bizarrely, the song was a top ten single for the Australian entertainer Rolf Harris in the 1990s. Harris had responded to an invitation to singers from the Australian alternative comedy show *The Money or the Gun* to perform the song in any way they wanted. *See also* ROCK GROUP NAMES.

Stake-out. A period of police surveillance over a defined area, as if one marked out with stakes.

Stakhanovite. In the former USSR a worker whose productivity exceeds the norm and who thus earns special privileges and rewards. The name is that of Aleksei Grigoryevich Stakhanov (1906–77), a Donbass coalminer who substantially increased his daily output by rationalization. His record output was 102 tons of coal in a 5¾ hour night shift on 30 August 1935, 14 times the norm. That same year STALIN held a conference of Stakhanovites in which he extolled the working man.

Stalin. The Soviet leader, who succeeded LENIN as head of the Communist Party, was born Iosif Vissarionovich Dzhugashvili (1879–1953), his surname being Georgian in origin. He adopted his well-known party name in 1913, from Russian *stal'*, 'steel', perhaps originally to indicate his unbroken spirit after repeated arrest, banishment and imprisonment. He had various other pen-names, including Soso, Koba (a short form of Yakoba, the name of a Georgian fictional patriotic hero), David, Nizheradze, Chizhikov and Ivanovich. *See also* UNCLE JOE.

Stalingrad. Formerly Tsaritsyn, on the Volga, renamed in 1925 to commemorate its defence by Stalin, in 1917, against the WHITE RUSSIANS. Stalin died in 1953 and in 1961 the name was changed to Volgograd. In 1943 it was the scene of the decisive defeat of the German 6th Army, a turning point of the Second World War. The ferocious battle for Stalingrad had begun in August 1942, with the Germans in the ascendant. In November, however, the Soviets launched 'Operation Uranus', encircling and trapping the German 6th Army which finally surrendered on 31 January 1943. The horrors of the battle were graphically recreated in Antony Beevor's best-selling book *Stalingrad* (1997).

Stalking. The following or pestering of a person, especially a celebrity, with whom the follower has become obsessed. The obsession may climax in violence to the victim. Although stalking has been recognized as an unpleasant fact of famous lives, most cases involve ordinary people who have fallen out with a partner, colleague or friend. The phenomenon became prominent in the 1990s.

Stalking horse. Originally in the 16th century a screen made in the shape of a horse behind which a hunter took concealment when stalking prey, the term later came to apply to any false pretext that concealed a person's true intention and specifically from the late 1980s to a candidate in an election for the leadership of a political party who stands simply in order to provoke the election and so allow a stronger candidate to come forward. Thus in 1999 Calum Miller was put forward as a 'stalking horse' to test the strength of the opposition in an election to replace Alex Salmond as leader of the SNP. In 1989 the media described Sir Anthony Meyer as the 'stalking donkey' in the first Conservative leadership challenge against Margaret Thatcher.

Stamping ground. A place where one regularly spends time; a favourite haunt; one's home territory or area of operation. The phrase originally referred to a location frequented by animals.

Stand-off. An uneasy deadlock or impasse, when each of two sides 'stands off' the other.

> Trouble erupted across Northern Ireland last night after security forces blocked the biggest Drumcree parade in its 191-year history and hundreds of Orangemen embarked on a stand-off that could last weeks.
>
> *The Times* (6 July 1998)

Stand on someone's shoulders, To. To base one's beliefs or principles on those of a successor. The image is of a person raised to greater heights by standing on the shoulders of another.

> [Karl Marx] came closer to foreseeing the 20th century than any of his contemporaries, and some of the best of his successors, such as Shaw and Wells, were standing on his shoulders.
>
> *The Times* (20 December 1999)

Stand up and be counted, To. To make one's presence known and one's views felt, often at some risk to oneself. The image is of rising to one's feet at a meeting when a count of supporters for a controversial motion is taken. The phrase is of US origin and dates from the early years of the 20th century.

Stand-up comedy. Comedy in the form of jokes told by a comedian standing on stage before an audience. The term dates from the 1960s, when comedians of this type first became familiar on television, although they were long familiar before this in the music hall. Examples of 20th-century stand-up comedians are Max Bygraves, Frankie Howerd and Ken Dodd, each of whom early found the knack of holding his audience in the hollow of his hand with his particular brand of humour.

Starsky and Hutch. A pair of US plain-clothes policemen, with the full names Dave Starsky and Ken Hutchinson, played by dark-haired Paul Michael Glaser and blond David Soul in the successful and popular television series named after them (1976–81). They spend much of the time jumping in and out of fast cars with squealing tyres in an unidentified US city that is presumed to be Los Angeles, on a mission to put ne'er-do-wells behind bars.

START. The Strategic Arms Reduction Talks that evolved from SALT. The first negotiations between the United States and the Soviet Union were in 1982. The Intermediate Nuclear Forces (INF) treaty was signed as a result in 1987, and the Strategic Arms Reduction Treaty in 1991. The talks continued after the disintegration of the Soviet Union in the latter year.

Starter home. A house or flat designed to suit a young couple or family buying their first home. The implication is that it is a start, and that they will move on to something bigger and better a few years later. There may also be a secondary allusion to their wish to start a family.

Star Trek. The cult US space fiction television series, first screened in 1966 and set in the future, tells how the crew of the Starship *Enterprise* reconnoitre the universe, finding monsters and mysteries at every turn. The best known crew member is Mr SPOCK, the Starship's first officer, and others include Captain Kirk (played by William Shatner) and Captain Picard (Patrick Stewart). The creator of the whole series was Gene Roddenberry (1921–91). Its many fans, or 'Trekkers' (earlier 'Trekkies'), express their rapturous devotion in conventions in both America and Britain, and eagerly await the latest Star Trek book, film or CD. In 1995 Paramount Pictures chose a fourth Star Trek series, *Voyager*, as the flagship programme of its new network, UPN, and in 1996 the eighth Star Trek movie, *First Contact*, was released.

> The five-year mission of the Enterprise has evolved into the 20th century's very own version of the quest myth – an epic story to rival the epic poetry of the Greeks.
>
> *Sunday Times* (12 February 1995)

Start-rite. The children's shoes so named evolved in 1921 as a patent design of the firm of Henry Quant and Son of Bury St Edmunds. The patent was later sold to James Smith of Norwich. The well-known advertisement depicting the Start-rite twins walking hand in hand down a long, tree-lined road dates from 1947 and was suggested by Rudyard Kipling's own illustration for his story 'The Cat that Walked by Himself' in the JUST SO STORIES (1902).

Star Wars. (1) The Strategic Defense Initiative (SDI) of the United States, first adumbrated by President Reagan in 1983 as a means of defending the United States against attack from Soviet intercontinental ballistic missiles (ICBMs). Because parts of the system proposed by the president would be based in space, the SDI was dubbed Star Wars in allusion to the space weaponry of the cult SCIENCE FICTION film of that name. The US government spent $30 million on the project before finally abandoning it in 1993, two years after the demise of the Soviet Union.

(2) The blockbuster movie *Star Wars* (1977), conceived, written and directed by George Lucas, was the first part of a trilogy, sequels being *The Empire Strikes Back* (1980) and *Return of the Jedi* (1983). It tells how a rebel princess in a distant galaxy escapes and with the help of her robots and a young farmer overcomes the threatening forces of evil. The strange names of the characters are more meaningful than they seem. That of the villainous Darth Vader may suggest 'Death Invader' but was intended to mean 'Dark Father'. The first name of the youthful hero Luke Skywalker evokes Greek *leukos*, 'light', appropriately for a boy who discovers the power of 'the Force' that can activate light sabres. The surname of the heroine, Princess Leia Organa, reflects the conflict of nature and technology seen in the forest-dwelling heroes ranged against 'the Empire'. The roughneck space pilot Han Solo has a name suggesting 'John' and 'solo', implying a 'loner' in an older world. The robot R2-D2 took his name from a sound editor's shorthand for 'Reel Two, Dialogue Two'. The hairy Wookiee, Chewbacca, has a name inspired by Lucas's malamute Indiana (who also gave the hero's name in his Indiana Jones films). The name of the ancient knighthood of the Jedi is based on that of Jed or Jeddak, the lords of Barsoom in Edgar Rice Burroughs' *A Princess of Mars* (1912). The Jedi knight Obi-Wan Kenobi takes the first part of his name from *obi*, a Japanese sash, and perhaps *san*, the Japanese honorary suffix. *Star Wars* was re-released using digital technology in 1997. A 'prequel', *The Phantom Menace*, followed in 1999 as Episode I of a new trilogy, so that *Star Wars* and its own two sequels are Episodes IV, V and VI.

Stasi. An abbreviation of German *Staatssicherheitsdienst*, 'State Security Service', as the name of the East German secret police. It was formed in 1950 and disbanded in 1990 following the reunification of East and West Germany. At its peak it employed some 85,000 full-time officers and kept files on 5 million East German citizens, roughly one in three of the population. It maintained close ties with the KGB in Moscow and had links with various terrorist organizations.

Statemented. Of a school pupil, having SPECIAL NEEDS. The statement is the legally binding assessment made by a local education authority defining the child's requirements. The process for statementing is fairly straightforward. The child is first referred to an educational psychologist for an assessment. After initial testing, other experts such as occupational therapists or social workers may be called in. The LEA then responds by issuing the statement detailing the extra help it intends to provide. The procedure was introduced by the Education Act of 1981.

State-of-the-art. Sophisticated and up-to-date. The phrase emerged in the 1970s as a general adoption of the narrower 1950s sense, as applied to the current conditions of practical or technological knowledge in a given field. 'Art' here is thus used in its broadest implication, relating to any creative or imaginative process.

> Aside from the luxury trimmings, the liner will also boast a state-of-the-art security system including trained guards and a heliport with a hi-tech cover hood.
>
> *heat* (18–24 November 1999)

Stateside. In (or towards) the United States, a term of US origin dating from the 1940s.

Status symbol. A term of US origin dating from the 1950s for a possession or asset that supposedly enhances a person's social prestige. Status symbols are most readily found in the world of business. Typical examples are a grossly outsize office desk or an ostentatiously displayed item of electronic equipment such as a MOBILE PHONE or laptop computer. Their owners would naturally claim that these were essential for their professional proficiency.

> It is a status symbol to have a bookmaker, even if you always ask him for Tote odds.
>
> GUY EGMONT: *The Art of Egmontese*, ch i (1961)

Stauffenberg Plot. *See* JULY BOMB PLOT.

Stay tuned. Watch or listen for further developments. The phrase originated as a formula spoken before a radio commercial. A printed equivalent is WATCH THIS SPACE.

Steady state theory. A theory explaining the origin of the universe, and contrasting with the more popular BIG BANG theory. It claims that the universe exists in time in a 'steady state', i.e. in such a way that the average density of matter does not vary with distance or time. Matter is thus continually being created in the space left by the receding stars and galaxies of the expanding universe. The theory was propounded in 1948 as the 'perfect cosmological principle' by three British scientists: Fred Hoyle, Hermann Bondi and Thomas Gold.

Stealth bomber. Designed specifically to evade radar detection at normal combat ranges, the Northrop Grumman B2 strategic bomber, of flying wing design, was launched in 1989 and grew out of the Stealth programme announced by the US government in 1980. B2 stealth bombers were in action in the 1999 Balkans conflict, flying 30-hour non-stop sorties from their bases in the United States to attack targets in Yugoslavia.

Steal the show, To. To be the centre of attraction. The expression dates from the 1930s and originated in theatre talk. The idea is that the person 'stole' the limelight from the rest of the cast.

Steam radio. Sound broadcasting, as the original basic medium, by contrast with the later and more sophisticated television. The expression evokes the steam age of rail travel, which preceded that of the diesel and electric train.

Steel Magnolia. A nickname given to Rosalynn Carter, wife of Jimmy Carter (b.1924), Democratic president of the USA (1977–81), on account of her 'steely' temperament and Southern origins (magnolia being associated with the South). *Steel Magnolias* is also the title of a popular play by US writer Robert Harling. Set in a Southern beauty salon, it was first performed in 1987 and turned into a film in 1989. The Steel Magnolias are also a rock group (with a name of the IRON BUTTERFLY type).

Sten gun. The lightweight sub-machine gun takes its name from the initials of its designers, R.V. Shepherd and H.J. Turpin, with the *-en* from the name of the BREN GUN. It was first in use in the Second World War.

Stepford wives. Uncannily perfect women, like those in Ira Levin's novel *The Stepford Wives* (1952), about the wives in Stepford, a commuter village outside New York, who to a newcomer seem all too good to be true. They are in fact computerized models, replaced by their husbands for the human originals. A film version appeared in 1974. In 1998 the Labour MP Brian Sedgemore notoriously compared NEW LABOUR's women MPs to Stepford wives, suggesting they had microprocessors implanted in their brains to keep them 'on-message' (*see* OFF-MESSAGE).

> 'Then there's the Stepford Wives,' veteran Left-winger Brian Sedgemore said in an outburst that earned him a rebuke from the party leadership. 'That's those female New Labour MPs who've had the chip inserted into their brains to keep them on-message.'
> *Sunday Express* (27 February 2000)

Step forward. Let me introduce ... Here now is ... Journalistic jargon for a person or organization forming the next or even the main topic of one's piece. The image is of inviting a person to step out of a group in order to be identified and introduced to the present company.

> There is always some corner of our operatic field that is forever esoteric. Step forward, the reformed Royal Opera House.
> *The Times* (2 November 1999)

Stepinfetchit. A US name dating from the 1960s for a supposedly typical shuffling, fawning, eye-rolling black servant or more generally for any servile black man. The term comes from Stepin Fetchit, the stage name of the black actor Lincoln Perry (d.1985), who before he became a film actor danced in a vaudeville as half of a team called 'Step 'n' Fetchit, the Two Dancing Fools from Dixie', taking the name of a horse that Perry had bet on and won. After the act split up, Perry kept the name for his solo act. The name itself spells out as 'step and fetch it', i.e. 'go and get it'.

> The driver, from a small town outside Houston, though white, seemed to have taken a course at the Stepin Fetchit school of etiquette. No matter what I said, or asked, his answer was the same: 'Yassuh.'
> *Maclean's* (March 1974)

Stepney wheel. A former type of spare wheel for a motor vehicle, in the form of an already inflated tyre on a spokeless metal rim, which could be temporarily clamped over a punctured wheel. The devices existed in the early years of the 20th century and took their name from Stepney Street, Llanelli, where they were first made. The name persists in the Indian subcontinent for any kind of spare wheel.

Step on it or **on the gas, To.** To speed up, as in a motor vehicle by putting one's foot on the accelerator. *See also* PUT ONE'S FOOT DOWN.

Step out of the shadows, To. To enter the public gaze from a position of obscurity or reticence; to speak out and clarify one's position.

> This morning ... the Prime Minister will step out of the shadows of the debate and publicly commit himself to abolishing the pound.
>
> *The Times* (14 October 1999)

Steptoe and Son. A classic television SITCOM running from 1964 to 1973 and centring on the relationship between a father and son in the rag-and-bone trade. The wilful and eccentric old father, Albert Steptoe, played by Wilfrid Brambell, and the perpetually exasperated son, Harold, played by Harry H. Corbett, invariably end up by thwarting each other's dearest aspirations. The genius of the series lay in its finely balanced blend of humour and pathos.

Stern Gang. A right-wing Zionist terrorist group founded in Palestine in 1940 by Abraham Stern (1907 42). Stern objected to the decision by the IRGUN to stop attacking the British in Palestine for the duration of the Second World War. One of the Stern Gang's most notorious acts was the assassination in 1948 of the United Nations mediator Count Folke Bernadotte (1895–1948), the nephew of King Gustaf VI of Sweden. The gang disbanded later in the same year. *See also* DEIR YASSIN.

Stick 'em up! Hands up! An armed robber's command that dates from the 1930s but that is now rarely heard in real life.

> Captain James P. O'Neill ... has arrested three Brits this year for spinning a yarn about being robbed. One said the thief told him to 'stick 'em up', but the cops saw through that. 'Nobody says that any more,' says O'Neill.
>
> *Sunday Times* (24 October 1999)

Stickies. A nickname for the 'Official' IRA, a faction which came into being as a result of a split in the ranks of the Irish Republican Army, mirrored by a similar split in the ranks of SINN FÉIN, in 1969. The Stickies were so named for their habit of affixing their Easter lilies (worn by Irish Republicans in memory of the 1916 EASTER RISING) to their lapels with gum, unlike

supporters of the Provisional IRA who used pins for the purpose (hence 'pinheads', a derisive nickname for the Provisionals). *See also* PROVOS.

Stick one's neck out, To. To take a rash risk; to ask for trouble. The expression is of US origin and dates from the early years of the 20th century, the reference probably being to a chicken that extends its neck in preparation for slaughter by decapitation.

Stick out like a sore thumb, To. To be very conspicuous. A sore thumb will be held out to avoid contact with the fingers, making it and its owner conspicuous. The simile dates from the 1930s.

Sticky Fingers. An album released by the ROLLING STONES in 1971. The key to its salacious title lies in the audacious cover, designed by the Pop artist Andy Warhol (1928–87) and featuring a pair of jeans with a real zip. The album includes the songs BROWN SUGAR, 'Wild Horses' and 'You Gotta Move'.

Sticky wicket. A tricky or awkward situation. The reference is to a cricket pitch that is drying after rain and is difficult for the batsman (in cricketing parlance also known as a 'sticky dog'). The expression dates from the Second World War. An amusing mis-explanation of the term is unintentionally offered by William and Mary Morris in their *Morris Dictionary of Words and Phrases* (1988). Having read somewhere that the allusion is to a soft pitch, they write: 'In cricket – so we are told – a soft pitch can cause the batsman more trouble than one smartly delivered.' The error results from an understanding of 'pitch' as it is used in baseball, meaning a delivery of the ball by the pitcher, corresponding to the bowl of a bowler.

Stig of the Dump. The name of a Stone Age man who is found living in a rubbish dump by a boy in a highly successful novel (1963) of the same name by Clive King (b.1924).

Stijl, De (Dutch, 'The Style'). The name of an organization of mainly Dutch artists founded in 1917 by Theo van Doesburg (1883–1931) and Piet Mondrian (1872–1944), as well as of the journal they published to announce their ideas. They hardly had any cohesive force and did not exhibit together but the particular 'style' they promoted was one of austere abstract clarity.

Sting, The. A film (1973) written by David S. Ward about an elaborate 'numbers racket' set up by two conmen to cheat a gangster out of a fortune. Starring Paul Newman and Robert Redford as the conmen and featuring the ragtime music of Scott Joplin, the film was a huge success and revived the word 'sting' (in disuse since the 1930s) as slang for a con trick or robbery. *See also* BUDDY MOVIE.

Stir-crazy. Mentally disturbed, especially as a result of being imprisoned. The expression is of US origin, although 'stir' is British 19th-century jargon for a prison, perhaps from Romany *sturbin*. *Stir Crazy* is the title of an American film of 1980 about two New Yorkers who plan their escape from prison when wrongly convicted of a bank robbery.

Stitch someone up, To. To betray a person by fabricating evidence against them; to manipulate a situation to one's own advantage. The idea is of completing a garment by sewing it up.

> Openshaw, 41, allegedly said on his arrest: 'I'm being stitched up.' The trial goes on.
> *Daily Mirror* (14 July 1989)

Stockbroker belt. A term for the area outside a city, and especially London, where wealthy stockbrokers live.

> Henk Huffener's house, off the Guildford–Dorking road, is not merely in the Surrey stockbroker belt – it is at its very buckle.
> *The Times* (1 March 1999)

Stockbrokers' Tudor. A facetious term coined in the 1930s by the writer and cartoonist Osbert Lancaster for a style of mock-Tudor architecture supposedly favoured by stockbrokers. *See also* TUDORBETHAN.

Stock car. A car that has been specially strengthened and modified for a form of racing in which the cars deliberately collide. Such cars have a standard or stock chassis, hence the name.

Stockholm syndrome. A term dating from the 1970s for the observed tendency of hostages to try to co-operate with their captors. The phenomenon takes its name from a robbery of the Sveriges Kreditbank in Stockholm in 1973, remarkable for the bonds formed between hostages and captors. The story of a woman suffering from Stockholm syndrome is the subject of the film *Blue Velvet* (1986), directed by David Lynch and starring Isabella Rossellini. The kidnapping of the heiress Patti Hearst by the SYMBIONESE LIBERATION ARMY in 1974 led to what may be described as an extreme example of the syndrome.

Stocking filler or **stuffer.** A small gift suitable for putting in a Christmas stocking.

Stoker Jim. *See* SUNNY JIM.

Stonewall. On the night of 27 June 1969, the day of Judy Garland's funeral, police from the Public Morals Section of the New York City Police raided the Stonewall Inn, a gay bar in Christopher Street, Greenwich Village. The operation was supposedly routine, since the bar had no liquor licence. Instead of passively accepting the situation, however, the patrons reacted angrily, taunting the police and sparking off a confrontation that lasted several days. The outcome was the birth of the gay liberation movement, and the name Stonewall was adopted worldwide by organizations campaigning for lesbian and gay rights. *See also* FRIEND OF DOROTHY.

Stop and search. The British police are empowered to stop and search people and vehicles if they have reasonable grounds for suspecting that they may find stolen goods, offensive weapons or implements that could be used for burglary. Senior police officers can further authorize stop and search operations in specified localities if they believe that serious incidents of violence may take place, or in order to prevent acts of terrorism. The practice is based on the 'stop and frisk' procedure carried out in the United States in the 1960s. One million 'stop and searches' were carried out by the police in Britain over the year 1998–9, of which 9 per cent were of black people.

Stormin' Norman. A nickname of General H. Norman Schwarzkopf (b.1934), US commander-in-chief of Allied forces during the 1991 GULF WAR. Also known as the Bear, the temperamentally unpredictable Schwarzkopf became a national hero after the war, was awarded an honorary knighthood by the Queen, and retired from the US Army later in 1991. As with the S in Harry S. Truman (*see* GIVE-'EM-HELL HARRY) the H in his name does not stand for anything. *See also* DESERT STORM; NMI.

Stormont. The eastern suburb of Belfast that is the location of Parliament House, built in 1928–32 in a Greek classical style and the seat of the Northern Ireland Parliament until the introduction of DIRECT RULE in 1972, and of Stormont Castle, the former official residence of the Northern Ireland prime minister, built in 1858 from the original house erected c.1830 by the Rev. John Cleland. In 1998, following the GOOD FRIDAY AGREEMENT, Parliament House became the seat of the Northern Ireland Assembly and Stormont House the office of the Northern Ireland first minister.

Story of my life. Said ruefully of a recurring misfortune, as: 'I was late for work again – that's the story of my life.' *The Story of My Life* is a standard title for an autobiography.

Strafe, To. This expressive verb, meaning to attack repeatedly with bombs or machine-gun fire from low-flying aircraft, is not English in origin but was derisively adopted from the German First World War catchphrase, *Gott strafe England*, 'May God punish England'. The source of this execration is uncertain, but it is in Alfred Funke's book *Schwert und Myrte* ('Sword and Myrtle') (1914).

Straight from the horse's mouth. Directly from the source; entirely reliable. The phrase applies to news, information and the like and comes from racing jargon. A racing tip that comes straight from the horse's own mouth must be dependable.

Straight man. The 'half' of a comedy duo whose lines and actions are designed to give his partner most of the laughs. Examples are Bud Abbot for Lou Costello or Dean Martin for Jerry Lewis in the cinema, or Ernie Wise for Eric Morecambe on television.

> Proud of what he had achieved, Wise was anxious to be appreciated as a comic in his own right, and disliked the term 'straight man'. He was, he insisted, a 'song and dance man'.
> *The Times* (Obituary of Ernie Wise) (22 March 1999)

Straight up. Truthfully; honestly. A phrase emphasizing that a statement is honest and genuine, since it is 'straight' or direct, not 'angled' or devious.

Strangers and Brothers. A novel (1940) by C.P. Snow, later Baron Snow (1905–80). It was reissued (1973) as *George Passant*, to allow the original title to encompass a sequence of 11 novels, reflecting the author's professional experiences over the years as scientist, academic and civil servant, and narrated by a kind of *alter ego*, the lawyer Lewis Eliot. The title indicates the divided world that Eliot enters: he and his brothers and two friends who have an almost fraternal relationship with him are the 'brothers', while other people are the 'strangers'.

Strangers on a train. A stock metaphor for a relationship that is doomed to end as suddenly as it began. Two strangers seated next to or opposite one another on a train may strike up a conversation and achieve a degree of intimacy, but the association will end when the train reaches its destination or when one of the two leaves the train before the other. The phrase itself was popularized by the title of Patricia Highsmith's first novel, a psychological thriller, *Strangers on a Train*

(1950), the story of two men who 'swap' murders, made into a classic film the following year by Alfred Hitchcock from a screenplay by Raymond Chandler. The image here is hardly romantic, but the phrase is now usually thought of in such terms. The situation itself has formed the basis for various literary works and has a pre-echo in David Lean's equally memorable film BRIEF ENCOUNTER (1945), set on a railway station.

> Strangers on a train, who brush their lives against each other for a while and then part. It is a popular and potent image, and in gloomy moments can be felt as summing up all that ever happens from first blink to last gasp.
> *The Times* (15 February 2000)

Strawberry Fields Forever. An innovatively recorded PSYCHEDELIC lyric by the BEATLES, credited to John Lennon and Paul McCartney and released in February 1967 as the B-side of PENNY LANE. The song evokes a lost world of childhood in a quasi-pastoral manner that was to become popular with a number of English pop groups of the late 1960s. Strawberry Fields is the name of an actual girls' reform school in Woolton, Liverpool.

Streaking. The act of running naked in a public place by way of a stunt, sometimes under the influence of a stimulant other than a bet or the buzz of bravado. The feat is usually staged out of doors, typically at a sporting venue, but may also be enacted in a public building such as a restaurant. The practice first emerged on US college campuses in the mid-1970s, and male streakers at first outnumbered female. According to John Ballard and Paul Suff's *Dictionary of Football* (1999) the first female streaker at a major football match was Variana Scotney, who ran on to the pitch at Highbury when Arsenal were playing Tottenham Hotspur in 1981. *See also* FAMOUS FOR 15 MINUTES.

> Abigail Saxon, 34, ... was challenged to streak twice around the fashionable Barca bar in Castlefield for £100.
> *The Times* (22 December 1998)

Stream of consciousness. A MODERNIST technique of novel writing, first deliberately employed by Dorothy Richardson (1873–1957) in *Pointed Roofs* (1915) and developed by James Joyce (1882–1941) and Virginia Woolf (1882–1941). By this technique the writer presents life as seen through a flow of thoughts and impressions in the mind of a single character. The term itself was coined by William James in *Principles of Psychology* (1890). *See also* MRS DALLOWAY; ULYSSES.

Streetcar Named Desire, A. A play (1947) by Tennessee Williams (1911–83) that was subsequently turned into a successful film, directed by Elia Kazan, starring Marlon Brando and Vivien Leigh. An intense drama about the relationship between faded Southern belle, Blanche DuBois, and her brother-in-law, Stanley Kowalski, the play had several titles before the final one, including *The Moth*, *Blanche's Chair in the Moon* and *The Poker Night*. The eventual title was inspired by a streetcar called 'Desire' (now preserved) that, together with another called 'Cemeteries', plied the main street in the district of New Orleans where Williams lived. The play is a leitmotif in Pedro Almodóvar's film *Todo Sobre Mi Madre* (*All About My Mother*) (1999). *See also* DESIRE STREET.

> They told me to take a streetcar named Desire, then transfer to one called Cemeteries.
>
> TENNESSEE WILLIAMS: *A Streetcar Named Desire*
> (Blanche's first line)

Street cred. In full, street credibility, or a 'persona grata' status among one's young urban peers. The expression arose in the popular music industry in the 1970s and embodies the tenet that the 'artist' must relate genuinely to the 'people', meaning the working-class youth of the streets and housing estates. Many police officers aim to gain 'street cred' for the greater efficiency of their duties.

> Crime writers and television producers have never doubted the value of the ageing detective with a well-worn patina of street cred.
>
> *The Times* (12 July 1999)

Street film. A type of silent film made in Germany during the 1920s. It laid emphasis on the depressing and dehumanizing aspects of urban life for the lower middle class and usually featured a sensitive individual seeking to rise above the limitations of his environment. The first such film was Carl Grune's *Die Strasse* ('The Street') (1923) and the best known is probably G.W. Pabst's *Die freudlose Gasse* ('Joyless Street') (1925).

Stressed out. Colloquially, exhausted or debilitated as a result of stress. The term emerged in the 1980s, an era when stress received recognition as a hazard of the pressures of modern life.

Stretch limo. A limousine that has been 'stretched' by the incorporation of an extended seating area. Such cars became associated with pop stars and other celebrities from the 1980s and originated in the United States.

Strictly for the birds. Unimportant; worthless. A phrase of US origin that became current in the 1950s. The reference is to horse manure, which is good only for picking over by birds.

Strife. A play (1909) by John Galsworthy (1867–1933) about the conflict between management and labour in the course of an industrial strike. A production of the play at the National Theatre in 1978 was especially poignant as the theatre was involved in a bitter dispute with its stage staff at the time.

Strikes again. Said tongue-in-cheek of someone or something repeating a characteristic action. The expression probably arose from a SCIENCE FICTION story involving an evil power. One of the six sequels to the comedy film *The* PINK PANTHER (1963), starring Peter Sellers as the incompetent Inspector CLOUSEAU, was *The Pink Panther Strikes Again* (1976).

> Dr David Jenkins has struck again. The former Bishop of Durham … has turned on the Government.
>
> *The Times* (8 September 1999)

Strine. According to the writer Alistair Morrison the brand of English spoken by Australians, a humorous survey of which is provided in *Let's Talk Strine* (1965), subtitled 'a lexicon of modern Strine usage'. The clipped tones of Australian speech are spelled out phonetically, with amusing and linguistically playful results. Thus 'Fried eye car nelpew' translates as 'I'm afraid I can't help you'; 'Hacker chufa get?' as 'How could you forget?'; and 'Nwotsa taller bat?' as 'What's it all about?'. 'Strine', of course, means 'Australian', and the baffling name of the book's supposed author, Professor Afferbeck Lauder (described as 'Professor of Strine Studies, University of Sinny; Fellow of the Yarnurdov Foundation') on closer examination turns out to be an Australian rendering of 'alphabetical order'. A later volume of Strine, *Nose Turn Unturned*, followed in 1966. *See also* FRAFFLY.

String along with someone, To. To accompany them generally or casually. The allusion is to a train of pack-mules, each 'strung' to the one in front. The expression dates from the 1920s.

> You may not be an angel
> 'Cause angels are so few,
> But until the day that one comes along
> I'll string along with you.
>
> AL DUBIN: 'You'll Never Be an Angel' (song) (1934)

Stringfellows. A famous London nightclub opened in 1980 by the self-proclaimed 'world's greatest disco owner' Peter Stringfellow (b.1940). It is brash and garish by comparison with ANNABEL'S or TRAMP but has several celebrities among its mostly middle-aged businessmen members.

String quartets. Many Western countries saw the creation of new string quartets in the 20th century, either to promote and popularize modern music or to concentrate on a particular period of music or even a particular composer. The following is a selection of some of the better known British quartets, with the date of their formation (and demise) and the origin of their name.

Aeolian Quartet (1944–82) (originally Stratton Quartet, from its leader, George Stratton): for Aeolus, Greek god of the winds, also the Aeolian harp, a stringed instrument named after him

Allegri Quartet (from 1953): after the Italian composer Gregorio Allegri (1582–1652)

AMADEUS QUARTET

Arditti Quartet (from 1974): from one of its original four members, Irvine Arditti

Blech Quartet (1934–50): from its leader, Harry Blech (b.1910)

Brodsky Quartet (from 1973): in honour of the Russian violinst Adolph Brodsky (1851–1929)

Brosa Quartet (1924–38): from its leader, Spanish-born Antonio Brosa (1894–1979)

Chilingirian Quartet (from 1971): founded by the Cypriot violinist Levon Chilingirian (b.1948)

Endellion Quartet (from 1979): after the Cornish village of St Endellion

Fitzwilliam Quartet (from 1975): after the 17th-century Fitzwilliam Virginal Book

Gabrieli Quartet (from 1966): after the Italian composer Giovanni Gabrieli (c.1554–1612)

Griller Quartet (1928–61): founded by Sidney Griller (1911–93)

London String Quartet (1908–35): London-based, and originally the New String Quartet

London String Quartet (1958–61): London-based, and originally the New London Quartet

Medici Quartet (from 1974): after the noted 17th-century Italian art patrons

Strip, The. The main street or central area of a US city, and especially Las Vegas, where the name is applied to the street where most of the gambling casinos are found.

> Not many performers can survive Las Vegas. … It got to Frank Sinatra; his years on the Strip gave him disastrous delusions of grandeur.
> *heat* (23–29 September 1999)

Strip city. A US term dating from the 1950s for a long, narrow stretch of urban development between two or more relatively distant cities.

> By 1980 or so, 80 per cent of us will live in cities, and the strip city – Boston to Washington, Los Angeles to San Diego, and Milwaukee to Cleveland – will have made its appearance.
> *Saturday Review* (13 January 1968)

Strippergram. A form of 'greetings telegram' delivered by a messenger who performs a STRIPTEASE for the benefit of the recipient. The show is typically enacted by a young woman wearing the uniform of a police-woman or traffic warden. *See also* KISSOGRAM.

Strip poker. A game of poker in which a player with a losing hand removes an item of clothing as a penalty or forfeit.

Strip search. A search of a person involving the removal of all their clothes. The aim is to find drugs or the like concealed in body cavities.

Striptease. A club or cabaret performance in which a woman or (less often) a man, slowly and provocatively undresses, i.e. teases by stripping. The person who does this, usually to music, is a stripper. Strip-tease is said to have originated at the *Bal des Quat'z Arts* held at midnight on 9 February 1893 at the Moulin Rouge in Paris, when a group of students rented the music hall for their celebrated Four Arts Ball. The event was notorious for its debauchery and drunkenness, and on this occasion the personal attractions of two girls were debated by their admirers. The young women then stood on tables for their ankles to be judged. Competition extended to their legs, thighs, hips, buttocks, breasts and shoulders, until one of the two ended up completely naked. News of the performance reached directors of other music halls, and on 13 March 1894 a short sketch entitled *Le Coucher d'Yvette* ('Yvette Goes to Bed') was staged at Le Divan Fayouau on the Rue des Martyrs. The act relied on the spectator's lubricious imagination being one jump ahead of actuality, so that when the actress reached the final stage of her gradual disrobing the audience would already see her as naked, although she had not yet removed her last drapes. The vogue caught on like wildfire, and soon every variety house in Paris had its own version of *Le Coucher d'Yvette* with titles such as *Le Bain de la Maid* ('The Maid Takes a Bath'), *Suzanne et la Grande Chaleur* ('Suzanne in a Heatwave') and *Liane chez le Médecin* ('Liane at the Doctor's').

Stroke City. A Northern Ireland nickname for the city of Derry/Londonderry, alluding to the stroke ('/') that separates the alternative names. The basic and historic name is Derry, from Irish *doire*, 'oak grove', but in 1609 James I granted a charter authorizing a plantation by merchants from London on the site of the city following its burning by the English. Hence the addition of the English name. Today, Derry is preferred by Catholics, and Londonderry by many Protestants. Official authorities, such as the Post Office, are generally non-committal when it comes to advising which of the two is 'correct', and entrance routes to the city have road signs showing both names. 'Stroke City' may be a partial pun on 'Stoke City' as the name of a football club. *See also* BOGSIDE.

Stroll on! Get away with you! You must be joking! An expression of astonishment or incredulity dating from the 1950s.

Strong silent type. A man of few words but effective action. The expression, now often used ironically, dates from the early 20th century when it was a taken up by various women novelists to describe a romantic male character of some kind.

Stroppy. Bad tempered and argumentative. The word dates from the 1950s and may derive from 'obstreperous', although there is perhaps also a suggestion of Greek *strophē*, 'a turning', 'a twisting'. (An older equivalent is 'wayward', which originally meant 'turned away'.) Hence 'strop' as a slang term for a bad mood or temper.

Strut one's stuff, To. To display one's ability; to show what one has to offer. The expression dates from the 1920s and has its origin in black slang for flaunting one's sexual attraction. Some birds literally 'strut their stuff' in their courting rituals.

> Groups simply register with the Shakespeare Centre, strut their stuff during April, then send a record of the event.
> *The Times* (28 December 1999)

Studs Lonigan. A trilogy (1935) by the US novelist James T. Farrell (1904–79), consisting of *Young Lonigan: a Boyhood on the Chicago Streets* (1932), *The Young*

Manhood of Studs Lonigan (1934) and *Judgment Day* (1935). The starting point was the story 'Studs' in *This Quarter* in 1930. William (Studs) Lonigan is the son of a lower-middle-class Irish Catholic family in Chicago. The trilogy, written in a naturalistic style, follows Lonigan from the age of 15 to his thirties, when pneumonia cuts short a life tainted by ill-fortune, dissipation and joblessness. An unpolished film version (1960) was directed by Irving Lerner.

Stuffed owl. An expression applied to poetry that treats trivial or inconsequential subjects in a grandiose manner. It comes from *The Stuffed Owl*, 'an anthology of bad verse' published by Percy Wyndham Lewis in 1930 and taking its title from a line by Wordsworth:

> The presence even of a stuffed Owl for her
> Can cheat the time; sending her out
> To ivied castles and to moonlight skies,
> Though he can neither stir a plume, nor shout;
> Nor veil, with restless film, his staring eyes.
> *Miscellaneous Sonnets*, III, xiii (1827)

Stuffed shirt. A pompous but vacuous person. The allusion is to a dummy displaying a dress shirt in a menswear store. The figure is pompous-looking but in fact hollow.

Stuff envelopes, To. To undertake basic secretarial work, which frequently involves inserting circulars, bills or advertising literature into envelopes for despatch to customers or the public. '

> She refused to stuff envelopes all day. 'I wanted to make sure that I was actually learning something. After all, I was paying to be there.'
> *The Times* (6 December 1999)

Stuff to give the troops. Just what is needed; exactly what should be given. Often occurring in the stock sentence 'That's the stuff to give the troops', the expression probably arose in the First World War but is first recorded only in the 1920s. 'Stuff' does not necessarily mean food.

> 'It's a very new Labour poem [by poet laureate Andrew Motion]. It's not exactly going to get [deputy prime minister] John Prescott sitting up and thinking this is the stuff to give the troops.'
> *The Times* (8 September 1999)

Stuka. The popular name (derived from the generic German term for a dive bomber, *Sturzkampfflugzeug*) of the Junkers Ju-87, which first entered service with the German LUFTWAFFE in 1937. It was tested successfully during the Spanish Civil War and became a key component of the BLITZKRIEG tactics that brought about rapid German victory in Poland in 1939 and Western Europe in 1940. The terror of its steep dive towards its targets was enhanced by the attachment of screaming sirens (*Jericho-Trompeten*, 'trumpets of Jericho'). The Stuka proved no match for British fighters such as the Spitfire and Hurricane, however, and was soon rendered obsolete. Nevertheless, it continued in service in some theatres, and production did not end until 1944.

Stunt girl. A US term for a woman reporter in the early years of the 20th century who went to great lengths, often in disguise, to get a story. The prime example was Winifred S. Black (1863–1936), who wrote under the pen-name 'Annie Laurie', from the popular song of this name. Her first major story was in 1890, when she faked an accident in order to be admitted to the San Francisco Receiving Hospital and so report on the rough treatment given to women vagrants there. In 1892 she secured an exclusive interview with President Benjamin Harrison by sneaking aboard his private train and hiding under a table. Her greatest story was in 1900, when she disguised herself as a boy to mingle among soldiers and write about a flood in Galveston, Texas.

Subbuteo. This popular game of table football dates from 1947 as the creation of Peter Adolph, who originally wanted to call it 'Hobby'. This name was not acceptable for registration purposes, however, so instead he took the Latin name of the hobby hawk, *Falco subbuteo*, adopting the second word of this by default. The suggestion of 'boot' in the name is thus fortuitous but apt.

Subsidiarity. A term used in politics for the principle that a central authority should have a subsidiary function and perform only those tasks which cannot be performed at a more local level. The word was first made familiar to the general public in 1990 as the result of controversy about the speed of progress towards European union, but is found in the narrow vocabulary of Eurocrats before this date and ultimately arose in the 1930s as a translation of German *Subsidiarität*, used in a paraphrase of Pope Pius XI's encyclical *Quadragesimo Anno* (1931). This articulated the modern Catholic social teaching that the best institutions for responding to a particular social task are those that are most proximate to it.

Subtext. The meanings or ideas that underlie the surface text of a literary work, drama or film. The term

originated in the 1950s as theatrical jargon for the unspoken in a play, and especially what was implied by a pause or by silence. In the cinema the subtext is often suggested by the juxtaposition of scenes or by background sound or music. The text of Ingmar Bergman's *The Virgin Spring* (1959), for instance, deals with the rape of a young girl and the revenge of her father, while the subtext elicits the viewer's awareness of the struggle of Christianity to overcome paganism and of the need for faith. The subtext of a work is always implicit, not explicit.

Subtopia. A word coined (from 'suburb' and 'Utopia') by the architectural journalist Ian Nairn to denote the sprawling suburban housing estates built to satisfy the town workers' yearning for country surroundings while clinging to the amenities of the town. The term includes all the paraphernalia of concrete posts, lamp standards, chain link fencing and other uglinesses associated with a disfigured landscape.

> There will be no real distinction between town and country. Both will consist of a limbo of shacks, bogus rusticities, wire and aerodromes, set in some fir-poled fields. ... Upon this new Britain the *Review* bestows a name in the hope that it will stick – *Subtopia*.
> IAN NAIRN: *Architectural Review*, cxvii (1955)

Such Sweet Thunder. The title of the Shakespearian suite by Duke Ellington (1899–1974), dating from 1957, comes from *A Midsummer Night's Dream* (IV.i):

> I was with Hercules and Cadmus once,
> When in a wood of Crete they bay'd the bear
> With hounds of Sparta: never did I hear
> Such gallant chiding; for, besides the groves,
> The skies, the fountains, every region near
> Seem'd all one mutual cry. I never heard
> So musical a discord, such sweet thunder.

In the series of vignettes Ellington matches Shakespearian characters to the individual style of his soloists: for example, Johnny Hodges on saxophone is a fervent Cleopatra and Jimmy Hamilton on clarinet a haughty Caesar, while Cat Anderson on trumpet reaches wildly high notes as Hamlet in 'Madness in Great Ones'. It was said that only a dog could hear his highest notes.

Sudetenland. An area, also called the Sudeten, in the north of what is now the Czech Republic. Formerly part of the Austro-Hungarian empire, it became part of the new state of Czechoslovakia following the Treaty of Saint Germain (1919). There were some

3.25 million German-speakers in the Sudetenland, and in the 1930s Hitler exploited the grievances of these people, sponsoring the formation of a quasi-NAZI Sudeten Party that agitated against the Czechoslovak government. The escalating violence led to the MUNICH AGREEMENT, by which Britain and France allowed Hitler to annex the Sudetenland (September 1938). The following year the Nazis occupied the whole of Czechoslovakia. At the end of the Second World War Czechoslovakia took back the Sudetenland and expelled the German-speaking population. *See also* PEACE FOR OUR TIME; SUDETEN SCOTS.

Sudeten Scots. A nickname for expatriate Scots in England who opposed DEVOLUTION, alluding to the German presence in Czech SUDETENLAND. The phrase, which happens to suggest 'southern Scots', was coined by William Ross, Baron Ross of Marnock (1911–88), secretary of state for Scotland (1964–70 and 1974–6).

Suedehead. A young person similar to a SKINHEAD but with slightly longer hair and smarter clothes.

Suez crisis. A brief conflict that erupted in 1956 following the nationalization of the Suez Canal by President Nasser of Egypt in retaliation for the withdrawal of financial support from the United States and Britain for the building of the Aswan dam. Israel attacked Egypt on 29 October 1956 and the following day Britain and France demanded that both sides withdraw from the canal. When Egypt refused, the British and French launched air attacks and landed troops. The action was strongly condemned by the United Nations, leading Britain and France to withdraw. The conflict is often referred to as simply 'Suez'.

> Suez – a smash and grab raid that was all smash and no grab.
> SIR HAROLD NICOLSON in conversation with Antony Jay (November 1956).

Suffer the little children. A media catchphrase frequently adopted to head a report of child ABUSE, a charity appeal or some similar item involving the suffering of children. The words are biblical, but with 'suffer', properly meaning 'allow', 'let', misapplied in its modern sense of 'experience pain': 'Jesus said, suffer little children, and forbid them not, to come to me' (Matthew 19:14).

Suffragette. The suffragette movement in Britain dates from the early 20th century, when women organized a campaign of demonstrations and militant action in their bid for a right to vote. The campaign was prompted by the repeated defeat of women's suffrage bills in Parliament in the 19th century, and was led by Mrs Emmeline Pankhurst (1858–1928) and her daughters Christabel (1880–1958) and Sylvia (1882–1960), who in 1903 founded the Women's Social and Political Union, with its motto 'Votes for Women'. Women over the age of 30 won the vote in 1918, and in 1929 the franchise was extended to all women of majority age, then 21. The word itself, first recorded in 1906, was the first in English to use the French feminine suffix -*ette*, and it spawned later terms such as usherette and drum majorette, where it is added to the masculine original. See also CAT AND MOUSE ACT.

> 'Very well ... Suffragettes if you like. To get an abuse listened to is the first thing; to get it understood is the next. Rather than not have our cause stand out clear and unmistakable before a preoccupied, careless world, we accept the clumsy label; we wear it proudly. And it won't be the first time in history that a name given in derision has become a badge of honour!'
> ELIZABETH ROBINS: *The Convert* (1907)

Sugar Bowl. The post-season American collegiate football game that has been played every New Year's Day at New Orleans, Louisiana, since 1935. It was originally played at the stadium of Tulane University but in 1976 moved to the Louisiana Superdome. The name alludes to 'Sugar State' as the nickname of Louisiana, so called from its many sugar plantations and sugar refineries. *See also* SUPER BOWL.

Sugar daddy. A rich, middle-aged or elderly man who lavishes expensive gifts on a much younger woman, usually in the hope of sexual favours. The expression is of US origin and arose in the 1920s. A derivation in rhyming slang 'sugar and honey' meaning 'money' has been proposed, but 'sugar' has long been a word associated with affection and luxury. *See also* TOY BOY.

> The morning papers had come aboard, reassuring citizens ... that sugar daddies were still being surprised in love-nests.
> P.G. WODEHOUSE: *The Luck of the Bodkins*, ch xxi (1935)

Sugar Ray Robinson. The US middleweight boxer (1921–89) was born Walker Smith. He became 'Ray Robinson' when he substituted for another boxer of that name, the word 'Sugar' being added later when his trainer was told that his boxer was 'sweet as sugar'. The US welterweight and middleweight boxer Ray Leonard (b.1956) took the name 'Sugar Ray' Leonard.

Suicide blonde. A woman with dyed blonde hair or peroxide blonde hair. The allusion may be to its 'killing' effect on men. *See also* PLATINUM BLONDE.

Suitable Boy, A. A novel (1993) by Vikram Seth (b.1952). The action begins in India in 1950, just after independence, and chiefly involves the members of four families. The central plot concerns the efforts of Mrs Mehta to find an appropriate husband ('a suitable boy') for her younger daughter, Lata. Lata finally makes her own choice from three men: a fellow student who is a Muslim, a factory manager and a poet, each of whom has good qualities. Subplots illustrate the general political situation at the time.

Sultans of Swing. A song written by Mark Knopfler and released by Dire Straits in 1979. It tells of the pleasures of being a part-time musician 'living it up for Friday night'. The wit of its lyrics and sinuous elegance of its music (particularly the accomplished guitar-playing of Mark Knopfler) contrasted with the contemporary fashion for the angry voice of PUNK.

Summerhill. A co-educational 'progressive' school set up near Leiston, Suffolk, in 1927 by A.S. Neill (1883–1973), a radical Scottish educationist. The basic tenet was that children need attend lessons only if they felt like it and that they themselves should formulate their rules of conduct. The scheme was seen as anarchic and degenerate by many, and the school has been criticized for its rudimentary facilities and poor academic standards. It was subsequently taken over by the founder's daughter, Zoe Redhead.

Summer of love. The summer of 1967, which saw the birth of the HIPPIE movement. Peace, love and flowers in the hair were particularly on display in San Francisco, although the phenomenon was apparent in other Western countries. As it was the height of the VIETNAM War, the slogan of the summer was 'Make love not war,' while the theme album was the Beatles' SERGEANT PEPPER'S LONELY HEARTS CLUB BAND. *See also* ALL YOU NEED IS LOVE; HASHBURY; LONG HOT SUMMER.

Summer pudding. The dessert so known, made of soft summer fruits such as redcurrants and raspberries with bread, has had this name only since the early 20th century. It was earlier known as 'hydropathic pudding', as it was served at health resorts where pastry was forbidden.

Summer's Lease. A novel (1988), part social comedy, part mystery story, by John Mortimer (b.1923). The plot centres on the villa in Tuscany on temporary lease for the summer holidays to an accident-prone, articulate family. The title is from Shakespeare:

> Shall I compare thee to a summer's day?
> Thou art more lovely and more temperate:
> Rough winds do shake the darling buds of May,
> And summer's lease hath all too short a date.
>
> Sonnet 18

Summer Time. The idea of making fuller use of the hours of daylight by advancing the clock originated with Benjamin Franklin (1706–90), but its introduction was due to its advocacy from 1907 by William Willett (1856–1915), a Chelsea builder. It was adopted in 1916 in Germany, then in Britain as a wartime measure, when clocks were advanced one hour. In Britain it became permanent by an Act of 1925. Summer Time, as it was called, began on the day following the third Saturday in April, unless that was Easter Day, in which case it was the day following the second Saturday in April. It ended on the day following the first Saturday in October. In 1961 Summer Time was extended by six weeks, beginning in March and ending in October, and similar extensions were made in 1962 and subsequent years. During the Second World War it ran from 25 February to 31 December in 1940 and from 1 January in the four years from 1941. In 1945 it ended in October. Double Summer Time (i.e. two hours in advance of GMT instead of one) was in force from 1941 to 1945 and in 1947 to save fuel. After the war Summer Time was in force in the years from 1948 to 1952 and 1961 to 1964. From 27 October 1969 until 31 October 1971, clocks were kept one hour ahead of GMT continuously in what was known as British Standard Time (BST). The end of Summer Time on the last Sunday in October has been marked since 1972 at Merton College, Oxford, with a backward procession round Fellows' Quad between 2 a.m. BST, as the moment when GMT is restored, and 2 a.m. GMT itself.

In the United States Summer Time (March to October) was in force in 1917 and 1918 and again from 1942 to 1945 (all the year round and known as War Time). The Uniform Time Act of 1967 re-introduced Summer Time from the last Sunday in April until the last Sunday in October while allowing individual states the right of option. The oil crisis of 1973 caused Congress to legislate for continuous Daylight Saving Time from 6 January 1974 to 26 October 1975. The Act was not renewed but in 1986 the start of Daylight Saving Time was moved to the first Sunday in April with effect from 5 April 1987.

Summertime Blues. A pop anthem by Eddie Cochran, released in 1958, concerning a teenager experiencing problems with his girfriend, his boss and his parents ('There ain't no cure for the Summertime Blues'). At one point in the song, a congressman responds to the tortured teenager 'I'd like to help you, son, but you're too young to vote.' 'Summertime Blues' is one of the first in a line of pop-music expressions of teenage angst that would later include The Who's MY GENERATION and (I CAN'T GET NO) SATISFACTION by the Rolling Stones. The Who in fact later sang a version of 'Summertime Blues' on their album *Live At Leeds*.

Sun Belt. The southern states of the United States, which are generally sunnier and drier than the northern. The name implies not merely a favourable climate, but a high standard of living, a high population density and generally conservative attitudes. The term was coined in 1969 by the US writer Kevin P. Phillips, who based it on 'corn belt' or BIBLE BELT. *See also* RUST BELT.

> That growth of small towns is distributed from region to region but national in scope: it is highest in the Sun Belt states of the West and South, lowest in the Middle West, but steady and substantial even in the Northeast, where the big cities are losing population.
> *Newsweek* (6 July 1981)

Sun City. The name of two very different communities, one for the elderly, the other for the young. Sun City, Arizona, was founded in 1960 as a residential suburb of Phoenix for retired people. By 1990 its population had grown to almost 40,000. Sun City in North-West Province, South Africa, was built in the early 1980s as a gambling, entertainment and sporting area in the former Bophuthatswana homeland, the aim being to attract tourists from the Rand area. The concept of a wealthy white man's playground in a predominantly impoverished black country is still grotesque. *See also* BANTUSTAN.

Sundae. The dish of ice cream with added ingredients first became popular at the turn of the 20th century. Its name remains of uncertain origin although appears to be associated with 'Sunday'. According to Harva Hachten, in *The Flavor of Wisconsin* (1981), it was the creation in 1881 of Ed Berners, owner of an ice cream parlour in Two Rivers, Michigan, and a customer called George Hallauer. Initially it had no distinctive name but was simply a 'chocolate-topped ice cream'. Another ice cream parlour then opened up in nearby Manitowoc, and its owner, George Giffy, began serving similarly embellished ice creams on Sundays. One weekday a little girl came in and ordered a dish of ice cream 'with stuff on it'. When told it was only served on Sundays, the young customer is reported to have said, 'Why, then, this must be Sunday, for it's the kind of ice cream I want.' Giffy gave it to her, and henceforth called the dish a 'Sunday'.

This does not explain the present spelling, however, which may have been made out of respect for Sunday churchgoers. In 1973 the State Historical Society of Wisconsin erected a marker at Two Rivers in recognition of its status as the birthplace of the confection, which is now traditionally served in a tall glass.

Sunday artist. An amateur artist, thought of as painting only on Sundays as a hobby.

Sunday driver. A person regarded as driving a car erratically or amateurishly, like one who drives only on Sundays for a 'spin', frequently slowing to see or point out the view.

Sunday lunch. The specially large midday meal served on Sundays. The British Sunday lunch has a traditional main dish of roast beef, Yorkshire pudding, Brussels sprouts, roast potatoes and gravy and is followed by a period of protracted inertia.

Sunday punch. A powerful or destructive blow. It is one's 'best', like a Sunday suit.

Sunningdale Agreement. An agreement in 1973 that resulted in the short-lived POWER-SHARING experiment in Northern Ireland, ended by a Protestant general strike in 1974. The agreement resulted from talks between the Irish and British premiers, Liam Cosgrave and Edward Heath, together with representatives from the Northern Ireland political parties. The talks were held at Sunningdale in Berkshire. *See also* DIRECT RULE.

Sunny or **Sonny Jim.** (1) A form of address to a man or boy, especially patronizingly or humorously. The name is obviously influenced by 'son' but specifically derives from Sunny Jim, a sprightly character adopted as a mascot by the manufacturers of Force breakfast cereal at the turn of the 20th century. It is believed that he arose as the winning entry of a competition run by the Force Food Company to find a character to promote their cereal, and it is known that his creator was a US schoolgirl named Ficken. The jingles that accompanied his antics were written by Minnie Hanff. The best known, as it appeared on a poster of 1903, was:

High o'er the fence leaps Sunny Jim,
　'Force' is the food that raises him.

(2) Sunny Jim was also a media nickname for the Labour politician James (now Lord) Callaghan (b.1912), chancellor of the exchequer (1964–7), home secretary (1967–70), foreign secretary (1974–6) and prime minister (1976–9). Callaghan was defeated in the 1979 general election after the far-from-sunny WINTER OF DISCONTENT. The nickname was awarded because of his continuing bland smile in the face of adversity. Another nickname for Callaghan was Stoker Jim, Callaghan having served in the Royal Navy during the Second World War, not as a stoker, but as a sub-lieutenant. Callaghan's successor as leader of the Labour Party, Michael Foot called him PC Callaghan, because of his work on behalf of the Police Federation, while the Beatle John Lennon called him Mr Caravans. *See also* GUMMIDGE, WORZEL.

Sunrise industry. A new and growing industry, typically in electronics or telecommunications. The term dates from the early 1980s. The converse, 'sunset industry', is less commonly found to denote traditional heavy industry. 'Sunrise' implies the dawn of a new era.

Sun, sea and sand. A travel agent's alliterative lure to the holidaymaker. Many southern European destinations can offer the required ingredients in abundance, notably Spain. The order of the second two nouns may be reversed in the phrase, and 'sex' is often implied as a further bait. *See also* SEA AND SANGRIA.

> Sun, sand and sea are no longer enough for the Yuppie generation of fun-seekers.
> *Observer* (26 June 1988)

Sunset Boulevard. A broad and handsome street in downtown Los Angeles, so called as it runs from the city centre westward to the Pacific. The section of the street to the west of HOLLYWOOD is known as the Sunset Strip, and is the centre of the city's night life. *Sunset Boulevard* is also the name of a successful romantic film of 1950 and of Andrew Lloyd Webber's musical of 1993 based on it.

Sunshine. A colloquial form of address to an unknown person, perhaps as an embellishment of 'son'.

Sunshine matinées. A series of ballet performances started in London in 1919 by Mrs Dorothy Claremont of the Sunshine Home for Blind Babies and the dance publicist Philip Richardson. The first performance was on 25 November that year at the Queen's Theatre,

London, and there were ten matinées altogether, with dancers including such famous names as Anton Dolin, Phyllis Bedells, Mary Wigman, Vera Trefilova, Ninette de Valois and Serafina Astafieva. The series ended in 1930, but meanwhile the All England Sunshine Dancing Competition had been started in 1922 as a contest for young dancers under the age of 22. This gave rise to the Sunshine Galas, the first of which was held in 1965, since when the Beryl Grey Award has been given annually to the best classical dancer.

Sunshine State. A nickname for New Mexico, which became the 47th state of the United States in 1912. The allusion is obvious, and the name also applies to other states, such as California and South Dakota.

Super Bowl. In American football the championship game of the National Football League, played by the winners of the league's American Football Conference and National Football Conference every January. The game resulted from the merger in 1966 of the American Football League (AFL) and older National Football League (NFL), and was originally called the AFL-NFL World Championship Game. The first game was played on 15 January 1967 in the Los Angeles Coliseum, with a win for the NFL's Green Bay Packers over the AFL's Kansas City Chiefs by 35–10. The present name, suggested by Lamar Hunt, owner of the Kansas City Chiefs, was based on that of the ROSE BOWL. *See also* SUGAR BOWL.

Supercalifragilisticexpialidocious. Amazing; wonderful. A fantastic invention popularized by the Walt Disney film *Mary Poppins* (1964) but apparently originating, although with different spelling, in an unpublished song title of 1949. If meaningful, the elements may perhaps be taken as *supercali* ('boiling hot') *fragilistic* ('inclined to fragility') *expialidocious* ('inclined to explode'), in other words very volatile. The word was still in use at the close of the 20th century. *See also* POPPINS, MARY.

> As far as we know, Sainsbury's offer more kinds of alliaceous vegetables (onions, shallots, garlic, leeks and chives) than any other supermarket. Which must make Sainsbury's the most supercalifragilisticexpialiaceous [*sic*] supermarket in the country.
> (Advertisement) (1997)

Supergirl. *See* SUPERMAN.

Superhooligans. A term for certain groups of football supporters with a reputation for violence towards fans from other clubs. They differ from ordinary fans because they typically sport no club colours, travel to matches by regular transport rather than 'football specials' and not infrequently leave 'calling cards' on their victims. Noted gangs of the 1980s were the 'Baby Squad' supporting Leicester City, the 'Bushwhackers' for Millwall, the 'Gooners' for Arsenal, the 'Head-hunters' for Chelsea, the 'Inter City Firm' for West Ham United and the 'Service Crew' for Leeds United.

Supermac. A nickname of the Conservative statesman Harold Macmillan, 1st earl of Stockton (1894–1986), prime minister from 1957 to 1963. The name was the creation of the political cartoonist 'Vicky' (Victor Weisz), who in a drawing for the *Evening Standard* of 6 November 1958 showed Macmillan dressed as SUPERMAN. The sobriquet was originally intended ironically, but as Macmillan's premiership evolved it came to apply more realistically to his particular style of relaxed showmanship. In the 1990s the *Guardian* cartoonist Steve Bell, in a back-handed homage to Vicky, depicted the Conservative prime minister John Major wearing his Y-FRONTS over his trousers as a weedy would-be Superman. *See also* MAC THE KNIFE.

Superman. A hypothetical superior human being of high intellectual and moral attainment, fancied as evolved from the normally existing type. The term (*Übermensch*) was invented by the German philosopher Friedrich Nietzsche (1844–1900), and was popularized in England by George Bernard Shaw's play, MAN AND SUPERMAN (1903). *See also* UNTERMENSCHEN.

In the world of American comics, Superman is one of the most popular heroes. He can fly, is invulnerable, has X-ray vision, and can move mountains single-handed. He is a refugee from the planet Krypton, and by day is the mild-mannered human newspaper reporter Clark Kent. When the occasion requires, however, he changes from his sober suit and spectacles into his blue tights and red cape and is 'up, up and away', soaring into the sky. He was the creation of two SCIENCE FICTION fans, Jerry Siegel and Joe Schuster, who introduced him in *Action Comics* in 1938. He has appeared in several films and a radio and television series, and there has even been a musical, *It's a Bird, It's a Plane, It's Superman* (a catch phrase from the radio series), turned into a television movie (1975).

The wide popularity of the term gave rise to many compounds, such as superwoman, superstar, SUPER-MODEL and the like, while Superman's cousin, Super-girl, has her own adventures, first appearing in *Action*

Comics in 1959. Her real name is Kara, alias Linda Lee Danvers. *See also* BATMAN.

Supermodel. A fashion model who has gained the status of a celebrity. In the 1990s many such models were seen as successors to the traditional film and pop stars, their glamour on a par with that of the silent movie stars of the 1920s. The genesis of the supermodel is usually dated to January 1990, when Peter Lindbergh's photograph of five models, Cindy Crawford, Linda Evangelista, Tatjana Patitz, Christy Turlington and Naomi Campbell, appeared on the cover of that month's British *Vogue* magazine. Since then stars such as Claudia Schiffer and Kate Moss have been added to the galaxy. *See also* MODELIZER.

Supreme sacrifice. To make the supreme sacrifice is to die for one's country in battle. The expression dates from the First World War and is first recorded in W.M. Clow's *The Evangel of the Strait Gate* (1916): 'These young men … have gone down not only to the horror of the battlefield but to the gates of death as they made the supreme sacrifice.' The phrasing may seem pompous now but was entirely appropriate for the spirit of its time.

Surfeit of Lampreys. A detective novel (1941; originally published in USA as *Death of a Peer*, 1940) by Ngaio Marsh (1899–1982). The charming but cash-strapped Lamprey family is notorious for its party games. When Uncle Gabriel Lamprey dies, Chief Detective Roderick Alleyn, named after the founder of Marsh's father's school, Dulwich College, is called in. A lamprey is an eel-like fish. According to the chronicler Robert Fabyan (d.1513), it was said that King Henry I of England died of eating a surfeit of them.

Surf the Net, To. To move from site to site on the INTERNET, especially in order to explore its diversities or sample its wares. The image is of riding on a surf-board. An alternate term for this computer activity is 'browsing'.

Surprise, surprise! A phrase said either when giving someone a surprise or, ironically, when something happens that was entirely predictable. The expression dates from the 1960s.

> 'You again!' he said. 'Surprise, surprise!' He'd been up and down the road four times, waiting for her.
>
> FAY WELDON: *The Heart of the Country* (1987)

Surrealism. A movement in art, literature and film that began in the mid-1920s and that flourished in the interwar years under the leadership of the poet André Breton (1896–1966). In painting it falls into two groups: hand-painted dream scenes as exemplified by Giorgio de Chirico (1888–1978), Salvador Dalí (1904–89) and René Magritte (1898–1967), and the creation of abstract forms by the practice of complete spontaneity of technique as well as subject matter by the use of contrast as with Jean Arp (1888–1966), Man Ray (1890–1976), Joan Miró (1893–1983) and Dalí. Prime examples of surrealist films are Man Ray's *L'Étoile de Mer* (1928) and Luis Buñuel and Dalí's *Un Chien Andalou* (1928). The latter includes shots of dead donkeys on pianos and opens shockingly with the slicing of a young woman's eyeball by a razor. *See also* CUBISM; DADAISM; FAUVISM; FUTURISM; ORPHISM; RURALISM; SYNCHROMISM; TACHISM; VORTICISM.

Surrogate mother. A woman who bears a child on behalf of another woman, either from her own egg fertilized by the other woman's partner, or from the implantation in her womb of a fertilized egg from the other woman. The ethics of surrogacy were a key factor in the BABY M case.

Surtitles. Captions projected onto a screen or otherwise displayed above the stage during the performance of an opera, either to translate the libretto or simply to enable the audience to follow the words being sung. The device, its name based on 'subtitles', was invented in 1983 by John Leberg as part of a move to popularize opera generally.

> And that was what much of the fuss was about. you simply couldn't hear half the words. [John] Tomlinson tells me that they will almost certainly use surtitles this time round. But this is opera in English. If the composer is doing his job properly, should they really be necessary?
> *The Times* (4 January 2000)

Survivalism. In its specialized sense, the practising of outdoor survival skills as a sport or hobby. By the late 1980s the term had become associated with the carrying of weaponry and, in the United States, with participation in paramilitary activity. The death by shooting of 16 people in Hungerford, Berkshire, in 1987 at the hands of a self-confessed survivalist, Michael Ryan, brought the term before a wide public and associated it with deranged behaviour and an obsession with militaria. *See also* HUNGERFORD MASSACRE.

Susie-Q. *See* SUZI-Q.

Sutch, Screaming Lord. *See* MONSTER RAVING LOONY PARTY.

Sutton Hoo treasure. An Anglo-Saxon ship burial of the early 7th century, discovered at Sutton Hoo near Woodbridge, Suffolk, in 1939. It is one of the richest ever found and the treasure, consisting of a sword and sheath, helmet, bowls and other objects in precious metals, is now in the British Museum. Further excavations were carried out on the site in the 1980s, and by 1992 six more mounds had come to light.

Suzanne. A lugubrious song by the Canadian poet, novelist and singer Leonard Cohen, released in 1968. First recorded by Judy Collins, the song appeared on Leonard Cohen's debut album *Songs of Leonard Cohen*. The Suzanne of the title, and Cohen's muse on this occasion, was a dancer whom Cohen once visited in her loft near the St Lawrence River in Montreal. The song's deeply personal lyrics include the line 'I touched her perfect body with my mind', and its baffling second verse has Jesus Christ walking on the waters of Montreal harbour.

Suzi-Q or **Susie-Q.** A dance of black American origin popular in the 1930s, in which the dancer interlaced fingers of both hands at chest height, then with elbows akimbo made a sawing motion across the body while performing cross-over footwork. The origin of the name is uncertain.

Suzuki method. A method of teaching the violin to very young children, typically in large groups. It was developed by the Japanese music teacher Shin'ichi Suzuki (1898–1998) and is based on his belief that any child can attain a high standard of ability as a violinist by adapting external stimuli.

Svengali. A person who exercises a controlling or mesmeric influence on another. The name is that of the musician in George du Maurier's novel *Trilby* (1894) who trains Trilby's voice and controls her stage singing by his sinister hypnotic powers.

> It's a mistake to write off [modern art patron Charles] Saatchi, or to view him as a Svengali figure, conjuring artists and movements out of the air.
> *Sunday Times* (22 August 1999)

SWALK. An acronym of 'sealed with a loving kiss', traditionally placed the back of envelopes, where the physical act of licking the flap approximates to the kissing of the loved addressee. The full phrase dates back to at least the 17th century. *See also* LOVERS' ACRONYMS.

Swallowers and stuffers. Customs officers' jargon for those who smuggle drugs into a country either by swallowing them sealed in a bag which is subsequently excreted or by concealing them in a body orifice such as the rectum or vagina. The terms date from the 1980s.

Swallows and Amazons. The first of a series of 12 children's novels by Arthur Ransome (1884–1967), writer, journalist and, briefly, husband of Evgenia Shelepin, Leon Trotsky's secretary. *Swallows and Amazons* (1930) is set in the English Lake District and, like the novels that followed it, deals with the adventures of children on holiday, reflecting its author's love of sailing and other outdoor pursuits. The Swallows are the four children of the Walker family, John, Susan, Titty and Roger, and they are named after their boat, *Swallow*; the Amazons are Nancy and Peggy Blackett, who are named after their boat, *Amazon*. The eleven novels that followed were, in order of publication: *Swallowdale* (1931), *Peter Duck* (1932), *Winter Holiday* (1933), *Coot Club* (1934), *Pigeon Post* (1936), *We Didn't Mean to Go to Sea* (1937), *Secret Water* (1939), *The Big Six* (1940), *Missee Lee* (1941), *The Picts and the Martyrs* (1943) and *Great Northern?* (1947). These later novels introduce new characters and settings as diverse as the Norfolk Broads, the North Sea, the South China Sea and the Outer Hebrides. A rather tame film version (1974) was directed by Claude Whatham.

> I have never read the Arthur Ransome classic but, if it is as dull as the film, I doubt I ever will. ... Everyone is frightfully prissy and well behaved.
> KEN RUSSELL: *Fire over England* (1994)

See also FIRST LINES OF NOVELS.

Swallow the dictionary, To. To say that someone has swallowed the dictionary is to accuse them of using long and recondite words. The expression is first recorded in the 1930s.

Swan. A theatre built in 1986 in Stratford-upon-Avon on the site of the original Shakespeare Memorial Theatre, built in 1879 but destroyed by fire in 1926. It stages works by Shakespeare's contemporaries, classics from all eras, and once a year a play by the Bard himself, the 'Swan of Avon'. Hence its name, which also reflects its riverside site and the swans on the Avon as well as commemorating the Swan Theatre that existed in London in Shakespeare's time.

Swan about or **around, To.** To move around aimlessly. The phrase is first recorded among troops in the Second World War to describe a tank moving apparently aimlessly across the battlefield, like a swan swimming idly about the waters or meandering with others in an aimless convoy. The tank's long gun barrel additionally evoked the bird's long neck. The expression caught on and is now variably directed, so that one can 'swan in', or enter in an ostentatiously relaxed way, and even 'swan out', or exit similarly.

> I play Kate. I'm a cocaine dealer and I swan in and seduce the hostess's husband and then tease him about it.
> *The Times* (12 January 2000)

Swastika. The fylfot, an elaborate cross-shaped design used as a charm to ward off evil and bring good luck. It was adopted by Hitler as the NAZI emblem about 1920, probably from the German Baltic Corps, who wore it on their helmets after service in Finland, where it was used as a distinguishing mark on Finnish aeroplanes. The word is from Sanskrit *svasti*, 'well-being'.

> The swastika was used in such a way that it represented something more than itself: a relic of an Aryan culture, peculiarly German and Indian and possessing special and exclusive virtues.
> PETER CALVOCORESSI in *Times Literary Supplement* (review of Malcolm Quinn, *The Swastika*) (16 December 1994)

Swatch. Nothing to do with a sample of fabric but a term for a disposable Swiss watch. The timepiece was developed in 1983 by the Swiss watchmakers Ernst Thonke, Jacques Müller and Elmer Mock and was the first integrated watch, in which the action was not a separate component from the case. The original model was the 'Delirium', and both it and later models gained cult status, in some cases even becoming collectors' items.

Sweat bullets, To. To suffer mental anguish; to work extremely hard. The allusion is to drops of perspiration the size of bullets. The Americanism dates from the 1950s.

Sweater girl. A dated term for a young woman with a generous bust, which is made apparent by the wearing of a tight sweater. The 'Sweater Girl' was the US film actress Lana Turner (1920–95), and her promotion by this name at the beginning of her career in the late 1930s popularized the expression.

Swedish massage. A particularly vigorous form of massage involving effleurage (stroking), friction and rubbing, petrissage (kneading and squeezing) and tapotement (slapping and pounding), all of which stimulates blood circulation through the soft tissues of the body. The term dates only from the 20th century but probably derives from the tradition established by the Swedish fencing master and pioneer of massaging techniques Peter Henrik Ling (1776–1839).

Sweeney. A shortening of 'Sweeney Todd', rhyming slang for FLYING SQUAD. The name is that of a fictitious barber who murdered his customers in George Dibdin's play *A String of Pearls, or the Fiend of Fleet Street* (1847), later known as *Sweeney Todd, the Demon Barber of Fleet Street*. The character's grim persona and grisly deeds doubtless appealed to the cockney coiners of the term, which dates from the 1930s. It was brought before a wide public by the television crime drama series *The Sweeney* (1975–82), centring on Detective Inspector Jack Regan, played by John Thaw, and his sidekick George Carter, played by Dennis Waterman. Both men regularly ignored the rule book, associated with villains, swore and drank to excess and generally presented an unflattering portrait of their templates in their pursuit of various villains and 'bad boys'.

Sweep something under the carpet, To. To conceal something embarrassing or unpleasant in the hope that it will be overlooked. One may hide household dust by sweeping it under the carpet but one will not have removed it. The figurative expression dates from the 1960s.

Sweet Fanny Adams. The phrase, meaning 'nothing at all', dates from the early 20th century. On 21 August 1867 eight-year-old Fanny Adams was raped and hacked to death in a hop garden at Alton, Hampshire. A 21-year-old solicitor's clerk, Frederick Baker, was tried soon after and hanged on Christmas Eve at Winchester. The Royal Navy, with grim humour, adopted her name as a synonym for tinned mutton, first issued at this time, with reference to its negligible nutritious value. Sweet Fanny Adams became, as a consequence, a phrase for anything worthless, and then for 'nothing at all'. The phrase is often abbreviated as 'Sweet FA' or simply 'SFA', the 'F' often being taken as the 'F-word'. *See* FOUR-LETTER WORD.

> Some of us [columnists] have to find ways of making our cursors dance merrily across our computer screens, even if there is sweet fanny adams to write about.
> *The Times* (28 December 1999)

Sweetheart arrangement. A secret business arrangement for mutual advantage, especially between employers and trade-union leaders and on terms that are beneficial to both these sides but not to the employees. The use of 'sweetheart' in this sense arose in the United States in the 1950s.

Sweetie-pie. A term of endearment that is first recorded in the 1920s but that was still in regular use at the end of the century. The allusion is to a tasty dish such as an apple pie. A person to whom one is attracted is similarly 'toothsome'. The phrase was punningly adopted for the name of the canary Tweety Pie pursued by the 'puddy tat' Sylvester in the long series of Warner Brothers cartoons screened from 1947 to 1964.

Sweet nothings. Sentimental trivia; formulaic phrases of amorous import. The expression dates from the turn of the 20th century. *See also* COOCHY COOCHY COO; GOO-GOO EYES.

Sweet spot. The point on a tennis racket believed by players to deliver the maximum power to the ball. In 1997 a physicist in Australia claimed to have disproved its existence. The term was originally used with reference to a golf club. In a broader sense the sweet spot is used of an especially fortunate or beneficial circumstance or factor. The term is first recorded in the 1970s.

Swing. With reference to JAZZ, swing is solo or ensemble playing over a regular pulse beat in such a way as to give the impression of a 'swinging' (forward-moving) rhythmic momentum. 'To swing' is to play jazz music in this particular way and the term, although not new, gained a wide currency in the early 1930s from a popular number beginning: 'It don't mean a thing if it ain't got that swing.' *See also* BOOGIE-WOOGIE.

Swing both ways, To. To be bisexual. The expression dates from the 1970s.

Swinging London. A nickname for London in the SWINGING SIXTIES, when it was regarded as the fashion and music capital of the world, with CARNABY STREET as its focus.

Swinging sixties. The 1960s, regarded as a period when all was lively, fashionable and exciting. The phrase reflects not only the general sense of freedom following the constraints and hardships of the postwar period but also the mood of rebellion among the young, who rose against the ESTABLISHMENT to demand peace and a 'brave new world'. *See also* SUMMER OF LOVE.

Swingometer. A device used to demonstrate the effect of a political swing at the time of an election. The best known was that first used in the mid-1960s by the BBC broadcaster Robert McKenzie. It was shaped like a large inverted metronome and pushed to left or right, marking the percentage swing in votes to one side or the other. Its function was soon taken over by computer analysis, but its sophisticated successor in the 1997 general election, demonstrated by the broadcaster Peter Snow, was still known by the name.

> Once again the BBC's swingometer will be our earliest guide to the likely outcome. From the moment the first seat is declared, its pendulum will instantly and automatically swing to the party that has gained the advantage over the other since the last election.
>
> PETER SNOW in *The BBC News General Election Guide* (1997)

Swings and roundabouts. A situation in which a gain in one direction is balanced by a loss in the other. The allusion is to the fairground owner's mixed fortunes on the two attractions. The expression 'to gain on the swings and lose on the roundabouts' dates from the early 20th century.

> For 'up an' down an' round', said 'e, goes all
>   appointed things,
> An' losses on the roundabouts means profits on the
>   swings!
>
> PATRICK CHALMERS: *Green Days and Blue Days* (1912)

Swing the lead, To. To malinger. A leadsman on a ship required skill rather than strength when taking soundings, so was taunted for not pulling his weight with the rest of the crew. The expression dates from the early 20th century.

Swiss army knife. A form of combat knife incorporating various gadgets and so noteworthy for its versatility. The term may be used figuratively for a 'Jack-of-all-trades' or other handy person.

> 'I call Patty my Swiss army knife because she is capable of doing almost anything.'
>
> *The Times* (12 January 2000)

Switched on. Well informed on contemporary fashionable and popular cults; thoroughly up to date and responsive to current trends and tendencies. The expression dates from the 1960s and is also applied to

someone under the influence of drugs. *See also* TURN SOMEONE ON.

Swoose. A cross between a swan and a goose. The hybrid name dates from the 1920s. Animal names of this kind have an ancient pedigree that includes the *camelopard* or giraffe, believed at one time to be a cross between a camel and leopard, and the *leopard* itself, thought to be half lion, half pard (male panther). The 20th century has seen the *tigon* as the offspring of a male tiger and a lioness, a *liger*, conversely, as that of a male lion and a tigress, a *shoat* as the fruit of a sheep and a goat, and its own opposite number, a *geep*. In livestock breeding there is the *beefalo*, a beast that is three-eighths bison and five-eighths domestic cow, and the much older *catalo*, as a cross between a cow ('cattle') and a buffalo. In another flight, the *Swoose* was the B17 bomber flown by Colonel Frank Kurtz, the most decorated US pilot of the Second World War, and he preserved the name in that of his actress daughter, Swoosie Kurtz (b.1943).

Sword Beach. The Allied code name for the stretch of beach on the Normandy coast running from the River Orne in the east to JUNO BEACH in the west. It was the easternmost of the Normandy landing beaches, and on D-DAY it was where the British 3rd Division came ashore. By the end of the day the British held a stretch of beach 6.5km (4 miles) wide and had penetrated the same distance inland.

Sword opera. A term of the 1990s for a television drama series set in ancient times, with much swordplay and other stylized action of a more or less violent nature. An example is *Xena: Warrior Princess*, first shown on satellite television in 1996, in which the title character campaigns against wicked warlords, man-eating centaurs and the like. The term itself is based on SOAP OPERA. *See also* XENA.

Sydney or the bush. All or nothing. An Australian phrase dating from the 1920s. Sydney, as Australia's largest city and chief port, is 'all', while the bush, as uncultivated or unsettled land, is 'nothing'. The bush to Australians is country as opposed to town, rural life as opposed to urban.

Sykes. A much-loved television SITCOM screened from 1960 to 1965 and 1971 to 1979, featuring the self-improving Sykes, played by Eric Sykes, and his twin sister Hattie, played by Hattie Jacques (in real life the wife of John le Mesurier of DAD'S ARMY fame), the two sharing a house at 24 Sebastopol Terrace, Suburbia. Early episodes opened with the arrival of some new gadget or new goods, but later plots centred on a series of domestic crises. Deryck Guyler played Corky, a pompous police constable, to add to the gentle humour.

Symbionese Liberation Army. A corps of US revolutionaries who first surfaced in 1973, when they killed a school official with cyanide-tipped bullets. The following year they gained worldwide notoriety following their kidnapping of the 19-year-old newspaper heiress Patricia Hearst, demanding that her parents distribute free food to the Californian poor. When they complied, Hearst joined her captors, took the name Tania, and participated in a bank robbery. She eventually married her SLA bodyguard. The name derives from the Greek for 'living together'. *See also* STOCK-HOLM SYNDROME.

Sympathy for the Devil. A controversial song by the ROLLING STONES, credited to Mick Jagger and Keith Richards and released in 1968. Mick Jagger sings in the persona of a knowing and sinisterly sophisticated Satan ('Pleased to meet you, hope you guess my name/ But what's puzzling you is the nature of my game'), chronicling his impact on the history of the human race to the demonic rhythms of electric guitar, bongo drums and maracas. The song appears on the album *Beggar's Banquet*. *See also* ALTAMONT.

Please allow me to introduce myself
I'm a man of wealth and taste
I've been around for a long, long year
Stole many a man's soul and faith.

Synchromism (Greek *sun*, 'with', and *khrōma*, 'colour'). A form of abstract art resembling ORPHISM begun in 1912 by two young American artists living in Paris, Morgan Russell (1886–1953) and Stanton Macdonald-Wright (1890–1973). It was characterized by movements of pure colour evolving by gradations or rhythms from the primaries to the intermediary colours. Russell's *Synchromy in Green* (1913) was the first painting to bear the name. *See also* CUBISM; DADAISM; FAUVISM; FUTURISM; RURALISM; SURREALISM; VORTICISM.

T

Tabloid. A nickname dating from the early 20th century for a newspaper having pages half the size of the average broadsheet. It is usually popular in style and dominated by huge headlines, a plethora of photographs and a slew of sensational stories. The name was originally a proprietary term, registered on 14 March 1884 by Messrs Burroughs, Wellcome & Co., for a medicine sold in the form of a tablet. The term then came to denote any medicinal tablet and finally the newspaper as described, which presents news in a reduced format and a 'concentrated', easily assimilable form. The name was first applied in this new sense to the *Daily Mail*, founded in 1896, referring not to its format (it was originally a broadsheet) but to its brief and pithy paragraphs, which it promoted as 'all the news in the smallest space'. *See also* HEAVIES; RED-TOPS.

Tachism (French *tache*, 'spot', 'splotch'). A style of abstract painting popular in the late 1940s and 1950s, characterized by the use of irregular dabs or splotches of colour. The term was first used in this sense in *c*.1951 by the French art critics Charles Estienne and Pierre Guéguen and it was given wider currency by Michel Tapié in his book *Un Art autre* (1952). The genre has affinities with ABSTRACT EXPRESSIONISM and leading exponents include Jean Fautrier (1898–1964), Georges Mathieu (b.1921) and Pierre Soulages (b.1919). *See also* CUBISM; DADAISM; FAUVISM; FUTURISM; RURALISM; SURREALISM; VORTICISM.

Tackle, Darren. The fictitious footballer who contributes a weekly column, 'The Diary of Darren Tackle', to the *Guardian* newspaper. He plays for a club called the Greens at their Daihatsu Studium [*sic*] and his writings chronicle the life of a professional First League player, including his drug-taking, gambling and would-be womanizing, in which he is invariably rejected. *See also* DARREN.

Tactical voting. The practice of transferring one's normal political allegiance to another party when voting at an election, the aim being to deny victory to a third party. The tactic was first widely in evidence during the general election of February 1974, when many people who would have voted Labour if there had been a full number of parties in their constituency, voted Liberal where the Labour candidate had little or no chance of winning, thus hoping to deny a win to the Conservatives.

Ta-da! Take a look at this! Presenting … . A phrase imitating a fanfare, drawing attention to a person or thing, as: 'Ta-da! How do you like my hairstyle?' The word dates from the 1970s.

Taffia. A network of influential Welsh people, especially those of marked nationalistic stance. The term is or was intended humorously as a blend of Taffy (a Welshman) and Mafia.

Taff Vale judgement. The verdict in a civil suit brought by the Taff Vale Railway Company in 1901 against the Amalgamated Society of Railway Workers. The judge granted the company £23,000 damages against the union as compensation for losses incurred by the company during a strike. The precedent established by the judgement potentially threatened the ability of unions to carry out industrial action, and resentment over this was a factor in the formation of the Labour Party in 1906. In the same year the Trades Dispute Act granted trade unions immunity from such actions.

Taft-Hartley Act. A controversial Act of Congress of 1947, limiting the power of trade unions in the USA. Sponsored by Senator Robert A. Taft of Ohio and

Representative Fred A. Hartley Jr of New Jersey it outlawed closed shops, proscribed the political use of union funds and allowed the government to bring injunctions against strikes that endangered national health or safety. The legislation was prompted by various factors, among them a fear of communist infiltration of the unions, the rapid growth in power and membership of the unions themselves, and a series of large-scale strikes, together leading to an anti-union climate in the United States after the Second World War.

Taggart. A television crime drama series first screened in 1983 and centring on the cases investigated by the Glasgow DCI Jim Taggart, played by Mark McManus. Following McManus' premature death in 1994, the series continued with Taggart's sidekick, DI Jardine, played by James McPherson, and WDC Jackie Reid, played by Blythe Duff, leading the investigations. McManus's dour anti-hero image left a lasting impression on the screen and the episodes without him were to a large extent imbued with his unseen presence.

Taig. A derogatory Protestant nickname for a Roman Catholic in Northern Ireland. It is an anglicized spelling of the Irish name *Tadhg* (English Teague), itself a nickname for an Irish person.

Tail-end Charlie. An RAF phrase in the Second World War for the rear gunner in the tail of an aircraft; also for the aircraft at the rear of a group, or the last ship in a flotilla.

Tail wags the dog, The. The less important or subsidiary factor dominates the situation, and the normal roles are thus reversed. The expression dates from the 1930s.

Take a bath, To. To suffer loss, especially in business, sport or gambling, The allusion is to being 'cleaned out'. The expression dates from the 1930s. *See also* TAKE SOMEONE TO THE CLEANERS.

> *Scream* distributor Miramax took a bath on *The Faculty* when it was released in December '98, so might be running scared this time.
> *heat* (7–13 October 1999)

Take a dim view of, To. To regard with disapproval. The expression dates from the 1930s and is of military origin.

Take a gander, To. To take a look. The reference is to the bird's long neck.

Take a leak, To. To urinate, of a male. The expression

dates from the early 20th century, although 'leak' in this sense goes back to at least the time of Shakespeare: 'Why, they will allow us ne'er a jordan, and then we leak in the chimney' (*Henry IV, Part I*, IV, i; 1598).

Take a page out of someone's book, To. To imitate them; to follow their example.

Take a powder, To. To leave quickly, especially in order to avoid a difficult situation. The American expression dates from the 1930s and is a shortening of 'to take a run-out powder', meaning to escape, with 'powder' probably alluding to the dust that one raises as one leaves.

Take a raincheck, To. To politely decline an offer while implying that one may take it up later. The phrase is of American origin, a raincheck being a voucher entitling one to see another baseball game if the original for which a ticket was purchased is rained off. The noun alone may be used figuratively for a courteous or diplomatic refusal of the type described.

> The opt-out negotiated by John Major at Maastricht may yet prove one of the most valuable rainchecks ever to be secured by British diplomacy in Europe.
> *The Times* (23 October 1999)

Take a running jump at yourself! An expression of contempt, dislike or indifference. The phrase may have a veiled sexual import, as 'jump' is an old word for sexual intercourse.

Take back the night. A slogan first used in the United States in the 1970s as a theme for a women's protest march at night through San Francisco's pornography STRIP. It was made in the cause of halting the tide of violence against women and of promoting their demand that the perpetrators of such violence should be held responsible for their actions. *See also* RECLAIM THE NIGHT.

> We have to take back the night every night, or the night will never be ours. And once we have conquered the dark, we have to reach for the light, to take the day and make it ours.
> ANDREA DWORKIN: *Take Back the Night* (1978)

Take care. Look after yourself. A general expression of goodwill on parting, signing off a letter, ending a telephone call or the like. There is normally no suggestion that the person needs to be particularly careful. The catchphrase became current in the late 1960s or early 1970s.

Take care of number one, To. To put oneself first, even if at the expense of others.

Take five, To. To take a short break, notionally one of five minutes. The expression arose in the Second World War.

Take it, To. To suffer mental or physical hardship without complaint. The expression is often found in the negative, as: 'I just can't take it any more.' The phrase dates from the 1930s.

Take It From Here. A radio comedy series that ran from 1948 to 1959, created by Frank Muir and Denis Norden. It blended skits, sketches and songs and its most popular item was 'The Glums', a comic SOAP OPERA about the everlasting engagement between the absurdly gormless Ron and the eternally optimistic Eth. The title of the series is a common phrase used in rehearsing a script.

Take it on the chin, To. To endure hardship and adversity without complaint. A metaphor from boxing dating from the 1920s.

Take some or **a bit of doing, To.** To require special effort or planning. The phrase dates from the 1930s.

Take someone for a ride, To. To trick or deceive them, especially for financial gain. The expression derives from American underworld slang of the 1920s, in which it was a euphemism for 'to kill'. Assassins would take their victim out in a car, kill them at some stage, then dump the body.

Take someone to the cleaners, To. To deprive them of their money or possessions, especially fraudulently. One 'cleans them out'. A later meaning of the phrase is to defeat or to criticize, as: 'The Dutch team were taken to the cleaners', 'She really took him to the cleaners over the loan.'

Take something in one's stride, To. To deal with something unpleasant or difficult as if it were part of one's normal routine. The figurative expression evolved at the turn of the 20th century from the literal, as applied to a horse that cleared an obstacle (jumped a fence) without checking its gallop.

Take the axe to something, To. To cut or prune it drastically and often unexpectedly.

> Marks & Spencer has taken the axe to its boardroom for the second time this year.
> *The Times* (1 October 1999)

Take the fifth, To. In American usage to refuse to testify to a US legislative committee under the protection of the Fifth Amendment to the US Constitution (1789), which states, in part, that: 'No person … shall be compelled in any criminal case to be a witness against himself … without due process of law.'

Take the heat off someone, To. To relieve the pressure on them. A phrase dating from the 1960s.

Take the mickey out of someone, To. To tease them. 'Mickey' probably represents 'Mickey Bliss', rhyming slang for 'piss', so that the expression is a euphemism for 'to take the piss'. This in turn alludes to the deflating of a person, as a bladder deflates when emptying.

Take or **hit the silk, To.** To bale out of an aircraft by parachute. The expression dates from the 1930s and although of American origin perhaps partly puns on the legal phrase 'to take silk', said of a barrister who becomes a Queen's (or King's) Counsel.

Take the weight off one's feet, To. To sit down; to relax. An expression dating from the 1930s.

Take to the hills, To. To run off; to disappear. The expression dates from the 1930s and derives from Western or adventure films. *See also* HEAD FOR THE HILLS.

> Some [Conservatives] want to become a real liberal party, allying social and personal liberty with economic freedom. Others see the party taking to the hills.
> *Sunday Times* (2 January 2000)

Taleban. *See* TALIBAN.

Talented Mr Ripley, The. A thriller (1956) by Patricia Highsmith (1921–95), the first of five about Tom Ripley, a plausible young man with a pathological criminal mind, who is not averse to murder in order to maintain a comfortable existence in his chateau near Fontainebleau. The beautifully shot film version (1999), with Matt Damon in the role of Ripley, was directed by Anthony Minghella. Highsmith's story was also the basis of the superior 1959 film *Plein Soleil* (*Purple Noon*), which was directed by René Clément and starred Alain Delon as Ripley.

Talent scout or **spotter.** A person who searches out individuals who seem to have potential in a field such as entertainment, sport, modelling, or the like. In the world of espionage a talent spotter is a person who alerts an intelligence officer to someone who is a potential agent. The officer will then gather background information on the proposed agent and if appropriate make an approach.

Tale of Peter Rabbit, The. A story for young children (1900) written and illustrated by Beatrix Potter (1866–1943), first published privately. It became the forerunner of many similar books, whose success is due not just to her story-telling ability and command of language, but also to her shrewd characterization and ecological accuracy. She was a noted botanical artist and a mycologist whose work was in 1897 wrongly dismissed by the Linnaean Society as non-sense, causing her to abandon any further attempt to publicize the findings of her scientific research. She wrote in her secret diary: 'It is odious to a shy person to be snubbed as conceited, especially when the shy person happens to be right.'

Taliban or **Taleban** (Persian, 'students'). A fundament-alist Muslim militia formed in Afghanistan in 1994 as a force of youthful fighters from religious schools in Pakistan. They pledged to replace with Islamic law the factionalism that had marked Afghan political life since the demise of the communist regime in 1992. Boosted by popular support and military success, they captured the capital, Kabul, within two years and by 1997 had come to control two thirds of Afghan-istan. They interpret Islamic law in the strictest terms, calling for public floggings and stoning to enforce social restrictions, banning music, television and even kite-flying, and prohibiting many activities by women, who may not attend school, work or appear in public unless accompanied by a male relative.

> Peace is not an option for Afghanistan, despite the near-conquest of the nation by Taleban, the strangest of many conquerors over the centuries.
> *The Times* (23 September 1998)

Talking head. A television presenter or speaker, who appears only in head-and-shoulders close-up, with-out any distracting background. The expression dates from the 1960s and has a derogatory tone, implying passivity rather than activity. By contrast *Talking Heads* (1988) was a series of six moving monologues for television by Alan Bennett. *See also under* ROCK GROUP NAMES.

> *Green and Pleasant Land* has rocked Sunday nights for the past two months – talking heads telling stories from pre-war rural Britain.
> *The Times* (17 December 1999)

Talks about talks. Preliminary discussions held before entering into formal negotiations. The expression dates from the 1970s and typically relates to political debates or labour disputes.

Tall, dark and handsome. Winningly good-looking. A stock phrase current from the 1930s and typically applied to an admired or romantically viewed film actor such as Cary Grant (1904–86).

> After sending the pop world into a dizzy fit last year with an excess of latinate wiggling, Ricky Martin looks to have turned his back on the whole Tall, Dark And Handsome act by bleaching his hair.
> *heat* (13–19 January 2000)

Tall Ships race. An international sailing race held in the summer every two years over different courses, such as Plymouth to Tenerife or Falmouth to Copen-hagen. The ships may be square-riggers (with sails set at right angles) or fore-and-afters (with sails set lengthwise) and half the crew must be trainees in order to prevent domination by the professionals. Most of the crews are young – at least two have been all-female – and entrants include navies, govern-ments, cadet training establishments and the like. The first such race was held in 1956. The term 'tall ship' for a high-masted ship dates from at least the 16th cen-tury, long predating the opening lines of John Mase-field's poem 'Sea Fever':

> I must go down to the sea again, to the lonely sea and
>   the sky,
> And all I ask is a tall ship and a star to steer her by.
> JOHN MASEFIELD: 'Sea Fever' (1902)

Tamagotchi. An electronic toy that was all the rage in Britain in 1997. It displayed a digital image of a creature that had to be looked after and responded to by its owner as if it were a pet. The original Tama-gotchi was ovoid. Hence its name, based on Japanese *tamago*, 'egg'.

> The egg-sized cyberpet has not deserted the classroom completely. … The fall of Tamagotchi can be used to demonstrate to five-year-olds how an object can lose its value.
> *The Times* (23 July 1999)

Tamil Tigers. The short name of the Liberation Tigers of Tamil Eelam (LTTE), a Sri Lankan guerrilla organ-ization formed in 1972 with the aim of establishing an independent state in the northeast of the country, where there is a Tamil majority. Its members display a tiger-like ferocity and strength in their determination. Eelam is the name of the desired Tamil homeland.

Tamla Motown. The first black-owned record com-pany in the United States, set up by Berry Gordy in Detroit (MOTOWN) in 1959. It was originally two separa-ate companies, Tamla and Motown, the former taking its name from the song 'Tammy' sung by Ray Evans in the film *Tammy and the Bachelor* (1957), in which Tammy is a tomboy played by Debbie Reynolds.

Tánaiste. *See* TAOISEACH.

Tank. The heavy armoured combat vehicle running on caterpillar tracks was first introduced on the battlefield by the British in the Battle of the SOMME (1916). It was called by the code name 'tank' in order not to arouse enemy suspicions. The term came about partly because the vehicle resembled a water tank, partly because it was supposedly designed for use in desert warfare. British tanks are usually given names beginning with C. Examples are the Churchill, Cromwell and Comet during the Second World War and the Centurion, Chieftain and Challenger after it.

> 'Tanks' is what these new machines are generally called, and the name has the evident official advantage of being quite undescriptive.
>
> *The Times* (18 September 1916)

Tankies. A derogatory nickname of the 1980s for members of the British Communist Party who supported hardline Soviet policies, and specifically that of military intervention using tanks, as in Afghanistan.

Tank top. The close-fitting sleeveless top, typically made of wool and worn over a shirt or blouse, came into fashion in the late 1960s. It was named after the tank suits of the 1950s, as one-piece bathing costumes worn in a tank (swimming pool), and is often known simply as a tank. *See also* BIKINI.

Tank up, To. To fill a vehicle's petrol tank; to drink copiously. The latter sense is typically found in the passive, as: 'By now he was really tanked up.' The expressions date from the 1930s.

Tante Yvonne (French, 'Aunt Yvonne'). A nickname of Yvonne de Gaulle, née Vendroux (1900–79), wife of Charles de Gaulle (1890–1970), president of France (1958–69). She was so named for her homeliness.

Taoiseach. The prime minister of the Republic of Ireland, from an Irish word meaning 'chief', 'leader'. In the 1937 constitution of Ireland (mainly the work of Éamon de Valera; *see* DEV) the *taoiseach* replaced the president of the executive council (the name given to the prime minister of the Irish Free State from 1922). *Tánaiste*, the name given to the deputy prime minister under the 1937 constitution, was in Gaelic Ireland a king or chief's designated successor. *See also* EIRE.

Tapiola. The terse and monothematic tone poem by Jean Sibelius (1865–1957) was composed in 1925. It was his last great orchestral work, as he gave up composition for the last thirty years of his life. Tapio was a god of the forests in Finnish mythology, and the following sunny lines are written at the head of the score:

> Wide-spread they stand, the Northland's dusky forests
> Ancient, mysterious, brooding savage dreams;
> Within them dwells the Forest's mighty God,
> And wood sprites in the gloom weave magic secrets.

Taras Bulba. A stirring rhapsody for orchestra by Leoš Janáček (1854–1928). Taras Bulba was a 15th-century Ukrainian Cossack leader who fought the Poles. Janáček was inspired by an 1835 story about him by Nikolai Gogol (1809–52).

Tardis. *See* DOCTOR WHO.

Targa roof. A type of roof hood on a sports car. The forward, rigid section can be detached, when it leaves a soft, convertible rear section and a central transverse roll-bar for structural support. The name comes from a model of Porsche car with this feature, introduced in 1965, and taking its own name from Italian *targa*, 'plate', 'shield', probably with reference to the *Targa Florio*, 'Florio Shield', a motor time-trial held annually in Sicily.

Tarka. The otter that is the subject of Henry Williamson's moving novel *Tarka the Otter* (1927), set in north Devon, telling the story of his life and concluding with his hunt to the death. A HERITAGE RAILWAY line in his home country has been named after him.

Tarmac. An ingenious nickname given to the Jamaican-born footballer John Barnes (b.1963) during his period at Liverpool Football Club in the late 1980s and early 1990s. 'Tarmac' is an extension of the nickname the 'Black Heighway', conferred on Barnes by Liverpool in recognition of his supposed similarity to Steve Heighway, a Liverpool star of the 1970s.

Tartan Army. Scottish football supporters, famed for following their team's fortunes wherever they play and for visibly and audibly advertising their national allegiance. A typical contingent will wear tartan costumes or bonnets, sport ginger wigs, paint blue St Andrew's saltires on their faces, and fearlessly flaunt the Scottish flag in the territory of the enemy. *See also* BARMY ARMY.

Tartan Tories. A dismissive former nickname for the Scottish National Party, the SNP, originating with Willie Ross (later Lord Ross of Marnock; 1911–88), secretary of state for Scotland (1964–70, 1974–6) at a time when the SNP was achieving significant electoral successes. Ross himself lost office over his opposition to DEVOLUTION. Since then the SNP has moved to the left.

Tart with a heart. A prostitute with a generous nature. The full form of the phrase is 'tart with a heart of gold'.

> Salma Hayek plays a stripper who just happens to be an angel – an unfamiliar twist on the old tart with a heart cliché – in director Kevin Smith's new film *Dogma*.
>
> *heat* (7–13 October 1999)

Tarzan. The famous foundling reared by apes in the African jungle was created in 1912 by Edgar Rice Burroughs (1875–1950). He has countless adventures in novels and films, in which he communes with animals, rescues damsels in distress and discovers lost civilizations. The first novel of 24 in which he appears is *Tarzan of the Apes* (1914). In the 'monkey language' that Burroughs invented for him, his name means 'white skin', from *tar*, 'white', and *zan*, 'skin'. He is given this name by his foster-mother, Kala the ape. The name came to be adopted for any apparent 'he-man' and was bestowed by the media on the Conservative politician Michael Heseltine (b.1933), not only for his height and blond hair but also with reference to an incident of 1976 when he brandished the House of Commons mace to protect it. Tarzana, now a suburban residential section of Los Angeles, was named in honour of Tarzan. *See also* HEZZA; SHEENA.

> The power that makes us respond to the wanderings of Odysseus is also at work in Burroughs' Tarzan, and the two great popular heroes speak openly to our most cherished fantasies.
>
> ERLING B. HOLTSMARK: *Tarzan and Tradition: Classical Myth in Popular Literature* (1981)

Task force. An armed force set up for a special operation, the latter being the 'task'. The term, of US origin and dating from the Second World War, was generally brought before the public in 1982 at the time of the FALKLANDS WAR, when the British government sent a naval task force to liberate the islands from the Argentinians.

TASS. The official news agency of the former Soviet Union, founded in 1925. The initials stand for *Telegrafnoe agentstvo Sovetskogo Soyuza* (Russian, 'Telegraphic Agency of the Soviet Union'). It had bureaux in many foreign countries (some used as covers for KGB activities), and Western analysts regarded its pronouncements as following the official Soviet line. In January 1992, shortly after the collapse of the Soviet Union, TASS became an independent commercial news agency, renaming itself ITAR (Information Telegraph Agency of Russia), although the name TASS was preserved for the domestic wire service. In Britain TASS was an acronym for the former Technical and Supervisory Staff union, now part of the MSF (Manufacturing, Scientific and Finance union).

Taste of Honey, A. A play (1958) by Shelagh Delaney (b.1939) about the experiences of a young working-class girl, Jo, who finds herself pregnant after a brief affair with a black naval rating. The film (1961), directed by Tony Richardson and starring Rita Tushingham as Jo, was admired as a fine example of KITCHEN SINK DRAMA. The title echoes a line in 1 Samuel 14:43: 'I did but taste a little honey with the end of the rod that was in mine hand, and, lo, I must die.'

Tate bricks. The name by which the installation entitled *Equivalent VIII*, by the American sculptor and poet Carl Andre (b.1935), has become popularly known. The installation, consisting of 120 firebricks arranged in a rectangle two bricks deep, was first created in 1966 and purchased by the Tate Gallery, London, in 1972. The work was vandalized in 1976 when a visitor threw dye over it in protest at what they considered to be a waste of public money.

Tautonym (Greek *tauto*, 'same'). In biological nomenclature this term indicates a taxonomic name in which the generic repeats the specific, as *Martes martes*, the pine marten. It could equally be applied, however, to the growing rank of designations, mainly in the business world, in which the generic word repeats a word that has become absorbed in an abbreviation whose original meaning is forgotten. A familiar example is 'PIN number', where 'number' repeats the word in 'personal identification number', the origin of the abbreviated 'PIN'. Other examples are 'ATM machine' (from 'automated teller machine'), 'APR rate' ('annual percentage rate'), 'TSB bank' ('Trustee Savings Bank') and, as its own official name, 'HSBC Bank' ('Hongkong and Shanghai Banking Corporation'). Also not uncommon in the media are 'AGM meeting' ('annual general meeting') and 'HIV virus' ('human immunodeficiency virus') (*see* HIV-POSITIVE).

Tawny Owl. *See* BROWN OWL.

Taxi Driver. A bleakly realistic film (1976), directed by Martin Scorsese, about an inarticulate VIETNAM veteran who becomes a taxi driver and who is dehumanized by the urban landscape of violent crime and brutality around him. The film starred Robert DeNiro and, controversially, 12-year-old Jodie Foster as the drug-addicted teenage whore, Iris.

Taxi squad. In American football a group of players who are not listed on a club's roster but who take part in practices and who are available as reserves for the team. The term owes its origin to Arthur McBride, founder of the Cleveland Browns football team, who also ran a taxi company, and who would give such players jobs with his business to support them and keep them available.

Taxman. A blues-influenced song by the BEATLES, credited to George Harrison, and released in the UK in August 1966. It refers to the raising of the top rate of income tax by the then Labour government to 19 shillings (95 pence) in the pound. The 'taxman' is thus the Labour prime minister of the time, Harold Wilson, but the lyric also includes a reference to the Conservative party leader, Edward Heath.

Tea and sympathy. Caring and hospitable behaviour towards a troubled person. The phrase comes from the title of Robert Anderson's play of 1953 about the problems faced by a sensitive teenage schoolboy accused of homosexuality. The 'tea and sympathy' in question is provided by the housemaster's wife. A film version followed in 1956.

> All you're supposed to do is every once in a while give the boys a little tea and sympathy.
> ROBERT ANDERSON: *Tea and Sympathy*, I (1953)

Tea boy. The boy whose job it is to make the tea. The designation is a paradigm for the lowliest employee in an organization, especially in the context of its chain of authority.

Teacher's pet. A person regarded with (undue) favour. The original sense, as applied to a teacher's favourite pupil, dates from the 1920s.

Teach-in. An American term for a series of lectures and discussions on a particular theme led by experts. The expression became current in England in the 1960s.

Teamster. An American term for a lorry driver, and specifically one who belongs to the Teamsters Union, the largest labour union in the United States. It was founded in 1903 as the International Brotherhood of Teamsters, Chauffeurs, Stablemen and Helpers of America but in 1940 'Stablemen' became 'Warehousemen'. It has had a chequered career, and between 1957 and 1988 three of its presidents were convicted of various criminal charges and sentenced to prison terms. Among their number was Jimmy Hoffa (1913–c.75), leader of the Teamsters from 1957, who was imprisoned in 1967 for the attempted bribery of a federal court judge after he was charged with corruption. Released by President Nixon in 1971, Hoffa disappeared in 1975 and is generally believed to have been murdered. His controversial career was the subject of a lengthy and tedious biopic, *Hoffa* (1992), starring Jack Nicholson.

Teapot Dome scandal. A corruption scandal that affected President Warren Harding's administration in the 1920s. For strategic reasons the government had acquired a number of US oil fields, and from 1921 the administration of these assets came under Albert B. Fall (1861–1944), secretary of the interior. Fall, in return for more than $300,000 (and a herd of cattle), secretly allowed the Mammoth Oil Company to drill on one of the government's oil fields, at Teapot Dome in Wyoming in 1922. He also did similar illegal deals with the Pan American Petroleum Company for the Elk Hills and Buena Vista Hills fields in California (the scandal is also called the Elk Hills scandal). Fall was eventually convicted and imprisoned.

Tear into someone, To. To attack or scold them; to attack them physically.

Tearjerker. A sentimental or romantic film evoking sadness, sympathy, yearning or the like. The term, of American origin and dating from the 1920s, can also apply to a novel, play, story, song or even person or event, such as a farewell occasion. Whatever it is, it can bring tears to the eyes. *See also* LOVE STORY.

Teasmade. The automatic tea-making machine of this name was invented by one Brenner Thornton in 1936 and the following year bought by the firm of Goblin, who made vacuum cleaners. The name is a neat pun on 'tea's maid' and 'tea's made', both indicating a personal service. Goblin's original model was rather more lavish than in later years, incorporating not only a clock and a bedside light but including two earthenware cups and saucers, a cream jug and a sugar basin.

Technicolor. Since the inception of the cinema filmmakers had sought to create a colour film. Early attempts were crude and unsatisfactory until 1922, when HOLLYWOOD produced its first Technicolor feature, a version of *Madama Butterfly* entitled *Toll of the Sea*. The process involved a camera containing two strips of film, one for red, the other for green, and a prism to split the incoming light into the primary colours. When the film was developed the two strips were combined, producing pleasing, natural results. The technique was further improved subsequently.

Techno. A type of popular music with a dance beat first appearing in the late 1980s, so called from its heavy use of technology in the form of synthesized sounds and electronic effects. TRANCE was a development.

Technobabble. Pretentious scientific or pseudo-scientific jargon, especially in the world of computers. The word is based on the earlier PSYCHOBABBLE, as the jargon of popular psychology.

Teddy bear. A child's toy bear, named after US President Theodore (Teddy) Roosevelt (1858–1919), who was fond of bear-hunting. Roosevelt was shown sparing the life of a bear-cub in a cartoon drawn by C.K. Berryman in 1902 as a spoof on the president's role as an ardent conservationist. In 1906 the *New York Times* published a humorous poem about the adventures of two bears named Teddy B and Teddy G in his honour. These names were then given to two bears newly presented to the Bronx Zoo and manufacturers seized on the event to put toy bears called teddy bears on the market. *See also* BRIDESHEAD REVISITED; TEDDY BEARS' PICNIC; WINNIE-THE-POOH.

Teddy bears' picnic. An occasion of innocent merriment. The phrase comes from the popular song of this name, which originated as a piece composed by John W. Bratton in 1907 as a tribute to President Theodore Roosevelt (*see* TEDDY BEAR). Words by Jimmy Kennedy were added in 1930 at the request of the publisher, B. Feldman and Co, for use in a Manchester pantomime. Val Rosing's famous recording with Henry Hall's Orchestra, made in 1932, was nominated by the 1933 International Radio Convention as ideal for testing broadcasting equipment.

> If you go down in the woods today
> You're sure of a big surprise
> If you go down in the woods today
> You'd better go in disguise.
> For every Bear that ever there was
> Will gather there for certain because,
> Today's the day the Teddy Bears have their Picnic.
> JIMMY KENNEDY: 'The Teddy Bears' Picnic' (1930)

Teddy Boys. A name arising in the 1950s for working-class youths who affected a style of dress and appearance supposedly reminiscent of the EDWARDIAN ERA, 'Teddy' being a pet form of the name Edward. Their costume typically consisted of a brightly coloured and velvet trimmed frock coat, an ornamental waistcoat, DRAINPIPES, and a narrow tie. Footwear could vary but often took the form of shiny lace-ups, BROTHEL CREEPERS or WINKLE-PICKERS. Hair styles were important, and were mostly based on a variant of the quiff. Two favourites were the DUCK'S ARSE and the so called 'elephant trunk', the latter being a large and long quiff swept forward over the face. Teds were often regarded as troublemakers, and the media carried stories of gang violence and antisocial behaviour. The flamboyance of dress and demeanour, however, to some extent compensated for the associated aggravation and aggressiveness, while it was the advent of the new pop music that took the teen cult into the mainstream. *See also* ROCK 'N' ROLL.

Teds. A colloquial name for TEDDY BOYS, dating almost from the first.

Teenage Mutant Ninja Turtles. A popular children's television cartoon series screened from 1988 to 1995. The characters were four turtles named Michelangelo, Raphael, Leonardo and Donatello, who with the aid of a ninja mask, as worn by Japanese ninjutsu, became swift martial arts experts. They were 'mutant' because when accidentally dropped down the New York sewer system they grew to human size and gained the power of speech. They were conceived in 1983 by Kevin Eastman and Peter Laird as a parody of the Japanese samurai-style heroes then prominent in comic strips.

Teenybopper. An American colloquialism applied in the 1960s and 1970s to girls in their early teens who adopted current fashions in dress and were devotees of pop music and the latest crazes generally. Although deriving from 'teen' the term has been influenced by 'teeny' (in the sense of small).

Tee-shirt. *See* T-SHIRT.

Teething troubles. Short-term problems that occur in the early stages of an enterprise. The expression dates from the 1930s and rather obviously alludes to the difficulty or discomfort sometimes experienced by young children when cutting or growing their teeth.

On one freezing morning just before Christmas, patrons ... were forced to queue for tickets *outside* the theatre for two hours, before being allowed to wait (for a further two hours) inside. Teething troubles? Perhaps.

The Times (4 January 2000)

Teflon. Properly a patent non-stick coating for cooking vessels marketed from the mid-1950s, the name has been taken up by the media to apply to anyone, but especially a politician, who is 'non-stick' in terms of blame, criticism, scandal and the like. In 1983 'Teflon-coated' was memorably applied by the Democratic Congresswoman Patricia Schroeder to President Reagan in this way. The word itself combines letters from the substance's scientific name, poly*tetra*fluoroethylene, with '-on' as in nylon or rayon.

Telecom Valley. A nickname for the Côte d'Azur in southeast France, as the location of several French and foreign telecommunications companies. The name is patterned on America's SILICON VALLEY.

Telecottage. Not usually a cottage in the normal sense but a room or building in a rural area containing computer equipment for the use of local people. The concept is of Swedish origin and the word translates Swedish *telestuga*. The first telecottage in Britain was opened in 1989 at a school in Warslow, Staffordshire.

Telethon. A mammoth television programme, or 'television marathon', especially one designed to raise money for charity. Telethons have been broadcast on independent television since the early 1980s, with viewers making donations by telephoned pledges. That of 1990 was a continuous live event lasting 27 hours and raising £24 million, but in 1992 the total fell to just over £15 million.

Teletourism. The last quarter of the 20th century saw the growth of television tourism, as the visiting of places where popular television programmes were filmed, especially SOAP OPERAS and dramatizations of novels. The places are invariably renamed in their televisual reincarnation, and this is part of the attraction for the fans, who as in the story itself are happy to blur the distinction between real and fictional. Even when the fictional place is unnamed, the location of filming still draws the crowds, as did Holmfirth, Kirklees, the setting of The LAST OF THE SUMMER WINE (1973–95). The following are some of the better known, fictional name first. *See also* COUNTRY.

Aidensfield (HEARTBEAT, from 1990): Goathland, North Yorkshire

Arnscote (*By the Sword Divided*, 1983, 1985): Rockingham Castle, Leicestershire

Beckindale (*Emmerdale*, from 1989): Esholt, Bradford

Brideshead (BRIDESHEAD REVISITED, 1981): Castle Howard, North Yorkshire

Cardale (*Peak Practice*, from 1993): Crich, Derbyshire

Darrowby (*All Creatures Great and Small*, 1978–90): Askrigg, North Yorkshire

Dibley (*The Vicar of Dibley*, from 1994): Turville, Buckinghamshire

Emmerdale (*Emmerdale Farm*, 1972–89): Arncliffe, North Yorkshire (*see also* Beckindale)

Fawlty Towers (FAWLTY TOWERS, 1975–9): Wooburn Grange, Bourne End, Buckinghamshire

Grantleigh Manor (*To the Manor Born*, 1979–81): Cricket House, Cricket St Thomas, Somerset

Home Farm (*The* DARLING BUDS OF MAY, 1991–3): Bliss Farm, Pluckley, Kent

Middlemarch (*Middlemarch*, 1994): Stamford, Lincolnshire

Millstone Manor (*Grace and Favour*, 1992): Chavenage House, Tetbury, Gloucestershire

Tannochbrae (1) (*Doctor Finlay's Casebook*, 1962–71): Callander, Scotland

Tannochbrae (2) (*Doctor Finlay*, from 1993): Auchtermuchty, Scotland

Tarrant (*Howards' Way*, 1985–90): Bursledon, Hampshire

Walmington-on-Sea (DAD'S ARMY, 1968–77): Thetford, Norfolk

Teletubbies. The four 'techno-babies', Tinky Winky, Dipsy, La La and Po, who first appeared on BBC children's television in 1997 as the creation of the children's television producer Anne Wood. They are distinctively coloured and resemble miniature spacemen, with aerials on their heads and televisions in their stomachs. They live in a magical land and have a friend in the Noo Noo, a vacuum cleaner character, who cleans up after them. They speak baby language and mostly run about, play, dance and eat custard and toast.

Their fans came to include both young viewers and students, the latter awarding them cult status, but many parents regarded them with disfavour because of their apparently deleterious effect on the speech-learning processes of their offspring.

Tell it like it is, To. To give the facts realistically or honestly. The expression originated from black English in the 1960s.

Tell me another! You can't expect me to believe that! The implication is that speaker is telling a lie or a joke rather than relating a fact.

Tell someone what to do with something, To. To reject something vehemently. 'What they can do with it' is stick it up their backside.

Tell someone where to get off or **where to go, To.** To scold them for interfering; to tell them off. 'Where they get off' or 'where they go' is hell.

> Someone suggested he [BBC chief political correspondent John Sergeant] present the late Sunday night God slot *Everyman*. Sergeant ... told his BBC bosses where to go.
>
> *The Times* (21 January 2000)

Telstar. The name given to the satellite launched by the United States in 1962 for relaying transatlantic telephone messages and television pictures. It was something of a pioneer of its time and that same year was even the subject of a popular musical hit by the British group the Tornados.

Tempest, The. A vivid expressionist painting by Oskar Kokoschka (1886–1980). Subtitled *The Bride of the Wind*, the work, painted in a broad painterly style somewhat reminiscent of the 16th-century Spanish painter El Greco, depicts a man and a woman swirling together in space. The painting, which dates from 1914, reflects the stormy relationship between Kokoschka and his mistress, Alma Mahler, the widow of the composer.

Temple, Paul. The English detective-novelist created by Francis Durbridge for the radio serial *Send for Paul Temple* (1938) and its many sequels broadcast over the next 30 years. He soon appeared in novels, the first of which appeared in the same year as the radio serial under the same title. Temple was the leading fictional detective on BBC radio in the Second World War, and he then graduated to films such as *Calling Paul Temple* (1948) and *Paul Temple Returns* (1952), all starring John Bentley.

Temporary gentleman. A nickname in the First World War for an officer commissioned only for the duration of the war. The allusion is to the hallowed phrase 'an officer and a gentleman'.

Temptation of Eileen Hughes, The. A novel (1981) by the Irish writer Brian (pronounced Bree-an) Moore (1921–99). At the centre of the narrative is Bernard McAuley, a materialist 'in search of a soul'. The title implies that he is the 'tempter', but Eileen herself is an object of temptation to Bernard, who finally commits suicide after Eileen has rejected the life he offers.

Ten Days that Shook the World. The title of a book (1919) by the US journalist John Reed (1887–1920), an eyewitness account of the BOLSHEVIK Revolution in Russia in November 1917. Reed, who came from a wealthy background, was one of the leading radical figures in the USA, became a friend of LENIN and helped to found the US Communist Party. Accused of treason in the USA, he fled to Soviet Russia, where he died of typhus. After his death the US Communist Party established many 'John Reed' clubs for writers and artists in US cities. His life is the subject of the film *Reds* (1981), directed by and starring Warren Beatty.

Tender Is the Night. A novel (1934) by F. Scott Fitzgerald (1896–1940). Written and rewritten under various titles several times, it in some respects complements the autobiographical novel, *Save Me the Waltz* (1932), by Fitzgerald's wife, Zelda (Sayre) (1900–48), whom he married in 1920 and who was from 1937 almost permanently in a home for the mentally ill. The novel charts the deterioration of a psychiatrist, Dick Diver, who marries one of his patients, a schizophrenic. The title comes from 'Ode to a Nightingale' by John Keats (1795–1821): 'Already with thee! Tender is the night,/And haply the Queen-Moon is on her throne.' A patchy film version (1961) was directed by Henry King.

Ten for 66 and All That. The title of the autobiography of the Australian leg-spin bowler Arthur Mailey (1886–1967) punning on the title of Sellar and Yeatman's celebrated 1066 AND ALL THAT and celebrating his feat of taking 10 wickets for 66 runs for the Australians against Gloucestershire in 1921.

Tenko. A grimly realistic television drama by Lavinia Warner running from 1981 to 1984 and telling of the trials and tribulations of a disparate group of British and Dutch women in a Japanese prison camp after the fall of Singapore in 1942. The title is the Japanese for 'rollcall'.

Ten Little Niggers. A detective novel (1939; as *And Then There Were None*, 1940; also published as *Ten Little Indians* and *The Nursery Rhyme Murders*) by Agatha Christie (1890–1976). The changes of title were largely due to POLITICAL CORRECTNESS. The references are to the familiar nursery rhyme, written as a song by Frank Green in 1868 or 1869: 'Ten little nigger boys went out to dine;/One choked his little self, and then there were

nine [etc]. … One little nigger boy living all alone; /
He got married, and then there were none.' It was
undoubtedly inspired by Septimus Winner's 'Ten
Little Injuns', published in England a short while
earlier, and still remembered in American nurseries.
A classic film version (1945), with some splendid acting cameos, was meticulously directed by René Clair
as an enjoyable black comedy.

10 out of 10. Complete success. A term of admiration
or approval for something perfectly done. The allusion is to 10 out of 10 marks in a piece of schoolwork,
'full marks'. Hence '10' as a colloquialism for the ideal
man or woman, reinforced by the film *10* (1979), in
which a sexually obsessed middle-aged composer
marks his girls one to 10 depending on their performance. The one awarded the maximum was played
by Bo Derek. Assessing a possible romantic or sexual
partner on such a scale is a common practice among
young people and is found in socializing settings such
as clubs, pubs, television dating shows and the like.

> One of my favourite things there is that the girls would
> always go '6, 7', something like that. The guys would
> always add on halves. They'd be like '8, 8 and a half'.
> And I'd go, 'What's the half for?' What's that about?
> *heat* (16 December 1999–5 January 2000)

1066 and all that. Britain's past history, popularly
viewed as explaining the nation's heterogeneous
heritage. The phrase is the title of W.C. Sellar and
R.J. Yeatman's humorous survey of British history,
published in 1930 as 'a subtle mixture of schoolboy
howlers, witty distortions and artful puns'. The book
was designed to satirize the smugness of the English
and the teaching of history by rote, but ironically itself
became a historical icon. A typical definition is 'The
Cavaliers (Wrong but Wromantic) and the Round-
heads (Right but Repulsive)'. 1066, as the date of the
Norman Conquest, probably still remains the best
known date in British history, 'all that' being the blur
of dates and events that occurred before and after it.

> The earl's own name undermined the solidity of
> his Anglo-Saxon lineage. Charles Francis Topham de
> Vere Beauclerk is an elision of British and French, a
> reminder of 1066 and all that.
> *The Times* (28 October 1999)

Ten to two. With one's hands on the steering wheel of
a car in the position of the hands of a clock showing
ten minutes to two. The phrase is equally used of a
person's feet so placed. The stated time is also that at
which clocks and watches are set when offered for

sale, the position of the hands supposedly representing a smile in order to encourage a purchase.

Tequila sunrise. A cocktail of tequila and grenadine,
popular in the 1970s. Its name alluded to its lurid hue,
which placed it in the lower range of the social scale.

Terminator, The. A film thriller (1984) about a lethal
cyborg robot that is sent back in time to the present
day in order to kill the mother of a future leader of
mankind in the battle against machines that seek to
take over the planet. Starring Arnold Schwarzenegger
as the 'Terminator', the film was followed by the
equally successful sequel *Terminator 2: Judgment Day*
(1991), which at $100 million was then the most
expensive film ever made. The films established
'terminator' as a stock phrase for any person hired
to kill or otherwise reduce the opposition, from assassins and mercenaries to officials and industrial
managers ordered to make cuts in staffing levels.

> Hasta la vista, baby.
> ARNOLD SCHWARZENEGGER: *Terminator 2*

Terminological inexactitude. A mock-pompous
euphemism for a downright lie, sometimes resorted
to in Parliament for this purpose. It was first so used
in a speech about labour contracts by Winston
Churchill:

> It cannot in the opinion of His Majesty's Government
> be classified as slavery in the extreme acceptance
> of the word without some risk of terminological
> inexactitude.
> *Hansard* (22 February 1906)

Terran. A SCIENCE FICTION name for an inhabitant of the
planet Earth, from Latin *terra*, 'earth'. The term dates
from the 1950s, with the spelling and capital dif-
ferentiating the word from the much earlier 'terrene',
as applied to the dry land or to the world in the sense
'secular'.

Terrence Higgins Trust. Britain's leading AIDS charity,
founded in 1982 in memory of one of the first British
gay men to die of the disease. Terrence Higgins had
joined the navy as an 18-year-old but sought release
on discovering his sexuality. Denied this legitimate
loophole, he painted hammer and sickle symbols all
over the ship on which he was serving and was finally
asked to leave. In the late 1960s he made his way to
SWINGING LONDON and spent much of his time party-
ing. Things began to go wrong in the early 1980s,
when he started to lose weight, and a collapse on the
dance floor resulted in his admission to hospital. He

discharged himself but was soon readmitted. Doctors diagnosed a parasitic pneumonia but were at a loss to identify its cause. Friends were expecting Higgins to make a full recovery but on 4 July 1982 death supervened.

Terrible beauty. *See* EASTER RISING.

Terriers. The Territorial Army was established in 1908 as part of the military reforms of Lord Haldane, then secretary of state for war, and within months had been semi-officially dubbed with the apt nickname. 'Terrors' and 'Torrals' were also considered but wisely rejected. The TA is now part of the wider Reserve Forces but has retained its identity and its sobriquet.

Terry Lee. *See* LEE, TERRY.

Tesco. *See* PILE IT HIGH, SELL IT CHEAP.

TESSA. The popular, friendly sounding Tax-Exempt Special Savings Account, introduced in 1991, allowed savers to invest a stated amount in a bank or building society and pay no tax on the interest, so long as the capital remained in the account for five years. Together with the PEP, it yielded to the blander ISA (Individual Savings Account) in 1999.

Test-tube baby. A baby conceived by *in vitro* fertilization. The world's first child to be born in this way was Louise Brown, delivered by Caesarian operation at Oldham District Hospital, Greater Manchester, on 26 July 1978. The embryo had been implanted in Mrs Brown's womb the previous November, after one of her eggs was fertilized in a test-tube by her husband's sperm. The procedure was the subject of considerable criticism at the time, both within the scientific establishment and from groups opposed on religious and ethical grounds.

Tet offensive. An attack carried out by North Vietnamese forces and VIET CONG in early 1968, during the VIETNAM War (1964–75). The offensive was aimed at major towns and cities throughout South Vietnam and was launched on 31 January, the Vietnamese Tet (new year) holiday, when many South Vietnamese troops were on leave. The communists managed to seize a number of symbolic targets in the South Vietnamese capital, Saigon, including the US embassy itself. Although through February US and South Vietnamese forces took a terrible toll of the Viet Cong, the determined and coordinated nature of the attack shocked many Americans, who viewed the fighting nightly on their television sets. The negative reaction of the American public persuaded President Johnson (*see* LBJ) to try to find a way out of the war.

Tetra Pak. The ubiquitous plastic-coated paper-board cartons for milk and other liquids were the invention in 1951 of the Swiss entrepreneur Dr Ruben Rausing, who chose the original tetrahedon shape that gave the name because it used a small amount of material to enclose a large volume. It was awkward to handle, however, and was superseded by several other configurations, including the 'Tetra Brik'. These were developed by the inventor's son, Gad Rausing, who bought the rights to the product in 1965 and together with his brother, Hans, built up the new business into the world's largest food packaging group.

Texas. The name of the American state has come to be used in various belittling culinary senses in the 20th century. Thus Texas butter is gravy made with flour and water in dripping, Texas strawberries are red beans and Texas toast is a thick slice of bread warmed (but not toasted) and spread with butter. Texas tea, however, is a nickname for marijuana, easily available in the state.

Texas Chainsaw Massacre, The. A notorious HORROR MOVIE (1974) written by Kim Henkel and Tobe Hooper in which a family of chainsaw-wielding unemployed slaughterhouse workers terrorize a Texas community, desecrating the local cemetery and decorating their house with human and animal remains. The title proclaimed the film's horror credentials, although it contains few scenes with much gore. It was loosely based upon the atrocities committed in real life by deranged Wisconsin farmer Ed Gein, whose bloodthirsty activities also influenced Alfred Hitchcock's PSYCHO. *See also* SPLATTER MOVIE.

TGIF. 'Thank God it's Friday', an utterance of relief from the world-weary worker. *See also* POET'S DAY.

TGV train. The first *train à grande vitesse* or French high-speed electric train ran from Paris to Lyon in 1981. Its cruising speed is about 300kph (185mph).

Thalidomide. A sedative and anti-sickness drug that was prescribed in West Germany and the UK between 1959 and 1962. However, it was found that if taken by pregnant women it badly affected the development of the foetus, leading to children being born with 'seal limbs' and other deformities. More than 2000 such children were born in West Germany, and around 500 in the UK, until the drug was withdrawn.

Thames and Hudson. A publishing house famous for its art books. It was founded in 1949 with offices in London and New York and initially hoped to attract an English-speaking readership on both sides of the Atlantic. Hence its name, from the rivers Thames and Hudson, on which London and New York respectively stand. The origin is also pictorially represented in its colophon of two dolphins, the upper one facing left or west, the lower right or east.

Thanks a million. Thank you very much. The usage is mostly ironic: 'Thanks a million, talking to you has made me late for work.' The same goes for variants such as 'Thanks a bunch'.

Thanks, but no thanks. I appreciate your offer but do not wish to accept it. A catchphrase from the 1970s. The implication is often that the offer is unacceptable rather than unwanted.

Thatcherism. A term for the policies and style of government of Margaret Thatcher (b.1925) as Conservative prime minister (1979–90). It denoted an emphasis on monetarism as a means of controlling the economy, the privatization of nationalized industries and trade union legislation. In a broader sense Thatcherism connoted a stress on individual responsibility and enterprise. *See also* IRON LADY.

> Her [Iris Murdoch's] journey from youthful illusion to disillusionment, from early support of the Communist Party to a kind of inchoate Thatcherism, was a model for her generation.
> *New Statesman* (12 February 1999)

Thatcher's Britain. A mainly derogative media nickname for Britain under the premiership of Margaret Thatcher (*see* THATCHERISM), especially as a society moulded or affected by the policies of her successive governments. The term was current for the whole of the 1980s.

Thatcher's children. The rising generation of the 21st century, especially the young Britons born in 1982, in the early days of THATCHERISM, and coming of age in the hallmark year 2000. Media pundits inevitably gave confused and conflicting interpretations of their attitudes and aspirations.

> They are confident, consumerist, content. But do Thatcher's children – proud of their country but unwilling to vote – have some nasty surprises in store?
> *Sunday Times Magazine* (2 January 2000)

That'll be the day. That will be worth waiting for. The usage is mainly ironic, implying that the day will never come. The phrase is of New Zealand origin and dates from the 1930s. 'That'll Be The Day' was the title of a song by Buddy Holly and the Crickets (1957), and

was also the title of a film (1975), starring David Essex, about a fairground worker's ascent to pop stardom.

That makes two of us. I quite agree; I know all about that. A catchphrase dating from the 1950s and typically said by someone who has experienced the same misfortune or unpleasantness as another.

That Obscure Object of Desire. A film, originally entitled *Cet obscur objet du désir* (1977), written and directed by the Spanish film director Luis Buñuel (1900–83), about a French businessman's obsessive love for a beautiful young Spanish woman called Conchita, the object of his desire. The obscurity of Conchita's character and her feelings for her admirer were cleverly emphasized by Buñuel's trick of casting two actresses, Carole Bouquet and Angela Molina, in the same role.

That's about the size of it. That's the way it looks. The phrase implies both an agreement and an assessment of a situation that is probably bad rather than good.

That's all I need. That is the last straw, on top of what I have already endured. The ironic phrase dates from the 1950s.

That's Life! A television programme broadcast by the BBC from 1973 to 1994. Presented by Esther Rantzen, it was a popular blend of consumer complaints, staged stunts and crudely comic street interviews.

That's the way the cookie crumbles. That's how things turn out. When you break or bite a cookie (biscuit) it may crumble anywhere. The American expression dates from the 1950s.

That Was The Week That Was. British television's first satirical show, screened by the BBC from 1962 to 1963. *TW3*, as it came to be known, was produced late on Saturday nights by Ned Sherrin and was characterized by a tone of irreverent informality. Features included revue sketches and songs, impromptu cartoons, and provocative monologues delivered from a high stool by Bernard Levin, who on one occasion was assaulted by an irate member of the audience. The presenter was David (now Sir David) Frost.

Theatre-in-the-round. A form of play presentation in which the audience is seated all round the acting area. It is one of the oldest forms of theatre but was revived in the 20th century as a conscious art form by those rebelling against the 'tyranny' of the proscenium arch, which can form a barrier between actors and audience. It was pioneered in the Soviet Union but then taken up elsewhere, some theatres being specifically designed for the purpose. *See also* ROUND HOUSE.

Theatreland. A name for the area of a city where many theatres are located. The designation is usually taken to apply to London, where the leading theatres are grouped in the West End between Oxford Street and the Strand. In this sense the name was introduced by the *Daily Chronicle* in its issue of 28 December 1905.

Theatre of Cruelty. A term for plays in which the dramatist seeks to communicate a sense of pain, suffering and evil through the portrayal of extreme violence. The expression translates French *théâtre de la cruauté*, coined by the French poet, actor and director Antonin Artaud in his *Manifeste du théâtre de la cruauté* (1932). Artaud's theory was that theatre should not be simply entertainment but genuine action with real effects on the real world, a typical scenario being a police raid on a RED-LIGHT DISTRICT, with prostitutes being rounded up on the streets and flushed out of brothels. All the ingredients of the genre are here, including not just violence but sexuality, social taboos and the eruption of dramatic action outside the safe confines of the stage.

Theatre of the Absurd. A term for a type of mainly French theatre portraying the futility and anguish of an individual's struggle in a meaningless and inexplicable world. *'L'absurde'* arose as Albert Camus's designation for the situation of modern humanity, a stranger in an inhuman universe. Samuel Beckett's play WAITING FOR GODOT (1955) typifies the genre and introduced the term to the public at large. It was seized on by journalists, who unfortunately confused it with the everyday sense of the word as applied to something outrageously comic. Other leading French absurdist dramatists are Arthur Adamov (1908–70), Eugène Ionesco (1912–94) and Jean Genet (1910–86), while the US theatre has Edward Albee (b.1928) and the British stage Harold Pinter (b.1930). A key study of the subject is Martin Esslin's *Theatre of the Absurd* (1961). *See also* BALD PRIMA DONNA; RHINOCEROS.

Thé dansant (French). An afternoon tea party with dancing. Such genteel entertainments were popular in the 1920s and 1930s.

> How restful to putt, when the strains of a band
> Announced a *thé dansant* was on at the Grand.
> JOHN BETJEMAN: *New Bats in Old Belfries*, 'Margate, 1940' (1945)

Thelma and Louise. *See* ROAD MOVIE.

them. A novel (1969), in the form of a social parable, by the US writer Joyce Carol Oates (b.1938). The message is whether and how members of a family that has been poverty-stricken for several generations can rise above the degradation they have experienced. The lower-case initial of the title emphasizes the low status of 'them'.

Theme music. A recurrent musical melody in a film, play or musical, often heard at the beginning of the work as a foretaste and serving as a final reprise at the end. It may relate to a specific character, as 'Tara's Theme' in Victor Fleming's film GONE WITH THE WIND (1939) and 'Lara's Theme' in David Lean's film DOCTOR ZHIVAGO (1965). *See also* SIGNATURE TUNE.

Theme park. An amusement park organized around a unifying idea ('theme') or group of ideas. The concept is American in origin and dates from the 1960s, taking its cue from DISNEYLAND. The realization first became popular in Europe in the 1980s. Most theme parks have a ROLLER COASTER as a leading attraction. The film JURASSIC PARK (1993) tells of the ordeal of a group of visitors in a theme park where the main attractions are genetically engineered dinosaurs.

There you go. Here you are. A phrase used when giving a person something, as change from a purchase. The suggestion is that you take it and go off with it.

Thermolactyl. *See* DAMART.

'They'. Those in authority, especially when seen as faceless and oppressive. The quotation marks emphasize their remoteness and express the speaker's implied criticism or resentment.

> This time 'they' may have gone too far. 'They' are putting the price of petrol up to £3.35 a gallon.
> FAY WELDON in *Sunday Times* (22 August 1999)

They shall not pass. The English version of French *Ils ne passeront pas*, a slogan of the French army at the defence of VERDUN in 1916. The words are variously attributed to Marshal Pétain and General Robert Nivelle and are first recorded in slightly different form in the latter's Order of the Day (23 June 1916) to his troops at the height of battle: *Vous ne les laisserez pas passer!* ('You will not let them pass!'). The actual inscription on the Verdun medal is *On ne passe pas* ('No one passes'). The words were adopted in the Spanish form *No pasarán* as a Republican watchword in the Spanish Civil War (1936–9) and ended a radio speech of 19 July 1936 by Dolores Ibarruri (La Pasionaria) calling on the women of Spain to help defend the Republic.

They Shoot Horses, Don't They? A film (1969) adapted by James Poe and Robert E. Thompson from a novel of the same title (1935) by Horace McCoy that depicts the hardships suffered during the era of the GREAT DEPRESSION. The action revolves around a Chicago dance marathon where the prize is three meals a day and $1500 in cash. The title occurs up in the script as the reply given when the drifter Robert, one of the dancers, is asked why he has murdered an opponent. It encapsulates the prevailing belief that when times are so hard there is little room for losers, who like horses with broken legs should be put out of their misery.

They think it's all over. Words spoken by the BBC television commentator Kenneth Wolstenholme in the closing seconds of the 1966 Wembley World Cup final, when England were leading West Germany by three goals to two. Wolstenholme's comment was prompted by the appearance on the pitch of England fans, who believed the match to be over. As he was speaking, the England forward Geoff Hurst scored a fourth goal for England, and Wolstenholme finished his sentence with the words 'it is now!' *They Think It's All Over* is also the title of an irreverent BBC TV sports quiz show, first screened in the 1990s. *See also* PHANTOM GOAL.

Thiefrow. A nickname for London's HEATHROW Airport, from its reputation for lax security and lost or purloined luggage.

Thiepval memorial. The Memorial to the Missing of the Battle of the SOMME, designed by Sir Edwin Lutyens (1869–1944) and constructed at Thiepval, northern France, in 1928–30. The battle of Thiepval Ridge, fought in September 1916, was one of the actions during the Somme offensive.

THIGMOO. A nickname for the British trade-union movement, being an acronym for 'this great movement of ours', a phrase used in many a speech.

Things Fall Apart. The first novel (1958) by the Nigerian writer Chinua Achebe (born Albert Chinualumogo; b.1930). Its theme is the mutual incomprehension between Ibo tribal communities and white officials in the 1890s, with more than a glance at changing attitudes within the tribe itself. Tribal taboos cause the downfall of the civil servant in *No Longer at Ease* (1960), who is the grandson of Okonkwo, the stubborn tragic hero of the earlier novel. The title comes from W.B. Yeats's poem 'The Second Coming' (1921):

Things fall apart; the centre cannot hold;
Mere anarchy is loosed upon the world,

The blood-dimmed tide is loosed, and everywhere
The ceremony of innocence is drowned.

Things that go bump in the night. Supernatural manifestations as a source of night-time terror. The phrase is part of the anonymous 'Cornish or West Country Litany' recorded in Francis T. Nettleinghame's *Polperro Proverbs and Others* (1926): 'From ghoulies and ghosties and long-leggety beasties/And things that go bump in the night,/Good Lord, deliver us!' The verse itself is obviously older than this but its precise date of origin remains uncertain.

[In the film *The Haunting*] there are plenty of things that go bump in the night. You'll go bump in the cinema as you slide to the floor in a deep sleep after the first hour of this torpid tale.
Sunday Times (26 September 1999)

Thingy. A shortening of 'thingummy' in vogue from the 1930s used to refer to a person or thing whose name one has forgotten, does not know, or prefers not to mention for some reason.

Mick Jagger, Liz Hurley, Camilla Parker-Bowles and Tamara Thingy [Beckwith] were among the guests, which gives you some idea about the tone.
The Times (27 November 1999)

Thinking man's crumpet. A nickname for the television presenter Joan Bakewell (b.1933), so ungallantly dubbed in the 1960s by the writer and broadcaster Frank Muir, implying an appeal both intellectual and sexual. The formula caught on, so that the writer and broadcaster Frank Delaney (b.1942) was referred to by the media in 1983 as 'the thinking man's Russell Harty', while the *Observer*, in its issue of 29 January 1998, described the youthful-looking television presenter Nick Ross (b.1947) as 'the thinking woman's newspaper boy'.

Think on one's feet, To. To react to a situation quickly and effectively, without prior planning. Much thinking is done in a leisurely way while seated, but here one thinks while working or walking. The expression dates from the 1930s and is often found in the world of business and commerce.

'We want people who can think on their feet and who want to fast-track their way to the board,' says Mr Stewart.
The Times (10 January 2000)

Think-tank. A popular term for a group of people with specialized knowledge and ability, set up to carry out research into particular problems (usually social, political and technological) and to provide ideas and possible solutions. The expression is of American origin and arose in the mid-20th century, although 50 years earlier it was already current to mean a brain.

All the classic signs of a once-great imperial institution in the throes of reform have engulfed Chatham House, home of Britain's most prestigious think tank. Grand plans to modernize the Royal Institute for Foreign Affairs, which has discreetly shaped government policies since the First World War, will be pushed aside tomorrow.

Sunday Times (5 September 1999)

Third age. Old age, regarded positively as an opportunity for travel, further education and the like. The expression translates French *troisième âge*, and was first current in Britain after 1983, when the University of the Third Age (U3A), founded in France 10 years earlier, was established to provide learning opportunities for retired people.

'Third Agers' will soon be so large a proportion of the population that they will exert huge influence on everything from politics to TV schedules.

The Times (23 July 1999)

Third Man, The. A thriller (1950) by Graham Greene (1904–91) from his own script for the stylish film (1949), directed by Carol Reed. Set in postwar Vienna, it concerns a US writer who arrives to stay with his friend, Harry LIME, only to discover that Lime has apparently been murdered. His chauffeur was driving the car that ran him down, and his doctor was on the scene. According to a witness, however, a third man was there when the body was moved. There are plots and a romantic sub-plot. The book has a happy outcome, and the film's ending is both poignant and scenic. In the film Lime was played by Orson Welles, who also contributed some of the dialogue. The film was influenced by the FILM NOIR, and one of its many memorable features was its atmospheric musical score performed on the zither by the Viennese composer/performer Anton Karas, which became know as 'The Harry Lime Theme'. The title 'the third man' was aped by the press in the early 1960s during the BURGESS AND MACLEAN spy scandal, in the course of which Kim Philby was thus identified.

Third Programme. The uncompromisingly highbrow service of broadcast speech and music introduced by the BBC in September 1946 and so named as the third station after the HOME SERVICE and LIGHT PROGRAMME.

It initially went out in the evenings only but in 1953 began broadcasting at 3 p.m. on Sundays. Other services such as Network Three and the Music Programme were subsequently added to the frequency, diminishing its impact, and in 1967 they all combined under the umbrella title of Radio 3. The Third Programme kept a separate editorial team until 1970, however, when it was absorbed into its new Radio 3 parent, the less esoteric parts of its speech output going to Radio 4. Whatever its designation it has always had a very tiny audience, some 2 per cent of the total, although Radio 3 controllers have latterly striven to make the service more 'listener-friendly'.

Third Reich. The German state under the rule of Hitler and the NAZI party (1933–45). The term was adopted from the title of Arthur Moeller van den Bruck's cultural study of Germany, *Das Dritte Reich* ('The Third Empire') (1923). In terms of German history the 'First Reich' was the Holy Roman Empire and the 'Second Reich' that under the Hohenzollern emperors (1871–1918). *See also* FOURTH REICH; THOUSAND-YEAR REICH.

Third wave. A term coined in the early 1980s by the American futurist Alvin Toffler (b.1928) to denote the age of information technology, as a development of the agrarian first wave and the industrial second wave.

Third way. A 'middle way' between the political left and right, especially as evolving through the moral, social or economic failure of either of these. The expression came to be particularly associated with the NEW LABOUR policies of Tony Blair after the 1997 general election. However, there were many 'third ways' long before this. Examples may be found in the FASCISM of the 1920s, in Harold Macmillan's 'capitalism with a human face' in the 1930s, in the path between capitalism and communism sought by the Socialist International in the 1950s, in the German GREEN PARTY in the 1970s, and in the Swedish Social Democrats in the 1980s. Tony Blair's 'third way' followed two decades of THATCHERISM on the one hand and the collapse of communism on the other.

Third wheel. An unwanted or superfluous person, often on the principle that 'two's company, three's a crowd'. Such a person is as desirable as a third wheel on a bicycle.

Third World (French *tiers monde*). An expression coined in 1952 by the French demographer Alfred Sauvy (1898–1990), when he compared the developing countries of Asia, Africa and Latin America to the pre-Revolutionary Third Estate (the bourgeoisie and working class) in France. The term was subsequently applied to these same countries regarded as distinct from the capitalist ('first') world and communist ('second') world. Sauvy's thesis was that 'the third world is nothing, but wants to be something'.

Third World War. The war that it was feared would break out between the USA and its NATO allies and the USSR and its WARSAW PACT allies as a result of the tensions of the COLD WAR. The term, first used in the late 1940s, is still used to refer to any hypothetical future global conflict, and is also used figuratively to describe a scene of extreme violence or mayhem.

Thirteen-point turn. A gradual manoeuvre to turn a vehicle in a confined space, as an extended form of the ideal three-point turn (forwards, backwards, and forwards again in a series of arcs).

> The chap behind me suggests I do a 13-point turn and go back the way I came. Since I am suddenly driving a tank instead of a Renault Espace, he guides me while I inch round and back until I'm clear.
> *The Times* (22 July 1999)

38th parallel. *See* KOREAN WAR.

Thirty-Nine Steps, The. A thriller (1915) by John Buchan (1875–1940), later, as Lord Tweedsmuir, Governor General of Canada (1935–40). Defined by Buchan himself as a 'shocker' and written while its author recovered from illness, it was originally have been called 'The Black Stone'. It is a picaresque story of a chase and marks the introduction of the character Richard Hannay, who reappears in other novels by Buchan. Against a background of German spy scares, Hannay has to prove his innocence when charged with murder as he is pursued by both the police and foreign spies the length and breadth of Britain. The resolution of the plot turns on Hannay's recognizing that a cryptic message about 'the thirty-nine steps' must refer to a set of steps down to the sea at a coastal town. Richard Hannay has been played by three different actors in film versions of the novel: Robert Donat in 1935, Kenneth More in 1959 and Robert Powell in 1978. The 1935 version was directed by Alfred Hitchcock, and the 1978 version was the first to be set in the correct EDWARDIAN ERA of Buchan's novel, and has a memorable scene in which Hannay clings to the clock hands of Big Ben in order to stop the detonation of a bomb. The site of the 'thirty-nine steps'

themselves is a genuine one in Kent, on the low cliffs not far from Broadstairs (whose own name means 'broad steps'). *See also* FIRST LINES OF NOVELS; GREENMANTLE; MR STANDFAST.

Thirtysomething. In one's 30s, an age when aims and ambitions crystallize and relationships 'make or break'. The expression was popularized by an American television series so titled, which from 1989 to 1992 recounted the stories of the family lives of a group of baby boomers (*see* BABY BOOM). The second part of the term is freely attached to any age decade.

> I suspect a generation gap has opened up between twentysomethings and the middle-aged babyboomers who thought *they* had created the sexual revolution.
> *The Times* (19 September 1998)

30-year rule. The rule in Britain that public records may be open to public inspection after a lapse of 30 years. The rule, introduced by the Public Records Act 1967, allows a fresh batch of material to become available at the Public Record Office on the first working day in each January. Some papers are regarded as too sensitive even for this delay and are subject to a longer restriction. A similar 50-year rule was earlier in force for much of the 20th century.

This is Spinal Tap. A spoof documentary (1984) written by Christopher Guest, Michael McKean, Harry Shearer and Rob Reiner about an ageing British HEAVY METAL band on a disastrous tour of the United States. The accuracy of this satire about the rock business fooled many into thinking that Spinal Tap was a real rock group. The wheel turned full circle when the band actually conducted a US tour with their second album *Break Like the Wind* in the early 1990s.

This is where we came in. We have come full circle; we are back where we started. The expression dates from the 1940s and refers to the former type of continuous cinema performance where one could enter at any point in the film and stay until the same point was reached in the next showing.

This Is Your Life. A long-running series of television programmes first broadcast in 1951 in each of which an unsuspecting victim, often but not exclusively a celebrity, is ambushed by the presenter in disguise and presented with a big red book encapsulating their life. They are then taken back to the studio to be faced with an unexpected succession of people from their often distant past. The programmes, combining sentiment and embarrassment in equal measure, were presented engagingly by Eamonn Andrews until his death in 1987, when Michael Aspel assumed his mantle.

This Ole House. A jaunty, country-influenced song released in 1954, written by Stuart Hamblen and performed by Rosemary Clooney (the aunt of George Clooney, heartthrob actor of the 1990s). The poignant inspiration for the song came from Hamblen's discovery, in the backwoods of rural Texas, of a deserted hut containing, along with heaps of broken furniture, the dead body of old man. The song describes how the house might have been during the last stages of the old man's life. A version of the song was released, successfully, by Shakin' Stevens in Britain in 1981.

This Sporting Life. The first novel (1960) by David Storey (b.1933). Rugby league football, which Storey played as a professional for Leeds, is the background of a story in which the conflict is between working-class origins and modern aspirations. That the title is intended ironically is revealed at the end of the book, when Arthur Machin, who has seen the game as a means to attain social position, realizes that it is only one facet of life. A moving film version (1963) was directed by Lindsay Anderson, with Richard Harris and Rachel Roberts in leading roles.

Thomas the Tank Engine. One of the 26 highly popular picture books in the 'Railway Series' for children by the Rev. W. Awdry (1911–97). Other titles in the series were *The Three Railway Engines* (1945), *James, the Red Engine* (1947) and *Tank Engine Thomas Again* (1948). Thomas, a shunting engine, is bossed about by the FAT CONTROLLER and attracts the disdain of other larger locomotives such as Gordon, the Big Engine, but eventually acquires his own branch line.

Thommo. The Australian cricketer Jeff Thomson (b.1950) who, with fellow fast bowler Dennis Lillee (b.1949), formed one of the most feared fast-bowling attacks in test cricket history. Their contribution to Australia's defeat of England in the 1974–5 Ashes series in Australia gave birth to the rhyme:

> Ashes to ashes, dust to dust –
> If Lillee don't get ya, Thommo must.
> *Sydney Telegraph* (1975)

Thought for the Day. A brief daily religious programme on BBC Radio 4 first broadcast in 1970, in which the speaker has three minutes to 'reflect on the events of the day from a perspective of faith'. Most of the regular speakers have been Christian, but Jewish speakers have also been heard and less often

those of other faiths. Prince Charles used the programme in 1995 to reflect on the 50th anniversary of VE DAY, and again on 1 January 2000 to consider the new MILLENNIUM.

Thousand-bomber raids. A name for the massive night-time bombing raids carried out by the RAF against German cities in the Second World War. The first such raid, Operation Millennium, took place on 30 May 1942, and the target was Cologne.

Thousand days. A term used by former members of his administration to refer to the period that President Kennedy held office (20 January 1961–22 November 1963). The phrase echoed President Roosevelt's HUNDRED DAYS and also suggested the tragic brevity and lost promise of the CAMELOT era. The phrase occurs in the title of Arthur Schlesinger's Pulitzer-winning inside account of the administration, *A Thousand Days: John F. Kennedy in the White House* (1965). *See also* JFK.

Thousand island dressing. A pink mayonnaise-based salad dressing flavoured with tomatoes, chilli, green peppers and the like. The name alludes to the multitude of ingredients and dates from the early 20th century, apparently being adopted from the Thousand Islands, a group of almost 2000 small islands in the St Lawrence River between the United States and Canada.

Thousand-Year Reich. Hitler's somewhat inaccurate description of his THIRD REICH, which, as it turned out, only managed to last a dozen years (1933–45).

Threatening Weather. The haunting painting by the Belgian SURREALIST René Magritte (1898–1967) was executed in 1928. In a clear blue sky over a calm bay appear three giant objects, a woman's naked torso, an inverted tuba and a cane-bottomed chair, all painted to look like clouds. The 'threat' suggested by the title may be sexual in nature.

Three-Cornered Hat, The. The popular ballet by Manuel de Falla (1876–1946) was based on a short novel, *El sombrero de tres picos* (1874), by Pedro de Alarcón. Alarcón's story satirizes the *corregidores*, the Spanish government officials or magistrates, often regarded as overbearing and prone to intrigue. Falla's first version of the music was in the form of a pantomime entitled *El corregidor y la molinera* ('The Magistrate and the Miller's Wife'), which was first performed in 1917. The ballet version with the present title was first staged by Diaghilev's BALLETS RUSSES in

1919, with choreography by Leonide Massine and costume designs by Pablo Picasso. Alarcón's story also forms the basis of the 1895 opera *Der Corregidor* by Hugo Wolf (1860–1903).

Three-day event. A horse-riding contest held over three days, originating in 1949 at Badminton House, the seat of the Duke of Beaufort in Gloucestershire. The first day is devoted to dressage, the second to cross-country riding and the third to show-jumping. The major annual contests are the European Championships at Burghley, near Stamford, Lincolnshire, the Badminton Horse Trials, and the British Open Horse Trials at Gatcombe Park, near Stroud, Gloucestershire.

Three-day week. The economic crisis of 1973 in Britain caused by labour disputes. It involved the coal mines, railways and power stations, and industry and commerce were restricted to three days' electricity consumption a week, obliging all television services to close at 10.30 p.m. It resulted in two general elections in 1974, both won by Labour with a narrow majority.

> If you are old enough to remember the three-day week, then [erotic novelist] Molly Parkin will need no introduction.
>
> *The Times* (24 April 1999)

3HO. A form of Sikhism practised mainly in North America. It was founded in 1969 by the Indian Sikh Yogi Bhajan and sometimes incorporates elements of yoga and vegetarianism. Full-time members of the group, who are almost always young Westerners, and often former HIPPIES, are readily distinguished by their traditional Sikh dress. The basic ideals of Sikhism are followed, so that only natural, pure foods are eaten, drugs and alcohol are banned, and males do not cut their hair. The name itself is an abbreviation of 'Happy, Healthy and Holy Organization'.

Three Mile Island. An island in the Susquehanna River near Harrisburg, Pennsylvania, that was the scene of the most serious accident in the history of the American nuclear power industry. At 4 a.m. on 28 March 1979 a valve in the nuclear reactor of the power station here closed in error, blocking the water supply to the main feedwater system and causing the reactor core to shut down. This was an automatic procedure that itself caused no hazard, but a series of equipment and instrument malfunctions, combined with human errors and mistaken decisions, led to a serious loss of water coolant from the reactor core. As a result the core was partially exposed and a quantity of hydrogen gas escaped into the reactor building. Though having negligible health consequences, the incident had profound effects on the American nuclear power industry, resulting in the closure of seven similar reactors and increased public fears about the safety of nuclear reactors in general. Coincidentally, 1979 also witnessed the release of The CHINA SYNDROME, a film in which an operational flaw in a nuclear power station is covered up by the authorities.

Threepenny Opera, The. The best known of the collaborations of the playwright Bertolt Brecht (1898–1956) and the composer Kurt Weill (1900–50). It was first performed in 1928. *Der Dreigroschenoper* (to give it its German title) is a modern version of John Gay's *The Beggar's Opera* (1728), the biggest musical hit of 18th-century London, and is set in the criminal underworld of Soho at the beginning of the 20th century. The German text of *The Threepenny Opera* is based on a translation of Gay by Gerhart Hauptmann, and some of the lyrics are drawn from Rudyard Kipling and from François Villon (the 15th-century criminal-poet). One of the best known songs is 'Mack the Knife', the name given by Brecht to Gay's original character, Macheath. *See also* MAC THE KNIFE.

Three Stooges. Three American knockabout comedians who appeared in hundreds of short films from the 1930s. They were Larry Fine (1911–75), Moe Howard (1895–1975) and Moe's brother Jerry (Curly) Howard (1906–52). In 1947 Curly was replaced by another brother, Shemp Howard (Samuel Howard) (1891–1955). Their form of slapstick was peculiarly violent.

Three strikes and you're out. A popular term for a law in the United States whereby a person convicted of three serious felonies is subject to mandatory life imprisonment. The phrase, often shortened to 'three strikes', is from baseball, in which a batter who has had three strikes, or three successive opportunities of hitting a fairly pitched ball without doing so, is out.

> California's controversial 'three strikes and you're out' law, which enforces life imprisonment on third-time-unlucky felons, has swollen jails to bursting point.
>
> *The Times* (17 January 2000)

Three Ws. The collective nickname given to the Barbados and West Indies cricketers Sir Frank Worrell (1924–67), Everton Weekes (b.1925) and Clyde Walcott (b.1926), all of whom were successful batsmen in the West Indies sides of the 1950s.

Thriller in Manila. A rhyming nickname given to the epic heavyweight boxing bout fought on 1 October 1975 in Manila, capital of the Philippines, between Joe Frazier and Muhammad Ali and won by the latter. *See also* RUMBLE IN THE JUNGLE.

Thrills and spills. The excitement of a dangerous sport or entertainment, especially as experienced by spectators. The 'spills' are the mishaps and accidents and possibly even deaths. (The original meaning of 'to spill' was in fact 'to kill', from Old English *spillan*.)

Throw a curve, To. To surprise or outwit someone; to act unexpectedly. An Americanism from baseball, in which a pitcher tries to fool the batter by means of a curve ball, i.e. one delivered with sufficient spin to make it deviate from its expected path.

Throw a wobbly, To. To display a fit of temper; to panic. The latter word relates to the person's uncontrolled deviation from the norm. The expression dates from the 1960s.

Throw one's weight about, To. To act arrogantly or aggressively, as if adding physical weight to any authority one has. The expression dates from the early 20th century.

Throw someone in at the deep end, To. To plunge them straight into a task or undertaking without any previous experience of it. The analogy is with a novice swimmer thrown in at the deep end of a swimming pool on a 'sink or swim' basis. The expression dates from the 1970s.

> What sort of induction process will be available? Do they intend to throw you in at the deep end or will there be a full induction programme?
>
> *The Times* (2 February 2000)

Throw someone to the wolves, To. To sacrifice a subordinate, friend or colleague in order to avert danger or diffficulties for oneself. The allusion is probably to stories of wolves in a pack pursuing travellers in a horse-drawn sleigh, one of whom to check the horde pushes a fellow-passenger off the vehicle. The expression dates from the 1920s.

Throw the baby out with the bathwater, To. To discard or reject what is essential or valuable along with the inessential or useless. The vivid expression dates from the turn of the 20th century and has its equivalent in German *das Kind mit dem Bade ausschütten*.

Throw the book at someone, To. To charge them with a particular offence; to inflict a severe punishment on them. The 'book' is an imaginary book of rules or of offences and their prescribed penalties. The expression dates from the 1930s and is of American origin.

Thumb a lift, To. To ask for or 'scrounge' a ride from a passing vehicle by holding out the hand with the thumb pointing in the direction of intended travel. The phrase and the practice are of American origin and date from the 1930s.

Thumb index. A series of rounded notches or indentations cut in the pages of a book showing initial letters or other particulars to enable the reader to find a reference easily. The device dates from the turn of the 20th century and in its issue for July 1903 *The Periodical* described the newly published *Oxford Thumb-Index Bible* as 'the latest novelty'.

Thumper. A nickname of the Labour politician John Prescott (b.1938), deputy prime minister from 1997. The allusion is not so much to his heavy figure and forceful manner but more subtly to Thumper, the rabbit in Walt Disney's cartoon film *Bambi* (1928), as a close colleague of Tony Blair, known as BAMBI. *See also* TWO JAGS.

Thunderbirds. A series of puppet films televised from 1965 to 1966 and depicting the explosive missions of the family-based members of International Rescue. The main characters are Jeff Tracey and his five sons, Scott (pilot of Thunderbird 1), Virgil (Thunderbird 2), Alan (Thunderbird 3), Gordon (co-pilot of Thunderbird 2, pilot of Thunderbird 4 for underwater work), and John (Thunderbird 5 space satellite), together with the blonde London agent Lady Penelope and her chauffeur Parker. The series, intended for children but annexed as cult adult viewing, was created by Gerry and Sylvia Anderson using their 'supermarionation' technique.

Thunder-thighs. A nickname for an overweight person, who has heavy thighs. The suggestion is that they cause the person's steps to crash like thunder, or more vividly that their ponderous rubbing together when walking resembles the collision of clouds, as the popular cause of thunder. The name was at one time applied, before she slimmed, to Christina Onassis (1951–88), daughter of the Greek millionaire shipowner Aristotle Onassis (1906–75).

Tiananmen Square. One of the largest squares in the world, situated in the centre of Beijing and famous as the site of pro-democracy demonstrations in May–June 1989, which were brutally suppressed by the Chinese authorities. The square takes its name from the Tiananmen ('Gate of Heavenly Peace') at the northern end of the square, which was once the entrance to the Imperial Palace. The pro-democracy movement had first come to the fore in April at the funeral of Hu Yaobang, who in 1987 had been forced to resign as secretary general of the Chinese Communist Party following student demonstrations demanding reform. At one point in May 1989 there were over a million demonstrators in Tiananmen Square, and many students established themselves there permanently. However, on 3–4 June tanks and troops entered the square, killing hundreds of demonstrators, and a period of harsh repression followed throughout China. The massacre and subsequent events were condemned by the international community.

Tib and fib. Medical jargon for a compound fracture of the tibia and fibula, or for a person who has suffered this. *See also* MEDICAL ABBREVIATIONS.

Tickety-boo. In good order; all right. The phrase, now somewhat dated, goes back to at least the 1930s and may be an elaboration of 'that's the ticket'. A putative source in Hindi *thik hai babu*, 'It's all right, sir', seems rather contrived.

Tickled pink. Highly amused. A tickled person goes red in the face. The phrase dates from the 1920s.

Tickle the dragon's tail, To. To undertake something dangerous or hazardous.

Tickle the ivories, To. To play the piano, especially idly or lightly. The allusion is to the ivory keys. The phrase dates from the 1940s.

Tie-in. A book, film or other product produced to take commercial advantage of a related work in another medium. A common example is the 'book of the film' as an antithesis to the established 'film of the book'. Some cult films or film series, such as STAR WARS and STAR TREK, generate a plethora of books, games, toys, models and artefacts of all kinds. *See also* AS SEEN ON TV.

Tiger, The. A nickname of Georges Clemenceau (1841–1929), Radical prime minister of France (1906–9, 1917–20). Prior to his return to the premiership he was a strident critic of successive French governments over their conduct of the First World War. He came to power in November 1917 at a time when France was polarized in its attitudes to the war in the wake of the disastrous 1917 spring offensive (*see* CHEMIN DES DAMES) and the subsequent mutinies in the French army. Clemenceau advocated 'war to the end', suppressed dissent and pacifist literature, and put several leading politicians on trial for treason. He insisted that the French army pursue a strategy of attack, and at the Paris Peace Conference was fierce in his demands of the defeated Germany, although the resulting TREATY OF VERSAILLES was not fierce enough for many in France. *See also* SPORTING NICKNAMES.

Tiger in one's tank. Energy; vitality; 'go'. The phrase comes from an advertising slogan of 1965 by the Esso Petroleum Co.: 'Put a tiger in your tank.' The words were made more memorable by the accompanying drawing of a pouncing tiger.

Tiger Tim. The mild little cartoon tiger, leader of the Bruin Boys, first appeared in the *Daily Mirror* in 1904 as the creation of the artist Julius Stafford Baker. For many years he and his chums appeared in the children's weekly comic *Rainbow* and subsequently in *Jack and Jill*, as well as various annuals.

Tigger. The toy tiger that, with WINNIE-THE-POOH, is one of the animal friends of CHRISTOPHER ROBIN in the children's stories by A.A. Milne. He makes his first appearance in *The House at Pooh Corner* (1928), in which three of the ten stories concern him. He suddenly shows up in the forest as 'a Very Bouncy Animal, with a way of saying How-do-you-do, which always left your ears full of sand'.

Tight ship. Literally a ship in which ropes, rigging and so on are tied and taut and ready for use, hence a strictly run ship. The expression is mostly used figuratively, as: 'He runs a tight ship.'

Tiki bar. A bar on a beach in the style of such a bar on one of the tropical islands of the South Pacific. The term comes from the Californian tourist industry. A tiki is an image of a human figure in the form of a small greenstone ornament. The word is of Maori origin.

Till Death Us Do Part. *See* GARNETT, ALF.

Till hell freezes over. Forever; endlessly. Hell will never freeze over. The expression dates from the early 20th century.

Tim. A Scottish Protestant nickname for a Roman Catholic, especially one who supports Glasgow Celtic football club. The name is simply the pet form of Timothy.

Time of the month. A common euphemism for a period of menstruation, a word itself implying 'month', from Latin *mensis*.

> Then, surprising herself as much as him, she drew back and away.
> 'I can't', she said.

'Time of the month?' he asked. 'I don't mind.' He didn't either, unlike Harry, whom menstruation made nervous.

FAY WELDON: *The Heart of the Country* (1987)

Time's arrow. The notion of time travelling from past to future as if in a physical dimension. The expression was coined by the astronomer Arthur Eddington. Martin Amis's novel *Time's Arrow* (1991) ingeniously plays with the concept.

Let us draw an arrow arbitrarily. If as we follow the arrow we find more and more of the random element in the world, then the arrow is pointing towards the future; if the random element decreases the arrow points towards the past. ... I shall use the phrase 'time's arrow' to express this one-way property of time which has no analogue in space.

ARTHUR EDDINGTON: *The Nature of the Physical World* (1928)

Time-sharing. The use of a property as a holiday home for a fixed limited time each year. The term was adopted in the 1970s from computer jargon, in which it denotes simultaneous access to a central processor by more than one user.

Times New Roman. *See* GILL SANS.

Times Square. A New York City square famous as one of the world's major entertainment centres. It is located in midtown Manhattan at the intersection of Seventh Avenue, 42nd Street and Broadway and was originally known as Longacre Square, but was renamed in 1903 when the *New York Times* set up its offices nearby. When the site of the original offices of the London *Times* at Printing House Square, Blackfriars, was redeveloped in the 1990s the location was renamed Times Square, partly to commemorate the newspaper but partly also to attract US corporate clients. *See also* CRICKET IN TIMES SQUARE.

Times They Are a Changin', The. A song and album by Bob Dylan, released in 1964. Its title refers both to the political change desired by 1960s radicals and also, possibly, to imminent changes in the direction of Dylan's music (the album is generally considered Dylan's last release as a purely folk artist). The song 'Only a Pawn in Their Game' makes reference to the assassination of the civil rights leader Medgar Evers (1925–63).

Time warp. An imaginary distortion of space in relation to time whereby people or objects of one period can be moved to another. The concept arose in the 1950s and originally applied to SCIENCE FICTION. The notion was later extended to anything 'out of time', especially a realistic 're-creation' or re-enactment of the past for the benefit of tourists or the pristine preservation of a particular location for the curiosity and edification of the present.

Duxford ... has been preserved in a time warp. Douglas Bader served here and the old RAF station is still alive with the ghosts of pilots pitching up at the beautiful original brick and sash-window guard house in their wire-wheeled MGs.

The Times (25 September 1999)

Tina. A nickname for Margaret Thatcher (b.1925), Conservative prime minister from 1979 to 1990, as an acronym of 'There is no alternative'. The words became a popular encapsulation of her response when government cuts in public spending were opposed. Her actual words were as follows:

We have to get our production and our earnings in balance. There's no easy popularity in what we are proposing, but it is fundamentally sound. Yet I believe people accept there is no real alternative.

MARGARET THATCHER: speech at Conservative Women's Conference (21 May 1980)

See also ATTILA THE HEN; LADY'S NOT FOR TURNING.

Tin Drum, The. The first novel (1962; in German as *Die Blechtrommel*, 1959) by Günter Grass (b.1927). It is the first of a picaresque trilogy, which begins in his native city of Langfuhr (Danzig) three years before he was born and reflects the growth of Nazism. The tin drum of the title is the metaphorical means whereby the dwarf Oskar Matzerath, from a mental hospital bed, 'drums up' experiences in his life. A film version (1979) was directed by Volker Schlöndorff. *See also* FIRST LINES OF NOVELS.

Tin ear. One who is tone deaf or unable to perceive subtleties in speech. Tin is a metal incapable of sensation. The phrase dates from the 1930s. *See also* CLOTH EAR.

Tin fish. Naval slang for a torpedo (which itself took its name from the fish known as the torpedo ray or electric ray).

Tin hat. A soldier's name for his protective metal helmet, dating from the turn of the 20th century. To 'put the tin hat' on something is to bring it to an abrupt and conclusive end.

Tinker, Tailor, Soldier, Spy. A spy thriller (1974) by John Le Carré (pen-name of David Cornwell; b.1931).

It is the first of a trilogy in which the enigmatic spymaster George SMILEY closes in on his adversary, the Russian Karla. The title reflects the children's fortune-telling rhyme when counting cherry stones or other small objects: 'Tinker, Tailor, Soldier, Sailor, Rich man, Poor man, Beggarman, Thief.'

Tin Lizzie. An old car; a jalopy or 'banger'. The name was originally an American nickname for the highly popular Model T Ford, launched in 1908. It was so called as it was sturdy, dependable and black, like the traditional Southern servant, called Elizabeth. Many people believed the car was made of tin, hence the descriptive, although its body was in fact of heavier-gauge sheet metal. The Irish pop group Thin Lizzy, formed in 1969, took its name from a robot cartoon character called Tin Lizzie in the comic BEANO. The band respelled both words, pointing out that many Irish do not pronounce the *h* in *th*.

Tinny. An Australian slang word for a can of beer, dating from the 1970s.

> While Sydneysiders are used to celebrating the festive season quietly with a turkey and a few 'tinnies' on the beach, their northern hemisphere cousins suffer an immediate metamorphosis when enveloped by the temptations of the Australian Christmas.
> *The Times* (21 December 1994)

Tin Pan Alley. The district of New York, originally in the area of Broadway and 14th Street, where popular music is published. In London, Denmark Street, off Charing Cross Road, was so called as the centre of the popular music industry. The name probably derives from the 19th-century musicians' nickname 'tin pan' for an old tinny piano. The 'Alley' is now largely deserted by song writers and music publishers who have moved to bigger premises.

Tinseltown. HOLLYWOOD, so dubbed for its superficial glamour and meretricious allure. The nickname first became popular in the 1970s and is said to have originated in a derisive remark made by the actor and composer Oscar Levant in the 1940s.

> British talent takes Tinseltown by storm.
> *Daily Telegraph* (headline) (23 March 1999)

Tintin. A cub reporter who is the main character of the comic strip stories by the Belgian artist Hergé (Georges Rémi; 1907–83). He has a constantly worried expression beneath his quiff of red hair, and is accompanied by his faithful dog, Milou (Snowy, in the English versions). He first appeared in 1929.

His name relates to French slang *tintin*, 'nothing at all'. *See also* 'Thompson Twins' *under* ROCK GROUP NAMES.

Tip and run raid. A phrase used in the Second World War to denote a hurried and often indiscriminate air raid when the enemy sped homeward after jettisoning their bombs. Its origin is in the light-hearted form of cricket in which the batsman is forced to run every time he hits ('tips') the ball.

Tip of the or **an iceberg.** The small perceptible part of a much larger situation or problem that remains hidden. Six-sevenths of an iceberg remain unseen below the surface. The expression dates from the 1960s.

> Since I began trying to find people who were abused … when they were evacuated, I have received many heartbreaking letters, and I am sure that I have uncovered only the tip of an iceberg.
> *The Times* (20 August 1999)

Tip one's hand, To. To reveal one's intentions inadvertently. The expression is of American origin and alludes to a hand of cards held in such a way that others can see them.

Tipperary. The perennially popular song 'It's a Long Way to Tipperary' is inseparably associated with the First World War. The music is credited to Jack Judge, of Oldbury, Birmingham, and the words to Harry Williams of Temple Balsall, Solihull. Judge subsequently claimed that he wrote both words and music, the credit to Williams being made in repayment for a loan. The song was actually composed one day early in 1912 at the New Market Inn in Stalybridge, Manchester, and sung by Judge at the Grand Theatre that evening. It was popularized in the music hall by Florrie Forde in a pantomime of 1914 and tells of an Irishman on a visit to London who longs to return to his homeland and his girl despite the lure of the legendary streets paved with gold.

> It's a long way to Tipperary,
> It's a long way to go;
> It's a long way to Tipperary,
> To the sweetest girl I know!
> Goodbye, Piccadilly,
> Farewell, Leicester Square;
> It's a long, long way to Tipperary,
> But my heart's right there!

Tiramisu. An Italian dessert of layers of sponge cake soaked in coffee and brandy or liqueur and filled with mascarpone cheese. The word represents Italian *tira* *mi sù*, literally 'pick me up', and gained its first foothold in English in the 1980s.

Tired and emotional. A humorous euphemism for 'drunk', said to have originated in *Private Eye* in 1965 with reference to the then foreign secretary, George Brown. The satirical magazine in question did much to popularize the phrase. An inebriated person easily falls asleep and readily becomes maudlin or 'weepy'.

Tiswas. A state of confusion of flustered excitement. To be 'all of a tiswas' is thus to be 'in a real state'. The word may be an elaboration of 'tizzy' or possibly a shortening of 'it is, it was', alluding to something that is no sooner present than it is gone. As the title of an anarchic Saturday morning television programme for young children, originally shown by ATV in the Birmingham area, *Tiswas* (1974–82) was proclaimed to mean 'This is Saturday Wear a Smile.'

Titanic. The British luxury passenger liner, the largest ship in the world when built, set sail from Southampton on 10 April 1912 on its maiden voyage to New York. In the early hours of 15 April it struck an iceberg off Newfoundland and sank with the loss of 1515 lives, including those of the captain and the ship's designer. Its 16 watertight compartments had been intended to make it unsinkable. In 1985 the wreck was located and explored by an unmanned submersible under the direction of American and French scientists. The tragedy inspired several re-creations and romantic fictions, such as the award-winning film *Titanic* (1997). *See also* LUSITANIA; NIGHT TO REMEMBER.

Titled trains. Many long-distance trains in Britain have gained names relating to their destinations or routes, or to the (royal) occasion of their first journey. Some Scotland-bound trains have names alluding to the novelist Sir Walter Scott. A few have historical titles. The following were running in 1999:

> *Armada*: Leeds–Plymouth
>
> *Atlantic Coast Express*: London–Newquay
>
> *Bristolian*: London–Bristol
>
> *Broadsman*: London–Norwich
>
> *Caledonian*: London–Glasgow
>
> *Cathedrals Express*: London–Oxford–Hereford–Worcester
>
> *Cornishman*: Edinburgh–Penzance
>
> CORNISH RIVIERA
>
> *Devonian*: Newcastle–Paignton
>
> *Devon Scot*: Aberdeen–Plymouth

> *Dorset Scot*: Edinburgh–Bournemouth
>
> *East Anglian*: London–Norwich
>
> FLYING SCOTSMAN
>
> *Golden Hind*: London–Plymouth
>
> *Highland Chieftain*: London–Inverness
>
> *Irish Mail*: London–Holyhead
>
> *Master Cutler*: Leeds–Sheffield
>
> *Mayflower*: London–Plymouth
>
> *Midland Scot*: Edinburgh–Birmingham
>
> *Norfolkman*: London–Norwich
>
> *Northern Lights*: London–Aberdeen
>
> *Pines Express*: Manchester–Poole
>
> *Red Dragon*: London–Swansea
>
> *Regatta Express*: London–Henley-on-Thames
>
> *Robin Hood*: London–Nottingham
>
> *Royal Duchy*: London–Penzance
>
> *Royal Scot*: London–Glasgow
>
> *St David*: London–Swansea
>
> *Sussex Scot*: Edinburgh–Brighton
>
> *Thames-Avon Express*: London–Stratford-upon-Avon
>
> *Torbay Express*: London–Torquay
>
> *Wessex Scot*: Edinburgh–Bournemouth
>
> *Y Ddraig Gymreig/The Welsh Dragon*: London–Holyhead

The following trains formerly ran under the names given below:

> *Aberdonian*: London–Aberdeen
>
> *Bournemouth Belle*: London–Bournemouth
>
> *Brighton Belle*: London–Brighton
>
> *Cambrian Coast Express*: London–Aberystwyth
>
> *Cheltenham Flyer*: London–Cheltenham
>
> *Clansman*: London–Perth
>
> *Coronation*: London–Edinburgh
>
> *Coronation Scot*: London–Glasgow
>
> *Devon Belle*: London–Plymouth/Ilfracombe
>
> *Elizabethan*: London–Edinburgh
>
> *Emerald Isle Express*: London–Holyhead
>
> *Fenman*: London–King's Lynn
>
> GOLDEN ARROW
>
> *Heart of Midlothian*: London–Edinburgh
>
> *Irishman*: Glasgow–Stranraer
>
> *Lakes Express*: London–Maryport
>
> *Lancastrian*: London–Manchester
>
> *Mancunian*: Manchester–London
>
> *North Briton*: Leeds–Edinburgh

Palatine: Manchester–Derby–London

Peak Express: London–Derby–Manchester

Ports-to-Ports Express: Newcastle–Barry

Queen of Scots: London–Glasgow

Royal Highlander: London–Aberdeen

Royal Wessex: London–Bournemouth

Silver Jubilee: London–Newcastle

Sunny South Express: Manchester–Hastings

Talisman: London–Edinburgh

Tynesider: London–Newcastle

Waverley: London–Edinburgh

White Rose: London–Leeds

Yorkshireman: London–Bradford

TLC. Tender loving care, as shown to a sick person being nursed back to health on the one hand or to a pampered pot plant on the other. The use of the abbreviation is now mostly facetious or ironic, but the phrase itself has a vaguely biblical ring: 'Remember, O Lord, thy tender mercies and thy loving kindnesses' (Psalm 25:6). *See also* MEDICAL ABBREVIATIONS.

TM. *See* TRANSCENDENTAL MEDITATION.

Toad Hall. The ancestral home of Mr Toad in Kenneth Grahame's children's novel *The* WIND IN THE WILLOWS (1908). It stands by the river that flows past River Bank, has every modern convenience and is an exceedingly comfortable gentleman's residence. Mr Toad himself, although basically kind-hearted, can seem conceited and boastful. He is given to short-lived enthusiasms for expensive or dangerous hobbies, the most recent of which is a passion for motorcars. Imprisoned for stealing a car, he contrives to escape and returns to Toad Hall only to find it occupied by a group of weasels, toads and ferrets from Wild Wood.

Tobacco baron. A prisoner who controls the supply of cigarettes to other prisoners and so dominates them. The term is more commonly used by the media than by inmates themselves.

Tobacco Road. A novel (1932) by the US writer Erskine Caldwell (1903–87) about a dysfunctional family who live in extreme poverty on Tobacco Road in rural Georgia. This slice of low life and earthy sex became a bestseller after its acquittal in a New York court of obscenity and the success of the dramatization (1934), which almost closed after a fortnight and then ran for over six years. An excellent but bowdlerized film version (1941) was directed by John Ford.

To Birmingham by way of Beachy Head. Metaphorically, a roundabout approach. It is a quotation from G.K. Chesterton's poem 'The Rolling English Road' (1914):

> A merry road, a mazy road, and such as we did tread
> The night we went to Birmingham by way of Beachy Head.

To bits. Very much, as: 'I was thrilled to bits', 'She loves him to bits', 'The kitten was mewing to bits'. The suggestion is of an action so intense that it 'shatters' the one involved.

> The man [rock musician Ian Dury] is sheer pounding, good-willed energy. New Boots and Panties!! was the best album of the late Seventies/early Eighties. We love him to bits.
>
> *Evening Standard* (Letter to the Editor)
> (27 September 1999)

Toblerone. The chocolate bars of this name were the creation in 1899 of the Swiss manufacturer Johann Tobler (1830–1905). This explains the main part of the name but not its modification, which is based on Italian *torrone*, a kind of nougat. The name was devised in 1908 by the firm's production manager, Emil Baumann, and was patented the following year. The triangular shape of the bar, with its practical serrations, is intended to suggest the peaks of Swiss mountains.

Toc H. The old telegraphy code for the letter T (*see* ROGER) and H, as the initials of Talbot House. The term was used in the First World War, when the first Talbot House was founded in December 1915 at Poperinghe, Belgium, in memory of Gilbert Talbot, third son of Edward Stuart Talbot (1844–1934), bishop of Winchester, who had been killed at Hooge earlier that year. The Rev. P.T.B. 'Tubby' Clayton made it a rest and recreation centre. In 1920 he founded a similar centre in London, also known as Toc H, which developed into an interdenominational association for Christian social service.

To die for. Said of something extremely good or desirable, as if worth dying for. The phrase was already current at the turn of the 20th century but suddenly came into vogue in the 1990s, when it was popularized by its punning use as the title of two films: the first British and released in 1994, about the ghost of a gay man's lover who had died of AIDS, the second American and first screened in 1996, about a small-town television weathergirl who murders her husband.

A few years ago there was a kind of fashion explosion in Antwerp and Belgium suddenly started producing to-die-for, avant-garde clothing.
Sunday Times (24 October 1999)

Toe-cover. An inexpensive and useless present. The term is the creation of the American writer Betty Mac-Donald in her book *The Plague And I* (1948) in which she describes it as a 'family word' and gives as an example of such a present a crocheted napkin ring.

Toe in the door. To have a toe in the door is to be in a position from which progress can be made. The expression dates from the 1970s. *See also* FOOT IN THE DOOR.

Toff, The. The suave but roguish hero of more than 50 crime novels by John Creasey, beginning with *Introducing the Toff* (1938). His real name is the Honourable Richard Rollison, and he is a young man 'down from Cambridge with half a million and a hatred of dullness'. He first appeared in *The Thriller* magazine in 1933, standing in for the SAINT.

Tokenism. The practice or policy of making merely a token effort or granting only minimal concessions, especially to minority or suppressed groups. The term is of American origin and dates from the 1960s.

To Kill a Mocking-Bird. A novel (1960) by the US writer Harper Lee (b.1926), which won the PULITZER PRIZE for fiction. The trial of a black man accused of raping a white woman, and the events that follow the trial, are seen through the eyes of Scout, the six-year-old daughter of the white defence lawyer, Atticus Finch. Although clearly innocent, the man is found guilty and is subsequently shot seventeen times by prison guards while, it is claimed, he was trying to escape. The editor of the local paper writes a courageous leader comparing the death to 'the senseless slaughter of songbirds by hunters and children'. A film version (1962) was directed by Robert Mulligan, with an OSCAR-winning performance by Gregory Peck as Finch.

Tokoism. The doctrine propounded by the Angolan missionary Simau Toko (1918–84). Raised in Luanda, and later a teacher in Baptist schools in Kibokolo and Bembo, Toko went in 1943 to the Belgian Congo (now Congo) to help bring aid to the Congolese. In 1949 he declared himself to be a prophet and began to preach his promise that Africans would throw off the status of slave and assume that of master. His words won many adherents, who formed groups of peaceful resistance to the Portuguese powers. In 1955 Toko was outlawed to the post of lighthouse keeper near Porto Alexandre (now Tombua) and in 1963 banished to the Azores. He died in his native Luanda.

Tokyo Rose. The name given by US servicemen to a woman broadcaster of propaganda from Japan during the Second World War. Several American-born Japanese women were suspected of taking part in these broadcasts but only one, Iva Ikuko Toguri d'Aquino (b.1916) was found guilty and in 1949 charged on eight counts of treason in San Francisco. She served six years in prison, but in 1977 was granted a pardon by President Gerald Ford. *See also* AXIS SALLY; HAW-HAW, LORD.

Tom and Jerry. The well-known cat and mouse cartoon characters first appeared in an animated cartoon called *Puss Gets the Boot* (1940), as the creations of the veteran animators, William Hanna and Joseph Barbera. Their names were chosen from hundreds of suggestions submitted by studio employees in a contest held at MGM, the film company that launched them. The names were not original, however, and existed earlier for the pair of roystering young men about town in Pierce Egan's *Life in London; or, The Day and Night Scenes of Jerry Hawthorn, Esq, and his Elegant Friend Corinthian Tom* (1821).

Tombeau de Couperin, Le. A piano suite by Maurice Ravel (1875–1937), written in 1917, and in which each of the six movements is dedicated to a friend killed in the First World War. The title means 'the tomb (or tombstone) of Couperin', referring to the great French composer and harpsichordist François Couperin (1668–1733). A number of 17th-century French composers used *tombeau* in the titles of works lamenting the death of some notable person; for example, Denis Gaultier's *Tombeau* for lute in memory of the lutenist de Lenclos. Ravel later orchestrated four of the six movements, which have provided music for two ballets.

Tom Keating's pictures. *See under* FAKES.

Tommy. *See* ATKINS, TOMMY.

Tommy gun. A Thompson short-barrelled sub-machine-gun, so named after its co-inventor (with John N. Blish), US General John T. Thompson (1860–1940), who patented it in 1920.

Tomorrow is the first day of the rest of your life. A thought-provoking truism dating from the late 1960s and said to have been coined by Charles Dederich, American founder of the Synanon drug and alcohol addiction centres. 'Today' sometimes replaces 'To-morrow'. The sentiment is similar to the less person-ally oriented 'Tomorrow is another day', the line that closes Margaret Mitchell's bestselling novel GONE WITH THE WIND (1936) and that originally was to have been its title.

Tom's Midnight Garden. A much-admired novel (1958) for children by the British writer Philippa Pearce (b.1920). Tom is sent away to stay with his aunt and uncle in a country house when his brother falls ill with measles. The 'Midnight garden' is a secret garden that appears only after the grandfather clock in the house has struck the 13th hour, and in it Tom makes the acquaintance of a Victorian family who formerly occupied the house.

Tom Swifties. A mildly amusing linguistic trick, in which an adverb relates both properly and punningly to a sentence of reported speech. An example is: '"What can I get you?" asked the waitress fetchingly.' The quip takes its name from Tom Swift, a boy's ad-venture hero created by the prolific American writer Edward L. Stratemeyer in the early 20th century. Tom Swift rarely passed a remark without a qualifying adverb, as 'Tom added eagerly' or 'Tom smiled rue-fully', and the wordplay arose as a pastiche of this.

Tono-Bungay. A novel (1909) by H.G. Wells (1866–1946), in which ideas about society are blended with scientific projections of the future. Wells himself described it as a 'social panorama in the vein of Balzac'. Tono-Bungay is a patent medicine, by means of which George Ponderevo's uncle Edward, having lost everything on the stock exchange, builds up a business empire, before going bankrupt again and being charged with forgery. In the meantime George has been designing aeroplanes and airships, in one of which he takes Edward to France to escape justice.

Tonton. A nickname of the French Socialist politician François Mitterrand (1916–96) when he was president of France (1981–95). 'Tonton' is a French child's word for 'uncle'.

Tonton Macoutes. Members of a notoriously brutal militia formed by President François PAPA DOC Duvalier of Haiti (1907–71) as a private force to terror-ize and liquidate alleged enemies of his regime. They were officially known as National Security Volunteers and were active from 1961 to 1986. The Haitian French name approximates to 'bogeymen'.

Ton-up. A speed of 100mph, especially on a motorcycle. A 'ton-up boy' is a rider who achieves this, or more generally a member of a motorcycle gang. The term dates from the 1950s.

> The BBC broadcast of 'Morning Service' from Keele University, Staffs, yesterday was interrupted when a record about 'ton-up' boys was heard above the hymn singing. A loud-speaker was found hidden behind a stage in the chapel.
> *Daily Telegraph* (25 January 1965)

Tony. The name of a number of awards made annually from 1947 in the American theatre in various categ-ories. The name is that of the American actress and manager Antoinette ('Tony') Perry (1888–1946). The word fortuitously echoes 'tony' in the colloquial sense of chic or sophisticated, literally having 'tone'.

Tony Curtis. A male hairstyle popular in the 1950s in which the hair at the sides of the head is combed back and that on the forehead combed forwards. The style takes its name from the US film actor Tony Curtis (b.1925), whose real name was Bernard Schwartz.

Tony's cronies. A derisive nickname for the INNER CABINET of Tony Blair, Labour prime minister from 1997, some of whom were supposedly appointed as personal friends rather than as skilful politicians, and by extension for the non-politicians courted by him. In 1998 the opposition leader, William Hague, accused NEW LABOUR of CRONYISM, his criticism centring on revelations about the supposedly corrupt activities of influential 'insiders'. *See also* BLAIR BABES.

> The growing power exercised by 'Tony's cronies' is threatening parliamentary democracy and undermin-ing the Civil Service by handing government over to an unaccountable new elite.
> *The Times* (25 February 2000)

Toodle-oo. Goodbye. The word is more likely to repres-ent a parting toot on a motor horn than to be a cor-ruption of French *à tout à l'heure*, 'see you soon', as sometimes explained. 'Toodle-pip' is a variant, and 'tooraloo' another.

Toon, The. A nickname for Newcastle upon Tyne, especially as the home of the celebrated football club Newcastle United, whose supporters, in their replica black-and-white team shirts, are known as the 'Toon Army' (*see also* TARTAN ARMY). 'Toon' is a northern dialect form of 'town'.

> Fervent supporters of Newcastle United have made the city the replica shirt capital of the world, dressing

children in the black and white of the Toon Army long before they can walk.

The Times (4 January 2000)

Tooth fairy. A desired or imaginary source of riches, as: 'Let's hope a tooth fairy can help with the funding.' The allusion is to the fairy said to take children's milk teeth after they have fallen out and to leave a coin under their pillow as payment.

'No doubt Solomon and David Morgan will continue to trap victims' … concluded MacIntyre. 'But perhaps after tonight they might find it a little more difficult.' If MacIntyre truly believes this, he probably believes in the tooth fairy, too.

The Times (1 December 1999)

Tootle along, To. To depart. The verb has become associated with a parting toot on a motor horn although it is more likely to be a variant of 'toddle'.

Too True to Be Good. A play (1932) by the Irish playwright George Bernard Shaw (1856–1950) in which a Burglar teams up with a Nurse in an attempt to steal an invalid's necklace but then befriends the intended victim to the extent that all three share the proceeds of the necklace's sale and set up home together on a tropical beach. The title results from a mangling of the proverbial 'too good to be true'.

Top banana. The leading comic in a performance; a chief or boss generally. The expression apparently derives from a skit involving the sharing of a banana. *See also* SECOND BANANA.

Top dog. A person who by skill, personality or violence obtains the mastery. The analogy is with a dog who is on top of another in a fight. The expression dates from the turn of the 20th century.

Top drawer. To be out of the top drawer is to have a high social status or be specially proficient. The allusion is to the uppermost drawer of a bureau or dresser, where jewellery and other valuables are kept.

'When you see people do things with a football like Di Canio did today, it's fantastic', Redknapp said. 'He's out of the top drawer.'

The Times (13 September 1999)

Top End. A laconic nickname for the northern part of Northern Territory, Australia, dating from the 1930s. The southern part of the state is sometimes known as 'the Centre', with Alice Springs as its 'capital', just as Darwin, the capital of the state as a whole, is specifically associated with the 'Top End'.

Top-of-the-range. The best there is of its kind. The term is typically applied to a manufactured article that is superior to all others of its type and that is frequently promoted as such.

'What started off as a hobby has given me all this,' he says, gesturing to the swimming pool and his beloved top-of-the-range £75,000 BMW 750 car.

The Times (3 January 2000)

Top shelf. The top shelf in a newsagent's shop, where pornographic magazines are placed to keep them out of view of the general public and out of reach of children. The phrase formerly denoted high quality or excellence, in the manner of 'top hole'.

Topsy and Tim. The names of two children used to represent gender stereotypes or the attitudes of a typical middle-class British family. The names are those of the small girl and boy who feature in a series of picture books for young children by Jean and Gareth Adamson, first published in 1959.

The subtext was pure *Topsy and Tim*: that as girls like long hair, fluffy teddy bears and elasticated bracelets made of sweets, women readers like books about love in the typing pool and Aga Sagas set in the Cotswolds.

The Times (30 October 1999)

Top 10. The 10 bestselling recordings of pop or rock music in the weekly charts. Attention usually focuses on the No. 1 spot. *See also* HIT PARADE.

Tora! Tora! Tora! A film about the Japanese attack on PEARL HARBOR, made in 1970 by a joint US-Japanese production team. Reconstructing events on both the American and Japanese sides, the film concentrates on the attack itself and the reasons why it was not prevented by the American military, rather than looking at the wider political context of the events of 7 December 1941. 'Tora, Tora, Tora' was the code name used by the Japanese to indicate the success of their mission. *Tora* is Japanese for 'tiger'.

Torch Song Trilogy. A trio of plays (1981) by the US playwright Harvey Fierstein (b.1954) in which the common link is a professional drag queen called Arnold. The title refers to the 'torch song' genre of intense love songs commonly delivered by singers in the bars and clubs that Arnold and his friends frequent.

Torrey Canyon. An oil tanker that on 18 March 1967 struck a reef between the Scilly Isles and Cornwall, resulting in one of Britain's worst environmental disasters, with some 130 km (80 miles) of Cornish coast being polluted by crude oil. The ship took its name from the Torrey Canyon Oil Company, one of three 'wildcatter' companies that in 1890 formed the Union Oil Company of California (now the Unocal Corporation). *See also* EXXON VALDEZ.

> This is the greatest ever peacetime threat to Britain.
> HAROLD WILSON, commenting on the *Torrey Canyon* disaster (30 March 1967)

Torschlusspanik. A German word, dating from the mid-20th century, designating a sense of alarm or anxiety at the passing of life's opportunities. The literal meaning of the word is 'door-closing panic', from the German words *Tor*, 'door', 'gate', *Schluss* 'closure', and *Panik* 'panic'.

Torvill and Dean. Jayne Torvill (b.1957) and Christopher Dean (b.1958) entranced the British public in the 1980s as a romantically dashing and talented pair of ice-skaters. They formed their partnership in 1975 and were soon setting new standards in the sport. They were six times British champions and won the grand slam of World, Olympic and European ice-dance titles in 1984, receiving a total of 136 perfect 'sixes', the highest award a judge can give. The high spot of their act was a haunting interpretation of Ravel's BOLÉRO. They later performed together in their own ice shows, and made a brief comeback to the sport at the 1994 Winter Olympics, in which they won bronze medals.

Torygraph. A media nickname for the *Daily Telegraph*, alluding to its more or less consistent support for the Conservative Party. The paper lost something of its political partisanism under the editorship of Max Hastings (1986–95) but visibly regained it under his successor, Charles Moore, a confirmed High Tory and former YOUNG FOGY, to the extent that even its news columns were slanted to suit the editorial line while its political coverage became blatantly propagandistic.

Tosca. The heroine of Puccini's opera that bears her name, premièred at Rome in 1900. The libretto, by Giuseppe Giacosa and Luigi Illica, is based on Victorien Sardou's drama *La Tosca* (1887). The story is set in Rome in June 1800. Baron Scarpia, chief of police, lusts after Tosca, the self-centred actress lover of the artist and republican loyalist, Mario Cavaradossi, who has aided the escape of Cesare Angelotti, former consul of the Roman Republic. He has Cavaradossi arrested and tortured until Tosca reveals Angelotti's hiding-place. Scarpia agrees to release Cavaradossi and provide both him and Tosca with a safe conduct after Cavaradossi has been subjected to a mock execution. Scarpia's price is Tosca herself. She agrees, but stabs him with a knife snatched from his desk when he begins to embrace her. Scarpia's so-called 'mock' execution squad turns out to have live bullets, and Cavaradossi is killed. By this time Scarpia's murder has been discovered, and in grief Tosca flings herself from the battlements.

Totes Meer. This is one of several paintings by Paul Nash (1889–1946) depicting the air war in the Second World War, during which he was an official war artist, as he had been in the First World War. The title is German for 'dead sea', and the picture shows a sea of shot-down German aeroplanes in which the wings become waves. Painted in 1940–41, the work was reproduced on a Royal Mail stamp in 1965 to commemorate the BATTLE OF BRITAIN (1940). The poet Anna Adams wrote of the painting: 'This clear eye records the waste, does not insist on pain.' *See also* WE ARE MAKING A NEW WORLD.

Totting up. A system introduced in 1988 by which penalty points for driving offences accumulate until they lead to disqualification. Originally three endorsements on a driver's licence led to this, but it is now the consequence if twelve points are incurred within three years. The number of points awarded for an offence is at the discretion of the court. For careless driving the figure may range from three to nine, while for speeding it is from three to six.

Touchy-feely. Expressing one's emotions openly and through physical contact. The phrase implies both senses of 'touch' (make physical contact, affect emotionally) and of 'feel' (perceive by touch, be emotionally affected). The term arose in the 1970s from the encounter groups of the 1960s, whose members sought physical benefit by close mutual contact.

> I [Labour MP Helen Brinton] am very touchy-feely with my constituents. If people break down during my surgery, I give them a hug.
> *The Times* (19 September 1998)

Tough act to follow. *See* HARD ACT TO FOLLOW.

Tough cookie. A tough person; a survivor. 'Cookie' here simply means 'person'. The phrase is of American origin and dates from the 1930s. The variant 'one tough cookie' is also found.

> Lisa Anderson is one tough cookie. You can hear it in her plummy, confident voice. You can see it in the set

of her mouth. If you want to know something, she will tell you straight.

Sunday Express (27 February 2000)

Tough love. A method of promoting the welfare of a person such as an addict or criminal by enforcing certain constraints on them or requiring them to take responsibility for themselves, stressing the importance of self-help rather than the indulgence of others. The American concept dates from the 1980s and was readily embraced by politicians seeking to restrict state benefits.

Tough shit or **titty**. So what; too bad. The crude American responses to express a lack of sympathy date from the 1950s, the mammary variant perhaps based on a black folk saying: 'It's tough titty, but the milk is good.'

'Even if you get away with it, you'll never be able to come home.'

'Well, so, tough titty.'

TRUMAN CAPOTE: *Breakfast at Tiffany's* (1958)

Tour de France. The world's first and best known cycle race was established in 1903 by the French cyclist and journalist Henri Desgrange (1865–1940) as a six-stage race of 2410km (1497 miles). This distance was later extended so that it is now about 4000km (2500 miles). The route now runs mainly through France and Belgium with occasional brief visits to Italy, Spain, Germany and Switzerland. In 1994 part of the race took place in England to mark the opening of the CHANNEL TUNNEL. From 1971 the race was restricted to 20 shorter stages. The winner of each stage is awarded the *maillot jaune* (yellow jersey) and the riders are accompanied by a vast fleet of official, press and support vehicles. The race has been won five times by Jacques Anquetil (France), Eddy Merckx (Belgium), Bernard Hinault (France) and Miguel Induráin (Spain). *See also* MILK RACE.

Towers of Trebizond, The. The last novel (1956) by Rose Macaulay (1881–1958), a witty account of a party of eccentric Anglo-Catholics attempting to spread the Christian faith in Turkey. The disused Byzantine churches of the ancient city of Trebizond (Trabzon) that they visit symbolize the nostalgia for the Christian faith in which the narrator indulges, having forfeited it by reason of her adulterous affair. The situation also reflects Macaulay's private grief. Her own 25-year affair with the Irish novelist Gerald O'Donovan (1871–1942) prevented

her from practising her strict Anglo-Catholicism. *See also* FIRST LINES OF NOVELS.

Town Like Alice, A. A novel (1949) by Nevil Shute (1899–1960). A young Englishwoman, who has, with her group, suffered incredible privations in Malaya during the Second World War at the hands of the Japanese, uses an inheritance to transform Midhurst, a depressed settlement in the Australian Gulf of Carpentaria country, into 'a town like Alice [Springs]'. A film version (1956), directed by Jack Lee and starring Peter Finch and Virginia McKenna, was freely adapted from the first part of the novel.

Toy boy. A young man who is 'kept' as a lover by an older woman. The term has also been used of gay relationships. A sort of converse is the 'boy toy', a young woman regarded as sexually attractive to young men. The rock star Madonna (b.1958) was so described in 1989. *See also* SUGAR DADDY.

Toytown. A name used figuratively of a thing that apparently or actually lacks real value or substance. The word originated in the 19th century in the literal sense of a model town for a child to play with. It subsequently became familiar as a proper name in a series of children's stories by the toymaker and illustrator S.G. Hulme Beaman (1886–1932), first in books, beginning with *The Road to Toytown* (1925), then from 1929 as radio plays on CHILDREN'S HOUR.

For us hacks following the Toytown mayoral race [London's mayoral elections] it is refreshing when a new name ... erupts.

The Times (4 December 1999)

Tracey. *See* TRACY.

Trachtenberg system. A system of speedy mathematical calculations based upon simple counting according to prescribed keys or formulae, which need to be memorized. There is no division or multiplication as such, and complicated calculations can be more easily and rapidly handled than by normal processes. The system was devised by Jakow Trachtenberg (1888–c.1960) during his seven long years in a NAZI concentration camp. He was born at Odessa and trained as an engineer and became a refugee in Germany after the Russian Revolution. The method still had its adherents at the turn of the 21st century.

Track record. Literally and originally, the record of an athlete or horse on a particular running track. This sense dates from the 1950s. The term was then adopted to denote the past record of a person or business, especially as a guide to likely future performance.

Tracy or **Tracey.** A female forename highly popular in the 1960s and 1970s. It was at one time a male forename, as were the surnames of other English noble families such as Clifford, Dudley and Stanley. As a female name it later took on overtones of a BIMBO or AIRHEAD, and when coupled with SHARON served subsequently to personify an ESSEX GIRL type. *See also* BIRDS OF A FEATHER.

Tracy, Dick. The newspaper comic-strip detective created by Chester Gould from 1931, and in his day one of the best known 'dicks' in the United States. He was played by Ralph Byrd in four film serials and later by Morgan Conway in two feature films before moving to television and to a stage musical in 1970. Of all the films in which he has appeared the most memorable was the lavishly produced *Dick Tracy* (1990), in which he was played by Warren Beatty.

Trade plates. Temporary number plates used by car dealers or manufacturers on unlicensed cars, and usually recognizable by their *ad hoc* fixing and red and white colours. Such cars are delivered for the motor trade by 'trade platers', who are generally paid the return train fare but who mostly find it advantageous to hitch-hike back. They are thus often seen brandishing their detached plates by a motorway slip road to this end.

Traduttori traditori. An early 20th-century Italian phrase, the literal meaning of which is 'translators (are) traitors', indicating that is impossible to translate without misrepresenting the original. The phrase is also found in the singular: *traduttore traditore*, (a) translator (is a) traitor.

Traffic calming. The deliberate slowing of traffic in a residential area by means of SLEEPING POLICEMEN and other measures. The technique was introduced to Britain in the late 1980s and the expression is a literal translation of German *Verkehrsberuhigung*.

Trahison des clercs (French, 'treason of the clerks'). The betrayal of standards by intellectuals influenced by politics. An early 20th-century French phrase, it originated in *La Trahison des Clercs* ('The Treachery of the Intellectuals'), a work (1927) by Julien Benda, in which he denounces as moral traitors those who betray truth and justice for racial and political considerations.

Trailer trash. An American term of the 1990s for poor whites who live in large stationary caravans ('trailers') and who are regarded as being unsociable, uncouth and unsightly. The expression came to be used generally as a term of scornful or semi-serious abuse.

> Eminem, aka Marshall Mathers, is white trailer trash, America's worst nightmare after black ghetto trash.
> *The Times* (31 December 1999)

Trainspotting. In the narrow sense, the collecting of railway locomotive numbers, a pursuit regarded by the uninvolved or uncomprehending as fit only for ANORAKS. The term subsequently broadened to apply to any obsessive occupation, especially one regarded as trivial or at best of minority interest. This second sense was popularized by the title of Irvine Welsh's cult novel of 1993, filmed to much acclaim in 1996. Written largely in a phonetic Scottish patois, Welsh's book consists of a series of loosely connected episodes illustrative of the lives of Edinburgh junkies, wideboys and psychopaths. On Leith Central Station 'an auld drunkard ... lurched up tae us, wine boatil in his hand. ... "What yis up tae, lads? Trainspottin, eh?" he sais, laughing uncontrollably at his ain fucking wit.' *See also* FIRST LINES OF NOVELS.

Tramp. A famous London nightclub opened in 1969 by Johnny Gold, who took its name from a television documentary describing Charlie Chaplin as 'the greatest tramp of them all'. Its 6000 members include many celebrities, some of whom still pay its original £10.50 entry fee. It has a rule 'no tramps without birds', meaning that male members must be accompanied by females, and despite some colourful incidents has always stayed away from controversy or scandal.

Trance. A type of electronic dance music evolving in the 1990s from TECHNO, so named from its hypnotic 'tribal' rhythms and sounds. The music was also seen as possessing a spiritual dimension.

Transcendental Meditation. A movement based on special techniques of meditation. TM, as it is usually known, was introduced to the West in the 1960s by the Maharishi Mahesh Yogi (b.1911) in his book *The Science of Being and Art of Loving*. It uses one of a number of Sanskrit mantras, each being a short word or phrase that is repeated in the mind to help the user quiet the activity of thought and so attain a deeper level of consciousness. This process, it is claimed, gives the practitioner deep relaxation, leading to inner joy, vitality and creativity. TM became particularly popular when the BEATLES embraced it for a few months in 1967. *See also* DEAR PRUDENCE.

Transit van. This general-purpose vehicle, despite its seemingly generic name, was launched by Ford in 1965 and was originally to have been called the 'V-series'. At the last minute, however, Sir William Batty, then chairman of Ford of Britain, decided that the name Transit would make the van more marketable. It was an immediate success, with a 'chunky' and businesslike look that its predecessor, the Thames, had lacked. Transits were soon being adapted for a wide range of tasks and the roomy and reliable vehicle was readily adopted for a host of transportation purposes.

Transport House. A former name for the leadership of the LABOUR PARTY, from its headquarters in SMITH SQUARE, London. The building was also the head office of the Transport and General Workers' Union. Hence its name. The Labour Party moved from Smith Square to Walworth Road in 1980 while the TGWU is now based in a new Transport House in Palace Street.

Travelogue. A film or illustrated lecture about travel. The word suggests a blend of 'travel' and 'monologue'. Travelogues were a staple of early silent cinema before the advent of the feature film and later became popular short films accompanying the main film. Their purpose was essentially to increase tourism, and many presented a glamorized and often vulgarized view of life in the country or region depicted.

Treasure of the Sierra Madre, The. A novel (1935; in German as *Der Schatz der Sierra Madre*, 1927) by the Polish-born German (or possibly Austrian) novelist B. Traven. Traven was the pen-name of Berick Traven Torsvan (c.1890–1969), whose name was originally Albert Otto Max Feige and who was also known as Ret Marut. Traven was an actor and anarchist, who settled in Mexico, where he was a union activist, eventually being listed as an enemy of the state. His best known book is an analysis of greed as three Americans search for a lost gold mine in the mountains of central Mexico. An unforgettable film version (1948) was directed by John Huston and starred Humphrey Bogart, Walter Huston and Tim Holt.

Treaty of Versailles. A treaty that brought a formal end to the First World War. It was signed in the Palace of Mirrors in the Palace of Versailles on 28 June 1919 by Lloyd George of Britain, Georges Clemenceau of France, Woodrow Wilson of the United States and Vittorio Orlando of Italy and took force on 10 January

1920. The treaty redivided the territory of the defeated CENTRAL POWERS, restricted Germany's armed forces, and established the LEAGUE OF NATIONS. It was bitterly criticized by the Germans, who complained that it had been 'dictated' to them, that it violated the spirit of the FOURTEEN POINTS and that it demanded intolerable sacrifices that would wreck their economy. It was subsequently revised and altered, mostly in Germany's favour. *See also* PEACE FOR OUR TIME.

Tree hugger. A contemptuous term for an environmental campaigner, typically regarded as hugging trees in order to love them and protect them.

Trekkie or **Trekker.** A fan of the cult American SCIENCE FICTION television programme STAR TREK.

Trench coat. A long, loose-belted, double-breasted raincoat in a military style, so called as originally worn by British army officers in the trenches during the First World War. It soon became fashionable among men and later also among women, and has more than once been revived in the latter style.

> The last time I coveted a trench coat I was 18, living in Paris and attempting to do an English take on the French take on le style anglais. ... Well, the trench is back, as part of the retro-YSL mood now sweeping through fashion, and boy is it good to see it again.
> LISA ARMSTRONG in *The Times* (7 February 2000)

Trench fever. A remittent or relapsing fever affecting men living in trenches, dugouts and the like, and transmitted by the excrement of lice. It first appeared in the First World War, in the static warfare on the WESTERN FRONT.

Trent's Last Case. A novel (1913) by E.C. Bentley (1875–1956), regarded as the prototype of the realistic detective story. Philip Trent, an artistic and literary figure with a gift for solving crimes, works on the mystery of the murder of an American millionaire. When the truth is finally revealed, he decides it is time to withdraw from being an amateur detective. Bentley was also the inventor of the CLERIHEW. A film version (1952) was directed by Herbert Wilcox.

Trial, The. A fragmentary novel (1937; in German as *Der Prozess*, 1925) by Franz Kafka (1883–1924). It concerns the tribulations of Josef K., arrested and imprisoned by an unnamed bureaucracy, and accused of a crime which is never specified. K's attempts to discover the reasons for his arrest came to nothing, and he is eventually led away by two men in black and executed by knifing. The novel has generally been interpreted as an allegory of existential guilt, and its depiction of a shadowy and menacing bureaucracy as an eerie premonition of the methods of 20th-century totalitarianism. Orson Welles directed a film version of the novel (1963). *See also* KAFKAESQUE.

Trial by television. The questioning of someone on a controversial matter in a television interview, especially when the questions are felt to be over-severe or unfair. The expression evokes 'trial by fire' and the experience involves a similar 'grilling'.

> Given that it [*The Spying Game*] involved at least two confrontations of alleged guilt ... why were there none of the ritual cries of protest from the Right about 'trial by television'?
>
> *The Times* (29 September 1999)

Triangle Shirtwaist fire. The most serious factory fire in the history of New York. It occurred on 25 March 1911 in the Asch building at the corner of Washington Street and Greene Street, where the Triangle Shirtwaist Company occupied the top three floors of 10. Some 500 young Jewish women and girls were employed there at the time and were unable to escape when fire broke out in the cutting room on the eighth floor. A total of 146 women died in less than 15 minutes, some as a result of jumping from open windows. The owners of the company, who had resisted government safety regulations, were charged with manslaughter but later acquitted.

Tribeca. A name adopted by property developers in the 1970s for an area of land at the West Side of New York City, as an acronym of 'triangle below Canal Street'. Dilapidated factories and warehouses have been converted to residential lofts, many of them inhabited by artists, and Tribeca is now a fashionable neighbourhood with a generally affluent population.

Tribute group or **band.** A group of amateur pop musicians who imitate a (usually well-known) band that has officially dissolved, partly to pay tribute to its former popularity, partly to please its nostalgic fans.

> The last time I reviewed Madness I suggested that they were beginning to sound like a tribute band. It's good to be able to report that this time they are back for real.
>
> *The Times* (28 December 1999)

Trick cyclist. A punning jocularism for a psychiatrist, who may indeed cultivate a delicate balancing act similar to that of the bicycling expert.

Trick or treat. A Halloween custom of American origin, in which children in fancy dress call at houses and threaten to play a prank ('trick') if they are not given sweets or a small gift ('treat'). In most cases the latter is usually proffered and the former rarely realized. A good example of the practice can be seen in the musical film *Meet Me in St Louis* (1944).

> This year the first group thump on the door at 6pm and we open it to an assorted bunch of mini-Supermans, a Pocahontas, two non-specific princesses and Po, the Teletubby, eagerly waving their plastic pumpkin buckets in expectation of sugar booty. 'Trick or treat', they chorus, as I produce the basket full of candycorn.
>
> *The Times* (4 November 1998)

Tricks of the trade. The ingenious devices or 'dodges' known only to the members of a craft or profession. There is no necessary implication of trickery.

Tricky Dicky. The nickname of Richard M. Nixon (1913–94), Republican vice-president (1953–61) and 37th president of the United States, so called from his combined political adroitness and evasiveness. The nickname was awarded to him long before his final disgrace and resignation over WATERGATE. It first appeared in 1950, when he was so dubbed by Helen Gahagan Douglas in the Californian *Independent Review* after Nixon, during his bid to become a senator, had inaccurately smeared his opponent as a communist fellow traveller. Various incidents in his subsequent career meant that the nickname stuck.

Once in the Senate, Nixon helped Joseph McCarthy's anti-communist witch-hunt (*see* McCARTHYISM). Allegations that he was secretly funded by Californian businessmen almost scuppered Nixon's successful bid to become Eisenhower's running-mate in the 1952 presidential election. He got out of this scrape by making a tear-jerking television speech in which he admitted accepting, as a gift for his children, a dog named Checkers. Nixon stood for the presidency against J.F. Kennedy (JFK) in 1960, and, perhaps boosted by his success with the Checkers speech, agreed to a televised debate with his opponent. However, Nixon refused to wear make-up, and his FIVE O'CLOCK SHADOW made him look shifty and shady. His next bid for the presidency, in 1968, was successful, and during his first term he moved towards ending US involvement in the VIETNAM War and pursued a policy of DÉTENTE with China and the Soviet Union. However, as the Watergate scandal broke in his second term, he fully lived up to his nickname, desperately trying to cover up his involvement in illegal activities.

The name Tricky Dicky is also used generally for any devious or manipulative person, especially a politician.

> Better a Tricky Dicky than a grey man in a grey suit.
> *Sunday Times* (Headline) (28 November 1999)

Trident. A type of US nuclear-armed SLBM (submarine-launched ballistic missile). The first version of Trident, which entered US service in the early 1980s, was based on its predecessor, the Poseidon 3, with the addition of a third-stage rocket motor. The name alludes to the trident wielded by Poseidon, the Greek god of the sea. Trident 2, the version adopted by Britain in the 1990s to replace its aged POLARIS missiles, has a range of 12,000km (7400 miles). The UK government's decision to go ahead with Trident, at enormous cost, was the subject of considerable controversy in Britain, particularly as the COLD WAR was by then over.

Trigger-happy. Ready or over-ready to shoot at anything at sight on the slightest provocation. The expression dates from the Second World War. *See also* BOMB-HAPPY.

Triple Alliance. *See* TRIPLE ENTENTE.

Triple Crown. An award or honour for winning a group of three events in various sports. In Britain the Triple Crown in rugby union denotes a victory in the Five Nations Championship (renamed the Six Nations Championship in 2000 when Italy joined the competition) by one of the four home countries over all the other three in the same season, as happened in 1998, when England won against Wales, Scotland and Ireland. In the United States the Triple Crown means a win in the Kentucky Derby, the Preakness and the Belmont Stakes, as famously occurred in 1919 when the chestnut colt Sir Barton swept the board, a feat that would not be repeated until 1930.

Triple Entente. A military alliance (1914–17) between Britain, France and Russia in the First World War. It was based on three earlier agreements: the Franco-Russian Alliance (1894), the ENTENTE CORDIALE between Britain and France (1904) and the Anglo-Russian Entente (1907). These agreements were drawn up in response to the Triple Alliance of Germany, Austria-Hungary and Italy formed in 1882, and the effect was to divide Europe into two armed camps. Romania allied itself with the Triple Alliance in 1883, and Italy withdrew in 1914 (see CENTRAL POWERS). Russia withdrew from the Triple Entente after the OCTOBER REVOLUTION in 1917. *See also* SARAJEVO.

Triple threat. An Americanism for a person adept in three skills or abilities. The expression comes from American football, in which a triple threat (to the opposition) is a player who is good at running, passing and kicking.

Triple-witching hour. In financial jargon the time when stock options, stock index futures and options on such futures all mature at once. Triple-witching hours occur quarterly and are usually accompanied by highly volatile trading. The allusion is to 'witching hour' as a term for midnight, the time when witches are active and magic takes place. The phrase derives from Shakespeare: ''Tis now the very witching time of night, / When churchyards yawn and hell itself breathes out /Contagion to this world' (*Hamlet*, III, ii). The term originated with reference to a one-day fall in share prices on Wall Street in September 1986, a year before BLACK MONDAY.

> This is triple-witching week in the money markets. Tomorrow, the Federal Reserve Open Market Committee meets in the US and on Thursday the European Central Bank is set to pronounce on euro interest rates and the Monetary Policy Committee on sterling rates.
> *The Times* (4 October 1999)

Trivial Pursuit. The commercially packaged quiz game of this name was born in 1979 when two Canadians, photo editor Chris Haney and sportswriter Scott Abbott, bought their eighth game of SCRABBLE, having worked through seven previous sets, and began to wonder how many other people had bought multiple copies of the game. The realization of a potential market led them to devise their own game, and as their job was reporting news it was natural for them to be interested in current affairs, and to present this from the time-honoured angles of 'who, what, when, where and why'. They originally planned to call the game 'Trivia Pursuit' but Haney's wife jokingly called it 'Trivial Pursuit', and this was the name adopted. Sales were initially discouraging, but a breakthrough came when the game was taken up by the American company Selchow and Righter, who gave it a major promotion at the 1983 New York Toy Fair. It is played with dice and question cards, the questions themselves falling into six colour categories: blue for geography, pink for entertainment, yellow for history, brown for art and literature, green for science and nature, orange for sport and leisure. *See also* PUB QUIZ.

Trolley dash. A consumer-oriented prize awarded by some competition organizers, commercial companies and the like. It consists in racing frenziedly around the aisles of a supermarket with a trolley and filling it with as many products as possible in a given time. The stunt usually attracts a cheering crowd of shoppers and brings welcome publicity to the sponsors right in the marketplace.

Trophy art. Works of art looted in time of war. The term particularly applies to art looted by the RED ARMY from NAZI Germany at the end of the Second World War and, conversely, to Russian art looted by the Germans. Russia's biggest loss of this type is generally considered to be the lavish Amber Room in the Yekaterinsky (Catherine's) Palace, Tsarskoye Selo (formerly Pushkin), destroyed by the Germans during the Nazi siege of LENINGRAD (now St Petersburg) (1941–4), during which many amber panels were looted. Much art of this type has still not been returned to its country of origin, and the Pushkin Museum, Moscow, continues to display a collection of Germany's Trojan gold, brought to the Soviet Union at the end of the war.

Trophy wife. A derogatory term for a person's wife regarded as a status symbol for her husband. She is typically seen as a BIMBO who has married an older man, often as his second wife. The arrangement is not without its rewards for the wife, who gains access to her husband's wealth. *See also* LADIES WHO LUNCH.

Tropic of Cancer. A semi-autobiographical novel (1934) in experimental form by Henry Miller (1891–1980). Unashamedly exhibitionistic, it covers his activities and other forms of low life in Paris during the 1930s. *Tropic of Capricorn* (1939) is a companion volume, reflecting his childhood and earlier life in the United States. Both books were banned in the United States until the 1960s. Of *Tropic of Cancer*, the poet and critic Ezra Pound (1885–1972) commented: 'At last an unprintable book which is readable.' The tropics of Cancer and Capricorn are two parallel lines of latitude between which the sun can be vertical over the earth's surface. Miller commented that 'Cancer is separated from Capricorn only by an imaginary line. … You live like a rock in the midst of the ocean; you are fixed while everything about you is in turbulent motion.' An unsatisfactory film version (1970) was directed by Joseph Strick.

Trot. A term of abuse in the 1960s for anyone vaguely left-wing and so politically suspect. The word is an abbreviation of 'Trotskyite' as a nickname for a radical socialist, especially one inspired by the political and economic principles of the Russian revolutionary Leon Trotsky (1879–1940), who advocated the establishment of world socialism by means of continuing revolution. *See also* HATTONISTAS; MILITANT TENDENCY.

Troubles. A term used for various periods of unrest in Irish history. In the 20th century the name became particularly associated with the Anglo-Irish War (War of Independence) of 1919–21 and the period of terrorism in Northern Ireland which began in the late 1960s. A novel entitled *Troubles* (1970), by J.G. Farrell (1935–79), uses the symbol of a rundown hotel (the ironically named 'Majestic'), to paint a vivid and tragicomic picture of events in southern Ireland in the stormy year of 1919, as British rule in southern Ireland began its final collapse. *The Troubles* (1996) was the title of an account of events in Northern Ireland since 1969 by Tim Pat Coogan. *See also* BIG FELLA; BOGSIDE; DIRECT RULE; FREE-STATERS; IRA; POWER-SHARING; ULSTER VOLUNTEER FORCE.

Troubleshooter. An American coinage for someone expert in locating and mending 'trouble', mechanical or otherwise. The original application at the turn of the 20th century was specifically to an engineer who traced and corrected faults on a telegraph or telephone line. The term was later adopted for a person brought into an industry to mend relations between employer and employee.

Trout Fishing in America. An experimental novel (1967) by Richard Brautigan (1935–84). It represents a quest for an alternative lifestyle, free from the constraints of modern living, in the form of a search for the perfect trout stream.

True Grit. A film WESTERN (1969) based on a novel (1968) of the same title by Charles Portis. The film starred John Wayne as an indomitable one-eyed marshal, 'Rooster' Cogburn, who is eventually persuaded to help a determined teenage girl avenge herself upon her father's murderers. According to Portis, he picked up the phrase while researching memoirs about the old West, in which all manner of heroes were praised for their 'grit' (meaning their determination or courage): 'I had never seen it in such profusion as in these books. There was grit, plain grit, plain old grit, clear grit, pure grit, pure dee grit (a euphemism for damned) and true grit. Thus the hard little word was in my head when I began the story.' He jotted the phrase down on the title page of his script for use within the text when it became appropriate, and then realized it would make a good title itself. Portis was not, as he admitted himself, the first writer to make use of the phrase, and as early as 1897 Bram Stoker quoted it in his novel *Dracula*.

Truman Doctrine. The pronouncement by US President Harry S. Truman on 12 March 1947 in which he declared immediate economic and military aid to the governments of Greece, threatened by communist insurrection, and Turkey, under pressure from Soviet expansion in the Mediterranean. Congress responded by promptly appropriating $400 million for this purpose. The move led to the establishment of the first American military bases abroad. *See also* EISENHOWER DOCTRINE.

Trustafarian. A vogue word of the 1990s for a young person from a wealthy background who affects the lifestyle and attitudes of the inner-city ghetto. The term combines 'trust fund', as a frequent means of support for such people, and RASTAFARIAN.

> A posh accent could be classed as a handicap in the employment market. ... Hence the Trustafarian's attempt to adopt Estuary English: 'Seriously cool, yah?'
>
> *Independent on Sunday* (28 November 1999)

Trust-busting. In 1902, as part of his SQUARE DEAL, President Theodore Roosevelt was determined to restrict the excessive power wielded by certain monopolies. Congress was reluctant to grant the necessary regulatory authority, but he circumvented the opposition by reviving the almost forgotten Sherman Anti-Trust Act (1890) and bringing successful suit against the Northern Securities Company. He pursued his policy of 'trust-busting' by bringing suit against 43 other major corporations over the next seven years.

Truth drug. A drug claimed to make a person tell the truth under questioning. An American doctor, R.E. House (1875–1930), used alkaloid scopolamine to induce a state of lethargic intoxication in which the patient lost many of his defences and spoke the truth concerning matters about which he would normally have lied or prevaricated. The value of this and other drugs in penology has by no means been established.

Truth or Consequences. The small American town and health resort of this name in New Mexico was originally called Hot Springs for its warm mineral waters. In 1950 the city council collaborated with the radio and television personality Ralph Edwards, host of the GAME SHOW *Truth or Consequences*, in a promotion effort to hold a yearly programme and fiesta there. Residents approved the new name, but it remains controversial and many still prefer Hot Springs.

T-shirt or **tee-shirt.** The familiar short-sleeved top, usually made of cotton, is so named as it has the shape of the letter T when spread out flat. The shirt is of American origin and first came into vogue in the 1940s when the US Navy introduced a knitted cotton undershirt of this style. It was initially worn by soldiers and marines but later evolved as a general garment, especially after being popularized by the film actor James Dean, who wore one in REBEL WITHOUT A CAUSE (1955).

Tsukahara. In gymnastics a style of vaulting consisting of a quarter or half turn onto the horse followed by one and a half back somersaults. It was introduced in international competition in 1970 by the Japanese gymnast Mitsuo Tsukahara (b.1947) and was a speciality of the teenage Romanian gymnast Nadia Comaneci in the late 1970s.

Tube Alloys. The Second World War code name for a section of the Department of Scientific and Industrial Research formed in 1940 to examine methods of producing an atomic bomb. The section was placed under the charge of William Akers, a director of ICI.

Tub of lard. An uncomplimentary nickname for a plump person. When the Labour politician Roy Hattersley failed to appear for the satirical television quiz programme HAVE I GOT NEWS FOR YOU an actual carton of lard was placed on the desk before his empty chair. *See also* HATTERJI.

Tudorbethan. An architectural style imitative of Tudor and Elizabethan. It was characteristic of the 1930s, when a rash of half-timbered suburban villas broke out in Britain. A similar term and style was Jacobethan, blending Jacobean and Elizabethan. *See also* STOCKBROKERS' TUDOR.

> The style in which Gothic predominates may be called, inaccurately enough, Elizabethan, and the style in which the classical predominates over the Gothic, equally inaccurately, may be called Jacobean. To save the time of those who do not wish to distinguish between these periods of architectural uncertainty, I will henceforward use the term 'Jacobethan'.
>
> JOHN BETJEMAN: *Ghastly Good Taste*, ch iv (1933)

Tug of love. A dispute over the custody of a child, who is thus torn between his or her parents, or between each of the adults who claims custody. This sense arose in the 1970s as a sort of punning converse of 'tug of war' although the expression is found earlier as the title of one of Israel Zangwill's *Ghetto Comedies* (1907).

> An explosion in 'tug-of-love' cases has seen hundreds of children abducted by one parent from another in the past five years.
>
> *The Times* (3 September 1999)

Tunnel of love. A fairground attraction of American origin designed for couples and consisting of a boat or train ride through a darkened tunnel. The concept has a certain sexual symbolism.

Tupamaros. A left-wing URBAN GUERRILLA group in Uruguay, founded as the Movimiento de Liberación Nacional (Spanish, 'National Liberation Movement') in around 1963 by Raúl Sendic (*c.*1925–89). Their terrorist activities escalated from around 1968, but they were ruthlessly crushed by the military regime that came to power in 1973. Following the restoration of democracy in 1985 thousands of imprisoned Tupamaros were released, including Sendic, who reorganized the Tupamaros as a legal political party. The name Tupamaro was derived from the native Peruvian Tupac Amaru II (originally José Gabriel Condorcanqui; *c.*1740–81), a descendant of Tupac Amaru, the last Inca ruler, who was executed by the Spanish in 1571. In 1780–81 Tupac Amaru II led an unsuccessful revolt against Spanish rule that spread from Peru to Bolivia and Argentina. Tupac Amaru II was captured, and forced to watch his wife and sons being killed before he himself was brutally put to death.

Tupperware. The plastic food containers take their name from Earl S. Tupper (1907–83), an American farmer's son from New Hampshire, who formed the Tupper Plastics Company in 1938. He developed methods to refine and purify polyethylene slag, until then regarded as a waste product, into a usable product that he called 'Poly-T'. He opened his first manufacturing plant in Farnumsville, Massachusetts, in 1942 and produced a range of dishes, bowls and cups to sell to hardware stores. The first sealed food storage containers followed in 1947, their waterproof and airtight lids based on an inverted paint tin lid. When sales slumped, Tupper took to selling his wares in people's homes. Tupperware 'parties' soon became staples of American life and a firmly established feature of suburban culture, opening economic as well as social doors for women.

Turandot. The opera by Giacomo Puccini of this name (1926) has a story that can be traced back to a tale given by Antoine Galland as part of his translation of *The Arabian Nights* (1704–8), but Puccini's libretto (written by Giuseppe Adami and Renato Simoni) was based on the play (1762) by the Italian dramatist Carlo Gozzi. The central character of the title is a Chinese princess who vows vengeance on all men for some past grievance but offers to marry any nobleman who can solve three riddles. If he cannot, she will kill him. A prince does solve them, but she refuses to marry him after all. A final change of heart, however, is also a change of mind. The opera is unpopular with many, who point to the torture and death of the loyal slave-girl Liu, the only genuinely good character. The princess's name is of Persian origin and means 'daughter of the Turanians', i.e. of the northern people (to the Arabians) who inhabit ancient Turkestan. The final '-dot' is related to English 'daughter'. Ferruccio Busoni also wrote an opera (1917) with this title, which was similarly based on Gozzi's play.

Turangalîla Symphony. The massive and mystical symphony by Olivier Messiaen (1908–92) was composed between 1946 and 1948 and first performed in 1949. *Turangalîla* is Sanskrit, the composer translating it as 'a love song, a hymn to joy, time, movement, rhythm, life and death'. Apparently the word should be pronounced with a heavy emphasis on the last two syllables. The music includes Indian influences and features parts for piano and ONDES MARTENOT, an early form of electronic keyboard.

Turf war. A dispute over territory between rival groups. The allusion is to the territory or 'patch' controlled by a street gang or criminal.

> The debate over mortgages has degenerated into a bitter turf war between the Treasury ... and the Department of Trade and Industry.
>
> *The Times* (6 January 2000)

Turing machine. A hypothetical computing machine for performing simple reading, writing and shifting operations in accordance with a prescribed set of rules. It is invoked in theories of computability and automata and takes its name from the British mathematician Alan Turing (1912–54), who described such a machine in 1936. During the Second World War Turing was one of the team that cracked the German ENIGMA code.

Turin Shroud. *See under* FAKES.

Turkey shoot. Anything very easy, and specifically a military situation where the attacker has an overwhelming advantage. The term is of American origin and alludes to former marksmanship contests in which a live turkey was tied behind a log with just its head showing as the target.

Turkey trot. A type of ballroom dance to ragtime music originating in the United States and popular in the early 20th century. The steps of the dancers suggest the stiff but rapid gait of a trotting turkey

Turner Prize. A prize established in 1984 by the Patrons of New Art to encourage the collection of contemporary British art. Since 1991 it has been restricted to artists aged under 50. In 1993 it was controversially awarded to Rachel Whiteread (b.1963) for her work *Untitled (House)*, a concrete cast of the interior of a house in London's East End. Later awards attracted similar debate, such as that of 1998, won by Chris Ofili (b.1968) for his work *The Adoration of Captain Shit and the Legend of the Black Star Part Two*, incorporating his 'trademark' elephant dung. The prize is named after the English painter J.M.W. Turner (1775–1851).

> J.M.W. Turner would be spinning in his grave at the thought of his name being used even remotely in connection with Ofili's complete lack of taste.
> *The Times* (Letter to the Editor) (19 December 1998)

Turn of the century. The beginning or end of a particular century. The turn of the 20th century is thus the period about the year 1900, when the 19th century turned into the 20th. The expression is first recorded in 1926.

Turn of the Screw, The. A ghostly psychological opera by Benjamin Britten (1913–76) with a libretto by Myfanwy Piper, based on the short story (1898) by Henry James (1843–1916). It was first performed in Venice in 1954. James's story, which concerns a governess who becomes convinced that her young charges are possessed, also inspired a film, *The Innocents* (1961), directed by Jack Clayton and with a screenplay by William Archibald and Truman Capote.

Turn on a sixpence or **a dime, To.** To turn a vehicle round in a tightly restricted area, represented by the American dime and the former English sixpence, both very small coins. The term is also figuratively applied to a business that can be similarly 'turned round' or reoriented at short notice.

> 'In the fashion business, you need to be able to turn on a sixpence.'
> *The Times* (3 November 1999)

Turn on, tune in, drop out. The epigrammatic title of a lecture of 1967 by the American drug-culture GURU Timothy Leary (1920–96). The sense is: 'Heighten your awareness through drugs (*see* TURN SOMEONE ON), set yourself on my wavelength, and reject conventional society' (*see* DROPOUT). Leary explored the theme further in his book *The Politics of Ecstasy* (1968).

Turn someone on, To. To excite them; to stimulate their interest, especially sexually. 'Whatever turns you on' is a stock response to a person's description of some unusual experience or plan, however mild. *See also* SWITCHED ON.

Turn the knife, To. *See* TWIST THE KNIFE.

Turn-up for the book. A completely unexpected result or occurrence, especially a welcome one. 'Turn-up' alludes to the turning up of a particular card in a game, while the 'book' is the one kept by a bookmaker on a racecourse. The expression dates from the 1940s.

Tutankhamun's curse. A legend arising from the death of the 5th earl of Carnarvon (1866–1923) following his sponsorship of the archaeologist Howard Carter and his assistance during the latter's excavations of the tomb of the pharaoh Tutankhamun (d.*c.*1352 BC). He died after an infection from a mosquito bite, but the writer Sir Arthur Conan Doyle, by then a convinced spiritualist, suggested that the death might be attributed to elementals created by the priests of Tutankhamun. Coincidentally there was a power failure at Cairo when Carnarvon died, and his dog in England expired at the same time. Carter survived until 1939.

Tweenies. (1) Children of primary school age, who are between toddlerhood and teenhood. A tweeny was originally a colloquialism for a between-maid, i.e. a maid between a cook and a housemaid.

> Let's start with the 'tweenie' market, the hugely successful ... enclave for six to 11-year-old girls and boys.
> *The Times* (17 December 1999)

(2) A highly popular television puppet show for three-to-five-year-old children, first screened in 1999. The characters are four brightly coloured rag doll 'children', Bella, Milo, Fizz and Jake, operated by actors. Bella and Fizz are two females who love ballet and dressing up, while Milo and Jake, the two males, enjoy dismantling toys. They were the creation of Iain Lauchlan, a former pantomime dame, and immediately threatened to eclipse the TELETUBBIES.

Twelve-tone system. *See* SERIALISM.

Twentieth-century blues. A feeling of despair or world weariness with regard to the 20th century, which opened with the golden glow of the EDWARD-

IAN ERA but went on to witness two world wars and, between them, the GREAT DEPRESSION. The *mal du siècle* was at its height in the latter period, and the phrase itself comes from a song in Noël Coward's musical play *Cavalcade*.

> Twentieth Century Blues
> Are getting me down.
> Who's
> Escaped those weary
> Twentieth Century Blues.
>
> NOËL COWARD: *Cavalcade*, 'Twentieth Century Blues' (1931)

Twenty-four carat. Entirely trustworthy; the finest. The purity of gold is measured in carats, 24 being the purest. The figurative use of the term dates from the 1930s. 'Twenty-two carat' is sometimes used similarly.

> Milne feels re-creating photo-realism is what computer animation was invented for. 'For me, this is the 24-carat use of the medium,' he says. 'I feel it is the correct purpose of computer graphics.'
>
> *Sunday Times* (26 September 1999)

Twenty-four-seven. Every day; all the time. The reference is to something that occurs or is available 24 hours a day, seven days a week, i.e. round the clock. The expression dates from the 1980s and sometimes appears in figures as 24–7 or 24/7.

> This is the city that never sleeps. New York is a veritable 24/7 souk.
>
> *The Times* (24 January 2000)

Twenty-six Counties. *See* SIX COUNTIES.

Twenty-three skiddoo. Go away; clear off. 'Skidoo' means 'skedaddle', but the reason for the particular number is uncertain. According to one theory, the reference is to air currents that would blow up women's skirts on the corner of Broadway and 23rd Street, New York. Police would shoo away gleeful male spectators with a shout of 'skiddoo!' Another source attributes the number to railway jargon, in which 23 denoted a message of urgency.

Twenty-twenty vision. Perfect vision. The term alludes to the Snellen chart used when measuring visual acuity. The patient reads rows of letters printed in successively decreasing sizes. Twenty-twenty (20/20) vision means that a row of letters near the bottom of the chart can be read at a distance of 20 feet. Measurements are now metric, so that the chart is placed 6 metres from the patient and normal vision is expressed as 6/6. If the patient can read only the letters

twice as large as those on the 6/6 line (which a normal eye could read at 12 metres) the acuity is said to be 6/12. The technical term gave 'twenty-twenty hindsight' to mean perfect understanding or appreciation of what has been seen. Hindsight, with its certain knowledge, is always superior to foresight.

Twiggy. The nickname that became the professional name of the 1960s model Lesley Hornby (b.1946). It referred to her unusually thin legs, which at school had similarly caused her to be dubbed Sticks. She later took up a career as a singer and dancer. In 1988 she married Leigh Lawson and has since performed as Lesley Lawson.

> Twiggy is a stupid name for a woman in her 40s, but it would be hard to drop. At least a full name makes me sound like a person, instead of a strange animal.
>
> LESLEY LAWSON interviewed in *Telegraph Magazine* (6 July 1991)

Twilight sleep. A state of semi-consciousness produced by injection of scopolamine and morphia in which a woman can undergo childbirth with comparatively little pain. *See also* TRUTH DRUG.

Twilight zone. The run-down area that sometimes develops around the central business district of a city. The expression took on a more general sense to mean any ambiguous or unsettled state between two opposing states and was popularized by the cult American SCIENCE FICTION television series *The Twilight Zone* (1959–63) created and often narrated by Rod Serling. Favourite themes in the 151 stories were TIME WARPS, Faustian pacts, doppelgangers and machines with minds of their own.

> There is a fifth dimension beyond that which is known to men. It is a dimension as vast as space and as timeless as infinity. It is the middle ground between light and shadow, between science and superstition, and it lies between the pit of man's fears and the summit of his knowledge. This is the dimension of imagination. It is an area we call The Twilight Zone.
>
> ROD SERLING: *The Twilight Zone*, Introduction (1959)

Twinkie. An American nickname for a male homosexual or effeminate man, also a young and sexually attractive person, a 'tempting teenager'. The allusion is apparently to the Twinkie, a type of cupcake with a soft centre, popular among young people.

Twinkie defence. An American colloquialism for an unlikely excuse, and originally for a legal defence of diminished responsibility in which the defendant's criminal behaviour is attributed to the effects of an unbalanced diet of convenience food, a typical example of which is the TWINKIE cupcake. The defence so known was first employed in 1979 in a San Francisco Supreme Court murder trial, the grounds being that the defendant's compulsive diet of candy bars, cupcakes and Cokes had built up an excessive sugar level which had aggravated a chemical imbalance in his brain. The defence was subsequently disallowed by the US Congress in 1981.

Twinkle or **gleam in one's eye.** A barely formed idea, and specifically that of a child that has not yet even been conceived. The expression dates from the 1960s.

Twin Peaks. This almost surreal television drama series, set in the lumber town of the title in the American Pacific Northwest, was screened to an intrigued audience from 1990 to 1991. The story centred on the question, 'Who killed Laura Palmer?', Laura being a beautiful high-school student. The main investigator was the FBI agent Dale Cooper, whose methods of detection included Tibetan mysticism, dreams and ESP. As the series progressed, viewers learned that Palmer was not the innocent she seemed and that Twin Peaks was a murky pool of drugs, adultery, pornography and satanism. Most of the town's inhabitants were cast as potential suspects before it was finally revealed that the culprit was Palmer's own father, possessed by the demonic 'Killer Bob'. Directed by David Lynch, *Twin Peaks* rapidly acquired cult status.

Twinset and pearls. A typicality of the older professional woman, especially in senior management. A twinset, as a matching cardigan and jumper, further symbolizes firm but bourgeois morality.

> Procter has left the publication she edited for a decade after an apparent war broke out amid the twinsets and pearls.
> *Sunday Times* (23 May 1999)

Twin town. A town in an overseas country that has established an official link with a town or community in one's own country. Many European towns set up such links after the Second World War as an earnest of the postwar mood of international amity and cooperation. Representatives of each place in the relevant country frequently make an annual visit to their opposite number in order to maintain the tie. Some twinnings are multiple, so that in 1991 the London

borough of Lambeth was twinned with Bluefields, Nicaragua (1984), Kenema, Sierra Leone (1989), Moskvoretsky, USSR (1962), Shinjuku, Japan (1989) and Vincennes, France (1954). Coventry twinned with Volgograd, USSR, in 1944, actually during the war.

Twist, The. A dance popular in the 1960s, so called from the contortions performed. 'The Twist', a rhythm-and-blues number by Hank Ballard and the Midnighters, released in 1959 as the B-side of 'Teardrops on Your Letter', soon afterwards became a major international hit for Chubby Checker.

Twist in the wind, To. To suffer protracted humiliation, regret or the like. The phrase presents the gruesome image of a hanging body in the open air. A variant includes 'slowly' after 'twist'.

Twist someone's arm, To. To compel them to do something against their will. The expression, which dates from the 1950s, is often used jocularly, as: 'Another drink?' 'You can twist my arm.'

Twist or **turn the knife, To.** To intensify a person's suffering deliberately. The image is of stabbing someone, then twisting the knife in the wound.

> An embattled Mr Hague stood his ground ... as Mr Blair twisted the knife in Tory wounds.
> *The Times* (14 October 1999)

Twitcher. A colloquialism for a birdwatcher, presumably so called from becoming 'twitchy' or nervously excited at the prospect of another sighting. There is also a suggestion of 'twitter' or 'tweeter', for the chirp that can equally indicate a bird's presence. The term dates from the 1970s.

Twitch the net curtains, To. To express puritanical disapproval. The allusion is to the genteel or prudish inhabitants of a respectable residential district who supposedly tweak aside the curtains preserving their privacy to peep at some scandalous scene, which then forms a topic of outraged gossip. The reaction is traditionally regarded as typical of MIDDLE ENGLAND.

> The Spice Girls rather put me in mind of sniping suburbanite matrons, twitching the net curtains and huffing with indignation when it turns out nobody's paying much attention to their own goings-on.
> *Sunday Times* (7 November 1999)

Two Brains. The nickname of the supposedly brilliant Conservative politician and ideologue David Willetts (b.1956), who worked as an adviser to Nigel Lawson and Margaret Thatcher and at the Thatcherite Centre for Policy Studies, before entering Parliament in 1992. He was known as 'the court philosopher' of John Major's government, and became paymaster general in 1996, although he had to resign the same year after it emerged that he had earlier attempted to influence the outcome of a Commons inquiry into the Neil Hamilton affair. He played an important role in the Tory election campaign of 1997 and after the landslide Labour victory sat on the Opposition front bench. *See also* TWO JAGS.

Twocking. The act of stealing a car, from the police acronym TWOCK, 'taking without owner's consent'. Those who commit such an offence, often disaffected teenagers, are thus twockers. The term dates from the early 1990s.

Two cultures. The existence in England, and to a great extent in western Europe, of two separate cultures with few points of contact between them, one based on the arts and the other on the sciences. The phrase gained immediate popularity after C.P. Snow's Rede Lecture, subsequently published as *The Two Cultures and the Scientific Revolution* (1959).

> I believe the intellectual life of the whole of western society is increasingly being split into two polar groups ... Literary intellectuals at one pole – at the other scientists, and as the most representative, the physical scientists. Between the two a gulf of mutual incomprehension.
>
> C.P. SNOW: *The Two Cultures and the Scientific Revolution* (1959)

Two fingers. A V-SIGN. To put two fingers up at (or to) a person or thing, or show two fingers to them, is thus to make this obscene gesture of scorn or defiance, literally or figuratively.

> He [Donald Sinden] is meant to be the play's 'giver of life', a genial Falstaff energetically showing two fingers to senility and death.
>
> *The Times* (10 September 1999)

Two Jags. A nickname applied to the Labour politician John Prescott (b.1938), deputy prime minister and secretary of state for transport and the regions in Tony Blair's government since 1997. The likeable but at times verbally challenged minister has struggled to bring forth transport policies that reduce the role of private cars. The barbed nickname derives from the fact that he has two official Jaguar cars at his disposal, one of which he used to carry himself and his wife a few hundred metres from his hotel to

the conference centre during the 1999 Labour Party conference. *See also* THUMPER.

Two left feet. To have two left feet is to be clumsy. Most people are right-footed in matters of stepping and kicking, so to have not just one left foot but (supposedly) two is to be anything but adroit. The expression dates from the early 20th century.

Two-minute silence. The cessation of traffic and all other activities for two minutes at 11 a.m. on 11 November to commemorate those who died in the First World War. First observed in 1919, it remained a central feature of REMEMBRANCE DAY. A special nationwide two-minute silence began at 8.38 p.m. (sunset) on 8 May 1995 to mark the 50th anniversary of VE DAY. *See also* ARMISTICE DAY.

> At the going down of the sun and in the morning
> We will remember them.
>
> LAURENCE BINYON: 'For the Fallen' (1914)

Twopenny Tube. A nickname for the Central London Railway, opened as part of the Underground network in 1900. The fare was originally 2d but the name lingered on for several years after it was raised to 3d in 1907.

2 Point 4 Children. A television SITCOM shown from 1991 to 1998 and centring on the life of the Porter family of East Chiswick. The series differed from the norm in that the main character was not the husband, Ben, played by Gary Olsen, but his wife, Bill, played by Belinda Lang, depicted not as a traditional wife and mother but as a person in her own right, unconfined by her family. The title refers to the supposed size of the average British family.

Two Ronnies, The. A television comedy series screened from 1971 to 1986, featuring the large and laid-back Ronnie Barker (b.1919) and the small and vivacious Ronnie Corbett (b.1930). The humour derived as much from the contrast between the two as from their mildly 'naughty' scripts. Each programme included a song by a female singer, a humorous monologue by the diminutive Corbett in a large armchair, and an episode of a spoof serial. Barker's tag-out line, 'It's goodnight from me, and it's goodnight from him', become something of a catchphrase.

Two sandwiches short of a picnic. Stupid; crazy; 'not all there'. The phrase dates from the 1980s. Similar expressions of identical meaning include the following:

> three bricks shy of a load
> several currants short of a bun
> a few trolleys short of a supermarket

a slice short of a full loaf

a nosebag short of a sack of oats

a few pence short of a first-class stamp

a few cans short of a six-pack

a sheaf short of a stook

three diamond clusters short of a tiara

one player short of a cricket team

2001: A Space Odyssey. A SCIENCE FICTION novel (1968, from his own screenplay) by Arthur C. Clarke (b.1917). While the novel demonstrates Clarke's ability to extrapolate from known data, it also represents a philosophical quest for the meaning of life and an investigation into the evolutionary process. The film version (1968), directed by Stanley Kubrick, was a masterly blend of technical wizardry and obscure symbolism, criticized by some for its tedium but praised by others for its moments of striking imagery. The music was by various composers but most memorable of all was the 'Sunrise' opening of Richard Strauss's *Also sprach Zarathustra* (1895). The film acquired cult status as a vision of the technological future, even if space exploration had not advanced nearly as far in reality by 2001. The film inspired a sequel (1984) directed by Peter Hyams under the title *2010*, but fans of the original movie were not impressed and gave it the alternative title *Ten Past Eight. See also* HAL.

Two-time, To. To deceive or betray, especially one's spouse or lover by consorting with someone else. The reference may be to having two lovers at a time or to 'making time' (sexually succeeding) with two at once. The term, of American origin, dates from the 1920s.

> He denied that he had imprisoned or attacked the two women, who had discovered they were being two-timed by the same man at a chance meeting in a nightclub.
> *The Times* (22 July 1999)

Two-Ton Tessie. The nickname of Tessie O'Shea (1914–95), an amply proportioned British music-hall singer, noted for her jollity and general 'full-of-fun' style. The name is sometimes applied to any plump or overweight person. Another such was 'Two-Ton Tony', otherwise Tony Galento (1910–79), an American heavyweight boxer noted for his adiposity.

> If you're worried about clogging your arteries or turning into a two-ton Tessie, have a wodge of heavenly butter on your toast only once in a while.
> *Sunday Times* (30 May 1999)

Two-up, two-down. A house with two reception rooms downstairs and two bedrooms upstairs. The term is first recorded in the 1950s but houses of this type date from at least the 19th century.

> In 1905, the pioneers of Letchworth, the first garden city, erected a row of show houses to demonstrate that a modest but adequate two-up, two-down worker's cottage could be built for no more than £150.
> *The Times* (2 August 1999)

Two-way mirror. A somewhat misleading name for a pane of glass which serves as a mirror one side but which can be seen through the other like a window. A person looking through from the second side can thus see or 'spy' without being seen.

Type A and Type B. The two types into which psychologists divide the personality. 'Type A' is characterized by ambition, impatience and competitiveness, but is susceptible to stress and heart disease; 'Type B' is easy-going and believed to have low susceptibility to stress. The two types thus posit specific links between a person's mental make-up and their physical condition.

Typhoid Mary. The nickname of Mary Mallon (1869–1938), an Irish-born carrier of typhoid fever in the New York area. Her case first arose in 1904, when an epidemic of typhoid spread over Oyster Bay and nearby towns on Long Island. The sources were traced to households where Mary had been a cook. She was apprehended, but escaped. She was eventually committed to an isolation centre and released only in 1910 on condition that she never worked with food again. But she resumed her occupation, and in 1914 a further epidemic broke out at Newfoundland, New Jersey, and at a Manhattan maternity hospital, both places where Mary had worked. Altogether 51 cases of typhoid, including three deaths, were directly attributed to her, although she herself was immune to the typhoid bacillus. The nickname became a metaphor for pollution and for the evil a single person can inflict on society.

Typhoo. The proprietary brand of tea was first produced by John Sumner in Birmingham in 1903 as 'Typhoo Tipps', the first word being a meaningless oriental-style creation, perhaps suggested by 'typhoon', the latter being a printer's misprint for 'tips', meaning the top leaves and buds of the tea plant that are picked to be dried, crushed and infused in boiling water to make the drink.

U

U and Non-U. A former semi-humorous mark of distinction between social classes in England based on the usage of certain words. 'U' is Upper Class and 'Non-U' is non-Upper Class. It is 'U' to say 'luncheon' for what 'Non-U' folk call 'lunch', 'U' to say 'napkin' instead of 'serviette', and 'U' to prefer 'cycle' to 'bike'. The terms owe their popularity to Nancy Mitford (1904–73), who quoted them in an article in the magazine *Encounter* in September 1955, but they were invented by Professor Alan Ross in 1954 and appeared in his article 'Linguistic class-indicators in present-day English' in the Finnish philological journal *Neuphilologische Mitteilungen*. A simplified and condensed version of this, entitled 'U and Non-U: An Essay in Sociological Linguistics', was later included in *Noblesse Oblige* (1956), edited by Nancy Mitford.

> No wonder show-jumping had recently attracted so many enthusiasts: it is the gypsy life of modern times, nomadic, transitory and glamorous, in which the gentry can take part as legitimately as the professional, where it is just as 'U' to sleep on straw in a horse-box as it is in the smartest hotel.
> MOYRA WILLIAMS: *Adventures Unbridled*, ch xi (1960)

U-bend. A section of piping or tubing in the form of a letter U, and particularly that of a waste pipe or toilet bowl outlet. The term has a figurative use for anything sinister, suspect or 'dirty'.

Übermenschen. *See* UNTERMENSCHEN.

UB 40. The designation of the card issued by the Department for Education and Employment to a person registered as unemployed, the initials standing for 'unemployment benefit'. Price concessions for such people, along with the young (under 16) and the old (over 60), are sometimes given in this form. UB 40 is also the name of a reggae group formed in 1979. The

name originally denoted the workless status of its members but they later promoted it positively as a political stance. Their record 'One in Ten' (1981) was thus a barbed comment on the level of British unemployment at the time.

U-boat. A German submarine. The term is adapted from German *Unterseeboot* ('underwater vessel'). *See also* E-BOAT.

UDI. The unilateral declaration of independence by the Rhodesian government of Ian Smith (b.1919), made on 11 November 1965. The declaration was made in the face of the demand of Britain, the colonial power, that independence was conditional on black majority rule. White minority rule continued illegally in Rhodesia, however, until the escalation of guerrilla activity forced the Smith government into talks in 1979, which resulted in the establishment of black majority rule and the independence of the country as Zimbabwe in 1980.

UFO. Unidentified flying object, the name given to objects claimed to have been sighted in the sky such as FLYING SAUCERS, or picked up on radar screens, the exact nature of which is uncertain. Study and observation of UFOs is termed ufology by enthusiasts. The peak of interest in such phenomena was in the 1950s and 1960s. By the close of the 20th century astronomers were generally agreed that there was no evidence for the visitation of earth by ALIENS and that obsession with UFOs had actually delayed legitimate research into the possibility of intelligent life elsewhere. *See also* CLOSE ENCOUNTER; LITTLE GREEN MEN.

Ugandan affairs or **practices.** A euphemism for sexual intercourse popularized by *Private Eye* in the 1970s. The term 'talking about Uganda' first appeared in a gossip item in the magazine's issue of 9 March

1973, describing a fashionable party held by Neal and Corinne Ascherson at which a former cabinet colleague of President Obote of Uganda had a 'meaningful confrontation' with the former features editor, Mary Kenny. In a letter to *The Times* of 13 September 1983 Corinne Ascherson, now Adam, identified the coiner of the phrase as the poet and critic James Fenton.

Ugli. The proprietary name of a hybrid citrus fruit, first produced in Jamaica by crossing a Seville orange, a grapefruit and a tangerine. The name was registered in 1938 and reflects the resulting fruit's unprepossessing appearance.

Ugly American. An American who behaves objectionably abroad. The expression derives from the title of William J. Lederer and Eugene Burdick's bestselling novel *The Ugly American* (1958), telling of tragic American misadventures in southeast Asia during the COLD WAR.

Uhu. The adhesive so named was first formulated in 1932 by Hugo and August Fischer in Bühl, southwest Germany. Their chemical company already produced goods with brandnames based on birds, such as *Pelikan* and *Schwan*, and for this new product they selected *Uhu*, 'eagle-owl', a bird found in the nearby Black Forest, its own name based on its cry.

UK plc. A jargonistic synonym for BRITAIN PLC.

Ulster Defence Regiment. The reserve force of soldiers, many of them part-time, that was established in 1970 in response to the upsurge of terrorism in Northern Ireland. Its predominantly Protestant membership made it controversial in any crisis caused by sectarian rivalry. In 1992 the UDR was merged with the two battalions of the Royal Irish Rangers to form a new Royal Irish Regiment, and for the first time it became a part of the regular British Army.

Ulster Unionist Party. Northern Ireland's largest political party, founded in 1905 to resist the threat of all-Ireland HOME RULE, is right-of-centre in orientation and advocates equality for Northern Ireland within the United Kingdom and so opposes union with the Republic of Ireland. It has the broadest support of any party in the province, reflecting the majority Protestant 'British' population of Northern Ireland, and has consistently won a large proportion of parliamentary and local seats. The UUP opposed the Anglo-Irish agreement of 1985 but cautiously welcomed the DOWNING STREET DECLARATION of

1993. Under David Trimble, its leader from 1995, it realistically supported the GOOD FRIDAY AGREEMENT of 1998. The party is sometimes known as the Official Unionist Party to distinguish it from the more hardline Democratic Unionist Party. *See also* PAISLEYITES.

Ulster Volunteer Force. The UVF was formed in 1913 by Sir Edward Carson, an ultra-Unionist Dublin barrister, with the military assistance of senior officers in the British Army, its aim being to provide military support for the resistance of Ulster's (Protestant) Loyalists to the third (Irish) HOME RULE Bill. During the First World War members of the UVF fought with the 36th (Ulster) Division on the battlefields of the SOMME, gaining a reputation for bravery which still resonates in the folk memory of Northern Ireland's Protestants. The UVF was active in sectarian warfare in Belfast during the early 1920s, but by the Second World War had virtually ceased to exist. Its veterans, however, formed the basis of the notorious B SPECIALS. The name was subsequently revived in the 1960s for a clandestine Protestant paramilitary force that was responsible for sectarian assassinations preceding the TROUBLES. The UVF was outlawed in the 1970s, when it remained less popular and active than the Ulster Defence Association (UDA), with which it frequently clashed. Its public image was boosted by the prominence of its long-imprisoned leader, Gusty Spence, in the announcement of the UVF ceasefire that followed the IRA ceasefire of 1994.

Ultra. *See* ENIGMA.

Ulysses. James Joyce's MODERNIST novel of 1922, regarded by many as the 20th century's most important work of fiction in the English language. The book was published by a small press in Paris in 1922, after three US judges had banned further publication of chapters in the United States. The narrative centres on a single day, 16 June 1904, the day on which Joyce had his first formal date with Nora Barnacle (1884–1951), a barmaid with whom in October that year he went to Zurich and then lived in Pola and Trieste. They married in 1931, after they had had a son in 1905 and a daughter in 1907. The book tells of a day in the life of its Jewish-Irish hero, Leopold Bloom, his wife, Molly, and Stephen Dedalus, the protagonist of the author's *A PORTRAIT OF THE ARTIST AS A YOUNG MAN* (1916). The structure of the book is intended to parallel that of Homer's *Odyssey*, with Odysseus's 19 years of wandering compared to Bloom's single day of roaming in Dublin. Bloom thus represents Odysseus

(Ulysses), Molly answers approximately to Penelope and Dedalus corresponds to Telemachus. The work is famous for its STREAM OF CONSCIOUSNESS style and for Molly's lengthy, unpunctuated monologue that concludes it. T.S. Eliot commented: 'James Joyce has no style but is the vacuum into which all styles rush.' The variety of styles and of narrative and typographical techniques in *Ulysses* express the different ways in which different people perceive. It was eventually cleared for publication in the USA, the judge concluding: 'whilst in many places the effect of *Ulysses* on the reader undoubtedly is somewhat emetic, nowhere does it tend to be an aphrodisiac.' *Ulysses* was published in the USA in 1934, and in Britain in 1936. *See also* BLOOMSDAY; FINNEGANS WAKE; FIRST LINES OF NOVELS.

Umpteen. Many; countless. The word is a blend of *umpty*, military slang for a dash in reading the Morse code, and *-teen* in the numbers 13 to 19.

Unabomber. The byname of Theodore Kaczynski, an American professor at the University of California at Berkeley, who in 1998 was given three life sentences for his 17-year reign of terror in the United States. He killed three people and injured 28 in a series of bomb attacks, although the reasons for these remained unclear. The main motivation seems to have been a conservation issue. The *una-* of the name refers to the *un*iversities and *a*irlines where his bombs first exploded.

Unacceptable face of capitalism. A phrase used by the Conservative prime minister, Edward Heath, in a speech on 15 May 1973 alluding to the so-called 'LONRHO affair'. This concerned a large payment made to the former Tory cabinet minister, Duncan Sandys, as compensation for leaving his consultancy post with the Lonrho Company, and in turn paid by him into an account in the Cayman Islands in order to avoid British tax. The expression subsequently came to apply to the 'unacceptable face' of almost anything. *See also* ACCEPTABLE FACE.

Unanswered Question, The. A short 'philosophical' orchestral work by Charles Ives (1874–1954). It was composed in 1906. The subtitle of the work is 'A Contemplation of a Serious Matter', and in it the two instrumental groups represent the Real and the Transcendental, and are obliged to deploy an element of improvisation. As Ives observed elsewhere: 'Beauty in music is too often confused with something that lets the ears lie back in an easy chair.'

Unbearable Bassington, The. A satirical novella (1912) by SAKI (H.H. Munro). The title of the book refers to Comus Bassington, who flouts his mother's attempts to marry him off in order to maintain her materialistic existence in the self-serving society of the EDWARDIAN ERA. Its bleak ending symbolizes the doomed generation who were shortly to lose their lives in the First World War, as Saki himself did.

Unbearable Lightness of Being, The. A novel (1984; in Czech as *Nesnesitelná lehkost bytí*, 1984) of the MAGIC REALISM school by Milan Kundera (b.1929) in which the fates of two couples are played out against a background of communist rule in Czechoslovakia. In such circumstances, there is an unbearable foreboding even when the 'sweet lightness of being' rises 'out of the depths of the future'. An unsatisfying film version (1987) was directed by Philip Kaufman.

Uncertainty principle. A principle in quantum mechanics enunciated in 1927 by the German physicist Werner Heisenberg (1901–76). The principle, also known as Heisenberg's uncertainty principle or the indeterminacy principle, states that it is not possible to measure accurately the position and momentum of a particle at any one time, as the very act of observing alters the outcome. Although the principle is significant only at the level of subatomic particles, it serves to undermine Newton's mechanistic account of the universe. It has important philosophical implications, not least because it casts doubt on the concept of causation. As a graffito seen in London in the 1970s has it, 'Heisenberg probably rules OK.'

Uncle Joe. A nickname for Joseph STALIN (1879–1953), supreme leader of the Soviet Union from 1929 until his death. The nickname was awarded to Stalin by his British allies during the Second World War, but his avuncular appearance belied the true nature of the tyrant responsible for the deaths of millions of his own people. More appropriate was his adopted name (he was born Iosif Vissarionovich Dzhugashvili): Stalin means 'man of steel'. *See also* FOUL-MOUTHED JOE.

Underclass. In the jargon of sociology a term for the lowest social stratum of society, mainly consisting of the poor, the uneducated and the unemployed, the latter in many cases being unemployable. The term dates from the 1960s as a translation of Swedish *underklass*.

It is hard to imagine that anyone from the 1990s

'underclass' will remember our current decade with much affection.

The Times (6 September 1999)

Under Milk Wood. A radio play by Dylan Thomas (1914–53), first broadcast on BBC Radio on 25 January 1954. The original title of the first part was LLAREGGUB ('bugger all' spelt backwards), the name of the Welsh seaside town in which the author introduces such characters as Myfanwy Price the dressmaker, her lover Mog Edwards the draper, the Rev. Eli Jenkins and Captain Cat. Friends persuaded the poet to opt for *Under Milk Wood* as the title, having convinced him that US readers would not understand his joke. Milk Wood is the wood above the town where Polly Garter has illicit meetings with the 'gandering hubbies' of other women. Laugharne, the Carmarthenshire town where Thomas is buried, is often identified as the model for his Llareggub.

> To begin at the beginning:
> It is spring, moonless night in the small town, starless and bible-black …
> DYLAN THOMAS: *Under Milk Wood* (opening lines)

Under one's own steam. Alone and unaided. The expression dates from the 1940s and alludes to the power provided by a steam engine.

Under starter's orders. Of racehorses or other runners, awaiting the starter's signal to depart. The expression dates from the 1960s. *See also* READY, STEADY, GO!

Under the counter. A phrase first current in the Second World War in connection with an illegal practice in some shops. Articles in short supply were kept out of sight, under the counter, for sale to favoured customers, often at inflated prices.

> Chief goods to 'go under the counter' are fully fashioned silk stockings, watches and silk handkerchiefs.
> *Evening Standard* (20 December 1945)

Under the Volcano. A novel (1947) by Malcolm Lowry (1909–57), intended to be one part of a Dante-esque novel sequence to be called 'The Voyage that Never Ends'. The first draft was written in Mexico in sight of the volcano Popocatepetl, after a spell in hospital in the United States, which failed to cure Lowry's alcoholism. The presence of the volcano looms over the account of a disillusioned British consul, destroyed by drink and drugs, during the Mexican Day of the Dead. A film version (1984), directed by John Huston, sacrificed the subtlety of the original in favour of a seemingly endless drunken monologue.

Underwhelmed. Unimpressed; disappointed. This facetious counterpart to 'overwhelmed' began to emerge in English from the 1950s. A typical use might be: 'I was distinctly underwhelmed by the standard of play.'

Under wraps. Concealed; hidden away. The term, which dates from the 1930s, is typically used of a new project, such as an innovative design or a new car model, which is kept secret until completion.

Uni. Student slang for a university, especially when of the REDBRICK variety.

> There's a whole group of us from uni. James, Emily, Alice, Lisa and Robin.
> *The Times* (15 May 1999)

Unilateral declaration of independence. *See* UDI.

Unilateral nuclear disarmament. The aim of CND and other anti-nuclear organizations, which believe that the world will be freed from the threat of a nuclear holocaust only if nuclear disarmament is started by one country; others will then follow. Unilateral nuclear disarmament or unilateralism has always been a topic of fierce debate within the British LABOUR PARTY. When a motion in favour came before the party conference in 1957 NYE Bevan, then shadow foreign secretary, famously declared: 'If you carry this resolution and follow out all its implications and do not run away from it you will send a Foreign Secretary, whoever he may be, naked into the conference chamber.' Unilateralism was briefly the policy of the Labour Party in 1960, and again in the 1980s until abandoned by party leader Neil Kinnock in 1987.

Unilever. The name of the manufacturers and sellers of a wide range of soaps and foods was created on 1 January 1930 as a result of a merger between the Dutch company Margarine Union and the British firm of Lever Brothers Ltd. The latter took its name from William Hesketh Lever (1851–1921), later Lord Leverhulme, a retail grocer's son born in Bolton, Lancashire, and his brother, James D'Arcy Lever, who set up Lever Brothers in 1885 to make and sell Sunlight Soap and, from 1894, Lifebuoy Carbolic Soap.

Unisex. Designed to be suitable for both sexes. The term arose in the late 1960s and particularly applied to dress, hairstyles and the like. Unisex clothing was pioneered by the French fashion designer André Courrèges (b.1923). By the end of the century unisex hairdressers were universal, although similar provision did not always extend to all areas of equal personal requirements.

Wendy Shillam, an architect with a reputation for speaking her mind on 'feminist' issues, initially laughed when I raised the topic. ... Her own preferred solution would be unisex loos.

The Times (6 September 1999)

UNITA. An acronym for the União Nacional para a Independência Total de Angola (Portuguese, 'National Union for the Total Independence of Angola'), a political and guerrilla group in Angola founded in 1966 by Jonas Savimbi (b.1934). UNITA played an important part in the struggle for independence against the colonial power, Portugal, along with two other liberation groups: the Movimento Popular de Libertação de Angola (MPLA; 'Popular Movement for the Liberation of Angola') and the Frente Nacional de Libertação de Angola (FNLA; 'National Front for the Liberation of Angola'). When Portugal suddenly withdrew from the country in November 1975 it left the capital, Luanda, in the hands of the Soviet-backed MPLA, while UNITA and the FNLA set up a rival government in Huambo. Civil war followed, with the MPLA being supported by a large Cuban force, while UNITA was helped by South African raids, and, from 1985, US military aid. Angola had become a pawn in the COLD WAR. By this time the FNLA had ceased to be a player. Eventually a cease-fire was agreed in 1991, and multiparty elections were held the following year. The MPLA beat UNITA in the elections, but Savimbi refused to accept the results, and civil war broke out again. Another peace agreement came in 1994, but Savimbi subsequently rejected the offer of the vice-presidency in a coalition government. In 1998 UNITA, which had supposedly been demilitarized, was expelled from the government for failing to hand over its weapons, and fighting broke out once more.

United Nations. The successor to the LEAGUE OF NATIONS as a world organization primarily concerned with the maintenance of peace but with numerous other functions and agencies. It sprang from the DUMBARTON OAKS talks (1944) between the United States, Britain and the Soviet Union and was formally inaugurated in 1945. Its headquarters is in New York City. The term 'United Nations' was originally used earlier in the Second World War as a name for the Allied nations, in particular the United States, the Soviet Union and members of the British Commonwealth, which united against the AXIS powers. In the *Supplement* (1945) to the massive fourth edition of his book *The American Language* (1936), the US linguistic

historian H.L. Mencken recounts the origin of the name as follows:

United Nations was coined by President Franklin Roosevelt. This was during Winston Churchill's visit to Washington at the end of December, 1941. He was a guest at the White House, and he and Churchill discussed the choice of a name for the new alliance. One morning, lying in bed, Roosevelt thought of *United Nations*, and at once sought Churchill, who was in his bath. 'How about *United Nations*?' he called through the door. 'That', replied Churchill, 'should do it'. And so it was.

United Reformed Church. The church formed in 1972 from the union of a large majority of the Congregational Church of England and Wales with the Presbyterian Church of England. It was joined in 1981 by the majority of the Disciples of Christ, a religious body set up among Scottish Presbyterians in the United States in the 19th century, and as some of these congregations were in Scotland took the name United Reformed Church in the United Kingdom.

Unit One. The name of a group of 11 avant-garde British artists formed in 1933, its creation being announced by Paul Nash (1889–1946) in a letter to *The Times* of 12 June that year. The name was intended to denote that while each artist was an individual unit, their common interests were one. The group consisted of seven painters: John Armstrong (1893–1973), John Bigge (1892–1973), Edward Burra (1905–76), Tristram Hillier (1905–83), Nash himself, Ben Nicholson (1894–1982) and Edward Wadsworth (1889–1949); two sculptors: Barbara Hepworth (1903–75) and Henry Moore (1898–1986); and two architects: Colin Lucas (1906–84) and Wells Coates (1895–1958). Hillier replaced Frances Hodgkins (1869–1947), who had been originally named in Nash's letter. Although Unit One was short lived, it had considerable impact in its promotion of abstract art and SURREALISM.

Universal Declaration of Human Rights. A document adopted by the General Assembly of the UNITED NATIONS in 1948 setting forth basic rights and fundamental freedoms to which all are entitled. They include the right to life, liberty, freedom from servitude, fair trial, marriage, ownership of property, freedom of thought and conscience, freedom of expression and the rights to vote, work and education.

University Challenge. A television student challenge quiz programme running from 1962 to 1987 on ITV and again from 1994 on BBC2. The questions are largely but not entirely academic and the answers sometimes embarrassingly naive. The quizmaster for the first series was the amiable Bamber Gascoigne, while the second series was presented somewhat more acerbically by Jeremy Paxman.

Unknown Warrior. The body of an unknown British soldier of the First World War brought home from one of the battlefields of the WESTERN FRONT and 'buried among the kings' in Westminster Abbey (11 November 1920). The inscription, in capital letters, begins: 'Beneath this stone rests the body of a British warrior unknown by name or rank brought from France to lie among the most illustrious of the land and buried here on Armistice Day.' Similar tombs were set up in the Arlington National Cemetery, Virginia, beneath the Arc de Triomphe at Paris, in the Unter den Linden at Berlin, and by the walls of the Kremlin in Moscow. In 1958 the bodies of two more unknown US servicemen were placed in the Tomb of the Unknown Soldier at Arlington, one who died in the Second World War and one who died in the KOREAN WAR (1950–53). Casualties of later conflicts have also been housed there. DNA testing has since confirmed that the VIETNAM 'Unknown' is US Air Force Lieutenant Michael J. Blassie, who was killed in action in 1972.

Unlimited Dream Company, The. A fantasy novel (1979) by J.G. Ballard (b.1930) in which a young man is reborn into the Thamesside suburban town of Shepperton (where Ballard lived), after crashing a stolen light aircraft. He can metamorphose himself into a beast or a bird, and he turns the town into an exotic garden. In the final chapter, entitled 'The Unlimited Dream Company', he expels from his body a human being whom he has absorbed. The title plays on the term 'limited company'.

Unpleasantness at the Bellona Club, The. A detective novel (1928) by Dorothy Sayers (1893–1957) in which the amateur detective Lord Peter WIMSEY and his imperturbable manservant Bunter investigate a murder in a men's club on Armistice Day.

Unspeakable Skipton, The. A novel (1959) by Pamela Hansford Johnson (1912–81) set in the town of Bruges in Belgium. Daniel Skipton, a scrounger and con-man, known by his circle in England as the 'unspeakable Skipton', is working on the great novel that will make his fortune. In the meantime he must depend on small handouts and dubious commissions. The character is loosely based on the novelist and essayist F.W. Rolfe

(1860–1913), an unfrocked Catholic priest who claimed to be Baron Corvo and who ended his days in Venice.

Untermenschen (German, 'subhumans'). A term applied by NAZI racial theorists to Jews, Slavs, gypsies and other groups regarded as inferior. The term thus served to help justify the appalling treatment inflicted on these peoples. The idea was in contrast to *Übermenschen* (German, 'supermen'), the Nazi ideal of powerful, physically perfect Nordic 'Aryans', who had the right to dominate and exploit lesser humans. The *Übermensch* was first conceived by the German philosopher Friedrich Nietzsche (1844–1900) as an elitist rather than racist idea: the superman is one of those rare humans who are capable of rising above the 'herd' to achieve the 'enhancement of life'. The 'will to power' Nietzsche talked about in relation to the *Übermensch* seems to have involved self-affirmation rather than the oppression of others. It seems that it was Nietzsche's sister who reinterpreted the philosopher's thinking in line with Nazi ideology. *See also* FINAL SOLUTION; HOLOCAUST; SUPERMAN.

Up and running. Operating; functioning. The phrase is particularly associated with computers that have been 'booted up' and that are running normally but has been extended to other activities requiring an initial opening or starting procedure.

> I arrive at 8.30am. … I go to reception to make sure it's up and running for 9am, and to see if I need to cover there today.
>
> *The Times* (28 July 1999)

Up for grabs. Easily obtainable; ready to be taken. The image is of something being tossed in the air for anyone to grasp or catch. The expression dates from the 1920s.

Up for it. Ready for any activity, especially when dangerous or exciting.

> If you thought Ibiza was simply a place where battalions of up-for-it clubbers go every summer to get out of it, think again.
>
> *heat* (6–12 January 2000)

Upside. The positive or advantageous aspect of something, as opposed to the 'downside', the negative or disadvantageous aspect. The term evolved in the 1960s and originally applied to the upward movement of share prices.

> While the upside [of part-time study] is the convenience and the ability to work full-time, the

downside is 'missing out' on the social side of university life.

The Times (24 August 1999)

Upside-down cake. A sponge cake that is turned out after baking so that the base becomes the top, displaying a decorative pattern composed of fruit. The name implies that the cake is the wrong side up, which of course is not the case. A number of culinary dishes involve an inversion from a mould or the like, such as a blancmange, and are 'right side up' when they emerge.

Upstairs, Downstairs. A highly regarded television series of period drama screened on ITV from 1971 to 1975. It was based on the sharp social divisions that existed in the EDWARDIAN ERA between a well-to-do household and its domestic staff, the respective 'upstairs' and 'downstairs' of the title. The 'downstairs' characters were much more roundly developed than the 'upstairs' Bellamy family, and included Hudson the butler, played by Gordon Jackson, Mrs Bridges the housekeeper, played by Angela Baddeley, and one of the housemaids, Rose, played by Jean Marsh, who together with Eileen Atkins devised the series as a whole.

Up the creek. In trouble; facing problems; pregnant. A fuller form is 'up the creek without a paddle'. One is thus in a difficult situation without the means of extricating oneself from it. *See also* SHIT.

Up the duff. Pregnant. 'Duff' has the sense of 'pudding'. The expression dates from the 1940s. *See also* BUN IN THE OVEN; IN THE CLUB.

> At 19, he was married ('only because she was up the duff' he explains gallantly).
>
> *Daily Telegraph* (26 September 1994)

Up there. On a level with others in high esteem. The phrase dates from the 1970s and is often expanded to 'up there with the best of them'. The image is almost of a 'board of honour' or a displayed notice of awards.

> Ten inches of pink plastic perfection with a wardrobe to die for, Barbie is up there with Coca-Cola and McDonald's as one of the icons of the last century.
>
> *heat* (6–12 January 2000)

Uptight. Nervous, tense; angry, irritated; straitlaced, conventional. All senses date from the 1960s and have the general idea of being 'wound up' and the converse of relaxed.

> What this ability to ridicule ourselves tells us about our national [British] character is reassuring. Cer-

tainly, it goes directly against the common view … that we are 'uptight'.

Sunday Express (27 February 2000)

Up to a point, Lord Copper. An expression of polite or deferential disagreement. It derives from Evelyn Waugh's novel *Scoop* (1938), in which Lord Copper is a newspaper proprietor: 'Mr Salter's side of the conversation was limited to expressions of assent. When Lord Copper was right he said, "Definitely, Lord Copper"; when he was wrong, "Up to a point".' *See also* FIRST LINES OF NOVELS.

> 'Pardoe's of Netherton, Theakston's of Masham, Adnam's of Southwold, Young's of Wandsworth … These are the great chateaux of British beer.' Well, up to a point, Lord Copper.
>
> *Sunday Times* (26 September 1999)

Up to here. As much as one can stand. The phrase dates from the 1940s and is usually found in a statement such as: 'I've had it up to here.' A gesture of the back of the hand to the chin, indicating that one is 'fed up' to that point, frequently accompanies the comment.

Up yours. A crude exclamation of contemptuous rejection, in spoken form often accompanied by a V-SIGN. The implied full phrase is 'Up your arse'. In May 1986 the *Sun* famously flaunted a front-page heading 'UP YOURS DELORS' for the benefit of Jacques Delors, President of the European Commission.

> [Australian radio show host John] Laws's response was typical of the man. It was basically, 'Up Yours'.
>
> *The Times* (30 July 1999)

Urban Cowboy. The nickname of Piers Adam (b.1964), owner of the Kartouche Club, London. The name puns on the title of a US film of 1980.

Urban guerrilla. A guerrilla operating in towns or cities and involved in kidnapping, bombing or the like. The term dates from the 1960s, 'urban' indicating the particular area of operations, as distinct from the more usual rural terrain. *See also* BAADER-MEINHOF GANG; RED BRIGADES; TUPAMAROS.

Urban legend or **myth.** A term current from the 1980s to describe a piece of modern folkore in the form of a widely known story, often macabre in nature. Such stories are called urban because they relate to modern urban society. They are largely apocryphal, but may contain elements of reality or plausibility, and usually take the form of an anecdote, told as if actually experienced by someone known to the teller or at any rate to 'a friend of a friend'. One of the best known is 'The Stolen Corpse', told in many variants but essentially involving a family holidaying in Spain who find one morning that their grandmother has died. Concerned about the formalities, they place the body in a hamper on the roof of the car and set off to find the British consul. On the way they stop for a snack, but on returning to the car find that it has been stolen, complete with the grandmother. Further examples are related in Roy Palmer's *Britain's Living Folklore* (1991) and in *The Vanishing Hitchhiker* (1988) by Jan Harold Brunvand.

URL. In computing the abbreviation of 'universal resource locator', an address system that gives each page on the WORLD WIDE WEB a unique location.

User-friendly. Easy to use or operate. The expression arose in the 1970s, originally with reference to computers, but its range of applications soon broadened, the second part of the term going on to give new formations such as 'environment-friendly', meaning not harmful to the environment.

Usher in violins, To. To plead one's case emotionally; to come up with a SOB STORY. The allusion is to a film with a strong love interest, in which melodramatic violin music traditionally heralds a romantic high spot.

> Without wanting to usher in violins, I feel that I all but gave up my twenties to this job.
> *The Times* (23 July 1999)

Utah Beach. The Allied code name for a stretch of beach on the east side of the Cotentin peninsula on the Normandy coast. On D-DAY the US 4th Infantry Division landed here. Utah is a state in the Rocky Mountains in the western USA.

Utility. The official term given during and after the Second World War to clothing, furniture and the like made according to government specification and sold at controlled prices. The name was a sign of the austerity of the times, practical qualities being more important than ornamentation. The goods bore a symbol consisting of two circles with a wedge removed from each, representing a reduction, and the figure 41, representing the year 1941, that of the scheme's introduction.

U-turn. A reversal of policy; a volte face, especially by a leading politician or even head of state. The expression dates from the 1950s and derives from the literal U-turn made by the driver of a motor vehicle when changing direction. A noted political U-turn was made by Edward Heath, Conservative prime minister from 1970 to 1974, when a growing economic crisis obliged him to switch from a conventional right-wing phase in 1970 to an unexpected left-wing stance in 1971. A successor, Margaret Thatcher, prime minister from 1979 to 1990, famously referred to the term in her speech at the Conservative Party Conference on 10 October 1980: 'To those waiting with bated breath for that favourite media catchphrase, the U-turn, I have only this to say: "You turn if you want; the LADY'S NOT FOR TURNING".'

> Yesterday the Tories undertook a breathtaking U-turn. John Redwood paraded in Parliament as a defender of the countryside.
> *The Times* (3 November 1999)

U-2. On 5 May 1960 President Khrushchev of the USSR told the Supreme Soviet that an American Lockheed U-2 aircraft had been shot down over Soviet territory on 1 May and its pilot captured. On 7 May the US government admitted it had been carrying out a spying mission. The incident was used by Khrushchev to humiliate the US president, Dwight D. Eisenhower, and to break up the summit conference in Paris on 17 May. The pilot, Gary Powers (1929–77), was convicted at a SHOW TRIAL in Moscow but in 1962 was released in exchange for Rudolf Abel, a Russian spy held by the USA. Powers published his view of the incident in *Operation Overflight* (1970).

UVF. *See* ULSTER VOLUNTEER FORCE.

V

V. The first novel (1963) by Thomas Pynchon (b.1937), an author of such reclusive habits that the only known photograph of him was taken in 1955. The title initial is the name under which a mysterious woman manifests herself at key moments of disaster that have contributed to the formation of modern Europe and America. The two human protagonists, among 200 named characters, are Herbert Stencil, obsessed with finding V, which he never does, and Benny Profane, an accident-prone realist. As Stencil's father notes in his journal: 'There is more behind and inside V than any of us had suspected. Not who, but what: what is she.'

Valentine State. A nickname of Arizona, so called with reference to the date of its entry into the Union, 14 February 1912, Valentine's Day.

Valium. A proprietary name for diazepam, an anti-anxiety drug, hypnotic and muscle relaxant. Together with LIBRIUM it was the notorious dependency sedative of the 1960s. The name may derive from Latin *valere*, 'to be strong'.

Valley Girl. A fashionable and affluent teenage girl from the San Fernando Valley, near Los Angeles, California, where VALSPEAK was spoken.

Valley of Ten Thousand Smokes. A volcanic valley in the region of Mount Katmai, Alaska. Shortly before Mount Katmai erupted on 6 June 1912 there were many bursts of molten matter in the valley, and these fissures have since discharged hot gases. It has been a National Monument since 1918.

Valley of the Dolls. A film (1967), based on a book of the same title (1966) by Jacqueline Susann (c.1918–74), about drug-taking among aspiring Hollywood film stars. The 'dolls' of the title are the pills on which the three main characters, all struggling actresses, are dependent. The expression 'valley of the dolls', a mainly US term for drug dependence, comes from the title of the book. The similarly titled film *Beyond the Valley of the Dolls* (1970) had little in common with the first film other than a theme of drug and alcohol addiction in show business.

Valspeak. Valspeak or Valleyspeak arose in the early 1980s as the jargon adopted by well-to-do teenagers in the San Fernando Valley near Los Angeles. It was specifically popularized by the rock musician Frank Zappa and his daughter, Moon Unit, in the novelty song 'Valley Girl' (1982), and its words and turns of phrase were characterized by sarcasm and exaggeration, as well as by an underlying ironic tone in expressions such as 'for sure' and 'as if'. Much of its content consisted of 'filler' words such as 'like' and 'totally', and it employed set phrases such as 'grody to the max' (grotty in the extreme). It was typically heard in the speech of the 'valley girl', with her disenchanted view of the world, and has been preserved in the dialogue of several novels and films. A good example of the latter is *Clueless* (1995), a clever re-working of Jane Austen's novel of manners *Emma* (1816), in which a BEVERLY HILLS teenager worries about losing her status as the most popular girl in the school and about winning the boy of her dreams. *See also* NOT!

Vamp. A shortening of vampire, as a word for a woman who uses her sexual wiles to attract men. The term arose in the early 20th century and became particularly identified with the US film actress Theda BARA, who first cast her sensual spell in the silent film *A Fool There Was* (1915), based on Kipling's poem 'The Vampire' (1897).

> A fool there was and he made his prayer
> (Even as you and I!)

To a rag and a bone and a hank of hair
(We called her the woman who did not care)
But the fool he called her his lady fair –
(Even as you and I!)
RUDYARD KIPLING: 'The Vampire' (1897)

Vanilla. Of a computer system: plain and basic, without BELLS AND WHISTLES. The reference is to a plain vanilla ice cream, the most common kind.

Vanishing cream. A cosmetic cream that is readily absorbed by the skin, i.e. it 'vanishes' into it. The name dates from the early 20th century.

Vanity plate. A personalized number plate on a private motor vehicle, as the US equivalent of a British CHERISHED NUMBER. The scope is greater, however, since any combination of letters or numbers can be used, provided it does not exceed six characters. This means that whole words can appear without any numbers at all. Thus Paul Rawden, of New Haven, Vermont, acquired a vanity plate reading simply 'PAULR'. Each plate also bears the name of the issuing state.

Vanity publishing. The publishing of a book in return for a fee from the author, resorted to by one desperate to see their name in print at any price. The cost is usually exorbitant, the quality of the finished product frequently inferior, and the writer often disappointed and disillusioned. The practice is generally discouraged by professional bodies and literary editors.

VAT. Value added tax, as essentially a sales tax on various goods and services. In practice it means that a tax is levied on a product each time it changes hands on its route to the point of sale. It was introduced in 1973, and in the late 1990s stood at 17½ per cent. There are inconsistencies. Newspapers and books are not subject to VAT, although the processes involved in their production are. Food and drink are generally not subject to VAT, but again there are anomalies. For example, a pie sold cold is not subject to VAT, but the same pie, heated by the vendor and sold as 'takeaway' food, is subject to the tax. Ice creams, chocolates, sweets, potato crisps and alcoholic drinks are also taxable. Further, while public transport in general is not subject to VAT, public transport designed to carry fewer than 12 people is. This means that standard bus and train journeys are zero-rated for VAT, but public minibus trips are not.

Vatican roulette. A nickname for the rhythm or calendar method of birth control, in which sexual intercourse is restricted to the times of the woman's menstrual cycle, when ovulation is least likely to occur. It is so called because it is permitted by the Roman Catholic Church and because, like Russian roulette, its efficacy is unpredictable.

Vatican II. The short name of Vatican Council II, as the 21st general or ecumenical council of the Roman Catholic Church, held from 11 October 1962 to 8 December 1965. It is regarded by many as the most significant religious event since the Reformation of the 16th century and certainly since Vatican Council I of 1869–70. The proposal to hold the council was apparently entirely due to Pope John XXIII, who attributed the idea of convening such an assembly to a sudden inspiration of the Holy Spirit. He defined its immediate task as the renewal of the life of the Church and of bringing up to date its teaching, discipline and organization, with the unity of all Christians as the ultimate goal. The consequences of the Council have been far-reaching, one being the almost complete replacement of Latin by the vernacular in the liturgy. Communion in both kinds was also extended to the laity, and the relationship with other Churches became warm rather than frigid as hitherto.

Va-va boom or **va-va voom.** A representation of a revving engine and rapid take-off, adopted in the 1960s to suggest sexual allure or 'go' generally. 'Vroom', or a variant of it, is also so used, while *Va Va Voom* is the title of a 'girlie' magazine published by Hugh Hefner, founder of PLAYBOY.

> Let us face it: [Conservative leader] William Hague doesn't have a lot of v-v-vroom.
> *The Times* (6 October 1999)

V-bomber. One of the three types of long-range jet bomber forming Britain's main nuclear weapons delivery system in the 1950s. The 'V' represents their respective names, as the Avro Vulcan, Handley Page Victor and Vickers Valiant. They were gradually superseded from the 1960s by submarine-based missiles, although some elderly Vulcans took part in the FALKLANDS WAR.

VC. *See* VICTOR CHARLIE.

V-chip. A device of the 1990s by which a television set can be programmed to block or encrypt a programme containing an unacceptable level of violence, sex or offensive language, usually with children in mind. The 'V' stands for 'viewer' but is popularly thought to represent 'violence'.

VE Day. 'Victory in Europe' Day. The end of hostilities in Europe after the Second World War, 8 May 1945.

France has an annual public holiday on this day called *Fête de la Liberté et de la Paix* (Freedom and Peace Day). *See also* ARMISTICE DAY; LIBERATION DAY; TWO-MINUTE SILENCE; VJ DAY.

Veganism. The adherence to a plant-based diet, avoiding all foods derived from animals, including meat, fish, poultry, eggs, milk and honey. In this strict regime vegans differ from vegetarians, some of whom eat dairy products. Veganism is often adopted in response to the exploitation of animals, although others become vegans for health, ecological or spiritual reasons.

Vegeburger. A flat savoury cake similar to a hamburger but containing vegetables instead of meat.

Vegemite. A proprietary name for a type of spread made from a concentrated yeast extract. It is regarded as a typical or even prototypical Australian foodstuff, on which all AUSSIES are weaned and reared. The name was coined from a blend of 'vegetable' and MARMITE.

Velcro. A proprietary name, registered in Britain in 1960, for a fabric made in narrow strips for use as a fastener. One strip has tiny loops and the other hooks so that they can be fastened by simply being pressed together and unfastened by being pulled apart. The fabric is particularly useful as a quick-release closure for outerwear and footwear such as waterproof jackets and children's shoes. The name is a shortening of French *velours croché*, 'hooked velvet'.

Velvet Fog. A nickname for the popular American singer Mel Tormé (b.1925), alluding to his soft and slightly husky voice and smooth CROONING style.

Velvet revolution. A non-violent political revolution. The phrase originally applied to the peaceful overthrow of communism in Czechoslovakia in 1989 under Václav Havel (b.1936) and is a translation of the Czech *sametová revoluce*, the former word being related to English 'samite'. The peaceful secession of Slovakia from Czechoslavakia, resulting in the creation of two separate states, the Slovak Republic and the Czech Republic, was referred to as the 'velvet divorce'.

Velvet Underground. *See under* ROCK GROUP NAMES.

Venture capitalist. A person engaged in investment, finance or business that is based on so called 'venture capital', now more usually known as risk capital, meaning capital invested in a highly speculative enterprise. The encouragement of small businesses in the 1980s produced a demand for high-risk investment in new ideas and entrepreneurs, with the result that venture capitalism became a regular feature in the world of finance rather than an occasional aspect of traditional financial trading.

Verbal diarrhoea. Excessive talk; meaningless monologizing. The phrase arose in the 1940s but 'diarrhoea' as a term for a prolix flow of words was current as early as the 17th century. 'Logorrhoea', based on it and having the same sense, dates from the early 20th century.

> He opens his mouth and lets this noise come out. It's not so much verbal diarrhoea as verbal incontinence.
> DERMOT BOLGER (ed.): *Finbar's Hotel*, 'The Test' (1997)

Verdun. A French garrison town some 200km (120 miles) east of Paris. During the First World War Verdun came to have an awful significance, as the town and its ring of fortresses (which had remained a French salient since 1914) became the site of the longest and bloodiest battle of the war, lasting from 21 February to 18 December 1916. The stated intention of the Germans in attacking Verdun was to 'bleed the French army white', knowing that the French would defend Verdun at all costs. In command of the German forces was Crown Prince Wilhelm, the LAUGHING MURDERER OF VERDUN, while the French were commanded by General (later Marshal) Philippe Pétain (*see* PÉTAINISTS).

The defence of Verdun became a national crusade in France of almost religious intensity, and both the government and the army high command forbade French withdrawal, despite two recommendations to do so from Pétain. In public Pétain famously promised '*Ils ne passeront pas*' ('They shall not pass'), and built up a major supply operation along the only road that remained open to Verdun. This small road, under constant German artillery bombardment, carried 90,000 French soldiers to the battle every week. Its popular name in France, *la Voie sacrée* ('the sacred way'), evoked the terrible sacrifices made by French soldiers, and entered French national mythology. Probably more than a quarter of a million Frenchmen died at Verdun, and the same number were wounded. The Germans suffered some 434,000 casualties, half of them killed. In the autumn the French retook the forts they had lost, and in all the Germans had only advanced a few kilometres. The main result of the battle was the terrible and irreplaceable toll of manpower on both sides. *See also* SOMME.

Verfremdungseffekt. *See* EPIC THEATRE.

Verlan. A French form of back slang which became, in the late 20th century, a popular type of talk among young people. It is formed by inverting the syllables or letters of a word and incorporating any spelling changes to facilitate pronunciation. Thus *pourri*, 'rotten', becomes *ripou*, *femme*, 'woman', is *meuf* and *chaud*, 'hot', is *auch*. The name itself is an inversion of *l'envers*, 'the other way round'.

Vermeer forgeries. *See under* FAKES.

Veronica. In bullfighting a movement in which the matador swings the cape in a slow circle round himself to encourage the charging bull to follow the cape rather than attack his person. The ploy is so called since the pose of the matador holding the cape out in his two hands resembles that in paintings of St Veronica holding out a towel to Christ for him to wipe his face as he proceeds on the road to Calvary.

Versailles, Treaty of. *See* TREATY OF VERSAILLES.

Vertigo. A suspense film (1958) directed by Alfred Hitchcock and starring James Stewart and Kim Novak, based on a novel *D'Entre Les Morts* by Pierre Boileau and Thomas Narcejac (the book was written specifically for Hitchcock to adapt). It concerns a detective with a fear of heights who falls in love with a woman who falls to her death. The detective is then startled to see what is apparently her double.

Vespa. An Italian make of motor scooter popular among the young and (reasonably) affluent in the 1950s and early 1960s. The name is Italian for 'wasp'.

Veteran car. *See* VINTAGE CAR.

Veterans Day. An annual holiday in the United States honouring veterans (ex-servicemen) of the armed forces and all men and women killed in the country's wars. It originated as ARMISTICE DAY, commemorating the end of the First World War on 11 November 1918. In 1954, after the KOREAN WAR, this date was officially designated Veterans Day. The day itself is usually observed with parades, speeches and the placing of floral tributes on servicemen's graves or at memorials. Special services are also held at Arlington National Cemetery, Virginia.

> They have this day, Veterans' Day, that all the jerks that graduated from Pency around 1776 come back and walk all over the place, with their wives and children and everybody.
>
> J.D. SALINGER: *The Catcher in the Rye* (1951)

V for Victory. On 14 January 1941 Victor de Lavaleye, a member of the exiled Belgian government in London, proposed in a broadcast to Belgium that the letter V, standing for Victory in many European languages, be substituted for the letters RAF, which were being chalked up on walls and other places in Belgium. The plan was immediately adopted, and the Morse code V (· · · –) was featured in every BBC broadcast to Europe, followed by the opening bar of Beethoven's 5th Symphony, which has the same rhythm. 'Colonel Britton' (D.E. Ritchie), director of the BBC European news service, was responsible for the diffusion of the V-sign propaganda, which gave hope to those under the NAZI yoke. Winston Churchill greatly popularized the sign of two upraised fingers in the form of a V, the palm facing outwards. This is now usually known as the peace sign. *See also* V-SIGN.

Viagra. A 'wonder drug' claimed to cure male impotence. It was launched by Pfizer in the United States in 1998 and almost immediately became the world's fastest selling prescription drug, although not all doctors favoured its use. The name is apparently arbitrary but does evoke 'Niagara'.

Vice anglais, Le (French, 'the English vice'). Flagellation or corporal punishment, regarded with some justification by the French as a typically English interest, especially of the upper classes. The phrase dates only from the 1940s, but the practice is much older and in English terms is particularly associated with Victorian times and the poems of Algernon Swinburne (1837–1909).

Vichy. A spa town in central France, on the River Allier, known for its bottled mineral water. It became notorious, however, as the seat of the French collaborationist government during the Second World War, popularly referred to as 'the Vichy government', or just 'Vichy'. Marshal Philippe Pétain, the last premier of the Third Republic, had agreed the German armistice terms at COMPIÈGNE (22 June 1940) after the fall of France and became head of state of the Vichy regime, formally known as *l'État français* ('French State'). While German forces occupied northern France, Vichy was left to administer the unoccupied south. Vichy regimes also held power in most of France's overseas colonies. The government was made up of a mixture of Catholic conservatives and far-right extremists and was authoritarian and quasi-fascist in character. As well as attempting to suppress resistance movements, the Vichy regime was involved in the deportation of

French Jews to the Nazi death camps. Pétain's position was gradually eroded, and Pierre Laval (1883–1945), who had been dismissed as Pétain's deputy in December 1940, was installed as head of government on German orders in April 1942. Vichy ceased to have any effective power in southern France in November 1942 when the Germans occupied the zone, following the Allied landings in northwest Africa. The Vichy regime finally dissolved when the Allies landed in Normandy in June 1944. *See also* MAQUIS; PÉTAINISTS; VERDUN.

Vichyssoise. The chilled potato and leek cream soup of this name was the creation in the early 20th century of the French chef Louis Diat in New York. He came from the Bourbonnais region of France, not far from Vichy, and the soup was based on a similar dish served by his mother, but hot. In the Second World War some French chefs in New York attempted to change the name to *Crème gauloise*, from their aversion to the VICHY government, but the original name was the one that prevailed.

Vick. The decongestant ointment of this name was the invention of an American pharmacist, Lunsford Richardson, born in 1854 in North Carolina. It began as one of his home remedies, the name coming partly from an advertisement for Vicks Seeds that he had seen in a magazine, partly from Vick, the name of his brother-in-law. The product is now marketed under the name 'Vicks VapoRub'.

Victor Charlie. US military slang for the VIET CONG, 'Victor' being the standard code word for 'V', and 'Charlie' for 'C'. The Viet Cong were also often referred to simply as the VC or Charlie (sometimes spelt Charley).

Victory Medal. A bronze medal with a winged figure of Victory on the obverse, awarded in 1919 to all Allied service personnel who had served in a theatre of war in the First World War, also to certain women's formations.

Victory roll. A rotational manoeuvre about a longitudinal axis performed by an aircraft as a sign of triumph. The term dates from the Second World War.

Video nasty. A video horror film or one depicting violence, sadism, killing or the like. The term became current from the early 1980s at a time when videos themselves, as a major new commercial activity, were beginning to incorporate dubious material that evaded normal censorship procedures. Videos

are now classified under a system similar to that for films. *See also* SNUFF MOVIE.

Viet Cong. The communist guerrilla force active in the VIETNAM War (1964–75) against the South Vietnamese government and US forces with the support of the North Vietnamese army. The name means 'Vietnamese communist'. *See also* HO CHI MINH TRAIL; TET OFFENSIVE; VIET MINH.

Viet Minh. The communist-dominated nationalist movement that led the struggle for Vietnamese independence from French rule. It was founded in China in 1941 by Ho Chi Minh (1890–1969), and many of its members supported the VIET CONG during the Vietnam War (1964–75). It takes its name from the first and last elements of *Viet-Nam Dôc-Lâp Dông-Minh*, 'Vietnamese Independence League'. *See also* DIEN BIEN PHU; HO CHI MINH TRAIL.

Vietnam. This southeast Asian country was the scene of almost continual conflict from 1945 to 1975. The wars in Vietnam constituted perhaps the 'hottest' manifestation of the COLD WAR, and witnessed the humiliation first of France and then of the USA. Indeed, the US failure in Vietnam was to leave a scar on the collective American consciousness for the remainder of the century.

Vietnam had been colonized by the French in the later 19th century. Nationalist resistance began in the 1930s, led by the communist Ho Chi Minh (1892–1969). During the Second World War it came under VICHY French rule, and then under Japanese occupation. The nationalists organized themselves as the VIET MINH, and when the Japanese surrendered in 1945 Ho Chi Minh declared the independence of Vietnam. However, French military forces returned to restore colonial rule, and the Viet Minh withdrew from the cities. All-out conflict began in 1950, and ended in May 1954 with the humiliating French defeat at DIEN BIEN PHU.

At the subsequent Geneva Accords in July 1954, Vietnam was divided into two independent countries, with Ho Chi Minh leading communist North Vietnam, while a Western-aligned government was established in South Vietnam. Shortly afterwards, US President Eisenhower (*see* IKE), fearing the extension of communist power in the region, sent military advisers to South Vietnam, and supported the South's refusal to participate in a referendum on reunification. The North, intent on reunification, supported communist guerrillas in the South (*see* VIET CONG), supplying them via the HO CHI MINH TRAIL. President Kennedy (*see* JFK) stepped up US military aid, but by 1963 much of the South was under Viet Cong control.

In 1964 President Johnson (*see* LBJ) used the North's attack on US warships in the Gulf of Tonkin as the pretext for the escalation of US military involvement. Subsequently some 2 million US troops saw service in Vietnam, and US bombers launched massive raids on the North. However, US forces proved incapable of defeating the guerrilla tactics of the Viet Cong, or of winning over the 'hearts and minds' of the South Vietnamese peasants who gave them support. Large numbers of US troops were conscripted unwillingly through the 'draft' and this, combined with atrocities against civilians (*see* MY LAI MASSACRE) and the military stalemate, led to the formation of a large antiwar movement in the USA. The nightly showing of uncensored newsreel footage of the war on US television also played its part. In the wake of the 1968 TET OFFENSIVE Johnson initiated peace talks.

Johnson's successor, Richard Nixon (*see* TRICKY DICKY), began US troop withdrawals, and at the same time authorized covert bombing raids and ground incursions into Cambodia (1970) and Laos (1971), aimed at the Ho Chi Minh Trail. Such actions strengthened antiwar sentiment in the USA. A ceasefire was agreed in 1973, and the USA completed its withdrawal. North Vietnamese forces renewed their offensive in 1975, and following the communist victory the two Vietnams were reunited. In all, 47,000 US servicemen died in the conflict, compared to 450,000 South Vietnamese civilians, and nearly 1 million Viet Cong and North Vietnamese troops.

View from the Bridge, A. A play (1955) by the US playwright Arthur Miller (b.1915) about a Brooklyn longshoreman who takes two illegal immigrants into his home but subsequently informs the authorities of their presence after one of them falls in love with his wife's niece, for whom he has a liking himself. The title reflects both the immediate environment of the play (the Brooklyn waterfront) and the detached observation of events as delivered by the local lawyer, Alfieri, who narrates the story.

View to a Kill, A. An unexciting film (1985) in the long-running series of James BOND secret agent movies based on the novels of Ian Fleming (1906–64). Roger Moore played Bond. Fleming's original story was published in 1960 with the rather more meaningful title 'From a View to a Kill', which may be been

suggested by Anthony Powell's novel *From a View to a Death* (1933), which in turn took the idea from the traditional foxhunting ballad 'D'ye ken John Peel', written in 1832 by John Woodcock Graves:

> Yes, I ken John Peel, and Ruby too,
> Ranter and Ringwood, Bellman and True,
> From a find to a check, from a check to a view,
> From a view to a death in the morning.

A 'check' in foxhunting language signifies a loss of scent, while a 'view' is the cry that signals the actual sighting of a fox.

Viking. The names of two unmanned US spacecraft launched respectively on 29 August and 9 September 1975. Ten months later they entered orbits round Mars and released landers to relay measurements of properties of the atmosphere and soil of the planet and colour photographs of its rocky surface. Experiments designed to detect evidence of life on Mars were inconclusive.

Vile Bodies. A novel (1930) by Evelyn Waugh (1903–66), satirizing the manners of the BRIGHT YOUNG THINGS in a recognizable but fantasized political and social setting. The 'vile bodies' are those of the characters who spend their time going from party to party, to the fury and puzzlement of their elders. The words have a biblical echo: 'Who shall change our vile body, that it may be fashioned like unto his glorious body' (Philippians 3:21).

Village England. Rural England, with its close-knit village communities that in the face of urban growth have retained their age-old associations of pubs, church bells and cricket matches. Many new estates at the close of the 20th century were being planned on the lines of such communities, one high-profile example being the MILLENNIUM Village at Greenwich in southeast London. There is a 'Gazetteer of Village England' listing various fictional locations in the novels and stories of P.G. Wodehouse in Geoffrey Jaggard's *Wooster's World* (1967).

> 'Village England's' charm and community are qualities that have been established over centuries, and have come about more through evolution than design.
> *Sunday Times* (10 May 1998)

Village idiot. A comparatively modern term for what was long seen as a regular feature of country life, in the form of a feeble-minded middle-aged or elderly man who supposedly resided in every village. He was traditionally thought of as sitting on a bench outside the village inn, where he readily regaled strangers with lurid local tales in return for a steady supply of ale. There may have been a germ of truth in this imagery, but the precise picture has now faded, leaving the term to persist as simply a light-hearted phrase for a slow or dim-witted person.

Vinegar Joe. A nickname of the acerbic American general Joseph Stilwell (1883–1946), as famous for his tongue-lashing as for his Second World War exploits in China, Burma, India and on the Japanese island of Okinawa. He earned the sobriquet when head of the Infantry School at Fort Benning, Georgia, between 1929 and 1933.

Vinland Map. *See under* FAKES.

Vintage car. An early style or model of motor car, specifically one made between 1917 and 1930. A veteran car is older and to a connoisseur is one made before 1916 or, in some logbooks, 1905.

Violon d'Ingres (French, 'Ingres' violin'). An activity or pastime for which a person is not primarily known. The French painter Ingres (1780–1867) was said to have been more proud of his violin-playing than of the paintings by which he made his name.

VIP. Very Important Person. This well-established abbreviation was popularized by a station commander of Transport Command in 1944 who was responsible for the movement of a plane-load of important individuals, including Lord Mountbatten, to the Middle East. He so described them in his movement orders to avoid disclosing their identity.

Virgin Soldiers, The. A novel (1966) by Leslie Thomas (b.1931). Set in Malaysia during the years 1948–52, it reflects the experiences of British soldiers garrisoned there to combat the threat of communist guerrillas: 'Some of this army were good soldiers; others were not.' A significant strand of the story concerns the sexual initiation of a 19-year-old private by a Chinese prostitute, with whom he falls in love. A film version (1969) was directed by John Dexter.

Virtual reality. A computer-generated simulation of a three-dimensional image or environment that can be interacted with in a seemingly real way by someone wearing a head-mounted display screen and special gloves. The term was originally used by computer programmers in the 1980s to describe any interactive technology but took on its present sense in 1989, when an American musician, Jaron Lanier, designed the equipment that allows users to participate in the simulation.

Vision thing. Idealism as opposed to pragmatism. The term usually relates to politicians who see themselves as managers rather than ideologists. It derives from President Bush's response, 'Oh, the vision thing', reported in *Time* on 26 January 1987, to the suggestion that he turn his attention from short-term campaign objectives and look to the longer term.

Visit, The. A play (1956) by the Swiss dramatist Friedrich Dürrenmatt (1921–90), in German *Der Besuch der alten Dame* ('The Old Lady's Visit'), about a millionairess who returns to her home town to wreak vengeance on those who wronged her in her youth. At her insistence, the town's leading citizen, her former lover, is publicly strangled, on which she hands over her money before ending her visit and leaving, to resounding cheers. The name of the town, Güllen, means 'liquid manure' in Swiss German. The drama typifies its author's fascination with black humour, and his grotesquely ironic style.

Visiting fireman. A US term current from the 1920s for a visitor who receives a cordial welcome. The concept is of one set of firemen visiting another fire station and receiving such a welcome.

Vital statistics. Properly, population statistics concerned with births, marriages, deaths, divorces and the like (Latin *vita*, 'life'). From the 1950s the term has been applied semi-seriously to a woman's bust, waist and hip measurements, usually given in inches.

> We are now privy to Ms Bailey's vital statistics (34–24–35), and the knowledge that she is a model aged 22, five foot seven, and buys her underwear from Marks and Spencer.
>
> *The Times* (4 December 1994)

Vitamin. The word as proposed in 1912 by the American biochemist Casimir Funk was originally 'vitamine', from Latin *vita*, 'life', and English 'amine', the latter referring to the amino acid that the substance was believed to contain. When it was found that this was not the case, the term was modified to its present spelling in 1920.

Vitamins are generally classified as water-soluble (B and C) or fat-soluble (A, D, E and K), and each of the letter-names has its chemical equivalent. Thus vitamin A is another name for retinol, vitamin B_1 is thiamine, vitamin B_2 is riboflavin, vitamin C is ascorbic acid, vitamin D_3 is cholecalciferol and so on.

Vive la différence (French, 'Long live the difference'). Hurray for the difference between the sexes. A humorous approval of diversity adopted by English from French in the 1960s.

Vivisector, The. A novel (1970) by the Australian writer Patrick White (1912–90), a rags-to-riches study of an eminent artist who as a child is bought from his parents by a wealthy couple. The course of his many relationships, some intense, some fleeting, is marred by the fact that he uses people dispassionately in the interests of his art, in the same way that a vivisector employs animals.

Viz. A coarsely humorous and rudely satirical comic aimed mainly at young and uninhibited readers. The first issue, published in November 1979, was launched in the bedroom of its founder, Chris Brown, for distribution around the pubs of his native Newcastle upon Tyne. By 1983 local sales had reached 3000 and steadily grew to reach a national peak of over a million in 1990. Its larger-than-life characters include the Fat Slags, two gross women; Johnny Fartpants, a crude juvenile; Billy the Fish, a libidinous OWN GOAL scorer; Roger Mellie, a foul-mouthed television anchorman; Biffa Bacon, a belligerent Geordie; Sid the Sexist, a happily chauvinist Geordie; and Finbarr Saunders, a purveyor of double entendres of the most sexually suggestive nature. The name comes from slang 'viz' meaning 'face' (visage).

VJ Day. 'Victory in Japan' Day. The end of hostilities in the Far East, 15 August 1945, and thus the end of the Second World War. *See also* VE DAY.

V-mail. A system of mail transmission in the United States during the Second World War. To conserve shipping space, a letter written on a letter sheet was reproduced in photographic microfilm and forwarded in this form to be enlarged on photographic paper for delivery. A 'V-letter' was a letter sent by this method. The 'V' is for 'Victory'.

> The same source made it evident that she received V-letters by the bale. They were always torn into strips like bookmarks.
>
> TRUMAN CAPOTE: *Breakfast at Tiffany's* (1958)

Vodafone. The proprietary name of a cellular radio system or the telephone that operates under this system, introduced in the mid-1980s. The name represents 'voice data phone'.

Vo-do-deo-do. A meaningless refrain appearing in popular jazz songs of the 1920s and 1930s and used subsequently to denote a style of singing or song characterized by speed, energy and an insistent rhythm. It

is first recorded in Jack Yellen's song 'Crazy Words, Crazy Tune' (1927): 'Sings the same words to ev'ry song. Vo-do-de-o. Vo-do-do-de-o-do.'

Voicemail. A system of US origin dating from the 1980s for electronically storing, processing and reproducing verbal messages left through the conventional telephone network.

Voice of the Turtle, The. A play (1943) by the Anglo-American playwright John Van Druten (1901–57) about a wartime romance between a young actress and a serviceman. The title is biblical in origin:

> Rise up, my love, my fair one, and come away. For, lo, the winter is past, the rain is over and gone; The flowers appear on the earth; the time of the singing of birds is come, and the voice of the turtle is heard in our land.
>
> Song of Solomon 2:10–12

Voie sacrée, La. *See* VERDUN.

Volvo. The first Swedish car of this name made its test run from Stockholm to Göteborg in 1926 and was produced by a company set up by two engineers, Assar Gabrielsson and Gustaf Larson. The name is Latin for 'I roll', although this did not originally apply to the car but to a subsidiary of the firm where the two men worked, SKF (Svenska Kullagerfabriken), a ball-bearing concern. The name is, however, equally applicable for a vehicle that 'rolls' or runs on wheels along the road.

V–1. A type of flying bomb sent against Britain by the Germans, June to August 1944, and subsequently against Antwerp. The V stood for *Vergeltungswaffe* ('reprisal weapon'). *See also* V-2.

Vorticism. An avant-garde art movement launched in Britain in 1914. It was related to CUBISM and FUTURISM and was mainly concerned with the visual arts but also embraced literature. Its designs were in straight lines and angular patterns, while machine-like forms were a frequent feature. Among its representatives, Wyndham Lewis (1882–1957) and Edward Wadsworth (1889–1949) were the most notable. The name was bestowed by the US poet Ezra Pound (1885–1972), for whom the vortex represented 'the point of maximum energy', an expression of the dynamism of modern life. *See also* DADAISM; FAUVISM; ORPHISM; RURALISM; SURREALISM; SYNCHROMISM; TACHISM.

Voss. A novel (1957) by the Australian writer Patrick White (1912–90). Johann Ulrich Voss, a German explorer who has affinities with Ludwig Leichhardt (1813–c.1848), sets out from Sydney to explore the Australian interior, having established an intense intellectual bond with Laura Trevelyan, the niece of one of his patrons. The disasters and sufferings that befall the party, and differing conceptions of Voss's contribution to history, have their counterparts in the experiences of Laura.

Vostok (Russian, 'east'). The first type of Soviet manned space rocket. On 12 April 1961 *Vostok 1* took Yuri Gagarin (1934–68) into space, where, in a 90-minute flight, he made a single orbit of the earth, the first ever manned space flight. Over the next two years there were a further five Vostok flights. The last, on 16 June 1963, carried Valentina Tereshkova (b.1937), the first woman in space.

Vote with one's feet, To. To indicate one's approval or disapproval of a thing by associating oneself with it (walking in) or dissociating oneself from it (walking out). The latter is the more usual interpretation. The expression dates from the 1960s.

> Britain's consumers are voting with their feet against high prices. Cheap has become chic.
> *Sunday Times* (20 June 1999)

Vox pop. A term for interviews with members of the public conducted by radio or television reporters. The expression is a shortening of Latin *vox populi*, 'voice of the people'.

> A few days ago, a BBC camera crew went round Washington collecting vox pops – close-ups of men in the street saying pithily what they think of things.
> *Listener* (8 February 1968)

Voyager. The name of two US unmanned space probes, which have sent back large amounts of new information about the outer planets, and discovered many new moons and planetary rings. Both were launched in 1977. *Voyager 1* passed Jupiter in March 1979 and Saturn in November 1980. *Voyager 2* passed Jupiter in July 1979, Saturn in August 1981, Uranus in January 1986 and Neptune in August 1989. Both probes are now heading beyond the Solar System, carrying information about their home planet.

Voyeurvision. A prurient form of television in which the private lives of young women are filmed continu-ously for entertainment. The genre arose in the United States in the 1990s and evolved from *Sliver* (1993), a video-surveillance film starring Sharon Stone. It subsequently became big business on the INTERNET, with such sites as *The Dolls' House* (1998), filming three North London flat-sharers around the clock, and the more explicit American *Voyeur-Dorm* (1997), in which 48 cameras capture the uncensored daily and nightly activities of seven girls.

VPL. An abbreviation of the 1980s phrase 'visible pantie line', indicating that the line of a person's underwear is perceptible through a tight skirt, dress or pair of trousers.

V-sign. A sign of the letter V made with the first two fingers pointing up and the back of the hand facing outwards. It is a crude gesture of abuse or contempt, and is not to be confused with the peace sign, which is made with the palm of the hand facing outwards (*see* V FOR VICTORY). The sign is sometimes said on somewhat dubious evidence to have originated in medieval battles between the English and the French, when English archers captured by the French would have their second and third fingers removed to ensure they would not draw the bow again. In defiance, the English soldiers stuck up their fingers at the French. *See also* HARVEY SMITH; TWO FINGERS; UP YOURS.

V-2. A long-range rocket with an explosive warhead, which was projected against Britain by the Germans in the autumn of 1944. V had the same origin as for the V-1.

Vulcan, The. The nickname of the Conservative politician John Redwood (b.1951), environment spokesman in William Hague's Shadow Cabinet, a post in which he was replaced (by Archie Norman) in 2000. His keen intelligence, piercing stare and pointed ears suggested a resemblance to Mr SPOCK in the television series STAR TREK, as a member of the race so named.

> In the end, even Vulcans die. John Redwood yesterday left the bridge of the Tory starship for perhaps the last time when William Hague beamed him off the Shadow Cabinet.
> *The Times* (2 February 2000)

W

Waac. The familiar name of a member of the Women's Army Auxiliary Corps, a body of women raised for non-combatant army service in the First World War. In the Second World War they were termed the ATS. This became the Women's Royal Army Corps (WRAC) in 1949. The WRAC was disbanded in 1992, when women wishing to enlist joined the regular army.

Waaf. The familiar name of a member of the Women's Auxiliary Air Force, or the force itself, which was originally set up in 1918 as the Women's Royal Air Force (WRAF). It was disbanded in 1920, but re-formed in 1939 as the WAAF. It once again became the WRAF in 1949 and was finally disbanded in 1994. Women are now able to enlist in the regular RAF.

WAC. In the Second World War the Women's Army Corps, the US equivalent of the British ATS. *See also* WAVES.

Waco. A town in Texas that in 1993 was the scene of an FBI siege of a compound containing armed and unarmed members of an extreme religious group, the Branch Davidian cult, led by David Koresh. The siege began on 18 February and ended on 19 April with the mass suicide of the 80 cult members still in the compound. The dead included Koresh himself and more than 17 children.

Waffen SS (German, 'Armed SS'). The combat units of the SS in NAZI Germany during the Second World War. They attempted to recruit British prisoners into an anti-Soviet unit known originally as the Legion of St George and later as the *Britische Freikorps* ('British Free Corps'). Few enlisted, and it was formed largely from Oswald Mosley's BLACKSHIRTS and British ex-servicemen with divided loyalties resulting from German parentage (*see also* MOSLEYITES).

Waggle dance. A distinctive movement or 'dance' performed by bees at the entrance to their nest or hive, said to be an indication to other bees of the site of a source of food. The term dates from the 1950s and translates German *Schwänzeltanz*, coined by the German zoologist Karl von Frisch in 1923. Hence Waggle Dance as the proprietary name of a brand of honey beer.

Wag one's finger, To. To reprimand or admonish, an action traditionally accompanied by the wagging of one's forefinger.

> Ms Liddell has no plans to wag her finger; she wants to charm her listeners in Paris.
> *The Times* (14 October 1999)

Wait and see. A phrase at one time humorously used with reference to the Liberal politician H.H. Asquith, 1st earl of Oxford and Asquith (1852–1928). Thus, 'What did Asquith say?' was formerly another way of saying 'Wait and see'. Asquith used the phrase in answer to a question in the House of Commons on 4 April 1910, and he took to repeating it subsequently when faced with an awkward question. Eventually the opposition took it up and chanted it back at him when questions were put to him. The same phrase was associated with the stalling policy of John Major when prime minister (1990–97) with regard to Britain's joining the SINGLE CURRENCY.

Waitangi Day. Since 1960 6 February has been celebrated as New Zealand's national day. It is a public holiday and commemorates the day on which the Treaty of Waitangi was made in 1840 by the British governor, William Hobson, with the Maori chiefs. They recognized British sovereignty in return for the tribes being guaranteed possession of their lands.

Wait for it! A parenthetical warning that what follows is a surprise or, ironically, is exactly what one was expecting. The allusion is to the drill sergeant's command on the parade ground to anyone showing signs of making the required move prematurely. The phrase dates from the 1930s.

> Lucy Gannon's new drama serial stars Kevin Whately as an overworked GP whose wife ... embarks on an affair with (wait for it) the window-cleaner.
>
> *The Times* (11 September 1999)

Waiting for Godot. A play, originally entitled *En attendant Godot*, by Samuel Beckett (1906–89). Perhaps the best known example of the THEATRE OF THE ABSURD, it was first performed in Paris in 1953 and opened to acclaim in Britain, in a translation from the French by the author, at the Arts Theatre, London, in August 1955. The performance was directed by Peter Hall. The play is ostensibly about a pair of tramps, Estragon and Vladimir, who wait interminably for the arrival of the mysterious Godot. The only other characters are Lucky, Pozzo and a Boy. Beckett cast doubt upon suggestions that Godot was in fact God ('If Godot were God, I would have called him that'), and there has been much debate over Godot's identity and significance. Because the play was written originally in French, other theories have suggested a link with the French *godillot* or *godasse* (slang words for 'boot'), as boots are discussed in the text, and with a tale that the author once came across a crowd watching the Tour de France cycle race and, on asking what they were doing, was informed, 'We are waiting for Godot' (that being the name of the slowest rider in the field). Alternatively, it was claimed, Beckett was once accosted by a prostitute while loitering in the Rue Godot de Mauroy in Paris and, on declining her advances, was asked impatiently what he was hanging about there for; was he perhaps 'waiting for Godot?' (as in the name of the street).

> Beckett's *Waiting for Godot* ... arrived in London ten years ago like a sword burying itself in an over-upholstered sofa.
>
> PENELOPE GILLIATT: review

Waiting for Lefty. A play (1935) by the US playwright Clifford Odets (1906–63) about the events that led up to a trade union vote to strike in the 1930s. The Lefty of the title is the leader of the union, whose arrival is impatiently expected. News eventually comes of Lefty's murder, and the decision to strike follows. Odets deliberately chose the name in order to try to break down traditional hostility towards the political left. It was published in Britain in 1937 by the LEFT BOOK CLUB.

> We're stormbirds of the working class. Workers of the world. ... And when we die they'll know what we did to make a new world.
>
> CLIFFORD ODETS: *Waiting for Lefty*

Wake-up call. In the figurative sense a person or thing that arouses people's awareness of an unsatisfactory situation and that prompts them to do something about it.

> Regarded by some as a powerful wake-up call, by others as sensationalist trash, Larry Clark's film [*Kids*] is one of the most controversial movies of recent years.
>
> *Sunday Times* (21 November 1999)

Waldorf salad. A salad made from apples, walnuts, lettuce and (or) celery and dressed with mayonnaise. It takes its name from the former Waldorf-Astoria Hotel on Fifth Avenue, New York, where it was first served in the early 20th century. The hotel was originally two separate hotels built by two feuding cousins: the Waldorf, built in 1893 by the US-born British financier William Waldorf Astor (1848–1919) on the site of his father's mansion, and the Astoria, erected in 1897 by John Jacob Astor IV (1864–1912) on the site of his mother's mansion to the north. The combined hotel was demolished in 1929 to make way for the Empire State Building. The present hotel of the same name on Park Avenue opened in 1931.

Walkabout. An informal stroll among a crowd by an important visitor. The word first gained public attention in this sense in March 1970 when Queen Elizabeth and the Duke of Edinburgh left their car when touring Wellington, New Zealand, and walked along the street to talk to local people. The event was immediately dubbed a royal 'walkabout' by Vincent Mulchrone of the *Daily Mail*. He in fact misused the term, which is Australian English in origin, meaning a periodic journey into the bush by an Aborigine in order to live in the traditional manner for a while and to make a temporary withdrawal from white society. This original sense was popularized by the highly rated Australian film *Walkabout* (1970), directed by Nicholas Roeg, telling how a group of small children trek among the Aborigines to safety after their father kills himself in the desert.

Walk away from, To. To escape with one's life, as when literally walking away from a road accident (*see*

WALKING WOUNDED). Also, casually or irresponsibly to abandon a situation with which one is supposed to be involved.

Walkies! A command to a dog (and sometimes a human) to get ready for a walk. The word became enduringly and endearingly associated with the animal trainer Barbara Woodhouse (1910–88) following her popular television series of 1980 on the training of dogs. Similar commands such as 'Sit!' and 'Wait!' were not far behind.

Walkie-talkie. A small radio transmitter and receiver that can be carried on the person to enable one to talk as one walks. The term arose from West Indian speech in the 1930s as US army slang and passed into other languages, the French preferred form being *talkie-walkie*, pronounced 'tokiwoki'. A walkie-talkie is also a type of doll that can walk and talk. *See also* WALKMAN.

> Using a walkie-talkie a 'meeting-edge executive' in a red jacket will always be obtainable.
> *The Times* (1 December 1999)

Walking on two legs. In modern China the use of small-scale, local methods in production and education, as distinct from large-scale or capital-intensive ones. The term translates the Chinese original and first became current in English in the 1960s.

Walking wounded. A term originating in the First World War for casualties able to make their own way on foot to the treatment stations, not needing to be carried there on a stretcher.

Walkman. The name of a make of personal stereo popular from the 1980s, so called because it could be played while walking (or cycling) along the street or riding in public transport, supposedly without disturbing others. A tinny hiss or rhythmic 'tish-tish-tish' was audible outside its headset, however, and irritated many. The first SONY Walkman was on sale in the West in 1979.

Walk on the Wild Side. A novel (1956) by Nelson Algren (1909–81), which is set in New Orleans during the GREAT DEPRESSION. It reflects the author's preoccupation with the criminal underworld and poverty-stricken vagrants, whose experiences he investigated and shared as a journalist. There is an emphasis on alternative sexual lifestyles. A dreary film version was directed by Edward Dmytryk in 1962, the most memorable part of the movie being the opening

credits. Lou Reed's hit song 'Walk on the Wild Side' (1972) was an ode to the denizens of Andy Warhol's films of the 1960s.

Walk the talk, To. To suit one's actions to one's words. An Americanism dating from the 1980s.

> It's essential that those in authority walk the talk or they risk being pilloried by an increasingly incredulous public.
> *Sunday Times* (2 January 2000)

Walk the wards, To. To gain experience as a medical student by accompanying a doctor or surgeon on his rounds in a hospital. The expression is now somewhat dated. 'To walk the hospitals' was an earlier equivalent.

Wallace and Gromit. These two puppet characters, an inventor and cheese fanatic and his clever dog, were developed by Nick Park and Aardman Animations, and first appeared in 1990 as the stars of a number of animated films made by the Claymation process, in which moulded clay models are filmed in a 'stop-action' technique, with minute movements given to the models in between each shot.

Wall of death. A fairground or amusement park sideshow in which a motorcyclist uses gravitational force to ride round the inside walls of a vertical cylinder. The act is often performed blindfold. *See also* WHEEL OF DEATH.

Wallpaper. In a figurative sense anything that provides a bland or undemanding background to an activity, such as MUSIC WHILE YOU WORK. In computer jargon wallpaper is an optional background pattern or picture on the screen.

> [After midnight] Channel 5 went with [the film] Emmanuelle, while FilmFour had Last Tango in Paris. At least the last two had the honesty to admit that they were probably just wallpaper for what most of their viewers were actually doing.
> *Sunday Times* (2 January 2000)

Wall Street Crash. The collapse of prices on the New York Stock Exchange on BLACK THURSDAY, leading to the GREAT DEPRESSION.

Wall-to-wall. When it arose in the 1950s this expression originally applied to fitted carpets that covered a whole floor from one wall to another. From the 1960s the term gained a figurative sense to describe anything extensive or even excessive, whether numerically countable or not, such as 'wall-to-wall piped music' or 'wall-to-wall customers'.

> After eight years spent in retirement in Gascony, I am delighted to have exchanged wall-to-wall sunshine for this country [Britain] where liberty, common courtesies and healthcare are free.
>
> *The Times* (Letter to the Editor) (25 October 1999)

Wally. A term for a stupid or inept person, first current in the 1960s. There are various stories accounting for the name. One tells of a person who lost his dog named Wally at a GLASTONBURY FESTIVAL. The owner walked around calling 'Wally!' and his cry was taken up by the crowd. Over the next few years the habit of calling 'Wally!' became established at rock concerts during a lull in the proceedings, in the manner of a MEXICAN WAVE at a sports event.

Walrus moustache. A large moustache overhanging the lips and so resembling the drooping whiskers of a walrus. Such moustaches, now considered old-fashioned, were fairly common in the late 19th and early 20th century. An example appears in Bruce Bairnsfather's drawing of Old Bill (*see* BETTER 'OLE).

Walter Mitty. A fantasist who daydreams of achievements he could never realize in ordinary life and who in some cases may try to gain them by illicit means. He was the creation of the US writer James Thurber and appears in his short story *The Secret Life of Walter Mitty* (1939).

> City Walter Mitty gambles away partners' £20m nest egg.
>
> *Sunday Times* (headline) (9 May 1999)

Walter Plinge. *See* PLINGE, WALTER.

WAMPAS baby stars. The 13 young US film actresses who were selected annually from 1922 to 1934 by the Western Association of Motion Picture Advertisers (WAMPAS) for showing signs of promise. Among those who fulfilled such promise were Clara Bow, selected in 1924, Mary Astor, Joan Crawford, Janet Gaynor and Fay Wray (1926), Jean Arthur and Loretta Young (1929), Joan Blondell (1931) and Ginger Rogers (1932). 'Baby' is simply an affectionate if somewhat belittling descriptive, since many of the women were at least 20 when chosen and already established in their careers. The enterprise received much publicity and aroused considerable attention among film fans.

Wannabe. A fan of a celebrity who aims to emulate their idol, or more generally anyone who seeks fame.

The word represents '(I) want to be' and originated in the United States in the 1980s among white youths who dressed and behaved like members of black gangs. The term subsequently became specifically associated with the rock star Madonna, who early in her career had many emulators and LOOKALIKES.

> Today, wannabes, already-ams and have-beens compete to be noticed more for what they don't wear than what they do.
>
> *Sunday Times* (7 November 1999)

Want to make something of it? Do you want to fight over it? A ritual challenge of US origin that arose in the 1930s. It is less menacing than it seems since it gives the other the chance to back down. A folksy variant is: 'Wanna make sumpin' of it?'

War and peace pudding. An austerity substitute for Christmas pudding promoted in Canada in the First World War and by the Ministry of Food in Britain in the Second World War. It was made by mixing flour, breadcrumbs, suet, dried fruit, grated raw carrot and bicarbonate of soda, turning all into a well-greased pudding bowl, and boiling or steaming the result for at least two hours. The meaning of the name is obvious, with a pun also implied on 'pease pudding'.

War baby. A baby born in wartime, especially the illegitimate offspring of a serviceman.

War Between the Tates, The. A clever and funny campus novel (1974) by Alison Lurie (b.1926). The Tate family consists of Brian, the academic husband, Erica, the domestic (by his choice, not hers) wife and two loutish teenage children, whom Erica has grown to hate. The playing out of the conflicts between them has parallels with the advance of the New Feminism and the Vietnam War (1964–75). The title alludes to both the couple and the war while simultaneously punning on the 'War Between the States' as a synonym for the American Civil War.

> Now Erica turns her head. For a moment their eyes meet; then both look down. Erica knows that Brian knows what she is thinking about, and he knows she knows he knows. This mutual knowledge is like a series of infinitely disappearing, darkening ugly reflections in two opposite mirrors. ... So they say nothing. There is nothing to say.
>
> ch iii

War bride. A soldier's foreign bride, met as a result of wartime postings or operations.

War chest. Originally and literally a chest or strong-box containing funds with which to fight a war, but later in the 20th century funds set aside by a political party or company for a campaign of some kind. The term is of American origin.

The news that the Prime Minister is insisting he keeps the 'lid' on a supposed £10 million 'war chest' has enraged those who dreamed that the money might be spent on schools, roads, hospitals and all the other things which … we supposed it to be in the 'gift' of the politicians.

Evening Standard (27 September 1999)

Wardour Street. A street in central London that was formerly famous for its antique dealers but that from the 1930s has contained the offices of several film companies. The name is thus sometimes used allusively for the British film industry. Because some of the antique dealers specialized in imitation antiques, the term 'Wardour-Street English' came into vogue at the turn of the 20th century for pseudo-archaic English, as typically found in historical romances.

Warm-up man. A man who 'warms up' an audience before a show or programme, especially one that is to be televised or recorded for television, by amusing them or entertaining them so that they are 'thawed' and more receptive to the material to come. The term dates from the 1960s.

Junior Simpson was the warm-up man for a comedy show I saw filmed two years ago, and when he stopped, mid-joke, to let the filming continue, the whole audience complained.

Sunday Times (20 February 2000)

Warner Brothers. The famous US film production company takes its name from the brothers Harry (1881–1958), Jack (1892–1978), Sam (1887–1927) and Albert (1884–1967) Warner. They were of Polish origin and were the sons of Benjamin, of unknown surname, and Pearl Eichelbaum, who emigrated to the United States in the 1880s and changed the family name to Warner in 1907. Harry was the leading light, beginning his career by opening a NICKELODEON, the first of a chain, in New Castle, Pennsylvania, in 1905. He abandoned film distribution for production in 1912, and his first film of note was *My Four Years in Germany* (1917). He set up studios in HOLLYWOOD in 1918 and with the cooperation of his brothers and himself as president incorporated the business as Warner Brothers Pictures in 1923. He was president until 1956, when Jack took over until 1966. The firm produced the

first *Don Juan* film with a synchronized musical score (1926), the first 'talkie', *The Jazz Singer* (1927), the first full-length all-talking picture, *Lights of New York* (1928), and the first all-talking colour movie, *On With the Show* (1929).

War of attrition. A war in which each side seeks to wear the other out by unremitting harassment. The expression dates from the First World War.

War of nerves. A conflict that employs psychological techniques rather than physical violence. Typical ingredients of a war of nerves are propaganda, threats, false rumours and SABOTAGE, all calculated to demoralize the enemy. The expression dates from the early part of the Second World War.

War poets. A term for those poets who served in the armed forces in the First World War and who wrote about their experiences, often in realistic and harrowing terms. The greatest of their number were Wilfred Owen (1893–1918), Siegfried Sassoon (1886–1967), Robert Graves (1895–1985), Isaac Rosenberg (1890–1918) and Edmund Blunden (1896–1974). Their condemnation of war, with its wholesale carnage and final futility, was coupled with a desire to disabuse the public of the aura of glamour that surrounded war as a cause to be fought and won for the honour of one's country and oneself, if need be as an 'ultimate sacrifice'. Many of the war poets had also been Georgian poets (*see* GEORGIAN POETRY), and at first there was no incompatibility between the celebration of the English countryside and the patriotic sentiment of the early years of the war. When the latter gave way to grim realism, however, the two schools became sharply distinguished. The poems of Rupert Brooke (1887–1915), although often about war, were in contrast largely devoted to the theme of idealistic self-sacrifice and thus do not place him among the war poets as generally understood. *See also* DULCE ET DECORUM EST.

Warren Commission. The official commission of inquiry into the assassination of President John F. Kennedy, who was shot in Dallas, Texas, on 22 November 1963. The seven-man commission was headed by Earl Warren (1891–1974), chief justice of the Supreme Court. The inquiry's report was published on 27 September 1964 and concluded that Lee Harvey Oswald (1939–63) had been a lone assassin. Oswald was not available for comment, as he had been shot dead a few days after the assassination by night-club owner Jack Ruby (1911–67) while in police custody. Critics have pointed to a number of pieces of evidence that cast doubt on the Commission's conclusion (*see* GRASSY KNOLL), and conspiracy theorists have come up with a range of culprits, the favourites being the CIA and the Mafia. *See also* JFK; KENNEDY CURSE.

War Requiem. A sombre, anti-war choral work by Benjamin Britten (1913–76), which combines nine poems by the WAR POET Wilfred Owen (1893–1918) with the words of the Latin requiem mass. The work was performed in the new COVENTRY Cathedral in 1962, which replaced the medieval cathedral destroyed in a German bombing raid in 1940. Britten, a lifelong pacifist, saw it as a work of reconciliation, and at the first performance the soloists were Galina Vishnevskaya (a Russian), Dietrich Fischer-Dieskau (a German) and Peter Pears (a Briton). Stravinsky described the requiem as 'Kleenex music'.

Warsaw Concerto. The stirringly romantic musical score written by Richard Addinsell (1904–77) for the film *Dangerous Moonlight* (1941). The film centres on a Polish pianist who escapes from the NAZIS, flies with the Polish Air Force in the BATTLE OF BRITAIN and loses his memory. This romantic melodrama was a huge hit with wartime audiences.

Warsaw Pact. The treaty signed in Warsaw in 1955 between the Soviet Union and the eastern bloc countries of Albania, Bulgaria, Czechoslovakia, Hungary, East Germany, Poland and Romania as the Soviet response to NATO. The pledge of friendship and collaboration was annulled in 1991 following the dissolution of eastern bloc Communism.

Warsaw risings. Two uprisings against the NAZIS in Warsaw, the Polish capital, during the Second World War. The first uprising, in April–May 1943, was by the Jews who had been confined in a sealed ghetto since 1940. Perhaps 100,000 Jews had died from starvation and disease, and hundreds of thousands had been deported to extermination camps. On 19 April a large SS force set about clearing the ghetto to make the city 'Jew-free' by the next day, the FÜHRER's birthday. However, they met with unexpectedly strong resistance. Two Jewish underground military organizations were in operation in the ghetto: the Farband (Jewish Military Union) and the communist ZOB (Jewish Fighting Organization). After the first day's fighting the Germans were forced to retreat, but over the next 20 days they gradually fought their way across the

ghetto, until all but 100 or so of the 60,000 Jews in the ghetto were dead.

The second Warsaw rising, code-named Operation Burza (Polish, 'storm') and initiated by the Home Army (the Polish resistance), broke out on 1 August 1944. With the Red Army having reached the far bank of the River Vistula, the Polish commander, General Tadeusz Bór-Komorowski, assumed he would receive Soviet support once the uprising got under way. However, after the long summer offensive STALIN ordered his forces to recuperate. It is almost certain that he also saw a political advantage in allowing the Home Army to be destroyed, as this would eliminate any possibility of Polish resistance to future Soviet occupation. The Poles were initially successful and had taken most of Warsaw by 4 August. However, the German counterattack began on 10 August. Two months of bitter fighting followed, in which between 150,000 and 180,000 Poles died before Bór-Komorowski surrendered on 5 October. When the Red Army did eventually enter Warsaw they found it virtually razed to the ground.

War to end war. A naively optimistic term applied to the First World War. The phrase may have been suggested by H.G. Wells's *The War That Will End War* (1914), as a prelude to the 'World State' that he envisaged.

Wash and brush-up. In the literal sense, dating from the turn of the 20th century, a quick wash and tidying of one's hair. The phrase later gained a metaphorical sense for any figurative cleaning or cleansing, as of the removal of offensive passages from a literary work.

> The fairy-tales which survived 18th and 19th-century gentility to become popular classics all tended to get a good narrative wash and brush-up on the way, ending up as straightforward morality tales, with the rough edges smoothed away.
> *The Times* (3 January 2000)

Wash one's hands, To. One of many euphemisms for visiting the lavatory, in this case dating from the 1930s. The expression does at least preserve the etymological origin of 'lavatory', in Latin *lavare*, 'to wash', and such a visit often concludes with the washing of one's hands in any case.

Wasp. A middle- or upper-class American white Protestant, regarded as highly influential in society. The word is an acronym of *white Anglo-Saxon Protestant*, originally used in statistical and sociological studies of US ethnic groups in the 1960s and a term which was popularized by the Philadelphia historian and sociologist E. Digby Baltzell (1915–96). The suggestion of the name of the stinging insect is in all likelihood not coincidental, since such people can wield their power as a 'weapon'.

> Brooks Brothers is the natural habitat of the W.A.S.P. The image of the store is synonymous with the white, Anglo-Saxon Protestant male – a virile but wholesome species flourishing in middle America.
> *Independent* (12 March 1988)

Wasp Factory, The. The first novel (1984) by Iain Banks (b.1954) is a study of insanity, which veers between psychological acuity and grotesque fantasy. The central character, 16-year-old Frank, has already been responsible for three violent murders. He lives with his father on a remote Scottish island, where he constructs a 'wasp factory' out of an old clock face to which he has added various tunnels and compartments, each with a special significance. From time to time he introduces a live wasp into this, using the route it takes and the fate it suffers as a prediction of the future. If it enters the fire compartments, for example, this means there will be a fire; if it enters the water compartments, there will be a drowning. The whole device is, up to a point, symbolic of Frank's own identity, which is eventually revealed to be that of Frances, a girl.

Waste Land, The. A densely allusive poem (1922) by T.S. Eliot (1888–1965) that is now recognized as one of the landmarks of literary MODERNISM. The title, like the poem itself, expresses the sense of futility and disillusion that followed in the wake of the First World War. More specifically, it refers to an incident in the second book of Malory's *Le Morte d'Arthur*, in which the knight Balyn deals King Pellam the 'Dolorous Stroke' that causes the 'Waste Land', a disaster that devastates three kingdoms and whose effects can only be alleviated by the quest for the Holy Grail. Many lines from the poem have become familiar as quotations (and misquotations), including its opening words, 'April is the cruellest month' (*see* CRUELLEST MONTH), and

> When lovely woman stoops to folly and
> Paces about her room again, alone,
> She smoothes her hair with automatic hand,
> And puts a record on the gramophone.

It has also furnished titles for several subsequent literary works, including Evelyn Waugh's novel *A Handful of Dust* (1934) and Iain M. Banks's novel *Consider Phlebas* (1987). In the years following its publication, the poem attracted numerous admirers, including university undergraduates, who allegedly chanted it from college windows as an act of artistic rebellion:

> After luncheon he stood on the balcony with a megaphone which had appeared surprisingly among the bric-a-brac of Sebastian's room, and in languishing tones recited passages from The Waste Land to the sweatered and muffled throng that was on its way to the river.
> EVELYN WAUGH: *Brideshead Revisited* (1945)

Watchful waiting. The phrase used by President Woodrow Wilson in 1913 to describe his policy of non-recognition of the Mexican Government of General Huerta. It did not last long, since the Americans occupied Vera Cruz in 1914. The words had been previously used by President Jackson in 1836.

Watch it! Be careful! A warning to watch one's words or actions before going too far. The phrase dates from the early 20th century.

> When summoning Cecil Beaton to photograph the Queen in 1968, he [Lord Charteris] wrote: 'I am under the legal obligation to remind you that under the terms of the Copyright Act of 1956, the copyright of all photographs taken at the sittings belongs to the Queen. So watch it!'
> *The Times* (Obituary of Lord Charteris of Amisfield) (27 December 1999)

Watch someone's back, To. To look after or protect them. A phrase dating from the 1950s.

> Robert Downey Jr recruits inmates to watch his back while he does time in America's deadliest jail.
> *heat* (23–29 September 1999)

Watch someone's smoke, To. To observe their activity; to see where they are going or what they are up to. The allusion is to a railway engine, whose passage in the days of steam could be followed by its smoke. The phrase usually occurs in the form 'Watch my smoke!' The expression is of US origin and dates from the turn of the 20th century.

Watch this space! Be alert for more news on this topic. The reference is properly to the section of a newspaper page that is reserved for a particular purpose, and especially for an advertisement, although the phrase is also used as a hint that more on a topic may follow in a later edition.

> It remains to be seen whether [rock musician Courtney] Love will shave her head. Watch this space.
>
> *The Times* (1 January 2000)

Watch with Mother. A highly regarded television series for pre-school children, running from 1950 to 1980. It soon settled into a regular routine of stories and puppets for each day of the week, with *Picture Book* on Monday, ANDY PANDY on Tuesday, *The Flowerpot Men* on Wednesday, *Rag, Tag and Bobtail* on Thursday and *The Woodentops* on Friday. Later contents were rather more varied. *See also* LISTEN WITH MOTHER; WOODENTOP.

Watergate. In the United States an area of flats and offices beside the River Potomac, Washington, D.C., which gave its name to a major political scandal. An illegal bugging attempt was made by Republicans at the Watergate headquarters of the Democratic Party during the 1972 elections, and this was followed by attempts to cover up the affair. The subsequent resignation and prosecution of senior White House officials and further evidence of corruption eventually led to the resignation of the Republican President Richard Nixon (1913–94, President 1968–74) when threatened with impeachment. *See also* ALL THE PRESIDENT'S MEN; DEEP THROAT; GATE; MAXIMUM JOHN; SMOKING GUN; TRICKY DICKY.

Watering hole. A pool where animals drink, or, in human terms, a favourite pub or bar. The latter sense dates from the 1970s.

> The 'Jampot' [Jamaica Wine House], one of the City's best-known watering-holes.
>
> *The Times* (29 December 1994)

Waterland. A regional novel (1983) by Graham Swift (b.1949), distinguished by its remarkably atmospheric evocation of the East Anglian Fens (Waterland) and for a technically intricate but skilfully handled plot involving incest, abortion and murder. Its central character, a history teacher, sets aside the syllabus and embarks on a historical and social survey of the Fens. Into this he weaves the dark details of his own family history and of himself and his wife. A glumly melodramatic film version (1992), starring Jeremy Irons, was directed by Stephen Gyllenhaal.

Waterloo. The irresistibly effervescent song (written by Benny Andersson, Stig Anderson and Björn Ulvaeus), with which the Swedish pop group Abba, clad in garb that hinted more than a little at the style of GLAM ROCK, won the EUROVISION SONG CONTEST in 1974. The song, which dramatically equates the lovelorn subordination of a besotted lover with the final defeat of Napoleon Bonaparte at the battle of Waterloo in 1815, is memorable for its thunderous piano chords, catchy melody, abysmal rhymes ('the history book on the shelf, is always repeating itself') and the group's audibly Scandinavian pronunciation of the song's English lyrics. It launched a career that would confer cult and gay-icon status on the Swedish foursome. *See also* ROCK GROUP NAMES.

Waterloo Sunset. A song about loneliness and isolation by the pop group the Kinks, released in 1967 and written by Ray Davies, in which the singer observes the world from his window. The song was originally intended to be entitled 'Liverpool Sunset', but 'Waterloo Sunset' was chosen because Davies had walked over Waterloo Bridge in London several times a week on his way to art school. The song appeared on the album *Something Else*.

Watershed. A media term for the time, usually understood as 9 p.m., after which television programmes regarded as unsuitable for children are broadcast. Complaints are sometimes made about unsuitable material transmitted 'before the watershed'. *See also* FAMILY HOUR.

> Scenes of a Valentine's Day killing on *EastEnders* were too graphic and macabre to be shown before the 9pm watershed, the Broadcasting Standards Commission ruled yesterday.
>
> *The Times* (27 May 1999)

Watership Down. An immensely popular animal novel (1972) by Richard Adams (b.1920). It concerns a community of rabbits who set out in search of a new home on the downs when their Berkshire warren is destroyed by construction workers, and can also be read as a political or environmental allegory. Adams created a complete world and convincing speech for his animal characters, particularly memorable among whom are HAZEL, Fiver and Bigwig. The title is the name of a part of the downs near Whitchurch, Hampshire, where Adams lives. A two-dimensional (in every sense) cartoon film version (1978) was directed by Tony Guy.

Watford. This Hertfordshire town, 26km (16 miles) northwest of London, is popularly reckoned to mark the outer limit of urban-based civilization, so that everything and everybody 'north of Watford' are in a supposed cultural wilderness. Watford was itself presumably chosen for this key role as it lies on the M1, the main thoroughfare to London. This Watford is sometimes confused, especially by non-motorists, with the Watford Gap, which is a service station, also on the M1, but north of Daventry in Northamptonshire. It lies in a broad valley at the northern end of the Cotswolds at the point where road, rail and canal routes run in parallel through the hills. It also has a 'border' role, and is sometimes regarded as the southern boundary of the Midlands.

> City types who would not usually dream of venturing north of Watford were yesterday falling over each other in their scramble to join in the excitement and buy a little piece of Knutsford.
>
> *The Times* (4 November 1999)

Watkinsland. An island off Latin America, or perhaps part of its mainland, as the imaginary setting of Doris Lessing's novel *Briefing for a Descent into Hell* (1971). It is named after Charles Watkins, a Cambridge professor of classics, who according to his own account was brought here by a porpoise after being shipwrecked in the South Atlantic. Watkinsland is peopled with various strange creatures, including a huge bird, a species of chimpanzee and a 'rat-dog', with the head of a monkey, coat of a dog and tail of a rat. Travellers are generally advised to proceed with caution.

Wave of the future. The inevitable future fashion or trend; the coming thing. The expression was popularized by the title of Anne Morrow Lindbergh's book *The Wave of the Future: A Confession of Faith* (1940), advocating that the advance of fascism should not be resisted.

Waves. Until 1942 the women's section of the US Naval Reserve or, since 1948, of the US Navy. The name is formed by the initial letters of Women Accepted for Volunteer Emergency Service.

Wave the flag, To. *See* SHOW THE FLAG.

Wavy Navy. The popular name for the former Royal Naval Volunteer Reserve (RNVR), whose officers wore gold distinction lace made in wavy lines instead of straight, as worn on the sleeves of regular officers belonging to the 'Straight Navy'. The RNVR lost its separate existence, after a fine wartime record, in 1957, when it was combined with the Royal Naval Reserve (RNR). *See also* WAVES; WRENS.

Wayne's World. *See* NOT!

Way off beam. Wholly incorrect; altogether on the wrong track. The phrase originated in the US Air Force in the Second World War, the allusion being to radio beams that guide aircraft.

> [Conservative culture spokesman Peter] Ainsworth said any suggestion that the series showed [BBC director-general Greg] Dyke was buttering up the Tory party would be 'way off beam'.
>
> *Sunday Times* (27 February 2000)

Way-out. Unusual; eccentric; avant-garde. A term that gained popularity in the SWINGING SIXTIES. 'Way-in' soon followed to mean 'conventional' or 'sophisticated'.

Way to go! Well done! A US exclamation of approval and encouragement, originally to athletes. It is short for 'That's the right way to go' and was first current in the 1940s, when it is said to have been coined for the film *Knute Rockne* (1940) (*see* GIPPER).

Wear another hat, To. To function in a different role or position. The allusion is to headgear worn for different occupations. The form of the phrase is variable, so that one can 'wear a different hat', 'wear two hats' and so on. The concept dates from the 1960s and arose as civil service jargon.

> Wearing his new 'economic overlord' hat the Prime Minister [Harold Wilson] summoned three key figures to Downing Street today.
>
> *Evening Standard* (29 August 1967)

We Are Making a New World. The stark painting by Paul Nash (1889–1946) has become as iconic of the wastefulness of war as the poems of Wilfred Owen or Siegfried Sassoon. After being injured in the First World War, Nash became an official war artist (a role he took on again in the Second World War). The title of this painting is heavily ironic: a low pale sun radiates tenuous beams of light over a shattered landscape of craters and splintered trees. The work, which dates from 1918, hangs in the Imperial War Museum, London. *See also* TOTES MEER.

Wear the trousers, To. To dominate. Said of a woman, and especially a wife, who assumes a domineering household role that was formerly believed to belong to the husband (who normally wears trousers). The expression dates from the 1930s. *See also* HER INDOORS.

Weary Willie and Tired Tim. A phrase still sometimes used for a pair of loafers or idlers. The names are those of two comical tramps, one fat, one thin, created by the cartoonist Tom Browne in 1896 for the weekly

Illustrated Chips. Their adventures continued on the front page of this paper until it ceased publication in 1953.

Weasel words. Words of convenient ambiguity, or a statement from which the original meaning has been sucked or retracted. Theodore Roosevelt popularized the term by using it in a speech in 1916 when criticizing President Wilson. A quotation from the speech provides a good example: 'You can have universal training, or you can have voluntary training, but when you use the word *voluntary* to qualify the word *universal*, you are using a weasel word; it has sucked all the meaning out of *universal*. The two words flatly contradict one another.'

Roosevelt was indebted to a story by Stewart Chaplin, 'Stained-glass Political Platform', which appeared in the *Century Magazine* in June 1900, and in which occurs the sentence: 'Why, weasel words are words that suck the life out of the words next to them, just as a weasel sucks the egg and leaves the shell.'

Weathermen. A terrorist group that evolved in 1969 from the US student organization Students for a Democratic Society, best known for its activity in the 1960s against the VIETNAM War. The Weathermen were the most radical of the factions, vowing to 'lead white kids into armed revolution'. They took their name from a line in Bob Dylan's song 'Subterranean Homesick Blues' (1965): 'You don't need a weatherman to know which way the wind blows.'

Wedgie. A nickname of the Labour politician Anthony Wedgwood Benn (b.1925), who in egalitarian fashion renounced his title of 2nd viscount Stansgate in 1963, and trimmed his name down to Tony Benn in the 1970s. He was minister for technology (1966–70), for industry (1974–5) and for energy (1975–9), since when he has been a prominent figure on the left of the party, generally opposing the leadership. His left-wing views have also earned him the hostile nickname Loony Benn (after 'loony bin', slang for a mental hospital). *See also* LOONY LEFT.

Wee Frees. A disparaging nickname for the minority of the Free Church of Scotland who in 1900 refused to unite with the United Presbyterian Church to form the United Free Church, which itself reunited with the Church of Scotland in 1929. The vestigial Free Church of Scotland, which is sternly Sabbatarian, remains strong in some parts of the Highlands and Islands.

Weekend warrior. A term for a person who engages in a part-time activity, whether literally at the weekend or not. The use of 'warrior' implies that the activity may be fairly strenuous.

> Don't be a 'weekend warrior'. If your job is sedentary, you must exercise a little in the week as well as at the weekend or the shock to your body could lead to strains and injuries.
> *The Times* (3 January 2000)

Week is a long time in politics. An epigram attributed to the Labour prime minister Harold Wilson (1916–95), and said to have been uttered by him on more than one occasion in the 1960s, the first time to lobby correspondents just after the 1964 general election. It has been taken to imply that politicians' policies and principles change with circumstances, and/or that unpopular actions are rapidly forgotten by the electorate. Wilson himself claimed that he meant that politicians, and the public, should take a longer term view than they normally do.

Wehrmacht (German, 'Defensive Force'). The German armed forces, and especially the army, from 1921 to the end of the Second World War.

Weight Watchers. An organization, in full Weight Watchers International Inc., founded in the United States in 1961 to promote dieting as a means of slimming and serving a similar purpose for compulsive eaters to that provided by ALCOHOLICS ANONYMOUS for compulsive drinkers.

Weimar Republic. The German federal republic established under the constitution of 1919, which lasted until it was overthrown by Hitler in 1933. It was so called from the Thuringian town, particularly associated with Goethe, where the constitution was adopted by the National Assembly. *See also* SPARTACISTS.

Weird and wacky. Unusual; eccentric; WAY-OUT. An epithet for any unconventional person or 'free spirit'. The phrase is of American origin and is a variant on the older 'weird and wonderful'.

> She studied drama at Bristol University, where fellow students remember her as 'weird and wacky. A bit of a hippy at heart'.
> *The Times* (11 November 1999)

Weirdstone of Brisingamen, The. This fantasy for children (1960; in USA as *The Weirdstone*) was the first novel by Alan Garner (b.1934). It is subtitled *A Tale of Alderley*, meaning Alderley Edge, the Cheshire village where Garner was born and from where the tradition of the story emanates. The story concerns the lost weirdstone, a piece of crystal shaped like a raindrop, which resurfaces in a bracelet, and involves two children with the Wizard of Alderley and his struggle against the forces of evil. A sequel, *The* MOON OF GOMRATH, was published in 1963.

Welcome mat. To put down the welcome mat for someone is to make them feel wanted or at home, especially after a period of absence away or a time when they were out of favour. The reference is to the doormat at the entrance to a house, which may actually have the word 'welcome' on it.

> Hague puts down welcome mat for Ken [Clarke].
> *Sunday Express* (headline) (27 February 2000)

Welfare state. A term applied to Britain after the implementation of the BEVERIDGE REPORT, providing for social security services for sickness, unemployment, retirement and the like, and essentially based on the National Insurance Act of 1946. The system depends on compulsory contributions and taxation and was built up on the less sweeping Liberal legislation of 1908–14. Many features were dismantled from 1979 under successive Conservative governments.

Well endowed. Having noticeably large genitals (of a man) or breasts (of a woman). The telling euphemism dates from the 1940s.

> Police hunting a naked swimmer … released security camera pictures in the hope that someone might recognize his 'distinctive features'. Detective Inspector Paul Chapman said of the intruder … 'He is extremely well-endowed.'
> *Sunday Times* (20 February 2000)

Well of Loneliness, The. A novel (1928) by Radclyffe Hall (pseudonym of Marguerite Radclyffe-Hall; 1880–1943). This study of lesbian love, written by a lesbian partly to demonstrate the isolation of those of similar sexuality, was banned in Britain for many years and finally published in a small, high-priced edition in a plain cover. Its heroine is the 'invert', Stephen Gordon, who is obliged to release her lovers to a conventional world while she herself remains trapped inside a 'well of loneliness'.

Welsh Windbag. A media nickname for the Welsh politician Neil Kinnock (b.1942), LABOUR PARTY leader from 1983 to 1992, alluding to his perceived verbosity and garrulousness. *See also* KINNOCKIO.

Welsh Wizard. (1) A nickname of the Liberal politician David Lloyd George (1863–1945). As chancellor of the exchequer (1908–15) he laid the foundations of the

WELFARE STATE and produced the PEOPLE'S BUDGET of 1909, and as prime minister (1916–22) he led Britain to a hard-won and costly victory in the First World War. The nickname referred to his powers as an orator and his inventive mind, while his enemies identified in him the supposedly pagan and magical qualities of cunning, deviousness and a lack of principles. Margot Asquith (1864–1945) observed, 'He couldn't see a belt without hitting below it,' and John Maynard Keynes (1883–1946) somewhat mysteriously stated, 'When he's alone in a room, there's nobody there.' *See also* LG.

(2) The nickname Welsh Wizard was also applied to the Welsh footballer Billy Meredith (1875–1958), likening his mercurial gifts to those of his famous countryman. The analogy was stated even more explicitly in one of Meredith's other nicknames, the Lloyd George of Welsh Football. He was also known as the Prince of Wingers.

Wendy. This girl's name was the invention of J.M. Barrie for his play PETER PAN. The poet and playwright W.E. Henley (1849–1903) was a friend of Barrie and used to address him as 'Friend'. Henley's young daughter, Margaret, copied this but pronounced the word 'Fwend' and duplicated it childishly as 'Fwendy-Wendy'. The latter half of this gave the name of Wendy Darling in the play. It soon caught on generally, as for the actresses Wendy Barrie (1912–78), Wendy Hiller (b.1912) and Wendy Toye (b.1917). Wendy Barrie, born Marguerite Wendy Jenkins, was Barrie's goddaughter and was named by him. She later took his surname as her stage name.

Wendy house. A toy house large enough for children to play in. It takes its name from the house built around the little girl WENDY Darling in J.M. Barrie's play PETER PAN. In prison slang 'wendy house' is the period of the day and the place in which prisoners are allowed to socialize.

We shall not be moved. The title of a labour and civil rights hymn of 1931, adapted from an earlier anonymous gospel hymn or spiritual. The words evoke a biblical verse: 'God is in the midst of her; she shall not be moved: God shall help her, and that right early' (Psalm 46:5).

We shall overcome. The title of a song originating from before the American Civil War (1861–5) and adopted for a hymn of 1901 by the Methodist minister C. Albert Tindley entitled 'I'll Overcome Some Day'. It was revived in 1946 as a protest song by black tobacco workers on picket lines in Charleston, South

Carolina, and again during the black civil rights campaign of 1963.

West Bank. A region on the west bank of the River Jordan, populated by Arabs and a base of Palestinian resistance since its capture by the Israelis in 1967. It was first taken by Jordan in 1948. Negotiations for the withdrawal of Israeli troops from Arab areas of the West Bank were settled by an agreement between Israel and the PLO in 1995 although the implementation of this to the satisfaction of both sides continued to remain a sticking point. *See also* GAZA STRIP.

Western. A distinct genre of film or novel in which life in the American West of the latter half of the 19th century is portrayed. The situations are usually formulaic and the characters stereotyped, with gun fights and cowboys predominant, but the genre nevertheless came to embody America's cultural history and helped to shape the nation's image of itself. It is the Western of the cinema rather than the novel that has become the most familiar, and its world has been additionally popularized through the medium of COUNTRY MUSIC. *See also* MAGNIFICENT SEVEN; STAGECOACH; WILD BUNCH.

Western Approaches. A mainly maritime name for the area of sea immediately to the west of the British Isles, and in particular for the western end of the English Channel. Admiral Sir Reginald Tupper was appointed Commander-in-Chief, Western Approaches, Queenstown, in 1919 and the name became familiar to many in the Second World War from the speeches of Winston Churchill and from radio news bulletins and newspaper reports. The film *Western Approaches* (1944), played to great documentary effect by men of the Allied navies, was a fictional story, telling how torpedoed merchantmen in the Atlantic were used by a U-BOAT as a decoy.

Western Front. The general term for the front in Belgium and northern France in both world wars. Erich Maria Remarque's anti-war novel *Im Westen nichts Neues* (1929), literally 'Nothing new in the west', became familiar in English translation as ALL QUIET ON THE WESTERN FRONT. The title was an ironic reproduction of a phrase repeatedly used in official communiqués relating to operations in France and Flanders.

Westland affair. A major political row during the Conservative administration of Margaret Thatcher, centring on the Westland helicopter company at Yeovil in Somerset. Michael Heseltine, then defence minister, favoured a rescue bid by a European consortium, but was opposed by Leon Brittan, trade and industry secretary, who sided with the Westland directors in preferring a deal with the US firm of Sikorski. In January 1986 Heseltine caused a sensation by resigning in the middle of a cabinet meeting when Mrs Thatcher insisted that ministerial statements on the affair should be approved by the Cabinet Office. A letter critical of Heseltine was subsequently leaked from the solicitor general. By the end of the month Brittan had also resigned, admitting he had approved the leak. The opposition claimed that the leak must have been ordered at a higher level, by the prime minister herself, but she stated that she had not been informed of the matter. The deal with Sikorski went through, and five years later Heseltine mounted a challenge for the Conservative leadership, starting a chain of events that brought Mrs Thatcher's premiership to an end in 1990.

West Side Story. The much performed musical by Leonard Bernstein (1918–90) has lyrics by Stephen Sondheim (b.1930). It was first staged in 1957. The story is an updated version of *Romeo and Juliet* set in New York's West Side dockland area, with the Montagues and Capulets replaced by rival teenage gangs, the Sharks and the Jets. The rivalry erupts into violence as a result of the love between Tony, one of the Jets, and Maria, the sister of the leader of the Sharks. The 1961 film version won an OSCAR for best picture.

West Wall (German *Westwall*). The extension of the SIEGFRIED LINE defences on Germany's western frontier, constructed following an order by Hitler in August 1944, as a belated part of his FORTRESS EUROPE. The West Wall incorporated parts of the MAGINOT LINE and was also built along the German North Sea coast between Denmark and the Netherlands.

Wet behind the ears. Inexperienced; naive; as innocent as a newborn child. When young animals are born, the last place to become dry after birth is the small depression behind each ear. The figurative expression dates from the 1920s.

> We are forever being told that we are on to a cushy number, jetting off to make films about the beaches of Goa or Mayan civilization. ... When I was a wet-behind-the-ears production secretary ten years ago it was a bit like that.
> *The Times* (23 July 1999)

Wets. This 19th-century term for a weak or spineless person, familiar from the talk of middle-class prep schoolboys, took on a new edge in the summer of 1979 when it came to be applied to members of Margaret Thatcher's Conservative cabinet and party who were opposed to the hard-line monetarist policies then being espoused. Many of those so dubbed actively embraced the name. Those who deviated less sharply from the line were known as Dries.

We Two Boys Together Clinging. This early painting by David Hockney (b.1937) dates from 1961. The homoerotic subject is executed in Hockney's distinctive early Pop art style (*see also* I SAW IN LOUISIANA A LIVE-OAK GROWING). Hockney himself has written about the painting in *David Hockney by David Hockney* (1976):

> We Two Boys Together Clinging is from Walt Whitman:
>
> > We two boys together clinging,
> > One the other never leaving …
> > Arm'd and fearless, eating, drinking, sleeping, loving.
>
> The emphasis of the painting is on 'clinging'; not only are the arms clinging but small tentacles help keep the bodies close together as well. At the time of the painting I had a newspaper clipping on the wall with the headline 'TWO BOYS CLING TO CLIFF ALL NIGHT'. There were also a few pictures of Cliff Richard pinned up nearby, although the headline was actually referring to a Bank Holiday mountaineering accident.

We wuz robbed! We've been cheated! The saying is attributed to the US boxing manager Joe Jacobs following Jack Sharkey's win on points over the German world heavyweight champion Max Schmeling, of whom Jacobs was manager, in the heavyweight title fight of 21 June 1932.

Wexford, Inspector. The rural police inspector, with full name Reginald Wexford, who appears in a series of detective novels by Ruth Rendell, starting with *From Doon with Death* (1965), in which he investigates gruesome murders in the sleepy country town of Kingsmarkham. He was memorably portrayed by George Baker in a television series based on the stories with the overall title *The Ruth Rendell Mysteries* (1987–92).

W.G. The nickname of the prodigiously bearded Gloucestershire and England cricketer Dr William Gilbert Grace (1848–1915), who single-handedly invented modern batsmanship. He was also known as the Doctor and the Champion.

Whaam! One of several paintings of jet fighters in action executed in enlarged comic-book style by Roy Lichtenstein (1923–97), the Peter Pan of POP ART. *Whaam!*, which dates from 1963, includes the words 'I pressed the fire control … and ahead of me rockets blazed through the sky … '. This results in the 'Whaam!' of the title as the enemy fighter explodes in flames. Similar works by Lichtenstein include *Blam* (1962). He also had a gentler side, and in such works as *Good Morning, Darling* (1964) drew on teenage romances for his inspiration. Hans Richter, the old Dadaist, recalled a conversation with Lichtenstein: 'His little son's schoolfellows asked him what his father was. An artist? What kind of artist? An abstract expressionist! Oh, said the children, somebody who paints abstracts because he's no good at drawing. Lichtenstein Junior came home crying and told his father he couldn't draw. Lichtenstein Senior assured him that this wasn't true and drew him a great big Mickey Mouse, just like in the comic strips. This didn't satisfy him: his father had to prove that he could draw people too. So Papa L. drew him a big George Washington in comic-strip style. That satisfied him! But the strange thing was that not only L. Junior, but L. Senior too, liked it.'

Wham, bam, thank you ma'am. A US encapsulation of an act of sexual intercourse performed perfunctorily and without compassion. The expression arose among US servicemen in the Second World War and may have been originally adopted from cowboy parlance.

What do you know? A US expression of surprise dating from the early years of the 20th century, as: 'Hey, what do you know? Steve's gotten himself a new car!'

What gives? What's the news? What's happening? An expression of US origin dating from the 1940s. Hence 'What gives with … ?' naming a person or thing, as: 'What gives with the bike?', i.e. 'How is the bike going?' The phrase probably derives from Yiddish *vi geht's?* 'how goes it?' (German *wie geht's?*) *See also* WHAT'S WITH?

What planet are you on? Didn't you know that? Do you really think that? A question put to someone clearly out of touch with reality, as if inhabiting a different planet from Earth. The concept can be variously expressed.

> 'The upper-class people are the multimillionaire people who … are such a strata [*sic*] above what I

have experienced in life as to be on a different planet.'

ERIC JACOBS and ROBERT WORCESTER: *We British*, ch xiii (1990)

What's My Line? One of the first British television panel games, originally screened from 1951 to 1963 and featuring some of Britain's earliest television personalities as its regular panellists: Lady Isobel Barnett (1918–81), David Nixon (1919–78), Gilbert Harding (1907–60) and Barbara Kelly (b.1924). The panel, chaired by Eamonn Andrews (1922–87), posed oblique questions to establish the occupation of each guest contestant. The programme was revived in 1973–4 and 1984–90.

What's that in aid of? What is the point of that? What is that all about? A stock query dating from the 1930s. The phrase 'in aid of', meaning 'in support of', is much older.

What's that supposed to mean? What is the exact sense of that? The question is usually put when a spoken word or phrase could have a critical or derogatory sense. A typical interchange might thus be: 'You're not exactly free of suspicion, are you?' 'What's that supposed to mean?'

What's with? What's the matter with? What's the reason for? A US phrase enquiring about something, as: 'What's with the hurry?' ('Why the hurry?') or 'What's with that guy?' ('What's wrong with that person?'). The phrase is also expanded to 'What is it with?' *See also* WHAT GIVES?

What is it with the super-rich? They rarely look as if life is worth living.

The Times (Letter to the Editor) (24 June 1999)

What's your poison? What would you like to drink? Alcohol actually is a poison, so the expression is not quite the euphemism it appears to be.

What the Butler Saw. A farcical comedy (1969) by the British playwright Joe Orton (1933–67) in which life in an asylum run by psychiatrist Dr Prentice is greatly disrupted by the errors and confusions arising from a range of sexual improprieties involving Prentice, his wife and sundry other characters. The title refers to the naughty seaside 'peepshow' machines, which often bore the legend 'What the Butler Saw'.

Wheeler-dealer. A person who 'wheels and deals'. 'Wheel' has its sense in the US expression BIG WHEEL. Hence one of great influence in a particular field (usually business or politics), a shrewd and influential operator and manipulator.

Wheelie. A stunt whereby the front wheel of a bicycle or motorcycle is lifted off the ground while being ridden.

Wheelie bin. A large refuse bin on wheels. Both the term and the object are of Australian origin, and the bins were first in use in Britain in the 1980s.

Wheel of death. A hazardous circus act, in which a performer spins in and on a large 'hamster wheel' as it is gradually lowered to the ground from a 15m (50ft) high wire. *See also* WALL OF DEATH.

The circus acrobat who fell to his death in front of hundreds of spectators was killed performing the same 'wheel of death' act that crippled his brother 18 months ago.

The Times (28 December 1994)

Wheel someone in or **on, To.** To introduce a person to a meeting, debate or broadcast programme simply to provide impersonal backing or to support an uncontroversial argument. The image is of wheeling in a dummy figure who can be manipulated accordingly.

The early news break meant that by the time Andrew Neil went on air … there had been plenty of time to wheel in the sort of guests who could flesh out the story and keep it moving.

The Times (27 November 1999)

Whelk stall. To say that someone could not even run a whelk stall is to indicate their complete organizational incompetence. The reason for the choice of this particular trade is uncertain, but as whelk stalls are normally found at seaside resorts the implication may be that little effort or expertise is required to make ready money from happy holidaymakers.

The leadership of Europe's most dynamic city is being fought between a tabloid novelist, a lobbyist with a taste for polygamy and a jokester who could not even run a whelk stall.

The Times (15 September 1999)

Wheneye. A slang term for a self-centred person who is forever reminiscing or recounting tales or experiences of past times, frequently with the opening words 'When I …'. The implication is usually that the speaker can outdo the (unwilling) listener.

When Harry Met Sally. A film comedy (1989), written by Nora Ephron, about a man and a woman (played by Billy Crystal and Meg Ryan) whose relationship changes over a number of years from antipathy to friendship and finally love. Remembered primarily for the much-imitated but never equalled restaurant scene in which Meg Ryan noisily demonstrates her skill at faking an orgasm, the film was originally to have been titled *It Had To Be You*, but this was dropped when it was discovered that another movie was being made with that title. Another suggestion was *Boy Meets Girl*.

I'll have what she's having.

ESTELLE REINER: as a diner at the restaurant

When push comes to shove. When it comes down to it; when matters become critical. If a simple push does not produce results, one must resort to a more forceful shove. The allusion may be specifically to rugby where, in a scrum, the opposing forwards huddle over the ball, trying to push each other off it in order to kick it out to their team-mates. When this 'push' comes to (becomes) 'shove', the game is under way. The expression is of US origin and dates from the 1950s.

The suspicion that [composer Percy] Grainger is, when push comes to shove, not really that important, still lingers.

Times Literary Supplement (6 August 1999)

When the balloon goes up. When the action starts; when the trouble begins. The expression dates from the First World War, when the artillery sent up a balloon as a signal for gunners to open fire, using this visual method as one more reliable than a courier or the field telephone.

When the fat lady sings. When everything is finally over. The expression implies that further action is still possible. Among the many variant full forms of the phrase one of the most recent and familiar is that quoted by Dan Cook in the *Washington Post* of 2 June 1978: 'The opera ain't over till the fat lady sings.' The reference is to the final act of the opera, in which the heroine often appears and then dies. Opera singers tend to be endowed with figures as full as their voices.

Where Angels Fear to Tread. A novel (1905) by E.M. Forster (1879–1970), the inspiration for which was a piece of gossip, overheard while he was in Italy, about an English tourist who formed a *mésalliance* with an Italian. The plot centres on the efforts of the members of an English family to 'rescue', from his Italian father, the baby whose mother, related to them by a former marriage, has died in childhood. The title is from

Alexander Pope (1688–1744): 'For Fools rush in where Angels fear to tread' (*An Essay on Criticism*, 1711). A disappointing film version (1991) was directed by Charles Sturridge.

Where Eagles Dare. A thriller (1967) by Alistair Maclean (1922–87). Seven men and a young woman are parachuted on to the side of a mountain in Germany in the Second World War. Their mission is to infiltrate themselves into an apparently inaccessible and impregnable castle on the heights, in which a US general in being held for questioning after an air crash. A predictable film version (1969) of the 'schoolboy adventure' type was directed by Brian G. Hutton.

Where it's at. The real thing; the true state of affairs. The phrase is typically applied to a centre of fashionable activity, where it is desirable to be seen.

Sydney is where it's at, the place to see if you are a sightseer, and the place to write about if you are a writer.

Sunday Times (8 August 1999)

Where's the beef? Where is the substance in what you say? The phrase has its origin in a television commercial first screened in the United States on 9 January 1984 by the Wendy International hamburger chain. In this, an outraged old lady, patronizing a non-Wendy establishment that served buns with salad and little else, demanded of the manager: 'Where's the beef?' The words were subsequently taken up by Walter Mondale in a televised debate with Gary Hart from Atlanta on 11 March that year: 'When I hear your new ideas I'm reminded of that ad, "Where's the beef?"'

Where's the fire? What's the hurry? Why are you going so fast? The phrase dates from the 1920s.

'Where's the fire, dear boy?' he drawled. 'Do we really have to run for it?'

J.F. STRAKER: *Final Witness*, ch xvi (1963)

Where the action is. In the centre of some important or fashionable activity; WHERE IT'S AT.

Whiffenpoofs. This was the name of a famous band of 'gentlemen songsters' at Yale University early in the 20th century, made up of the best singers in the senior class. Their key piece was 'The Whiffenpoof Song', with words by two Yalemen, Meade Minnigerode and Guy S. Pomeroy, that were a part-parody of Rudyard Kipling's poem 'Gentlemen-Rankers' from his *Barrack Room Ballads* (1892). The music was by Guy H. Scull of Harvard in an adaptation by Tod B. Galloway of Amherst. The song itself was composed in 1909 and took its name from the Whiffenpoof, an imaginary fish in Victor Herbert's operetta *Little Nemo* (1908). The Whiffenpoofs still exist, although now their number is limited to 14 seniors.

Whilst. An alternative form of 'while', dating from medieval times and found in Shakespeare but in modern usage favoured in official documents, letters to the press and the like as bearing a greater degree of formality than its common equivalent. It mostly occurs in the sense 'although' or 'whereas' rather than 'during the time that', and the following opening sentences of letters to the *The Times* (11 August 1999) are typical of the usage: 'Whilst I hold no brief for new Labour …', 'Whilst I agree that "The Church is people, not old stones" …'.

Whirlybird. A US nickname for a helicopter, dating from the 1950s. The colloquialism linguistically mirrors the standard word, which translates literally from the Greek as 'spiral wing'.

Whisky Galore. A novel (1947) by Compton Mackenzie (born Edward Montague Compton; 1883–1972). Said by him to be based loosely on the wreck of the SS *Cabinet Minister* off Eriskay with a cargo of whisky, it is a satire on Scottish life, manners, religion and superstitions, whose starting point is a wreck in similar circumstances during a grave shortage during the Second World War of *uisge beatha* (water of life). A wonderful film version (1948), fast paced and excellently acted, was directed by Alexander Mackendrick.

Whispering campaign. A deliberate dissemination of derogatory rumours about someone, specifically a candidate for political election. The expression is of American origin and dates from the 1920s.

> [Ramón] Pajares's job [as managing director] was made even more difficult by the fact that he had to face a nasty whispering campaign that was, at times, little short of racist in tone.
> *The Times* (3 January 2000)

Whispering Death. A nickname for the Jamaica, West Indies, Lancashire and Derbyshire cricketer Michael Holding (b.1954). A fast bowler, his smooth and silent run-up produced deliveries of terrifying velocity. He is particularly remembered for an over bowled in 1981 to the England opening batsman Geoffrey Boycott (a master of defensive play), in which he defeated Boycott with a succession of unplayable balls before clean bowling him.

Whistle-blower. A person who informs on someone who is engaged in an illicit activity. *See also* BLOW THE WHISTLE ON.

> Some of Britain's biggest train companies are refusing to back plans for a national 'whistle-blower' scheme allowing staff to report safety defects confidentially.
> *The Times* (22 October 1999)

Whistle Down the Wind. A film (1961) adapted by Keith Waterhouse and Willis Hall from a novel of the same title by Mary Hayley Bell about three motherless children in rural Lancashire who find a fugitive criminal in their barn and become convinced he is Jesus Christ. The film starred Hayley Mills (the author's daughter), Bernard Lee and Alan Bates, who played the fugitive. The title (generally interpreted as to talk or argue purposelessly) comes from a proverbial saying connected with falconry, referring to the releasing of a hawk down wind.

Whistle in the dark, To. To hazard a guess; to speculate wildly; to appear more confident than one really is. The expression dates from the 1930s.

Whistle-stop tour. A fast tour with only brief pauses on the way. A whistle-stop is a US term for a minor station, which trains approach with a whistle signal, not calling unless a flag or lamp is displayed. In political parlance a whistle-stop tour became the term for a full-scale tour of the United States by a presidential candidate, during which stops were made at communities with a whistle-stop. The train had private cars, and the candidate addressed the assembled crowd from the platform of the rear car. Harry S. Truman was the last presidential candidate to undertake a full whistle-stop tour, in 1948. Later candidates have undertaken abbreviated tours, such as that made by Jimmy Carter in 1976. Britain's equivalent is a campaign by BATTLEBUS.

Whitbread Prize. This literary award was founded in 1971 and named after its sponsors, the brewers and distillers Whitbread plc. Awards are made in two stages. First, nominations are selected in the four categories of novel, first novel, biography and poetry. One of these is then voted by the panel of judges as Whitbread Book of the Year. The novelist William Trevor won the prize for the third time in 1994. Attempts by the Inland Revenue to tax the award have so far failed.

White Album. The name generally used to describe a double album by the BEATLES, officially entitled

The Beatles and released in November 1968. It acquired the name the White Album because of the stark simplicity of its plain white cover. The album's 30 tracks include BACK IN THE USSR, DEAR PRUDENCE, 'The Continuing Story Of Bungalow Bill', HAPPINESS IS A WARM GUN, 'Rocky Racoon', 'Sexy Sadie' and HELTER-SKELTER. The extraordinary eight-minute track 'Revolution 9' represents the Beatles at their most avant-garde.

White Army. A name for the Russian counter-revolutionary or anti-BOLSHEVIK forces that opposed the RED ARMY in the Russian Civil War of 1918–20. The main groups were the army commanded on the southern front by General Anton I. Denikin, the forces of Admiral Alexander V. Kolchak in Siberia and the troops of General Pyotr N. Wrangel in the Crimea. The Red Army were the eventual victors.

White Australia policy. A policy that had its roots in the 19th-century Australian gold rushes, which attracted numerous Chinese workers. The presence of these immigrants led to resentment among white Australians, who feared competition and a lowering in their standard of living. Other resented immigrants included Japanese, Pacific islanders and East Indians. The desire for uniform immigration laws to exclude Asian immigrants was one of the factors that brought the colonies together into the Commonwealth of Australia in 1901. Federal laws soon followed to implement the White Australia policy. For decades immigration was almost entirely from the British Isles, although after the Second World War large numbers of non-English-speaking Europeans were welcomed. Immigration restrictions against non-Europeans began to be relaxed from 1966, and the White Australia policy was formally abandoned in 1973.

White City. A famous stadium in Shepherd's Bush, northwest London, completed in 1908 as part of a complex for the Franco-British Exhibition. That same summer it staged the fourth Olympic Games, and it was here that the modern length of the marathon was fixed at 26 miles 385 yards (42.195km). The length was originally planned at 26 miles (41.84km), but the extra yards were added to bring the finishing line before the royal box. Greyhound racing began at White City in 1927, and until its demolition in the 1980s it was the site of the Greyhound Derby. The name alludes to its white-stuccoed buildings and continues in use for the surrounding area, which at the close of the 20th century was scheduled for development as a vast new shopping centre.

White cliffs of Dover. The chalk cliffs near Dover, Kent, serving as a patriotic or nostalgic landmark for those returning home from abroad. They were popularized from a morale-boosting song sung by the FORCES' SWEETHEART, Vera Lynn, in the Second World War:

> There'll be bluebirds over
> The white cliffs of Dover,
> Tomorrow, just you wait and see.
>
> NAT BURTON: 'The White Cliffs of Dover' (1941)

White-collar worker. A professional or clerical worker, whose calling demands or at one time demanded a certain nicety of attire, typified by the wearing of a white collar. The term dates from the 1920s. *See also* BLUE-COLLAR WORKER; GREY-COLLAR WORKER; PINK-COLLAR WORKER.

White goods. Originally a term for household linens, such as sheets and towels, which are, of course, not necessarily white. The term later came to apply to electrical goods that are conventionally white, such as washing machines and refrigerators.

Whitehall Warrior. A nickname for an officer in the armed forces employed as a civil servant, typically on retirement, rather than on active service. His 'battle' is thus with administrative matters rather than military. Whitehall in London is the location of several government offices.

White hat. A US colloquialism for a good man or hero, dating from the 1970s. The reference is to the white hats worn by the 'Goodies' in early Western films, as distinct from the black ones worn by the 'Baddies'. *See also* GOODIES.

White hope. A person expected to bring success to a team or organization. The term dates from the early years of the 20th century and originally applied to a white boxer who might have been able to beat Jack Johnson (1878–1946), the first black to be world heavyweight champion (1908–15).

White Horse Final. In footballing history a nickname for the Cup Final of 1923 between Bolton Wanderers and West Ham United at Wembley. Thousands of fans spilled on to the pitch before the start of the game, and it required mounted police, and in particular Constable George Scorey on his 13-year-old white horse, Billy, to clear it before the match could begin. Although Scorey was only one of several mounted policemen on duty that day, his conspicuous white horse gave the name by which the final has always been referred to since.

White Hotel, The. A novel (1981) by D.M. Thomas (b.1935), whose starting point is a poem narrated by an imaginary patient of the psychoanalyst Sigmund Freud (1856–1939). She is revealed as a half-Jewish opera singer, Lisa Erdman. One of her numerous sexual hang-ups is that her promiscuous mother died with her lover, Lisa's uncle, in a hotel fire. Lisa later has a brief happy marriage in Russia, only to die in the BABY YAR massacre of Ukrainian Jews in 1941. The underlying theme of the novel is thus the conflict between sex and death, with the former expressed in terms of a Utopia and a regression towards the womb, the 'white hotel' of the title.

White knight. A champion or rescuer, especially one who comes to the aid of a company in financial difficulties. The expression dates from the 1980s and appears to derive not from the enthusiastic but ineffectual White Knight in Lewis Carroll's *Through the Looking-Glass* (1871) but from the KNIGHT IN SHINING ARMOUR on a white charger who rescues a DAMSEL IN DISTRESS. *See also* BLACK KNIGHT.

> The independent directors of Waddington group are seeking a white knight to head off the £330 million takeover offer from the packaging industry veteran Stuart Wallis.
> *The Times* (17 January 2000)

White-knuckle ride. A fairground or amusement park ride aiming to give a 'thrill of a lifetime' to its intrepid travellers, who grasp the rail before them so tightly that their knuckles turn white. The expression can be figuratively used of any similar stressful experience.

> Bluewater … is a shoppers' theme park in which the only white-knuckle ride you will experience will take place four weeks later when you open your credit card bills.
> *The Times* (15 September 1999)

White label. A musical recording for which the fully printed commercial label is not yet available. It has thus been supplied with a plain white label before any general release of the recording, either for promotional purposes or as a limited-edition pressing to test the market. The term dates from the 1920s.

> Ibiza is … a musical melting pot which attracts producers from all over Europe, who turn up with white labels of their latest tune and distribute them to DJs in the island's innumerable bars and clubs.
> *heat* (6–12 January 2000)

White list. The opposite of a black list, as a list of people or products viewed with approval. The term dates from the turn of the 20th century.

> There was for the first time in a major British political campaign a 'whitelist': media with invitations. There was a blacklist: media without invitations. The Times had three journalists on the latter.
> *The Times* (15 October 1999)

White man's burden. In the days of imperialism the duty supposed to be imposed upon the white races, especially the British, to govern and to educate the more 'backward' coloured peoples. The expression was the creation of Kipling, the original reference being specifically to the role of the United States in the Philippines.

> Take up the White Man's burden –
> Send forth the best ye breed –
> Go bind your sons to exile
> To serve your captives' need.
> RUDYARD KIPLING: 'The White Man's Burden' (1899)

White Mischief. *See* HAPPY VALLEY.

White Noise. A comic novel (1985) by Don DeLillo (b.1936), centring on an 'airborne toxic event' and the manufacture of an experimental drug to cure the fear of death. White noise is the term for inexplicable electronic signals that are present in the atmosphere.

White Pelé. A nickname applied to two Brazilian footballers: Tostão (Eduardo Gonçalves de Andrade: b.1947), a member of his country's World Cup-winning team in 1970; and Zico (Artur Antunes Coimbra; b.1953), a formidable successor to Pelé in the Brazilian national sides of the 1970s and 80s. *See also* BLACK PELÉ; BRAZILIAN FOOTBALLERS; EUROPEAN PELÉ.

Whiter shade of pale, A. Paler in complexion than usual. The phrase was popularized by the song of this name performed by the pop group Procol Harum in the late 1960s, with lyrics by Keith Reid and music by Gary Brooker. Its title comes from a phrase used by the song's producer Guy Stevens while talking to his exhausted wife. The song, a worldwide hit, was released in 1967 during the SUMMER OF LOVE. Its melody evokes that of J.S Bach's so-called *Air on a G String* (from his Orchestral Suite No. 3 in D Major), an impression increased by the prominent use of an organ. The lyrics, including references to '16 vestal virgins' and Chaucer's *Miller's Tale*, represent the pop lyric of the 1960s at its most obscurely allusive and, some might say, pretentious.

> And it was later, as the Miller told his tale,
> That her face, at first just ghostly,
> Turned a whiter shade of pale.
> KEITH REID: 'A Whiter Shade of Pale' (1967)

Whiter than white. Free from taint; beyond reproach; absolutely pure and innocent. The phrase dates from the 1920s and was popularized as a slogan for Persil soap powder.

> As Mr Hague put it, the Conservative Party had to be 'whiter than white' on this question.
> *The Times* (25 November 1999)

White Russian. An inhabitant of White Russia or Belorussia (now Belarus; Russian *bely*, 'white'), a former republic of the USSR. White Russian is also a term for a counter-revolutionary or *émigré* at the time of the BOLSHEVIK revolution, and their army was known as the WHITE ARMY, in direct contrast to the Communist RED ARMY.

White settlers. A term applied by some Scots to English people living in Scotland. The term is also used elsewhere of incomers. The implication is that such people take advantage of their wealth to buy up the best property and have no concern for the local people. The term, which came into popular use in the 1990s, contains within it an echo of the resentment of European settlers that was felt by their subjects in the colonial era.

White van man. A man with an anonymous white van who undertakes various errands and who is generally regarded, mostly quite without justification, as a 'shady character' and as a notoriously bad driver given to ROAD RAGE. The term came to be applied indiscriminately to repair men and delivery men in general, as well as to plumbers and decorators, whether qualified and competent or simply bungling COWBOYS. The individual described is also known as 'man with a white van' or simply 'man with a van', its colour being implicit.

> [In the television documentary *White Van Man*] we meet three examples of WVM who only approximately fit the stereotype. ... All are described as 'fifty, failed and free', but not all are intent on overtaking illegally, driving too close to your rear bumper or carving you up at roundabouts.
> *The Times* (27 November 1999)

Whitewall. A style of haircut in which the sides of the head are shaved and the top and back left longer. The appearance is that of a whitewall tyre, which has a white stripe round the outside.

Whitewater Affair. A US government scandal based on the alleged dealings of President Clinton and his wife Hillary before Clinton became president in 1993. The action began in 1978 when the Clintons and their partners, James McDougal and his wife Susan, bought a plot of land in the OZARK COUNTRY north of Little Rock, Arkansas, and set up the Whitewater Development Corporation to build holiday homes. The enterprise failed when McDougal went bankrupt and was charged with bank fraud, although he was subsequently acquitted. There was no evidence that the Clintons were aware of any wrongdoing, but critics made much of Clinton's association with McDougal at a time when the future president was state attorney-general in Arkansas. The scandal surfaced when Clinton became president and resulted in the resignation of his aides.

White wedding. A traditional wedding at which the bride wears a long white dress. The term dates only from the 1940s, although white, as a symbol of purity, has been the customary colour for the bridal gown since the 18th century.

White Wednesday. *See* BLACK WEDNESDAY.

Whizz or **whiz kid.** A highly intelligent young person, one who achieves rapid success, the onomatopoeic word 'whizz' being the sound of something moving through the air with great rapidity. The term has probably also been influenced by 'wizard'. Punningly, a 'gee-whizz kid' is a naive novice, who reacts in disbelief at every innovation or turn of event.

> Is Mr Blair really still the 'gee-whizz kid' of gossip, unable quite to believe it is all real?
> *The Times* (29 September 1999)

Who dares wins. The motto of the SAS from 1942, adopted from that of Brigadier Robert Yerburgh, Lord Alvingham (1889–1955).

Whodunit. A colloquialism originating in the United States for a detective story. The word is said to have been coined by Donald Gordon in the American *News of Books* of 10 July 1930 in which he described Milward Kennedy's novel *Half-Mast Murder* as 'a satisfactory whodunit'. *See also* WHYDUNIT.

The detective story is easily identifiable, because despite the ingenuity of writers who prevent the

reader from guessing 'Whodunit', it has only one plot, basically: the solution of a mystery, usually murder.
JERRY PALMER in H.R.F. KEATING (ed.), *Whodunit? A Guide to Crime, Suspense & Spy Fiction* (1982)

Who Framed Roger Rabbit? A film (1988) in which animated and live action were cleverly combined to tell the story of a private detective (played by Bob Hoskins) who is hired to investigate the private life of Roger Rabbit's sexy wife Jessica (both cartoon characters). Hence the widely repeated alternative title 'Who Rogered Jessica Rabbit?' When the film was shown in Golders Green, the heart of London's Jewish community, a storm allegedly damaged the title on display at the local cinema so that it read 'Who Framed Roger Rabbi?'

Who he? An editorial query written by the name of a supposedly little-known person. The expression is particularly associated with Harold Ross, editor of the *New Yorker* (1925–51). It was subsequently popularized by its use in the satirical magazine *Private Eye*, while Jonathan Goodman's *Who He?* (1984) is an entertaining 'Dictionary of the Unknown Famous'.

Whole ball of wax. Absolutely everything; 'the works'. The US expression dates from the 1950s but is of uncertain origin. According to one theory, the reference may be to a former method of distributing the land of an estate to heirs, in which the amount of each portion was concealed in a ball of wax. This was then drawn out of a hat in a sort of lottery.

Whole megillah. A long or tedious story; a 'rigmarole'. The Megillah, from the Hebrew for 'scroll', is any of the five of the Hebrew scriptures (Song of Solomon, Ruth, Lamentations, Ecclesiastes and Esther) appointed to be read on certain Jewish feast-days. The phrase, dating from the 1950s, alludes to the length of the books and translates Yiddish *a gantse Megillah*.

Whole new ball game. A totally new or revised situation. The term comes from baseball, in which it is used to mean a sharp turn of events, as when the team that was ahead falls behind. The expression dates from the 1960s.

This makes molecular anthropology 'a whole new ball game', says Zegura.
New Scientist (11 July 1998)

Whole nine yards. *See* GO THE WHOLE NINE YARDS.

Whoop-de-do. A motorcycling term for a very bumpy road, inspired by the exclamation of the rider.

Whoopee cushion. A joke cushion that makes a sound like the breaking of wind when someone sits on it. The allusion is to 'making whoopee' as a synonym for boisterous merry-making. The device was first put to use in the 1960s.

Who's Afraid of Virginia Woolf? A play (1962) by US playwright Edward Albee (b.1928) depicting the tense relationship between a sharp-tongued college professor and his embittered wife. Filmed in 1966 with Richard Burton and Elizabeth Taylor in the two main roles, the play owed its memorable title to a line of graffiti scribbled in soap on a mirror in a bar in New York's Greenwich Village that the author happened to visit in the 1950s. The quip, evidently derived from the song title 'Who's Afraid of the Big Bad Wolf' from the Disney cartoon *The Three Little Pigs* (1933), was later redefined by Albee as meaning 'who's afraid of living without false illusions'.

Whose Line Is It Anyway? A popular television show of improvised comedy first screened in 1988, in which under the sceptical eye of chairman Clive Anderson a team of ALTERNATIVE comedians improvise various scenarios, some suggested by members of the audience. The title puns on that of Brian Clark's play *Whose Life Is It Anyway?* (1977).

Who's he when he's at home? A semi-humorous enquiry about a person's identity, especially when one feels one should really know the answer. The pronoun is obviously variable.

The question on everybody's lips must be: hang on, who's this Geoff Hoon when he's at home?
Sunday Times (28 November 1999)

Why? A single written query often accompanying a floral tribute at the scene of a fatal accident. The implication is twofold: why did the accident happen, and why did the person have to die.

The congregation ... filed slowly ... across the road to look at the ... floral tributes. ... Many bore cards asking simply: 'Why?'
The Times (11 October 1999)

Why Didn't They Ask Evans? A detective novel (1934) by Agatha Christie (1890–1976), the starting point of which is the discovery by a golfer, who has sliced his ball over a cliff, of a dying man, whose last words are, 'Why didn't they ask Evans?'

Whydunit. A mystery novel, play or film that deals primarily with the motivation for the crime, as distinct from the WHODUNIT, which concentrates on establishing the identity of the perpetrator.

[Sean] Connery takes over the interrogation and in the process beats the man to death. This much we know almost from the beginning, so the film [*The Offence*] is less of a whodunit than a whydunit.

Time (4 June 1973)

Wicca. The religious cult of modern witchcraft. It was founded in Britain in the mid-20th century and claims to originate from pre-Christian pagan religions. The word is Old English for 'witch', meaning originally a man (not a woman) who practises witchcraft.

Wide boy. A man who lives by his wits, usually dishonestly; a SPIV or petty criminal. 'Wide' here has its former slang sense of 'sharp', meaning wide awake and alert. The phrase gained popular currency in the Second World War.

The wide boys in white socks are back. Estate agents, never a much-loved breed, have been misbehaving again in scenes reminiscent of the 1980s.

The Times (25 September 1999)

Wide Sargasso Sea. A novel (1966) by Jean Rhys (pseudonym of Ella Gwendoline Rees Williams; 1890–1979). Set in Dominica, where Rhys was born and lived until she was 16 years old, Jamaica and, the last of three parts, in England, it is the story of the mad wife of Mr Rochester in *Jane Eyre* by Charlotte Brontë, from her childhood in Jamaica to the moment of truth of the conflagration at Thornfield Hall. The Sargasso Sea is a part of the Atlantic full of seaweed to the north of the West Indies. A lush Australian film version (1992), directed by John Duigan, recast the subtle original as a saga of sex and revenge.

Wifelet. A girlfriend, regarded as fulfilling the role of a wife without having the actual status of one. The word is particularly associated with the sexual partners of Alexander Thynn, the idiosyncratic 7th Marquess of Bath (b.1932), whose residence at Longleat, Wiltshire, is adorned with his own portraits of around 70 such women. Thynn apparently invented the term, its *-let* suffix doubtless intended to denote affection but equally capable of being understood as diminishing or dismissive. *See also* LOINS OF LONGLEAT.

'The wifelet is a flexible definition. If somebody is a girlfriend but hasn't been sexually active for some years, I still count them in.'

ALEXANDER THYNN interviewed in *Sunday Times Magazine* (29 August 1999)

Wigan Pier. There are fine piers in several British seaside resorts, notably Eastbourne, Brighton, Blackpool, Weston-super-Mare and Southend. Wigan, however, is an inland town and does not have a pier as such. What passes for a pier is the remains of a gantry, now little more than a few iron girders, protruding from a wall by the Liverpool–Leeds canal. As such, it is a curiosity and a tourist attraction in its own right. The story goes that the name arose when a trainload of miners was delayed in Wigan next to a coal-wagon gantry. The area was flooded at the time, and when a miner asked a local where they were, the facetious reply came: 'Wigan pier.' The tale spread and was soon picked up by music-hall performers who used it to mock the middle classes and their holidays at resorts that had proper piers. George ORWELL's *The* ROAD TO WIGAN PIER (1937) is an account of industrial poverty in Wigan, Sheffield and Barnsley.

Wightman Cup. The trophy awarded to the winner of tennis matches held annually between teams of women from Britain and the USA. It was donated in 1923 by the US tennis champion Hazel Hotchkiss Wightman (1886–1974), and the first contest was held at Forest Hills, New York, on 11 and 13 August 1923 with a win for the Americans. Matches are played in the USA in odd-numbered years and in Britain in even-numbered years.

Wilco. Military jargon for '(I) will comply', denoting acceptance of a message received by radio or telephone. The phrase became familiar from its use by the RAF in the Second World War.

Wild blue yonder. The far distance; a remote place. The metaphor is aeronautical and derives from Robert Crawford's song 'The Army Air Corps' in Moss Hart's musical *Winged Victory* (1943), the official show of the US Air Force.

Off we go into the wild blue yonder,
Climbing high into the sun.

Wild Bunch, The. An elegiac, blood-soaked WESTERN (1969) directed by Sam Peckinpah and starring William Holden, Warren Oates, Ernest Borgnine and Robert Ryan. Set in the twilight years of the Wild West and on the eve of the Mexican Revolution, the film was considered exceptionally violent at the time of its release. The 'Wild Bunch' are a group of ageing outlaws who move into a southern Texan town to carry out a robbery, but are set up and ambushed by bounty hunters (among whose number is a former member of the bunch, forced to pursue his former accomplices or face a life behind bars). Pursued by the bounty hunters, the bunch flee to Mexico where they become involved with a corrupt and vicious Mexican general who enlists their help in stealing a consignment of US Army weapons. When the youngest member of the bunch is captured and tortured for stealing weapons to supply revolutionaries in his home village, the bunch decide to do battle with the Mexicans to rescue their stricken friend. The words of the bunch's leader, 'I wouldn't have it any other way,' precipitate a final shootout of quite extraordinary ferocity.

Wild card. An unpredictable person or thing. More specifically in computing a wild card is a character than will match one or more characters in searches for files that share a common specification. The term comes from card games, especially poker, where it refers to a card that can have any value, suit or colour chosen by the player that holds it.

Wild child. An unconventional or 'rebellious' young person. The expression is typically associated with the FLOWER PEOPLE of the SWINGING SIXTIES, although the type at its most positive and beguiling is rather more than this. A fine literary example is the figure of Hazel Woodus in Mary Webb's *Gone to Earth* (1917), a gypsy's daughter who 'stands for unadulterated nature in all its bounty and beauty' (Patricia Craig in *Times Literary Supplement*, 24 December 1999).

> Were you a Sixties wild child? Do you remember the days of miniskirts and false eyelashes, Mini Coopers and flower power?
>
> *Sunday Times* (29 August 1999)

Wilderness of mirrors. A phrase descriptive of the confusing world of espionage. It is said to have been first used in this sense by James J. Angleton (1917–87), the leading counter-intelligence specialist of the CIA, who described it as the 'myriad of stratagems, deceptions, artifices and all the other devices of disinformation which the Soviet bloc and its coordinated intelligence services use to confuse and split the West'. The term originally comes from T.S. Eliot's poem 'Gerontion' (1920). It was also used by David C. Martin as the title of his book about Angleton, *Wilderness of Mirrors* (1980).

Wild One, The. A film (1953) adapted by John Paxton from a story, 'The Cyclists' Raid', by Frank Rooney about the chaos that ensues after a gang of motorbike riders, led in the film by Marlon Brando (the 'wild one' of the title), descends on a small country town. The plot was based on an actual incident that took place during the Fourth of July weekend of 1947, when 4000 bikers occupied the small town of Hollister, California, and destroyed it.

> *Murphy*: What are you rebelling against?
> *Brando*: What have you got?

William. The grubby-kneed, 11-year-old schoolboy William Brown is the hero of an engaging series of 38 books by Richmal Crompton (1890–1969). He and his pals 'the Outlaws', Ginger, Henry and Douglas, bring a note of welcome anarchy into the select middle-class setting in which they live. Together with William's dog, Jumble, they are involved in a variety of escapades in which they frequently fall foul of adult authority. William also has an ongoing love-hate relationship with Violet Elizabeth Bott, a precious, lisping six-year-old who is forever threatening to 'thcream an' thcream an' thcream till I'm thick'. The first story of his exploits was 'Rice-Mould', which was published in *Home Magazine* in February 1919. The series of novels opened with *Just – William* (1922) and closed posthumously with *William the Lawless* (1970). Illustrations by Thomas Henry did much to enhance the lively text.

Willie. An affectionate nickname for William Whitelaw (1918–99), the Tory grandee who served as deputy prime minister (1979–88) to Margaret Thatcher, the IRON LADY. When he was elevated to the House of Lords as Viscount Whitelaw in 1983 Thatcher memorably observed that 'every prime minister should have a Willie', apparently in reference to his ability to spot and avoid political BANANA SKINS. *See also* WOBBLING WILLIE.

Wilshire Boulevard. A broad street that passes through the centre of Los Angeles and leads to the Pacific coast in the region of Santa Monica. It is famous for its Miracle Mile, close to HOLLYWOOD, a glamorously glittering stretch of stores, boutiques, hotels, restaurants and nightclubs, and takes its name from a local developer, H.G. Wilshire (1861–1927).

Wimmin. A respelling of 'women', adopted by some feminists from the late 1970s as a means of avoiding the undesirable '-men'. The term became particularly associated with the 'peace women' at GREENHAM COMMON.

> We have spelt it this way because we are not wo*men* neither are we *female*. ... You may find it trivial – it's just another part of the deep, very deep rooted sexist attitudes.
>
> *This Magazine Is For, About, and By Young Wimmin* (August 1979)

Wimp. A weak or ineffectual person, especially a male. The word may have originated in an Oxford University slang term for a female student and derive from a blend of 'woman' and 'whimperer'. In computer jargon a WIMP, suggesting this word, is an acronym of *w*indows, *i*cons, *m*ice and *p*ull-down menus, devices designed to help the novice or the faint-hearted.

Wimpy. A proprietary name for a hamburger, as served in a Wimpy restaurant. The name comes from that of J. Wellington Wimpy, a character who was always portrayed eating a hamburger in Elzie C. Segar's POPEYE comic strip. The name was patented in the United States in 1935.

Wimsey, Lord Peter. The aristocratic private detective is the central character of the crime novels of Dorothy L. Sayers (1893–1957). He first appears in *Whose Body?* (1923), and in many of his manners is similar to Bertie WOOSTER. He has a manservant, Mervyn Bunter, a private income and a number of acquaintances among the idle rich. Film versions about Wimsey followed, and he was played on television by Ian Carmichael in *Lord Peter Wimsey* (1972–9) and by Edward Petherbridge in *A Dorothy L. Sayers Mystery* (1987). He is said to be based on the travel writer Eric Whelpton (1894–1981). *See also* GAUDY NIGHT; NINE TAILORS.

Winchester Three. In 1988 three young Irish people, Martina Shanahan, Finbar Cullen and John McCann, were sentenced at Winchester Crown Court to 25 years' imprisonment on charges of conspiracy to murder Tom King, then secretary of state for Northern Ireland. They were freed on appeal in 1990. *See also* BIRMINGHAM SIX; BRIDGEWATER THREE; GUILDFORD FOUR.

Wind in the Willows, The. An animal fantasy (1908) by Kenneth Grahame (1859–1932). The book was developed from stories told by Grahame to his son Alastair, born in 1900, and inspired by the river and wood at Cookham Dean, Berkshire, where Grahame was brought up by his grandmother. Opinion is divided as to whether the character of Toad, 'the motor-car snatcher, the prison-breaker, the Toad who always escapes', was created as a means of deflating his rather bumptious son or served as an imaginative extension of the outwardly quiet, respectable Bank of England executive that Grahame was. On its publication the anonymous reviewer in *The Times Literary Supplement* reported: 'As a contribution to natural history the work is negligible.' The story was originally called *The Mole and the Water-Rat* in the author's first draft. It

was then retitled *The Wind in the Willows*, itself the original title of the chapter called 'The Piper at the Gates of Dawn', in which Mole and Rat have a vision of Pan. Grahame finally decided in favour of the alliterative title, itself evocative of his earlier lyrical essays on the English countryside. A disappointing film version (1996), directed by Terry Jones, turned the original into little more than a pantomime. *See also* TOAD HALL.

Windmill Theatre. A theatre in Soho that was famous in the 1930s and during the Second World War for its shows with nude women, who were allowed to appear so long as they remained still. The logic behind this was that movement would have given them a sexual import, whereas if they posed stationary they were regarded as artistic displays. The Windmill remained open right through the war, leading it to boast the proud slogan, 'We never closed'. It closed in 1964, and although reopening for a time in the 1980s for 'nude entertainment' was taken over for television productions in 1990.

Wind of change. A new current of opinion; a reformist trend. The phrase was popularized by Harold Macmillan (1894–1986) in his speech to the South African Parliament (3 February 1960), with reference to the social and political ferment in the African continent. *Winds of Change* was also the title of the first book (1966) of his seven volumes of memoirs, completed in 1975. *See also* AT THE END OF THE DAY.

> The wind of change is blowing through this continent, and, whether we like it or not, this growth of [African] national consciousness is a political fact.

Window of opportunity. A favourable opportunity for doing something that must be acted on instantly if it is not to be missed. The image is of seeing an opportunity through an open window and seizing it before it shuts. The expression dates from the 1970s. 'Window' alone was in earlier use in the 1960s for an interval in which atmospheric and astronomical circumstances were favourable for the launch of a spacecraft. Earlier still, in the Second World War, the word 'Window' was a code name for 'chaff', strips of metal foil which were released from aircraft to obstruct radar detection.

> 'I knew we had a window of opportunity,' said Burt. 'If we didn't move now, that window would be shut and it would be shut forever.'
> *Sunday Times* (26 September 1999)

Window shopping. The pastime of looking at goods displayed in shop windows without actually buying any of them. The phrase is of US origin and dates from the 1920s.

Wind someone up, To. To tease or irritate them. The image is of winding up a spring mechanism to increase the tension. An act of teasing in this way is thus a 'wind-up'.

Windsor. The name of the British royal family dates from 17 July 1917 when, in a climate of revulsion against all things German, George V (1865–1936) changed his German title, Saxe-Coburg-Gotha, inherited from his grandfather, Prince Albert (1819–61), consort of Queen Victoria, to a more British-sounding Windsor. He adopted this title partly because Edward III (1312–77) had used it but chiefly as a symbolic reflection of the importance of Windsor Castle, a royal residence since William the Conqueror chose the site for a fortress after his conquest of England in 1066. In 1960 Queen Elizabeth II declared that those of her descendants not entitled to the style of Royal Highness or of Prince or Princess would in future use the surname Mountbatten-Windsor, so linking the surname of her husband (before their marriage the Duke of Edinburgh was known as Lieutenant Philip Mountbatten) with their descendants without changing the name of the house established by her grandfather. The first use of the new name on an official document was at the marriage of Princess Anne to Captain Mark Phillips on 14 November 1973. *See also* GOTHA RAIDS.

Windsor knot. A large loose knot in a tie, as sported in the 1950s by the Duke of Windsor, formerly Edward VIII (1894–1972).

Winkle one's way, To. To worm one's way; to insinuate oneself.

Winkle-pickers. Shoes with very elongated and pointed toes, affected by TEDDY BOYS in the 1950s. The allusion is to the use of a pin for picking winkles out of their shells.

Winnie. A fond if slightly patronizing nickname given to Winston Churchill (1874–1965) during his last period as prime minister (1951–5), when his powers were visibly failing. His attempts to revive the 'special relationship' with the USA led to a cartoon in which President Eisenhower (*see* IKE) was portrayed as Hiawatha and Churchill as 'Winniehaha' (playing on Minnehaha).

Winnie-the-Pooh. The 'Bear of Very Little Brain' who appears in the nursery verses and children's stories by A.A. Milne (1882–1956). He made his bow in 1924 and has gained near cult status since. He had his genesis in a TEDDY BEAR named Winnie belonging to Milne's young son, CHRISTOPHER ROBIN, who also appears in the narratives. 'Pooh' was a nickname for a swan that the little boy fed every morning. The original Winnie was an American black bear, the mascot of a Canadian regiment. When the regiment was sent to France in 1914 Winnie was left in the care of the Royal Zoological Society and lived in London Zoo until her death in 1934. The popular Russian versions of the stories have Winnie-the-Pooh as *Vinni-Pukh* and by a linguistic quirk *pukh* happens to mean 'swansdown'. *See also* HEFFALUMP; PADDINGTON BEAR; POOHSTICKS; TIGGER.

> Pooh woke up suddenly with a sinking feeling. He had had that sinking feeling before, and he knew what it was. *He was hungry.*
> A.A. MILNE: *Winnie-the-Pooh*, ch v (1926)

Win on points, To. To succeed but only just. The term comes from boxing, in which one of the contestants wins by scoring more points than his opponent rather than winning by a knockout.

Winslow Boy, The. A play (1946) by the British playwright Terence Rattigan (1911–77) about the trial of a young naval cadet who has been accused of stealing a postal order and whose father is determined to clear his name at any cost. The play was based on a real case, that of George Archer-Shee, a cadet who was expelled from Osborne Naval College in 1908 on charges of petty theft. He was found not guilty of the charges thanks largely to the brilliant defence of Sir Edward Carson and received £7000 compensation from the Admiralty. He died at Ypres during the First World War.

Winter of discontent. The winter of 1978–9, marked in Britain by serious strikes. The phrase is from Shakespeare's *Richard III* (1592) and was originally applied in this sense in January 1979 by the political journalist Peter Jenkins. It was then taken up a month later in a television interview by the Labour prime minister, James Callaghan (*see* SUNNY JIM). The strikes are generally believed to have been a determining factor in the fall of the Labour government and the election of Margaret Thatcher's first Conservative administration in May 1979.

Winter War. The war between Finland and the USSR (30 November 1939–12 March 1940), fought in the appalling conditions of the Arctic winter, for which the Finns were much better equipped than the Soviets. The war is also called the Russo–Finnish War or the Soviet–Finnish War. Despite the Nazi–Soviet Non-Aggression Pact of August 1939, Stalin was still fearful of a German attack. To protect the Baltic approaches to the USSR, and to Leningrad (St Petersburg) in particular, the Soviets drew up demands for certain Finnish territories, including part of the Karelian isthmus and a naval base at Hangö, in exchange for a large area of Soviet territory. Negotiations broke down, and the Red Army attacked. However, the Finnish forces under Marshal Mannerheim (1867–1951) put up a stiff resistance that cost the Soviets dearly, and it was not until March 1940 that the Red Army broke through the so-called Mannerheim Line across the Karelian isthmus. The mooted expeditionary force from Britain and France never materialized, and the Finns were obliged to agree to the Soviet peace terms, ceding western Karelia and giving the USSR a 30-year lease on the Hangö peninsula. Soviet casualties in the conflict were 200,000, while the Finns lost 25,000 men.

Win–win situation. A situation in which each party benefits in some way from an outcome. The phrase arose as business jargon in the 1990s.

> Mr Bealey said afterwards: 'I am very pleased with the result. I am just very grateful to the many former pupils who have supported me. I don't think there are any win-win situations in something like this.'
> *The Times* (24 February 2000)

Wipers. A nickname for the town of Ypres in Belgium, from the pronunciation of its name by British servicemen in the First World War. The town was the site of three significant battles involving great loss of life, and the name must have become subconsciously associated with 'wipe (out)'. Some of the men may also have been familiar with the old town fort known as the Ypres Tower at Rye, Sussex. This was originally the Badding Tower but was later renamed when it was sold to a John de Ypres. It now houses a museum as part of Rye Castle. *See also* FIRST WORLD WAR SLANG; MENIN GATE; PASSCHENDAELE.

Wipe the smile off someone's face, To. To make them stop smiling; to 'sober' them by means of a serious remark or action. The expression dates from the turn of the 20th century.

A young accountant thought it a hoot to see how much beer he could spray on to a newly painted ceiling. The smile was wiped off his face when he saw the estimate for repainting.
The Times (13 October 1999)

Wirewalkers. Not funambulists but boys employed by the Post Office in the BLITZ to walk round the City of London as roving post offices. They could take telegrams ('wires'), charge customers and give change, and to announce their services they wore signs saying 'Telegrams Accepted'. The general aim was to maintain a semblance of normality with BUSINESS AS USUAL.

Wise man. A colloquial term for a special adviser or expert, especially one consulted or brought in by a government department or a business.

> Scotland Yard is planning to appoint a team of 'wise men' to look for fresh leads in the hunt for [television presenter] Jill Dando's killer.
> *The Times* (10 May 1999)

Wish book. A US term for a mail order catalogue.

Wishful thinking. A desire or hope for something impractical or unfeasible. The term arose from Freudian psychology in the 1920s and translates German *Wunschdenken*.

Wish list. A mental or written list of objects of desire, especially as planned and in many cases realized by the well-off. The term and concept date from the 1970s.

> My wish list had on it various things I had fallen in love with in the autumn, but which were too expensive for there to be any hope of owning them unless I got a lucky break in sale time.
> *The Times* (7 January 2000)

Wish me luck. Said when one is about to embark on a risky or difficult enterprise. The expression was popularized by Gracie Fields' song (written by Phil Park and Harry Parr Davies), 'Wish me luck as you wave me goodbye', which she first sang in the film *Shipyard Sally* (1939) and which went well into the years of the Second World War.

Wish you were here. A phrase dating from the EDWARDIAN ERA, when it was conventionally written on a SEASIDE POSTCARD and sent to one's family or friends at home. The words have had various applications since then, and *Wish You Were Here* (1987) was the title of a film about the GROWING PAINS of a teenage girl in a seaside town in the 1950s, with Emily Lloyd in the central role.

With a bang. Abruptly or spectacularly, as if accompanied by an explosion, as: 'His words brought me down to earth with a bang', 'The holiday began with a bang.' *See also* GO WITH A BANG.

> This is the way the world ends
> Not with a bang but a whimper.
> T.S. ELIOT: *Poems 1909–1925*, 'The Hollow Men' (1925)

With a capital. A speaker or writer may emphasize a word by referring to it as if spelt 'with a capital', as: 'She is musical with a capital M', 'He's a failure with a capital F.' *See also* CONSERVATIVE WITH A SMALL 'C'.

> He is not a personality with a capital P, not flamboyant, not it seems an angry man.
> NESTA WYN ELLIS: *John Major*, ch iii (1991)

With a Little Help from My Friends. A song by the BEATLES, credited to John Lennon and Paul McCartney, sung by Ringo Starr, and released on the album SERGEANT PEPPER'S LONELY HEARTS CLUB BAND in June 1967. The mildly narcotic sentimentality of 'With a Little Help from My Friends' epitomizes the communal spirit of the SUMMER OF LOVE, of which it became a favourite anthem. The song's enduring popularity has led to the recording of around 100 cover versions by performers as diverse as Count Basie and Ike and Tina Turner.

> What do you see when you turn out the light?
> I can't tell you but I know it's mine.

Withdrawal symptoms. A term dating from the 1920s for the unpleasant physiological reactions resulting from the process of ceasing to take an addictive drug. *See also* COLD TURKEY.

With it. Fashionable; up to date; trendy; au fait. The phrase dates from the 1930s and came into its own in the SWINGING SIXTIES. It is now itself less 'with it' than it was.

With knobs on. The same to you and more so. A schoolboy retort dating from the 1920s. A fuller version is: 'the same to you with brass knobs on.' The reference is to an embellishment and perhaps specifically to the brass knobs at the head and foot of an old-fashioned iron bedstead.

Without batting an eyelid. Showing no concern or emotion; remarking nothing abnormal. 'Batting' is 'blinking'. The expression dates from the turn of the 20th century.

Wizard of Dribble. The nickname of Sir Stanley Matthews (1915–2000), the renowned English footballer, whose paramount gift on the field lay in dribbling. His almost magical skill carried him clean past the best defenders in over a quarter of a century of world football.

Wizard of Earthsea, A. The first (1968) in a trilogy of fantasies for young adults by Ursula Le Guin (b.1929), set in an invented world called EARTHSEA, which consists of a vast and elaborate group of islands. Magic abounds, but though the perils may be inventions, the adventures and predicaments are real. A fourth fantasy, *Tehanu: the Last Book of Earthsea* (1990) was added later.

Wizard of Ooze. A nickname for Senator Everett M. Dirksen (1896–1969) of Illinois, famous for his flamboyant oratory and colourful phrases. He once upbraided a colleague with the words, 'That idea has as much effect as a snowflake on the bosom of the Potomac', and in a floor debate, when an opponent started to filibuster, said that he would 'invoke upon him every condign imprecation'. His motto was: 'The oilcan is mightier than the sword.'

Wizard of Oz. The central figure in the popular children's book, *The Wonderful Wizard of Oz* (1900), by L. Frank Baum, a US journalist. The musical comedy of the same name (1901) was a great success, which was repeated in the film of 1939. *See also* FIRST LINES OF NOVELS; OZ; YELLOW BRICK ROAD.

> We're off to see the Wizard,
> The wonderful Wizard of Oz.
> We hear he is a whiz of a wiz
> If ever a wiz there was.
> 'Yellow Brick Road', sung in film by Dorothy, the Cowardly Lion, the Scarecrow and the Tin Man

Wobblies. The Industrial Workers of the World (IWW) were so nicknamed. This US revolutionary labour organization was formed in 1905 at a meeting of labour activists in Chicago and reached its peak before the First World War but largely petered out after it. They aimed to gather the country's poorest and most exploited workers into 'one big union' that would ultimately challenge capitalism itself, and they drew their main support from migratory farmers, textile workers and dockers. Their songs include 'The Preacher and the Slave' (*see* PIE IN THE SKY) and Harry McClintock's 'Hallelujah, I'm a Bum'. They were also known as the Bummery. Wobbly may be from a Chinese-American pronunciation of IWW as 'I-wobbly-wobbly'.

Wobbling Willie. A media nickname for the Conservative politician William Whitelaw (1918–99), current in 1983 when he was made a viscount and had to fend off embarrassing questions from the LABOUR PARTY. *See also* WILLIE.

Wobbly bits. A colloquialism or euphemism for the male genitalia or female breasts. *See also* NAUGHTY BITS.

> Once upon a time actresses used to show off their wobbly bits to attract the attention of the press.
> *The Times* (15 September 1999)

Wog. A derogatory colloquial name applied to blacks, Arabs, Egyptians and other non-whites. It is possibly a contraction of 'golliwog', but in popular naval parlance is held to stand for 'wily oriental gentleman'. Another assertion is that it was formerly applied by the British army to its Egyptian labourers and is an abbreviation of 'workers on government service'. The chauvinistic catchphrase 'Wogs begin at Calais' first made itself evident after the Second World War.

Wolf Cub. The long-established and original name for a member of the junior branch of the BOY SCOUT Movement, now called Cub Scouts (age range 8–10½ years). The conception owes much to Rudyard Kipling's *Jungle Books* (1894, 1895). *See also* AKELA.

Wolf pack. A term applied in the Second World War to German submarines in a group.

Wolf whistle. A whistle made by a male at the sight of a female, expressing sexual admiration. It usually consists of two notes, one rising, the other descending. The name implies that the male is 'hungry', like a wolf. The expression dates from the 1950s. *See also* PHWOAH!

> Local builders wolf-whistled as [actress] Catherine Zeta Jones took to the Old Course in St Andrews with golf-loving Michael Douglas.
> *heat* (14–20 October 1999)

Wolves of Willoughby Chase, The. A fantasy (1962) for children by Joan Aiken (b.1924), daughter of the American poet Conrad Aiken (1889–1973). The story is set in the north of England in an imaginary period in the 1830s, when wolves from Europe and Russia have entered the country through the recently opened Channel Tunnel. Willoughby Chase is the home of Sir Willoughby Green, father of Bonnie, the book's main character. A entertaining film version (1988) was directed by Stuart Orme.

Woman in Black, The. A ghost story (1983) by Susan Hill (b.1942), in a timeless, period setting. A ghost takes revenge for the death of her child by taking the lives of other children. The title recalls that of the Victorian mystery story, *The Woman in White* (1860) by Wilkie Collins.

Womanist. A black feminist. The word was originally in use in the 17th century as a term for a womanizer. This meaning then became obsolete, and the term was adopted in its modern sense in the 1970s by the black American novelist Alice Walker (b.1944) as being more relevant to black people than 'feminist' and also for its suggestion of 'womanish'.

Woman's Hour. A weekday radio programme for women, first broadcast in 1946. It has gradually but radically changed its content over the years, keeping pace with the equally radical changes in women's lives. It has openly explored formerly taboo subjects on radio, typically on sexual matters, but has never quite shaken off its middle-class Home Counties tone. A serialized book has always been a popular feature. The programme long went out at 2 p.m, an hour when women were presumed to be at home and have some time to themselves. In 1990 the schedulers of Radio 4 ruffled the feathers of more than a few when it was moved to 10.30 a.m. and subsequently 10.00 a.m.

Wombles. Small, hairy, bear-like creatures who live underground, originally beneath Wimbledon Common in London. Individually they are Great Uncle Bulgaria, Orinoco, Wellington, Bungo, Tomsk, Madame Cholet, Miss Adelaide and the eccentric inventor Tobermory. They were the creation of Elisabeth Beresford, and after making their bow in the children's book *The Wombles* (1968) they went on to be popular in animated form on television. They are dedicated conservationists and make ingenious use of the litter left by humans. The cult for the cuddly creatures was raised to greater heights by a pop group of the same name who dressed the part and took the charts by storm in 1974 with hits such as 'The Wombling Song' and 'Remember You're a Womble'.

Women's lib. A trivializing abbreviation of 'women's liberation', a militant feminist movement arising in the 1960s to campaign for the liberation of women from subservient social status and all forms of sexism. The term was gradually abandoned from the 1970s to be replaced by 'feminism'. Women themselves prefer 'women's movement'.

Wonderbra. The proprietary name of a type of lacy low-cut brassiere introduced by the US company Gossard in 1968, replacing the earlier cumbersome 'bra-slip'. It was an instant bestseller and remained an object of desire for many young women for the next 20 years. The name may have been intended as a pun on German *wunderbar*, 'wonderful'.

Wonder State. The official nickname of the state of Arkansas, introduced in 1923 to mask its prevalent chronic unemployment and economic backwardness. The recent rapid growth of private enterprise has to some extent justified the earlier optimistic description.

Woodbine Willie. The Rev. G.A. Studdert Kennedy (1883–1929) was so called from the popular brand of small cigarettes named Woodbines, which he gave to the men in the trenches in the First World War when serving as chaplain to the forces (1916–19). *See also* PACKET OF WOODBINES.

Wooden cross. A wooden cross on the grave of a serviceman killed in action. Hence an ironic term for death in action, regarded as an 'award of merit'. The phrase arose in the First World War.

Woodentop. A nickname for a policeman or a slow-witted person, the former being disparagingly regarded as the latter, by comparison with sharp-witted detectives. Both terms date from the 1980s and may have been suggested by the children's television puppet programme *The Woodentops* (1955–8).

Woods are full, The. A 20th-century Americanism denoting an abundance, as: 'The woods are full of computer magazines these days.' The imagery is from hunting.

Woodstock. A small town near Albany in the state of New York, which gave its name to a huge rock festival held nearby in the summer of 1969. In 1994 a 25th anniversary restaging of the original event, commercially sponsored, attracted some 350,000 young (and not so young) people.

Woolton pie. A vegetable dish of carrots, parsnips, turnips and potatoes, covered with white sauce and pastry, named after Frederick James Marquis, 1st Earl Woolton (1883–1964), minister of food during the Second World War. Woolton encouraged British housewives to make use of whatever foodstuffs were available but his pie mostly failed to excite the already jaded domestic appetite.

> The London crowd shuffled past, surfeited with tea and Woolton pies.
> EVELYN WAUGH: *Officers and Gentlemen*, Pt II, ch vi (1955)

Woolworth Building. A 60-storey, neo-Gothic office building on New York's Broadway, erected in 1911 by the chain-store magnate F.W. Woolworth (1852–1919), effectively as a monument to himself. It was the tallest building in the world until it was surpassed by the Chrysler Building in 1926. It is popularly known as the Cathedral of Commerce, a term used of it at the time of its dedication.

Woomera. The name of the rocket testing range in south Australia, appropriately an Aborigine word for a spear-throwing stick.

Woop Woop. In Australian usage a humorous name for a remote outback town or district. It probably imitates a typical Aboriginal place-name with its characteristic duplication, such as Wagga Wagga, although according to one theory it derives from the 'geelorious town o' Woop-Up' in E.L. Wheeler's *Deadwood Dick on Deck* (1878) in which 'Whoop-Up' is the name of a back-country US mining town. The term itself is first recorded only in the 1920s, however.

Wooster, Bertie. The amiable young man-about-town who, with his manservant JEEVES, has various comic and amorous adventures in the stories and novels by P.G. Wodehouse, of which he is the narrator. He is as vacuous as Jeeves is clever, and his speech is a goldmine of fashionable pre-1914 slang. His indolent existence is marred chiefly by his fearsome aunts. He made his literary début in the short story 'The Artistic Career of Corky' (1916) and is said to be based on John Wodehouse Kimberley, 3rd earl of Kimberley (1883–1941), Wodehouse's cousin.

> It is no use telling me that there are bad aunts and good aunts. At the core they are all alike. Sooner or later, out pops the cloven hoof.
> P.G. WODEHOUSE: *The Code of the Woosters*, ch ii (1938).

Wop. In the original US slang usage this meant an uncouth or aggressive person. The term was later used as a derogatory name for Italians and those of similar complexion. It is probably derived from southern Italian dialect *guappo*, 'braggart', 'dandy', itself from Spanish *guapo*.

Worcester woman. The archetype of what POLICY WONKS and SPIN DOCTORS regard as the key British voter around the turn of the MILLENNIUM. She is comfortably middle-class, probably reads the *Daily Mail*, is from a well-off part of southern England but not the metropolis, represents the values of MIDDLE ENGLAND and almost certainly voted for Labour (in its NEW LABOUR incarnation) for the first time in the 1997 general election. Worcester itself reverted to Conservative control in the local-government elections of May 2000. *See also* ESSEX MAN; ISLINGTON MAN; ORPINGTON MAN; SELSDON MAN.

Words of one syllable. To speak to someone in words of one syllable is to say what one means plainly and directly, even bluntly. Most so-called FOUR-LETTER WORDS are monosyllabic. The expression dates from the 1920s.

Words of the 20th century. In 1997 Collins English Dictionaries produced a list of 100 words that were new in their day and that, when taken together, were said to define the 20th century. The words themselves are effectively a random selection, but they first entered common usage, or appeared in reference books and dictionaries, in the year stated, so have some claim to the role. They are as follows, many having their own entries in the present book:

radioactivity (1896)

aspirin (1897)

krypton (1898)

gamine (1899)

LABOUR PARTY (1900)

fingerprint (1901)

TEDDY BEAR (1902)

tarmac (1903)

FIFA (Fédération internationale de football association; 1904)

SINN FÉIN (1905)

SUFFRAGETTE (1906)

ALLERGY (1907)

BORSTAL (1908)

JAZZ (1909)

GIRL GUIDE (1910)

AIR RAID (1911)

schizophrenia (1912)

isotope (1913)

VORTICISM (1914)

TANK (the military vehicle; 1915)

dada (1916) (*see* DADAISM)

Cheka (1917) (*see* KGB)

BOLSHIE (1918)

FASCISM (1919)

ROBOT (1920)

CHAPLINESQUE (1921)

gigolo (1922)

SPOONERISM (1923; but *see* entry)

SURREALISM (1924)

British Summer Time (1925; *see* SUMMER TIME)

television (1926)

talkie (1927)

PENICILLIN (1928)

MAGINOT LINE (1929)

PLUTO (the planet) (1930)

OSCAR (the Academy award; 1931)

neutron (1932)

GESTAPO (1933)

BELISHA BEACON (1934)

ALCOHOLICS ANONYMOUS (1935)

MICKEY MOUSE (1936)

surreal (1937; *see* SURREALISM)

NYLON (1938)

WALTER MITTY (1939)

JEEP (1940)

RADAR (1941)

robotics (1942; *see* ROBOT)

DAM BUSTERS (1943)

DOODLEBUG (1944)

TUPPERWARE (1945)

BIKINI (1946)

FLYING SAUCER (1947)

SCRABBLE (1948)

BIG BROTHER (1949)

NATO (1950)

discotheque (1951)

stoned (1952)

ROCK 'N' ROLL (1953)

TEDDY BOY (1954)

LEGO (1955)

ANGRY YOUNG MAN (1956)

PSYCHEDELIC (1957)

silicon chip (1958; *see* SILICON VALLEY)

HOVERCRAFT (1959)

LASER (1960)

CATCH-22 (1961)

MONTEZUMA'S REVENGE (1962)

RACHMANISM (1963)

MOOG SYNTHESIZER (1964)

MINISKIRT (1965)

CULTURAL REVOLUTION (1966)

pulsar (1967)

FOSBURY FLOP (1968)

moon buggy (1969)

BUTTERFLY EFFECT (1970; but *see* entry)

WORKAHOLIC (1971)

WATERGATE (1972)

VAT (value-added tax; 1973)

Ceefax (1974)

fractal (1975)

PUNK ROCK (1976)

ERM (the European exchange-rate mechanism; 1977)

TEST-TUBE BABY (1978)

RUBIK'S CUBE (1979)

SOLIDARITY (the Polish trade-union movement; 1980)

SDP (Social Democratic Party) (1981)

CD (compact disc) (1982)

AIDS (acquired immune deficiency syndrome; 1983)

YUPPIE (young upwardly mobile professional; 1984)

GLASNOST (1985)

MEXICAN WAVE (1986)

PEP (Personal Equity Plan; 1987)

ACID HOUSE (1988)

VELVET REVOLUTION (1989)

CROP CIRCLE (1990)

ETHNIC CLEANSING (1991)

clone (1992)

information superhighway (1993)

National Lottery (1994)

ROAD RAGE (1995)

ALCOPOP (1996)

Blairite (1997; *see* BLAIRISM)

Workaholic. A compulsive worker, who is addicted to work as an alcoholic is to drink. The term, first recorded in 1968, is the earliest of the '-aholics', and was coined by Wayne Oates, an American pastoral counsellor, who popularized it in his *Confessions of a Workaholic* (1971). It was followed in due course by the chocaholic, shopaholic and similar obsessives.

Working girl. A young woman who goes out to work rather than remaining at home. The term can have disparaging overtones and is also one of many euphemisms for a prostitute. The latter is the sense in the film *Working Girls* (1986), about a prostitute in a New York brothel, but not in *Working Girl* (1988), about a secretary who outsmarts her female boss in business and in love.

Never having enjoyed the company of Sophie Rhys-Jones [Countess of Wessex], as this working girl no longer wishes to be known, I cannot gainsay those who testify to her gamesome charm.
The Times (21 September 1999)

World According to Garp, The. A novel (1978), in experimental narrative form, by the US novelist John Irving (b.1942). It follows the unorthodox life of T.S. Garp from conception to assassination, interspersed with extracts from his mother's autobiography, a posthumous biography of himself, his own story and his last novel. Violence and sex, and sometimes both together, obtrude. A somewhat uneasy film version (1981), directed by George Roy Hill, failed to convey the drama of the original. *See also* FIRST LINES OF NOVELS.

World Bank. The informal name for the International Bank for Reconstruction and Development, a specialized agency of the Unitied Nations that was set up in 1945. Its purpose is to use capital investment to aid development, especially in poorer countries, but it has been criticized in a similar way to its sister organization, the IMF.

World first. An occurrence that has never taken place anywhere in the world before.

'We're performing a 30-minute version of every Shakespeare play and we've got more than 1,000 children involved,' he explains. 'We think it's a world first.'
The Times (28 December 1999)

World music. The traditional music of Africa, Latin America and Asia. It emerged as a distinct genre at the first annual World of Music, Arts and Dance Festival (WOMAD), held at Pilton near Shepton Mallet, Somerset, in the summer of 1982 and came to embrace everything from field recordings of isolated peoples to new urban styles, traditional revivals to NEW AGE explorations.

'World Music' – What Is It? The dawning of a new musical 'global village' or an unfocused, unsuccessful marketing ploy? The realization of time-honoured cultural traditions or cynical pop exploitation and New Age natterings? Old field recordings or brave new electronic blends? It may, in fact, be all those things, none of them, and perhaps something more.
CHRIS HEIM in *Britannica Book of the Year* (1998)

World's policeman. *See* NEW WORLD ORDER.

World Wide Web. The information system on the INTERNET emerged in 1994 as the world's largest example of HYPERTEXT. The Web, familiar as the 'www' of Internet addresses such as the BBC's 'http://www.bbc.co.uk', consists of many thousands of pages or 'Websites'. Users can move from page to page in search of information by using a 'browser', a program providing a window on a computer screen on which the pages are displayed. The more specialized the Website, the longer its address. One for R.D. Blackmore's novel *Lorna Doone* (1869), for example, is 'http://src.doc.ic.ac.uk/media/literary/collection/ project-gutenberg/gutenberg/etext97/lorna10.txt'. The World Wide Web itself, with its cumbersome name, was the invention in 1990 of the English computer scientist Tim Berners-Lee (b.1955), who also devised the URL and wrote the two protocols 'http' and 'html' (*see* HYPERTEXT).

Worm. In computer jargon a self-replicating program able to propagate itself across a network, usually with disastrous results. It is not a virus, since it does not need human help to wreak its mischief. In 1999 the so-called 'Explore' worm caused widespread and expensive damage in the United States, wiping out years of work in thousands of databases. The term was introduced in this sense in *The Shockwave Rider*, a novel by the US SCIENCE FICTION writer John Brunner.

> I'm just assuming that you have the biggest-ever worm loose in the net, and that it automatically sabotages any attempt to monitor a call to the ten nines.
>
> JOHN BRUNNER: *The Shockwave Rider*, II (1975)

Worry beads. A string of beads that one can manipulate as a means of occupying one's hands and calming one's nerves. They date from the 1960s and originated among the Greeks.

> 'Pardon?' said the foreigner, ... and the man replied, 'Ah, and there was me thinking you were Greek. It was the way you were using the worry beads. Between the middle fingers, just like a Greek, but I suppose that you are French.'
>
> LOUIS DE BERNIÈRES, 'Greek Legends', in *The Times Magazine* (8 January 2000)

Worse for wear. In its literal sense, dating from the 18th century, the expression means showing signs of damage or deterioration by being worn. It is now commonly used as a euphemism for 'drunk' or 'suffering from a hangover'.

> The team leaves for its 'awayday' on Friday afternoon and returns on Saturday – usually feeling the worse for wear.
>
> *The Times* (13 October 1999)

Worst-case scenario. A possibility characterized by circumstances of the worst foreseeable type. The expression was popularized by military bureaucrats during the COLD WAR.

Worzel Gummidge. *See* GUMMIDGE, WORZEL.

Woy. A *Private Eye* nickname for Roy Jenkins (later Lord Jenkins of Hillhead; b.1920) on account of his inability to pronounce the letter 'r'. Jenkins, known for his fondness for claret and Europe, served in Labour governments as chancellor of the exchequer (1967–70) and home secretary (1974–6) before becoming president of the European Commission (1977–81), where he was punningly known as Le Roi Jean Quinze. On returning to Britain he co-founded and was the first leader of the Social Democratic Party.

WRAC. *See* WAAC.

WRAF. *See* WAAF.

Wrap one's car round something, To. To crash it. The image is of a wrecked car encircling a tree or pole, although the phrase is used for even a minor collision or 'encounter'. The expression is American in origin and dates from the 1950s.

> I crash on a weekly basis. Even if I really concentrate, I manage to wrap the car around something – a pillar, a traffic cone, even a cat once.
>
> *Sunday Times* (26 September 1999)

Wrap up, To. To be quiet; to shut up. The image is of parcelling up one's words. The phrase dates from the 1940s.

Wrens. Members of the Women's Royal Naval Service, formed in 1917. It was temporarily disbanded between the wars, then finally disbanded in 1993, when women were able to enlist in the regular Royal Navy. Wrens were long restricted to shore duties and first went to sea only in 1990, when 16 joined the crew of HMS *Brilliant* for five weeks' operational training. The Wrens' quarters was often jocularly known as 'The Wrennery' and their barracks at Devonport, in the manner of the Royal Navy, was given the ship's name HMS *Impregnable*, punning somewhat salaciously on the contrary senses of the word. See *also* WAAC; WAAF.

Wright brothers. *See* KITTY HAWK.

Write one's own ticket, To. To stipulate one's own conditions; to dictate one's own terms. 'Ticket' here has its basic sense of a document that gives its holder a particular right, such as admission to a show or authority to travel. The US expression dates from the 1920s.

Writer's block. A periodic lack of inspiration that can descend on the most experienced of writers and that results in an almost pathological inability to put pen to paper.

> Family and friends had claimed that she [novelist Iris Murdoch] was the victim of 'serious writer's block'.
> *The Times* (9 February 1999)

Write the book on something, To. To be an expert on it, as: 'Does he know anything about microlights?' 'He wrote the book on microlights.' The phrase is American in origin.

Wrong side of the tracks. To be on the wrong side of the tracks is to be socially inferior. The expression is of American origin, dating from the 1930s, and alludes to the fact that poor and industrial areas in many towns were at one time located to one side of the main railway line, partly because the prevailing wind would carry smoke into them, away from the better-off neighbourhoods. The poorer districts of British cities are similarly often found east of the centre, since the prevailing wind is usually west or southwest. A familiar example is London's East End.

> I thought at first that she was from the wrong side of the railroad tracks, but she seems to have settled down to being a nice little lady and a good war worker.
> SINCLAIR LEWIS: *Cass Timberlane*, ch xxxiv (1945)

WVS. The Women's Voluntary Service, set up in 1938, primarily to help with air raid precautions. It became the WRVS (Women's Royal Voluntary Service) in 1949. It continues to do valuable social and welfare work with the aged and infirm and gives help in emergencies. It is particularly noted for its 'meals on wheels' service.

Wysiwyg. Computer slang for 'What you see is what you get', i.e. what you see on the screen is exactly what will appear on the print-out. The word, pronounced 'wiziwig', is also used for a person or thing taken 'warts and all'. In 1992 it was adopted as the title of a children's SCIENCE FICTION television comedy series, in which it is the name of a reporter from outer space.

> Look at Ken Clarke. He is a classic 'wysiwyg' politician. Anyone with a computer knows about wysiwyg: it stands for 'what you see is what you get'. … Click on Ken Clarke, and you get exactly what you see.
> *The Times* (29 October 1999)

X

X. At one time a classification for 'adult' films, meaning in the main those of a specifically sexual or violent nature. The designation was replaced in Britain in 1983 by '18', the legal age of majority, and in the United States in 1990 by 'NC-17', i.e. 'no children under 17'. *See also* X-RATED.

X, Malcolm. *See* MALCOLM X.

X-craft. A code name for the Royal Navy's midget submarines that were in action against the German battleship *Tirpitz* in 1943. Each submarine was designated 'X' followed by a distinguishing number.

> Of the six attacking craft X9 was lost on passage and X8 … had to be scuttled. X10 found that *Scharnhorst* had left the fiord and X5 was sunk by gunfire, leaving X6 … and X7 to make their way up Altenfiord.
>
> *The Times* (Obituary of Rear-Admiral Godfrey Place)
> (30 December 1994)

Xena. The feisty fighter who sets forth in quest of wicked warlords, man-eating centaurs and the like in the television series *Xena: Warrior Princess*, first screened on satellite television in 1996. She is played by the New Zealand actress Lucy Lawless and has a sidekick in the sharp-tongued runaway Gabrielle, played by Renee O'Connor. *See also* SWORD OPERA.

Xerox. A proprietary name, registered in 1952, for a make of photocopiers. The name itself is based on a respelling of Greek *xeros*, 'dry', in allusion to xerography, the dry copying process that such copiers employ. From the 1960s the name became virtually generic to mean both 'a photocopy' and 'to photocopy', a development that the manufacturing company rigorously resisted but was powerless to prevent, since one cannot stop people using words in any way they choose.

X-Files, The. A television series in which a pair of fictional FBI agents, Fox Mulder and Dana Scully, played respectively by David Duchovny and Gillian Anderson, investigate the paranormal. It was first screened in 1993 and soon attracted a cult following.

X marks the spot. This is the place; this is the exact location. The reference is to the marking of a location on a map or the scene of a crime in a plan or photograph with a cross or 'X'. The catchphrase dates from the 1920s.

X-rated. Indecent; pornographic, as 'X-rated humour'. The allusion is to the former x film classification.

XXXX. The tradename of a brand of Australian lager, pronounced 'four-x'. It was later taken up as a humorous euphemism for a FOUR-LETTER WORD (typically as in 'I don't give a XXXX').

XYZ. 'Examine your zip', an initialism serving as a caution to a man before he steps forth.

Y

Yackety-yack. A phrase imitative of incessant chatter dating from the 1950s.

Yah boo! An exclamation of derision or scorn, originating from children's slang in the 1920s. 'Yah boo sucks!' is a later expansion. The phrase has gained some currency to express an attitude of mocking superiority.

> In the late 20th century ... a distinct yah-boo-sucks attitude has developed on the part of celebrity tyrants towards the politicians who seek to court them.
> *The Times* (6 November 1999)

Yahoo! This search engine for the INTERNET was set up in 1994 by two American electrical engineering graduate students at Stanford University, David Filo and Jerry Yang, initially to track their favourite sites on the burgeoning WORLD WIDE WEB. The name is supposed to be an acronym for 'Yet Another Hierarchical Officious Oracle', but Filo and Wang claimed that they regarded themselves as yahoos (rude, noisy or violent people). More appropriately, the word is an exclamation of joy or excitement, as on making a happy discovery or thinking a happy thought.

> We started off with a few extra-size beers ... I let out a yahoo. The night was on.
> JACK KEROUAC: *On the Road*, Pt I, ch ix (1957)

Yalta Conference. A meeting between Winston Churchill of Britain, Franklin D. Roosevelt of the United States and Joseph Stalin of the Soviet Union from 4 to 11 February 1945 at Livadiya, a Black Sea resort 3km (2 miles) from Yalta in the Crimea. The BIG THREE heads of government planned the final stages of the Second World War and agreed the subsequent division of the defeated countries of eastern Europe. It had already been decided that Germany would be divided into occupied zones administered by British, French, US and Soviet forces.

Yardie. A member of a Jamaican or West Indian gang that is engaged in organized crime worldwide, especially in illegal drug-trafficking. The name comes from the Jamaican use of 'yard' to mean a house or home. 'Yard' was adopted by Jamaicans in England and elsewhere as a term for their home country.

Yarg. The name of a full-cream cow's milk cheese first produced in 1983 in Cornwall by a couple named Gray. Hence its name, as reversal of theirs. Names formed in this particular way usually indicate an inferior version of the original, as 'Klim', a type of powdered milk available in the Second World War, or even 'yob', as a 'backward' boy. But this does not apparently apply with Yarg.

Years young. A coy substitution for 'years old' in stating the age of older people, designed to emphasize their youthfulness of spirit if not of body. A television documentary on centenarians in Britain was predictably titled *100 Years Young* (1999). The term dates from the turn of the 20th century.

> To the lovely women, sixty years young, whose noble womanhood wins beauty from the passing years, this book is inscribed in loving esteem and admiration.
> ELLA ADELIA FLETCHER: *The Woman Beautiful*, Dedication (1900)

Yellow brick road. A metaphorical road to happiness. The allusion is to the Yellow Brick Road along which Dorothy and her friends go on their way to the WIZARD OF OZ. The pop singer Elton John released a highly successful song and album entitled 'Goodbye Yellow Brick Road' in 1973.

> The road to the City of Emeralds is paved with yellow brick.
> L. FRANK BAUM: *The Wonderful Wizard of Oz* (1900)

Yellow card. In football a card shown by the referee as a caution to a player who has committed an offence. A repetition of the offence, or a more serious infringement, is likely to result in a RED CARD. The system is based on the amber and red traffic light signals and was introduced on 2 October 1976. The yellow card was withdrawn by the Football Association in January 1981 but reinstated in 1987.

Yellow dog contract. A US term dating from the early 20th century for an employee's work contract (now illegal) that forbids membership of a trade union. 'Yellow dog' was formerly a term for a contemptible person or thing, ultimately referring to a mongrel with a dingy tawny coat.

Yellow Pages. The registered tradename of a classified telephone directory. It originated in the United States in the early 20th century as the name of an index printed on yellow paper, as at the back of a mail order catalogue. The name's application to the telephone directory dates from the 1950s. Subscribers are listed alphabetically by their product, occupation or service – e.g. (under B) Baby goods, Background music, Bags, Bailiffs, Bait merchants, Ballet shoes.

Yellow peril. A scare, originally raised in Germany in the late 1890s, that the yellow races of China and Japan would rapidly increase in population and overrun the territories occupied by the white races with fearful consequences.

> But Japan was Asia, part of the Yellow Peril, poised like a descending pendulum above Australia's rich, empty, underpopulated pit.
>
> COLLEEN MCCULLOUGH: *The Thorn Birds*, ch xv (1977)

Yellow press. The sensationalist newspapers. The term derives from an 1895 issue of Joseph Pulitzer's *New York World* containing a comic strip by Richard Outcault whose central figure was a child in a yellow dress, 'The Yellow Kid'. This experiment in colour printing was Pulitzer's shot in the circulation war against William Randolph Hearst's recently published *New York Journal*. The rivalry was dubbed 'yellow journalism' and came to be characterized by scare headlines, sensational articles, lavish illustrations, comic features, Sunday supplements and the like.

Yellow ribbon. A tradition has evolved in the United States of using yellow ribbons to decorate the home or home town of a person or group of people returning from danger. The custom was publicized worldwide by the media in 1981 following the safe return of 52 US

embassy hostages from Iran. The observance goes back to the days when a yellow ribbon, a decoration on US cavalrymen's tunics, was given to a sweetheart as a favour.

Yellow Submarine. A comic song by the BEATLES, credited to John Lennon and Paul McCartney and released in August 1966. It was originally written as a children's song, and involves an array of amusing nautical effects, including bubbles and rattling chains. An animated film *Yellow Submarine* was released in July 1968, and a soundtrack album with songs by the Beatles and an instrumental score appeared in 1969.

> In the town where I was born
> Lived a man who sailed to sea
> And he told us of his life
> In the land of submarines.

Yerma. A play (1934) by the Spanish playwright Federico García Lorca (1898–1935) about a woman trapped in a loveless marriage. Yerma, which means 'barren' in Spanish, is the name of the wife whose husband Juan has no interest in having children, ignoring the fact that she longs to be a mother:

> A woman who doesn't bear children is as useless as a bunch of thistles – something fit for God's rubbish heap.

Yes, Minister. An enjoyable BBC television comedy series, written by Anthony Jay and Jonathan Lynn, that combined farce with satire. It was broadcast from 1980 to 1982 and follows the respective struggles to gain and retain power of an unscrupulous senior civil servant, Sir Humphrey Appleby, played by Nigel Hawthorne, and his ineffectual but occasionally wily minister, Rt Hon James Hacker, MP, played by Paul Eddington. The plot lines are suitably convoluted and the dialogue wittily credible for its ESTABLISHMENT setting. Hacker eventually becomes prime minister, as depicted in a subsequent series, *Yes, Prime Minister* (1986–8).

Yesterday. A song by the BEATLES in which the singer (Paul McCartney) reflects on a lost love. Credited to John Lennon and Paul McCartney, it was released in the UK in August 1965. McCartney's voice is accompanied on the song by a guitar and string quartet. The song had the very unromantic working title of 'Scrambled Eggs'. John Lennon makes a bitter reference to the song in a track on his 1971 album *Imagine*, where the lyrics of 'How Do You Sleep' include the line 'The only thing you done was Yesterday', a decidedly unjust allusion to the supposed paucity of McCartney's creative input into the Beatles' songs.

Yesterday's men. Men, especially politicians, whose career is over or past its peak. The expression was popularized (but not invented) by a LABOUR PARTY slogan of 1970, 'Yesterday's men (they failed before!)', referring to the Conservatives. It was later turned against them by the television programme *Yesterday's Men* (1971), a sardonic documentary on Labour cabinet ministers who had lost office in the 1970. The style and content of the programme, written and presented by David Dimbleby, led to the threat of lawsuits, a major political row and the setting up of the Broadcasting Complaints Commission (now Broadcasting Standards Commission).

Yes, Virginia. A cliché sometimes prefixed to a reply to a naïve or childish question, as: 'Yes, Virginia, tea does contain caffeine, just as coffee does.' It originated in the United States in December 1897, when Francis P. Church, an editor on the New York *Sun*, received a letter from eight-year-old Virginia O'Hanlon asking about Santa Claus, who many of her friends had said did not exist. Church's reply contained the words, 'Yes, Virginia, there is a Santa Claus'. The line became a favourite with readers and was reprinted annually by the *Sun* until the paper went out of business in 1949. Virginia O'Hanlon went on to become a headteacher and throughout her life received a steady stream of correspondence about her Santa Claus letter. She died on 13 May 1971, aged 81.

Yes, We Have No Bananas. The memorable title of a song of 1923 by Frank Silver and Irving Cohen, the latter of whom apparently heard the remark from the lips of a Greek fruit seller. *Punch*, in its issue of 1 August 1923, described the title as 'the latest catchword', and the banana importers Elders and Fyffes distributed 10,000 hands of bananas to music sellers with the slogan, 'Yes! We have no bananas! On sale here'. The words work well in other languages to the notes of Cohen's tune, as French *Si, on n'a pas d'bananes*, German *Ja, wir hab'n kein' Bananen* and even Russian *Da, u nas nyet bananov*.

Y-fronts. The proprietary name, registered in 1953, of a make of boys' or men's underpants in the form of close-fitting briefs with a front opening within an inverted Y-shape. The first trial Y-front was produced in 1934 by Coopers Inc of Kenosha, USA, under the name 'Brief Style 1001', and the style itself was suggested by a pair of swimming trunks worn by a bather

on the French Riviera that one of the firm's senior vice-presidents had seen in a magazine photograph.

Yippies. Members of the Youth International Party, an anarcho-absurdist organization that in 1968 together with Students for a Democratic Society (*see* WEATHERMEN) led a demonstration in Chicago against the Vietnam War, racism and other blights of a blinkered US government.

Yogi Bear. The cartoon bear who starred in the American animated television series named after him, screened from 1958 to 1963 and produced by the Hanna-Barbera team. He lives in Jellystone Park and has a little friend in Boo-Boo. There have been Yogi Bear comics, and a feature-length cartoon film, *Hey There! It's Yogi Bear!*, was released in 1964.

Yom Kippur War. The Israeli and common Western name for the 1973 Arab–Israeli War. The name is not particularly acceptable in the Arab world, as Yom Kippur is a Jewish religious holiday, the Day of Atonement. In 1973 Yom Kippur fell on the 6 October, and it was on this day that Egypt and Syria launched a surprise attack on Sinai and the GOLAN HEIGHTS, territories that had been seized by Israel during the 1967 SIX-DAY WAR. Fierce fighting continued for two weeks, during which the Israelis established a bridgehead on the west bank of the Suez Canal, while the Egyptians crossed in the opposite direction to take part of Sinai. On 22 October a ceasefire was arranged through the mediation of the United Nations, the USA and the Soviet Union.

Yonks. The slang word meaning 'a long time', especially in the phrase 'for yonks', first emerged in general use in the 1960s. Its origin is uncertain, although it may relate to 'donkey's years'.

Yoof culture. The cultural scene of young people in the raw mass, especially as experienced in the field of broadcasting. The use of 'yoof' for 'youth', originally reflecting a non-standard pronunciation, soon gained a veneer of disparagement. It was particularly associated with the MOCKNEY speech of the television producer and presenter Janet Street-Porter (b.1946), who was appointed BBC commissioning editor for youth television in 1988.

> As long ago as 1987 Channel 4 had a 'desert island' strand in its groundbreaking 'yoof' TV show *Network 7*.
> *heat* (13–19 January 2000)

Yorkshire Rasputin. A nickname given by the press corps to Bernard Ingham (b.1932), former journalist and Labour candidate, who was press secretary to the IRON LADY, Margaret Thatcher, throughout her premiership (1979–90). His nickname derives from the Mad Monk, RASPUTIN, who had such a powerful and supposedly sinister influence over the last tsar of Russia, Nicholas II, and his wife. The nickname was earned by Ingham's mastery of the 'black arts' of spin doctoring (*see* SPIN DOCTOR), which he combined with a rebarbative, no-nonsense Yorkshire style that kept both press and government ministers in order.

Yorkshire Ripper. A media nickname for Peter Sutcliffe (b.1946), murderer of some 13 women over a five-year period from 1975. The name was based on that of Jack the Ripper, the unknown murderer of several prostitutes in the East End of London in the late 1880s, the term relating to the gross mutilation of the bodies.

Yosser. A nickname for a MOONLIGHTER, from Yosser Hughes, one of the main characters in Alan Bleasdale's black television comedy *The Boys from the Black Stuff* (1982), about a gang of unemployed tarmac layers in wasteland Liverpool. Hughes drives himself into a psychotic state as he begs for work and his often-repeated pleas 'Gissa job' and 'I could do that' became national catchphrases, not least because of the political situation of the time.

> Black day for Yossers as Lord goes on a ghost hunt.
> *The Times* (headline) (11 November 1999)

You ain't seen nothing yet. A US catchphrase dating from the 1920s. In its variant form, 'You ain't heard nothing yet', it was spoken by Al Jolson in the first full-length movie *The Jazz Singer* (1927), in which he was actually promoting the title of one of his songs, recorded in 1919. Ronald Reagan used the 'seen' version during his successful presidential campaign of 1984.

You can say that again. You are stating the obvious. The expression is often ironically used to refer to an unintentional understatement. The phrase dates from the 1930s.

> The advert [for a director of rail communications] first appeared on Friday, three days after the Paddington [rail] disaster, in the magazine PR Week, which made it the publication's 'job of the week'. You can say that again.
> *Sunday Times* (10 October 1999)

You can't get there from here. The problem is too hard to solve. The phrase can have a literal sense, meaning that the place you want to go to is hard or impossible to get to from here.

You can't win. A stock expression said, usually in exasperation, when one realizes or feels that whatever one does one will not succeed or manage to please a particular person or people. The phrase dates from the 1920s and is the title of Jack Black's novel *You Can't Win* (1926).

> An electric wheelchair would really help, but my local authority won't pay for one because I'm not disabled enough. You can't win.
> *Sunday Times Magazine* (2 January 2000)

You can't win 'em all. You cannot succeed every time. The phrase is a standard expression of comfort to someone who has lost or been unsuccessful, especially after a promising beginning.

You could have fooled me. You can't expect me to believe that. A comment expressing scepticism or mild contradiction dating from the 1970s.

You don't know the half of it. There's more to it than that. The expression dates from the 1930s and implies that the speaker knows everything about a situation, whereas the other does not.

You guessed it. There is no need for me to tell you. A journalistic tag preceding a piece of information or an outcome that the reader is likely to expect or deduce.

> Many people are throwing their resources into another scheme that upsets the townies: to turn the old cattle market into – you've guessed it – a multiplex.
> *The Times* (4 August 1999)

You heard! Don't pretend you didn't hear what I said! The phrase, dating from the 1950s, is typically addressed to someone who pretends not to have heard a particular statement or question.

You'll never walk alone. This song by Oscar Hammerstein II in the musical *Carousel* (1945) was taken up by fans of Liverpool Football Club and adopted as its anthem. The words of the title appear on the gates of the club's home ground at Anfield.

You must be joking. You can't expect me to believe that. The expression dates from the 1960s and exists in variants such as 'You've got to be joking' or simply 'You're joking'.

You name it. Whatever you can think of. A formula dating from the 1960s to express the extent or variety of something, in a typical fuller form: 'You name it, we've got it.'

> Brooms, sink plungers, dustbins, newspapers, match-

boxes – you name it and they'll knock, rip or scrape some sort of rhythmic sense out of the thing.
heat (18–24 November 1999)

Young Adolf. A black comic novel (1978) by Beryl Bainbridge (b.1934), written with touches of hilarious hindsight, in which a young Adolf Hitler (1889–1945) visits his sister-in-law in Bainbridge's native city of Liverpool in the 1920s. *See also* BIRTHDAY BOYS.

Young fogy. A young or youngish person who has the outlook and mannerisms of an OLD FOGY. The stance was adopted by some in the 1980s as a 'throwback' to the 1950s generation. The novelist and biographer A.N. Wilson (b.1950) is generally regarded as an archetypal young fogy.

Young Guard. A group of young Russian guerrilla fighters based in Krasnodon in German-occupied Ukraine in the Second World War. They were 91 in number, including factory workers, students and government employees, and had four radio receivers, an underground printing press, weapons and explosives at their disposal. They distributed hundreds of anti-NAZI leaflets and on the eve of the 25th anniversary of the October Revolution set up eight Soviet flags in the city. Other operations included the blowing up of German troop-carrying vehicles and the burning down of the Nazi labour exchange with its lists of local people earmarked for transportation to Germany. On 15 November 1942 they freed 70 Soviet prisoners of war from a concentration camp and evacuated a further 20 from hospital. They were planning to blow up the German garrison when their activities were revealed by one of their company, as a result of which they were captured and tortured and 71 of their number were thrown, alive or dead, down a 53m (174ft) mineshaft. Five of the original ringleaders were shot in a nearby forest on 9 February 1943, and only 11 escaped. Their dramatic story was retold by Alexander Fadeyev in his novel *Molodaya gvardiya* ('The Young Guard') (1946), and the new town of Molodogvard-eysk, founded in 1954, was named in their honour.

Young gun. An assertive and aggressively self-confident young man, as if making his way in life by shooting with a gun. 'Young Guns (Go For It)' was a hit for the pop group Wham! in late 1982.

Wrinklies like the [Rolling] Stones and Elton [John] lead the rich list but young guns are gaining.
Heat (10–19 January 2000)

Young hopeful. A young or youngish person who is deemed likely to succeed.

Young Ones, The. The first real showing of undiluted ALTERNATIVE comedy on television, featuring the chaotic antics of a group of four students sharing a squat in a rambling house. There is no story line to speak of, simply a series of grotesque situations, some verging on the offensive. The four consist of the loud-mouthed Cliff Richard fan Rick, played by Rick Mayall, the dim-witted HIPPIE Neil, nicely evoked by Nigel Planer, the stud-headed, spiky-haired PUNK Vivien, played by Adrian Edmondson, and the rather remote Mike, personified by Christopher Ryan. There were two series, the first in 1982, the second in 1984. *The Young Ones* (1961) was also the title of a film starring Cliff (now Sir Cliff) Richard and featuring a song of the same name.

Young thing. A young person, especially one seen to possess any or all of the desirable characteristics of youth, as verve, style, good looks, physical prowess and the like. The expression is typically used of the socially advantaged, and the BRIGHT YOUNG THINGS and FLAPPERS of the 1920s and 1930s were prominent on the social scene for their exuberance and often outrageous behaviour.

In best bachelor form, Prince Andrew slipped into Spencer House. It being an NSPCC bash, the Prince looked after the interests of young things.
The Times (24 June 1999)

Young Turks. A Turkish reforming party seeking to transform the decadent Ottoman Empire into a modern European state and to give it a parliamentary constitution. It had its origins in a committee formed at Geneva in 1891, and the party, considerably supported by students, raised the standard of revolt at Salonika in 1908, deposed Sultan Abdul Hamid and replaced him by his brother as Mohammed V (1909). Their 'liberalism' was not dominant, but they remained the major force in Turkish politics until the end of the First World War, when the party was dissolved. Turkey was proclaimed a republic in 1923. 'Young Turks' is also used generally for young people eager for radical change to the established order.

You Only Live Twice. The fifth film (1967) in the long-running series of James BOND films based on the secret agent novels of Ian Fleming (1906–64). Scripted by Roald Dahl and starring Sean Connery as Bond, the film derived its title from the proverbial 'you only live once' tag, as used in a Fritz Lang crime thriller as early as 1937. It is justified within the script by Bond faking his own death and then reappearing to thwart the plans of arch-villain Donald Pleasence.

Your actual. The real or genuine thing specified, as: 'This is your actual vintage Rolls Royce.' The turn of phrase became popular following its use in the dialogue of two gay characters, Julian and Sandy, in the radio comedy *Round the Horne* (1965–9). Typically, they would introduce some French phrase into their lines and then say: 'That's your actual French, you know.' *See also* YOUR AVERAGE.

Your average. The average or typical thing specified, 'your' implying that the reader or listener will be familiar with it. The expression may equally be used of people. *See also* YOUR ACTUAL.

> *Black on White* is not your usual concert, nor is it your average piece of performance art.
> *The Times* (5 July 1999)

Your Country Needs You. *See* KITCHENER'S ARMY.

You're a poet and you don't know it. A catchphrase said, with appropriate variation of pronoun, when someone makes an unwitting rhyme, as: 'If it comes on to rain we can go on the train.'

You're telling me. There is no need to tell me that, I am aware of it already. The phrase expressing agreement dates from the 1930s and may owe something to a 1932 song by Gus Kahn so titled.

You're the doctor. You know best; whatever you say. A catchphrase dating from the early 20th century. *See also* JUST WHAT THE DOCTOR ORDERED.

Your guess is as good as mine. I don't know either. A phrase dating from the 1930s.

Your King and Country need you. A British recruitment slogan in the First World War, coined by Eric Field in 1914.

Your place or mine? A stock phrase evolving among young people in the 1970s as the key question after a period of time engaged in 'chat'. The implication is of a more intimate engagement.

You've lost me. I don't follow what you're saying. The idea is that your reasoning or narrative is so tortuous that I have lost the thread. The phrase dates from the 1960s.

You win. Said when conceding agreement to another's demand or choice, usually after a discussion or even argument, as: 'All right, you win, we'll go there later.' *See also* YOU CAN'T WIN.

Yo-yo. The familiar toy that falls and rises on an adroitly manipulated string is first recorded in 1915 as a Fili-

pino device of this type. The word was registered as a tradename in Canada in 1932, and it was then that a sudden craze for the toy spread through the Western world. Subsequent vogues followed in the 1950s and late 1990s. The origin of the name is uncertain, although a meaning 'come-come' is adduced in some dictionaries.

Ypres. *See* WIPERS; MENIN GATE.

Yuck or **yuk.** A word expressive of disgust or distaste, as an imitative variant of 'ugh'. Hence 'yucky' to denote anything unpleasant or cloyingly sentimental. *See also* YUCKIES.

Yuckies. A term for a couple in an embarrassingly close or 'clonish' relationship, of the kind that makes one say YUCK, especially when each was formerly idolized as a media or sports figure. The expression, based on YUPPIES, dates from the late 1990s.

> It's a rare thing even to see them apart. ... Hip as they may try to be, Posh [of the SPICE GIRLS] and Becks [footballer David Beckham] are sadly what's known as Yuckies.
> *Sunday Times* (29 August 1999)

Yuk. *See* YUCK.

Yuppie flu. A slighting nickname for the malady known more formally as chronic fatigue syndrome and medically as myalgic encephalomyelitis (ME). The condition, supposedly typical among YUPPIES, usually occurs after a viral infection and involves fever, aching and tiredness and depression. The diagnosis became more frequent in the late 1980s as a result of media publicity. Much debate surrounds the cause, which some have ascribed to hysteria or even hyperventilation.

Yuppies. Young urban (or upwardly mobile) professional people. A popular acronym from the 1980s, and of American origin. *See also* SOCIONYMS.

> 'The Yuppie Handbook' [1984] defined the yuppie as a fast-track baby-boomer between 25 and 46 residing in or near a major city and living on aspirations of glory and power or 'anyone who brunches on the weekend or works out after work'.
> *International Herald Tribune* (March 1986)

Yvette. Canadian slang for an old-fashioned French Canadian woman or girl, as the name of a character in a Quebec school primer. Its use in this sense was popularized by Lise Payette, a Parti Québecois cabinet minister, during the campaign leading up to the referendum of 1980 on economic union between Canada and an independent Quebec.

Z

Zapata moustache. A thick moustache that curves down around the edges of the mouth, like that worn by the Mexican revolutionary Emiliano Zapata (1879–1919).

Zapper. A colloquial term for a remote-control unit for a television or video recorder, with which one 'zaps' to effect an instant change of channel or programme or simply to switch on or off.

Zazie dans le Métro. A novel (1959; in English as *Zazie in the Metro*, 1960) by Raymond Queneau (1903–76). The mind of the philosopher–poet is behind the clowning in this ostensibly light novel, in which a provincial girl's ambition to travel on the Paris Métro is thwarted by a typical French one-day strike. A film version (1960), directed by Louis Malle, is full of comic action, with a zestful young Catherine Demongeot in the title role.

Z-Cars. A seminal television drama series screened from 1962 to 1978. It was set in the docklands of Liverpool and depicted in gritty detail the professional lives of a squad of PANDA CAR drivers, some of whom, controversially for the day, were depicted as fallible human beings. Thus the first episode showed one policeman beating his wife and another asking for the result of a horse race. Many of the actors, such as Colin Welland, Brian Blessed and Leonard Rossiter, became household names, and a spin-off was the police drama *Softly, Softly* (*see* SOFTLY-SOFTLY). The cars used were Ford Zephyrs. Hence the 'Z'.

Zebra crossing. A type of road crossing marked by broad black and white stripes on the road, accompanied by BELISHA BEACONS at the side of the road. The term dates from the early 1950s. *See also* PELICAN CROSSING; PUFFIN CROSSING.

Zeppelin. The imposing German airship used during the First World War for reconnaissance and bombing and after the war for passenger transport. It took its name from its constructor, Count Ferdinand von Zeppelin (1838–1917). The *Graf Zeppelin* was completed in 1928 and was in commercial passenger service for 10 years, making 590 flights before being decommissioned in 1937. In the latter year the *Hindenburg*, the largest Zeppelin ever built, suddenly exploded while landing at Lakehurst, New Jersey, at the end of a transatlantic crossing, killing 36 of its 97 passengers. The disaster was attributed by some to anti-NAZI saboteurs. A second *Graf Zeppelin* was completed in 1938 and was the most advanced commercial airship ever built. It was used by the Germans for surveillance in the months before the Second World War but was grounded after the outbreak of war. Both of the *Graf Zeppelin* airships were broken up in 1940 when Goering, head of the LUFTWAFFE, wanted their aluminium for combat aircraft.

Zero hour. A military term, first used in the First World War, for the exact time at which an attack or operation is to be begun. From this are timed the subsequent operations, e.g. zero + 3 means 3 minutes after zero hour. The term was succeeded in the Second World War by H-hour.

Zero option. A disarmament proposal by one side to reduce the number of nuclear missiles, or not to deploy them, if the other will do the same. The expression originated in the early 1980s with specific reference to the American proposal that if the Soviet Union would withdraw its medium-range SS-20 missiles from Europe, the United States would abandon its plan to deploy Pershing and cruise missiles there. The expression itself evolved from the *Null-lösung*, 'zero solution', put forward in 1981 by the German Chancellor Helmut Schmidt. 'Zero' implies reduction to nothing.

Zero-sum game. A game in which the sum of the winnings of all the players is always zero and hence any situation in which an advantage to one participant necessarily leads to a disadvantage to one or more of the others. The expression was introduced by the American economists John von Neumann and Oscar Morgenstern in their influential study *Theory of Games and Economic Behavior* (1944).

> Other parties [than the Liberal Democrats] have opposed arbitrary power. Usually, this has tended to be part of the zero-sum game of class-based politics.
> *The Times* (22 September 1999)

Zero tolerance. The total non-acceptance of antisocial behaviour, with laws or penalties applied rigorously to even minor infringements. The policy was introduced in the United States in the early 1980s to cover a crackdown on even the mildest forms of street crime, such as graffiti, vandalism, obstruction, aggressive begging or spitting. The concept crossed to Britain in the 1990s.

> The world's largest cruise lines, buffeted by allegations of sexual assaults, declared yesterday a policy of zero tolerance towards crimes at sea.
> *The Times* (28 July 1999)

Ziegfeld Follies. The American theatrical producer Florenz Ziegfeld (1867–1932) first mounted his *Follies* revue in 1907 at the New York Theatre Roof, his name becoming a permanent part of the title in 1911. The show was loosely based on the Parisian *Folies Bergère*, but knowing that he could not display the dancing nudes of his French counterpart, Ziegfeld posed the near naked 'girls' in what he called 'living tableaux', or motionless poses. He thus adroitly blurred the distinction between art on the one hand and soft pornography on the other. The extravagantly staged shows ran continuously to his death and then periodically until 1957.

Zigger-zagger. The onomatopoeic nickname of the large rattle that football fans formerly brandished at matches. As it was swung round a handle it made a loud rasping or clacking sound. Peter Terson's play *Zigger Zagger* (1967) is about a football fan named Zigger and a football crowd.

Ziggy Stardust. An alien hermaphrodite with blood-red hair, the *alter ego* of the rock singer David Bowie.

Ziggy Stardust appears on the CONCEPT ALBUM *The Rise and Fall of Ziggy Stardust and the Spiders from Mars*, released in 1972, at the height of Bowie's GLAM ROCK phase. The basis of the album resided in the idea of a supergroup (the Spiders) with a five-year lifespan. The concept, with its undertones of SCIENCE FICTION and androgyny, was a feeble one, but many of the songs on the album, such as 'Moonage Daydream', 'Starman', 'Rock and Roll Suicide' and 'Suffragette City', were critically acclaimed. The Spiders from Mars also appeared on the album *Aladdin Sane* (1973).

Zillions. A very large number. The word emerged in the 1940s as a fanciful alteration of 'millions', 'billions' and the like, with 'z' perhaps representing the sound of 'x' (as in 'xylophone') in its mathematical role as an unknown number, or even as itself in this role. *See also* SQUILLIONS.

Zimmer frame. The make of walking frame for elderly or disabled people takes its proprietary name from its manufacturing company, Zimmer Orthopaedic Ltd. The company's own name comes from Mongolian *zhima*, a sledge drawn by a *zho*, a hybrid of a yak and a cow, which was guided by a man walking at the rear holding an upright frame.

Zimmermann Telegram. On 16 January 1917 Arthur Zimmermann (1864–1940), German foreign secretary, sent a telegram to the German minister in Mexico with the terms of an alliance between Mexico and Germany by which Mexico was to attack the United States with German and Japanese assistance in return for the US states of New Mexico, Texas and Arizona. The telegram, originally sent in code, was decoded by British Admiralty intelligence and made available to President Woodrow Wilson, who published it on 1 March 1917. In convincing the Americans of German hostility towards the United States, the telegram became one of the principal factors leading to the US declaration of war against Germany five weeks later.

Zinoviev Letter. *See under* FAKES.

Zionist. The Jewish movement for the establishment of the 'national home' in Palestine. The Zionist movement was founded in 1895 by the Austrian Theodor Herzl (1860–1904), and the BALFOUR DECLARATION of 1917 recognized Zionist aspirations. From 1920 to 1948 Palestine was a British MANDATE, administered under great difficulties arising from the friction between Jews and Arabs. The independent state of Israel was established in 1948. The Palestine Liberation

Organization (PLO), founded in 1964, has fought constantly, often at bitter cost, to regain some kind of Palestinian representation in what it regards as Israeli-occupied territory.

Zip code. In the United States the system introduced in 1963 to facilitate the sorting and delivery of mail, based on five-digit (or, since the late 1970s, nine-digit) numbers. The first three of the five digits identified the section of the country to which the item was destined, and the last two the specific post office or zone of the addressee. The word 'Zip', while suggesting speed, is an acronym of Zone Improvement Plan, the formal name of the system. The British POSTCODE is similar.

Zone 14. In football the area in front of the penalty arc identified by analysts of the game as critical for creating goal-scoring opportunities. The area was identified by scientists at the Research Institute for Sport and Exercise Sciences at the John Moores University, Liverpool, who divided each half of the pitch into 18 zones. By analysing matches at the 1998 World Cup finals, they found that winning teams made more passes from zone 14 than losing teams, and also that the passes were more often played forward, from the zone into the penalty area.

Zoo daddy. An American colloquialism dating from the 1970s for a divorced or separated father who rarely sees his children. On occasions when he does see them, he frequently seeks to hold their interest and affection for the brief time available by taking them to the zoo or some other place of public entertainment. Hence 'Disneyland daddy' as an American alternative for the situation.

Zoo Story, The. A one-act play (1959) by the US playwright Edward Albee (b.1928) about a chance meeting between two men on a public bench that culminates in one of them being knifed to death after they clash over possession of the bench. The title refers to the visit one of the men has just made to a zoo, although it is the 'human zoo' that is really under discussion:

> You have everything in the world you want; you've told me about your home, and your family, and your own little zoo. You have everything, and now you want this bench. Are these the things men fight for?

Zoot suit. An exaggerated style of clothing adopted in the late 1930s by followers of fashionable SWING music. It usually consisted of baggy trousers caught in at the bottom, a long coat resembling a frock coat, a broad-brimmed hat and a flowing tie, all in vivid

colours. An essential adjunct was a long watch chain looping across the trousers. The outfit made a comeback in the 1990s and was complemented by a feminine version. 'Zoot' is simply a rhyming jingle on 'suit'.

> 'If you see a hand, whaddya do?' instructed Simon, dapper in a chocolate brown zoot suit.
> *The Times* (4 December 1999)

Zoo TV. A type of television programme that encourages emotional and often uncontrolled reactions from the participants, as a debate before a live audience or a scene involving personal disclosures. A typical example is *The Jerry Springer Show*, an American talk show first screened in 1991 that evolved to include outrageous topics and physical fisticuffs among the guests. The analogy is with the untrammelled behaviour of zoo animals, especially monkeys, before the gaze of visitors.

> A gaggle of teenagers whooping and hollering in full 'zoo' TV mode.
> *heat* (20–26 January 2000)

Zorba the Greek. A novel (1952; in Greek as *Vios kai Politeia tou Alexi Zormpa*, 'The Life and Times of Alexis Zorbas', 1946) of the MAGIC REALISM school by the Greek writer Nikos Kazantzakis (1883–1957). The character of the passive, contemplative narrator, contrasts with that of the larger than life Greek of the old tradition, whose actions are unpremeditated and often irrational.

> 'I went off all of a sudden, got hold of the boss, who had come that day to inspect the place, and just beat him up.'
> 'But what had he done to you?'
> 'Nothing at all. ....'
> 'Well?'
> '... It just came over me. You know the tale of the miller's wife? Well, you don't expect to learn spelling from her backside, do you. The backside of the miller's wife, that's human reason.'

An enjoyable film version (1964), with memorable music by Mikis Theodorakis, was directed by Michael Cacoyannis.

Zorbing. An EXTREME SPORT that emerged in New Zealand in the mid-1990s and that consists in hurling oneself down hills or fast-flowing streams in a 'zorb', a large perspex ball.

Zorro. The black-masked, black-caped master swordsman and avenger of old California was the creation of

Johnston McCulley. He first appeared in 1919 in the magazine story 'The Curse of Capistrano'. His 'trademark' is the letter Z, which he slashes on the clothes or skin of his enemies. He soon transferred to the cinema screen, where he was played by such actors as Douglas Fairbanks in *The* MARK OF ZORRO (1920) and Tyrone Power in the 1940 version of this. His name is Spanish for 'fox', from a word that originally meant 'cunning'.

Zuleika Dobson. The only novel (1911) by Max Beerbohm (1872–1956), essayist, critic, parodist, and caricaturist. Subtitled *An Oxford Love Story*, it describes delicately and wittily the passionate and ultimately apocalyptic response of the undergraduate population to Zuleika DOBSON, the beautiful and predatory niece of the head of one of the colleges.

Zuppa inglese (Italian, 'English soup'). Not a soup but a rich Italian dessert resembling trifle. The dish was first familiar to the English themselves in the 1970s.

Zut alors! An expression of surprise, annoyance, impatience etc, supposedly typical of the French. It represents *zut*, an imitative word approximating to English 'tut' or 'tch', and *alors*, 'then'.

> Zut alors! You British can have your secrets back.
> *Sunday Times* (headline) (12 December 1999)

Zyklon-B. A tradename for hydrogen cyanide, the quick-acting, lethal gas used by the NAZIS to kill millions of Jews and other 'UNTERMENSCHEN' during the Second World War. The effectiveness of Zyklon-B in achieving the FINAL SOLUTION was first demonstrated at the Bełżec extermination camp in Poland in August 1942 and subsequently employed on an industrial scale at AUSCHWITZ and elsewhere. *See also* HOLOCAUST.

Zzz. A representation of the sound of a person sleeping or snoring, typically found in cartoons and comics. The choice of the last letter of the alphabet for this is apt in both sound and sense, since sleeping implies a 'closing down' of activity.